Access® 2010 Bible

Michael R. Groh

WILEY

Wiley Publishing, Inc.

Access® 2010 Bible

Published by
Wiley Publishing, Inc.
10475 Crosspoint Boulevard
Indianapolis, IN 46256
www.wiley.com

Copyright © 2010 by Wiley Publishing, Inc., Indianapolis, Indiana

Published simultaneously in Canada

Library of Congress Control Number: 2010924560

ISBN: 978-0-470-47534-8

Manufactured in the United States of America

10 9 8 7 6 5 4 3 2 1

For general information on our other products and services or to obtain technical support, please contact our Customer Care Department within the U.S. at (877) 762-2974, outside the U.S. at (317) 572-3993 or fax (317) 572-4002.

Trademarks: Wiley and related trade dress are registered trademarks of Wiley Publishing, Inc., in the United States and other countries, and may not be used without written permission. Access is a registered trademark of Microsoft Corporation in the United States and/or other countries. All other trademarks are the property of their respective owners. Wiley Publishing, Inc., is not associated with any product or vendor mentioned in this book.

Wiley also publishes its books in a variety of electronic formats. Some content that appears in print may not be available in electronic books.

About the Author

Michael R. Groh is a well-known author, writer, and consultant specializing in Windows database systems. His company, PC Productivity Solutions, provides information-management applications to companies across the country. Over the last 25 years, Mike has worked with a wide variety of programming languages, operating systems, and computer hardware, ranging from programming a DEC PDP-8A using the Focal interpreted language to building distributed applications under Visual Studio .NET and Microsoft SharePoint.

Mike was one of the first people outside of Microsoft to see Access in action. He was among a select group of journalists and publishers invited to preview the Access 1.0 beta (then called Cirrus) at the 1992 Windows World Conference in Chicago. Since then, Mike has been involved in every Microsoft Access beta program, both as an insider and as a journalist reporting on the evolution of this fascinating product.

Mike has authored parts of more than 20 different computer books and is a frequent contributor to computer magazines and journals. He has written more than 200 articles and editorials over the last 15 years, mostly for Advisor Media. He has frequently spoken at computer conferences virtually everywhere in the world, and is technical editor and contributor to periodicals and publications produced by Advisor Media.

Mike holds a master's degree in clinical chemistry from the University of Iowa and an MBA from Northeastern University.

Mike can be reached at AccessBible@mikegroh.com. Please prefix the e-mail subject line with "Access Bible:" to get past the spam blocker on this account.

About the Technical Editor

Doug Steele has been working with computers, both mainframe and PC, for almost 40 years. (Yes, he did use punch cards in the beginning!) For over 30 years, Doug has worked for a large international oil company. Databases and data modeling have been his focus for most of that time, although recently he has been working on a desktop project that will roll out Windows 7 to about 100,000 computers worldwide. Doug has authored numerous articles on Access, and has been recognized by Microsoft as an MVP (Most Valuable Professional) for more than ten years.

Doug holds a master's degree in system design engineering from the University of Waterloo, where his research centered around designing user interfaces for nontraditional computer users. This research stemmed from his background in music. (He holds an associateship in piano performance from the Royal Conservatory of Music in Toronto.) Doug can be reached at `AccessHelp@rogers.com`.

Credits

Acquisitions Editor
Katie Mohr

Project Editor
Elizabeth Kuball

Technical Editor
Doug Steele

Copy Editors
Elizabeth Kuball, Linda Morris, Susan Pink

Editorial Manager
Jodi Jensen

Vice President & Executive Group Publisher
Richard Swadley

Vice President and Publisher
Andy Cummings

Editorial Director
Mary C. Corder

Project Coordinator
Patrick Redmond

Graphics and Production Specialists
Jennifer Mayberry
Ronald G. Terry

Media Development Assistant Project Manager
Jenny Swisher

Media Development Associate Producer
Doug Kuhn

Media Development Quality Assurance
Marilyn Hummel

Proofreading and Indexing
Sossity R. Smith
Infodex Indexing Services, Inc.

Contents at a Glance

Acknowledgments xxxiii

Introduction xxxv

Part I: Access Building Blocks. 1
Chapter 1: An Introduction to Database Development 3
Chapter 2: Creating Access Tables 25
Chapter 3: Designing Bulletproof Databases 91
Chapter 4: Selecting Data with Queries...129
Chapter 5: Using Operators and Expressions in Access 171
Chapter 6: Working with Datasheet View 215
Chapter 7: Creating Basic Access Forms..251
Chapter 8: Working with Data on Access Forms..289
Chapter 9: Presenting Data with Access Reports 319

Part II: Programming Microsoft Access 375
Chapter 10: VBA Programming Fundamentals..377
Chapter 11: Mastering VBA Data Types and Procedures 417
Chapter 12: The Access Event Model...451
Chapter 13: Accessing Data with VBA Code 473
Chapter 14: Debugging Your Access Applications..523
Chapter 15: Using Access Data Macros 551

Part III: More-Advanced Access Techniques 577
Chapter 16: Working with External Data..579
Chapter 17: Importing and Exporting Data..609
Chapter 18: Advanced Access Query Techniques 637
Chapter 19: Advanced Access Form Techniques..679
Chapter 20: Advanced Access Report Techniques..709
Chapter 21: Building Multiuser Applications 751
Chapter 22: Integrating Access with Other Applications 789
Chapter 23: Handling Errors and Exceptions...819

Part IV: Professional Database Development **839**

Chapter 24: Optimizing Access Applications 841
Chapter 25: Advanced Data Access with VBA 881
Chapter 26: Bulletproofing Access Applications..897
Chapter 27: Using the Windows Application Programming Interface 939
Chapter 28: Object-Oriented Programming with VBA 969
Chapter 29: Customizing Access Ribbons..1009
Chapter 30: Using Access Macros 1049
Chapter 31: Distributing Access Applications 1083

Part V: Access and Windows SharePoint Services **1101**

Chapter 32: Understanding Windows SharePoint Services 1103
Chapter 33: Integrating Access with SharePoint..1117
Chapter 34: Understanding Access Services...1135
Chapter 35: Deploying Access Applications to SharePoint 1145

Part VI: Access as an Enterprise Platform **1181**

Chapter 36: Client/Server Concepts...1183
Chapter 37: SQL Server as an Access Companion..1199
Chapter 38: Upsizing Access Databases to SQL Server 1223

Part VII: Appendixes **1243**

Appendix A: Access 2010 Specifications 1245
Appendix B: What's New in Access 2010..1253
Appendix C: What's on the CD-ROM 1267

Index 1271

Contents

Acknowledgments .... **xxxiii**

Introduction .... **xxxv**

Part I: Access Building Blocks   1

Chapter 1: An Introduction to Database Development 3

The Database Terminology of Access 4
    Databases 4
    Tables 6
    Records and fields 8
    Values 8
Relational Databases...8
Access Database Objects 10
    Datasheets 10
    Queries 10
    Data-entry and display forms 11
    Reports...12
    Database objects..12
A Five-Step Design Method...12
    Step 1: The overall design — from concept to reality 13
    Step 2: Report design 14
    Step 3: Data design...16
    Step 4: Table design 19
    Step 5: Form design 22
Summary 23

Chapter 2: Creating Access Tables 25

Getting Started with Access...25
    The Templates section...26
    The Office Backstage View 27
Creating a Database...28
The Access 2010 Environment...33
    The Navigation Pane 33
    The ribbon 36
    Other relevant features of the Access environment 37

Contents

Creating a New Table...39
  Designing tables...40
  Using the Design tab..45
  Working with fields..47
Creating tblCustomers..55
  Using AutoNumber fields...55
  Completing tblCustomers...55
Changing a Table Design...56
  Inserting a new field..56
  Deleting a field...56
  Changing a field location...57
  Changing a field name..57
  Changing a field size..57
  Handling data conversion issues...57
  Assigning field properties..58
Understanding tblCustomers Field Properties..73
Setting the Primary Key...76
  Choosing a primary key...76
  Creating the primary key...77
  Creating composite primary keys..78
Indexing Access Tables..78
  The importance of indexes...80
  Multiple-field indexes..81
  When to index tables..83
Printing a Table Design...84
Saving the Completed Table..85
Manipulating Tables..85
  Renaming tables...86
  Deleting tables..86
  Copying tables in a database...86
  Copying a table to another database...87
Adding Records to a Database Table...88
Understanding Attachment Fields..88
Summary..90

Chapter 3: Designing Bulletproof Databases **91**
Building Bulletproof Databases...92
Data Normalization...94
  First normal form...95
  Second normal form...97
  Third normal form..102
  Denormalization..102
Table Relationships...104
  Connecting the data...105
  One-to-one..107

Contents

One-to-many 108

Many-to-many 110

Integrity Rules 112

No primary key can contain a null value 113

All foreign key values must be matched by corresponding primary keys 114

Keys 114

Deciding on a primary key 115

The benefits of a primary key 117

Designating a primary key 118

Creating relationships and enforcing referential integrity 119

Viewing all relationships 125

Deleting relationships 126

Application-specific integrity rules 126

Summary 127

Chapter 4: Selecting Data with Queries 129

Introducing Queries 130

What queries are 130

Types of queries 133

What queries can do 134

What queries return 134

Creating a Query 135

Adding Fields 138

Adding a single field 138

Adding multiple fields 139

Displaying the Recordset 140

Working with Fields 141

Selecting a field in the QBE grid 142

Changing field order 142

Resizing columns in the QBE grid 143

Removing a field 144

Inserting a field 144

Providing an alias for the field name 144

Showing a field 145

Changing the Sort Order 147

Displaying Only Selected Records 149

Understanding selection criteria 149

Entering simple string criteria 150

Entering other simple criteria 151

Printing a Query's Recordset 153

Saving a Query 153

Creating Multi-Table Queries 153

Viewing table names 155

Adding multiple fields 156

Multi-table query limitations 156

Overcoming query limitations 157

Contents

Working with the Table Pane...158
   Looking at the join line 158
   Manipulating Field Lists 159
   Moving a table...159
   Removing a table..159
   Adding more tables 160
Creating and Working with Query Joins 160
   Using ad hoc table joins 161
   Specifying the type of join...162
   Deleting joins..164
Understanding Table Join Types 165
   Working with inner joins (equi-joins) 165
   Understanding outer joins...166
   Working with self-joins...167
   Creating a Cartesian product 169
Summary 170

Chapter 5: Using Operators and Expressions in Access 171

Introducing Operators 171
   Looking at the types of operators 172
   Operator precedence 185
Using Operators and Expressions in Queries...................................187
   Using query comparison operators.....................................188
   Understanding complex criteria 189
   Using functions in select queries 192
   Referencing fields in select queries.....................................192
Entering Single-Value Field Criteria 193
   Entering character (Text or Memo) criteria.........................193
   The Like operator and wildcards...195
   Specifying non-matching values 198
   Entering numeric criteria...199
   Entering true or false criteria 200
   Entering OLE object criteria 201
Using Multiple Criteria in a Query 201
   Understanding an Or operation..201
   Specifying multiple values with the Or operator..................202
   Using the Or cell of the QBE pane.......................................202
   Using a list of values with the In operator 203
   Using And to specify a range 204
   Using the Between...And operator 205
   Searching for Null data..206
Entering Criteria in Multiple Fields..208
   Using And and Or across fields in a query...........................208
   Specifying Or criteria across fields of a query 209

Using And and Or together in different fields...211
A complex query on different lines...212
Summary 213

Chapter 6: Working with Datasheet View. 215
Understanding Datasheets...215
Looking at the Datasheet Window..217
    Moving within a datasheet...218
    Using the Navigation buttons...218
    Examining the Datasheet ribbon 219
Opening a Datasheet 221
Entering New Data...221
    Saving the record 223
    Understanding automatic data-type validation 224
    Knowing how properties affect data entry 225
Navigating Records in a Datasheet 227
    Moving between records 227
    Finding a specific value 228
Changing Values in a Datasheet 230
    Manually replacing an existing value 230
    Changing an existing value...231
Using the Undo Feature 232
Copying and Pasting Values...232
Replacing Values..233
Adding New Records 234
Deleting Records..234
Displaying Records 235
    Changing the field order 235
    Changing the field display width..237
    Changing the record display height..238
    Changing display fonts...239
    Displaying cell gridlines and alternate row colors...239
    Aligning data in columns..241
    Hiding and unhiding columns...241
    Freezing columns..242
    Saving the changed layout..242
    Saving a record...242
Sorting and Filtering Records in a Datasheet 242
    Sorting your records with QuickSort..243
    Filtering a selection 243
    Filtering by form 246
Focusing on Special Features of Datasheets...247
Printing Records 248
    Printing the datasheet...249
    Using the Print Preview window 249
Summary 249

Contents

Chapter 7: Creating Basic Access Forms **251**

    Formulating Forms 252
        Creating a new form..253
        Looking at special types of forms 257
        Resizing the form area 263
        Saving your form...263
    Working with Controls..264
        Categorizing controls 264
        Adding a control 266
        Selecting and deselecting controls 271
        Manipulating controls 272
    Introducing Properties..282
        Displaying the Property Sheet 282
        Getting acquainted with the Property Sheet...283
        Changing a control's property setting..284
        Naming control labels and their captions 285
    Summary 287

Chapter 8: Working with Data on Access Forms **289**

    Using Form View...289
        Looking at the Home ribbon tab 291
        Navigating among fields 294
        Moving among records in a form...294
    Changing Values in a Form..295
        Knowing which controls you can't edit 296
        Working with pictures and OLE objects..296
        Entering data in the Memo field 297
        Entering data in the Date field..298
        Using option groups..298
        Using combo boxes and list boxes..299
        Switching to Datasheet view 300
        Saving a record...300
    Printing a Form...300
    Working with Form Properties 301
        Changing the title bar text with the Caption property 303
        Creating a bound form..304
        Specifying how to view the form 304
        Removing the Record Selector 305
        Looking at other form properties..305
    Adding a Form Header or Footer 311
    Changing the Layout...312
        Changing a control's properties...312
        Setting the Tab Order..313
        Aligning controls..314
        Modifying the format of text in a control..314
        Using the Field List to add controls...314

Creating a Calculated Control 316
Converting a Form to a Report 317
Summary 317

Chapter 9: Presenting Data with Access Reports 319

Introducing Reports 319
    Identifying the different types of reports...320
    Distinguishing between reports and forms 322
Creating a Report, from Beginning to End...323
    Defining the report layout 323
    Assembling the data 324
    Creating a report with the Report Wizard..324
    Printing or viewing the report 338
    Saving the report 340
Banded Report Design Concepts 340
    The Report Header section 343
    The Page Header section 343
    The Group Header section 343
    The Detail section...344
    The Group Footer section 344
    The Page Footer section 344
    The Report Footer section 345
Creating a Report from Scratch 345
    Creating a new report and binding it to a query 347
    Defining the report page size and layout 348
    Placing controls on the report 350
    Resizing a section 351
    Working with text boxes 352
    Changing label and text-box control properties...............................359
    Growing and shrinking text-box controls..360
    Sorting and grouping data 361
    Sorting data within groups 363
    Adding page breaks..366
Improving the Report's Appearance 367
    Adjusting the page header 368
    Creating an expression in the group header 369
    Enhancing the Detail section 370
    Creating a report header...371
Summary 373

Part II: Programming Microsoft Access   375

Chapter 10: VBA Programming Fundamentals 377

Introducing Visual Basic for Applications..378
Understanding VBA Terminology...379
Starting with VBA Code Basics 380

Contents

Migrating from Macros to VBA...381
    Knowing when to use macros and when to use VBA 382
    Converting your existing macros to VBA 382
    Using the Command Button Wizard 385
Creating VBA Programs...386
    Events and event procedures..387
    Modules 389
Understanding VBA Branching Constructs 401
    Branching..401
    Looping...404
Working with Objects and Collections..406
    An object primer..406
    The With statement..408
    The For Each statement...409
Looking at Access Options for Developers 410
    The Editor tab of the Options dialog box 410
    The Project Properties dialog box 412
    Command-line arguments..414
Summary 416

Chapter 11: Mastering VBA Data Types and Procedures. 417

Introducing the Access VBA Editor 418
Using Variables 421
    Naming variables...422
    Declaring variables 423
Working with Data Types 427
    Comparing implicit and explicit variables 430
    Forcing explicit declaration 431
    Using a naming convention 431
    Understanding variable scope and lifetime 432
Understanding Subs and Functions...435
    Understanding where to create a procedure 436
    Calling VBA procedures 437
    Creating subs 437
Creating Functions...441
    Handling parameters..442
    Calling a function and passing parameters 443
    Creating a function to calculate sales tax 445
Simplifying Code with Named Arguments 447
Summary 449

Chapter 12: The Access Event Model 451

Programming Events...452
    Understanding how events trigger VBA code..452
    Creating event procedures...453

Identifying Common Events 454
    Form event procedures 456
    Control event procedures...459
    Report event procedures..460
    Report section event procedures..462
Paying Attention to Event Sequence 465
    Looking at common event sequences 465
    Writing simple form and control event procedures 466
Summary 471

Chapter 13: Accessing Data with VBA Code 473
Understanding SQL 473
    Viewing SQL statements in queries 474
    A SQL primer 475
Working with Data 485
Understanding ADO Objects..488
    The ADO Connection object 489
    The ADO Command object 492
    The ADO Recordset object 494
Understanding DAO Objects..499
    The DAO DBEngine object 501
    The DAO Workspace object 501
    The DAO Database object 502
    The DAO TableDef object 502
    The DAO QueryDef object 503
    The DAO Recordset object 505
    The DAO Field objects (recordsets)..506
Writing VBA Code to Update a Table...508
    Updating fields in a record using ADO 509
    Updating a calculated control...513
    Adding a new record 517
    Deleting a record...517
    Deleting related records in multiple tables...............................518
Summary 521

Chapter 14: Debugging Your Access Applications 523
Testing Your Applications..524
Using the Module Options...525
    Auto Syntax Check...525
    Require Variable Declaration 527
    Auto List Members 528
    Auto Quick Info 528
    Auto Data Tips 529
    Break on All Errors...529
    Compile on Demand 530

Contents

Organizing VBA Code 530
Compiling VBA Code 532
Traditional Debugging Techniques 534
    Using MsgBox 534
    Using Debug.Print 537
Using the Access Debugging Tools 538
    Running code with the Immediate window 538
    Suspending execution with breakpoints 539
    Looking at variables with the Locals window 544
    Setting watches with the Watches window 545
    Using conditional watches 547
    Using the Call Stack window 548
Summary 549

Chapter 15: Using Access Data Macros. 551
Introducing Data Macros 551
Looking at How Data Macros Are Created 553
    Using the Macro Designer 553
    Using the Action Catalog 557
Discovering Table Events 562
    Before events 562
    After events 564
Building Macros 566
    Adding macro items 566
    Manipulating macro items 569
    Moving macro items 572
    Collapsing macro items 573
    Saving a macro as XML 574
Recognizing the Limitations of Data Macros 575
Summary 576

Part III: More-Advanced Access Techniques   577

Chapter 16: Working with External Data. 579
Looking at How Access Works with External Data 580
    Types of external data 580
    Ways of working with external data 581
Linking External Data 584
    Linking to external database tables 585
    Limitations of linked data 587
    Linking to other Access database tables 588
    Linking to ODBC data sources 590
    Linking to xBase files 591
    Linking to non-database data 591

Working with Linked Tables...597
   Setting view properties..598
   Setting relationships..598
   Optimizing linked tables...598
   Deleting a linked table reference 599
   Viewing or changing information for linked tables......................................599
Using Code to Link Tables in Access..600
   The Connect and SourceTableName properties..600
   Checking links 606
Summary 608

Chapter 17: Importing and Exporting Data 609
Looking at Your Options for Importing and Exporting...609
Importing External Data..611
   Importing from another Access database 611
   Importing from an Excel spreadsheet 614
   Importing a SharePoint list..618
   Importing data from text files..618
   Importing an XML document 623
   Importing an HTML document 627
   Importing Access objects other than tables...628
   Importing an Outlook folder 630
   Importing dBase tables 631
   Troubleshooting import errors 633
Exporting to External Formats 634
   Exporting objects to other Access databases 634
   Exporting through ODBC drivers..635
   Functionality exclusive to exports 636
Summary 636

Chapter 18: Advanced Access Query Techniques. 637
Using Calculated Fields..638
Calculated Fields and the Expression Builder...640
Counting Records in a Table or Query 642
Finding the Top (*n*) Records in a Query..644
How Queries Save Field Selections..646
   Hiding (not showing) fields..647
   Renaming fields in queries 647
Query Design Options 649
Setting Query Properties 651
Creating Queries That Calculate Totals 653
   Showing and hiding the Total row in the QBE pane....................................654
   The Total row options 654
   Performing totals on all records...657
   Performing totals on groups of records...659

Contents

Specifying criteria for a total query...662
Creating expressions for totals...664
Creating Crosstab Queries...666
Understanding the crosstab query...666
Creating the crosstab query...667
Understanding Action Queries..671
Types of action queries...671
Creating action queries...671
Troubleshooting action queries..676
Summary..677

Chapter 19: Advanced Access Form Techniques **679**

Setting Control Properties..679
Customizing default properties..681
Manipulating controls at runtime..682
Reading control properties...685
Working with Subforms..686
Designing Forms..688
Using the Tab Stop property...688
Tallying check boxes..688
Adding animation...688
Using SQL for a faster refresh..690
Selecting data for overtyping...690
Toggling properties with Not...690
Creating an auto-closing form..691
Setting up combo boxes and list boxes.....................................691
Determining whether a form is open...693
Tackling Advanced Forms Techniques...694
Using the Page Number and Date/Time controls.....................694
Using the Image control..695
Morphing a control..695
Using the Format Painter..696
Offering more end-user help..697
Adding background pictures...697
Fine-tuning your form's behavior with form events.................699
Using the Tab Control...700
Using Dialog Boxes to Collect Information.....................................703
Composing the SQL statement...704
Adding a default button..706
Setting a Cancel button...706
Removing the control menu..706
Closing the form...707
Summary..707

Chapter 20: Advanced Access Report Techniques **709**

Grouping and Sorting Data 710
    Grouping data alphabetically 710
    Grouping on date intervals 714
    Hiding repeating information 716
    Hiding a page header 719
    Starting a new page number for each group 719
Formatting Data 720
    Creating numbered lists 720
    Adding bullet characters 723
    Adding emphasis at runtime 725
    Avoiding empty reports 728
    Avoiding null values in a tabular report 728
    Inserting vertical lines between columns 729
    Adding a blank line every *n* records 731
    Even-odd page printing 733
    Using different formats in the same text box 735
    Centering the title 736
    Easily aligning control labels 736
    Micro-adjusting controls 736
Adding Data 737
    Adding more information to a report 737
    Adding the user's name to a bound report 738
Trying More Techniques 739
    Displaying all reports in a combo box 739
    Fast printing from queried data 740
    Hiding forms during Print Preview 741
    Using snaking columns in a report 741
    Exploiting two-pass report processing 747
    Assigning unique names to controls 749
Summary 750

Chapter 21: Building Multiuser Applications **751**

Working on a Network 752
    Network performance 752
    File location 753
    Data sources 754
Considering the Options for Opening a Database 756
Splitting a Database for Network Access 759
    Detailing the benefits of splitting a database 759
    Knowing where to put which objects 761
    Using the Database Splitter add-in 762
Finding the Key to Locking Issues 764
    Access's built-in record-locking features 765
    Record-lock error handling 768

Contents

Reducing Multiuser Errors with Unbound Forms...780
    Creating an unbound form...781
    Making an unbound form work 781
  Summary 788

Chapter 22: Integrating Access with Other Applications 789

Using Automation in Access..790
    Understanding how Automation works..790
    Creating Automation references 791
    Binding your VBA object variables to objects in the Automation interface 792
    Creating an instance of an Automation object 795
    Getting an existing object instance 797
    Working with Automation objects 799
    Closing an instance of an Automation object 800
Looking at an Automation Example Using Word 800
    Creating an instance of a Word object..805
    Making the instance of Word visible 805
    Creating a new document based on an existing template...806
    Inserting data 806
    Activating the instance of Word 806
    Moving the cursor in Word 807
    Discarding the Word object instance 807
    Inserting pictures by using bookmarks..807
    Using Office's macro recorder 808
Collecting Data with Microsoft Outlook..811
    Creating an e-mail 811
    Managing replies 815
  Summary 818

Chapter 23: Handling Errors and Exceptions. 819

Dealing with Errors..820
    Logical errors 820
    Runtime errors 821
Identifying Which Errors Can Be Detected..824
    What an error handler is 824
    How to set a basic error trap 825
Trapping Errors with VBA..826
    The Err object 827
    VBA error-handling statements...829
    The Error event 836
    The ADO Errors collection 837
  Summary 838

Part IV: Professional Database Development   839

Chapter 24: Optimizing Access Applications 841

Understanding Module Load on Demand 841
   Organizing your modules...842
   Pruning the call tree 842
Using the .accdb Database File Format...844
Distributing .accde Files...846
Understanding the Compiled State...848
   Putting your application's code into a compiled state 849
   Losing the compiled state 850
   Distributing applications in a compiled or uncompiled state 851
Improving Absolute Speed 854
   Tuning your system..856
   Getting the most from your tables 856
   Getting the most from your queries 858
   Getting the most from your forms and reports 859
   Getting the most from your modules 862
   Increasing network performance 866
Improving Perceived Speed...867
   Using a splash screen 867
   Loading and keeping forms hidden 868
   Using the hourglass...868
   Using the built-in progress meter 869
   Creating a progress meter as a pop-up form 870
   Speeding up the progress meter display 872
Working with Large Access Databases..872
   Understanding how databases grow in size 873
   Recognizing that compiling and compacting may not be enough 874
   Using the decompile option 876
   Detecting an uncompiled database and automatically recompiling.........................877
   Making small changes to large databases 879
Summary 879

Chapter 25: Advanced Data Access with VBA 881

Adding an Unbound Combo Box to a Form to Find Data 881
   Using the FindRecord method...883
   Using a bookmark..885
Filtering a Form 888
   With code 888
   With a query 889
Summary 895

Contents

Chapter 26: Bulletproofing Access Applications **897**

Introducing Bulletproofing..898
Looking at the Characteristics of Bulletproofed Applications............................898
Identifying the Principles of Bulletproofing...899
    Building to a specification 900
    Becoming one with documentation 902
    Considering your users 903
    Getting the application to the users 905
    Enabling the users to actually use the application...907
    Controlling the flow of information...912
    Keeping the user informed 915
    Tracking down problems 919
    Securing the environment 923
    Protecting your database 927
    Continuing to improve the product...938
Summary 938

Chapter 27: Using the Windows Application Programming Interface . . . **939**

What the Windows API Is..939
Reasons to Use the Windows API...940
    Common code base...941
    Tested and proven code 941
    Cross-platform compatibility...941
    Smaller application footprint 941
    Application consistency...941
DLL Documentation 942
    Finding the documentation 942
    Making sense of the documentation 942
    Recognizing what you can't do with the API...945
How to Use the Windows API...946
    The Declare statement 946
    Wrapper functions 949
API Examples...950
    Retrieving system information...952
    Going over general-purpose Windows API functions 960
    Manipulating application settings with the Windows API...............................962
Summary 967

Chapter 28: Object-Oriented Programming with VBA **969**

Introducing Object-Oriented Programming 970
    Getting to know objects 970
    Defining objects with class modules...972
    Looking at a simple class module 973
    Adding a class module to a database 974

Creating simple product properties 975
Creating methods 976
Using the product object 978
Creating bulletproof property procedures 980
Recognizing the Benefits of Object-Oriented Programming 981
Encapsulating functionality 982
Simplifying programming tasks 982
Managing a class's interface 983
Using Property Procedures 986
Looking at the types of property procedures 986
Exploring property-value persistence 989
Heeding property procedure rules 990
Modifying the Product Class 991
Retrieving product details 992
Looking at the new ProductID property 993
Adding a new property to provide extra information 994
Adding a new method to the product class 995
Learning about Class Events 997
The Class_Initialize event procedure 997
The Class_Terminate event procedure 998
Adding Events to Class Modules 999
Learning about events in Access 1000
Recognizing the need for events 1000
Creating custom events 1001
Raising events 1002
Trapping custom events 1003
Passing data through events 1004
Exploiting Access class module events 1005
Summary 1008

Chapter 29: Customizing Access Ribbons 1009
Why Replace Toolbars and Menus? 1009
New controls for Access ribbons 1013
SplitButton 1013
DropDown 1014
Gallery 1014
SuperTips 1015
Working with the Access Ribbon 1015
Tabs 1016
Groups 1016
Controls 1017
Managing the ribbon 1017
Working with the Quick Access Toolbar 1018
Editing the Default Access Ribbon 1020

Contents

Developing Custom Access Ribbons...1023
 The ribbon creation process 1023
 Using VBA callbacks...1023
The Ribbon Hierarchy...1025
Getting Started with Access Ribbons..1026
 Step 1: Design the ribbon and build the XML......................................1026
 Step 2: Write the callback routines..1027
 Step 3: Create the USysRibbons table 1029
 Step 4: Add XML to USysRibbons 1030
 Step 5: Specify the custom ribbon property..1032
The Basic Ribbon XML..1033
Adding Ribbon Controls..1035
 Specifying imageMso...1035
 The Label control 1037
 The Button control 1038
 Separators 1038
 Check boxes...1039
 The DropDown control..1040
 The SplitButton Control 1041
Using Visual Web Developer...1042
Managing Ribbons 1045
Completely Removing the Access Ribbon...1046
Summary 1047

Chapter 30: Using Access Macros. 1049
An Introduction to Macros..1049
 Creating a macro..1050
 Assigning a macro to an event 1052
Multi-Action Macros 1054
Submacros 1057
Conditions..1061
 Opening reports using conditions 1061
 Multiple actions in conditions 1064
Temporary Variables..1065
 Enhancing a macro you've already created 1065
 Using temporary variables to simplify macros 1066
 Using temporary variables in VBA...1068
Error Handling and Macro Debugging 1069
 The OnError action 1071
 The MacroError object 1073
 Debugging macros..1074
Embedded Macros 1075
Macros versus VBA Statements..1077
 Choosing between macros and VBA 1078
 Converting existing macros to VBA 1078
Summary 1081

Chapter 31: Distributing Access Applications **1083**

Defining the Current Database Options 1084
  Application options 1085
  Navigation options 1089
  Ribbon and toolbar options 1090
  Name AutoCorrect Options 1091
Testing the Application before Distribution 1092
Polishing Your Application 1094
  Giving your application a consistent look and feel 1094
  Adding common professional components 1095
Bulletproofing an Application 1098
  Using error trapping on all Visual Basic procedures 1099
  Separating tables from the rest of the application 1099
  Documenting the application 1100
Summary 1100

Part V: Access and Windows SharePoint Services   1101

Chapter 32: Understanding Windows SharePoint Services **1103**

Introducing SharePoint 1104
Reviewing Various Types of SharePoint Sites 1106
Working with SharePoint Lists 1107
Looking at a SharePoint Web Site 1108
  Editing SharePoint list items 1110
  Creating SharePoint lists 1112
Summary 1115

Chapter 33: Integrating Access with SharePoint **1117**

Introducing SharePoint as a Data Source 1118
Sharing Access Data with SharePoint 1119
  Linking to SharePoint lists 1119
  Exporting Access tables to SharePoint 1123
  Moving Access tables to SharePoint 1127
Using SharePoint Templates 1131
Summary 1134

Chapter 34: Understanding Access Services **1135**

Explaining Managed Applications 1136
Looking at Web Publishing in Access 1137
  Why SharePoint? 1137
  Leveraging SharePoint features 1137
  Publishing Access applications to SharePoint 1138
Understanding Access Services 1140

Contents

Examining Access Web Application Limits 1141

Not public-facing 1141

Fewer than 20,000 rows of data 1143

Modest transactional requirements 1143

Summary 1144

Chapter 35: Deploying Access Applications to SharePoint 1145

Looking at SharePoint Deployment Options 1146

Enhanced table exporting option 1146

Publishing to SharePoint option 1156

Dealing with Compatibility Checker Problems 1174

General errors 1174

Relationship and lookup errors 1174

Form and report errors 1175

Query errors 1176

Macro errors 1177

Schema errors 1178

Summary 1179

Part VI: Access as an Enterprise Platform   1181

Chapter 36: Client/Server Concepts 1183

Looking at the Parts of Client/Server Architecture 1184

Applications 1186

The back office 1187

Making Sense of Multi-Tier Architecture 1192

Two-tier systems 1193

Three-tier systems 1193

Putting It All Together: Access, Client-Server, and Multiple Tiers 1194

Access as a database repository 1195

Access as an Internet database 1197

Summary 1197

Chapter 37: SQL Server as an Access Companion 1199

Connecting to SQL Server 1201

Introducing connection strings 1201

Connecting to SQL Server from Access 1203

Working with SQL Server Objects 1214

Using SQL Server tables from Access 1215

Views 1217

Stored procedures 1219

Triggers 1221

Summary 1221

Contents

Chapter 38: Upsizing Access Databases to SQL Server **1223**

Introducing SQL Server Express 1224

Upsizing Access and the Upsizing Wizard..1225

    Before upsizing an application...1226

    Running the Upsizing Wizard 1227

    Working with an Access ADP file 1233

    Comparing Access to SQL Server data types...1235

Summary 1240

Part VII: Appendixes   1243

Appendix A: Access 2010 Specifications **1245**

Microsoft Access Database Specifications 1247

Microsoft SQL Server Express Specifications 1249

Appendix B: What's New in Access 2010 . . . . **1253**

The User Interface...1253

Publish Access to the Web 1258

Tables 1258

Datasheet View 1259

Forms 1261

Reports 1263

Macros 1263

Security 1265

SharePoint 1265

Summary 1266

Appendix C: What's on the CD-ROM **1267**

System Requirements..1267

Using the CD 1268

What's on the CD 1268

    Example files..1268

    eBook version of Access 2010 Bible..1269

Troubleshooting...1269

Index **1271**

Acknowledgments

When I first saw Access in July 1992, I was instantly sold on this new-generation database management and access tool. I've spent the last 15 years using Access virtually every day. In fact, I eat, breathe, live, and sleep Access!

The fact that it's possible to earn a living working principally with a single product is a tribute to the Microsoft Access designers. This product has changed the productivity of corporations and private citizens of the world. More people use this product to run their businesses, manage their affairs, track the most important things in their lives, and manage data in their work and play than any other product ever written. It is a privilege to be part of this worldwide community.

The *Microsoft Office Access 2010 Bible* has been completely rewritten for Access 2010, with many new examples and more in-depth coverage. I've covered every new feature I could think of for the beginning and intermediate users and especially enhanced the programming section. Over 500,000 copies of *Access Bibles* have been sold for all versions of Microsoft Access; for this, I thank all those loyal readers.

My first acknowledgment is to all the users of Access who have profited and benefited beyond everyone's wildest dreams.

There are many people who assisted me in writing this book; I'd like to recognize each of them.

To Katie Mohr, Jodi Jensen, Tiffany Ma, and the editorial and administrative staff at Wiley. Thanks for the opportunity to work on this book!

A very big thanks to Doug Steele for his excellent technical editing of the *Access 2010 Bible*. Doug is a highly regarded member of the Access community and has been recognized by Microsoft as an MVP as far back as I can remember. Doug and I go way back to the days when every version of Access was a new game, and I am honored to have Doug onboard as technical editor. Doug's long, long experience with Access shows on every single page of this book. He let me get away with nothing — he caught problems in examples that I've used many, many times as an Access instructor for AppDev (Application Developer's Training Company) and presenter at the Advisor conferences. Doug's well-known sense of humor never left him as he labored over the chapters in this book, and I learned a lot from his suggestions and guidance.

I can never thank enough Elizabeth Kuball, my sorely neglected project editor on both the *Access 2007 Bible* and now the *Access 2010 Bible*. Elizabeth made countless corrections to my prose, catching hundreds of misspellings and grammatical errors, and suggesting better ways to convey complex concepts. Elizabeth did her level best to keep me on schedule, and made sure deadlines did not slip any more than humanly possible. Elizabeth never seems to sleep, and even though we are

Acknowledgments

separated by three time zones, she responded to my e-mails within minutes every time. This book is much, much better for her hard work and diligence.

To Carole McClendon, the very best literary agent in the business, and all the folks at Waterside Productions for being my agent.

Thanks also to Rob Tidrow. Years ago, Rob and I worked together at New Riders Publishing in Indianapolis, and it was he who recommended me as the lead author of the *Access Bible*. Thanks, Rob!

A special thank-you to Clint Covington, Kerry Westphal, Steve Greenberg, Greg Lindhorst, Ryan McMinn, Suraj Poozhiyill, Russell Sinclair, Wouter Steenbergen, Chris Downs, Eran Megiddo, and the rest of the Microsoft Access 2010 team! You've built a terrific product, and I thank you! Thank you for your irreplaceable help getting this book done on time.

As an Access developer, I strongly suggest you visit the Access Team Blog (`http://blogs.msdn.com/access/`) every few days. The Access development team frequently updates this site with white papers, articles, and news on what's happening with Microsoft Access. All too often, we think of Microsoft as a huge, faceless corporation that doesn't listen to user feedback, but I promise you that the Access team really, really wants to hear from you. The Access Team Blog is not a marketing Web site; instead, it is a gathering place for Access enthusiasts and supports a strong peer-to-peer exchange between Access developers in the field (that's you!) and the people who actually write the specifications and code for each new version of Microsoft Access. I've met the Access team members on many occasions, and I'm always impressed with their dedication and desire to learn more about how people use Microsoft Access.

Thanks to these wonderful people, I'm able to deliver a quality book to my readers.

Finally, I dedicate this book to Pam. You are the one. *Vos es panton volo.*

—Mike Groh

Introduction

Welcome to the *Microsoft Access 2010 Bible,* your personal guide to a powerful, easy-to-use database-management system. This book is in its eleventh revision and has been totally rewritten for Microsoft Access 2010 with new text, new pictures, and a completely new and improved set of example files.

This book examines Access 2010 with more examples than any other Access 2010 book. I strongly believe that Microsoft Access is an excellent database manager and the best desktop and workgroup database-development system available today. My goal with this book is to share what I know about Access and, in the process, help make your work and your life easier.

This book contains everything you need in order to learn Microsoft Access to a mid-advanced level. The book starts off with database basics and builds, chapter by chapter, on topics previously covered. In places where it's essential that you understand previously covered topics, I present the concepts again and review how to perform specific tasks before moving on. Although each chapter is an integral part of the book as a whole, each chapter can also stand on its own and has its own example files. You can read the book in any order you want, skipping from chapter to chapter and from topic to topic. (Note that this book's index is particularly thorough; you can refer to the index to find the location of a particular topic you're interested in.)

The examples in this book have been well thought out to simulate the types of tables, queries, forms, and reports most people need to create when performing common business activities. There are many notes, tips, and techniques (and even a few secrets) to help you better understand Microsoft Access.

This book easily substitutes for the online help included with Access. It guides you through each task you need to perform with Access, and it follows a much more structured approach than the Microsoft Access online help, going into more depth on almost every topic and showing many different types of examples. You'll also find much more detail than in most other books on Microsoft Access.

Is This Book for You?

I wrote this book for beginning, intermediate, and even advanced users of Microsoft Access 2010. With any product, most users start at the beginning. If you're already familiar with Microsoft Access and comfortable building Access applications, you may want to start with the later parts of this book. Of course, starting at the beginning of a book is usually a good idea so you don't miss out on the secrets and tips in the early chapters.

I believe that this book covers Microsoft Access 2010 in detail better than any other book currently on the market. I hope you'll find this book helpful while working with Access and that you enjoy the innovative style of a Wiley book.

Yes — If you have no database experience

If you're new to the world of database management, this book has everything you need to get started with Microsoft Access 2010. It also offers advanced topics for reference and learning. Beginning developers should pay particular attention to Part I, where I cover the essential skills necessary for building successful and efficient databases. Your ability as a database designer is constantly judged by how well the applications you build perform, and how well they handle data entrusted to them by their users. The chapters in Part I won't necessarily make you an expert database designer, but I guarantee that you'll be a better developer if you carefully read this material.

Yes — If you've used other database managers like FileMaker

If you've been working with another database system (such as FileMaker, Paradox, or FoxPro) or you're upgrading from an earlier version of Access, this book is for you. You'll have a head start because you're already familiar with database managers and how to use them. With Microsoft Access, you will be able to do all the tasks you've performed with other database systems — without programming or getting lost. This book takes you through every subject step by step.

Yes — If you want to learn the basics of Visual Basic for Applications (VBA) programming

I understand that a very large book is needed to properly cover the VBA programming language, but I took the time to put together many chapters that build on what you learn in the forms chapters (primarily Chapters 7, 8, and 19) of this book. The VBA programming chapters use the same examples you'll be familiar with by the end of the book. Part II of this book explains the nuts and bolts, with a lot of gritty technical details, of writing VBA procedures and building Access applications around the code you add to your databases. Part II provides everything you need (other than a lot of practice!) to become a bona fide VBA programmer.

Yes — If you are an Access 2007 developer

Access 2007 and 2010 have much in common. For the most part, the user interfaces are the same, with most of the differences in the arrangement of controls in the ribbon and the addition of the Backstage in Access 2010. With the exception of the chapters on data macros (Chapter 15) and publishing Access applications to SharePoint (Chapters 34 and 35), the material in this book should run as described in Access 2007.

That said, Microsoft has made some changes in the format of the `.accdb` data file. You may have some difficulty opening some of this book's example databases in Access 2007. This does not mean that the file is necessarily corrupted — it just means that Access 2007 is unable to work with the additional objects (such as data macros) that may be present in an Access 2010 database file.

However, all the other chapters on database design, queries, forms, reports, VBA programming, optimization, and so on, are equally applicable to Access 2007 and 2010 application development.

Pardon My Dust!

It almost goes without saying that this book was written during the Access 2010 beta testing phase, months before the release of Office 2010. It's possible that a few of the figures in this book don't exactly match what you see when you open Access 2010, or that the terminology will have changed from the time I wrote the book to the time you install Access 2010 on your computer. Please bear with me. Microsoft has done a great job of documenting its plans and expectations for Access 2010 and, as an author, I've done my best to explain the many changes in Access 2010. I hope that any differences you encounter between my descriptions and explanations and your experience with Access 2010 are minor and don't impact your workflow.

Please feel free to drop me an email at `AccessBible@mikegroh.com` if you have a question or comment about the material in the *Microsoft Access 2010 Bible*. Also, contact me if you have a more general question about development with Access or SQL Server, and I'll try to help you out. Please be sure to prefix the subject line of your e-mail with "Access Bible" to get past the spam blocker on this account.

Several of the chapter folders on the book's CD include a `readme` file. Please be sure to check the contents of this file because it contains information that became available after the book was sent for publication or helps explain how to use the example in the chapter's folder.

Conventions Used in This Book

I use the following conventions in this book:

- When you're instructed to press a key combination (press and hold down one key while pressing another key), the key combination is separated by a plus sign. Ctrl+Esc, for example, indicates that you must hold down the Ctrl key and press the Esc key; then release both keys.

- *Point the mouse* refers to moving the mouse so that the mouse pointer is on a specific item. *Click* refers to pressing the left mouse button once and releasing it. *Double-click* refers to pressing the left mouse button twice in rapid succession and then releasing it. *Right-click* refers to pressing the right mouse button once and releasing it. *Drag* refers to pressing and holding down the left mouse button while moving the mouse.

- I use *italics* for new terms and for emphasis.

- I use **bold** for material that you need to type directly into the computer.

- I use monofont for information you see on-screen — error messages, expressions, and formulas, for example.

Icons and Alerts

You'll notice special graphic symbols, or icons, used in the margins throughout this book. These icons are intended to alert you to points that are particularly important or noteworthy. I use the following icons in this book:

Note
This icon highlights a special point of interest about the topic under discussion.

Tip
This icon points to a useful hint that may save you time or trouble.

Caution
This icon alerts you that the operation being described can cause problems if you're not careful.

Cross-Reference
This icon points to a more complete discussion in another chapter of the book.

On the CD-ROM
This icon highlights information for readers who are following the examples and using the sample files included on the disc accompanying this book.

New Feature
This icon calls attention to new features of Access 2010.

Sidebars

Throughout this book, you'll notice material placed in gray boxes. This material offers background information, an expanded discussion, or a deeper insight about the topic under discussion. Some sidebars offer nuts-and-bolts technical explanations, and others provide useful anecdotal material.

How This Book Is Organized

This book contains 38 chapters and three appendixes, divided into seven parts.

Part I: Access Building Blocks

Part I consists of nine chapters that cover virtually every aspect of Access development. For many Access developers, these chapters are all that you'll ever need. The chapters in this part cover basic database design, referential integrity, constructing tables and queries, building forms and reports, and using the new features in Access 2010.

Chapters 1 through 3 contains great conceptual material on understanding the basic elements of data, introduces you to the keywords of database management, and teaches you how to plan tables and work with Access data types. Chapter 4 through 6 teaches you Access queries, expressions, and working with Datasheet view. Much has changed in Access 2007 and 2010, and even experienced Access users are easily confused by the new user interface.

Chapters 7 through 9 take you on a tour of various types of forms and give you a complete understanding of form controls. These chapters drill into the process of creating great-looking and effective forms and reports. You'll learn how to take best advantage of the new features in Access 2010.

Part II: Programming Microsoft Access

Virtually every serious Access application uses VBA code to perform operations not possible with macros, or to make using the application easier and more reliable. Learning VBA programming is often a daunting task, so the six chapters in this part take extra care to explain the principles behind VBA programming, and show you how to take advantage of this powerful programming language.

In these chapters, you'll learn not only the fundamental skills required to become proficient in VBA, but also many "insider" tricks and techniques to apply to your Access application development projects. You'll come to understand and appreciate the complex object and event models that drive Access applications, and how to construct the VBA code necessary to take advantage of this rich programming environment.

Part III: More-Advanced Access Techniques

After you've gotten through the basics of building Access applications, you'll want your database development skills to extend and enhance your Access applications. Part III is made up of eight chapters that cover virtually every aspect of advanced Access development, including importing and exporting data, exchanging data with other Windows applications, and handling application errors and exceptions.

The techniques in Part III would normally take most Access developers several years to master. I've carefully selected a potpourri of techniques that have proven valuable to me in the relevant development efforts. Each chapter is accompanied by an example database that demonstrates the techniques documented in the chapter.

Part IV: Professional Database Development

Over the years, Access has grown in its features and capabilities. Although most Access developers never have to use the techniques and features documented in Part IV, I've included these techniques to make the *Microsoft Access 2010 Bible* the most comprehensive reference possible.

Part IV includes eight chapters covering a wide range of professional-level Access techniques. In these chapters, you'll read about advanced features such as object-oriented programming in Access, using the Windows API, and customizing the Access 2010 ribbons. Much of the information in Part IV has been added for this edition of the *Microsoft Access Bible,* and reflects the growth and expansion of Access's capabilities.

Part V: Access and Windows SharePoint Services

Microsoft has made a huge investment in Windows SharePoint Services. SharePoint is Microsoft's premier collaborative computing system and is widely used in small and large companies as a data and information sharing platform.

Integration with SharePoint has grown over the last few versions of Microsoft Access. Versions prior to Access 2007 could display, but not edit, SharePoint data. Access 2007 introduced edit capabilities to its relationship with SharePoint, greatly enhancing Access's stature as a front end to SharePoint data.

With Access 2010, Microsoft has extended SharePoint integration capabilities to include publishing Access tables, forms, and reports on SharePoint sites. Although somewhat limited when compared to strictly Access applications, publishing Access objects to the SharePoint platform provides a powerful way of sharing Access data with remote users.

Part VI: Access as an Enterprise Platform

Access is often employed in "enterprise" environments as a front end to data stored in a variety of server database systems, such as Microsoft SQL Server and Oracle. The three chapters in Part V cover a variety of topics that are of interest to developers working in enterprise environments, particularly those using SQL Server as a database engine. In these chapters, you'll learn the fundamental technologies behind SQL Server and how Access integrates with server databases hosted in Microsoft SQL Server.

You'll also learn how to upsize Access applications to SQL Server. Access 2010 seamlessly integrates with SQL Server, either as a simple consumer of SQL Server data or as a direct interface to a SQL Server database. The chapters in Part VI cover this important technology in detail.

Part VII: Appendixes

The last part contains three appendixes. Appendix A documents the Access 2010 specifications, including maximum and minimum sizes of databases and many of the controls in Access. Appendix B briefs you on what's new with Access 2010. Appendix C describes the contents of this book's CD-ROM.

Guide to the Examples

The examples in the *Microsoft Access 2010 Bible* are specially designed to maximize your learning experience. Throughout this book, you'll see many examples of good business table design and implementation, form and report creation, and module coding in Visual Basic. You'll see examples that use both Jet and ACE (the database engines built into Microsoft Access 2007 and 2010), as well as examples that connect to SQL Server databases. You'll also see forms that work with SharePoint data located in remote locations on intranets and the Internet.

As every developer knows, it's important to understand what you're creating and programming from the application standpoint. In this book, I've chosen a simple example that I hope any business or developer can relate to. More important, in this or any book you must relate to it successfully in order to learn. When developing systems, you often find yourself analyzing applications that you don't have a lot of experience with. In a book such as the *Microsoft Access 2010 Bible*, it helps to have a relatively simple database that illustrates database design and implementation principles.

Many of the examples in this book use a fictitious company named Collectible Mini Cars (CMC). Collectible Mini Cars sells model cars, trucks, and other vehicles to retailers and consumers. The example database contains the necessary tables, queries, forms, reports, and module code to facilitate CMC's business needs.

Not every example described in this book's chapters is taken from the Collectible Mini Cars database. I used whatever example I had or could devise that best illustrates the concepts presented in each chapter. As with real-life database development, this book uses a number of different database designs, each with an important message for Access developers.

Note

Within this guide I use some terms that haven't been thoroughly explained yet. Feel free to skip over them and return to this guide often as you start new chapters that use these forms and reports.

Tip

Although professional developers will always split program and data objects into two separate database files, it's a common development practice to combine all the objects into one database and split them when development is nearing completion. When you're working in a front-end database and you're linked to your data file, you must load the back-end database file before you can make changes to the table design. You'll learn more about this in several places in this book.

The main Switchboard menu

When you load the completed example file (`CollectibleMiniCars.accdb`), you'll see the main Switchboard menu shown in Figure FM.1. This Switchboard contains buttons that display the main areas of the system.

The Collectible Mini Cars main Switchboard menu, which allows users to open various forms and reports

These main areas include

- **Products:** All the products sold by Collectible Mini Cars. The models are separated by category (cars, trucks, motorcycles, and so on), and include a description, make, model year, and other details, such as the color and model scales (1:24, 1:32, and so on).

- **Sales:** This button displays an Invoice form that lets CMC enter sales information. The Sales table (`tblSales`) allows for an unlimited number of line items on an invoice, and each item is selected from information stored in the Products table.

- **Reports:** Any good application contains a number of reports. This button opens a second form showing all the reports available in the CMC database.

Data tables

Data is the most important part of any system and in Access (as well as every other database-management system), data is arranged into data structures known as *tables*. Tables help define the arrangement of the data, as well as hold the data itself. Tables are related to each other in order to pass data back and forth and to help assemble the chaos of data into well-defined and well-formatted information.

The diagram in Figure FM.2 displays the table schema in the Collectible Mini Cars example. As you'll learn in Part I of this book, the lines, arrows, and symbols between the tables mean something important and communicate to the developer how the data interacts. You'll learn terms like *table, field, record, relationship, referential integrity, normalization, primary keys,* and *foreign keys* as you begin to understand how tables work within a database.

FIGURE FM.2

The Collectible Mini Cars relationship diagram

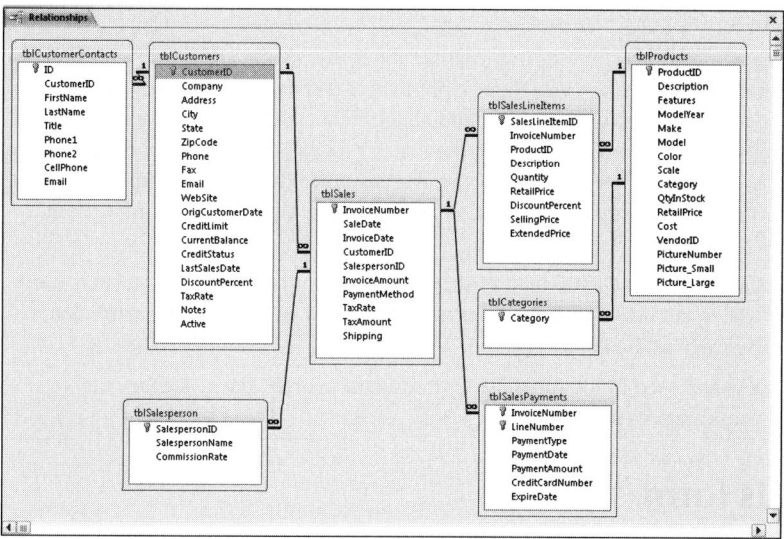

The example database consists of the eight core tables shown in Figure FM.2. Many of the smaller tables are *lookup tables,* the sole purpose of which is to provide a list of valid selections. The larger tables hold data used by the database application itself. All these tables include a number of data fields that are used as the definitions of the data. The lines between the tables show how tables are related:

- **tblSales** contains the primary sales information, including the sale date, the invoice number, the buyer ID (which links to **tblContacts** to retrieve information about the buyer), and various other financial information.

- **tblSalesLineItems** contains fields for the individual line items that make up a sale. A sale may contain a variety of items. Several products may be sold to a single buyer at one time, or a shipment may be sent to an alternate address. The sales form (**frmSales**) provides data entry of an invoice and an unlimited number of line items stored in this table.

  The data fields in **tblSalesLineItems** include the invoice number, which links the invoice to the line items as well as the quantity purchased. The **ProductID** field (which links to **tblProducts**) is used to retrieve product information, including the item description, list price, and wholesale cost.

Cross-Reference

You learn more about relational database theory and how to build tables in Part I of this book

- **tblSalesPayments** contains fields for the individual payment lines. The invoice may be paid for by a variety of methods. The customer may make a deposit for the sale with a check, and then split the remaining amount owed with a variety of credit cards. By having unlimited payment lines in the Invoice form you can do this.

  The data fields in tblSalesPayments include the invoice number that's used to link to tblSales. There is also a field for the payment type to allow the entry of the payment type (credit card, cash, and so on).

- **tblCustomerContacts** contains information about the people and companies that do business with Collectible Mini Cars. Names, physical and shipping addresses, phone and fax numbers, e-mail addresses, Web sites, and all the financial information are stored in this table. Unlike tblSalesLineItems, the contact data is linked from an Invoice form and is not copied to any other table. This way, if a customer changes her address or phone number, any invoice that is related to the contact data instantly shows the updated information.

- **tblProducts** is one of the main tables used in this book. The Products form is used to teach nearly all form development lessons in the book so you should pay particular attention to its design and construction.

- **tblCategories** is used to lookup a list of product categories. Each category includes the category name and description.

The Products form

frmProducts, shown in Figure FM.3, illustrates one approach for building Access forms. It's also one of the forms used most frequently through the book. The Products form was developed with many of the Microsoft Access form control types that handle data types such as text, currency, date, yes/no, memo, and OLE pictures.

You need a good understanding of the use of the form as well as the technical details of how it's built. The form contains information about each product and is bound (tied to) tblProducts. As you enter information into frmProducts, it's stored in the tblProducts table.

The top of frmProducts contains a control that allows you to quickly find a record. This Quick Find is programmed using VBA code behind a combo box selection. The bottom of the form contains a series of command buttons demonstrating how to create new records, delete existing records, and display Search and Print dialog boxes.

FIGURE FM.3

The Collectible Mini Cars Products form, which allows data entry for all products in inventory

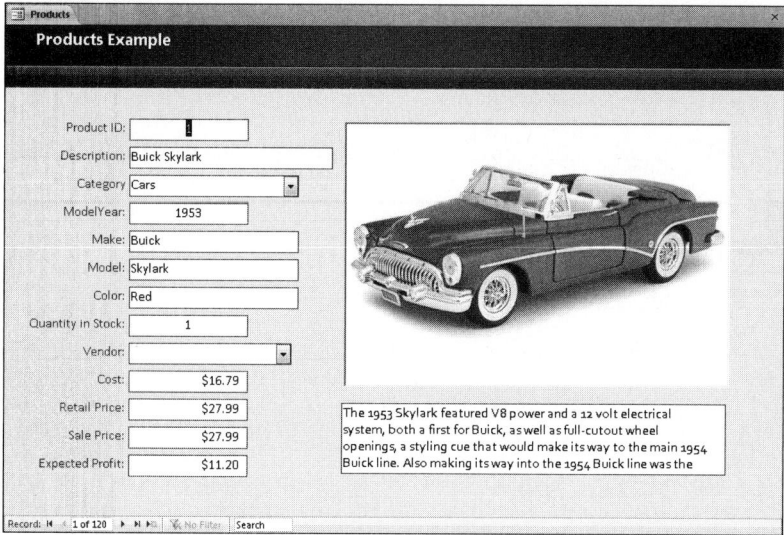

The Invoice form

frmInvoice, shown in Figure FM.4, demonstrates some more-advanced form concepts. Unlike the other forms, the Invoice form contains a subform that uses a *one-to-many relationship* to join to data on the main form; this means that there may be one or more records in the subform related to the record displayed on the main form. In this example, an invoice sells one or more products to a buyer.

This form also demonstrates calculations on the form. All the items in the Amount column have to be totaled to yield the subtotal. All this is happening using fields in the Invoice Line Items (fsub-SalesLineItems) subform.

The Invoice form also shows several other important techniques, including displaying values from other forms. Each line item and payment can be deleted using a button. The bottom of the invoice form contains buttons to create a new record a fill in any defaults, as well as to delete an unneeded invoice and to display Search and Print dialog boxes.

Introduction

The Collectible Mini Cars Invoice form used to show multiple linked subforms and totals

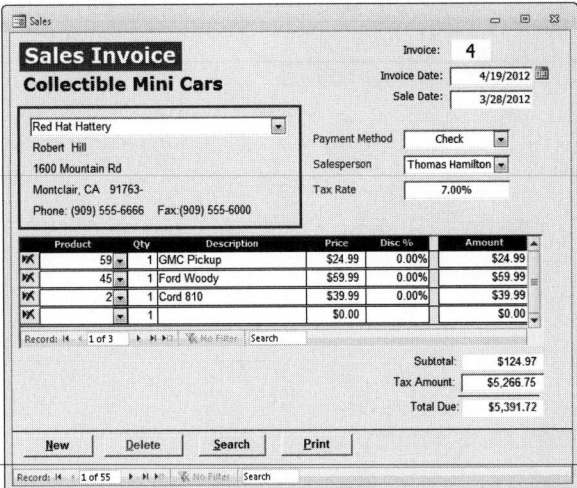

Part I

Access Building Blocks

Each part of this book builds on previous parts, and the chapters in each part contain examples that draw on techniques explained in previous parts and chapters. As a developer, your applications will benefit from the skills you acquire by reading the chapters and practicing the examples contained in this book.

But everyone has to start somewhere when approaching a new discipline, and Part I of this book presents the essential skills necessary for anyone to succeed at database development with Microsoft Access. The topics covered in this part explain the skills and techniques that are necessary to successfully use the Microsoft Access capabilities documented in the remaining parts of this book.

The chapters in this part provide the information that you'll need to build strong Microsoft Access applications. These chapters go well beyond simply describing how to build tables, forms, and reports with Access. They give you the skills necessary to normalize data and plan and implement effective tables. Primary among these essential skills is choosing the data types for the fields in your tables and providing strong, descriptive names for these important database objects. You'll also examine the steps necessary to properly create relationships between tables and specify the characteristics that govern those relationships.

IN THIS PART

Chapter 1
An Introduction to Database Development

Chapter 2
Creating Access Tables

Chapter 3
Designing Bulletproof Databases

Chapter 4
Selecting Data with Queries

Chapter 5
Using Operators and Expressions in Access

Chapter 6
Working with Datasheet View

Chapter 7
Creating Basic Access Forms

Chapter 8
Working with Data on Access Forms

Chapter 9
Presenting Data with Access Reports

An Introduction to Database Development

In this chapter, you learn the concepts and terminology of databases and how to design the tables that your Access application's forms and reports will use.

Database development is quite unlike most other ways you work with computers. Unlike Microsoft Word or Excel, where the approach to working with the application is easy to understand, good database development requires prior knowledge. A beginning user opening Access for the first time likely has no idea where to start. Although the opening user interface helps you create your first database, from that point on, you're pretty much on your own. Unlike Word or Excel, you can't just start typing things in at the keyboard and see any results.

The fundamental concept underlying Access databases is that data is stored in *tables*. Tables are comprised of rows and columns of data, much like an Excel worksheet. In a properly designed database, each table represents a single entity, such as a person or product. Each row within a table describes a single instance of the entity, such as one person or an individual product. Each column in an Access table contains a single type of data, such as text or date/time.

As you work with Access, you'll spend considerable time designing and refining the tables in your Access applications. Table design and implementation are two processes that distinguish database development from most other computer activities you may pursue. Unlike a word processor, where you can dive right in and start typing words and sentences, building a database table requires some prior knowledge of how databases work.

IN THIS CHAPTER

Examining the differences between databases, tables, records, fields, and values

Discovering why multiple tables are used in a database

Creating Access database objects

Designing a database system

On the CD-ROM

All the examples presented in this chapter can be found in the sample database `CollectibleMiniCars`. `accdb` on this book's CD-ROM. If you haven't yet copied this database to your hard drive, please do so now.

After you understand the basic concepts and terminology, the next important lesson to learn is good database design. Without a good design, you may have to constantly rework your tables, queries will be difficult to write, and you may not be able to extract the information you want from your database. Throughout this book, you learn how to use the basic components of Access applications, including queries, forms, and reports. You also learn how to design and implement each of these objects. Although the Collectible Mini Cars case study provides invented examples, the concepts illustrated by this simple application are not fictitious.

Some of this chapter's concepts are somewhat complex, especially to people new to Access or database development.

Cross-Reference

If your goal is to get right into Access, you might want to skip to Chapter 2 and read about building tables. If you're fairly familiar with Access but new to designing and creating tables, read the current chapter before starting to create tables.

The Database Terminology of Access

Before examining the table examples in this book, it's a good idea to have a firm understanding of the terminology used when working with databases — especially Access databases. Microsoft Access follows most, but not all, traditional database terminology. The terms *database, table, record, field,* and *value* indicate a hierarchy from largest to smallest. These same terms are used with virtually all database systems, so you should learn them well.

Databases

Generally, the word *database* is a computer term for a collection of information concerning a certain topic or business application. Databases help you organize this related information in a logical fashion for easy access and retrieval. Some older database systems used the term *database* to describe individual tables. Current use of *database* applies to all elements of a database system.

Databases aren't only for computers. There are also manual databases; we sometimes refer to these as *manual filing systems* or *manual database systems*. These filing systems usually consist of people, papers, folders, and filing cabinets — paper is the key to a manual database system. In a real manual database system, you probably have in/out baskets and some type of formal filing method. You access information manually by opening a file cabinet, taking out a file folder, and finding the correct piece of paper. Users fill out paper forms for input, perhaps by using a keyboard to input information that is printed on forms. You find information by manually sorting the papers or by copying information from many papers to another piece of paper (or even into an Excel spreadsheet). You may use a spreadsheet or calculator to analyze the data or display it in new and interesting ways.

An Access database is nothing more than an automated version of the filing and retrieval functions of a paper filing system. Access databases store information in a carefully defined structure. Access tables store a variety of different kinds of data, from simple lines of text (such as name and address) to complex data such as pictures, sounds, or video images. Storing data in a precise format enables a database management system (DBMS) like Access to turn data into useful information.

Tables serve as the primary data repository in an Access database. Queries, forms, and reports provide access to the data, enabling a user to add or extract data, and presenting the data in useful ways. Most developers add macros or Visual Basic for Applications (VBA) code to forms and reports to make their Access applications easier to use.

A relational database management system (RDBMS), such as Access, stores data in *related* tables. For example, a table containing employee data (names and addresses) may be related to a table containing payroll information (pay date, pay amount, and check number). *Queries* allow the user to ask complex questions (such as "What is the sum of all paychecks issued to Jane Doe in 2012?") from these related tables, with the answers displayed as onscreen forms and printed reports.

In fact, one of the fundamental differences between a relational database and a manual filing system is that, in a relational database system, data for a single individual person or item may be stored in separate tables. For example, in a patient management system, the patient's name, address, and other contact information is likely to be stored in a different table than the table holding patient treatments. In fact, the treatment table holds all treatment information for all patients, and a patient identifier (usually a number) is used to look up an individual patient's treatments in the treatment table.

In Access, a *database* is the overall container for the data and associated objects. It's more than the collection of tables, however — a database includes many types of objects, including queries, forms, reports, macros, and code modules.

Access works a single database at a time. As you open an Access database, the objects (tables, queries, and so on) in the database are presented for you to work with. You may open several copies of Access at the same time and simultaneously work with more than one database, if needed.

Many Access databases contain hundreds, or even thousands, of tables, forms, queries, reports, macros, and modules. With a few exceptions, all the objects in an Access database reside within a single file with an extension of .accdb, .accde, or .adp.

Cross-Reference

The .adp file format is a special database format used by Access to act as a front end to work with SQL Server data. Chapter 37 covers Access Data Projects in detail.

Tables

A table is just a container for raw information (called *data*), similar to a folder in a manual filing system. Each table in an Access database contains information about a single entity, such as a person or product, and the data in the table is organized into rows and columns.

Figure 1.1 shows the Products table from the Collectible Mini Cars database application. The Products table is typical of the tables found in Access applications. Each row defines a single product. In Figure 1.1, the row containing information on the die-cast model of a 2003 Volkswagen Beetle is selected.

FIGURE 1.1

The Collectible Mini Cars products table

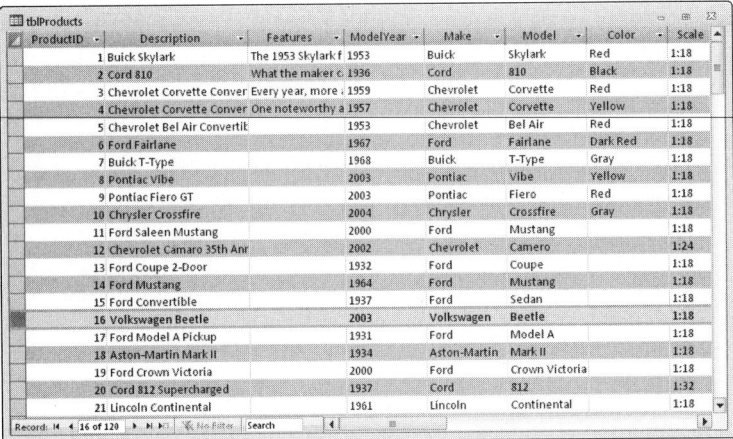

In the "A Five-Step Design Method" section, later in this chapter, I show you a successful technique for planning Access tables.

Cross-Reference

In Chapters 2 and 3, you learn the very important rules governing relational table design and how to incorporate those rules into your Access databases. These rules and guidelines ensure your applications perform with the very best performance while protecting the integrity of the data contained within your tables.

In fact, it's very important that you begin to think of the objects managed by your applications in abstract terms. Because each Access table defines an entity, you have to learn to think of the table *as* the entity. As you design and build Access databases, or even when working with an existing application, you must think of how the tables and other database objects represent the physical entities managed by your database and how the entities relate to one another.

After you create a table, you view the table in a spreadsheet-like form, called a *datasheet*, comprising rows and columns (known as *records* and *fields*, respectively — see the following section, "Records and fields"). Figure 1.2 shows the Datasheet view of the customers table in the Collectible Mini Cars application. Although a datasheet and a spreadsheet are superficially similar, a datasheet is a very different type of object. Chapter 6 discusses Access datasheets, and the differences between datasheets and spreadsheets are explained in detail.

FIGURE 1.2

A table displayed as a datasheet

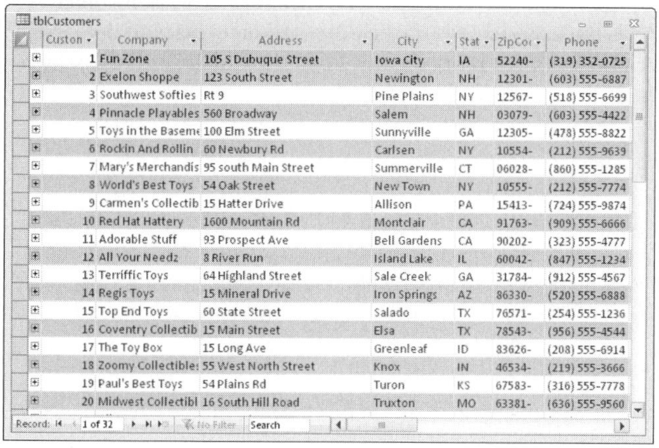

tblCustomers

Custon	Company	Address	City	Stat	ZipCo	Phone
1	Fun Zone	105 S Dubuque Street	Iowa City	IA	52240-	(319) 352-0725
2	Exelon Shoppe	123 South Street	Newington	NH	12301-	(603) 555-6887
3	Southwest Softies	Rt 9	Pine Plains	NY	12567-	(518) 555-6699
4	Pinnacle Playables	560 Broadway	Salem	NH	03079-	(603) 555-4422
5	Toys in the Baseme	100 Elm Street	Sunnyville	GA	12305-	(478) 555-8822
6	Rockin And Rollin	60 Newbury Rd	Carlsen	NY	10554-	(212) 555-9639
7	Mary's Merchandis	95 south Main Street	Summerville	CT	06028-	(860) 555-1285
8	World's Best Toys	54 Oak Street	New Town	NY	10555-	(212) 555-7774
9	Carmen's Collectib	15 Hatter Drive	Allison	PA	15413-	(724) 555-9874
10	Red Hat Hattery	1600 Mountain Rd	Montclair	CA	91763-	(909) 555-6666
11	Adorable Stuff	93 Prospect Ave	Bell Gardens	CA	90202-	(323) 555-4777
12	All Your Needz	8 River Run	Island Lake	IL	60042-	(847) 555-1234
13	Terriffic Toys	64 Highland Street	Sale Creek	GA	31784-	(912) 555-4567
14	Regis Toys	15 Mineral Drive	Iron Springs	AZ	86330-	(520) 555-6888
15	Top End Toys	60 State Street	Salado	TX	76571-	(254) 555-1236
16	Coventry Collectib	15 Main Street	Elsa	TX	78543-	(956) 555-4544
17	The Toy Box	15 Long Ave	Greenleaf	ID	83626-	(208) 555-6914
18	Zoomy Collectible:	55 West North Street	Knox	IN	46534-	(219) 555-3666
19	Paul's Best Toys	54 Plains Rd	Turon	KS	67583-	(316) 555-7778
20	Midwest Collectibl	16 South Hill Road	Truxton	MO	63381-	(636) 555-9560

Record: 1 of 32 No Filter Search

The customers table represents people who work with Collectible Mini Cars. Notice how the table is divided into horizontal (left-to-right) rows, and vertical (top-to-bottom) columns of data. Each row (or *record*) defines a single customer, while each column (or *field*) represents one type of information associated with customers.

For example, the top row in `tblCustomers` contains data describing Fun Zone, including the address, and phone number. Each bit of information describing Fun Zone is a field (`CompanyName`, `Address`, `Phone`, and so on). Fields are combined to form a record, and records are grouped to build the table. (Each row in a table constitutes a record.)

Each field in an Access table includes many properties that specify the type of data contained within the field, and how Access should handle the field's data. These properties include the name of the field (`Company`) and the type of data in the field (`Text`). A field may include other properties as well. For example, the Address field's `Size` property tells Access the maximum number of characters allowed for the address.

Cross-Reference

You learn much more about fields and field properties in Chapter 2.

Records and fields

As Figure 1.2 shows, the datasheet is divided into rows (called *records*) and columns (called *fields*), with the first row (the heading on top of each column) containing the names of the fields in the database. In Figure 1.2, the fields are named `CustomerID`, `Company`, `Address`, `City`, `State`, and so on. Each row is a single record containing fields that are related to that record. In a manual system, the rows are individual forms (sheets of paper), and the fields are equivalent to the blank areas on a printed form that you fill in.

Note

When working with Access, the term field is used to refer to an attribute stored in a record. In many other database systems, including SQL Server, column is the expression you'll hear most often in place of field. Field and column mean the same thing. The exact terminology used relies somewhat on the context of the database system underlying the table containing the record.

Values

At the intersection of a record and a field is a *value* — the actual data element. For example, Fun Zone, the company name in the first record, represents one data value. Certain rules (discussed in Chapters 2 and 3) govern how data is contained in an Access table. For example, in a properly designed database, the Fun Zone record occurs only once because each row in a table must be unique in some way. A table may contain more than one company named Fun Zone, but *something* about each company (such as the address) must be different. If rows in a table are not unique, Access has no way to distinguish between the duplicate rows, and the data can't be trusted or managed properly.

Relational Databases

Microsoft Access is a relational database development system. Access data is stored in related tables, where data in one table (such as customers) is related to data in another table (such as orders). Access maintains the relationships between related tables, making it easy to extract a customer and all the customer's orders, without losing any data or pulling order records not owned by the customer.

Note

In the following sections (in fact, in the rest of this book), you'll see references to things such a "the customers table" or "the `tblCustomers` table." In the former, "the customers table" refers to the database table containing customer data, while "the `tblCustomers` table" (or just "`tblCustomers`") refers to the database table named `tblCustomers`. Different developers have different ways of naming things. For example, in my database, I may use `tblCustomers` as the name of the customers table, while another person might use Customers as the name for the same table. When working with a database it's very important to understand exactly which object is referenced by a name or description.

Multiple tables simplify data entry and reporting by decreasing the input of redundant data. By defining two tables for an application that uses customer information, for example, you don't need to store the customer's name and address every time the customer purchases an item.

After you've created the tables, they need to be related to each other. For example, if you have a customers table (tblCustomers) and a sales table (tblSales), you must relate tblCustomers to tblSales in order to see all the sales records for a customer. If you had only one table, you would have to repeat the customer name and address for each sale record. Two tables let you look up information in tblCustomers for each sale by using the related fields CustomerID (in tblCustomers) and CustomerID (in tblSales). This way, when a customer changes address, for example, the address changes only in one record in tblCustomers. When sales information is onscreen, the correct contact address is always visible.

Separating data into multiple tables within a database makes the system easier to maintain because all records of a given type are within the same table. By taking the time to properly segment data into multiple tables, you experience a significant reduction in design and work time. This process is known as *normalization*.

Cross-Reference
You can read about normalization in Chapter 3.

Later in this chapter, in the section titled "A Five-Step Design Process," you can work through a case study for Collectible Mini Cars that consists of five tables.

Why create multiple tables?

The prospect of creating multiple tables almost always intimidates beginning database users. Most often, beginners want to create one huge table that contains all the information they need — for example, a customer table with all the sales placed by the customer and the customer's name, address, and other information. After all, if you've been using Excel to store data so far, it may seem quite reasonable to take the same approach when building tables in Access.

A single large table for all customer information quickly becomes difficult to maintain. You have to input the customer information for every sale a customer makes (repeating the name and address information over and over again in every row). The same is true for the items purchased for each sale when the customer has purchased multiple items as part of a single purchase. This makes the system more inefficient and prone to data-entry mistakes. The information in the table is inefficiently stored — certain fields may not be needed for each sales record, and the table ends up with a lot of empty fields.

You want to create tables that hold the minimum of information while still making the system easy to use and flexible enough to grow. To accomplish this, you need to consider making more than one table, with each table containing fields that are only related to the focus of that table. Then, after you create the tables, you link them so that you're able to glean useful information from them. Although this process sounds extremely complex, the actual implementation is relatively easy.

Access Database Objects

If you're new to databases (or even if you're an experienced database user), you need to understand a few key concepts before starting to build Access databases. The Access database contains six types of top-level objects, which consist of the data and tools that you need to use Access:

- **Table:** Holds the actual data.
- **Query:** Searches for, sorts, and retrieves specific data.
- **Form:** Lets you enter and display data in a customized format.
- **Report:** Displays and prints formatted data.
- **Macro:** Automates tasks without programming.
- **Module:** Contains programming statements written in the Visual Basic for Applications (VBA) programming language.

Datasheets

Datasheets are one of the many ways by which you can view data in Access. Although not a permanent database object, a datasheet displays a table's content in a row-and-column format similar to a Microsoft Excel worksheet. A datasheet displays a table's information in a raw form, without transformations or filtering. The Datasheet view is the default mode for displaying all fields for all records. (Figures 1.1 and 1.2 earlier in this chapter are Datasheet views of Access tables.)

You scroll through the datasheet using the directional keys on your keyboard. You can also display related records in other tables while in a datasheet. In addition, you can make changes to the displayed data.

Caution
Be careful when you're making changes or allowing a user to modify data in Datasheet view. When a datasheet record is updated, the data in the underlying table is permanently changed.

Queries

Queries extract information from a database. A query selects and defines a group of records that fulfill a certain condition. Most forms and reports are based on queries that combine, filter, or sort data before it's displayed. Queries are often called from macros or VBA procedures to change, add, or delete database records.

An example of a query is when a person at the sales office tells the database, "Show me all customers, in alphabetical order by name, who are located in Massachusetts and bought something over the past six months." or "Show me all customers who bought Chevrolet car models within the past six months and display them sorted by customer name and then by sale date."

Instead of asking the question in English words, a person uses the query by example (QBE) method. When you enter instructions into the Query Designer window and run the query, the query translates the instructions into Structured Query Language (SQL) and retrieves the desired data.

Cross-Reference

Chapter 4 discusses the Query Designer window and building queries.

In the first example, the query first combines data from `tblSales` and `tblCustomers`, using `CustomerID` as a link between the tables. Next, it retrieves the customer name, address, and any other data you want to see. Access then filters the records, selecting only those in which the sales date is within six months of the current date. The query sorts the resulting records by the customer's name. Finally, the resulting records are displayed as a datasheet. Figure 1.3 shows just such a query in Design view. In this figure, the user is requesting all customers from Connecticut who've placed an order in the previous six months.

FIGURE 1.3

A typical Access query

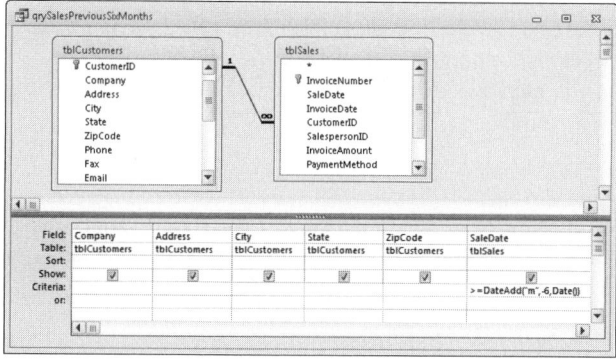

After you run a query, the resulting set of records may be used in a form that is displayed onscreen or printed on a report. In this way, user access is limited to the data that meets the criteria in the returned records.

Data-entry and display forms

Data-entry forms help users get information into a database table quickly, easily, and accurately. Data-entry and display forms provide a more structured view of the data than what a datasheet provides. From this structured view, database records can be viewed, added, changed, or deleted. Entering data through the data-entry forms is the most common way to get the data into the database table.

Data-entry forms restrict access to certain fields within the table. Forms can also check the validity of your data before it's added to the database table.

Most users prefer to enter information into data-entry forms rather than Datasheet views of tables. Forms often resemble familiar paper documents and can aid the user with data-entry tasks. Forms make data-entry easy to understand by guiding the user through the fields of the table being updated.

Read-only screens and forms are often used for inquiry purposes. These forms display certain fields within a table. Displaying some fields and not others means that you can limit a user's access to sensitive data while allowing access to other fields within the same table.

Reports

Reports present your data in printed format. Access supports several different types of reports. A report may list all records in a given table (such as a customers table) or may contain only the records meeting certain criteria, such as all customers living in Arizona. You do this by basing the report on a query that selects only the records needed by the report.

Reports often combine multiple tables to present complex relationships among different sets of data. An example is printing an invoice. The customers table provides the customer's name and address (and other relevant data) and related records in the sales table to print the individual line-item information for each product ordered. The report also calculates the sales totals and prints them in a specific format. Additionally, you can have Access output records into an *invoice report,* a printed document that summarizes the invoice.

Tip
When you design your database tables, keep in mind all the types of information that you want to print. Doing so ensures that the information you require in your various reports is available from within your database tables.

Database objects

To create database objects, such as tables, forms, and reports, you first complete a series of *design* tasks. The better your design is, the better your application will be. The more you think through your design, the faster and more successfully you can complete any system. The design process is not some necessary evil, nor is its intent to produce voluminous amounts of documentation. The sole intent of designing an object is to produce a clear-cut path to follow as you implement it.

A Five-Step Design Method

Figure 1.4 is a version of a common design method modified especially for use with Microsoft Access. This five-step method is a top-down approach, starting with the overall system design and ending with the forms design.

FIGURE 1.4

The five-step design flowchart. This design methodology is particularly well-suited for Access databases.

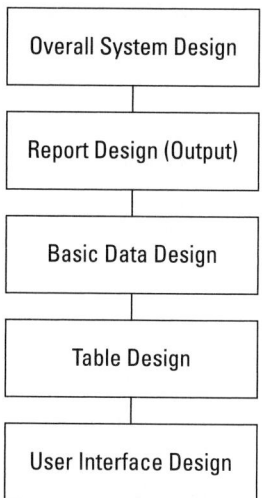

These five design steps, along with the database system illustrated by the examples in this book, teach a great deal about Access and provide a great foundation for creating database applications — including tables, queries, forms, reports, macros, and simple VBA modules.

The time you spend on each step depends entirely on the circumstances of the database you're building. For example, sometimes users give you an example of a report they want printed from their Access database, and the sources of data on the report are so obvious that designing the report takes a few minutes. Other times, particularly when the users' requirements are complex, or the business processes supported by the application require a great deal of research, you may spend many days on Step 1.

As you read through each step of the design process, *always* look at the design in terms of outputs and inputs. Although you see actual components of the system (products, customers, and transactions), remember that the focus of this chapter is how to move through each step. As you watch the Collectible Mini Cars database being designed, pay particular attention to the design process, not the actual system.

Step 1: The overall design — from concept to reality

All software developers face similar problems, the first of which is determining how to meet the needs of the end user. It's important to understand the overall user requirements before zeroing in on the details.

The five-step design method shown in Figure 1.4 helps you to create the system that you need, at an affordable price (measured in time or dollars). The Collectible Mini Cars database, for example, allows the client to sell items (vehicles and parts) to customers and supports the following tasks:

- Entering and maintaining customer information (name, address, and financial history)
- Entering and maintaining sales information (sales date, payment method, total amount, customer identity, and other fields)
- Entering and maintaining sales line-item information (details of items purchased)
- Viewing information from all the tables (sales, customers, sales line items, and payments)
- Asking all types of questions about the information in the database
- Producing a monthly invoice report
- Producing a customer sales history
- Producing mailing labels and mail-merge reports

These eight tasks have been described by the users. You may need to consider other tasks as you start the design process.

Most of the information that is necessary to build the system comes from the users. This means that you need to sit down with them and learn how the existing process works. To accomplish this you must do a thorough *needs analysis* of the existing system and how you might automate it.

One way to accomplish this is to prepare a series of questions that give insight to the client's business and how the client uses his data. For example, when considering automating any type of business, you may consider asking these questions:

- What reports and forms are currently used?
- How are sales, customers, and other records currently stored?
- How are billings processed?

As you ask these questions and others, the client will probably remember other things about the business that you should know.

A walkthrough of the existing process is also helpful to get a feel for the business. You may have to go back several times to observe the existing process and how the employees work.

As you prepare to complete the remaining steps, keep the client involved — let the users know what you're doing and ask for input on what to accomplish, making sure it's within the scope of the user's needs.

Step 2: Report design

Although it may seem odd to start with reports, in many cases, users are more interested in the printed output from a database than they are in any other aspect of the application. Reports often include every bit of data managed by an application. Because reports tend to be comprehensive, reports are often the best way to gather important information about a database's requirements. In the case of the Collectible Mini Cars database, the printed reports contain detailed and summarized versions of most of the data in the database.

After you've defined the Collectible Mini Cars' overall systems in terms of what must be accomplished, you can begin report design.

When you see the reports that you'll create in this section, you may wonder, "Which comes first — the chicken or the egg?" Does the report layout come first, or do you first determine the data items and text that make up the report? Actually, these items are considered at the same time.

It isn't important how you lay out the data in a report. The more time you take now, however, the easier it will be to construct the report. Some people go so far as to place gridlines on the report so that they know exactly where they want each bit of data to be.

The reports in Figures 1.5 and 1.6 were created with two different purposes. The report in Figure 1.5 displays information about the Collectible Mini Cars products while the report in Figure 1.6 is an invoice with billing and customer information. The design and layout of each report is driven by the report's purpose and the data it contains.

FIGURE 1.5

A product information report

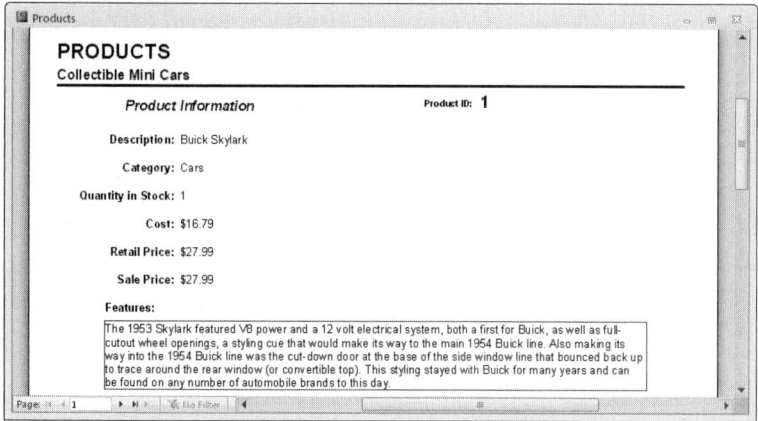

Cross-Reference

You can read more about the reports for the Collectible Mini Cars database in this book's introduction and in Chapters 9 and 20.

FIGURE 1.6

A sales invoice report containing sales information

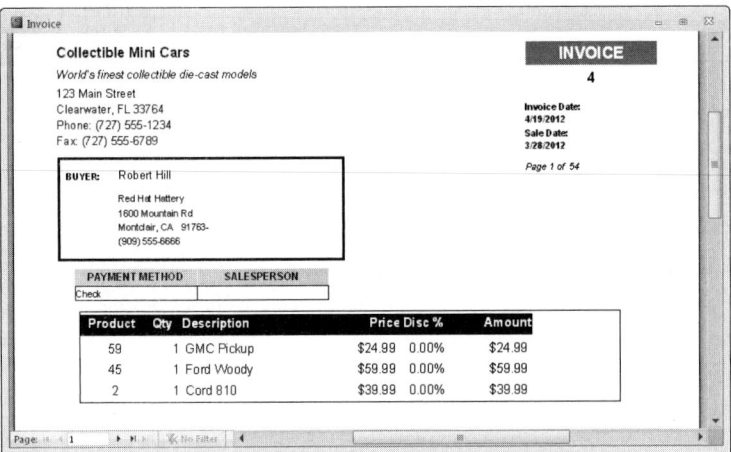

Step 3: Data design

The next step in the design phase is to take an inventory of all the information needed by the reports. One of the best methods is to list the data items in each report. As you do so, take careful note of items that are included in more than one report. Make sure that you keep the same name for a data item that is in more than one report because the data item is really the same item.

Another method is to separate the data items into a logical arrangement. Later, these data items are grouped into table structures and then mapped onto data-entry screens (forms). You should enter customer data, for example, as part of a customers table process, not as part of a sales entry.

Customer information

First, look at each report you've roughed out for your database. For the Collectible Mini Cars database, start with the customer data and list the data items, as shown in Table 1.1.

TABLE 1.1

Customer-Related Data Items Found in the Reports

Customers Report	Invoice Report
Customer Name	Customer Name
Street	Street
City	City
State	State

Customers Report	Invoice Report
ZIP Code	ZIP Code
Phone Numbers	Phone Number
E-Mail Address	
Web Site Information	
Discount Rate	
Customer Since	
Last Sales Date	
Sales Tax Rate	
Credit Information (four fields)	

As you can see by comparing the type of customer information needed for each report, there are many common fields. Most of the customer data fields are found in both reports. Table 1.1 shows only some of the fields that are used in each report — those related to customer information. Because the related row and the field names are the same, you can easily make sure that you have all the data items. Although locating items easily is not critical for this small database, it becomes very important when you have to deal with large tables containing many fields.

Sales information

After extracting the customer data, you can move on to the sales data. In this case, you need to analyze only the Invoice report for data items that are specific to the sales. Table 1.2 lists the fields in the report that contain information about sales.

TABLE 1.2

Sales Data Items Found in the Reports

Invoice Report	Line Item Data
Invoice Number	
Sales Date	
Invoice Date	
Payment Method	
Salesperson	
Discount (overall for sale)	
Tax Location	
Tax Rate	

continued

TABLE 1.2 (continued)	
Invoice Report	**Line Item Data**
Product Purchased (multiple lines)	Product Purchased
Quantity Purchased (multiple lines)	Quantity Purchased
Description of Item Purchased (multiple lines)	Description of Item Purchased
Price of Item (multiple lines)	Price of Item
Discount for each item (multiple lines)	Discount for Each Item
Payment Type (multiple lines)	
Payment Date (multiple lines)	
Payment Amount (multiple lines)	
Credit Card Number (multiple lines)	
Expiration Date (multiple lines)	

As you can see when you examine the type of sales information needed for the report, a few items (fields) are repeating (for example, the Product Purchased, Quantity Purchased, and Price of Item fields). Each invoice can have multiple items, and each of these items needs the same type of information — number ordered and price per item. Many sales have more than one purchased item. Also, each invoice may include partial payments, and it's possible that this payment information will have multiple lines of payment information, so these repeating items can be put into their own grouping.

Line-item information

You can take all the individual items that you found in the sales information group in the preceding section and extract them to their own group for the invoice report. Table 1.2 shows the information related to each line item.

Looking back at the report in Figure 1.6, you can see that the data from Table 1.2 doesn't list the calculated field amount. The amount is dynamically calculated as the report prints, rather than storing the value in the database.

Tip
Unless a numeric field needs to be specifically stored in a table, simply recalculate it when you run the report (or form). You should avoid creating fields in your tables that can be created based on other fields — calculated data can be easily created and displayed in a form or report.

Cross-Reference
As you'll read in Chapter 2, storing calculated values in database tables leads to data maintenance problems.

Step 4: Table design

Now for the difficult part: You must determine what fields are needed for the tables that make up the reports. When you examine the multitude of fields and calculations that make up the many documents you have, you begin to see which fields belong to the various tables in the database. (You already did much of the preliminary work by arranging the fields into logical groups.) For now, include every field you extracted. You'll need to add others later (for various reasons), although certain fields won't appear in any table.

It's important to understand that you don't need to add every little bit of data into the database's tables. For example, users may want to add vacation and other out-of-office days to the database to make it easy to know which employees are available on a particular day. However, it's very easy to burden an application's initial design by incorporating too many ideas during the initial development phases. Because Access tables are so easy to modify later on, it's probably best to put aside noncritical items until the initial design is complete. Generally speaking, it's not difficult to accommodate user requests after the database development project is under way.

After you've used each report to display all the data, it's time to consolidate the data by purpose (for example, grouped into logical groups) and then compare the data across those functions. To do this step, first look at the customer information and combine all its different fields to create a single set of data items. Then you do the same thing for the sales information and the line-item information. Table 1.3 compares data items from these three groups of information.

TABLE 1.3

Comparing the Data Items

Customer Data	Invoice Data	Line Items
Customer Company Name	Invoice Number	Product Purchased
Street	Sales Date	Quantity Purchased
City	Invoice Date	Description of Item Purchased
State	Payment Method	Price of Item
ZIP Code		Discount for Each Item
Phone Numbers (two fields)	Discount (overall for this sale)	Taxable?
E-Mail Address	Tax Rate	
Web Site	Payment Type (multiple lines)	
	Payment Date (multiple lines)	
Discount Rate	Payment Amount (multiple lines)	
Customer Since	Credit Card Number (multiple lines)	
Last Sales Date	Expiration Date (multiple lines)	
Sales Tax Rate		
Credit Information (four fields)		

Consolidating and comparing data is a good way to start creating the individual table definitions for Collectible Mini Cars, but you have much more to do.

As you learn more about how to perform a data design, you also learn that the customer data must be split into two groups. Some of these items are used only once for each customer, while other items may have multiple entries. An example is the Sales column — the payment information can have multiple lines of information.

You need to further break these types of information into their own columns, thus separating all related types of items into their own columns — an example of the *normalization* part of the design process. For example, one customer can have multiple contacts with the company. One customer may make multiple payments toward a single sale. Of course, I've already broken the data into three categories: customers, invoices, and sales line items.

Keep in mind that one customer may have multiple invoices, and each invoice may have multiple line items on it. The invoice category contains information about individual sales and the line items category contains information about each invoice. Notice that these three columns are all related; for example, one customer can have multiple invoices and each invoice may require multiple detail lines (line items).

The relationships between tables can be different. For example, each sales invoice has one and only one customer, while each customer may have multiple sales. A similar relationship exists between the sales invoice and the line items of the invoice.

Cross-Reference
I cover creating and understanding relationships and the normalization process in Chapter 3.

Database table relationships require a unique field in both tables involved in a relationship. A unique identifier in each table helps the database engine to properly join and extract related data.

Only the sales table has a unique identifier (`InvoiceNumber`), which means that you need to add at least one field to each of the other tables to serve as the link to other tables. For example, adding a `CustomerID` field to `tblCustomers`, adding the same field to the invoice table, and establishing a relationship between the tables through `CustomerID` in each table. The database engine uses the relationship between customers and invoices to connect customers with their invoices. Relationships between tables is done through *key* fields.

Cross-Reference
Creating relationships is explained in Chapter 3.

With an understanding of the need for linking one group of fields to another group, you can add the required key fields to each group. Table 1.4 shows two new groups and link fields created for each group of fields. These linking fields, known as *primary keys* and *foreign keys*, are used to link these tables together.

The field that uniquely identifies each row in a table is the *primary key*. The corresponding field in a related table is the *foreign key*. In our example, CustomerID in tblCustomers is a primary key, while CustomerID in tblInvoices is a foreign key.

Let's assume a certain record in tblCustomers has 12 in its CustomerID field. Any records in Invoices with 12 as its CustomerID is "owned" by customer 12.

Cross-Reference

As you'll see in Chapters 2 and 3, special rules apply to choosing and managing keys. The notion of primary and foreign keys is the single most important concept behind relational databases.

TABLE 1.4

Tables with Keys

Customers Data	Invoice Data	Line Items Data	Sales Payment Data
CustomerID	InvoiceID	InvoiceID	InvoiceID
Customer Name	CustomerID	Line Number	Payment Type
Street	Invoice Number	Product Purchased	Payment Date
City	Sales Date	Quantity Purchased	Payment Amount
State	Invoice Date	Description of Item Purchased	Credit Card Number
ZIP Code	Payment Method	Price of Item	Expiration Date
Phone Numbers (two fields)	Salesperson	Discount for Each Item	
E-Mail Address			
Web Site Information			
Discount Rate			
Customer Since			
Last Sales Date			
Sales Tax Rate	Tax Rate		

With the key fields added to each table, you can now find a field in each table that links it to other tables in the database. For example, Table 1.4 shows CustomerID in both the customers table (where it's the primary key) and the Invoice table (where it's a foreign key).

You've identified the core of the three primary tables for your system, as reflected by the first three columns in Table 1.4. This is the general, or first, cut toward the final table designs. You've also created an additional table to hold the sales payment data. Normally, payment details (such as the credit card number) are not part of a sales invoice.

Taking time to properly design your database and the tables contained within it is arguably the most important step in developing a database-oriented application. By designing your database efficiently, you maintain control of the data — eliminating costly data-entry mistakes and limiting your data entry to essential fields.

Although this book is not geared toward teaching database theory and all its nuances, this is a good point to briefly describe the art of database normalization. You'll read the details of normalization in Chapter 3, but in the meantime you should know that *normalization* is the process of breaking data down into constituent tables. Earlier in this chapter you read about how many Access developers add dissimilar information, such as customers, invoice data, and invoice line items, into one large table. A large table containing dissimilar data quickly becomes unwieldy and hard to keep updated. Because a customer's phone number appears in every row containing that customer's data, multiple updates must be made when the phone number changes.

Step 5: Form design

After you've created the data and established table relationships, it's time to design your forms. *Forms* are made up of the fields that can be entered or viewed in Edit mode. Generally speaking, your Access screens should look a lot like the forms used in a manual system.

When you're designing forms, you need to place three types of objects onscreen:

- Labels and text-box data-entry fields. The fields on Access forms and reports are called *controls.*
- Special controls (multiple-line text boxes, option buttons, list boxes, check boxes, business graphs, and pictures).
- Graphical objects to enhance the forms (colors, lines, rectangles, and three-dimensional effects).

Ideally, if the form is being developed from an existing printed form, the Access data-entry form should resemble the printed form. The fields should be in the same relative place on the screen as they are in the printed counterpart.

Labels display messages, titles, or captions. Text boxes provide an area where you can type or display text or numbers that are contained in your database. Check boxes indicate a condition and are either unchecked or checked. Other types of controls available with Access include list boxes, combo boxes, option buttons, toggle buttons, and option groups.

Cross-Reference
Chapter 7 covers the various types of form controls available in Access.

In this book, you create several basic data-entry forms:

- **Clusters:** Contains several different types of controls
- **Sales:** Combines data from multiple tables
- **Products:** Adds products to the Collectible Mini Cars database

You'll encounter each of these forms as you read through the following chapters. Although Collectible Mini Cars is just one small example of an Access database application, the principles you learn building the Collectible Mini Cars tables, queries, forms, reports, and other database objects are applicable to virtually any other Access project.

Summary

This chapter introduces the concepts and considerations driving database development. There is no question that data is important to users. Most companies simply can't operate without their customer and product lists, accounts receivable and accounts payable, and payroll information. Even very small companies must efficiently manage their business data.

Good database design means much more than sitting down and knocking together a few tables. Very often, poor database design habits come back to haunt developers and users in the form of missing or erroneous information on screens and printed reports. Users quickly tire of reentering the same information over and over again, and business managers and owners expect database applications to *save* time and money, not contribute to a business's overhead.

Creating Access Tables

In this chapter, you learn how to create a new Access database and its tables. You establish the database container to hold your tables, forms, queries, reports, and code that you build as you learn Access. Finally, you create the actual tables used by the Collectible Mini Cars database.

Note
This chapter uses the examples in the database named `Chapter02.accdb`. If you haven't yet copied this file from the book's CD, please do so now.

Getting Started with Access

As you open Access 2010, the default startup screen, called the Backstage, is revealed (see Figure 2.1). I'll examine the Backstage in more detail later in this chapter, but you should understand the major components of the user interface as you get started using Access 2010. Even experienced Access developers are surprised at how different Access 2010 looks from previous versions.

Each time you open Access, the welcome screen may or may not look different, depending on whether you've elected to have Office Online periodically update the user interface. In an effort to provide a high level of support for Microsoft Office users, Microsoft has equipped each of the Office applications with the ability to communicate directly with Microsoft's Web servers and download new content to the user's desktop.

IN THIS CHAPTER

Introducing Microsoft Access

Opening a new database

Getting acquainted with the Access environment

Adding tables to a database

Creating a new table

Modifying the design of a table

Working with field properties

Specifying the primary key

Adding indexes

Documenting a table's design

Saving a new table

Working with tables

Adding data to a table

Using attachment fields

FIGURE 2.1

The opening Access screen provides a number of ways to start working with Access.

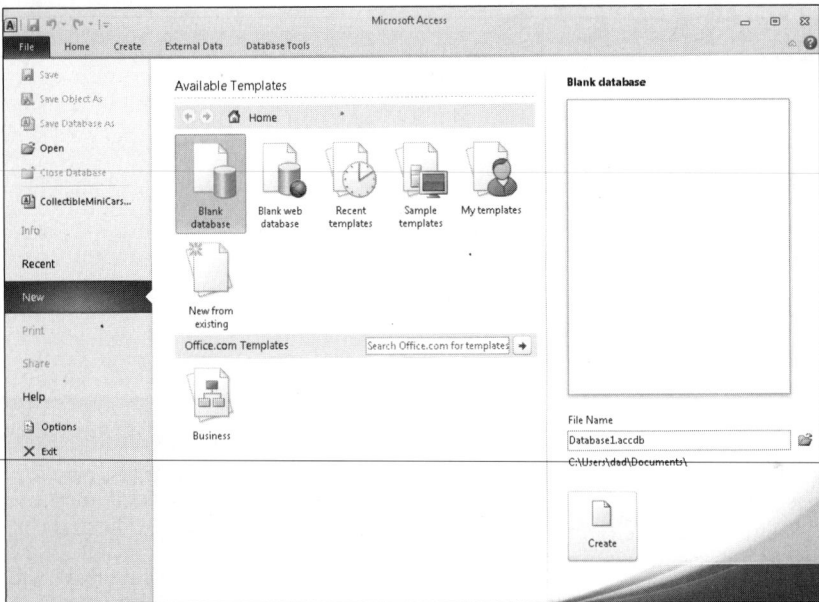

The center of the screen is dominated by the Microsoft Office Online templates, which are described in the next section. The right side of the screen contains a list of recently opened databases, while the left side of the screen contains a number of tabs for revealing other options for working with Access.

The Templates section

When you start Microsoft Access, you see the initial welcome screen (refer to Figure 2.1). For users with a live Internet connection, the content of the welcome screen changes from time to time as Microsoft updates the online templates available on the Microsoft Web site.

I'll show you how to create a new database in the "Creating a Database" section of this chapter. In the meantime, let's take a look at the purpose of online templates. Microsoft has long been concerned that building Access databases is too difficult for many people. Not everyone takes the time to understand the rules governing database design, or to learn the intricacies of building tables, queries, forms, and reports.

Microsoft established the online templates repository as a way to provide beginners and other busy people the opportunity to download partially or completely built Access applications. The template databases cover many common business requirements such as inventory control and sales management. You might want to take a moment to explore the online templates, but they aren't covered in this book.

The Office Backstage View

Our main interest at the moment is the rectangular button (labeled `File`) in the upper-left corner of the main Access screen. This button opens the Office Backstage view (shown in Figure 2.2), which is the gateway to a number of options for creating, opening, or configuring Access databases. The Backstage is shared by all the Office 2010 applications and it features similar options in Access, Word, Excel, and Outlook. The Backstage options include activities that infrequently are used when you're working within the main Access window, but that are necessary for saving, printing, or maintaining Access databases. Putting these options into the Backstage area means they don't have to appear anywhere on the ribbon as you're working with Access.

In Figure 2.2, the Recent tab is selected. Notice that a list of recently opened databases appears to the right of commands in the Backstage. Near the bottom of the Recent Databases list is a spin button for selecting the number of databases you'd like to see in the list to the left of Recent Databases. Each database in the list is accompanied by a button that lets you pin the database to the recent list so that it's always available as you work with Access.

Instead of discussing each of the other Backstage commands at the moment, I'll cover each command in detail as we work through the Access user interface. For the moment, notice the `New` command near the middle of the menu on the left side of the Backstage. You'll use this button to create a new Access database in the next section.

Note

Some confusion exists over the name of the rectangular button you see in the upper-left corner of the main Access window. Most users call this button the File button, and the drop-down that appears when this button is clicked, the File menu. However, in Access 2007, Microsoft referred to this button as the Microsoft Office Button. In Access 2010, the button's name has returned to its earlier name, and it's once again called the File button. As mentioned earlier, the screen you see when the File button is clicked in Access 2010 is the Backstage — it's no longer referred to as the File menu.

FIGURE 2.2

The File menu contains many important commands.

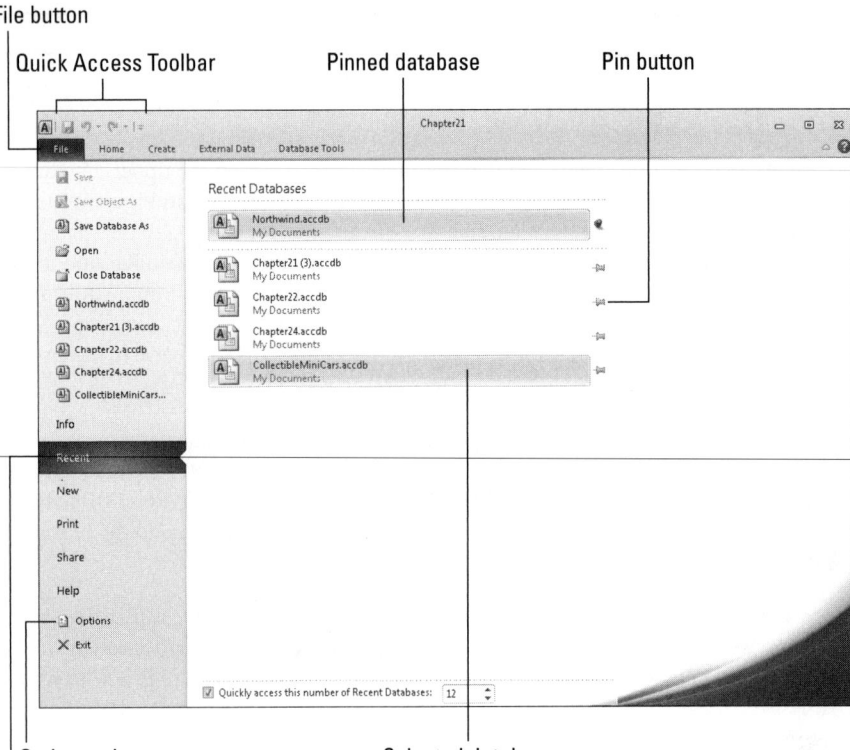

File button

Quick Access Toolbar   Pinned database   Pin button

Options tab   Selected database

Recent tab

Creating a Database

There are many ways to create a new database file. Selecting the New tab in the Backstage area opens the new database screen (see Figure 2.3). This is where you either create an entirely new database or open a new database based on a template (for more on templates, see "The Templates section," earlier in this chapter). You can even create a new database from the design of an existing Access application.

FIGURE 2.3

The new database screen provides many options for creating Access databases.

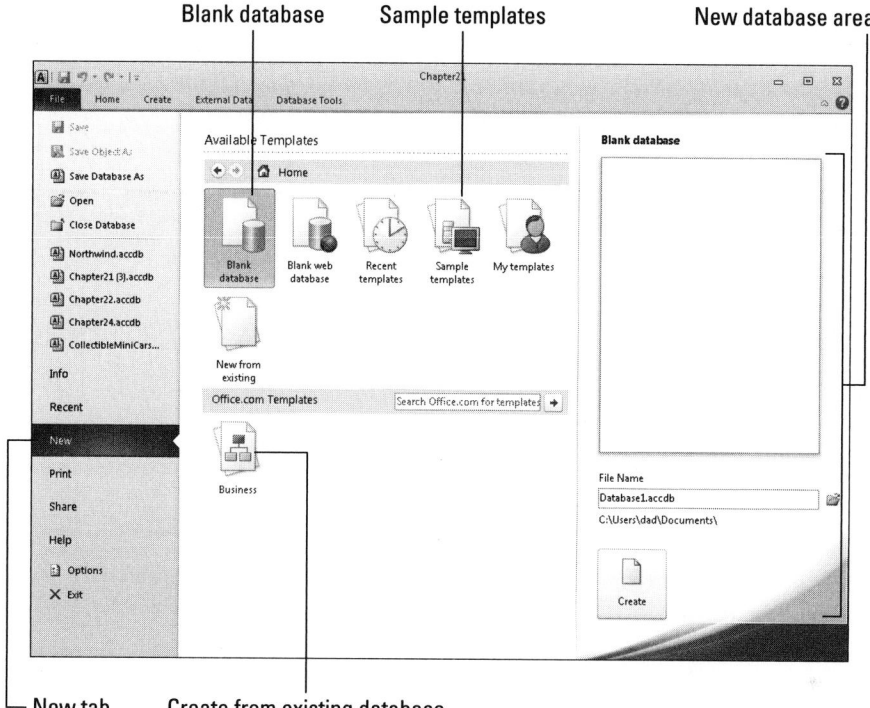

Blank database   Sample templates   New database area

New tab   Create from existing database

Clicking the Blank Database button transforms the new database area at the right side of the new database screen (see Figure 2.4). Figure 2.4 actually shows this area after the Marketing Projects database template has been selected as the source of a new Access database. When selecting the Blank Database button, the picture area above the File Name box is, quite literally, blank.

Enter the name of the new database in the File Name box in the Blank Database area. By default, Access creates the new database file in the folder specified in the Access options screen. (The Access options are discussed throughout this book.) By default, Access selects your My Documents folder as the new database's destination. If you want to use a different folder, use the browse button (it looks like a Windows Explorer folder) to the right of the File Name box to browse to the location you want to use.

FIGURE 2.4

Enter the name of the new database in the File Name box.

Default database location

New database name

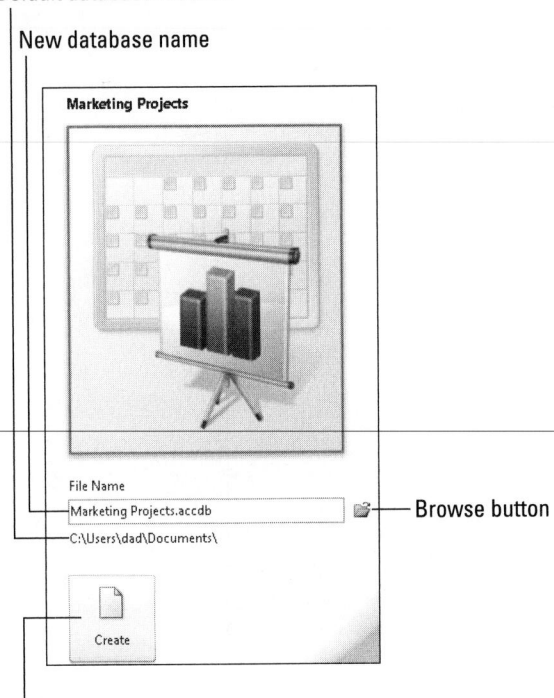

Marketing Projects

File Name

Marketing Projects.accdb — Browse button

C:\Users\dad\Documents\

Create

Create button

Access provides a default name of Database1.accdb for new databases. Be sure to provide a name that you'll recognize. In Figure 2.5, the new database is named MyCollectibleMiniCars.accdb. (Entering the extension .accdb is optional — Access automatically supplies it if you don't.)

When the new database is created, Access automatically opens it for you. In Figure 2.5, notice that Access opens the new database with a blank table already added to the database, ready to be filled in with fields and other design details.

FIGURE 2.5

The new MyCollectibleMiniCars database is created.

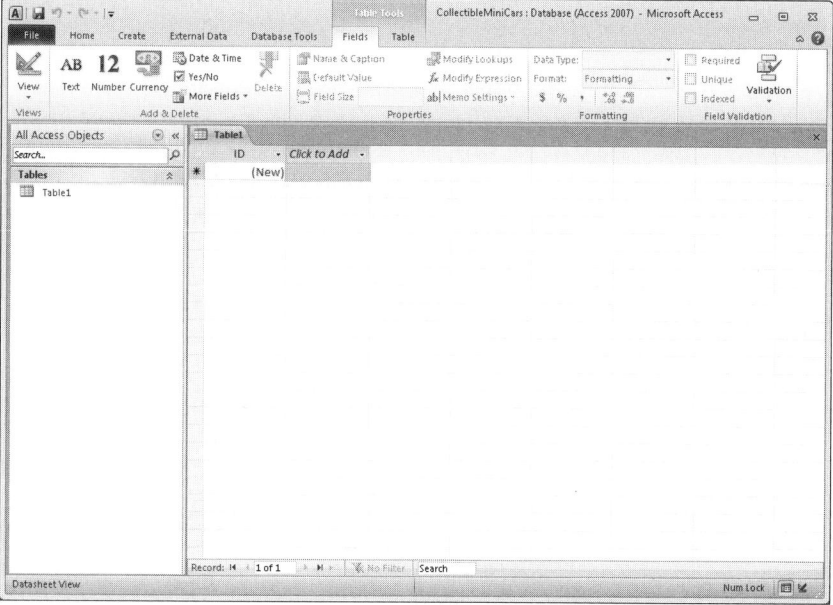

Note

Access 2010 recognizes all previous versions of Access database files. By default, the 2007 format (with an .accdb extension) is used, but you can specify Access 2000, 2002–2003, or 2007 as the default format. Choose File ⇨ Options ⇨ General, select the Default File Format option, and choose whichever format you prefer. For example, if much of your Access 2010 work is performed on Access 2000 databases, you should choose the 2000 format to preserve backward compatibility. Users still working with Access 2000 aren't able to open Access files created in the .accdb format.

If you choose to use an older Access database format, you won't be able to use the features that are only supported by the .accdb format.

This book uses a mix of Access file formats for its examples. All the Collectible Mini Cars files on the CD-ROM are in Access 2010 format, but other examples may be in Access 2000 or 2002–2003 formats.

How Access works with data

Microsoft Access works with data in numerous ways. For simplicity, most of the examples in this book use data stored in local tables. A *local table* is contained within the Access .accdb file that's open in front of you. This is how you've seen examples so far.

In many professionally developed Microsoft Access applications, the actual tables are kept in a database (usually called the *back end*) separate from the other interface objects (forms, reports, queries, pages, macros, and modules). The back-end data file stays on a file server on the network, and each user has a copy of the front-end database (containing the forms and reports) on his computer. This is done to make the application more maintainable. By separating the data and their tables into another database, maintenance work (building new indexes, updating reports, and so on) is more easily done without affecting the remainder of the system.

For example, you may be working with a multiuser system and find a problem with a form or report in the database. If all the data and interface objects are in the same database, you have to shut down the system while repairing the broken form or report — other users can't work with the application while you repair the form or report.

By separating data from other objects, you can fix the errant object while others are still working with the data. After you've fixed the problem, you deliver the new changes to everyone, and they import the form or report into their local databases. Splitting a database also makes it much easier to back up an application's data without affecting the application's user interface.

You may want to first develop your application with the tables within the .accdb database. Then, later, you can use the Database Splitter Wizard to automatically move the tables in your .accdb file to a separate Access .accdb file. This process is explained in Chapter 16.

Access 2010 works directly with Access 2000, 2002–2003, and Access 2007 .accdb databases. Earlier Access database files (such as Access 97 or 95) must be converted to 2000, 2002–2003, or 2007 before they can be used in Access 2010. Access examines the database file you're opening and, if the file must be converted, presents you with the Database Enhancement dialog box (shown in Figure 2.6).

Clicking Yes in the Database Enhancement dialog box opens a second dialog box (not shown), which asks for the name of the converted database. Clicking No in the Database Enhancement dialog box opens the obsolete database in read-only mode, enabling you to view, but not modify, objects in the database; this process is sometimes referred to as *enabling* the obsolete database. Choosing to enable an obsolete database is sometimes necessary when you must understand the design of an old database, but users are still working with the old database and it can't be upgraded to Access 2010 format.

If you're following the examples in this book, note that I've chosen MyCollectibleMiniCars. accdb as the name of the database file you create as you complete this chapter. This database is for the hypothetical business, Collectible Mini Cars. After you enter the filename, Access creates the empty database.

FIGURE 2.6

Opening an obsolete Access data file invokes the Database Enhancement dialog box.

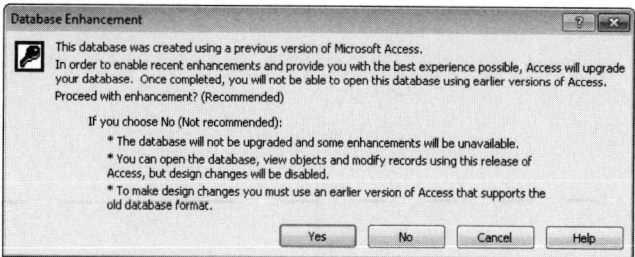

On the CD-ROM

The CD-ROM that comes with this book contains multiple database files. The completed file containing all the data and other database objects is named `CollectibleMiniCarsData.accdb`**.**

The CD-ROM also contains a single example database file for most chapters in this book. The example file for a chapter is named `ChapterXX.accdb or ChapterXX.mdb`**, where XX is a chapter number. If a chapter uses files where the data is split from the other objects, the names are usually** `ChapterXX_FrontEnd.accdb` **and** `ChapterXX_BackEnd.accdb`**. This chapter describes building a single database file named** `MyCollectibleMiniCars.accdb`**.**

The Access 2010 Environment

The initial Access screen, after creating a new database, is shown in Figure 2.5. Across the top of the screen is the Access ribbon, which was new at Access 2007 and replaces the toolbars and menus seen in previous versions of Access. The ribbon is divided into a number of *groups*. I show you each of the groups and the controls in each group in the next several chapters.

The Navigation Pane

The Navigation Pane, at the left of the screen, is your primary navigation aid when working with Access. By default, the list is filled with the names of tables in the current database, but it can also display other types of objects by clicking on the drop-down list in the Navigation Pane's title bar to reveal the navigation options (shown in Figure 2.7).

The Navigation Pane shows queries, forms, reports, and other Access object types. It can even display a combination of different types of objects.

FIGURE 2.7

Choosing an alternate display for the Navigation Pane

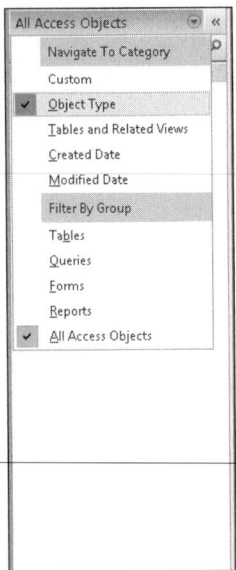

Here are the navigation options:

- **Custom:** The Custom option creates a new tab in the Navigation Pane. This new tab is titled Custom Group 1 by default and contains objects that you drag and drop into the tab's area. Items added to a custom group still appear in their respective "object type" view, as described in the next bullet.

Tip

Custom groups are a great way to group dissimilar objects (like tables, queries, and forms) that are functionally related. For example, you could create a Customers custom group, and add all the database objects related to customer activities. Items contained in a custom group can appear in other groups as well.

- **Object Type:** The Object Type setting is most similar to previous versions of Access. When selected, Object Type transforms the selection list to display the usual Access object types: tables, queries, forms, reports, and so on.

- **Tables and Related Views:** The Tables and Related Views setting requires a bit of explanation. Access tries very hard to keep the developer informed of the hidden connections between objects in the database. For example, a particular table may be used in a number of queries, or referenced from a form or report. In previous versions of Access, these relationships were very difficult to determine, and no effective tool was built into Access helping you understand these relationships.

Figure 2.8 shows how the Tables and Related Views works. The Categories group has been expanded to show that nine other in the Northwind Traders database are all related to the Categories table. This information helps a developer to understand that changing the Categories table affects a number of other objects in the database.

FIGURE 2.8

The Tables and Related Views setting is a powerful tool for analyzing an Access database.

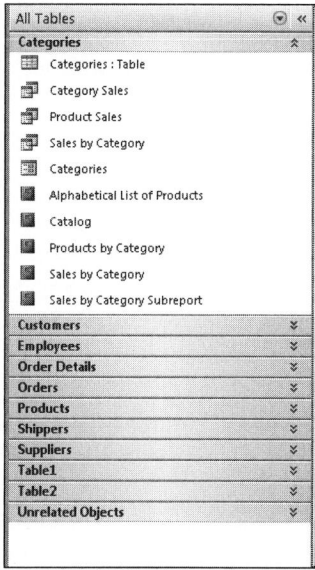

In addition to the Categories group, there are several other table-related groups, such as Customers, Employees, Order Details, and so on.

- **Created Date and Modified Date:** These options group the database objects by either the created date or the modified date. These settings are useful when you need to know when an object was either created or last modified.

- **Filter By Group:** The Filter By Group option filters the selected object type (tables, forms, and so on) by a number of grouping options. The grouping option is determined by the navigation category chosen in Navigate To Category selected at the top of the Navigation Pane (refer to Figure 2.7). For example, selecting Created Date changes the options under Filter By Group to the following options: Today, Yesterday, Last Week, Two Weeks Ago, and so on.

Tip

The `Filter By Group` option is really only helpful when you have a fairly large number of objects in your Access database. If you have an Access database containing several hundred different forms, you'll find it very useful to filter by forms that were modified within the last week or so. But when there are only a few objects in a database, the Filter By Group option has little effect.

- **Tables, Queries, Forms, Reports:** These are the major types of Access objects. You filter the objects shown in the Navigation Pane by selecting a single object type. Some Access databases contain dozens of each type of object, and these options enable you to view only a single type of object (such as tables) in the Navigation Pane.

- **All Access Objects:** By default the Navigation Pane shows all objects in the current database. Select All Access Objects when you have been working with one of the filtered view and want to see every object in the database.

The ribbon

The Access ribbon occupies the top portion of the main Access screen. The ribbon replaces the menus and toolbars seen in previous versions of Access. The ribbon's appearance changes depending on what task you're working on in the Access environment. Figure 2.9 shows the Home ribbon tab you see when you're working with Access tables in Datasheet view. A very different ribbon appears when working with forms or reports in Design view.

The Home tab of the Access 2010 ribbon

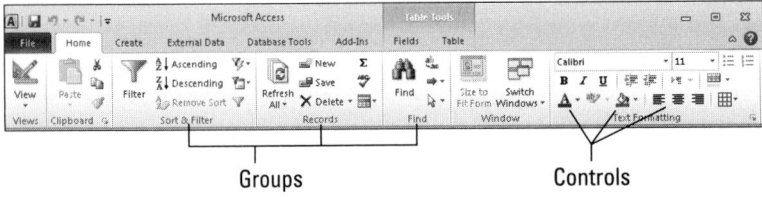

The ribbon is divided into a number of groups, each containing any number of controls. The Sort and Filter group, for example, includes options for sorting a datasheet's contents in ascending or descending order, while the Find group contains commands for searching through records within the datasheet.

The other groups on the ribbon — `Views`, `Clipboard`, `Records`, `Window`, and `Text Formatting` — contain controls that perform other tasks commonly associated with Access datasheets. For example, The `View` control in the `Views` group changes the Datasheet view of the table to Design view, making it easy to update the table's design.

Instead of explaining each of the groups and controls within groups on the ribbon, I'll introduce you to each relevant ribbon command in the proper context in this chapter and the chapters that follow.

Other relevant features of the Access environment

The Access environment includes a number of other important features. In the far-right lower corner are two buttons that enable you to quickly change the selected object in the middle of the screen from Design view to the object's Normal view. For example, in the case of an Access table, the Normal view is to display the table as a datasheet, while a report's Normal view is to display the report in Print Preview.

Figure 2.10 illustrates one of the more interesting changes for Access 2007 and 2010. A common complaint among some developers with earlier versions of Access was the fact that, when multiple objects were simultaneously opened in the Access environment, the objects would often overlap and obscure each other, making it more difficult to navigate between the objects. For example, in Access 2000, you might have a form open in Design view and, at the same time, a table open in Datasheet view. Invariably, one of these objects would overlap the other, and, depending on how large the object was, could completely obscure the other object.

FIGURE 2.10

The tabbed interface is a welcome addition to Access.

Form view buttons

Microsoft has added a tabbed document interface to Access, preventing objects from obscuring other objects that are open at the same time. In Figure 2.10, the Northwind Employees form is currently in use. Three other database objects (the Employees table, the Orders form, and the Invoices report) are also opened in the Access work area. Clicking on a tab associated with an object activates the tab and brings the object to the top.

When an object such as the Employees form is put into Design view by right-clicking the tab, and selecting `Design View` from the shortcut menu, the form view is replaced with the Form Designer (shown in Figure 2.11). The Access environment is highly adaptable to whichever tasks you're currently performing in your database.

FIGURE 2.11

The Access environment adapts to your workflow.

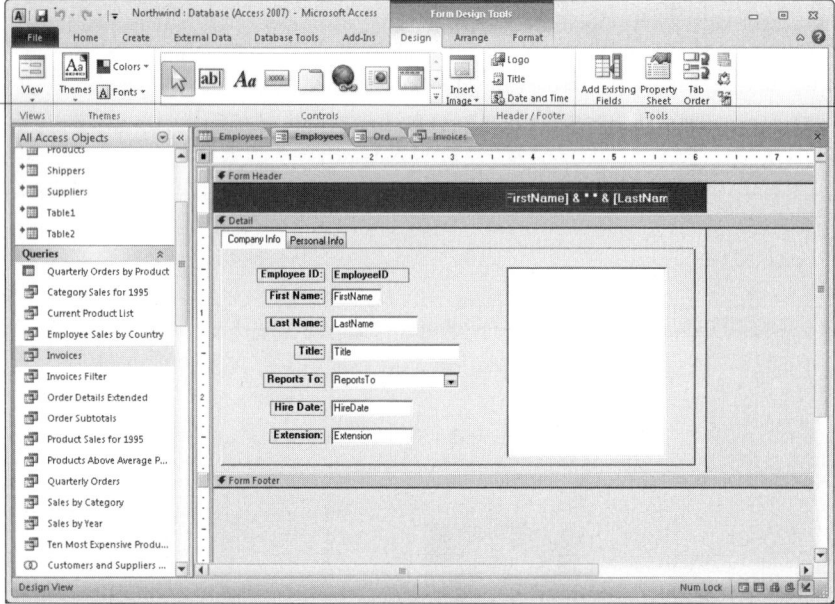

Tip

If you decide that you don't care for the tabbed interface, click the File button, and select the Options tab near the bottom of the Backstage. Then select the Current Database tab, and change the Document Window Options from `Tabbed Documents` to `Overlapping Windows`.

Creating a New Table

Creating database tables is as much art as it is science. Acquiring a good working knowledge of the user's requirements is a fundamental step for any new database project.

Cross-Reference
Chapter 3 covers the details of applying database design rules to the creation of Access tables.

In this chapter, I show you the steps required to create basic Access tables. In the following sections, you'll study the process of adding tables to an Access database, including the relatively complex subject of choosing the proper data type to assign to each field in a table.

It's always a good idea to plan tables on paper first, before you use the Access tools to add tables to the database. Many tables, especially small ones, really don't require a lot of forethought before adding them to the database. After all, not much planning is required to design a table holding lookup information, such as the names of cities and states. However, more complex entities, such as customers and products, usually require considerable thought and effort to implement properly.

Although you can create the table interactively without any forethought, carefully planning a database system is a good idea. You can make changes later, but doing so wastes time; generally, the result is a system that's harder to maintain than one that you've planned well from the beginning.

In the following sections, I explore the new, blank table added to the `Chapter02.accdb` database. It's important to understand the steps required to add new tables to an Access database. Because the steps required to add tables have changed so dramatically from earlier versions of Access, even experienced Access developers will want to read the following sections.

The importance of naming conventions

Most Access developers eventually adopt a naming convention to help identify database objects. Most naming conventions are relatively simple and involve nothing more than adding a prefix indicating an object's type to the object's name. For example, an employees form might be named `frmEmployees`.

As your databases grow in size and complexity, the need to establish a naming convention for the objects in your databases increases. Even with the `Name AutoCorrect` option turned on (click the File button and choose `Options`⇨`Current Database`⇨`Name AutoCorrect`), Access only corrects the most obvious name changes. Changing the name of a table breaks virtually every query, form, and report that uses the information from that table. Your best defense is to adopt reasonable object names, use a naming convention early on as you begin building Access databases, and stick with the naming convention throughout the project.

Access imposes very few restrictions on the names assigned to database objects. Therefore, it's entirely possible to have two distinctly different objects (for example, a form and a report, or a table and a macro) with the same name. (You can't, however, have a table and a query with the same name, because tables and queries occupy the same namespace in the database.)

continued

continued

Although simple names like Contacts and Orders are adequate, as a database grows in size and complexity, you might be confused about which object a particular name refers to. For example, later in this book, you'll read about manipulating database objects through code and macros. When working with Visual Basic for Applications (VBA), the programming language built into Access, there must be no ambiguity or confusion between referenced objects. Having both a form and a report named Contacts might be confusing to you *and* your code.

The simplest naming convention is to prefix object names with a three- or four-character string indicating the type of object carrying the name. Using this convention, tables are prefixed with `tbl` and queries with `qry`. The generally accepted prefixes for forms, reports, macros, and modules are `frm`, `rpt`, `mcr`, and `bas` or `mod`, respectively.

In this book, most compound object names appear in mixed case: `tblBookOrders`, `tblBookOrderDetails`, and so on. Most people find mixed-case names easier to read and remember than names that appear in all-uppercase or all-lowercase characters (such as `TBLBOOKORDERDETAILS` or `tblbookorderderdetails`).

Also, at times, I use informal references for database objects. For example, the formal name of the table containing contact information in the previous examples is `tblContacts`. An informal reference to this table might be "the Contacts table."

In most cases, your users never see the formal names of database objects. One of your challenges as an application developer is to provide a seamless user interface that hides all data-management and data-storage entities that support the user interface. You can easily control the text that appears in the title bars and surfaces of the forms, reports, and other user-interface components to hide the actual names of the data structures and interface constituents.

Take advantage of the long object names that Access permits to give your tables, queries, forms, and reports descriptive, informative names. There is no reason why you should confine a table name to `ConInfo` when `tblContactInformation` is handled just as easily and is much easier to understand.

Descriptive names can be carried to an extreme, of course. There's no point in naming a form `frmUpdateContactInformation` if `frmUpdateInfo` does just as well. Long names are more easily misspelled or misread than shorter names, so use your best judgment when assigning names.

Finally, although Access lets you use spaces in database object names, you should avoid spaces at all costs. Spaces don't add to readability and can cause major headaches, particularly when upsizing to client/server environments or using OLE automation with other applications. Even if you don't anticipate extending your Access applications to client/server or incorporating OLE or DDE automation into your applications, get into the habit of not using spaces in object names.

Designing tables

Designing a table is a multistep process. By following the steps in order, your table design can be created readily and with minimal effort:

1. Create the new table.

2. Enter field names, data types, properties, and (optionally) descriptions.

3. Set the table's primary key.

4. Create indexes for appropriate fields.

5. Save the table's design.

Generally speaking, some tables are never really finished. As users' needs change, or the business rules governing the application change, you might find it necessary to open an existing table in Design view. This book, like most books on Access, describes the process of creating tables as if every table you ever work on is brand-new. The truth is, however, that most of the work that you do on an Access application is performed on existing objects in the database. Some of those objects you've added yourself, while other objects may have been added by another developer at some time in the past. However, the process of maintaining an existing database component is exactly the same as creating the same object from scratch.

Tip

Just a quick note about modifying tables once they're built: Adding a new field to a table almost never causes problems. Existing queries, forms, and reports, and even VBA code, will continue using the table as before. After all, these objects won't reference the new field because the field was added after their creation. Therefore, you can add a new field and incorporate the field where needed in your application, and everything works as expected.

The trouble comes when you remove or rename a field in a table. Even with AutoCorrect turned on, Access won't update field-name references in VBA code, in control properties, and in expressions throughout the database. Changing an existing field (or any other database object, for that matter) is always a bad idea. You should always strive to provide your tables, fields, and other database objects with good, strong, descriptive names when you add them to the database, instead of planning to go back later and fix them.

Tip

Many Access developers routinely turn off AutoCorrect. (Use the File tab to access the Backstage, selection Options, then Current Database. In the Name Autocorrect Options, make sure Track Name AutoCorrect Info is unchecked.) The AutoCorrect feature negatively affects performance because it constantly watches for name changes in an application, and takes corrective action when needed. Furthermore, because AutoCorrect never quite corrects all the names in an application, there is always more work to perform when you change the name of a database object.

Begin by selecting the Create tab on the ribbon at the top of the Access screen. The Create tab (shown in Figure 2.12) contains all the tools necessary to create not only tables, but also forms, reports, and other database objects.

On the CD-ROM

The following examples use the Chapter02.accdb database found on this book's CD.

FIGURE 2.12

The Create tab contains tools necessary for adding new objects to your Access database.

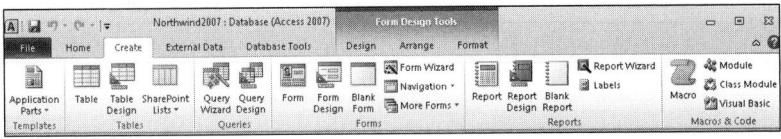

There are two main ways to add new tables to an Access database, both of which are invoked from the Tables group on the Create tab:

- **Clicking on the Table button:** Adds a complete new table to the database
- **Clicking on the Table Design button:** Adds a table in Design view to the database.

For this example, I'll be using the Table Design button, but first, let's take a look at the Table button.

Clicking the `Table` button adds a new table to the Access environment. The new table appears in Datasheet view in the area to the right of the Navigation Pane. The new table is shown in Figure 2.13. Notice that the new table appears in Datasheet view, with an ID column already inserted, and a Click to Add column to the right of the ID field.

FIGURE 2.13

The new table in Datasheet view

ID field   New field

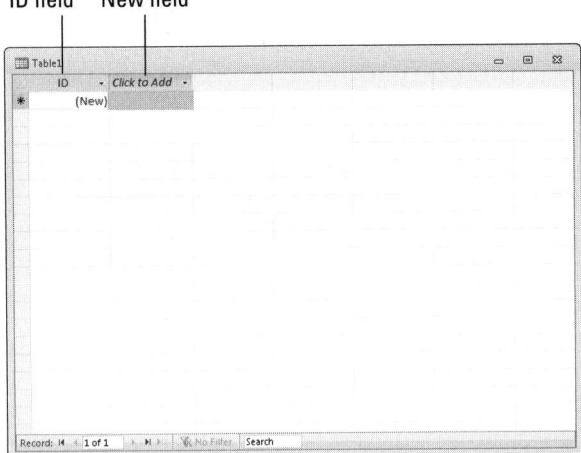

The `Click to Add` column is intended to permit users to quickly add tables to an Access database. All that you have to do is begin entering data in the `new` column. You assign the field a name by right-clicking the field's heading, selecting Rename Column, and entering a name for the field. In other words, building an Access table can be very much like creating a spreadsheet in Microsoft Excel.

Note

This approach was usually referred to as "creating a table in Datasheet view" in previous versions of Microsoft Access.

Once you've added the new column, the tools in the Fields ribbon tab (shown in Figure 2.14) allow you to set the specific data type for the field, and its formatting, validation rules, and other properties.

FIGURE 2.14

Field design tools are located in the Fields ribbon tab.

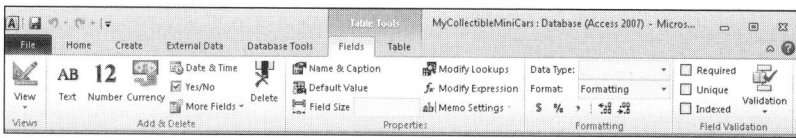

There are good reasons *not* to use the Datasheet view method of building tables. Relational database systems such as Access are constructed by breaking data into constituent entities, and then building a table for each entity. The tables in an Access database should carefully and accurately reflect the entities they describe. Seemingly small issues, such as deciding which data type to assign to a field, have a dramatic impact on the utility, performance, and integrity of the database and its data.

Every table added to an Access database, and the fields added to tables, should have a purpose in the overall database design. Even when adding tables using the Table button, it's far too easy to add tables that don't conform to the rules described in Chapter 3, and that don't fit well into the database's design.

The second method of adding new tables is to click the Table Design button in the Tables group on the Create tab. Access opens a new table in Design view, allowing you to add fields to the table's design. Figure 2.15 shows a new table's design after a few fields have been added. Table Design view provides a somewhat more deliberate approach to building Access tables.

The Table Designer is quite easy to understand, and each column is clearly labeled. At the far left is the `Field Name` column, where you input the names of fields you add to the table. You assign a data type to each field in the table, and (optionally) provide a description for the field.

FIGURE 2.15

A new table added in Design view

Field Name   Data Type

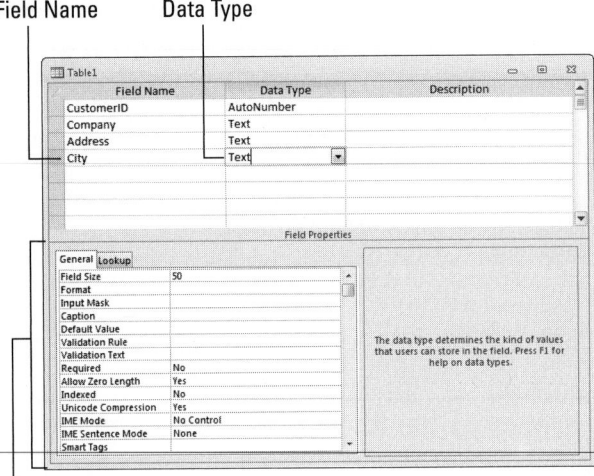

Field Properties

For this exercise, you create the Customers table for the Collectible Mini Cars application. The basic design of this table is outlined in Table 2.1. I cover the details of this table's design in the "Creating tblCustomers" section, later in this chapter.

TABLE 2.1

The Collectible Mini Cars Customers Table

Field Name	Data Type	Description
CustomerID	AutoNumber	Primary key
Company	Text 50	Contact's employer or other affiliation
Address	Text 50	Contact's address
City	Text 50	Contact's city
State	Text 50	Contact's state
ZipCode	Text 50	Contact's zip code
Phone	Text 50	Contact's phone
Fax	Text 50	Contact's fax
Email	Text 100	Contact's e-mail address
WebSite	Text 100	Contact's Web address

Field Name	Data Type	Description
OrigCustDate	DateTime	Date the contact first purchased something from Collectible Mini Cars
CreditLimit	Currency	Customer's credit limit in dollars
CurrentBalance	Currency	Customer's current balance in dollars
CreditStatus	Text	Description of the customer's credit status
LastSalesDate	DateTime	Most recent date the customer purchased something from Collectible Mini Cars
TaxRate	Number (Double)	Sales tax applicable to the customer
DiscountPercent	Number (Double)	Customary discount provided to the customer
Notes	Memo	Notes and observations regarding this customer
Active	Yes/No	Whether the customer is still buying or selling to Collectible Mini Cars

Some of the fields in the preceding table are rather generous in the amount of space allocated for the field's data. For example, it's unlikely that anyone's name occupies 50 characters, but there is no harm in providing for very long names. Access only stores as many characters as are actually entered into a text field. Therefore, allocating 50 characters doesn't actually use 50 characters for every name in the database.

Looking once again at Figure 2.15, you see that the Table Design window consists of two areas:

- **The field entry area:** Use the field entry area, at the top of the window, to enter each field's name and data type. You can also enter an optional description.

- **The field properties area:** The area at the bottom of the window is where the field's properties are specified. These properties include field size, format, input mask, and default value, among others. The actual properties displayed in the properties area depend upon the data type of the field. You learn much more about these properties in the "Assigning field properties" section, later in this chapter.

Tip
You can switch between the upper and lower areas of the table designer by clicking the mouse when the pointer is in the desired pane or by pressing F6.

Using the Design tab

The Design tab on the Access ribbon (shown in Figure 2.16) contains many controls that assist in creating a new table definition.

The Design tab of the ribbon

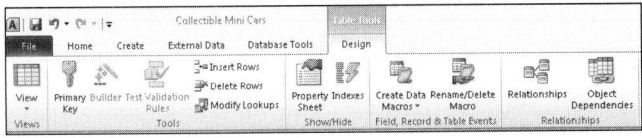

The controls in the Design tab affect the import table design considerations. Only a few of the controls shown in Figure 2.16 are described in the following sections. You'll learn much more about the other buttons in the "Creating tblCustomers" section, later in this chapter, and in subsequent chapters of this book.

Primary Key

Click this button to designate which of the fields in the table you want to use as the table's primary key. Traditionally, the primary key appears at the top of the list of fields in the table but could appear anywhere within the table's design. Moving a field is easy: Simply left-click on the gray selector to the left of the field's name to highlight the field in the Table Designer, and drag the field to its new position.

Insert Rows

Although it makes very little difference to the database engine, many developers are fussy about the sequence of fields in a table. Also, particularly when assigning an index or composite index to a table, you want the fields to be next to each other in the table's field list.

Cross-Reference

Composite keys, consisting of multiple fields combined as a single key, are discussed in detail in Chapter 3.

The Insert Rows button inserts a blank row just *above* the position occupied by the mouse cursor. For example, if the cursor is currently in the second row of the Table Designer, clicking the Insert Row button inserts an empty row in the second position, moving the existing second row to the third position.

Delete Rows

Conversely, the Delete Rows button removes a row from the table's design.

Caution

Access doesn't ask you to confirm the deletion before actually removing the row.

Property Sheet

The Property Sheet button opens the table's Property Sheet (shown in Figure 2.17). These properties enable you to specify important table characteristics, such as a validation rule to apply to the entire table, or an alternate sort order for the table's data.

FIGURE 2.17

The Property Sheet

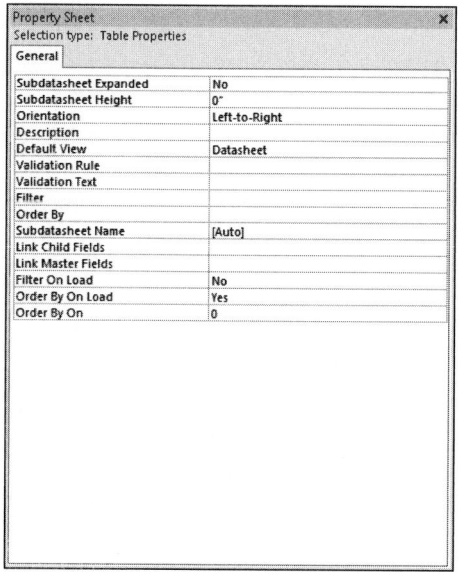

Indexes

Indexes are discussed in much more detail in the "Indexing Access Tables" section, later in this chapter. Clicking the Indexes button opens the Indexes dialog box (shown in Figure 2.28, later in this chapter), enabling you to specify the details of indexes on the fields in your table.

Working with fields

Fields are created by entering a field name and a field data type in the upper entry area of the Table Design window. The (optional) Description property indicates the field's purpose. The description appears in the status bar at the bottom of the screen during data entry and may be useful to people working with the application. After entering each field's name and data type, you can further specify how each field is used by entering properties in the property area.

Naming a field

A field name should be descriptive enough to identify the field to you as the developer, to the user of the system, and to Access. Field names should be long enough to quickly identify the purpose of the field, but not overly long. (Later, as you enter validation rules or use the field name in a calculation, you'll want to save yourself from typing long field names.)

To enter a field name, position the pointer in the first row of the Table Design window under the Field Name column. Then type a valid field name, observing these rules:

- Field names can be from 1 to 64 characters.
- Field names can include letters, numbers, and many special characters.
- Field names can't include a period (.), exclamation point (!), brackets ([ ]), or accent grave (`).
- You can't use low-order ASCII characters — for example Ctrl+J or Ctrl+L (ASCII values 0 through 31).
- You can't start with a blank space.
- You can't use a double quotation mark ("") in the name of a Microsoft Access project file.

You can enter field names in uppercase, lowercase, or mixed case. If you make a mistake while typing the field name, position the cursor where you want to make a correction and type the change. You can change a field name at any time, even if the table contains data.

Note

Access is not case sensitive, so the database itself doesn't care whether you name a table tblCustomers or TblCustomers. Choosing uppercase, lowercase, or mixed case characters is entirely your decision and should be aimed at making your table names descriptive and easy to read.

Caution

After your table is saved, if you change a field name that is also used in queries, forms, or reports, you have to change it in those objects as well. One of the leading causes of errors in Access applications stems from changing the names of fundamental database objects such as tables and fields, but neglecting to make all the changes required throughout the database. Overlooking a field name reference in the control source of a control on the form or report, or deeply embedded in VBA code somewhere in the application, is far too easy.

Specifying a data type

The next step is to actually create your tables and define your fields for those tables. You must also decide what type of data each of your fields will hold. In Access, you can choose any of several data types (these data types are detailed in the "Assigning field data types" section, later in this chapter):

- Text: Alphanumeric characters; up to 255 characters
- Memo: Alphanumeric characters; very long strings up to 65,538 characters
- Number: Numeric values of many types and formats. The different numeric options are described in the "Number data type" section, later in this chapter.
- Date/Time: Date and time data
- Currency: Monetary data
- AutoNumber: Automatically incremented numeric counter
- Yes/No: Logical values; Yes/No, True/False

- `OLE Object`: Pictures, graphs, sound, video, word processing, and spreadsheet files
- `Hyperlink`: A field that links to a picture, graph, sound, video, word processing, or spreadsheet file

One of these data types must be assigned to each of your fields. You may also want to specify the `Field Size` property for the `Text` fields, or accept the default of 255 characters. The `Field Size` property specifies the maximum number of characters that a `Text` data type field may contain.

Specifying data validation rules

The last major design decision concerns data validation, which becomes important as users enter data. You want to make sure that only good data (data that passes certain defined tests) gets into your system. You have to deal with several types of data validation. You can test for known individual items, stipulating that the `Gender` field can accept only the values `Male`, `Female`, or `Unknown`, for example. Or you can test for ranges, specifying that the value of `Weight` must be between 0 and 1,500 pounds. You'll read more about validation rules in the "Validation Rule and Validation Text" section, later in this chapter.

Assigning field data types

After you name a field, you must decide what type of data the field holds. Before you begin entering data, you should have a good grasp of the data types that your database uses. Access supports ten basic data types (see Table 2.2). Some data types (such as numbers) have several options.

TABLE 2.2

Data Types Available in Microsoft Access

Data Type	Type of Data Stored	Storage Size
Text	Alphanumeric characters	255 characters or less
Memo	Alphanumeric characters	65,536 characters or less
Number	Numeric values	1, 2, 4, or 8 bytes, 16 bytes for Replication ID (GUID)
Date/Time	Date and time data	8 bytes
Currency	Monetary data	8 bytes
AutoNumber	Automatic number increments	4 bytes, 16 bytes for Replication ID (GUID)
Yes/No	Logical values: Yes/No, True/False	1 bit (0 or –1)
OLE Object	Pictures, graphs, sound, video	Up to 1GB (disk space limitation)
Hyperlink	Link to an Internet resource	64,000 characters or less
Attachment	A special field that enables you to attach external files to an Access database.	Varies by attachment
Lookup Wizard	Displays data from another table	Generally 4 bytes

Figure 2.18 shows the Data Type drop-down list used to select the data type for the field you just created.

FIGURE 2.18

The Data Type drop-down list

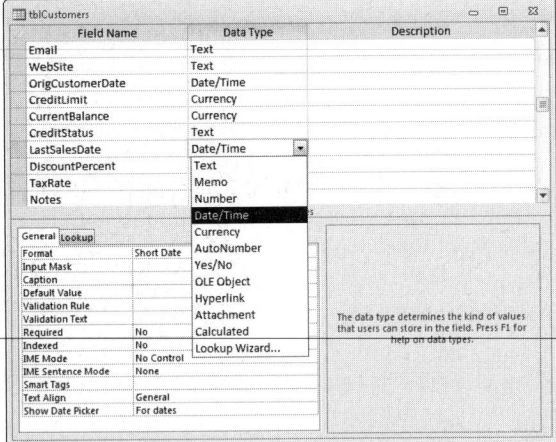

Here are the basic rules to consider when choosing the data type for new fields in your tables:

- **The data type should reflect the data stored in the field.** For example, you should select one of the numeric data types to store numbers like quantities and prices. Do not store data like phone numbers or Social Security numbers in numeric fields, however. Your application won't be performing numeric operations like addition or multiplication on phone numbers, and this data should not be stored in numeric fields. Instead, use text fields for common data, such as Social Security numbers and phone numbers.

Note
Numeric fields never store leading zeros. Putting a zip code such as 02173 into a numeric field means only the last four digits (2173) are actually stored.

- **Consider the storage requirements of the data type you've selected.** Although you can use a Long Integer data type in place of a Simple Integer or Byte Value, the storage requirements of a Long Integer (4 bytes) is twice that of a Simple Integer. This means that twice as much memory is required to use and manipulate the number and twice as much disk space is required to store its value. Whenever possible, use Byte or Integer data types for simple numeric data.

- **Will you want to sort or index the field?** Because of their binary nature, Memo and OLE Object fields can't be sorted or indexed. Use Memo fields sparingly. The overhead required to store and work with Memo fields is considerable.

- **Consider the impact of data type on sorting requirements.** Numeric data sort differently from text data. Using the numeric data type, a sequence of numbers will sort as expected: 1, 2, 3, 4, 5, 10, 100. The same sequence stored as text data will sort like this: 1, 10, 100, 2, 3, 4, 5. If it's important to sort text data in a numeric sequence, you'll have to first apply a conversion function to the data before sorting.

Tip

If it's important to have text data representing numbers to sort in the proper order, you might want to prefix the numerals with zeros (001, 002, and so on). Then the text values will sort in the expected order: 001, 002, 003, 004, 005, 010, 100.

- **Is the data text or date data?** When working with dates, you're almost always better off storing the data in a Date/Time field than as a Text field. Text values sort differently from date data (dates are stored internally as numeric values), which can upset reports and other output that rely on chronological order.

  Don't be tempted to store dates in one Date/Time field and time in another Date/Time field. The Date/Time field is specifically designed to handle both dates and times, and, as you'll see throughout this book, it's quite easy to display only the date or time portion of a Date/Time value.

  A Date/Time field is also meant to store a discrete date and time, and not a time interval. If keeping track of durations is important, you should use two Date/Time fields — one to record the start and the other at the end of a duration.

- **Keep in mind the reports that will be needed.** You won't be able to sort or group memo or OLE data on a report. If it's important to prepare a report based on memo or OLE data, add a Tag field like a date or sequence number, which can be used to provide a sorting key, to the table.

Text data type

The Text data type holds information that is simply characters (letters, numbers, punctuation). Names, addresses, and descriptions are all text data, as are numeric data that are not used in a calculation (such as telephone numbers, Social Security numbers, and zip codes).

Although you specify the size of each Text field in the property area, you can enter no more than 255 characters of data in any Text field. Access uses variable length fields to store text data. If you designate a field to be 25 characters wide and you use only 5 characters for each record, then only enough room to store 5 characters is used in your database.

You'll find that the .accdb database file might quickly grow quite large, but text fields are not the usual cause. However, it's good practice to limit Text field widths to the maximum you believe is likely for the field. Names can be quite tricky because fairly long names are common in some cultures. However, it's a safe bet that a postal code might be less than 12 characters, while a U.S. state abbreviation is always 2 characters. By limiting a Text field's width, you also limit the number of characters users can enter when the field is used in a form.

Memo data type

The Memo data type holds a variable amount of data from 0 to 65,536 characters for each record. So, if one record uses 100 characters, another requires only 10, and yet another needs 3,000, you use only as much space as each record requires.

You don't specify a field size for the Memo data type. Access allocates as much space as necessary for the memo data.

Number data type

The Number data type enables you to enter *numeric* data — that is, numbers that will be used in mathematical calculations or represent scalar quantities such as inventory counts. (If you have data that will be used in monetary calculations, you should use the Currency data type, which performs calculations without rounding errors.)

The exact type of numeric data stored in a number field is determined by the Field Size property. Table 2.3 lists the various numeric data types, their maximum and minimum ranges, the decimal points supported by each numeric data type, and the storage (bytes) required by each numeric data type.

TABLE 2.3

Numeric Field Settings

Field Size Setting	Range	Decimal Places	Storage Size
Byte	0 to 255	None	1 byte
Integer	–32,768 to 32,767	None	2 bytes
Long Integer	–2,147,483,648 to 2,147,483,647	None	4 bytes
Double	-1.797×10308 to 1.797×10308	15	8 bytes
Single	-3.4×1038 to 3.4×1038	7	4 bytes
Replication ID	N/A	N/A	16 bytes
Decimal	1–28 precision	15	8 bytes

Caution

Many errors are caused by choosing the wrong numeric type for number fields. For example, notice that the maximum value for the Integer data type is 32,767. I once saw a database that ran perfectly for several years and then started crashing with overflow errors. It turned out that the overflow was caused by a particular field being set to the Integer data type, and when the company occasionally processed very large orders, the 32,767 maximum was exceeded.

Be aware that overflow may occur simply by adding two numbers together, or performing any mathematical operation that results in a value too large to be stored in a field. Some of the most difficult bugs occur only when circumstances (such as adding or multiplying two numbers) cause an overflow condition at runtime.

Design your tables very conservatively, and allow for larger values than you ever expect to see in your database. This is not to say that using the `Double` data type for all numeric fields is a good idea. The `Double` data type is very large (8 bytes) and might be somewhat slow when used in calculations or other numeric operations. Instead, the `Single` data type is probably best for most floating-point calculations, and `Long Integer` is a good choice where decimal points are irrelevant.

Date/Time data type

The `Date/Time` data type is a specialized number field for holding dates or times (or dates *and* times). When dates are stored in a `Date/Time` field, it's easy to calculate days between dates and other calendar operations. Date data stored in `Date/Time` fields sort and filter properly as well. The `Date/Time` data type holds dates from January 1, 100, to December 31, 9999.

Currency

The `Currency` data type is another specialized number field. Currency numbers are not rounded during calculations and preserve 15 digits of precision to the left of the decimal point and 4 digits to the right. Because `Currency` fields use a fixed-decimal-point position, they're faster in numeric calculations than doubles.

AutoNumber

The `AutoNumber` field is another specialized `Number` data type. When an `AutoNumber` field is added to a table, Access automatically assigns a long integer (32-bit) value to the field (beginning at 1) and increments the value each time a record is added to the table. Alternatively (determined by the `New Values` property), the value of the `AutoNumber` field is a random integer that is automatically inserted into new records.

Only one `AutoNumber` field can appear in a table. Once assigned to a record, the value of an `AutoNumber` field can't be changed programmatically or by the user. `AutoNumber` fields are equivalent to the `Long Integer` data type and occupy 4 bytes, but they display only positive values. The range of possible values for `AutoNumber` fields is from 1 to 4,294,967,296 — more than adequate as the primary key for most tables.

Note

An `AutoNumber` **field is not guaranteed to generate a continuous, unbroken set of sequential numbers. For example, if the process of adding a new record is interrupted (such as the user pressing the Esc key while entering the new record's data) an** `AutoNumber` **field will "skip" a number.** `AutoNumber` **fields should not be used to provide a stream of sequential numbers. Instead, sequential numbers can be easily added to a table through a data macro (data macros are explained in Chapter 15) or VBA code.**

Yes/No

`Yes/No` fields accept only one of two possible values. Internally stored as 1 (Yes) or 0 (No), the `Yes/No` field is used to indicate yes/no, on/off, or true/false. A `Yes/No` field occupies a single bit of storage.

OLE Object

The `OLE Object` field stores OLE data, highly specialized binary objects such as Microsoft Word documents, Excel spreadsheets, sound or video clips, and images. The OLE object is created by an application that Windows recognizes as an OLE Server, and can be linked to the parent application or embedded in the Access table. OLE objects can only be displayed in bound object frames in Access forms and reports. OLE objects can be as large as 1GB or more in size. OLE fields can't be indexed.

Attachment

The `Attachment` data type was introduced Access 2007. In fact, the `Attachment` data type is one of the reasons Microsoft changed the format of the Access data file. The older `.mdb` format is unable to accommodate attachments.

The `Attachment` data type is relatively complex, compared to the other type of Access fields, and requires a special type of control when displayed on Access forms. For details on this interesting type of field, turn to "Understanding Attachment Fields," later in this chapter.

Hyperlink data type

The `Hyperlink` data type field holds combinations of text and numbers stored as text and used as a hyperlink address. It can have up to three parts:

- The text that appears in a control (usually underlined).
- The Internet address — the path to a file or Web page.
- Any sub-address within the file or page. An example of a sub-address is a picture on a Web page. Each part of the hyperlink's address is separated by the pound sign (#).

Access hyperlinks can even point to forms and reports in other Access databases. This means that you can use a hyperlink to open a form or report in an external Access database and display the form or report on the user's computer.

Lookup Wizard

The `Lookup Wizard` data type inserts a field that enables the end user to choose a value from another table or from the results of a SQL statement. The values may also be presented as a combo box or list box. At design time, the Lookup Wizard leads the developer through the process of defining the lookup characteristics when this data is assigned to a field.

As you drag an item from the `Lookup Wizard` field list, a combo box or list box is automatically created on the form. The list box or combo box also appears on a query data sheet that contains the field.

Entering a field description

The field description is completely optional; you use it only to help you remember a field's uses or to let another developer understand the field's purpose. Often, you don't use the Description column at all, or you use it only for fields whose purpose is not obvious. If you enter a field description, it appears in the status bar whenever you use that field in Access — in the datasheet or in a form. The field description can help clarify a field whose purpose is ambiguous or give the user a more complete explanation of the appropriate values for the field during data entry.

Creating tblCustomers

Working with the different data types, you should be ready to create the final working copy of tblCustomers. When creating the table, you must add a field that is used to link this table to two other tables (tblSales and tblContactLog) in the Collectible Mini Cars application.

Using AutoNumber fields

Access gives special considerations to AutoNumber fields. You can't change a previously defined field from another type to AutoNumber if any data has been added to the table. If you try to change an existing field an AutoNumber, you'll see an error that says

```
Once you enter data in a table, you can't change the data type of
    any field to AutoNumber, even if you haven't yet added data to
    that field.
```

You'll have to add a new AutoNumber field and begin working with it instead of changing an existing field to AutoNumber.

Note
Only one AutoNumber field can be added to an Access table. Generally speaking, it's better to use AutoNumber fields where their special characteristics are needed by an application.

Completing tblCustomers

With tblCustomers in Design view, you're ready to finalize its design. Table 2.1, shown earlier in this chapter, lists the field definitions for tblCustomers. Enter the field names and data types as shown in Table 2.1. The next few pages explain how to change existing fields (which includes rearranging the field order, changing a field name, and deleting a field).

Here are the steps for adding fields to a table structure:

1. Place the cursor in the Field Name column in the row where you want the field to appear.

2. Enter the field name and press Enter or Tab to move to the Data Type column.

3. Select the field's data type from the drop-down list in the Data Type column.

4. If desired, add a description for the field in the Description column.

Repeat each of these steps to create each of the data entry fields for tblCustomers. You can press the down-arrow (↓) key to move between rows, or use the mouse and click on any row. Pressing F6 switches the focus from the top to the bottom of the table design window, and vice versa.

Changing a Table Design

Even the best planned table will require changes from time to time. You might find that you want to add another field, remove a field, change a field name or data type, or simply rearrange the order of the field names.

Although a table's design can be changed at any time, special considerations must be given to tables containing data. Be careful of making changes that damage data in the table, such as making text fields smaller or changing the `Field Size` property of `Number` fields. You can always add new fields to a table without problems, but changing existing fields might be an issue. And, with very few exceptions, it's almost always a bad idea to change a field's name after a table has been put into use in an application.

Inserting a new field

To insert a new field, in the Table Design window, place your cursor on an existing field and right-click on a field in the table's design surface and select Insert ➪ Rows, or click the Insert Rows button in the ribbon. A new row is added to the table, and existing fields are pushed down. You can then enter a new field definition. Inserting a field does not disturb other fields or existing data. If you have queries, forms, or reports that use the table, you might need to add the field to those objects as well.

Deleting a field

There are three ways to delete a field. While the table is in Design view:

- Select the field by clicking the row selector and pressing Delete.
- Right-click on the selected field and choose Delete Rows from the shortcut menu.
- Select the field and click the Delete Rows button from the Tools group on the ribbon's Design tab.

When you delete a field containing data, you'll see a warning that you'll lose data in the table for the selected field. If the table contains data, make sure that you want to eliminate the data for that field (column). You'll also have to delete the same field from queries, forms, reports, macros, and VBA code that use the field name.

Tip
When you delete a field, you can immediately click the Undo button and return the field to the table. But you must undo changes before you save the table's definition or make any other changes to the table's design.

Tip
If you try to delete a field that's part of a relationship (a primary or secondary key field), Access informs you that you can't delete the field until you remove the relationship in the Relationships window.

Cross-Reference
Table relationships and the Relationships window are discussed in Chapter 3.

If you delete a field, you must also fix up all references to that field throughout Access. Because you can use a field name in forms, queries, reports, and even table-data validation, you must examine your system carefully to find any instances where you might have used the specific field name.

Changing a field location

The order of your fields, as entered in the table's Design view, determines the left-to-right column sequence in the table's Datasheet view. If you decide that your fields should be rearranged, click on a field selector and use the mouse to drag the field to its new location.

Changing a field name

You change a field's name by selecting the field's name in the Table Design window and entering a new name; Access updates the table design automatically. As long as you're creating a new table, this process is easy.

Changing a field size

Making a field size larger is simple in a table design. However, only text and number fields can be increased in size. You simply increase the `Field Size` property for text fields or specify a different field size for number fields. You must pay attention to the decimal-point property in number fields to make sure that you don't select a new size that supports fewer decimal places than you currently have.

Caution
When you want to make a field size smaller, make sure that none of the data in the table is larger than the new field width. Choosing a smaller field size may result in data loss.

Tip
Remember that each text field uses only the number of characters actually entered in the field. You should still try to make your fields only as large as the largest value so that Access can stop someone from entering a value that might not fit on a form or report.

Handling data conversion issues

If, in spite of your best efforts, it becomes necessary to change the data type of a field containing data, you might suffer data loss as the data-type conversion occurs. You should be aware of the effects of a data-type conversion on existing data:

- **Any data type to** `AutoNumber`: Can't be done. The `AutoNumber` field type must be created fresh in a new field.

- `Text` to `Number`, `Currency`, `Date/Time`, or `Yes/No`: In most cases, the conversion will be made without damaging the data. Inappropriate values are automatically deleted. For instance, a `Text` field containing "January 28, 2012" will be faithfully converted to a `Date/Time` field. If, however, you change a field containing "January 28, 2012" to a `Yes/No` data type, its value will be deleted.

- `Memo` to `Text`: A straightforward conversion with no loss or corruption of data. Any text longer than the field size specified for the `Text` field is truncated and lost.

- `Number` to `Text`: No loss of information. The number value is converted to text using the General Number format.

- `Number` to `Currency`: Because the `Currency` data type uses a fixed decimal point, some precision may be lost as the number is truncated.

- `Date/Time` to `Text`: No loss of information. Date and time data are converted to text with the General Date format.

- `Currency` to `Text`: No loss of information. The currency value is converted to text without the currency symbol.

- `Currency` to `Number`: Simple, straightforward conversion. Some data may be lost as the currency value is converted to fit the new number field. For example, when converting `Currency` to `Long Integer`, the decimal portion is truncated (cut off).

- `AutoNumber` to `Text`: Conversion occurs without loss of data, except in a case where the width of the text field is inadequate to hold the entire `AutoNumber` value. In this case, the number is truncated.

- `AutoNumber` to `Number`: Simple, straightforward conversion. Some data may be lost as the `AutoNumber` value is converted to fit the new number field. For example, an `AutoNumber` larger than 32,767 will be truncated if it is converted to an `Integer` field.

- `Yes/No` to `Text`: Simple conversion of `Yes/No` value to text. No loss of information.

Note
The `OLE Object` data type **can't be converted to any other type of data.**

Assigning field properties

The field properties built into Access tables are powerful allies that can help you manage the data in your tables. In most cases, the field property is enforced by the database engine, which means the property is consistently applied wherever the field's value is used. For example, if you've set the `Default Value` property in the table design, the default value is available in the table's Datasheet view, on forms, and in queries.

In fact, field properties are among the many differences between Access tables and Excel worksheets. Understanding field properties is just one of several skills necessary to begin using Access tables to store data, rather than Excel worksheets.

Each field data type has its own set of properties. For example, Number fields have a Decimal Places property, and Text fields have a Text Align property. Although many data types share a number of properties (such as Name) in common, there are enough different field properties to make it easy to become confused or to incorrectly use the properties. The following sections discuss some of the more important and frequently used field properties.

Note

The following sections include many references to properties, and property settings in the Access Table Designer. The formal name for a property (such as DefaultValue) never contains a space, while the property's expression in the Table Designer usually contains a space for readabilty (Default Value). These relative minor differences become important when referencing properties in expressions, VBA code, and macros. When making a formal reference to a property in code or a macro, always use the "spaceless" version of the property's name, not the property reference you see in the Access user interface.

Common properties

Here is a list of all the general properties (note that they may not all be displayed, depending on which data type you chose):

- **Field Size:** When applied to Text fields, limits the size of the field to the specified number of characters (1–255). The default is 50.

- **New Values:** Applies to AutoNumber fields. Allows specification of Increment or Random type.

- **Format:** Changes the way data appears after you enter it (uppercase, dates, and so on). There are many different types of formats that may be applied to Access data. Many of these differences are explained in the "Format" section, later in this chapter.

- **Input Mask:** Used for data entry into a predefined format (phone numbers, zip codes, Social Security numbers, dates, customer IDs). Applicable to both Number and Text data types.

- **Decimal Places:** Specifies the number of decimal places for the Currency and the Single, Double, and Decimal Number data types.

- **Caption:** Optional label for form and report fields. Access uses the Caption property instead of the field name in these situations.

- **Default Value:** The value automatically provided for new data entry into the field. This value can be any value appropriate for the field's data type. A default is no more than an initial value; you can change it during data entry. To specify a default value, simply enter the desired value into the DefaultValue property setting. A default value can be an expression, as well as a number or a text string.

Note

Because the Default Value for Number and Currency data types is set to 0 by default, these fields are set automatically to 0 when you add a new record. In many situations, such as medical test results and many financial applications, 0 is not an appropriate default value for numeric fields. Be sure to verify that 0 is an appropriate default value in your Access applications.

- **Validation Rule:** Ensures that data entered into the field conforms to some business rule, such as "greater than zero," "date must occur after January 1, 2000," and so on.

- **Validation Text:** Displays a message when data fails validation.

- **Required:** Specifies whether you must enter a value into a field.

- **Allow Zero Length:** Determines whether you may enter an empty string (" ") into a text field to distinguish it from a null value.

- **Indexed:** Speeds up data access and (if desired) limits data to unique values. Indexing is explained in greater detail later in this chapter.

- **Unicode Compression:** Used for multi-language applications. Requires about twice the data storage, but enables Office documents, including Access reports, to be displayed correctly no matter what language or symbols are used. Generally speaking, Unicode is of no value unless the application is likely to be used in Asian environments.

- **IME Mode:** Also known as the Kanji conversion mode property, this is used to show whether the Kanji mode is maintained when the control is lost. The setting has no relevance in English or European-language applications.

- **IME Sentence Mode:** Used to determine the Sequence mode of fields of a table or controls of a form that switch when the focus moves in or out of the field. The setting has no relevance in English or European-language applications.

- **Smart Tags:** Used to assign a specific action to obtain data in this field. For example, the Financial Symbol Smart Tag obtains recent stock quotes from MSN Money Central.

Format

The Format property specifies how the data contained in table fields appears whenever the data is displayed or printed. When set at the table level, the format is in effect throughout the application. There are different format specifiers for each data type.

Access provides built-in format specifiers for most field data types. The exact format used to display field values is influenced by the Regional Settings in the Windows Control Panel.

The Format property affects only the way a value is displayed and not the value itself or how the value is stored in the database.

If you elect to build a custom format, construct a string in the field's Format property box. There are a number of different symbols you use for each data type. Access provides global format specifications to use in any custom format specifier:

- **(space):** Display spaces as characters.

- **"SomeText":** Display the text between the quotes as literal text.

- **! (exclamation point):** Left-aligns the display.

- *** (asterisk):** Fills empty space with the next character.

- **\ (backslash):** Displays the next character as literal text. Use the backslash to display characters that otherwise have special meaning to Access.

- **[color]:** Displays the output in the color (black, blue, green, cyan, red, magenta, yellow, or white) indicated between the brackets.

The `Format` property takes precedence when both a format specifier and an input mask have been defined.

Number and Currency field formats

There is a wide variety of valid formats for `Number` and `Currency` fields. You can use one of the built-in formats or construct a custom format of your own:

- **General Number:** The number is displayed in the format in which it was entered. (This is the default format for numeric data fields.)

- **Currency:** Add a thousands separator (usually a comma), use a decimal point with two digits to the right of the decimal, and enclose negative numbers in parentheses. A Currency field value is shown with the currency symbol (such as a dollar or euro sign) specified by the Regional and Language Options in Control Panel.

- **Fixed:** Always display at least one digit to the left and two digits to the right of the decimal point.

- **Standard:** Use the thousands separator with two digits to the right of the decimal point.

- **Percent:** The number value is multiplied by 100 and a percent sign is added to the right. Percent values are displayed with two decimal places to the right of the decimal point.

- **Scientific:** Scientific notation is used to display the number.

- **Euro:** Prefixes the euro currency symbol to the number, and uses spaces instead of commas as the thousands delimiter.

The built-in numeric formats are summarized in Table 2.4.

TABLE 2.4

Numeric Format Examples

Format Type	Number as Entered	Number as Displayed	Format Defined
General	987654.321	987654.3	######.#
Currency	987654.321	$987,654.32	$###,##0.00
Euro	987654.321	€987,654.32	€###,##0.00
Fixed	987654.321	987654.32	######.##
Standard	987654.321	987,654.32	###,###.##
Percent	.987	98.7%	###.##%
Scientific	987654.321	9.88E+05	###E+00

All the previous formats are the default formats based on setting the Decimal Places property to AUTO. The exact format applied also depends on the region settings on the user's computer.

Custom numeric formats

Custom formats are created by combining a number of symbols to create a format specifier. The symbols used with Number and Currency fields are listed here:

- **. (period):** Specifies where the decimal point should appear.
- **, (comma):** The thousands separator.
- **0 (zero):** A placeholder for 0 or a digit.
- **# (pound sign):** A placeholder for nothing or a digit.
- **$ (dollar sign):** Displays the dollar sign character.
- **% (percent sign):** Multiplies the value by 100 and adds a percent sign.
- **E- or e-:** Uses scientific notation to display the number. Uses a minus sign to indicate a negative exponent and no sign for positive exponents.
- **E+ or e+:** Uses scientific notation to display the number. Uses a plus sign to indicate positive exponent.

You create custom formats by composing a string made up of one to four sections separated by semicolons. Each section has a different meaning to Access:

- **First section:** The format specifier for positive values
- **Second section:** The format specifier for negative values
- **Third section:** The format specifier for 0 values
- **Fourth section:** The format specifier for null values

Each section is a combination of a numeric formatting string and an optional color specification. Here's an example of a custom format:

```
0,000.00[Green];(0,000.00)[Red];"Zero";"—"
```

This format specifies showing the number with zeros in all positions (even if the number is less than 1,000), using the comma thousands separator, enclosing negative numbers in parentheses, using "Zero" to indicate zero values, and using three dashes for null values.

Date/Time field formats

Access includes a wide variety of built-in and custom formats applicable to Date/Time fields. You can create a custom format to display date and time data in virtually any format imaginable.

Built-in Date/Time formats

The following are the built-in Date/Time formats (these examples are based on the "English (United States)" regional settings in the Control Panel.):

- **General Date:** If the value contains a date only, don't display a time value and vice versa. Dates are displayed in the built-in Short Date format (mm/dd/yy), while time data is displayed in the Long Time format.
- **Long Date:** Sunday, May 13, 2012.
- **Medium Date:** 13-May-12.
- **Short Date:** 5/13/12.
- **Long Time:** 9:21:17 AM.
- **Medium Time:** 09:21 AM.
- **Short Time:** 09:21.

Date and time formats are influenced by the Regional Settings in the Windows Control Panel.

Custom Date/Time formats

Custom formats are created by constructing a specification string containing the following symbols:

- **: (colon):** Separates time elements (hours, minutes, seconds)
- **/ (forward slash):** Separates date elements (days, months, years)
- c: Instructs Access to use the built-in General Date format
- d: Displays the day of the month as one or two digits (1–31)
- dd: Displays the day of the month using two digits (01–31)
- ddd: Displays the day of the week as a three-character abbreviation (Sun, Mon, Tue, Wed, Thu, Fri, Sat)
- dddd: Uses the full name of the day of the week (Sunday, Monday, Tuesday, Wednesday, Thursday, Friday, Saturday)
- ddddd: Uses the built-in Short Date format
- dddddd: Uses the built-in Long Date format
- w: Uses a number to indicate the day of the week
- ww: Shows the week of the year
- m: Displays the month of the year using one or two digits
- mm: Displays the month of the year using two digits (with leading 0 if necessary)
- mmm: Displays the month as a three-character abbreviation (Jan, Feb, Mar, Apr, May, Jun, Jul, Aug, Sep, Oct, Nov, Dec)
- mmmm: Displays the full name of the month (for example, January)
- q: Displays the date as the quarter of the year
- y: Displays the day of the year (1 through 366)
- yy: Displays the year as two digits (for example, 12)
- yyyy: Displays the year as four digits (2012)

- h: Displays the hour using one or two digits (0–23)
- hh: Displays the hour using two digits (00–23)
- n: Displays the minutes using one or two digits (0–59)
- nn: Displays the minutes using two digits (00–59)
- s: Displays the seconds using one or two digits (0–59)
- ss: Displays the seconds using two digits (00–59)
- tttt: Uses the built-in Long Time format
- AM/PM: Uses a 12-hour format with uppercase AM or PM
- am/pm: Uses a 12-hour format with lowercase am or pm
- A/P: Uses a 12-hour format with uppercase A or P
- a/p: Uses a 12-hour format with lowercase a or p
- AMPM: 12-hour format using the morning or after designator specified in the Regional Settings in the Windows Control Panel

Text and Memo field formats

When applied to Text fields, format specifiers help clarify the data contained within the fields. tblCustomers uses several formats. The State text field has a > in the Format property to display the data entry in uppercase. The Active field has a Yes/No format with lookup Display Control property set to Text Box.

Text and Memo fields are displayed as plain text by default. If a particular format is to be applied to Text or Memo field data, use the following symbols to construct the format specifier:

- @: A character or space is required.
- &: A character is optional (not required).
- <: Force all characters to their lowercase equivalents.
- >: Force all characters to their uppercase equivalents.

The custom format specifier may contain as many as three different sections, separated by semicolons:

- **First section:** Specifier for fields containing text
- **Second section:** Format for fields containing zero-length strings
- **Third section:** Format for fields containing null values

If only two sections are given, the second section applies to both zero-length strings and null values. For example, the following specifier displays None when no string data is contained in the field and Unknown when a null value exists in the field. Otherwise, the simple text contained in the field is displayed:

```
@;"None";"Unknown"
```

Several examples of custom text formats using the "English (United States)" regional settings are presented in Table 2.5.

TABLE 2.5

Format Examples

Format Specified	Data as Entered	Formatted Data as Displayed
>	Adam Smith	ADAM SMITH
#,##0;(#,##0);0;None	15, -15, 0, No Data	15, (15), 0, None
Currency	12345.67	$12,345.67
"Acct No." 0000	271	Acct No. 0271
mmm yy	9/17/12	Sep 12
Long Date	9/17/12	Thursday, September 17, 2012

The second example in this table requires a bit of explanation. A field's `Format` property accepts a semicolon-delimited string with as many as four elements. The first two elements are the specifiers when the field's value is positive or negative, respectively, while the last two are the specifications for zero and null values. In row two of Table 2.5, the format string specifies that negative values are to be enclosed in parentheses, while null values are represented by `None`.

Yes/No field formats

A `Yes/No` field displays `Yes`, `No`, `True`, `False`, `On`, or `Off`, depending on the value stored in the field and the setting of the `Format` property for the field. Access predefines these rather obvious format specifications for the `Yes/No` field type:

- **Yes/No:** Displays `Yes` or `No`
- **True/False:** Displays `True` or `False`
- **On/Off:** Displays `On` or `Off`

`Yes`, `True`, and `On` all indicate the same "positive" value, while `No`, `False`, and `Off` indicate the opposite ("negative") value.

Access stores `Yes/No` data in a manner different from what you might expect. The `Yes` data is stored as −1, whereas `No` data is stored as 0. You'd expect it to be stored as 0 for `No` and 1 for `Yes`, but this isn't the case. Without a format setting, you must enter −1 or 0, and it will be stored and displayed that way.

You're also able to specify a custom format for `Yes/No` fields. For example, assume you've got a table with a field that indicates whether the employee has attended an orientation meeting. Although a yes or no answer is appropriate, you might want to get a little fancy with the field's display. By default, a check box is used to indicate the value of the `Yes/No` field (checked means

Yes). To customize the appearance of the Yes/No field, set its Format property according to the following pattern:

```
;"Text for Yes values";"Text for No values"
```

Notice the placeholder semicolon at the front of this string. Also, notice that each text element must be surrounded by quotes. In the case of the employee table, you might use the following Format property specifier:

```
;"Attendance OK";"Must attend orientation"
```

You must also set the Yes/No field's Display Control property to Text Box in order to change the default check box display to text.

Hyperlink data-type format

Access also displays and stores hyperlink data in a manner different from what you would expect. The format of this type is composed of up to three parts, separated by pound signs (#):

- **Display Text:** The text that is displayed as a hyperlink in the field or control
- **Address:** The path to a file (UNC) or page (URL) on the Internet
- **Sub-Address:** A specific location within a file or page

The Display Text property is the text that is visible in the field or control, while the address and sub-address are hidden. In the following example, "Microsoft MSN Home Page" is the displayed text, while http://www.msn.com is the hyperlink's address.

```
Microsoft MSN Home Page#http://www.msn.com
```

Input Mask

The Input Mask property makes it easier for users to enter the data in the correct format. An input mask limits the way the user inputs data into the application. For example, you can restrict entry to only digits for phone numbers, Social Security numbers, and employee IDs. An Input Mask for a Social Security number might look like "000-00-0000." This mask requires input into every space, restricts entry to digits only and does not permit characters or spaces.

A field's input mask is applied anywhere the field appears (query, form, report).

The Input Mask property value is a string containing as many as three semicolon-separated sections:

- **First section:** Contains the mask itself, composed of the symbols shown later.
- **Second section:** Tells Access whether to store the literal characters included in the mask along with the rest of the data. For example, the mask might include dashes to separate the parts of the Social Security number, while a phone number might include parentheses and dashes. Using a 0 tells Access to store the literal characters as part of the data while 1 tells Access to store only the data itself.

- **Third section:** Defines the "placeholder" character that tells the user how many characters are expected in the input area. Many input masks use pound signs (#) or asterisks (*) as placeholders.

The following characters are used to compose the Input Mask string:

- 0: A digit is required, and plus (+) and (–) minus signs are not permitted.
- 9: A digit is optional, and plus (+) and (–) minus signs are not permitted.
- #: Optional digit or space. Spaces are removed when the data is saved in the table. Plus and minus signs are allowed.
- L: A letter from A to Z is required.
- ?: A letter from A to Z is optional.
- A: A character or digit is required.
- a: A character or digit is optional.
- &: Permits any character or space (required).
- C: Permits any character or space (optional).
- . (period): Decimal placeholder.
- , (comma): Thousands separator.
- : (colon): Date and time separator.
- ; (semicolon): Separator character.
- – (dash): Separator character.
- / (forward slash): Separator character.
- < (less-than sign): Converts all characters to lowercase.
- > (greater-than sign): Converts all characters to uppercase.
- ! (exclamation point): Displays the input mask from right to left. Characters fill the mask from right to left.
- \ (back slash): Displays the next character as a literal.

The same specifiers are used on a field's Property Sheet in a query or form.

An Input Mask is ignored when importing data or adding data to a table with an action query.

An Input Mask is overridden by the Format property assigned to a field. In this case, the Input Mask is in effect only as data is entered and reformatted according to the format specifier when the entry is complete.

The Input Mask Wizard

Although you can manually enter an Input Mask, you can easily create an Input Mask for Text or Date/Time type fields with the Input Mask Wizard. When you click the Input Mask property, a Builder button (three periods) appears in the property's input box. Click the Builder button to start the wizard. Figure 2.19 shows the first screen of the Input Mask Wizard.

FIGURE 2.19

The Input Mask Wizard for creating input masks for Text and Date field types

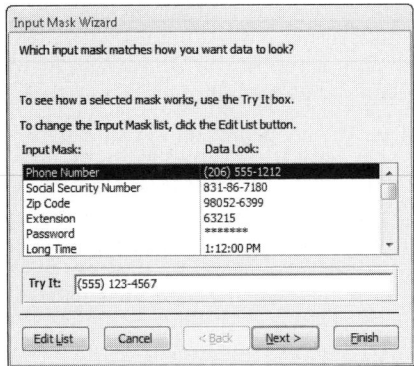

The Input Mask Wizard shows not only the name of each predefined Input Mask, but also an example for each name. You can choose from the list of predefined masks. Click in the Try It text box and enter a test value to see how data entry will look. After you choose an Input Mask, the next wizard screen enables you to refine the mask and specify the placeholder symbol (perhaps a # or @). Another wizard screen enables you to decide whether to store special characters (such as the dashes in a Social Security number) with the data. When you complete the wizard, Access adds the Input Mask characters in the field's Property Sheet.

Tip

You can create your own Input Mask properties for Text and Date/Time fields by simply clicking the Edit List button in the Input Mask Wizard, and entering a descriptive name, Input Mask, placeholder character, and sample data content. Once created, the new mask will be available the next time you use the Input Mask Wizard.

Enter as many custom masks as you need. You can also determine the international settings so that you can work with multiple country masks.

Caption

The Caption property determines what appears in the default label attached to a control created by dragging the field from the field list onto a form or report. The caption also appears as the column heading in Datasheet view (table or query) that include the field.

Caution

Be careful using the Caption property. Because the caption text appears as the column heading in Datasheet view, you might be misled by a column heading in a query's Datasheet view. When the field appears in a query, you don't have immediate access to the field's properties, so you must be aware that the column heading is actually determined by the Caption property and may not reflect the field's name. To be even more confusing, the caption assigned in the table's Design view and the caption assigned in a field's Property Sheet in the Query Design view are different properties and can contain different text.

Captions can be as long as 2,048 characters, more than adequate for all but the most verbose descriptions.

Validation Rule and Validation Text

The `Validation Rule` property establishes requirements for input into the field. Enforced by the Jet database engine, the `Validation Rule` ensures that data entered into the table conforms to the requirements of the application.

Validation properties are a great way to enforce business rules, such as ensuring that a product is not sold for zero dollars, or requiring that an employee review date comes after her hire date. And, like other field properties, validation rules are enforced wherever the field is used in the application.

The value of the `Validation Rule` property is a string containing an expression that is used to test the user's input. The expression used as a field's `Validation Rule` property can't contain user-defined functions or any of the Access domain or aggregate functions (`DCount`, `DSum`, and so on). A field's `Validation Rule` property can't reference forms, queries, or other tables in the application. (These restrictions don't apply to validation rules applied to controls on a form, however.) Field validation rules can't reference other fields in the table, although a rule applied to a record in a table can reference fields in the same table (a record-level validation rule is set in the table's Property Sheet, rather than on an individual field).

The `Validation Text` property contains a string that is displayed in a message box when the user's input doesn't satisfy the requirements of the `Validation Rule` property. The maximum length of the `Validation Text` property value is 255 characters.

When using the `Validation Rule` property, you should always specify a `Validation Text` value to avoid triggering the generic message box Access displays when the rule is violated. Use the `Validation Text` property to provide users with a helpful message that explains acceptable values for the field. Figure 2.20 shows the message box displayed when the value specified by the `Validation Rule` attached to the `CreditLimit` field is exceeded.

FIGURE 2.20

A data-validation warning box. This appears when the user enters a value in the field that does not match the rule specified in the design of the table.

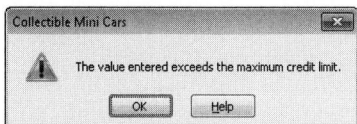

The `Validation Rule` property doesn't apply to check boxes, option buttons, or toggle buttons within an option group on a form. The option group itself has a `Validation Rule` property that applies to all the controls within the group.

Validation properties are often used to ensure that certain dates fall after other dates (for example, an employee's retirement date must fall after his starting date), that nonnegative numbers are entered for values such as inventory quantities, and that entries are restricted to different ranges of numbers or text.

Dates in a `Validation Rule` property are surrounded, or *delimited,* by pound signs (#) when used in Access expressions. If you want to limit the `LastSalesDate` data entry to dates between January 1, 2012, and December 31, 2013, enter **Between #1/1/2012# and #12/31/2013#**.

Tip
If you want to limit the upper end to the current date, you can enter a different set of dates, such as Between #1/1/2010# and Date(). Date() **is a built-in VBA function that returns the current date; it's completely acceptable as part of a validation rule or other expression.**

When a field is dragged onto a form, the `Validation Rule` property of the new control is not set to the field's `Validation Rule`. Unless you enter a new `Validation Rule` value in the control's Property Sheet, Access enforces the rule set at the table level.

Field and control `Validation Rule` properties are enforced when the focus leaves the table field or form control. `Validation Rule` properties applied to both a field and a control bound to the field are enforced for both entities. The table-level rule is applied as data is edited on the bound control and as focus leaves the control.

You can't create table-level `Validation Rule` properties for linked "foreign" tables, such as FoxPro, Paradox, or dBASE. Apply `Validation Rule` properties to controls bound to fields in linked foreign tables.

Required
The `Required` property instructs Access to require input into the field. When set to `Yes`, input is required in the field within a table or in a control on a form bound to the field. The value of a required field can't be Null.

The `Required` property is invalid for `AutoNumber` fields. By default, all `AutoNumber` fields are assigned a value as new records are created.

The Access database engine enforces the `Required` property. An error message is generated if the user tries to leave a text box control bound to a field with its `Required` property set to `Yes`.

The `Required` property can be used in conjunction with the `Allow Zero Length` property to determine when the value of a field is unknown or doesn't exist.

AllowZeroLength
The `AllowZeroLength` property specifies whether you want a zero-length string (" ") to be a valid entry for a `Text` or `Memo` field. `AllowZeroLength` accepts the following values:

- `Yes`: A zero-length string is a valid entry.
- `No`: The table will not accept zero-length strings, and instead, inserts a Null value into the field when no valid text data is supplied.

You can also use Visual Basic for Applications (VBA) code to set a field's AllowZeroLength property.

Combining the AllowZeroLength and Required properties enables you to differentiate between data that doesn't exist (which you'll probably want to represent as a zero-length string) and data that is unknown (which you'll want to store as a null value). In some cases, you'll want to store the proper value in the Text or Memo field.

An example of data that doesn't exist is the case of a customer who doesn't have an e-mail address. The e-mail address field should be set to an empty (zero-length) string indicating that you know the user has an e-mail address, but you don't know what it is. Another customer who is entirely new to the company should have a Null value in the e-mail address field, indicating that you don't know whether the customer has an e-mail address.

An Input Mask can help your application's users distinguish when a field contains a Null value. For example, the Input Mask could be set to display Ask customer when the field contains a zero-length string, and Unknown when the value is Null.

The Required property determines whether a Null value is accepted by the field, while the AllowZeroLength property permits zero-length strings in the field. Together, these independent properties provide the means to determine whether a value is unknown or absent for the field.

The interaction between Required and AllowZeroLength can be quite complicated. Table 2.6 summarizes how these two properties combine to force the user to input a value, or to insert either a Null or zero-length string into a field.

TABLE 2.6

Required and AllowZeroLength Property Combinations

AllowZeroLength	Required	Data Entered by User	Value Stored in Table
No	No	Null	Null
No	No	Space	Null
No	No	Zero-length string	Disallowed
Yes	No	Null	Null
Yes	No	Space	Null
Yes	No	Zero-length string	Zero-length string
No	Yes	Null	Disallowed
No	Yes	Space	Disallowed
No	Yes	Zero-length string	Disallowed
Yes	Yes	Null	Disallowed
Yes	Yes	Space	Zero-length string
Yes	Yes	Zero-length string	Zero-length string

Indexed

The Indexed property tells Access that you want to use a field as an index in the table. Indexed fields are internally organized to speed up queries, sorting, and grouping operations. If you intend to frequently include a certain field in queries (for example, the employee ID or Social Security number) or if the field is frequently sorted or grouped on reports, you should set its Indexed property.

The valid settings for the Indexed property are as follows:

- No: The field is not indexed (default).
- Yes (Duplicates OK): The field is indexed and Access permits duplicate values in the column. This is the appropriate setting for values such as names, where it is likely that names like Smith will appear more than once in the table.
- Yes (No Duplicates): The field is indexed and no duplicates are permitted in the column. Use this setting for data that should be unique within the table, such as Social Security numbers, employee IDs, and customer numbers.

Indexes are discussed in more detail later in this chapter.

In addition to the primary key, you can index as many fields as necessary to provide optimum performance. Access accepts as many as 32 indexes per table. Keep in mind that each index extracts a small performance hit as new records are added to the table. Access dynamically updates the indexing information each time a new record is added. If a table includes an excessive number of indexes, a noticeable delay might occur as each new record is added.

The Indexed property is set in the field's Property Sheet or on the table's Property Sheet. You must use the table's Property Sheet to set multi-field indexes.

Cross-Reference

Using the table indexes Property Sheet is discussed in Chapter 3.

The AutoIndex option

The Access Options dialog box (File ⇨ Access Options ⇨ Object Designers) contains an entry (AutoIndex on Import/Create) that directs Access to automatically index certain fields as they're added to a table's design. By default, fields that begin or end with ID, key, code, or num (for example, EmployeeID or TaskCode) are automatically indexed as the field is created. Every time a new record is added to the table, the field's value is added to the field's index. If there are other field name patterns you'd like Access to automatically index, add new values to the Auto Index on Import/Create checkbox on the Object Designers tab in the Access Options dialog box (see Figure 2.21).

FIGURE 2.21

The Table Design View area on the Options screen contains options for setting the AutoIndex on Import/Create specifier.

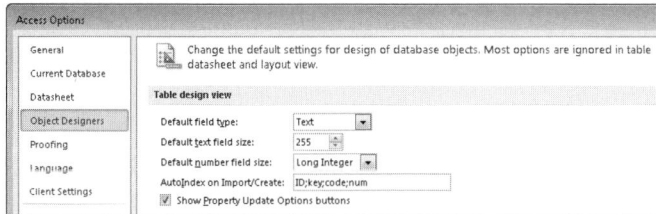

When to index

Generally speaking, you should index fields that are frequently searched or sorted. Remember that indexes slow down certain operations such as inserting records and some action queries.

Memo and OLE Object fields can't be indexed. It would be impossible for Access to maintain an index on these complete data types.

An index should not be used if a field contains very few unique values. For example, you won't see a significant benefit from indexing a field containing a person's sex or state, or Yes/No fields. Because there is a limited range of values in such fields, Access easily sorts the data in these fields.

Use a multiple-field index in situations where sorts are often simultaneously performed on multiple fields (for example, first and last names). Access will have a much easier time sorting such a table.

Understanding tblCustomers Field Properties

After you enter the field names, data types, and field descriptions, you may want to go back and further refine each field. Every field has properties, and these are different for each data type. In tblCustomers, you must enter properties for several data types. Figure 2.22 shows the property area for the field named CreditLimit. Notice that there are two tabs on the property box — General and Lookup.

Tip

Figure 2.22 shows 11 properties available for the CreditLimit Currency **field. Other types, such as** Number **and** Date/Time, Text, **or** Yes/No **show more or fewer options.**

FIGURE 2.22

The property area for the `Currency` field named `CreditLimit`

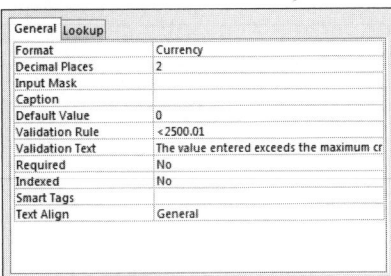

General	Lookup	
Format	Currency
Decimal Places	2
Input Mask	
Caption	
Default Value	0
Validation Rule	<2500.01
Validation Text	The value entered exceeds the maximum cr
Required	No
Indexed	No
Smart Tags	
Text Align	General

Pressing F6 switches between the field entry pane and the property pane (you may have to press F6 several times before you reach the desired pane). You can also move between panes by clicking the desired pane. Some properties display a list of possible values, along with a downward-pointing arrow when you move the pointer into the field. When you click the arrow, the values appear in a drop-down list.

The Field Properties pane of the Table Design window has a second tab: the Lookup tab. After clicking this tab, you may see a single property, the `Display Control` property. This property is used for `Text`, `Number`, and `Yes/No` fields.

Figure 2.23 shows the Lookup Property window for the `Active Yes/No` field where `Display Control` is the only property. This property has three choices: `Check Box`, `Text Box`, and `Combo Box`. Choosing one of these determines which control type is used when a particular field is added to a form. Generally, all controls are created as text boxes except `Yes/No` fields, which are created as check boxes by default. For `Yes/No` data types, however, you may want to use the Text Box setting to display `Yes/No`, `True/False`, or another choice that you specifically put in the format property box.

Cross-Reference
You learn about combo boxes in Chapter 7 and again in Chapter 19.

If you're working with `Text` fields instead of a `Yes/No` field and know a certain `Text` field can only be one of a few combinations, select the combo box choice for the display control. Figure 2.24 shows the Lookup tab when combo box has been selected as the display control for the `Credit Status` field. There are only two acceptable values for `Credit Status`: `OK` and `Not OK`. These two values (separated by a semicolon) are specified as the combo box's `Row Source`, and the `Row Source Type` is set to `Value List`.

FIGURE 2.23

The Lookup tab for a Yes/No field

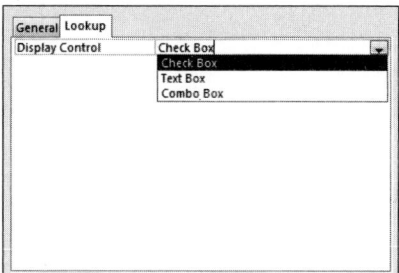

FIGURE 2.24

Setting up a combo box as the display control for Credit Status

Combo box is selected

Display Control	Combo Box
Row Source Type	Value List
Row Source	OK;Not OK
Bound Column	1
Column Count	1
Column Heads	No
Column Widths	
List Rows	16
List Width	Auto
Limit To List	No
Allow Multiple Values	No
Allow Value List Edits	No
List Items Edit Form	
Show Only Row Source Values	No

Values displayed for this field

Although Figure 2.24 shows a combo box using a value list for its items, you could also specify a query or SQL statement as the combo box's row source.

Figure 2.25 shows how the Credit Status field appears when tblCustomers is displayed as a datasheet. The user can select only OK or Not OK as the credit status, and the same combo box appears when the field is added to an Access form.

The properties for a Lookup field are different for each data type. The Yes/No data type fields differ from Text fields or Number fields. Because a Lookup field is really a combo box, the standard properties for a combo box are displayed when you select a Lookup field data type.

FIGURE 2.25

Using a combo box as a lookup control to restrict user input on a field

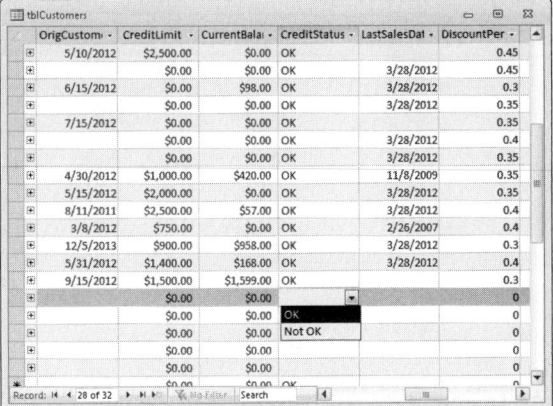

Setting the Primary Key

Every table should have a *primary key* — one or a combination of fields with a unique value for each record. (This principle is called *entity integrity* in the world of database management.) In tblCustomers, the CustomerID field is the primary key. Each customer has a unique CustomerID value so that the database engine can distinguish one record from another. CustomerID 17 refers to one and only one record in the Contacts table. If you don't specify a primary key (unique value field), Access can create one for you.

Choosing a primary key

Without the CustomerID field, you'd have to rely on another field or combination of fields for uniqueness. You couldn't use the Company field because two customers could easily have the same company name. In fact, you couldn't even use the Company and City fields together (in a multi-field key), for the same reason — it's entirely possible two customers with the same name exist in the same city. You need to come up with a field or combination of fields that makes every record unique.

The easiest way to solve this problem is to add an AutoNumber field to serve as the table's primary key. The primary key in tblCustomers is CustomerID, an AutoNumber field.

If you don't designate a field as a primary key, Access can add an AutoNumber field and designate it as the table's primary key. AutoNumber fields make very good primary keys because Access creates the value for you, the number is never reused within a table, and you can't change the value of an AutoNumber field.

Good primary keys

- Uniquely identify each record.
- Cannot be null.
- Must exist when the record is created.
- Must remain stable — you should never change a primary key value once it's established.
- Should be simple and contain as few attributes as possible.

In addition to uniquely identifying rows in a table, primary keys provide other benefits:

- A primary key is always an index.
- An index maintains a presorted order of one or more fields that greatly speeds up queries, searches, and sort requests.
- When you add new records to your table, Access checks for duplicate data and doesn't allow any duplicates for the primary key field.
- By default, Access displays a table's data in the order of its primary key.

By designating a field such as CustomerID as the primary key, data is displayed in a meaningful order. In our example, because the CustomerID field is an AutoNumber, its value is assigned automatically by Access in the order that a record is put into the system.

Although all the tables in the Collectible Mini Cars application use AutoNumber fields as their primary keys, you should be aware of the reasons why AutoNumber fields make such excellent primary keys.

The ideal primary key is, then, a single field that is immutable and guaranteed to be unique within the table. For these reasons, the Collectible Mini Cars database uses the AutoNumber field exclusively as the primary key for all tables.

Creating the primary key

The primary key can be created in any of three ways. With a table open in Design view:

- Select the field to be used as the primary key and click the Primary Key button (the key icon) in the Tools group in the ribbon's Design tab.
- Right-click on the field to display the shortcut menu and select Primary Key.
- Save the table without creating a primary key, and allow Access to automatically create an AutoNumber field.

After you designate the primary key, a key icon appears in the gray selector area to the left of the field's name to indicate that the primary key has been created.

Creating composite primary keys

You can designate a combination of fields to be used as a table's primary key. Such keys are often referred to as *composite primary keys*. As indicated in Figure 2.26, select the fields that you want to include in the composite primary key, then click the key icon in the Tools ribbon tab. It helps, of course, if the fields lie right next to each other in the table's design.

Creating a composite primary key

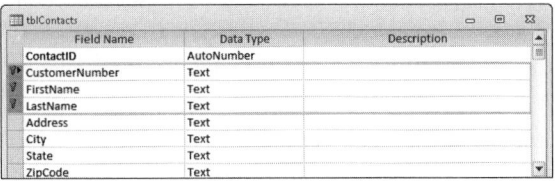

Composite primary keys are primarily used when the developer strongly feels that a primary key should be comprised of data that occurs naturally in the database. There was a time when all developers were taught that every table should have a *natural primary key* (data that occurs naturally in the table).

The reason that composite primary keys are seldom used these days is because developers have come to realize that data is highly unpredictable. Even if your users promise that a combination of certain fields will never be duplicated in the table, things have a way of turning out differently than planned. Using a *surrogate primary key* (a surrogate primary key is a key field that does not naturally occur in the table's data, such as a Social Security Number or Employee ID), such as an AutoNumber, separates the table's design from the table's data. The problem with natural primary keys is that, eventually, given a large enough data set, the values of fields chosen as the table's primary key are likely to be duplicated.

Furthermore, when using composite keys, maintaining relationships between tables becomes more complicated because the fields comprising the primary key must be duplicated in all the tables containing related data. Using composite keys simply adds to the complexity of the database without adding stability, integrity, or other desirable features.

Indexing Access Tables

Data is rarely, if ever, entered into tables in a meaningful order. Usually, records are added to tables in random order (with the exception of time-ordered data). For example, a busy order-entry system will gather information on a number of different customer orders in a single day. Most often, this data will be used to report orders for a single customer for billing purposes or for extracting order quantities for inventory management. The records in the Orders table, however, are in chronological order, which is not necessarily helpful when preparing reports detailing customer orders. In that case, you'd rather have data entered in customer ID order.

To further illustrate this concept, consider the Rolodex card file many people use to store names, addresses, and phone numbers. Assume for a moment that the cards in the file were fixed in place. You could add new cards, but only to the end of the card file. This limitation would mean that "Jones" might follow "Smith," which would in turn be followed by "Baker." In other words, there is no particular order to the data stored in this file.

An unsorted Rolodex like this would be very difficult to use. You'd have to search each and every card looking for a particular person, a painful and time-consuming process. Of course, this is not how you use address card files. When you add a card to the file, you insert it into the Rolodex at the location where it *logically* belongs. Most often, this means inserting the card in alphabetical order, by last name, into the Rolodex.

Records are added to Access tables as described in the fixed card file example earlier. New records are always added to the end of the table, rather than in the middle of the table where they may logically belong. However, in an order-entry system, you'd probably want new records inserted next to other records on the same customer. Unfortunately, this isn't how Access tables work. The *natural order* of a table is the order in which records were added to the table. This order is sometimes referred to as *entry order* or *physical order* to emphasize that the records in the table appear in the order in which they were added to the table.

Using tables in natural order is not necessarily a bad thing. Natural order makes perfect sense if the data is rarely searched or if the table is very small. Also, there are situations where the data being added to the table is highly ordered to start with. If the table is used to gather sequential data (like readings from an electric meter) and the data will be used in the same sequential order, there is no need to impose an index on the data.

But for situations where natural order does not suffice, Microsoft Access provides *indexing* to help you find and sort records faster. You specify a *logical* order for the records in a table by creating an *index* on that table. Access uses the index to maintain one or more internal sort orders for the data in the table. For example, you may choose to index the `LastName` field that will frequently be included in queries and sorting routines.

Microsoft Access uses indexes in a table as you use an index in a book: To find data, Access looks up the data's location in the index. Most often, your tables will include one or more *simple indexes*. A simple index is one that involves a single field in the table. Simple indexes may arrange the table's records in ascending or descending order. Simple indexes are created by setting the field's `Indexed` property to one of the following values:

- `Yes (Duplicates OK)`
- `Yes (No Duplicates)`

By default, Access fields are not indexed, but it's hard to imagine a table that doesn't require some kind of index. The next section discusses why indexing is important to use in Access tables.

The importance of indexes

Microsoft's data indicates that more than half of all tables in Access databases contain *no* indexes. This number doesn't include the tables that are improperly indexed — it includes only those tables that have no indexes at all. It appears that a lot of people don't appreciate the importance of indexing the tables in an Access database.

On the CD-ROM

As a demonstration of the power and value of indexes, this book's CD includes a database named `IndexTest.accdb`. This database includes two identical tables containing approximately 355,000 random words. One table is indexed on the `Word` field, and the other is not. A small form (shown in Figure 2.27) lets you query either the indexed or unindexed table, and shows the number of milliseconds the search takes.

FIGURE 2.27

`frmIndexTest` provides a quick and easy way to verify the importance of indexes.

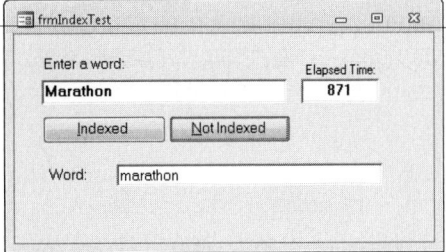

In a number of repeated tests, the indexed table consistently finds a word in less than 1 millisecond, while the unindexed search takes between 400 and 800 milliseconds. Displaying the results you see in Figure 2.27 takes almost no time at all and doesn't contribute to the overall time required to run the query. It goes without saying that the actual time required to run a query depends very much on the computer's hardware, but performance enhancements of 500 percent and more are not at all uncommon when adding an index to a field.

Because an index means that Access maintains an internal sort order on the data contained in the indexed field, you can see why performance is enhanced by an index. You should index virtually every field that is frequently involved in queries or is frequently sorted on forms or reports.

Without an index, Access must search each and every record in the database looking for matches. This process is called a *table scan* and is analogous to searching through each and every card in Rolodex file to find all the people who work for a certain company. Until you reach the end of the deck, you can't be sure you've found every relevant card in the file.

As mentioned earlier in this chapter, a table's primary key field is always indexed. This is because the primary key is used to locate records in the table. Indexing the primary key makes it much easier for Access to find the required tables in either the current table or a foreign table related to the current table. Without an index, Access has to search all records in the related table to make sure it has located all the related records.

Tip

The performance losses due to unindexed tables can have a devastating effect on the overall performance of an Access application. Anytime you hear a complaint about the performance of an application, consider indexing as a possible solution.

Multiple-field indexes

Multiple-field indexes (also called *composite indexes*) are easy to create. In Design view, click on the Indexes toolbar button or select the Indexes command on the View menu. The Indexes dialog box (shown in Figure 2.28) appears, allowing you to specify the fields to include in the index.

FIGURE 2.28

Multifield (composite) indexes can enhance performance.

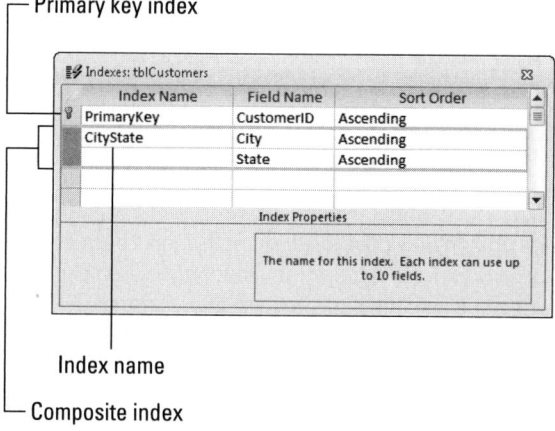

Enter a name for the index (`CityState` in Figure 2.28) and tab to the Field Name column. Use the drop-down list to select the fields to include in the index. In this example `City` and `State` are combined as a single index. Any row appearing immediately below this row that does not contain an index name is part of the composite index. Access considers both these fields when creating the sort order on this table, speeding queries and sorting operations that include both the `City` and `State` fields.

As many as ten fields can be included in a composite index. As long as the composite index is not used as the table's primary key, any of the fields in the composite index can be empty.

Figure 2.29 shows how to set the properties of an index. The cursor is placed in the row in the Indexes dialog box containing the name of the index. Notice the three properties appearing below the index information in the top half of the Indexes dialog box.

FIGURE 2.29

It's easy to set the properties of an index.

Selected index

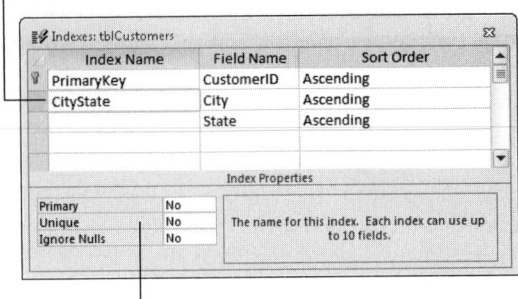

Index properties

The index properties are quite easy to understand (these properties apply to single-field and composite indexes equally):

- **Primary:** When set to Yes, Access uses this index as the table's primary key. More than one field can be designated as the primary key, but keep the rules governing primary keys in mind, particularly those requiring each primary key value to be unique and that no field in a composite primary key can be empty. The default for the Primary property is No.

- **Unique:** When set to Yes, the index must be unique within a table. A Social Security number field is a good candidate for a unique index because the application's business rules may require one and only one instance of a Social Security Number in the table. In contrast, a last name field should not be uniquely indexed, because many last names, like Smith and Jones, are very common, and having a unique index on the last name field will only cause problems.

  When applied to composite keys, the *combination* of field values must be unique — each field within the composite key can duplicate fields found within the table.

- **Ignore Nulls:** If a record's index field contains a Null value (which happens in a composite index only if all fields in the composite index are Null) the record's index won't contribute anything to the overall indexing. In other words, unless a record's index contains some kind of value, Access doesn't know where to insert the record in the table's internal index sort lists. Therefore, you might want to instruct Access to ignore a record if the index value is null. By default, the Ignore Nulls property is set to No, which means Access inserts records with a Null index value into the indexing scheme along with any other records containing Null index values.

You should test the impact of the index properties on your Access tables and use the properties that best suit the data handled by your databases.

A field can be both the primary key for a table and part of a composite index. You should index your tables as necessary to yield the highest possible performance without worrying about over-indexing or violating some arcane indexing rules. For example, in a database such as Collectible Mini Cars, the invoice number in `tblSales` is frequently used in forms and reports, and should be indexed. In addition, there are many situations in which the invoice number is used in combinations with other fields, such as the sales date or salesperson ID. You should consider adding composite indexes combining the invoice number with sales date, and salesperson ID, to the sales table.

When to index tables

Depending on the number of records in a table, the extra overhead of maintaining an index may not justify creating an index beyond the table's primary key. Though data retrieval is somewhat faster than it is without an index, Access must update index information whenever you enter or change records in the table. In contrast, changes to nonindexed fields do not require extra file activity. You can retrieve data from nonindexed fields as easily (although not as *quickly*) as from indexed fields.

Generally speaking, it's best to add secondary indexes when tables are quite large, and when indexing fields other than the primary key speeds up searches. Even with large tables, however, indexing can slow performance if the records in tables will be changed often or new records will be added frequently. Each time a record is changed or added, Access must update all indexes in the table.

Given all the advantages of indexes, why not index everything in the table? What are the drawbacks of indexing too many fields? Is it possible to over-index tables?

First, indexes increase the size of the Access database somewhat. Unnecessarily indexing a table that doesn't really require an index eats up a bit of disk space for each record in the table. More important, indexes extract a performance hit for each index on the table every time a record is added to the table. Because Access automatically updates indexes each time a record is added (or removed), the internal indexing must be adjusted for each new record. If you have ten indexes on a table, Access makes ten adjustments to the indexes each time a new record is added or an existing record is deleted, causing a noticeable delay on large tables (particularly on slow computers).

Sometimes changes to the data in records cause adjustments to the indexing scheme. This is true if the change causes the record to change its position in sorting or query activities. Therefore, if you're working with large, constantly changing data sets that are rarely searched, you may choose *not* to index the fields in the table, or to minimally index by indexing only those few fields that are likely to be searched.

As you begin working with Access tables, you'll probably start with the simplest one-field indexes and migrate to more complex ones as your familiarity with the process grows. Do keep in mind, however, the tradeoffs between greater search efficiency and the overhead incurred by maintaining a large number of indexes on your tables.

It's also important to keep in mind that indexing does not modify the physical arrangement of records in the table. The natural order of the records (the order in which the records were added to the table) is maintained after the index is established.

Note

A compact and repair cycle on an Access database forces Access to rebuild the indexes in all the tables, and physically rearranges tables in primary key order in the `.accdb` file. The maintenance operations ensure that your Access databases operate at maximum efficiency.

Printing a Table Design

You can print a table design by clicking the Database Documenter button in the Analyze group on the ribbon's Database Tools tab. The Analyze group contains a number of tools that make it easy to document your database objects. When you click the Database Documenter button, Access shows you the Documenter dialog box, which lets you select objects to print. In Figure 2.30, `tblCus-tomers` is selected in the documenter's Tables tab.

FIGURE 2.30

The Documenter dialog box

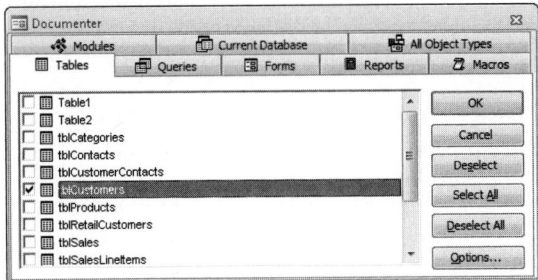

You can also set various options for printing. When you click the Options button, the Print Table Definition dialog box (shown in Figure 2.31) appears, enabling you to select which information from the Table Design to print. You can print the various field names, all their properties, the indexes, and even network permissions.

Caution

Don't select too many options in the Print Table Definition dialog box. Printing every detail of a table's design can take many pages to output. It's probably best to print just a few items for a table, and add to the options when necessary.

After you select which data you want to view, Access generates a report. You can view the report in a Print Preview window or send it to a printer. You may want to save the report within the database as part of the application's documentation.

FIGURE 2.31

Printing options in the Print Table Definition dialog box

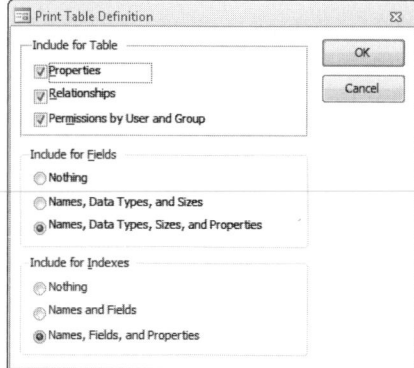

Tip

The Database Documenter creates a table of all the objects and object properties you specify. You can use this utility to document such database objects as forms, queries, reports, macros, and modules.

Saving the Completed Table

You can save the completed table design by choosing File⇨ Save or by clicking the Save button in the Quick Access toolbar in the upper-left corner of the Access environment. If you're saving the table for the first time, Access asks for its name. Table names can be up to 64 characters long and follow standard Access object-naming conventions — they may include letters and numbers, cannot begin with a number, and can't include punctuation. You can also save the table when you close it.

If you've saved this table before and you want to save it with a different name, choose File⇨ Save Object As and enter a different table name. This action creates a new table design and leaves the original table with its original name untouched. If you want to delete the old table, select it in the Navigation Pane and press the Delete key.

Manipulating Tables

As you add many tables to your database, you may want to use them in other databases or make copies of them as backups. In many cases, you may want to copy only the table's design and not include all the data in the table. You can perform many table operations in the Navigation Pane, including

- Renaming tables
- Deleting tables

- Copying tables in a database
- Copying a table to another database

You perform these tasks by direct manipulation or by using menu items.

Renaming tables

Rename a table by following these steps:

1. Select the table name in the Navigation Pane.
2. Click once on the table name, and press F2.
3. Type the new name of the table and press Enter.

You can also rename the table by right-clicking on its name in the Navigation Pane and selecting Rename from the shortcut menu. After you change the table name, it appears in the Tables list, which re-sorts the tables in alphabetical order.

Caution

If you rename a table, you must change the table name in any objects in which it was previously referenced, including queries, forms, and reports.

Deleting tables

Delete a table by selecting the table in the Navigation Pane and pressing the Delete key. Another method is to right-click the table and select Delete from the shortcut menu. Like most delete operations, you have to confirm the delete by clicking Yes in a confirmation box.

Caution

Be aware, however, that holding down the Shift key while pressing the Delete key deletes the table (or any other database object, for that matter) without confirmation. You'll find the Shift+Delete key combination useful for removing items, but also dangerous if not carefully applied.

Copying tables in a database

The copy and paste options in the Clipboard group on the Home tab allow you to copy any table in the database. When you paste the table back into the database, the Paste Table As dialog box appears, asking you to choose from three options:

- **Structure Only:** Clicking the Structure Only button creates a new table, an empty table with the same design as the copied table. This option is typically used to create a temporary table or an archive table to which you can copy old records.
- **Structure and Data:** When you click Structure and Data, a complete copy of the table design and all its data is created.

- **Append Data to Existing Table:** Clicking the Append Data to Existing Table button adds the data of the selected table to the bottom of another table. This option is useful for combining tables, such as when you want to add data from a monthly transaction table to a yearly history table.

Follow these steps to copy a table:

1. Right-click the table name in the Navigation Pane and choose Copy from the shortcut menu, or click the Copy button in the Clipboard group on the Home tab.
2. Choose Paste from the shortcut menu, or click the Paste button in the Clipboard group on the Home tab.
3. Enter the name of the new table.

   When you're appending data to an existing table (see the next step), you must type the name of an existing table.
4. Choose one of the Paste options — Structure Only, Structure and Data, or Append Data to Existing Table — from the Paste Table As dialog box.
5. Click OK to complete the operation.

Figure 2.32 shows the Paste Table As dialog box where you make these decisions.

FIGURE 2.32

Pasting a table opens the Paste Table As dialog box.

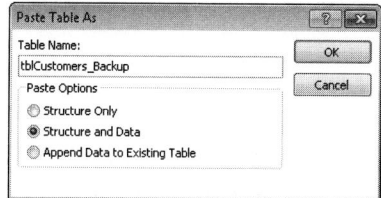

Copying a table to another database

Just as you can copy a table within a database, you can copy a table to another database. There are many reasons why you may want to do this. Maybe you share a common table among multiple systems, or you may need to create a backup copy of your important tables within the system.

When you copy tables to another database, the relationships between tables are not copied. Access copies only the table design and the data to the other database. The method for copying a table to another database is essentially the same as for copying a table within a database:

1. Right-click the table name in the Navigation Pane and choose Copy from the shortcut menu, or click the Copy button in the Clipboard group on the Home tab.

2. Open the other Access database and choose Edit Paste from the shortcut menu, or click the Copy button in the Clipboard group on the Home tab.

3. Provide the name of the new table and choose one of the Paste options (Structure Only, Structure and Data, or Append Data to Existing Table).

4. Click OK to complete the operation.

Adding Records to a Database Table

Adding records to a table is as simple as clicking the table in the Navigation Pane to open the table in Datasheet view. Once the table is opened, enter values for each field. Figure 2.33 shows adding records in datasheet mode to the table.

You can enter information into all fields except CustomerID. AutoNumber fields automatically provide a number for you.

FIGURE 2.33

Using Datasheet view to add records to a table

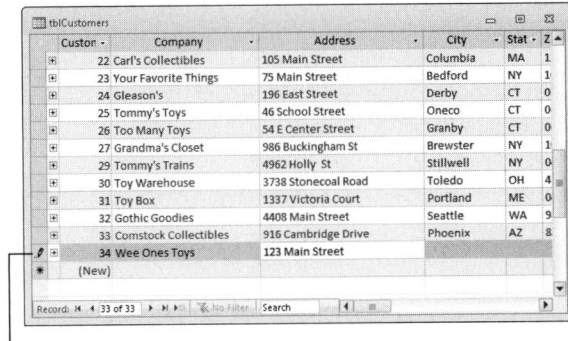

New record

Although you can add records directly into the table through the Datasheet view, it isn't the most efficient way. Adding records using forms is better because code behind a form can dynamically provide default values (perhaps based on data already added to the form) and communicate with the user during the data entry process.

Understanding Attachment Fields

Microsoft recognizes that database developers must deal with many different types of data. Although the traditional Access data types (Text, Currency, OLE Object, and so on) are able to handle many different types of data, until recently there was no way to accommodate *complete files* as Access data without performing some transformation on the file (such as conversion to OLE data).

New Feature

Access 2010 includes the `Attachment` data type, enabling you to bring entire files into your Access database as "attachments" to a table. When you click on an attachment field, Access opens a small Attachments dialog box (shown in Figure 2.34), enabling you to locate files to attach to the table.

FIGURE 2.34

Managing attachments in an Attachment field

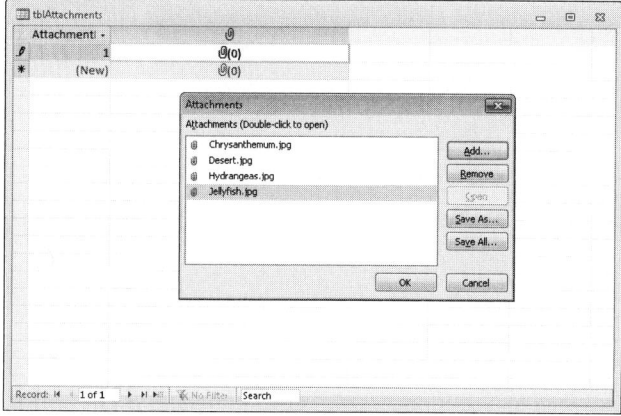

The Add button in Figure 2.34 opens the familiar Windows Choose File dialog box, enabling you to search for one or more files to attach to the field. The selected files are added to the list you see in Figure 2.34. Notice also that the Attachments dialog box includes buttons for removing attachments from the field, and for saving attachments back to the computer's disk.

The significant thing to keep in mind about the `Attachment` data type is that a single attachment field in a table can contain multiple files of different types. It's entirely possible to store a Word document, several audio or video clips, and a number of photographs, within a single attachment field.

Cross-Reference

In Chapter 19, you'll see how `Attachment` fields are used on Access forms.

Caution

Obviously, because the attached data is incorporated into the database, the `.accdb` file will quickly grow if many attachments are added. You should use the `Attachment` data type only when its benefits outweigh the burden it places on an Access application.

Summary

This chapter has covered the important topics of creating new Access databases and adding tables to Access databases. Although I've covered these topics from the perspective of creating brand-new databases and tables, the operations you performed in this chapter are identical to the maintenance procedures you perform on existing databases and tables.

The next chapter drills into the very important topics of data normalization, referential integrity, creating relationships, and other operations and procedures required to protect the integrity and reliability of data in your Access databases. Unless you have a very firm understanding of these important issues, you should take the time to study the material in Chapter 3 and understand how Access supports professional database design.

Designing Bulletproof Databases

IN THIS CHAPTER

Understanding bulletproof database design

Normalizing database data

Looking at common table relationships

Understanding integrity rules

Adding key fields to tables

I've already covered one of the most basic assumptions about relational database systems — that is, that data is spread across a number of tables that are related through primary and foreign keys (see Chapters 1 and 2 for a review). Although this basic principle is easy to understand, it can be much more difficult to understand why and when data should be broken into separate tables.

Because the data managed by a relational database such as Access exists in a number of different tables, there must be some way to connect the data. The more efficiently the database performs these connections, the better and more flexible the database application as a whole will function.

Although databases are meant to model real-world situations, or at least manage the data involved in real-world situations, even the most complex situation is reduced to a number of relationships between pairs of tables. As the data managed by the database becomes more complex, you may need to add more tables to the design. For example, a database to manage employee affairs for a company will include tables for employee information (name, Social Security number, address, hire date, and so on), payroll information, benefits programs the employee belongs to, and so on.

This chapter uses a variety of data from different business situations, including Northwind Traders (the traditional Access example database), a small bookstore, and the Collectible Mini Cars application used in other chapters of this book. Each data set has somewhat different objectives from the others and is used to emphasize different aspects of relational theory. All the tables described in this chapter are contained in the `Chapter03.accdb` database.

When working with the actual data, however, you concentrate on the relationship between two tables at a time. You might create the employees and payroll tables first, connecting these tables with a relationship to make it easy to find all the payroll information for an employee.

On the CD-ROM

This chapter uses a variety of data from the database named `Chapter03.accdb`. If you haven't already copied it onto your machine from the CD, you'll need to do so now. If you're following the examples, you can use the tables in this database or create the tables yourself in another database.

Building Bulletproof Databases

In Chapters 1 and 2, you saw examples of common relationships found in many Access databases. By far the most common type of table relationship is the one-to-many. The Collectible Mini Cars application has many such relationships: Each record in the Customers table is related to one or more records in the Sales table (each contact may have purchased more than one item through Collectible Mini Cars). (I cover one-to-many relationships in detail in the "Table Relationships" section, later in this chapter.)

You can easily imagine an arrangement that would permit the data contained in the Customers and Sales tables to be combined within a single table. All that would be needed is a separate row for each order placed by each of the contacts. As new orders come in, new rows containing the customer and order information would be added to the table.

The Access table shown in Figure 3.1 is an example of such an arrangement. In this figure, the `OrderID` column contains the order number placed by the contact (the data in this table has been sorted by `CustomerID` to show how many orders have been placed by each contact). The table in Figure 3.1 was created by combining data from the Customers and Orders tables in the Northwind Traders sample database and is included in the `Chapter03.accdb` database file on this book's CD-ROM.

Notice the `OrderID` column to the right of the `CompanyName` column. Each contact (like Alfreds Futterkiste) has placed a number of orders. Columns to the far right in this table (beyond the right edge of the figure) contain more information about each contact, including address and phone numbers, while columns beyond the company information contain the specific order information. In all, this table contains 24 different fields.

The design shown in Figure 3.1 is what happens when a spreadsheet application such as Excel is used for database purposes. Because Excel is entirely spreadsheet oriented, there is no provision for breaking up data into separate tables, encouraging users to keep everything in one massive spreadsheet.

FIGURE 3.1

An Access table containing customer *and* orders data

Such an arrangement has several problems:

- **The table quickly becomes unmanageably large.** The Northwind Traders Contacts table contains 11 different fields, while the Orders table contains 14 more. One field — `OrderID` — overlaps both tables. Each time an order is placed, all 24 data fields in the combined table would be added for each record added to the table, including a lot of data (such as the `Contact Name` and `Contact Title`) not directly relevant to an order.

- **Data are difficult to maintain and update.** Making simple changes to the data in the large table — for example, changing a contact's phone or fax number — involves searching through all records in the table, changing every occurrence of the phone number. It's easy to make an erroneous entry or miss one or more instances. The fewer records needing changes, the better off the user will be.

- **A monolithic table design is wasteful of disk space and other resources.** Because the combined table contains a huge amount of redundant data (for example, a contact's address is repeated for every sale), a large amount of hard disk space is consumed by the redundant information. In addition to wasted disk space, network traffic, computer memory, and other resources would be poorly utilized.

A much better design — the relational design — moves the repeated data into a separate table, leaving a field in the first table to serve as a reference to the data in the second table. The additional field required by the relational model is a small price to pay for the efficiencies gained by moving redundant data out of the table.

A second huge advantage of normalizing data, and applying strict database design rules to Access applications is that the data becomes virtually bulletproof. In an appropriately designed and managed database, users are ensured that the information displayed on forms and reports truly reflects the data stored in the underlying tables. Poorly designed databases are prone to data corruption, which means that records are sometimes "lost" and never appear on forms and reports, even though users added the data to the application, or the wrong data is returned by the application's queries. In either case, the database can't be trusted because users are never sure that what they're seeing in forms and reports is correct.

Users tend to trust what they see on the screen and printed on paper. Imagine the problems that would occur if a customer were never billed for a purchase, or inventory were incorrectly updated. Nothing good can come from a weak database design. As database developers, we're responsible for making sure the applications we design are as strong and resilient as possible. Building bullet-proof databases that resist data entry errors and always correctly return data as expected is the theme of this chapter.

Data Normalization

The process of splitting data across multiple tables is called *normalizing* the data. There are several stages of normalization; the first through the third stages are the easiest to understand and implement and are generally sufficient for the majority of applications. Although higher levels of normalization are possible, they're usually ignored by all but the most experienced and fastidious developers.

To illustrate the normalization process, I'll use a little database that a book wholesaler might use to track book orders placed by small bookstores in the local area. This database must handle the following information:

- Book title
- ISBN
- Author
- Publisher
- Publisher address
- Publisher city
- Publisher state
- Publisher zip code
- Publisher phone number
- Publisher fax
- Customer name
- Customer address
- Customer city
- Customer state
- Customer zip code
- Customer phone number

Although this data set is very simple, it's typical of the type of data you might manage with an Access database application, and it provides a valid demonstration of normalizing a set of data.

First normal form

The initial stage of normalization, called first normal form (abbreviated *1NF*), requires that the table conform to the following rule:

> Each cell of a table must contain only a single value and the table must not contain repeating groups of data.

A table is meant to be a two-dimensional storage object, and storing multiple values within a field or permitting repeating groups within the table implies a third dimension to the data. Figure 3.2 shows the first attempt (`tblBookOrders1`) at building a table to manage bookstore orders. Notice that some bookstores have ordered more than one book. A value like 7 `Cookie Magic` in the `BookTitles` field means that the contact has ordered seven copies of the cookbook titled *Cookie Magic*. Storing both a quantity and the item's name in the same cell is just one of several ways that this table violates first normal form.

FIGURE 3.2

An unnormalized `tblBookOrders` table

The table in Figure 3.2 is typical of a *flat-file* approach to building a database. Data in a flat-file database is stored in two dimensions (rows and columns) and neglects the third dimension (related tables) possible in a relational database system such as Microsoft Access.

Notice how the table in Figure 3.2 violates the first rule of normalization. Many of the records in this table contain multiple values in the `BookTitle` field. For example, the book titled *Smokin' Hams* appears in records 7 and 8. There is no way for the database to handle this data easily — if you want to cross-reference the books ordered by the bookstores, you'd have to parse the data contained in the `BookTitle` field to determine which books have been ordered by which contacts.

A slightly better design is shown in Figure 3.3 (`tblBookOrders2`). The books' quantities and titles have been separated into individual columns. Each row still contains all the data for a single order. This arrangement makes it somewhat easier to retrieve quantity and title information, but the repeating groups for quantity and title continue to violate the first rule of normalization. (The row height in Figure 3.3 has been adjusted to make it easier to see the table's arrangement.)

FIGURE 3.3

Only a slight improvement over the previous design

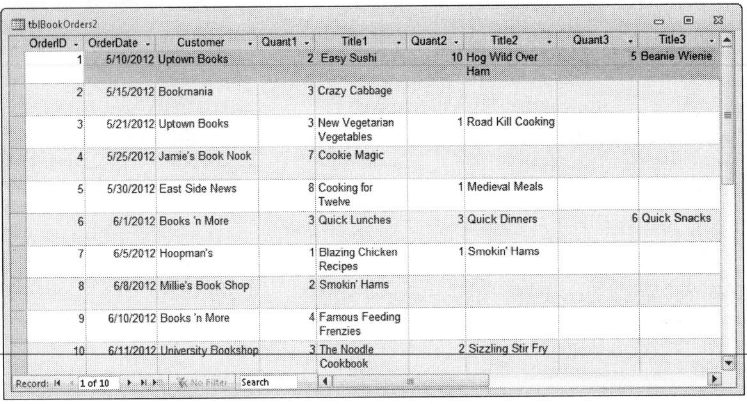

tblBookOrders2

OrderID	OrderDate	Customer	Quant1	Title1	Quant2	Title2	Quant3	Title3
1	5/10/2012	Uptown Books	2	Easy Sushi	10	Hog Wild Over Ham	5	Beanie Wienie
2	5/15/2012	Bookmania	3	Crazy Cabbage				
3	5/21/2012	Uptown Books	3	New Vegetarian Vegetables	1	Road Kill Cooking		
4	5/25/2012	Jamie's Book Nook	7	Cookie Magic				
5	5/30/2012	East Side News	8	Cooking for Twelve	1	Medieval Meals		
6	6/1/2012	Books 'n More	3	Quick Lunches	3	Quick Dinners	6	Quick Snacks
7	6/5/2012	Hoopman's	1	Blazing Chicken Recipes	1	Smokin' Hams		
8	6/8/2012	Millie's Book Shop	2	Smokin' Hams				
9	6/10/2012	Books 'n More	4	Famous Feeding Frenzies				
10	6/11/2012	University Bookshop	3	The Noodle Cookbook	2	Sizzling Stir Fry		

Record: 1 of 10 No Filter Search

The design in Figure 3.3 is still clumsy and difficult to work with. The columns to hold the book quantities and titles are permanent features of the table. The developer must add enough columns to accommodate the maximum number of books that could be purchased by a bookstore. For example, let's assume that the developer anticipates that no bookstore will ever order more than 50 books at a time. This means that 100 columns are added to the table (two columns — `Quantity` and `Title` — are required for each book title ordered). If a bookstore orders a single book, 98 columns would sit empty in the table, a very wasteful and inefficient situation.

Based on the design shown in Figure 3.3, it would be exceedingly difficult to query `tblBookOrders2` to get the sales figure for a particular book. The quantity sold for any book is scattered all over the table, in different rows and different columns, making it very difficult to know where to look for in a book's sales data.

Also, if any book order exceeds 100 books, the table has to be redesigned to accommodate the two additional columns needed by the order. Of course, the user might add a second row for the order, making the data in the table more difficult to work with than intended.

Figure 3.4 shows `tblBookOrders3`, a new table created from the data in Figure 3.3 in first normal form. Instead of stacking multiple book orders within a single record, in `tblBookOrders3` each record contains a single book ordered by a customer. More records are required, but the data is handled much more easily. First normal form is much more efficient because the table contains no unused fields. Every field is meaningful to the table's purpose.

FIGURE 3.4

First normal form at last!

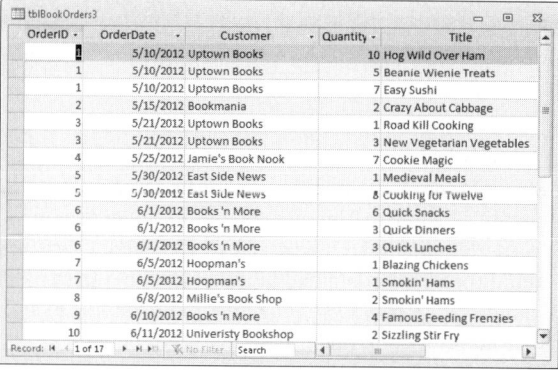

The table in Figure 3.4 contain the same data as shown in Figure 3.2 and Figure 3.3. The new arrangement, however, makes it much easier to work with the data. For example, queries are easily constructed to return the total number of a particular book ordered by contacts, or to determine which titles have been ordered by a particular bookstore.

Tip

Your tables should always be in first normal form. Make sure each cell of the table contains a single value, don't mix values within a cell, and don't have repeating groups (as you saw in Figure 3.3).

The table design optimization is not complete at this point, however. Much remains to be done with the BookOrders data and the other tables in this application. In particular, the table shown in Figure 3.4 contains a lot of redundant information. The book titles are repeated each time customers order the same book, and the order number and order date are repeated for all the rows for an order.

A more subtle issue is the fact that the OrderID can no longer be used as the table's primary key. Because the OrderID is duplicated for each book title in an order, it can't be used to identify individual records in the table. Instead, the OrderID field is now a key field for the table and can be used to locate all the records relevant to a particular order. The next step of optimization corrects this situation.

Second normal form

A more efficient design results from splitting the data in tblBookOrders into two different tables to achieve *second normal form* (2NF). The first table contains the order information (for example, the OrderID, OrderDate, and Customer), while the second table contains the order details (Quantity and Title). This process is based on the second rule of normalization:

Data not directly dependent on the table's primary key is moved into another table.

This rule means that a table should contain data that represents a single entity. `tblBookOrders3` violates this rule of normalization because the table contains information about two different entities — books and orders. The individual book titles do not depend on the table's key field, `OrderID`. Only the order date, customer, and quantity depend on the `OrderID`. (For the meantime, I'm ignoring the fact that this table does not contain a primary key. I'll be adding primary keys in the "Keys" section, later in this chapter.)

At first glance, it might appear as though the book titles are indeed dependent on the Order ID. After all, the reason the book titles are in the table is because they're part of the order. However, a moment's thought will clarify the violation of second normal form. The title of a book is completely independent of the book order in which it is included. The same book title appears in multiple book orders; therefore, the `OrderID` has nothing to do with how a book is named. Given an arbitrary `OrderID`, you can't tell anything about the books contained in the order other than looking at the Orders table. Similarly, given a book title, there is nothing that binds the title to a specific order. (This is what is meant by *dependency* — a book title is not dependent on an `OrderID`.)

The `OrderDate`, however, is *completely* dependent on the `OrderID`. For each `OrderID` there is one and only one `OrderDate`. Therefore, any `OrderDate` is dependent on its associated `OrderID`. An `OrderDate` may be duplicated in the table, of course, because multiple orders may be received on the same day. For each `OrderID`, however, there is one and only one valid `OrderDate` value.

Second normal form often means breaking up a monolithic table into constituent tables, each of which contains fewer fields than the original table. In this example, second normal form is achieved by breaking the table containing books and orders data into separate `Orders` and `Order Details` tables.

The order-specific information (such as the order date, customer, payment, and shipping information) goes into the Orders table, while the details of each order item (book, quantity, selling price, and so on) is contained by the Order Details table. (Not all this data is shown in the example tables.)

The new tables are shown in Figure 3.5. The `OrderID` is the primary key for the `tblBookOrders4` table. The `OrderID` field in the `tblBookOrderDetails` is a foreign key (see Chapter 1) that references the `OrderID` primary key field in `tblBookOrders4`. Each field in `tblBookOrders4` — `OrderDate` and `Customer` — is said to be dependent on the table's primary key.

`tblBookOrders4` and `tblBookOrderDetails` are joined in a one-to-many relationship. `tblBookOrderDetails` contains as many records for each order as are necessary to fulfill the requirements of the order. The `OrderID` field in `tblBookOrders4` is now a true primary key. Each row in `tblBookOrders4` contains a unique `OrderID`, and none of the rows has a blank `OrderID`.

FIGURE 3.5

Second normal form: The `OrderID` field connects these tables together in a one-to-many relationship.

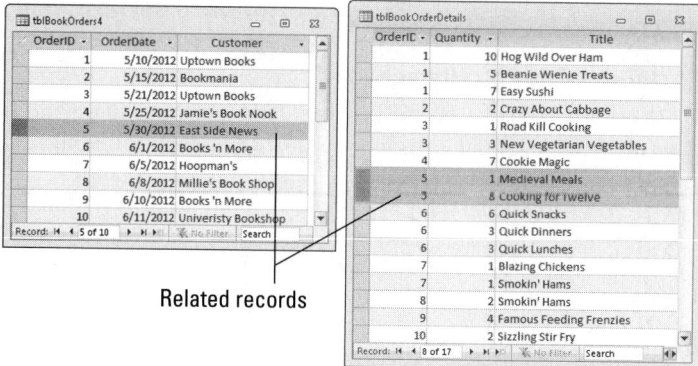

Related records

Each field in `tblBookOrders4` is dependent on the `OrderID` field and appears only once for each order that is placed. The `OrderID` field in `tblBookOrderDetails` does not serve as the primary key for `tblBookOrderDetails`; instead, it's a foreign key. In fact, `tblBookOrder-Details` doesn't even have a primary key, but one could be easily added.

The data in `tblBookOrders4` and `tblBookOrderDetails` can be easily updated. If a bookstore cancels a particular book title in an order, the corresponding record is deleted from `tblBookOrderDetails`. If, on the other hand, a bookstore adds more books to an order, new records are added to `tblBookOrderDetails` to accommodate the additional titles, or the `Quantity` field can be modified to increase or decrease the number of books ordered.

Breaking a table into individual tables, each of which describes some aspect of the data, is called *decomposition*. Decomposition is a very important part of the normalization process. Even though the tables appear smaller than the original table (refer to Figure 3.2), the data contained within the tables is the same as before.

It's easy to carry decomposition too far — creating only as many tables as are required to fully describe the data set managed by the database. When decomposing tables, be careful not to lose data. For example, if the `tblBookOrders4` table contained a `SellingPrice` field, you'd want to make sure that field was moved into `tblBookOrderDetails`.

A developer working with the bookstore tables is able to use queries to recombine the data in `tblBookOrders4` and `tblBookOrderDetails` in new and interesting ways. It'd be quite easy to determine how many books of each type have been ordered by the different customers, or how many times a particular book has been ordered. When coupled with a table containing information such as book unit cost, book selling price, and so on, the important financial status of the book wholesaler becomes clear.

Notice also that the number of records in tblBookOrders4 has been reduced. This is one of several advantages to using a relational database. Each table contains only as much data as is necessary to represent the entity (in this case, a book order) described by the table. This is far more efficient than adding duplicate field values (refer to Figure 3.2) for each new record added to a table.

Further optimization: Adding tables to the scheme

The design shown in Figure 3.5 is actually pretty good. Yet, I could still do more to optimize this design. Consider the fact that the entire name of each customer is stored in tblBookOrders4. Therefore, a customer's name appears each time the customer has placed an order. Notice that Uptown Books has placed two orders during the period covered by tblBookOrders4. If the Uptown Books bookstore changed its name to Uptown Books and Periodicals, you'd have to go back to this table and update every instance of Uptown Books to reflect the new name.

Overlooking an instance of the customer's name during this process is called an *update anomaly* and results in records that are inconsistent with the other records in the database. From the database's perspective, *Uptown Books* and *Uptown Books and Periodicals* are two completely different organizations, even if I know that they're the same store. A query to retrieve all the orders placed by Uptown Books and Periodicals will miss any records that still have Uptown Books in the Customer field because of the update anomaly.

Also, the table lacks specific information about the customers. No addresses, phone numbers, or other customer contact information are contained in tblBookOrders4. Although you could use a query to extract this information from a table named tblBookStores containing the addresses, phone numbers, and other information about the bookstore customers, using the customer name (a text field) as the search key is much slower than using a numeric key in the query.

Figure 3.6 shows the results of a refinement of the database design: tblBookOrders5 contains a foreign key named CustomerID that relates to the CustID primary key field in the tblCustomers table. This arrangement uses tblCustomers as a lookup table to provide customer-related information to a form or report.

Part of the performance improvement is due to the fact that the CustomerID field in tblBookOrders5 is a long integer (4-byte) value instead of a text field. This means that Access has to manipulate only 4 bytes of memory when looking for records in tblCustomers. The Customer field in tblBookOrders4 was a text field with a width of 50 characters. This means that Access might have to consider as many as 50 bytes of memory when searching for matching records in tblCustomers.

A second advantage of removing the customer name from the orders table is that the name now exists in only one location in the database. If Uptown Books changes its name to Uptown Books and Periodicals, I now only have to change its entry in the tblBookStores table. This single change is reflected throughout the database, including all forms and reports that use the customer name information.

FIGURE 3.6

The numeric `CustomerID` field results in faster retrievals from `tblCustomers`.

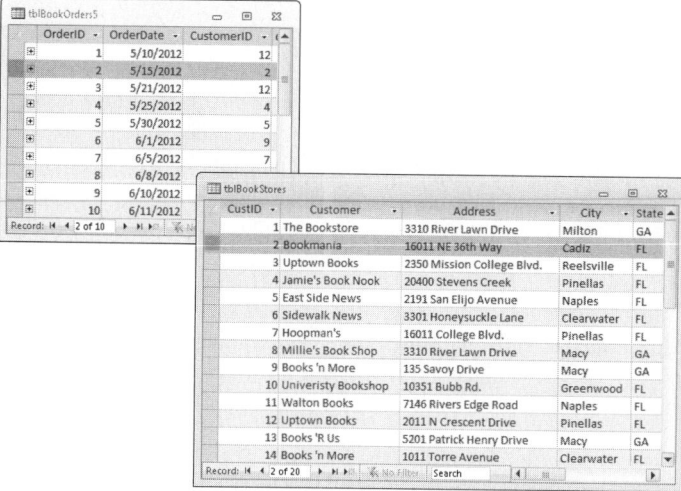

In some situations, you might want the database to keep track of the names of its customers, particularly if the names change frequently. If this is the case, it's a relatively simple task to add another table containing a `CustomerID` field pointing to `tblCustomers`, a text field to hold the old customer name, and, perhaps, a `Date/Time` field showing when the old name was retired and the new name went into effect (the new name, of course, is kept in `tblCustomers`). History tables are quite common in many database applications and are usually quite easy to implement.

In Figure 3.6, `tblBookOrders5` should contain all the order-specific information, including the shipping and payment methods, the salesperson identity, and any other information you want to track for orders. Also, given the `CustomerID` in `tblBookStores`, it's quite easy to add tables to the application for tracking promotions, preferences, and other information related to individual customers.

Breaking the rules

From time to time, you might find it necessary to break the rules. For example, let's assume the bookstores are entitled to discounts based on the volume of purchases over the last year. Strictly following the rules of normalization, the discount percentage should be included in the `tblBook-stores` table. After all, the discount is dependent on the customer, not on the order.

But maybe the discount applied to each order is somewhat arbitrary. Maybe the book wholesaler permits the salespeople to cut special deals for valued customers. In this case, you might want to include a `Discount` column in the table containing book orders information, even if it means duplicating information in many records. You could store the traditional discount as part of the customer's record in `tblBookstores`, and use it as the default value for the `Discount` column but permit the salesperson to override the discount value when a special arrangement has been made with the customer.

Third normal form

The last step of normalization, called third normal form (abbreviated *3NF*), requires removing all fields that can be derived from data contained in other fields in the table or other tables in the database. For example, assume the sales manager insists that you add a field to contain the total value of an order in the orders table. This information, of course, would be calculated from the `Quantity` field in `tblBookOrderDetails` and the book unit price from the book information table.

It's not really necessary to add the new `OrderTotal` field to the `Orders` table. Access easily calculates this value from data that is available in the database. The only advantage of storing order totals as part of the database is to save the few milliseconds required for Access to retrieve and calculate the information when the calculated data is needed by a form or report.

Removing calculated data has little to do with maintaining the database. The main benefits are saving disk space and memory, and reducing network traffic. Depending on the applications you build, you might find good reasons to store calculated data in tables, particularly if performing the calculations is a lengthy process, or if the stored value is necessary as an audit check on the calculated value printed on reports. It might be more efficient to perform the calculations during data entry (when data is being handled one record at a time) instead of when printing reports (when many thousands of records are manipulated to produce a single report).

As you'll read in the "Denormalization" section, later in this chapter, there are some good reasons why you might choose to include calculated fields in a database table. As you'll read in this section, most often the decision to denormalize is based on a need to make sure the same calculated value is stored in the database as is printed on a report.

Tip

Although higher levels of normalization are possible, you'll find that, for most database applications, third normal form is more than adequate. At the very least, you should always strive for first normal form in your tables by moving redundant or repeating data to another table.

Denormalization

After hammering you with all the reasons why normalizing your databases is a good idea, let's consider when you might deliberately choose to denormalize tables or use unnormalized tables.

Generally speaking, you normalize data in an attempt to improve the performance of your database. For example, in spite of all your efforts, some lookups will be time-consuming. Even when using carefully indexed and normalized tables, some lookups require quite a bit of time, especially when the data being looked up is complicated or there's a large amount of it.

More on anomalies

This business about update anomalies is important to keep in mind. The whole purpose of normalizing the tables in your databases is to achieve maximum performance with minimum maintenance effort.

Three types of errors can occur from an unnormalized database design. Following the rules outlined in this chapter will help you avoid the following pitfalls:

- **Insertion anomaly:** An error occurs in a related table when a new record is added to another table. For example, let's say you've added the `OrderTotal` field described in the previous section. After the order has been processed, the customer calls and changes the number of books ordered or adds a new book title to the same order. Unless you've carefully designed the database to automatically update the calculated `OrderTotal` field, the data in that field will be in error as the new data is inserted into the table.

  If insertion anomalies are a problem in your applications, you may be able to utilize data macros (see Chapter 15) to help synchronize the data in your tables when changes are made.

- **Deletion anomaly:** A deletion anomaly causes the accidental loss of data when a record is deleted from a table. Let's assume that the `tblBookOrders3` table contains the name, address, and other contact information for each bookstore. Deleting the last remaining record containing a particular customer's order causes the customer's contact information to be unintentionally lost. Keeping the customer contact information in a separate table preserves and protects that data from accidental loss. Avoiding deletion anomalies is one good reason not to use cascading deletes in your tables. (See the "Table Relationships" section, later in this chapter, for more on cascading deletes.)

- **Update anomaly:** Storing data that is not dependent on the table's primary key causes you to have to update multiple rows anytime the independent information changes. Keeping the independent data (such as the bookstore information) in its own table means that only a single instance of the information needs to be updated. (For more on update anomalies, see "Further optimization: Adding tables to the scheme" earlier in this chapter.)

Similarly, some calculated values may take a long time to evaluate. You may find it more expedient to simply store a calculated value than to evaluate the expression on the fly. This is particularly true when the user base is working on older, memory-constrained, or slow computers.

Be aware that most steps to denormalize a database schema result in additional programming time required to protect the data and user from the problems caused by an unnormalized design. For example, in the case of the calculated `OrderTotal` field, you must insert code that calculates and updates this field whenever the data in the fields underlying this value change. This extra programming, of course, takes time to implement and time to process at runtime.

Caution

Make sure that denormalizing the design does not cause other problems. If you know you've deliberately denormalized a database design and you're having trouble making everything work (particularly if you begin to encounter any of the anomalies discussed in the previous section), look for workarounds that permit you to work with a fully normalized design.

Finally, always document whatever you've done to denormalize the design. It's entirely possible that you or someone else will be called in to provide maintenance or to add new features to the application. If you've left design elements that seem to violate the rules of normalization, your carefully considered work may be undone by another developer in an effort to "optimize" the design. The developer doing the maintenance, of course, has the best of intentions, but he may inadvertently reestablish a performance problem that was resolved through subtle denormalization.

One thing to keep in mind is that denormalization is almost always done for reporting purposes, rather than simply to maintain data in tables. Consider a situation in which a customer has been given a special discount that doesn't correspond to his traditional discount. It may be very useful to store the actual amount invoiced to the customer, instead of relying on the database to calculate the discount each time the report is printed. Storing the actual amount ensures that the report always reflects the amount invoiced to the customer, instead of reporting a value that depends on other fields in the database that may change over time.

Table Relationships

Many people start out using a spreadsheet application like Excel or Lotus 1-2-3 to build a database. Unfortunately, a spreadsheet stores data as a two-dimensional worksheet (rows and columns) with no easy way to connect individual worksheets together. You must manually connect each cell of the worksheet to the corresponding cells in other worksheets — a tedious process at best.

Two-dimensional storage objects like worksheets are called *flat-file databases* because they lack the three-dimensional quality of relational databases. Figure 3.7 shows an Excel worksheet used as a flat-file database.

FIGURE 3.7

An Excel worksheet used as a flat-file database

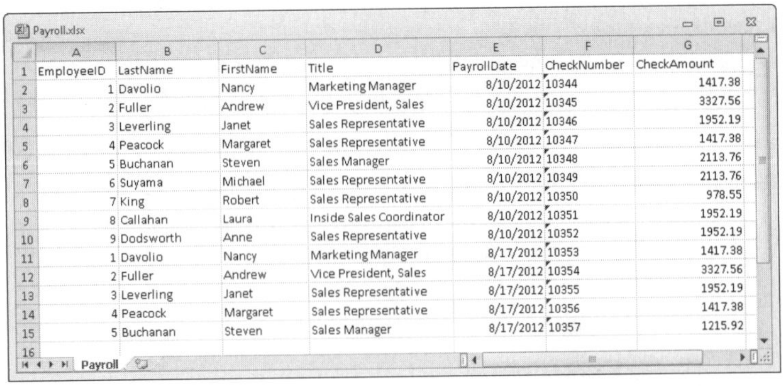

EmployeeID	LastName	FirstName	Title	PayrollDate	CheckNumber	CheckAmount
1	Davolio	Nancy	Marketing Manager	8/10/2012	10344	1417.38
2	Fuller	Andrew	Vice President, Sales	8/10/2012	10345	3327.56
3	Leverling	Janet	Sales Representative	8/10/2012	10346	1952.19
4	Peacock	Margaret	Sales Representative	8/10/2012	10347	1417.38
5	Buchanan	Steven	Sales Manager	8/10/2012	10348	2113.76
6	Suyama	Michael	Sales Representative	8/10/2012	10349	2113.76
7	King	Robert	Sales Representative	8/10/2012	10350	978.55
8	Callahan	Laura	Inside Sales Coordinator	8/10/2012	10351	1952.19
9	Dodsworth	Anne	Sales Representative	8/10/2012	10352	1952.19
1	Davolio	Nancy	Marketing Manager	8/17/2012	10353	1417.38
2	Fuller	Andrew	Vice President, Sales	8/17/2012	10354	3327.56
3	Leverling	Janet	Sales Representative	8/17/2012	10355	1952.19
4	Peacock	Margaret	Sales Representative	8/17/2012	10356	1417.38
5	Buchanan	Steven	Sales Manager	8/17/2012	10357	1215.92

The problems with flat-file databases should be immediately apparent from viewing Figure 3.7. Notice that the employee information is duplicated in multiple rows of the worksheet. Each time a payroll check is issued to an employee, a new row is added to the worksheet. Obviously, this worksheet would rapidly become unmanageably large and unwieldy.

Consider the amount of work required to make relatively simple changes to the data in Figure 3.7. For example, changing an employee's title requires searching through numerous records and editing the data contained within individual cells, creating many opportunities for errors.

Through clever programming in the Excel VBA language, it would be possible to link the data in the worksheet shown in Figure 3.7 with another worksheet containing the order detail information. It would also be possible to programmatically change data in individual rows. But such Herculean efforts are needless when you harness the power of a relational database such as Microsoft Access.

Connecting the data

A table's *primary key* uniquely identifies the records in a table. In a table of employee data, the employee's Social Security number, a combination of first and last names, or an employee ID might be used as the primary key. Let's assume the employee ID is selected as the primary key for the employees table. When the relationship to the payroll table is formed, the `EmployeeID` field is used to connect the tables together. Figure 3.8 shows this sort of arrangement (see the "One-to-many" section, later in this chapter).

Cross-Reference

Some of the issues related to using natural keys (such as Social Security number) are discussed in the section titled "Natural versus surrogate primary keys," later in this chapter.

FIGURE 3.8

The relationship between the `tblEmployees` and `tblPayroll` tables is an example of a typical one-to-many relationship.

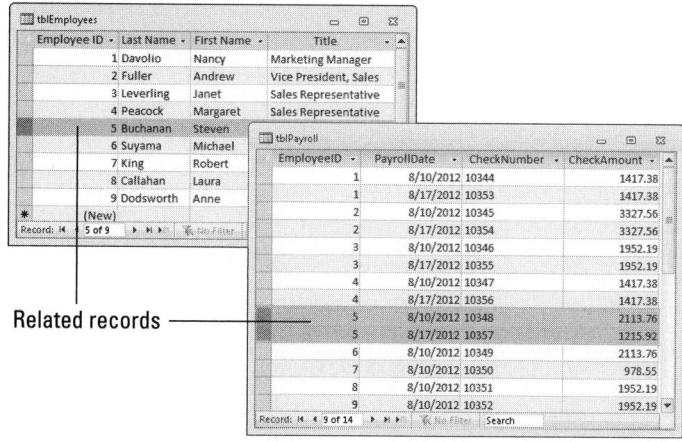

Related records

Although you can't see the relationship in Figure 3.8, Access knows it's there because a formal relationship has been established between tblEmployees and tblPayroll (this process is described in the "Creating relationships and enforcing referential integrity" section, later in this chapter). Because of the relationship between these tables, Access is able to instantly retrieve all the records from tblPayroll for any employee in tblEmployees.

The relationship example shown in Figure 3.8, in which each record of tblEmployees is related to several records in tblPayroll, is the most common type found in relational database systems, but it's by no means the only way that data in tables is related. This book, and most books on relational databases such as Access, discuss the three basic types of relationships between tables:

- One-to-one

- One-to-many

- Many-to-many

Figure 3.9 shows most of the relationships in the Collectible Mini Cars database.

FIGURE 3.9

Most of the Collectible Mini Cars table relationships

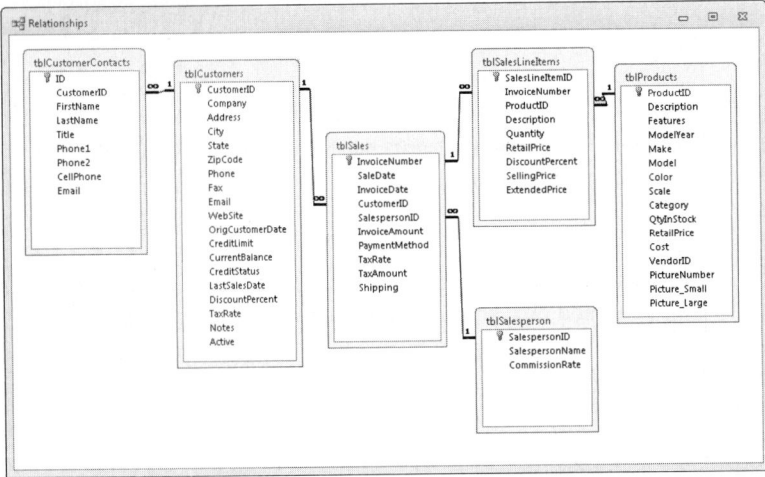

Notice that there are several one-to-many relationships between the tables (for example, tbl-Sales-to-tblSalesPayments, tblSales-to-tblSalesLineItems, and tblCustomers-to-tblSales). The relationship that you specify between tables is important. It tells Access how to find and display information from fields in two or more tables. The program needs to know whether to look for only one record in a table or look for several records on the basis of the relationship. tblSales, for example, is related to tblCustomers as a many-to-one relationship. This is because the focus of the Collectible Mini Cars system is on sales. This means that there will *always* be only one customer related to every sales record. That is, many sales can be associated with a single customer. In this case, the Collectible Mini Cars system is actually using `tblCustomers` as a lookup table.

Note

Relationships can be very confusing — they depend upon the focus of the system. For example, when working with `tblCustomers` and `tblSales`, you can always create a query that has a one-to-many relationship to `tblSales` from `tblCustomers`. Although the system is concerned with sales (invoices), sometimes you'll want to produce reports or views that are buyer related instead of invoice related. Because one buyer can have more than one sale, there will always be one record in `tblCustomers` and at least one record in `tblSales`. In fact, there could be many related records in `tblSales`. So Access knows to find only one record in the Customers table and to look for any records in the Sales table (one or more) that have the same customer number.

One-to-one

A one-to-one relationship between tables means that for every record in the first table, one and only one record exists in the second table. Figure 3.10 illustrates this concept.

FIGURE 3.10

A one-to-one relationship

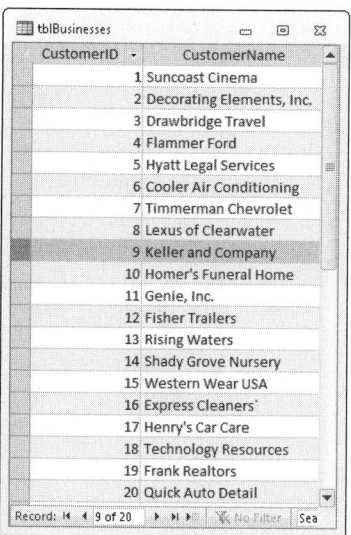
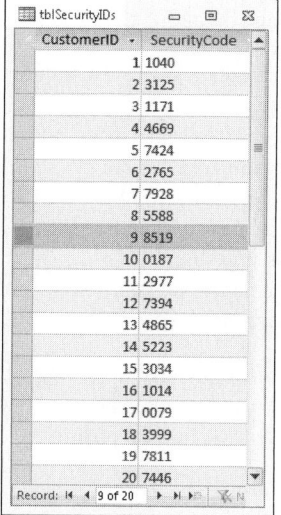

Pure one-to-one relationships are not common in relational databases. In most cases, the data contained in the second table is most often included in the first table. As a matter of fact, one-to-one relationships are generally avoided because they violate the rules of normalization. Following the rules of normalization, data should not be split into multiple tables if the data describes a single entity. Because a person has one and only one birth date, the birth date should be included in the table containing a person's other data.

There are times, however, when it's not advisable to store certain data along with other data in the table. For example, consider the situation illustrated in Figure 3.10. The data contained in `tblSe-curity` is confidential. Normally, you wouldn't want anyone with access to the public customer information (name, address, and so on) to have access to the confidential security code that the customer uses for purchasing or billing purposes. If necessary, `tblSecurity` could be located on a different disk somewhere on the network, or even maintained on removable media to protect it from unauthorized access.

Another instance of a one-to-one relationship is a situation in which the data in a table exceeds the 255-field limit imposed by Access. Although rare, there could be cases in which you might have too many fields to be contained within a single table. The easiest solution is simply to split the data into multiple tables and connect the tables in a 1:1 relationship through the primary key (using the same key value, of course, in each table).

Although situations where normalized data exceeds 255 columns, there are times when perfectly normalized data exceeds 255 columns. Consider an engineering study on a new car engine. The engineers might want to capture test measurements (temperatures, pressures, vibration, and so on) from several dozen sensors during the test. Each sensor might generate several hundred measurements in a few minutes' time. Although there are many ways to store the data, it would be possible to capture the data as a series of tables in a 1:1 relationship with one another, each table row representing one sensor, and each column containing the measurement at a particular time.

Yet another situation is one in which data is being transferred or shared among databases. Perhaps the shipping clerk in an organization doesn't need to see all of a customer's data. Instead of including irrelevant information such as job titles, birth dates, alternate phone numbers, and e-mail addresses, the shipping clerk's database contains only the customer's name, address, and other shipping information. A record in the customer table in the shipping clerk's database has a one-to-one relationship with the corresponding record in the master customer table located on the central computer somewhere within the organization. Although the data is contained within separate `.accdb` files, the links between the tables can be *live* (meaning that changes to the master record are immediately reflected in the shipping clerk's `.accdb` file).

Tables joined in a one-to-one relationship will almost always have the same primary key — for example, `OrderID` or `EmployeeNumber`. There are very few reasons you would create a separate key field for the second table in a one-to-one relationship.

One-to-many

A far more common relationship between tables in a relational database is the one-to-many. In one-to-many relationships, each record in the first table (the *parent*) is related to one or more records in the second table (the *child*). Each record in the second table is related to one and only one record in the first table.

Without a doubt, one-to-many relationships are the most common type encountered in relational database systems. Examples of one-to-many situations abound:

- **Customers and orders:** Each customer (the "one" side) has placed several orders (the "many" side), but each order is sent to a single customer.

- **Teacher and student:** Each teacher has many students, but each student has a single teacher (within a particular class, of course).

- **Employees and paychecks:** Each employee has received several paychecks, but each paycheck is given to one and only one employee.

- **Patients and treatments:** Each patient receives zero or more treatments for a disease, but each treatment is given to multiple patients.

As I discuss in the "Creating relationships and enforcing referential integrity" section, later in this chapter, Access makes it very easy to establish one-to-many relationships between tables. A one-to-many relationship is illustrated in Figure 3.11. This figure, using tables from the Northwind Traders database, clearly demonstrates how each record in the `Customers` table is related to several different records in the `Orders` table. An order can be sent to only a single customer, so all requirements of one-to-many relationships are fulfilled by this arrangement.

FIGURE 3.11

The Northwind Traders database contains many examples of one-to-many relationships.

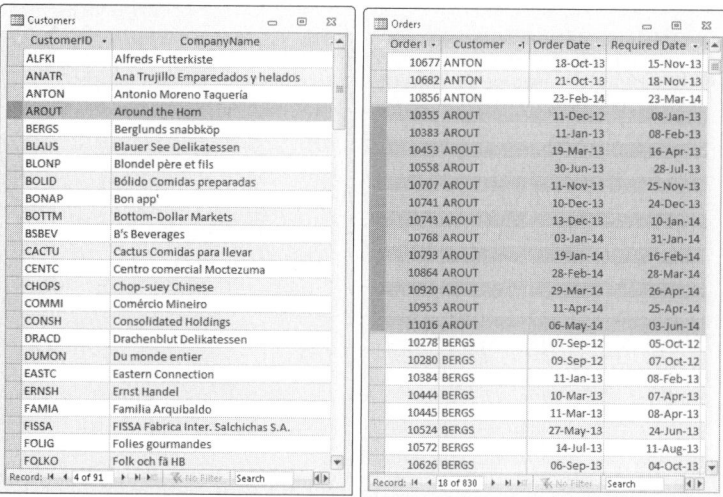

Although the records on the "many" side of the relationship illustrated in Figure 3.11 are sorted by the `CustomerID` field in alphabetical order, there is no requirement that the records in the many table be arranged in any particular order.

Note

Although parent-child is the most common expression used to explain the relationship between tables related in a one-to-many relationship, you may hear other expressions used, such as master-detail applied to this design. The important thing to keep in mind is that the intent of referential integrity is to prevent lost records on the "many" side of the relationship. Referential integrity guarantees that there will never be an orphan (a child record without a matching parent record). As you work with related tables, it's important to keep in mind which table is on the "one" side and which is on the "many" side.

Notice how difficult it would be to record all the orders for a customer if a separate table were not used to store the order's information. The flat-file alternative discussed earlier in this section, requires much more updating than the one-to-many arrangement shown in Figure 3.11. Each time a customer places an order with Northwind Traders, a new record is added to the `Orders` table. Only the `CustomerID` (for example, AROUT) is added to the `Orders` table as the foreign key back to the `Customers` table. Keeping the customer information is relatively trivial because each customer record appears only once in the `Customers` table.

Many-to-many

You'll come across many-to-many situations from time to time. In a many-to-many arrangement, each record in both tables can be related to zero, one, or many records in the other table. An example is shown in Figure 3.12. Each student in `tblStudents` can belong to more than one club, while each club in `tblClubs` has more than one member.

FIGURE 3.12

A database of students and the clubs they belong to is an example of a many-to-many relationship.

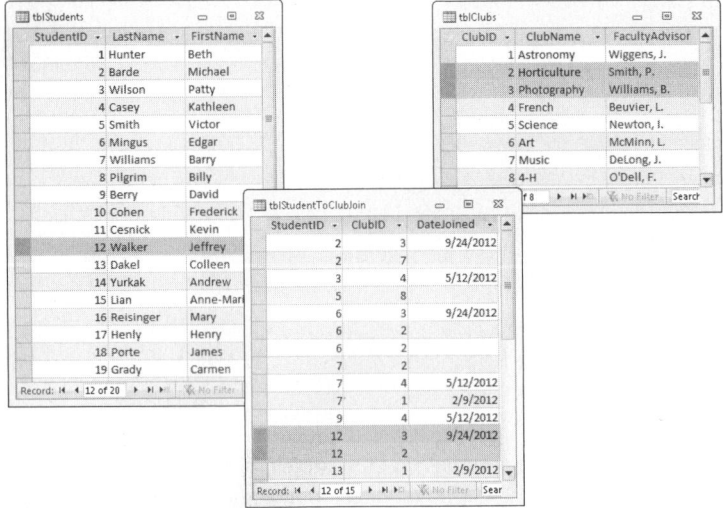

As indicated in Figure 3.12, many-to-many relationships are somewhat more difficult to understand because they can't be directly modeled in relational database systems like Access. Instead, the many-to-many relationship is broken into two separate one-to-many relationships, joined through a linking table (called a *join table*). The join table has one-to-many relationships with both of the tables involved in the many-to-many relationship. This principle can be a bit confusing at first, but close examination of Figure 3.12 soon reveals the beauty of this arrangement.

In Figure 3.12, you can see that student ID 2 (Michael Barde) belongs to the music club (Club ID = 7), while student ID 12 (Jeffrey Wilson) is a member of the horticulture club (Club ID = 2). Both Michael Barde and Jeffrey Wilson belong to the photography club (Club ID = 3). Each student belongs to multiple clubs, and each club contains multiple members.

Because of the additional complication of the join table, many-to-many relationships are often considered more difficult to establish and maintain. Fortunately, Access makes such relationships quite easy to establish, if a few rules are followed. These rules are explained in various places in this book. For example, in order to update either side of a many-to-many relationship (for example, to change club membership for a student), the join table must contain the primary keys of both tables joined by the relationship.

Many-to-many relationships are quite common in business environments:

- **Lawyers to clients (or doctors to patients):** Each lawyer may be involved in several cases, while each client may be represented by more than one lawyer on each case.

- **Patients and insurance coverage:** Many people are covered by more than one insurance policy. For example, if you and your spouse are both provided medical insurance by your employers, you have multiple coverage.

- **Video rentals and customers:** Over a year's time, each video is rented by several people, while each customer rents more than one video during the year.

- **Magazine subscriptions:** Most magazines have circulations measured in the thousands or millions. Most people subscribe to more than one magazine at a time.

The Collectible Mini Cars database has a many-to-many relationship between tblCustomers and tblSalesPayments, linked through tblSales. Each customer might have purchased more than one item, and each item might be paid for through multiple payments. In addition to joining contacts and sales payments, tblSales contains other information, such as the sale date and invoice number. The join table in a many-to-many relationship often contains information regarding the joined data.

Given how complicated many-to-many joins can be to construct, it's fortunate that many-to-many relationships are quite a bit less common than straightforward one-to-many situations.

Although Figure 3.12 shows a join table with just two fields — StudentID and ClubID — there is no reason that the join table can't contain other information. For example, the tblStudent-ToClubJoin table might include fields to indicate membership dues collected from the student for each club.

Integrity Rules

Access permits you to apply referential integrity rules that protect data from loss or corruption. *Referential integrity* means that the relationships between tables are preserved during updates, deletions, and other record operations. The relational model defines several rules meant to enforce the referential integrity requirements of relational databases. In addition, Access contains its own set of referential integrity rules that are enforced by the Jet database engine.

Imagine a payroll application that contained no rules regulating how data in the database is used. It'd be possible to issue payroll checks that aren't linked to an employee, for instance. From a business perspective, issuing paychecks to "phantom" employees is a very serious situation. Eventually, the issue will be noticed when the auditors step in and notify management of the discrepancy.

Referential integrity operates strictly on the basis of the tables' key fields. Referential integrity means that the database engine checks each time a key field (whether primary or foreign) is added, changed, or deleted. If a change to a value in a key field invalidates a relationship, it is said to violate referential integrity. Tables can be set up so that referential integrity is automatically enforced.

Figure 3.13 illustrates one of several relationships in the Collectible Mini Cars database. The Products table is related to the `Sales Lines Item` table through the `ProductID` field. The `ProductID` field in the `Products` table is the primary key, while the `ProductID` field in the `Sales Line Items table` is a foreign key. The relationship connects each product with a line item on a sales invoice. In this relationship, the `Products table` is the parent table, while the `Sales Line Items table` is the child table.

FIGURE 3.13

A typical database relationship

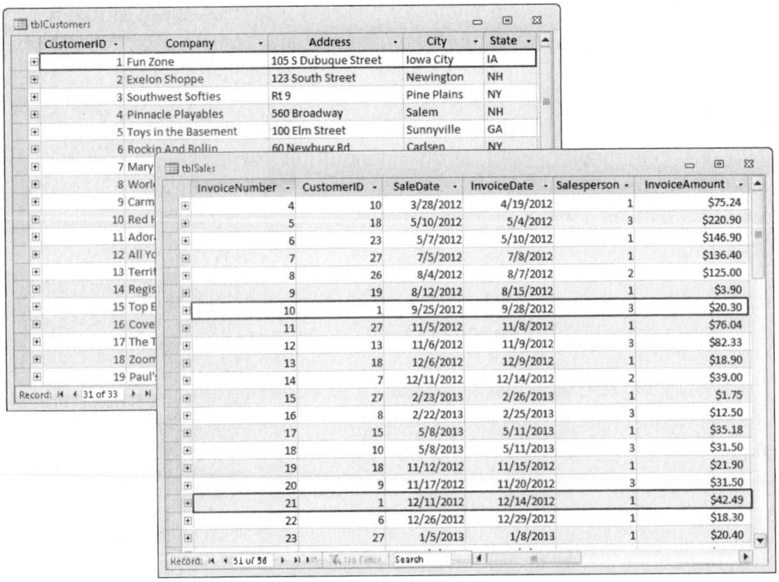

tblCustomers

CustomerID	Company	Address	City	State
1	Fun Zone	105 S Dubuque Street	Iowa City	IA
2	Exelon Shoppe	123 South Street	Newington	NH
3	Southwest Softies	Rt 9	Pine Plains	NY
4	Pinnacle Playables	560 Broadway	Salem	NH
5	Toys in the Basement	100 Elm Street	Sunnyville	GA
6	Rockin And Rollin	60 Newbury Rd	Carlsen	NY
7	Mary			
8	Worl			
9	Carm			
10	Red H			
11	Ador			
12	All Yo			
13	Terri			
14	Regis			
15	Top E			
16	Cove			
17	The T			
18	Zoom			
19	Paul'			

Record: 31 of 33

tblSales

InvoiceNumber	CustomerID	SaleDate	InvoiceDate	Salesperson	InvoiceAmount
4	10	3/28/2012	4/19/2012	1	$75.24
5	18	5/10/2012	5/4/2012	3	$220.90
6	23	5/7/2012	5/10/2012	1	$146.90
7	27	7/5/2012	7/8/2012	1	$136.40
8	26	8/4/2012	8/7/2012	2	$125.00
9	19	8/12/2012	8/15/2012	1	$3.90
10	1	9/25/2012	9/28/2012	3	$20.30
11	27	11/5/2012	11/8/2012	1	$76.04
12	13	11/6/2012	11/9/2012	3	$82.33
13	18	12/6/2012	12/9/2012	1	$18.90
14	7	12/11/2012	12/14/2012	2	$39.00
15	27	2/23/2013	2/26/2013	1	$1.75
16	8	2/22/2013	2/25/2013	3	$12.50
17	15	5/8/2013	5/11/2013	1	$35.18
18	10	5/8/2013	5/11/2013	3	$31.50
19	18	11/12/2012	11/15/2012	1	$21.90
20	9	11/17/2012	11/20/2012	3	$31.50
21	1	12/11/2012	12/14/2012	1	$42.49
22	6	12/26/2012	12/29/2012	1	$18.30
23	27	1/5/2013	1/8/2013	1	$20.40

Record: 31 of 56 Search

Orphaned records are very bad in database applications. Because sales information is almost always reported as which products were sold to which customers, a sales invoice that is not linked to a valid customer will not be discovered under most circumstances. It's easy to know which products were sold to Fun Zone, but given an arbitrary sales record, it may not be easy to know that there is no valid customer making the purchase. In Figure 3.13, the invoice records related to Fun Zone are indicated by boxes drawn around the data in `tblSales`.

Because the referential integrity rules are enforced by the Access database engine, data integrity is ensured wherever the data appears in the database: in tables, queries, or forms. Once you've established the integrity requirements of your applications, you don't have to be afraid that data in related tables will become lost or disorganized.

I can't overemphasize the need for referential integrity in database applications. Many developers feel that they can use VBA code or user interface design to prevent orphaned records. The truth is that, in most databases, the data stored in a particular table may be used in many different places within the application. Also, given the fact that many database projects extend over many years, and among any number of developers, it's not always possible to recall how data should be protected. By far, the best approach to ensuring the integrity of data stored in any database system is to utilize the power of the database engine to enforce referential integrity.

The general relational model referential integrity rules ensure that records contained in relational tables are not lost or confused. For obvious reasons, it's important that the primary keys connecting tables be protected and preserved. Also, changes in a table that affect other tables (for example, deleting a record on the "one" side of a one-to-many relationship) should be rippled to the other tables connected to the first table. Otherwise, the data in the two tables will quickly become unsynchronized.

No primary key can contain a null value

The first referential integrity rule states that no primary key can contain a null value. A *null value* is one that simply does not exist. The value of a field that has never been assigned a value (even a default value) is `Null`. No row in a database table can have `Null` in its primary key field because the main purpose of the primary key is to guarantee uniqueness of the row. Obviously, null values cannot be unique and the relational model would not work if primary keys could be `Null`.

Furthermore, Access can't evaluate a null value. Because a null value doesn't exist, it can't be compared with any other value. It isn't larger or smaller than any other value; it simply doesn't exist. Therefore, a null value can't be used to look up a record in a table, or to form a relationship between two tables.

Access automatically enforces the first referential integrity rule. As you add data to tables, you can't leave the primary key field empty without generating a warning (one reason the `AutoNumber` field works so well as a primary key). Once you've designated a field in an Access table as the primary key, Access won't let you delete the data in the field, nor will it allow you to change the value in the field so that it duplicates a value in another record.

When using a composite primary key made up of several fields, all the fields in the composite key must contain values. None of the fields is allowed to be empty. The combination of values in the composite primary key must be unique.

All foreign key values must be matched by corresponding primary keys

The second referential integrity rule says that all foreign key values must be matched by corresponding primary keys. This means that every record in a table on the "many" (or *child*) side of a one-to-many relationship must have a corresponding record in the table on the "one" (or *parent*) side of the relationship. A record on the "many" side of a relationship without a corresponding record on the "one" side is said to be *orphaned* and is effectively removed from the database schema. Identifying orphaned records in a database can be very difficult, so you're better off avoiding the situation in the first place.

The second rule means that

- **Rows cannot be added to a "many" side table (the child) if a corresponding record does not exist on the "one" side (the parent).** If a child record contains a `ParentID` field, the `ParentID` value *must* match an existing record in the parent table.
- **The primary key value in a "one" side table cannot be changed if the change would create orphaned child records.**
- **Deleting a row on the "one" side must not orphan corresponding records on the "many" side.**

For example, in the sales example, the foreign key in each record in `tblSales` (the "many" side) must match a primary key in `tblEmployees`. You can't delete a record in `tblCustomers` (the "one" side) without deleting the corresponding records in `tblSales`.

One of the curious results of the rules of referential integrity is that it is entirely possible to have a parent record that is not matched by any child records. Intuitively, this makes sense. A company may certainly have employees who haven't yet been issued paychecks. Or, the Collectible Mini Cars company may hire a new employee who hasn't made any sales yet. Eventually, of course, most parent records are matched by one or more child records, but this condition is not a requirement of relational databases.

As you'll see in the next section, Access makes it easy to specify the integrity rules you want to employ in your applications. You should be aware, however, that not using the referential integrity rules means that you might end up with orphaned records and other data integrity problems.

Keys

When you create database tables, like those created in Chapter 2, you should assign each table a primary key. This key is a way to make sure that the table records contain only one unique value; for example, you may have several contacts named Michael Heinrich, and you may even have more than one Michael Heinrich (for example, father and son) living at the same address. So, in a case like this, you have to decide how you can create a record in the Customer database that will let you identify each Michael Heinrich separately.

Uniquely identifying each record in a table is precisely what a primary key field does. For example, using the Collectible Mini Cars as an example, the CustomerID field (a unique number that you assign to each customer placing an order) is the primary key in tblCustomers — each record in the table has a different CustomerID number. (No two records have the same number.) This is important for several reasons:

- You don't want to have two records in tblCustomers for the same customer, because this can make updating the customer's record virtually impossible.

- You want assurance that each record in the table is accurate, so that the information extracted from the table is accurate.

- You don't want to make the table (and its records) any larger than necessary. Adding redundant or duplicate fields and records just complicates the database without adding value.

The ability to assign a single, unique value to each record makes the table clean and reliable. This is known as *entity integrity*. By having a different primary key value in each record (such as the CustomerID in tblCustomers), you can tell two records (in this case, customers) apart, even if all other fields in the records are the same. This is important because you can easily have two individual customers with a common name, such as Fred Smith, in your table.

Theoretically, you could use the customer's name and address, but two people named Fred D. Smith could live in the same town and state, or a father and son (Fred David Smith and Fred Daniel Smith) could live at the same address. The goal of setting primary keys is to create individual records in a table that *guarantees* uniqueness.

If you don't specify a primary key when creating Access tables, Access asks whether you want one. If you say yes, Access uses the AutoNumber data type to create a primary key for the table. An AutoNumber field is automatically inserted each time a record is added to the table, and can't be changed once its value has been established. Furthermore, once an AutoNumber value has appeared in a table, the value will never be reused, even if the record containing the value is deleted and the value no longer appears in the table. In fact, because an AutoNumber field is added to a new record before any of the other data, if the new row is not saved for some reason, the new AutoNumber is never used in the table at all.

Deciding on a primary key

As you learned previously, a table normally has a unique field (or combination of fields) — the primary key for that table — which makes each record unique. The primary key is an identifier that is often a text or AutoNumber data type. To determine the contents of this ID field, you specify a method for creating a unique value for the field. Your method can be as simple as letting Access automatically assign an AutoNumber value or using the first letter of the real value you're tracking along with a sequence number (such as A001, A002, A003, B001, B002, and so on). The method may rely on a random set of letters and numbers for the field content (as long as each field has a unique value) or a complicated calculation based on information from several fields in the table.

However, there is no reason why the primary key value has to be *meaningful* to the application. A primary key exists in a table solely to ensure uniqueness for each row and to provide an anchor for table relationships. Many Access developers routinely use `AutoNumber` fields as primary keys simply because they meet all the requirements of a primary key without contributing to an application's complexity.

Table 3.1 lists the Collectible Mini Cars tables and describes one *possible* plan for deriving the primary key values in each table. As this table shows, it doesn't take a great deal of work (or even much imagination) to derive a plan for key values. Any rudimentary scheme with a good sequence number always works. Access automatically tells you when you try to enter a duplicate key value. To avoid duplication, you can simply add the value of 1 to the sequence number.

TABLE 3.1

Deriving the Primary Key

Table	Possible Derivation of Primary Key Value
tblCustomers	Companies: AutoNumber field assigned by Access
tblSales	Invoice Number: AutoNumber field
tblSalesLineItems	Invoice Number (from Sales) and an AutoNumber field
tblProducts	Product Number, entered by the person putting in a new product
tblSalesPayments	Invoice Number (from Sales) and an AutoNumber field
tblSalesperson	Sales Person ID: AutoNumber field
tblCategories	Category of Items: Entered by the person putting in a new record

Even though it is not difficult to use logic (implemented, perhaps, though VBA code) to generate unique values for a primary key field, by far the simplest and easiest approach is to use `AutoNumber` fields for the primary keys in your tables. The special characteristics of the `AutoNumber` field (automatic generation, uniqueness, the fact that it cannot be changed, and so on) make it the ideal candidate for primary keys. Furthermore, an `AutoNumber` value is nothing more than a 4-byte integer value, making it very fast and easy for the database engine to manage. For all these reasons, the Collectible Mini Cars exclusively uses `AutoNumber` fields as primary keys in its tables.

You may be thinking that all these sequence numbers make it hard to look up information in your tables. Just remember that, in most case, you never look up information by an ID field. Generally, you look up information according to the *purpose* of the table. In `tblCustomers`, for example, you would look up information by customer name — last name, first name, or both. Even when the same name appears in multiple records, you can look at other fields in the table (zip code, phone number) to find the correct customer. Unless you just happen to know the customer ID number, you'll probably never use it in a search for information.

The benefits of a primary key

Have you ever placed an order with a company for the first time and then decided the next day to increase your order? When you call the people at the order desk, they may ask you for your customer number. You tell them that you don't know your customer number. Next, they ask you for some other information — generally, your zip code and last name. Then, as they narrow down the list of customers, they ask your address. Once they've located you in their database, they can tell you your customer number. Some businesses use phone numbers or e-mail addresses as starting points when searching for customer records.

Cross-Reference
Primary and foreign keys are discussed in Chapter 1, but, because these concepts are so important in database applications, they are covered again in this chapter.

Database systems usually have more than one table, and the tables are related in some manner. For example, in the Collectible Mini Cars database, tblCustomers and tblSales are related to each other through the CustomerID field. Because each customer is *one* person, you only need one record in tblCustomers.

Each customer can make many purchases, however, which means you need to set up a second table to hold information about each sale — tblSales. Again, each invoice is *one* sale (on a specific day at a specific time). CustomerID is used to relate the customer to the sales.

The *primary key* in the parent table (CustomerID in tblCustomers) is related to a *foreign key* in the child table (the CustomersID field in the tblSales table).

Besides being a common link field between tables, the primary key field in an Access database table has these advantages:

- Primary key fields are always indexed, greatly speeding up queries, searches, and sorts that involve the primary key field.
- Access forces you to enter a value (or automatically provides a value, in the case of AutoNumber fields) every time you add a record to the table. You're guaranteed that your database tables conform to the rules of referential integrity.
- As you add new records to a table, Access checks for duplicate primary key values and prevents duplicates entries, thus maintaining data integrity.
- By default, Access displays your data in primary key order.

Tip
An index is a special internal file that is created to put the records in a table in some specific order. For example, the primary key field in the tblCustomers table is an index that puts the records in order by CustomerID field. Using an indexed table, Access using the index to quickly find record within the table.

Designating a primary key

From the preceding sections, you're aware that choosing a table's primary key is an important step toward bulletproofing a database's design. When properly implemented, primary keys help stabilize and protect the data stored in your Access databases. As you read the following sections, keep in mind that the cardinal rule governing primary keys is that the values assigned to the primary key field within a table must be unique. Furthermore, the ideal primary key is stable.

Single-field versus composite primary keys

Sometimes, when an ideal primary key doesn't exist within a table as a single value, you may be able to combine fields to create a *composite* primary key. For example, it's unlikely that a first name or last name alone is enough to serve as a primary key, but by combining first and last names with birth dates, you may be able to come up with a unique combination of values to serve as the primary key. As you'll see in the "Creating relationships and enforcing referential integrity" section, later in this chapter, Access makes it very easy to combine fields as composite primary keys.

There are several practical considerations when using composite keys:

- **None of the fields in a composite key can be null.**
- **Sometimes composing a composite key from data naturally occurring within the table can be difficult.** Sometimes records within a table differ by one or two fields, even when many other fields may be duplicated within the table.
- **Each of the fields can be duplicated within the table, but the combination of composite key fields cannot be duplicated.**

However, as with so many other issues in database design, composite keys have a number of issues:

- **Composite keys tend to complicate a database's design.** If you use three fields in a parent table to define the table's primary key, the same three fields must appear in every child table.
- **Ensuring that a value exists for all the fields within a composite key (so that none of the fields is null) can be quite challenging.**

Tip

Most developers avoid composite keys unless absolutely necessary. In many cases, the problems associated with composite keys greatly outweigh the minimal advantage of using composite keys generated from data within the record.

Natural versus surrogate primary keys

Many developers maintain that you should use only natural primary keys. A *natural primary key* is derived from data already in the table, such as a Social Security number or employee number. If no single field is enough to uniquely identify records in the table, these developers suggest combining fields to form a *composite primary key*.

However, there are many situations where no "perfect" natural key exists in database tables. Although a field like `SocialSecurityNumber` may seem to be the ideal primary key, there are a number of problems with this type of data:

- **The value is not universal.** Not everyone has a Social Security number.

- **The value may not be known at the time the record is added to the database.** Because primary keys can never be null, provisions must be made to supply some kind of "temporary" primary key when the Social Security number is unknown, and then other provisions must be made to fix up the data in the parent and child tables once the value becomes known.

- **Values such as Social Security number tend to be rather large.** A Social Security number is at least nine characters, even omitting the dashes between groups of numbers. Large primary keys unnecessarily complicate things and run more slowly than smaller primary keys.

- **Legal and privacy issues inhibit its use.** A Social Security number is considered "personally identifiable information" and (in the United States) its use is limited under the Social Security Protection Act of 2005.

Caution

By far the largest issue is that adding a record to a table is impossible unless the primary key value is known at the time the record is committed to the database. Even if temporary values are inserted until the permanent value is known, the amount of fix-up required in related tables can be considerable. After all, unless Cascade Update is enabled on the relationship, you can't change the value of a primary key if related child records exist in other tables.

Although an `AutoNumber` value does not naturally occur in the table's data, because of the considerable advantages of using a simple numeric value that is automatically generated and cannot be deleted or changed, in most cases an `AutoNumber` is the ideal primary key candidate for most tables.

Creating primary keys

A primary key is created by opening a table in Design view, selecting the field (or fields) that you want to use as a primary key, and clicking the Primary Key button on the toolbar (the button with the key on it). If you're specifying more than one field to create a composite key, hold down the Ctrl key while using the mouse to select the fields before clicking on the Primary Key toolbar button.

Cross Reference

Setting a table's primary key is covered in detail in Chapter 2.

Creating relationships and enforcing referential integrity

The Relationships window Database Ribbon icon lets you specify the relationships and referential integrity rules you want to apply to the tables involved in a relationship. Creating a permanent, managed relationship that ensures referential integrity between Access tables is easy:

1. Select Database Tools ⇨ Relationships.

   The Relationships window appears.

2. Click on the Show Table ribbon button, or right-click on the Relationships window and select Show Table from the shortcut menu. The Add Table dialog box appears, as shown in Figure 3.14.

FIGURE 3.14

Double-click to add tables to the Relationships window.

3. Add `tblBookOrders5` and `tblOrderDetails` to the Relationships window (double-click each table in the Show Table dialog box, or select each table and click the Add button).

4. You create a relationship by dragging the primary key field in the one-side table and dropping it on the foreign key in the many-side table. Alternatively, drag the foreign key field and drop it on the primary key field.

   For this example, drag `OrderID` from `tblBookOrders5` and drop it on `OrderID` in `tblBookOrderDetails`. Access immediately opens the Edit Relationships dialog box (shown in Figure 3.15) to enable you to specify the details about the relationship you intend to form between the tables. Notice that Access recognizes that the relationship between the `tblBookOrders5` and `tblBookOrderDetails` as a one-to-many.

5. Specify the referential details you want Access to enforce in the database.

   In Figure 3.15 notice the Cascade Delete Related Records check box. If this check box is left unchecked, Access will not permit you to delete records in `tblBookOrders5` (the one-side table) until all the corresponding records in `tblBookOrderDetails` (the many-side table) were first deleted. With this box checked, deletions across the relationship "cascade" automatically. Cascading deletes can be a dangerous operation because the deletions in the many-side table occur without confirmation.

FIGURE 3.15

You enforce referential integrity in the Edit Relationships dialog box.

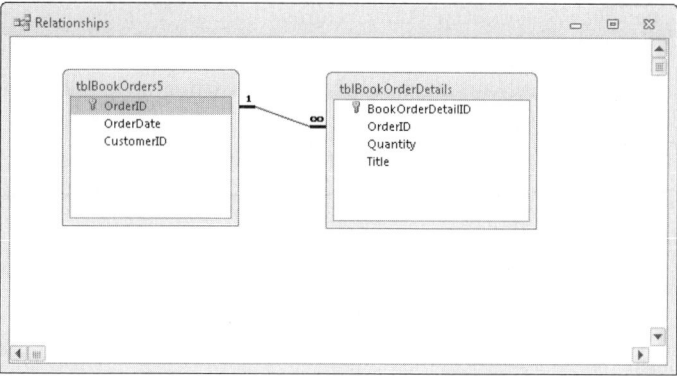

6. Click the Create button.

   Access draws a line between the tables displayed in the Relationships window, indicating the type of relationship. In Figure 3.16, the 1 symbol indicates that `tblBookOrders5` is the "one" side of the relationship while the infinity symbol (∞) designates `tblBookOr-derDetails` as the "many" side.

FIGURE 3.16

A one-to-many relationship between `tblBookOrders5` and `tblBookOrderDetails`

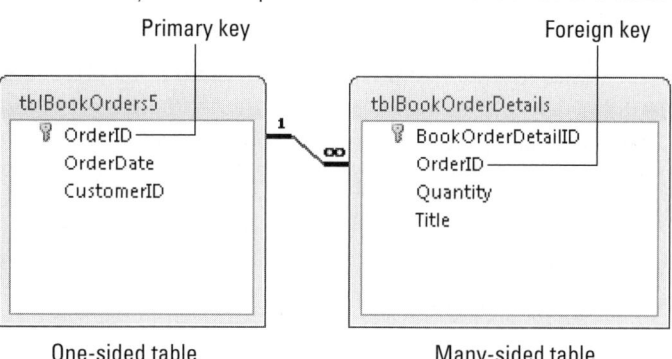

Specifying the Join Type between tables

The right side of the Edit Relations window has four buttons:

- **Create:** Clicking the Create button returns you to the Relationships window with the changes specified.

- **Cancel:** The Cancel button cancels the current changes and returns you to the Relationships window.

- **Join Type:** The Join Type button opens the Join Properties dialog box.

- **Create New:** The Create New button lets you specify an entirely new relation between the two tables and fields.

By default, when you process a query on related tables, Access only returns records that appear in both tables. Considering the payroll example from the "Integrity Rules" section, earlier in this chapter, this means that you would only see employees that have valid paycheck records in the paycheck table. You would not see any employees who have not yet received a paycheck. Such a relationship is sometimes called an *equi-join* because the only records that appear are those that exist on *both* sides of the relationship.

However, the equi-join is not the only type of join supported by Access. Click on the Join Type button to open the Join Properties dialog box. The alternative settings in the Join Properties dialog box allow you to specify that you prefer to see all the records from either the parent table or child table, regardless of whether they're matched on the other side. (It's possible to have an unmatched child record as long as the foreign key in the child table is null.) Such a join (called an *outer join*) can be very useful because it accurately reflects the state of the data in the application.

In the case of the Collectible Mini Cars example, seeing all the customers, regardless of whether they have records in the Sales table, is what you're shooting for. To specify an outer join connecting customers to sales, perform these steps:

1. From the Relationships window, add `tblCustomers` and `tblSales`. Click the Join Type button.

   The Join Properties dialog box appears (see Figure 3.17).

2. Select the `Include ALL Records from 'tblCustomers' and Only Those Records from 'tblSales' Where the Joined Fields Are Equal` check box.

3. Click OK.

   You're returned to the Edit Relationships dialog box.

4. Click OK.

   You're returned to the Relationships window. The Relationships window should now show an arrow going from the `Contacts` table to the `Sales` table. At this point, you're ready to set referential integrity between the two tables on an outer join relationship.

FIGURE 3.17

The Join Properties dialog box, used to set up the join properties between `tblCus-tomers` and `tblSales`. Notice that it specifies all records from the Customers table.

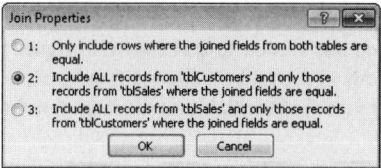

Given the join properties shown in Figure 3.17, any time the customers and sales tables are involved in a query, all the customer records are returned, even if a customer has not yet placed any orders. This setting ought to give a more complete impression of the company's customer base instead of restricting the returned records to customers who've placed orders.

Establishing a join type for every relationship in your database is not absolutely necessary. In the following chapters, you'll see that you can specify outer joins for each query in your application. Many developers choose to use the default equi-join for all the relationships in their databases, and to adjust the join properties on each query to yield the desired results.

Enforcing referential integrity

After using the Edit Relationships dialog box to specify the relationship, verify the table and related fields, and specify the type of join between the tables, you should set referential integrity between the tables. Select the Enforce Referential Integrity check box in the lower portion of the Edit Relationships dialog box to indicate that you want Access to enforce the referential integrity rules on the relationship between the tables.

Caution

If you choose not to enforce referential integrity, you can add new records, change key fields, or delete related records without warnings about referential integrity violations — thus, making it possible to change critical fields and damaging the application's data. With no integrity active, you can create tables that have orphans (Sales without a Contact). With normal operations (such as data entry or changing information), referential integrity rules should be enforced.

Enforcing referential integrity also enables two other options (cascading updates and cascading deletes) that you may find useful. These options are near the bottom of the Edit Relationships dialog box (refer to Figure 3.15).

Note

You might find, when you select Enforce Referential Integrity and click the Create button (or the OK button if you've reopened the Edit Relationships window to edit a relationship), that Access will not allow you to create a relationship and enforce referential integrity. The most likely reason for this behavior is that you're asking Access to create a relationship that violates referential integrity rules, such as a child table with orphans in it. In such a case, Access warns you by displaying a dialog box similar to that shown in Figure 3.18. The warning happens in this example because there are some records in the `Sales` table with no matching value in the `Salesperson` table. This means that Access can't enforce referential integrity between these tables because the data within the tables already violates the rules.

A dialog box warning that referential integrity cannot be enforced because of integrity violations

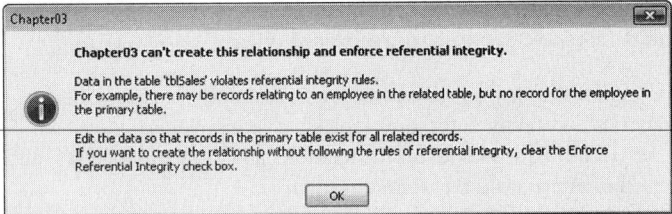

Tip

To solve any conflicts between existing tables, you can create a Find Unmatched query by using the Query Wizard to find the records in the many-side table that violate referential integrity. Then you can convert the Unmatched query to a Delete query to delete the offending records or add the appropriate value to the `SalespersonID` field.

You could remove the offending records and return to the Relationships window and set referential integrity between the two tables. Whether it's appropriate to clean up data by deleting records depends entirely on the business rues governing the application. Deleting orders just because referential integrity can't be enforced would be considered a bad idea in most environments.

Choosing the Cascade Update Related Fields option

If you specify Enforce Referential Integrity in the Edit Relationships dialog box, Access enables the Cascade Update Related Fields check box. This option tells Access that, as a user changes the contents of a related field (the primary key field in the primary table — `CustomerID`, for example), the new `CustomerID` is rippled through all related tables.

Note

If the primary key field in the primary table is a related field between several tables, this option must be selected for all related tables or it won't work.

Generally speaking, however, there are very few reasons why the value of a primary key may change. The example I give in the "Connecting the data" section, earlier in this chapter, of a missing Social Security number is one case where you may need to replace a temporary Social Security number with the permanent Social Security number after employee data has been added to the database. However, when using an AutoNumber or another surrogate key value, there is seldom any reason to have to change the primary key value once a record has been added to the database.

Choosing the Cascade Delete Related Records option

The Cascade Delete Related Records option instructs Access to delete all related child records when a parent record is deleted. Although there are instances in which this option can be quite useful, as with so many other options, cascading deletes comes with a number of warnings.

For example, if you've chosen Cascade Delete Related Records and you try to delete a particular customer (who moved away from the area), Access first deletes all the related records from the child tables — Sales and SalesLineItems — and then deletes the customer record. In other words, Access deletes all the records in the sales line items for each sale for each customer — the detail items of the sales, the associated sales records, and the customer record — with one step.

Perhaps you can already see the primary issue associated with cascading deletes. If all of a customer's sales records are deleted when the customer record is deleted, you have no way of properly reporting sales for the period. You could not, for instance, reliably report on the previous year's sales figures because all the sales records for "retired" customers have been deleted from the database. Also, in this particular example, you would lose the opportunity to report on sales trends, product category sales, and a wide variety of other uses of the application's data.

It would make much better sense to use an Active field (Yes/No data type) in the Customers table to indicate which customers are still active. It would be quite easy to include the Active field in queries where only current customers are needed (Active = Yes), and ignore the Active field in queries where all sales (regardless of the customer's active status) are required.

Tip

To use this option, you must specify Cascade Delete Related Records for all the table's relationships in the database. If you don't specify this option for all the tables in the chain of related tables, Access won't cascade deletions.

In general, it's probably not a good idea to enable cascading deletes in a database. It's far too easy to accidentally delete important data. Consider a situation where a user accidentally deletes a customer, wiping out the customer's entire sales history, including payments, shipping, backorders, promotions, and other activities. There are very few situations where users should be permitted to delete many different types of data as a single action.

Viewing all relationships

With the Relationships dialog box open, select View ➪ All Relationships to see all the relationships in the database. If you want to simplify the view you see in the Relationships window, you can "hide" a relationship by deleting the tables you see in the Relationships window. Click on a table, press the Delete key, and Access removes the table from the Relationships window. Removing a table from the Relationships window doesn't delete any relationships between the table and other tables in the database.

When building database tables, make sure that the Required property of the foreign key field in the related table (in the case of `tblBookOrders5` and `tblBookOrderDetails`, the foreign key is `OrderID` in `tblBookOrderDetails`) is set to `Yes`. This action forces the user to enter a value in the foreign key field, providing the relationship path between the tables.

The relationships formed in the Relationships window are permanent and are managed by Access. When you form permanent relationships, they appear in the Query Design window by default as you add the tables (queries are discussed in detail in Chapter 4). Even without permanent relationships between tables, you form temporary relationships any time you include multiple tables in the Query Design window.

Cross-Reference

If you connect to a SQL Server back-end database or use the Microsoft Database Engine and create an Access Data Project, the Relationships window is different. You can find more about this subject in Chapters 37 and 38.

Deleting relationships

From time to time, you might find it necessary to delete relationships between tables. The Relationships window is simply a picture of the relationships between tables. If you open the Relationships window, click on each of the tables in the relationship, and press the Delete key, you delete the picture of the tables in the relationship, but not the relationship itself. You must first click on the line connecting the tables and press Delete to delete the relationship, and then delete each of the table pictures to completely remove the relationship.

Application-specific integrity rules

In addition to the referential integrity rules enforced by the Jet database engine, you can establish a number of business rules that are enforced by the applications you build in Access. In many cases, your clients or users will tell you the business rules that must be enforced by the application. It's up to you as the developer to compose the Visual Basic code, table design, field properties, and so on that implement the business rules expected by your users.

Typical business rules include items such as the following:

- The order-entry clerk must enter his ID number on the entry form.
- Quantities can never be less than zero.
- The unit selling price can never be less than the unit cost.
- The order ship date must come after the order date.

Most often, these rules are added to a table at design time. Enforcing such rules goes a long way toward preserving the value of the data managed by the database. For example, in Figure 3.19, the ValidationRule property of the Quantity field (>=0) ensures that the quantity can't be a negative number. If the inventory clerk tries to put a negative number into the Quantity field, an error message box pops up containing the validation text: Must not be a negative number.

FIGURE 3.19

A simple validation rule goes a long way toward preserving the database's integrity.

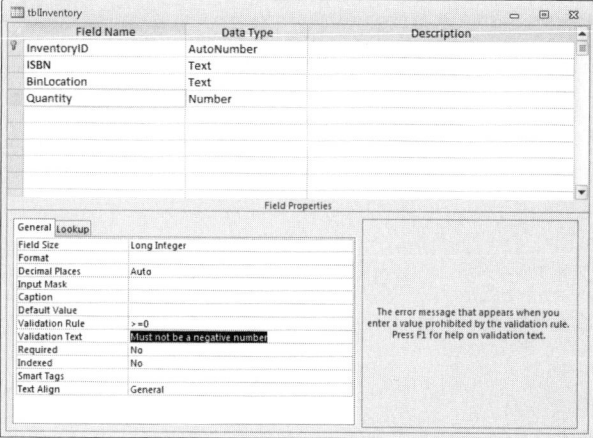

You can also establish a tablewide validation rule that provides some protection for the data in the table. Unfortunately, only one rule can be created for the entire table, making it difficult to provide specific validation text for all possible violations.

Cross-Reference

You can read examples of using VBA to enforce business rules in many different chapters in this book.

Summary

This chapter examines the relationships between tables in an Access database, and how you normalize the data for the best performance. I also covered the important topic of ensuring data security through the built-in integrity rules that are enforced by the Jet database engine. Most Access databases are built without adequate safeguards; make sure your database applications provide adequate protection for your user's data.

You're now ready to begin exploring using all that data. The next chapter takes on the challenging topic of constructing powerful, useful queries that return the data in a variety of ways. As you'll soon see, building queries in Microsoft Access is about much more than simply asking the database to return data to you. You'll learn how to control the sort order, combine data from multiple tables, and include expressions and other techniques that extend the flexibility of your queries.

Later, Chapter 5 explains the confusing topic of combining query operators such as AND and OR to achieve the desired results in a query. Access uses the same operators in a number of different places (such as VBA code and form and report design), so a firm understanding of this important topic extends well beyond query construction.

Selecting Data with Queries

Q ueries are an essential part of any database application. Queries are the tools that enable you and your users to extract data from multiple tables, combine it in useful ways, and present it to the user as a datasheet, on a form, or as a printed report.

You may have heard the old cliché, "Queries convert data to information." To a certain extent, this statement is true — that's why it's a cliché. The data contained within tables is not particularly useful because, for the most part, the data in tables appears in no particular order. Also, in a properly normalized database, important information is spread out among a number of different tables. Queries are what draw these various data sources together and present the combined information in such a way that users can actually work with the data.

In this chapter, you learn how to create and enhance queries. Using the Sales (tblSales), Customers (tblCustomers), Contacts (tblContacts), Sales Line Items (tblSalesLineItems), Categories (tblCategories), and Products (tblProducts) tables, you create several types of queries for the Collectible Mini Cars database.

On the CD-ROM

This chapter uses the Chapter04.accdb database. **If you haven't already copied it onto your machine from the CD, you should do so now.**

The data returned by Access queries is often used to populate forms and reports. As you read this chapter, keep in mind that the transformations and conversions imposed on data returned by a query apply whether the data is viewed in a datasheet, in a form, or in a report. One of the underlying principles of queries is that the work performed by a query is independent of how

IN THIS CHAPTER

Understanding what queries are and what they can do for you

Creating queries

Specifying the fields in a query

Displaying a query's results

Adding and removing fields from a query's design

Sorting a query's results

Filtering records returned by a query

Printing records returned by a query

Saving a query

Including more than one table in a query

Adding, deleting, and moving tables in a query

Joining tables in a query's design

Understanding the options for joining tables in a query

the query's data is used. In many cases it makes more sense to include logic such as transformations, combinations, and sorting in a query, instead of performing these actions at the form or report level.

Introducing Queries

A database's primary purpose is to store and extract information. Information can be obtained from a database immediately after the data is added, or days, weeks, or even years later. Of course, retrieving information from database tables requires knowledge of how the database is designed.

For example, consider printed reports kept in a traditional filing cabinet, arranged by date and by a sequence number that indicates when the report was produced. To find a specific report, you must know its year and sequence number. In a good filing system, you might have a cross-reference book to help you find a specific report. This book might have all reports categorized alphabetically by type of report and, perhaps, by date. Such a book can be helpful, but if you know only the report's topic and approximate date, you still have to search through all the sections of the book to find out where to get the report.

Unlike manual filing systems, databases like Microsoft Access quickly and easily retrieve information to meet virtually any criteria you specify.

This is the real power of a database — the capacity to examine the data in more ways than you can imagine. Queries, by definition, ask questions about the data stored in the database. Most queries are used to drive forms, reports, and graphical representations of the data contained in a database.

What queries are

Let's start with the basics. The word *query* comes from the Latin word *quaerere,* which means "to ask or inquire." Over the years, the word *query* has become synonymous with *quiz, challenge, inquire,* or *question.*

A Microsoft Access query is a question that you ask about the information stored in Access tables. You build queries with the Access query tools, and then save it as a new object in the Access database. Your query can be a simple question about data in a single table, or it can be a more complex question about information stored in several tables. After you submit the question, Microsoft Access returns only the information you requested.

Using queries this way, you might ask the Collectible Mini Cars database to show you only trucks that were sold in the year 2012. To see the *types* of trucks sold for the year 2012, you need information from three tables: tblSales, tblSalesLineItems, and tblProducts. Figure 4.1 shows just such a query in the Access query designer. Although it might look complex, it's actually very simple and easy to understand.

FIGURE 4.1

A typical three-table select query

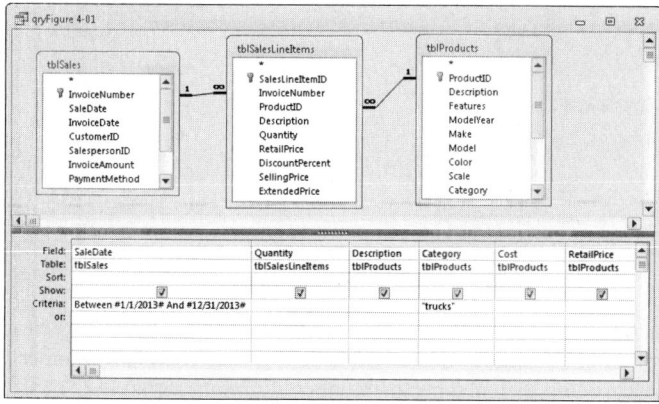

After you create and run a query, Microsoft Access retrieves and displays the requested records as a datasheet. This set of records returned by a query is called a *recordset*. As you've seen in Chapters 1 and 2, a datasheet looks just like a spreadsheet, with rows of records and columns of data. The Datasheet view of the recordset can display many records simultaneously.

You can easily filter information from a single table using the Search and Filter capabilities of a table's Datasheet view (Filter by Selection and Filter by Form).

Cross-Reference
I discuss datasheets in detail in Chapter 6.

Clicking the Datasheet View button on the ribbon runs the query and returns the records shown in Figure 4.2. This query is relatively easy to design when you understand how to use the Access query designer. This simple query has many elements that demonstrate the power of the Access query engine: sorting a result set of records, specifying multiple criteria, and even using a complex Or condition in one of those fields.

You can build very complex queries using the Access query designer. Suppose, for example, that you want to send a notice to all previous buyers of multiple products in the past year. This type of query requires getting information from four tables: tblCustomers, tblSales, tblSalesLineItems, and tblProducts. The majority of the information you need is in tblCustomers and tblProducts.

FIGURE 4.2

The results of the query shown in Figure 4.1

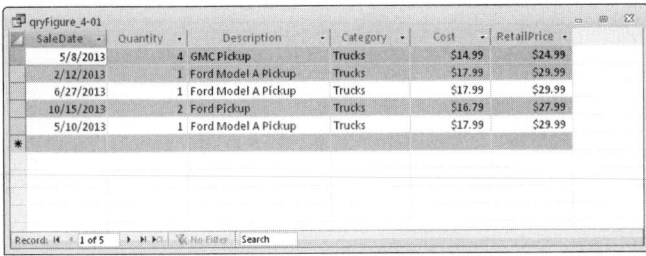

In this case, you want Access to show you a datasheet of all customer names and addresses meeting the query's criteria (multiple products purchased in 2012). In this case, Access retrieves customer names and cities from `tblCustomers` and then obtains the number of products from the `tbl-Products` table, and the year of sale from the `tblSales` table. Figure 4.3 shows this relatively complex query.

FIGURE 4.3

A more complex query returning customers that purchased more than one car in 2012

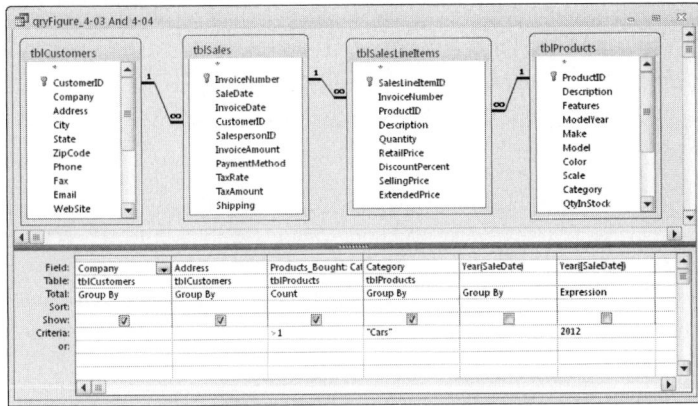

Access takes the information specified by the criteria, combines it, and displays in a single data-sheet. This datasheet is the result of a query that draws from `tblCustomers`, `tblSales`, `tbl-SalesLineItems`, and `tblProducts`. The database query performs the work of assembling all the information for you. Figure 4.4 shows the resulting datasheet.

FIGURE 4.4

The resulting datasheet of the query shown in Figure 4.3

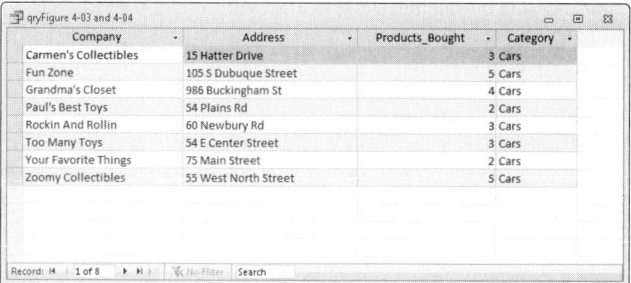

In Figure 4.4, notice that you can't tell which table provided the data in each column. In most cases your users won't know, nor will they care, where the data they see in an application comes from. In this case, you know that the data is taken from four different tables, but the complexity of the query is hidden from users. Access does an excellent job of connecting users to data, as this query example shows.

Types of queries

Access supports many different types of queries, grouped into six basic categories:

- **Select:** The most common type of query is the select query. As its name implies, a select query selects information from one or more tables, creating a recordset. Generally speaking, the data returned by a select query is updatable and is often used to populate forms and reports.

- **Total:** A total query is a special type of select query. Total queries provide sums or other calculations (such as count) from the records returned by a select query. Selecting this type of query adds a Total row in the Query by Example (QBE) grid.

- **Action:** An action query (Make-Table, Delete, Update, or Append) enables you to create new tables or change data in existing tables. Action queries affect many records as a single operation.

- **Crosstab:** A crosstab query can display summary data in cross-tabular form like a spreadsheet, with row and column headings based on fields in the table. The individual cells of the recordset are computed or calculated from data in the underlying tables.

- **Specialized queries:** There are three specialized query types — union, pass-through, and data definition. These queries are used for advanced database manipulation, such as working with client/server SQL databases like SQL Server or Oracle. You create these queries by writing SQL statements that are specific to the server database.

- **Top(n):** Top(n) queries enable you to specify a number or percentage of records you want returned from any type of query (select, total, and so on).

What queries can do

Queries are flexible. They allow you to look at your data in virtually any way you can imagine. Most database systems are continually evolving and changing over time. Very often, the original purpose of a database is very different from its current use.

Here is just a sampling of what you can do with Access queries:

- **Choose tables.** You can obtain information from a single table or from many tables that are related by some common data. Suppose you're interested in seeing the customer name along with the items purchased by each type of customer. When using several tables, Access combines the data as a single recordset.

- **Choose fields.** Specify which fields from each table you want to see in the recordset. For example, you can select the customer name, zip code, sales date, and invoice number from tblCustomers and tblSales.

- **Provide criteria.** Record selection is based on selection criteria. For example, you might want to see records for only a certain category of products.

- **Sort records.** You might want to sort records in a specific order. For example, you might need to see customer contacts sorted by last name and first name.

- **Perform calculations.** Use queries to perform calculations such as averages, totals, or counts of data in records.

- **Create tables.** Create a brand-new table based on data returned by a query.

- **Display query data on forms and reports.** The recordset you create from a query might have just the right fields and data needed for a report or form. Basing a form or report on a query means that, every time you print the report or open the form, you see the most current information contained in the tables.

- **Use a query as a source of data for other queries (subquery).** You can create queries that are based on records returned by another query. This is very useful for performing ad hoc queries, where you might repeatedly make small changes to the criteria. In this case, the second query filters the first query's results.

- **Make changes to data in tables.** Action queries modify multiple rows in the underlying tables as a single operation. Action queries are frequently used to maintain data, such as archiving stale records or deleting obsolete information.

What queries return

Access combines a query's records and, when executed, displays them in a datasheet by default. The set of records returned by a query is commonly called (oddly enough) a *recordset*. A recordset is a dynamic set of records. The recordset returned by a query is not stored within the database, unless you have directed Access to build a table from those records.

Cross-Reference

You can read much more about datasheets in Chapter 6.

When using an action query, the query's recordset is gone when the query ends. Action queries perform an action on the records specified by the query's design, but no records are returned to display on a form or report.

When you save a query, only the structure of the query is saved, not the returned records. Consider these benefits of *not* saving the recordset to a physical table:

- A smaller amount of space on a storage device (usually a hard disk) is needed.
- The query uses updated versions of records.

Every time the query is executed, it reads the underlying tables and re-creates the recordset. Because recordsets themselves are not stored, a query automatically reflects any changes to the underlying tables made since the last time the query was executed — even in a real-time, multiuser environment. Depending on your needs, a query's recordset can be viewed as a datasheet, or in a form or report. When a form or report is based on a query, the query's recordset is re-created and bound to the form or report each time it's opened.

Creating a Query

After you create your tables and place data in them, you're ready to work with queries. To begin a query, choose the Create ribbon, and click on the Query Design button in the Other group. Access opens the query designer in response.

Figure 4.5 shows two windows. The underlying window is the query designer. Floating on top of the designer is the Show Table dialog box. The Show Table dialog box is *modal,* which means that you must do something in the dialog box before continuing with the query. Before you continue, you add the tables required for the query. In this case, tblProducts is highlighted and ready to be added.

FIGURE 4.5

The Show Table dialog box and the query design window

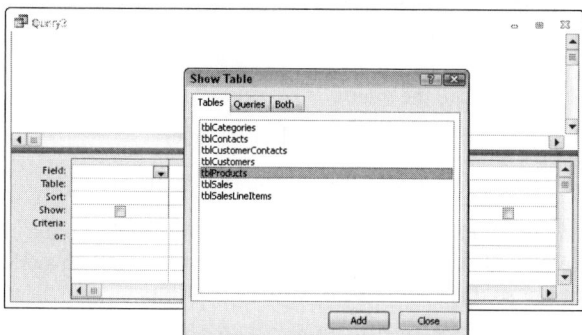

The Show Table dialog box (refer to Figure 4.5) displays all tables and queries in your database. Double-click on tblProducts to add it to the query design, or highlight tblProducts in the list and click the Add button. Close the Show Table dialog box after adding tblProducts. Figure 4.6 shows tblProducts added to the query.

FIGURE 4.6

The query design window with tblProducts added

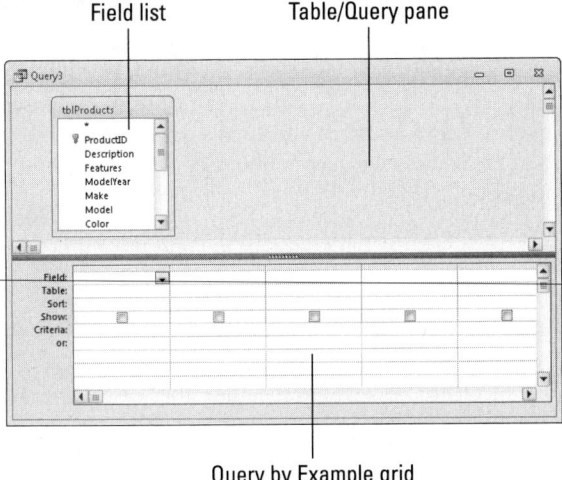

To add additional tables to the query, right-click on the anywhere in the upper portion of the query designer and select Show Table from the shortcut menu that appears. Alternatively, drag tables from the Navigation Pane to the upper portion of the query designer. There is also a Show Table button on the Design ribbon tab.

Removing a table from the query designer is easy. Just right-click on the table in the query designer and select Remove Table from the shortcut menu.

The query window has three primary views:

- **Design view:** Design view is where you create the query.
- **Datasheet view:** Datasheet view displays the records returned by the query.
- **SQL View:** The SQL View window displays the SQL statement behind a query.

The Field List window (or, more simply, the Field List) contains the names of all the fields in the selected table or query. A Field List can be resized by clicking on the edges and dragging it to a different size. You may want to resize a Field List so that all of a table's fields are visible.

The Query Designer consists of two sections:

- **The table/query pane (top):** This is where tables or queries and their fields are added to the query's design.
- **The Query by Example (QBE) design grid (bottom):** The QBE grid holds the field names involved in the query and any criteria used to select records. Each column in the QBE grid contains information about a single field from a table or query contained within the upper pane.

The two window panes are separated horizontally by a pane-resizing bar (refer to Figure 4.6). Use the mouse to move the bar up or down to change the relative sizes of the upper and lower panes.

Switch between the upper and lower panes by clicking the desired pane or by pressing F6 to switch panes. Each pane has horizontal and vertical scrollbars to help you move around.

You actually build the query by dragging fields from the upper pane to the QBE grid.

Figure 4.6 displays an empty QBE grid at the bottom of the Query Designer. The QBE grid has six labeled rows:

- **Field:** This is where field names are entered or added.
- **Table:** This row shows the table the field is from. This is useful in queries with multiple tables.
- **Sort:** This row enables sorting instructions for the query.
- **Show:** This row determines whether to display the field in the returned recordset.
- **Criteria:** This row consists of the criteria that filter the returned records.
- **or:** This row is the first of a number of rows to which you can add multiple query criteria.

You learn more about these rows as you create queries in this chapter.

The Query Design ribbon (shown in Figure 4.7) contains many different buttons specific to building and working with queries. Although each button is explained as it's used in the chapters of this book, here are the main buttons:

FIGURE 4.7

The Query Design ribbon

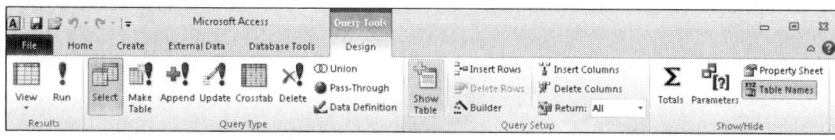

- **View:** Switches between the Datasheet view and Design view in the query window. The View drop-down control also enables you to display the underlying SQL statement behind the query.

- **Run:** Runs the query. Displays a select query's datasheet, serving the same function as selecting Datasheet View from the View button. However, when working with action queries, the Run button performs the operations (append, make-table, and so on) specified by the query.

- **Select:** Clicking the Select button opens a new select query in the Query Designer.

- **Make Table, Append, Update, and Crosstab:** Each of these buttons specifies the type of query you're building. In most cases, you transform a select query into an action query by clicking one of these buttons.

- **Show Table:** Opens the Show Table dialog box.

- **Save (in the Quick Access Toolbar):** Saves the query. It's a good idea to save your work often, especially when creating complex queries.

The remaining buttons are used for creating more-advanced queries, printing the contents of the query, and displaying a query's Property Sheet.

Adding Fields

There are several ways to add fields to a query. You can add fields one at a time, select and add multiple fields, or select all the fields in a field list.

Adding a single field

You add a single field in several ways. One method is to double-click the field name in the table in the top pane of the query designer. The field name immediately appears in the first available column in the QBE pane. Alternatively, drag a field from a table in the top pane of the query designer, and drop it on a column in the QBE grid. Dropping a field between two fields in the QBE grid pushes other fields to the right.

Another way to add fields to the QBE grid is to click an empty field cell in the QBE grid, and select the field's name from the drop-down list in the cell, or type the field's name into the cell. Figure 4.8 shows selecting the Cost field from the drop-down list. Once the field is selected, simply move to the next field cell and select the next field you want to see in the query.

Each cell in the Table row of the QBE grid contains a drop-down list of the tables contained in the upper pane of the query designer.

After selecting the fields, run the query by clicking the Datasheet button or the Run button on the ribbon. Click the Design View button on the ribbon to return to the query design window.

FIGURE 4.8

Adding fields in the QBE grid. Clicking the down arrow in the field box reveals a drop-down list from which you select a field.

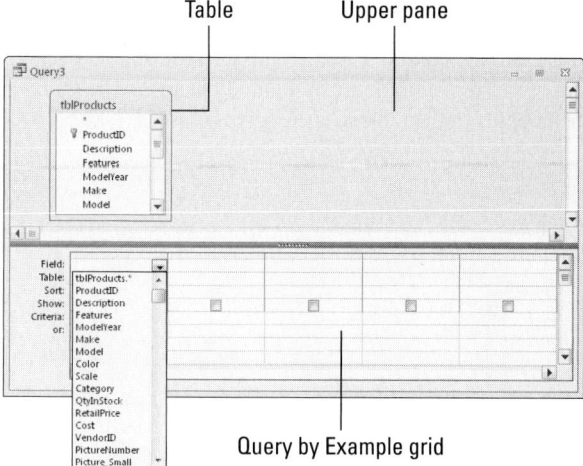

Query by Example grid

Adding multiple fields

You can add multiple fields in a single action by selecting the fields from the Field List window and dragging them to the QBE grid. The selected fields don't have to be contiguous (one after the other). Hold down the Ctrl key while selecting multiple fields. Figure 4.9 illustrates the process of adding multiple fields.

FIGURE 4.9

Selecting multiple fields to add to the QBE grid

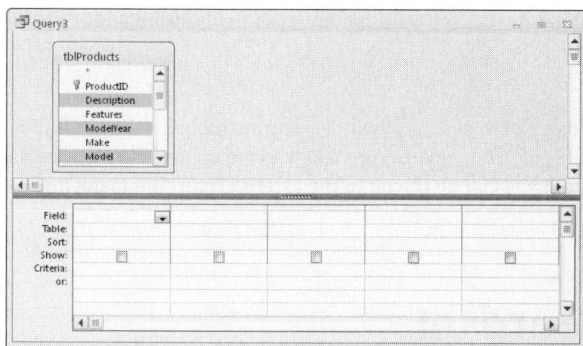

The fields are added to the QBE grid in the order in which they occur in the table.

You can also add all the fields in the table by clicking on the Field List's header (where it says tblProducts in Figure 4.10) to highlight all the fields in the table. Then drag the highlighted fields to the QBE grid.

Alternatively, click and drag the asterisk (*) from the Field List to the QBE grid (or double-click the asterisk to add it to the QBE grid). Although this action doesn't add all the fields to the QBE grid, the asterisk directs Access to include all fields in the table in the query.

FIGURE 4.10

Adding the asterisk to the QBE grid selects all fields in the table.

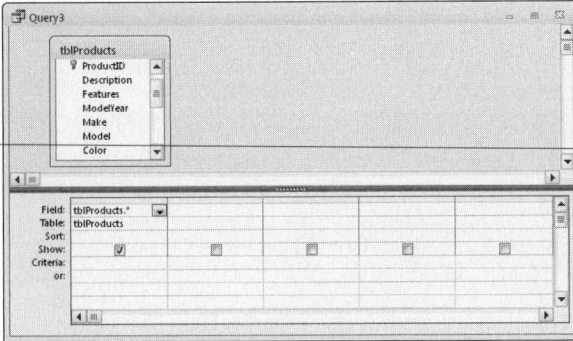

Tip

Unlike selecting all the fields, the asterisk places a reference to all the fields in a single column. When you drag multiple columns, as in the preceding example, you drag names to the QBE grid. If you later change the design of the table, you also have to change the design of the query. The advantage of using the asterisk for selecting all fields is that changes to the underlying tables don't require changes to the query. The asterisk means to select all fields in the table, regardless of the field names or changes in the number of fields in the table.

Caution

The downside of using the asterisk to specify all fields in a table is that the query, as instructed, returns all the fields in a table, regardless of whether every field is used on a form or report. Retrieving unused data can be a very inefficient process. Very often, performance problems can be traced to the asterisk returning many more fields than necessary to a form or report.

Displaying the Recordset

Click the Run button or the Datasheet button to view the query's results (see Figure 4.11).

FIGURE 4.11

The datasheet view of the query

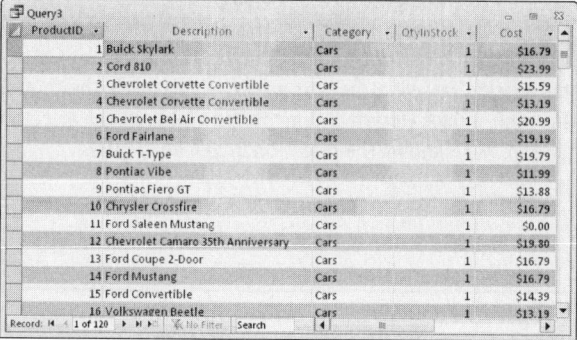

Cross-Reference

Working with records in Datasheet view is covered in detail in Chapter 6.

Filtering, sorting, rearranging, and searching within a datasheet is quite easy. My simple select query didn't transform the data in any way, so the data shown in Figure 4.11 is completely editable. I can modify existing data, delete rows, and even add new records to this data set, if I want.

When you're working with data in the datasheet, all the table and field properties defined at the table level are in effect. Therefore, validation rules, default values, and other properties assert themselves even though the datasheet is the result of a query.

Note

Earlier versions of Access referred to an updatable datasheet as a Dynaset. This term emphasized the fact that the datasheet was dynamically linked to its underlying data sources. However, the term has fallen by the way-side because, very often, the data in a query's datasheet is not updatable. You'll see data transformations later in this chapter and in many other chapters in this book.

At any time, clicking the Design View button on the ribbon returns you to Query Design view.

Working with Fields

Sometimes you'll want to work with the fields you've already selected — rearranging their order, inserting a new field, or deleting an existing field. You may even want to add a field to the QBE grid without showing it in the datasheet. Adding a field without showing it enables you to sort on the hidden field, or to use the hidden field as criteria.

Selecting a field in the QBE grid

Before you can move a field's position, you must first select it. To select it, you will work with the field selector row.

The *field selector* is the thin gray area at the top of each column in the QBE grid at the bottom of the query designer. Each column represents a field. To select the Category field, move the mouse pointer until a small selection arrow (in this case, a dark downward arrow) is visible in the selector row and then click and drag the column. Figure 4.12 shows the selection arrow above the Category column just before it's selected.

Selecting a column in the QBE grid. The pointer changes to a downward-pointing arrow when you move over the selection row.

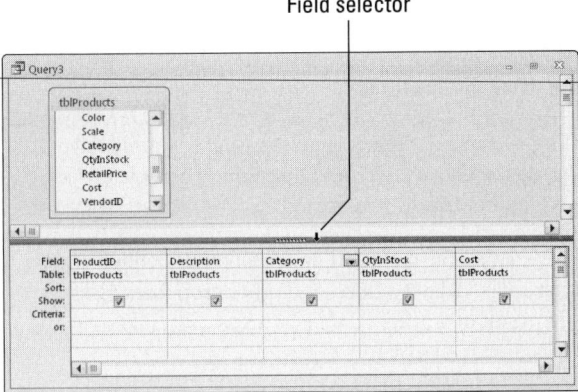

Field selector

Tip

Select multiple contiguous fields by clicking the first field you want to select, and then dragging across the field selector bars of the other fields.

Changing field order

The left-to-right order in which fields appear in the QBE grid determines the order in which they appear in Datasheet view. You might want to move the fields in the QBE grid to achieve a new sequence of fields in the query's results. With the fields selected, you can move the fields on the QBE design by simply dragging them to a new position.

Left-click on a field's selector bar, and, while holding down the left mouse button, drag the field into a new position in the QBE grid.

Figure 4.13 shows the `Category` field highlighted. As you move the selector field to the left, the column separator between the fields `ProductID` and `Description` changes (gets wider) to show you where `Category` will go.

Moving the `Category` field to between `ProductID` and `Description`. Notice the QBE field icon below the arrow near the `Description` column.

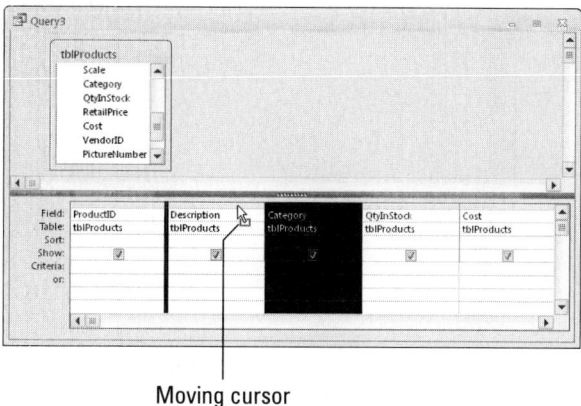

Moving cursor

Tip

The field order in a query is irrelevant to how the data appears on a form or report. Normally, you'll arrange the controls on a form or report in response to user requirements.

Resizing columns in the QBE grid

The QBE grid generally shows five or six fields in the viewable area of your screen. The remaining fields are viewed by moving the horizontal scroll bar at the bottom of the window.

You might want to shrink some fields to be able to see more columns in the QBE grid. You adjust the column width to make them smaller (or larger) by moving the mouse pointer to the margin between two fields, and dragging the column resizer left or right (see Figure 4.14).

Tip

An easier way to resize columns in the QBE grid is to double-click on the line dividing two columns in the grid. Access auto-sizes the column to fit the data displayed in the column.

The width of a column in the QBE grid has no affect on how the field's data is displayed in a datasheet, form, or report. The column width in the QBE grid is just a convenience to you, the developer. Also, QBE column width is not preserved when you save and close the query.

FIGURE 4.14

Resizing columns in the QBE grid

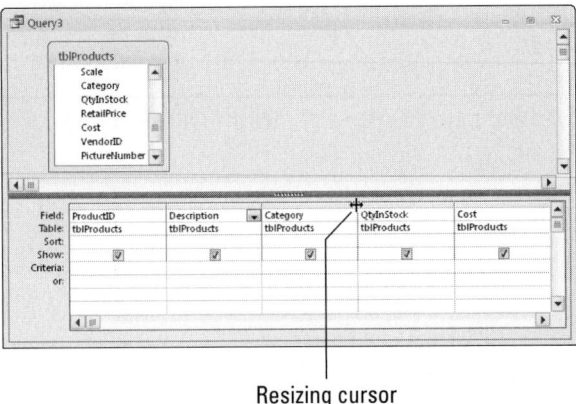

Resizing cursor

Removing a field

Remove a field from the QBE grid by selecting the field (or fields) and pressing the Delete key. You can also right-click on a field's selector bar and choose Cut from the shortcut menu.

Inserting a field

Insert new fields in the QBE grid by dragging a field from a Field List window in the tables pane above the QBE grid and dropping it onto a column in the QBE grid. The new column is inserted to the left of the column on which you dropped the field. Double-clicking a field in a Field List adds the new column at the far-right position in the QBE grid.

Providing an alias for the field name

To make the query datasheet easier to read, you can provide aliases for the fields in your query. An alias becomes the field's heading in the query's datasheet, but it doesn't affect the field's name or how the data is stored and used by Access. Aliases are sometimes useful to help users better understand the data returned by a query. As you can see in Chapter 18, data in queries are often transformed by performing simple operations such as combining a person's first and last name as a single field. In these situations, aliases are very useful because they provide an easily recognizable reference to the transformed data.

To follow along with this example, create a query using the fields from the tblProducts (refer to Figure 4.13). Follow these steps to establish an alias for the ProductID and Description fields:

1. Click to the left of the *P* of the ProductID column in the top row of the QBE grid.

2. Type **ProductNumber:** to the left of ProductID.

3. Click to the left of the *D* in the Description column and enter **ProductDescription:** to the left of the field name.

    When you run the query, the aliases you created appear as the column headings. Figure 4.15 shows both the query in Design view and the query's datasheet. Notice that the `ProductID` and `Description` column sport their new aliases instead of their respective field names.

FIGURE 4.15

Aliases can help users understand data.

Alias

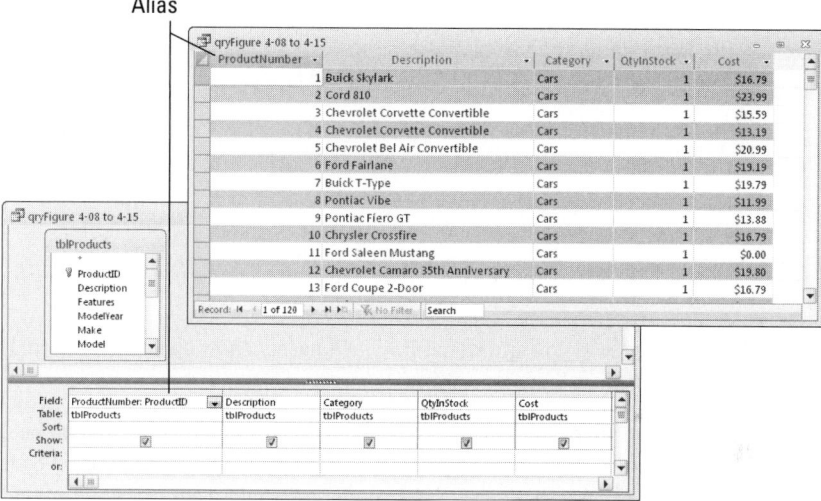

Caution

Use aliases with caution. Because an alias masks the name of the field underlying a datasheet, it's easy to become confused about which column headings are aliases and which are field names. It is a complete waste of time looking for a field named `ProductDescription`, based on a datasheet column heading. It would be nice if Access somehow distinguished between aliases and field names in Datasheet view, but the only way to know for sure is to examine the query's design. Also, the alias is how the field is named when used in a form or report.

Showing a field

While you're performing queries, you might want to show only some of the fields in the QBE grid. Suppose, for example, you've chosen `FirstName`, `LastName`, `Address`, `City`, and `State`. Then you decide that you want to temporarily look at the same data, without the State field. You could start a new query adding all the fields except `State`, or you could simply "turn off" the `State` field by unchecking the Show check box in the State column (see Figure 4.16).

FIGURE 4.16

The Show check box is unchecked for the `State` field.

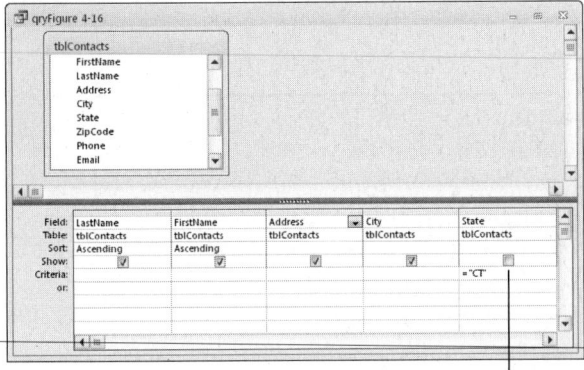

Unchecked Show box

By default, every field you add to the QBE grid has its Show check box selected.

In Figure 4.17 notice that the `State` field does not appear in the query's results. In many cases, especially with a query such as the one illustrated in Figure 4.16, you don't need to see a field that is used as the query's criteria. You already know that every record returned by the query will have CT in the `State` field, so you can save a little screen space and a tiny bit of time to run the query by removing the `State` field from the query results.

FIGURE 4.17

The unchecked field does not appear in the query's results.

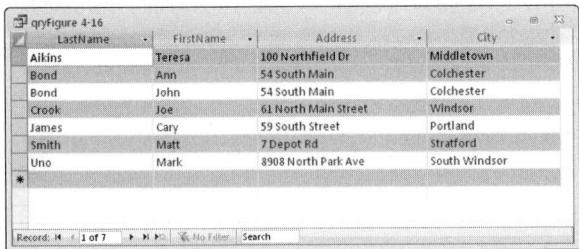

Access still considers the State field because it contains the query's criteria, but otherwise the field is ignored.

A common reason to hide a field in the query is because the field is used for sorting, but its value is not needed in the query. For example, consider a query involving the invoices from the Collectible Mini Cars database. For a number of reasons, the users might want to see the invoices sorted by the order date, even though the actual order date is irrelevant for this particular purpose. Simply include the OrderDate field in the QBE grid, set the sort order for the OrderDate field, and uncheck its Show box. Access sorts the data by the OrderDate field even though the field is not shown in the query's results.

Caution

If you save a query that has an unused field (its Show box is unchecked and no criteria or sort order is applied to the field), Access eliminates the field from the query as part of the query-optimization process. The next time you open the query, the field won't be included in the query's design.

Changing the Sort Order

When viewing a recordset, you often want to display the data in a sorted order. You might want to sort the recordset to make it easier to analyze the data (for example, to look at all the tblProducts sorted by category).

Sorting places the records in alphabetical or numeric order. The sort order can be ascending (0 to 9 and A to Z) or descending (9 to 0 and Z to A). You can sort on a single field or multiple fields.

You input sorting directions in the Sort row in the QBE grid. To specify a sort order on a particular field (such as LastName), perform these steps:

1. Position the cursor in the Sort cell in the LastName column.
2. Click the drop-down list that appears in the cell, and select the sort order (Ascending or Descending) you want to apply.

   Figure 4.18 shows the QBE grid with ascending sorts specified for the LastName and FirstName fields. Notice that the LastName field is still showing the sort options available. Also notice that the word *Ascending* is being selected in the field's Sort cell.

Note

You can't sort on a Memo or an OLE object field.

FIGURE 4.18

An ascending sort has been specified for the `LastName` and `FirstName` fields.

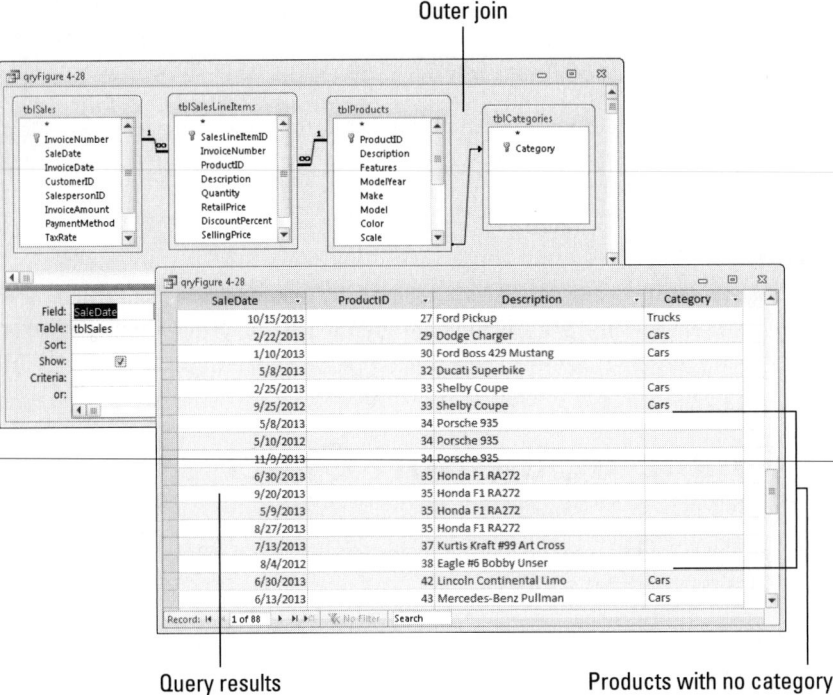

Query results   Products with no category

The left-to-right order in which fields appear in the QBE grid is important when sorting on more than one field. Not only do the fields appear in the datasheet in left-to-right order, but they're sorted in the same order; this is known as *sort order precedence*. The leftmost field containing sort criteria is sorted first, the first field to the right containing sort criteria is sorted next, and so on. In the example shown in Figure 4.18, the `LastName` field is sorted first, and then the `FirstName` field.

Figure 4.19 shows the results of the query shown in Figure 4.18. Notice that the data is sorted by `LastName`, and then by `FirstName`. This is why Ann Bond appears before John Bond, and John Jones appears before Kevin Jones in the query's data.

FIGURE 4.19

The order of the fields in the QBE grid is critical when sorting on multiple fields.

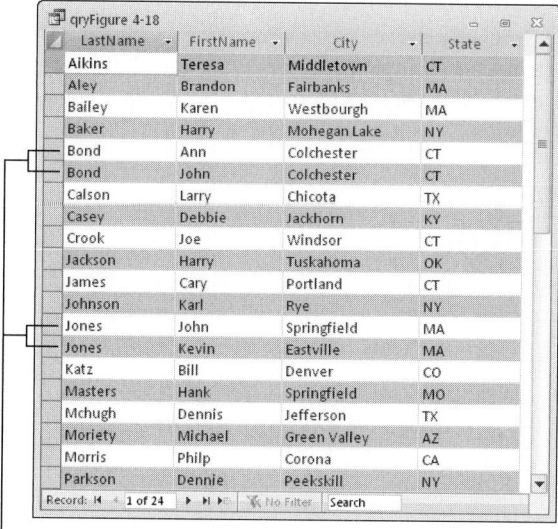

LastName	FirstName	City	State
Aikins	Teresa	Middletown	CT
Aley	Brandon	Fairbanks	MA
Bailey	Karen	Westbourgh	MA
Baker	Harry	Mohegan Lake	NY
Bond	Ann	Colchester	CT
Bond	John	Colchester	CT
Calson	Larry	Chicota	TX
Casey	Debbie	Jackhorn	KY
Crook	Joe	Windsor	CT
Jackson	Harry	Tuskahoma	OK
James	Cary	Portland	CT
Johnson	Karl	Rye	NY
Jones	John	Springfield	MA
Jones	Kevin	Eastville	MA
Katz	Bill	Denver	CO
Masters	Hank	Springfield	MO
Mchugh	Dennis	Jefferson	TX
Moriety	Michael	Green Valley	AZ
Morris	Philp	Corona	CA
Parkson	Dennie	Peekskill	NY

qryFigure 4-18

Record: 1 of 24   No Filter   Search

Records showing sorting precedence

Displaying Only Selected Records

So far, most of the queries described in this chapter return all the records in the `tblCustomers` and `tblProducts` tables. Most often users want to work only with records conforming to some criteria. Otherwise, too many records may be returned by a query, causing serious performance issues. For example, you might want to look only at customers who have not bought any products within the last six months. Access makes it easy for you to specify a query's criteria.

Understanding selection criteria

Selection criteria are filtering rules applied to data as they're extracted from the database. Selection criteria instruct Access which records you want to look at in the recordset. A typical criterion might be "all sellers," or "only those vehicles that are not trucks," or "products with retail prices greater than $75."

Selection criteria limit the records returned by a query. Selection criteria aid the user by selecting only the records a user wants to see, and ignoring all the others.

You specify criteria in the Criteria row of the QBE grid. You designate criteria as an expression. The expression can be as a simple example (like "trucks" or "not trucks"), or it can take the form of complex expressions using built-in Access functions.

Proper use of query criteria is critical to an Access database's success. In most cases, the users have no idea what data is stored in a database's tables and accept whatever they see on a form or report as truthfully representing the database's status. Poorly chosen criteria might hide important information from the application's users, leading to bad business decisions or serious business issues later on.

Entering simple string criteria

Character-type criteria are applied to Text-type fields. Most often, you'll enter an example of the text you want to retrieve. Here is a small example that returns only product records where the product type is "Cars":

1. Add `tblProducts` and choose the `Description`, `Category`, and `Cost` fields.

2. Type **CARS** into the Criteria cell under the `Category` column.

3. Run the query.

   Only cars are displayed in the query's results (see Figure 4.20). Notice that you did not enter an equal sign or place quotes around the sample text, yet Access added double quotes around the value. Access, unlike many other database systems, automatically makes assumptions about what you want.

FIGURE 4.20

Specifying "Cars" as the query's criteria

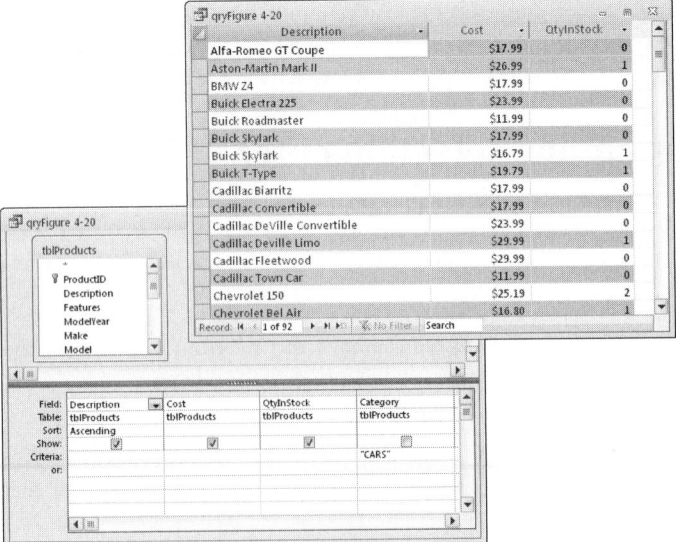

Figure 4.20 shows both the query design and the datasheet resulting from the query. This figure also illustrates one reason you might want to hide a column in a query. There's no point in displaying "Cars" in every row in the third column. In fact, because this query only returns information about cars, the user can very well assume that every record references a car, and there's no need to display a product category in the query. Unchecking the `Category` field's Show box in the query's design removes Category from the datasheet, making the data easier to understand.

You could enter the criteria expression in any of these other ways:

CARS   = CARS   "CARS"   = "Cars"

By default, Access is *not* case sensitive, so any form of the word *cars* works just as well as this query's criteria.

Figure 4.20 is an excellent example for demonstrating the options for various types of simple character criteria. You could just as well enter "Not Cars" in the criteria column, to return all products that are not cars (trucks, vans, and so on).

Generally, when dealing with character data, you enter equalities, inequalities, or a list of acceptable values.

This capability is a powerful tool. Consider that you have only to supply an example, and Access not only interprets it but also uses it to create the query recordset. This is exactly what *Query by Example* means: You enter an example and let the database build a query based on the example.

To erase the criteria in the cell, select the contents and press Delete, or select the contents and right-click Cut from the shortcut menu that appears.

Entering other simple criteria

You can also specify criteria for `Numeric`, `Date`, and `Yes/No` fields. Simply enter the example data in the criteria field just as you did for text fields. In almost every case, Access understand the criteria you enter and adjusts to correctly apply the criteria to the query's fields.

It is also possible to add more than one criteria to a query. For example, suppose that you want to look only at contacts who live in Connecticut and have been customers since January 1, 2012 (where `OrigCustDate` is greater than or equal to January 1, 2012). This query requires criteria in both the `State` and `OrigCustDate` fields. To do this, it's critical that you place both examples on the same criteria row. Follow these steps to create this query:

1. Create a new query starting with `tblCustomers`.

2. Add `ContactType`, `FirstName`, `LastName`, `State`, and `OrigCustDate` to the QBE grid.

3. Enter **"ct" or "CT"** in the Criteria cell in the `State` column.

4. Enter **>= 01/01/2012** in the Criteria cell in the `OrigCustDate` column.

   Access adds pound sign characters (#) around the date in the criteria box.

5. Run the query.

Figure 4.21 shows how the query should look.

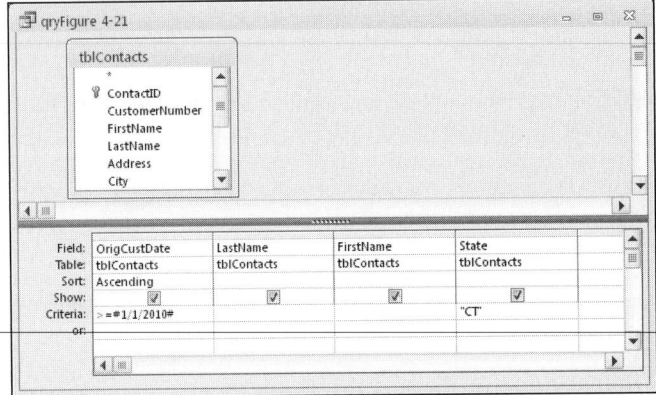

FIGURE 4.21

Specifying text and date criteria in the same query

Access displays records of customers that live in Connecticut and who became customers after January 1,, 2012.

Cross-Reference
Advanced queries are covered in depth in Chapter 18.

Access uses comparison operators to compare Date fields to a value. These operators include less than (<), greater than (>), equal to (=), or a combination of these operators.

Notice that Access automatically adds pound sign (#) delimiters around the date value. Access uses these delimiters to distinguish between date and text data. The pound signs are just like the quote marks Access added to the "Cars" criteria. Because OrigCustDate is a DateTime field, Access understands what you want and inserts the proper delimiters for you.

Be aware that Access interprets dates according to the Regional and Language Options (Windows XP) or the Region and Language settings (Windows 7) in the Windows Control Panel. For example, in most of Europe and Asia, #5/6/2012# is interpreted as June 5, 2012, while in the United States this date is May 6, 2012. It is very easy to construct a query that works perfectly but returns the wrong data because of subtle differences in regional settings.

Cross-Reference
Operators and precedence are covered more in Chapter 5.

Printing a Query's Recordset

After you create your query, you can easily print all the records in the recordset. Although you can't specify a type of report, you can print a simple matrix-type report (rows and columns) of the recordset created by your query.

You do have some flexibility when printing a recordset. If you know that the datasheet is set up just as you want, you can specify some options as you follow these steps:

1. Use the query you just created for Connecticut customers who've been active since January 1, 2012.

2. If you aren't in the Datasheet view, run the query by clicking the Run button in the Results group on the ribbon.

3. Choose File ➪ Print from the Query Datasheet window's ribbon.

4. Specify the print options that you want in the Print dialog box and click OK.

The printout reflects all layout options in effect when you print the dataset. Hidden columns don't print, and gridlines print only if the Gridlines option is on. The printout reflects the specified row height and column width.

Saving a Query

To save your query, click the Save button in the Quick Access toolbar at the top of the Access screen. Access asks you for the name of the query if this is the first time the query has been saved.

After saving the query, Access returns you to the mode you were working in. Occasionally, you'll want to save and exit the query in a single operation. To do this, click the Close Window button in the upper-right corner of the query designer. Access always asks you to confirm saving the changes before it actually saves the query.

Creating Multi-Table Queries

Using a query to get information from a single table is common; often, however, you need information from several related tables. For example, you might want to obtain a buyer's name and product purchased by the customer. This query requires four tables: `tblCustomers`, `tblSales`, `tblSalesLineItems`, and `tblProducts`.

Cross-Reference

In Chapter 3, you learned the importance of primary and foreign keys and how they link tables together. You learned how to use the Relationships window to create relationships between tables. Finally, you learned how referential integrity affects data in tables.

After you create the tables for your database and decide how the tables are related to one another, you're ready to build multiple-table queries to obtain information from several related tables. A multi-table query presents data as if it existed in one large table.

The first step in creating a multiple-table query is to add the tables to the Query window:

1. Create a new query by clicking the Query Design button in the Create ribbon tab.
2. Add `tblCustomers`, `tblSales`, `tblSalesLineItems`, and `tblProducts` by double-clicking each table's name in the Show Table dialog box.
3. Click the Close button in the Show Table dialog box.

Note

You can also add each table by highlighting the table in the list separately and clicking Add.

Figure 4.22 shows the top pane of the query design window with the four tables you just added. Because the relationships were set at table level, the join lines are automatically added to the query.

FIGURE 4.22

The query design window with four tables added. Notice that the join lines are already present.

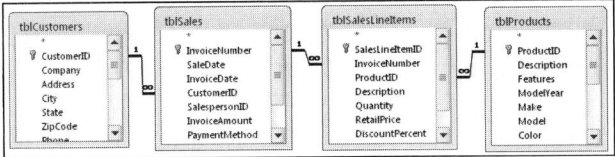

Note

You can add more tables, at any time, by choosing Query ⇨ Show Table from the Query Design ribbon.

You add fields from more than one table to the query in exactly the same way as you do when you're working with a single table. You can add fields one at a time, multiple fields as a group, or all the fields from a table.

Caution

If you type a field name in an empty field cell that has the same name in more than one table, Access enters the field name from the first table that it finds containing the field name.

Selecting a field from the drop-down list in the field cell first adds the table's name, followed by a period and the field name. For example, the `ProductID` in `tblSalesLineItems` is displayed as `tblSalesLineItems.ProductID`. This helps you select the correct field name. Using this method, you can select a common field name from a specific table.

Tip

The easiest way to select fields is still to double-click the field names in the top half of the query designer. To do so, you might have to resize the Field List windows to see the fields that you want to select.

Viewing table names

When you're working with multiple tables in a query, the field names in the QBE grid can become confusing. You might find yourself asking, for example, just which table the `Description` field is from.

Access automatically maintains the table name that is associated with each field displayed in the QBE grid. Figure 4.23 shows the query designer with the name of each table displayed under the field name in the QBE grid.

FIGURE 4.23

The QBE grid with table names displayed. Notice that it shows all four table names.

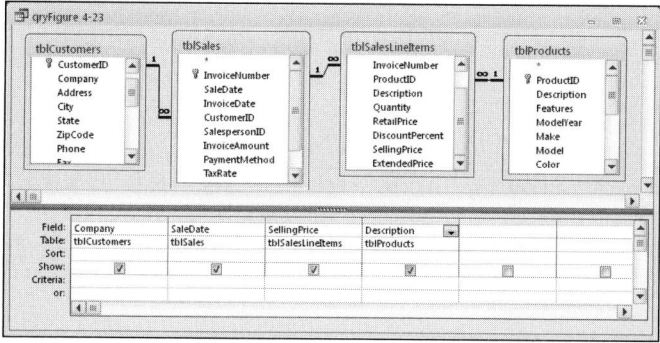

After you add fields to a query, you can run the query. Figure 4.24 shows the data returned by the query in Figure 4.23.

FIGURE 4.24

The Datasheet view of data from multiple tables

Adding multiple fields

The process of adding multiple fields in a multi-table query is identical to adding multiple fields in a single-table query. When you're adding fields from several tables, you must add them from one table at a time. The easiest way to do this is to select multiple fields and drag them together down to the QBE grid.

Select multiple contiguous fields by clicking the first field of the list and then clicking the last field while holding down the Shift key. You can also select noncontiguous fields in the list by holding down the Ctrl key while clicking individual fields.

Caution

Selecting the asterisk (*) does have one drawback: You can't specify criteria on the asterisk column itself. You have to add an individual field from the table and enter the criterion. If you add a field for a criterion (when using the asterisk), the query displays the field twice — once for the asterisk field and a second time for the criterion field. Therefore, you might want to deselect the Show cell of the criterion field.

Multi-table query limitations

When you create a query with multiple tables, there are limits to which fields can be edited. Generally, you can change data in a query's recordset, and your changes are saved in the underlying tables. The main exception is a table's primary key — a primary key value can't be edited if referential integrity is in effect and if the field is part of a relationship.

To update a table from a query, a value in a specific record in the query must represent a single record in the underlying table. This means that you can't update a field that transforms data, such as combining first and last names. Each field in a transformed recordset usually represents multiple fields in the underlying tables. There is no way to change the data in a transformed field and have it reflected in the underlying tables.

In Access, the records in your tables might not always be updateable. Table 4.1 shows when a field in a table is updateable. As Table 4.1 shows, queries based on one-to-many relationships are updateable in both tables (depending on how the query was designed).

TABLE 4.1

Rules for Updating Queries

Type of Query or Field	Updateable	Comments
One table	Yes	
One-to-one relationship	Yes	
Results contains `Memo` field	Yes	Memo field updateable.
Results contain a hyperlink	Yes	Hyperlink updateable.
Results contain an OLE object	Yes	OLE object updateable.
One-to-many relationship	Usually	Restrictions based on design methodology (see text).
Many-to-one-to-many relationship	No	Can update data in a form or data access page if Record Type = Recordset.
Two or more tables with no join line	No	Must have a join to determine updateability.
Crosstab	No	Creates a snapshot of the data.
Totals query (Sum, Avg, and so on)	No	Works with grouped data creating a snapshot.
Unique Value property is Yes	No	Shows unique records only in a snapshot.
SQL-specific queries	No	Union and pass-through work with ODBC data.
Calculated field	No	Will recalculate automatically.
Read-only fields	No	If opened read-only or on read-only drive (CD-ROM).
Permissions denied	No	Insert, replace, or delete are not granted.
ODBC tables with no unique identifier	No	A unique identifier must exist.
Paradox table with no primary key	No	A primary key file must exist.
Locked by another user	No	Can't be updated while a field is locked by another.

Overcoming query limitations

Table 4.1 shows that there are times when queries and fields in tables are not updateable. As a general rule, any query that performs aggregate operations or uses an Open DataBase Connectivity (ODBC) data source is not updateable; most other queries can be updated. When your query has more than one table and some of the tables have a one-to-many relationship, some fields might not be updateable (depending on the design of the query).

Updating a unique index (primary key)

If a query uses two tables involved in a one-to-many relationship, the query must include the primary key from the one-side table. Access must have the primary key value so that they can find the related records in the two tables.

Replacing existing data in a query with a one-to-many relationship

Normally, all the fields in the many-side table (such as the tblSales table) are updateable in a one-to-many query. All the fields (*except* the primary key) in the one-side table (tblCustomers) can be updated. Normally, this is sufficient for most database application purposes. Also, the primary key field is rarely changed in the one-side table because it is the link to the records in the joined tables.

Updating fields in queries

If you want to add records to both tables of a one-to-many relationship, include the foreign key from the many-side table and show the field in the datasheet. After doing this, records can be added starting with either the one-side or many-side table. The one side's primary key field is automatically copied to the many side's join field.

If you want to add records to multiple tables in a form (covered in Chapters 7 and 8), remember to include all (or most) of the fields from both tables. Otherwise, you won't have a complete set of the record's data on your form.

Working with the Table Pane

The upper (table) pane of the query designer contains information that is important to your query. Understanding the table pane and how to work with field lists is critically important to building complex queries.

Cross-Reference

These lines were pre-drawn because you already set the relationships between the tables as described in Chapter 3.

Looking at the join line

A *join line* connects tables in the query designer (refer to Figure 4.22). The join line connects the primary key in one table to the foreign key in another table. The *join line* represents the relationship between two tables in the Access database. In this example, a join line goes from tblSales to tblCustomers, connecting ContactID in the tblCustomers table to the Buyer field in tblSales. The join line is added by Access because relationships were set in the relationship builder.

If referential integrity is set on the relationship, Access uses a somewhat thicker line for the join connecting to the table in the query designer. A one-to-many relationship is indicated by an infinity symbol (∞) on the many-side table end of the join line.

Access auto-joins two tables if the following conditions are met:

- Both tables have fields with the same name.
- The same-named fields are the same data type (text, numeric, and so on).
- One of the fields is a primary key in its table.

Manipulating Field Lists

Each Field List begins at a fixed size, which shows a number of fields and several leading characters of each field name. Each Field List window is resizable and can be moved within the query designer. If there are more fields than will show in the Field List window, a scroll bar enables you to scroll through the fields.

Note

After a relationship is created between tables, the join line remains between the two fields. As you move through a table selecting fields, the line moves relative to the linked fields. For example, if you scroll downward, towards the bottom of the window in `tblCustomers`, the join line moves upward with the customer number, eventually stopping at the top of the table window.

When you're working with many tables, these join lines can become confusing as they cross or overlap. As you scroll through the table, the line eventually becomes visible, and the field it is linked to becomes obvious.

Moving a table

Move the Field Lists by grabbing the title bar of a Field List window (where the name of the table is) with the mouse and dragging the Field List window to a new location. You may want to move the Field Lists for a better working view or to clean up a confusing query diagram.

You can move and resize the Field Lists anywhere in the top pane. Access saves the arrangement when you save and close the query. Generally speaking, the Field Lists will appear in the same configuration the next time you open the query.

Removing a table

You might need to remove tables from a query. Use the mouse to select the table you want to remove in the top pane of the query window and press the Delete key. Or right-click on the Field List window and choose `Remove Table` from the shortcut menu.

Removing a table from a query's design does not remove the table from the database, of course.

Caution

When you remove a table from a query design, join lines to that table are deleted as well. There is no warning or confirmation before removal. The table is simply removed from the screen, along with any of the table's fields added to the QBE grid. Be aware, however, that deleted tables referenced in calculated fields (calculated fields are discussed in detail in Chapter 18) will not be removed. The "phantom" table references may cause errors when you try to run the query.

Adding more tables

You might decide to add more tables to a query or you might accidentally delete a table and need to add it back. You accomplish this task by clicking on the Show Table button on the Query Setup group in the Design ribbon. The Show Table dialog box appears in response to this action.

Creating and Working with Query Joins

By default, an Access query returns only records where data exists on both sides of a relationship. This means, for instance, that a query that extracts data from the Contacts table and the Sales table only returns records where contacts have actually placed sales, and will not show contacts who haven't yet placed a sale. If a contact record is not matched by at least one sales record, the contact data is not returned by the query. This means that, sometimes, the query might not return all the records you expect.

The situation described in the preceding paragraph is called an *inner join* or an *equi-join*. Although this is the most common join type between tables in a query, users sometimes want to see all the data in a table (like the tblCustomers table in the preceding example), regardless of whether those records are matched in another table. In fact, users often want to specifically see records that are *not* matched on the other side of the join. Consider a sales department that wants to know all the contacts who have *not* made a sale in the last year. You must modify the default query join characteristics in order to process this type of query.

You can create joins between tables in these three ways:

- By creating relationships between the tables when you design the database.
- By selecting two tables for the query that have a field in common that has the same name and data in both tables. The field is a primary key field in one of the tables.
- By modifying the default join behavior.

The first two methods occur automatically in the query design window. Relationships between tables are displayed in the query designer when you add the related tables to a query. It also creates an automatic join between two tables that have a common field, as long as that field is a primary key in one of the tables and the Enable Auto Join choice is selected (by default) in the Options dialog box.

If relationships are set in the relationship builder, you might not see the auto-join line if:

- The two tables have a common field, but it isn't the same name.
- A table isn't related and can't be logically related to the other table (for example, tblCustomers can't directly join the tblSalesLineItems table).

If you have two tables that aren't related and you need to join them in a query, use the query design window. Joining tables in the query design window does *not* create a permanent relationship between the tables; instead, the join (relationship) applies only to the tables while the query operates.

Tables in a query have to be joined in some way. Including two tables with nothing in common (for example, a query based on tblCustomers and tblProducts) means that Access has no way to know which records in the tblCustomers table match which records in the tblProducts table. Unless there is some way to relate the tables to one another, the query returns unusable data.

Caution

As a general rule, all tables in a query should be joined to at least one other table. If, for example, two tables in a query aren't joined in some way, the query produces a Cartesian product (also known as the cross-product) of the two tables. (This subject is discussed in the "Creating a Cartesian product" section, later in this chapter.) For now, note that a Cartesian product means that if you have five records in Table 1 and six records in Table 2, the resulting query will have 30 records (5 × 6) that will probably be useless.

Using ad hoc table joins

Figure 4.25 shows a simple query containing tblSales, tblSalesLineItems, tblProducts, and tblCategories. Notice that the join line between tblProducts and tblCategories is thinner than the other join lines, and does not include the 1 and infinity (∞) symbols. This is an ad hoc join, formed when the Categories table was added to the query.

No formal relationship yet exists between tblProducts and tblCategories. However, Access found the Category field in both the tables, determined that the Category data type is the same in both tables, and that the Category field in tblCategories is the primary key. Therefore, Access added an ad hoc join between the tables.

Note

Tables are not joined automatically in a query if they aren't already joined at the table level, if they don't have a common named field for a primary key, or if the AutoJoin option is off.

If Access had not auto-joined tblProducts and tblCategories (perhaps because the Category field was named differently in the tables), you can easily add an ad hoc join by dragging the Category field from one table and dropping it on the corresponding field in the other table.

FIGURE 4.25

An ad hoc join between `tblProducts` and `tblCategories`

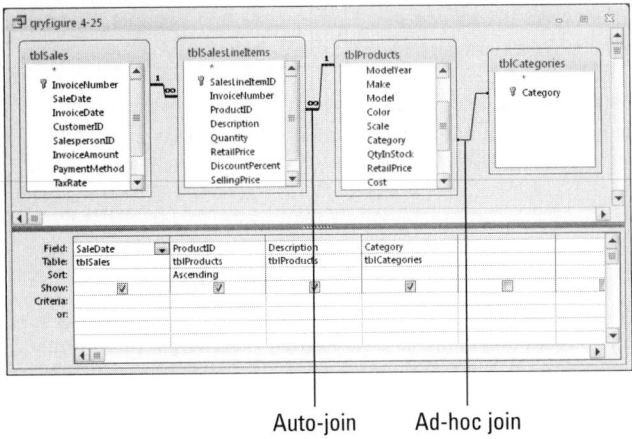

Auto-join   Ad-hoc join

Specifying the type of join

The problem with most joins is that, by default, they exhibit equi-join behavior as the query executes. In the case of the query in Figure 4.25, if a product record exists that doesn't have an assigned category (for example, a car that was never assigned to a category), the query doesn't return any records where a product record is not matched by a category. Figure 4.26 shows the result of this query.

FIGURE 4.26

You can't tell that records are missing from this query.

SaleDate	ProductID	Description	Category
8/12/2012	1	Buick Skylark	Cars
8/4/2012	1	Buick Skylark	Cars
2/23/2013	1	Buick Skylark	Cars
7/5/2012	2	Cord 810	Cars
1/16/2013	2	Cord 810	Cars
12/6/2012	2	Cord 810	Cars
5/13/2013	2	Cord 810	Cars
11/22/2013	2	Cord 810	Cars
3/28/2012	2	Cord 810	Cars
7/13/2013	2	Cord 810	Cars
5/10/2012	3	Chevrolet Corvette Convertible	Cars
1/6/2013	4	Chevrolet Corvette Convertible	Cars
3/11/2013	4	Chevrolet Corvette Convertible	Cars
5/10/2012	4	Chevrolet Corvette Convertible	Cars
11/5/2012	5	Chevrolet Bel Air Convertible	Cars
5/10/2012	5	Chevrolet Bel Air Convertible	Cars
6/27/2013	6	Ford Fairlane	Cars

Record: 1 of 78   No Filter   Search

The problem in Figure 4.26 is that you can't even tell records are missing. The only way you'd ever determine that there should be more than 78 records returned by this query is by carefully examining the sales records, by composing another query that counts all sales, or by performing some other audit operation.

You must modify the join characteristics between `tblProducts` and `tblCategories` to get an accurate picture of the Collectible Mini Cars sales. Carefully right-click on the thin join line between `tblProducts` and `tblCategories`, and select the Join Properties command from the shortcut menu. This action opens the Join Properties dialog box (see Figure 4.27), enabling you to specify an alternate join between the tables.

Selecting an outer join for the query

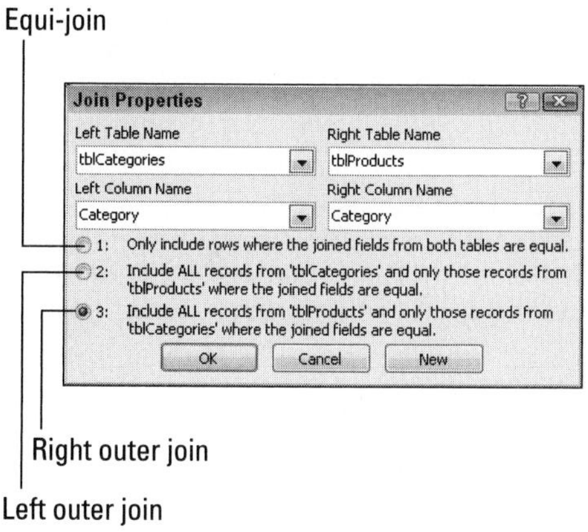

Equi-join

Right outer join

Left outer join

In Figure 4.27, the third option (Include All Records from 'tblProducts' . . .) has been selected (the first option is the default). Options 2 and 3 are called *outer joins* and direct Access to retrieve all records from the left (or right) table involved in the join, regardless of whether those records are matched on the other side of the join.

Figure 4.28 shows the result of the new join. In the lower-right corner of this figure you see how an outer join appears in the Access query design, while the rest of the figure shows the recordset returned by the query.

An outer join is represented by a join line with an arrow pointing at one of the tables involved in the join. In Figure 4.28, `tblProducts` is right-joined to `tblCategories`, which means all records from `tblProducts` are shown, regardless of whether there are matching records in `tbl-Categories`. A blank cell in the Category column indicates a product for which no category has been assigned.

FIGURE 4.28

A right outer join corrects the "missing products" problem in Figure 4.27.

The lower portion of Figure 4.28 shows the recordset from the query. Notice that 88 records are now returned, and that several rows in the recordset have no `Category` value. The query now accurately reports the number of sales records.

Of course, you can easily create joins that make no sense, but when you view the data, it'll be pretty obvious that you got the join wrong. If two joined fields have no values in common, you'll have a datasheet in which no records are selected.

Note

You can select either table first when you create a join.

You would never want to create a meaningless join. For example, you wouldn't want to join the `City` field from the `tblCustomer` table to the `tblSalesDate` of `tblSales`. Although Access enables you to create this join, the resulting recordset will have no records in it.

Deleting joins

To delete a join line between two tables, select the join line and press the Delete key. Select the join line by placing the mouse pointer on any part of the line and clicking once.

Caution

If you delete a join between two tables and the tables remain in the query window unjoined to any other tables, the solution will have unexpected results because of the Cartesian product that Access creates from the two tables. The Cartesian product is effective for only this query. The underlying relationship remains intact.

Access enables you to create multiple-field joins between tables (more than one line can be drawn). The two fields must have data in common; if not, the query won't find any records to display.

Understanding Table Join Types

In Chapter 3, you learned about table relationships and relating two tables by a common field. Access understands all types of table and query relations, including:

- One-to-one
- One-to-many
- Many-to-one
- Many-to-many

When you specify a relationship between two tables, you establish rules for the type of relationship, not for viewing the data based on the relationship.

To view data in two tables, they must be joined through common fields in the two tables. Tables with established relationships are automatically joined through the relationship. Within a query, you can create ad hoc joins or change existing joins, and as you've already seen, Access often auto-joins tables for you. Just as there are different types of relationships, there are different types of joins. In the following sections, you learn about a number of different types of joins:

- Inner joins (equi-joins)
- Outer joins
- Self-joins
- Cartesian (cross-product) joins

Working with inner joins (equi-joins)

The default join in Access is known as an *inner join* or *equi-join*. It tells Access to select all records from both tables that have the same value in the fields that are joined.

Note

The Access manuals refer to the default join as both an equi-join and inner join (commonly referred to as an inner join in database relational theory). The Access Help system refers to it as an inner join. The terms equi-join and inner join are interchangeable; however, in the remainder of this chapter they are referred to as inner joins.

If records are found in one table that don't have matching records in the other table, they're excluded from the returned recordset and aren't shown in the datasheet. Thus, an inner join between tables is simply a join where records are selected when matching values exist in the joined field of both tables.

You can create an inner join between the tblCustomers and tblSales tables by bringing these two tables into a new query and clicking on the join line to activate the Join Property dialog box and selecting the first choice: Only Include Rows Where the Joined Fields from Both Tables Are Equal.

It's possible to have a buyer in `tblCustomers` who has no sales. With referential integrity controlling the relationship, it's impossible, to have a sale with no buyer. If you create a query to show contacts and their sales, any record of a contact without a sale is not shown in the returned recordset.

Understanding outer joins

The query design window should now display two tables in the top pane of the query window — `tblCustomers` and `tblSales`, with four fields selected to display. If your query window does not have these two tables, create a new query and add them. The following sections use these tables as examples to explain how inner and outer joins operate.

Unlike inner joins (equi-joins), *outer joins* show all records in one table and any matching records in the other. The table or query that does not have a matching record simply displays an empty cell for the unmatched data when the recordset is displayed.

When you've created an outer join, the join line points to one of the tables. The base of the arrow is attached to the "main" table — the one that returns all records. The arrow points to the right-joined (or left-joined) table — the one that might be missing a matching record (see Figure 4.29).

So far, the outer-join examples you've seen have involved tables with no formal relationships. Figure 4.29 shows the results of an inner join between contacts and sales. Not all customers have placed sales with Collectible Mini Cars — perhaps they've called for product quotes, but haven't placed an order yet.

The recordset contains all customers, regardless of whether they've placed sales.

Once in the query design, again double-click the join line between the `tblCustomers` and `tblSales` tables. Select the second choice from the Join Properties dialog box (Include All Records from tblCustomers) and click the OK button. The join line now has an arrow pointing to the right toward `tblSales`; this is a *right outer join*. (If the arrow points to the left in the top pane, the join is known as a *left outer join*.)

If you create this right outer join query between the tables and select the Datasheet button to display the recordset, you see that you have a few more records than in an inner-join query. This means that there are at least a few records in `tblCustomers` without sales.

A sales record without a customer is called an *orphan* record. Referential integrity can't be set in the Relationships window if orphan records exist. If you can't set referential integrity between tables, you'll have to identify and remove orphan records before trying again.

FIGURE 4.29

A datasheet with a right outer join. It shows all customers, including those with no sales.

All records returned from this table

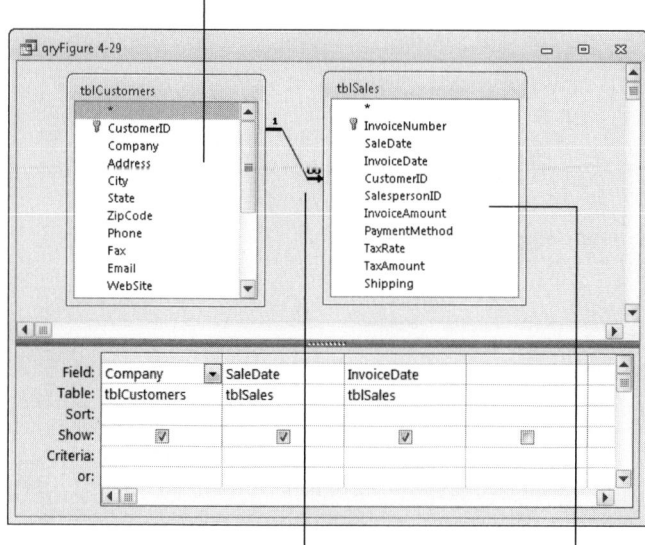

Outer join line   This table may be missing records

Working with self-joins

A self-join is a very special type of join that is quite easy to understand, particularly when given a simple example. A self-join occurs when a field in a table is related to another, or the same, field in the table. The classic example of a self-join is a table containing employee records. Very often this table will include a field specifying an individual's supervisor. But, because supervisors are also employees, the supervisor records are contained in the same table.

The Collectible Mini Cars database does not include any examples of self-joined tables, so I have to borrow the Employees table from the Northwind Traders example database. The Northwind Employees table uses EmployeeID as the primary key, and includes a field named ReportsTo that specifies each employee's supervisor.

Creating a self-join query is easy. In this case, add the Northwind Employees table *twice* to a new query. The first time it is added, Access uses the default heading (Employees) for the Field List. The second time the table is added Access uses Employees_1 as the Field List heading. No join line is added to the query design because Access has no idea why you've added the same table twice. You must explicitly establish a join line by dragging the ReportsTo field from Employees and dropping it on the EmployeeID field in Employees_1 (see Figure 4.30).

FIGURE 4.30

A query with a self join involving the Employees table

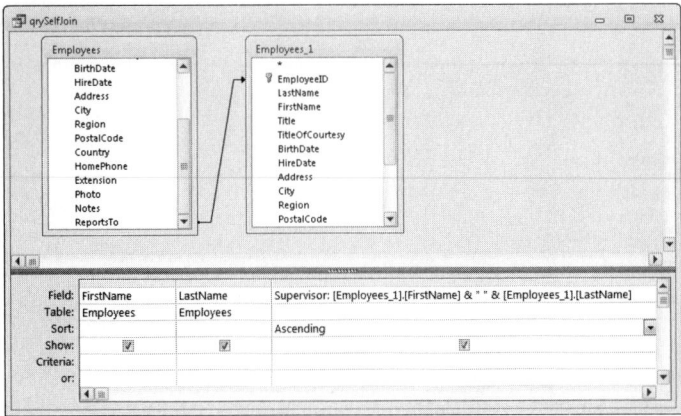

Notice in Figure 4.30 that a right outer join has been established between the Field Lists in the tables pane. This join means that all records in Employees are returned by the query, even if they are not joined to a record in Employees_1. In the Northwind Employees table, supervisors do not report to anyone, so they will have no matching records in Employee_1. The outer join is necessary to see supervisors in the query's results.

The recordset returned by qrySelfJoin is shown in Figure 4.31. Several employees (like Laura Callahan) report to Andrew Fuller, while others report to Steven Buchanan. Steven Buchanan, in turn, reports to Andrew Fuller. Andrew Fuller is the only employee who has no supervisor.

FIGURE 4.31

All Northwind employees and their supervisors

True self-joins are relatively rare in most databases. But, it's good to know that Access handles self-joined tables with no trouble. Keep in mind that you must use an outer join in the self-joined query design when it is important to see all of the records from one side or the other of the self-join.

Creating a Cartesian product

Adding `tblCustomers` and `tblSales` to a query without specifying a join between the tables causes Access to combine *every* `tblCustomers` record with *every* `tblSales` record. Combining all records in one table with all record in another table results in a *Cartesian product* (cross-product) of the tables. Cartesian products contain thousands of records for even small tables and are not useful to an application's users.

Figure 4.32 shows a query design that results in a Cartesian product. In this particular example, Access adds a join line between `tblCustomers` and `tblSales` because a formal relationship exists between these tables in the Collectible Mini Cars database. For the purpose of this demonstration, I manually deleted the join line before adding several fields to the QBE grid.

FIGURE 4.32

A query that returns a Cartesian product set of records

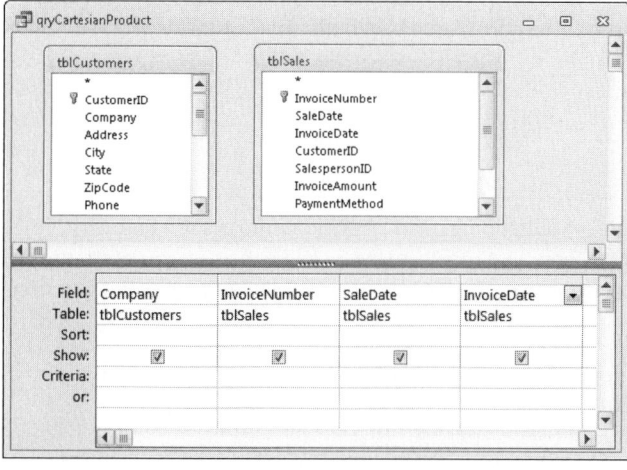

Figure 4.33 shows a portion of the recordset returned by `qryCartesianProduct`. Notice that every customer is included in the customer column, while the InvoiceNumber, SaleDate, and InvoiceDate are repeated for every customer. In all, 1485 rows are returned, in spite of the relatively small set of data in these tables.

A Cartesian product recordset

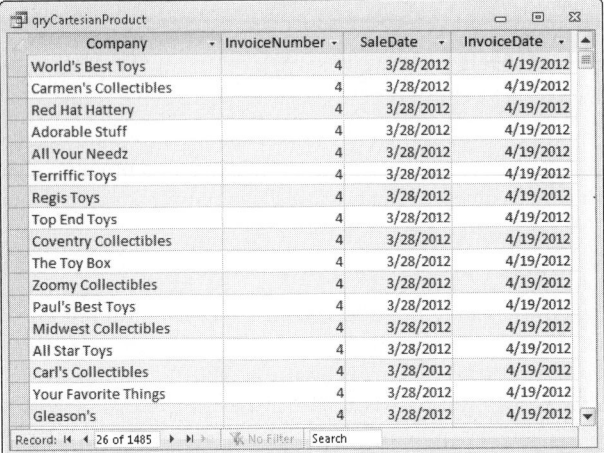

Company	InvoiceNumber	SaleDate	InvoiceDate
World's Best Toys	4	3/28/2012	4/19/2012
Carmen's Collectibles	4	3/28/2012	4/19/2012
Red Hat Hattery	4	3/28/2012	4/19/2012
Adorable Stuff	4	3/28/2012	4/19/2012
All Your Needz	4	3/28/2012	4/19/2012
Terriffic Toys	4	3/28/2012	4/19/2012
Regis Toys	4	3/28/2012	4/19/2012
Top End Toys	4	3/28/2012	4/19/2012
Coventry Collectibles	4	3/28/2012	4/19/2012
The Toy Box	4	3/28/2012	4/19/2012
Zoomy Collectibles	4	3/28/2012	4/19/2012
Paul's Best Toys	4	3/28/2012	4/19/2012
Midwest Collectibles	4	3/28/2012	4/19/2012
All Star Toys	4	3/28/2012	4/19/2012
Carl's Collectibles	4	3/28/2012	4/19/2012
Your Favorite Things	4	3/28/2012	4/19/2012
Gleason's	4	3/28/2012	4/19/2012

Record: 26 of 1485 — No Filter — Search

In virtually every instance, the data returned by a Cartesian product query is worthless. Because data is duplicated for every row in both tables, there is no useful information that can be derived from the query.

Summary

This chapter has taken on the major topic of building select queries. Without a doubt, query creation is a daunting task, and one that takes a lot of practice. Even simple queries can return unexpected results, depending on the characteristics of the join between tables, and the criteria used to filter data in the underlying tables.

Queries are an integral and important part of any Access database application. Queries drive forms, reports, and many other aspects of Access applications.

Users always assume the data they see in a form or report is correct. Most often, data in a form or report is provided by a query. As you read in this chapter, it's quite easy to produce a query that returns only part of the data expected by users, or transforms data in unpredictable ways. You should always carefully test your queries and verify that they're working as expected.

Your best bet for mastering Access queries is to try increasingly difficult queries, and to *always* check your work. In the case of improperly joined tables, Access queries almost always under-report the data in the tables. You'll discover the missing records only by carefully examining the data to ensure that your query is working properly.

Using Operators and Expressions in Access

In previous chapters, you created queries using selected fields from one or more tables. You also sorted the data and set criteria to limit the results of a query. This chapter focuses on using operators and expressions to calculate information, compare values, and display data in a different format — using queries to build examples.

This chapter uses queries to demonstrate the use of operators and functions, but the principles in this chapter's exercises apply anywhere operators and expressions appear in Access.

On the CD-ROM

This chapter uses the `Chapter05.accdb` database. If you haven't already copied it onto your machine from the CD, you'll need to do so now.

Cross-Reference

For more on using operators and expressions in forms, reports, and VBA, see Chapters 7, 8, 9, and 13. Using the VBA programming language is discussed in Chapters 10 and 11.

IN THIS CHAPTER

Understanding operators in expressions

Creating complex queries

Building queries with simple criteria

Using multiple criteria in a query

Composing complex query criteria

Introducing Operators

Operators let you add numbers, compare values, put text strings together, format data, and perform a wide variety of tasks. You use operators to instruct Access to perform a specific action against one or more *operands*. The combination of operators and operands is known as an *expression*.

Note

You'll see the term *evaluate* a lot in this chapter. When you present Access with a field, expression, variable, and so on, Access evaluates the item and (internally) represents the item as a value. It's very important to compose expressions in such a way that Access evaluates them as we expect. If Access incorrectly evaluates an expression, the application will not perform as expected. Understanding how Access evaluates a query's criteria or an expression used in VBA code is critically important to success as an Access developer.

You'll use operators every time you create an equation in Access. For example, operators specify data validation rules in table properties, create calculated fields in forms and reports, and specify criteria in queries.

Operators indicate that an operation needs to be performed on one or more items. Here are some common examples of operators:

| = | & | And | Like | + |

Looking at the types of operators

Operators can be grouped into the following types:

- Mathematical operators
- Comparison operators
- String operators
- Boolean (logical) operators
- Miscellaneous operators

Mathematical operators

Mathematical operators are also known as *arithmetic* operators, because they're used for performing numeric calculations. By definition, you use mathematical operators to work with numbers as operands. When you work with mathematical operators, numbers can be any numeric data type. The number can be a constant value, the value of a variable, or a field's contents. You use these numbers individually or combine them to create complex expressions.

Note

Some of the examples in this section may seem complex, but trust me: You don't need a graduate degree in mathematics to work through them.

There are seven basic mathematical operators:

+	Addition
–	Subtraction
*	Multiplication
/	Division
\	Integer division
^	Exponentiation
Mod	Modulo

I cover each of these operators in detail in the following sections.

The addition operator: +

If you want to create a calculated field in a query for adding the value of tax to the price, use an expression similar to (calculated fields are covered in detail in Chapter 18):

```
[TaxAmt]+[tblSalesLineItems].[Price]
```

To use this expression, you would have to create a calculated field in the query named [TaxAmt] using the multiplication operator:

```
TaxAmt: [tblSales].[TaxRate] * [tblSalesLineItems].[Price]
```

You could also create a form for adding the values, such as GrossAmount and Tax, in which case you would use [GrossAmount] + [Tax]. This simple expression uses the addition operator to add the contents of both fields and display the result in the object containing the expression.

Note

In this example, specifying the table name isn't necessary because your tables have only one field named FirstName and one field named LastName. However, it's good practice to specify the table containing the field, using a period as the separator.

Caution

Although you can concatenate (join) text strings by using the addition operator, you should use the ampersand (&) operator to avoid confusing Access. When you use the plus sign (+), Access initially interprets the operands as numeric values and only switches behavior when it determines that the operands are strings. You can very easily introduce side-effect bugs into an application when using overloaded operators like the plus sign. You can read more about concatenation and other operations in the "String operators" section, later in this chapter.

The subtraction operator: –

The minus sign (–) performs simple subtraction, such as calculating a final invoice amount by subtracting a discount from the price:

```
[Price] - ([Price] * [DiscountPercent])
```

The parentheses around [Price] * [DiscountPercent] instruct Access to perform this operation before subtracting the multiplication result from [Price]. Without parentheses, Access may process expressions from left to right, which would return an incorrect result. In this particular case, because the order of precedence means that the multiplication takes place before subtraction, but that may not always be the case. In most cases, it's better to wrap operations you want to occur first within parentheses, as shown in this example.

Note

Although parentheses are not mathematical operators, they play an important role in many expressions, as discussed in the "Operator precedence" section, later in this chapter.

The multiplication operator: *

A simple example of when to use the multiplication operator is to calculate the total price of several items. You could design a query to display the number of items purchased and the price for each item. Then you could add a calculated field containing the value of the number of items purchased times the price per item. In this case, expression would be

    [tblSalesLineItems].[Quantity] * [tblSalesLineItems].[Price]

Note

The standard Access notation for dealing with table names and field names in an expression is to enclose each name in square brackets, and separate them with a period. For example:

    [TableName].[FieldName]

Tip

Notice that you use the table name before the field name in the preceding example. Because only one table has a field named Price and one other table has a field named Quantity, you could have skipped the table names. However, specifying the name of the table containing the field and using a period to separate the table name from the field name are good practices.

The division operator: /

Use the division operator to divide two numbers. Suppose, for example, that a pool of 212 people win a $1,000,000 lottery. The expression to determine each individual's payoff of $4,716.98 is

    1000000 / 212

Note

Notice that the 1000000 value does not contain commas. Access is not able to perform a mathematical operation on numeric values containing punctuation.

The integer division operator: \

The integer division operator takes any two numbers (number1 and number2), rounds them up or down to integers, divides the first by the second (number1 / number2), and then drops the decimal portion, leaving only the integer value. Here are some examples of how integer division differs from normal division:

Normal Division	Integer Conversion Division
100 / 6 = 16.667	100 \ 6 = 16
100.9 / 6.6 = 15.288	100.9 \ 6.6 = 14
102 / 7 = 14.571	102 \ 7 = 14

Note

Access rounds whole numbers based on a principle known as "banker's rounding" or "round half to even." Rounding is always done to the nearest even number: 6.5 becomes 6, and 7.5 becomes 8. This is only an issue, of course, when the rounded value is exactly midway between two whole numbers. 6.51 rounds (as you'd expect) to 7, and 6.49 rounds to 6.

The exponentiation operator: ^

The exponentiation operator (^) raises a number to the power of an exponent. Raising a number simply means multiplying a number by itself. For example, multiplying the value 4 x 4 x 4 (that is, 4³) is the same as entering the formula 4^3.

The exponent does not have to be a whole number; it can even be negative. For example, 2^2.1 returns 4.28709385014517, and 4^–2 is 0.0625.

The modulo division operator: Mod

The modulo operator (Mod) takes any two numbers (number1 and number2), rounds them up or down to integers, divides the first by the second (number1 / number2), and then returns the remainder. Here are some examples of how modulo division compares to normal division:

Normal Division	Modulo Division	Explanation
10 / 5 = 2	10 Mod 5 = 0	10 is evenly divided by 5
10 / 4 = 2.5	10 Mod 4 = 2	10 / 4 = 2 with a remainder of 2
22.24 / 4 = 5.56	22.24 Mod 4 = 2	22 / 4 = 5 with a remainder of 2
22.52 / 4 = 5.63	22.52 Mod 4 = 3	23 / 4 = 5 with a remainder of 3

The tricky thing about modulo division is that the returned value is the remainder after integer division is performed on the operands. The Mod operator is often used to determine whether a number is even or odd by performing modulo division with 2 as the divisor:

```
5 Mod 2 = 1
4 Mod 2 = 0
```

If Mod returns 1, the dividend is odd. Mod returns 0 when the dividend is even.

Comparison operators

Comparison operators compare two values or expressions in an equation. There are six basic comparison operators:

=	Equal
<>	Not equal
<	Less than
<=	Less than or equal to
>	Greater than
>=	Greater than or equal to

The expressions built from comparison operators always return True, False, or Null. Null is returned when the expression can't be evaluated.

As you read the following descriptions, please keep in mind that Access is case-insensitive in most situations. When comparing strings, for example, "CAR," "Car," and "car" are the same to Access.

Note

Access actually returns a numeric value for comparison operator expressions. Access uses −1 to represent True and 0 to represent False.

If either side of an equation is a Null value, the result is always Null.

The equal operator: =

The equal operator (=) returns True if the two expressions are the same. For example,

[tblProducts].[Category] = "Car"	Returns True if Category is a car. It returns False for any other Category.
[tblSales].[SaleDate] = Date()	Returns True if the date in SaleDate is today and False for any other date.

The not-equal operator: <>

The not-equal operator (<>) is the opposite of the equal operator. For example,

[tblProducts].[Category] <> "Car"	Returns True if Category is anything but car and False only when Category is car.

The less-than operator: <

The less-than operator (<) returns a logical `True` if the left side of the equation is less than the right side, as in this example:

`[tblSalesLineItems].[Price] < 1000`   Returns `True` if the `Price` field contains a value of less than 1,000 and `False` whenever `Price` is greater than 1,000.

Interestingly, the less-than operator (in fact, the same is true for most comparison operators) is easily applied to string values. For example, the following expression is `False`:

`"Man" > "Woman"`

Without getting philosophical about the expression, what actually happens is that Access does a character-by-character comparison of the strings. Because *M* appears before *W* in the alphabet, the word *Man* is not greater than *Woman*. The ability to compare strings can be of significant value when sorting string data or arranging names in a particular order.

Again, because Access string comparisons are not case sensitive, *XYZ* is not greater than *xyz*.

The less-than-or-equal-to operator: <=

The less-than-or-equal-to operator (<=) returns `True` if the operand on the left side of the equation is either less than or equal to the right-side operand, as in this example:

`[tblSalesLineItems].[Price] <= 2500`   Returns `True` if `Price` equals 2500 or is less than 2500, and `False` for any `Price` that is more than 2500.

Caution

Comparison operators must be composed properly. Access reports an error if you enter =<. The order of the characters in this operator is important. It must be less than or equal to: <=.

The greater-than operator: >

The greater-than operator (>) is the opposite of less than. This operator returns `True` when the left-side operand is greater than the operand on the right side. For example,

`[tblSales].[TaxRate] > 3.5`   Returns `True` if `TaxRate` is greater than `3.5`, and `False` whenever `TaxRate` is less than or equal to `3.5`.

The greater-than-or-equal-to operator: >=

The greater-than-or-equal-to operator (>=) returns `True` if the left side is either greater than or equal to the right side. For example,

`[tblSales].[TaxRate] >= 5`   Returns `True` if `TaxRate` is 5 or greater.

String operators

Access has three string operators for working with strings. Unlike the mathematical and logical operators, the string operators are specifically designed to work with the string data type:

`&`	Concatenates operands
`Like`	Operands are similar
`Not Like`	Operands are dissimilar

The concatenation operator: &

The concatenation operator joins two or more strings into a single string. In some ways, concatenation is similar to addition. Unlike addition, however, concatenation always returns a string:

```
[FirstName] & [LastName]
```

However, there is no space between the names in the returned string. If `[FirstName]` is "Fred" and `[LastName]` is "Smith," the returned string is `FredSmith`. If you want a space between the names, you must explicitly add a space between the strings, as follows:

```
[FirstName] & " " & [LastName]
```

The concatenation operator easily joins a string with a numeric- or date-type value. Using the & eliminates the need for special functions to convert numbers or dates to strings.

Suppose, for example, that you have a number field (`HouseNumber`) and a text field (`StreetName`), and you want to combine both fields:

```
[HouseNumber] & " " & [StreetName]
```

If `HouseNumber` is "1600" and `StreetName` is "Pennsylvania Avenue N.W.," the returned string is

```
"1600 Pennsylvania Avenue N.W."
```

Note
Quotes are added around the returned string to clarify the result.

Maybe you want to print the `OperatorName` and current date at the bottom of a report page. This can be accomplished with the following:

```
"This report was printed " & Now() & " by " & [OperatorName]
```

Notice the spaces after the word *printed* and before and after the word *by*. If the date is March 21, 2012, and the time is 4:45 p.m., this expression looks like:

```
This report was printed 3/21/12 4:45:40 PM by Jim Rosengren
```

The addition operator (+) also concatenates two character strings. For example, to combine FirstName and LastName from tblContacts to display them as a single string, the expression is

```
[tblContacts].[FirstName] + " " + [tblContacts].[LastName]
```

Tip

Knowing how the concatenation operator works makes maintaining your database expressions easier. If you always use the concatenation operator (&) — instead of the addition operator (+) — when working with strings, you won't have to be concerned with the data types of the concatenation operands. Any expression that uses the concatenation operator converts all operands to strings for you. Using the addition operator to concatenate strings can sometimes lead to unpredictable results because Access must decide whether the operands are numbers or strings, and act accordingly. The concatenation operator forces Access to treat the operands as strings and always returns a string as a result.

Although the ampersand and plus sign both serve as concatenation operators, using the plus sign might exhibit unexpected results in some situations. The ampersand *always* returns a string when concatenating two values. The operands passed to the ampersand operator may be strings, numeric or date/time values, field references, and so on, and a string is always returned.

Because it always returns a string, the ampersand is often used to prevent Invalid use of null errors when working with data that might be null. For example, let's assume a particular text box on an Access form may or may not contain a value because we can't be sure the user has entered anything into the text box. When assigning the contents of the text box to a variable (variables are discussed in detail in Chapter 10), some developers concatenate an empty string to the text box's contents as part of the assignment:

```
MyVariable = txtLastName & ""
```

The ampersand ensures that, even if the text box contains a null value, the variable is assigned a string and no error is raised.

The plus sign, on the other hand, returns a null value when one of the operands is null:

```
MyVariable = txtLastName + ""
```

In this case, if txtLastName is truly null, the user may encounter an Invalid use of null error because the result of the concatenation is null (assuming, once again, that txtLastName contains a null value).

Most experienced Access developers reserve the plus sign for arithmetical operations and always use the ampersand for string concatenation.

The Like and Not Like operators

The Like operator, and its opposite, the Not Like operator, compare two string expressions. These operators determine whether one string matches, or doesn't match, the pattern of another string. The returned value is `True`, `False`, or `Null`. The `Like` and `Not Like` operators are case-insensitive.

The `Like` operator uses the following syntax:

```
expression Like pattern
```

`Like` looks for the expression in the pattern; if it is present, the operation returns `True`. For example:

`[FirstName] Like "John"`	Returns `True` if the first name is `John`.
`[LastName] Like "SMITH*"`	Returns `True` if the last name is `Smith`, `Smithson`, or any other name beginning with `"Smith,"` regardless of capitalization. (Wildcards like * are discussed in the "Using wildcards" sidebar.)
`[State] Not Like "NY"`	Returns `True` for any state other than New York.

Note

If either operand in a `Like` operation is `Null`, the result is `Null`.

The `Like` and `Not Like` operators provides powerful and flexible tools for string comparisons. Wildcard characters extend the flexibility of the `Like` operator.

Boolean (logical) operators

Boolean operators (also referred to as *logical operators*) are used to create multiple conditions in expressions. Like comparison operators, these operators always return `True`, `False`, or `Null`. Boolean operators include the following:

And	Logical And
Or	Inclusive Or
Not	Logical Not

The And operator

Use the *And* operator to perform a logical *conjunction* of two expressions. The operator returns `True` if both expressions are `True`. The general syntax of And is

```
Expression1 And Expression2
```

For example:

`[tblContacts].[State] = "MA" And` `[tblContacts].[ZipCode] = "02379"`	Returns `True` only if both expressions are `True`.

Using wildcards

Table 5.1 shows the five wildcards you can use with the Like operator:

TABLE 5.1

Wildcards Used by the Like Operator

Wildcard	Purpose
?	A single character (0–9, Aa–Zz)
*	Any number of characters (0–n)
#	Any single digit (0–9)
[list]	Any single character in the list
[!list]	Any single character not in the list

Both [list] and [!list] can use the hyphen between two characters to signify a range.

Here are some wildcard examples:

[tblContacts].[LastName] Like "Mc*"	Returns True for any last name that begins with "Mc" or "MC," such as "McDonald," "McJamison," and "MCWilliams." Anything that doesn't start with "Mc" or "MC" returns False.
[Answer] Like "[A-D]"	Returns True if the Answer is A, B, C, D, a, b, c, or d. Any other character returns False.
"AB1989" Like "AB####"	Returns True because the string begins with "AB" and is followed by four digits.
[LastName] Not Like "[A,E,I,O,U]*"	Returns True for any last name that does not begin with a vowel. "Smith" and "Jones" return True while "Adams" and "O'Malley" return False.
[City] Like "?????"	Returns True for any city that is exactly five characters long.

Tip

If the pattern you're trying to match contains a wildcard character, you must enclose the wildcard character in brackets. In the example:

```
"AB*Co" Like "AB[*]C*"
```

The [*] in the pattern treats asterisks in the third position as data. Since the asterisk character is enclosed in brackets, it won't be mistaken for a asterisk wildcard character.

The logical And operator depends on how the two operands are evaluated by Access. Table 5.2 describes all the possible results when the operands are True or False. Notice that And returns True only when *both* operands are True.

TABLE 5.2

And Operator Results

Expression1	Expression2	Expression1 And Expression2
True	True	True
True	False	False
True	Null	Null
False	True	False
False	False	False
False	Null	False
Null	True	Null
Null	False	False
Null	Null	Null

The Or operator

The Or operator performs a logical *disjunction* of two expressions. Or returns True if *either* condition is True. The general syntax of Or is

```
Expression1 Or Expression2
```

The following examples show how the Or operator works:

[LastName] = "Casey" Or [LastName] = "Gleason"	Returns True if LastName is either Casey or Gleason.
[TaxLocation] = "TX" Or [TaxLocation] = "CT"	Returns True if TaxLocation is either TX or CT.

The Or operator (like And) returns True or False depending on how Access evaluates its operands. Table 5.3 shows all possible combinations with two operands. Notice that Or returns False only when *both* operands are False.

TABLE 5.3

Or Expression Results

Expression1	Expression2	Expression1 Or Expression2
True	True	True
True	False	True
True	Null	True
False	True	True
False	False	False
False	Null	Null
Null	True	True
Null	False	Null
Null	Null	Null

The Not operator

The Not operator negates a numeric or Boolean expression. The Not operator returns the True if the expression is False, and False if the expression is True. The general syntax of Not is

```
Not [numeric|boolean] expression
```

The following examples show how to use the Not operator:

Not [Price] <= 100000	Returns True if Price is greater than 100,000.
If Not (City = "Seattle") Then	Returns True for any city that is not Seattle.

If the operand is Null, the Not operator returns Null. Table 5.4 shows all the possible values.

TABLE 5.4

Not Operator Results

Expression	Not **Expression**
True	False
False	True
Null	Null

Miscellaneous operators

Access has three very useful miscellaneous operators:

Between...And	Range
In	List comparison
Is	Reserved word

The Between...And operator

Between...And determines whether an expression's value falls within a range of values:

```
expression Between value1 And value2
```

If the value of the expression falls within *value1* and *value2*, or is the same as *value1* or *value2*, the result is True; otherwise, it's False.

The following examples show how to use the Between...And operator:

[TotalCost] Between 10000 And 19999	Returns True if the TotalCost is between 10,000 and 19,999, or equal to 10,000 or 19,999.
[SaleDate] Between #1/1/2012# And #12/31/2012#	Returns True when the SaleDate occurs within the year 2012.

The Between...And operator can also be used with Not operator to negate the logic:

Not [SaleDate] Between #1/1/2012# And #3/31/2012#	Returns True only when SaleDate is *not* within the first quarter of 2012.

The In operator

The In operator determines whether an expression's value is the same as any value within a list. The general syntax of In is:

```
Expression In (value1, value2, value3, ...)
```

If the expression's value is found within the list, the result is True; otherwise, the result is False.

The following example uses the In operator as a query's criteria in the Category column:

```
In ('SUV','Trucks')
```

This query displays only those models that are SUVs or trucks.

The In operator is also used in VBA code:

```
If [tblCustomers].[City] In("Seattle", "Tacoma") Then
```

In this case the body of the If...Then...Else statement executes only if the City field is either Seattle or Tacoma.

The return value of the In operator can be negated with Not:

```
If strCity Not In ("Pittsburgh", "Philadelphia") Then
```

In this case, the body of the If...Then...Else statement executes only if strCity is not set to either Pittsburgh or Philadelphia.

The Is operator

The Is operator is used only with the keyword Null to determine whether the value of an object is null:

```
expression Is Null
```

The following example uses the Is operator:

```
[LastName] Is Null      Returns True if the LastName field is Null.
```

It is important to note that the Is operator applies only to objects and object variables, such as fields in tables. The Is operator can't be used with simple variables such as strings or numbers.

Operator precedence

When you work with complex expressions that have many operators, Access must determine which operator to evaluate first, and then which is next, and so forth. Access has a built-in predetermined order for mathematical, logical, and Boolean operators, known as *operator precedence.* Access always follows this order unless you use parentheses to override its default behavior.

Operations within parentheses are performed before operations outside the parentheses. Within parentheses, Access follows the default operator precedence.

Precedence is determined first according to category of the operator. The operator rank by order of precedence is

1. Mathematical
2. Comparison
3. Boolean

Each category contains its own order of precedence, which I explain in the following sections.

The mathematical precedence

Mathematical operators follow this order of precedence:

1. Exponentiation
2. Negation
3. Multiplication and/or division (left to right)

4. Integer division

5. Modulus division

6. Addition and/or subtraction (left to right)

7. String concatenation

The comparison precedence

Comparison operators observe this order of precedence:

1. Equal

2. Not equal

3. Less than

4. Greater than

5. Less than or equal to

6. Greater than or equal to

7. Like

Precedence order

Simple arithmetic provides an example of order of precedence. Remember that Access performs operations within parentheses before operations that are not in parentheses. Also remember that multiplication and division operations are performed before addition or subtraction operations.

For example, what is the answer to this simple equation?

$x = 10 + 3 * 4$

If your answer is 52, you need a better understanding of precedence in Access. If your answer is 22, you're right. If your answer is anything else, you need a calculator!

Multiplication is performed before addition by the rules of mathematical precedence. Therefore, the equation $10 + 3 * 4$ is evaluated in this order: $3 * 4$ yields 12. Then 12 is added to 10, which returns 22.

Look at what happens when you add parentheses to the equation. What is the answer to this simple equation?

$x = (10 + 3) * 4$

Now the answer is 52. Within parentheses, the values 10 and 3 are added first, and then the result (13) is multiplied by 4, which yields 52.

The Boolean precedence

The Boolean operators follow this order of precedence:

1. Not
2. And
3. Or
4. Xor
5. Eqv
6. Imp

Using Operators and Expressions in Queries

One of the most common uses of operators and expressions is when building complex query criteria. A thorough understanding of how these constructs work can ease the process of building sophisticated, useful queries. This section deals specifically with building query criteria using operators and expressions. Some of the information in the remainder of this chapter parallels earlier discussions, but the context is specifically query design.

Knowing how to specify criteria is critical to designing and writing effective queries. Although queries can be used against a single table for a single criterion, many queries extract information from several tables using more complex criteria.

Because of this complexity, your queries are able to retrieve only the data you need, in the order that you need it. You might, for example, want to select and display data from the Collectible Mini Cars database to get the following information:

- All buyers of Chevy car or Ford truck models
- All buyers who have purchased something during the past 60 days
- All sales for items greater than $90
- The number of customers in each state
- Customers that have made comments or complaints

As your database system evolves, you'll want to retrieve subsets of information like these examples. Using operators and expressions, you create complex select queries to limit the number of records returned by the query. This section discusses select queries that use operators and expressions. Later, you'll apply this knowledge when working with forms, reports, and VBA code.

Cross-Reference
Chapter 4 gives an in-depth explanation of working with queries.

Using query comparison operators

When working with select queries, you may need to specify one or more criteria to limit the scope of information shown. You specify criteria by using comparison operators in equations and calculations. The categories of operators are mathematical, relational, logical, and string. In select queries, operators are used in either the Field or Criteria cell of the Query by Example (QBE) pane.

Table 5.5 shows the most common operators used with select queries.

TABLE 5.5

Common Operators Used in Select Queries

Mathematical	Relational	Logical	String	Miscellaneous
* (multiply)	= (equal)	And	& (concatenate)	Between...And
/ (divide)	<> (not equal)	Or	Like	In
+ (add)	> (greater than)	Not	Not Like	Is Null
– (subtract)	< (less than)			Is Not Null

Using these operators, you can ferret out groups of records like these:

- Product records that include a picture
- A range of records, such as all sales between November and January
- Records that meet both And *and* Or criteria, such as all records that are cars and are not either a truck or SUV
- All records that do *not* match a value, such as any category that is not a car

When you add criteria to a query, use the appropriate operator with an example of what you want. In Figure 5.1, the example is Cars. The operator is equal (=). Notice that the equal sign is *not* shown in the figure because it's the default operator for select queries.

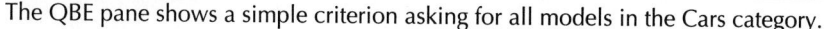

FIGURE 5.1

The QBE pane shows a simple criterion asking for all models in the Cars category.

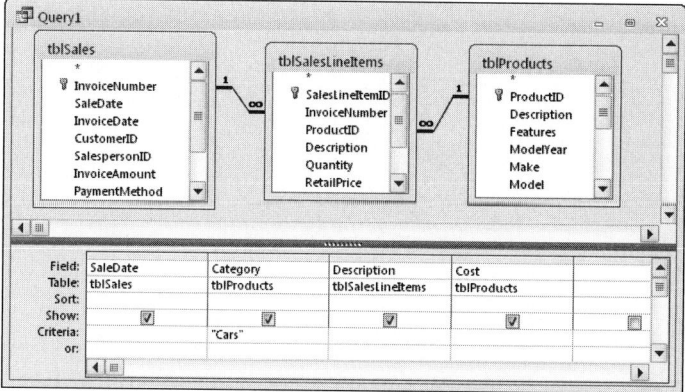

Understanding complex criteria

You build complex query criteria using any combination of the operators shown in Table 5.5. For many queries, complex criteria consist of a series of Ands and Ors, as in these examples:

- State must be Connecticut *or* Texas.
- City must be Sunnyville *and* state must be Georgia.
- State must be MA *or* MO *and* city must be Springfield.

These examples demonstrate the use of both logical operators: And/Or. Many times, you can create complex criteria by entering example data in different cells of the QBE pane, as shown in Figure 5.2. In Figure 5.2, criteria is specified in both the State and Category columns. Within the State column, the criteria specifies "either California or Arizona," while the additional criteria in the Category column adds "not Cars." When combined, the criteria in the two columns limits the returned records to those where the customer state is either California or Arizona, and the product category is not cars.

However, using explicit Boolean operators is not the only way to select records based on multiple criteria. Figure 5.3 demonstrates a common Access technique using complex criteria without entering the operator keywords And/Or at all. In this example, the criteria "stacked" within a single column specifies Or. For example, in the State column, the criteria is interpreted as "CA" Or "AZ". The presence of criteria in another column in the QBE grid implies And. Therefore, the criteria in the Category column is combined with the state criteria is interpreted as:

```
(State = "CA" And Category <> "Cars") Or (State = "AZ" And Category
    <> "Cars")
```

FIGURE 5.2

Using And and Or criteria in a query

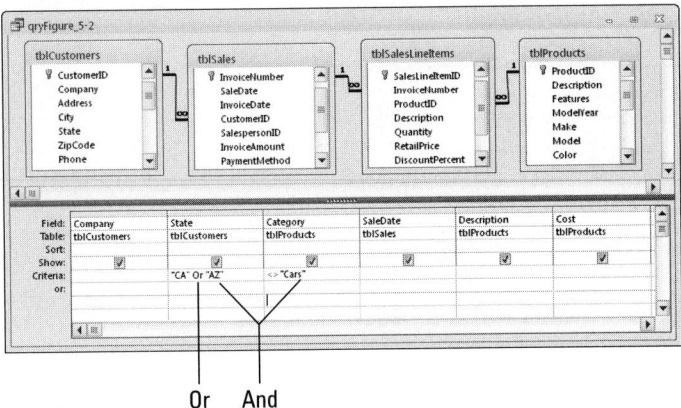

Or   And

FIGURE 5.3

Creating complex criteria without using the And/Or operators

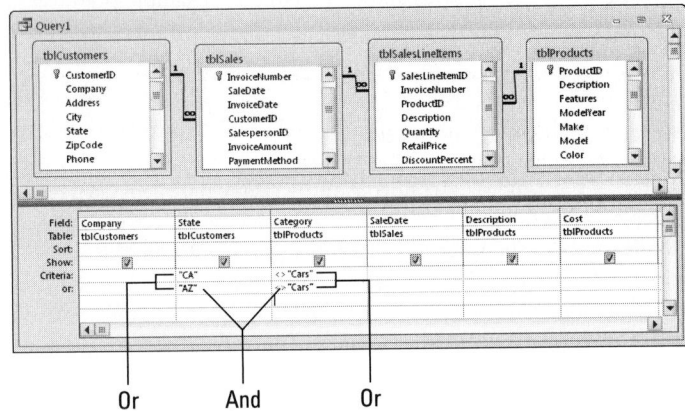

Or   And   Or

In any case, the queries in Figures 5.2 and 5.3 are equivalent and return the same data.

One confusing aspect about the query in Figure 5.3 is that the criteria in the Category column must appear twice, once for each value in the State column. If the Category criteria appeared only once, perhaps in the same row as "AZ" in the State column, the combined criteria would be interpreted as:

```
(State = "AZ" and Category <> "Cars") Or (State = "CA")
```

You learn how to create this type of complex query in the "Entering Criteria in Multiple Fields" section, later in this chapter.

Tip

In the QBE pane, enter `And` **criteria in the same row and** `Or` **criteria in different rows.**

Access takes your graphical query and creates a single SQL `SELECT` statement to actually extract the information from your tables. Click the drop-down in the ribbon's View group and select SQL View to change the window's contents to display the SQL `SELECT` statement (shown in Figure 5.4), which Access creates from the fields and criteria placed in the QBE pane in Figure 5.3.

FIGURE 5.4

The SQL view for the query in Figure 5.3. Notice that it contains a single `OR` and two `AND` operators (in the `WHERE` clause).

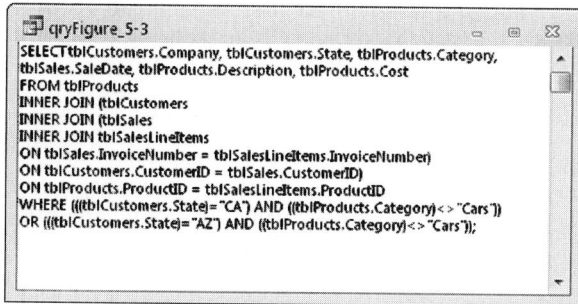

```
qryFigure_5-3                                            _  ▣  ☒

SELECT tblCustomers.Company, tblCustomers.State, tblProducts.Category,
tblSales.SaleDate, tblProducts.Description, tblProducts.Cost
FROM tblProducts
INNER JOIN (tblCustomers
INNER JOIN (tblSales
INNER JOIN tblSalesLineItems
ON tblSales.InvoiceNumber = tblSalesLineItems.InvoiceNumber)
ON tblCustomers.CustomerID = tblSales.CustomerID)
ON tblProducts.ProductID = tblSalesLineItems.ProductID
WHERE (((tblCustomers.State)="CA") AND ((tblProducts.Category)<>"Cars"))
OR (((tblCustomers.State)="AZ") AND ((tblProducts.Category)<>"Cars"));
```

The SQL statement in Figure 5.4 has been slightly rearranged by the author for clarification purposes. When you switch to SQL View in your database, you'll see one long multi-line statement with no breaks between sections.

An expression for this query's criteria is

```
(tblCustomers.State = "CT" AND tblProducts.Category <> "Cars") OR
    (tblCustomers.State = "MA" AND tblProducts.Category <> "Cars")
```

You must enter the category criteria (`<> "Cars"`) for each state in the QBE pane, as shown in Figure 5.3. In the "Entering Criteria in Multiple Fields" section, later in this chapter, you learn to use the `And/Or` operators in a Criteria cell of the query, which eliminates the redundant entry of these fields.

Tip

In this example, you looked for all models that didn't contain cars in the `Category` **field. To find records that do match a value, drop the** `<>` **operator with the value. For example, enter Cars to find all records with Cars as the category. You don't have to use the equal sign in the QBE pane when working with select queries.**

The `And/Or` operators are the most common operators when working with complex criteria. The operators consider two different expression (one on each side of the `And/Or` operators) and then determine whether the expressions are `True` or `False`. Then the operators compare the results of the two expressions against each other for a logical `True/False` answer. For example, take the first `And` statement in the expression given in the preceding paragraph:

```
(tblCustomers.State = "CA" AND tblProducts.Category <> "Cars")
```

The right side of the criteria (`tblProducts.Category <> "Cars"`) evaluates to `True` if `Category` is anything other than `Cars`. The `And` operator compares the logical `True/False` from the left and right expressions to return `True/False` answer.

Note

A field has a `Null` value when it has no value at all. Null indicates the lack of entry of information in a field. `Null` is neither `True` nor `False`, nor is it the same as a space character or 0. Null simply has no value. If you never enter a name in the `City` field and just skip it, Access leaves the field empty (unless a default value is provided in the table's design). This state of emptiness is known as `Null`.

When the result of an `And/Or` operation is `True`, the overall condition is `True`, and the query displays the records meeting the `True` condition.

Notice that the result of an `And` operation is `True` only when *both* sides of the expression are `True`, whereas the result of an `Or` operation is `True` when *either* side of the expression is `True`. In fact, one side can be a `Null` value, and the result of the `Or` operation will still be `True` if the other side is `True`. This is the fundamental difference between `And/Or` operators.

Using functions in select queries

When you work with queries, you might want to use built-in Access functions to display information. For example, you might want to display items such as:

- The day of the week (Sunday, Monday, and so forth) for sales dates
- All customer names in uppercase
- The difference between two date fields

You can display all this information by creating calculated fields for the query.

Cross-Reference

I discuss calculated fields in depth in detail in Chapter 18 (and in many other places in this book).

Referencing fields in select queries

When you work with a field's name in queries, most often you should enclose the name in square brackets (`[]`). Access requires brackets around any field name that's used as a query's criteria and around field names that contain spaces or punctuation characters. An example of a field name in brackets is

```
[tblSales].[SaleDate] + 30
```

In this example, 30 days is added to the `SaleDate` field in `tblSales`.

Caution

If you omit the brackets (`[ ]`) around a field name in the QBE grid, Access might place quotes around the field name and treat it as literal text instead of a field name.

Entering Single-Value Field Criteria

You'll encounter situations in which you want to limit the query records returned on the basis of a single field criterion, such as in these queries:

- Customer (buyer) information for customers living in New York state

- Sales of truck models

- Customers who bought anything in the month of January

Each of these queries requires a single-value criterion. Simply put, a *single-value criterion* is the entry of only one expression in the QBE grid. The expression can be example data, such as "CA", or a function, such as `DatePart("m",[SaleDate]) = 1`. Criteria expressions can be specified for virtually any data type: Text, Numeric, Date/Time, and so forth. Even OLE Object and Counter field types can have criteria specified.

Entering character (Text or Memo) criteria

You use character criteria for Text or Memo data-type fields. These are either examples or patterns of the contents of the field. To create a query that returns customers who live in New York state, for example, follow these steps:

1. Open a new query in Design view based on `tblCustomers` and add the `FirstName`, `LastName`, and `State` fields to the QBE pane.

2. Click the Criteria cell for `State` field.

3. Type **NY** in the cell.

    Your query should look like Figure 5.5. Notice that only one table is open and only three fields are selected. Click the Datasheet View button in the Home ribbon's Views group to see this query's results.

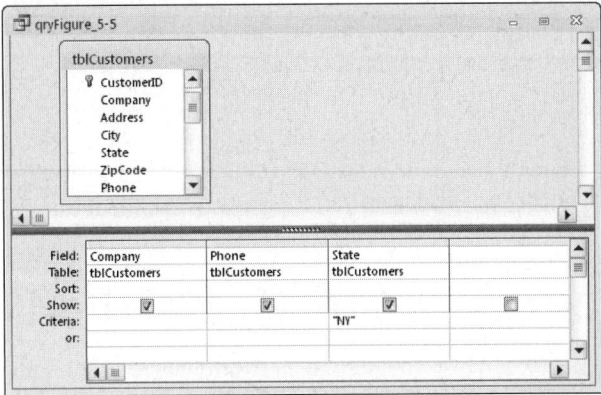

FIGURE 5.5

The query design window showing `tblCustomers` open

You don't have to enter an equal sign before the literal word NY because this is a select query. To see all states except NY, you must enter either the <> (not equal) or the Not operator before NY.

You also don't have to type quotes around the word NY. Access assumes that you're using a literal string NY and adds the quotes for you automatically.

Tip

If you type quotation marks, you should use the double quotation mark to surround literals. Access normally uses the single quotation mark as a remark character in its programming language. However, when you use the single quotation mark in the Criteria cell, Access interprets it as a double quotation mark.

Special considerations apply when data in the field contains quotation marks. For example, consider a query to find a person whose name is given as Robert "Bobby" Jones. Ideally, the contacts table would include a nickname field to capture "Bobby," but, in the absence of a nickname field, the data entry clerk may enter the first name as Robert "Bobby," using the quotation marks around "Bobby."

In this case, Access sees the double-quotation characters as data, and you may want to include the quotes in the criteria. The simplest solution is to use a criteria expression such as the following:

```
'Robert "Bobby"'
```

Notice the single quotes surrounding the criteria string. Access correctly interprets the single quotes as delimiting characters, and understands that the double quotes within the single quote are just data. You should not use an expression such as the following:

```
"Robert 'Bobby'"
```

This is, of course, the opposite use of quotation marks as the previous example. In this case, Access expects to find single quotes around "Bobby" in the first name field, and no records will be returned.

The Like operator and wildcards

In previous sections, you worked with *literal* criteria. You specified the exact field contents for Access to find, which was NY in the previous example. Access used the literal to retrieve the records. Sometimes, however, you know only a part of the field contents, or you might want to see a wider range of records on the basis of a pattern.

For example, you might want to see all product information for items with "convertible" in the description. Many different makes and models may be convertibles, and there's no field where "convertible" will work by itself as the query's criteria. You'll need to use wildcards to make sure you successfully select all records containing "convertible" in the description.

Here's another example: Suppose you have a buyer who has purchased a couple of red models in the last year. You remember making a note of it in the Notes field about the color, but you don't remember which customer it was. To find these records, you're required to use a wildcard search against the Notes field in tblCustomers to find records that contain the word *Red*.

Use the Like operator in the Criteria cell of a field to perform wildcard searches against the field's contents. Access searches for a pattern in the field; you use the question mark (?) to represent a single character or the asterisk (*) for several characters. In addition to ? and *, Access uses three other characters for wildcard searches. Table 5.1 lists the wildcards that the Like operator can use.

The question mark (?) stands for any single character located in the same position as the question mark in the example expression. An asterisk (*) stands for any number of characters in the same position in which the asterisk is placed. The pound sign (#) stands for a single digit (0–9) found in the position occupied by the pound sign. The brackets ([ ]) and the list they enclose stand for any single character that matches any one character in the list located within the brackets. Finally, the exclamation point (!) inside the brackets represents the Not operator for the list — that is, any single character that does *not* match any character in the list.

These wildcards can be used alone or in conjunction with each other. They can even be used multiple times within the same expression.

To create an example using the Like operator, let's suppose you want to find the customer who likes red model cars. You know that Red is used in one of the Notes field in tblCustomers. To create the query, follow these steps:

1. Add tblCustomers, tblSales, tblSalesLineItems, and tblProducts to the query.

2. Add Company and Notes from tblCustomers, SalesDate from tblSales, and Description from tblProducts to the QBE pane.

3. Click the Criteria cell of the `Notes` field and enter * **red** * as the criteria.

   Be sure to put a space between the first asterisk and the *r* and the last asterisk and the *d* — in other words, put spaces before and after the word *red*.

Tip

In the preceding steps, you put a space before and after the word red. If you didn't, Access would find all words that have the word red in them — like aired, bored, credo, fired, geared, restored, and on and on. By placing a space before and after the word red, Access is being told to look for the word red only.

There is, however, one issue with this example. Notice that the criteria (`"* red *"`) requires a space after the word *red*. This means that a record containing the following note will not be returned by this query:

Customer wants any model of car, as long as it's red!

Because there is no space immediately after *red*, this record will be missed. The proper criteria to use is

```
Like "* red[ ,.!?]"
```

The brackets around " ,.!?" instruct Access to select records when the Notes field ends with the word *red*, followed by a space or punctuation character. Obviously, there may be other characters to consider within the brackets, and you must have a good idea of the variety of data in the queried field.

When you click outside the Criteria cell, Access automatically adds the `Like` operator and the quotation marks around the expression. Your query QBE pane should look like Figure 5.6.

FIGURE 5.6

Using the `Like` operator in a select query

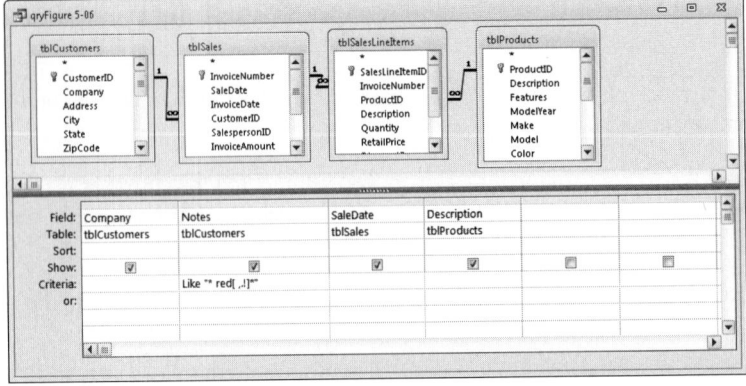

After creating this query, click on the Datasheet View command to view the query's results. It should look like Figure 5.7.

FIGURE 5.7

The results of using the `Like` operator with a select query in a `Memo` field. The query looks for the word *red* in the `Features` field.

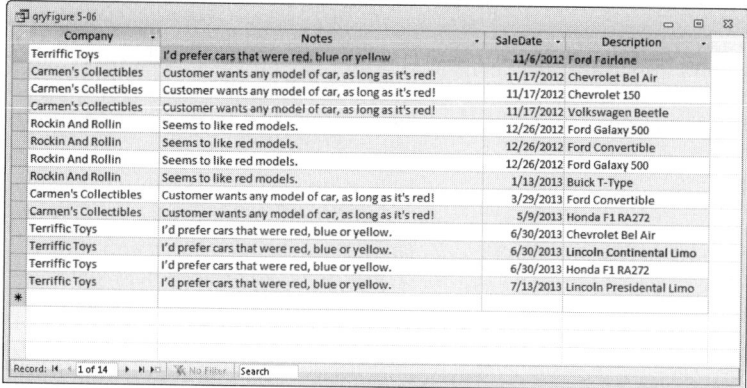

Clicking on the Datasheet View command on the ribbon, you see that a number of records match your query's criteria. The recordset returned by this query includes redundant information in the Company and Notes columns, but the redundancy is the result of asking for this information along with the sales and product data.

Access automatically adds the `Like` operator and quotation marks if you meet these conditions:

- Your expression contains no spaces.
- You use only the wildcards ?, *, and #.
- You use brackets ([ ]) inside quotation marks (" ").

If you use the brackets without quotation marks, you must supply the `Like` operator and the quotation marks.

Using the `Like` operator with wildcards is the best way to perform pattern searches through memo fields. It's just as useful in text and date fields as the examples in Table 5.6 demonstrate.

TABLE 5.6

Using Wildcards with the Like Operator

Expression	Field Used In	Results of Criteria
Like "Ca*"	tblCustomers.LastName	Finds all records of contacts whose last name begin with Ca (for example, Carson and Casey).
Like "* red *"	tblProducts.Features	Finds all records of products with the word *red* anywhere within the Features field.
Like "C*"	tblSales.PaymentMethod	Finds all sales that were paid for by check or credit card.
Like "9/*/2012"	tblSales.SaleDate	Finds all records of sales for the month of September 2012.
Like "## South Main"	tblCustomers.Address	Finds all records of contacts with houses containing house numbers between 10 and 99 inclusively (for example, 10, 22, 33, 51 on South Main).
Like "[CDF]*"	tblCustomers.City	Finds all records of contacts for customers who live in any city with a name beginning with C, D, or F.
Like "[!EFG]*"	tblCustomers.City	Finds all records of contacts who do not live in any city that begins with the letters E, F, or G; all other city records are displayed.

Table 5.6 shows several examples that can be used to search records in the tables of the Collectible Mini Cars database.

Specifying non-matching values

To specify a non-matching value, you simply use either the Not or the <> operator in front of the expression that you don't want to match. For example, you might want to see all contacts who have purchased a vehicle, but you want to exclude buyers from New York state. Follow these steps to see how to specify this non-matching value:

1. Open a new query in Design view, and add tblCustomers.
2. Add Company and State from tblCustomers.
3. Click in the Criteria cell of State.

4. Type **Not NY** in the cell.

Access automatically places quotation marks around NY if you don't do so before you leave the field. You can also use <> instead of the word Not. The query should look like Figure 5.8. The query selects all records *except* those for buyers who live in the state of New York.

FIGURE 5.8

Using the Not operator in criteria

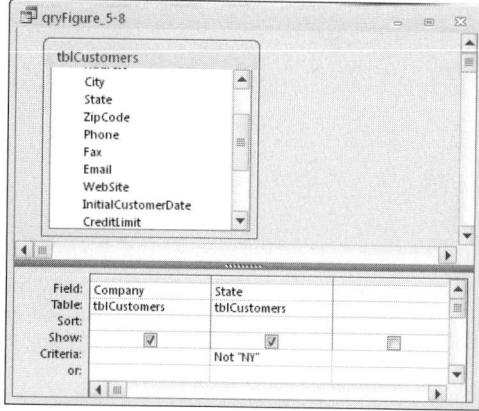

Note

You can use the <> operator instead of Not in Step 4 of the previous instructions to exclude New York (NY). The result is the same with either operator. These two operators are interchangeable except with the use of the keyword Is. You can't say Is <> Null. Instead, you must say Not Is Null or more accurately Is Not Null.

Entering numeric criteria

You use numeric criteria with numeric or currency data-type fields. You simply enter the numbers and the decimal symbol — if required — following the mathematical or comparison operator (but don't use commas!). For example, you might want to see all sales where the product's inventory count is less than 6:

1. Open a new query in Design view, and add tblProducts.

2. Add ProductID, Description, Make, Model, and QtyInStock from tbl-Products to the QBE grid.

3. Click in the Sort cell for Make and select Ascending from the drop-down list.

4. Click in the Criteria cell for QtyInStock and enter **<10** in the cell.

Your query looks like Figure 5.9. When working with numeric data, Access doesn't enclose the expression with quotes, as it does with string criteria.

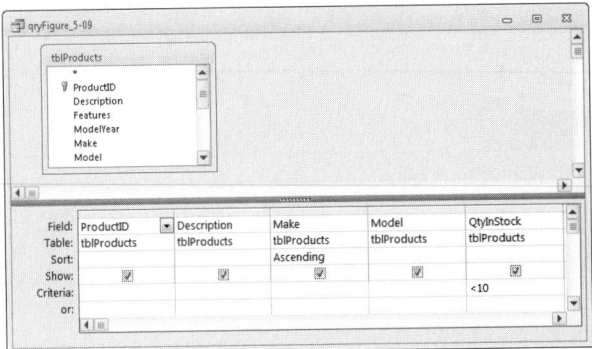

FIGURE 5.9

Criteria set for products with low inventory

The criteria applied to numeric fields usually includes comparison operators, such as less than (<), greater than (>), or equal to (=). If you want to specify a comparison other than equal, you must enter the operator as well as the value. Remember that Access defaults to equal when running a select query. That's why you needed to specify <10 in the QtyInStock column in the example shown in Figure 5.9.

Access does not surround the criteria with quotes because QtyInStock is numeric and requires no delimiter.

Entering true or false criteria

True and false criteria are used with Yes/No type fields. The example data that you supply as criteria must evaluate to True or False. You can also use the Not and the <> operators to signify the opposite, but the Yes/No data also has a Null state that you might want to consider. Access recognizes several forms of true and false.

Thus, instead of typing **Yes**, you can type any of these in the Criteria: cell: **On, True, Not No, <> No, <No, or –1**.

Note

A Yes/No **field can have three states:** Yes, No, **and** Null. Null **only occurs when no default value was set in a table and the value has not yet been entered. Checking for "Is Null" displays only records containing Null in the field, and checking for "Is Not Null" always displays all records with** Yes **or** No **in the field. After a** Yes/ No **field check box is checked (or checked and then deselected), it can never be** Null. **It must be either** Yes **or** No **(–1 or 0).**

Entering OLE object criteria

You can specify criteria for OLE objects: `Is Null` or `Is Not Null`. For example, suppose you don't have pictures for all the products and you want to view only those records that have a picture — that is, those in which the picture is not null. You specify the `Is Not Null` criterion for the `Picture` field of `tblProducts`.

Tip
Although `Is Not Null` **is the correct syntax, you can also use Not Null in the QBE grid and Access supplies the** `Is` **operator for you.**

Using Multiple Criteria in a Query

In previous sections of this chapter, you worked with single-condition criteria on a single field. As you learned in those sections, you can specify single-condition criteria for any field type. In this section, you work with multiple criteria based on a single field. For example, you might be interested in seeing all records in which the buyer comes from New York, California, or Arizona. Or maybe you want to view the records of all the products sold during the first quarter of the year 2012.

The QBE pane has the flexibility to solve these types of problems. You can specify criteria for several fields in a select query. Using multiple criteria, for example, you can determine which products were sold for the past 90 days. Either of the following expressions could be used as criteria in the SaleDate field's criteria:

```
Between Date() And Date() - 90
Between Date() And DateAdd("d",-90,Date())
```

Of these, the expression using the `DateAdd` function is less ambiguous and more specific to the task.

Understanding an Or operation

You use an `Or` operator in queries when you want a field to meet either of two conditions. For example, you might want to see all the records where the customer lives in either New York or California. In other words, you want to see all records where a customer lives in NY, in CA, or both. The general expression for this operation is

```
[State] = "NY" Or [State] = "CA"
```

If either side of this expression is `True`, the resulting answer is also `True`. To clarify this point, consider these conditions:

- Customer 1 lives in NY — the expression is `True`.
- Customer 2 lives in CA — the expression is `True`.

- Customer 3 lives in NY and CA — the expression is `True`.
- Customer 4 lives in CT — the expression is `False`.

Specifying multiple values with the Or operator

The `Or` operator is used to specify multiple values for a field. For example, you use the `Or` operator if you want to see all records of buyers who live in CT or NJ or NY. To do this, follow these steps:

1. Open a new query in Design view, and add `tblCustomers` and `tblSales`.
2. Add `Company` and `State` from `tblCustomers` and `SalesDate` from `tblSales`.
3. Click in the Sort cell of `State`.
4. Select Ascending from the drop-down list.
5. Click in the Criteria cell of `State`.
6. Type **AZ Or CA Or NY** in the cell.

   Your QBE pane should resemble the one shown in Figure 5.10. Access automatically places quotation marks around your example data — AZ, CA, and NY.

FIGURE 5.10

Using the `Or` operator. Notice the two `Or` operators under the `State` field — AZ Or CA Or NY.

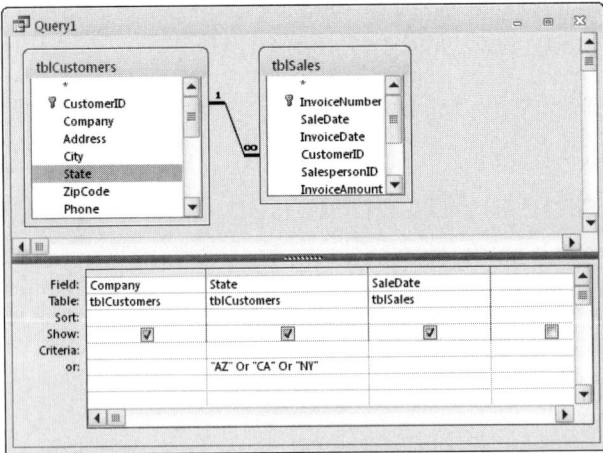

Using the Or cell of the QBE pane

Besides using the literal `Or` operator as a single expression on the Criteria row under the `State` field, you can supply individual criteria for the field vertically on separate rows of the QBE pane, as shown in Figure 5.11.

FIGURE 5.11

Using the Or cell of the QBE pane. You can place criteria vertically in the QBE grid.

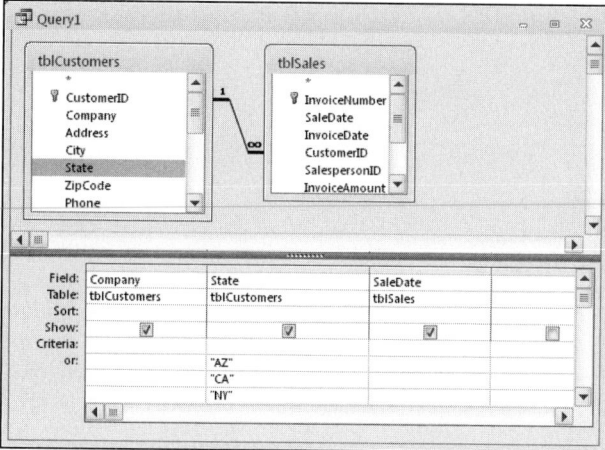

Tip

Access allows up to nine Or cells for each field. If you need to specify more Or conditions, use the Or operator between conditions (for example, AZ Or CA Or NY Or PA).

Access rearranges the design shown in Figure 5.11 when the query is saved to match the query in Figure 5.10. In fact, when you open qryFigure_5-11 in the Chapter05.accdb example database, you'll see that it is exactly the same as qryFigure_5-10 because of the way Access rearranged the criteria when qryFigure_5-11 was originally saved. When you build a query using "vertical" Or criteria, Access optimizes the SQL statement behind the query by placing all the Or criteria into a single expression.

Note

Access doesn't allow periods in the names of objects, so I've used hyphens instead.

Using a list of values with the In operator

Another method for specifying multiple values of a single field is using the In operator. The In operator finds a value from a list of values. For example, use the expression IN(AZ, CA, NY) under the State field in the query used in Figure 5.11. The list of values in the parentheses becomes an example criterion. Your query should resemble the query shown in Figure 5.12.

Access automatically adds quotation marks around AZ, CA, and NY.

Note

When you work with the In operator, each value (example data) must be separated from the others by a comma.

FIGURE 5.12

Using the In operator to find all records for buyer state being either AZ, CA, or NY

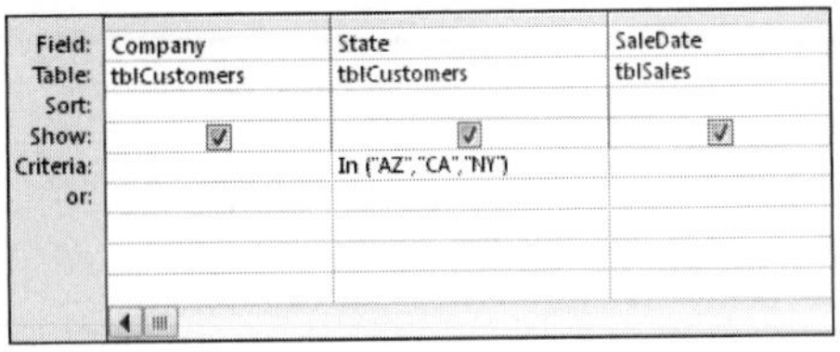

Field:	Company	State	SaleDate
Table:	tblCustomers	tblCustomers	tblSales
Sort:			
Show:	☑	☑	☑
Criteria:		In ("AZ","CA","NY")	
or:			

Using And to specify a range

The And operator is frequently used in fields that have numeric or date/time data types. It's seldom used with text data types, although it can be this way in some situations. For example, you might be interested in viewing all buyers whose names start with the letters *d, e,* or *f*. The And operator can be used here (> "Cz" And <"G"), although the Like operator is better (Like "[DEF]*") because it's much easier to understand.

You use the And operator in queries when you want a field to meet two or more conditions that you specify. For example, you might want to see records of buyers that have purchased products between October 1, 2012, and March 31, 2013. In other words, the sale had to have occurred during the last quarter of the year 2012 and the first quarter of 2013. The general expression for this example is

        (SaleDate >= 10/1/2012) And (SaleDate <= 3/31/2013)

Note

Parentheses are included in this example for clarity.

Unlike the Or operation (which has several conditions under which it is True), the And operation is True only when *both* sides of the expression are True. To clarify use of the And operator, consider these conditions:

- SaleDate (9/22/2012) is not greater than 10/01/2012 but is less than 3/31/2013 — the result is False.

- SaleDate (4/11/2013) is greater than 10/01/2012 but is not less than 3/31/2013 — the result is False.

- SaleDate (11/22/2012) is greater than 10/01/2012 and is less than 3/31/2013 — the result is True.

Using an And operator with a single field sets a range of acceptable values in the field. Therefore, the key purpose of an And operator in a single field is to define a range of records to be viewed. For example, you can use the And operator to create a range criterion to display all buyers who have purchased products between October 1, 2012, and March 31, 2013, inclusively. To create this query, follow these steps:

1. Create a new query using tblCustomers and tblSales.
2. Add Company from tblCustomers and SaleDate from tblSales.
3. Click in the Criteria cell of SaleDate.
4. Type >= #10/1/2012# And <= #3/31/2013# in the cell.

   The query should resemble Figure 5.13.

FIGURE 5.13

Using an And operator to specify complex query criteria.

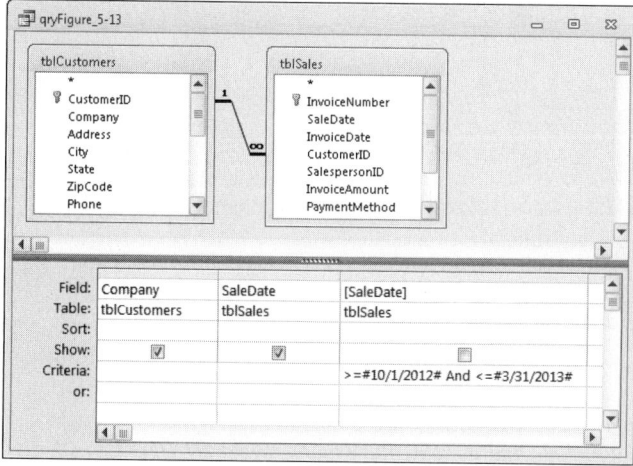

Notice the pound signs (#) used to delimit the dates in the expressions on both sides of the And operator. Access recognizes pound signs as delimiters for date and time values. Without the pound signs, Access evaluates the date values as numeric expressions (10 divided by 1 divided by 2012, for example).

Using the Between...And operator

You can request a range of records using another method — the Between...And operator. With Between...And, you can find records that meet a range of values — for example, all sales where the list price of the product was $50 and $100. Using the previous example, create the query shown in Figure 5.14.

FIGURE 5.14

Using the `Between...And` operator. The results are the same as the query in Figure 5.13.

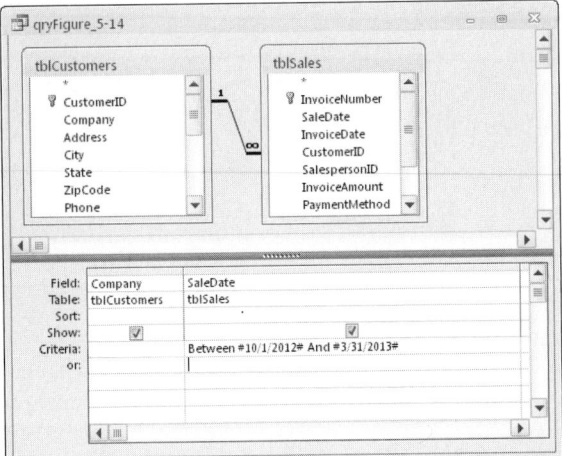

The operands for the `Between...And` operator are inclusive. This means that sales on 10/1/2012 and 3/31/2013 are included in the query results.

Searching for Null data

A field might have no contents for several reasons: For example, perhaps the value wasn't known at the time of data entry, or the person who did the data entry simply forgot to enter the information, or the field's information was removed. Access does nothing with this field. Unless a default value is specified in the table design, the field simply remains empty. (A field is said to be *null* when it's truly empty.)

What is a null value?

Databases must work with all kinds of information. We're all familiar with text, numeric, date, and other types of data, and in most cases, the value is known. For example, we almost certainly know a new employee's first and last name, but we may not yet know their middle name. How does a database represent a value that is unknown, and which may, in fact, not exist? That's where *null* comes in. By default, most fields in a database table are null until a value is provided. The value may come from a user entering a value on a form, or may be provided through the field's default value property. If we learn the employee does not have a middle name, we may enter an empty string (" ") in the field holding the middle name. In this case, an empty string means that there is no middle name. But, as long as the value is unknown, the field is *null*.

Logically, a `Null` is neither `True` nor `False`. A `Null` field is not equivalent to all spaces or to 0. A `Null` field simply has no value.

Access lets you work with `Null` value fields by means of two special operators:

> `Is Null` `Is Not Null`

You use these operators to limit criteria based the `Null` state of a field. Earlier in this chapter, you learned that a `Null` value can be used to query for products having a picture on file. In the next example, you look for buyers that don't have the `Notes` field filled in:

1. Create a new query using `tblCustomers` and `tblSales`.
2. Add `Notes` and `Company` from `tblCustomers`, and `SaleDate` from `tblSales`.
3. Enter `Is Null` as the criteria in the `Notes` field.
4. Uncheck the `Show` box in the `Notes` field.

Your query should look like Figure 5.15. Select the Datasheet View command to see the records that don't have a value in the `Notes` field.

You unchecked the `Show` box because there is no need to display the `Notes` field in the query results. The criteria selects only those rows where `Notes` is null, so there is, quite literally, nothing to see in the `Notes` field and no reason to display it in the results.

FIGURE 5.15

Use `Is Null` to select rows containing fields that contain no data.

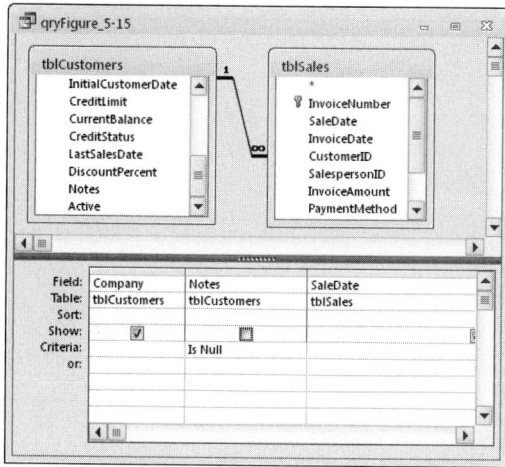

Tip

When using the `Is Null` and `Is Not Null` operators, you can enter `Null` or `Not Null` and Access automatically adds the `Is` to the `Criteria` field.

Entering Criteria in Multiple Fields

Earlier in this chapter, you worked with single and multiple criteria specified in single fields. In this section, you work with criteria across several fields. When you want to limit the records based on several field conditions, you do so by setting criteria in each of the fields that will be used for the scope. Suppose you want to search for all sales of models to resellers in Kansas (KS). Or suppose you want to search for motorcycle model buyers in Massachusetts or Connecticut. Or suppose you want to search for all motorcycle buyers in Massachusetts or trucks in Connecticut. Each of these queries requires placing criteria in multiple fields and on multiple lines.

Using And and Or across fields in a query

To use the And operator and the Or operator across fields, place your example or pattern data in the Criteria cells (for the And operator) and the Or cells of one field relative to the placement in another field. When you want to use And between two fields, you place the example or pattern data across the same row in the QBE pane. When you want to use Or between two fields, you place the criteria on different rows in the QBE pane. Figure 5.16 shows the QBE pane and a rather extreme example of this placement.

FIGURE 5.16

The QBE pane with And/Or criteria between fields using the Criteria and Or rows

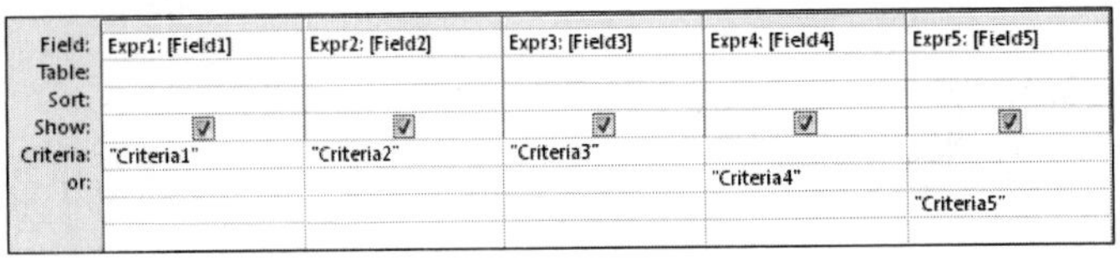

Field:	Expr1: [Field1]	Expr2: [Field2]	Expr3: [Field3]	Expr4: [Field4]	Expr5: [Field5]
Table:					
Sort:					
Show:	☑	☑	☑	☑	☑
Criteria:	"Criteria1"	"Criteria2"	"Criteria3"		
or:				"Criteria4"	
					"Criteria5"

Figure 5.16 shows that if the only criteria fields present were `Criteria1`, `Criteria2`, and `Criteria3` (with `Criteria4` and `Criteria5` removed), all three would be And-ed between the fields. If only the criteria fields `Criteria4` and `Criteria5` were present (with `Criteria1`, `Criteria2`, and `Criteria3` removed), the two would be Or-ed between fields. As it is, the

expression for this example is (Criteria1 And Criteria2 And Criteria3) Or Criteria4 Or Criteria5. Therefore, this query displays a record if a value matches any of these criteria:

- Criteria1 And Criteria2 And Criteria3 (all must be True)
- Criteria4 (this can be True and either/both of the other two lines can be False)
- Criteria5 (this can be True and either/both of the other two lines can be False)

As long as one of these three criteria is True, the record appears in the query's results.

Here's the SQL statement behind the query in Figure 5.16:

```
SELECT Table1.Field1, Table1.Field2,
Table1.Field3, Table1.Field4, Table1.Field15
FROM Table1
WHERE (Table1.Field1="Criteria1"
AND Table1.Field2="Criteria2"
AND Table1.Field3="Criteria3")
OR (Table1.Field4="Criteria4")
OR (Table1.Field5="Criteria5")
```

The locations of the parentheses in this SQL statement are significant. One set of parentheses surrounds the criteria for Field1, Field2, and Field3, while parentheses surround each of the criteria applied to Field4 and Field5. This means, of course, that Criteria1, Criteria2, and Criteria3 are applied as a group, while Criteria4 and Criteria5 are included individually.

Specifying Or criteria across fields of a query

Although the Or operator isn't used across fields as commonly as the And operator, occasionally Or is very useful. For example, you might want to see records of any models bought by contacts in Connecticut or you might want to see records on truck models, regardless of the state they live in. To create this query, follow these steps:

1. Add tblCustomers, tblSales, tblSalesLineItems, and tblProducts to a new query.

2. Add Company and State from tblCustomers, and Description and Category from tblProducts.

3. Enter **CT** as the criteria for State.

4. Enter **Trucks** in the Or cell under Category.

   Your query should resemble Figure 5.17. Notice that the criteria entered are not in the same row of the QBE pane for State and Category. When you place criteria on different rows in the QBE grid, Access interprets this as an Or between the fields. This query returns customers who either live in Connecticut or who have bought truck models.

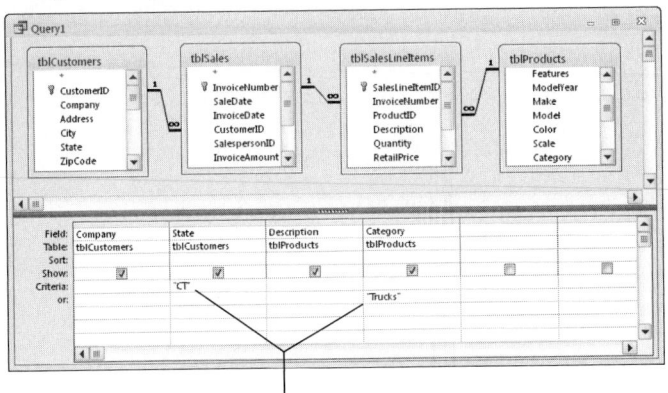

FIGURE 5.17

Using the `Or` operator between fields.

"Or" because criteria are in different rows

Here's the SQL statement behind the query in Figure 5.17:

```
SELECT tblCustomers.Company, tblCustomers.State,
tblProducts.Description, tblProducts.Category
FROM tblProducts
INNER JOIN (tblCustomers
INNER JOIN (tblSales INNER JOIN tblSalesLineItems
ON tblSales.InvoiceNumber = tblSalesLineItems.InvoiceNumber)
ON tblCustomers.CustomerID = tblSales.CustomerID)
ON tblProducts.ProductID = tblSalesLineItems.ProductID
WHERE (tblCustomers.State="CT") OR (tblProducts.Category="Trucks")
```

Notice the placement of parentheses in the WHERE clause. Either condition (State = "CT" or Category="Trucks") can be true, and the record is returned by the query.

Moving "Trucks" to the same row as "CT" in the QBE grid changes the query's logic to return customers who live in Connecticut *and* have bought truck models. The rearranged query is shown in Figure 5.18.

Here's the SQL statement for this minor rearrangement:

```
SELECT tblCustomers.Company, tblCustomers.State,
tblProducts.Description, tblProducts.Category
FROM tblProducts
INNER JOIN (tblCustomers
INNER JOIN (tblSales INNER JOIN tblSalesLineItems
ON tblSales.InvoiceNumber = tblSalesLineItems.InvoiceNumber)
ON tblCustomers.CustomerID = tblSales.CustomerID)
ON tblProducts.ProductID = tblSalesLineItems.ProductID
WHERE (tblCustomers.State="CT") AND (tblProducts.Category="Trucks")
```

FIGURE 5.18

A simple rearrangement in the QBE grid results in a very different query.

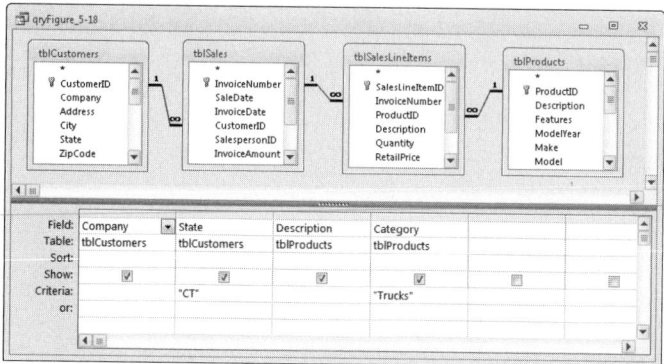

The difference is significant because the rearrangement is considerably more restrictive when returning records. Only one record is returned by qryFigure_5-18, while qryFigure5-17 returns 17 rows.

Using And and Or together in different fields

After you've worked with And and Or separately, you're ready to create a query using And and Or in different fields. In the next example, the query displays records for all buyers of motorcycle models in Connecticut and buyers of truck models in New York:

1. Use the query from the previous example, emptying the two criteria cells first.
2. Enter **CT** in the Criteria row in the State column.
3. Enter **NY** in the or row under CT in QBE grid.
4. Type **Motorcycles** as criteria in the Category field.
5. Enter **Trucks** under Motorcycles in the Category field.

    Figure 5.19 shows how the query should look. Notice that CT and Motorcycle are in the same row; NY and Trucks are in another row. This query represents two Ands across fields, with an Or in each field.

The important thing to notice about this query is that Access returns, essentially, two sets of data: motorcycle model owners in Connecticut and truck model owners in New York. All other customers and model combinations are ignored.

FIGURE 5.19

Using Ands and Ors in a select query

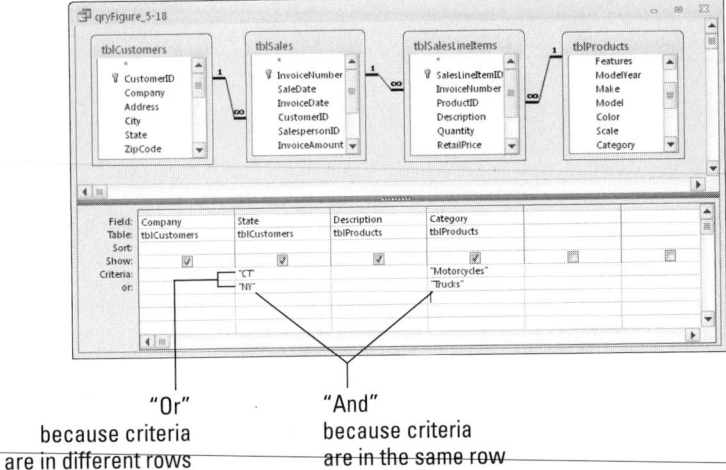

"Or"
because criteria
are in different rows

"And"
because criteria
are in the same row

A complex query on different lines

Suppose you want to view all records of Chevy models bought in the first six months of 2012 where the buyer lives in Massachusetts, or any type of vehicle from buyers in California. In this example, you use three fields for setting criteria: tblCustomers.State, tblSales. SaleDate, and tblProducts.Description. Here's the expression for setting these criteria:

```
((tblSales.SaleDate Between #1/1/2012# And #6/30/2012#) And
    (tblProducts.Description = Like "*Chev*" ) And (tblCustomers.
    State = "MA")) OR (tblCustomers.State = "CA")
```

The query design is shown in Figure 5.20.

Note

You can enter the date 1/1/12 instead of 1/1/2012, and Access processes the query exactly the same. The Regional and Language settings in the Windows Control Panel determine how dates are interpreted. By default, two-digit years from 00 to 30 are interpreted as 2000 to 2030, while all two-digit years between 31 and 99 are taken to be as 1931 to 1999. This is one reason why consistently using four-digit years during data entry is always a good idea.

FIGURE 5.20

Using multiple `Ands` and `Ors` across fields. This is a rather complex `Select` query.

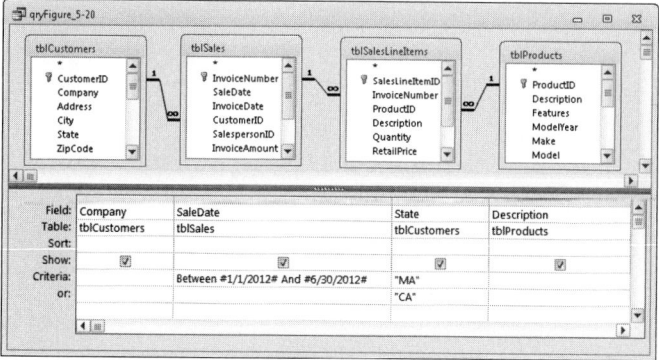

Summary

In this chapter, you learned how to use various operators to create expressions in Access. You used mathematical operations to perform arithmetic calculations, relational operators to compare values, string operators to concatenate and match text patterns using wildcards, and Boolean operators to perform logical operations. You also used `Is`, `Not`, and `Between...And` operators.

You implemented these operators in queries to see them in action. You created simple and complex criteria by creating expressions using the various types of operators. You learned the difference between using `And` and `Or` in your queries and how to set the QBE pane to get the desired results.

Working with Datasheet View

I n Chapter 2, you created a database named
`MyCollectableMiniCars.accdb` to hold the tables, queries, forms,
reports, and macros you'll create as you learn Access. You also created a
table named `tblContacts` using the Access table designer.

In this chapter, you'll use a datasheet to enter data into an Access table and
display the data many different ways. Using Datasheet view allows you to see
many records at once, in the familiar spreadsheet-style format. In this chapter, you'll work with `tblContacts` and `tblProducts` to add, change,
and delete data, as well as learn about different features available in
Datasheet view.

On the CD-ROM
This chapter uses the database named `Chapter06.accdb`. If you haven't
already copied it onto your computer from the CD, you'll need to do so now.

Understanding Datasheets

Using a datasheet is just one of the ways to view data in Access. A datasheet
is similar to a spreadsheet in that it displays data as a series of rows and columns. Figure 6.1 shows a typical Datasheet view of a table. Each row represents a single record, and each column represents a single field in the table.
Scroll up or down in the datasheet to see the rows (records) that don't fit on
the screen; scroll left or right to see the columns (fields) that don't fit.

IN THIS CHAPTER

Understanding datasheets

**Looking at the datasheet
window**

Opening a datasheet

Entering new data

Navigating records

Changing values in a datasheet

Using the undo feature

**Copying and pasting values in
a datasheet**

Replacing values in a datasheet

Adding records in datasheet

Deleting records in datasheet

**Displaying records in a
datasheet**

Sorting and filtering records

**Focusing on special features of
datasheets**

Printing records

Note

Many of the behaviors described in this chapter apply equally to Access forms. Most Access forms display data from a single record at a time, and interacting with the data on such a form is much like working with data in a single row of a datasheet.

Datasheets are completely customizable, which allows you to view data in many ways. Changing the font size, column widths, and row heights makes more or less of the data fit on the screen. Rearranging the order of the rows and/or columns lets you organize the records and fields logically. Locking columns makes them stay in position as you scroll to other parts of the datasheet, and hiding columns makes them disappear. Filtering the data hides records that don't match specific criteria.

Note

Datasheet view displays data from a number of different data sources: tables, queries, and forms displayed as datasheets. Depending on the data source, some of the datasheet behaviors described in this chapter may not work exactly as described. This is particularly true when the underlying data source is a query or form. With these data sources, you might frequently find the datasheet is read-only.

FIGURE 6.1

A typical Datasheet view. Each row represents a single record in the table; each column represents a single field (like `Description` or `RetailPrice`) in the table.

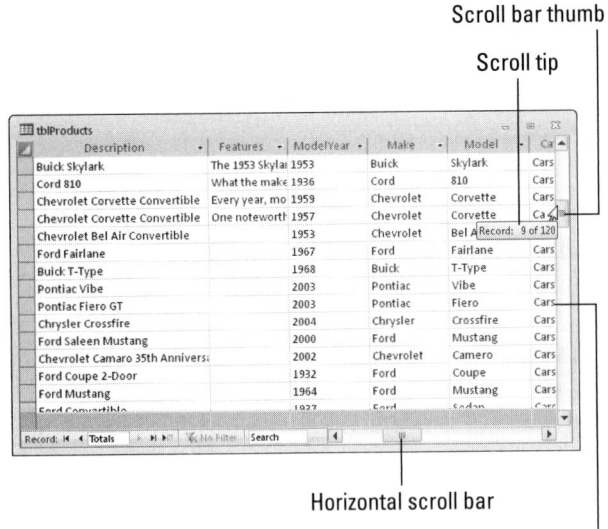

A quick review of records and fields

A *table* is a container for storing related information — patient records, a card list (birthday, holiday), birthday reminders, payroll information, and so on. Each table has a formal structure comprised of fields, each with a unique name to identify and describe the stored information and a specific data type — text, numeric, date, time, and so on — to limit what users enter in these fields. When displayed in a *datasheet* (a two-dimensional sheet of information), Access displays these fields in columns.

The table is composed of records, which hold information about a single entity (like a single customer or a single product). One record is made up of information stored in all the fields of the table structure. For example, if a table has three fields — name, address, and phone number — then the first record only has one name, one address, and one phone number in it. The second record also has one name, one address, and one phone number in it. A datasheet is an ideal way of looking at all the table's contents at once. A single record appears as a row in the datasheet; each row contains information for that specific record. The fields appear as columns in the datasheet; each column contains an individual field's contents. This row-and-column format lets you see lots of data at once.

Looking at the Datasheet Window

A datasheet typically appears in the center of the main Access window. The datasheet arranges the records initially by primary key and arranges the fields by the order in the table design.

At the top of the Access window, you see the title bar (displaying the database filename), the Quick Access toolbar, and the ribbon. At the bottom of the Access window, you see the status bar, which displays information about the datasheet. For example, it might contain field description information, error messages, warnings, or a progress bar.

Generally, error messages and warnings appear in dialog boxes in the center of the screen rather than in the status bar. If you need help understanding the meaning of a button in the toolbar, move the mouse over the button, hovering over it, and an explanatory tooltip appears with a one- or two-word explanation.

The right side of the Datasheet window contains a scroll bar for moving vertically between records. As you scroll between records, a scrolltip (shown in Figure 6.1) tells you precisely where the scroll bar takes you. The size of the scroll bar "thumb" (the small rectangle on the scroll bar) gives you a proportional look at how many of the total number of records are being displayed. The bottom of the Datasheet window also contains a scroll bar for moving among fields (left to right). The Navigation buttons for moving between records also appear in the bottom-left corner of the Datasheet window.

Moving within a datasheet

You easily move within the Datasheet window using the mouse to indicate where you want to change or add to your data — just click a field within a record. In addition, the ribbons, scroll bars, and Navigation buttons make it easy to move among fields and records. Think of a datasheet as a spreadsheet without the row numbers and column letters. Instead, columns have field names, and rows are unique records that have identifiable values in each cell.

Table 6.1 lists the navigational keys you use for moving within a datasheet.

TABLE 6.1

Navigating in a Datasheet

Navigational Direction	Keystrokes
Next field	Tab
Previous field	Shift+Tab
First field of current record	Home
Last field of current record	End
Next record	Down arrow ($\downarrow$)
Previous record	Up arrow ($\uparrow$)
First field of first record	Ctrl+Home
Last field of last record	Ctrl+End
Scroll up one page	PgUp
Scroll down one page	PgDn

Using the Navigation buttons

The *Navigation buttons* (shown in Figure 6.2) are the six controls located at the bottom of the Datasheet window, which you click to move between records. The two leftmost controls move you to the first record or the previous record in the datasheet. The three rightmost controls position you on the next record, last record, or new record in the datasheet. If you know the record number (the row number of a specific record), you can click the record-number box, enter a record number, and press Enter.

Note

If you enter a record number greater than the number of records in the table, an error message appears stating that you can't go to the specified record.

FIGURE 6.2

The Navigation buttons of a datasheet

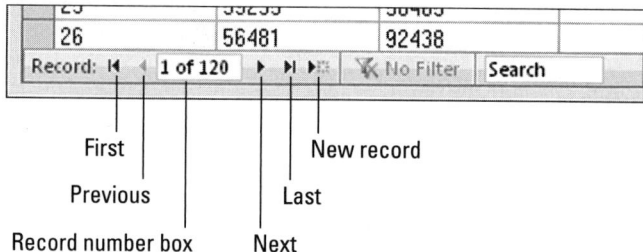

Examining the Datasheet ribbon

The Datasheet ribbon (shown in Figure 6.3) provides a way to work with the datasheet. The Home ribbon has some familiar objects on it, as well as some new ones. This section provides an overview of the groups on the ribbon; the individual commands are described in more detail later in this chapter.

Cross-Reference

I explain ribbons in Chapter 29.

FIGURE 6.3

The Datasheet ribbon's Home tab

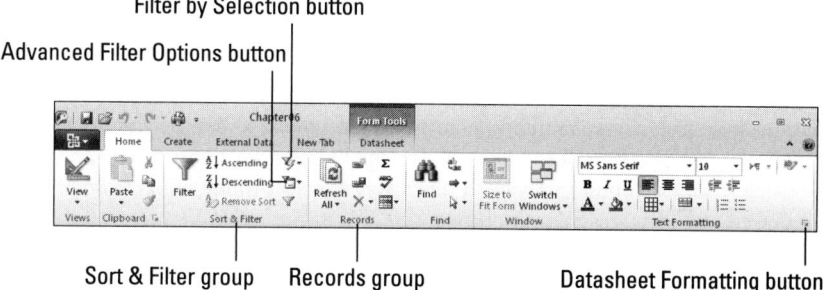

Views

The Views group allows you to switch between Datasheet view, PivotTable view, PivotChart view, and Design view. You can see all four choices by clicking the View command's downward-pointing arrow. Clicking Design View permits you to make changes to the object's design (table, query, and so on). Clicking Datasheet View returns you to the datasheet.

Clipboard

The Clipboard group contains the Cut, Copy, and Paste commands. These commands work like the commands in other applications (such as Word and Excel). The Paste command's down arrow gives you three choices: Paste, Paste Special, and Paste Append. Paste Special gives you the option of pasting the contents of the Clipboard in different formats (Text, CSV, Records, and so on). Paste Append pastes the contents of the Clipboard as a new record — as long as a row with a similar structure was copied to the Clipboard.

Sort & Filter

The Sort & Filter group lets you change the order of the rows as well as limit the rows being displayed — based on criteria you want.

Records

The Records group lets you save, delete, or add a new record to the datasheet. It also contains commands to show totals, check spelling, freeze and hide columns, and change the row height and cell width.

Find

The Find group lets you find and replace data and go to specific records in the datasheet. Use the Select command to select a record or all records.

Window

The Window group includes two buttons that help you control the items (forms, reports, tables, and so on) that are open in the main Access window:

- **Size to Fit Form:** The Size to Fit Form button resizes the form in the window to fit the size set when the form was created. By default, Access forms have a sizeable border, which means the user might drag the form to a new size. The Size to Fit Form button restores a form to the size specified at design time.

- **Switch Windows:** The Switch Windows button lets you choose a different open window to work with. A form or report needed by the user might be under another form or report, and the Switch Windows button provides a quick way to select which object is on top of the other objects in the Access main window.

Text Formatting

The Text Formatting group lets you change the look of text fields in the datasheet. Use these commands to change the font, size, bold, italic, color, and so on. Selecting a font attribute (such as bold) applies the attribute to all fields in the datasheet (see the Note just below this paragraph for the only exception to this rule). Use the Align Left, Align Right, and Align Center commands to justify the data in the selected column. Click the Gridlines command to toggle gridlines on and off. Use the Alternate Fill/Back Color command to change the colors of alternating rows or to make them all the same. All the controls in the Text Formatting group are disabled when the focus is on a field that is not either the Text or Memo data types.

Note

The controls in the text formatting group behave differently when the currently selected field in the datasheet happens to be the Memo data type. When a memo field is selected, you can change the font attributes (bold, underline, italics, and so on) of individual characters and words in the field, but only if the Text Format property is set to Rich Text. The Text Format property (which applies only to the Memo data type) is set to Plain Text by default.

Opening a Datasheet

Follow these steps to open a datasheet from the Database window:

1. Using the `Chapter06.accdb` database from the CD, click Tables in the Navigation Pane.

2. Double-click the table name you want to open (in this example, `tblProducts`).

An alternative method for opening the datasheet is to right-click on `tblProducts` and select Open from the pop-up menu.

Tip

If you're in any of the design windows, click on the Datasheet View command in the ribbon's View group to view your data in a datasheet.

Entering New Data

All the records in your table are visible when you first open it in Datasheet view. If you just created your table, the new datasheet doesn't contain any data. Figure 6.4 shows an empty datasheet and a portion of the Modify Fields ribbon tab. When the datasheet is empty, the first row contains an asterisk (*) in the record selector — indicating it's a new record.

The Modify Fields ribbon tab includes virtually all the tools needed to build a complete table. You can specify the data type, default formatting, indexing, field and table validation, and other table construction tasks from the controls in the Modify Fields tab.

The new row appears at the bottom of the datasheet when the datasheet already contains records. Click the New Record command in the ribbon's Record group, or click the new record button in the group of navigation buttons at the bottom of the datasheet to move the cursor to the new row — or simply click on the last row, which contains the asterisk. The asterisk turns into a pencil when you begin entering data, indicating that the record is being edited. A new row — containing an asterisk — appears below the one you're entering data into. The new-record pointer always appears in the last row of the datasheet. Figure 6.5 shows adding a new record to `tblProducts`.

FIGURE 6.4

An empty datasheet. Notice that the first record is blank and has an asterisk in the record selector.

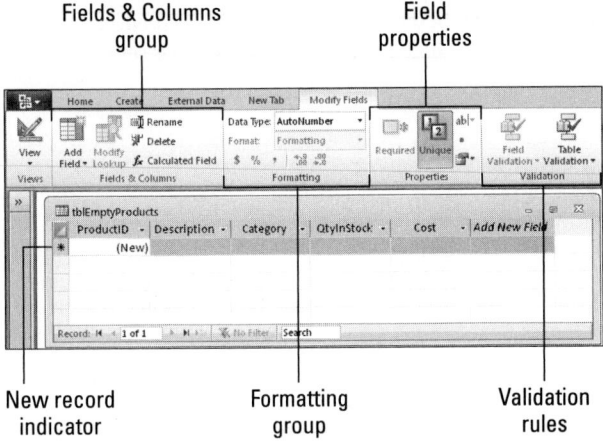

New record indicator   Formatting group   Validation rules

FIGURE 6.5

Entering a new record into the Datasheet view of tblProducts

Edit indicator

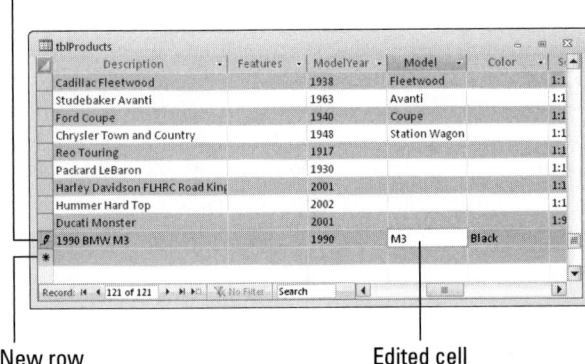

New row   Edited cell

To add a new record to the open Datasheet view of the tblProducts, follow these steps:

1. Click the New Record button.

2. Type in values for all fields of the table, moving between fields by pressing the Enter key or the Tab key.

When adding or editing records, you might see three different record pointers:

- **Record being edited:** A pencil icon
- **Record is locked (multiuser systems):** A padlock icon
- **New record:** A pencil icon

Caution

If the record contains an `AutoNumber` field, Access shows the name (New) in the field. You can't enter a value in this type of field; instead, simply press the Tab or Enter key to skip this field. Access automatically puts the number in when you begin entering data.

Saving the record

Moving to a different record saves the record you're editing. Tabbing through all the fields, clicking on the Navigation buttons, clicking Save in the ribbon's Record group, and closing the table all write the edited record to the database. You'll know the record is saved when the pencil disappears from the record selector.

To save a record, you must enter valid values into each field. The fields are validated for data type, uniqueness (if indexed for unique values), and any validation rules that you've entered into the `Validation Rule` property. If your table has a primary key that's not an `AutoNumber` field, you'll have to make sure you enter a unique value in the primary key field to avoid the error message shown in Figure 6.6. One way to avoid this error message while entering data is to use an `AutoNumber` field as the table's primary key.

FIGURE 6.6

The error message Access displays when attempting to save a record with a duplicate primary key value entered into the new record. Use an `AutoNumber` field as your primary key to avoid this error.

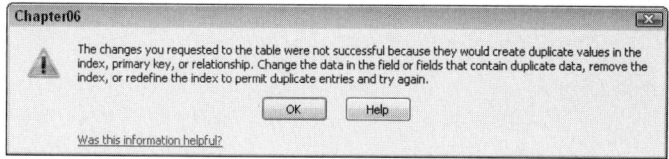

Tip

The Undo button in the Quick Access toolbar reverses changes to the current record and to the last saved record. After you change a second record, you can't undo the saved record.

Tip

You can save the record to disk without leaving the record by pressing Shift+Enter.

Now you know how to enter, edit, and save data in a new or existing record. In the next section, you learn how Access validates your data as you make entries into the fields.

Understanding automatic data-type validation

Access validates certain types of data automatically. Therefore, you don't have to enter any data-validation rules for these data types when you specify table properties. The data types that Access automatically validates include

- Number/Currency
- Date/Time
- Yes/No

Access validates the data type when you move off the field. When you enter a letter into a Number or Currency field, you don't initially see a warning not to enter these characters. However, when you tab out of or click on a different field, you get a warning like the one shown in Figure 6.7. This particular warning lets you choose to enter a new value or change the column's data type to Text. You'll see this message if you enter other inappropriate characters (symbols, letters, and so on), enter more than one decimal point, or enter a number too large for the specified numeric data type.

FIGURE 6.7

The warning Access displays when entering data that doesn't match the field's data type. Access gives you a few choices to correct the problem.

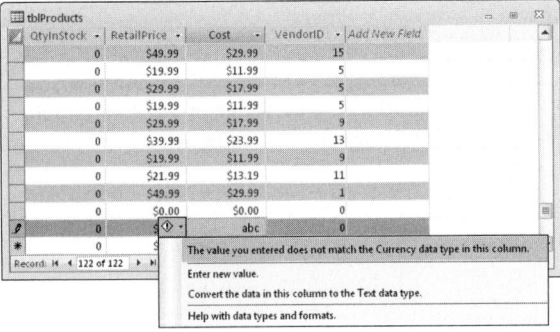

Access validates Date/Time fields for valid date or time values. You'll see a warning similar to the one shown in Figure 6.7 if you try to enter a date such as 14/45/05, a time such as 37:39:12, or an invalid character in a Date/Time field.

Yes/No fields require that you enter one of these defined values:

- **Yes:** Yes, True, –1, or a number other than 0 (which displays as –1)
- **No:** No, False, Off, or 0

Of course, you can define your own acceptable values in the Format property for the field, but generally these values are the only acceptable ones. If you enter an invalid value, the warning appears with the message to indicate an inappropriate value.

Tip

Display a check box in Yes/No fields to prevent users from entering invalid data.

Knowing how properties affect data entry

Because field types vary, you use different data-entry techniques for each type. In the "Saving the record" section, earlier in this chapter, you learned that some data-type validation is automatic. Designing tblContacts, however, means entering certain user-defined format and data-validation rules. The following sections examine the types of data entry.

Standard text data entry

The first field — ContactID — in tblContacts is an AutoNumber field, while other fields in the table are Text fields. After skipping ContactID, you simply enter a value in each field and move on. The ZipCode field uses an input mask (00000\-9999;0;) for data entry. The Phone and Fax fields also use an input mask (!\(999") "000\-0000;0;). Text fields accept any characters, unless you restrict them with an input mask.

Tip

To enter multiple lines in a Text or Memo field, press Ctrl+Enter to add a new line. This is useful, for example, in large text strings for formatting a multiple-line address field.

Date/Time data entry

The OrigCustDate and LastSalesDate fields in tblContacts are Date/Time data types, which both use a Short Date format (3/16/2012). However, you could've defined the format as Medium Date (16-Mar-12) or Long Date (Friday, March 16, 2012). Using either of these formats simply means that no matter how you type in the date — using month and year; day, month, and year; or month, day, and year — the date always displays in the specified format (short date [3/16/12], medium date [16-Mar-12], or long date [Friday, March 16, 2012]). Therefore, if you type 4/8/13 or 8 Apr 13, Access displays the value in the specified format as you leave the field. Dates are actually stored in the database without any formatting, so the format you select on a form doesn't affect how the data is stored.

Tip

Formats only affect the display of the data. They don't change storage of data in the table.

Warning

In general, it isn't a good idea to apply an input mask on Date/Time data. Microsoft Access does a more-than-adequate job of validating date and time values. You're far more likely to encounter data-entry problems with an input mask on a date-containing control than you are to avoid trouble by using an input mask.

Number/Currency data entry with data validation

The CreditLimit field in tblContacts has a validation rule assigned to it. It has a Validation Rule property to limit the amount of credit to $250,000. If the rule is violated, a dialog box appears with the validation text entered for the field. If you want to allow a contact to have more than $250,000 credit, change the validation rule in the table design.

The exact currency character used by Access (in this case, the dollar sign) is determined by the regional options set in the Control Panel's Regional Settings.

OLE object data entry

You can enter OLE (Object Linking and Embedding) Object data into a datasheet, even though you don't see the object. An OLE Object field holds many different item types, including:

- Bitmap pictures
- Sound files
- Business graphs
- Word or Excel files

Any object that an OLE server supports can be stored in an Access OLE Object field. OLE objects are generally entered into a form so you can see, hear, or use the value. When OLE objects appear in datasheets, you see text that tells what the object is (for example, you may see Bitmap Image in the OLE Object field). You can enter OLE objects into a field in two ways:

- Pasting from the Clipboard
- Right-clicking on the OLE Object field and clicking on Insert Object from the pop-up menu

Memo field data entry

The second-to-last field in the table is Notes, which is a Memo data type. This type of field allows up to 65,536 characters of text for each field. Recall that you entered a long string (about 260 characters) into the Memo field. As you entered the string, however, you saw only a few characters at a time — the rest of the string scrolled out of sight. Pressing Shift+F2 displays a Zoom window with a scroll bar (see Figure 6.8) that lets you to see more characters at a time. Click the Font button at the bottom of the window to view all the text in a different font or size. (The font in Figure 6.8 has been enlarged considerably over the 8-point default font size for the Zoom window.)

When you first display text in the Zoom window, all the text is selected and highlighted. You can deselect the text by clicking anywhere in the window. If you accidentally delete all the text or change something you didn't want to, click Cancel to exit back to the datasheet with the field's original data.

Tip

Use the Zoom window (Shift+F2) when designing Access objects (tables, forms, reports, queries) to see text that normally scrolls out of view.

FIGURE 6.8

The Zoom window. Notice that you can see a lot more of the field's data — not all 65,536 characters, but still quite a lot.

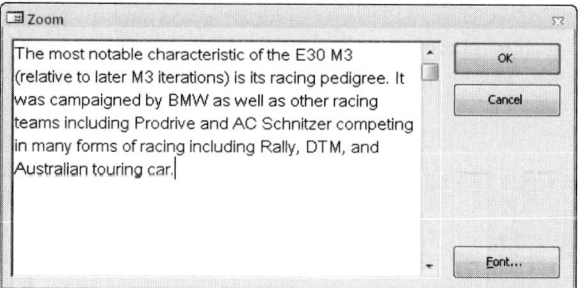

Navigating Records in a Datasheet

Wanting to make changes to records after you've entered them is not unusual. You might want to change records for several reasons:

- You receive new information that changes existing values.
- You discover errors in existing values.
- You need to add new records.

When you decide to edit data in a table, the first step is to open the table — if it isn't already open. From the list of tables in the Navigation Pane, double-click on tblProducts to open it in Datasheet view. If you're already in Design view for this table, click the Datasheet View button to switch views.

When you open a datasheet in Access that has related tables, a column with a plus sign (+) is added to indicate the related records, or subdatasheets. Click a row's plus sign to open the sub-datasheet for the row.

Moving between records

You can move to any record by scrolling through the records and positioning your cursor on the desired record. With a large table, scrolling through all the records might take a while, so you'll want to use other methods to get to specific records quickly.

Use the vertical scroll bar to move between records. The scroll-bar arrows move one record at a time. To move through many records at a time, drag the scroll box or click the areas between the scroll thumb and the scroll-bar arrows.

Tip

Watch the scrolltips when you use scroll bars to move to another area of the datasheet. Access does not update the record-number box until you click a field.

Use the five Navigation buttons (refer to Figure 6.2) to move between records. You simply click these buttons to move to the desired record. If you know the record number (the row number of a specific record), click the record-number box, enter a record number, and press Enter.

Also use the Go To command in the ribbon's Find group to navigate to the First, Previous, Next, Last, and New records.

Finding a specific value

Although you can move to a specific record (if you know the record number) or to a specific field in the current record, usually you'll want to find a certain value in a record. You can use one of these methods for locating a value in a field:

- Select the Find command (a pair of binoculars) from the ribbon's Find group.
- Press Ctrl+F.
- Use the Search box at the bottom of the datasheet window.

The first two methods display the Find and Replace dialog box (shown in Figure 6.9). To limit the search to a specific field, place your cursor in the field you want to search before you open the dialog box. Change the Look In combo box to the table name to search the entire table for the value.

FIGURE 6.9

The Find and Replace dialog box. The fastest way to activate it is to simply press the Ctrl+F key combination.

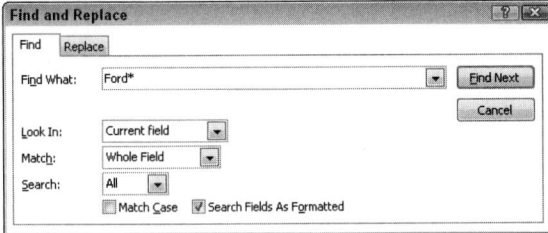

Tip

If you highlight the entire record by clicking the record selector (the small gray box next to the record), Access automatically searches through all fields.

The Find and Replace dialog box lets you control many aspects of the search. Enter the value you want to search for in the Find What combo box — which contains a list of recently used searches. You can enter a specific value or choose to use three types of wildcards:

* (any number of characters)

? (any one character)

(any one number)

To look at how these wildcards work, suppose that you want to find all the rows with Ford at the beginning of the `Description` field in `tblProducts`. Using `Ford*` in the Find What box will find rows beginning with Ford. Then, suppose that you want to search for values ending with Mustang; you'd use *Mustang. If you want to search for any value that begins with Ford, ends with Mustang, and contains any number of characters in between, use Ford*Mustang.

Cross-Reference
For more information on using wildcards, see Chapter 5.

The Match drop-down list contains three choices that eliminate the need for wildcards:

- **Any Part of Field:** If you select Any Part of Field, Access searches to see whether the value is contained anywhere in the field. This search finds the Ford anywhere in the field, including values like Ford Mustang, 2008 Ford F-150, and Ford Galaxy 500.

- **Whole Field:** The default is Whole Field, which finds fields containing exactly what you've entered. For example, the Whole Field option finds Ford only if the value in the field being searched is exactly Ford, and nothing else.

- **Start of Field:** A search for Ford using the Start of Field option searches from the beginning of the field, and returns all the rows containing Ford as the first four characters of the description.

In addition to these combo boxes, you can use two check boxes at the bottom of the Find and Replace dialog box:

- **Match Case:** Match Case determines whether the search is case-sensitive. The default is not case-sensitive (not checked). A search for SMITH finds smith, SMITH, or Smith. If you check the Match Case check box, you must then enter the search string in the exact case of the field value. (The data types Number, Currency, and Date/Time don't have any case attributes.)

  If you've checked Match Case, Access doesn't use the value Search Fields As Formatted (the second check box), which limits the search to the actual values displayed in the table. (If you format a field for display in the datasheet, you should check the box.)

- **Search Fields As Formatted:** The Search Fields As Formatted check box, the selected default, finds only text that has the same pattern of characters as the text specified in the Find What box. Clear this box to find text regardless of the formatting. For example, if you're searching the `Cost` field for a value of $16,500, you must enter the comma if Search Fields as Formatted is checked. Uncheck this box to search for an unformatted value (16500.)

Caution

Checking Search Fields As Formatted may slow the search process.

The search begins when you click the Find Next button. If Access finds the value, the cursor highlights it in the datasheet. To find the next occurrence of the value, click the Find Next button again. The dialog box remains open so that you can find multiple occurrences. Choose one of three search direction choices (Up, Down, or All) in the Search drop-down list to change the search direction. When you find the value that you want, click Close to close the dialog box.

Use the search box at the bottom of the Datasheet window (refer to Figure 6.1) to quickly search for the first instance of a value. When using the search box, Access searches the entire datasheet for the value in any part of the field. If you enter FORD in the search box, the datasheet moves to the closest match as you type each letter. First, it finds a field with *F* as the first character, then it finds *FO* and so on. Once it finds the complete value, it stops searching. To find more than one instance, use the Find Next button in the upper-left corner of the Find and Replace dialog box.

Changing Values in a Datasheet

If the field that you're in has no value, you can type a new value into the field. When you enter new values into a field, follow the same rules as for a new-record entry.

Manually replacing an existing value

Generally, you enter a field with either no characters selected or the entire value selected. If you use the keyboard (Tab or Arrow keys) to enter a field, you select the entire value. (You know that the entire value is selected when it's displayed in reverse video.) When you begin to type, the new content replaces the selected value automatically.

When you click in a field, the value is not selected. To select the entire value with the mouse, use any of these methods:

- Click just to the left of the value when the cursor is shown as a large plus sign.
- Click to the left of the value, hold down the left mouse button, and drag the mouse to select the whole value.
- Click in the field and press F2.

Tip

You may want to replace an existing value with the value from the field's Default Value property. To do so, select the value and press Ctrl+Alt+Spacebar. To replace an existing value with that of the same field from the preceding record, press Ctrl+' (single quote mark). Press Ctrl+; (semicolon) to place the current date in a field.

Caution

Pressing Ctrl+– (minus sign) deletes the current record.

Changing an existing value

If you want to change an existing value instead of replacing the entire value, use the mouse and click in front of any character in the field to activate Insert mode; the existing value moves to the right as you type the new value. If you press the Insert key, your entry changes to Overstrike mode; you replace one character at a time as you type. Use the arrow keys to move between characters without disturbing them. Erase characters to the left by pressing Backspace, or to the right of the cursor by pressing Delete.

Table 6.2 lists editing techniques.

TABLE 6.2

Editing Techniques

Editing Operation	Keystrokes
Move the insertion point within a field	Press the right-arrow (→) and left-arrow (←) keys
Insert a value within a field	Select the insertion point and type new data
Select the entire field	Press F2
Replace an existing value with a new value	Select the entire field and type a new value
Replace a value with the value of the previous field	Press Ctrl+' (single quote mark)
Replace the current value with the default value	Press Ctrl+Alt+Spacebar
Insert a line break in a Text or Memo field	Press Ctrl+Enter
Save the current record	Press Shift+Enter or move to another record
Insert the current date	Ctrl+; (semicolon)
Insert the current time	Ctrl+: (colon)
Add a new record	Ctrl++ (plus sign)
Delete the current record	Ctrl+– (minus sign)
Toggle values in a check box or option button	Spacebar
Undo a change to the current field	Press Esc or click the Undo button
Undo a change to the current record	Press Esc or click the Undo button a second time after you undo the current field

Fields that you can't edit

Some fields can't be edited, such as:

- **AutoNumber fields:** Access maintains AutoNumber fields automatically, calculating the values as you create each new record. AutoNumber fields can be used as the primary key.

- **Calculated fields:** Forms or queries may contain fields that are the result of expressions. These values are not actually stored in your table and are not editable.

- **Locked or disabled fields:** You can set certain properties in a form to prevent editing for a specific field.

- **Fields in multiuser locked records:** If another user locks the record, you can't edit any fields in that record.

Using the Undo Feature

The Undo button on the Quick Access toolbar is often dimmed because there's nothing to undo. As soon as you begin editing a record, however, you can use this button to undo the typing in the current field. You can also undo a change with the Esc key; pressing Esc cancels either a changed value or the previously changed field. Pressing Esc twice undoes changes to the entire current record.

After you type a value into a field, click the Undo button to undo changes to that value. After you move to another field, you can undo the change to the preceding field's value by clicking the Undo button. You can also undo all the changes to an unsaved current record by clicking the Undo button after you undo a field. After you save a record, you can still undo the changes by clicking the Undo button. However, after the next record is edited, changes to the previous record are permanent.

Caution

Don't rely on the Undo command to save you after you edit multiple records. When working in a datasheet, changes are saved when you move from record to record and you can only undo changes to the current record.

Copying and Pasting Values

Copying or cutting data to the Clipboard is a Microsoft Windows task; it isn't a specific function of Access. After you cut or copy a value, you can paste into another field or record by using the Paste command in the ribbon's Clipboard group. You can cut, copy, or paste data from any Windows application or from one task to another in Access. Using this technique, you can copy entire records between tables or databases, and you can copy datasheet values to and from Word and Excel.

The Paste command's down arrow gives you three choices:

- **Paste:** Paste inserts the contents of the Clipboard into one field.
- **Paste Special:** Paste Special gives you the option of pasting the contents of the Clipboard in different formats (text, CSV, records, and so on).
- **Paste Append:** Paste Append pastes the contents of the Clipboard as a new record — provided a row with a similar structure was copied.

Tip

Select a record or group of records using the record selector to cut or copy one or more records to the Clipboard. Then use Paste Append to add them to a table with a similar structure.

Replacing Values

To replace an existing value in a field, you can manually find the record to update or you can use the Find and Replace dialog box. Display the Find and Replace dialog box using these methods:

- Select the Replace command from the ribbon's Find group.
- Press Ctrl+H.

This dialog box allows you to replace a value in the current field or in the entire datasheet. Use it to find a certain value and replace it with a new value everywhere it appears in the field or table.

After the Find and Replace dialog box is active, you should first click the Replace tab and type in the value that you want to find in the Find What box. After you've selected all the remaining search options (turn off Search Fields As Formatted, for example), click the Find Next button to find to the first occurrence of the value. To change the value of the current found item (under the cursor), enter a value in the Replace With box and click the Replace button. For example, Figure 6.10 shows that you want to find the value Mini Vans in the `Category` field of `tblProducts` and change it to Minivans.

FIGURE 6.10

The Find and Replace dialog box with the Replace tab showing. In this case, you want to replace Mini Vans with Minivans.

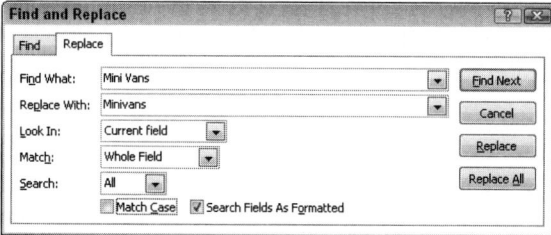

You can select your search options in the Find tab and then click the Replace tab to continue the process. However, it's far easier to simply do the entire process using the Replace tab. Enter the value you want to find and the value that you want to replace it with. After you've completed the dialog box with all the correct information, select one of the command buttons on the side:

- **Find Next:** Finds the next field that has the value in the Find What field.
- **Cancel:** Closes the form and performs no find and replace.
- **Replace:** Replaces the value in the current field only. (*Note:* You must use the Find Next button first.).
- **Replace All:** Finds all the fields with the Find What value and replaces them with the Replace With value. Use this if you're sure that you want to replace all the values; double-check the Look In box to make sure you don't replace the values in the entire datasheet if you don't want to.

Adding New Records

There are a number of ways to add a record to the datasheet:

- Click on the datasheet's last line, where the record pointer is an asterisk.
- Click the new record Navigation button (the furthest button on the right).
- Click the New command from the ribbon's Records group.
- Choose Go To ⇨ New from the ribbon's Find group.
- Move to the last record and press the down-arrow (↓) key.
- Press Ctrl++ (plus sign).

Once you move to a new record, enter data into the desired fields and save the record.

Deleting Records

To delete records, select one or more records using the record selectors, and then press the Delete key or click the Delete command in the ribbon's Records group. The Delete command's drop-down list contains the Delete Record command, which deletes the current record, even if it's not selected. When you press Delete or choose the ribbon command, a dialog box asks you to confirm the deletion (see Figure 6.11). If you select Yes, the records are deleted; if you select Cancel, no changes are made.

Caution

The Default value for this dialog box is Yes. Pressing the Enter key automatically deletes the records. If you accidentally erase records using this method, the action can't be reversed.

FIGURE 6.11

The Delete Record dialog box warns you that you're about to delete a specific number of records — the default response is Yes (okay to delete) so be careful when deleting records.

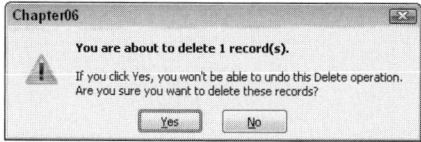

Caution

If you have relations set between tables and checked Enforce Referential Integrity — for example, the tblContacts (Customer) **table is related to** tblSales — **then you can't delete a parent record (**tblContacts**) that has related child records (in** tblSales**) unless you also check the Cascade Delete check box. Otherwise, you receive an error message dialog box that reports** The record can't be deleted or changed because the table '<tablename>' includes related records.

To select multiple contiguous records, click the record selector of the first record that you want to select and drag the mouse to the last record that you want to select. Or click to select the first record, and then hold Shift and click on the last record that you want in the selection.

Displaying Records

A number of techniques can increase your productivity when you add or change records. Change the field order, hide and freeze columns, change row height or column width, change display fonts, and change the display or remove gridlines to make data entry easier.

Changing the field order

By default, Access displays the fields in a datasheet in the same order that they appear in a table or query. Sometimes, you want to see certain fields next to each other in order to better analyze your data. To rearrange your fields, select a column by clicking the column heading, and then drag the column to its new location (as shown in Figure 6.12).

FIGURE 6.12

Selecting and dragging a column to change the field order

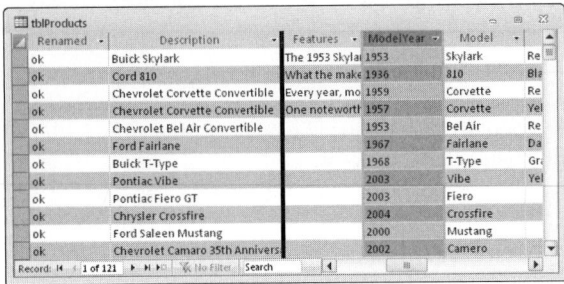

You can select and drag columns one at a time, or select multiple columns to move at the same time. Suppose you want QtyInStock to appear before Description in the tblProducts datasheet. Follow these steps to make this change:

1. Position the mouse pointer over the QtyInStock column heading.

   The cursor changes to a down arrow.

2. Click to select the column.

   The entire QtyInStock column is now highlighted.

3. Release the mouse button.

4. Click the mouse button on the column heading again.

   The pointer changes to an arrow with a box under it.

5. Drag the column to the left edge of the datasheet between the Description and Features fields.

   A thin black column appears between them (see Figure 6.12).

6. Release the mouse button.

   The column moves in front of the Description field of the datasheet.

With this method, you can move any individual field or contiguous field selection. To select multiple fields, click and drag the mouse across multiple column headings. Then you can move the fields left or right or past the right or left boundary of the window.

Note

Moving fields in a datasheet does not affect the field order in the table design.

Changing the field display width

You can change the *field display width* (column width) either by specifying the width in a dialog box (in number of characters) or by dragging the column border. When you drag a column border, the cursor changes to the double-arrow symbol.

To widen a column or to make it narrower, follow these steps:

1. Place the mouse pointer between two column names on the field separator line.

   The mouse pointer turns into a small line with arrows pointing to the left and right — if you have it in the correct location.

2. Drag the column border to the left to make the column smaller or to the right to make it larger.

Tip
You can instantly resize a column to the best fit (based on the longest visible data value) by double-clicking the right column border after the cursor changes to the double arrow.

Note
Resizing the column doesn't change the number of characters allowed in the table's field size. You're simply changing the amount of viewing space for the data contained in the column.

Alternatively, you can resize a column by right-clicking the column header and selecting Column Width from the pop-up menu to display the Column Width dialog box, as shown in Figure 6.13. Set the Column Width box to the number of characters you want to fit in the column or click the Standard Width check box to set the column to its default size. Click on Best Fit to size the column to the widest visible value.

FIGURE 6.13

The Column Width dialog box

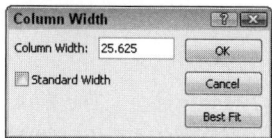

Caution
You can hide a column by dragging the column gridline to the gridline of the next column to the left, or by setting the column width to 0 in the Column Width dialog box. If you do this, you must choose More ⇨ Unhide Columns in the ribbon's Records group to redisplay the hidden columns.

Changing the record display height

You might need to increase the row height to accommodate larger fonts or text data displays of multiple lines. Change the record (row) height of all rows by dragging a row's border to make the row height larger or smaller, or you can choose More ⇨ Row Height in the ribbon's Records group.

When you drag a record's border, the cursor changes to the vertical two-headed arrow you see at the left edge of Figure 6.14.

Changing a row's height. Position the mouse as shown, and drag to the desired height.

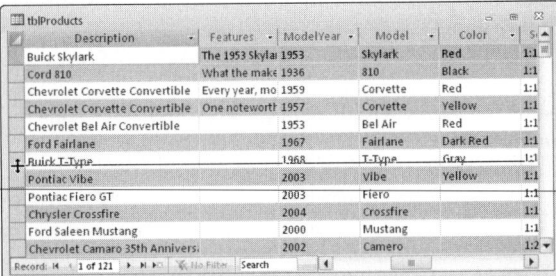

To increase or decrease a row's height, follow these steps:

1. Place the mouse pointer between record selectors of two rows.

   The cursor changes to the double-pointing arrow (up and down).

2. Drag the row border upward to shrink all row heights, or drag the border downward to increase all row heights.

Note

The procedure for changing row height changes the row size for all rows in the datasheet. You can't have rows with different heights.

You can also resize rows by choosing More ⇨ Row Height in the ribbon's Records group. The Row Height dialog box appears; there you enter the row height in point size. Check the Standard Height check box to return the rows to their default size.

Caution

If you drag a record's gridline up to meet the gridline immediately above it in the previous record, all rows are hidden. This also occurs if you set the row height close to 0 (for example, a height of 0.1) in the Row Height dialog box. In that case, you must use the Row Height dialog box to set the row height to a larger number to redisplay the rows.

Changing display fonts

By default, Access displays all data in the datasheet in the Calibri 11-point Regular font. Use the commands and drop-down lists in the ribbon's Text Formatting group (shown in Figure 6.15) to change the datasheet's text appearance.

FIGURE 6.15

Changing the datasheet's font directly from the ribbon. Choose font type style, size, and other font attributes for the entire datasheet.

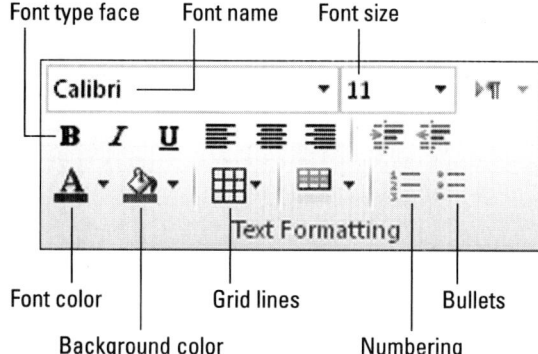

Setting the font display affects the entire datasheet. If you want to see more data on the screen, you can use a very small font. You can also switch to a higher-resolution display size if you have the necessary hardware. If you want to see larger characters, you can increase the font size or click the Bold button.

Displaying cell gridlines and alternate row colors

Normally gridlines appear between fields (columns) and between records (rows). You can set how you want the gridlines to appear using the Gridlines command in the ribbon's Text Formatting group (shown in Figure 6.15). Choose from the following options in the Gridlines drop-down list:

- Gridlines: Both
- Gridlines: Horizontal
- Gridlines: Vertical
- Gridlines: None

Use the Fill Color and Alternate Fill/Back Color drop-down lists to change the background colors of the datasheet. The Fill Color palette changes the color of the odd-numbered rows in the datasheet. The Alternate Fill/Back Color palette changes the color of the even-numbered rows. If you don't want alternating row colors, select No Color from the Alternate Fill/Back Color palette and the even-numbered rows will match the odd-numbered rows.

After changing the gridline settings or alternate row colors, Access will ask whether to save the changes to the datasheet's layout. Be sure to click the Yes button to make the changes permanent.

The Datasheet Formatting dialog box (shown in Figure 6.16) gives you complete control over the datasheet's look. Open this dialog box using the Datasheet Formatting command in the bottom-right corner of the ribbon's Text Formatting group. Use the Flat, Sunken, and Raised radio buttons under Cell Effect to change the grid to a 3-D look. Click the Horizontal and Vertical check boxes under Gridlines Shown to toggle which gridlines you want to see. Change the Background Color, Alternate Background Color, and Gridline Color using the available color palettes. The sample in the middle of the dialog box shows you a preview of changes.

FIGURE 6.16

The Datasheet Formatting dialog box. Use this dialog box to customize the look of the datasheet.

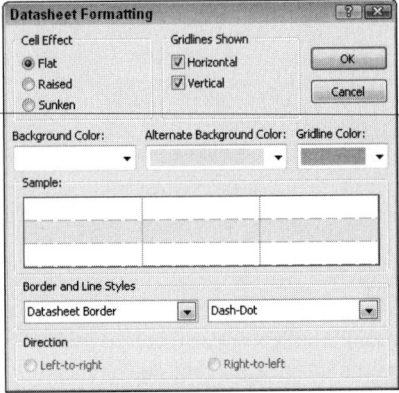

Use the Border and Line Styles drop-down lists to change the look of the gridlines. You can change the styles for the Datasheet Border and the Column Header Underline. Choose a different line style for each of the selections in the first drop-down list. The different line styles you can select from include

- Dash-Dot
- Dash-Dot-Dot
- Dashes
- Dots
- Double Solid
- Short Dashes
- Solid
- Sparse Dots
- Transparent Border

Figure 6.17 shows a datasheet with dots instead of solid lines and a higher contrast between alternating rows. You can use the various colors and styles to customize the datasheet's look to your liking.

FIGURE 6.17

Different line styles and row colors for the datasheet

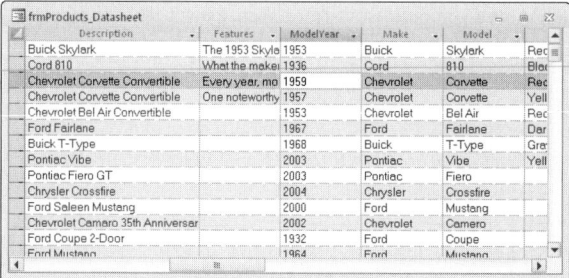

Aligning data in columns

Align the data to the left or right, or center it within a column using the alignment buttons. Choose alignments different from the default alignments Access chooses based on a field's data type (text aligns left, numbers/dates align right). Follow these steps to change the alignment of the data in a column:

1. Position the cursor anywhere within the column that you want to change the alignment.

2. Click on the Align Left, Align Center, or Align Right commands in the ribbon's Text Formatting group (refer to Figure 6.15) to change the alignment of the column's data.

Hiding and unhiding columns

Hide columns by dragging the column gridline to the preceding field or by setting the column width to 0:

1. Position the cursor anywhere within the column that you want to hide.

2. Choose More ➪ Hide Columns in the ribbon's Records group.

   The column disappears because the column width is simply set to 0. You can hide multiple columns by first selecting them and then choosing More ➪ Hide Columns.

After you've hidden a column, you can redisplay it by choosing More ➪ Unhide Columns in the ribbon's Records group. This action displays a dialog box that lets you selectively unhide columns by checking next to each field. Click Close to return to the datasheet showing the desired columns. Also use this dialog box to hide one or more columns by unchecking the check box next to each field you want to hide.

Freezing columns

When you want to scroll left and right among many columns but want to keep certain columns from scrolling out of view, choose More ⇨ Freeze in the ribbon's Records group. With this command, for example, you can keep the ProductID and Description fields visible while you scroll through the datasheet to find the product's features. The frozen columns are visible on the far-left side of the datasheet while other fields scroll horizontally out of sight. The fields must be contiguous if you want to freeze more than one at a time. (Of course, you can first move your fields to place them next to each other.) When you're ready to unfreeze the datasheet columns, simply choose More ⇨ Unfreeze.

Tip
When you unfreeze columns, the column doesn't move back to its original position. You must move it back manually.

Saving the changed layout

When you close the datasheet, you save all your data changes but you might lose all your layout changes. As you make all these display changes to your datasheet, you probably won't want to make them again the next time you open the same datasheet. If you make any layout changes, Access prompts you to save the changes to the layout when you close the datasheet. Choose Yes to save the changes. You can also save the layout changes manually by clicking Save on the Quick Access toolbar.

Caution
If you're following the example, don't save the changes to tblProducts.

Saving a record

Access saves each record when you move off it. Pressing Shift+Enter or selecting Save from the ribbon's Records group saves a record without moving off it. Closing the datasheet also saves a record.

Sorting and Filtering Records in a Datasheet

The ribbon's Sort & Filter group (shown in Figure 6.18) lets you rearrange the order of the rows and reduce the number of rows. Using the commands in this group, you'll display the records you want in the order you want to see them. The following sections demonstrate how to use these commands.

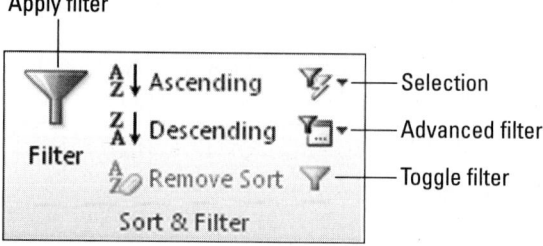

FIGURE 6.18

The Sort & Filter group lets you change the record order and narrow the number of rows.

Sorting your records with QuickSort

Sometimes you might simply want to sort your records in a desired order. The QuickSort ribbon commands let you sort selected columns into either ascending or descending order. To use these commands, click in a field you want to sort by, and then click Ascending (A–Z) or Descending (Z–A). The data redisplays instantly in the sorted order. Right-clicking on a column and selecting either Sort A to Z or Sort Z to A also sorts the data.

To sort your data on the basis of values in multiple fields, highlight more than one column: Highlight a column (see the "Changing the field order" section, earlier in this chapter), hold down the Shift key, and drag the cursor to the right. When you select one of the QuickSort commands, Access sorts the records into major order (by the first highlighted field) and then into orders within orders (based on subsequent fields). If you need to select multiple columns that aren't contiguous (next to each other), you can move them next to each other (see the "Changing the field order" section, earlier in this chapter).

Tip
To display the records in their original order, use the Remove Sort command in the Sort & Filter ribbon group.

Filtering a selection

Filter by Selection lets you select records on the basis of the current field value. For example, using `tblProducts`, move your cursor to the `Category` column and click the Ascending (A to Z) command. Access sorts the data by the vehicle's category. Now place your cursor in a row containing Trucks in the `Category` column. Press the Selection command in the ribbon's Sort & Filter group and choose `Equals "Trucks"`. Access filters the datasheet to show only those records where the `Category` is trucks.

Access gives you four choices when you click the Selection command:

- Equals "Trucks"
- Does Not Equal "Trucks"

- Contains "Trucks"
- Does Not Contain "Trucks"

The area to the right of the Navigation buttons — at the bottom of the Datasheet window — tells you whether the datasheet is currently filtered; in addition, the Toggle Filter command on the ribbon is highlighted, indicating that a filter is in use. When you click this command, it removes the filter. The filter specification does not go away; it's simply turned off. Click the Toggle Filter command again to apply the same filter.

Filtering by selection is additive. You can continue to select values, each time pressing the Selection command.

Tip
Right-click the field content that you want to filter by and then select from the available menu choices.

If you want to further specify a selection and then see everything that *doesn't* match that selection (for example, where the Make field is not Chevrolet), move the cursor to the field (the Make field where the value is Chevrolet), right-click on the datasheet, and then select Does Not Equal "Chevrolet" from the filter options that appear in the right-click shortcut menu.

When using the Selection command on numeric or date fields, select Between from the available command to enter a range of values. Enter the smallest and largest numbers or oldest and newest dates to limit the records to values that fall in the desired range.

Imagine using this technique to review sales by salespeople for specific time periods or products. Filtering by selection provides incredible opportunities to drill down into successive layers of data. Even when you click the Toggle Filter command to redisplay all the records, Access still stores the query specification in memory. Figure 6.19 shows the filtered datasheet, with the Filter by Select list still open on the Category field.

When a datasheet is filtered, each column has an indicator in the column heading letting you know if a filter is applied to that column. Hover the mouse over the indicator to see a tooltip displaying the filter. Click on the indicator to specify additional criteria for the column using the pop-up menu shown in Figure 6.20. Click on the column heading's down-arrow for an unfiltered column to display a similar menu.

The menu contains commands to sort the column ascending or descending, clear the filter from the field, select a specific filter, and check values you want to see in the datasheet. The available commands change based on the data type of the column. In this case, Text Filter lets you enter a criterion that filters the data based on data you type in.

FIGURE 6.19

Using Filter by Selection. In this case, you see all trucks that are not Chevrolet models.

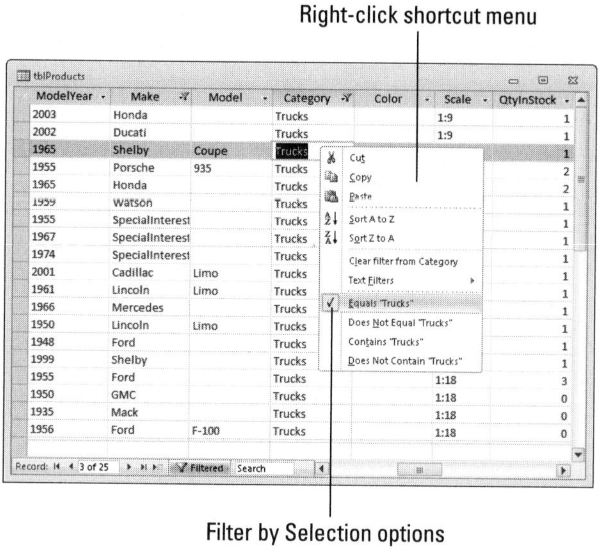

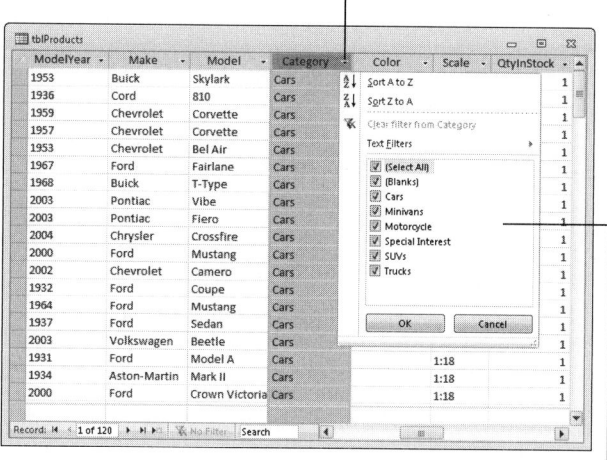

Right-click shortcut menu

Filter by Selection options

FIGURE 6.20

Filtering the Category field. Use the column filter menu to select criteria for a field.

Filter by Selection button

Filter by Selection IB+

The check boxes in this menu contain data that appears in the column. In this case, the choices are: (Select All), (Blanks), Minivans, Cars, SUV, Trucks, Motorcycles, and SpecialInterest. Click (Select All) to see all the records regardless of this field's value. Click (Blanks) to see the records that don't contain data. Select any of the data values to limit the records where the field contains the selected values. Click on Minivans and Cars to display the records where `Category` is equal to Minivans or Cars.

If you want to filter data but you can't find the value that you want to use and you know the value, click the Text Filters (or Number Filters, Date Filters, and so on) command and choose one of the available commands (Equals, Does Not Equal, Begins With, and so on) to display a dialog box where you type in the desired value.

Filtering by form

Filter by Form lets you enter criteria into a single row on the datasheet. Clicking the Filter by Form button transforms the datasheet into a single row containing a drop-down list in every column. The drop-down list contains all the unique values for the column. An Or tab at the bottom of the window lets you specify *OR* conditions for each group. Choose Advanced ➪ Filter by Form in the ribbon's Sort & Filter group to enter Filter by Form mode, shown in Figure 6.21.

Select values from the combo boxes or type values you want to search for in the field. If you want to see records where the `Category` is Trucks or SUVs, select Trucks from the `Category` drop-down list, click the Or tab at the bottom of the window, and then select SUVs from the `Category` drop-down list. To see records where `Category` is SUV and `QtyInStock` is 1, select SUV from the `Category` drop-down and type 1 in `QtyInStock`. Once you enter the desired criteria, click the Toggle Filter command to apply the filter. (The Toggle Filter button is shown back in Figure 6.3.)

FIGURE 6.21

Using Filter by Form lets you set multiple conditions for filtering at one time. Notice the Or tab at the bottom of the window.

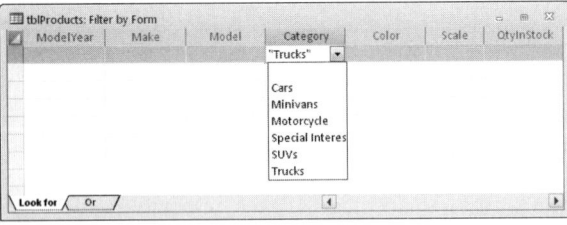

Enter as many conditions as you need using the Or tab. If you need even more advanced manipulation of your selections, you can choose Advanced ➪ Advanced Filter/Sort from the ribbon's Sort & Filter group to get an actual QBE (Query by Example) screen that you can use to enter more-complex criteria.

Cross-Reference
Chapters 4 and 5 discuss queries and using operators and expressions.

Focusing on Special Features of Datasheets

Historically, Access datasheets have always borne a close resemblance to Excel worksheets. Not only do worksheets and datasheets look alike, but in many ways they work alike as well. As you've seen in this chapter, Access datasheets support sorting, searching, freezing columns, and other features mirrored in Excel worksheets. But, until recently, there was little else that was common between Access datasheets and Excel worksheets.

Unlike Excel worksheets, Access datasheets haven't supported row and column summation and other types of data aggregation. Beginning with Access 2007, and continued in Access 2010, Access datasheets support a Totals row at the bottom of datasheets (see Figure 6.22). The Totals row is opened by clicking on the Totals button in the ribbon's Records group on the Home tab (the Totals button is marked with a Greek sigma character, much like the AutoSum button in Excel). Each column in the totals row can be set to a different aggregate calculation (Sum, Average, Minimum, Maximum, Count, Standard Deviation, and Variance).

To use the Totals row, open a table or form in Datasheet view and click on the Totals button in the Records group on the ribbon's Home tab. Access adds a Totals row at the bottom of the datasheet, just below the New row.

FIGURE 6.22

The datasheet Totals row

New row

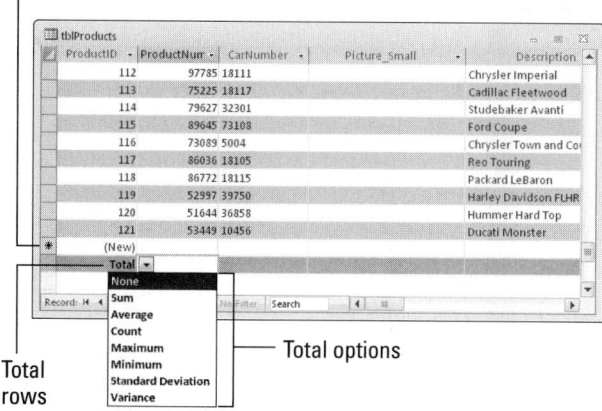

Total rows

Total options

Clicking on a column in the Totals row transforms the datasheet cell to a drop-down list. The items in the drop-down list are specific for the column's data type. For example, in text columns the drop-down list shows only None and Count, while a numeric column contains a full complement of totals calculations (Sum, Average, Count, and so on). DateTime columns include None, Average, Count, Minimum, and Maximum.

The Totals calculation you choose is dynamic. As you change data in the datasheet or underlying table, the calculation results displayed in the Totals row are automatically updated after a very short delay. Recalculating a lot of totals extracts a small performance penalty, so you might want to hide the Totals row (described below) when its special features aren't needed.

The Totals options you choose for the columns in a datasheet persist. If you close the datasheet and report it, the Totals row is still there.

To remove the Totals row, open the datasheet and click the Totals button in the Records group on the ribbon. One interesting behavior of the Totals row is, if you choose to remove it, you can restore it later on (by clicking the Totals button again) and the row is restored to its original setting.

Printing Records

You can print all the records in your datasheet in a simple row-and-column layout. In Chapter 9, you learn to produce formatted reports. For now, the simplest way to print is to click the Print icon in the Quick Access toolbar. This prints the datasheet to the Windows default printer. Click on the Microsoft Office Button to view other print options, shown in Figure 6.23.

FIGURE 6.23

The Microsoft Office Print menu

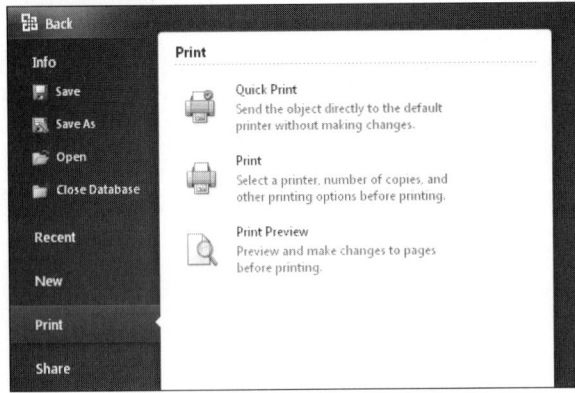

The printout reflects all layout options that are in effect when the datasheet is printed. Hidden columns don't print. Gridlines print only if the cell gridline properties are on. The printout also reflects the specified row height and column width.

Only so many columns and rows can fit on a page; the printout takes up as many pages as required to print all the data. Access breaks up the printout as necessary to fit on each page. For example, the tblProducts printout might be six pages — three pages across are needed to print all the fields in tblProducts, and each record requires three pages in length. Each record of tblContacts might need four pages in length. The number of pages depends on your layout and your printer.

Printing the datasheet

You can also control printing from the Print dialog box, which you open by clicking the Microsoft Office Button, and then clicking on Print. From the Print dialog box, customize your printout by selecting from several options:

- **Print Range:** Prints the entire datasheet or only selected pages or records
- **Copies:** Determines the number of copies to be printed
- **Collate:** Determines whether multiple copies are collated

You can also click the Properties button and set options for the selected printer or select the printer itself to change the type of printer. The Setup button allows you to set margins and print headings.

Using the Print Preview window

Although you may have all the information in the datasheet ready to print, you may be unsure of whether to change the width or height of the columns or rows, or whether to adjust the fonts to improve your printed output. To preview your print job, click the Print Preview command under the Print menu to display the Print Preview window. The default view is the first page in single-page preview. Use the ribbon commands to select different views and zoom in and out. Click Print to print the datasheet to the printer. Click the Close Print Preview command on the right side of the ribbon to return to Datasheet view.

Summary

In this chapter, you learned how to open and navigate around in a datasheet using the keyboard, ribbons, and navigation buttons. You learned to enter new records and edit data in existing records, as well as how to undo changes you made to the data. You saw what happens when Access validates each field based on its data type.

You also customized the fonts, colors, column widths, row heights, and other visual aspects of the datasheet. You froze and unfroze columns and hid them from view. You limited the number of records using different types of filters and sorted the records using the QuickSort commands. I also covered printing datasheets and some of the printing options available to you when working with Datasheet view.

Creating Basic Access Forms

Forms provide the most flexible way for viewing, adding, editing, and deleting your data. They're also used for *switchboards* (forms with buttons that provide navigation), for dialog boxes that control the flow of the system, and for messages. Controls are the objects on forms such as labels, text boxes, buttons, and many others. In this chapter, you learn how to create different types of forms. I also fill you in on the types of controls that are used on a form. This chapter also discusses form and control properties, and how you determine the appearance and behavior of an Access interface through setting or changing property values.

The forms you add to an Access database are a critical aspect of the application you create. In most situations, users should not be permitted direct access to tables or query datasheets. It's far too easy for a user to delete valuation information or incorrectly input data into the table. Forms provide a valuable tool for managing the integrity of a database's data. Because forms can contain VBA code or macros, a form can verify data entry or confirm deletions before they occur. Also, a properly designed form can reduce training requirements by helping the user understand what kind of data is required by displaying a message as the user tabs into a control. Or, a form can provide default values or perform calculations based on data input by the user or retrieved from a database table.

IN THIS CHAPTER

Creating different types of forms

Adding controls to a form

Working with the Property Sheet

On the CD-ROM

In this chapter, you use `tblProducts`, `tblCustomers`, **and other tables in** `Chapter07.accdb`.

Formulating Forms

Use the Forms group on the Create tab of the ribbon to add forms to your database. The commands in the Forms group — shown in Figure 7.1 — let you create the following different types of forms and ways to work with Access forms:

FIGURE 7.1

Use the Form group on the ribbon's Create tab to add new forms to your database.

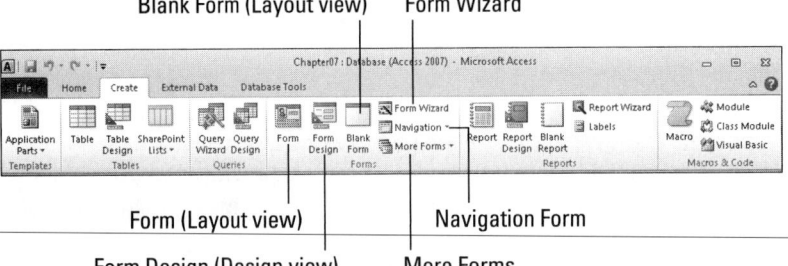

- **Form:** Creates a new form that lets you enter information for one record at a time. You must have a table, query, form, or report open or selected to use this command. When you click on the Form button with a table or query highlighted in the Navigation Pane, Access binds the new form to the data source and opens the form in Layout view.

- **Form Design:** Creates a new blank form and displays it in Design view. If a table or query is selected in the Navigation Pane when the Form Design button is clicked, the new form is automatically bound to the data source.

- **Blank Form:** Instantly creates a blank form with no controls. The new form is not bound to a data source, and it opens in Layout view. You must specify a data source (table or query) and build the form by adding controls from the data source's Field List.

- **Form Wizard:** Access features a simple wizard to help you get started building forms. The wizard asks for the data source, provides a screen for selecting fields to include on the form, and lets you choose from a number of very basic layouts for the new form.

- **Navigation Form:** The Access navigation form is a specialized form intended to provide user navigation through an application. Navigation forms are discussed in detail later in this chapter.

New Feature

The navigation form is new to Access 2010.

- **More Forms:** The More button in the Forms group drops down a gallery containing a number of other form types.

- **Multiple Items:** This is a simple tabular form that shows multiple records bound to the selected data source.

- **Datasheet:** Creates a form that is displayed as a datasheet.

- **Split Form:** Creates a split form, which shows a datasheet in the upper, lower, left, or right area of the form, and a traditional form in the opposite section for entering information on the record selected in the datasheet.

- **Modal Dialog:** Provides a template for a modal dialog form. A modal dialog form (often called a *dialog box*) stays on the screen until the user provides information requested by the dialog, or is dismissed by the user.

- **PivotChart:** Instantly creates a PivotChart form.

- **Pivot Table:** Creates a form consisting of a PivotTable.

If any of the terminology in the preceding bullets is new to you, don't worry — each of these terms is discussed in detail in this chapter. Keep in mind that the Access ribbon and its contents are very context dependent, so every item may not be available at the time you access the Create tab.

Creating a new form

Like many other aspects of Access development, Access provides multiple ways of adding new forms to your application. The easiest is to select a data source, such as a table, and click the Form command in the Create ribbon tab. Another is to use the Form Wizard and allow the wizard to guide you through the process of specifying a data source and other details of the new form.

Using the Form command

Use the Form command in the ribbon's Form group to automatically create a new form based on a table or query selected in the Navigation Pane.

Note

This process was called AutoForm in previous versions of Access.

To create a form based on tblProducts, follow these steps:

1. Select tblProducts in the Navigation Pane.

2. Select the Create tab on the ribbon.

3. Click on the Form command in the Form group.

   Access creates a new form containing all the fields from tblProducts displayed in Layout view, shown in Figure 7.2. Layout view lets you see the form's data while changing the layout of controls on the form. (The form shown in Figure 7.2 is included in the Chapter07.accdb example database as tblProducts_AutoForm.)

FIGURE 7.2

Use the Form command to quickly create a new form with all the fields from a table or query.

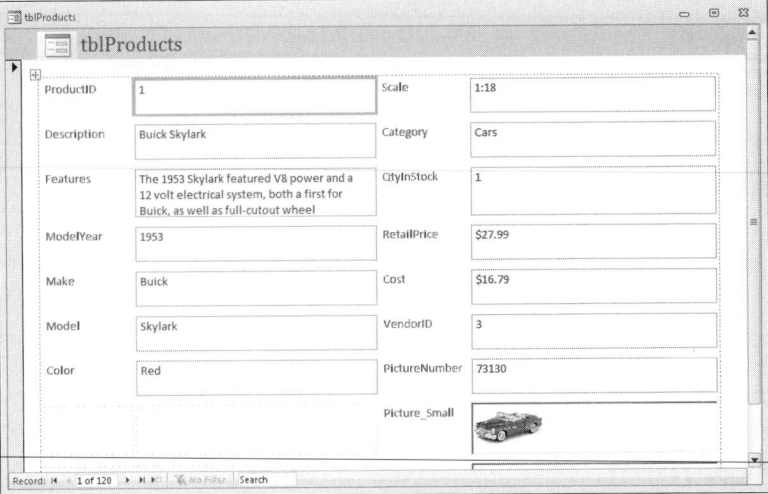

The new form is opened in Layout view, which is populated with all the controls in the underlying data source. Layout view gives you a good idea how the controls appear relative to one another, but it can't be used for resizing controls or moving controls about on the form. Right-click on the form's title bar and select Design View to rearrange controls on the form.

The Form Design button in the Forms group does essentially the same thing as the Form button, except that no controls are added to the form's design surface and the form is opened in Design view. Form Design is most useful when you're creating a new form that might not use all the fields in the underlying data source, and you want more control over control placement from the start.

Similarly, the Blank Form option opens a new empty form, but this time in Layout view. You add controls to the form's surface from the Field List, but you have little control over control placement. The Blank Form option is most useful for quickly building a form with bound controls with little need for precise placement. A new blank form can be produced in less than a minute.

Using the Form Wizard

Use the Form Wizard command in the Forms group to create a form using a wizard. The Form Wizard visually walks you through a series of questions about the form that you want to create and then creates it for you automatically. The Form Wizard lets you select which fields you want on the form, the form layout (Columnar, Tabular, Datasheet, Justified), the form style (Access 2003, Access 2010, Apex, and so on), and the form title.

To start the Form Wizard based on tblCustomers, follow these steps:

1. Select tblCustomers in the Navigation Pane.
2. Select the Create tab on the ribbon.
3. Click on the Form Wizard button in the Forms group.

   Access starts the Form Wizard shown in Figure 7.3.

FIGURE 7.3

Use the Form Wizard to create a form with the fields you choose.

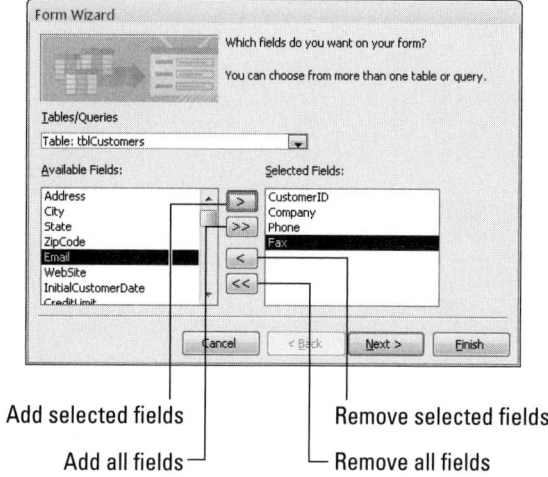

Add selected fields · Add all fields · Remove selected fields · Remove all fields

The wizard is initially populated with fields from tblCustomers, but you can choose another table or query with the Tables/Queries drop-down list above the field selection area. Use the buttons in the middle of the form to add and remove fields to the Available Fields and Selected Fields list boxes.

Note

You can also double-click any field in the Available Fields list box to add it to the Selected Fields list box.

The series of buttons at the bottom of the form let you navigate through the other steps of the wizard. The types of buttons available here are common to most wizard dialog boxes:

- **Cancel:** Cancel the wizard without creating a form.
- **Back:** Return to the preceding step of the wizard.
- **Next:** Go to the next step of the wizard.
- **Finish:** End the wizard using the current selections.

Caution

If you click Next or Finish without selecting any fields, Access tells you that you must select fields for the form before you can continue.

Clicking Next opens the second wizard dialog box (shown in Figure 7.4) where you specify the overall layout and appearance of the new form.

FIGURE 7.4

Select the overall layout for the new form.

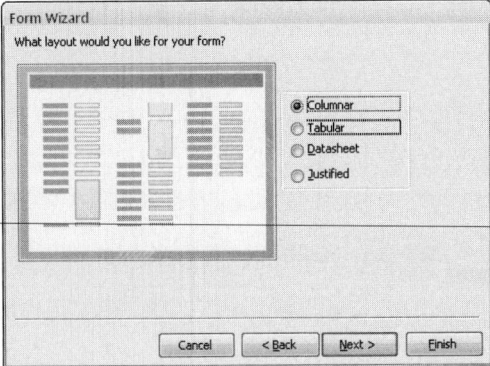

The Columnar layout is the wizard default, but you can also choose the Tabular, Datasheet, or Justified options. Clicking Next takes you to the last wizard dialog box (shown in Figure 7.5), where you provide a name for the new form.

FIGURE 7.5

Saving the new form

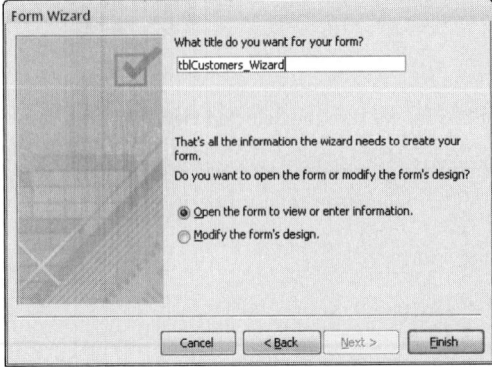

The main advantage of using the Form Wizard is that it binds the new form to a data source and adds controls for the selected fields. In most cases, however, you still have considerable work to do after the Form Wizard has finished.

Looking at special types of forms

When working with Access, the word *form* can mean any of several different things, depending on context. This section discusses several different ways that "forms" are used in Access, and presents an example of each usage.

Navigation forms

New Feature

Access 2010 introduces an entirely new form intended specifically as a navigation tool for users. Navigation forms include a number of tabs that provide instant access to any number of other forms in a form/subform arrangement. The Navigation ribbon button offers a number of button placement options (shown in Figure 7.6). Horizontal Tabs is the default.

FIGURE 7.6

The Navigation button provides a number of tab placement options.

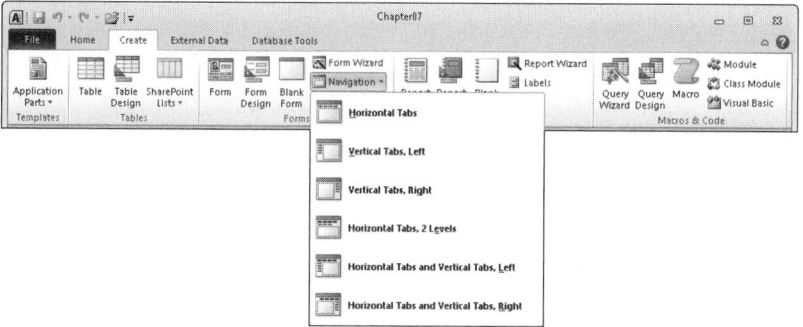

Selecting a tab placement in the Navigation drop-down list opens the new navigation form in Design view (see Figure 7.7). The new form includes a row of tabs along the top and a large area under the tabs for embedding subforms. You type the tab's label (like Products) directly into the tab, or add it through the tab's Caption property. As you complete the tab's label, Access adds a new, blank tab to the right of the current tab.

In Figure 7.7, the Horizontal Tabs option was selected when choosing a navigation form template. The alternatives to Horizontal Tabs (Vertical Tabs, Left, Vertical Tabs, Right, and so on) are shown in Figure 7.6.

FIGURE 7.7

The Navigation form features a large area for embedding subforms.

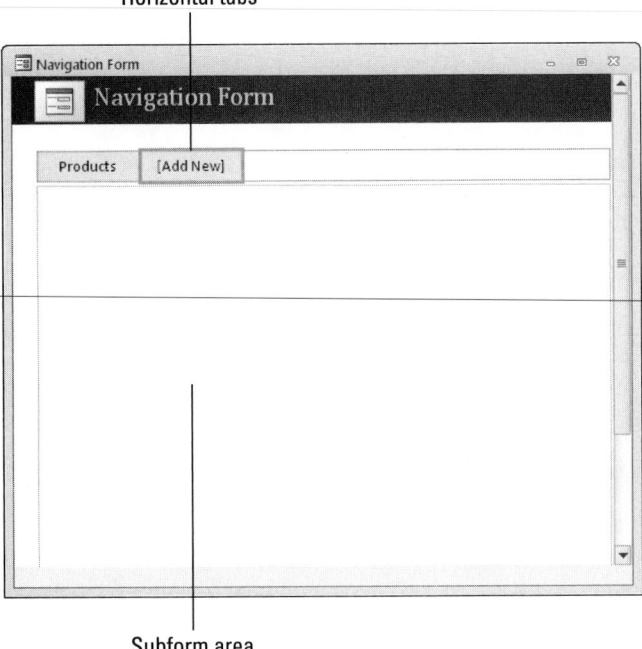

Horizontal tabs

Subform area

The tab's Property Sheet (shown in Figure 7.8) includes the Navigation Target Name property for specifying the Access form to use as the tab's subform. Select a form from the drop-down list in the Navigation Target Name property, and Access creates the association to the subform for you.

FIGURE 7.8

Use the `Navigation Target Name` property to specify the tab's subform.

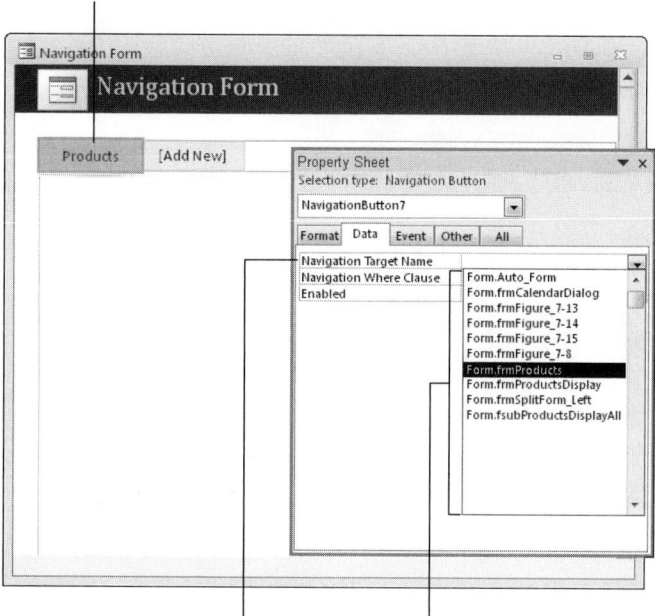

Selected tab

Navigation Target Name property   List of all forms in database

The completed navigation form is shown in Figure 7.9. The auto-generated navigation form makes extravagant use of screen space. There are a number of things that could be done to enhance this form, such as removing the navigation form's header section and reducing the empty space surrounding the subform. `frmProducts` shown in Figure 7.9 is included in the `Chapter07.accdb` example database.

FIGURE 7.9

A navigation form is a quick and easy way to provide basic navigation features.

Tabs   Navigation form header

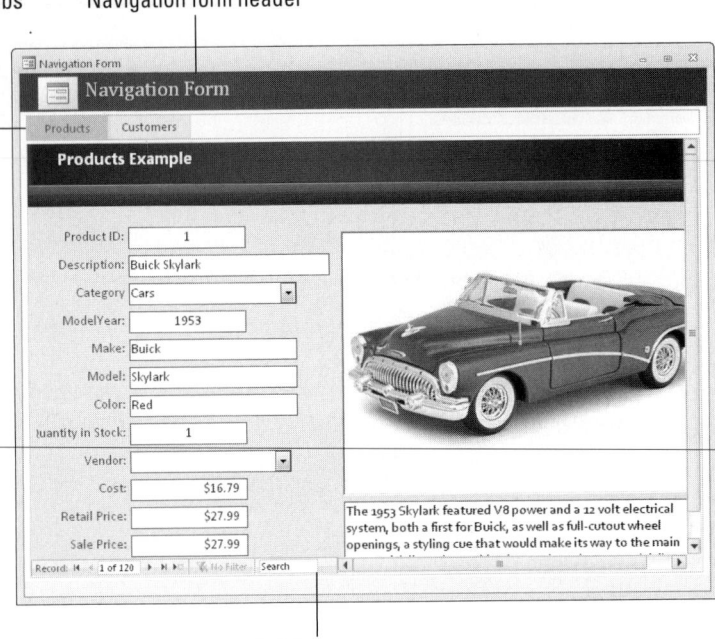

Subform area

Multiple-items forms

Click the `More Forms` button in the ribbon's Form group, and then click the Multiple Items button, to create a tabular form based on a table or query selected in the Navigation Pane. A tabular form is much like a datasheet, but it's much more attractive than a plain datasheet.

Cross-Reference

Chapter 6 discusses datasheets in detail.

Because the tabular form is truly an Access form, you can convert the default text box controls on the form to combo boxes, list boxes, and other advanced controls. Because tabular forms display multiple records at one time, they're very useful when you're reviewing or updating multiple records. To create a multiple-items form based on `tblProducts`, follow these steps:

1. Select `tblProducts` in the Navigation Pane.
2. Select the Create tab on the ribbon.
3. Click the More Forms button and click Multiple Items.

Access creates a new multiple-items form based on `tblProducts` displayed in Layout view (as shown in Figure 7.10). Although the form looks similar to a datasheet, you can only resize the rows and columns in Design view and Layout view.

Create a multiple-items form when you want to see data similar to Datasheet view.

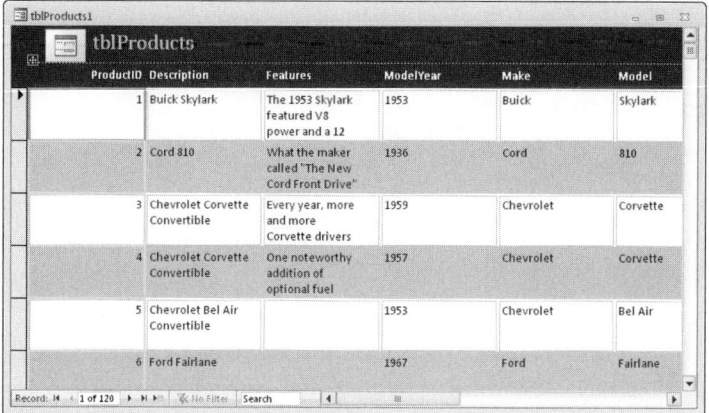

Split forms

Click the `More Forms` button in the ribbon's Form group, and then click the Split Form button, to create a split form based on a table or query selected in the Navigation Pane. The split-form feature gives you two views of the data at the same time, letting you select a record from a datasheet in the upper section and edit the information in a form in the lower section.

To create a split form based on `tblProducts`, follow these steps:

1. Select `tblProducts` in the Navigation Pane.
2. Select the Create tab on the ribbon.
3. Click the More Forms button and click Split Form.

    Access creates a new split form based on `tblCustomers` displayed in Layout view (shown in Figure 7.11). Resize the form and use the splitter bar in the middle to make the lower section completely visible.

The `Split Form Orientation` property determines whether the datasheet is on the top, bottom, left, or right of the form area. The default is as shown in Figure 9-11, with the datasheet area on the bottom. `frmCustomers_SplitForm` (shown in Figure 7.11) is included in the `Chapter07.accdb` example database.

FIGURE 7.11

Create a split form when you want to select records from a list and edit them in a form. Use the splitter bar to resize the upper and lower sections of the form.

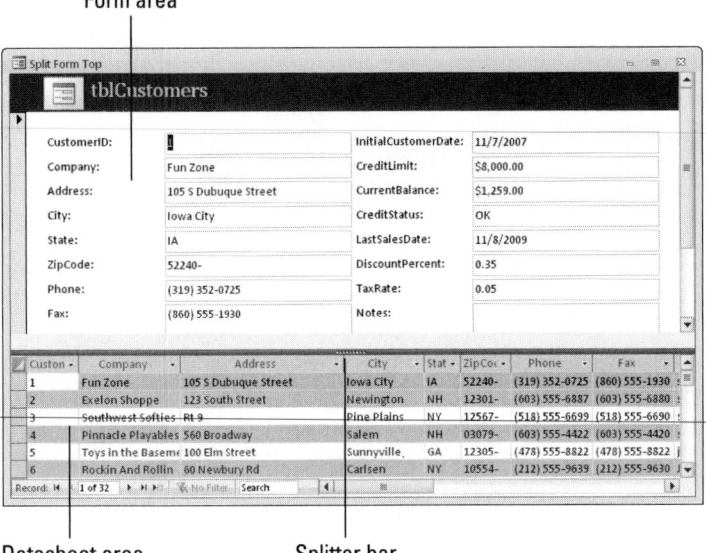

Datasheet forms

Click the More Forms button in the ribbon's Form group, and then click the Datasheet button, to create a form that looks like a table or query's datasheet. A datasheet form is useful when you want to see the data in a row and column format, but you want to limit which fields are displayed and editable.

To create a datasheet form based on tblProducts, follow these steps:

1. Select tblProducts in the Navigation Pane.

2. Select the Create tab on the ribbon.

3. Click the Form group's More Forms button and click Datasheet.

   You can view any form you create as a datasheet by selecting Datasheet View from the ribbon's View drop-down. A datasheet form appears in Datasheet View by default when you open it.

Tip

You can prevent users from viewing a form as a datasheet by setting the form's properties. You'll learn more about form properties in the "Introducing Properties" section, later in this chapter.

Resizing the form area

The white area of the form is where you work. This is the size of the form when it's displayed. Resize the white area of the form by placing the cursor on any of the area borders and dragging the border of the area to make it larger or smaller. Figure 7.12 shows a blank form in Design view being resized.

FIGURE 7.12

Design view of a blank form. Resize the form area by dragging the bottom-right corner.

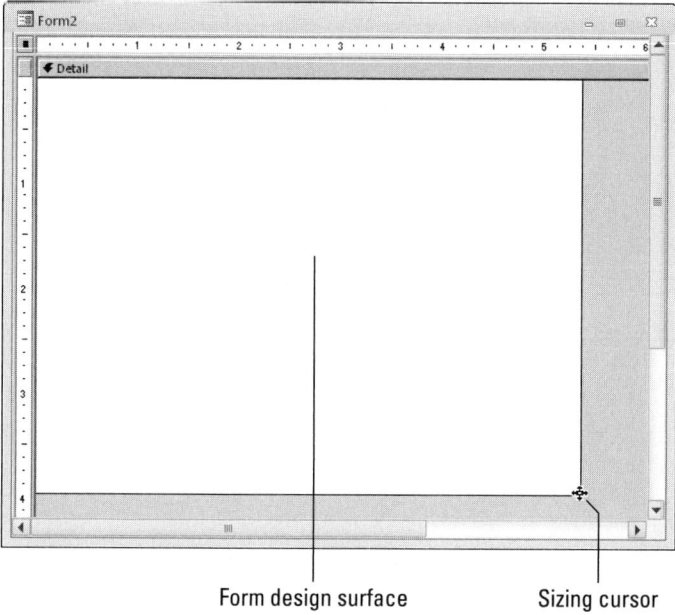

Form design surface   Sizing cursor

Saving your form

You can save the form at any time by clicking on the Save button in the Quick Access toolbar. When you're asked for a name for the form, give it a meaningful name (for example, frmProducts, frmCustomers, frmProductList.) Once you've given the form a name, you won't be prompted the next time you click Save.

When you close a form after making changes, Access asks you to save it. If you don't save a form, all changes since you opened the form (or since you last clicked Save) are lost. You should frequently save the form while you work if you're satisfied with the results.

Tip

If you're going to make extensive changes to a form, you might want to make a copy of the form. For example, if you want to work on the form frmProducts, you can copy and then paste the form in the Navigation Pane, giving it a name like frmProductsOriginal. Later, when you've completed your changes and tested them, you can delete the original copy.

Working with Controls

Controls and properties form the basis of forms and reports. It's critical to understand the fundamental concepts of controls and properties before you begin to apply them to custom forms and reports.

Note
Although this chapter is about forms, you'll learn that forms and reports share many common characteristics, including controls and what you can do with them. As you learn about controls in this chapter, you'll be able to apply nearly everything you learn when you create reports.

The term *control* has many definitions in Access. Generally, a control is any object on a form or report, such as a label or text box. These are the same sort of controls used in any Windows application, such as Access, Excel, or Web-based HTML forms, or those that are used in any language, such as .NET, Visual Basic, C++, or C#. Although each language or product has different file formats and different properties, a text box in Access is similar to a text box in any other Windows product.

You enter data into controls and display data using controls. A control can be bound to a field in a table (when the value is entered in the control, it's also saved in some underlying table field), or data can be unbound and displayed in the form but not saved when the form is closed. A control can also be an object, such as a line or rectangle.

Some controls that aren't built into Access are developed separately — these are ActiveX controls. ActiveX controls extend the basic feature set of Access and are available from a variety of vendors.

Whether you're working with forms or reports, essentially the same process is followed to create and use controls. In this chapter, I explain controls from the perspective of a form.

Categorizing controls

Forms and reports contain many different types of controls. You can add these controls to forms using the Controls group on the Design tab, shown in Figure 7.13. Hovering the mouse over the control displays a tooltip telling you what the control is.

FIGURE 7.13

The Design tab lets you add and customize controls in a form's Design view.

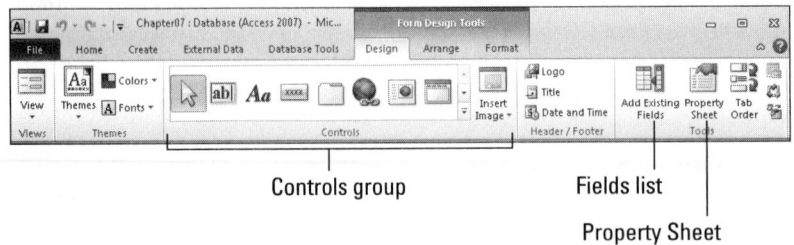

Table 7.1 briefly describes the basic Access controls.

TABLE 7.1

Controls in Access Forms

Control	What It Does
Text Box	Displays and allows users to edit data.
Label	Displays static text that typically doesn't change.
Button	Also called a command button. Calls macros or runs VBA code when clicked.
Combo Box	A drop-down list of values. Combo boxes include a text box at the top for inputting values that are not included in the drop-down list.
List Box	A list of values that is always displayed on the form or report.
Subform/Subreport	Displays another form or report within the main form or report.
Line	A graphical line of variable thickness and color, which is used for separation.
Rectangle	A rectangle can be any color or size or can be filled in or blank; the rectangle is used for emphasis.
Image	Displays a bitmap picture with very little overhead.
Option Group	Holds multiple option buttons, check boxes, or toggle buttons.
Check Box	A two-state control, shown as a square that contains a check mark if it's on and an empty square if it's off.
Option Button	Also called a radio button, this button is displayed as a circle with a dot when the option is on.
Toggle Button	This is a two-state button — up or down — which usually uses pictures or icons instead of text to display different states.
Tab Control	Displays multiple pages in a file folder type interface.
Page	Adds a page on the form or report. Additional controls are added to the page, and multiple pages may exist on the same form
Chart	This chart displays data in a graphical format.
Unbound Object Frame	This frame holds an OLE object or embedded picture that isn't tied to a table field and can include graphs, pictures, sound files, and video.
Bound Object Frame	This frame holds an OLE object or embedded picture that is tied to a table field.
Page Break	This is usually used for reports and indicates a physical page break.
Hyperlink	This control creates a link to a Web page, a picture, an e-mail address, or a program.
Attachment	This control manages attachments for the Attachment data type. Attachment fields (see Chapter 2) provide a way to *attach* external files (such as music or video clips or Word documents) to Access tables.

The Use Control Wizards button, revealed by expanding the Controls group by clicking on the More button in the lower-right corner of the group, doesn't add a control to a form. Instead, the `Use Control Wizards` button determines whether a wizard is automatically activated when you add certain controls. The Option Group, Combo Box, List Box, Subform/Subreport, Bound and Unbound Object Frame, and Command Button controls all have wizards to help you when you add a new control. You can also use the ActiveX Controls button (also found at the bottom of the expanded Controls group) to display a list of ActiveX controls, which you can add to Access.

There are three basic categories of controls: bound, unbound, and calculated.

Bound controls

These are controls that are bound to a field in the data source underlying the form. When you enter a value into a bound control, Access automatically updates the field in the current record. Most of the controls used for data entry can be bound. Controls can be bound to most data types, including `Text`, `Date/Time`, `Number`, `Yes/No`, `OLE Object`, and `Memo` fields.

Unbound controls

Unbound controls retain the entered value, but they don't update any table fields. You can use these controls for text label display, for controls such as lines and rectangles, or for holding unbound OLE objects (such as bitmap pictures or your logo) that aren't stored in a table but on the form itself. Very often, VBA code is used to work with data in unbound controls and directly update Access data sources.

Cross-Reference
Turn to Chapters 13 and 19 for details on using VBA control to manipulate forms and controls and working with unbound data.

Calculated controls

Calculated controls are based on expressions, such as functions or calculations. Calculated controls are unbound because they don't directly update table fields. An example of a calculated control is `=[SalePrice] - [Cost]`. This control calculates the total of two table fields for display on a form but is not bound to any table field. The value of an unbound calculated control may be referenced by other controls on the form, or used in an expression in another control on the form or in VBA in the form's module.

Adding a control

You add a control to a form in one of three ways:

- **By clicking a button in the Design ribbon's Controls group and drawing a new unbound control on the form:** Use the control's `ControlSource` property to bind the new control to a field in the form's data source.

- **By dragging a field from the Field List to add a bound control to the form:** Access automatically chooses a control appropriate for the field's data type and binds the control to the selected field.

- **By double-clicking a field in the Field List to add a bound control to the form:** Double-clicking works just like dragging a field from the Field List to the form. The only difference is that, when you add a control by double-clicking a field, Access decides where to add the new control to the form. Usually the new control is added to the right of the most-recently added control, and sometimes below it.

Using the Controls group

When you use the buttons in the Controls group to add a control, you decide which type of control to use for each field. The control you add is *unbound* (not attached to the data in a table field) and has a default name such as `Text21` or `Combo11`. After you create the control, you decide what table field to bind the control to, enter text for the label, and set any properties. You'll learn more about setting properties later in this chapter.

You can add one control at a time using the Controls group. To create three different unbound controls, perform these steps:

1. With the form created earlier open in Design view, click the Text Box button (ab|) in the Controls group.

2. Move the mouse pointer to the Form Design window, and click and drag the new control onto the form's surface in its initial size and position.

3. Click the Option button in the Controls group, click on the form's surface, and drag the Option button to its initial position and size on the form.

4. Click the Check Box button in the Controls group and add it to the form as you added the other controls.

   When you're done, your screen should resemble Figure 7.14.

Tip

Clicking the Form Design window with a control selected creates a default-size control. If you want to add multiple controls of the same type, double-click on the icon in the Controls group to lock it down, and then draw as many controls as you want on the form. Click the selector control (the arrow) to unlock the control and return to normal operation.

FIGURE 7.14

Unbound controls added from the Controls group

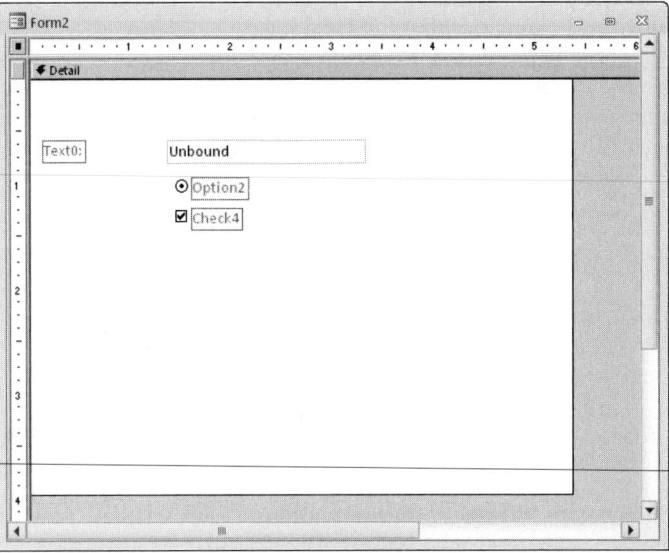

Using the Field List

The Field List displays a list of fields from the table or query the form is based on. Open the Field List by clicking the Add Existing Fields button in the Tools group on the ribbon's Design tab (refer to Figure 7.13).

Drag fields from the Field List and drop them on the form to create bound controls. Select and drag them one at a time, or select multiple fields by using the Ctrl key or Shift key:

- **To select multiple contiguous fields,** hold down the Shift key and click the first and last fields that you want.

- **To select multiple noncontiguous fields,** hold down the Ctrl key and click each field that you want.

By default, the Field List appears docked on the right of the Access window, shown in Figure 7.15. The Field List window is movable and resizable and displays a vertical scrollbar if it contains more fields than can fit in the window.

Most often, dragging a field from the Field List adds a bound text box to the Design window. If you drag a Yes/No field from the Field List window, Access adds a check box. Optionally, you can select the type of control by selecting a control from the Controls group and dragging the field to the Design window.

FIGURE 7.15

Click Add Existing Fields in the Tools group to show the Field List.

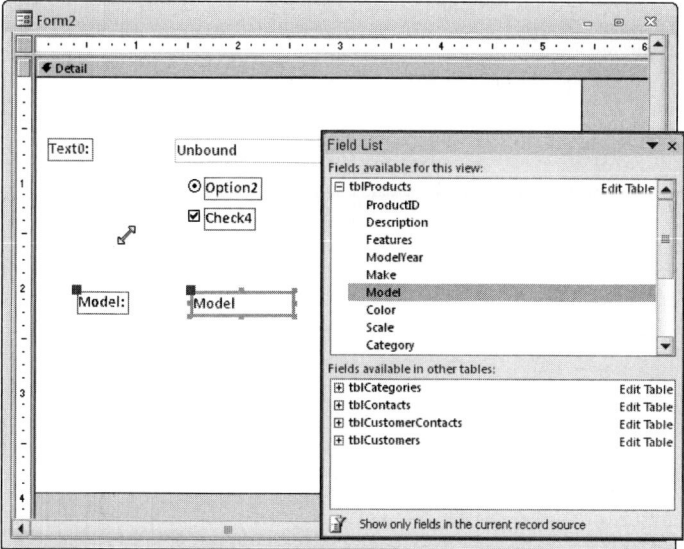

Caution

When you drag fields from the Field List window, the first control is placed where you release the mouse button. Make sure that you have enough space to the left of the control for the labels. If you don't have enough space, the labels slide under the controls.

You gain several distinct advantages by dragging a field from the Field List window:

- The control is automatically bound to the field.
- Field properties inherit table-level formats, status-bar text, and data-validation rules and messages.
- The label control and label text are created with the field name as the caption.
- The label control is attached to the field control, so they move together.

Select and drag the Description, Category, RetailPrice, and Cost fields from the Field List window to the form, as shown in Figure 7.16. Double-clicking a field also adds it to the form.

FIGURE 7.16

Drag fields from the Field List to add bound controls to the form.

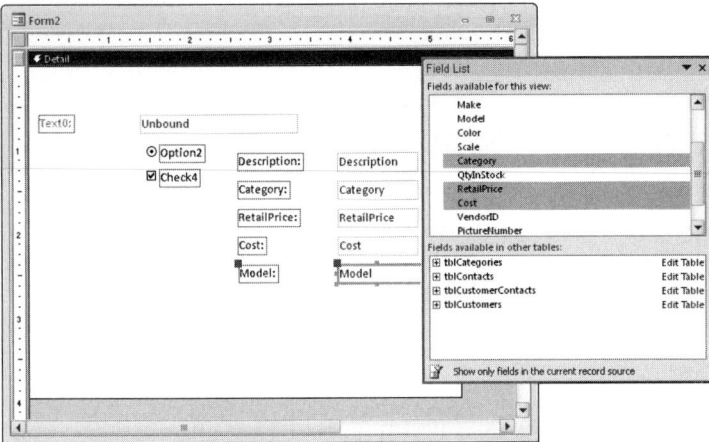

You can see four new controls in the form's Design view — each one consists of a Label control and a Text Box control (Access attaches the Label control to the text box automatically). You can work with these controls as a group or independently, and you can select, move, resize, or delete them. Notice that each control has a label with a caption matching the field name, and the Text Box control displays the bound field name used in the text box. If you want to resize just the control and not the label, you must work with the two controls (label and associated text box) separately.

Close the Field List by clicking the Add Existing Fields command in the ribbon's Tools group or the Close button on the Field List.

Tip

In Access, you can change the type of control after you create it; then you can set all the properties for the control. For example, suppose that you add a field as a Text Box control and you want to change it to a List Box. Right-click the control and select Change To from the pop-up menu to change the control type. However, you can change only from some types of controls to others. You can change almost any type of control to a Text Box control, while option buttons, toggle buttons, and check boxes are interchangeable, as are List Box and Combo Box controls.

In the "Introducing Properties" section, later in this chapter, you learn how to change the control names, captions, and other properties. Using properties speeds the process of naming controls and binding them to specific fields. If you want to see the differences between bound and unbound controls, switch to Form view using the View command in the ribbon's View group. The `Description`, `Category`, `RetailPrice`, and `Cost` controls display data because they're bound to `tblProducts`. The other three controls don't display data because they aren't bound to any data source.

Note

As you add controls from the Field List, Access builds the form's `RecordSource` property as a SQL statement. The `RecordSource` after adding these four fields is

```
SELECT tblProducts.Model, tblProducts.Description, tblProducts.Category,
    tblProducts.RetailPrice, tblProducts.Cost FROM tblProducts;
```

Selecting and deselecting controls

After you add a control to a form, you can resize it, move it, or copy it. The first step is to select one or more controls. Depending on its size, a selected control might show from four to eight *handles* (small squares called *moving and sizing handles*) around the control — at the corners and midway along the sides. The move handle in the upper-left corner is larger than the other handles and you use it to move the control. You use the other handles to size the control. Figure 7.17 displays some selected controls and their moving and sizing handles.

FIGURE 7.17

A conceptual view of selecting controls and their moving and sizing handles

Moving handle

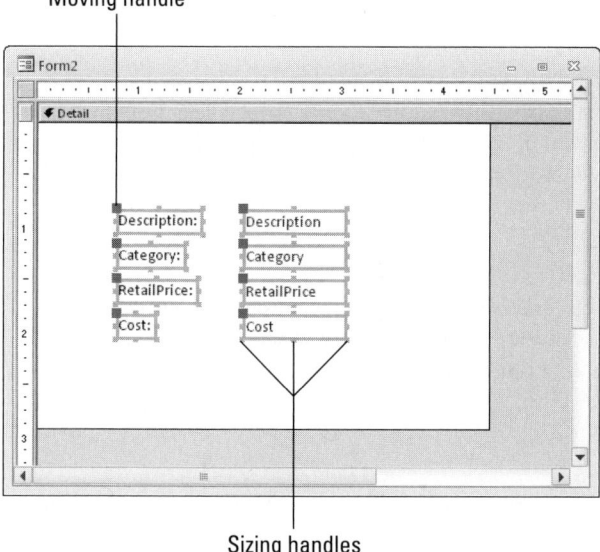

Sizing handles

The Select command (which looks like an arrow) in the Controls group must be chosen in order for you to select a control. If you use the Controls group to create a single control, Access automatically reselects the pointer as the default.

Selecting a single control

Select any individual control by clicking anywhere on the control. When you click a control, the sizing handles appear. If the control has an attached label, the move handle for the label also appears in the upper-left corner of the control. If you select a label control that is associated with another control, all the handles for the label control are displayed, and only the move handle appears in the associated control.

Selecting multiple controls

You select multiple controls in these ways:

- Click each control while holding down the Shift key.
- Drag the pointer through or around the controls that you want to select.
- Click and drag in the ruler to select a range of controls.

Figure 7.17 shows the result of selecting the multiple bound controls graphically. When you select multiple controls by dragging the mouse, a rectangle appears as you drag the mouse. Be careful to drag the rectangle only through the controls you want to select. Any control you touch with the rectangle or enclose within it is selected. If you want to select labels only, make sure that the selection rectangle only encloses the labels.

Tip

If you find that controls are not selected when the rectangle passes through the control, you may have the global selection behavior property set to `Fully Enclosed`. This means that a control is selected only if the selection rectangle completely encloses the entire control. Change this option by clicking the Microsoft Office Button and selecting Access Options. Then select Object Designers and set the Forms/Reports Selection behavior to `Partially Enclosed`.

Tip

By holding down the Shift or `Ctrl` key, you can select several noncontiguous controls. This lets you select controls on totally different parts of the screen. Click on the form in Design view and then press `Ctrl+A` to select all the controls on the form. Press `Shift` or `Ctrl` and click on any selected control to remove it from the selection.

Deselecting controls

Deselect a control by clicking an unselected area of the form that doesn't contain a control. When you do so, the handles disappear from any selected control. Selecting another control also deselects a selected control.

Manipulating controls

Creating a form is a multistep process. The next step is to make sure that your controls are properly sized and moved to their correct positions. The Layout tab of the ribbon — shown in Figure 7.18 — contains commands used to assist you in manipulating controls.

FIGURE 7.18

The Arrange tab lets you move and resize controls, as well as manipulate the form's overall layout.

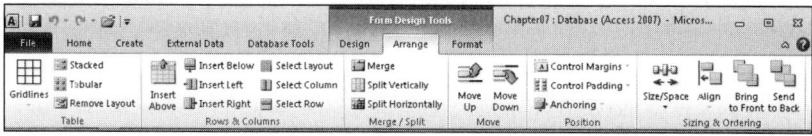

Resizing a control

You *resize* controls using any of the smaller handles in the upper, lower, and right edges of the control. The sizing handles in the control corners let you drag the control larger or smaller in both width and height — and at the same time. Use the handles in the middle of the control sides to size the control larger or smaller in one direction only. The top and bottom handles control the height of the control; the left and right handles change the control's width.

When the mouse pointer touches a corner handle of a selected control, the pointer becomes a diagonal double arrow. You can then drag the sizing handle until the control is the desired size. If the mouse pointer touches a side handle in a selected control, the pointer changes to a horizontal or vertical double-headed arrow. Figure 7.19 shows the Description control after being resized. Notice the double-headed arrow in the corner of the Description control.

FIGURE 7.19

Resizing a control

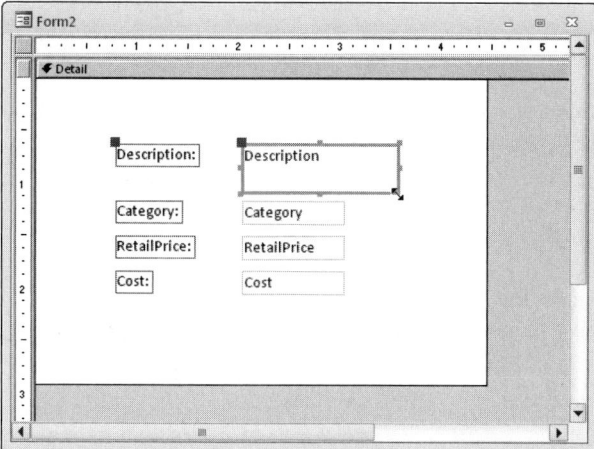

Tip

You can resize a control in very small increments by holding the Shift key while pressing the arrow keys (up, down, left, and right). This technique also works with multiple controls selected. Using this technique, a control changes by only 1 pixel at a time (or moves to the nearest grid line if Snap to Grid is selected in the Layout ribbon's Control Layout group).

When you double-click on any of the sizing handles, Access resizes a control to a best fit the text contained in the control. This feature is especially handy if you increase the font size and then notice that the text is cut off either at the bottom or to the right. For label controls, note that this best-fit sizing adjusts the size vertically and horizontally, though text controls are resized only vertically. This is because when Access is in Form Design mode, it can't predict how much of a field to display — the field name and field contents can be radically different. Sometimes, Access doesn't correctly resize the label and you must manually change its size.

Sizing controls automatically

The Size and Ordering group on the Arrange ribbon tab has several commands that help the arrangement of controls:

- **To Fit:** Adjusts control height and width for the font of the text they contain.
- **To Tallest:** Makes selected controls the height of the tallest selected control.
- **To Shortest:** Makes selected controls the height of the shortest selected control.
- **To Grid:** Moves all sides of selected controls in or out to meet the nearest points on the grid.
- **To Widest:** Makes selected controls the width of the widest selected control.
- **To Narrowest:** Makes selected controls the height of the narrowest selected control.

Tip

You can access many commands by right-clicking after selecting multiple controls. When you right-click on multiple controls, a shortcut menu displays choices to size and align controls.

Moving a control

After you select a control, you can easily move it, using either one of these methods:

- Click on the control and hold down the mouse button; the cursor changes to a four-directional arrow. Drag the mouse to move the control to a new location.
- Click once to select the control and move the mouse over any of the highlighted edges; the cursor changes to a four-directional arrow. Drag the mouse to move the control to a new location.
- Select the control and use the arrow keys on the keyboard to move the control. Using this technique, a control changes by only 1 pixel at a time (or moves to the nearest grid line if Snap to Grid is selected in the Layout ribbon's Control Layout group).

Figure 7.20 shows a Label control that has been separately moved to the top of the Text Box control. The four-directional arrow cursor indicates that the controls are ready to be moved together. To see this cursor, the control(s) must already be selected.

FIGURE 7.20

Moving a control

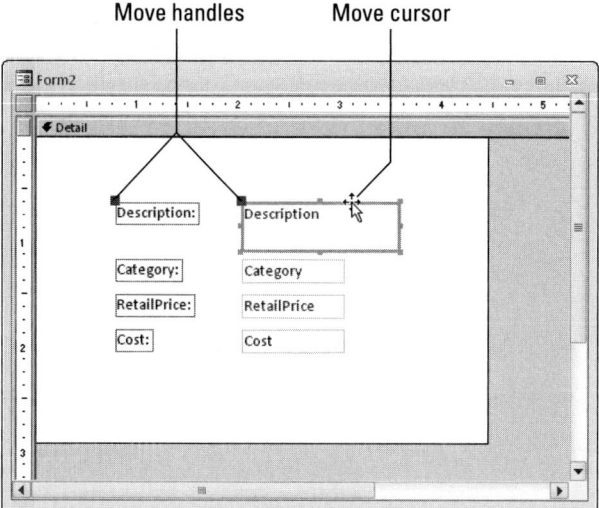

Press Esc before you release the mouse button to cancel a moving or a resizing operation. After a move or resizing operation is complete, click the Undo button on the Quick Access toolbar to undo the changes, if needed.

Aligning controls

You might want to move several controls so that they're all aligned. The Sizing and Ordering group on the Arrange tab contains the following alignment commands:

- **Left:** Aligns the left edge of the selected controls with the leftmost selected control.
- **Right:** Aligns the right edge of the selected controls with the rightmost selected control.
- **Top:** Aligns the top edge of the selected controls with the topmost selected control.
- **Bottom:** Aligns the bottom edge of the selected controls with the bottommost selected control.
- **To Grid:** Aligns the top-left corners of the selected controls to the nearest grid point.

You can align any number of selected controls by selecting an align command. When you choose one of the align commands, Access uses the control that is the closest to the desired selection as the model for the alignment. For example, suppose that you have three controls and you want to left-align them. They're aligned on the basis of the control farthest to the left in the group of the three controls.

Figure 7.21 shows several sets of controls. The first set of controls is not aligned. The label controls in the middle set of controls have been left-aligned while the text box controls in the right-side set have been right-aligned.

An example of unaligned and aligned controls on the grid

Each type of alignment must be done separately. In this example, you can left-align all the labels or right-align all the text boxes at once.

The sizing grid has been turned off in Figure 7.21. By default, Access displays a series of small dots across the entire surface of a form while it's in Design view. The grid can assist you in aligning controls. Hide or display the grid by selecting the Grid command from the Size/Space gallery under the Sizing & Ordering group in the Arrange ribbon tab. You can also hide or display the ruler using the Ruler command in the same gallery.

Use the Snap to Grid command in the Size/Space gallery to align controls to the grid as you draw or place them on a form. This also aligns existing controls to the grid when you move or resize them.

As you move or resize existing controls, Access lets you move only from grid point to grid point. When Snap to Grid is off, Access ignores the grid and lets you place a control anywhere on the form or report.

Tip

You can temporarily turn Snap to Grid off by pressing the Ctrl key before you create a control (or while sizing or moving it). You can change the grid's fineness (number of dots) from form to form by using the Grid X and Grid Y form properties. (Higher numbers indicate greater fineness.)

Cross-Reference
You'll learn more about form properties in Chapter 8.

The Arrange tab's Sizing & Ordering group contains commands to adjust spacing between controls. The spacing commands adjust the distance between controls on the basis of the space between the first two selected controls. If the controls are across the screen, use horizontal spacing; if they're down the screen, use vertical spacing. The spacing commands are

- **Equal Horizontal:** Makes the horizontal space between selected controls equal. You must select three or more controls in order for this command to work.

- **Increase Horizontal:** Increases the horizontal space between selected controls by one grid unit.

- **Decrease Horizontal:** Decreases the horizontal space between selected controls by one grid unit.

- **Equal Vertical:** Makes the vertical space between selected controls equal. You must select three or more controls in order for this command to work properly.

- **Increase Vertical:** Increases the vertical space between selected controls by one grid unit.

- **Decrease Vertical:** Decreases the vertical space between selected controls by one grid unit.

Tip
Aligning controls aligns the only the controls themselves. If you want to align the text within the controls (also known as justifying the text), you must use the Format tab's Font group and click the Left, Right, or Center buttons.

Modifying the appearance of a control
To modify the appearance of a control, select the control and click on commands that modify that control, such as the options in the Font or Controls group. Follow these steps to change the text color and font of the Description label:

1. Click the Description label on the form.
2. In the Format tab's Font group, change Font Size to 14, click the Bold button, and change Font Color to blue.
3. Resize the Description label so the larger text fits.

   Remember: You can double-click any of the sizing handles to autosize the label.

To modify the appearance of multiple controls at once, select the controls and click on commands to modify the controls, such as commands in the Font or Controls group. To change the text color and font of the Description, Category, and Cost labels and text boxes, follow these steps:

1. Select the three labels and three text boxes by dragging a selection box through them (refer to Figure 7.11).

2. In the Format tab's Font group, change the Font Size to 14, click the Bold button, and change Font Color to blue.

3. Resize the labels and text boxes so the larger text fits.

   Remember: You can double-click any of the sizing handles to autosize the controls.

   As you click the commands, the controls' appearances change to reflect the new selections (shown in Figure 7.22). The fonts in each control increase in size, become bold, and turn blue. Any changes you make apply to all selected controls.

FIGURE 7.22

A typical form containing multiple controls.

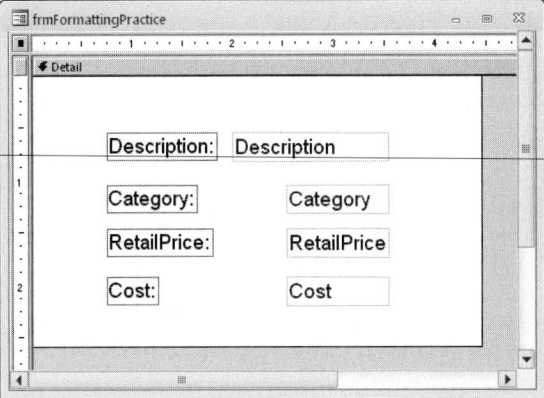

When multiple controls are selected, you can also move the selected controls together. When the cursor changes to the four-directional arrow, click and drag to move the selected controls. You can also change the size of all the controls at once by resizing one of the controls in the selection. All the selected controls increase or decrease by the same number of units.

Grouping controls

If you routinely change properties of multiple controls, you might want to group them together. To group controls together, select the controls by holding down the Shift key and clicking them or dragging the selection box through them. After the desired controls are selected, select the Group command from the Arrange tab's Size/Space group. A box appears around the selected controls, as shown in Figure 7.23, indicating that they're grouped together.

After you've grouped the controls together, whenever you click any of the controls inside the group, the entire group is selected. Double-click on a control to select just that one control. After a single control in the group is selected, you can click on any other control to select it.

FIGURE 7.23

Grouping multiple controls together

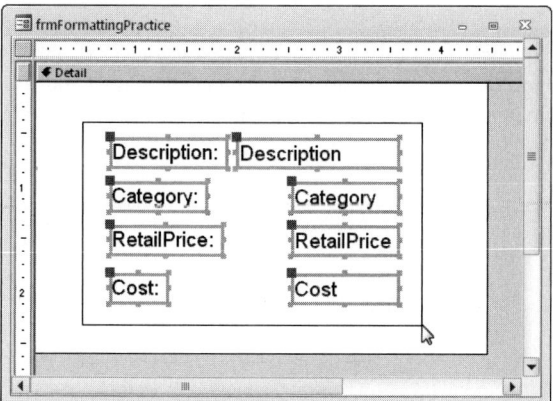

To resize the entire group, put your mouse on the side you want to resize. After the double arrow appears, click and drag until you reach the desired size. Every control in the group changes in size. To move the entire group, click and drag the group to its new location. With grouped controls, you don't have to select all the controls every time you change something about them.

To remove a group, select the group by clicking any field inside the group, and then select the Ungroup command from the Layout ribbon's Control Layout group.

Attaching (and reattaching) a label to a control

If you accidentally delete a label from a control, you can reattach it. To create and then reattach a label to a control, follow these steps: Later in this chapter, in the "Naming control labels and their captions" section, you'll learn about the special relationship between a control and its label. By default, Access controls include a label when the control is added to a form, and moves around with the control as you reposition the control on the form. The "Naming control labels and their captions" section describes these behaviors and how to work with control labels.

1. Click the Label button on the Controls group.

2. Place the mouse pointer in the Form Design window.

   The mouse pointer becomes the Text Box button.

3. Click and hold down the mouse button where you want the control to begin; drag the mouse to size the control.

4. Type **Description:** and click outside the control.

5. Select the Description label control.

6. Select Cut from the Home ribbon's Clipboard group.

7. Select the `Description` text box control.

8. Select Paste from the Home ribbon's Clipboard group to attach the label control to the text-box control.

Another way to attach a label to a control is to click the informational icon next to the label, shown in Figure 7.24. This informational icon lets you know that this label is unassociated with a control. Select the Associate Label with a Control command from the menu, and then select the control you want to associate the label with.

Associating a label with a control

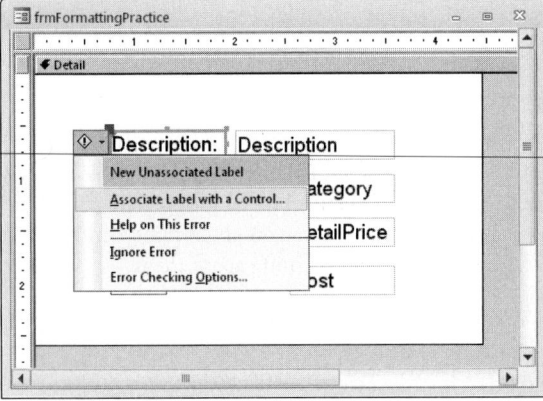

Changing a control's type

In Figure 7.25, the `Complete` control is a check box. Although there are times you may want to use a check box to display a Boolean (yes/no) data type, there are other ways to display the value, such as a toggle button. A toggle button is raised if it's true and depressed (or at least very unhappy) if it's false.

Use these steps to turn a check box into a toggle button:

1. Select the `Complete` label control (just the label control, not the check box).

2. Press Delete to delete the label control because it isn't needed.

3. Right-click the `Complete` check box, and choose Change To ⇨ Toggle Button from the pop-up menu.

4. Resize the toggle button and click inside it to get the blinking cursor; then type **After** on the button as its caption (shown on the right of Figure 7.25).

FIGURE 7.25

Become a magician and turn a check box into a toggle button.

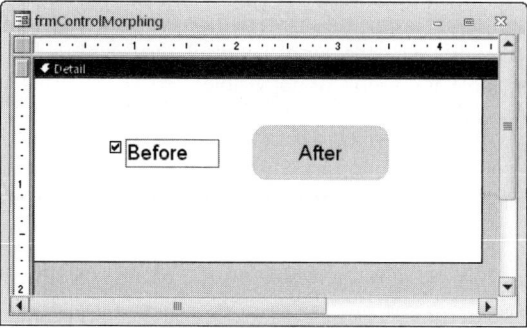

Copying a control

You can create copies of any control by copying it to the Clipboard and then pasting the copies where you want them. If you have a control for which you've entered many properties or specified a certain format, you can copy it and revise only the properties (such as the control's name and bound field name) to make it a different control. This capability is useful with a multiple-page form when you want to display the same values on different pages and in different locations, or when copying a control from one form to another.

Deleting a control

You can delete a control by simply selecting it in the form's Design view and pressing the Delete key on your keyboard. The control and any attached labels will disappear. You can bring them back by immediately selecting Undo from the Quick Access toolbar. You can also select Cut from the Home ribbon's Clipboard group or Delete from the Home ribbon's Records group.

You can delete more than one control at a time by selecting multiple controls and pressing Delete. You can delete an entire group of controls by selecting the group and pressing Delete. If you have a control with an attached label, you can delete only the label by clicking the label itself and then selecting one of the delete methods. If you select the control, both the control and the label are deleted.

To delete only the label of the Description control, follow the next set of steps (this example assumes that you have the `Description` text box control in your Form Design window):

1. Select the `Description` label control only.
2. Press Delete to remove the label from the form.

Introducing Properties

Properties are named attributes of controls, fields, or database objects that are used to modify the characteristics of a control, field, or object. Examples of these attributes are the size, color, appearance, or name of an object. A property can also modify the behavior of a control, determining, for example, whether the control is read-only or editable and visible or not visible.

Properties are used extensively in forms and reports to change the characteristics of controls. Each control on the form has properties. The form itself also has properties, as does each of its sections. The same is true for reports; the report itself has properties, as does each report section and individual control. The label control also has its own properties, even if it's attached to another control.

Everything that you do with the ribbon commands — from moving and resizing controls to changing fonts and colors — can be done by setting properties. In fact, all these commands do is change properties of the selected controls.

Displaying the Property Sheet

Properties are displayed in a Property Sheet (sometimes called a Property window). To display the Property Sheet for the Description text box, follow these steps:

1. Drag `Description`, `Category`, `RetailPrice`, and `Cost` from the Field List to the form's Design view.

2. Click the `Description` text box control to select it.

3. Click the Property Sheet command in the Design ribbon's Tools group, or press F4 to display the Property Sheet.

   The screen should look like the one shown in Figure 7.26. In Figure 7.26, the Description text box control has been selected and the Format tab in the Property Sheet is being scrolled to find the margin properties associated with a text box.

Because the Property Sheet is a window, it can be undocked, moved, and resized. It does not, however, have Maximize or Minimize buttons.

There are several ways to display a control's Property Sheet if it's not visible:

- Select a control and click the Property Sheet command in the Design tab's Tools group.
- Double-click any control.
- Right-click any control and select Properties from the pop-up menu.
- Press F4 while any control is selected.

FIGURE 7.26

Change an object's properties with the Property Sheet.

Selected control   Tabs

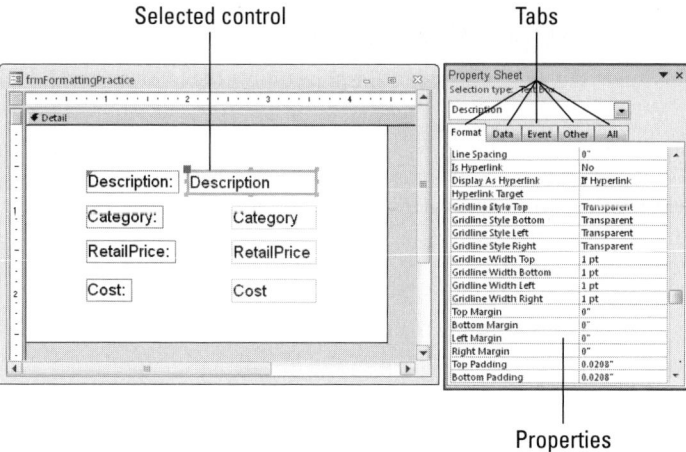

Properties

Getting acquainted with the Property Sheet

With the Property Sheet displayed, click on any control in Design view to display the properties for that control. Select multiple controls to display similar properties for the selected controls. The vertical scroll bar lets you move between various properties.

The Property Sheet has an All tab that lets you see all the properties for a control. Or you can choose another tab to limit the view to a specific group of properties. The specific tabs and groups of properties are as follows:

- **Format:** These properties determine how a label or value looks: font, size, color, special effects, borders, and scroll bars.

- **Data:** These properties affect how a value is displayed and the data source it is bound to: control source, input masks, validation, default value, and other data-type properties.

- **Event:** Event properties are named events, such as clicking a mouse button, adding a record, pressing a key for which you can define a response (in the form of a call to a macro or a VBA procedure), and so on.

- **Other:** Other properties show additional characteristics of the control, such as the name of the control or the description that displays in the status bar.

Cross-Reference

The number of properties available in Access has increased greatly since early versions of Access. The most important properties are described in various chapters of this book. For a discussion of Event properties and Event procedures, see Part II.

Figure 7.26 shows the Property Sheet for the Description text box. The first column lists the property names; the second column is where you enter or select property settings or options.

Changing a control's property setting

There are many different methods for changing property settings, including the following:

- Enter or select the desired value in a Property Sheet.
- For some properties, double-clicking the property name in the Property Sheet cycles through all the acceptable values for the property.
- Change a property directly by changing the control itself, such as changing its size.
- Use inherited properties from the bound field or the control's default properties.
- Enter color selections for the control by using the ribbon commands.
- Change label text style, size, color, and alignment by using the ribbon commands.

You can change a control's properties by clicking a property and typing the desired value.

In Figure 7.27, you see a down arrow and a button with three dots to the right of the Control Source property-entry area. Some properties display a drop-down arrow in the property-entry area when you click in the area. The drop-down arrow tells you that Access has a list of values from which you can choose. If you click the down arrow in the Control Source property, you find that the drop-down list displays a list of all fields in the data source — tblProducts. Setting the Control Source property to a field in a table creates a bound control.

FIGURE 7.27

Setting a control's Control Source property

Drop-down button

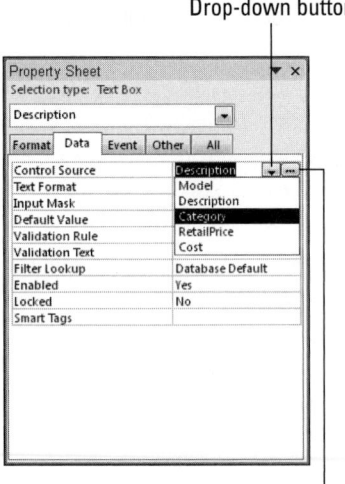

Builder button

Some properties have a list of standard values such as Yes or No; others display varying lists of fields, forms, reports, or macros. The properties of each object are determined by the control itself and what the control is used for.

A nice feature in Access is the ability to cycle through property choices by repeatedly double-clicking on the choice. For example, double-clicking on the Display When property alternately selects Always, Print Only, and Screen Only.

The Builder button contains an ellipsis (...) and opens one of the many builders in Access — including the Macro Builder, the Expression Builder, and the Module Builder. When you open a builder and make some selections, the property is filled in for you. You'll learn about builders later in this book.

Each type of object has its own property window and properties. These include the form itself, each of the form sections, and each of the form's controls. You display each of the property windows by clicking on the object first. The property window will instantly change to show the properties for the selected object.

Naming control labels and their captions

You might notice that each of the data fields has a label control and a text-box control. Normally, the label's Caption property is the same as the text box's Name property. The text box's Name property is usually the same as the table's field name — shown in the Control Source property. Sometimes, the label's Caption is different because a value was entered into the Caption property for each field in the table.

When creating controls on a form, it's a good idea to use standard naming conventions when setting the control's Name property. Name each control with a prefix followed by a meaningful name that you'll recognize later (for example, txtTotalCost, cboState, lblTitle). Table 7.2 shows the naming conventions for form and report controls. You can find a very complete, well-established naming convention online at www.xoc.net/standards.

The properties displayed in Figure 7.27 are the specific properties for the Description text box. The first two properties, Name and Control Source, are set to Description.

The Name is simply the name of the field itself. When a control is bound to a field, Access automatically assigns the Name property to the bound field's name. Unbound controls are given names such as Field11 or Button13. However, you can give the control any name you want.

With bound controls, the Control Source property is the name of the table field to which the control is bound. In this example, Description refers to the field with the same name in tblProducts. An unbound control has no control source, whereas the control source of a calculated control is the actual expression for the calculation, as in the example =[SalePrice] - [Cost].

TABLE 7.2

Form/Report Control-Naming Conventions

Prefix	Object
frb	Bound object frame
cht	Chart (graph)
chk	Check box
cbo	Combo box
cmd	Command button
ocx	ActiveX custom control
det	Detail (section)
gft[n]	Footer (group section)
fft	Form footer section
fhd	Form header section
ghd[n]	Header (group section)
hlk	Hyperlink
img	Image
lbl	Label
lin	Line
lst	List box
opt	Option button
grp	Option group
pge	Page (tab)
brk	Page break
pft	Page footer (section)
phd	Page header (section)
shp	Rectangle
rft	Report footer (section)
rhd	Report header (section)
sec	Section
sub	Subform/subreport
tab	Tab control
txt	Text box
tgl	Toggle button
fru	Unbound object frame

Summary

In this chapter, you learned how to add different types of forms to your database using the Create ribbon's Form group. You learned about the different types of controls and how to add them to the form. Then you learned how to move and resize these controls.

You also learned how properties are the building blocks of an object. The Property Sheet contains every attribute of the control, from where it's located on the form to what data it displays to what font it's displayed in. You learned how to display the Property Sheet and how to change a few properties, including the Name property, using naming conventions.

Working with Data on Access Forms

In Chapter 7, you learned about the tools necessary to create and display a form — Design view, bound and unbound controls, the Field list, and the ribbon's Controls group. In this chapter, you learn how to work with data on the form, view and change the form's properties, and use Access's Layout view.

An Access application's user interface is made up of forms. Forms display and change data, accept new data, and interact with the user. Forms convey a lot of the personality of an application, and a carefully designed user interface dramatically reduces the training required of new users.

Most often, the data displayed on Access forms is bound (either directly or indirectly) to Access tables. Changes made to a form's data affect the data stored in the underlying tables.

On the CD-ROM

In this chapter, you use `tblProducts`, `tblSales`, and `tblContacts` in the `Chapter08.accdb` database to provide the data necessary to create the examples.

IN THIS CHAPTER

Viewing and modifying data in Form view

Editing form data

Printing Access forms

Understanding form properties

Adding form headers and footers

Adjusting a form's layout

Adding calculated controls to a form

Converting a form to a report

Using Form View

Form view is where you actually view and modify data. Working with data in Form view is similar to working with data in a table or query's Datasheet view. Form view presents the data in a user-friendly format, which you create and design.

Cross-Reference

For more information on working in Datasheet view, see Chapter 6.

To demonstrate the use of the Form view, follow these steps to create a new form based on `tbl-Products`:

1. Select `tblProducts` in the Navigation pane.
2. Click the Create tab on the ribbon.
3. Click the Form command in the Form group.
4. Click the Form view button on the Home tab's Views group to switch from Layout view to Form view.

Figure 8.1 shows the Access window with the newly created form displayed in Form view. This view has many of the same elements as Datasheet view. At the top of the screen, you see the Access title bar, the Quick Access toolbar, and the ribbon. The form in the center of the screen displays your data, one record at a time.

FIGURE 8.1

A form in Form view

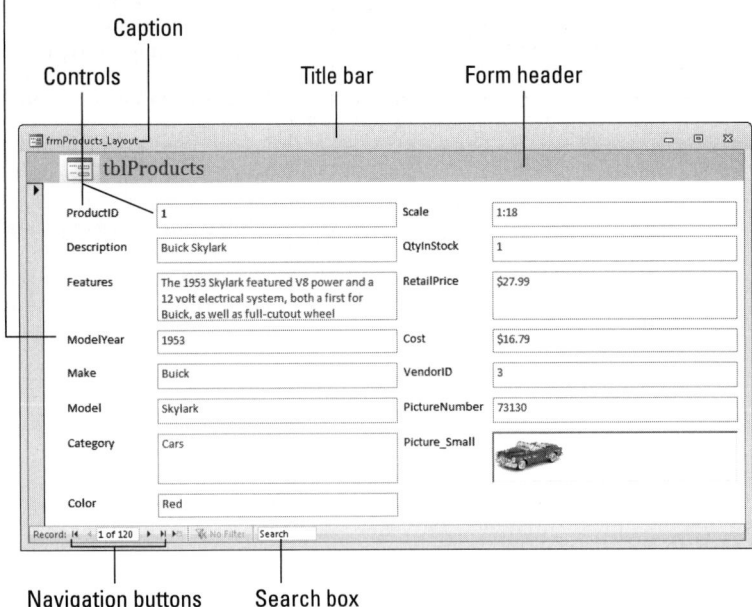

Tip

If the form contains more fields than can fit on-screen at one time, Access automatically displays a horizontal and/or vertical scroll bar that you can use to see the remainder of the data. You can also see the rest of the data by pressing the PgDn key. If you're at the bottom of a form, or the entire form fits on the screen without scrolling, and you press PgDn, you'll move to the next record.

The status bar at the bottom of the window displays the active field's Description property that you defined when you created the table (or form). If no Description exists for a field, Access displays "Form View" in the status bar. Generally, error messages and warnings appear in dialog boxes in the center of the screen (rather than in the status bar). The navigation controls, search box, and view shortcuts are found at the bottom of the screen. These features lets you move from record to record, quickly find data, or switch views.

Looking at the Home ribbon tab

The Home ribbon tab (shown in Figure 8.2) provides a way to work with the data. The Home ribbon tab has some familiar objects on it, as well as some new ones. This section provides an overview of the form's Home tab. The individual commands are described in more detail later in this chapter. Keep in mind that the Access ribbon and its controls is very context-sensitive. Depending on your current task, one of more of the commands may be grayed out or not visible. Although this behavior can be confusing, Microsoft's intent is to simplify the ribbon as much as possible to allow you to focus on the task at hand, and not have to deal with irrelevant commands as you work.

FIGURE 8.2

The Form ribbon's Home tab

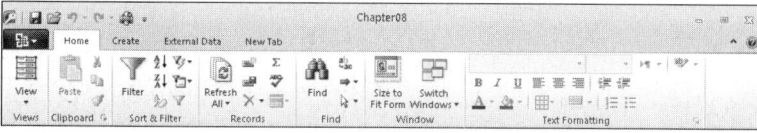

The Views group

At the far left is the Views group, which allows you to switch among the following views, which you can see by clicking the button's down-arrow.

- **Form view:** Form view lets you manipulate data on the form.
- **Datasheet view:** Datasheet view shows the data in the row-and-column format.

Cross-Reference

Turn to Chapter 6 for information on the row-and-column format.

- **PivotTable view:** PivotTable view lets you display a form's data as a pivot table.

- **PivotChart view:** PivotChart view lets you display a form's data as pivot charts.
- **Layout view:** Layout view lets you change the form's design while viewing data.
- **Design view:** Design View permits you to make changes to the form's design.

Note
All these commands may not be available on all forms. By setting the form's properties, you can limit which views are available. You'll learn more about form properties in the "Working with Form Properties" section, later in this chapter.

The Clipboard group

The Clipboard group contains the Cut, Copy, Paste, and Format Paint commands. These commands work like the same commands in other applications (like Word and Excel). The Clipboard is a resource provided by Windows and is shared by virtually all Windows applications. Items you copy or cut from Excel, for example, can be pasted into Access if the *context* is appropriate. For example, you could copy a VBA procedure from an Excel worksheet and paste it into an Access VBA code module because the contexts are the same. But you could not copy an Excel spreadsheet and paste it into Access, because Access has no way of working with an Excel spreadsheet.

The Paste command's down arrow gives you three choices:

- **Paste:** The Paste button inserts whatever item has been copied to the Windows Clipboard into the current location in Access. Depending on the task you're working on, the pasted item might be plain text, a control, a table or form, or some other object.
- **Paste Special:** Paste Special gives you the option of pasting the contents of the Clipboard in different formats (Text, CSV, Records, and so on).
- **Paste Append:** Paste Append pastes the contents of the Clipboard as a new record — as long as a record with a similar structure was copied to the Clipboard. Obviously, Paste Append remains disabled for any operation that does not involve copying and pasting a database table record.

The other controls in the Clipboard ribbon group include

- **Cut:** The Cut operation removes the item from its current place in the application, and puts it onto the Windows Clipboard. The item is not destroyed by removing it from its current location, but it must be pasted before a second item is copied to the Clipboard because a cut or copied item overwrites whatever is on the Clipboard.
- **Copy:** Whatever item or object that currently has the focus is copied to the Clipboard. Copy can be applied to plain text, but it also applies to controls on a form or report (with the form or report in Design view, of course), database records, entire tables, queries, and other database objects, and so on. The Windows Clipboard accepts virtually anything that is copied to it.
- **Format Painter:** The Format Painter (the icon that looks like a brush or paint brush) is a special tool to use when working with Access forms and reports in Design view. The concept of Format Painter is quite simple: You copy the *format* of an item (such as its font settings) and *paint* the formatting onto another item.

Tip

The Format Painter is a huge time-saver when working with many controls on a form or report. Set a control (such as a text box) to look exactly the way you want all the text boxes to look, select the text box, and then click (or double-click) the Format Painter. Then, as you click on another text box, the first text box's formatting is applied to the second text box. Double-clicking the Format Painter "locks" it so that you can paint the format onto multiple items. (Click once on the Format Painter to unlock it.)

The Sort & Filter group

The Sort & Filter group lets you change the order of the records, and, based on your criteria, limit the records shown on the form.

The Records group

The Records group lets you save, delete, or add a new record to the form. It also contains commands to show totals, check spelling, freeze and hide columns, and change the row height and cell width while the form is displayed in Datasheet view.

The Find group

The Find group lets you find and replace data and go to specific records in the datasheet. Use the Select command to select a record or all records.

The Window group

The Window group contains two controls:

- **Size to Fit Form:** When you work with a form in Design view, Access "remembers" the size (height and width) of the form at the moment you save it. When working with the overlapping windows interface, a user may resize a form by dragging its borders to a new size and shape. The Size to Fit Form returns the form to the dimension set at design time.

- **Switch Windows:** Switch Windows provides a handy way to see all the objects (forms, reports, tables, and so on) that are currently open in the main Access windows. You can change to another object by selecting it from the drop-down list that appears when you click on Switch Windows.

The Text Formatting group

The Text Formatting group lets you change the look of the datasheet in Datasheet view. Use these commands to change the font, size, bold, italic, color, and so on. Use the Align Left, Align Right, and Align Center commands to justify the data in the selected column. Click the Gridlines option to toggle gridlines on and off. Use Alternate Fill/Back Color to change the colors of alternating rows, or make them all the same. When modifying text in a Memo field with the `Text Format` property set to `Rich Text`, you can use these commands to change the fonts, colors, and so on.

Navigating among fields

Navigating a form is nearly identical to moving around a datasheet. You can easily move around the form by clicking the control that you want and making changes or additions to your data. Because the form window displays only as many fields as can fit on-screen, you need to use various navigational aids to move within your form or between records.

Table 8.1 displays the navigational keys used to move between fields within a form.

TABLE 8.1

Navigating in a Form

Navigational Direction	Keystrokes
Next field	Tab, right-arrow (→) or down-arrow (↓) key, or Enter
Previous field	Shift+Tab, left-arrow (←), or up-arrow (↑)
First field of current record	Home or Ctrl+Home
Last field of current record	End or Ctrl+End
Next page	PgDn or Next Record
Previous page	PgUp or Previous Record

If you have a form with more data that can fit on the screen at one time, a vertical scroll bar displays. You can use the scroll bar to move to different pages on the form. You can also use the PgUp and PgDn keys to move between form pages. You can move up or down one field at a time by clicking the scroll-bar arrows. With the scroll-bar button, you can move past many fields at once.

Moving among records in a form

Although you generally use a form to display one record at a time, you still need to move between records. The easiest way to do this is to use the Navigation buttons, shown in Figure 8.3.

The Navigation buttons are the six controls located at the bottom-left corner of the Form window. The two leftmost controls move you to the first record and the previous record in the form. The three rightmost controls position you on the next record, last record, or new record in the form. If you know the record number (the row number of a specific record), you can click the Record Number box, enter a record number, and press Enter.

FIGURE 8.3

The Navigation buttons of a form

Record: I◄ ◄ 5 of 100 ► ►I ►✷

The record number displayed in the Navigation controls is just an indicator of the current record's position in the recordset and changes every time you filter or sort the records. To the right of the record number is the total number of records in the current view. The record count may not be the same as the number of records in the underlying table or query. The record count changes when you filter the data on the form.

Changing Values in a Form

Earlier in this book, you learned datasheet techniques to add, change, and delete data within a table. These techniques are the same ones you use on an Access form. Table 8.2 summarizes these techniques.

TABLE 8.2

Editing Techniques

Editing Technique	Keystrokes
Move insertion point within a control	Press the right-arrow ($\rightarrow$) and left-arrow ($\leftarrow$) keys
Insert a value within a control	Select the insertion point and type new data
Select the entire contents of a control	Press F2
Replace an existing value with a new value	Select the entire field and enter a new value
Replace a value with value of the preceding field	Press Ctrl+' (single quotation mark)
Replace the current value with the default value	Press Ctrl+Alt+Spacebar
Insert the current date into a control	Press Ctrl+; (semicolon)
Insert the current time into a control	Press Ctrl+: (colon)
Insert a line break in a Text or Memo control	Press Ctrl+Enter
Insert a new record	Press Ctrl++ (plus sign)
Delete the current record	Press Ctrl+– (minus sign)
Save the current record	Press Shift+Enter or move to another record
Toggle values in a check box or option button	Spacebar
Undo a change to the current control	Press Esc or click the Undo button
Undo a change to the current record	Press Esc or click the Undo button a second time after you Undo the current control

Knowing which controls you can't edit

Some controls, including the following, can't be edited:

- **Controls displaying AutoNumber fields:** Access maintains AutoNumber fields automatically, calculating the values as you create each new record.

- **Calculated controls:** Access may use calculated control in forms or queries. Calculated values are not actually stored in your table.

- **Locked or disabled fields:** You can set certain form and control properties to prevent changes to the data.

- **Controls in multiuser locked records:** If another user locks the record, you can't edit any controls in that record.

Working with pictures and OLE objects

OLE (Object Linking and Embedding) objects are objects not part of an Access database. OLE objects commonly include pictures but may be any number of other data types, such as links to Word documents, Excel spreadsheets, and audio files. You can also include video files such as `.mpg` or `.avi` files.

In Datasheet view, you can't view a picture or an OLE object without accessing the OLE server (such as Word, Excel, or the Windows Media Player). In Form view, however, you can size the OLE control area to be large enough to display a picture, business graph, or other OLE objects. You can also size text-box controls on forms so that you can see the data within the field — you don't have to zoom in on the value, as you do with a datasheet field.

The Access OLE control supports many types of objects. As with a datasheet, you have two ways to enter OLE fields into a form:

- Copy the object (such as an `.mp3` file) to the Clipboard and paste it from the controls in the ribbon's Clipboard group.

- Right-click on the OLE control and click Insert Object from the shortcut menu to display the Insert Object dialog box, shown in Figure 8.4.

FIGURE 8.4

The Insert Object dialog box

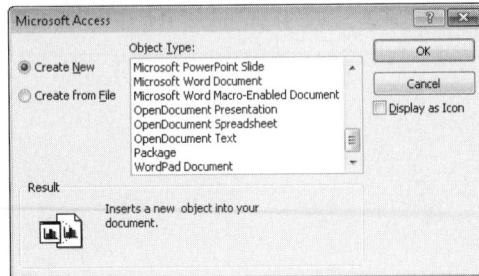

Use the Insert Object dialog box to add a new object to the OLE field, or add an object from an existing file. The Create from File option button adds a picture or other OLE object from an existing file.

When displaying a picture in an OLE control, set the `Size Mode` property to control how the image representing the OLE object is displayed. The settings for this property are

- **Clip:** Keeps the image at its original size and cuts off parts of the picture that don't fit in the control.
- **Zoom:** Fits the image in the control and keeps it in its original proportion, which may result in extra white space.
- **Stretch:** Sizes image to fit exactly between the frame borders. The stretch setting may distort the picture.

Entering data in the Memo field

The `Features` field in the form shown in Figure 8.1 is a Memo data type. This type of field contains up to 65,535 bytes of text. The first two sentences of data appear in the text box. When you click in this text box, a vertical scroll bar appears, allowing you to view all the data in the control.

Better yet, you can resize the Memo control in the form's Design view if you want to make it larger to show more data. With the memo field's text box selected, you can press Shift+F2 and display a Zoom dialog box, as shown in Figure 8.5, to see more data. The text in the Zoom dialog box is fully editable. You can add new text or change text already in the control.

FIGURE 8.5

The Zoom dialog box

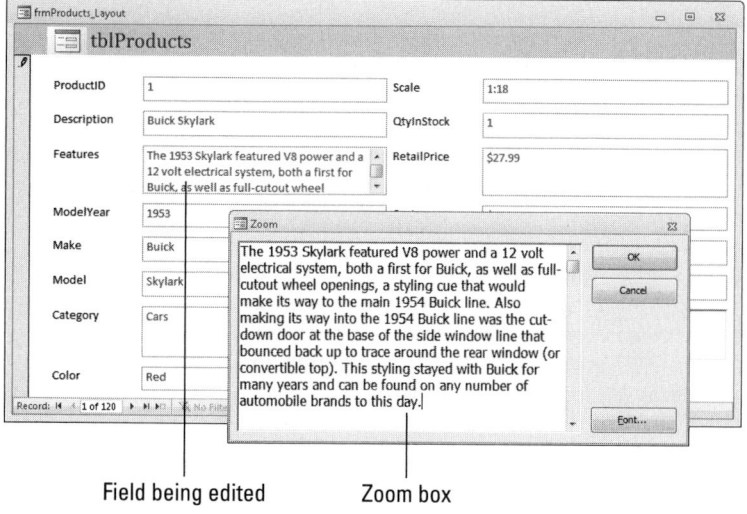

Field being edited   Zoom box

Entering data in the Date field

The SaleDate field in the frmSales_Layout form shown in Figure 8.5 is a Date/Time data type. This field is formatted to accept and show date values. When you click in this text box, a Date Picker icon automatically appears next to it, as shown in Figure 8.6. Click the Date Picker to display a calendar from which you can choose a date.

FIGURE 8.6

Using the Date Picker control

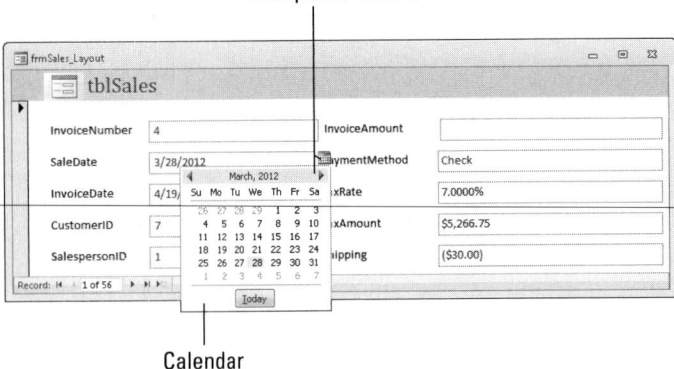

Calendar

If the Date Picker doesn't appear, switch to Design view and change the control's Show Date Picker property to For dates. Set the Show Date Picker property to Never if you don't want to use the Date Picker.

Using option groups

Option groups let you choose from a number of option buttons (sometimes called radio buttons). Option buttons let you select one value while deselecting all the other values. Option groups work best when you have a small number of mutually exclusive choices to select from. Figure 8.7 shows an option group next to the Follow-Up Date text box. Option groups also work with toggle buttons and check boxes.

The easiest and most efficient way to create option groups is with the Option Group Wizard. You can use it to create option groups with multiple option buttons, toggle buttons, or check boxes. When you're through, all your control's property settings are correctly set. To create an option group, switch to Design view and select the Option Group button from the Design tab's Controls group. Make sure the Use Control Wizards command is selected.

Using an option group to select a mutually exclusive value

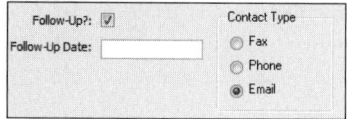

Tip

Option groups can be bound only to numeric fields. When creating an option group for a Yes/No field (which is actually stored as a number), set the `Yes` value to –1 and the `No` value to 0.

Using combo boxes and list boxes

Access has two types of controls — *list boxes* and *combo boxes* — for showing lists of data from which a user can select. The list box is always open and ready for selection, whereas the combo box has to be clicked to open the list for selection. Also, the combo box enables you to enter a value that is not on the list and takes up less room on the form.

Because combo boxes are very efficient of space on the surface of a form, you may want to use (for example) a combo box containing values from `tblCustomers`, as shown in Figure 8.8. The easiest way to do this is with the Combo Box Wizard. This wizard walks you through the steps of creating a combo box that looks up values in another table. To create a combo box, switch to Design View and select the Combo Box command from the Design tab's Controls group. Make sure the Use Control Wizards command is selected.

Using a combo box to select a value from a list

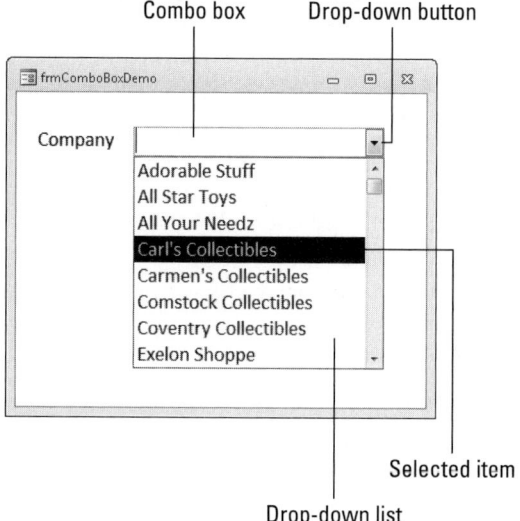

After you create the combo box, examine the Row Source Type, Row Source, Column Count, Column Heads, Column Widths, Bound Column, List Rows, and List Width properties. Once you become familiar with setting these properties, you can right-click a text box, choose Change To⇨Combo Box, and set the combo box's properties manually.

Switching to Datasheet view

With a form open, switch to Datasheet view by using one of these methods:

- Click the Datasheet View command in the Home tab's Views group.
- Click the Datasheet View button in the View Shortcuts section at the bottom-right of the Access window.
- Right-click on the form's title bar — or any blank area of the form — and choose Datasheet View from the pop-up menu.

The datasheet is displayed with the cursor on the same field and record that it occupied while in the form. Moving to another record and field and then redisplaying the form in Form view causes the form to appear with the cursor on the field occupied in Datasheet view.

To return to Form view — or any other view — select the desired view from the Views group, the View Shortcuts, or the pop-up menu.

Saving a record

Access automatically saves each record when you move off it. Pressing Shift+Enter or selecting Save from the ribbon's Records group saves a record without moving off it. Closing the form also saves a record.

Warning
Because Access automatically saves changes as soon as you move to another record, you may inadvertently change the data in the underlying tables. And, because you can't undo changes to an Access database, there is no easy way to revert to the record's previous state.

Printing a Form

You can print one or more records in your form exactly as they appear on-screen. (You learn how to produce formatted reports in Chapter 9.) The simplest way to print is to click the Print button in the Backstage area to print the form on the Windows default printer. Click on the Microsoft Office Button to view other print options.

Printing a form is like printing anything else. Windows is a WYSIWYG ("What You See Is What You Get") environment, so what you see on the form is what you get in the printed hard copy. If you added page headers or page footers, they would be printed at the top or bottom of the page. The printout contains any formatting that you specified in the form (including lines, boxes, and shading) and converts colors to grayscale if you're using a monochrome printer.

The printout includes as many pages as necessary to print all the data. If your form is wider than a single printer page, you need multiple pages to print your form. Access breaks up the printout as necessary to fit on each page.

You can also control printing from the Print dialog box, which you open by clicking the Microsoft Office Button, and then clicking on Print. Customize your printout by selecting from several options:

- **Print Range:** Prints the entire form or only selected pages or records
- **Copies:** Determines the number of copies to be printed
- **Collate:** Determines whether copies are collated

You can also click the Properties button and set options for the selected printer or select a different printer. The Setup button allows you to set margins and print headings.

Tip

Although you may have a form ready to print, you may not be sure whether that information will print on multiple pages or fit on a single page. Click the Print Preview command under the Print menu to display the Print Preview window. The default view is the first page to show in single-page preview. Use the ribbon commands to select different views and zoom in and out. Click Print to print the form to the printer. Click the Close Print Preview command on the right side of the ribbon to return to Form view.

Working with Form Properties

You use form properties to change the way the form is displayed. Property settings include the form's background color or picture, the form's width, and so on. Tables 8.3 through 8.5 in this chapter discuss some of the more important properties. Changing default properties is relatively easy: You select the property in the Property Sheet and set a new value.

On the CD-ROM

The examples in this section use `frmProducts` from the `Chapter08.accdb` example database.

Note

The form selector is the area where the rulers meet while the form is in design or layout view. A small black square appears when the form is selected, as shown in Figure 8.9.

To set a form's properties, you have to show the Property Sheet for the form. Switch to Design or Layout view and display the form's Property Sheet:

- Click the form selector so a small black square appears, and then click the Property Sheet button in the Design tab's Tools group.

- Click the Property Sheet command in the Design tab's Tools group, and then select Form from the drop-down at the top of the Property Sheet.

- Double-click the form selector.

- Right-click the form selector and select Properties from the pop-up menu or by pressing F4 while the form is in Design or Layout view.

FIGURE 8.9

Using the form selector to display the form's Property Sheet

Form selector

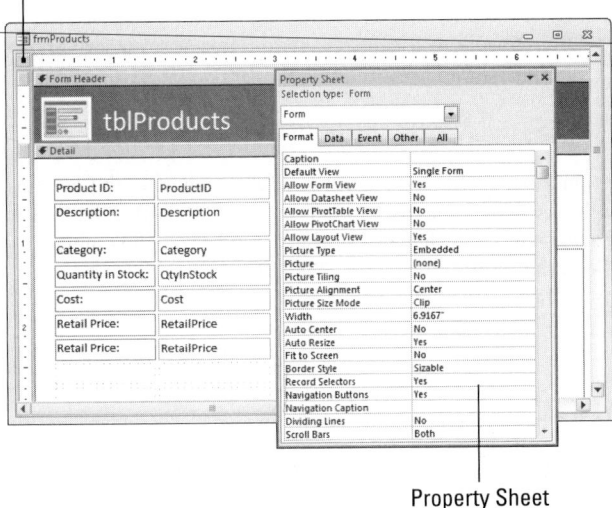

Property Sheet

By default, the form's Property Sheet appears docked to the right side of the Access window. Because the Property Sheet is a window, it can be undocked, moved, and resized. In Figure 8.9, the Property Sheet has been undocked and dragged to a position overlying frmProducts. Notice that the Property Sheet window does not have Maximize or Minimize buttons.

Cross-Reference

Chapter 7 has more information on working with the Property Sheet.

Changing the title bar text with the Caption property

Normally, a form's title bar shows the name of the form after it's saved. The form's Caption property specifies the text displayed in the title bar when the form is in Form view. Follow these steps to change the title bar text:

1. Click the form selector to make sure the form itself is selected.

2. Click the Property Sheet button in the Design tab's Tools group, or press F4 to open the Property Sheet.

3. Click the Caption property in the Property Sheet and enter **Products** in the property's text box, as shown in Figure 8.10.

FIGURE 8.10

Change the Caption property in the form's Property Sheet.

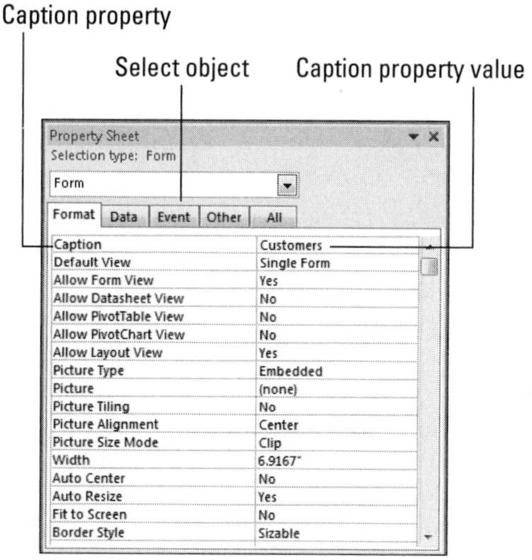

Caption property

Select object   Caption property value

Property Sheet	▼ ✕
Selection type: Form	
Form	▼

Format	Data	Event	Other	All

Caption	Customers
Default View	Single Form
Allow Form View	Yes
Allow Datasheet View	No
Allow PivotTable View	No
Allow PivotChart View	No
Allow Layout View	Yes
Picture Type	Embedded
Picture	(none)
Picture Tiling	No
Picture Alignment	Center
Picture Size Mode	Clip
Width	6.9167"
Auto Center	No
Auto Resize	Yes
Fit to Screen	No
Border Style	Sizable

4. Click any other property or press Enter to move off of the Caption property.

Switch to Form view to see the form's new title bar text. The caption you enter in the form's properties overrides the name of the saved form.

Note

Obviously, using a property to change a form's caption is a trivial exercise. This exercise is designed simply to show you how easily you manipulate a form's appearance by changing its properties. As you work your way through this book you'll encounter, literally, hundreds of examples of using the design tools provided by Access to enhance your application and make them more useful to your users.

Creating a bound form

A *bound form* is directly connected to a data source, such as a table or query. Bound forms usually automatically update data in the bound data source when the user moves to a new record in the form.

To create a bound form, you must specify a data source in the form's `Record Source` property. In Figure 8.10, the Data tab of the Property Sheet contains the properties controlling what and how data is displayed on the form. Although not shown here, the `Record Source` property is at the very top of the Property Sheet's Data tab.

The data source can be one of three choices:

- **Table:** The name of a table in the current database file. The table can be a local table (stored in the database itself) or can be linked to another Access database or an external data source such as SQL Server.
- **Query:** The name of a query that selects data from one or more database tables.
- **SQL Statement:** A SQL `SELECT` statement that selects data from a table or query.

When a form is unbound — the `Record Source` property is blank and the data is obtained with VBA code — you can't have bound controls on the form. (Bound controls have their `Control Source` property set to a field in a table.)

Cross-Reference

For more information on adding bound controls with the Field List, see Chapter 7.

Specifying how to view the form

Access uses several properties to determine how a form is viewed. The `Default View` property determines how the data is displayed when the form is initially opened:

- **Single Form:** Displays one record at a time. Single Form is the default and displays one record per form page, regardless of the form's size.
- **Continuous Forms:** Shows more than one record at a time. Continuous Forms tells Access to display as many detail records as will fit on-screen. Figure 8.11 shows a continuous form displaying five records.
- **Datasheet:** Row and column view like a spreadsheet or the standard query Datasheet view.
- **PivotTable:** A datasheet with movable columns that can be swapped with rows. A PivotTable form displays a form's fields horizontally or vertically and then calculates the total of the row or column.
- **PivotChart:** A graph made from a pivot table. The PivotChart setting displays a graphical analysis of data stored in a table, query, or form.

- **Split Form:** Provides two views of the data at the same time, letting you select a record from a datasheet in the upper section and edit the information in the lower section of the split form.

FIGURE 8.11

The Continuous Forms setting of the Default view property shows multiple records at once.

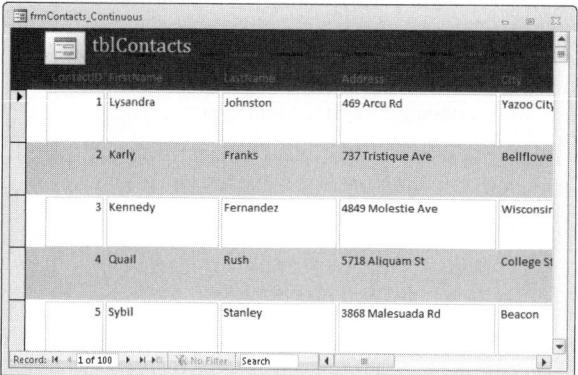

There are five separate properties to allow the developer to determine if the user can change the default view. These include `Allow Form View`, `Allow Datasheet View`, `Allow PivotTable View`, `Allow PivotChart View`, and `Allow Layout View`. The default setting is `Yes` for all these properties. If you set the `Allow Datasheet View` property to `No`, the Datasheet view commands (in the ribbon's Views group, the form's View Shortcuts, and right-click pop-up menu) won't be available and the data can be viewed only as a form. If you set the `Allow Form View` property to `No`, the Form view commands won't be available, and the data can be viewed only as a datasheet.

Removing the Record Selector

The `Record Selectors` property determines whether the Record Selector (the vertical bar shown in Figure 8.11 on the left side of a form with a right-pointing arrow indicating the selected record) is displayed. The Record Selector is important in multiple-record forms or datasheets because it points to the current record. A pencil icon in the Record Selector indicates that the record is being edited. Though the Record Selector is important for datasheets, you probably won't want it for a single record form. To remove the Record Selector change the form's `Record Selectors` property to `No`.

Looking at other form properties

Tables 8.3 through 8.5 list the most commonly used form properties and offers a brief description of each. You'll learn more about most of these properties when they're used in examples in this chapter and other chapters throughout this book.

TABLE 8.3

Form Format Properties

Property	Description	Options
Caption	Text that is displayed in the form's title bar.	N/A
Default View	Determines the initial view when the form is opened.	Single Form: One record per page (default).
		Continuous Forms: As many records per page as will fit.
		Datasheet: Row and column view.
		PivotTable: Displays values horizontally or vertically; then calculates the total of the row or column.
		PivotChart: Graphical data display.
		Split Form: Displays a datasheet in the upper portion and a form in the lower portion.
Allow Form View	Form view allowed.	Yes/No
Allow Datasheet View	Datasheet view allowed.	Yes/No
Allow PivotTable View	PivotTable view allowed.	Yes/No
Allow PivotChart View	PivotChart view allowed.	Yes/No
Allow Layout View	Layout view allowed.	Yes/No
Scroll Bars	Determines whether any scroll bars are displayed.	Neither: No scroll bars are displayed.
		Horizontal Only: Displays only horizontal scroll bar.
		Vertical Only: Displays only vertical scroll bar.
		Both: Displays both horizontal and vertical scroll bars.
Record Selectors	Determines whether the Record Selector is displayed.	Yes/No
Navigation Buttons	Determines whether navigation buttons are visible.	Yes/No
Dividing Lines	Determines whether lines between form sections are visible.	Yes/No

Property	Description	Options
Auto Resize	Form automatically resizes to display a complete record.	Yes/No
Auto Center	Centers form on-screen when it's opened.	Yes/No
Border Style	Determines the form's border style.	None: No border or border elements (scroll bars, navigation buttons).
		Thin: Thin border, not resizable.
		Sizable: Normal form settings.
		Dialog: Thick border, title bar only, cannot be sized; use for dialog boxes.
Control Box	Determines whether control menu (Restore, Move Size) is available.	Yes/No
Min Max Buttons	Specifies whether the Min and Max buttons appear in the form's title bar	None: No buttons displayed in upper-right corner of form.
		Min Enabled: Displays only Minimize button.
		Max Enabled: Displays only Maximize button.
		Both Enabled: Displays Minimize and Maximize buttons.
Close Button	Determines whether to display Close button in upper-right corner and a close menu item on the control menu.	Yes/No
Width	Displays the value of the width of the form (in inches). Width can be entered or Access sets it as you adjust the width of the form.	N/A
Picture	Enter the name of a bitmap file to use as the background of the entire form.	N/A
Picture Type	Determines whether the form's picture is embedded or linked.	Embedded: Picture is embedded in the form and becomes a part of the form.
		Linked: Picture is linked to the form. Access stores the location of the picture and retrieves it every time the form is opened.
Picture Size Mode	Determines how the form's picture is displayed.	Clip: Displays the picture at its actual size.
		Stretch: Fits picture to form size (non-proportional).
		Zoom: Fits picture to form size (proportional); this may result in the picture not fitting in one dimension (height or width).

continued

TABLE 8.3	(continued)	
Property	**Description**	**Options**
Picture Alignment	Determines the form's picture alignment.	Top Left: The picture is displayed in the top-left corner of the form.
		Top Right: The picture is displayed in the top-right corner.
		Center: (Default) The picture is centered.
		Bottom Left: The picture is displayed in the bottom-left corner.
		Bottom Right: The picture is displayed in the bottom-right corner.
		Form Center: The form's picture is centered horizontally and vertically.
Picture Tiling	Used when you want to overlay multiple copies of a small bitmap. For example, a single brick can become a wall.	Yes/No
Grid X	Displays setting for number of points per inch when X grid is displayed.	N/A
Grid Y	Displays setting for number of points per inch when Y grid is displayed.	N/A
Layout for Print	Determines whether form uses screen fonts or printer fonts.	Yes: Printer Fonts. No: Screen Fonts.
Sub-datasheet Height	Determines the height of a sub-datasheet when expanded.	N/A
Sub-datasheet Expanded	Determines the saved state of all sub-datasheets in a table or query.	Yes: The saved state of sub-datasheets is expanded. No: The saved state of sub-datasheets is closed.
Palette Source	The palette for a form or report.	(Default): Indicates the default Access color palette. You can also specify other Windows palette files (`.pal`), `.ico`, `.bmp`, `.db`, and `.wmf` files.
Orientation	Determines view orientation.	Right-to-Left: Appearance and functionality move from right to left. Left-to-Right: Appearance and functionality move from left to right.
Moveable	Determines whether the form can be moved.	Yes/No

Property	Description	Options
Split Form Orientation	Determines the look of a form in Split Form view.	Datasheet on Top: Datasheet appears at the top of the form.
		Datasheet on Bottom: Datasheet appears at the bottom of the form.
		Datasheet on Left: Datasheet appears to the left of the form.
		Datasheet on Right: Datasheet appears to the right of the form.
Split Form Datasheet	Determines whether data can be edited in the datasheet of a Split Form.	Allow Edits: Edits are allowed.
		Read Only: Data is read-only and cannot be changed.
Split Form Splitter Bar	Determines whether there's a splitter bar on a Split Form.	Yes/No
Save Splitter Bar Position	Determines whether the position of the Splitter Bar should be saved.	Yes/No
Split Form Size	Size of the form part of the Split Form.	N/A
Split Form Printing	Determines which section of a Split Form to print.	Form Only: Prints the form portion.
		Datasheet Only: Prints the datasheet section.
Navigation Caption	Overrides the word *Record* in the form's navigation buttons.	N/A

TABLE 8.4

Form Data Properties

Property	Description	Options
Record Source	Specifies the source of data displayed on the form.	N/A
Filter	Used to specify a subset of records to be displayed when a filter is applied to a form. Can be set in the form properties, with a macro, or through VBA.	N/A
Filter on Load	Apply filter at form/report startup.	Yes/No
Order By	Specifies the field(s) used to order the data in the view.	N/A
Order By on Load	Apply sort at form/report start-up.	Yes/No

continued

TABLE 8.4	*(continued)*	
Property	**Description**	**Options**
Allow Filters	Determines whether a user will be able to display a filtered form.	Yes/No
Allow Edits	Determines whether a user will be able to edit data, making the form editable or read only.	Yes/No
Allow Deletions	Determines whether a user will be able to delete records.	Yes/No
Allow Additions	Determines whether a user will be able to add records.	Yes/No
Data Entry	Determines whether form opens to a new blank record, not showing any saved records.	Yes/No
Recordset Type	Used to determine whether multi-table forms can be updated.	Dynaset: Only default table field controls can be edited.
		Dynaset (Inconsistent Updates): All tables and fields are editable.
		Snapshot: No fields are editable (same as read-only)
Record Locks	Used to determine default multiuser record locking on bound forms.	No Locks: Record is locked only as it's saved.
		All Records: Locks entire form's records while using the form.
		Edited Record: Locks only current record during an edit.
Fetch Defaults	Determines whether default values should be retrieved.	Yes/No

TABLE 8.5		

Form "Other" Properties

Property	**Description**	**Option Definition**
Pop Up	Form is a pop-up that floats above all other objects.	Yes/No
Modal	User must close the form before doing anything else. Disables other windows. When Pop Up set to Yes, Modal disables menus and toolbar, creating a dialog box.	Yes/No

Property	Description	Option Definition
Cycle	Determines how Tab works in the last field of a record.	All Records: Tabbing from the last field of a record moves to the next record.
		Current Record: Tabbing from the last field of a record moves to the first field of that record.
		Current Page: Tabbing from the last field of a record moves to the first field of the current page.
Menu Bar	Used to specify an alternate menu bar.	N/A
Toolbar	Use this property to specify the toolbar to use for the form. You can create a toolbar for your form by selecting the Customize option under the Toolbar command in the View menu.	N/A
Custom Ribbon ID	Name of custom ribbon to apply on open.	N/A
Shortcut Menu	Determines whether shortcut (right-click) menus are available.	Yes/No
Shortcut Menu Bar	Specifies the name of an alternate shortcut menu bar.	N/A
Fast Laser Printing	Prints rules instead of lines and rectangles.	Yes/No
Help File	Name of compiled Help file to assign custom help to the form.	N/A
Help Context Id	ID of context-sensitive entry point in the Help file to display.	N/A
Tag	Use this property to store extra information about your form.	N/A
Has Module	Use this property to show if your form has a class module. Setting this property to No removes the VBA code module attached to the form.	N/A
Use Default Paper Size	Use the default paper size when printing.	Yes/No

Adding a Form Header or Footer

Although the form's Detail section usually contains the majority of the controls that display data, there are other sections in a form that you can add:

- **Form Header:** Displayed at the top of each page when viewed and at the top when the form is printed.

- **Form Footer:** Displayed at the bottom of each page when viewed and at the bottom of the form when the form is printed.

The form header and footer remain on the screen, while any controls in the Detail section can scroll up and down.

You select the header and footer options in the Header/Footer group on the Design ribbon tab (with the form open in Design view, of course).

Changing the Layout

In this section, you'll learn how to change a form's layout using Layout view. You'll add, move, and resize controls, as well as change a few other characteristics while viewing the form's data.

With a form open in Design view, select the Arrange tab in the Form Design Tools area of the ribbon. The Arrange tab includes controls for selecting a form's initial layout, including the default positions of controls on the form. The Arrange tab is highly context sensitive. The view you see in Figure 8.12 is the result of selecting a number of controls on the form. A somewhat different view may be seen if other controls or form sections (header, footer, and so on) are selected.

FIGURE 8.12

The Form ribbon's Arrange tab

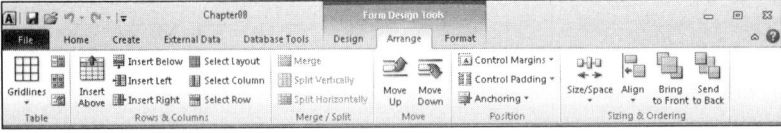

Changing a control's properties

In previous versions of Access, you had to make changes to the form in Design view. In Layout view, you can change these properties while looking at data instead of empty controls. Click the Property Sheet command in the Layout tab's Tools group to display the Property Sheet for the selected control.

Cross-Reference

For more information on changing control properties with the Property Sheet, see Chapter 7.

Setting the Tab Order

You may notice that when you use the Tab key to move from control to control, the cursor jumps around the screen. The route taken by the Tab key may seem strange, but that's the original order in which the controls were added to the form.

The tab order of the form is the order in which the focus moves from control to control as you press Tab. The form's default tab order is always the order in which the controls were added to the form. Moving controls around on the form means you'll need to change the form's tab order. Even though you may make heavy use of the mouse when designing your forms, most data entry people use the keyboard, rather than the mouse, to move from control to control.

Select Tab Order from the Design tab's Tools group to display the Tab Order dialog box, shown in Figure 8.13. This dialog box shows the controls in the form arranged in the current tab order. Controls such as labels, lines, and other non-data controls don't appear in the Tab Order dialog box.

FIGURE 8.13

The Tab Order dialog box

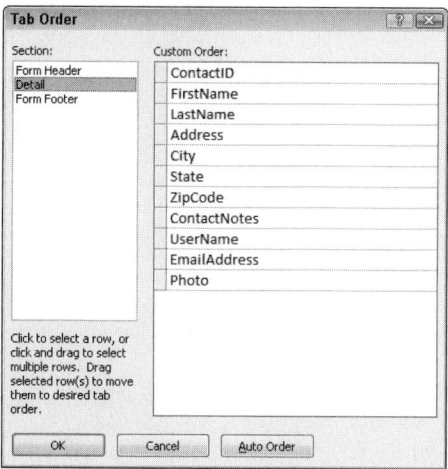

The Tab Order dialog box lets you select either one or more rows at a time. Multiple contiguous rows are selected by clicking the first control and dragging to select multiple rows. After highlighting rows, the selected rows can be dragged to their new positions in the tab order.

The Tab Order dialog box has several buttons at the bottom. Auto Order places the controls in order from left to right and from top to bottom, according to their position in the form. This button is a good starting place when the tab order is very disorganized. The OK button applies the changes to the form, while the Cancel button closes the dialog box without changing the tab order.

Each control has two properties related to the Tab Order dialog box. The Tab Stop property determines whether pressing the Tab key lands you on the control. The default is Yes. Changing the Tab Stop property to No removes the control from the tab order. When you set the tab order, you're setting the Tab Index property values. Moving the fields around in the Tab Order dialog box changes the Tab Index properties of those (and other) controls.

Aligning controls

You may want to move several controls so that they're all *aligned* (lined up). With multiple controls selected, the Layout ribbon's Control Alignment group has several options for aligning controls: Left, Right, Top, and Bottom. These commands work the same as the Control Alignment commands described in Chapter 7, with the exception of aligning controls to the grid, which is not available in Layout view.

Modifying the format of text in a control

To modify the formatting of text within a control, select the control by clicking it, and then select a formatting style to apply to the control. The Layout view ribbon's Design tab (shown in Figure 8.14) contains additional commands for changing the format of a control.

FIGURE 8.14

The Form ribbon's Format tab

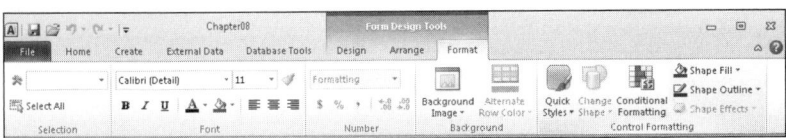

To change the fonts for the Category control, make sure you're in Layout view, and then follow these steps:

1. Select the Category text box control by clicking on it.

2. Change the Font Size to 14, and then click on the Bold button in the Format tab's Font group.

   The control does not automatically resize when changing its font properties. If you see only a portion of the text box, the control may require resizing to display all the text.

Using the Field List to add controls

The form's Field List displays a list of fields from the table or query on which the form is based. Use the Add Existing Fields button on the Design tab to open it if the Field List is not currently visible. Drag fields from the Field List to the form's surface to add bound controls to the form. Select and drag them one at a time, or select multiple fields by using the Ctrl key or Shift key. The Field List in Layout view works the same as the Field List in Design view, which is described in detail in Chapter 7.

Click the Add Existing Fields command in the Design tab's Controls group to display the Field List. By default, the Field List appears docked on the right of the Access window, shown in Figure 8.15. This window is movable and resizable and displays a vertical scrollbar if it contains more fields than can fit in the window.

Access adds a control that's appropriate for the data type of the bound field. For example, dragging a text field to the form's surface adds a text box, while an OLE data field adds a Bound OLE Object control.

To add fields from the Field List to a new form, follow these steps:

1. Select `tblProducts` in the Navigation Pane.

2. Click the Create tab on the ribbon, and then select the Blank Form command in the Form group to open a new form in Layout view. The new form is bound to `tblProducts`.

3. If the Field List isn't displayed, click on the ribbon's Design tab, and then select Add Existing Fields from the Controls group.

4. While holding down the Shift key, click the `ProductID` and `Cost` fields in the Field List.

5. Drag the selected fields to the form, as shown in Figure 8.15.

FIGURE 8.15

Adding fields from the Field List in a form's Layout view

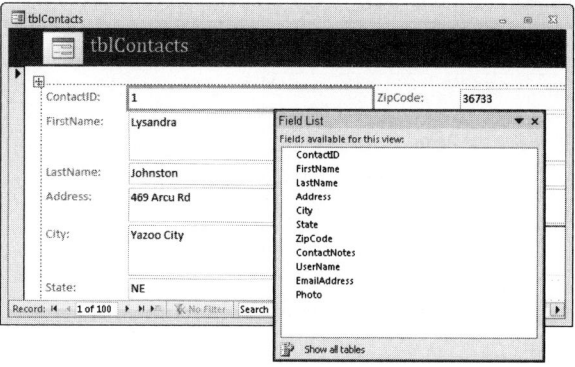

Tip

You can select noncontiguous fields in the list by clicking each field while holding down the Ctrl key. The selected fields can be dragged (as part of the group) to the form's design surface.

Creating a Calculated Control

Unbound controls may use an expression as their `ControlSource` property. As the form loads, Access evaluates the expression and populates the control with the value returned by the expression. The following example demonstrates creating an unbound calculated control:

1. Select `tblProducts` in the Navigation Pane.
2. Click the Create tab on the ribbon, and then click on the Blank Form command in the Form group to display a new form in Layout view.
3. Drag `Cost` and `SalePrice` from the Field List onto the form's surface.
4. Switch the form to Design view.
5. Click on Text Box in the Controls group and draw a new text box on the form.
6. Set the `Name` property to `txtProfit` and set its `Control Source` property to: `=[SalePrice]-[Cost]`.
7. Change the `Format` property to `Currency` and its `Decimal Places` to 2.
8. Change the label's `Caption` property to `Profit:`.
9. Switch to Form view to test the expression.

    Your screen should look like Figure 8.16. `txtProfit` shows the difference between the `SalePrice` and `Cost`.

FIGURE 8.16

Creating a calculated control

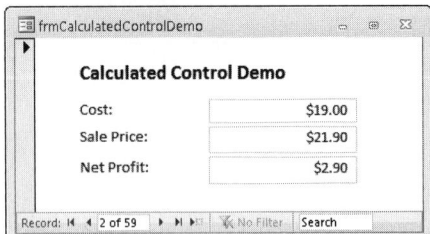

Converting a Form to a Report

By opening a form in Design view, clicking the Microsoft Office Button, and selecting Save As, you can save a form as a report. The entire form is saved as the report. If the form has form headers or footers, these are used as the report's header and footer sections. If the form has page headers or page footers, these are used as the report's Page Header and Page Footer sections. You can now use the report in Design view, adding groups and other features without having to re-create general layout all over again. You'll learn more about reports in later chapters.

Summary

In this chapter, you learned that working with data in Form view is similar to working with data in a table or query's Datasheet view. You learned how to navigate among fields and records and how to use controls such as option groups and combo boxes to facilitate data entry.

You also learned about a form's properties, including the different groupings and each property setting. You learned how setting some of these properties affects a form's appearance. You added a form header and footer and worked with the new Layout view, which lets you manipulate a form and its controls while viewing live data.

Throughout this book, you'll learn how to enhance basic Access forms with additional features and advanced controls. You'll also find out how to automate a form's features with macros and VBA code.

Forms are the primary user interface for your Access applications. The time you spend designing and implementing your forms benefits your users every time they work with your applications.

Presenting Data with Access Reports

It's hard to underestimate the importance of reports in database applications. Many people who never work with an Access application in person use reports created by Access. A lot of maintenance work on database projects involves creating new and enhancing existing reports. Access is well known and respected for its powerful reporting features.

Reports provide the most flexible way of viewing and printing summarized information. They display information with the desired level of detail, while enabling you to view or print your information in many different formats. You can add multilevel totals, statistical comparisons, and pictures and graphics to a report.

In this chapter, you learn to use the Report Wizard as a starting point. You also learn how to create reports and what types of reports you can create with Access.

On the CD-ROM

In this chapter, you create new reports using the Report Wizard and by creating a blank report without using a wizard. You use tables created in previous chapters. The `Chapter09.accdb` database file on the book's CD-ROM contains the completed reports described in this chapter.

Introducing Reports

Reports present a customized view of your data. Report output is viewed on-screen or printed to provide a hard copy of the data. Very often reports provide summaries of the information contained in the database. Data can be grouped and sorted in any order and can be used to create totals that perform statistical operations on data. Reports can include pictures and other graphics as well as memo fields in a report. If you can think of a report you want, Access probably supports it.

IN THIS CHAPTER

Looking at the different types of Access reports

Creating reports with a Report Wizard

Creating a report from scratch

Improving the form's appearance

Identifying the different types of reports

Four basic types of reports are used by most businesses:

- **Tabular reports:** These reports print data in rows and columns with groupings and totals. Variations include summary and group/total reports.
- **Columnar reports:** These reports print data and can include totals and graphs.
- **Mailing-label reports:** These reports create multicolumn labels or snaked-column reports.

Tabular reports

Tabular reports are similar to a table displaying data in rows and columns. Figure 9.1 is a typical tabular report (rptProductsSummary) displayed in Print Preview.

Unlike forms or datasheets, tabular reports often group data by one or more fields. Often, tabular reports calculate and display subtotals or statistical information for numeric fields in each group. Some reports include page totals and grand totals. You can even have multiple snaked columns so that you can create directories (such as telephone books). These types of reports often use page numbers, report dates, or lines and boxes to separate information. Reports may have color and shading and display pictures, business graphs, and memo fields. A special type of summary tabular report can have all the features of a detail tabular report but omit record details.

FIGURE 9.1

A tabular report (rptProductsSummary) displayed in Print Preview

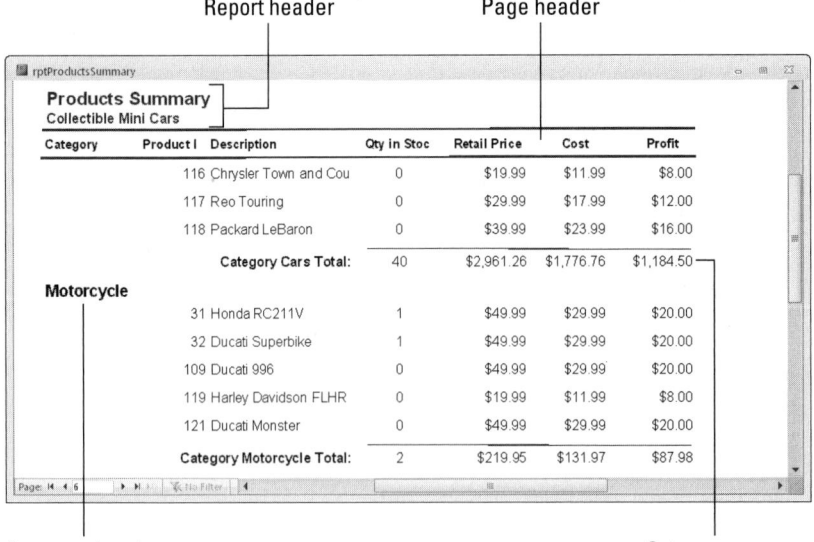

Columnar reports

Columnar reports generally display one or more records per page, but they do so vertically. Columnar reports display data very much as a data-entry form does, but they're used strictly for viewing data and not for entering data. Figure 9.2 shows part of a columnar report (rptProducts) in Print Preview.

A columnar report showing report controls distributed throughout the entire page

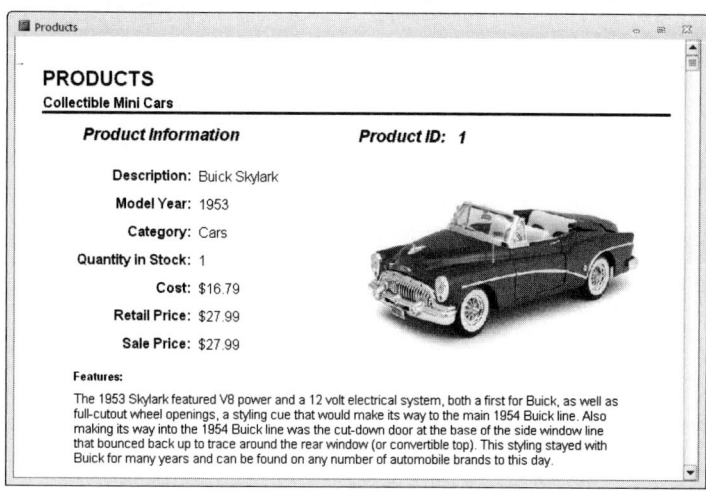

Another type of columnar report displays one main record per page (like a business form) but can show many records within embedded subforms. An invoice is a typical example. This type of report can have sections that display only one record and at the same time have sections that display multiple records from the *many* side of a one-to-many relationship — and even include totals.

Figure 9.3 shows an invoice report (rptInvoice) from the Collectible Mini Cars database system in Report view.

In Figure 9.3, the information in the top portion of the report is on the "main" part of the report, whereas the product details near the bottom of the figure are contained in a subreport embedded within the main report.

FIGURE 9.3

An invoice report (`rptInvoice`)

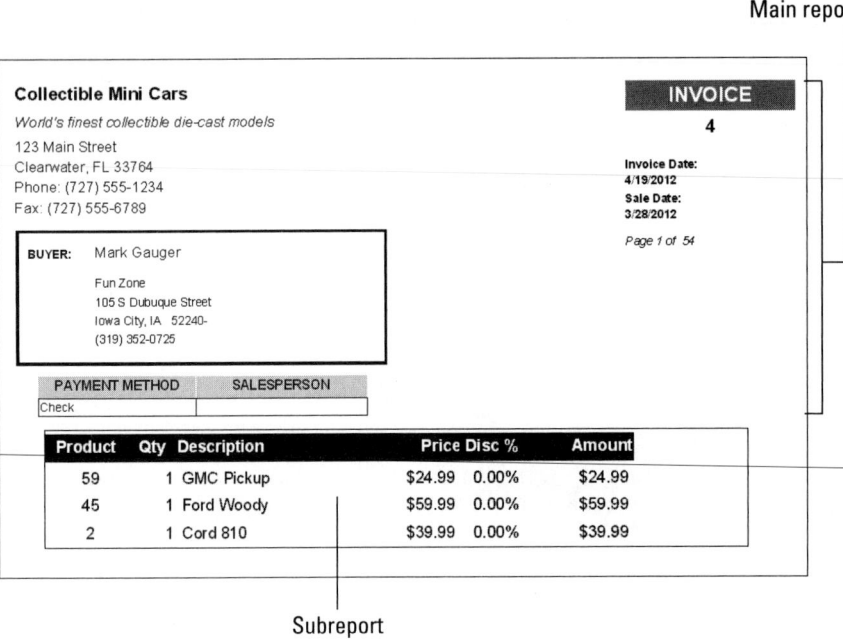

Subreport

Mailing-label reports

Mailing labels (shown in Figure 9.4) are also a type of report. Access includes a Label Wizard to help you create this type of report. The Label Wizard enables you to select from a long list of label styles. Access accurately creates a report design based on the label style you select. You can then open the report in Design mode and customize it as needed.

Distinguishing between reports and forms

The main difference between reports and forms is the intended output. Whereas forms are primarily for data entry and interaction with the users, reports are for viewing data (either onscreen or in hard-copy form). Calculated fields can be used with forms to display an amount based on other fields in the record. With reports, you typically perform calculations on groups of records, a page of records, or all the records included in the report. Anything you can do with a form — except input data — can be duplicated by a report. In fact, you can save a form as a report and then refine it in the Report Design window.

FIGURE 9.4

rptCustomerMailingLabels, a typical mailing-label report

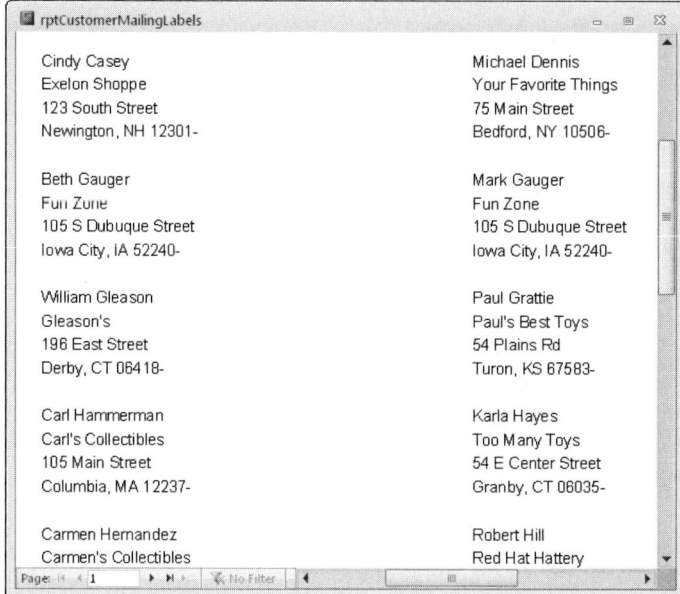

Creating a Report, from Beginning to End

The report process begins with your desire to view data, but in a way that differs from a form or datasheet display. The purpose of the report is to transform raw data into a meaningful set of information. The process of creating a report involves several steps:

1. Defining the report layout
2. Assembling the data
3. Creating the report with the Access Report Wizard
4. Printing or viewing the report
5. Saving the report

Defining the report layout

You should begin by having a general idea of the layout of your report. You can define the layout in your mind, on paper, or interactively using the Report Designer.

Tip

Very often, an Access report is expected to duplicate an existing paper report or form used by the application's consumers.

Assembling the data

After you have a general idea of the report layout, assemble the data needed for the report. Access reports use data from two primary sources:

- A single database table
- A recordset produced by the query

You can join many tables in a query and use the query's recordset as the record source for your report. A query's recordset appears to an Access report as if it were a single table.

As you learned in Chapter 4, you use queries to specify the fields, records, and sort order of the records stored in tables. Access treats a recordset data as if it were a single table (for processing purposes) in datasheets, forms, and reports. When the report is run, Access matches data from the recordset or table against the fields specified in the report and uses the data available at that moment to produce the report.

Note

Reports do not follow the sort order specified in an underlying query. Most often reports are sorted at the report level, either in the detail section or in a group section. Very often, it's a waste of time to sort data in a query that is used solely to populate a report because the data is resorted and rearranged by the report itself.

In the following example, you use data from `tblProducts` to create a relatively simple tabular report.

Creating a report with the Report Wizard

Access enables you to create virtually any type of report. Some reports, however, are easier to create than others, especially when a Report Wizard is used as a starting point. Like form wizards, the Report Wizard gives you a basic layout for your report, which you can then customize.

The Report Wizard simplifies laying out controls by stepping you through a series of questions about the report that you want to create. In this chapter, you use the Report Wizard to create tabular and columnar reports.

Creating a new report

The Access ribbon contains several commands for creating new reports for your applications. That Create tab of the ribbon includes a grouping called Reports containing several options such as Report, Labels, and Report Wizard. For this exercise, click the Report Wizard button in the Reports group of the Create ribbon tab. The first screen of the Report Wizard (shown in Figure 9.5) appears.

FIGURE 9.5

The first screen of the Report Wizard after selecting a data source and fields

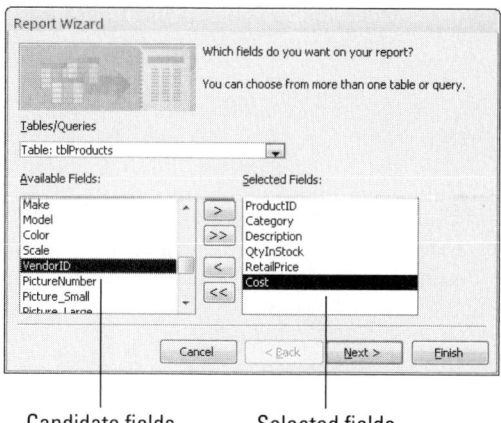

Candidate fields   Selected fields

In Figure 9.5, `tblProducts` has been selected as the data source for the new report. Under the Tables/Queries drop-down list is a list of available fields. When you click on a field in this list and click the right pointing arrow, the field moves from the Available Fields list to the report's Selected Fields list. For this exercise, select Product ID, Category, Description, QtyInStock, RetailPrice, and Cost.

Tip

Double-clicking any field in the Available Fields list adds it to the Selected Fields list. You can also double-click any field in the Selected Fields list to remove it from the box.

You're limited to selecting fields from the original record source you started with. You can select fields from other tables or queries by using the Tables/Queries drop-down list in the Report Wizard. As long as you've specified valid relationships so that Access properly links the data, these fields are added to your original selection and you use them on the report. If you choose fields from unrelated tables, a dialog box asks you to edit the relationship and join the tables. Or you can return to the Report Wizard and remove the fields.

After you've selected your data, click Next to go to the next wizard dialog box.

Selecting the grouping levels

The next dialog box enables you to choose which field(s) to use for grouping data. Figure 9.6 shows the Category field selected as the data grouping field for the report. The field selected for grouping determines how data appears on the report, and the grouping fields appear as group headers and footers in the report.

Groups are most often used to combine data that are logically related. The classic example is grouping all products by product category. A very practical example is choosing to group on CustomerID so that each customer's sales history appears as a group on the report. You use the report's group headers and footers to display the customer name and any other information specific to each customer.

The Report Wizard lets you specify as many as four group fields for your report. You use the Priority buttons to change the grouping order on the report. The order you select for the group fields is the order of the grouping hierarchy.

Select the Category field as the grouping field and click the > button to specify a grouping based on category values. Notice that the picture changes to show Category as a grouping field, as shown in Figure 9.6. Each of the other fields (ProductID, Description, QtyInStock, RetailPrice, and SalesPrice) selected for the report will appear within the Category groups.

FIGURE 9.6

Specifying the report's grouping

Grouping field

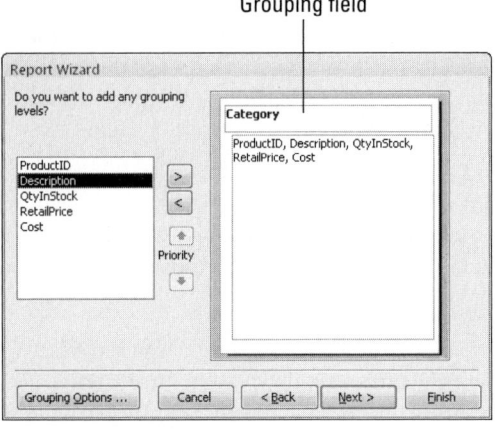

Defining the group data

After you select the group field(s), click the Grouping Options button at the bottom of the dialog box to display the Grouping Options dialog box, which enables you to further define how you want groups displayed on the report.

For example, you can choose to group by only the first character of the grouping field. This means that all records with the same first character in the grouping field are grouped. If you group a customers table on CustomerName, and then specify grouping by the first character of the CustomerName field, a group header and footer appears for all customers whose name begins with the same character. This specification groups all customer names beginning with the letter A, another group for all records with customer name beginning with B, and so on.

The Grouping Options dialog box enables you to further define the grouping. This selection can vary in importance, depending on the data type.

The Grouping Intervals list box displays different values for various data types:

- **Text:** Normal, 1st Letter, 2 Initial Letters, 3 Initial Letters, 4 Initial Letters, 5 Initial Letters
- **Numeric:** Normal, 10s, 50s, 100s, 500s, 1000s, 5000s, 10000s, 50000s, 100000s
- **Date:** Normal, Year, Quarter, Month, Week, Day, Hour, Minute

Normal means that the grouping is on the entire field. In this example, use the entire CustomerName field.

Notice that the grouping options simplify creating reports grouped by calendar months, quarters, years, and so on. This means that you can easily produce reports showing sales, payroll, or other financial information needed for business reporting.

If you displayed the Grouping Options dialog box, click the OK button to return to the Grouping Levels dialog box, and then click the Next button to move to the Sort Order dialog box.

Selecting the sort order

By default, Access automatically sorts grouped records in an order meaningful to the grouping field(s). For example, after you've chosen to group by Customer Name, Access arranges the groups in alphabetical order by Customer Name. However, for your purposes, it might be useful to specify a sort within each group. As an example, your users might want to see the customer records sorted by Order Date in descending order so that the newest orders appear near the top for each customer group.

In this example, Access sorts data by the Category field. As Figure 9.7 shows, the data is also sorted by Description within each group.

FIGURE 9.7

Selecting the field sorting order

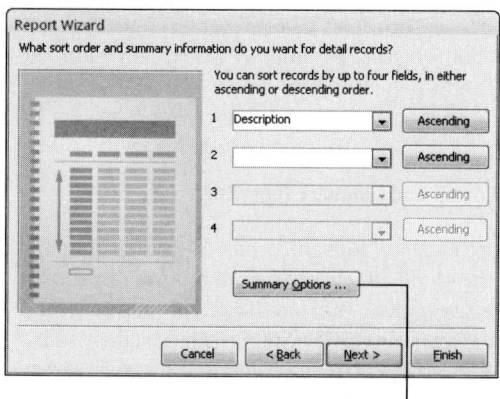

Opens Summary Options dialog box

Sort fields are selected by the same method you use for selecting grouping fields. You can select sorting fields that haven't been chosen for grouping. The fields chosen in this dialog box affect only the sorting order in the data displayed in the report's Detail section. Select ascending or descending sort by clicking the button to the right of each sort field.

Selecting summary options

Near the bottom of the sorting screen of the Report Wizard is a Summary Options button. Clicking this button displays the Summary Options dialog box (shown in Figure 9.8), which provides additional display options for numeric fields. All the numeric and currency fields selected for the report are displayed and may be summed. Additionally, you can display averages, minimums, and maximums.

FIGURE 9.8

Selecting the summary options

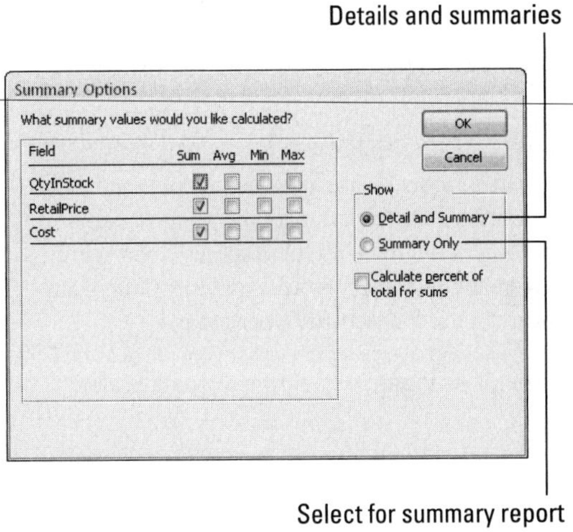

Details and summaries

Select for summary report

You can also decide whether to show or hide the data in the report's Detail section. If you select Detail and Summary, the report shows the detail data, whereas selecting Summary Only hides the Detail section and shows only totals in the report.

Cross-Reference

In Chapter 20, you'll learn how to programmatically control detail and summary reporting options.

Finally, checking the Calculate Percent of Total for Sums box adds the percentage of the entire report that the total represents below the total in the group footer. If, for example, you have three products and their totals are 15, 25, and 10, respectively, 30%, 50%, and 20% shows below their total (that is, 50) — indicating the percentage of the total sum (100%) represented by their sum.

Clicking the OK button in this dialog box returns you to the sorting screen of the Report Wizard. There you can click the Next button to move to the next wizard screen.

Selecting the layout

Two more dialog boxes affect the look of your report. The first (shown in Figure 9.9) enables you to determine the basic layout of the data. The Layout area provides six layout choices that tell Access whether to repeat the column headers, indent each grouping, and add lines or boxes between the detail lines. As you select each option, the picture on the left changes to show how the choice affects the report's appearance.

You choose between Portrait (up-and-down) and Landscape (across-the-page) layout for the report in the Orientation area. Finally, the `Adjust the Field Width So All Fields Fit` on a Page check box enables you to cram a lot of data into a little area. (A magnifying glass may be necessary!)

For this example, choose Stepped and Portrait, as shown in Figure 9.9. Then click the Next button to move to the next dialog box.

FIGURE 9.9

Selecting the page layout

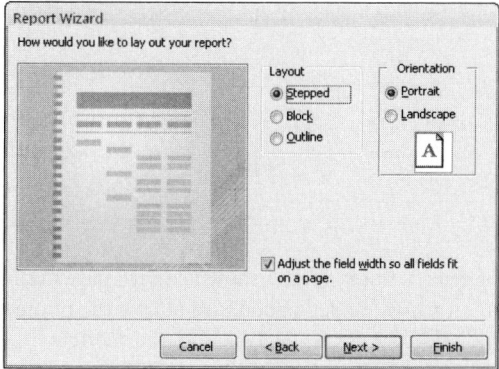

Opening the report design

The final Report Wizard screen contains a checkered flag, which lets you know that you're at the finish line. The first part of the screen enables you to enter a title for the report. This title appears only once, at the very beginning of the report, not at the top of each page. The report title also serves as the new report's name. The default title is the name of the table or query you initially specified as the report's data source. The report just created in the `Chapter09.accdb` example is named `rptProducts_Wizard`.

Next, choose one of the option buttons at the bottom of the dialog box:

- Preview the report
- Modify the report's design

For this example, leave the default selection intact to preview the report. Click Finish and the report displays in Report view (see Figure 9.10).

rptProducts_Wizard displayed in Report view

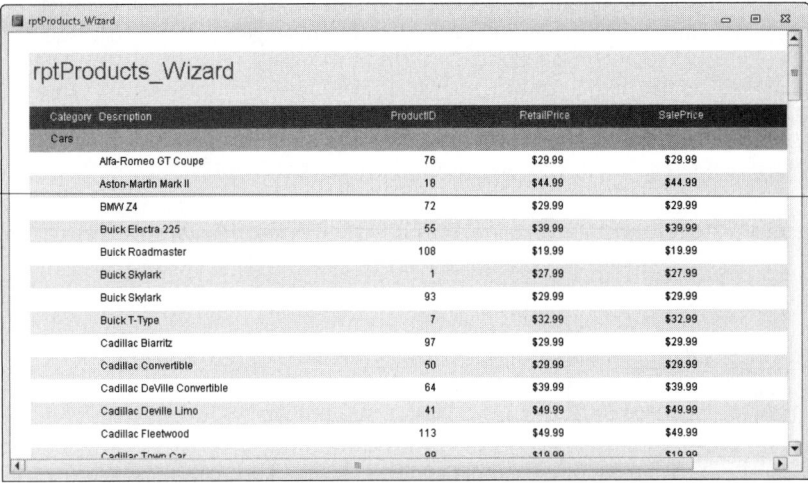

Report view provides an overall presentation of the report, but it doesn't show margins, page numbering, and how the report will look when printed on paper. To get a good idea of how the printed report will look, right-click the report's title bar and select Print Preview from the shortcut menu.

Adjusting the report's layout

There are a few small issues with the report you see in Figure 9.10. The Access Report Wizard has chosen the fonts and overall color scheme, which may not be what you had in mind. Also, the Description column isn't quite wide enough to show the information in this product field.

The Report Wizard displays the new report in Report view. Right-click on the report's title bar and select Layout View from the shortcut menu. The new report in Layout view is shown in Figure 9.11.

In Figure 9.11, the Description column has been resized to allow more room to show descriptions without clipping. Resizing the Description column has pushed the other columns to the right, but the report's width accommodates these changes.

FIGURE 9.11

Layout view is useful for resizing controls in a columnar report.

Reference lines

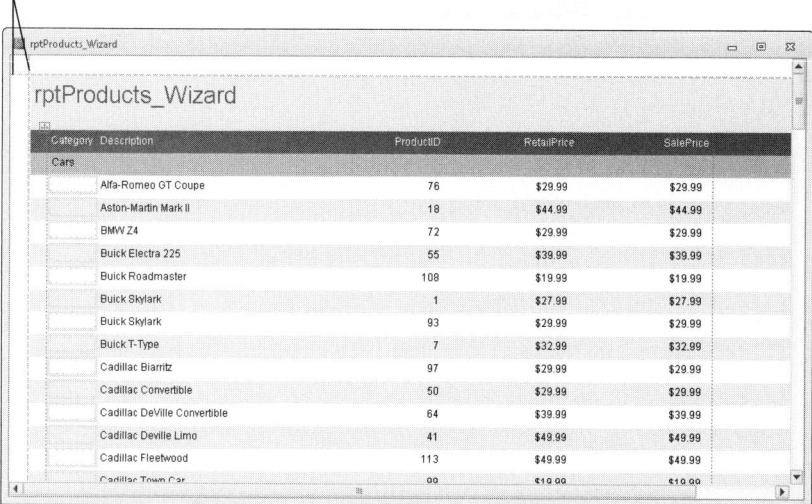

Choosing a theme

After you adjust the layout, you can use controls in the Themes group on the ribbon's Design tab to change the report's colors, fonts, and overall appearance. The Themes button opens a gallery containing several dozen themes (see Figure 9.12).

Themes are an important concept in Access 2010. A theme sets the color scheme, selected font face, font colors, and font sizes for Access 2010 forms and reports. As you hover the mouse over the theme icons in the gallery, the report open in Layout view behind the gallery instantly changes to show you how the report would look with the selected theme.

Each theme has a name, like Office, Apex, Flow, Paper, and Metro. Theme names are useful when you want to refer to a particular theme in the application's documentation or in an e-mail or other correspondence. Themes are stored in a file with a `.thmx` extension, in the `Program Files\` `Microsoft Office\Document Themes 14` folder. Themes apply to all the Office 2010 documents (Word, Excel, and Access), making it easy to determine a style to apply to all of a company's Office output.

FIGURE 9.12

Choosing a theme for the report

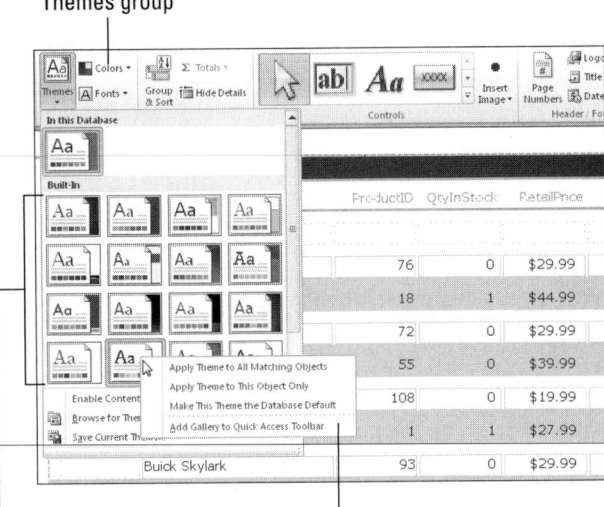

Themes group

Themes gallery   Right-click menu

Note

Access 2007 users may be wondering what happened to the AutoFormat feature in 2007. For a number of reasons, Microsoft decided to replace AutoFormat with themes in Office 2010. AutoFormat applied to individual controls, which meant a lot of work when building a complicated form or report. AutoFormat also tended to be all or nothing, making it difficult to apply an AutoFormat and then alter the colors and fonts to controls on a form or report. Themes are much more flexible. They even allow you to save a completed form or report as a new theme (see the `Save Current Theme` option at the bottom of the theme gallery in Figure 9.12). There was no way to create a custom AutoFormat in Access 2007.

As the right-click menu in Figure 9.12 indicates, you can apply the selected theme just to the current report (`Apply Theme to this Object Only`), all reports (`Apply Theme to All Matching Objects`), or all forms *and* reports in the application (`Make This Theme the Database Default`). There's even an option to add the theme as a button to the Quick Access toolbar, an extremely useful option for selectively applying the theme to other objects in the database.

Tip

It's very tempting to try out every reporting style and option when building Access forms and reports. Unfortunately, when carried too far, your Access application may end up looking like a scrapbook of design ideas rather than as a valuable business tool. Professional database developers tend to use a minimum of form and report styles and use them consistently throughout an application. Be considerate of your users and try not to overwhelm them with a lot of different colors, fonts, and other user interface and reporting styles.

For the purposes of this exercise, the Concourse theme was selected for the new products report.

Creating new theme color schemes

Access 2010 provides several dozen default themes, with each theme consisting of a set of complementary colors, fonts, and font characteristics. In addition, you can set up entirely new color and font themes and apply them to your forms and reports. Creating a custom color theme is a great way to apply a company's corporate color scheme to the forms and reports in an application.

With a form or report open in Design view, follow these steps:

1. Click the Colors button in the Themes group on the Design ribbon tab.

   The color theme list opens.

2. Select the Create New Theme Colors command at the very bottom of the list of color themes.

   The Create New Theme Colors dialog box (shown in Figure 9.13) appears, showing the currently selected color theme.

FIGURE 9.13

Setting up a custom color theme

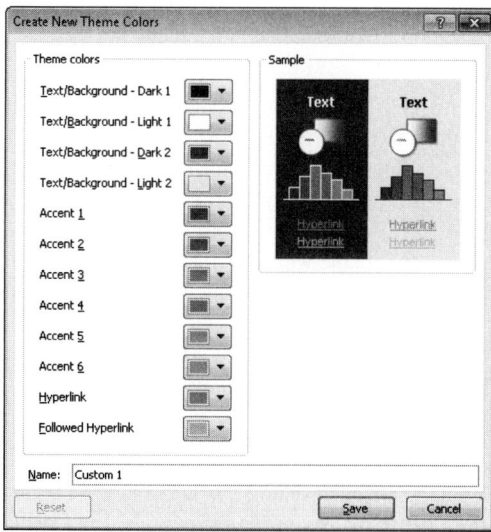

Modifying a color theme requires a considerable amount of work. As you can see from Figure 9.13, each color theme includes 12 different colors. Each of the 12 buttons on the Create New Theme Colors dialog box opens a color palette (shown in Figure 9.14) where you select a theme element's color, such as the color for the Text/Background – Light 2 element.

FIGURE 9.14

Selecting a theme element's color

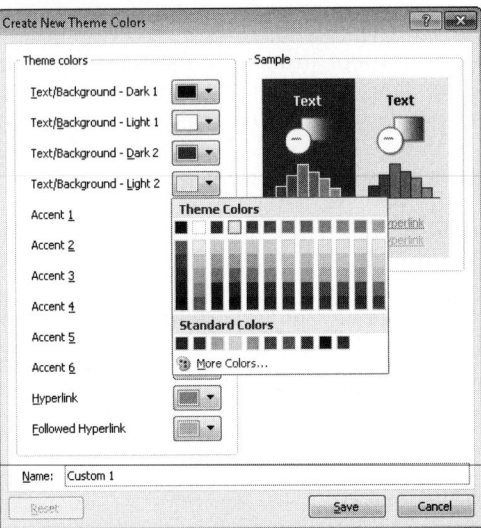

3. When the color customization is complete, assign a name for the custom color theme and click Save.

    When you close the Create New Theme Colors dialog box, you'll see that the custom color theme has been applied to the form or report currently open in Design view. If you want to apply the new color theme to all the forms or reports in the application, open the color theme list, right-click on the name of a custom color theme at the top of the list (see Figure 9.15), and select Apply Color Scheme to All Matching Objects. If you have a report open in Design view, the theme will be applied to all reports in the application. If, on the other hand, you have a form open in Design view, all the forms in the application receive the new color theme.

Even after applying a color theme, you can adjust the colors of individual items on a report (or form, for that matter). Open the report in Design view, select the item to change, and choose its new color(s) in the Property Sheet.

Although not described or shown here, a similar dialog box is available (Create New Theme Fonts) in the Fonts drop-down list in the Themes group on the Design tab. The Create New Theme Fonts dialog box enables you to set up a custom font theme (heading and body fonts, and so on) to apply to forms and reports. Creating custom fonts themes works just like adding your own color themes to an application. Save the theme with a name you'll recognize, and apply the font theme to forms and reports as needed.

FIGURE 9.15

Applying a color theme to all matching objects in an application

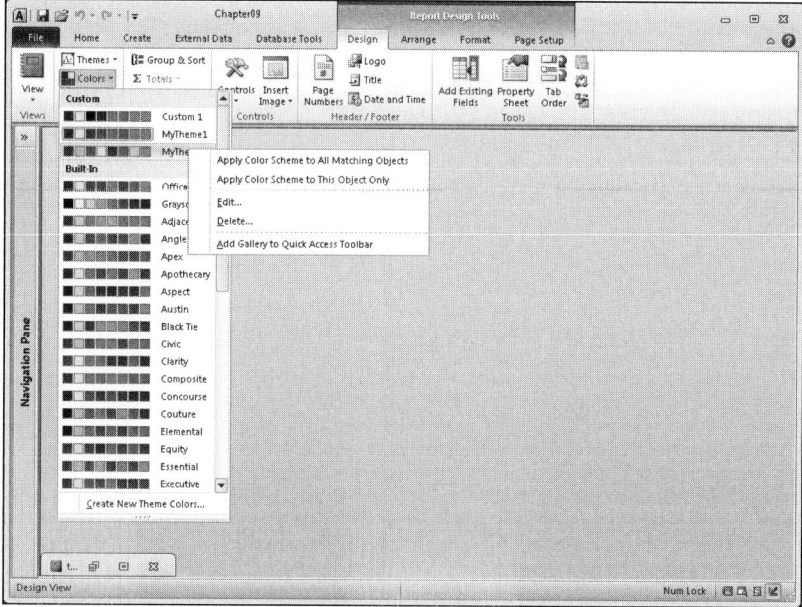

Using the Print Preview window

Figure 9.16 shows the Print Preview window in a zoomed view of rptProducts_Wizard. This view displays your report with the actual fonts, shading, lines, boxes, and data that will be used on the report when printed to the default Windows printer. Clicking the left mouse button on the report's surface changes the view to a page preview that shows the entire page.

The Access ribbon transforms to display controls relevant to viewing and printing the report. The Print Preview ribbon tab includes controls for adjusting the size, margins, page orientation (Portrait or Landscape), and other printing options. The print options are stored with the report when you save the report's design. The Print Preview tab also includes a Print button for printing the report, and another button for closing Print Preview and returning to the report's previous view (Design, Layout, or Report view).

You can move around the page by using the horizontal and vertical scrollbars, or use the Page controls (at the bottom-left corner of the window) to move from page to page. The Page controls include DVD-like navigation buttons to move from page to page or to the first or last page of the report. You can also go to a specific page of the report by entering a value in the text box between the Previous and Next controls.

FIGURE 9.16

Displaying `rptReport_Wizard` in the zoomed preview mode

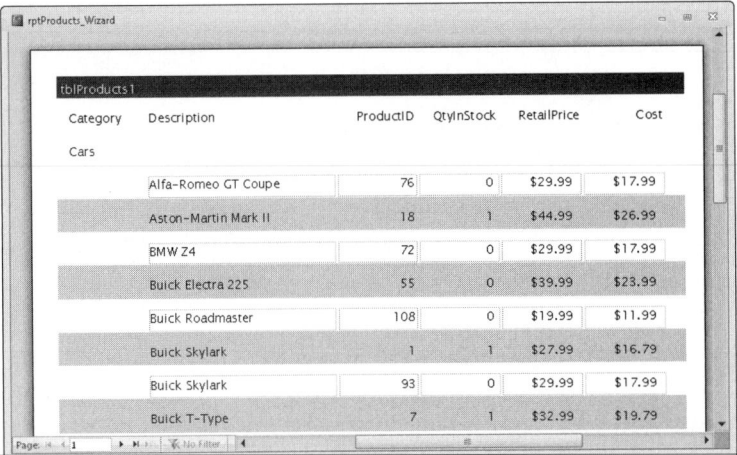

Right-clicking on the report and selecting the Multiple Pages option, or using the controls in the Zoom group in the Print Preview ribbon tab, lets you view more than one page of the report in a single view. Figure 9.17 shows a view of the report in the Print Preview's two-page mode. Use the navigation buttons (in the lower-left section of the Print Preview window) to move between pages, just as you would to move between records in a datasheet. The Print Preview window has a toolbar with commonly used printing commands.

FIGURE 9.17

Displaying multiple pages of a report in Print Preview's page preview mode

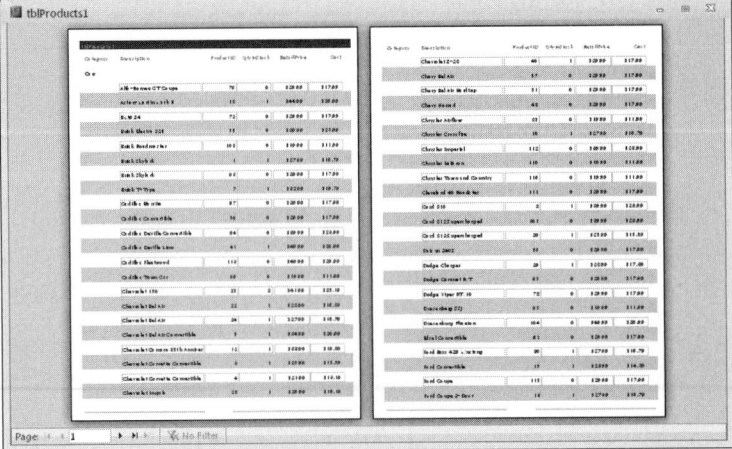

If, after examining the preview, you're satisfied with the report, click the Printer button on the toolbar to print the report. If you're dissatisfied with the design, select the Close button to switch to the Report Design window and make further changes.

Publishing in alternate formats

An important feature of the Print Preview tab is the ability to output the Access report in a number of common business formats, including PDF, XPS (XML Paper Specification), HTML, and other formats.

Clicking the PDF or XPS button in the Data ribbon group opens the Publish as PDF or XPS dialog box (shown in Figure 9.18). This dialog box provides options for outputting in standard PDF format or in a condensed version (for use in a Web context). You also specify the destination folder for the exported file.

FIGURE 9.18

Access 2010 provides powerful options for publishing reports.

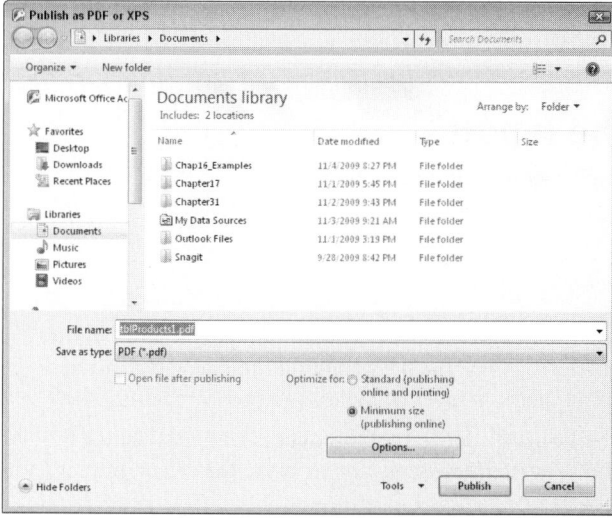

The PDF or XPS view of an Access report is indistinguishable from the report when viewed in Access. Either format is common in many business environments these days.

Viewing the Report Design window

Right-clicking the report's title bar and selecting Design View opens the Access Report Designer on the report. As shown in Figure 9.19, the report design reflects the choices you made using the Report Wizard.

FIGURE 9.19

The Report Design window

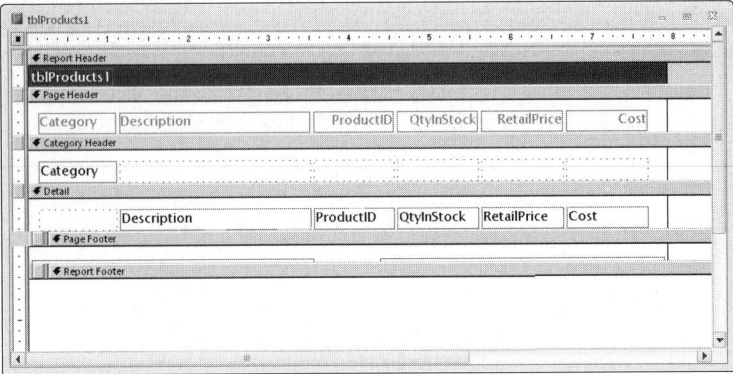

Return to the Print Preview mode by clicking the Print Preview button on the Report Design toolbar or by choosing File ⇨ Print Preview. You can also select File ⇨ Print or File ⇨ Page Setup. The File menu also provides options for saving your report.

Printing or viewing the report

The final step in the process of creating a report is printing or viewing it.

Printing the report

There are several ways to print your report:

- **Choose File ⇨ Print in the main Access window (with a report highlighted in the Navigation Pane).** Choosing File ⇨ Print opens the standard Print dialog box. You use this dialog box to select the print range, number of copies, and print properties.

- **Click the Print button on the Print Preview tab of the Access ribbon.** Clicking the Print button in the Access ribbon immediately sends the report to the default printer without displaying a Print dialog box.

Viewing the report

You can view a report in four different views: Design, Report, Layout, and Print Preview. (Layout view is described in the next section.) You can also print a report to the default Windows printer. You've already seen various preview windows in previous chapters. This chapter focuses on the Report Design window.

The Report Design window is one of two places where you create and modify reports. You began working with a new report by selecting a table or query to serve as the new report's data source. Click the Blank Report button in the Create tab of the main Access ribbon. By default, the new report appears in Layout view, as shown in Figure 9.20.

FIGURE 9.20

Layout view of a new report based on `tblProducts`

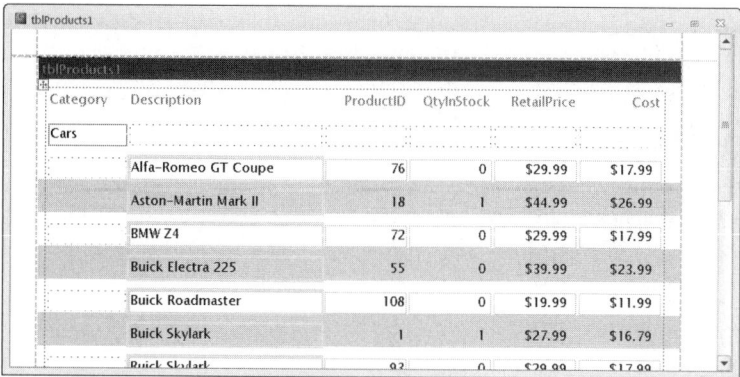

Layout view enables you to see the relative positions of the controls on the report's surface, as well as the margins, page headers and footers, and other report details.

The main constraint of Layout view is that you can't make fine adjustments to a report's design unless you put the report in Design view. Layout view is primarily intended to allow you to adjust the relative positions of controls on the report and is not meant for moving individual controls around on the report. For example, the icon that appears in the upper-left corner of the report shown in Figure 9.17 can be deleted by clicking on the icon and pressing the Delete button, or moved to another location by dragging it to a better location on the report's surface.

While in Layout view, you can also right-click any control and select Properties from the shortcut menu. The Property Sheet allows you to modify the default settings for the selected control.

Figure 9.21 shows the Access ribbon while a report is open in Layout view. Not surprisingly, the options on the ribbon are mostly involved with adjusting the appearance of the controls on the report.

FIGURE 9.21

The Access ribbon while a report is open in Layout view

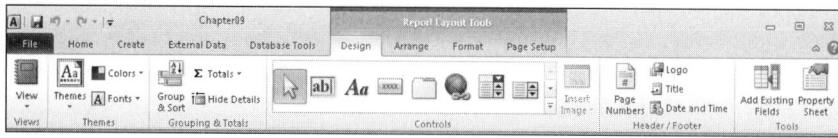

In Figure 9.21 notice that you can't adjust the fine details of a control, such as its height or width, but you can adjust the font used for the control, the font size, the BackColor, and the ForeColor of a report control. To adjust a control's height and width, click on the control and drag its margins to the new height or width.

Note
Layout view first became available in Access 2007. Versions earlier than 2007 do not support Layout view.

Saving the report

Save the report design at any time by choosing File ⇨ Save, File ⇨ Save As, or File ⇨ Export from the Report Design window, or by clicking the Save button on the Quick Access toolbar. The first time you save a report (or any time you select Save As or Export), a dialog box enables you to select or type a name.

Tip
You might find it useful to save a copy of a report before beginning maintenance work on the report. Reports tend to be pretty complicated, and it's easy to make a mistake on a report's design and not remember how to return the report to its previous state. A backup provides a valuable safeguard against accidental loss of a report's design.

Banded Report Design Concepts

Access reports support a "banded" approach to design. The banded report design is an important concept and must be mastered by Access developers. In an Access report, data is processed one record at a time. Individual fields may be placed in different places on report and can even appear more than once in a report, if needed.

Many first-time Access developers are confused by a report's appearance in Design view. Some people expect to see a "page" that is decorated by adding fields in a large design surface, much like how forms are built. However, because Access processes report data one record at a time, Design view is meant to help you specify how each row is laid out on the printed page. In addition, Design view shows you elements such as a page's header and footer, and areas occupied by group headers and footers. Each area occupied by controls plays a vital role in the report's appearance when printed.

Reports are divided into *sections*, known as *bands* in most report-writing software packages. (In Access, these are simply called *sections*.) Access processes each record in the underlying data set, processing each section in order and deciding (for each record) whether to process fields or text in that section. For example, the report footer section is processed only after the last record is processed in the recordset.

In Figure 9.22 (`rptProductsSummary`), is shown in Print Preview. Notice that the data on the report is grouped by `ProductCategory` (Cars, Trucks, and so on). Each group has a *group header* containing the category name. Each group also has a footer displaying summary information for the category. The *page header* contains column descriptions (Product ID, Description, and so on). The group footer that ends each group contains summary data for several columns in each group.

A portion of `rptProductsSummary`, a grouped report containing summary data

Group header   Page header

Group footer   Column totals

Page number

The following Access sections are available:

- **Report header:** Prints only at the beginning of the report; used for the title page.
- **Page header:** Prints at the top of each page.
- **Group header:** Prints before the first record of a group is processed.
- **Detail:** Prints each record in the table or recordset.
- **Group footer:** Prints after the last record of a group is processed.
- **Page Footer:** Prints at the bottom of each page.
- **Report footer:** Prints only at the end of a report after all records are processed.

Figure 9.23 shows rptProductSummary open in Design view. As you can see, the report is divided into as many as seven sections. The group section displays data grouped by categories, so you see the sections Category Header and Category Footer. Each of the other sections is also named for the type of processing it performs.

FIGURE 9.23

rptProductSummary in Design view

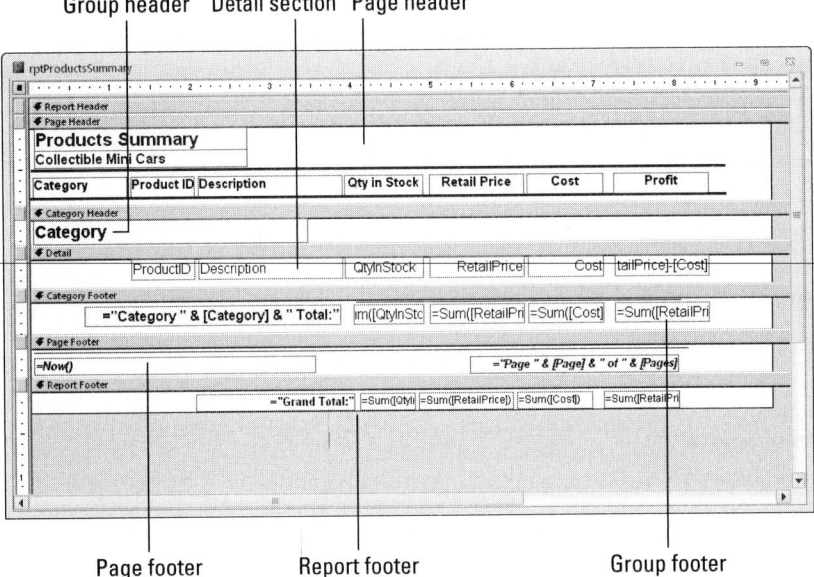

You can place any type of text or text-box controls in any section, but Access processes the data one record at a time. It also takes certain actions (based on the values of the group fields or current section of the page being processed) to make the bands or sections active. The example in Figure 9.20 is typical of a report with multiple sections. As you learned, each section in the report has a different purpose and different triggers.

Note

Page and report headers and footers are added as pairs. To add one without the other, resize the section you don't want to a height of 0 or set its Visible property to No.

Caution

If you remove a header or footer section, you also lose the controls in those sections.

The Report Header section

Controls in the Report Header section are printed only once, at the beginning of the report. A common use of a Report Header section is as a cover page or a cover letter or for information that needs to be communicated only once to the user of the report.

You can also have controls in the Report Header section print on a page that is separate from the rest of the report, which enables you to create a title page and include a graphic or picture in the Report Header. The `Force New Page` property in the Report Header section can be set to `After Section` to place the information in the report header in a separate page.

In Figure 9.23, the Report Header section is not used. Notice that the Report Header's height is 0.

Note
Only data from the first record can be placed in a report header.

The Page Header section

Controls in the Page Header section normally print at the top of every page. If a report header on the first page is not on a page of its own, the information in the Page Header section prints just below the report header information. Typically, page headers contain column headers in group/total reports. Page headers often contain a title for the report that appears on every page.

The `Page Header` section shown in Figure 9.23 contains horizontal lines above and below the label controls. Each label control can be moved or sized individually. You can also change special effects (such as color, shading, borders, line thickness, font type, and font size) for each control.

Both the Page Header and Page Footer sections can be set to one of four settings (found in the Report's properties, not the section properties):

- **All Pages:** The page header and page footer print on every page.
- **Not with Report Header:** Neither the page header nor footer prints on a page with the report header.
- **Not with Report Footer:** The page header does not print with the report footer. The report footer prints on a new page.
- **Not with Report Header/Footer:** Neither the page header nor the footer prints on a page with the report header or footer.

The Group Header section

A Group Header section normally displays the name of the group, such as "Trucks" or "Motorcycles." Access knows when all the records in a group have been displayed in a Detail section when the group name changes. In this example, the detail records are all about individual products. The Category control in the Category Header tells you that the products within the group belong to the indicated category (trucks or motorcycles). Group Header sections immediately precede Detail sections.

You can have multiple levels of group headers and footers. In this report, for example, the data is only for categories. However, in some reports you might have groups of information with date values. You could group your sections by year or by month and year, and within those sections by another group such as category.

Note

To set group-level properties such as Group On, Group Interval, Keep Together, or something other than the default, you must first set the `Group Header` and `Group Footer` property (or both) to `Yes` for the selected field or expression. You learn about these later in the chapter.

The Detail section

The Detail section processes *every* record in the data and is where each value is printed. The Detail section frequently contains calculated fields such as profit that is the result of a mathematical expression. In this example, the Detail section simply displays information from the `tblProduct` table except for the last control. The profit is calculated by subtracting the cost from the SalePrice.

Tip

You can tell Access whether you want to display a section in the report by changing the section's `Visible` property in the Report Design window. Turning off the display of the Detail section (or by excluding selected group sections) displays a summary report with no detail or with only certain groups displayed.

The Group Footer section

You use the Group Footer section to calculate summaries for all the detail records in a group. In the Products Summary report, the expression = `Sum([RetailPrice] - [Cost])` adds a value calculated from all the records within a category. The value of this text-box control is automatically reset to 0 every time the group changes.

Cross-Reference

You learn more about expressions and summary text boxes in Chapters 5 and 20.

Tip

You can change the way summaries are calculated by changing the `Running Sum` property of the text box in the Report Design window.

The Page Footer section

The Page Footer section usually contains page numbers or control totals. In very large reports, such as when you have multiple pages of detail records with no summaries, you might want page totals as well as group totals. For the Products Summary Report, the page number is printed by combining the text page, and built-in page number controls. These controls show Page *x* of *y* where *x* is the current page number and *y* is the total number of pages in the report. A text-box control with the following expression in the Control Source property can be used to display page-number information that keeps track of the page number in the report:

```
="Page: " & [Page] & " of " & [Pages]
```

You can also print the date and the time printed. You can see the page number text box in the Page Footer section in Figure 9.23. The Page Footer in rptProductsSummary also contains the current date and time at the left side of the Page Footer section.

The Report Footer section

The Report Footer section is printed once at the end of the report after all the detail records and group footer sections are printed. Report footers typically display grand totals or other statistics (such as averages or percentages) for the entire report. The report footer for the Products Summary report uses the expression = Sum with each of the numeric fields to sum the amounts.

Note
When there is a report footer, the Page Footer section is printed after the report footer.

The Report Writer in Access is a two-pass report writer, capable of preprocessing all records to calculate the totals (such as percentages) needed for statistical reporting. This capability enables you to create expressions that calculate percentages as Access processes those records that require foreknowledge of the grand total.

Creating a Report from Scratch

Fundamental to all reports is the concept that a report is another way to view records in one or more tables. It's important to understand that a report is bound to either a single table or a query that brings together data from one or more tables. When you create a report, you must select which fields from the query or table you want to see in your report. Unless you want to view all the records from a single table, bind your report to a query. Even if you're accessing data from a single table, using a query lets you create your report on the basis of a particular search criterion and sorting order. If you want to access data from multiple tables, you have almost no choice but to bind your report to a query. In the examples in this chapter, all the reports are bound to queries (even though it's possible to bind a report to a table).

It may be obvious, but it bears mentioning that the data in a printed report is static and only reflects the state of data in the database at the moment the report is printed. For this reason, every report should have a "printed" date and time somewhere on the report (often in the report header or footer area) to document exactly when the report was printed.

Note

Access lets you create a report without first binding it to a table or query, but you'll have no controls on the report. This capability can be used to work out page templates with common text headers or footers such as page numbering or the date and time, which can serve as models for other reports. You can add controls later by changing the underlying control source of the report.

Throughout the rest of this chapter, you learn the tasks necessary to create the Product Display Report (a part of a page is shown in Figure 9.24). In these sections, you design the basic report, assemble the data, and place the data in the proper positions.

FIGURE 9.24

The Product Display report

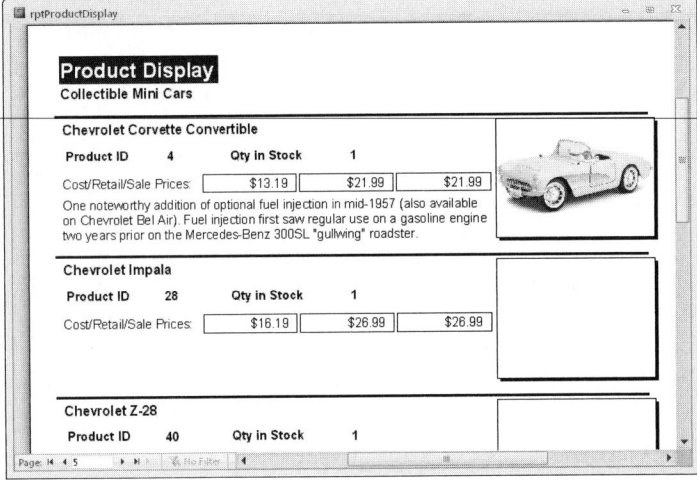

Tip

As with almost every task in Access, there are many ways to create a report without wizards. It is important, however, to follow some type of methodology, because creating a good report involves a fairly consistent approach. You should create a checklist that is a set of tasks that will result in a good report every time. As you complete each task, check it off your list. When you're done, you'll have a great-looking report. The following section outlines this approach.

Creating a new report and binding it to a query

The first step is to create a new, empty report and bind it to `tblProducts`. Creating a blank report is quite easy:

1. Select the Create tab of the main Access ribbon.

2. Click the Blank Report button in the Reports ribbon group.

   Access opens a blank report in Layout view, and positions a Field List dialog box on top of the new report (see Figure 9.25).

FIGURE 9.25

A blank report in Layout view

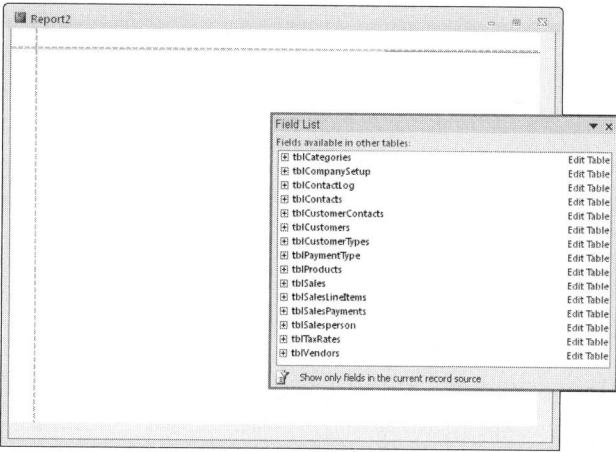

At this point, you have two different paths for adding controls to the report: continue working in Layout view, or switch to Design view. Each of these techniques has advantages, but for the purposes of this exercise I'll use Design view because it better demonstrates the process of building Access reports.

3. Right-click the report's title bar, and select Design view from the shortcut menu.

   The Report window transforms to the traditional Access banded Report Designer, as shown in Figure 9.26. This figure also shows the Field List open on `tblProducts`, allowing you to track fields from the list to the appropriate section on the new report.

   In Figure 9.26, the Description field has been dragged onto the Detail section of the report.

Building the new report in Design view

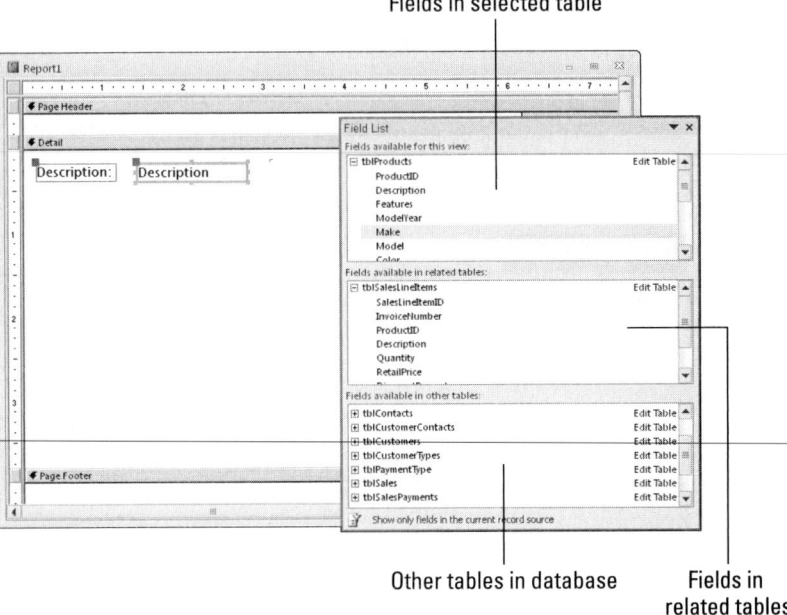

Fields in selected table

Other tables in database

Fields in related tables

Defining the report page size and layout

As you plan your report, consider the page-layout characteristics as well as the kind of paper and printer you want to use for the output. As you make these decisions, you use several dialog boxes and properties to make adjustments. These specifications work together to create the desired output.

Click the Page Setup tab in the Access ribbon to select the report's margins, orientation, and other overall characteristics. Figure 9.27 shows a portion of the Access screen with the Page Setup tab selected, and the Margins option open.

Notice that the Page Setup tab includes options for setting the paper size, the report's orientation (Portrait or Landscape), its margins, and other details. Dropping down either the Size or Margins option reveals a tab containing common settings for each of these options.

rptProductDisplay is to be a portrait report, which is taller than it is wide. You want to print on letter size paper (8½ x 11 inches), and you want the left, right, top, and bottom margins all set to 0.25 inches. In Figure 9.27 notice that the Narrow margins option is selected, which specifies exactly 0.25 inches for all four margin settings.

FIGURE 9.27

Setting a report's margins

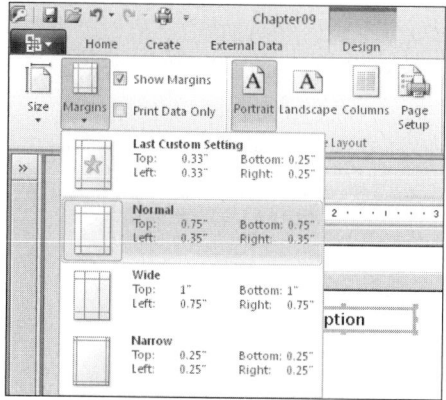

If the margins you need for your particular report are not shown in the Margins options, click the small button in the lower-right corner of the Page Layout group to open the common Windows Page Setup dialog box. This dialog box enables you to specify the margins, orientation, and other page-layout specifications as you would in Microsoft Word or any other Windows application.

To set the right border for the Product Display report to 7½ inches, follow these steps:

1. Click the right edge of the report body (where the white page meets the gray background).

   The mouse pointer changes to a double-headed arrow.

2. Drag the edge to the 7½-inch mark.

Note

Your units of measure may be different, depending on the regional settings in Control Panel.

If the ruler isn't displayed in the Report Designer, select the Layout tab, move to the Show/Hide group, and click the ruler icon.

Note

You can also change the Width property in the Property window for the report.

Tip

If you run your report and every other page is blank, it's a sign that the width of your report exceeds the width of your page. To fix this problem, decrease the left and right margin size or reduce the report's width. Sometimes, when you move controls around, you accidentally make the report width larger than you originally intended. For example, in a portrait report, if your left margin plus report width plus right margin is greater than 8½ inches, you'll see blank pages.

Placing controls on the report

Access takes full advantage of drag-and-drop capabilities of Windows. The method for placing controls on a report is no exception:

1. Click the Add Existing Fields button in the Tools group of the Design ribbon tab.

   The Field List window appears.

2. Choose a control in the Toolbox if you want to use something other than the default control types for the fields.

3. Select each field that you want on your report and then drag them to the appropriate section of the Report Design window.

   Select multiple fields by holding down the Ctrl key as you click on fields in the Field List. Depending on whether you choose one or several fields, the mouse pointer changes shape to represent your selection as you drag fields onto the report.

   The fields appear in the detail section of the report, as shown in Figure 9.28. Notice that for each field you dragged onto the report, there are two controls. When you use the drag-and-drop method of placing fields, Access automatically creates a label control with the field name attached to the Text control to which the field is bound.

FIGURE 9.28

The report with several fields added

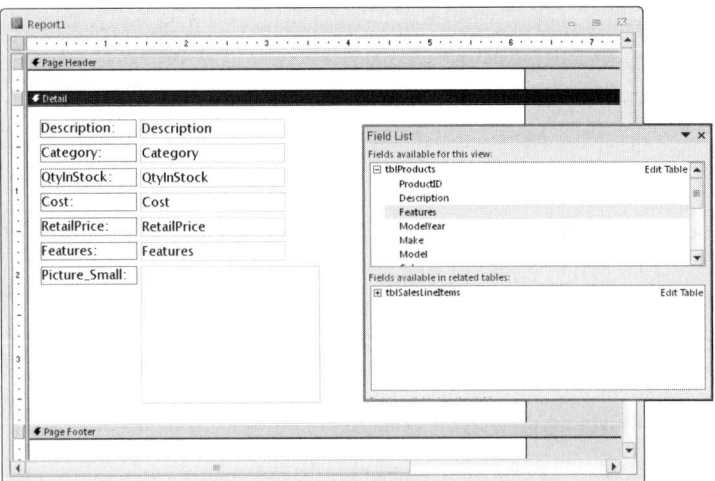

Note

Notice the Bound Object Frame control for the `Small_Picture` field. Access always creates a Bound Object Frame control for an OLE-type object found in a table. Also notice that the Detail section automatically resizes itself to fit all the controls. Above the Bound Object Frame control is the control for the memo field Features.

Controls are needed for the customer information in the page header section. Before you do this, however, you must resize the page header to leave room for a title you'll add later.

Resizing a section

To make room on the report for the title information in the page header, you must resize it. You resize by using the mouse to drag the bottom of the section you want to resize. The mouse pointer turns into a vertical double-headed arrow as it's positioned over the bottom of a report section. Drag the section border up or down to make the section smaller or larger.

Resize the Page Header section to make it about ¾ inch high by dragging the bottom margin of the page header downward. Use the Controls group on the Design ribbon tab to drag labels to the report. Add two labels to the Page Header section, and enter **Product Display** as the Caption property of one label, and **Collectible Mini Cars** for the other.

The labels you just added are unattached; they aren't related to any other controls on the report. When you drag a field from the Field List, Access adds not only a text box to contain the field's data, but also a label to provide an identifier for the text box. Labels that you drag from the Controls group on the Access ribbon are unattached and not related to text boxes or any other control on the report.

You may notice the Page Header section expanding to accommodate the label controls that you dragged into the section. All the fields needed for the Product Display report are now placed in their appropriate sections.

Tip

To create a multiple-line label entry, press Ctrl+Enter to force a line break where you want it in the control.

Tip

If you enter a caption that is longer than the space in the Property window, the contents scroll as you type. Otherwise, open a Zoom box that gives you more space to type by pressing Shift+F2.

Modifying the appearance of text in a control

To modify the appearance of the text in a control, select the control by clicking its border (not in the control itself). You can then select a formatting style to apply to the label by clicking the appropriate button on the Formatting toolbar.

To make the titles stand out, follow these steps to modify the appearance of label text:

1. Click the newly created report heading Product Display label.

2. Click the Formatting ribbon tab, and select the Bold button in the Font group on the ribbon.

3. From the Font Size drop-down list, select 18.

4. Repeat for the Collectible Mini Cars label, using a 12 pt Arial font and Bold.

   The size of the labels may not fit their displayed text. To tighten the display or to display all the text when a label isn't big enough, double-click any of the sizing handles, and Access chooses an appropriate size for the label.

   Figure 9.29 shows these labels added, resized, and formatted in the report's Page Header section.

FIGURE 9.29

Adding unbound labels to the report

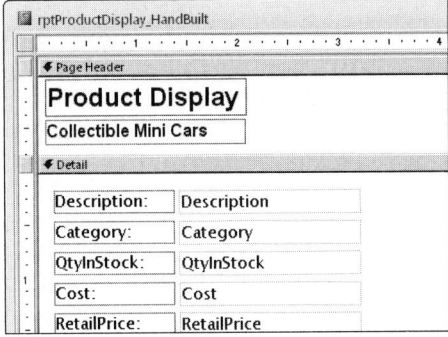

Working with text boxes

So far, you added controls bound to fields in the tables and unbound label controls used to display titles in your report. There is another type of text-box control that is typically added to a report: unbound text boxes that are used to hold expressions such as page numbers, dates, or a calculation.

Adding and using text-box controls

In reports, text-box controls serve two purposes:

- They enable you to display stored data from a particular field in a query or table.

- They display the result of an expression.

Expressions can be calculations that use other controls as their operands, calculations that use Access functions (either built in or user defined), or a combination of the two.

Entering an expression in a text control

Expressions enable you to create a value that is not already in a table or query. They can range from simple functions (such as a page number) to complex mathematical computations.

Cross-Reference

Chapter 5 discusses expressions in greater detail.

A function is a small program that, when run, returns a single value. The function can be one of many built-in Access functions or it can be user defined.

The following steps show you how to use an unbound text box to add a page number to your report:

1. Click in the middle of the Page Footer section, and resize the page footer so that it is ½ inch in height.

2. Drag a text-box control from the Controls group on the Design ribbon tab and drop it into the Page Footer area. Make the text box about three-quarters of the height of the Page Footer section and about ½ inch wide.

3. Select the text box's attached label and change its contents to say **Page:**.

4. Select the text box control (it says "Unbound") and enter **= Page** directly into the text box.

   Alternatively, you could open the Property Sheet (press F4) and enter **= [Page]** as the text box's `ControlSource` property.

5. Drag the new text-box control until it's near the right edge of the report's page, as shown in Figure 9.30.

   You may want to also move the text box's label so that it's positioned close to the text box. The upper-left handle on the label moves the label independently of the text box.

FIGURE 9.30

Adding a page-number expression in a text-box control

Tip
You can always check your result by clicking the Print Preview button on the toolbar and zooming in on the Page Footer section to check the page number.

Sizing a text-box control or label control

You select a control by clicking it. Depending on the size of the control, from three to seven sizing handles appear — one on each corner except the upper-left corner and one on each side. Moving the mouse pointer over one of the sizing handles changes the mouse pointer to a double-headed arrow. When the pointer changes, click the control and drag it to the size you want. Notice that, as you drag, an outline appears indicating the size the label control will be when you release the mouse button.

If you double-click any of the sizing handles, Access resizes a control to best fit for text in the control. This feature is especially handy if you increase the font size and then notice that the text no longer fits the control.

Note that, for label controls, the *best-fit sizing* resizes both vertically and horizontally, although text controls resize only vertically. The reason for this difference is that in Report Design mode, Access doesn't know how much of a field's data you want to display. Later on, the field's name and contents might be radically different. Sometimes label controls are not resized correctly, however, and have to be adjusted manually.

Tip
You can also choose Arrange ⇨ Size/Space ⇨ To Fit to change the size of the label control text automatically.

Before continuing, you should check how the report is progressing. You should also save the report frequently as you make changes to it. You could send a single page to the printer, but it's probably easier to view the report in Print Preview. Right-click the report's title bar, and select Print Preview from the shortcut menu. Figure 9.31 shows a print preview of the report's current appearance. The page header information is at the very top of the page, and the first product record appears below the header.

As you move the mouse over the print preview, the cursor changes to a magnifying glass. Click any portion of the view to zoom in so that can closely examine the report's layout. Only one record per page appears on the report because of the vertical layout. In the next section, you move the controls around and create a more horizontal layout.

Deleting and cutting attached labels from text controls

To create the report shown in Figure 9.31, you must move the text-box labels from the Detail section to the Page Header section. Once moved, these controls appear as headings above each column of data and are repeated on each page of the report.

FIGURE 9.31

A print preview of the report so far

Controls in page header

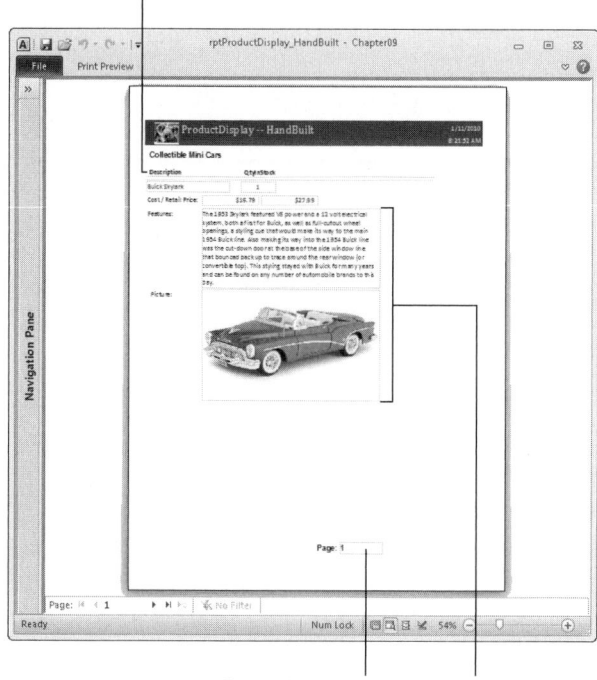

Controls in page footer   Detail section

You can easily delete one or more attached controls in a report. Simply select the desired controls and press Delete. However, if you want to *move* the label to the Page Header section (rather than simply deleting it), you can cut the label instead of deleting it. When removing attached controls, there are three choices:

- Delete only the label control.
- Cut the label control to the Clipboard.
- Delete or cut the label and the text-box control.

Oddly enough, you can't simply drag a label from the Detail section to the page header. Dragging an attached label from the Detail section drags its text box along with it. You must cut the label from the Detail section and paste it into the Page Header section.

If you select the label control and cut it by pressing Ctrl+X, only the label control is removed. If you select the text-box control and cut or delete it, the label and the text-box controls are removed.

To cut an attached label control (in this case, the label attached to the Description text box), follow these steps:

1. Click the Close button on the toolbar to exit Print Preview mode.

2. Select the Description label in the Detail section.

3. Press Ctrl+X (Cut).

   After you've cut the label, you may want to place it somewhere else. In this example, place it in the Page Header section.

Pasting labels into a report section

It's as easy to cut labels from controls placed in the Detail section and paste them into the page header as it is to delete the labels and create new ones in the page header. Regardless, you now paste the label you cut in the previous steps:

1. Click anywhere in or on the Page Header section.

2. Press Ctrl+V (Paste).

   The Product ID label appears in the page header.

3. Repeat for the Quantity in Stock labels.

   If you accidentally selected the data text-box control and both controls are cut or deleted, click the Undo toolbar button, or press Ctrl+Z, to undo the action.

Tip

If you want to delete only the text-box control and keep the attached label control, right-click the label control and select Copy from the shortcut menu. Next, to delete the text-box control and the label control, select the text-box control and press the Delete key. Finally, right-click anywhere on the form and select Paste from the shortcut menu to paste only the copied label control to the report.

Moving label and text controls

Before discussing how to move label and text controls, it's important to review a few differences between attached and unattached controls. When an attached label is created automatically with a text control, it's called a *compound control*. In a compound control, whenever one control in the set is moved, the other control moves along with it. This means that, moving either the label or the text box also moves the related control.

To move both controls in a compound control, select either of the pair of controls with the mouse. As you move the mouse pointer over either of the objects, the pointer turns into a hand. Click the controls and drag them to their new location. As you drag, an outline for the compound control moves with your pointer.

To move only one of the controls in a compound control, drag the desired control by its moving handle (the large square in the upper-left corner of the control). When you click a compound control, it looks like both controls are selected, but if you look closely, you see that only one of the two controls (text box or label) is selected (as indicated by the presence of both moving and sizing handles). The unselected control displays only a moving handle. A pointing finger indicates that you've selected the move handles and can now move one control independently of the other. To move either control individually, select the control's move handle and drag it to its new location.

Cross-Reference

To move a label that isn't attached, simply click any border (except where there is a handle) and drag it.

To make a group selection, click with the mouse pointer anywhere outside a starting point and drag the pointer through (or around) the controls you want to select. A gray, outlined rectangle appears, showing the extent of the selection. When you release the mouse button, all controls the rectangle surrounds are selected. You can then drag the group of controls to a new location.

Tip

The Selection Behavior option (choose File ⇨ Options ⇨ Object Designers ⇨ Form/Reports ⇨ Selection Behavior) determines how controls are selected with the mouse. You can enclose them fully (the rectangle must completely surround the selection) or partially (the rectangle must touch only the control), which is the default.

Make sure you also resize all the controls as shown in the figure. Change the size and shape of the Features memo field and the OLE picture field Picture. The OLE picture field displays as a rectangle with no field name in Design view. (It's to the right in Figure 9.32.)

Place all the controls in their proper position to complete the report layout. Figure 9.32 shows one possible layout of the controls. You make a series of group moves by selecting several controls and positioning them close to where you want them. Then, if needed, you can fine-tune their position by dragging individual controls.

Use Figure 9.32 as a guide to placing on the report. Notice that the Cost label in the Detail section has been renamed to Cost/Retail Prices.

At this point, you're about halfway done. The screen should look something like Figure 9.32. Remember that these screenshots are taken with the Windows screen resolution set to 1,024 x 768. If you're using a lower resolution, or you have large fonts turned on in the Windows Display Properties (in the Control Panel), you have to scroll the screen to see the entire report.

These steps complete the rough design for this report. There are still properties, fonts, and sizes to change. When you make these changes, you have to move controls around again. Use the designs in Figure 9.32 only as a guideline. How it looks to *you*, as you refine the look of the report in the Report window, determines the final design.

FIGURE 9.32

Rearranging the controls on the report

Modifying the appearance of multiple controls

The next step is to apply bold formatting to all the label controls in the Page Header section directly above the section separator. The following steps guide you through modifying the appearance of text in multiple label controls:

1. Select all label controls in the bottom of the Page Header section by clicking them one at a time while holding down the Shift key.

   Alternatively, click in the vertical ruler immediately to the left of the labels in the Page Header. Access selects all controls to the right of where you clicked in the vertical ruler. There are four label controls to select (refer to Figure 9.32).

   Alternatively, you can drag a bounding box around the label controls in the page header.

2. Click the Bold button on the toolbar.

   After you make the final modifications, you're finished, except for fixing the picture control. To do this, you need to change properties, which you do in the next section.

Note

This may seem to be an enormous number of steps because the procedures were designed to show you how laying out a report design can be a slow process. Remember, however, that when you click away with the mouse, you don't realize how many steps you're doing as you visually design the report layout. With a WYSIWYG (What You See Is What You Get) layout tool like the Access Report Designer, you might need to perform many tasks, but it's still easier and faster than programming. Figure 9.32 shows the final version of the design layout as seen in this chapter. In the next chapter, you continue to improve this report layout.

Changing label and text-box control properties

To change the properties of a text or label control, you need to display the control's Property Sheet. If it isn't already displayed, perform one of these actions to display it:

- Double-click the border of the control (anywhere except a sizing handle or move handle).
- Select a control and press F4.
- Right-click the control with the mouse and select Properties.
- Press F4 to open the Properties window, and use the drop-down list at the top of the window to select the form or control on the form.

The Property Sheet enables you to look at and edit a control's property settings. Using tools on the Design ribbon, such as the formatting windows and text-formatting buttons, also changes the property settings of a control. Clicking the Bold button in the Design tab, for example, sets the control's Font Weight property to Bold. It's usually easier and more intuitive to use the controls on the Design ribbon, but many properties are not accessible through the ribbon. Plus, objects often have more options available through the Property Sheet.

The Size Mode property of an OLE object (bound object frame), with its options of Clip, Stretch, and Zoom, is a good example of a property that is available only through the Property Sheet.

The image control, which is a bound object frame, presently has its Size Mode property set to Clip, which is the default. With Clip, the picture is displayed in its original size and may be too large to fit in the frame. With Size Mode set to Clip, Access simply cuts off the picture at the edge of its control. In this exercise, you change the setting to Stretch so that the picture is automatically sized to fit the picture frame.

Follow these steps to change the property for the bound object frame control that contains the picture:

1. Click the frame control of the picture bound object.
2. Click the Size Mode property and click the arrow to display the drop-down list box.
3. Select Stretch.

You might also consider changing the Border Style property to Transparent. When set to Transparent, no boxes are drawn around the picture and the picture blends into the report's surface.

These steps complete the changes to your report so far. A print preview of the first few records appears in Figure 9.33. If you look at the pictures, notice how the picture is properly displayed and the product's Features text box now appears across the bottom of each Detail section.

FIGURE 9.33

The report displayed in Print Preview

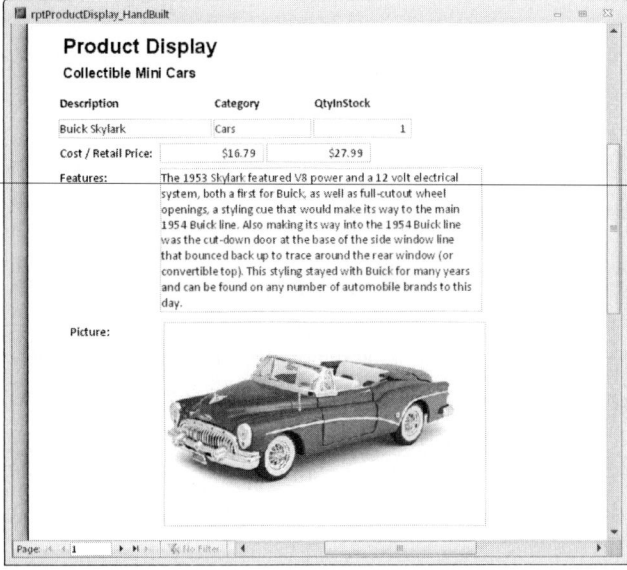

Growing and shrinking text-box controls

When you print or print-preview controls that can have variable text lengths, Access provides options for enabling a control to grow or shrink vertically, depending on the exact contents of a record. The Can Grow and Can Shrink properties determine whether a text control resizes its vertical dimension to accommodate the amount of text contained in its bound field. Although these properties are usable for any text control, they're especially helpful for text-box controls.

Table 9.1 explains the acceptable values for these two properties.

TABLE 9.1

Text Control Values for Can Grow and Can Shrink

Property	Value	Description
Can Grow	Yes	If the data in a record uses more lines than the control is defined to display, the control resizes to accommodate additional lines.
Can Grow	No	If the data in a record uses more lines than the control is defined to display, the control does not resize. Rather, it truncates the data in the control.
Can Shrink	Yes	If the data in a record uses fewer lines than the control is defined to display, the control resizes to eliminate blank space. The Can Shrink property of all controls in the section must be set to Yes before the section can shrink.
Can Shrink	No	If the data in a record uses fewer lines than the control is defined to display, the control does not resize to eliminate blank space.

To change the Can Grow settings for a text control, follow these steps:

1. Select the Features text-box control.
2. Display the Property window.
3. Click the Can Grow property, click the arrow, and select Yes.

Note

The Can Grow and Can Shrink properties are also available for report sections. Use a section's Property Sheet to modify these values. Setting a report section's Can Grow and Can Shrink affects only the section, not the controls contained within the section. However, you must set the section's Can Grow to Yes to allow the control within the section to grow. If the section's Can Grow is not set, the control can only expand as far as the section's border permits.

The report is starting to look good, but you may want to see groups of like data together and determine specific orders of data. To do this, you use sorting and grouping.

Sorting and grouping data

You can often make the data on the report more useful to users by grouping the data in informative ways. Suppose that you want to list your products first by category and then by description within each category. To do this, you use the Category and Description fields to group and sort the data.

Creating a group header or footer

Grouping on a field in the report's data adds two new sections — Group Header and Group Footer — to the report. In the following steps, you use the group header to display the name of the product category above each group of records. You won't use the Category group footer in this example because there are no totals by category or other reasons to use a group footer.

Follow these steps to create a Category group header:

1. Click the Sort & Group button in the Grouping and Totals group of the Design ribbon tab. You should see that the report's data already sorted by Description and Category.

2. Click the Add a Group button in the Group, Sort, and Total area.

3. Select Category from the field list, and Access adds Group on Category with A on top of the Group, Sort, and Total area.

   Access adds Category Header and Category Footer sections to the report's design as soon as you select the Category field for grouping. The Category Header section appears between the Page Header and Detail sections. If you define a group footer, it appears below the Detail section, and above the Page Footer area. If a report has multiple groupings, each subsequent group becomes the one closest to the Detail section. The groups defined first are farthest from the Detail section.

The Group Properties pane (displayed at the bottom of the Sorting and Grouping box) contains these properties:

- **Group Header:** Yes creates a group header. No removes the group header.
- **Group Footer:** Yes creates a group footer. No removes the group footer.
- **Group On:** Specifies how you want the values grouped. The options you see in the drop-down list box depend on the data type of the field on which you're grouping. If you group on an expression, you see all grouping options.

For Text data types, there are two choices:

- **Each Value:** The same value in the field or expression.
- **Prefix Characters:** The same first n number of characters in the field.

For Date/Time data types, there are additional options:

- **Each Value:** The same value within the field or expression.
- **Year:** Dates within the same calendar year.
- **Qtr:** Dates within the same calendar quarter.
- **Month:** Dates within the same month.
- **Week:** Dates within the same week.
- **Day:** Dates on the same date.
- **Hour:** Times within the same hour.
- **Minute:** Times within the same minute.

Currency, or Number data types provide three options:

- **Each Value:** Includes the same value in the field or expression.
- **Interval:** Includes values falling within the interval you specify.
- **Group Interval:** Specifies any interval that is valid for the values in the field or expression you're grouping on. The Group Interval has its own options:
  - **Keep Together:** Controls widows and orphans so that you don't have a header at the bottom of a page without detail until the next page.
  - **Whole Group:** Prints header detail and group footer on one page.
  - **With First Detail:** Prevents the contents of the group header from printing without any following data or records on a page.
  - **No:** Does not keep data together.

Sorting data within groups

Sorting enables you to determine the order in which the records are viewed on the report, based on the values in one or more controls. This order is important when you want to view the data in your tables in a sequence other than that of your input. For example, new products are added to tblProducts as they're needed on an invoice. The physical order of the database reflects the date and time a product is added. Yet, when you think of the product list, you probably expect it to be in alphabetical order by Product ID, and you want to sort it by Description of the cost of the product. By sorting in the report itself, you don't have to worry about the order of the data. Although you can sort the data in the table by the primary key or in a query by any field you want, there are good reasons to do it in the report. This way, if you change the query or table, the report is still in the correct order.

In the case of the products report, you want to display the records in each category group sorted by description. Follow these steps to define a sort order based on the Description field within the Category grouping:

1. Click the Grouping button in the Design ribbon tab to display the Group, Sort, and Total area, if it isn't already open.

   You should see that the Category group already exists in the report.

2. Click the Add a Sort button in the Group, Sort, and Total area.

3. Select Description in the Field List.

   Notice that Sort Order defaults to Ascending.

4. Close the Group, Sort, and Total area by clicking the X in the upper-right corner.

   The Group, Sort, and Total section should now look like Figure 9.34.

FIGURE 9.34

The Group, Sort, and Total area completed

With A on Top button

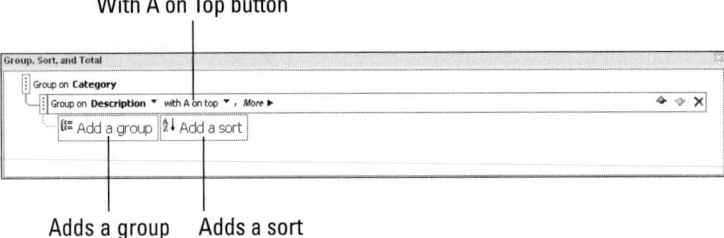

Adds a group   Adds a sort

Although in this example you used a field, you can also sort (and group) with an expression. To enter an expression, click the Add a Sort or Add a Group button in the Group, Sort, and Total area and click the Expression button at the bottom of the field list. The Expression Builder dialog box opens, enabling you to enter any valid Access expression, such as in = [**RetailPrice**]-[**Cost**].

To change the sort order for fields in the Field/Expression column, simply click the drop-down arrow to the right of the With A on Top button (see Figure 9.34) to display the Sort Order list. Select Descending from the sort options that appear.

Removing a group header or footer

To remove a group header or footer, display the Group, Sort, and Total area, select the group or sort specifier to delete, and press the Delete key. Any controls in the group header or footer will be removed.

Hiding a section

Access also enables you to hide headers and footers so that you can break data into groups without having to view information about the group itself. You can also hide the Detail section so that you see only a summary report. To hide a section, follow these steps:

1. Click the section you want to hide.

2. Display the section's Property Sheet.

3. Click the Visible property and select No from the drop-down list in the property's text box.

Note

Sections are not the only objects in a report that can be hidden; controls also have a Visible property. This property can be useful for expressions that trigger other expressions.

Sizing a section

Now that you've created the group header, you might want to put some controls in the section, move some controls around, or even move controls between sections. Before you start manipulating controls within a section, you should make sure the section is the proper height.

To modify the height of a section, drag the top border of the section below it. If, for example, you have a report with a page header, Detail section, and page footer, change the height of the Detail section by dragging the top of the Page Footer section's border. You can make a section larger or smaller by dragging the bottom border of the section.

For this example, change the height of the group header section to ⅛ inch by following these steps:

1. Move your mouse pointer to the bottom of the Category section.

   The pointer changes to a horizontal line split by two vertical arrows.

2. Select the top of the Detail section (which is also the bottom of the Category Header section).

3. Drag the selected band lower until three dots appear in the vertical ruler (⅜") and release the mouse button when you have the band positioned.

   The gray line indicates where the top of the border will be when you release the mouse button.

Moving controls between sections

You now want to move the Category control from the Detail section to the Category Header section. You can move one or more controls between sections by simply dragging the control with your mouse from one section to another or by cutting it from one section and pasting it to another section:

1. Select the Category control in the Detail section and drag it up to the Category Header section as shown in Figure 9.35.

   You should now perform the following steps to complete the report design:

2. Delete the Category label from the page header.

3. Move the ProductID control and its associated label after the Description control and its associated label, as shown in Figure 9.35.

4. Move the Description control and its associated label to the left so that it starts just to the right of the start of the Category control in the Category Header control.

   By offsetting the first control in the Detail section slightly to the right of the start of the control in the Group Header section, you show the hierarchy of the data presented in the report. It now shows that each group of products is for the category listed in the group header.

5. Lengthen the Description control so that it approaches the ProductID control.

Figure 9.35 shows this property window and the completed report design. The Property Sheet is opened in this figure so that you can see how the Force New Page property is set for the Category Header section.

FIGURE 9.35

Completing the Group Header section and forcing a page break before the Category Header section

In Figure 9.35 notice that the group header is named Category. You name a report section by selecting the section bar (such as GroupHeader0) and provide a name for the section in the Property Sheet.

Adding page breaks

Access enables you to force page breaks based on groups. You can also insert forced breaks within sections, except in Page Header and Page Footer sections.

In some report designs, it's best to have each new group begin on a different page. You can achieve this effect easily by using the Force New Page property of a group section, which enables you to force a page break every time the group value changes.

The four `Force New Page` property settings are

- **None:** No forced page break (the default)
- **Before Section:** Starts printing the current section at the top of a new page every time there is a new group
- **After Section:** Starts printing the next section at the top of a new page every time there is a new group
- **Before & After:** Combines the effects of Before Section and After Section

To force a page break before the Category group:

1. Click anywhere in the Category header, or click the Category Header bar above the section.
2. Display the Property Sheet and select `Before Section` in the `Force New Page` property's drop-down list.

Tip

Alternatively, you can set the `Force New Page` property to `After Section` in the Category Footer section.

Sometimes, you want to force a page break, but not on the basis of a grouping. For example, you might want to split a report title across several pages. The solution is to use the Page Break control from the ribbon's Controls group. Drag the Page Break control and drop it on the report where you want a page break to occur each time the page prints.

Note

Be careful not to split data in a control. Place page breaks above or below controls without overlapping them.

Improving the Report's Appearance

As you near completion of testing your report design, you should also test the printing of your report. Figure 9.36 shows the first page of the Product Display report. There are a number of things still to do to complete the report.

The report is pretty boring and plain. If your goal is to just look at the data, this report is done. However, you need to do more before you're really done.

Although the report has good, well-organized data, it isn't of professional quality. To make a report more visually appealing, you generally add a few graphic elements like lines and rectangles, and possibly some special effects such as shadows or sunken areas. You want to make sure sections have distinct areas separate from each other using lines or colors. Make sure controls aren't touching each other (because text might eventually touch if a value is long enough). Make sure text is aligned with other text above or below and to the right or left.

In Figure 9.36, you can see opportunities for improvements.

The report is pretty plain and uninteresting at this point.

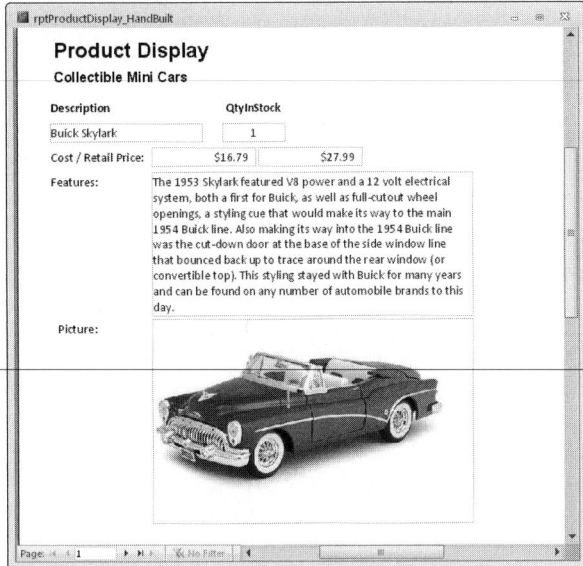

Adjusting the page header

The page header contains several large labels positioned far apart from each other. The column headers are small and just hanging there. They could be made one font size larger. The entire page header should be separated from the Detail section by a horizontal line.

If you wanted to add some color to your report, you could make the report name a different color. Be careful not to use too many colors unless you have a specific theme in mind, though. Most serious business reports use one or two colors, and rarely more than three with the exception of graphs and charts. Furthermore, colors are not much use when printed on most laser printers. Color laser printers are just becoming widely available, so adding a lot of color to your Access reports may not be appreciated by your users.

Figure 9.37 shows these changes. The Product Display label has been changed to a blue background color with white foreground text. This is done by first selecting the control and then selecting Blue for the background. They've also been placed under each other and left aligned. The rectangle around each of the controls was also properly sized by double-clicking each control's sizing handles.

The next step is to add a nice thick line separating the Page Header section from the Category Group Header section:

1. Select the Line tool in the Controls ribbon group.

2. Place the mouse cursor near the far left side of the Page Header, just to the right and above the 1-inch mark on the vertical toolbar, as shown in Figure 9.37.

FIGURE 9.37

Adjusting controls in the page header

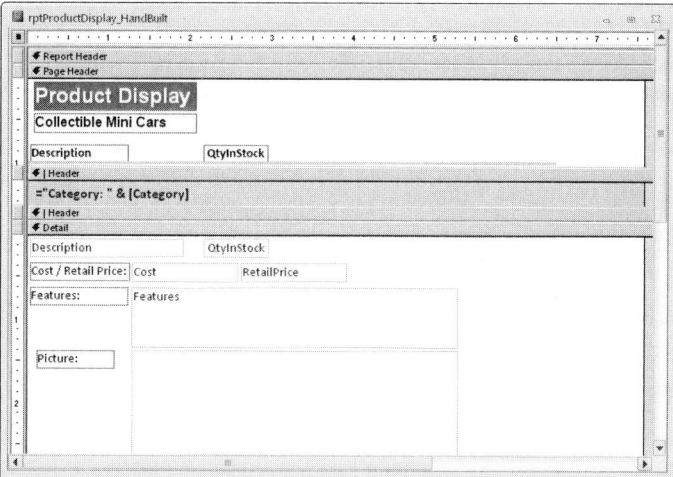

3. Hold down the Shift key and drag the mouse across the page header, releasing it just to the left of the 7½-inch mark.

   Holding down the Shift key forces a nice, straight, horizontal line.

4. Select the line and select the 2 pt Border Width property from the line's property window.

Creating an expression in the group header

Figure 9.37 also shows that the Category field has been replaced by an expression. If you place the value of the category in the Group Header section, it looks out of place and may not be readily identifiable. Most data values should have some type of label to identify what they are.

The expression ="Category: " & [Category] displays Category: followed by a space and the value of the Category field (such as Category: Cars) in the text box. The & symbol (the concatenation operator) joins strings. Make sure you leave a space after the colon or the value won't be separated from the label. The text control has been bolded and underlined, and the font point size has been increased as well.

You may find that Access complains about a circular reference on the `Category` text box after you change the control's `ControlSource`. This happens because the name of the control is `Category`, and the text box is bound to a field named Category. Access doesn't understand that [Category] in the expression you entered as the `ControlSource` actually refers to the field, not the text box. (A text box's value can't be based on the text box's contents — that's the definition of *circular reference*.) The solution is to rename the text box to `txtCategory` to distinguish it from its bound field.

Caution

When you create a bound control, it uses the name of the data field as the default control name. Using the control in an expression without changing the name of your control, causes circular references. You must manually rename the control to something other than the original field name. This is another reason why a simple naming convention, such as prefixing text boxes with `txt`, is such a good idea. You'll avoid a lot of nagging problems by adopting a naming convention for the controls on your Access reports.

Follow these steps to complete the expression and rename the control:

1. Select the `Category` control in the Category Group Header section and display the property window for the control.

2. Change the `ControlSource` property to `="Category: " & [Category]`.

3. Change the `Name` property to `txtCategoryDisplay`.

Enhancing the Detail section

The Detail section is in fairly good shape. Make sure the Description control is slightly indented from the Category expression in the Group Header. A label should be created, as shown in Figure 9.37, identifying the values in the `Cost` and `Retail Price` controls.

A line is also good to add to this Detail section to separate one record from another. This is often done when records occupy varying space within a group. Some records are shorter than others, and the separation between records might not be obvious to users.

Because you don't want two lines at the bottom of each page (you add a line to the Page Footer next), you put this line at the top of the Detail section:

1. Select the Line tool in the Controls ribbon group.

2. Place the cursor near the far left side of the Detail section, just to the right and above the ⅛-inch mark on the vertical toolbar.

    You may have to reposition controls in the Detail section to make room for the horizontal line.

3. Hold down the Shift key and drag the line across the page header, releasing the mouse button just to the left of the 7½-inch mark.

4. Select the line and set `BorderWidth` property to 1 pt or 2 pt.

Numeric data controls are right-aligned by default. Because they're next to each other horizontally and not above each other vertically, they can be left or center aligned. Although the repeating groups of records are above each other, they're separated by a wide space and left alignment is okay.

One task to complete is to change the picture control to make the picture fit within the control and to add a shadow to dress up the picture and give it some depth. Follow these steps to complete these tasks:

1. Select the Picture control in the Detail section.

2. Change the control's `Size Mode` property to `Stretch`.

3. Select `Shadowed` as the `Special Effect` property.

Creating a report header

The Report Header section is printed only once for the entire report. The report header is the logical place to put things such as the report's title, a logo, and the print date and time. Having this information in the report header makes it easy for any user of the report to know exactly what's in the report and when the report was printed.

With the report open in Design view, the ribbon includes a Design tab. Within the Header/Footer group on the Design tab are a number of controls that help you add important features to the report's header and footer.

For example, click on the Logo button, and Access opens the Insert Picture dialog box (shown in Figure 9.38) for browsing to an image file to insert as the report's logo. Virtually any image file (`.jpg`, `.gif`, `.bmp`, and so on) is a candidate for inclusion as the report's logo.

FIGURE 9.38

Browsing to an image file to use as the report's logo

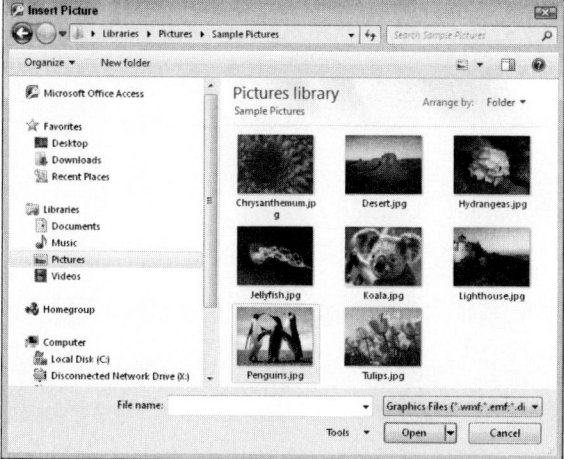

The Title button in the Header/Footer group adds the report's name as the report header's title, and positions the edit cursor within the title label to make it easy for you to adjust the report's title.

Finally, the Date and Time button opens the Date and Time dialog box (shown in Figure 9.39). Specify the date and time format you'd like to use for the date control by selecting the Date and Time control in the Header/Footer group in the ribbon's Design tab.

FIGURE 9.39

Specifying the date and time format

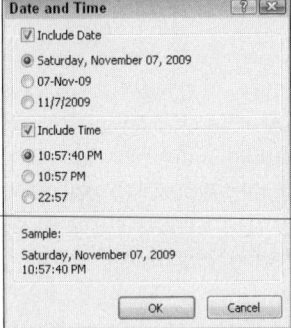

The completed report in Print Preview is shown in Figure 9.40. The report header in this figure was created in less than a minute using the tools built into Access 2010.

Caution

If every even-numbered page is blank, you accidentally widened the report past the 8-inch mark. If you move a control to brush up against the right page-margin border or exceed it, the right page margin increases automatically. When it's past the 8-inch mark, it can't display the entire page on one piece of paper. The blank page you get is actually the right side of the preceding page. To correct this, make sure that all your controls are within the 8-inch right margin; then drag the right page margin back to 8 inches.

As you close the report, Access will prompt you for the report's name.

FIGURE 9.40

The completed report in Print Preview

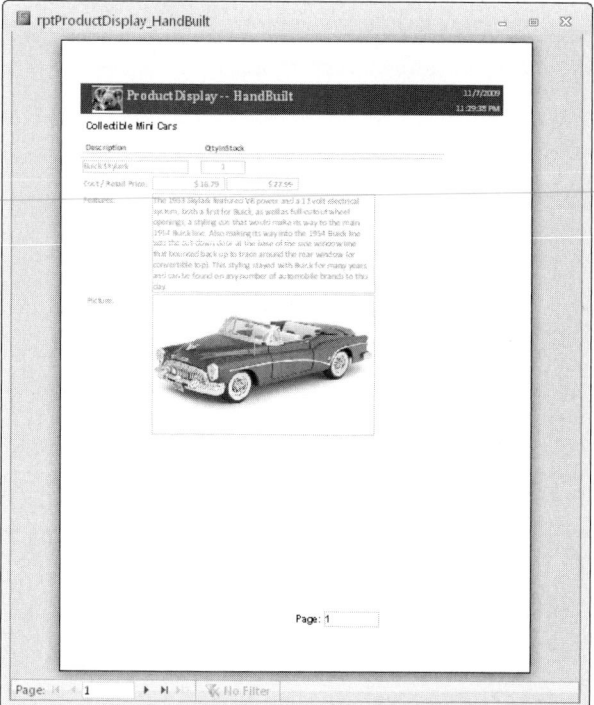

Summary

Reports are an important part of most Access applications. Reports are the most widely used feature of many Access applications, and they're seen by people who never work with the Access application running on a computer.

Access is endowed with an outstanding Report Designer. This long chapter has surveyed the wealth of report-creation tools available to the Access developer. As long as this chapter is, it has only scratched the surface and presented the fundamental capabilities of the Access Report Designer.

In this chapter, you read about the different types of Access reports, learned how to use the Access Report Wizard to build reports, and then created reports from scratch. You also read about the many different ways to provide a report with data, and to display data on the report. This chapter also discussed a number of techniques for summarizing data on Access reports.

Chapter 20 revisits reports and discusses a number of advanced report design techniques.

Part II

Programming Microsoft Access

art II explains the art and science of Visual Basic for Applications (VBA) and introduces macro programming. Very few professional-quality Access applications have been written without liberal use of either the VBA programming language or macros, or a combination of both. VBA provides you with powerful tools for adding capabilities and flexibility to your applications.

As you'll see in this part, VBA is a large and somewhat complex programming language. If you aren't already using VBA, you'll want to carefully study the chapters in this part and work the examples until you're comfortable creating VBA modules and composing programming statements.

These chapters provide you with the essential skills necessary to become comfortable writing VBA code. You'll learn where VBA code lives within an Access application, how to compose VBA statements, and how to hook up VBA code to your forms and reports.

It's hard to exaggerate how important VBA programming skills are to professional database developers. Because VBA is used in so many different platforms (Access, Word, Excel, and more), your programming skills are transferable to many situations beyond Access database development. Also, the VBA programming language is very similar to the languages used in Microsoft Visual Studio. Quite frankly, there is no limit to what you can accomplish with the skills you develop in learning Access VBA.

IN THIS PART

Chapter 10
VBA Programming Fundamentals

Chapter 11
Mastering VBA Data Types and Procedures

Chapter 12
The Access Event Model

Chapter 13
Accessing Data with VBA Code

Chapter 14
Debugging Your Access Applications

Chapter 15
Using Access Data Macros

VBA Programming Fundamentals

Most Access developers use macros now and then. Although macros provide a quick and easy way to automate an application, writing Visual Basic for applications (VBA) modules is the best way to create applications. VBA provides data access, looping and branching, and other features that macros simply don't support — or at least don't support with the flexibility most developers want. In this chapter, you learn how to use VBA to extend the power and usefulness of your applications.

On the CD-ROM
Use the database file `Chapter10.accdb` in this chapter.

Note
Although many readers of this book are experienced Access developers and are comfortable working with VBA, this chapter and the other chapters in this part of the book assume that you have no experience with VBA. I include these chapters to provide you with a firm foundation for many of the techniques I discuss in later chapters. As you'll see in Part III and beyond, many advanced Access techniques simply can't be implemented without the use of VBA code.

IN THIS CHAPTER

Working with VBA

Reviewing VBA terminology

Understanding VBA code basics

Moving from macros to VBA

Writing VBA code

Adding branching constructs

Understanding objects and collections

Understanding developer options

The limitations of macros

For a number of reasons, this book doesn't extensively cover Access macro creation. To begin with, there are enough important topics that I had to choose which topics to cover in detail. Plus, macros are pretty easy to learn on your own and they're well documented in the Access online help. There are, however, two areas where macros can't be beat: data macros in tables and embedded macros on forms and controls. The ability to embed macros in tables and forms make macros much more attractive than in versions prior to Access 2007.

But, by far, the biggest reason I don't document macros is that macros are guaranteed to be non-portable to other applications. You can't use an Access macro anywhere other than in Access. VBA code, on the other hand, is very portable to Word, Excel, Outlook, Visio, and even Visual Studio .NET (with changes).

It's impossible to tell where an Access application might end up. Very often, Access apps are upsized and upgraded to SQL Server and Visual Studio .NET. The VBA code in your Access applications is readily converted to Visual Basic .NET, and many Access procedures can be used (perhaps with a few changes) in Word or Excel. VBA is a very portable, useful language, and VBA skills are applicable in many situations other than building Access applications.

I don't mean to imply that macros have no place in Access applications, or that macros are necessarily inferior to VBA code. Microsoft has issues related to previous versions of Access macros. In particular, macros in Access 2007 and 2010 include variables and simple error handling (mostly jumping to a named location when an error occurs). These updates to the Access macro engine are significant, but, in the opinion of many Access developers, they aren't enough to justify using macros instead of VBA in professional applications.

Introducing Visual Basic for Applications

Visual Basic for Applications (VBA) is the programming language built into Microsoft Access. VBA is shared among all the Microsoft Office applications, including Word, Excel, Outlook, PowerPoint, and even Visio. If you aren't already a VBA programmer, learning the VBA syntax and how to hook VBA into the Access event model is a definite career builder.

VBA is a key element in most professional Microsoft Access applications. Microsoft provides VBA in Access because VBA provides significant flexibility and power to Access database applications. Without a full-fledged programming language like VBA, Access applications would have to rely on the somewhat limited set of actions offered by Access macros. Although macro programming also adds flexibility to Access applications, VBA is much easier to work with when you're programming complex data-management features or sophisticated user-interface requirements.

Cross-Reference

If you want more information on macros, turn to Chapter 30.

What's in a name?

The name Visual Basic is a source of endless confusion for people working with the Microsoft products. Microsoft has applied the name Visual Basic to a number of different products and technologies. For more than a decade, Microsoft marketed a stand-alone product named Visual Basic that was, in many ways, comparable to and competitive with Microsoft Access. Visual Basic was folded into Visual Studio in its very first version. In 1995, Microsoft added the Visual Basic for Applications (VBA) programming language to Access, Word, and Excel in Microsoft Office. The name Visual Basic for Applications was chosen because the VBA syntax is identical in Access, Word, and Excel.

Although the VBA language used in Access is very similar to Visual Basic .NET, they aren't exactly the same. You can do some things with VB .NET that can't be done with Access VBA, and vice versa.

In this book, the expressions "VBA" and "Visual Basic" refer to the programming language built into Access and should not be confused with the Microsoft VB .NET product.

If you're new to programming, try not to become frustrated or overwhelmed by the seeming complexity of the VBA language. As with any new skill, you're much better off approaching VBA programming by taking it one step at a time. You need to learn exactly what VBA can do for you and your applications, along with the general syntax, statement structure, and how to compose procedures using the VBA language.

This book is chock-full of examples showing you how to use the VBA language to accomplish useful tasks. Each of the procedures you see in this book has been tested and verified to work correctly. If you find that a bit of code in this book doesn't work as expected, take the time to ensure that you've used the example code exactly as presented in this book. Very often, the most difficult problems implementing any programming technique stem from simple errors, such as misspelling or forgetting to include a comma or parentheses where required.

Note

A programming language is much like a human language. Just as humans use words, sentences, and paragraphs to communicate with one another, a computer language uses words, statements, and procedures to tell the computer what you expect it to do. The primary difference between human and computer languages is that a computer language follows a very strict format. Every word and sentence must be precisely composed because a computer doesn't understand context or nuance. Every task must be carefully defined for the computer, using the syntax supported by the programming language.

Understanding VBA Terminology

Before you plunge into my VBA coverage, here's a review of some basic VBA terminology:

- **Keyword:** A word that has special meaning in VBA. For example, in the English language, the word *now* simply indicates a point in time. In VBA, Now is the name of a built-in VBA function that returns the current date and time.

- **Statement:** A single VBA word or combination of words that constitutes an instruction to be performed by the VBA engine.

- **Procedure:** A collection of VBA statements that are grouped together to perform a certain task. You might, for example, write a complex procedure that extracts data from a table, combines the data in a particular way, and then displays the data on a form. Or, you might write three smaller procedures, each of which performs a single step of the overall process.

  There are two types of VBA procedures: *subs* (subroutines) and *functions:*

  - **Subroutines** perform a single task and then just go away.

  - **Functions** perform a task and then return a value, such as the result of a calculation.

  The example described earlier, where the procedure extracts data from a table, is actually a subroutine. It performs a specific task; then, when it ends, the procedure just goes away.

  The example where the operation is split into three smaller procedures includes a function. In this case, the first procedure that opens the database and extracts data most likely returns the data as a recordset, and the recordset is passed to the other procedures that perform the data combination and data display.

- **Module:** Procedures live in *modules*. If statements are like sentences and procedures are like paragraphs, modules are the chapters or documents of the VBA language. A module consists of one or more procedures and other elements combined as a single entity within the application.

- **Variable:** Variables are sometimes tricky to understand. Because Access is a database development tool, it makes sense that VBA code has to have some way of managing the data involved in the application. A variable is nothing more than a name applied to represent a data value. In virtually all VBA programs, you create and use variables to hold values such as customer names, dates, and numeric values manipulated by the VBA code.

VBA is appropriately defined as a *language*. And, just as with any human language, VBA consists of a number of words, sentences, and paragraphs, all arranged in a specific fashion. Each VBA sentence is a *statement*. Statements are aggregated as *procedures,* and procedures live within *modules*. A *function* is a specific type of procedure — one that returns a value when it's run. For example, `Now()` is a built-in VBA function that returns the current date and time, down to the second. You use the `Now()` function in your application whenever you need to capture the current date and time, such as when assigning a timestamp value to a record.

Starting with VBA Code Basics

Each statement in a procedure is an instruction you want Access to perform.

There are, literally, an infinite number of different VBA programming statements that could appear in an Access application. Generally speaking, however, VBA statements are fairly easy to read and understand. Most often, you'll be able to understand the purpose of a VBA statement based on the keywords (such as `DoCmd.OpenForm`) and references to database objects in the statement.

Each VBA statement is an instruction that is processed and executed by the VBA language engine built into Microsoft Access. Here's an example of a typical VBA statement that opens a form:

```
DoCmd.OpenForm "frmMyForm", acNormal
```

Notice that this statement consists of an action (OpenForm) and a noun (frmMyForm). Most VBA statements follow a similar pattern of action and a reference either to the object performing the action or to the object that's the target of the action.

DoCmd is a built-in Access object that performs numerous tasks for you. Think of DoCmd as a little robot that can perform many different jobs. The OpenForm that follows DoCmd is the task you want DoCmd to run, and frmMyForm is the name of the form to open. Finally, acNormal is a modifier that tells DoCmd that you want the form opened in its "normal" view. The implication is that there are other view modes that may be applied to opening a form; these modes include Design (acDesign) or Datasheet (acFormDS) view, and Print Preview (acPreview, when applied to reports).

Note

Writing programming statements and code usually requires more work than the alternatives, such as using macros or the Access Command Button Wizard. Very often, the VBA code you write refuses to work as expected. And, sometimes the things you want to do with VBA are just too difficult or might be impossible to accomplish with VBA. At the same time, VBA programming skills are a great addition to a developer's résumé. The ability to efficiently program complex business rules or use code to clean up data before they're added to a database are valuable skills.

Although this and the following chapters provide only the fundamentals of VBA programming, you'll learn more than enough to be able to add advanced features to your Access applications. You'll also have a good basis for deciding whether you want to continue studying this important programming language.

Migrating from Macros to VBA

Should you now convert all the macros in your applications to VBA? The answer depends on what you're trying to accomplish. The fact that Access includes VBA doesn't mean that Access macros are no longer useful; it simply means that Access developers should learn VBA and add it to their arsenal of tools for creating Access applications.

VBA isn't always the answer. Some tasks, such as creating global key assignments, can be accomplished only via macros. You can perform some actions more easily and effectively by using a macro than by writing VBA code.

Note

An Access macro is a stepwise list of actions that you compose using the Access macro editor. Microsoft Word and Excel use the word macro to refer to procedures written in the VBA programming language, often through the use of the Word or Excel macro recorder. When working within the Access environment, a macro always refers to the stepwise set of instructions composed using the Access macro editor. Most Access developers refer to VBA code as either procedures or modules, and virtually never refer to these objects as macros.

Knowing when to use macros and when to use VBA

In Access, macros often offer a great way to take care of many details, such as opening reports and forms. Macros can usually be created very quickly because the arguments for each macro action are displayed in the macro editor. You don't have to remember complex or difficult syntax.

You can accomplish many things with the VBA code and with macros:

- **Create and use your custom functions.** In addition to using built-in Access functions, VBA enables you to create and work with your own reusable functions.

- **Respond to errors.** Both macros and VBA handle errors quite well. However, macros are limited to jumping to a set of macro actions in response to the error, while VBA error handlers can examine what caused the error, take corrective action, and repeat the statement(s) that caused the error. Macro error handling is quite good, but not quite as strong as when working with VBA code.

- **Use automation to communicate with other Windows applications.** You can write VBA code to see whether a file or some data or value exists before you take some action, or you can communicate with another Windows application (such as a spreadsheet), passing data back and forth.

- **Use the Windows Application Programming Interface (API).** VBA enables you to hook into many resources provided by Windows, such as determining the user's Windows login name, or the name of the computer the user is working on. The Windows API provides a virtually unlimited number of ways to enhance your Access applications.

Cross-Reference
Turn to Chapter 27 for more on the Windows API.

- **Maintain the application.** Unlike macros, code can be built into a form or report, making maintaining the form or report more efficient. Plus, if you move a form or report from one database to another, the event procedures built into the form or report travel with it.

- **Create or manipulate objects.** In most cases, you'll find that you need to work with an object in Design view. In some situations, however, you might want to manipulate the definition of an object in code. Using VBA, you can manipulate all the objects in a database, including the database itself.

Access supports embedded macros in forms, reports, and controls. An embedded macro lives within its host object (form, report, or control), and travels with the object if it is copied to another Access database. This is a huge improvement over the old Access macro model where it was very difficult to know which macros were related to which forms and reports. Even then, however, embedded macros suffer from the performance issues associated with external macros, and they aren't portable to any other applications, like Word or Excel.

Converting your existing macros to VBA

As you become comfortable with writing VBA code, you might want to rewrite existing macros as VBA procedures. As you begin this process, you quickly realize how challenging the effort can be as you review every macro in your macro libraries. You can't cut and paste a macro into a VBA code module. You have to analyze the task accomplished by each macro action, and then add the equivalent VBA statements to your code.

Fortunately, Access provides a feature to convert macros to VBA code automatically. One of the options in the Save As dialog box is Save As Module. You can use this option when a macro file is highlighted in the Macros object area of the Solution Explorer. This option enables you to convert an entire macro group to a VBA module in seconds.

To try the conversion process, save the `mcrOpenContacts` macro in the `Chapter10.accdb` database as a module by following these steps:

1. Open the Macros section of the Navigation Pane, and s elect the `mcrOpenContacts` macro.

2. Click the File button in the upper-left corner of the main Access window to open the Backstage, and select Save As from the command list.

   The Save As dialog box appears, as shown in Figure 10.1.

FIGURE 10.1

Saving a macro as a module

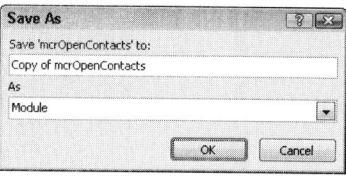

3. Select Module from the drop-down list on the Save As dialog box.

   Access assigns a default name for the new module as `Copy of` followed by the macro name. Oddly enough, when you save a macro as a VBA module, Access doesn't use the name displayed in the Save As dialog box, nor does it use any name that you enter in the Save As dialog box.

   The Convert Macro dialog box appears, as shown in Figure 10.2.

FIGURE 10.2

The Convert Macro dialog box

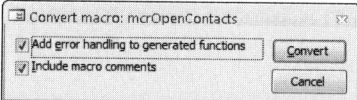

4. Select the options that include error handling and comments, and click Convert.

   Access briefly displays each new procedure in the VBA editor window as it's converted. When the conversion process completes, the Conversion Finished! message box appears.

Figure 10.3 shows the newly created VBA module, Converted Macro–mcrOpenContacts. Notice that the module and the function within the module are named after the converted macro, regardless of any other name you might have entered in the Save As dialog box.

FIGURE 10.3

The converted module

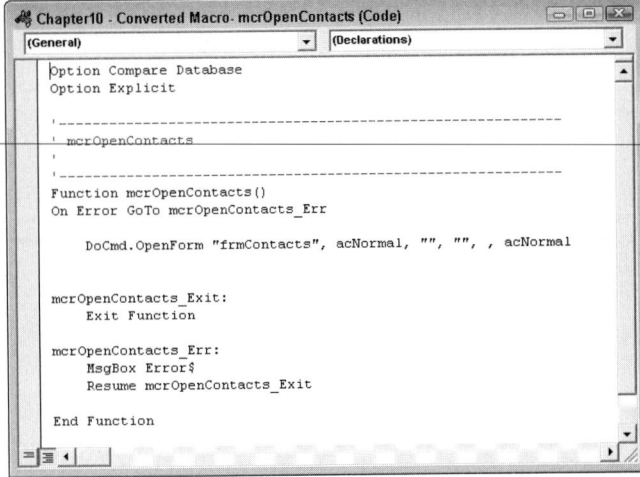

When you specify that you want Access to include error processing for the conversion, Access automatically inserts an On Error statement as the first statement in the procedure, telling Access to branch to an error handler that displays an appropriate message and then exit the function.

Cross-Reference
Handling errors is covered in Chapter 23.

The statement beginning with DoCmd is the code that Access created from the macro's actions. DoCmd methods mimic macro actions and perform important tasks such as opening forms and reports and setting the values of controls.

Using the Command Button Wizard

One option when adding a button to an Access form is to use the Command Button Wizard. When Access creates a command button with a wizard, it adds an embedded macro attached to the button. The embedded macro performs whatever action (open form, open report, and so on) that you specified when you worked with the wizard. You can open the embedded macro in the macro editor (described in Chapters 15 and 30) and modify it to fit your needs.

Access supports more than 30 types of command buttons through the Command Button Wizard. These buttons include finding or printing records, as well as applying a filter to a form's data. Run this wizard by adding a command button to a form with the Use Control Wizards option selected in the Design tab of the Access ribbon. (You have to expand the controls palette to see the Use Control Wizards option.) Figure 10.4 shows a Go To Next Record command button being created. Notice that the Command Button Wizard even shows a preview of the image it selects for the button in the panel at the left side of the wizard dialog box.

FIGURE 10.4

The Command Button Wizard

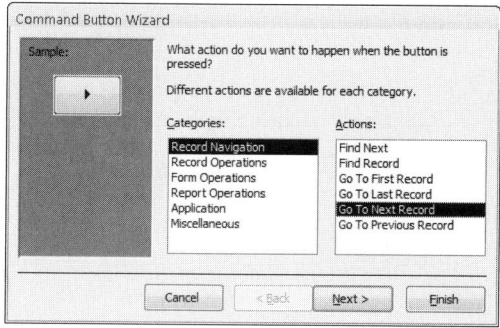

The `Chapter10.accdb` example database includes a form named `frmButtonWizardSamples_Macros`. This form, shown in Figure 10.5 in Design mode, contains a dozen command buttons created with the Command Button Wizard. Review the procedures for the buttons on this form to see how powerful Access macros can be. The buttons on this form don't actually do anything because there is no data on the form, and the macros have nothing to actually work with, but they show the variety of actions supported by the command button wizard.

Figure 10.6 shows the code for the Go To First Record command button.

The macro produced by the Command Button Wizard is very simple but effective.

FIGURE 10.5

Examples of Command Button Wizard buttons

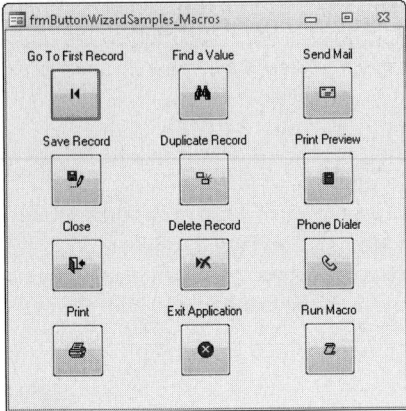

FIGURE 10.6

The Go To First Record button's On Click procedure

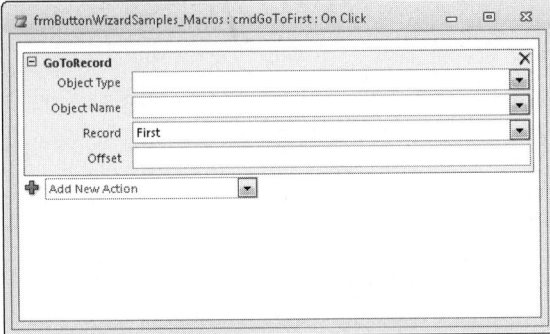

Creating VBA Programs

Access has a wide variety of tools that enable you to work with tables, queries, forms, and reports without ever having to write a single line of code. At some point, you might begin building more sophisticated applications. You might want to "bulletproof" your applications by providing more intensive data-entry validation or implementing better error handling.

Some operations can't be accomplished through the user interface, even with macros. You might find yourself saying, "I wish I had a way to . . ." or "There just has to be a function that will let me. . . ." At other times, you find that you're continually putting the same formula or expression in a query or filter. You might find yourself saying, "I'm tired of typing this formula into . . ." or "Doggone it, I typed the wrong formula in this. . . ."

For situations such as these, you need the horsepower of a high-level programming language such as VBA. VBA is a modern, structured programming language offering many of the programming structures available in most programming languages. VBA is *extensible* (capable of calling Windows API routines) and can interact through ActiveX Data Objects (ADO), through Data Access Objects (DAO), and with any Access or VBA data type.

Getting started with VBA programming in Access requires an understanding of its event-driven environment.

Events and event procedures

In Access, unlike old-fashioned programming environments, the user controls the actions and flow of the application. The user determines what to do and when to do it, such as changing information in a field or clicking a command button. The user determines the flow of action and, through *events,* the application determines what action to take or ignore.

In contrast, procedural programming languages require that the programmer determine the flow of actions that the user must follow. In fact, the programmer must accommodate all possibilities of user intervention — for example, keystrokes a user might enter in error — and must determine what actions to take in response to the user.

Using macros and event procedures, you implement the responses to these actions. Access provides *event properties* for each control you place on a form. By attaching a VBA procedure to a control's event property, you don't have to worry about the order of actions a user might take on a particular form.

In an event-driven environment such as Access, the objects (forms, reports, and controls) respond to events. Basically, an event procedure is VBA code that executes when an event (such as a button click) occurs. The code is directly attached to the form or report containing the event being processed. An Exit command button, for example, closes the form when the user clicks the button. Clicking the command button triggers its `Click` event. The event procedure is the VBA code attached to the `Click` event. The event procedure automatically runs every time the user clicks the command button.

There are two types of procedures: subprocedures (often called subs) and functions.

Sub and function procedures are grouped and stored in *modules.* The Modules object button in the Navigation Pane contains the common global, or *standard,* modules that any form or report can access. You *could* store all your procedures in a single module, but that wouldn't be a good idea. You'll probably want to group related procedures into separate modules, categorizing them by the nature of the operations they perform. For example, an `Update` module might include procedures for adding and deleting records from a table.

Subprocedures

A subprocedure (or *sub*) is the simplest type of procedure in a VBA project. A subprocedure is nothing more than a container for VBA statements that typically perform a task such as opening a form or report or running a query. The code in a subprocedure simply executes and then goes away without leaving a trace other than whatever work it performed.

All Access event procedures are subs. Clicking on a command button triggers the button's Click event, for example.

These VBA statements within a sub are the code you want to run every time the procedure is executed. The following example shows an Exit command button's subprocedure:

```
Sub cmdExit_Click()
   DoCmd.Close
End Sub
```

The first line of this procedure notifies the VBA engine that the procedure is a sub and that its name is cmdExit_Click. If *parameters* (data passed to the procedure) are associated with this sub, they appear within the parentheses.

There is only one VBA statement within this sub: DoCmd.Close. The End Sub statement at the bottom ends this procedure. The cmdExit_Click () subprocedure is attached to the Exit button's Click event. The event procedure closes the form when the user clicks the Exit command button.

Functions

A function is very similar to a subprocedure with one major exception: A function returns a value when it ends. A simple example is the built-in VBA Now() function, which returns the current date and time. Now() can be used virtually anywhere your application needs to use or display the current date and time. An example is including Now() in a report header or footer so that the user knows exactly when the report was printed.

Now() is just one of several hundred built-in VBA functions. As you'll see throughout this book, the built-in VBA functions provide useful and very powerful features to your Access applications.

In addition to built-in functions, you might add custom functions that perform tasks required by your applications. An example is a data transformation routine that performs a mathematical operation (such as currency conversion or calculating shipping costs) on an input value. It doesn't matter where the input value comes from (table, form , query, and so on). The function always returns exactly the correct calculated value, no matter where the function is used.

Within the body of a function, you specify the function's return value by assigning a value to the function's name (and, yes, it does look pretty strange to include the function's name within the function's body). You then can use the returned value as part of a larger expression. The following function calculates the square footage of a room:

```
Function nSquareFeet(Height As Double, _
    Width As Double) As Double
  'Assign this function's value:
  nSquareFeet = Height * Width
End Function
```

This function receives two parameters: `Height` and `Width`. Notice that the function's name, `nSquareFeet`, is assigned a value within the body of the function. The function is declared as a Double data type, so the return value is recognized by the VBA interpreter as a Double.

The main thing to keep in mind about functions is that they return values. The returned value is often assigned to a variable or control on a form or report:

```
dblAnswer = nSquareFeet(Height, Width)
txtAnswer = nSquareFeet(Height, Width)
```

If the function (or subroutine, for that matter) requires information (such as the `Height` and `Width` in the case of the `nSquareFeet function`) the information is passed as arguments within the parentheses in the function's declaration.

You'll read much more about subroutines and functions in the remaining chapters of this book. You'll also see many more examples of passing arguments to procedures, returning values from functions, and using subs and functions to perform complicated work in Access applications.

One last point: Notice the underscore character at the end of the `nSquareFeet` function's declaration. A space followed by an underscore at the end of a VBA statement (called a *continuation character*) instructs the VBA engine to include the next line as part of the same statement.

Modules

Modules and their procedures are the principal objects of the VBA programming language. The code that you write is added to procedures that are contained in *modules*.

Looking at the types of modules

There are two types of VBA code modules in most Access applications. The first type is a freestanding, independent module that might be accessed by any other object (such as forms and reports) within the application. These modules are often called *standard* or *global* modules. The second type of module exists with (or behind, if you prefer) the forms and reports in an application and is normally accessible only to the form or report and its controls. This second type of module is usually referred to as *form* and *report modules*.

As you create VBA procedures for your Access applications, you use both types of modules.

Cross-Reference

In addition to standard and the modules behind form and reports, Access supports a third type of VBA code module. Chapter 28 discusses class modules, and the object-oriented programming techniques supported by all versions of Access since Access 97. Object-oriented programming is an important concept and can lead to simplified programming and efficient code-reuse.

Standard modules

Standard modules are independent from forms and reports. Standard modules store code that is used from anywhere within your application. By default, these procedures are often called *global* or *public* because they're accessible to all elements of your Access application.

Use public procedures throughout your application in expressions, macros, event procedures, and other VBA code. To use a public procedure, you simply reference it from VBA code in event procedures or any other procedure in your application.

Tip

Procedures run; modules contain. Procedures are executed and perform actions. Modules, on the other hand, are simple containers, grouping procedures and declarations together. A module can't be run; instead, you run the procedures contained within the module.

Standard modules are stored in the Module section of the Navigation Pane. Form and report modules (see the next section) are attached to their hosts and are accessed through the Form Property Sheet or Report Property Sheet.

Tip

Generally speaking, you should group related procedures into modules, such as putting all of an application's data conversion routines into a single module. Logically grouping procedures make maintenance much easier because there is a single place in the application for all the procedures supporting a particular activity. Plus, most modules contain procedures that are related in some way.

Form and report modules

All forms and reports support events. The procedures associated with form and report events can be macros or VBA code. Every form or report you add to your database contains a VBA code module (unless its Has Module property is set to No). This form or report module is an integral part of the form or report; it's used as a container for the event procedures you create for the form or report. The module attached to each form or report is a convenient way to place all the object's event procedures in a single location.

Cross-Reference

For more on events, turn to Chapter 12.

Adding VBA event procedures to a form module is very powerful and efficient. Because the module is an integral and permanent part of the form or report, all the event procedures travel with the object when it's exported to another Access database.

Modifying a control's event procedure is easy: Simply click the builder button (with the ellipsis: . . .) in the Property Sheet next to the event property name, to open the form's code module. Figure 10.7 illustrates accessing the Click event procedure of the Delete button on the Contacts form.

FIGURE 10.7

Accessing a control's event procedure from the Property Sheet

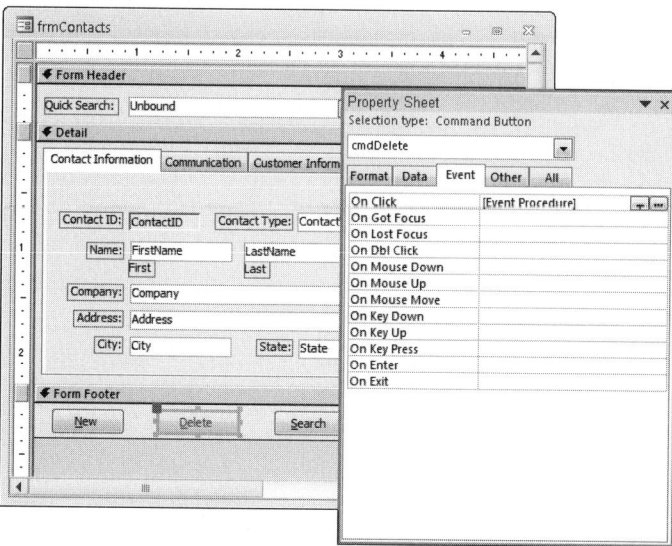

Notice the [Event Procedure] in the control's On Click property. It tells you that there is code attached to the control's Click event. Clicking on the builder button (with the ellipsis, or . . .) in the On Click property opens a dialog box where you can choose to build a macro or VBA code, or create an expression for the event. Choosing the Code Builder option opens the VBA code editor, displaying the event procedure.

Tip

Many Access developers prefer to routinely use VBA code for their procedures. You can instruct Access to always use VBA code by selecting the Always Use Event Procedures check box in the Form/Report Design view section under Object Designers in the Access Options screen (found in the Backstage).

Caution

Event procedures that directly work with a form or report belong in the module of the form or report. A form's module should contain only the declarations and event procedures needed for that form and its controls (buttons, check boxes, labels, text boxes, combo boxes, and so on). Placing procedures shared with other forms in a form's module really doesn't make sense and should be avoided.

Creating a new module

Using the Modules section of the Navigation Pane, you create and edit VBA code contained in standard modules. You could, for example, create a Beep procedure that makes the computer beep as a warning or notification that something has happened in your program.

Think of a module as a collection of procedures. Your Access databases can contain thousands of modules, although most Access applications include only a few dozen standard modules.

Cross-Reference

You'll see many examples of creating functions and procedures in Chapters 11 through 14.

For this example, you can use the `Chapter10.accdb` database or open a new blank database. Add a new module by selecting the Create tab of the Access ribbon, and then clicking on the Module button in the Other ribbon group (see Figure 10.8).

FIGURE 10.8

Adding a new module to an Access database

Access opens the VBA editor and adds a new module with a default name (see Figure 10.9).

FIGURE 10.9

The newly opened module in the VBA editor

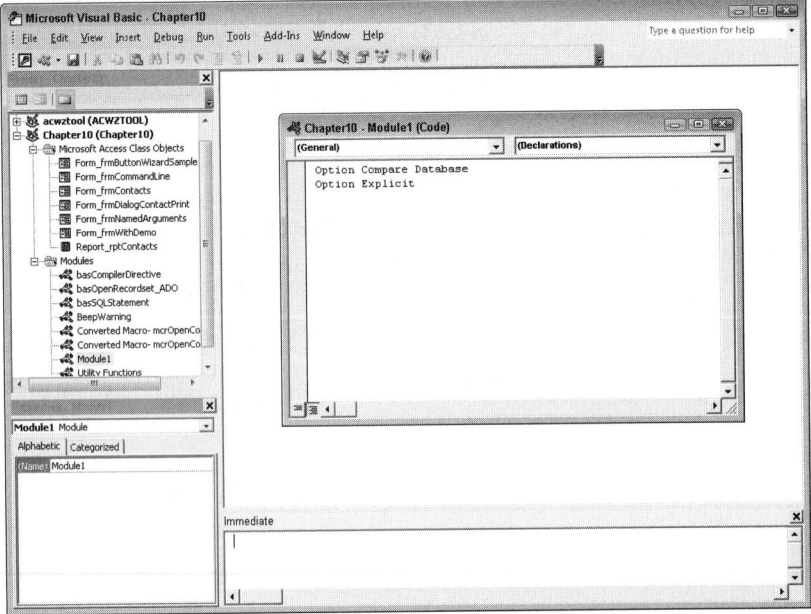

Working in the code window

Whenever you work on VBA procedures in your Access applications, you edit each module in a separate editor window. Although the code window may be confusing at first, it's easy to understand and use after you learn how each part works.

Note

Notice that the Access code window doesn't use the ribbon. Instead, the code window appears much as it has in every version of Access since Access 2000. Therefore, in this book you'll see references to the code window's toolbar and menu whenever I describe working with Access VBA modules. Don't confuse references to the code editor's toolbar with the main Access window's ribbon.

When you enter Design mode of a module — whether it's via a form or report module or the Modules group on the Navigation Pane — the VBA editor and its menu and toolbar open to enable you to create or edit your procedures.

When you display VBA code within a form (or report) module, the Object and Procedure drop-down lists at the top of the code window contain the form's controls and events. You select these objects and events to create or edit event procedures for the form. Form and report modules can also include procedures that are not related to a control's events.

The Object drop-down list for a standard module offers only one choice: General. The Procedure drop-down list contains only the names of existing procedures within the standard module.

The code window's toolbar (shown in Figure 10.9) helps you create new modules and their procedures quickly. The toolbar contains buttons for the most common actions you use to create, modify, and debug modules.

The code window — the most important area of the VBA editor — is where you create and modify the VBA code for your procedures. The code window has the standard Windows features to resize, minimize, maximize, and move the window.

Tip

You can split the code window into two independent edit panes by dragging down the splitter bar (the little horizontal bar at the very top of the vertical scroll bar at the right edge of the code window). Splitting the window enables simultaneous editing of two sections of code. Each section of a split VBA code window scrolls independently, and changes you make in one pane of a split window show up in the other pane. Double-click the splitter bar to return the window to its former state, or grab the splitter bar with the mouse and drag it to the top of the code editor window to close the second edit pane. (Microsoft Word and Excel feature a similar splitter button, making it very easy to edit different parts of the same Word document or Excel worksheet.)

The Immediate window (shown at the bottom of Figure 10.9) enables you to try a procedure while you're still in the module. See the "Checking your results in the Immediate window" section later in this chapter for an example.

Cross-Reference

You'll read much more about the Immediate window and the other debugging tools in Chapter 14.

Each VBA code module includes two or more sections:

- A declarations section at the top of the module
- A section for each procedure

The declarations section

You can use the declarations section at the top of a VBA module to declare (define) variables used in the module's procedures. A variable is a way to temporarily store values as your code runs. Examples of variables include

- `intCounter` (an integer)
- `curMySalary` (a currency)
- `dtmDate` (a date/time)

The three-character prefixes (`int`, `cur`, `dtm`) in these variable names constitute a simple naming convention and are entirely optional. Naming conventions are routinely used by most Access developers to help document a variable's data type (integer, currency, and datetime, respectively, in this case). Anything you can do to document your application helps reduce maintenance costs and make your code easier to modify later on.

The name you give a variable doesn't determine the type of data contained within the variable.

Caution

You might have noticed the `Option Explicit` line at the top of the VBA modules in this chapter's figures and example database. `Option Explicit` is a directive that instructs the VBA compiler to require every variable to be "explicitly" declared within the module. This means that every variable must be declared as a specific data type (integer, string, and so on).

Explicit variable declaration is always a good idea because it prevents stray variables from creeping into an application and causing bugs. Without the `Option Explicit` directive at the top of the module, every time you type in an identifier that the VBA compiler doesn't recognize, it automatically creates a new variable by that name. This means that, when using "implicit" variable declarations, if you've been using a variable named `strLastName` and type it in incorrectly (for example, `strLstName`), the VBA compiler creates a new variable named `strLstName` and begins using it. Bugs caused by simple misspellings can be very difficult to detect, because the application doesn't raise any errors, and the only way to detect the cause of the bug is to go through the code one line at a time until you find the misspelling.

You aren't required to declare every variable used in a module within the declarations section, because variables are also declared within procedures. But be aware that all the variables defined in the declarations section are shared by all the procedures within the module.

Cross Reference

Variable scope (the term that describes where a variable can be used in an application) is described in Chapter 11.

Creating a new procedure

After you complete any declarations for the module, you're ready to create a procedure. Follow these steps to create a procedure called `BeepWarning`:

1. Open the `Module1` module you previously created, as shown in Figure 10.9.
2. Go to any empty line in the code window.
3. Type the code in *exactly* as shown in Figure 10.10.

FIGURE 10.10

Entering a new procedure in the code window

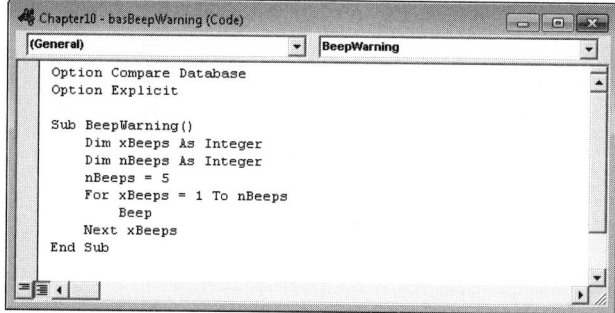

4. Save the module (the save button is in the VBA editor's toolbar), naming it `basBeepWarning`.

Notice that, as you entered the first line of the procedure, Access automatically added the `End Sub` statement to the procedure.

In this example, you're running the program five times. The completed function should look like the one shown in Figure 10.10.

When `BeepWarning` actually runs, the five beeps will almost certainly blend together as a single beep from your computer's speaker.

If you enter the name of a function you previously created in this module (or in another module within the database), Access informs you that the function already exists. Access doesn't enable you to create another procedure with the same name.

Using IntelliSense

Suppose that you know you want to use a specific command, but you can't remember the exact syntax. Access features two types of IntelliSense to help you create each line of code:

- **Auto List Members:** Auto List Members is a drop-down list that is automatically displayed when you type the beginning of a keyword that has associated objects, properties, or methods. For example, if you enter DoCmd.Open, a list of the possible options displays, as shown in Figure 10.11. Scroll through the list box and press Enter to select the option you want.

FIGURE 10.11

Access Auto List Members help in a module

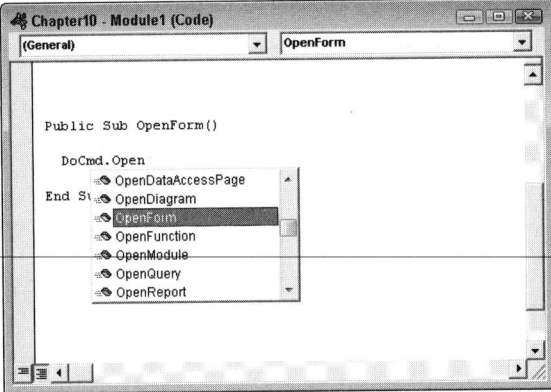

In this example, the OpenForm method is selected (actions associated with an object are called *methods*). After choosing an item in the list, more Auto List Members help is displayed. Or, if parameters are associated with the keyword, the other type of module help, Auto Quick Info (see the next bullet), is displayed, as shown in Figure 10.12.

FIGURE 10.12

Access Auto Quick Info help in a module

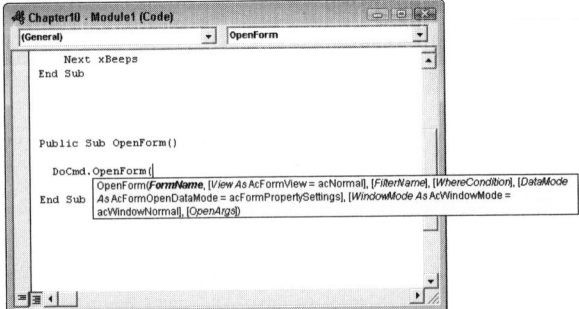

- **Auto Quick Info:** Auto Quick Info guides you through all the options (called *parameters*) for the specific item. The bold word (FormName) is the next parameter available for the DoCmd object. Figure 10.12 shows that there are many parameters available for the OpenForm command. The parameters are separated by commas. As each parameter is entered the next parameter is highlighted in bold. The position of parameters is significant; they can't be rearranged without causing problems. Press the Esc key to hide Auto List Members help.

  Not every parameter is required for every VBA command. Parameters surrounded by square brackets (such as View in Figure 10.12) are optional. Access provides reasonable defaults for all optional arguments that are omitted from the statement using the command.

Compiling procedures

After code has been written, you should compile it to complete the development process.

The compilation step converts the English-like VBA syntax to a binary format that is easily executed at runtime. Also, during compilation, all your code is checked for incorrect syntax and other errors that will cause problems when the user works with the application.

If you don't compile your Access applications during the development cycle, Access compiles the code whenever a user opens the application and begins using it. In this case, errors in your code might prevent the user from using the application, causing a great deal of inconvenience to everyone involved.

Compile your applications by choosing Debug ➪ Compile from the code window. An error window appears if the compilation is not successful.

Note

Access compiles all procedures in the module, and all modules in the Access database, not just the current procedure and module.

Saving a module

When you finish creating a procedure, you save it by saving the module. Save the module by choosing File ➪ Save, or simply close the code editor to save the module automatically. Access prompts you for a name to apply to the module if no name has yet been assigned. If the code you're working on is part of a form or report's module, the form or report is saved along with the module.

Creating procedures in the form or report design window

All forms, reports, and their controls may have *event procedures* associated with their events. While you're in a form or report's Design view, you can add an event procedure in any of three ways:

- Choose Build Event from the shortcut menu (see Figure 10.13).
- Choose Code Builder in the Choose Builder dialog box when you click the builder button to the right of an event in the Property dialog box.

FIGURE 10.13

The shortcut menu for a control in the form design window

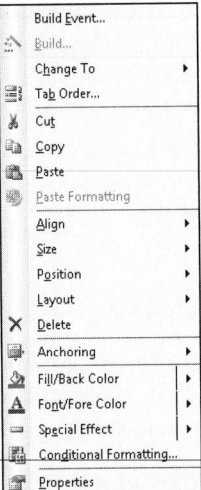

- Type [**Event Procedure**] into the event property, or select it from the top of the event drop-down list (see Figure 10.14).

FIGURE 10.14

The Property Sheet in the form design window

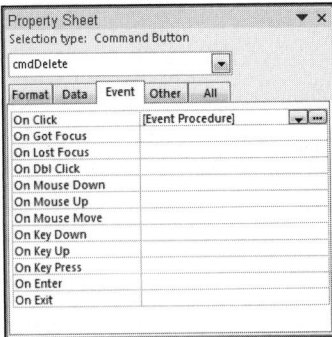

Whether you choose Build Event from the shortcut menu or click the builder button in the Property dialog box (or press F7, for that matter), the Choose Builder dialog box appears.

Choosing the `Code Builder` item opens the VBA code editor, as shown in Figure 10.15. Clicking the View Microsoft Access button in the code window's toolbar toggles between the form designer and the VBA code window.

FIGURE 10.15

A form module open in Design view

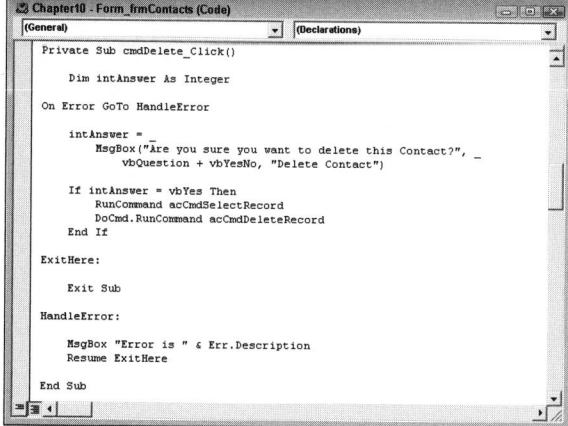

Editing an existing procedure

There a number of ways to access existing code behind a form or report. These are by far the most common:

- Click the `View Code` button in the Tools group in the Access ribbon (with the form or report open in Design view, of course).
- Select an event procedure from a control's event property (refer to Figure 10.7).

Opening a standard module is even easier. Simply select `Modules` in the Navigation Pane; then right-click on a module and select Design View from the shortcut menu (see Figure 10.16).

Checking your results in the Immediate window

When you write code for a procedure, you might want to try the procedure while you're in the module, or you might need to check the results of an expression. The Immediate window (shown in Figure 10.17) enables you to try your procedures without leaving the module. You can run the module and check variables. You could, for example, type **?** and the name of the variable.

Press Ctrl+G to view the Immediate window, or choose View ➪ Immediate Window in the VBA code editor.

FIGURE 10.16

Selecting a module to edit

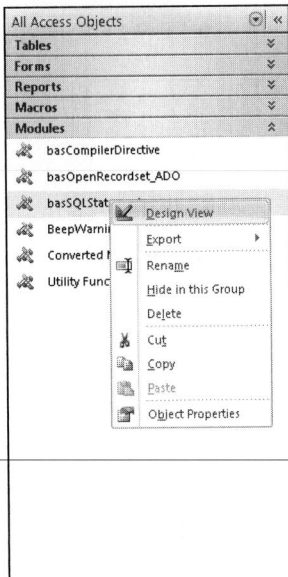

FIGURE 10.17

The Immediate window

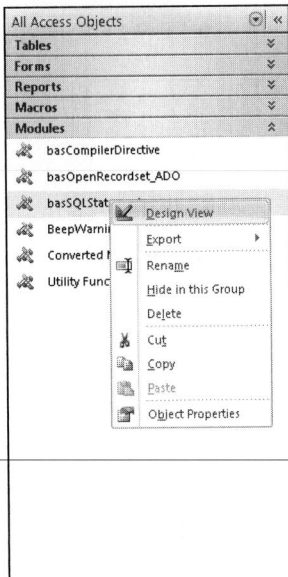

Running the BeepWarning procedure is easy. Simply type **BeepWarning** into the Immediate window and press Enter. You might hear five beeps or only a continuous beep because the interval between beeps is short.

Figure 10.10, earlier in this chapter, also shows the VBA code for this subprocedure.

Cross-Reference
You'll see many more examples of using the Immediate window in Chapter 14.

Understanding VBA Branching Constructs

The real power of any programming language is its capability to make a decision based on a condition that might be different each time the user works with the application. VBA provides two ways for a procedure to execute code conditionally: branching and looping.

Branching

Often, a program performs different tasks based on some value. If the condition is True, the code performs one action. If the condition is False, the code performs a different action. An application's capability to look at a value and, based on that value, decide which code to run is known as *branching* (or conditional processing).

The procedure is similar to walking down a road and coming to a fork in the road; you can go to the left or to the right. If a sign at the fork points left for home and right for work, you can decide which way to go. If you need to go to work, you go to the right; if you need to go home, you go to the left. In the same way, a program looks at the value of some variable and decides which set of code should be processed.

VBA offers two sets of conditional processing statements:

- If...Then...Else...End If
- Select Case...End Select

The If...Then...Else...End If construct

The If...Then...End If and If...Then...Else...End If construct checks a condition and, based on the evaluation, perform an action. The condition must evaluate to a Boolean value (True or False). If the condition is True, the program moves to the line following the If statement. If the condition is False, the program skips to the statement following the Else statement, if present, or the End If statement if there is no Else clause.

In Figure 10.18, the code examines the value of the ContactType, and if the value is "Buyer", the Customer page is made visible; otherwise, the Customer page is made invisible.

FIGURE 10.18

The VBA code decides whether to display the Customer page of a tab control.

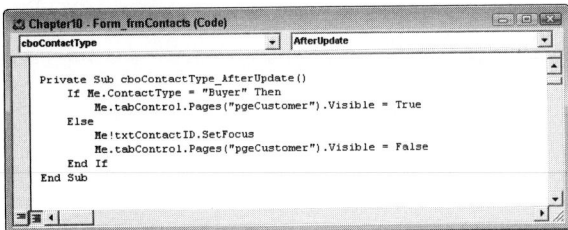

The Else statement is optional. Use Else to perform an alternative set of actions when the If condition is False:

```
If Condition Then
    [Action to perform when Condition is True]
Else
    [Action to perform when Condition is False]
End If
```

The Then and Else clauses can contain virtually any valid VBA statements, including another If... Then... Else...End If:

```
If Condition1 Then
    [Action to perform when Condition1 is True]
Else
    If Condition2 Then
        [Action to perform when Condition2 is True]
    Else
        [Action to perform when Condition2 is False]
    End If
End If
```

Needless to say, nested If... Then... Else...End If constructs can become quite complicated and confusing. The ElseIf clause sometimes helps reduce this confusion:

```
If Condition1 Then
    [Action to perform when Condition1 is True]
ElseIf Condition2 Then
    [Action to perform when Condition2 is True]
Else
    [Action to perform when Condition2 is False]
End If
```

In this example, notice that there is only one End If statement at the bottom of the construct.

When you have many conditions to test, the `If...Then...ElseIf...Else` conditions can get rather unwieldy. A better approach is to use the `Select Case...End Select` construct.

The Select Case...End Select statement

VBA offers the `Select Case` statement to check for multiple conditions. Following is the general syntax of the `Select Case` statement:

```
Select Case Expression
    Case Value1
        [Action to take when Expression = Value1]
    Case Value2
        [Action to take when Expression = Value2]
    Case ...
    Case Else
        [Default action when no value matches Expression]
End Select
```

Notice that the syntax is similar to that of the `If...Then` statement. Instead of a Boolean condition, the `Select Case` statement uses an expression at the very top. Then, each `Case` clause tests its value against the expression's value. When a `Case` value matches the expression, the program executes the block of code until it reaches another `Case` statement or the `End Select` statement. VBA executes the code for only one matching `Case` statement.

Note

If more than one `Case` statement matches the value of the test expression, only the code for the first match executes. If other matching `Case` statements appear after the first match, VBA ignores them.

Figure 10.19 shows `Select...Case` used by `frmDialogContactPrint` to decide which of several reports to open.

FIGURE 10.19

Using the `Select Case` statement

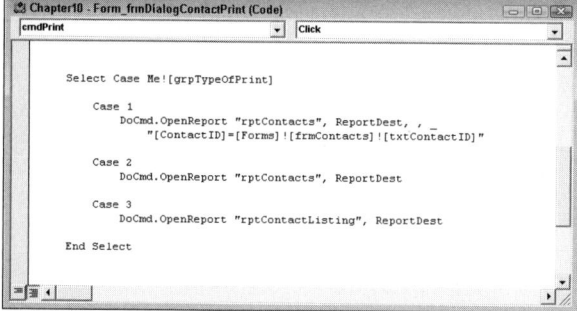

Using the Case Else statement is optional, but it's always a good idea. The Case Else clause is always the last Case statement of Select Case and is executed when none of the Case values matches the expression at the top of the Select Case statement.

In some procedures, you might want to execute a group of statements more than one time. VBA provides some constructs for repeating a group of statements.

Looping

Another very powerful process that VBA offers is repetitive looping — the capability to execute a single statement or a group of statements over and over. The statement or group of statements is repeated until some condition is met.

VBA offers two types of looping constructs:

- Do...Loop
- For...Next

Loops are commonly used to process records within a recordset, change the appearance of controls on forms, and a number of other tasks that require repeating the same VBA statements multiple times.

The Do...Loop statement

Do...Loop is used to repeat a group of statements *while* a condition is True or *until* a condition is True. This statement is one of the most commonly used VBA looping constructs:

```
Do [While | Until Condition]
    [VBA statements]
    [Exit Do]
    [VBA statements]
Loop
```

Alternatively, the While (or Until) may appear at the bottom of the construct:

```
Do
    [VBA statements]
    [Exit Do]
    [VBA statements]
Loop [While | Until Condition]
```

Notice that Do...Loop has several options. The While clause causes the VBA statements within the Do...Loop to execute as long as the condition is True. Execution drops out of the Do... Loop as soon as the condition evaluates to False.

The Until clause works in just the opposite way. The code within the Do...Loop executes only as long as the condition is False.

Placing the While or Until clause at the top of the Do...Loop means that the loop never executes if the condition is not met. Placing the While or Until at the bottom of the loop means that the loop executes at least once because the condition is not evaluated until after the statements within the loop has executed the first time.

Exit Do immediately terminates the Do...Loop. Use Exit Do as part of a test within the loop:

```
Do While Condition1
    [VBA statements]
    If Condition2 Then
        Exit Do
    End If
    [VBA statements]
Loop
```

Exit Do is often used to prevent endless loops. An endless loop occurs when the condition's state (True or False) never changes within the loop.

In case you're wondering, *Condition1* and *Condition2* in this example may be the same. There is no requirement that the second condition be different from the condition used at the top of the Do...Loop.

Figure 10.20 illustrates how a Do loop may be used. In this particular example, a recordset has been opened and each record is processed within the Do loop. In this example, the company's name is printed in the Immediate window, but the data is not modified or used in any way.

FIGURE 10.20

Using the Do...Loop statement

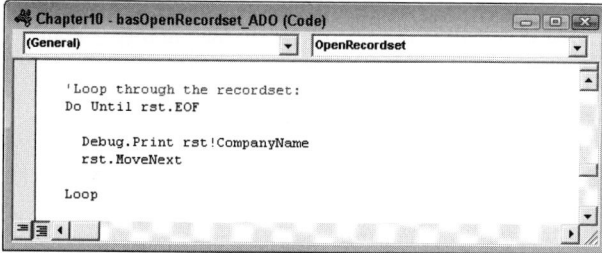

The While and Until clauses provide powerful flexibility for processing a Do...Loop in your code.

The For...Next statement

Use For...Next to repeat a statement block a set number of times. The general format of For...Next is

```
For CounterVariable = Start To End
    [Statement block]
Next CounterVariable
```

We already saw an example of the For...Next loop. Earlier in this chapter, you saw a procedure named BeepWarning that looks like this:

```
Sub BeepWarning()
    Dim xBeeps As Integer
    Dim nBeeps As Integer
    nBeeps = 5
    For xBeeps = 1 To nBeeps
        Beep
    Next xBeeps
End Sub
```

In this procedure, xBeeps is the counter variable, 1 is the start, and nBeeps is the end. In this example, xBeeps starts at 1 and is incremented at the bottom of the For...Next loop at the Next xBeeps statement.

An alternate form of For...Next is

```
For CounterVariable = Start To End Step StepValue
    [Statement block]
Next CounterVariable
```

The only difference here is the StepValue added to the first statement. The Step keyword followed by an increment causes the counter variable to be incremented by the step value each time the loop executes. For example, if *Start* is 10 and *End* is 100 and *StepValue* is 10, the counter variable starts at 10 and increments by 10 each time the loop executes.

Most of the time, a For...Next loop counts upward, starting at an initial value and incrementing the counter variable by the amount specified by the step value. In some cases, however, you might need a loop that starts at a high start value and steps downward to an end value. In this case, use a negative number as the step value.

The following section explains the special syntax to use when working with objects instead of simple variables.

Working with Objects and Collections

Very often, you have to work with objects such as the controls on a form or a recordset object containing data extracted from the database. VBA provides several constructs specifically designed to work with objects and collections of objects.

An object primer

Although Microsoft Access is not object oriented, it's often referred to as *object based*. Many of the things you work with in Access are objects and not just simple numbers and character strings. Generally speaking, an *object* is a complex entity that performs some kind of job within an Access application. Access uses *collections* to aggregate similar objects as a single group.

For example, when you build an Access form, you're actually creating a `Form` object. As you add controls to the form, you're adding them to the form's `Controls` collection. Even though you might add different types of controls (such as buttons and text boxes) to the form, the form's `Controls` collection contains all the controls you've added to the form.

You'll see many, many examples of working with individual objects and collections of objects in this book. Understanding how objects differ from simple variables is an important step to becoming a proficient Access developer.

Each type of Access object includes its own properties and methods, and shares many other properties (such as `Name`) and methods with many other Access objects.

Collections, however, have just a few properties and methods. These are the most important properties associated with Access collections:

- `Name`: The name of the collection. Most collection names are capitalized and are the plural form of the type of object contained within the collection. For example, a form's controls are contained within the form's `Controls` collection.

- `Count`: The number of items contained with the collection. A collection with a `Count` of 0 is empty. Collections can contain virtually any number of items, but performance degrades when the `Count` becomes very large (in excess of 50,000 objects).

- `Item`: Once you have objects stored in a collection, you need a way to reference individual objects in the collection. The `Item` property points to a single item within a collection.

The following example demonstrates setting a property on just one item in a collection:

```
MyCollection.Item(9).SomeProperty = Value
```

or:

```
MyCollection.Item("ItemName").SomeProperty = Value
```

where *MyCollection* is the name assigned to the collection, *SomeProperty* is the name of a property associated with the item, and *Value* is the value assigned to the property.

This small example demonstrates a couple of important concepts regarding collections:

- **There are different ways to reference the items stored in a collection.** In most cases, each item stored in a collection (such as a form's `Controls` collection) has a name and can be referenced using its name:

  ```
  MyForm.Controls("txtLastName").FontBold = True
  ```

  As a consequence, each object's name within a collection must be unique. You can't, for example, have two controls with the same name on an Access form.

  The alternate way to reference an object in a collection is with a number that indicates the item's ordinal position within the collection. The first item added to a collection is item 0 (zero), the second is item 1, and so on.

- **A collection might contain many thousands of objects.** Although performance suffers when a collection contains several tens of thousands of objects, a collection is a handy way to store an arbitrary number of items as an application runs. You'll see several examples of using collections as storage devices in this book.

The With statement

The `With` statement enables you to loop through all the members of an object collection, setting or changing the properties of each member. Any number of statements can appear between the `With` and `End With` statements. `With` statements can be nested.

As an example, consider the code using the following `For...Next` looping construct. This code loops through all members of a form's `Controls` collection, examining each control. If the control is a command button, the button's font is set to 10 point, Bold, Times New Roman:

```
Private Sub cmdOld_Click()
    Dim i As Integer
    Dim c As Control
    For i = 0 To Me.Controls.Count - 1
        Set c = Me.Controls(i) 'Grab a control
        If TypeOf c Is CommandButton Then
            'Set a few properties of the control:
            c.FontName = "Times New Roman"
            c.FontBold = True
            c.FontSize = 12
        End If
    Next
End Sub
```

Don't be confused by the different expressions you see in this example. The heart of this procedure is the `For...Next` loop. The loop begins at zero (the start value) and executes until the `i` variable reaches the number of controls on the form minus one. (The controls on an Access form are numbered beginning with zero. The `Count` property tells you how many controls are on the form.) Within the loop, a variable named `c` is pointed at the control indicated by the `i` variable. The `If TypeOf` statement evaluates the exact type of control referenced by the `c` variable.

Within the body of the `If...Then` branch, the control's properties (`FontName`, `FontBold`, and `FontSize`) are adjusted. You'll frequently see code such as this when it's necessary to manipulate all the members of a collection.

Notice that the control variable is referenced in each of the assignment statements. Referencing control properties one at a time is a fairly slow process. If the form contains many controls, this code executes relatively slowly.

An improvement on this code uses the `With` statement to isolate one member of the `Controls` collection and apply a number of statements to that control. The following code uses the `With` statement to apply a number of font settings to a single control.

```
Private Sub cmdWith_Click()
  Dim i As Integer
  Dim c As Control
  For i = 0 To Me.Controls.Count - 1
    Set c = Me.Controls(i)   'Grab a control
    If TypeOf c Is CommandButton Then
      With c
        'Set a few properties of the control:
        .FontName = "Arial"
        .FontBold = True
        .FontSize = 8
      End With
    End If
  Next
End Sub
```

The code in this example (cmdWith_Click) executes somewhat faster than the previous example (cmdOld_Click). Once Access has a handle on the control (With c), it's able to apply all the statements in the body of the With without having to fetch the control from the controls on the form as in cmdOld_Click.

In practical terms, however, it's highly unlikely that you'll notice any difference in execution times when using the With construct as shown in this example. However, when working with massive sets of data, the With statement might contribute to overall performance. In any case, the With statement reduces the wordiness of the subroutine, and makes the code much easier to read and understand.

Think of the With statement as if you're handing Access a particular item and saying "Here, apply all these properties to *this* item." The previous example said, "Go get the item named *x* and apply this property to it" over and over again. The speed difference in these commands is considerable.

The For Each statement

The code in cmdWith_Click is further improved by using the For Each statement to traverse the Controls collection. For Each walks through each member of a collection, making it available for examination or manipulation. The following code shows how For Each simplifies the example.

```
Private Sub cmdForEach_Click()
  Dim c As Control
  For Each c In Me.Controls
    If TypeOf c Is CommandButton Then
      With c
        .FontName = "MS Sans Serif"
        .FontBold = False
        .FontSize = 8
      End With
    End If
  Next
End Sub
```

The improvement goes beyond using fewer lines to get the same amount of work done. Notice that you no longer need an integer variable to count through the Controls collection. You also don't have to call on the Controls collection's Count property to determine when to end the For loop. All this overhead is handled silently and automatically for you by the VBA programming language.

The code in this listing is easier to understand than in either of the previous procedures. The purpose of each level of nesting is obvious and clear. You don't have to keep track of the index to see what's happening, and you don't have to worry about whether to start the For loop at 0 or 1. The code in the For...Each example is marginally faster than the With...End With example because no time is spent incrementing the integer value used to count through the loop and Access doesn't have to evaluate which control in the collection to work on.

On the CD-ROM

The Chapter10.accdb **example database includes** frmWithDemo **(see Figure 10.21), which contains all the code discussed in this section. Each of the three command buttons along the bottom of this form uses different code to loop through the** Controls **collections on this form, changing the font characteristics of the controls.**

FIGURE 10.21

frmWithDemo is included in Chapter10.accdb.

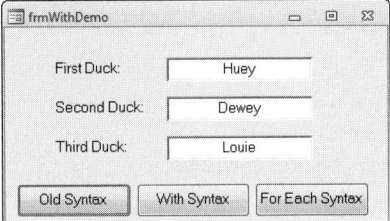

Looking at Access Options for Developers

Many of the most important features in Access affect only developers. These features are hidden from end users and benefit only the person building the application. Spend some time exploring these features so that you fully understand their benefits. You'll soon settle on option settings that suit the way you work and the kind of assistance you want as you write your VBA code.

The Editor tab of the Options dialog box

The Options dialog box contains several important settings that greatly influence how you interact with Access as you add code to your applications. These options are accessed by opening a module in the VBA code editor, and choosing Tools ⇨ Options.

Auto Indent

Auto Indent causes code to be indented to the current depth in all successive lines of code. For example, if you inserted four spaces (or tabs) in front of the current line of code, each line of code following the current line will be automatically indented four spaces.

Auto Syntax Check

When the Auto Syntax Check option is selected, Access checks each line of code for syntax errors as you enter it in the code editor. Many experienced developers find this behavior intrusive and prefer to keep this option disabled, instead letting the compiler point out syntax errors. Most of the syntax errors caught by Auto Syntax Check are the most obvious spelling errors, missing commas, and so on.

Break on all Errors

Break on All Errors causes Access to behave as if On Error GoTo 0 is always set, regardless of any error trapping you might set up in code. When this option is selected, Access stops on every error, making it easier to debug the code.

Require Variable Declaration

This setting automatically inserts the Option Explicit directive into all VBA modules in your Access application. This option is *not* selected by default in recent versions of Access.

Tip

When you get used to having Option Explicit set on every module (including global and class modules), the instances of rogue and unexplained variables (which, in reality, are almost always misspellings of declared variables) disappear. With Option Explicit set in every module, your code is more self-explanatory and easier to debug and maintain because the compiler catches every single misspelled variable.

Compile on Demand

Compile on Demand instructs Access to compile modules only when their procedures are required somewhere else in the database. When this option is unchecked, all modules are compiled anytime any procedure is called.

Auto List Members

This option pops up a list box containing the members of an object's object hierarchy in the code window. In Figure 10.11, the list of Application objects appeared as soon as I typed as the period following Application in the VBA statement. You select an item from the list by continuing to type it in or scrolling the list and pressing the spacebar.

Auto Quick Info

When Auto Quick Info has been selected Access pops up syntax help (refer to Figure 10.12) when you enter the name of a procedure (function, subroutine, or method) followed by a period, space,

411

or opening parenthesis. The procedure can be a built-in function or subroutine or one that you've written yourself in Access VBA.

Auto Data Tips

The Auto Data Tips option displays the value of variables when you hold the mouse cursor over a variable with the module in break mode. Auto Data Tips is an alternative to setting a watch on the variable and flipping to the Debug window when Access reaches the break point.

Cross-Reference

Debugging Access VBA is described in Chapter 14.

The Project Properties dialog box

All the code components in an Access application, including all the modules, procedures, variables, and other elements are aggregated as the application's VBA project. The VBA language engine accesses modules and procedures as members of the project. Access manages the code in your application by keeping track of all the code objects that are included in the project, which is different than and separate from the code added into the application as runtime libraries and wizards.

Each Access project includes a number of important options. The Project Properties dialog box (shown in Figure 10.22) contains a number of settings that are important for developers. Open the Project Properties dialog box by opening a module in the code window, and choosing Tools ➪ *Project Name* Properties (where *Project Name* is the name of your database's project).

FIGURE 10.22

The Project Properties dialog box contains a number of interesting options.

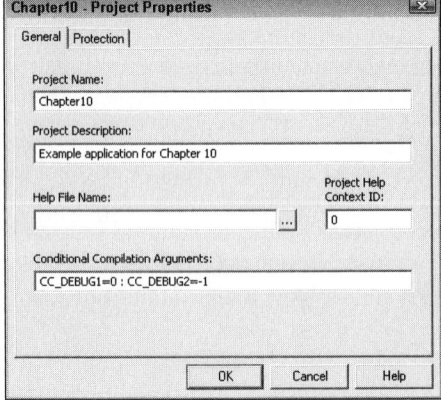

Project Name

Certain changes in an application's structure require Access to recompile the code in the application. For example, changing the code in a global module affects all statements in other modules using that code, so Access must recompile all the code in the application. Until the code is recompiled, Access "decompiles" the application by reverting to the plain-text version of the code stored in the .accdb file and ignoring the compiled code in the .accdb. This means that each line of the code must be interpreted at runtime, dramatically slowing the application.

Sometimes insignificant modifications, such as changing the name of the project itself, are sufficient to cause decompilation. This happens because of the hierarchical nature of Access VBA. Because all objects are "owned" by some other object, changing the name of a high-level object might change the dependencies and ownerships of all objects below it in the object hierarchy.

Access maintains a separate, independent project name for the code and executable objects in the application. Simply changing the name of the .accdb file is not enough to decompile the code in an Access application. By default, the project name is the same as the name of the .accdb, but it's not dependent on it. You can assign a unique name to the project with the Project Name text box in the General tab of the Project Properties dialog box.

Project Description

The project description is, as its name implies, a description for the project. Because this area is so small, it isn't possible to add anything of significance that might be helpful to another developer.

Conditional Compilation Arguments

Compiler directives instruct the Access VBA compiler to include or exclude portions of code, depending on the value of a constant established in the module's declarations section.

One of the limitations of using compiler directives is that the constant declaration is local to the module. This means that you have to use the #Const compiler directive to set up the constant in every module that includes the #If directive. This limitation can make it difficult to remove all the #Const compiler directives to modify the code at the conclusion of development.

For example, consider a situation in which you want to use conditional compilation to include certain debugging statements and functions during the development cycle. Just before shipping the application to its users, you want to remove the compiler directives from the code so that your users won't see the message boxes, status-bar messages, and other debugging information. If your application consists of dozens of forms and modules, you have to make sure you find every single instance of the #Const directive to make sure you successfully deactivated the debugging code. (This is why it's such a good idea to apply a naming convention to the identifiers you use with the #Const directive.)

Fortunately, Access provides a way for you to set up "global" conditional compilation arguments. The General tab of the Project Properties dialog box contains the Conditional Compilation Arguments text box, where you can enter arguments to be evaluated by the conditional compilation directives in your code.

As an example, assume you've set up the following sort of statements in all the modules in your application:

```
#If CC_DEBUG2 Then
   MsgBox "Now in ProcessRecords()"
#End If
```

Instead of adding the constant directive (#Const CC_DEBUG2 = True) to every module in the application, you might enter the following text into the Conditional Compilation Arguments text box:

```
CC_DEBUG2 = -1
```

This directive sets the value of CC_DEBUG2 to -1 (True) for all modules (global and form and report class modules) in the application. You need to change only this one entry to CC_DEBUG2=0 to disable the debugging statements in all modules in the application.

Note
You don't use the words True or False when setting compiler constants in the Project Properties dialog box, even though you do use these values within a VBA code module. You must use -1 for True and 0 for False in the Project Properties dialog box.

Separate multiple arguments with colons — for example: CC_DEBUG1=0 : CC_DEBUG2=-1.

Command-line arguments

The Options dialog box you open from the File menu (click on the large round Microsoft Office Button in the upper-left corner of the main Access window, and choose File ⇨ Access Options) provides a number of interesting options. Select the Advanced tab and scroll down to the Advanced section near the bottom of the dialog box. Notice the Command-Line Arguments text box at the very bottom of the Advanced section.

Many applications use command-line arguments to influence how the application behaves at runtime. You could, for example, add a command-line argument to an Access database application that indicates whether the user was an experienced or novice user. The application might display help and other assistance that is appropriate for the user's experience level. (Use the Command function to return the arguments portion of the command-line used to start Access or the Access runtime environment.)

Passing a Windows application command-line arguments during development has always been difficult. Windows requires command-line arguments to be passed as text in the Target text box of a program icon's Property Sheet. Figure 10.23 shows such a Property Sheet. The text /User Novice in the Target text box is the command-line argument passed to the Access application as it starts up.

Before the `Command-Line Arguments` option was available, there was no easy way to test the effect of command-line arguments in your application. Use this option to test and debug the command-line argument code you build into your applications.

Adding a command-line argument to a shortcut pointing to a Windows application

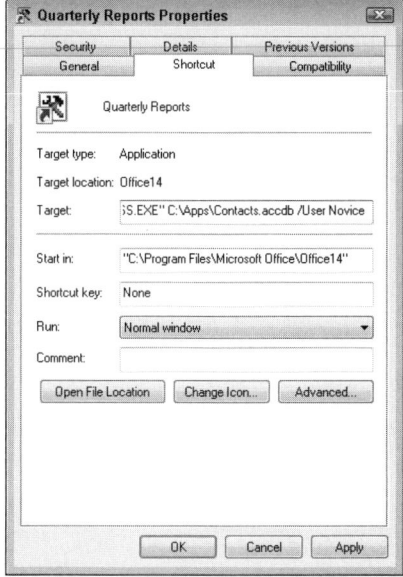

Caution

Don't forget to remove the text from this option before distributing your application to end users. The text you enter in this option setting is persistent and will remain there until it's removed or changed.

On the CD-ROM

Use the `Command` function to return the arguments portion of the command line used to start Access or the Access runtime environment. The `Chapter10.accdb` example database includes `frmCommandLine` (see Figure 10.24), a demonstration of the `Command` function. Use the Options dialog box to set some command-line arguments for `Chapter10.accdb`; then click on the button on `frmCommandLine` to see how the `Command` function retrieves the arguments.

FIGURE 10.24

`Chapter10.accdb` includes `frmCommandLine` to demonstrate using command-line arguments in your applications.

Summary

This chapter reviewed some of the important topics as you work with Access VBA. I showed you the fundamental concepts of creating VBA modules and procedures and touched on the important topic of event-driven programming in Microsoft Access.

You also read that Access provides a large number of options and settings that influence how you work with your modules and procedures. The good news is that you have a lot of options controlling the appearance and behavior of the Access code editor. There is *no* bad news about writing code in Microsoft Access!

The `With...End, With,` and `For Each` constructs make it easy and efficient to traverse the members of object collections. Named arguments give you a lot more flexibility in passing parameters to functions and subroutines.

You continue your exploration of the VBA programming language in the next several chapters. In Chapters 11 through 15 you learn virtually every fundamental skill necessary to succeed as a VBA programmer. One important aspect of VBA programming is that it's a skill with no barriers — your abilities as an Access VBA programmer are completely transferable to any of the other Microsoft Office products like Word and Excel.

Mastering VBA Data Types and Procedures

A ll VBA applications require *variables* to hold data while the program executes. Variables are like a white board where important information can be temporarily written and read later on by the program. For example, when a user inputs a value on a form, you'll most often use a variable to temporarily hold the value until it can be permanently stored in the database or printed on a report. Simply put, a variable is the name you've assigned to a particular bit of data in your application. In more technical terms, a variable is a named area in memory used to store values during program execution.

Variables are transient and do not persist after an application stops running. And, as you'll read in the "Understanding variable scope and lifetime" section, later in this chapter, a variable may last a very short time as the program executes or may exist as long as the application is running.

In most cases, you assign a specific data type to each of the variables in your applications. For example, you may create a string variable to hold text data such as names or descriptions. A currency variable, on the other hand, is meant to contain values representing monetary amounts. You shouldn't try to assign a text value to a currency variable because a runtime error may occur as a result.

The variables you use have a dramatic effect on your applications. You have many options when it comes to establishing and using variables in your Access programs. Inappropriately using a variable can slow an application's execution or potentially cause data loss.

This chapter contains everything you need to know about creating and using VBA variables. The information in this chapter helps you use the most efficient and effective data types for your variables while avoiding the most common problems related to VBA variables.

IN THIS CHAPTER

Naming and declaring variables

Looking at the VBA data types

Working with subs and functions

Building functions

In addition to variables, I take a look at code editor options, working with VBA procedures and passing parameters to procedures.

Introducing the Access VBA Editor

Because I'll be writing quite a bit of code in this chapter, and in the following chapters, this seems a good place to discuss a few options when using the VBA code editor and writing VBA code.

The Access code editor supports a number of important features to help you write and manage VBA code. For example, any line of code ending in an underscore character preceded by a space is recognized as a statement that is continued on the next line, making it easy to see all the parts of very long VBA statements. Notice the statement that starts out `If SysCmd` in Figure 11.1. This statement actually occupies two lines of code: the one containing the `If` statement and the line immediately under it.

FIGURE 11.1

The continuation character is a welcome feature in the Access VBA Editor.

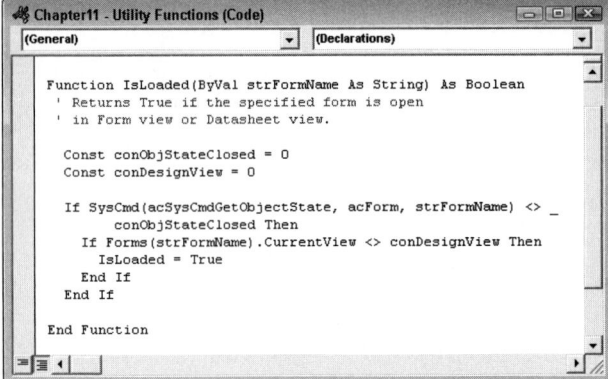

```vba
Function IsLoaded(ByVal strFormName As String) As Boolean
    ' Returns True if the specified form is open
    ' in Form view or Datasheet view.

    Const conObjStateClosed = 0
    Const conDesignView = 0

    If SysCmd(acSysCmdGetObjectState, acForm, strFormName) <> _
            conObjStateClosed Then
        If Forms(strFormName).CurrentView <> conDesignView Then
            IsLoaded = True
        End If
    End If

End Function
```

Tip

When you use continuation characters, it is a good idea to indent the continued lines of code. Being able to recognize continued lines of code without having to keep track of the continuation characters is important.

The Access VBA statement continuation is quite powerful. You can split long declarations such as Windows API declares, and you can even split long strings into multiple lines.

Cross-Reference

The Windows API is discussed in detail in Chapter 27.

One particularly powerful use of the continuation character is illustrated later in this chapter (in Figure 11.14). In Figure 11.14, a long SQL statement is split across a number of lines of code. All that's needed on each subsequent line is the concatenation character (&) and as much of the string as you want to add on the line. Each portion of the SQL statement must be surrounded by double quotes, and you must preserve spaces between words in the statement. Splitting long SQL statements this way makes it easy to see what's in the statement and, therefore, what fields end up in the resulting recordset.

Most often, however, continuation characters are used to break up long, complex statements. Figure 11.2 shows an example of this use of the continuation character. In this figure, a long VBA statement that opens a new recordset is split into five lines of code. The continuation characters are placed after the commas separating the elements contained in the complex statement, making the statement easier to read and understand.

FIGURE 11.2

Use the continuation character to split long strings into multiple lines.

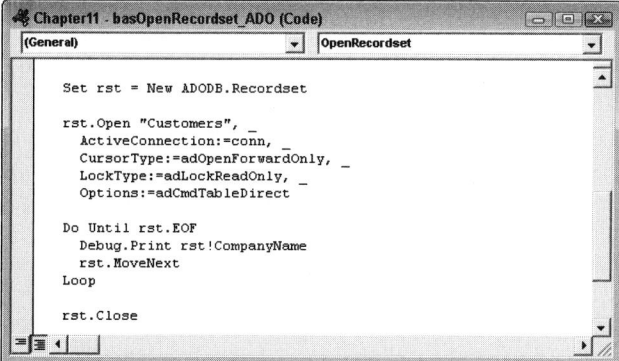

Continuation characters can be inserted almost anywhere within a VBA statement. (You can't split individual words in a statement with continuation characters.) It makes sense, therefore, to insert the continuation character sequence in places (such as in Figure 11.2) that add to the readability of long statements. In Figure 11.2, inserting a continuation after each comma breaks the statement into logical sections. Putting continuations anywhere else in this statement would make it harder to read.

Another powerful feature of the Access code editor is the text colors used to set aside comments, keywords, and identifiers. Although it's not obvious in this book's figures, the comments in Figure 11.1 and Figure 11.2 appear in a green font, while the VBA keywords like Function, Const, and If are blue. Identifiers like conObjStateClosed and conDesignView, as well as the procedure name IsLoaded in Figure 11.1, are black.

Tip

You can adjust the editor font and text colors to suit your particular style. In the code editor, choose Tools ➪ Options to open the Options dialog box. Select the Editor Format tab (shown in Figure 11.3), and you see all the options for the font, font size, and colors for various parts of the VBA syntax.

FIGURE 11.3

The Options dialog box contains plenty of settings that affect the VBA code window.

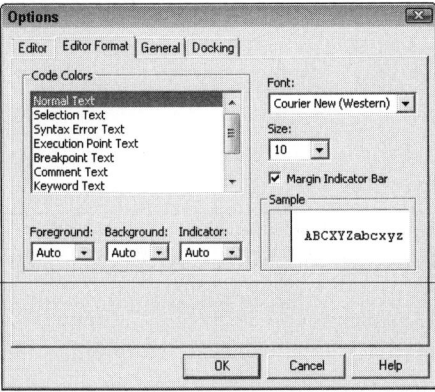

Another terrific feature of the Access code window is that the object drop-down list (shown in Figure 11.4) is alphabetically sorted. If you use a naming convention in your Access code, all the controls will be grouped by the control type. For example, by using cmd as the prefix for command buttons, all the command buttons are sorted together in the object list.

FIGURE 11.4

The object list in the Access code window is sorted alphabetically.

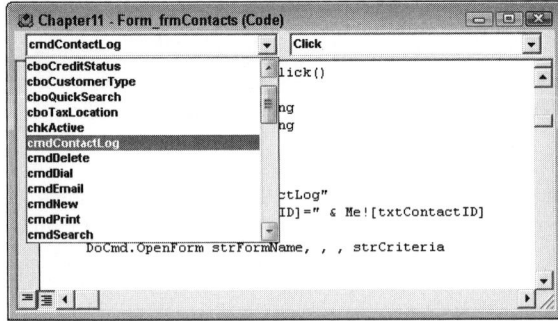

Using Variables

One of the most powerful concepts in programming is the variable. A *variable* is a temporary storage location for some value and is given a name. You can use a variable to store the result of a calculation, hold a value entered by the user, or read from a table, or you can create a variable to make a control's value available to another procedure.

To refer to the result of an expression, you use a variable's name to store the result. To assign an expression's result to a variable, you use the = operator. Here are some examples of expressions that assign values to variables:

```
counter = 1

counter = counter + 1

today = Date()
```

Figure 11.5 shows a simple procedure using several different variables. Although this is a very simple example of using variables, it effectively demonstrates just about everything you need to know about using VBA variables:

FIGURE 11.5

Variable declarations appear at the top of VBA procedures.

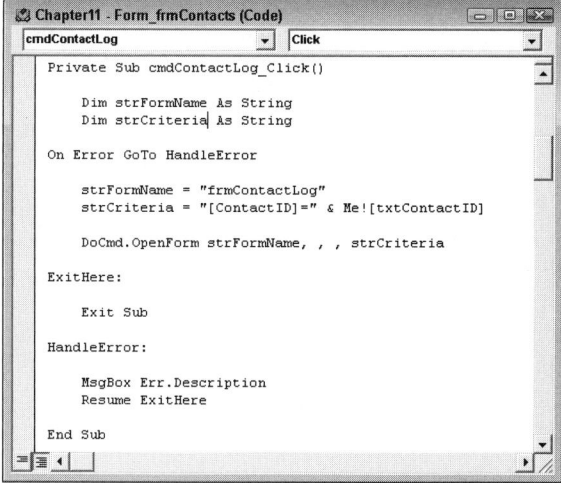

```
Chapter11 - Form_frmContacts (Code)

cmdContactLog                    Click

Private Sub cmdContactLog_Click()

    Dim strFormName As String
    Dim strCriteria As String

On Error GoTo HandleError

    strFormName = "frmContactLog"
    strCriteria = "[ContactID]=" & Me![txtContactID]

    DoCmd.OpenForm strFormName, , , strCriteria

ExitHere:

    Exit Sub

HandleError:

    MsgBox Err.Description
    Resume ExitHere

End Sub
```

- The Dim keyword establishes the new variables — strDocName and strCriteria — within a procedure.

- You provide a meaningful name for the variable as part of the `Dim` statement. In Figure 11.5, the variable names are `strDocName` and `strLinkCriteria`, indicating how the variables are used by the procedure.

- The `Dim` statement includes the data type of the new variable. In Figure 11.5, both variables are declared as the `string` data type.

- Different techniques can be used to assign a value to a variable. Figure 11.5 uses the `=` operator to assign a literal value — `frmContactLog` — to `strDocName`. Notice that `frmContactLog` is surrounded by quotation marks, making it a "literal" value. A value pulled from the `txtContactID` text box on the form's surface is combined with a literal string — `"[ContactID]="` — and assigned to the `strCriteria` variable. The data assigned to variables should always be appropriate for the variable's data type.

- Variables are manipulated with a variety of operators. Figure 11.5 uses the VBA concatenation operator (`&`) to combine `[ContactID]=` and the value in `txtContactID`.

There are a number of ways to perform each of the tasks you see in Figure 11.5. For example, as you'll read in the "Declaring variables" section, later in this chapter, the `Dim` statement is not the only way to establish a variable. And, as you'll see throughout this book, the `=` operator is not the only way to assign a value to a variable. Also, you don't need to use a variable like `strCriteria` to temporarily hold the value generated by combining two values. The two values could just as easily be combined on the fly within the `DoCmd.OpenForm` statement:

```
DoCmd.OpenForm "frmContactLog", _
    "[ContactID] = " & Me![txtContactID]
```

There are very few rules governing how you declare and use your variables. You should always strive for readability in your VBA code. In the small example shown in Figure 11.5, you can easily see that `strFormName` holds the name of a form, especially because it's used as part of the `DoCmd.OpenForm` statement.

Naming variables

Every programming language has its own rules for naming variables. In VBA, a variable name must meet the following conditions:

- It must begin with an alphabetical character.

- It must not contain an embedded period.

- It must have a unique name. The variable's name cannot be used elsewhere in the procedure or in modules that use the variables.

- It must not contain spaces or punctuation characters.

- It must not be a reserved word, such as `Sub`, `Module`, or `Form`.

- It must be no longer than 64 characters.

Although you can make up almost any name for a variable, most programmers adopt a standard convention for naming variables. Some common practices include the following:

- Using a mix of uppercase and lowercase characters, as in `TotalCost`.

- Using all lowercase characters, as in `counter`.

- Separating the parts of a variable's name with underscores, as in `Total_Cost`.

- Preceding the name with the data type of the value. A variable that stores a number might be called `intCounter`, while a variable holding a string might be named `strLastName`.

Note

One source of endless confusion to Access developers is the fact that Access object names (tables, queries, forms, and so on) may contain spaces, while variable names never include spaces. One reason not to use spaces in Access object names is to eliminate confusion when mixing different naming conventions within a single application. You're really better off being consistent in how you apply names to your Access objects, variables, procedures, and other application entities.

Tip

When creating variables, you can use uppercase, lowercase, or both to specify the variable or call it later. VBA variables are not case-sensitive. This fact means that you can use the `TodayIs` variable later without having to worry about the case that you used for the name when you created it; `TODAYIS`, `todayis`, and `tOdAyIs` all refer to the same variable. VBA automatically changes any explicitly declared variables to the case that was used in the declaration statement (the `Dim` statement).

When you need to see or use the contents of a variable, you simply reference its name. When you specify the variable's name, the computer program goes into memory, finds the variable, and gets its contents for you. This process means, of course, that you need to be able to remember and correctly reference the name of the variable.

Declaring variables

There are two principle ways to add variables to your applications. The first method — called *implicit declaration* — is to let VBA automatically create the variables for you. As with most things that are not carefully controlled, you'll find that letting VBA prepare your variables for you is not a particularly good idea and can lead to performance issues or efficiency in your programs (see the "Comparing implicit and explicit variables" section, later in this chapter).

Implicit declaration means that VBA automatically creates a `variant`-type variable for each identifier it recognizes as a variable in an application. (Variants are discussed in the "Working with Data Types" section, later in this chapter.) In the following, there are two implicitly declared variables — `strFirstName` and `strLastName` In this example, two string variables (`strFirstName` and `strLastName`) are assigned the text contained in two text boxes (`txtFirstName` and `txtLastName`), and a third string variable (`strFullName`) is assigned the combination of `strFirstName` and `strLastName`, with a space between them.

```
Private Sub Combine_Implicit()
  strFirstName = txtFirstName
  strLastName = txtLastName
  txtFullName = strFirstName & " " & strLastName
End Sub
```

The second approach is to *explicitly* declare them with one of the following keywords: Dim, Static, Private, or Public (or Global). The choice of keyword has a profound effect on the variable's scope within the application and determines where the variable can be used in the program. (Variable scope is discussed in the "Understanding variable scope and lifetime" section, later in this chapter.)

The syntax for explicitly declaring a variable is quite simple:

```
Dim VariableName As DataType

Static VariableName As DataType

Private VariableName As DataType

Public VariableName As DataType
```

In each case, the name of the variable and its data type are provided as part of the declaration. VBA reserves the amount of memory required to hold the variable as soon as the declaration statement is executed. Once a variable is declared, you can't change its data type, although you can easily convert the value of a variable and assign the converted value to another variable.

The following example shows the Combine_Implicit sub rewritten to use explicitly declared variables:

```
Private Sub Combine_Explicit()
  Dim strFirstName As String
  Dim strLastName As String
  strFirstName = txtFirstName.Text
  strLastName = txtLastName.Text
  txtFullName = strFirstName & " " & strLastName
End Sub
```

So, if there's often very little difference between using implicit and explicit variables, why bother declaring variables at all? The following code demonstrates the importance of using explicitly declared variables in your applications:

```
Private Sub Form_Load()
  Department = "Manufacturing"
  Supervisor = "Joe Jones"
  Title = "Senior Engineer"
  'Dozens of lines of code go here
  txtDepartment = Department
  txtSupervisor = Superviser
  txtTitle = Title
End Sub
```

In this example code, the `txtSupervisor` text box on the form is always empty and is never assigned a value. A line near the bottom of this procedure assigns the value of an implicitly declared variable named `Superviser` to the `txtSupervisor` text box. Notice that the name of the variable (`Superviser`) is a misspelling of the intended variable (`Supervisor`). Because the source of the assignment appears to be a variable, VBA simply creates a new variant named `Superviser` and assigns its value (which is, literally, `nothing`) to the `txtSupervisor` text box to it. And, because the new `Superviser` variable has never been assigned a value, the text box always ends up empty. Misspellings such as this are very common and easy to overlook in long or complex procedures.

Furthermore, the code shown in this example runs fine, and causes no problem. Because this procedure uses implicit variable declaration, Access raises no error because of the misspelling, and the problem isn't detected until someone notices the text box is always empty. Imagine the problems you'd encounter in a payroll or billing application if variables went missing because of simple spelling errors!

When you declare a variable, Access sets up a location in the computer's memory for storing a value for the variable ahead of time. The amount of storage allocated for the variable depends on the data type you assign to the variable. More space is allocated for a variable that will hold a currency amount (such as $1,000,000) than for a variable that will never hold a value greater than, say, 255. This is because a variable declared with the `currency` data type requires more storage than another variable declared as a `byte data type`. (Data types are discussed later in this chapter, in the "Working with Data Types" section.)

Even though VBA doesn't require you to declare your variables before using them, it does provide various declaration commands. Getting into the habit of declaring variables is good practice. A variable's declaration assures that you can assign only a certain type of data to it — always a numeric value or only characters, for example. In addition, you attain real performance gains by pre-declaring variables.

Tip

A programming best practice is to explicitly declare variables at the top of the procedure; this makes the program easier for other programmers to work with later on.

The Dim keyword

To declare a variable, you use the `Dim` statement. (*Dim* is an abbreviation of the archaic *Dimension* programming term — because you're specifying the dimension of the variable.) When you use the `Dim` statement, you must supply the variable name that you assign to the variable. Here's the format for the `Dim` keyword:

```
Dim [VariableName] [As DataType]
```

The following statement declares the variable `xBeeps` as an integer data type:

```
Dim xBeeps As Integer
```

Notice that the variable name follows the Dim statement. In addition to naming the variable, use As *Data Type* to specify a data type for the variable. The data type is the kind of information that will be stored in the variable — string, integer, currency, and so on. The default data type is variant; it can hold any type of data.

When you use the Dim statement to declare a variable in a procedure, you can refer to that variable only within that procedure. Other procedures, even if they're stored in the same module, don't know anything about the variable declared within a procedure. Such a variable is often described as *local* because it's declared *locally* within a procedure and is known only by the procedure that owns it. (You can read more about variable scope in the "Understanding variable scope and lifetime" section, later in this chapter.)

Variables also can be declared in the declarations section of a module. Then all the procedures in the module can access the variable. Procedures *outside* the module in which you declared the variable, however, can't read or use the variable.

The Public keyword

To make a variable available to all modules in the application, use the Public keyword when you declare the variable. Figure 11.6 illustrates declaring a public variable.

FIGURE 11.6

Declaring a public variable

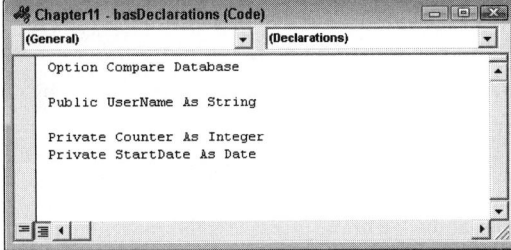

Caution

You can't declare a variable public within a procedure. It must be declared in the declarations section of a module. If you try to declare a variable public within a procedure, you get an error message.

Although you can declare a public variable in any module, it seems logical to declare public variables only within the module that will use them the most. The exceptions to this rule are true global variables that you want to make available to all procedures across modules and that are not specifically related to a single module. Some programmers declare global variables in a single standard module so that you can find them easily.

Tip

You can declare public variables in the code module attached to a form or report. Referencing these public variables from another module is a little bit different than referencing public variables declared in standard modules. To reference the value of a public variable declared behind a form or report from another module, you must qualify the variable reference, using the name of the form or report object. `frmMainForm.MyVariable`, for example, accesses a form named `frmMainForm` and obtains the value of the public variable `MyVariable` declared in the form's code module. Public variables declared within a form or report's module cannot be referenced unless the form or report is open.

The Private keyword

The declarations section in Figure 11.6 shows the use of the `Dim` and `Private` statements to declare variables. Technically, there is no difference between `Private` and `Dim`, but using `Private` at the module level to declare variables that are available to only that module's procedures is a good idea. Declaring private variables contrasts with

- `Dim`, which *must* be used at the procedure level, distinguishing where the variable is declared and its scope (`Module` versus `Procedure`)
- `Public`, the other method of declaring variables in modules, making understanding your code easier

Tip

You can quickly go to the declarations section of a module while you're working on code in a form's module by selecting `(Declarations)` from the Procedure drop-down list in the code editor. Another way to move to the declarations section is to select `(General)` in the Object drop-down list in the code editor. (Refer to the Module window combo boxes in Figure 11.6.) The Declarations item is not available when a control, or the form, is selected in the Object drop-down list.

When you declare a variable, you use the `AS` clause to specify a data type for the new variable. Because Access is a database development system, it's not surprising that variable data types are similar to field data types in an Access database table.

Working with Data Types

When you declare a variable, you also specify the data type for the variable. Each variable has a data type. The data type of a variable determines what kind of information can be stored in the variable.

A `string` variable — a variable with a data type of `string` — can hold character values ranging from A to Z, a to z, and 0 to 1, as well as formatting characters (#, -, !, and so on). Once created, a `string` variable can be used in many ways: comparing its contents with another string, pulling parts of information out of the string, and so on. If you have a variable defined as a string, however, you cannot use it to do mathematical calculations.

Table 11.1 describes the 12 fundamental data types supported by VBA.

TABLE 11.1

VBA Data Types

Data Type	Range	Description
Boolean	True or false	2 bytes
Byte	0 to 255	1-byte binary data
Currency	–922,337,203,685,477,5808 to 922,337,203,685,477,5807	8-byte number with fixed decimal point
Decimal	+/–79,228,162,514,264,337,593,543,950,335 with no decimal point +/–7.9228162514264337593543950335 with 28 places to the right of the decimal; smallest nonzero number is +/–0.0000000000000000000000000001	14 bytes
Date	01 Jan 100 to 31 Dec 9999	8-byte date/time value
Double	–1.79769313486231E308 to –4.94065645841247E–324 for negative values and 4.94065645841246544E-324 through 1.79769313486231570E+308 for positive values	8-byte floating-point number
Integer	–32,768 to 32,767	2-byte integer
Long	–2,147,483,648 to 2,147,483,647	4-byte integer
Object	Any object reference	4 bytes
Single	–3.402823E38 to –1.401298E–45 for negative values and 1.401298E–45 to 3.402823E38 for positive values	4-byte floating-point number
String (variable length; 10 bytes plus length of string)	0 to approximately 2,000,000,000	Varies by size of data
String (fixed length)	1 to approximately 65,400	Length of string
Variant (with numbers)	Any numeric value up to the range of the double data type (see earlier in this table)	16 bytes
Variant (with characters; 22 bytes plus length of string)	0 to approximately 2,000,000,000	Varies by size of data

Most of the time, you use the string, date, integer, and currency or double data types. If a variable always contains whole numbers between –32,768 and 32,767, you can save bytes of memory and gain speed in arithmetic operations if you declare the variable an integer data type.

Note

How big is a string variable? As shown in Table 11.1, string variables can contain quite a bit of data. How much text data could be stored in a single VBA string? The Oxford English Dictionary (OED) is widely accepted as the definitive reference of the English language. Although not the world's largest dictionary (the Dutch Woordenboek de Nederlandsche Taal is considerably longer) the OED is quite impressive. Containing more than 301,000 main entries, 22,000 pages, and 59,000,000 individual words, the OED is available as a 20-volume printed edition.

As large as it is, the OED is only 540MB of data. A single VBA string variable, therefore, could contain almost four complete copies of the OED!

When you want to assign the value of an Access field to a variable, you need to make sure that the type of the variable can hold the data type of the field. Table 11.2 shows the corresponding VBA data types for Access field types.

TABLE 11.2

Access and VBA Data Types

Access Field Data Type	VBA Data Type
AutoNumber (Long Integer)	Long
AutoNumber (Replication ID)	—
Currency	Currency
Computed	—
Date/Time	Date
Memo	String
Number (Byte)	Byte
Number (Integer)	Integer
Number (Long Integer)	Long
Number (Single)	Single
Number (Double)	Double
Number (Replication ID)	—
OLE object	String
Text	String
Hyperlink	String
Yes/No	Boolean

Now that you understand variables and their data types, you're ready to learn how to use them when writing procedures.

Comparing implicit and explicit variables

The default data type for VBA variables is the `variant`. This means that, unless you specify otherwise, every variable in your application will be a variant. As you read earlier in this chapter, although useful, the `variant` data type is not very efficient. Its data storage requirements are greater than the equivalent simple data type (a `string`, for instance) and the computer spends more time keeping track of the data type contained in a variant than for other data types.

Here's an example of how you might test for the speed difference when using implicitly declared `variant` variables and explicitly declared variables. This code is found behind `frmImplicit-Test` in Chapter11.accdb:

```
'Use a Windows API call to get the exact time:
Private Declare Function GetTickCount _
    Lib "kernel32" () As Long
Private Sub cmdGo_Click()
  Dim i As Integer
  Dim j As Integer
  Dim sExplicit As Single
  txtImplicitStart = GetTickCount()
  For o = 1 To 10000
    For p = 1 To 10000
      q = i / 0.33333
    Next p
  Next o
  txtImplicitEnd = GetTickCount()
  txtImplicitElapsed = txtImplicitEnd - txtImplicitStart
  DoEvents   'Force Access to complete pending operations
  txtExplicitStart = GetTickCount()
  For i = 1 To 10000
    For j = 1 To 10000
      sExplicit = i / 0.33333
    Next j
  Next i
  txtExplicitEnd = GetTickCount()
  txtExplicitElapsed = txtExplicitEnd - txtExplicitStart
  DoEvents
End Sub
```

In this small test, the loop using implicitly declared variables required approximately 7.2 seconds to run while the loop with the explicitly declared variables required only 5.6 seconds. This is a performance enhancement of approximately 20 percent just by using explicitly declared variables.

The actual execution time of this — or, any — VBA procedure depends largely on the relative speed of the computer and the tasks the computer is executing at the time the procedure is run. Desktop computers vary a great deal in CPU, memory, and other resources, making it quite impossible to predict how long a particular bit of code should take to execute.

Forcing explicit declaration

Access provides a simple *compiler directive* that forces you to always declare the variables in your applications. The Option Explicit statement, when inserted at the top of a module, instructs VBA to require explicit declaration of all variables in the module. If, for example, you're working with an application containing a number of implicitly declared variables, inserting Option Explicit at the top of each module results in a check of all variable declarations the next time the application is compiled.

Because explicit declaration is such a good idea, it may not come as a surprise that Access provides a way to automatically ensure that every module in your application uses explicit declaration. The Editor tab of the Options dialog box (shown in Figure 11.7) includes a Require Variable Declaration check box. This option automatically inserts the Option Explicit directive at the top of every module created from this point in time onward.

FIGURE 11.7

Requiring variable declaration is a good idea in most Access applications.

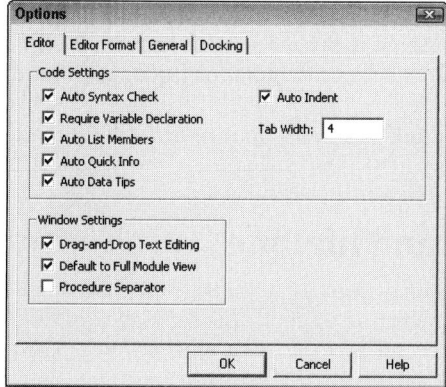

The Require Variable Declaration option doesn't affect modules already written. This option applies only to modules created *after* this option is selected, so you'll have to insert the Option Explicit statement in existing modules. Require Variable Declaration is not set by default in current versions of Access. You must set this option yourself to take advantage of having Access add Option Explicit to all your modules.

Using a naming convention

Like most programming languages, applications written in VBA tend to be quite long and complex, often occupying many thousands of lines of code. Even simple VBA programs may require hundreds of different variables. VBA forms often have dozens of different controls on them, including text boxes, command buttons, option groups, and other controls. Keeping track of the variables, procedures, forms, and controls in even a moderately complicated VBA application is a daunting task.

One way to ease the burden of managing the code and objects in an application is through the use of a naming convention. A *naming convention* applies a standardized method of supplying names to the objects and variables in an application.

The most common naming convention used in Access applications uses a three- or four-character prefix (a *tag*) attached to the base name of the objects and variables in a VBA application. For example, a text box containing a person's last name might be named txtLastName, while a command button that closes a form would be named cmdClose or cmdCloseForm.

The names for variables follow a similar pattern. The string variable holding a customer name might be named strCustomer and a Boolean variable indicating whether the customer is currently active would be either boolActive or fActive (the f indicates a *flag* value).

Using a naming convention is not difficult. Most of the code in this book uses one- and three-character prefixes exclusively. In some cases, when the use of the variable is obvious, a one-character prefix is used (for example, sLastName) to keep code examples short and simple. In longer procedures, three-character prefixes are used on most variables. Most of the controls on the Access forms in the projects on this book's CD use three-character prefixes.

This simple naming convention helps you select the most logical name to apply to the variables and objects in your applications. In most cases, you'll assign a name to a variable or object based on how that item is used in the application. In other words, using a naming convention encourages names based on the functionality provided by the variables and objects in your applications. After all, you shouldn't be adding to an application variables and objects that don't have specific jobs to perform.

Understanding variable scope and lifetime

A variable is more than just a simple data repository. Every variable is a dynamic part of the application and may be used at different times during the program's execution. The declaration of a variable establishes more than just the name and data type of the variable. Depending on the keyword used to declare the variable and the placement of the variable's declaration in the program's code, the variable may be visible to large portions of the application's code. Alternatively, a different placement may severely limit where the variable can be referenced in the procedures within the application.

Examining scope

The visibility of a variable or procedure is called its *scope*. A variable that can be seen and used by any procedure in the application is said to have *public scope*. A variable that is usable by a single procedure is said to have scope that is *private* to that procedure.

There are many analogies for public and private scope. For example, a company is likely to have a phone number that is quite public (the main switchboard number) and is listed in the phone book and on the company's Web site; each office or room within the company might have its own extension number that is private within the company. A large office building has a public street address that is known by anyone passing by the building; each office or suite within that building will has a number that is private within that building.

Variables declared within a procedure are local to that procedure and can't be used or referenced outside of that procedure. Most of the listings in this chapter have included a number of variables declared within the procedures in the listings. In each case, the Dim keyword was used to define the variable. Dim is an instruction to VBA to allocate enough memory to contain the variable that follows the Dim keyword. Therefore, Dim intMyInt As Integer allocates less memory (2 bytes) than Dim dblMyDouble As Double (8 bytes).

The Public (or Global) keyword makes a variable visible throughout an application. Public can only be used at the module level and can't be used within a procedure. Most often, the Public keyword is used only in standard (standalone) modules that are not part of a form. Figure 11.8 illustrates variables declared with three very different scopes.

FIGURE 11.8

Variable scope is determined by the variable's declaration.

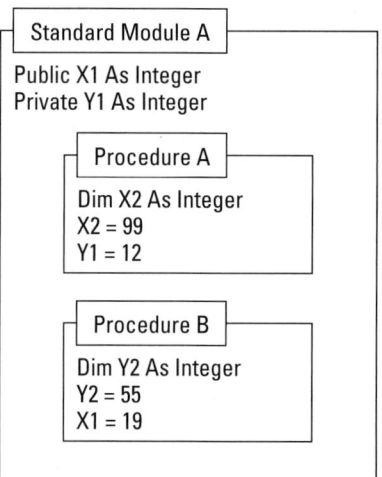

Every variable declared in the general section of the standard module is public throughout the application unless the Private keyword is used. Private restricts the visibility of a variable to the module in which the variable is declared. In Figure 11.8, the X1 integer declared with Public scope at the top of the module will be seen everywhere in the application while the Private Y1 integer declared in the next statement is accessible only within the module.

Misunderstanding variable scope is a major cause of serious bugs in many Access applications. It's entirely possible to have two same-named variables with different scopes in an Access VBA project. When ambiguity exists, Access always uses the "closest" declared variable.

Consider two variables named `MyVariable`. One of these variables is global (`public`) in scope, while the other is a module-level variable declared with the `Private` keyword. In any procedure Access uses one or the other of these variables. In a module where `MyVariable` is *not* declared, Access uses the `public` variable. The `private` variable is used only within the module containing its declaration.

The problem comes when multiple procedures use a variable with the same name as the multiply-declared `MyVariable`. Unless the developer working on one of these procedures has diligently determined which variable is being used, a serious error may occur. All too easily, a procedure might change the value of a `public` variable that is used in dozens of places within an application. If even one of those procedures changes the `public` variable instead of a more local variable, a very difficult-to-resolve bug occurs.

A bit farther down in Figure 11.8, you see two procedures (A and B). Each procedure declares a variable that is usable only from within the procedure. In Procedure A, you see a variable named `X2` declared as an integer and assigned the value `99`. Just below this assignment is a reference to the `Y1` variable defined at the top of the module. This is the variable that is accessible only from within the module. Procedure B defines an integer variable named `Y2` and assigns it a value of `55`. The `X1` variable in Procedure B that is assigned the `19` value is the public `X1` variable declared at the top of the module.

Determining a variable's lifetime

Variables are not necessarily permanent citizens of an application. Just as their visibility is determined by the location of their declaration, their *lifetime* is determined by their declaration as well. A variable's lifetime determines when it is accessible to the application.

By default, procedure-level variables exist only while the procedure is executing. As soon as the procedure ends, the variable is removed from memory and is no longer accessible. As already discussed, the scope of procedure-level variables is limited to the procedure and cannot be expanded beyond the procedure's boundaries.

A variable declared in the declarations section of a form's module exists as long as the form is open. All the procedures within the form's module can use the module-level variables as often as they need, and they all share the value assigned to the variable. When the form is closed and removed from memory, all its variables are removed as well.

The greatest variable lifetime is experienced by the variables declared in public (standard) modules. These variables are available as soon as the VBA application starts up, and they persist until the program is shut down and removed from memory. Therefore, public variables retain their values throughout the application and are accessible to any of the procedures within the program. Private variables (declared with the `Private` keyword) declared at the top of standard modules endure throughout the application, but following the rules of variable scope, they're accessible only from within the module.

There is one major exception to the general rule that procedure-level variables persist only as long as the procedure is running. The `Static` keyword makes a procedure-level variable persist between calls to the procedure. Once a value has been assigned to a static variable, the variable retains its value until it's changed in another call to the procedure.

An alternative to using static variables is to declare a global or module-level variable and use it each time a particular procedure is called. The problem with this approach is that a global or module-level variable is accessible to other procedures that are also able to modify its value. You can experience undesirable side-effect bugs by unwittingly changing the value of a widely-scoped variable without realizing what has happened. Because of their procedure-limited scope, static variables are one way to avoid side-effect bugs.

Incidentally, declaring a procedure with the `Static` keyword makes all variables in the procedure static as well. In the following listing, both variables — `intStatic` and `intLocal` — in the `StaticTest2` sub are static, in spite of their local declarations within the procedure. The `Static` keyword used in the procedure's heading makes both variables static in nature.

```
Private Static Sub StaticTest2()
  Dim intStatic As Integer
  Dim intLocal As Integer
  intStatic = intStatic + 1
  intLocal = intLocal + 1
  txtStatic = intStatic
  txtLocal = intLocal
End Sub
```

Understanding Subs and Functions

The code in a VBA application lives in containers called *modules*. As you learned in Chapter 10, modules exist behind the forms in an Access application as well as in standalone modules. The modules themselves contain many procedures, variable and constant declarations, and other directives to the VBA engine.

The code within the modules is composed of procedures. There are two main types of procedures in VBA: *subroutines* or *subprocedures* (often called *subs*) and *functions*.

The general rules for procedures include the following:

- **You must give the procedure a unique name within its *scope* (see "Understanding variable scope and lifetime," earlier in this chapter).** Although it isn't a good idea — because of the chance of confusing the VBA engine or another person working with your code — it is possible to have more than one procedure with the same name, as long as the name is unique within each procedure's scope.

- **The name you assign to a procedure can't be the same as a VBA keyword or the name of a built-in VBA procedure.**

- **A procedure and a module cannot have the same name.** This is one place where a naming convention can be very useful. If you always prefix module names with `bas` or `mod`, you don't run the risk of an error occurring from having a procedure and module with the same name.

- **A procedure can't contain other procedures within it.** A procedure can, however, call another procedure and execute the code in the other procedure at any time.

Because of the rules governing procedure scope, you can't have two public procedures both named MyProcedure, although you could have two private procedures, both named MyProcedure, or one public procedure named MyProcedure and one private procedure named MyProcedure. The reason it's a bad idea to use the same procedure name for multiple procedures, even when the procedures have different scopes, should be obvious.

The following sections cover some of the specifics regarding VBA procedures. Planning and composing the procedures in your modules is the most time-consuming part of working with VBA, so it's important to understand how procedures fit into the overall scheme of application development.

Subroutines and functions both contain lines of code that you can run. When you run a subroutine or function, you *call* it. *Calling, running,* and *invoking* are all terms meaning *to execute* (or run) the statements (or lines of code) within the procedure or function. All these terms can be used interchangeably (and they will be, by different developers). No matter how you invoke a VBA procedure — using the Call keyword, referencing the procedure by its name, or running it from the Immediate window — they all do the same thing, which is to cause lines of code to be processed, run, executed, or whatever you want to call it.

The only real difference between a procedure and a function is that, when it's called, a function returns a value — in other words, it generates a value when it runs, and makes the value available to the code that called it. You can use a Boolean function to return a True or False value indicating, for example, where the operation the procedure performed was successful. You could see if a file exists, if a value was greater than another value, or anything you choose. Functions return dates, numbers, or strings; functions can even return complex data types such as recordsets.

A subprocedure does not return a value. However, although a function directly returns a value to a variable created as part of the function call, there are other ways for functions and subprocedures to exchange data with form controls or declared variables in memory.

Understanding where to create a procedure

You create procedures in one of two places:

- **In a standard VBA module:** You create a subprocedure or function in a standard module when the procedure will be shared by code in more than one form or report or by an object other than a form or report. For example, queries can use functions to handle very complex criteria.
- **Behind a form or report:** If the code you're creating will be called only by a single procedure or form, the subprocedure or function should be created in the form or report's module.

Note

A module is a container for multiple subprocedures and functions.

Calling VBA procedures

VBA procedures are called in a variety of ways and from a variety of places. They can be called from events behind forms and reports, or they can be placed in module objects and called by simply using their name or by using the `Call` statement. Here are some examples:

```
SomeSubRoutineName

Call SomeSubRoutineName

Somevalue = SomeFunctionName
```

Only functions return values that may be assigned to variables. Subprocedures are simply called, do their work, and end. Although functions return a single value, both subprocedures and functions can place values in tables, in form controls, or even in public variables available to any part of your program. You can see several examples of different ways to use subprocedures and functions throughout this chapter.

The syntax used for calling subprocedures with parameters is variable. For example, when using the `Call` keyword to call a subprocedure that includes arguments, the arguments must be enclosed in parentheses:

```
Call SomeSubRoutineName(arg1, arg2)
```

However, when the same call without the `Call` keyword requires no parentheses:

```
SomeSubRoutineName arg1, arg2
```

Also, using the `Call` keyword with a function tells Access your code is not capturing the function's return value:

```
Call SomeFunctionName
```

or, when arguments are required:

```
Call SomeFunctionName(arg1, arg2)
```

In this case, the function is treated as if it is a subroutine.

Creating subs

Conceptually, subroutines are easy to understand. A *subroutine* (usually called a *sub* and sometimes called a *subprocedure*) is a set of programming statements that is executed as a unit by the VBA engine. VBA procedures can become complex, so this elementary description of subroutines is quickly overwhelmed by the actual subroutines you'll compose in your Access applications.

Figure 11.9 shows a typical subroutine. Notice the `Sub` keyword that begins the routine, followed by the name of the subroutine. The declaration of this particular subroutine includes the `Private` keyword, which restricts the availability of this subroutine to the module containing the subroutine.

FIGURE 11.9

A typical subroutine in an Access application

The subroutine you see in Figure 11.9 contains most of the components you'll see in almost every VBA sub or function:

- **Declaration:** All procedures must be *declared* so that VBA knows where to find them. The name assigned to the procedure must be unique within the VBA project. The `Sub` keyword identifies this procedure as a subroutine.

- **Terminator:** All procedures must be terminated with the `End` keyword followed by the type of procedure that is ending. In Figure 11.9, the terminator is `End Sub`.

- **Declarations area:** Although variables and constants can be declared within the body of the procedure, good programming conventions require variables to be declared near the top of the procedure where they'll be easy to find.

- **Statements:** A VBA procedure can contain many statements. Usually, however, you'll want to keep your VBA procedures small to make debugging as painless as possible. Very large subroutines can be difficult to work with, and you'll avoid problems if you keep them small. Instead of adding too many features and operations in a single procedure, place operations in separate procedures and call those procedures when those operations are needed.

At the conclusion of a subroutine, program flow returns to the code or action that originally called the sub. The subroutine shown in Figure 11.9 runs in response to the form's Load event, so control is returned to that event.

As an example of a useful VBA subroutine, the next several paragraphs describe building an event procedure for a control on an Access form. This procedure retrieves several values from the cboBuyerID combo box columns and uses them in the form. The RowSource of the cboBuyerID combo box contains six active columns, which are as follows:

VBA Column Number	Value
0	Name: tblContacts.LastName & ", " & : tblContacts.FirstName
1	Company (from tblContacts)
2	DiscountPercent (from tblTaxRates)
3	TaxRate (from tblTaxRates)
4	TaxLocation (from tblContacts)
5	ContactID (from tblContacts). This is the bound column of this combo box.

Note

Combo-box row sources start with column 0, so column 2 is the third column in the row source.

The objective of this exercise is to learn about procedures, but it also serves to teach you some additional VBA commands. The code is added to the form as cboBuyerID AfterUpdate event.

To create an event procedure in a form, follow these steps:

1. Select the cboBuyerID control in frmSales Design view.
2. Press F4 to display the Property window for the control.
3. Click in the After Update event property in the Event tab of the property sheet and select [Event Procedure] from the event's drop-down list.
4. Press the builder button (...) to open the VBA code editor.
5. Enter the following code into the cboBuyerID_AfterUpdate event procedure, as shown in Figure 11.10. The following code goes between Private Sub cboBuyerID_AfterUpdate() and End Sub in the VBA code editor.

```
Me.Recalc
If Not IsNull(cboBuyerID) Then
    'Verify that the DiscountPercent is valid:
    If Not IsNull(cboBuyerID.Column(2)) Then
      'Get the DiscountPercent from Column 2:
      txtDiscountRate = _
          Format(cboBuyerID.Column(2),"Percent")
      'Get the Tax Location from Column 4:
      txtTaxLocation = cboBuyerID.Column(4)
      'Get the Tax Rate from Column 3:
      txtTaxRate = cboBuyerID.Column(3)
    End If
  Else
    'Invalid data found in the combo box,
    'so set all the text boxes to Null:
    txtDiscountRate = Null
    txtTaxLocation = Null
    txtTaxRate = Null
End If
```

6. Select Compile Chapter11 from the Debug menu in the code editor to check your syntax.

7. Close the VBA window and return to the frmSales form.

The code first performs a Recalc on the form to update any values that may be in an incomplete state, like a buyer ID in the process of being selected or a line item that was in the process of being selected when the combo box was used.

Tip
Anytime you're doing data entry and you need code to run to perform some process, it's a good idea to first run the form's Recalc command.

The Me. refers to the current form and substitutes in this example for Forms!frmSales!.

The first IF statement checks to make sure a buyer ID was selected by making sure the current value of the combo box's bound column — ContactID — is not null. If it isn't null (meaning, a valid value was selected in the combo box), a second IF statement checks to make sure not only that the value of cboBuyerID is valid but also that the value of the third column — DiscountPercent — is not null.

If the DiscountPercent column (column 2) is valid, the values from that and other combo-box columns are used to fill controls on the form.

Figure 11.10 shows the procedure created in the code editor after entering the procedure described earlier. After you finish entering these statements, press the Save button on the toolbar to save your code before closing the VBA window.

FIGURE 11.10

The `frmSales` `cboBuyerID_AfterUpdate` event procedure in the VBA code window

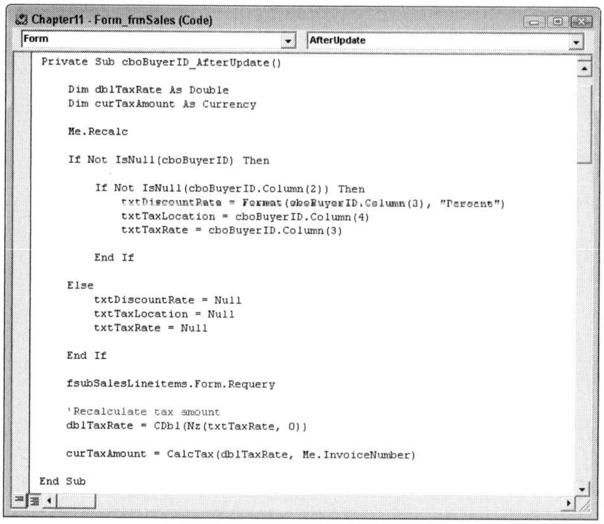

```
Chapter11 - Form_frmSales (Code)
Form                                    AfterUpdate

    Private Sub cboBuyerID_AfterUpdate()

        Dim dblTaxRate As Double
        Dim curTaxAmount As Currency

        Me.Recalc

        If Not IsNull(cboBuyerID) Then

            If Not IsNull(cboBuyerID.Column(2)) Then
                txtDiscountRate = Format(cboBuyerID.Column(3), "Percent")
                txtTaxLocation = cboBuyerID.Column(4)
                txtTaxRate = cboBuyerID.Column(3)

            End If

        Else
            txtDiscountRate = Null
            txtTaxLocation = Null
            txtTaxRate = Null

        End If

        fsubSalesLineitems.Form.Requery

        'Recalculate tax amount
        dblTaxRate = CDbl(Nz(txtTaxRate, 0))

        curTaxAmount = CalcTax(dblTaxRate, Me.InvoiceNumber)

    End Sub
```

The procedure behind this form runs each time the user selects a different buyer in `cboBuyerID`. This code updates the value of the tax location and tax rate.

Creating Functions

Functions differ from subprocedures in that functions return a value. In the examples in this section, you'll see functions that calculate the extended price (quantity × price) for a line item, create a function to calculate the total of all the taxable line items, and then apply the current tax rate to the total.

Although functions can be created behind individual forms or reports, usually they're created in modules. This first function will be created in a new module that you'll name `basSalesFunctions`. Putting this function in a standard module makes it available to all parts of the application. To do this, follow these steps:

1. Select the Modules tab in the Navigation Pane.

2. Right-click the `basSalesFunctions` module and select Design view from the context menu.

   The VBA window is displayed with the title basSalesFunctions (Code) in the title bar.

3. Move to the bottom of the module, and enter the following code:

```
Public Function CalcExtendedPrice( _
    Quantity As Integer, _
    Price As Currency, _
    Discount As Double _
    ) As Currency
    Dim ExtendedPrice As Currency
    ExtendedPrice = Quantity * Price
    CalcExtendedPrice = ExtendedPrice - (ExtendedPrice * Discount)
End Function
```

The first statement declares the variable `ExtendedPrice` as the `currency` data type. `ExtendedPrice` is used in an intermediate step in the function. The next line of code performs a calculation assigning the product of two variables, `Quantity` and `Price`, to the `ExtendedPrice` variable. You might notice that the `Quantity` and `Price` variables are not declared within the function; these variables are explained in the next section, "Handling parameters."

Finally, the last line of code performs one more calculation to apply any discount to `ExtendedPrice`. The function's name is treated as if it were a variable and is assigned the value of the calculation. This is how a function gets the value that it returns to the calling program.

Handling parameters

Now, the question you should be asking is: Where did the `Quantity`, `Price`, and `Discount` variables come from? The answer is simple. They're the parameters passed from another procedure, as you may have already guessed.

Parameters (often called *arguments*) passed to a procedure are treated like any other variable by the procedure. Parameters have a name and a data type and are used as a way to send information to a procedure. Parameters are often used to get information back from a procedure, as well.

The following table shows the names and data types of the arguments used in the `CalcExtendedPrice` function.

Parameter Name	Data Type
Quantity	Integer
Price	Currency
DiscountPercent	Double

These parameter names can be anything you want them to be. Think of them as variables you would normally declare. All that's missing is the `Dim` statement. They don't have to be the same name as the variables used in the call to the function. Very often, you'll pass the names of fields in a table or controls on a form or variables created in the calling procedure as parameters to a procedure.

The completed `CalcExtendedPrice` function is shown in Figure 11.11. Notice how this function's parameters are defined in the function's declaration statement. The parameters are separated by continuation characters (a space followed by an underscore) to make the code easier to read.

FIGURE 11.11

The completed `CalcExtendedPrice` function

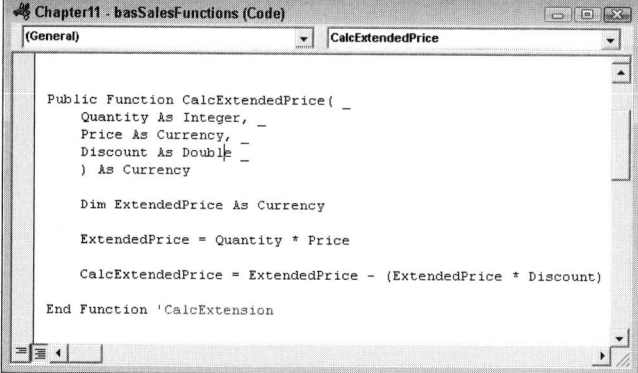

Calling a function and passing parameters

Now that you've completed the function, it's time to test it.

Normally, a function call comes from a form or report event or from another procedure, and the call passes information as parameters. The parameters passed to a procedure are often variables or data taken from a form's controls. You can test this function by going to the Immediate window and using hand-entered values as the parameters.

Follow these steps to test the function:

1. Press Ctrl+G to display the Immediate window.
2. Enter **? CalcExtendedPrice(5, 3.50, .05)**.

   This statement passes the values as 5, 3.50, and .05 (5 percent) to the `Quantity`, `Price`, and `DiscountPercent` parameters, respectively. `CalcExtendedPrice` returns 16.625 using those values, as shown in Figure 11.12.
3. Close the Immediate window and the VBA window and return to the Database window.

FIGURE 11.12

Testing the `CalcExtendedPrice` function in the Immediate window

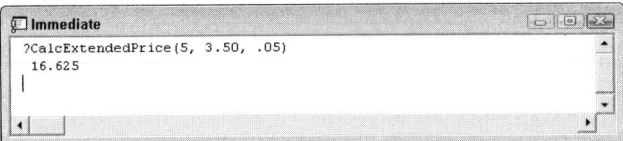

The next task is to use the function to calculate the extended price (price multiplied by quantity) of each item included in a sales invoice. You can add a call to the function from the Amount box on `fsubSalesLineItems`. This is a subform embedded on `frmSales`. Follow these steps:

1. Display the `frmSales` form in Design view.

2. Click into the `fsubSalesLineitems` subform.

3. Click into the `txtAmount` control in the subform.

4. Display the Property window and enter the following into the `Control Source` property, as shown in Figure 11.13: **=CalcExtendedPrice (Nz(txtQuantity,0),Nz(txtPrice,0), Nz(txtDiscountPercent,0))**.

   This expression passes the values from three controls — `txtQuantity`, `txtPrice`, and `txtDiscountPercent` — in the subform to the `CalcExtendedPrice` function in the module and returns the value back to the control source of the `txtAmount` control each time the line is recalculated or any of the parameters change. The references to `txtQuantity`, `txtPrice`, and `txtDiscountPercent` are enclosed in calls to the `Nz` function, which converts null values to zero. This is one way to avoid `Invalid use of null` errors that would otherwise occur.

FIGURE 11.13

Adding a function call to the `Control Source` of a control

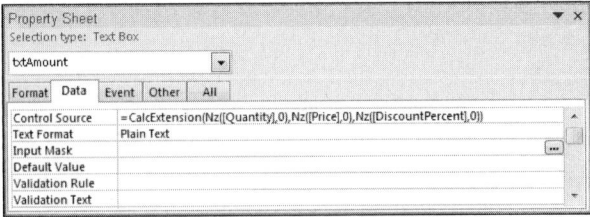

The sales form (`frmSales`) enforces a business rule that the extended price is always recalculated any time the user changes the quantity, price, or discount on the sales form.

In Figure 11.13, notice that the `Control Source` property for `txtAmount` simply calls the `CalcExtendedPrice` function. The call does not specify the module that contains the function. Because `CalcExtendedPrice` was declared with the `Public` keyword, Access easily finds it and passes the required arguments to it.

Tip

The `CalcExtendedPrice` **example illustrates an important aspect of Access development: Add a public function in a single location anywhere in the application's code and use the function anywhere it's needed. The ability to reuse a procedure in multiple places reduces maintenance. Changing the single instance of the function is reflected everywhere the public procedure is used.**

Creating a function to calculate sales tax

In the Collectible Mini Cars application, whenever you add a line item to a sales invoice, you specify whether the item is taxable. The sales form adds up the extended prices for all the taxable line items to determine the sales tax for the sale. This total can then be multiplied by the tax rate to determine the tax.

The Collectable Mini Cars sales form (`frmSales`) includes a text-box control for the tax amount. You could simply create an expression for the control's value such as:

```
=fSubSalesLineitems.Form!txtTaxableTotal * txtTaxRate
```

This expression references `txtTaxableTotal` in the subform (`fSubSalesLineitems`) and multiplies it by the tax rate (`txtTaxRate`) from the main form (`frmSales`).

However, although this expression displays the tax amount, the expression entered into the `txtTaxAmount` control would make the `txtTaxAmount` control read-only because it contains an expression. You wouldn't be able to override the calculated amount if you wanted to. The tax applied to a sale is one of the fields that needs to be changed once in a while for specific business purposes.

Better than using a hard-coded expression is creating a function to calculate a value and then place the value of the calculation in the control. This way, you can simply type over the calculated value if needed.

You could enter the following lines of code at the end of the `cboBuyerID_AfterUpdate` event code you created before. This way, each time you choose a new contact on the sales form, the tax is recalculated after the contact's tax rate is retrieved on the `frmSales` form.

```
txtTaxAmount = _
   fSubSalesLineitems.Form!txtTaxableTotal * txtTaxRate
```

You could also add these lines of code to the `AfterUpdate` events behind the `txtQuantity`, `txtPrice`, `txtDiscountPercent`, and `chkTaxable` controls. Each time the value in any of these controls changes, the value of the tax is updated.

Actually, better would be to place this statement in the `AfterUpdate` event of `fsubSalesLineitems`. This way, the tax is recalculated each time a value is updated in any record of this form. Because `fsubSalesLineitems` is displayed as a datasheet, the `AfterUpdate` event fires as soon as the user moves to another line in `fsubSalesLineitems`.

Although you can use a simple expression that references controls on forms and subforms, this technique only works behind the form containing the code. Suppose you also need to calculate tax in other forms or in reports. There's a better way than relying on a form.

This is an old developer's expression: "Forms and reports lie; tables never lie." This means that the controls of a form or report often contain expressions, formats, and VBA code that may make a value seem to be one thing when the table actually contains a completely different value. The table containing the data is where the real values are stored and it's where calculations and reports should retrieve data from.

You can easily use VBA code to extract data from a table, use the data in a complex calculation, and return the result to a control on a form, on a report, or to another section of code.

Figure 11.14 shows the completed `CalcTax` function.

FIGURE 11.14

The `CalcTax` function

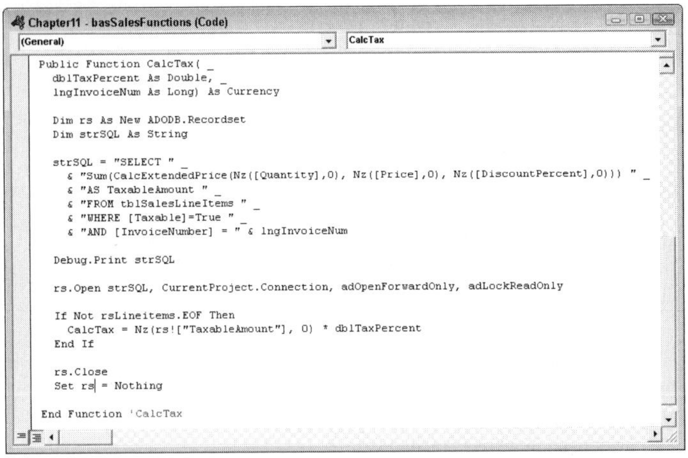

The function is called from the `AfterUpdate` events behind the `txtQuantity`, `txtPrice`, or `txtDiscountPercent` controls in the subform. The `CalcExtendedPrice` function calculates the sum of the taxable line items from the `tblSalesItems` table. The `SQLstatement` combined with a bit of ADO code to determine the total. The calculated total amount is then multiplied by the `dblTaxPercent` parameter to calculate the tax. The tax is set to the variable `CalcTax` (the name of the expression).

An important feature of this example code is that it combines data extracted from a database table (`Price`, `DiscountPercent`) with data passed as parameters (`dblTaxPercent`, `lngInvoiceNum`). All the extraction and calculations are automatically performed by the code, and the user is never aware of how the tax amount is determined.

Tip

Functions and subprocedures are important to the concepts of reusable code within an application. You should try to use functions and subprocedures and pass them parameters whenever possible. A good rule is this: The first time you find yourself copying a group of code, it's time to create a procedure or function.

Simplifying Code with Named Arguments

Another significant feature of Access VBA is the use of named arguments for procedures. Without named arguments, the arguments passed to procedures must appear in the correct left-to-right order. With named arguments, you provide the name of each parameter passed to a subroutine or function, and the subroutine or function uses the argument based on its *name* rather than on its *position* in the argument list.

Also, because every parameter passed to a procedure is explicitly named, you can omit an unused parameter without causing an error. Named arguments are a great way to clean up your code while making it much easier to read and understand.

Assume your application includes the function shown here:

```
Function PrepareOutput(sStr1 As String, sStr2 As String, _
    sStr3 As String) As String
  PrepareOutput = sStr1 & " " & sStr2 & " " & sStr3
End Function
```

This function, of course, does nothing more than concatenate sStr1, sStr2, and sStr3 and return it to the calling routine. The next example shows how this function might be called from another procedure:

```
Private Sub cmdForward_Click()
  txtOutput = PrepareOutput(txtFirstName, _
      txtLastName, txtHireDate)
End Sub
```

The arguments required by `PrepareOutput()` must be passed in left-to-right order. The results of this function are shown in Figure 11.15. The text in the Function Output text box on this form shows the arguments in the order in which they appear in the text boxes on the left side of this form.

Each argument can be specified by its name as you pass it to functions. Naming arguments makes them position-independent.

FIGURE 11.15

`frmNamedArguments` demonstrates the value of using named arguments in VBA procedures.

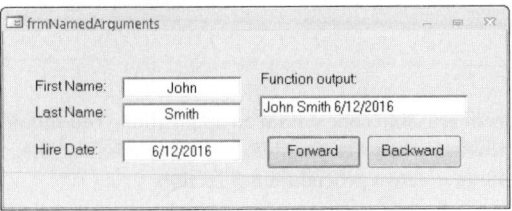

Examine the code in the following listing to see how named arguments work:

```
Private Sub cmdBackward_Click()
    txtOutput = PrepareOutput(sStr2:=txtLastName, _
        sStr3:=txtFirstName, sStr1:=txtHireDate)
End Sub
```

The thing to notice in `cmdBackward_Click` is that the arguments are not passed to `PrepareOutput()` in the order specified by the procedure's argument list. As long as the name used for an argument matches an argument in `PrepareOutputs`'s argument list, Access VBA correctly uses the arguments in `PrepareOutput()`.

On the CD-ROM

The `Chapter11.accdb` **example database includes the** `frmNamedArguments` **you see in Figure 11.15 and Figure 11.16. The two buttons below the Function Output text box pass the text from the First Name, Last Name, and Hire Date text boxes to the** `PrepareOutput()` **function using positional and named arguments.**

FIGURE 11.16

`PrepareOutput()` is able to use arguments submitted in any order as long as they're named.

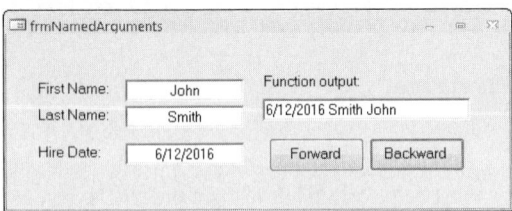

Summary

Building on the VBA programming fundamentals presented in Chapter 10, this chapter took a closer look at using VBA to build subprocedures and functions. You also saw many more ways to use VBA variables and data types in your Access applications.

We looked at some of the differences between subprocedures (or subroutines, if you prefer) and functions, passing parameters to procedures, and returning values from functions. Mastering the skills necessary to create strong VBA procedures and correctly using the many different VBA variable types are essential steps to building bulletproof Access applications.

The Access Event Model

W hen working with a database system, the same tasks may be performed repeatedly. Instead of doing the same steps each time, you can automate the process with VBA or macros.

Database management systems continually grow as you add records in a form, build new queries, and create new reports. As the system grows, many of the database objects are saved for later use — for a weekly report or monthly update query, for example. You tend to create and perform many tasks repetitively. Every time you add contact records, you open the same form. Likewise, you print the same form letter for contacts that have purchased a vehicle in the past month.

You can add VBA code throughout your application to automate these tasks. The VBA language offers a full array of powerful commands for manipulating records in a table, controls on a form, or just about anything else. This chapter continues the previous chapters' discussions of working with procedures in forms, reports, and standard modules.

On the CD-ROM

In this chapter, you'll use the database file `Chapter12.accdb`. Copy this database file from the book's CD if you want to follow along with the examples presented in this chapter.

This chapter focuses on the Access event model, a vitally important aspect of Access development. As you'll see in this chapter, Access provides a wide variety of events to trigger your code in response to user actions.

IN THIS CHAPTER

Mastering Access event programming

Reviewing common events

Understanding event sequences

Programming Events

An Access event is the result or consequence of some user action. An Access event occurs when a user moves from one record to another in a form, closes a report, or clicks on a command button on a form. Even moving the mouse generates a continuous stream of events.

Access applications are event-driven and Access objects respond to many types of events. Access events are hooked into specific object properties. For example, checking or unchecking a check box triggers a MouseDown, a MouseUp, and a Click event. These events are hooked into the check box through the OnMouseDown, OnMouseUp, and OnClick properties, respectively. You use VBA to compose event procedures that run whenever the user clicks on the check box.

Access events can be categorized into seven groups:

- **Windows (form, report) events:** Opening, closing, and resizing
- **Keyboard events:** Pressing or releasing a key
- **Mouse events:** Clicking or pressing a mouse button
- **Focus events:** Activating, entering, and exiting
- **Data events:** Changing the current row, deleting, inserting, or updating
- **Print events:** Formatting and printing
- **Error and timing events:** Happening after an error has occurred or some time has passed

In all, Access supports more than 50 different events that can be harnessed through VBA event procedures.

Of these types of events, by far the most common are the keyboard and mouse events on forms. As you'll see in the following sections, forms and most controls recognize keyboard and mouse events. In fact, exactly the same keyboard and mouse events are recognized by forms and controls. The code you write for a mouse-click event on a command button is exactly the same sort of code that you might write for the mouse-click on a form.

In addition, most Access object types have their own unique events. The following sections discuss the most commonly programmed events, but Microsoft has a habit of introducing new event capabilities with each new version of Access. Also, many ActiveX controls you might use in your Access applications may have their own unique and special events. When using an unfamiliar control or a new type of object in your Access applications, be sure to check out what events and properties are supported by the control or object.

Understanding how events trigger VBA code

You can create an event procedure that runs when a user performs any one of the many different events that Access recognizes. Access responds to events through special form and control properties. Reports have a similar set of events, tailored to the special needs and requirements of reports.

Figure 12.1 shows the Property Sheet for `frmProducts`. This form has many event properties. Each form section (page header, form header, detail, page footer, form footer) and every control on the form (labels, text boxes, check boxes, and option buttons, for example) has its own set of events.

The Property Sheet for `frmProducts` with the Events tab open.

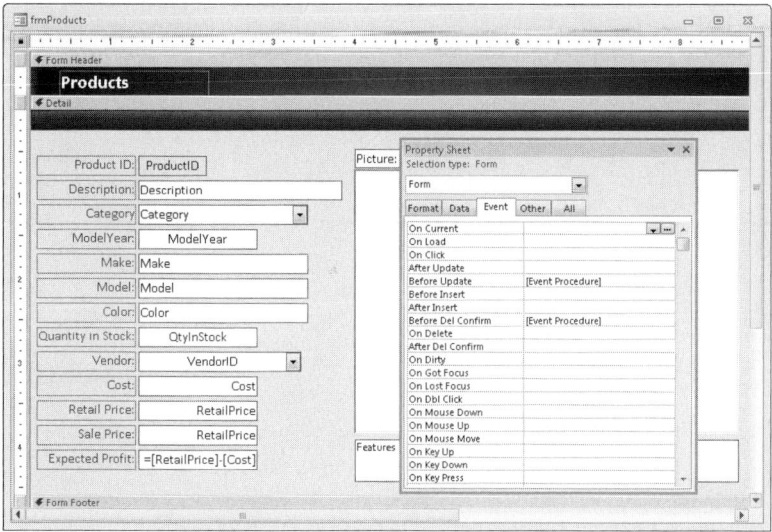

In Figure 12.1, notice that the Property Sheet is open on the Event tab. Access forms include more than 50 events, and each form section includes a number of events, as well as each control on the form. As you select a form section or a control on the form, the Event tab in the Property Sheet changes to show you the offense for that object.

In Figure 12.1, all the events with existing event procedures contain [Event Procedure], which indicates that the property has associated VBA code that executes whenever this event is triggered.

Creating event procedures

In Access, you execute event procedures through an object's event properties.

Access provides event properties you use to tie VBA code to an object's events. For example, the On Open property is associated with a form or report opening on the screen.

Note

Access event procedures, as seen in the Property Sheet, often contain spaces. For instance, the Open event appears as the On Open event procedure. The event itself, of course, is Open. Many, but not all, event property names begin with On.

You add an event procedure to a form or report by selecting the event property (Before Update, for this example) in the object's Property Sheet. If no event procedure currently exists for the property, a drop-down arrow and builder button appear in the property's box, as shown in the Before Update event property in Figure 12.1.

The drop-down button exposes a short list that contains [Event Property]. Selecting this option and then clicking on the builder button, takes you to the VBA code editor with an event procedure template already in place (see Figure 12.2).

FIGURE 12.2

An empty event procedure template for the form's BeforeUpdate event.

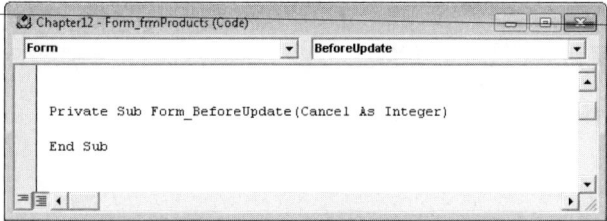

Notice the general format of the event procedure's declaration:

```
Private Sub Object_Event()
```

The *Object* portion of the procedure's name is, of course, the name of the object raising the event, while the *Event* portion is the specific event raised by the object. In Figure 12.2, the object is Form and the event is BeforeUpdate. Some events support arguments, which appear within the parentheses at the end of the declaration.

In case you're wondering, you can't change the name, or the arguments, of an event procedure and expect it to continue working. Access VBA relies on the Object_Event naming convention to tie a procedure to an object's event.

Identifying Common Events

Certain events are raised by many different Access objects. Microsoft has taken great care that these events behave exactly the same way, regardless of the object raising them. Table 12.1 lists several of the events most commonly used by Access developers. Most of these events apply to forms and all the different controls you might add to an Access form.

TABLE 12.1

Events Common to Multiple Object Types

Event	Event Type	When the Event Is Triggered
Click	Mouse event	When the user presses and releases (clicks) the left mouse button on an object
DblClick	Mouse event	When the user presses and releases (clicks) the left mouse button twice on an object
MouseDown	Mouse event	When the user presses the mouse button while the pointer is on an object
MouseMove	Mouse event	When the user moves the mouse pointer over an object
MouseUp	Mouse event	When the user releases a pressed mouse button while the pointer is on an object
MouseWheel	Mouse event	When the user spins the mouse wheel
KeyDown	Keyboard event	When the user presses any key on the keyboard when the object has focus or when the user uses a SendKeys macro action
KeyUp	Keyboard event	When the user releases a pressed key or immediately after the user uses a SendKeys macro action
KeyPress	Keyboard event	When the user presses and releases a key on an object that has the focus or when the user uses a SendKeys macro action

Not surprisingly, these events are all associated with the mouse and the keyboard because these are the user's primary means of inputting information and giving directions to an application. Not every object responds to every one of these events, but when an object responds to any of these events, the event exhibits exactly the same behavior.

Tip

Many developers simply copy and paste VBA code from one event procedure to the same event procedure on another object. For example, you might want to do some fancy formatting on a text box when the user clicks into the box. You can copy the code performing the fancy formatting into another control's Click event procedure to get the same effect without having to retype the code. Even though you'll have to fix up the pasted code with the second text box's name, it's much less work than retyping the entire procedure.

Access supports many, many different events. In fact, one of Access's fundamental strengths is the wide variety of events available to developers. You can control virtually every aspect of an Access application's behavior and data management through event procedures. Although Microsoft makes no formal distinction between types of events, the following sections categorize events and event procedures into groups based on the type of object (forms, reports, and so on) that raise the events within the group.

Tip

Access supports a very, very rich event model. Not many Access developers master every Access event, nor is there need to. Virtually every Access developer learns and uses the events that are important for the applications he's building and then learns other events as he goes. You don't need to worry about memorizing all these events — instead, just be aware that Access supports many different types of events and that they're there when you need them.

Form event procedures

When you work with forms, you can create event procedures based on events at the form level, the section level, or the control level. If you attach an event procedure to a form-level event, whenever the event occurs, the action takes effect against the form as a whole (such as when you move to another record or leave the form).

To have your form respond to an event, you write an event procedure and attach it to the event property in the form that recognizes the event. Many properties can be used to trigger event procedures at the form level.

Note

When I refer to form events, I'm talking about events that happen to the form as a whole — not about an event that can be triggered by a specific control on a form. Form events execute when moving from one record to another or when a form is being opened or closed. I cover control events in the "Control event procedures" section, later in this chapter.

Essential form events

Access forms respond to many, many events. You'll never write code for most of these events because of their specialized nature. There are, however, some events that you'll program over and over again in your Access applications. Table 12.2 lists some of the most fundamental and important Access form events. Not coincidentally, these are also the most commonly programmed Access form events.

In Table 12.2, notice how many events are related to data (`Current`, `BeforeInsert`, and so on). Because Access forms are usually involved in working with data (adding new data, editing, and so on), Access forms include these events to provide you with a high level of control over data management.

TABLE 12.2

Essential Form Events

Event	When the Event Is Triggered
Open	When a form is opened, but the first record is not displayed yet
Load	When a form is loaded into memory but not yet opened
Resize	When the size of a form changes
Unload	When a form is closed and the records unload, and before the form is removed from the screen
Close	When a form is closed and removed from the screen
Activate	When an open form receives the focus, becoming the active window
Deactivate	When a different window becomes the active window, but before it loses focus
GotFocus	When a form with no active or enabled controls receives the focus
LostFocus	When a form loses the focus
Timer	When a specified time interval passes. The interval (in milliseconds) is specified by the TimerInterval property.
BeforeScreenTip	When a screen tip is activated

Form mouse and keyboard events

Access forms also respond to a number of mouse and keyboard events, as shown in Table 12.3.

TABLE 12.3

Form Mouse and Keyboard Events

Event	When the Event Is Triggered
Click	When the user presses and releases (clicks) the left mouse button
DblClick	When the user presses and releases (clicks) the left mouse button twice on a form
MouseDown	When the user presses the mouse button while the pointer is on a form
MouseMove	When the user moves the mouse pointer over an area of a form
MouseUp	When the user releases a pressed mouse button while the pointer is on a form
MouseWheel	When the user spins the mouse wheel
KeyDown	When the user presses any key on the keyboard when a form has focus or when the user uses a SendKeys macro action
KeyUp	When the user releases a pressed key or immediately after the user uses a SendKeys macro action
KeyPress	When the user presses and releases a key on a form that has the focus or when the user uses a SendKeys macro

In addition, the `KeyPreview` property is closely related to form keyboard events. This property (which is found only in forms) instructs Access to allow the form to see keyboard events before the controls on the form. By default, the controls on an Access form receive events before the form. For example, when you click on a button on a form, the button — not the form — sees the click, even though the form supports a `Click` event. This means that a form's controls mask key events from the form, and the form can never respond to those events. You must set the `KeyPreview` property to `Yes` (true) before the form responds to any of the key events (`KeyDown`, `KeyUp`, and so on).

Form data events

The primary purpose of Access forms is to display data. Not surprisingly then, Access forms have a number of events that are directly related to a form's data management. You'll see these events programmed over and over again in this book, and you'll encounter event procedures written for these events virtually every time you work on an Access application. These events are summarized in Table 12.4.

TABLE 12.4

Form Data Events

Event	When the Event Is Triggered
Current	When you move to a different record and make it the current record
BeforeInsert	After data is first entered into a new record, but before the record is actually created
AfterInsert	After the new record is added to the table
BeforeUpdate	Before changed data is updated in a record
AfterUpdate	After changed data is updated in a record
Dirty	When a record is modified
Undo	When a user has returned a form to clean state (the record has been set back to an unmodified state); the opposite of `OnDirty`
Delete	When a record is deleted, but before the deletion takes place
BeforeDelConfirm	Just before Access displays the Delete Confirm dialog box
AfterDelConfirm	After the Delete Confirm dialog box closes and confirmation has happened
Error	When a runtime error is produced
Filter	When a filter has been specified, but before it is applied
ApplyFilter	After a filter is applied to a form

The `Current` event fires just after the data on a form is refreshed. Most often this occurs as the user moves the form to a different record in the recordset underlying the form. The `Current` event is often used to perform calculations based on the form's data or to format controls. For example, if a certain numeric or date value is outside of an expected range, the `Current` event can be used to change the text box's `BackColor` property so the user notices the issue.

The BeforeInsert and AfterInsert events are related to transferring a new record from the form to an underlying data source. BeforeInsert fires as Access is about to transfer the data, and AfterInsert is triggered after the record is committed to the data source. For example, you could use these events to perform a logging operation that keeps track of additions to a table.

The BeforeUpdate and AfterUpdate events are frequently used to validate data before it's sent to the underlying data source. As you'll see later in this chapter, many form controls also support BeforeUpdate and AfterUpdate. A control's update is triggered as soon as the data in the control is changed.

Tip

A form's Update event fires much later than the BeforeInsert or AfterInsert events. The Update event occurs just as the form prepares to move to another record. Many developers use the form's BeforeUpdate event to scan all the controls on the form to ensure that all the data in the form's controls is valid. A form's BeforeUpdate event includes a Cancel parameter that, when set to True, causes the BeforeUpdate event to terminate. Canceling an update event is an effective way to protect the integrity of the data behind an Access application.

Tip

Users often want to be notified of pending updates before they move off a record to another record. By default, Access forms automatically update a form's underlying data source as the user moves to another record or closes the form. The Dirty event fires whenever the user changes any of the data on a form. You can use the Dirty event to set a module-level Boolean (true/false) variable (let's call it boolDirty) so that other controls on the form (such as a close button) know that pending changes exist on the form. If boolDirty is True when the close button is clicked or when the BeforeUpdate event fires, you can display an Are you sure? message box to confirm the user's intention to commit the changes to the database.

Control event procedures

Controls also raise events. Control events are often used to manipulate the control's appearance or to validate data as the user makes changes to the control's contents. Control events also influence how the mouse and keyboard behave while the user works with the control. A control's BeforeUpdate event fires as soon as focus leaves the control (more precisely, BeforeUpdate fires just before data is transferred from the control to the recordset underlying the form, enabling you to cancel the event if data validation fails), whereas a form's BeforeUpdate does not fire until you move the form to another record. (The form's BeforeUpdate commits the entire record to the form's data source.)

This means that a *control's* BeforeUpdate is good for validating a single control while the *form's* BeforeUpdate is good for validating multiple controls on the form. The form's BeforeUpdate would be a good place to validate that values in two different controls are in agreement with each other (such as a zip code in one text box, and the city in another text box), instead of relying on the BeforeUpdate in each of the controls.

You create event procedures for control events in exactly the same way you create procedures for form events. You select [Event Procedure] in the Property Sheet for the event, and then add

VBA code to the event procedure attached to the event. Table 12.5 shows each control event property, the event it recognizes, and how it works. As you review the information in Table 12.5, keep in mind that not every control supports every type of event.

TABLE 12.5

Control Events

Event	When the Event Is Triggered
BeforeUpdate	Before changed data in the control is updated to the underlying recordset
AfterUpdate	After changed data is transferred to the form's recordset
Dirty	When the contents of a control change
Undo	When the form is returned to a clean state
Change	When the contents of a text box change or a combo box's text changes
Updated	When an ActiveX object's data has been modified
NotInList	When a value that isn't in the list is entered into a combo box
Enter	Before a control receives the focus from another control
Exit	Just before the control loses focus to another control
GotFocus	When a nonactive or enabled control receives the focus
LostFocus	When a control loses the focus
Click	When the left mouse button is pressed and released (clicked) on a control
DblClick	When the left mouse button is pressed and released (clicked) twice on a control or label
MouseDown	When a mouse button is pressed while the pointer is on a control
MouseMove	When the mouse pointer is moved over a control
MouseUp	When a pressed mouse button is released while the pointer is on a control
KeyDown	When any key on the keyboard is pressed when a control has the focus or when a SendKeys macro action is used
KeyPress	When a key is pressed and released on a control that has the focus or when a SendKeys macro action is used
KeyUp	When a pressed key is released or immediately after a SendKeys macro is used

Report event procedures

Just as with forms, reports also use event procedures to respond to specific events. Access reports support events for the overall report itself and for each section in the report. Individual controls on Access reports do not raise events.

Attaching an event procedure to the report runs code whenever the report opens, closes, or prints. Each section in a report (header, footer, and so on) also includes events that run as the report is formatted or printed.

Several overall report event properties are available. Table 12.6 shows the Access report events. As you can see, the list of report events is much shorter than the form event list.

TABLE 12.6

Report Events

Event Property	When the Event Is Triggered
Open	When the report opens but before printing
Close	When the report closes and is removed from the screen
Activate	When the report receives the focus and becomes the active window
Deactivate	When a different window becomes active
NoData	When no data is passed to the report as it opens
Page	When the report changes pages
Error	When a runtime error is produced in Access

Even though users do not interact with reports as they do with forms, events still play a vital role in report design. Opening a report containing no data generally yields erroneous results. The report may display a title and no detail information. Or, it may display #error values for missing information. This situation can be a little scary for the user. Use the NoData event to inform the user that the report contains no data. NoData fires as a report opens and there is no data available in the report's RecordSource. Use the NoData event procedure to display a message box describing the situation to the user and then cancel the report's opening. Figure 12.3 shows a typical NoData event procedure.

FIGURE 12.3

Running a NoData event procedure when there is no data for a report

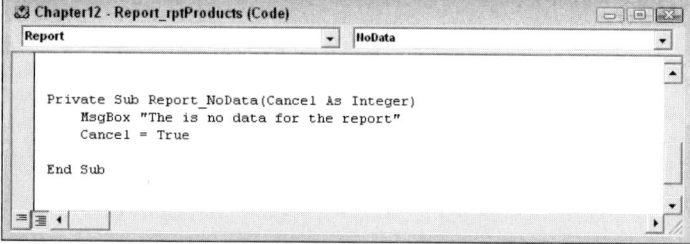

The `Report_NoData` event illustrated in Figure 12.3 first displays a message box to advise the user that the report contains no data. Then the event procedure cancels the report's opening by setting the `Cancel` parameter to `True`. Because the `Cancel` parameter is set to `True`, the report never appears on the screen and is not sent to the printer.

Many Access events are accompanied by parameters, such as the `Cancel` parameter you see in Figure 12.3. In this case, setting `Cancel` to `True` instructs Access to simply ignore the process that triggered the event. Because `NoData` was triggered as part of the report's opening process, setting `Cancel` to `True` prevents the report from being sent to the printer or being displayed on the screen. You'll see many examples of event property procedure parameters throughout this book.

Report section event procedures

In addition to the event properties for the form itself, Access offers three specialized event properties to use with report sections. Table 12.7 shows each property, the event it recognizes, and how it works.

TABLE 12.7

Report Section Events

Event	When the Event Is Triggered
Format	When the section is pre-formatted in memory before being sent to the printer. This is your opportunity to apply special formatting to controls within the section.
Print	As the section is sent to the printer. It is too late to format controls in a report section when the Print event fires.
Retreat	After the Format event but before the Print event. Occurs when Access has to back up past other sections on a page to perform multiple formatting passes. Retreat is included in all sections except headers and footers.

The Format event

Use the `Format` event to apply special formatting to controls within a section before the section is printed. `Format` is useful, for example, to hide controls you don't want to print because of some condition in the report's data. The event procedure runs as Access lays out the section in memory but before the report is sent to the printer.

You can set the `On Format` and `On Print` event properties for any section of the report. However, `OnRetreat` is not available for the page header or page footer sections. Figure 12.4 shows the Property Sheet for the report's `On NoData` event property. Notice that the drop-down list at the top of the Property Sheet shows that the report is selected, so the events in the Event tab relate to the report itself and not an individual control on the report.

FIGURE 12.4

Specifying an event procedure for a report's Detail section

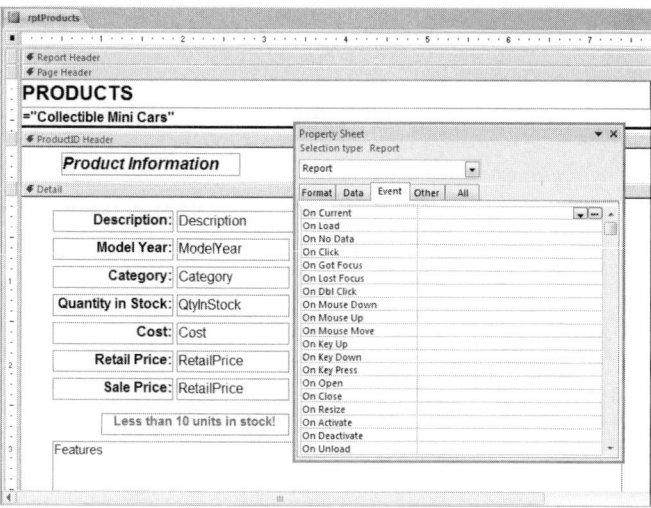

In addition to the NoData event, other report events are frequently programmed. Figure 12.5 shows how to add code to a report's Format event to control the visibility of controls on the report.

FIGURE 12.5

Running an event procedure to display or hide a control on a report

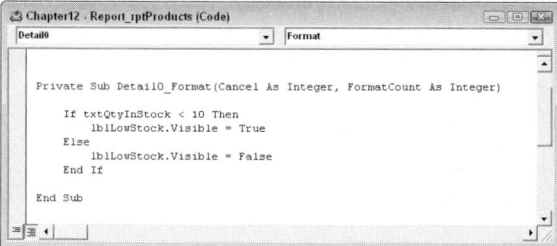

The Detail0_Format event procedure illustrated in Figure 12.5 first checks the value of the txtQtyInStock control. If the value of txtQtyInStock is less than 10, lblLowStock is displayed; otherwise, the warning control is hidden.

You'll see many examples of using events and event procedures to manipulate forms, reports, and controls throughout this book.

Form PivotTable events

The more recent versions of Access include the ability to create pivot tables that display data in interesting ways. Although this book does not discuss pivot tables in detail, you might encounter pivot tables as you work with Microsoft Access. Because of the special requirements imposed by pivot tables, Access forms include a number of events, as shown in Table 12.8.

An Access pivot table is actually a special view of a table, created by selecting PivotTable View from the View group in the Home tab while a table is open in Datasheet view. A pivot chart is created from a table open in Datasheet view by clicking on the PivotChart button in the Forms group on the Create tab of the Access ribbon.

TABLE 12.8

Form PivotTable Events

Event	When the Event Is Triggered
Timer	When a specified time interval passes
TimerInterval	When the interval is specified in milliseconds
BeforeScreenTip	When a screen tip is activated
CmdEnabled	When a command has become enabled in a pivot chart or pivot table
CmdChecked	When a pivot chart or pivot table command has been selected
CmdBeforeExecute	When a PivotChart or PivotTable command has been selected from the ribbon, but not yet executed
CmdExecute	Immediately after a pivot table or pivot chart command has been executed
DataChange	When a pivot table or pivot chart's data is changed or refreshed
DataSetChange	When a new data set for the chart changes (for example, when filtered)
PivotTableChange	Whenever the list field, field set, or total is added or deleted in a pivot table
SelectionChange	When a user makes a new selection; cannot be canceled
ViewChange	When a different PivotTable view of the current data is opened
Connect	When a pivot table connects to the underlying recordset
Disconnect	When a pivot table disconnects from the underlying recordset
BeforeQuery	When a pivot table is about to get a new data object
Query	When the pivot table receives a new data object
AfterLayout	When the pivot chart has already been laid out but before any rendering is done
BeforeRender	When the pivot chart is about to paint itself on the screen (before drawing begins)
AfterRender	When the object has been rendered in the pivot chart
AfterFinalRender	When all the chart objects have been rendered

Paying Attention to Event Sequence

Sometimes even a fairly simple action on the part of the user raises multiple events in rapid succession. As an example, every time the user presses a key on the keyboard, the KeyDown, KeyPress, and KeyUp events are raised. Similarly, pressing the left mouse button fires the MouseDown and MouseUp events, as well as a Click event. It's your prerogative as a VBA developer to decide which events you program in your Access applications.

Events don't occur randomly. Events actually fire in a predictable fashion, depending on which control is raising the events. Sometimes the trickiest aspect of working with events is keeping track of the order in which events occur. It may not be intuitive, for example, that the Enter event occurs before the GotFocus event (see Table 12.2) or that the KeyDown event occurs before the KeyPress event (see Table 12.3).

Looking at common event sequences

Here are the sequences of events for the most frequently encountered form scenarios:

- **Opening and closing forms**
    - When a form opens: Open (form) → Load (form) → Resize (form) → Activate (form) → Current (form) → Enter (control) → GotFocus (control)
    - When a form closes: Exit (control) → LostFocus (control) → Unload (form) → Deactivate (form) → Close (form)
- **Changes in focus**
    - When the focus moves from one form to another: Deactivate (form1) → Activate (form2)
    - When the focus moves to a control on a form: Enter → GotFocus
    - When the focus leaves a form control: Exit → LostFocus
    - When the focus moves from control1 to control2: Exit (control1) → LostFocus (control1) → Enter (control2) → GotFocus (control2)
    - When the focus leaves the record in which data has changed, but before entering the next record: BeforeUpdate (form) → AfterUpdate (form) → Exit (control) → LostFocus (control) → Current (form)
    - When the focus moves to an existing record in Form view: BeforeUpdate (form) → AfterUpdate (form) → Current (form)
- **Changes to data**
    - When data is entered or changed in a form control and the focus is moved to another control: BeforeUpdate → AfterUpdate → Exit → LostFocus
    - When the user presses and releases a key while a form control has the focus: KeyDown → KeyPress → KeyUp

- When text changes in a text box or in the text-box portion of a combo box: KeyDown → KeyPress → Change → KeyUp

- When a value that is not present in the drop-down list is entered into a combo box's text area: KeyDown → KeyPress → Change → KeyUp → NotInList → Error

- When data in a control is changed and the user presses Tab to move to the next control:

    Control1: KeyDown → BeforeUpdate → AfterUpdate → Exit → LostFocus

    Control2: Enter → GotFocus → KeyPress → KeyUp

- When a form opens and data in a control changes: Current (form) → Enter (control) → GotFocus (control) → BeforeUpdate (control) → AfterUpdate (control)

- When a record is deleted: Delete → BeforeDelConfirm → AfterDelConfirm

- When the focus moves to a new blank record on a form and a new record is created when the user types in a control: Current (form) → Enter (control) → GotFocus (control) → BeforeInsert (form) → AfterInsert (form)

- Mouse events

    - When the user presses and releases (clicks) a mouse button while the mouse pointer is on a form control: MouseDown → MouseUp → Click

    - When the user moves the focus from one control to another by clicking the second control:

        Control1: Exit → LostFocus

        Control2: Enter → GotFocus → MouseDown → MouseUp → Click

    - When the user double-clicks a control other than a command button: MouseDown → MouseUp → Click → DblClick → MouseUp

Writing simple form and control event procedures

Writing simple procedures to verify a form or control's event sequence is quite easy. Use the preceding information to determine which event should be harnessed in your application. Very often unexpected behavior can be traced to an event procedure attached to an event that occurs too late — or too early! — to capture the information that is needed by the application.

The Chapter12.accdb example database includes a form named frmEventLogger that prints every event for a command button, a text box, and a toggle button in the Debug window. This form is provided to demonstrate just how many Access events are triggered by minor actions. For example, clicking the command button one time, and then tabbing to the text box and pressing one key on the keyboard fires the following events:

- cmdButton_MouseDown
- cmdButton_MouseUp

- `cmdButton_Click`
- `cmdButton_KeyDown`
- `cmdButton_Exit`
- `cmdButton_LostFocus`
- `txtText1_Enter`
- `txtText1_GotFocus`
- `txtText1_KeyPress`
- `txtText1_KeyPress`
- `txtText1_KeyUp`
- `txtText1_KeyDown`
- `txtText1_KeyPress`
- `txtText1_Change`
- `txtText1_KeyUp`

You'll have to open the code editor and display the Immediate window to see these events displayed. From anywhere in the Access environment, press Ctrl+G and the code editor instantly opens with the Immediate window displayed. Then, Alt+Tab back to the main Access screen, open the form, and click on the various controls and type something into the text box. You'll see a long list of event messages when you use Ctrl+G to return to the Immediate window.

Obviously, this is far more events than you'll ever want to program. Notice that, on the command button, both the `MouseDown` and `MouseUp` events fire before the `Click` event. Also, a `KeyDown` event occurs as the Tab key is pushed, and then the command button's `Exit` event fires before its `LostFocus` event. (The focus, of course, moves off the command button to the text box as the Tab key is pressed.)

Also, notice that the text box raises *two* `KeyPress` events. The first is the `KeyPress` from the Tab key, and the second is the `KeyPress` that occurs as a character on the keyboard is pressed. Although it may seem strange that the Tab key's `KeyPress` event is caught by a text box and not by the command button, it makes sense when you consider what is happening under the surface. The Tab key is a directive to move the focus to the next control in the tab sequence. Access actually moves the focus before passing the `KeyPress` event to the controls on the form. This means that the focus moves to the text box, and the text box receives the `KeyPress` raised by the Tab key.

Keep in mind that you only write code for events that are meaningful to your application. Any event that does not contain code is ignored by Access and has no effect on the application.

Also, it's entirely likely that you'll occasionally program the wrong event for a particular task. You may, for example, be tempted to change the control's appearance by adding code to a control's `Enter` event. (Many developers change a control's `BackColor` or `ForeColor` to make it easy for the user to see which control has the focus.) You'll soon discover that the `Enter` event is an unreliable indicator of when a control has gained focus. The `GotFocus` and `LostFocus` events are specifically provided for the purpose of controlling the user interface, while the Enter and Exit events are more "conceptual" in nature and are not often programmed in Access applications.

This small example helps explain, perhaps, why Access supports so many different events. Microsoft has carefully designed Access to handle different *categories* of events, such as data or user-interface tasks. These events provide you with a rich programming environment. You'll almost always find exactly the right control, event, or programming trick to get Access to do what you need.

Opening a form with an event procedure

Most applications require multiple forms and reports to accomplish the application's business functions. Instead of requiring the users of the application to browse the database container to determine which forms and reports accomplish which tasks, an application generally provides a switchboard form to assist users in navigating throughout the application. The switchboard provides a set of command buttons labeled appropriately to suggest the purpose of the form or report it opens. Figure 12.6 shows the switchboard for the Collectible Mini Cars application.

FIGURE 12.6

Using a switchboard to navigate through the forms and reports of an application

The Collectible Mini Cars switchboard includes five command buttons. Each command button runs an event procedure when the button is clicked. The Products button (cmdProducts), for example, runs the event procedure that opens frmProducts. Figure 12.7 shows the Properties window for cmdProducts. Figure 12.8 shows the VBA code for the Click event of cmdProducts.

FIGURE 12.7

Specifying an event procedure for a control event

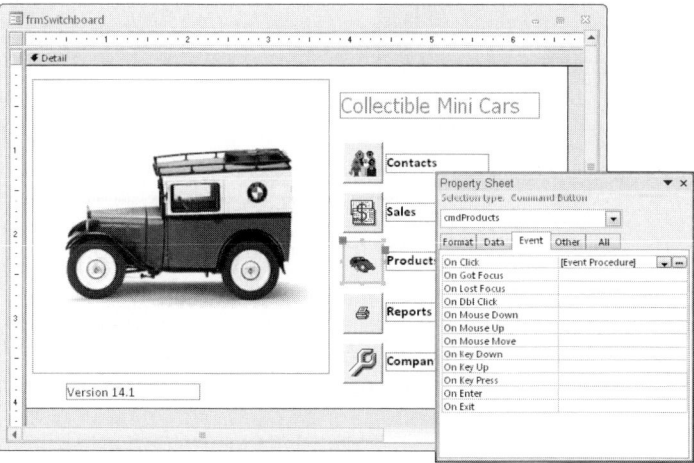

FIGURE 12.8

Using an event procedure to open a form

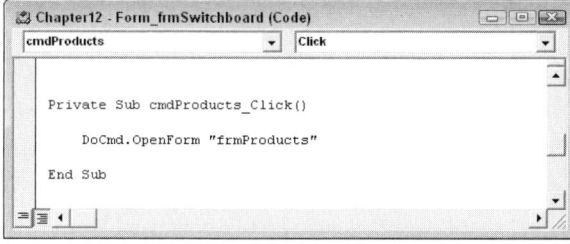

Running an event procedure when closing a form

Sometimes, you'll want to perform some action when you close or leave a form. For example, you might want Access to keep a log of everyone using the form, or you might want to close the form's Print dialog box every time a user closes the main form.

To automatically close `frmDialogProductPrint` every time `frmProducts` is closed, create an event procedure for the `frmProducts Close` event. Figure 12.9 shows this event procedure.

FIGURE 12.9

Running an event procedure when a form closes

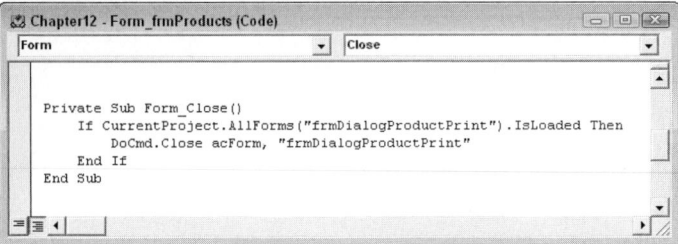

The `Form_Close` event illustrated in Figure 12.9 first checks to see if the form `frmDialogProductPrint` is open. If it is open, the statement to close it executes. Although trying to close a form that isn't currently open doesn't cause an error, it's a good idea to check to see if an object is available before performing an operation on the object.

Using an event procedure to confirm record deletion

Although you can use the Access Form View ribbon to delete a record in a form, a better practice is to provide a Delete button on the form. A Delete button is more user-friendly because it provides a visual cue to the user as to how to delete a record. Plus, a command button affords more control over the delete process because you can include code to verify the deletion before it's actually processed. Or you might need to perform a referential integrity check to ensure that deleting the record doesn't cause a connection to the record from some other table in the database to be lost.

Use the `MsgBox()` function to confirm a deletion. `cmdDelete`'s event procedure uses `MsgBox()` to confirm the deletion, as shown in Figure 12.10.

When the `cmdDelete_Click()` event procedure executes, Access displays a message box prompt, as shown in Figure 12.11. Notice that the message box includes two command buttons: Yes and No. Access displays the prompt and waits for the user to make a selection. The record is deleted only when the user confirms the deletion by clicking the Yes button.

Caution

Before the `RunCommand acCmdDeleteRecord` statement executes, it automatically checks to see if deleting the record violates referential integrity rules that you've set up in the Relationships diagram. If a violation occurs, an Access error message displays and the deletion is canceled.

Cross-Reference

See Chapter 2 for more information on setting up referential integrity in a database.

Cross-Reference

The `MsgBox` function is discussed in detail in Chapter 26.

FIGURE 12.10

Using the MsgBox( ) function to confirm a deletion

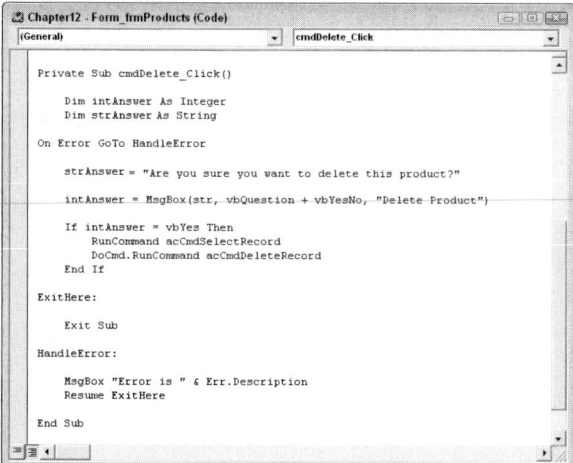

FIGURE 12.11

A confirmation dialog box before deleting a record

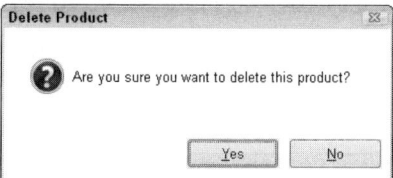

Summary

A thorough understanding of the Access event model is an essential skill for serious Access developers. Access is unusually well equipped with events that enable developers to respond to virtually every move made by users. In addition, the data-driven events provide virtually total control over how Access works with and manages data.

The next chapter continues exploring the many uses of the VBA programming language. There you'll learn many more details of adding powerful VBA procedures to Access forms and reports.

Accessing Data with VBA Code

IN THIS CHAPTER

Examining SQL statements

Working with Access data

Examining the ADO object model

Looking at DAO objects

Updating a table with VBA code

Data access and data management are at the core of any database application. Although you can do a fine job building applications with bound forms, using Visual Basic for Applications (VBA) code to access and manipulate data directly provides far greater flexibility than a bound application can. Anything that can be done with bound forms and controls can be done with a bit of VBA code using ActiveX Data Objects (ADO) or Data Access Objects (DAO) to retrieve and work with data.

The VBA language offers a full array of powerful commands for manipulating records in a table, providing data for controls on a form, or just about anything else. This chapter provides some in-depth examples of working with procedures that use SQL and ADO to manipulate database data.

On the CD-ROM

In the `Chapter13.accdb` database, you'll find a number of forms to use as a starting point and other completed forms to compare to the forms you change in this example.

Understanding SQL

Many of the VBA procedures that you write for working with Access data utilize Structured Query Language (SQL) statements to retrieve data from a database, add new data to a database, or update records in a database. When you use the Access Query Designer to create a query, Access converts the query's design into a SQL statement. The SQL statement is what Access actually executes when the query runs.

SQL is a fairly standard language for querying and updating database tables, and it's used by many relational databases. Although Access SQL does not comply with ANSI SQL-92 (the generally accepted specification for SQL language implementations), Access SQL shares many similarities with all SQL implementations. Your Access SQL statements run with very few changes in SQL Server or many other database systems.

Although forms and reports do have the ability to work with queries that are stored in an Access database, many times you'll find that creating a query on the fly in your code is quicker, easier, and more flexible than working with Access queries. SQL is relatively easy to understand and work with. This is a quick overview of SQL statements and how to create them in Access.

Viewing SQL statements in queries

To view the SQL statement that Access creates while building a query, choose View⇨SQL View from the tab on the Access ribbon. Figure 13.1 shows a typical SQL statement that returns the product description, company name, and state for products purchased by contacts in Connecticut or New York.

Don't be put off by the apparent complexity of the SQL statement in Figure 13.1. The same query in Design view is shown in Figure 13.2. As you can see, the Access Query Designer hides much of the complexity of the underlying SQL statement.

FIGURE 13.1

The SQL statement behind the `qryProductsSold_NY_CT` query in the SQL view window

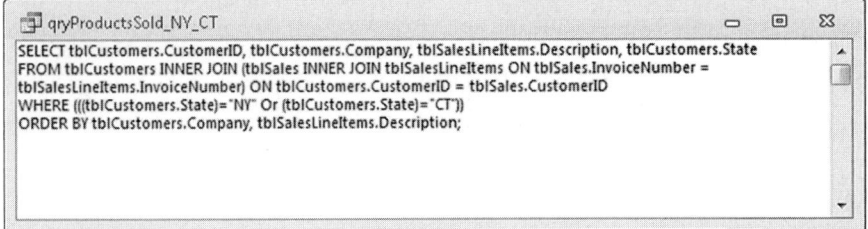

FIGURE 13.2

The same query in Design view

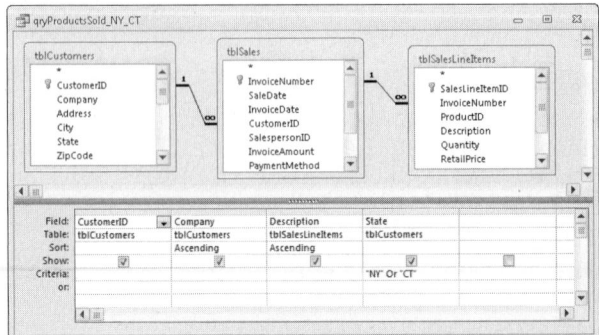

As you add tables and choose fields in the Access Query Designer, behind the scenes, Access composes a SQL statement that is stored within the database file. Anything you can do in the Query Designer can be expressed using the Access SQL syntax. Opening a query actually instructs Access to retrieve the SQL statement and compose the representation of the SQL statement you see in the Query Designer.

You can make changes to the query using either the Design window or the SQL window. As you work with the query, you can alternate between view modes using the View drop-down menu in the Access ribbon. The changes you make in either view are immediately reflected in the alternative view. On occasion, however, changes in the SQL view cannot be viewed directly in the Design window because the Design window cannot display a representation of every possible SQL statement. These queries still run as expected but can only be designed in the SQL window.

Tip

If you're proficient in creating SQL queries on your own, you can even create a new query directly in the SQL window. To add new lines to the SQL statement, simply press Enter, or add additional SQL text to the existing statement, while working in the SQL view window.

A SQL primer

One way to learn SQL syntax is to build a query in Design view; then view the corresponding SQL statement in the SQL view window. The example in Figure 13.1 uses the four most common SQL commands. Table 13.1 shows each command and explains its purpose. Each of these commands is discussed in detail in the following sections.

TABLE 13.1

Four Common SQL Keywords

Keyword	Purpose in SQL Statement
SELECT	This keyword starts a SQL statement. It's followed by the names of the fields that are selected from the table or tables (if more than one is specified in the FROM clause). SELECT is a required keyword for queries that extract data from tables.
FROM	FROM is followed by the name(s) of the table(s) containing the fields specified in the SELECT command. FROM is a required keyword for SELECT queries. If more than one table is used, you must also specify a JOIN type so that Access knows how the data in the tables are related.
WHERE	The WHERE keyword specifies conditions used to filter (limit) the records that are returned by the SELECT. The WHERE keyword is optional and is used when you want to select only specific records from the underlying data source.
ORDER BY	ORDER BY specifies the order in which you want the selected records to be sorted. The ORDER BY clause is optional and used when you want records returned in a specific sequence. Without an ORDER BY clause, Access returns records in an unpredictable order determined by the database engine (Jet).

Using these four basic keywords, you can build very powerful SQL statements to use in your Access forms and reports.

Note

By convention, SQL keywords are entered in all uppercase. This is not a requirement, however, because Jet, the database engine built into Microsoft Access, is case-insensitive.

Also, SQL statements may span many, many lines. The Jet database engine doesn't care how long a SQL statement is, or whether it spans multiple lines, as long as the SQL syntax (spaces, commas, and so on) is correct.

SELECT

The SELECT keyword is the first keyword used in two query types: in a Select query or a Make-Table query. SELECT specifies the field(s) you want displayed in the result data.

After specifying the keyword SELECT, specify the fields you want included and displayed by the query. The general syntax is:

```
SELECT Field_one, Field_two, Field_three [,...]
```

where *Field_one*, *Field_two*, and so on, are replaced with the names of the table fields. As many as 255 fields may be included in the SELECT statement.

Notice that commas separate each field in the list from the others. For example, use the following SELECT clause to specify Company Name and City fields in the Customers table:

```
SELECT [Company Name], City
```

The last field name in the list is not followed by a comma.

Note

The field name Company Name needs square brackets around it because it has a space in the name (see the "Using brackets around field names" sidebar for more information).

If you need to view fields from more than one table, specify the name of the tables in which to find the fields. The SELECT statement would, for example, look like this to select fields from both the Customers and Sales tables:

```
SELECT tblCustomers.Company, tblCustomers.City, tblSales.SaleDate,
    tblSales.InvoiceNumber
```

The dot between tblCustomers and Company is an operator that indicates that Company is contained within tblCustomers. In this context, the dot separates a table from a field name. This is an example of how context determines how Access interprets operators.

Using brackets around field names

A field or table name that contains spaces requires the use of brackets ([ ]). The brackets serve as delimiters to let the SQL parser know that you're referring to a specific field or table. A field or table name that contains special characters requires the use of brackets. (Spaces are considered special characters.) If the name doesn't contain spaces or special characters, you don't need to use brackets. Access may insert brackets around field and table names, but they're generally unnecessary.

The square brackets surround just the field name (tblMyTable.[My Field Name]), not the table and field name ([tblMyTable.My Field Name]). Think of the square brackets as marking the beginning and end of an identifier.

When you build a query using the Query Designer, Access automatically includes the table's name before the field name even when the table name is optional. The table name is required only when more than one table in the SQL statement has fields with exactly the same name. For example, a field named Invoice Number appears in both the Sales and Sales Line Items tables. If you want to select an invoice number field in your SQL statement, you must specify which of these to use — the one in Sales or the one in Sales Line Items.

The following SQL SELECT statement illustrates how the table name is used to specify which table supplies Invoice Number:

```
SELECT tblCustomers.Company, tblCustomers.City, _
    tblSales.SaleDate, tblSales.InvoiceNumber
```

Tip
Although table names are not required for non-duplicate fields in a SQL statement, it's a good idea to use them for clarity. Anyone viewing your SQL statements will immediately know where each field is found in the database.

You can use the asterisk wildcard (*) to specify that all fields in a table should be selected. If you're going to select all fields from more than one table, include the table name, a period (.), and the asterisk for each table:

```
SELECT tblCustomers.*, tblCustomers.*, tblSales.*, tblSales.*
```

Caution
Generally speaking, it isn't a good idea to use the asterisk to select all fields within a table. Your queries are guaranteed to run more slowly than necessary if you routinely extract more data than needed in your queries. By all means, select all the fields that are necessary to satisfy the user's requirements, but don't make a habit of selecting all columns from all tables. Keep in mind that queries pull everything specified by the SQL statement, regardless of whether a query's data is displayed on a form or report.

When you create a SQL SELECT statement, several *predicates* are available for the SELECT clause:

- ALL
- DISTINCT
- DISTINCTROW
- TOP

A *predicate* modifies how the SELECT command works. It works in conjunction with the WHERE clause (actually, in SQL terminology, the WHERE condition) of a SQL statement.

ALL

As its name implies, the ALL predicate means return all records matching the query's criteria. ALL is the default for Select queries.

DISTINCT

Use the DISTINCT predicate when you want to retrieve only one instance of duplicated data in the fields specified in the SELECT statement. For example, assume you want to know all the different cities where the Collectible Mini Cars customers live. The following SQL statement queries tblCustomers for the distinct City values:

```
SELECT DISTINCT City
FROM tblCustomers
```

Adding an ORDER BY clause ensures the returned data is properly sorted:

```
SELECT DISTINCT City
FROM tblCustomers
ORDER BY City
```

By default, a query containing the DISTINCT clause is sorted by the selected fields, but it's always a good idea to include an explicit ORDER BY clause.

I'll ignore everything past the first line of this query for the meantime. Notice the DISTINCT clause that follows the SELECT keyword. The addition of the DISTINCT keyword has a profound effect on the records returned by this query.

The DISTINCT predicate tells Access to show only one record if the values in the *selected* fields are duplicates (in this case the selected field is City). Other fields that are not included in the query may be different. DISTINCT eliminates duplicates based on the fields selected by the query.

The DISTINCT predicate is added to an Access query's SQL statement by setting the query's Unique Values property. Right-click in the upper portion of the Access Query Designer, and select Properties. Then, set the Unique Values property to Yes (see Figure 13.3). Access adds the DISTINCT predicate to the SQL statement underlying the query for you.

FIGURE 13.3

Setting the Unique Values property

Unique Values property

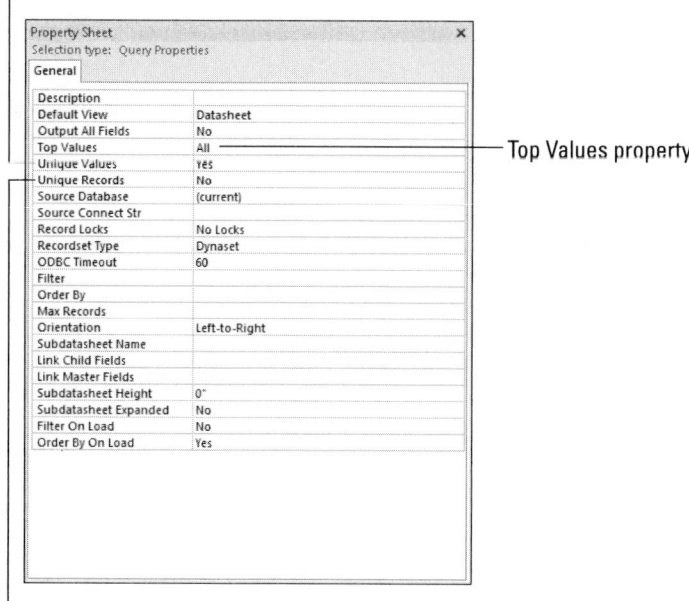

Top Values property

Unique Records property

Records returned by a query that includes the DISTINCT predicate are not updateable. Each record in the result set represents one or more records in the underlying tables, and there is no way for Access to know which records to update. Therefore, the data returned by a DISTINCT query is read-only.

DISTINCTROW

The DISTINCTROW predicate is unique to Access. It works much like DISTINCT, with one big difference: It looks for duplicates on the basis of *all* fields in the table(s) underlying the query, not just the fields selected by the query.

Generally speaking, Access queries behave as if DISTINCTROW were always included in the SQL statement. The only time you'll see a query with DISTINCTROW return different records than a query without DISTINCTROW is when all the tables underlying the query contain exactly the same records. Because all the tables in a normalized database include a primary key that uniquely identifies each row, it's unlikely that a DISTINCTROW query will find identical records in tables joined by a query.

The DISTINCTROW predicate is added to a query's SQL statement by setting the query's Unique Records property to Yes. Unique Values (DISTINCT) and Unique Records (DISTINCTROW) are mutually exclusive and both cannot be set to Yes at the same time. The Chapter13.accdb example database includes qryUsing_DISTINCTROW, a query that demonstrates the DISTINCTROW predicate.

TOP

The TOP predicate enables you to restrict the number of records returned to the TOP <number> of values. For example, the following SELECT statement displays the first five contact records (see qryTop_5_Sales in Chapter13.accdb):

```
SELECT TOP 5
tblSales.InvoiceNumber, tblSales.SaleDate, tblSales.CustomerID,
    tblSales.InvoiceAmount
FROM tblSales;
```

You must use the ORDER BY clause in conjunction with the TOP predicate. This example (qryCustomersMostRecentSales) uses the ORDER BY clause with the TOP predicate to answer a business question (which five companies most recently place orders):

```
SELECT TOP 5 Company, LastSalesDate
FROM tblCustomers
ORDER BY LastSalesDate DESC
```

This example returns a list of companies with the five most recent sales dates. In other words, the query lists all the companies and orders them by their last sales date in descending order (so that the most recent sales are at the top of the list), and then picks the first five companies in the ordered list. A TOP query does not always return exactly the number of records specified. The criteria used may return fewer records than requested, or more records may be returned if multiple records match the criteria and the "tied" records push the count record count over the requested number.

The TOP predicate has an optional keyword, PERCENT, that displays the top number of records on the basis of a percentage rather than a number. To see the top 10 percent of your contacts, you use a SELECT statement like this example (qryCustomersTop10PercentSales):

```
SELECT TOP 10 PERCENT Company, LastSalesDate
FROM tblCustomers
ORDER BY LastSalesDate DESC
```

FROM

As the name suggests, the FROM clause specifies the tables (or queries) that contain the fields named in the SELECT statement. The FROM clause is required for SELECT queries. The FROM clause tells SQL where to find the records. If you fail to include a FROM clause in a SELECT statement, you'll receive an error.

When you're working with one table, the FROM clause simply specifies the table name:

```
SELECT Company, City
FROM tblCustomers
```

When you're working with more than one table, you can supply a table expression to the FROM clause to specify how to retrieve data from the multiple tables. The FROM clause is where you set the relationship between two or more tables for the SELECT statement. The table expression can be one of three types:

- INNER JOIN...ON
- RIGHT JOIN...ON
- LEFT JOIN...ON

Use INNER JOIN...ON to specify the Access default inner or *equijoin*. To join two tables, you link them using a field that both tables have in common. For example, the Contacts and Sales tables have a common field that identifies the buyer. To join the Sales and Contacts tables, the table expression syntax is as follows (see qryInvoicesAndCustomers in Chapter13.accdb):

```
SELECT tblSales.InvoiceDate, tblSales.InvoiceNumber,
tblCustomers.Company
FROM tblCustomers
INNER JOIN tblSales
ON tblCustomers.CustomerID = tblSales.CustomerID;
```

Notice that the FROM clause specifies the first table to use: tblCustomers. Then the INNER JOIN clause specifies the second table to use: tblSales. Finally, the ON keyword specifies which field(s) — CustomerID, in this case — are used to join the table. The results of this little query are shown in Figure 13.4.

FIGURE 13.4

A query using the default INNER JOIN clause

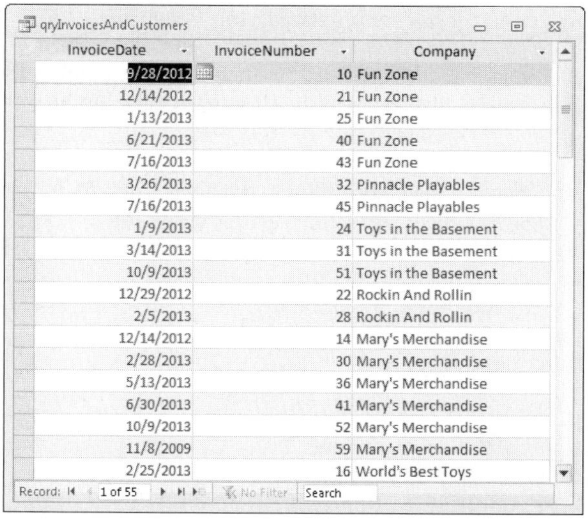

InvoiceDate	InvoiceNumber	Company
9/28/2012	10	Fun Zone
12/14/2012	21	Fun Zone
1/13/2013	25	Fun Zone
6/21/2013	40	Fun Zone
7/16/2013	43	Fun Zone
3/26/2013	32	Pinnacle Playables
7/16/2013	45	Pinnacle Playables
1/9/2013	24	Toys in the Basement
3/14/2013	31	Toys in the Basement
10/9/2013	51	Toys in the Basement
12/29/2012	22	Rockin And Rollin
2/5/2013	28	Rockin And Rollin
12/14/2012	14	Mary's Merchandise
2/28/2013	30	Mary's Merchandise
5/13/2013	36	Mary's Merchandise
6/30/2013	41	Mary's Merchandise
10/9/2013	52	Mary's Merchandise
11/8/2009	59	Mary's Merchandise
2/25/2013	16	World's Best Toys

Record: 1 of 55   No Filter   Search

In the case of an inner join, it really makes no difference which table is specified first in the FROM clause. Because records are selected only when values exist on *both* sides of the join (for example, when CustomerID joins tblCustomers and tblSales), Access gets data from both tables, regardless of which table is specified in the FROM clause.

Note

In Figure 13.4 notice that the Customer ID is not shown in the query results. There is no need to display the Customer ID in this particular query because, even though the Customer ID is used as the join field, it isn't required by the users in the query's output.

The inner join requirement that the same value (in our case, the same CustomerID value) appears in both tables causes a lot of trouble for Access developers. Because matching records must appear in *both* tables before data from either table appears in the query's results, always keep in mind that the default join in an Access query is an inner join, and it's possible that more records are available in the tables than are indicated by the query results.

The LEFT JOIN and RIGHT JOIN work exactly the same, except that they specify an *outer* join instead of an *inner* join. You use outer joins when you want to return records from a parent table even if the dependent table does not contain any records with matching values specified in the ON clause. The following example (qryCustomersAndInvoiceNumbers) shows a query coded as an outer join:

```
SELECT tblCustomers.Company, tblSales.InvoiceNumber
FROM tblCustomers
LEFT JOIN tblSales
ON tblCustomers.CustomerID = tblSales.CustomerID;
```

In this example, the query includes *all* the company names and the invoice numbers associated with customers. All company names are included in the results, even those that have not placed an order. The Invoice Number field is null when the customer has not yet placed a sale (see Figure 13.5).

Most of the rows in Figure 13.5 include an InvoiceNumber value, but there are several null cells in the query's datasheet. These rows indicate customers who are in the Customers table but haven't placed orders.

If you'd like to see all customers who haven't placed a sale, add a filter to the query's design. In this case (qryCustomersWithNoInvoiceNumbers), the query selects records where the InvoiceNumber is Null:

```
SELECT tblCustomers.Company, tblCustomers.Address,
tblCustomers.City, tblCustomers.State,
tblCustomers.ZipCode, tblCustomers.Phone
FROM tblCustomers
LEFT JOIN tblSales
ON tblCustomers.CustomerID = tblSales.CustomerID
WHERE (((tblSales.InvoiceNumber) Is Null));
```

FIGURE 13.5

A query using a LEFT JOIN clause

Notice that InvoiceNumber is not included in the SELECT clause. In this example, there is no reason to include the InvoiceNumber as part of the SELECT clause because it will be blank (Null) in every record returned by the query. (This query's results are shown in Figure 13.6.) However, InvoiceNumber is included in the WHERE clause, of course. The WHERE clause could also include a criteria limiting the results to customers who haven't placed an order in the last few months, instead of returning all customers who haven't ever placed an order. The WHERE clause is discussed in detail in the next section.

FIGURE 13.6

All customers who have not yet placed an order

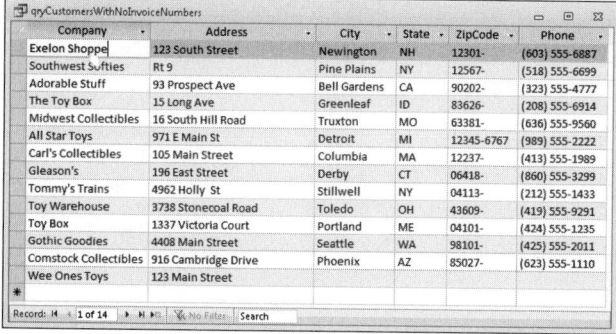

The query in Figure 13.6 is an excellent example of a typical business requirement. In this case, these results could be used by the sales department to follow up with cold calls or marketing materials.

WHERE

Use the WHERE clause of the SQL statement only when you want to restrict returned records based on a condition. Unlike SELECT and FROM, the WHERE clause is optional.

The SQL statement shown in Figure 13.1 specifies the following WHERE clause:

```
WHERE (tblCustomers.State="NY") Or (tblCustomers.State="CT")
```

The WHERE condition can be any valid Boolean (True or False) expression. It can be an evaluation on a single field, as in the previous example, or a complex expression based on several criteria.

Note

If you use the WHERE condition, it must follow the FROM clause of the SQL statement.

You'll see many, many examples of WHERE clauses throughout this book, so there is no need to show a lot of examples at this time.

ORDER BY

The ORDER BY clause is how the returned data is sorted. A query sorts the returned data by the field(s) you specified in the ORDER BY clause, in ascending or descending order. Using the example in Figure 13.1, the query was sorted by two of the fields in the SELECT clause:

```
ORDER BY tblCustomers.Company, tblSalesLineItems.Description;
```

The fields in the ORDER BY clause appear in the same left-to-right order that they appear in the QBE grid in the query's design. The data is sorted by the fields in the ORDER BY clause in left-to-right order. In this case, the returned data is first sorted by company, then by description. Be sure to specify a sort order that makes sense for your data.

Specifying the end of a SQL statement

Because a SQL statement can be as long as 64,000 characters, a way is needed to tell the database language that you've finished creating the statement. By default, a semicolon (;) indicates the end of a SQL statement, but the semicolon is not required by Access.

Access is very forgiving about the ending semicolon. If you forget to place one at the end of a SQL statement, Access assumes that it should be there and runs the SQL statement. On the other hand, if you accidentally place a semicolon inside a SQL statement, Access reports an error and tries to tell you where it occurred.

The fields specified in the ORDER BY clause do not have to be the same fields specified in the SELECT clause. You can sort by any of the fields in the tables specified in the FROM clause. In fact, the fields in the ORDER BY clause don't have to be included in the query's results. Uncheck the Show checkbox in the QBE grid to exclude the field from the query's results.

Working with Data

The first thing to note when discussing data access objects is that the DAO and ADO object models are separate from the Access object model. DAO and ADO represent the objects managed and "owned" by the Access database engines (ACE or Jet), which are software components installed along with Office. In the past, Excel (with the MSQuery add-on) and Visual Basic (the stand-alone application development product) could directly use the Jet database engine or access it through open database connectivity (ODBC) or Microsoft Query.

Using Access VBA enables you to manipulate your database objects behind the scenes, giving you a great amount of flexibility within your applications. Access provides two different object models for working with data: ADO and DAO.

ADO (ActiveX Data Objects) is the newer of the two syntaxes. It's based on Microsoft's ActiveX technology, which provides the basis for independent objects that perform complex tasks without input from their hosts. When applied to ADO, the ActiveX objects are able to perform a wide variety of data access tasks without hampering Access in any way. Because ADO objects are quite powerful, the ADO object model (meaning, the ADO object hierarchy) is fairly sparse. Only a few objects are needed to perform virtually all data access tasks in Access applications.

The older data access object model supported by Access is DAO (Data Access Objects). Unlike ADO, DAO objects are simple and direct, and require a bit more VBA code to establish and maintain. DAO is widely used and was the only data access methodology in Access for many years.

The distinction between Access and DAO is important because Access's user interface tends to blur the line between objects belonging to Access and those belonging to the database engine. There are some features available in code that you may *think* are data access objects but are really features of Access, and vice versa. In code, you'll have to develop with this distinction in mind. For example, ADO and DAO objects have many built-in properties and methods; other properties are added by Access.

In any case, working with ADO and DAO in VBA procedures provides you with much greater flexibility than dealing strictly with forms and reports bound to queries and tables. As you'll see in the rest of this chapter, relatively few lines of ADO or DAO code perform complex operations on data, such as updating or deleting existing records, or adding new records to tables. Using VBA code means that an application can respond to current conditions on a form, such as missing or incorrect values. It's quite easy to perform ad hoc queries against data that would otherwise require complex queries with many parameters.

Entire books — *big* books — have been written on the topics covered in the remainder of this chapter. All I can do in this chapter is provide you with some fundamental examples of using ADO and DAO in Access applications, and, coupled with the material in the other chapters in this book, you should be well prepared to incorporate VBA-based data management in your Access applications.

Note

ADO and DAO are not equivalent in every regard. Both syntaxes enable you to add to or modify the data in tables, build recordsets, work with data in recordsets, and populate forms with data. However, ADO has a distinct edge when it comes to working with external data sources. As you'll soon see, ADO requires a provider that defines the data source used by the ADO objects in an application. ADO providers are specific to the data source, such as SQL Server or Access. The provider endows the ADO objects with special abilities (such as the ability to test the connection to the data source), depending on the underlying data sources. DAO, on the other hand, is a more generic data access syntax and is not specific to any one data source. ADO is the logical choice where advanced data access tasks must be performed, while DAO is very good at routine querying, updating, and other data tasks.

The following sections describe each of these objects and explain how each object adds to the ADO data access capabilities.

Although Access is not strictly object oriented, it is most certainly object *based.* The remainder of chapter describes the *object models* you use in VBA code to perform data-management tasks in your Access applications. An object model is simply the arrangement of the objects that perform the data-management tasks. A sound understanding of the ADO and DAO object models is an essential requirement when using VBA code to manage Access data.

Many of the objects described in this chapter contain a *collection* of zero or more objects. A collection is a container holding all the members of a certain type of object. (A collection is, itself, an object.)

A collection is like a stack of baseball cards. Each card in the stack is different from all the other cards, but all baseball cards have certain characteristics (like size, the statistics printed on the back, and so on) in common. In Access, a *recordset* object (either ADO or DAO) contains a collection of *field* objects. Every recordset object shares certain characteristics with all other recordset objects, and every field object is similar to all other fields in certain ways.

The name of a collection is almost always the plural of the object type within the collection. Therefore, a `Fields` collection contains a number of different `Field` objects.

Note

It's important to know when a term applies to an object of the same name or is just the name of a general category of database items. In this book, a capitalized word like Field refers to a `Field` object, in contrast to field (lowercase), which is a generic reference to any field in any table. Similarly, Fields means a `Fields` collection, while fields refers to a number of different fields.

Each ADO or DAO object comes with a collection of properties and methods. Each property or method provides you with a way to define the object, or represents an action you use to direct the object to perform its job.

An object's `Properties` collection is made up of a number of `Property` objects. Each `Property` object has its *own* set of properties. Properties can be referenced directly, created through the Access interface, or created by a user and added to the `Properties` collection. You generally refer to a property in this way: *ObjectName.PropertyName*. For example, to refer to the Name property of a field, the syntax would be as follows:

```
MyField.Name
```

Methods are a little different. A method is an *action* an object can perform, or is an action performed *on* an object. The purpose of a data access object is to manipulate or display data in a database; therefore, each object must have some way to act upon that data. You can't add or delete methods in the ADO or DAO objects. (This is one of the several ways that Access is not truly object oriented.) You can only invoke the method on the object. For example, the following code places the record pointer of the recordset `MyRecordset` at the next record:

```
MyRecordset.MoveNext
```

Like properties, every ADO and DAO object has a set of methods applicable to that object.

If you ever need to know more about an ADO or DAO object, use the Object Browser (shown in Figure 13.7). Open the Object Browser from within the VBA Editor by pressing F2 or choosing View⇨Object Browser from the menu in the VBA editor window. The Object Browser lets you examine each object's methods and properties and the arguments you can expect when using them. The Object Browser is used by all Microsoft applications that feature VBA as their language engine.

FIGURE 13.7

The Object Browser provides a view into an object's properties and methods.

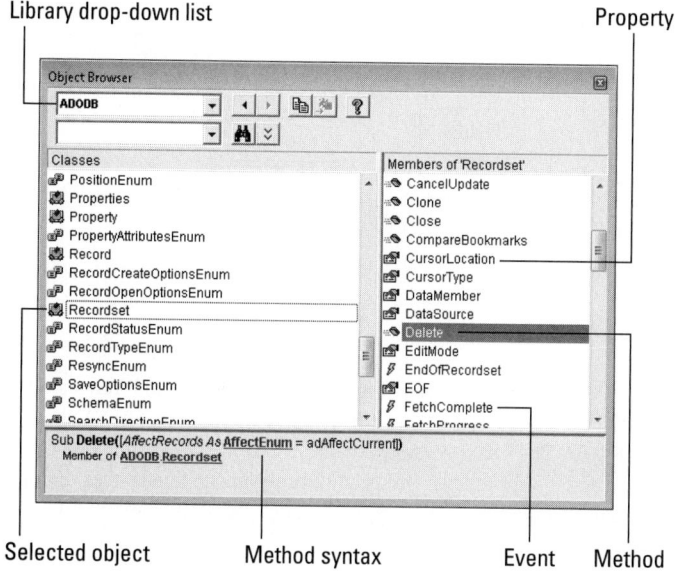

The Object Browser is easy to use. Select a library (ADODB, for example) from the drop-down list in the upper-left corner; then scroll through the object list on the left side of the browser to find an object of interest. Selecting an object fills the right-side list with the object's properties, methods, and events (if applicable). Clicking on a property, method, or event reveals the item's syntax in the area below the lists.

Although the Object Browser doesn't show specific code examples, very often seeing the syntax associated with property, method, or event may be enough to get you started writing VBA code, or to clarify the object's details.

Understanding ADO Objects

I'll begin my explanation of the ActiveX Data Objects by examining the ADO object model, and describing the purpose of each object. Then I'll look at a number of code examples that use the ADO objects to perform common database tasks.

The ADO object model is shown in Figure 13.8. As you can see, the ADO object model is quite simple and includes only a few types of objects. Notice that the ADO object model is not hierarchical. Each object stands alone and is not subordinate to another object in the model.

FIGURE 13.8

The ADO object model

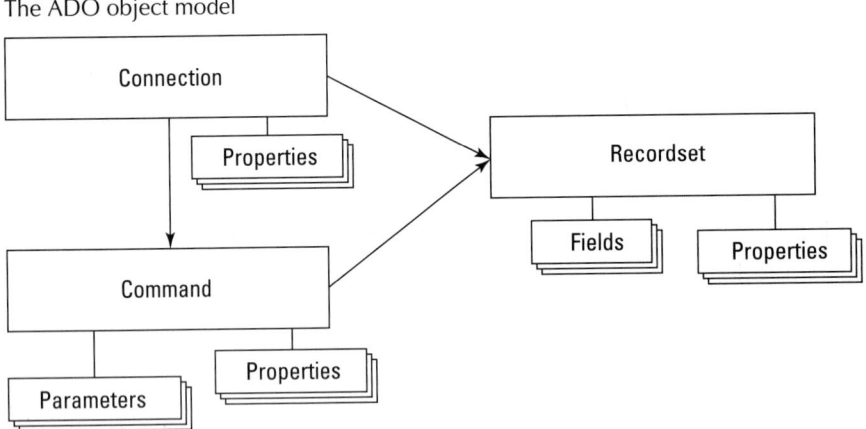

Using ADO objects requires a reference to the ADO library. Figure 13.9 shows the References dialog box (opened by choosing Tools ⇨ References in the VBA editor window) with the ADO library (Microsoft ActiveX Data Objects) selected. The exact version of the ADO library installed on your machine may vary, and, in fact, there may be more than one ADO library in the References dialog box. Select the highest-numbered library to make sure you have the latest version available to Access.

FIGURE 13.9

Referencing the ADO library

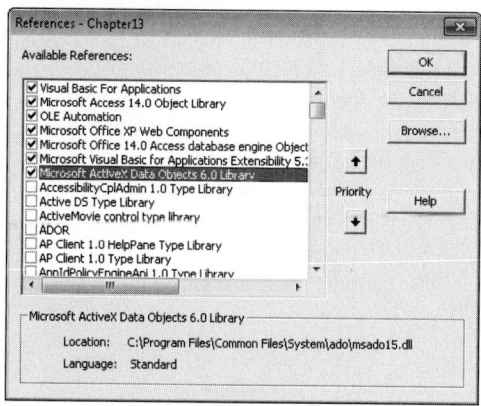

In the following code examples, notice that all the ADO object variables are referenced as ADODB object types. Although not entirely necessary, prefixing object type names with a library reference clears up any ambiguity that Access might have regarding the type of object referenced by the VBA statements. For example, both ADO and DAO support a Recordset object. Unless the object type declaration is prefixed with either ADODB or DAO, Access may misunderstand *which* type of recordset is referenced in a VBA statement.

The ADO Connection object

As its name suggests, the Connection object provides a connection to a data source. Access to a data source is necessary for any data operation, so the Connection object is required in virtually any scenario involving ADO.

After the ADO library has been referenced, creating a Connection object is simple (the ADO library is referenced as ADODB in VBA code):

```
Dim cnn as ADODB.Connection
Set cnn = New ADODB.Connection
```

These two statements are typical of VBA's approach to object-oriented programming. In the first statement, an object variable (cnn) is established as an ADODB.Connection object type. This means that VBA recognizes cnn as a Connection, with all the properties and methods associated with Connection objects, as defined by the ADO library. However, at this point cnn is just a placeholder — it doesn't yet exist in memory.

The second statement instantiates the cnn object variable. As this statement executes, VBA creates a Connection object in the computer's memory, points the cnn variable to the object in memory, and prepares it for use.

The Connection must be opened before it can be used. The following statement is the easiest way to open an ADO Connection:

```
cnn.Open CurrentProject.Connection
```

In this case, the Connection connects to the current database. As you'll soon see, a Connection object requires a number of properties to be set before it can successfully open, but opening a Connection on the current database's Connection property provides all those settings. CurrentProject.Connection is actually a long string (specifically, a *connection string*) that includes all the information needed about the current database. A typical Connection property setting is as follows:

```
Provider=Microsoft.ACE.OLEDB.12.0;User ID=Admin;
Data Source=C:\Data\Chapter13.accdb;
Mode=Share Deny None;Extended Properties="";
Jet OLEDB:System database=C:\...\Access\System.mdw;
Jet OLEDB:Registry Path=...\Access Connectivity Engine;
Jet OLEDB:Database Password="";
Jet OLEDB:Engine Type=6;
Jet OLEDB:Database Locking Mode=1;
Jet OLEDB:Global Partial Bulk Ops=2;
Jet OLEDB:Global Bulk Transactions=1;
Jet OLEDB:New Database Password="";
Jet OLEDB:Create System Database=False;
Jet OLEDB:Encrypt Database=False;
Jet OLEDB:Don't Copy Locale on Compact=False;
Jet OLEDB:Compact Without Replica Repair=False;
Jet OLEDB:SFP=False;
Jet OLEDB:Support Complex Data=True
```

Note
Line breaks have been added above for clarity, and some lines have been shortened.

This is actually considerably more than the Connection object actually needs, but Microsoft wanted to make sure nothing was missing.

Notice the Data Source portion of the ConnectionString property. This is the part that points to a specific .accdb file. Changing this path means the Connection object can open virtually any Access database as long as the path is valid and terminates at an .accdb file.

The following procedure opens a Connection against the current database, prints the Connection object's Provider property, and then closes and discards the Connection object:

```
Public Sub OpenConnection()
    Dim cnn As ADODB.Connection
    Set cnn = New ADODB.Connection
    cnn.Open CurrentProject.Connection
    ' Connection is open
```

```
        Debug.Print cnn.Provider
        cnn.Close
        Set cnn = Nothing
    End Sub
```

When working with ADO, it's very important to close an object (if the object supports a `Close` method) and set it to `Nothing` when your code is done with the object. ADO objects tend to stay in memory once they've been opened, and must be explicitly closed and discarded (set to `Nothing`) to clear them from memory. If an ADO object is not properly terminated, it may remain in memory causing problems for users.

A `Connection` object requires the provider information and the data source. The provider specifies which ADO provider (essentially a driver) to attach to the `Connection` object. For example, there is a provider for SQL Server databases: one for the Jet database engine, and another for the ACE database engine. Each provider knows how to connect to a different type of data, and endows the `Connection` object with features specific to the data source.

The downside to the `Connection` object, and one that causes a lot of problems for Access developers, is the correct syntax to use for the `Connection` object's `ConnectionString` property. The `ConnectionString` must be properly composed and must reference a provider that is installed on the local machine.

There is a little trick to discovering the `ConnectionString` to use against an ADO provider. Start by creating an empty text file, and change its extension from `.txt` to `.udl` (universal data link). Next, double-click on the empty file, and Windows opens the Data Link Properties dialog box (shown in Figure 13.10). Use this dialog box to select a provider (on the Provider tab) and a data source (on the Connection tab); then close the dialog box.

FIGURE 13.10

Use the Data Link Properties dialog box to set up a connection string.

Provider tab   Connection tab

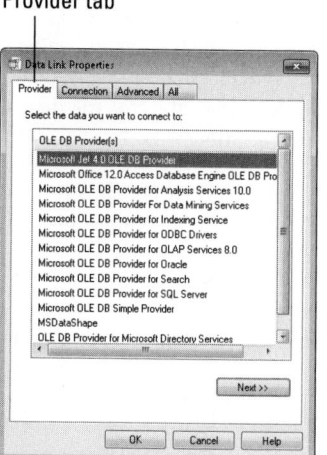
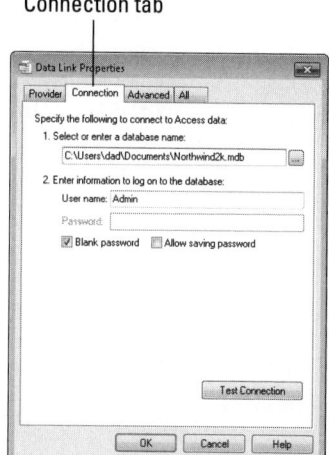

Finally, open the .udl file in Notepad and copy the connection string from the file's contents and paste into your VBA program. The connection string in the following procedure was generated using this trick:

```
Public Sub OpenConnection()
    Dim cnn As ADODB.Connection
    Dim strCnn As String
    Set cnn = New ADODB.Connection
    ' The exact path to the database may
    ' vary in the following statement:
    strCnn = "Provider=Microsoft.Jet.OLEDB.4.0;" _
        & "Data Source=C:\Northwind.mdb;" _
        & "Persist Security Info=False"
    cnn.ConnectionString = strCnn
    cnn.Open CurrentProject.Connection
    ' Connection is open
    Debug.Print cnn.Provider
    cnn.Close
    Set cnn = Nothing
End Sub
```

The reason this trick works is that a .udl file is recognized by Windows as a container for an ADO connection string. Double-clicking on the file opens the Data Link Properties dialog box, which is the default editor for .udl files. You specify all the attributes needed in an ADO connection string through the Data Link Properties dialog box, and those attributes are added to the .udl file.

The Provider tab in the Data Link Properties dialog box shows all the providers currently installed on the local machine. ADO is a local process, so the provider must be installed locally for ADO to work. The ADO providers you see in Figure 13.10 were installed either along with Windows 7 or as part of Office 2010.

The ADO Command object

The second major ADO topic is the Command object. As its name implies, a Command object executes a command against the data source opened through a Connection. The command can be as simple as the name of an Access query, or as complex as a long SQL statement that selects dozens of fields and includes WHERE and ORDER BY clauses. In fact, the Command object is the most common way to execute SQL Server stored procedures from Access applications.

As you'll see later in this chapter, the output from executing a Command object can be directed into a recordset. The data in the recordset can then be used to populate a form or controls such as text boxes, combo boxes, and list boxes.

There are many, many ways to use Command objects. The following procedure is just one example of using a Command object. In this case, the Command object populates a recordset with data taken directly from tblCustomers. (Recordsets are discussed in the next section.) The following procedure (ExecuteCommand1) is included in basADO_Commands in the Chapter 13.accdb example database.

```
Public Sub ExecuteCommand1
    Dim rst As ADODB.Recordset
    Set rst = New ADODB.Recordset
    Dim cmd As ADODB.Command
    Set cmd = New ADODB.Command
    cmd.ActiveConnection = CurrentProject.Connection
    cmd.CommandText = "tblCustomers"
    Set rst = cmd.Execute
    Debug.Print rst.GetString
    rst.Close
    Set rst = Nothing
End Sub
```

Notice the following actions in this procedure:

- A Recordset and a Command object are both declared and instantiated.

- The Command object's ActiveConnection property is set to the current project's Connection property.

- The Command object's CommandText property is set to the name of a table in the database.

- The recordset is populated by setting it to the value returned when the Command object is executed.

Notice the recordset's GetString method. GetString is a handy way to output everything that's in the recordset. Figure 13.11 shows the output from ExecuteCommand1 in the Debug window.

Cross-Reference

The Debug window is thoroughly discussed in Chapter 14.

FIGURE 13.11

GetString is a convenient way to see what's in a recordset.

This little example illustrates almost everything you need to know about ADO Command objects. A Command object must be attached to an available Connection through its ActiveConnection property. The ActiveConnection can be a connection string or an open Connection object. It doesn't make any difference where the Connection is pointing — an Access or SQL Server database, Oracle or any other data source. The Command object uses the Connection's special knowledge of the data source to get at the data.

Command objects are most valuable when working with parameterized queries. Each Command object includes a Parameters collection containing, naturally, Parameter objects. Each parameter corresponds to a parameter required by the query or stored procedure referenced by the Command's CommandText property.

Very often the CommandText property is set to a SQL statement that includes parameters:

```
SELECT * FROM tblCustomers
WHERE State = 'NY' OR State = "NJ"
```

You'll see many examples of using the ADO Command object to populate recordsets and perform actions on data throughout this book.

The ADO Recordset object

The ADO Recordset is a very versatile object. Most often, it's populated by executing a Command, or directly through its Open method. OpenADORecordset1 illustrates how easily the Recordset object opens an Access table (Open_ADO_Recordset1 is included in basADO_ Recordsets in the Chapter13.accdb example database):

```
Public Sub Open_ADO_Recordset1()
    Dim rs As ADODB.Recordset
    Set rs = New ADODB.Recordset
    rs.Open "SELECT * FROM tblCustomers", _
        CurrentProject.Connection
    Debug.Print rs.GetString
    rs.Close
    Set rs = Nothing
End Sub
```

In this example, the recordset is populated by opening the Customers table. Notice that a SQL statement is used to select records from tblCustomers. The SQL statement could include WHERE or ORDER BY clauses to filter and sort the data as it's selected.

An alternate way to write this procedure is to use a separate statement for assigning the ActiveConnection property:

```
Public Sub Open_ADO_Recordset2()
    Dim rs As ADODB.Recordset
    Set rs = New ADODB.Recordset
    rs.ActiveConnection = CurrentProject.Connection
    rs.Open "SELECT * FROM tblCustomers"
    Debug.Print rs.GetString
    rs.Close
    Set rs = Nothing
End Sub
```

The Open_ADO_Recordset1 procedure is included in basADO_Recordsets in the Chapter13.accdb example database.

Many developers prefer the approach in OpenRecordset2 because it's easier to see exactly what's happening to the Recordset object and where its properties are being set. Although these very small procedures are easily understood, in larger code segments finding all the references to an object like rst can be challenging, especially when the VBA statements become long and complex.

As with the other ADO objects, a Recordset object must be declared and instantiated. Like the Command object, if the Open method is used to populate a Recordset object, an open connection must be provided as an argument to the Open method.

Recordset objects are used in many different places in this book. Depending on context, the most commonly used Recordset methods include Open, Close, MoveFirst, MoveNext, MovePrevious, and MoveLast.

Navigating Recordsets

Recordsets wouldn't be much use if all you could do is open and close them, or if the GetString method was the only way to use the data in a recordset. Depending on context, the word *recordset* means several different things:

- The rows of data returned by a query
- The data bound to an Access form
- The object filled with data as the result of an ADO operation

In all cases, however, a recordset is a data structure containing rows and columns of data. The rows, of course, are *records,* while the columns are *fields.*

It makes sense that Access provides ways to *navigate* through a recordset. When viewing a table or query results as a datasheet, you can use the vertical and horizontal scroll bars or arrow keys to move up and down, left and right, through the datasheet view of the recordset. It's not surprising, then, that ADO Recordset objects support methods for moving through the records contained in a recordset.

The following procedure demonstrates the fundamental ADO recordset navigation methods. (As you'll see in the "Understanding DAO Objects" section, later in this chapter, DAO recordsets support identically named methods.)

```
Public Sub RecordsetNavigation()
    Dim rs As ADODB.Recordset
    Set rs = New ADODB.Recordset
    rs.ActiveConnection = CurrentProject.Connection
    rs.CursorType = adOpenStatic
    rs.Open "Select * from tblCustomers"
    Debug.Print rs!CustomerID, rs!Company
    rs.MoveNext
    Debug.Print rs!CustomerID, rs!Company
    rs.MoveLast
    Debug.Print rs!CustomerID, rs!Company
    rs.MovePrevious
```

```
        Debug.Print rs!CustomerID, rs!Company
        rs.MoveFirst
        Debug.Print rs!CustomerID, rs!Company
        rs.Close
        Set rs = Nothing
    End Sub
```

This procedure begins by opening a Recordset object populated with data from tblCus-tomers. It immediately displays the CustomerID and Company from the very first record; then it moves around the recordset a few rows at a time, displaying the CustomerID and Company for each record along the way. It ends by returning to the first record and displaying its data. The output produced by RecordsetNavigation is shown in Figure 13.12.

FIGURE 13.12

Demonstrating recordset navigation

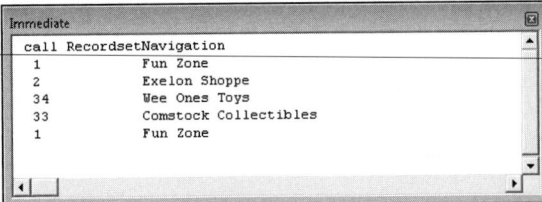

Obviously, this is a trivial example meant to demonstrate how easily ADO recordsets can be navigated. As a developer, you're free to work with any record in the recordset, moving up and down the rows as needed.

Access recordsets support the concept of a *current record pointer*. Only one record within a recordset is *current* at a time. When you make changes to a recordset or navigate through its rows, your code affects only the current record.

The RecordsetNavigation procedure also demonstrates how to reference individual fields within a record. After moving to a row, individual fields are referenced as members of the recordset. Access works on just one record at a time, so any reference to a field evaluates to the field within the current record.

Understanding CursorType

In the RecordsetNavigation procedure, notice the recordset's CursorType property. In this example, it's set to adOpenStatic. There are several settings for CursorType; adOpenStatic means to open the recordset with a static type cursor. Access uses a cursor to keep track of the current record in a recordset. A static cursor means that the data in the recordset is static, and new records can't be added to the recordset. Static cursors are ideal when the purpose of the recordset is to review data in the underlying tables and adding new records is not necessary.

Table 13.2 shows the permissible values for `CursorType`.

TABLE 13.2

CursorType Values

Value	Effect of CursorType
adOpenDynamic	A dynamic cursor supports all navigation methods, and the recordset is completely editable. New records can be added and existing records can be edited. Changes made by other users are reflected in the recordset currently in memory.
adOpenForwardOnly	The recordset is opened as a static copy of the underlying data, and new records can't be added. The recordset will also not reflect changes made to the underlying tables by other users. Most important, only the `MoveNext` and `MoveLast` methods are valid against a forward-only recordset.
adOpenKeyset	Supports full navigation and records are editable. However, records added or deleted by other users are not seen.
adOpenStatic	Opens a static recordset that does not show changes made to the underlying tables by other users. Similar to a forward-only cursor, except that all navigation methods are valid.

Each type of cursor has a specific effect on the data contained in a recordset. For example, you wouldn't want to use a forward-only cursor on data where the user expects to be able to move forward and backward through the data. A forward-only recordset is most often used for updating records as a bulk operation, such as updating area codes or tax rates in a number of records.

On the other hand, it doesn't make sense to use a dynamic cursor (`adOpenDynamic`) for simple tasks such as scanning a recordset for updates. A dynamic cursor keeps track of changes by the current user and changes in the underlying tables. A dynamic cursor is, therefore, slower and requires memory and CPU cycles than a simpler forward-only cursor.

Detecting the recordset end or beginning

The `MovePrevious` and `MoveNext` methods move the current record pointer one row through the recordset. If the pointer is at the very first or very last record, these methods move the pointer off the beginning or end of the recordset without raising an error. When you're navigating a recordset, you need to be sure the current record pointer is resting on a valid record before referencing data or executing an action on the record.

The ADO `Recordset` object support two Boolean properties, `EOF` and `BOF`, that indicate when the current record pointer is at the end or beginning (respectively) of the recordset. (*EOF* and *BOF* are acronyms for *end of file* and *beginning of file*.) `EOF` and `BOF` are both `False` when the record pointer is on a valid record. `EOF` is `True` only when the record pointer is off the end of the recordset, and `BOF` is `True` only when the pointer is off the beginning of the recordset. `EOF` and `BOF` are both `True` *only* when the recordset contains no records at all.

The Use_EOF_BOF procedure illustrates using EOF and BOF in an ADO Recordset:

```
Public Sub Use_EOF_BOF()
    Dim rs As ADODB.Recordset
    Set rs = New ADODB.Recordset
    rs.ActiveConnection = CurrentProject.Connection
    rs.CursorType = adOpenStatic
    rs.Open "SELECT * FROM tblCustomers " _
        & "WHERE State = 'NY' " _
        & "ORDER BY Company"
    Do Until rs.EOF
        Debug.Print rs!Company
        rs.MoveNext
    Loop
    rs.MoveLast
    Do Until rs.BOF
        Debug.Print rs!Company
        rs.MovePrevious
    Loop
    rs.Close
    Set rs = Nothing
End Sub
```

Previous examples in this chapter have included code like this. The main differences are checking EOF and BOF state before executing the MoveLast and MovePrevious methods. Notice that these properties change to True only *after* these methods have executed. When moving toward the end of the recordset, the EOF value is checked after MoveNext has executed (at the top of the Do Until loop).

Counting records

It's often very useful to know how many records are in a recordset before beginning operations that may take a long time. Otherwise, a user may unwisely select criteria that return too many records to handle efficiently. Fortunately, ADO Recordset objects provide a RecordCount property that tells you exactly how many records are present in the recordset:

```
Dim rs As ADODB.Recordset
Set rs = New ADODB.Recordset
rs.ActiveConnection = CurrentProject.Connection
rs.CursorType = adOpenStatic
rs.Open "SELECT * FROM tblCustomers"
Debug.Print "RecordCount: " & rs.RecordCount
```

The RecordCount property is not valid for forward-only recordsets. Notice that the CursorType is set to adOpenStatic in this code fragment. If it's set to adOpenForwardOnly, the RecordCount property is set to −1 and does not change while the recordset is in memory.

RecordCount is a convenient way to determine whether a recordset contains any records at all. The only issue with RecordCount is that, on large recordsets, RecordCount penalizes performance. The Recordset object actually counts the number of records it contains, halting execution until the count is complete.

A much faster way to detect an empty recordset is determining whether EOF and BOF are both True:

```
If rs.BOF = rs.EOF Then
    Debug.Print "No records to process"
    Exit Sub
End If
```

BOF and EOF are the same value only when the recordset contains no records. (In this case, both are True at the same time.)

Cross-Reference

ADO Recordset objects include many capabilities not covered in this chapter. Many of the remaining recordset features are covered in Chapter 25, while others are documented in various other chapters of this book. The ADO Recordset object is a powerful tool for Access developers, and deserves careful study in a variety of contexts.

Understanding DAO Objects

Data Access Objects (DAO) is the older Access data access object model. DAO has been included in Access since the very beginning, and, although not the focus of this book, it's frequently used in Access applications.

Unlike ADO, DAO objects are arranged in a hierarchical fashion. Certain objects are subordinate to other objects, and they can't exist without an instance of the superior object. The father of all DAO objects is DBEngine. DBEngine is at the head of the DAO family tree, and all other objects are descendants of DBEngine (see Figure 13.13).

Each of the most frequently used DAO objects is described later in this section.

Generally speaking, the DAO hierarchy closely follows the arrangement of Access database objects. For example, an Access table (which is a TableDef object) contains fields (each of which is a Field object). A field has a set of properties you use to specify the details of its data type, the default value, validation rules, and so on.

Note

For clarity's sake, the set of properties associated with each DAO object is left out of Figure 13.13. But, you can safely assume that every object in Figure 13.13 includes an attached set of property objects.

FIGURE 13.13

The DAO object model

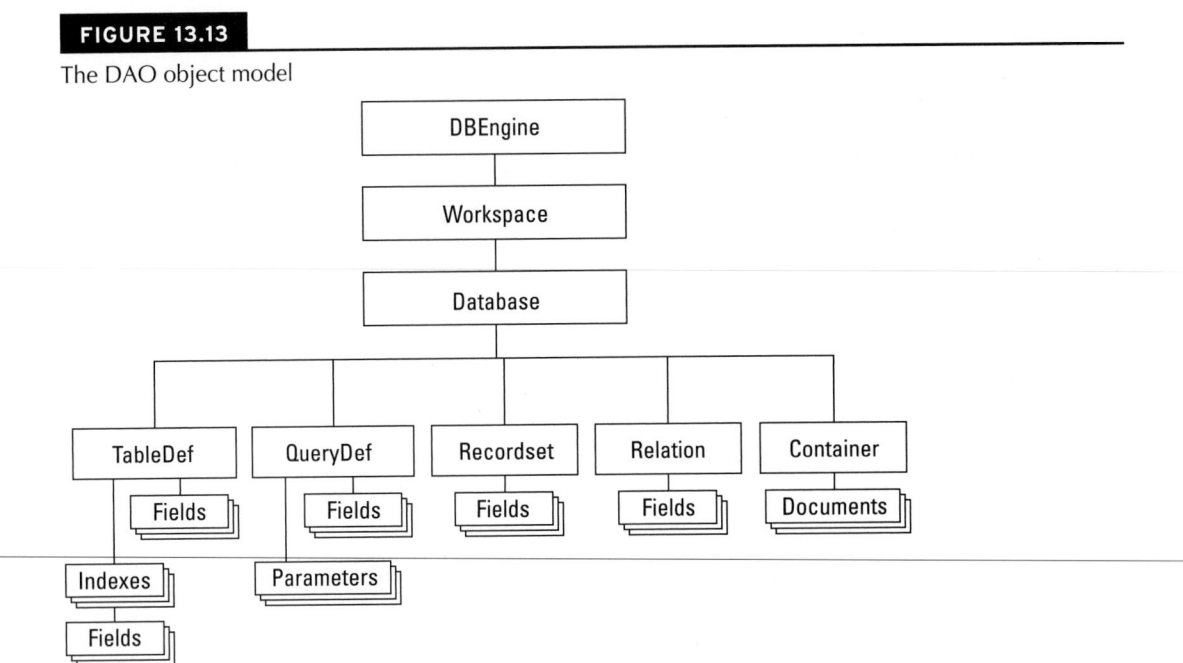

Each DAO object also has a collection of properties appropriate for its object type. A TableDef object may have some properties in common with a QueryDef, but each object has properties that are unique to its object type. A QueryDef has a Name property, as does a TableDef, but a QueryDef has a SQL property and a TableDef cannot. The same is true of methods. Each DAO object has actions that only it can perform. For example, an action query defined by a QueryDef has an Execute method but a TableDef does not. Learning which properties and methods apply to each DAO object is perhaps the biggest challenge facing Access developers.

Note

As you read through the following sections, you'll notice that details have been omitted from the discussions of each type of data access object. Because of the numerous properties and methods associated with each DAO object, and the many ways these objects are used in Access applications, it's not possible to present a detailed description of the entire DAO object model in a single chapter. Instead, examples of specific ways to use DAO (and ADO) are given throughout this book. Please refer to the index to find the chapters and sections in this book discussing particular data access objects.

Note

Microsoft Access 2007 introduced ACE (Microsoft Access Engine), a new database engine for the Microsoft Office products. ACE is the reason why Access 2007 and 2010 support advanced features such as attachment and multi-value fields. Because of the new data types, ACE required an updated version of DAO (called ACEDAO) to support the new capabilities. The biggest differences between DAO and ACEDAO is the introduction of the `Recordset2` and `Field2` objects, plus new properties and methods required to support the features introduced with Access 2007. Access 2010 continues to support DAO 3.6, the most recent version of "traditional" DAO. Although this section describes traditional DAO, all the explanations and examples in this section apply equally to ACEDAO as well. The Access 2010 `.mdb` format only supports DAO 3.6, and not ACEDAO.

The DAO DBEngine object

The `DBEngine` object, which is the object representing the Jet engine, is at the very top of the DAO hierarchy. It isn't a member of any collection, and all collections are children of `DBEngine`. There is only one instance of this object, and it's one of the few data access objects that you can't create yourself. You open the `DBEngine` object when you start Access and issue a DAO operation. It has very few properties and methods. For property changes to take effect, they must be issued *before* a data access object operation has been performed; otherwise, you'll receive an error. Because `DBEngine` is at the top of the hierarchy, you almost always begin a DAO code sequence with `DBEngine`.

The DAO Workspace object

A `Workspace` object represents an open, active session for each user working with Access. All databases are opened within a workspace, either as a default database session or one that has been created using the `CreateWorkspace` method of the `DBEngine` object.

Tip

If you choose to use transaction tracking (`BeginTrans...EndTrans`) within your application, these statements include all recordsets opened within the current workspace. If you don't want to use transactions with a particular recordset, create a new workspace and open the recordset within the new `Workspace` object.

Security is also implemented from `Workspace` objects (but, only for the `.mdb` file format). The security methods available to `Workspace` objects allow you to create your own security interfaces and routines. If necessary, you can create users or groups using the `CreateUser` or `CreateGroup` methods of the `Workspace` object.

Note

User-level security is not discussed in this book. Refer to the Access 2007 Bible for a discussion of user-level security as applied to Access 2007 and 2010.

The DAO Database object

A `Database` object represents a data source and is analogous to an ADO `Connection` object. Access is able to directly open a number of different database formats. When working directly with the ACE or Jet database engines, a database could be any number of sources: a dBASE file, a FoxPro file, another .mdb, or even an ODBC data source. The distinguishing feature is how you set your database object variables.

The following code refers to the currently open Microsoft Access database:

```
Dim db As DAO.Database
Set db = CurrentDb
```

`CurrentDb` is a method of the Access `Application` object, which represents the entire Access environment and all its objects. `CurrentDb` is a fast, easy way to open the database that the user is currently working with.

It's also possible to open an Access database *outside* of the current database:

```
Dim db As DAO.Database
Set db = OpenDatabase("C:\Northwind.mdb")
```

Notice that the `OpenDatabase` method accepts the path to an existing .mdb or .accdb file. The `OpenDatabase` method may fail, depending on whether the external Access database is available, or whether its current state prevents opening from another Access application.

As with ADO objects, be sure to prefix DAO object type declarations with DAO so that Access is clear as to which library to use when setting up the object.

Note
ACEDAO objects use DAO as the prefix, just as DAO 3.6 objects do.

The DAO TableDef object

The DAO `TableDef` object represents a table in an Access database. The table may be local or linked to the current database. The following procedure (which is included in the Chapter13. accdb example database) creates a new table named MyTempTable, adds three text fields to it, and adds the table to the current database's `TableDefs` collection.

```
Public Sub CreateNewTableDef()
    Dim db As DAO.Database
    Dim tdfNew As DAO.TableDef
    ' The next statement instructs Access
    ' to ignore errors that may occur if
    ' the table does not already exist:
    On Error Resume Next
    'Delete the new table if it exists:
    db.TableDefs.Delete "MyTempTable"
    ' Return to default error handling:
```

```
        On Error GoTo 0
        Set db = CurrentDb
        Set tdfNew = db.CreateTableDef("MyTempTable")
        With tdfNew
            ' Create fields and append them to the tdfNew:
            .Fields.Append .CreateField("FirstName", dbText)
            .Fields.Append .CreateField("LastName", dbText)
            .Fields.Append .CreateField("Phone", dbText)
        End With
        ' Append the new TableDef object to the current database:
        db.TableDefs.Append tdfNew
        db.Close
    End Sub
```

Running this code in the Chapter13.accdb database creates a new table named
MyTempTable, a permanent addition to the database. Notice that the CreateNewTableDef
procedure deletes this table if it exists, before creating it as a new TableDef. Access won't be able
to append the new TableDef object to its TableDefs collection if a table with the same name
already exists in the database.

Cross-Reference

The CreateNewTableDef procedure includes two statements that control how Access handles errors in this
code. Chapter 23 discusses the VBA error handling statements, and explains why you'd use On Error Resume
Next and On Error GoTo 0 in a procedure such as this.

TableDef objects are stored in the TableDefs collection. The following procedure displays the
names of all TableDef objects (including hidden and system tables) in the current database:

```
    Public Sub DisplayAllTableDefs()
        Dim db As DAO.Database
        Dim tdf As DAO.TableDef
        Set db = CurrentDb
        With db
          Debug.Print .TableDefs.Count _
              & " TableDefs in " & .Name
          For Each tdf In .TableDefs
             Debug.Print "  " & tdf.Name
          Next tdf
        End With
    End Sub
```

The DAO QueryDef object

A QueryDef object represents a saved query in an Access database. Using VBA code, you can
point a QueryDef object variable at an existing query (or, create a new query), and change the
query's SQL statement, populate parameters used by the query, and execute the query. The query
could be a select query that returns a recordset, or an action query that modifies code in the tables
underlying the query.

Creating a `QueryDef` in code is similar to creating a `TableDef` except that the new `QueryDef` doesn't have to be explicitly appended to the database's `QueryDefs` collection:

```
Public Sub CreateNewQueryDef()
    Dim db As DAO.Database
    Dim qdf As DAO.QueryDef
    Set db = CurrentDb
    Set qdf = db.CreateQueryDef("MyQueryDef", _
        "SELECT * FROM tblCustomers")
    db.Close
End Sub
```

In fact, as soon at the `CreateQueryDef` method is executed, Access adds the new `QueryDef` to the database. You must explicitly delete the `QueryDef` if you don't want it to appear in the Navigation Pane:

```
CurrentDb.TableDefs.Delete "QueryDefName"
```

You could, if desired, create a `QueryDef` without a name. In this case, the new `QueryDef` is not saved and does not show up in the Navigation Pane. This technique might be useful, for instance, if you're filling a combo box or list box with data and you don't want to create a permanent `QueryDef` because the criteria changes every time the code is executed.

One time-honored advanced Access technique is dynamically changing an existing `QueryDef` object's SQL statement. Once the SQL property has been changed, the query returns the recordset specified by the new SQL statement:

```
Public Sub ChangeQueryDefSQL()
    Dim qdf As DAO.QueryDef
    Set qdf = CurrentDb.QueryDefs("MyQueryDef")
    qdf.SQL = "SELECT * FROM tblProducts"
End Sub
```

Notice that the `ChangeQueryDefSQL` procedure uses `CurrentDb` instead of declaring and instantiating a `Database` object. Using `CurrentDb` in this fashion is easier than writing the more formal method; it also eliminates the need to close the `Database` object at the end of the procedure.

It's very easy to populate a DAO `Recordset` object directly from a `QueryDef` (see the next section for more on the `Recordset` object). Notice how much simpler this procedure is than the equivalent ADO process:

```
Public Function GetRecordset() As DAO.Recordset
    Dim rs As DAO.Recordset
    Dim qdf As DAO.QueryDef
    Set qdf = CurrentDb.QueryDefs("MyQueryDef")
    ' Open Recordset with QueryDef:
    Set rs = qdf.OpenRecordset(dbOpenSnapshot)
    rs.MoveLast
```

```
        Debug.Print "Number of records: " & rs.RecordCount
        Set GetRecordset = rs
        rs.Close
    End Sub
```

Notice that the locally declared `Recordset` object (`rs`) is assigned to the function just before the function ends. This is one way for a procedure to build recordsets without having to duplicate the code setting up the recordset and running the `QueryDef` every place a recordset is needed by an application.

The DAO Recordset object

`Recordset` objects are declared and set to a particular table, query, or ODBC data source within your application. Using a `Recordset` object's methods you can update, edit, and delete records, move forward and backward within the recordset, or locate specific records using the `Find` and `Seek` methods.

A `Recordset` object can be a `Table`, a `Dynaset`, or a `Snapshot` type; the type you specify depends on your needs. For example, suppose you only wanted to scan through a table to search for a particular value of a field. A `Snapshot`, which is a read-only view of your data, would probably be a good choice. Or maybe you'd like to query a table on the fly, but the query depends on user input. In this case, you might build a SQL statement based on an input value, and use the SQL statement to build a `Dynaset`-type recordset.

You specify the type of recordset using the `dbOpenTable`, `dbOpenDynaset`, and `dbOpen-Snapshot` constants as arguments of the `OpenRecordset` method of a `Database` object. The following example shows how to open a `Snapshot`-type recordset based on a SQL string.

```
    Dim db As DAO.Database
    Dim rs As DAO.Recordset
    Dim strSQL As String
    strSQL = "SELECT * FROM tblCustomers"
    Set db = CurrentDb
    Set rs = db.OpenRecordset(strSQL, dbOpenSnapshot)
```

If you don't explicitly choose a type of `Recordset`, Access uses what it believes to be the most efficient method. You can't open an ODBC data source using the `dbOpenTable` option. Instead, you must use the `dbOpenDynaset` and `dbOpenSnapshot` constants.

As you'll see in many different places in this book, there are a number of different ways to open DAO recordsets. The following procedure illustrates just one of these techniques. In this particular example, the recordset is created directly against `tblCustomers`, and each field in every row in the table is displayed in the debug window (the `Field` object and `Fields` collection are discussed in the next section):

```
Public Sub OpenDAORecordset1()
    Dim db As Database
    Dim rs As Recordset
    Dim i As Long
    Set db = CurrentDb
    'Open recordset directly against a table:
    Set rs = db.OpenRecordset("tblCustomers")
    Do While Not rs.EOF
        For i = 0 To rs.Fields.Count - 1
            Debug.Print rs.Fields(i).Name _
                & " " & rs.Fields(i).Value
        Next i
        Debug.Print
        rs.MoveNext
    Loop
    rs.Close
    Set rs = Nothing
    db.Close
End Sub
```

The DAO Field objects (recordsets)

Field objects within recordsets represent a column of data from a table or returned by a query. Recordset Field objects differ from their TableDef and QueryDef counterparts in that they actually contain a data value. Each TableDef object contains a Fields collection containing the data held within the table represented by the TableDef.

You'll see many, many references to DAO (and ADO) fields in this book, so there isn't much to discuss at this point. In the meantime, it's enough to know that the DAO Field object supports many more properties than are visible in the Access Table Designer. The Chapter13.accdb example database includes the following procedure that enumerates all the "valid" properties of the Company field in tblCustomers:

```
Public Sub DisplayFieldProperties()
    Dim db As DAO.Database
    Dim tdf As DAO.TableDef
    Dim fld As DAO.Field
    Dim prop As DAO.Property
    Set db = CurrentDb
    Set tdf = db.TableDefs("tblCustomers")
    Set fld = tdf.Fields("Company")
    Debug.Print "Properties in Company field:"
    On Error Resume Next
    For Each prop In fld.Properties
        On Error Resume Next
        Debug.Print "  " & prop.Name & " = " & prop.Value
        On Error GoTo 0
    Next prop
    db.Close
End Sub
```

Deciding between ADO and DAO

Given the obvious similarities between ADO and DAO, you might be confused as to which syntax to choose for new Access applications. (I'm assuming that existing Access application already specify either ADO or DAO.) After all, Microsoft continues to support ADO and DAO, and it has introduced ACEDAO, an Access 2007/2010-specific version of DAO. So, which is best for *your* applications?

As with everything else in database development, the answer depends on your specific situation. In spite of its more complex object model, DAO is somewhat faster and easier for certain tasks. Because DAO doesn't require a connection string, DAO code tends to be simple and easy to write. Very often a successful DAO procedure can be written strictly from memory, without having to look up the syntax in a book or online. DAO is also somewhat faster than ADO, especially when working with small data sets.

ADO, on the other hand, excels when connecting to external databases, whether the data source is another Access application or a SQL Server database. Depending on the referenced provider, ADO connections include properties that tell you the connection's state (open, connecting, disconnected, and so on). This information can be extremely valuable in some situations.

Tip

There is no problem including both ADO and DAO code in the same application — but you cannot use DAO and ACEDAO in the same project. Just be sure to prefix object references with DAO (or ACEDAO), or ADODB, depending on the object syntax you're using.

In many cases, the decision to use DAO or ADO depends on the example code you might find to use in your application. There are, literally, thousands of VBA code examples available using either DAO or ADO. From a purely technical standpoint, there is no compelling reason to use either DAO or ADO. The only exception is when working with SQL Server data. Because Microsoft provides a native ADO provider for SQL Server, ADO is clearly the better choice when working with SQL Server. Once a connection is established to the SQL Server database, the ADO Command object is the ideal way to invoke a stored procedure or run an ad hoc query against SQL Server tables. In a SQL Server context, ADO will almost always be faster and more efficient than DAO because DAO's access to SQL Server is limited to using an OLEDB data source pointing to the SQL Server database.

Cross-Reference

OLEDB is covered in Chapter 37.

In case you're wondering, ACEDAO is the default data access library in Access 2010. Every new Access 2010 database is created with a reference set to the Microsoft Office 14.0 Access Database Engine Object Library (ACEDAO) already in place. If you want to use ADO in your Access 2010 applications, you'll have to manually add a reference to the Microsoft ActiveX Data Objects 6.0 Library.

Not every property associated with a Field object is *valid* at a particular time. Some properties are only set after the field contains data, or when the field is involved in an index. For example, the Value property of the Field object cannot be referenced directly from code. Instead, you set or get the value of a field only through the field's membership in a Recordset object. The On Error Resume Next statement allows this code to run, in spite of invalid properties. The errors that may occur when invalid properties are referenced by this code are ignored.

Writing VBA Code to Update a Table

Updating data in a table by using a form is easy. You simply place controls on the form for the fields of the table that you want to update. For example, Figure 13.14 shows frmSales. The controls on frmSales update data in tblSales, tblSalesLineitems, and tblSalesPayments. because these fields are directly bound to controls on frmSales.

Using a form to update data in tables

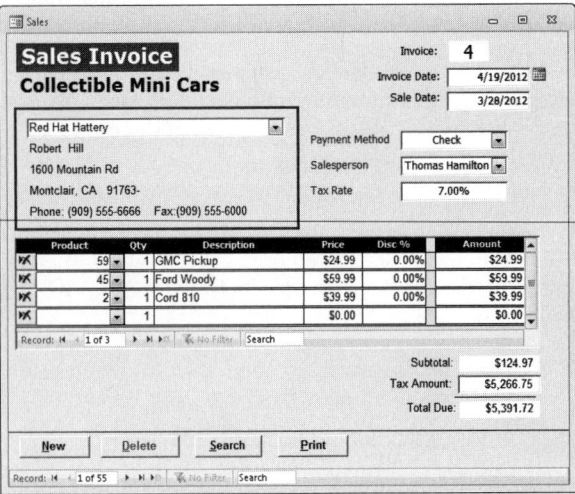

Sometimes, however, you want to update a field in a table that isn't displayed on the form. When information is entered in frmSales, for example, the field for the last sales date (LastSalesDate) in tblCustomers should be updated to reflect the most recent date on which the contact purchased a product. When you enter a new sale, the value for the LastSalesDate field is the value of the txtSaleDate control on frmSales.

Because the contact's last sales date refers to the txtSaleDate control on frmSales, you don't want the user to have to enter it twice. Theoretically, you could place the LastSalesDate field as a calculated field that is updated after the user enters the Sale Date, but displaying this field would be confusing and is irrelevant to the items for the current sale.

The best way to handle updating the LastSalesDate field in tblCustomers is to use a VBA procedure. You can use VBA code to update individual fields in a record, add new records, or delete records.

Updating fields in a record using ADO

Use the `AfterUpdate` event procedure to update `LastSalesDate` (see Figure 13.15). This procedure uses ADO syntax to operate directly on `tblCustomers`.

Using ADO to update a table

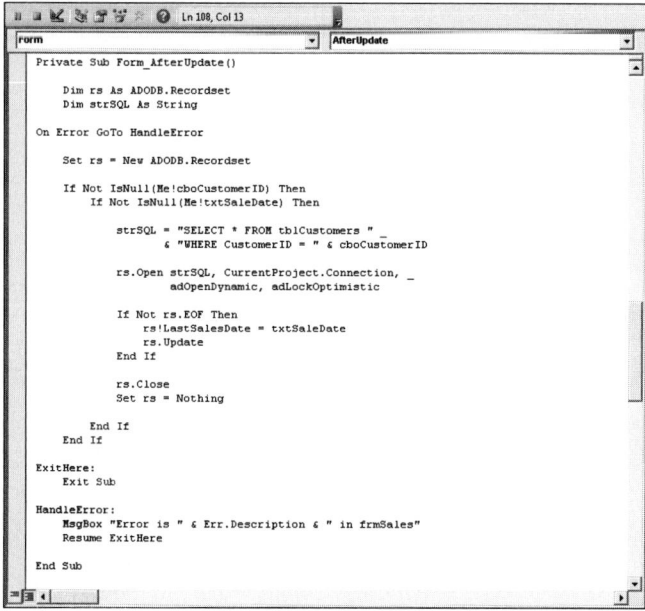

```
Private Sub Form_AfterUpdate()

    Dim rs As ADODB.Recordset
    Dim strSQL As String

On Error GoTo HandleError

    Set rs = New ADODB.Recordset

    If Not IsNull(Me!cboCustomerID) Then
        If Not IsNull(Me!txtSaleDate) Then

            strSQL = "SELECT * FROM tblCustomers " _
                & "WHERE CustomerID = " & cboCustomerID

            rs.Open strSQL, CurrentProject.Connection, _
                adOpenDynamic, adLockOptimistic

            If Not rs.EOF Then
                rs!LastSalesDate = txtSaleDate
                rs.Update
            End If

            rs.Close
            Set rs = Nothing

        End If
    End If

ExitHere:
    Exit Sub

HandleError:
    MsgBox "Error is " & Err.Description & " in frmSales"
    Resume ExitHere

End Sub
```

The programming syntax used to access and manipulate the data in an Access database is ADO. ADO defines a number of different objects, each with a set of properties and methods for performing a variety of data-oriented operations.

ADO is not a programming language. Instead, it's a VBA syntax specifically designed for data access. Syntax simply refers to the words and phrases you use in your VBA code to accomplish a particular task.

ADO is a versatile means of accessing data from various locations. The Collectible Mini Cars examples you've seen so far show you how to use Access to update data in a local Access database. All tables, queries, forms, and reports are stored in a single Access database file located either in a folder on your desktop or on a file server. But Access, as a generic database development tool, can interact with all kinds of databases. You can develop forms and reports in one Access database that get their data from another Access database that may be on your local desktop or on a remote file server. You can even link to non-Access server databases, like Oracle and SQL Server, just as easily as you can link to an Access database.

As a data access interface, ADO allows you to write programs to manipulate data in local or remote databases. Using ADO, you can perform database functions including querying, updating, data-type conversion, indexing, locking, validation, and transaction management.

Here is a fragment of a procedure showing how to use the ADO `Recordset` object to open a table:

```
Dim rs As ADODB.Recordset
Set rs = New ADODB.Recordset
rs.ActiveConnection = CurrentProject.Connection
rs.Source = "tblCustomers"
rs.CursorType = adOpenDynamic
rs.LockType = adLockOptimistic
rs.Open
```

The ADO `Recordset` object provides the `Open` method to retrieve data from a table or query. A recordset is simply a set of records from a database table or the set of records returned by a query.

The `Open` method has four parameters:

- `Source`: The data source to open. `Source` can be the name of a table (as in this example), the name of a query, or a SQL statement that retrieves records. When referencing a table, the table can be a local or linked table.

- `ActiveConnection`: Refers to a connection to a database. A connection is a communication line into the database. `CurrentProject.Connection` refers to the current Access database.

- `CursorType`: ADO supports a number of different cursor types. A *cursor* is a pointer, or set of pointers, to records. Think of a cursor the way ADO keeps track of records. Depending on the property settings used to retrieve data, ADO cursors can move only *forward* through records (`adOpenForwardOnly`), or permit forward and backward movement (`adOpenDynamic`). A dynamic cursor (`adOpenDynamic`) allows movement in both directions, while `adOpenForwardOnly` permits only forward movement. (The `CursorType` property is explained in detail in the "Understanding `CursorType`" section, earlier in this chapter.)

- `LockType`: Determines how ADO locks records when updating. `adLockOptimistic` allows other users to work with a record that is locked by the ADO code, while `adLock-Pessimistic` completely locks other users out of the record while changes are made to the record's data.

This same ADO statement can be rewritten in a somewhat more condensed fashion:

```
Dim rs As ADODB.Recordset
Set rs = New ADODB.Recordset
rs.Open "tblCustomers", CurrentProject.Connection, _
  adOpenDynamic, adLockOptimistic
```

In this example, the recordset properties are set as part of the Open statement. Either syntax is correct; it's completely the choice of the developer. Also, because we are directly accessing the table, there is no way to specify an ORDER BY for the data. The data is likely to be returned in an unpredictable order.

Here is another example extracting a single record, based on a CustomerID:

```
Dim rs As ADODB.Recordset
Set rs = New ADODB.Recordset
rs.ActiveConnection = CurrentProject.Connection
rs.Source = _
   "SELECT * FROM tblCustomers WHERE CustomerID = 17"
rs.CursorType = adOpenDynamic
rs.LockType = adLockOptimistic
rs.Open
```

Notice that, in Figure 13.15 rather than specifying a table, the Source property is a SQL SELECT statement. The SQL statement used to extract records returns a single record, based on the CustomerID. In this case, because the LockType property is set to adLockOptimistic, the data in the record can be changed by the user.

Both CursorType and LockType are optional. If you don't specify a CursorType or LockType, ADO creates the recordset as an adOpenForwardOnly/adLockReadOnly type recordset by default. This type of recordset is not updatable. If you need to make changes to the data in the recordset, you need an understanding of the various CursorType and LockType combinations and how they affect the capabilities of a recordset.

When you use ActiveX Data objects, you interact with data almost entirely through Recordset objects. Recordsets are composed of rows containing fields, just like database tables. Once a recordset has been opened, you can begin working with the values in its rows and fields.

You've seen recordsets many times in this book. The records returned by a query are delivered as a recordset. Actually, when you open an Access table, Access arranges the table's records as a recordset, and presents it in Datasheet view. You never really "see" an Access table — you see only a representation of the table's data as a recordset displayed in Datasheet view.

When you open an updatable recordset — by using the adOpenDynamic or adOpenKeySet cursor type, and specifying the adLockOptimistic lock type — the recordset opens in edit mode.

One major difference between a table open in Datasheet view and an ADO recordset is that a recordset provides no visual representation of the data it contains. A datasheet provides you with rows and columns of data, and even includes column headings so you know the names of the fields in the underlying table.

An ADO (or DAO, for that matter) recordset exists only in memory. There is no easy way to visualize the data in a recordset. As a developer you must always be aware of the field names, row count, and other data attributes that are important to your application.

When working with datasheets and recordsets only one record is active. In a datasheet the active record is indicated by a color difference in the row. Recordsets have no such visual aid, so you must always be aware of which record is current in a recordset.

Fortunately, both ADO and DAO provide a number of ways to keep track of records in a recordset, and different techniques for moving around within a recordset. It's also quite easy to learn the field names in a recordset and to modify the data within each field.

This chapter, and many of the chapters that follow, demonstrate many of the data management techniques available through the VBA language. As an Access developer, you'll almost certainly learn new and more effective ways to work with data every time you work on an Access application.

Before you change data in any of the recordset's fields, however, you need to make sure that you're in the record you want to edit. When a recordset opens, the current record is the first record in the set. If the recordset contains no records, the recordset's EOF property is `True`.

Caution

A runtime error occurs if you try to manipulate data in a recordset that contains no records. Be sure to check the value of the EOF property immediately after opening a recordset:

```
Set rs = new ADODB.Recordset
rs.Open "tblCustomers".... etc.
If rs.EOF <> True Then
     'Okay to process records
End If
```

Errors will occur if the code moves past either EOF (MoveNext) or BOF (MovePrevious). Your code should always check the EOF and BOF property after executing a move method.

To update a field in the current record of the recordset, in an ADO recordset, you simply assign a new value to the field. When using DAO, you must execute the `Recordset` object's `Edit` method before assigning a new value. In the `Form_AfterUpdate` procedure in Figure 13.15, you assign the value of `txtSaleDate` on the `frmSales` form to the recordset's `LastSaleDate` field.

After you change the record, use the recordset's `Update` method to commit the record to the database. The `Update` method copies the data from the memory buffer to the recordset, overwriting the original record. The entire record is replaced, not just the updated field(s). Other records in the recordset, of course, are not affected by the update.

Changes to an ADO recordset are automatically saved when you move to another record or close the recordset. In addition, the edited record is also saved if you close a recordset or end the procedure that declares the recordset or the parent database. However, you should use the `Update` method for better code readability and maintainability.

Use the record's `CancelUpdate` method to cancel pending changes to an ADO recordset. If it's important to undo changes to a record, you must issue the `CancelUpdate` method before moving to another record in an ADO recordset because moving off of a record commits the change and an undo is no longer available.

The `rsCustomers.Close` statement near the end of the `Form_AfterUpdate` procedure closes the recordset. Closing recordsets when you're done with them is good practice. In Figure 13.15, notice also that the `Recordset` object is explicitly set to nothing (`Set rsCustomers = Nothing`) to clear the recordset from memory. Omitting this important step can lead to "memory leaks" because ADO objects tend to persist in memory unless they're explicitly set to `Nothing` and discarded.

Updating a calculated control

In the `frmSales` example, the `txt.TaxAmount` control displays the tax to collect at the time of the sale. The tax amount's value is not a simple calculation. The tax amount is determined by the following items:

- The sum of the item amounts purchased that are taxable
- The customer's tax rate in effect on the sale date
- The value in `txtOtherAmount` and whether the `txtOtherAmount` is a taxable item

When the user changes information for the current sale, any one or all three of these factors can change the tax amount. The tax amount must be recalculated whenever any of the following events occur in the form:

- Adding or updating a line item
- Deleting a line item
- Changing the buyer to another customer
- Changing `txtTaxLocation`
- Changing `txtOtherAmount`

You use VBA procedures to recalculate the tax amount when any of these events occurs.

Recalculating a control when updating or adding a record

Figure 13.16 shows the code for adding or updating a line item on `frmSales`.

FIGURE 13.16

Recalculating a field after a form is updated

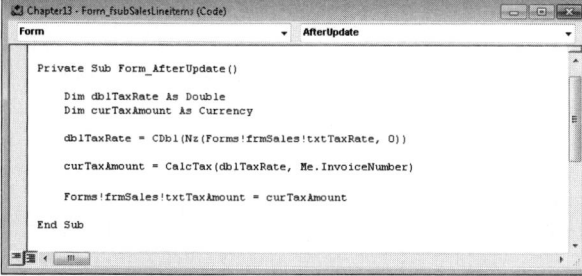

A single event can handle recalculating the tax amount when new line items are added or when a line item is changed — when an item's price or quantity is changed, for example. In any case, you can use the subform's AfterUpdate event to update the sales tax. AfterUpdate occurs when a new record is entered or when any value is changed for an existing record.

The Form_AfterUpdate procedure for fsubSalesLineItems executes when a line item is added to the subform, or when any information is changed in a line item. The Form_ AfterUpdate procedure recalculates the tax amount control (txtTaxAmount) on frmSales. The dblTaxRate variable holds the customer's tax rate (the value of txtTaxRate on frm- Sales) and curTaxAmount stores the value returned by the CalcTax() function. CalcTax() calculates the actual tax amount. When the After_Update procedure calls CalcTax(), it passes two parameters: the value of dblTaxRate and the current line item's invoice number (Me. InvoiceNumber). Figure 13.17 shows the CalcTax() function.

FIGURE 13.17

CalcTax() uses ADO to determine sales tax.

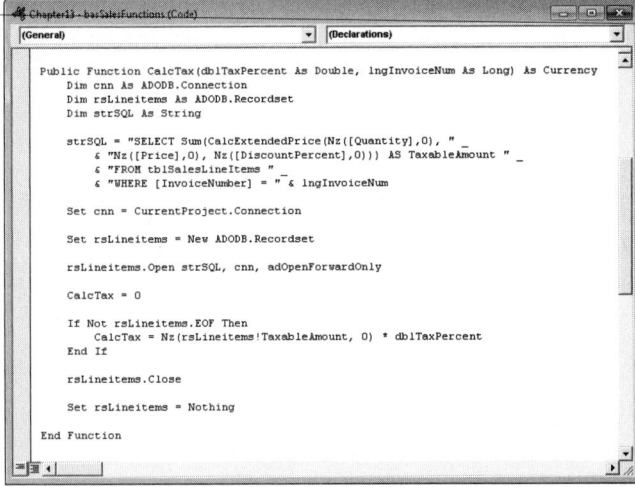

CalcTax() uses ADO syntax to create a recordset that sums the quantities and prices for the taxable items in tblSalesLineItems for the current sale. The function receives two parameters: the tax rate (dblTaxPercent) and the invoice number (lngInvoiceNum). The function's return value is initially set to 0 (zero) at the top of the function. The ADO code checks to see if the recordset returned a record. If the recordset is at the end of the field (EOF), the recordset did not find any line items for the current sale — and CalcTax remains set to 0. If the recordset does contain a record, the return value for CalcTax is set to the recordset's TaxableAmount field times the tax rate (dblTaxPercent).

At the end of the procedure, `txtTaxAmount` is set to the `curTaxAmount` value.

When the Buyer, Tax Location, or Tax Rate controls are changed in `frmSales`, you use the `AfterUpdate` event for the individual control to recalculate the tax amount. Figure 13.18 shows the code for the `txtTaxRate_AfterUpdate` event.

FIGURE 13.18

Recalculating a control after a control is updated

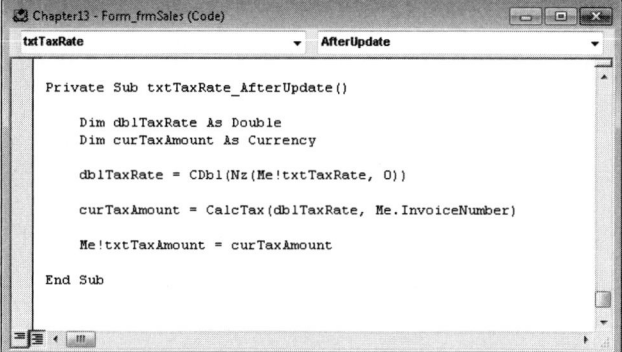

The logic implemented in `txtTaxRate_AfterUpdate` is identical to the logic in `fsubSales-LineItems_AfterUpdate`. In fact, you can use the same code for the Buyer and Tax Location controls as well. The only difference between the code in Figure 13.16 and the code in Figure 13.18 is that the procedure in Figure 13.16 runs whenever a change occurs in the sales line items subform, while the code in Figure 13.18 runs whenever a change is made to `txtTaxRate` on the main form.

Checking the status of a record deletion

Use the form's `AfterDelConfirm` event to recalculate the `txtTaxAmount` control when deleting a line item. The form's `AfterDelConfirm` event (shown in Figure 13.19) is similar to the code for the subform's `AfterUpdate` event. Notice however, that `txtTaxAmount` on the main sales form is set by this procedure, even though this code runs in `fsubSalesLineItems` subform embedded on `frmSales`.

Access always confirms deletions initiated by the user. Access displays a message box asking the user to confirm the deletion. If the user affirms the deletion, the current record is removed from the form's recordset and temporarily stored in memory so that the deletion can be undone if necessary. The `AfterDelConfirm` event occurs after the user confirms or cancels the deletion. If the `BeforeDelConfirm` event isn't canceled, the `AfterDelConfirm` event occurs after the delete confirmation dialog box is displayed. The `AfterDelConfirm` event occurs even if the `BeforeDelConfirm` event is canceled.

FIGURE 13.19

Recalculating a control after a record is deleted

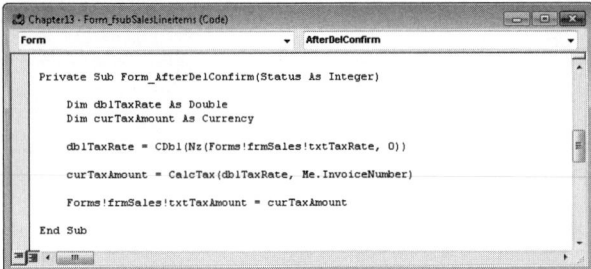

The `AfterDelConfirm` event procedure returns status information about the deletion. Table 13.3 describes the deletion status values.

TABLE 13.3

Deletion Status Values

Status value	Description
acDeleteOK	Deletion occurred normally
acDeleteCancel	Deletion canceled programmatically
acDeleteUserCancel	User canceled deletion

The `Status` argument for the `AfterDelConfirm` event procedure can be set to any of these values within the procedure. For example, if the code in the `AfterDelConfirm` event procedure determines that deleting the record may cause problems in the application, the `Status` argument should be set to `acDeleteCancel`:

```
If <Condition_Indicates_a_Problem> Then
  Status = acDeleteCancel
  Exit Sub
Else
  Status = acDeleteOK
End If
```

The `Status` argument is provided to enable your VBA code to override the user's decision to delete a record if conditions warrant such an override. In the case that `Status` is set to `acDeleteCancel`, the copy of the record stored in the temporary buffer is restored to the recordset, and the delete process is terminated. If, on the other hand, `Status` is set to `acDeleteOK`, the deletion proceeds and the temporary buffer is cleared after the user moves to another record in the recordset.

Adding a new record

You can use ADO to add a record to a table just as easily as updating a record. Use the AddNew method to add a new record to a table. The following shows an ADO procedure for adding a new customer to tblCustomers:

```
Private Sub AddNewCustomer(FName As String, LName As String)
    Dim rs As ADODB.Recordset
    Set rs = New ADODB.Recordset
    rs.Open "tblCustomers", CurrentProject.Connection, _
        adOpenDynamic, adLockOptimistic
    With rs
        .AddNew   'Add new record
        'Add data:
        ![LastName] = LName
        ![LastName] = FName
        .Update   'Commit changes
    End With
    rs.Close
    Set rs = Nothing
End Sub
```

As you see in this example, using the AddNew method is similar to using ADO to edit recordset data. AddNew creates a buffer for a new record. After executing AddNew, you assign values to fields in the new record. The Update method adds the new record to the end of the recordset, and then to the underlying table.

Deleting a record

To remove a record from a table, you use the ADO method Delete. The following code shows an ADO procedure for deleting a record from tblCustomers.

```
Private Sub DeleteContact(CustomerID As Long)
    Dim rs As ADODB.Recordset
    Dim strSQL as string
    Set rs = New ADODB.Recordset
    'Select single record from tblCustomers:
    strSQL = "SELECT * FROM tblCustomers " _
        & "WHERE [CustomerID] = " & CustomerID
    rs.Open strSQL, CurrentProject.Connection, _
        adOpenDynamic, adLockOptimistic
    With rs
        If not .EOF Then
            .Delete   'Delete the record
        End If
    End With
    rs.Close
    Set rs = Nothing
End Sub
```

Note

Notice that you don't follow the `Delete` method with `Update`. As soon as the `Delete` method executes, the record is permanently removed from the recordset.

Deleting records using ADO doesn't trigger the deletion confirmation dialog box. Generally speaking, changes made to data with ADO code are not confirmed because confirmation would interrupt the user's workflow. This means that, as the developer, you're responsible for making sure that deletions are appropriate before proceeding. Once the record is deleted, there is no way to undo the change to the underlying table.

Deleting related records in multiple tables

When you write ADO code to delete records, you need to be aware of the application's relationships. The table containing the record that you're deleting may be participating in a one-to-many relationship with another table.

Take a look at the relationships diagram (see Figure 13.20) for the tables used in the `frmSales` example. `tblSales` has two dependent tables associated with it: `tblSalesLineItems` and `tblSalesPayments`.

Examining the tables of a one-to-many relationship

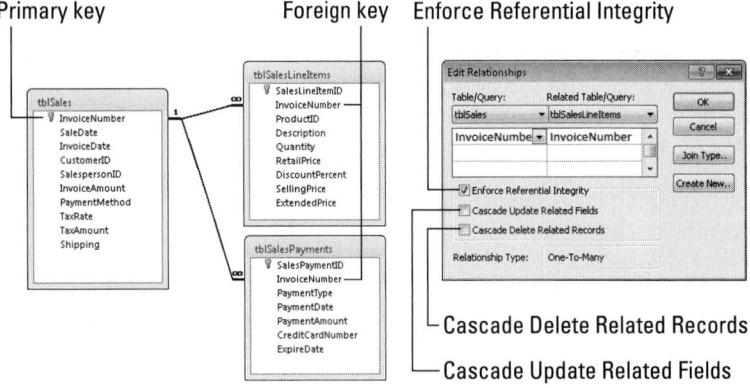

The Edit Relationships dialog box shows how the relationship is set up between `tblSales` and `tblSalesLineItems`. The relationship type is a one-to-many (1:M) and referential integrity is enforced. A one-to-many relationship means that each record in the parent table (`tblSales`) may have one or more records in the child table (`tblSalesLineItems`). Each record in the parent table must be unique — you can't have two sales records with exactly the same `InvoiceNumber`, `SalesDate`, and other information.

In a one-to-many relationship each child record (in tblSalesLineItems) *must* be related to one record (and, *only* one record) in the parent table (tblSales). But, each sales record in tbl-Sales may be related to more than one record in tblSalesLineItem.

When you enforce referential integrity on a one-to-many relationship, you're telling Access that a record in tblSales *can't* be deleted if records with the same invoice number value exist in tbl-SalesLineItems. If Access encounters a delete request that violates referential integrity, Access displays an error message and the delete will be canceled, unless cascading deletes have been enabled un the Edit Relationships dialog box (refer to Figure 13.20).

As you'll recall from Chapter 3, you have the option of setting Cascade Update Related Fields and Cascade Delete Related Fields in the Edit Relationships dialog box. By default, these options are not enabled — and for good reason. If cascading deletes is turned on, when you use VBA code to delete a sales record, all the related records in tblSalesLineItems and tblSalesPayments are also deleted. Depending on the situation, this may or may not be a good thing. In the case of a canceled sales order, there is probably no harm done by deleting the unsold sales line items. However, when working on a canceled order where payment has been made, deleting the customer's payment history may be an issue. Surely, they'll expect a refund of payments made on the order, but Access just deleted the payment records.

In most cases, you're far better off using an Active field (Yes/No data type) to indicate a parent record's status. The Active field is set to Yes when the order is placed, and only set to No when the order has been canceled or completed. You might also consider adding a CancellationDate field to tblSales, and set it to the date on which an order is canceled. If CancellationDate is null, the order has not been canceled.

When you write ADO code to delete a record, you need to first check to see if there are any one-to-many relationships between the table containing the record to delete and any other tables in the database. If there are dependent tables, the records in the dependent tables need to be deleted before Access allows you to delete the record in the parent table.

Fortunately, you can write a single procedure using ADO code to delete records in both the dependent table(s) and the parent table. Figure 13.21 shows the code for the cmdDelete command button in frmSales.

The cmdDelete_Click event procedure deletes records in tblSalesPayments, tblSales-LineItems, and tblSales that have an invoice number matching the current invoice number.

The first statement in cmdDelete_Click (If Me.NewRecord Then) uses the NewRecord property to see if the current sales record is new. If the record is new, Me.Undo rolls back changes to the record and the procedure ends (Exit Sub). If the current record is not new, the procedure displays a message box to confirm that the user really wants to delete the record. If the user clicks the Yes button, the procedure deletes the records from the tables.

`strSQL` holds a SQL statement for locating and deleting records in `tblSalesPayments` with an invoice number that matches the invoice number on `frmSales`. `strSQL` is passed as a parameter to the `Execute` method of the current project's (`CurrentProject`) connection. You can pass either the name of a query or a SQL statement as a parameter to the `Execute` method. The `Execute` method simply runs the specified query or SQL statement.

FIGURE 13.21

Using ADO code to delete multiple records

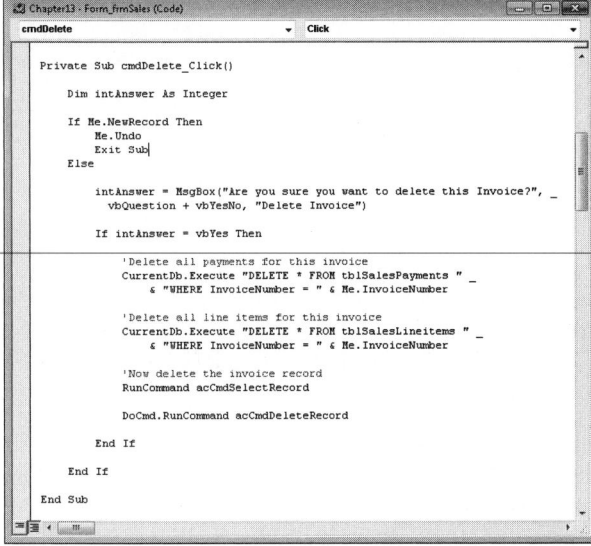

Note

If the query or SQL statement contains a `WHERE` clause and the `Execute` method does not find any records that meet the `WHERE` condition, no error occurs. If the query or SQL statement contains invalid syntax or an invalid field or table name, however, the `Execute` method fails and an error is raised.

The same process is used to delete records in `tblSalesLineItems`.

After the `tblSalesLineItems` records are deleted, the `tblSales` record can then be deleted. The following listing shows a slightly different way to write the `cmdDelete_Click` procedure.

```
Private Sub cmdDelete_Click()
    Dim intAnswer As Integer
    Dim strSQL As String
    If Me.NewRecord Then
        Me.Undo
        Exit Sub
    End If
```

```
     intAnswer = MsgBox("Are you sure you " _
       & " want to delete this invoice?", _
       vbQuestion + vbYesNo, "Delete Invoice")
     If intAnswer = vbNo Then
       Exit Sub
     End If
     'Delete payments for this invoice:
     strSQL = "DELETE * FROM tblSalesPayments " _
       & "WHERE InvoiceNumber = " & Me.InvoiceNumber
     CurrentProject.Connection.Execute strSQL
     'Delete line items:
     strSQL = "DELETE * FROM tblSalesLineItems " _
       & "WHERE InvoiceNumber = " & Me.InvoiceNumber
     CurrentProject.Connection.Execute strSQL
     'Delete invoice record:
     RunCommand acCmdSelectRecord
     RunCommand acCmdDeleteRecord
   End Sub
```

This procedure uses SQL statements to explicitly delete records in the child tables (`tblSalesLineItems` and `tblSalesPayments`) before deleting the parent record in `tblSales`.

Notice that this procedure includes two different `Exit Sub` statements. The first is executed if the current record happens to be a new record. Presumably, there is no reason to delete a new record, and, in fact, an attempt to delete a new record raises an error.

The second `Exit Sub` executes if the user chooses not to delete the record (the `MsgBox` function returns vbNo, in this case) after clicking the Delete button. If the user confirms the deletion (the value of `MsgBox`, in this case, is vbYes), the code proceeds to delete the invoice records matching the current `InvoiceNumber`, and then deletes the current record displayed on `frmSales`.

Many developers prefer using `Exit Sub` (or `Exit Function`) to jump out of a procedure as soon as the code determines there is no need to continue. An `Exit Sub` statement provides an explicit end to the procedure and is easily understood by anyone reviewing the code. When using nested `If` statements, particularly when the procedure is quite long and involved, the `End If` statement ending the `If` may be easily missed or misunderstood.

Summary

In the previous few chapters, you learned the basics of programming, reviewed some of the built-in functions, and experienced the various logical constructs. You learned about ADO and how to access data in tables and queries through SQL recordsets. You also learned a lot about forms and queries in previous chapters. In this chapter, you used all this knowledge and learned how to display selected data in forms or reports using a combination of techniques involving forms, VBA code, and queries.

You'll see many other examples that use ADO and DAO to manipulate data in Access tables and recordsets throughout this book. A little bit of VBA code, coupled with either the ADO or DAO syntax, is able to perform complex operations without the use of queries or other database objects. Whenever possible, the examples in this book are written in a generic fashion that is easily modified to fit other situations by replacing the names of fields, tables, and other objects. You should use VBA code whenever complex data-management tasks are required by your applications, or in situations in which users require more flexibility than is provided by queries and forms alone.

Debugging Your Access Applications

Many Access applications rely on significant amounts of VBA (Visual Basic for Applications) code in forms and reports, and as stand-alone modules. Because of its power and flexibility, VBA is used for all aspects of application development, from communicating with the user to massaging and transforming data on its way from tables and queries to forms and reports.

Because VBA code is often complicated (or at least, seems complicated!) debugging an error or problem in an application can be difficult and time-consuming. Depending on how well organized the code is, and whether simple conventions, such as providing descriptive names for variables and procedures, were followed, tracking down even a small coding bug can be a frustrating experience.

Fortunately, Access provides a full complement of debugging tools to make your life easier. These tools not only save time by helping you pinpoint where a coding error occurs, but can help you better understand how the code is organized and how execution passes from procedure to procedure.

Note

This chapter largely ignores the errors caused by poor design — misrepresentation of data caused by ill-designed queries, update and insert anomalies caused by inappropriate application of referential integrity rules, and so on. For the most part, these problems occur because of issues such as failing to conform to proper design disciplines, misunderstanding Access query design, and so on. What I can help you with, however, are the bugs that creep into your VBA code, particularly those bugs that cause noticeable problems with the data or user interface in your applications.

IN THIS CHAPTER

Verifying an application's features

Identifying where errors come from and how to avoid them

Setting up code module options

Getting help with your VBA code

Debugging the traditional way, with MsgBox **and** Debug. Print

Taking advantage of the debugging tools available in Access

Cross-Reference

Chapter 23 contains valuable information about adding error handling to your Access applications. You can't exclude every type of problem from your Access databases, but you can, at least, prepare for the inevitable issues that arise in database applications.

Note

This chapter assumes that you're comfortable designing and implementing the data structures in your applications and that the tables, queries, and other structural components of your databases are not a source of problems.

On the CD-ROM

This chapter is a departure from the other example files you've used in the book. The sample database file (Chapter14.accdb) contains the basic example code shown throughout this chapter. The code in Chapter14.accdb does not necessarily do anything useful. It's provided mostly as a "test bench" for practicing with the Access debugging tools rather than as a good example of practical VBA code.

Many of the statements in the examples have been commented out because they contain syntax errors and other types of problems. You may have to remove the single quotes in front of some of the example statements to experience the error or view the assistance already built into Microsoft Access.

Finally, there are many more examples in Chapter14.accdb than are described in the text of this chapter. After you read the chapter, go back through the examples and try them out. You'll learn more about debugging than you probably ever wanted to know, but the experience will serve you well as you develop and debug your programs.

Testing Your Applications

Testing Access applications is an ongoing process. Each time you switch a form or report from Design view to Normal view, or leave the VBA Editor to run a bit of code, you're testing your application. Every time you write a line of code and move to another line, the VBA syntax parser checks the code you just wrote. Each time you change a property in a form or report and move your cursor to another property or another control, you're testing the property you've changed.

Testing is the time to see if your application runs the way you intend, or even if it runs at all. When you run an application and it doesn't work, you've found a *bug*. Fixing problems is most often referred to as *debugging*. This term dates back to the earliest electro-mechanical computers. Legend has it that a moth shorted out an electrical circuit. The late Admiral Grace Hopper, an early pioneer in computing, coined the term *debugging* to describe the process of removing the moth.

You've already learned a lot about testing and debugging. When you run a report and no data appears, you've had to check the report's RecordSource property to ensure that the report is pulling the correct data. You may have viewed the data in a query or table to see if the data source is the problem. If you run a form and you see #Name or #Error in individual controls, you've learned to check the control's ControlSource property. Perhaps you have an incorrect reference to a table field or you spelled something wrong and Access is unable to evaluate the reference.

Maybe you have too many parentheses in an expression, or you've used a control name in a formula that conflicts with an Access keyword. Each time you had this problem, you may have asked someone with more experience than you what the problem was, or perhaps you looked it up online or in a book, or you researched the syntax of the formula.

Most problems with query, form, and report design are pretty obvious. You know you have a problem when a query returns the wrong data, or a form or report fails to open or displays an error message as it opens. Behind the scenes, Access does a great deal to help you notice and rectify problems with your application's design. When you run forms and reports, Access often reports an error if it finds something seriously and obviously wrong.

It's much more difficult for Access to help you with incorrectly written code. Very often, a problem in VBA code exists for months or even years before a user notices it. Even poorly written code can run without throwing errors or exhibiting obvious problems. However, determining exactly where a bug exists in VBA code — and figuring out what to do to repair the bug — can be very challenging. When you create VBA code, you're pretty much on your own when it comes to detecting and resolving problems. Fortunately, a wide variety of tools have been built into the editor to help you.

Tip

Testing and debugging takes quite a bit of time. Many good developers easily spend a third of their time designing a program, another third writing code, and another third testing and debugging. Having someone other than the developer test a program's operation is often a good idea. A person who is unfamiliar with an application is more likely to do something the developer never expected, leading to new and surprising bugs and instability issues.

Using the Module Options

Many VBA errors are very easy to either prevent, or to handle once they occur. The VBA code editor features a number of options designed to help you avoid errors in your VBA code, and to help make your code easier to read and understand. Figure 14.1 shows the Editor tab of the Options dialog box (Tools ⇨ Options while the VBA code editor window is open). The Code Settings area in the upper half of this dialog box contains a number of important options that help you write and debug the VBA code in your applications.

The Editor tab in the Options dialog box (see Figure 14.1) contains a number of options that are important to the integrity of your VBA code. These options are summarized in the following sections.

Auto Syntax Check

By far the most common error when writing VBA code is a syntax error. Syntax errors are caused by using the VBA language incorrectly, much like mispronouncing a sentence in a foreign language. By far, the most common bug in Access VBA code is the simple syntactical error caused by misspelling a keyword or a variable name or misusing a procedure, property, or method.

The Editor tab of the Options dialog box contains a number of important VBA coding options.

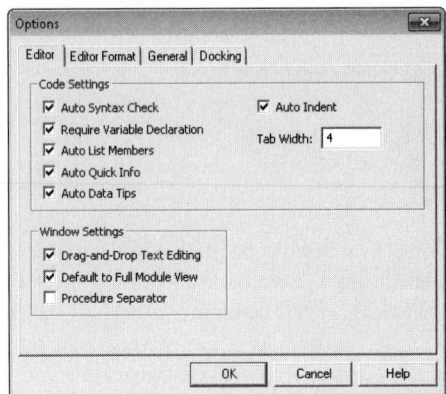

These errors are so easy to detect and correct that Access includes an option to automatically check for syntactical errors. When you select the Auto Syntax Check option, Access checks each line of code for syntax errors as you enter it in the code editor. Most of the syntax errors caught by Auto Syntax Check are the most obvious spelling errors, missing commas, and so on. It will not catch more subtle errors such as data type mismatch, and, of course, Auto Syntax Check won't catch logical errors.

If you enable Auto Syntax Check, a message box pops up over your code whenever Access detects a syntax error in your VBA statements. Regardless of whether you enable Auto Syntax Check, Access also turns the erroneous statement to red to indicate a problem.

Tip

Most developers find that turning the statement to red is enough of an indication of a problem, and they don't want to be interrupted by the message box, so they leave Auto Syntax Check unselected.

Notice the Auto Syntax Check check box in the Code Settings area. This option causes Access to check your code for syntactical errors line by line as you type it into the code editor window. Figure 14.2 illustrates automatic syntax checking. In this figure, the MsgBox statement contains an error. Do you see the error?

Notice the stray comma right after the "sSQL:" portion of the MsgBox line. No comma is needed here because these arguments to the MsgBox statement are not separated with commas. Access detects the stray comma and displays the statement in a red typeface to tell you that there's a problem on that line.

Tip

If you don't like red, you can change the color of syntax error text in the Code Colors area of the Editor Format tab of the Options dialog box.

FIGURE 14.2

Automatic syntax checking can save you from simple bugs.

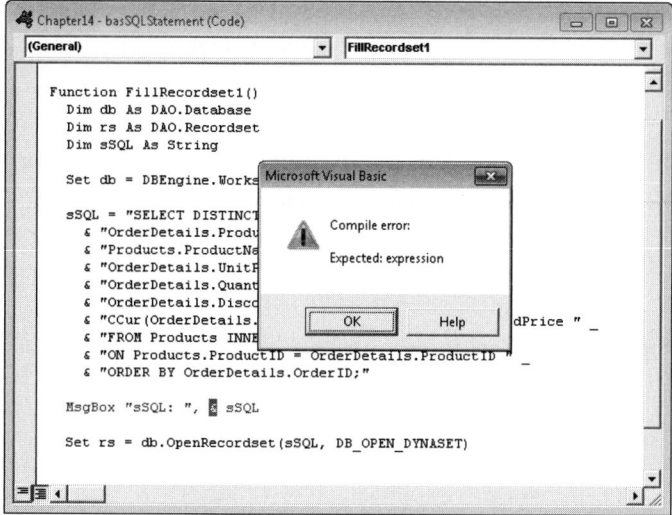

Fixing syntactical errors is straightforward: Simply examine the line for misspellings, stray characters, missing quotation marks, and so on. Very often, syntax errors are introduced by using parentheses where they aren't needed (or omitting them when they're necessary!), improperly placing square brackets, and so on.

Tip

Many syntactical errors can be avoided by adhering to the naming conventions frequently mentioned in this book: Avoid spaces in object names, use mixed-case names to make them easier to read, and so on. Anything you can do to make your code easier to understand goes a long way toward avoiding silly syntactical errors.

Require Variable Declaration

The Require Variable Declaration setting automatically inserts the `Option Explicit` directive into all VBA modules in your Access application. This means, of course, that all variables must be explicitly declared (with a `Dim`, `Private`, `Public`, or `Static` keyword) before they're used. The Require Variable Declaration option is selected by default and is preferred by most experienced Access developers.

Caution

Without `Option Explicit`, variables don't have to be declared, so it's easy to fall into a habit of using variables without carefully considering appropriate data types, naming conventions, or the impact of variable scope. Code written without the benefit of `Option Explicit` can get ugly pretty fast.

A common bug in applications with poor control over variables occurs when a variable is used out of context. It's easy to mistake one variable (like `LastName`) for another variable (like `LName`), particularly in large or complex applications. Bugs like this can be extremely difficult to resolve because the code may run fine even though data is being mishandled. By using the `Option Explicit` directive in every code module, you can be sure every variable is properly declared, making it much less likely you'll use `LastName` as a variable in one procedure, and `LName` in another procedure.

The Require Variable Declaration setting affects only new code modules added to the application. You'll have to manually add this directive to the top of existing module before variable declaration is enforced throughout the application.

Auto List Members

This option pops up a list box containing the members of an object's object hierarchy in the code window. In Figure 14.3, you can see the list of `Application` objects that appeared as soon as I typed the period following `Application` in the VBA statement. Use the up and down arrow keys to locate an item in this list and select it or continue typing in the object reference.

FIGURE 14.3

Auto List Members makes it easy to recall the members of an object's hierarchy.

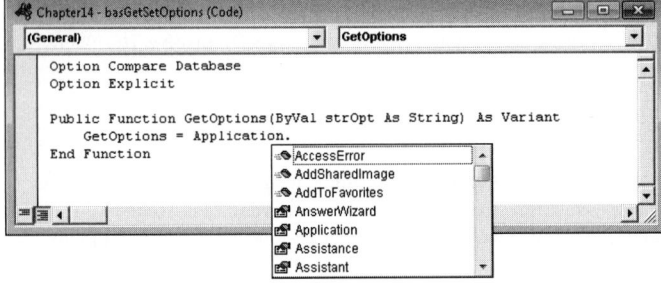

Auto Quick Info

When you select Auto Quick Info, Access pops up syntax help (see Figure 14.4) when you enter the name of a procedure (function, subroutine, or method) followed by a period, space, or opening parenthesis. The procedure can be a built-in function or subroutine or one that you've written yourself in Access VBA. This option helps you learn and understand the proper syntax of each command and method.

FIGURE 14.4

Auto Quick Info provides syntax reminders in the module window.

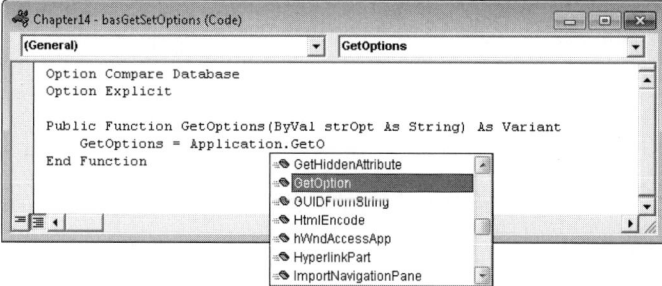

Auto Data Tips

Figure 14.5 shows Auto Data Tips in action. This option displays the value of variables when you hold the mouse cursor over a variable with the module in break mode. Auto Data Tips is an alternative to setting a watch on the variable and flipping to the Immediate window when Access reaches the break point. (You can find out more about watches in the "Setting watches with the Watches window" section, later in this chapter.)

FIGURE 14.5

Auto Data Tips reveals the value of a variable wherever the variable is used.

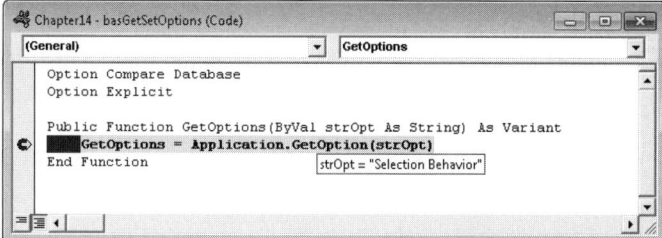

Break on All Errors

In addition to the settings on the Editor tab, the General tab on the Options dialog box includes some powerful settings (see Figure 14.6). These settings are geared more to how VBA operates in Access, rather than how the code looks or behaves in the VBA code editor.

Break on All Errors forces Access stops at each and every error (regardless of the error handling you may have added to your application) to allow you to debug the statement generating the error. During the development process, you'll want to see errors as they occur instead of relying on the error handling you built into your code to make sure you understand what's generating the errors.

The Options dialog box's General tab contains some valuable options.

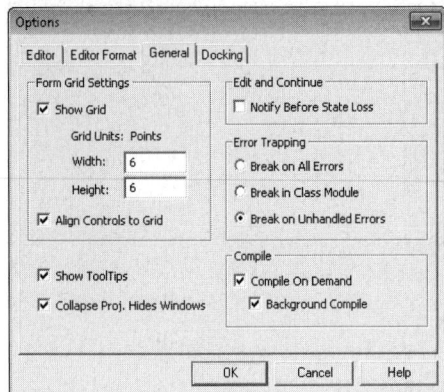

Remember

Be sure to turn this option off before distributing the application to end users.

Compile on Demand

Compile on Demand instructs Access to compile modules only when their procedures are required somewhere else in the database. When this option is unchecked, all modules are compiled any time any procedure is called. Unchecking this option makes sure that you see all errors that are detected by the compiler each time you make changes to the modules in your application. If you leave this option selected, the Access compiler won't recompile all the code in the application, which means that some errors may slip through and only be discovered at runtime.

Organizing VBA Code

It shouldn't come as any surprise that your coding habits have a lot to do with the errors you encounter in your applications. Very often, the adoption of simple coding conventions eliminates all but the toughest syntactical and logical errors in VBA code.

One convention you should follow is to put each variable declaration in its own line of code. Consider the code shown in Figure 14.7. Although bunching multiple variable declarations together as a single Dim statement is perfectly permissible, you have to scan the entire line of code to find the declaration of each of the variables. The problem in Figure 14.7 is that it's far too easy to overlook a variable or to misunderstand the data type assigned to a variable. You can easily create a logical bug by assigning a variable an incorrect value.

FIGURE 14.7

Putting multiple declarations on one line makes finding a variable's Dim statement difficult.

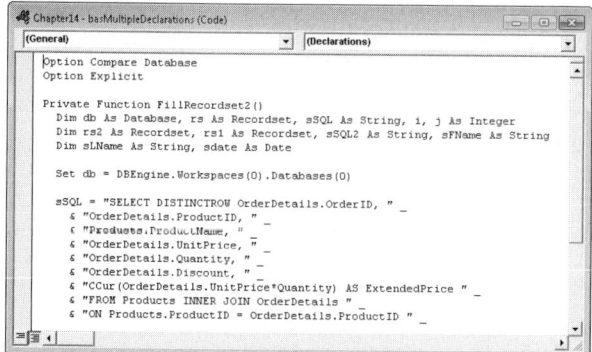

Other errors may be caused by using a variable in an inappropriate context, such as using a string variable in a mathematical expression. In this particular case, VBA will use a numeric value stored in the string variable without throwing an error, but a runtime error is thrown if the string variable contains a text value (such as a person's name).

The long declaration in Figure 14.7 contains another, more subtle error. Notice that the declaration contains i, j As Integer at the end of the statement. Presumably the programmer intended for both i and j to be the Integer data type, but this isn't what actually happens. VBA requires the As *DataType* clause for *each* variable declaration. If the As *DataType* is omitted (as it is for the i variable), the variable is established as a Variant data type. Although the code you see in Figure 14.7 runs without errors, because the i variable is a Variant, the code runs somewhat more slowly than it would if i were an Integer.

Figure 14.8 shows the same declarations reconfigured as multiple Dim statements. You can much more easily see the data type of the rs1 variable in Figure 14.8. Let your eye run down the list of variable names until you reach rs1 and see that it's a Recordset type variable. This is another reason why short, descriptive variable names are preferred over long, descriptive names.

A second, less obvious change in Figure 14.8 is the fact that variables are grouped by data type. All the Recordset variables are grouped together as are the Integer variables. You could carry this grouping one step farther by sorting the variables alphabetically by data type.

Spreading out your variable declarations doesn't appreciably affect compile times or runtimes. There is no difference in code module size after the code has been reduced to a binary format by the Access VBA compiler. In other words, you gain little by condensing variable declarations into a few lines of code. Spreading out variable declarations makes them much easier to read without sacrificing execution or compilation speed.

FIGURE 14.8

Single-variable `Dim` statements are easier to work with than several variables declared as a single VBA statement.

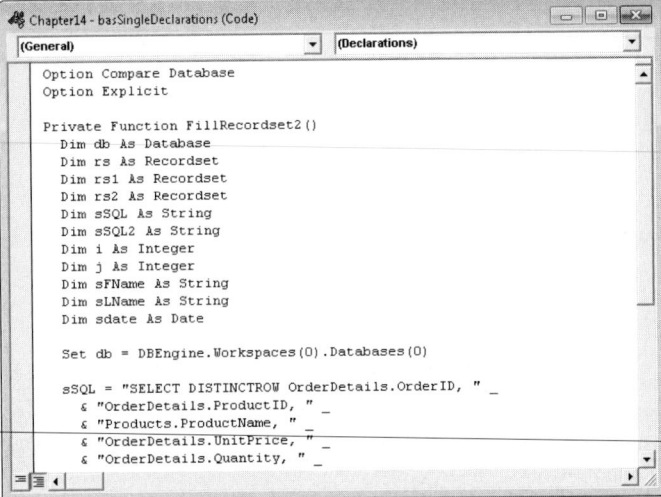

Compiling VBA Code

After you create a subprocedure or function and want to make sure that all your syntax is correct, you should compile your procedures by choosing Debug➪Compile *Project Name* from the VBA code editor window menu (where *Project Name* is the name of the project set in the Project dialog box, accessed from the Tools menu). Figure 14.9 shows the Debug menu opened in the editor window.

The compile action checks your code for errors and also converts the programs to a form that your computer can understand. If the compile operation is not successful, an error window appears, as shown in Figure 14.10.

This level of checking is more stringent than the single-line syntax checker. Variables are checked for proper references and type. Each statement is checked for all proper parameters. All text strings are checked for proper delimiters ,such as the quotation marks surrounding text string. Figure 14.10 illustrates a typical compile-time error. In this case, the name of a method (GetOption) has been misspelled, and the compiler is unable to resolve the misspelled reference.

Access compiles all currently uncompiled procedures, not just the one you're currently viewing. If you receive a compilation error, immediately modify the code to rectify the problem. Then try to compile the procedure again. If there are further compile errors, you'll see the next error.

Note

Unfortunately, the VBA compiler reports compilation errors one at a time. Most other compilers (such as the compilers in Visual Studio .NET) show you as many errors as they find during compilation.

FIGURE 14.9

The Debug menu in the VBA code editor window contains valuable debugging tools.

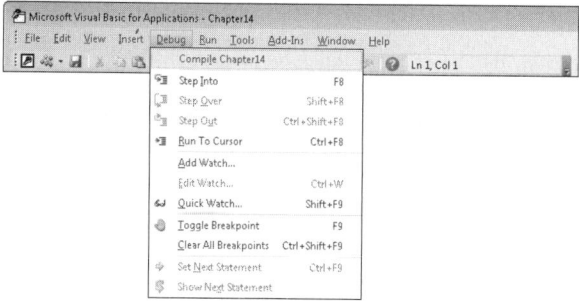

FIGURE 14.10

Viewing a compile error

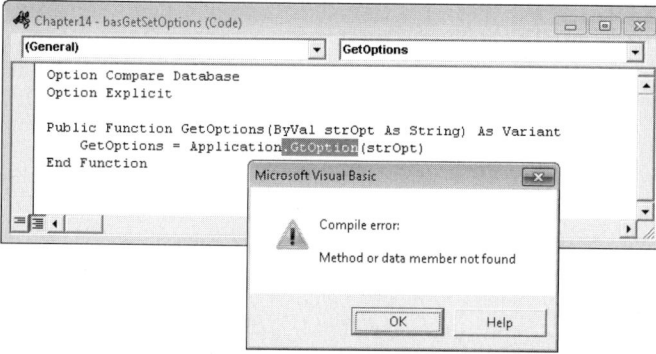

Tip

After compiling your application, you can't choose Debug➪Compile (it's grayed out). Before implementing an application, you should make sure that your application is compiled.

Your database is named with a standard Windows name, such as Chapter14.accdb, but Access uses an internal project name to reference the VBA code in your application. You'll see this name when you compile your database. When the database file is first created, the project name and the Windows filename will be the same. The project name isn't changed when you change the Windows filename of the .accdb file. You can change the project name by choosing Tools➪ *Project Name* Properties (where *Project Name* is the current internal project name). (The Project Name property is shown in Figure 14.13, a little later in this chapter.)

Compiling your database only makes sure that you have no syntax errors. The compiler can check only for language problems by first recognizing the VBA statement and then checking to see that you specify the correct number of options and in the right order. The VBA compiler can't detect logical errors in your code, and it certainly can't help with runtime problems.

Tip

After you compile your program, be sure to compact your database. Every time you make a change to your program, Access stores both the changes and the original version. When you compile your program, it may double in size as the compiled and uncompiled versions of your code are stored. Compacting the database can reduce the size of the database by as much as 80 percent to 90 percent, because it eliminates all previous versions internally.

Traditional Debugging Techniques

Two widely used debugging techniques have been available since Access 1.0. The first is to insert `MsgBox` statements to display the value of variables, procedure names, and so on. The second common technique is to insert `Debug.Print` statements to output messages to the Immediate window.

Using MsgBox

Figure 14.11 shows an example of a message box displaying a long SQL statement to enable the developer to verify that the statement was properly composed by the application. The example in Figure 14.11 is found in the `basUsingMsgBox` module in the `Chapter14.accdb` example database.

FIGURE 14.11

The `MsgBox` statement makes a satisfactory debugging tool (with some limitations).

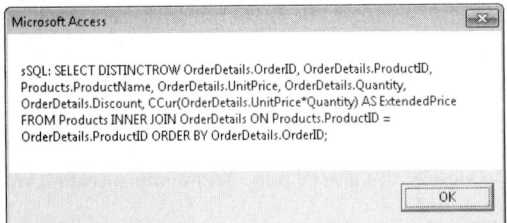

Here are the advantages of using the `MsgBox` statement:

- The `MsgBox` statement is simple and easy to use and only occupies a single line of code.
- The `MsgBox` statement can output many types of data.
- The message box itself pops up right on the user interface, and you don't have to have the Immediate window open or flip to the Immediate window to view the message box.
- `MsgBox` halts code execution, and because you know where you've put the `MsgBox` statements, you know exactly where the code is executing.

There are also some problems associated with `MsgBox` statements:

- There is nothing about the `MsgBox` statement to prevent it from popping up in front of an end user, causing all kinds of confusion and other problems.

Caution

Never, ever forget to remove all `MsgBox` statements from your code before shipping to end users!

- Message boxes are modal, which means you can't flip to the code editor window or Immediate window (discussed in the "Running code with the Immediate window" section, later in this chapter) to examine the value of variables or examine the code underlying the application. Using the `MsgBox` statement is an all-or-nothing proposition (with the one exception described in the "Compiler directives" sidebar).

Compiler directives

A refinement of the `MsgBox` technique is to use compiler directives to suppress the `MsgBox` statements, unless a special type of constant has been set in the code or within the Access environment. Examine the code in the following figure. Notice the `#Const` compiler directive above the `MsgBox` statement and the `#If` and `#End If` directives surrounding the `MsgBox` statement.

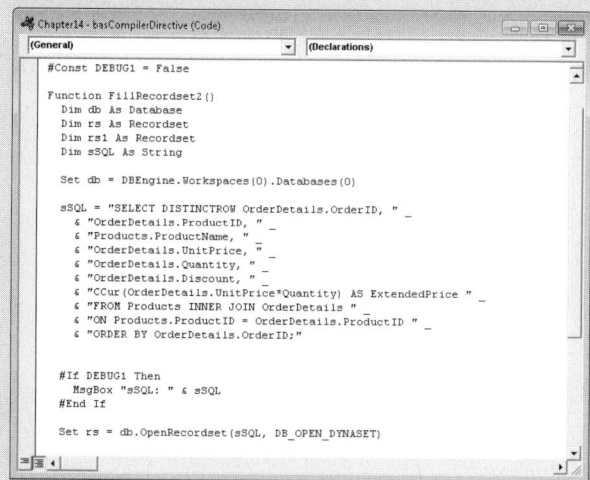

```
Chapter14 - basCompilerDirective (Code)
(General)                          (Declarations)

#Const DEBUG1 = False

Function FillRecordset2()
  Dim db As Database
  Dim rs As Recordset
  Dim rs1 As Recordset
  Dim sSQL As String

  Set db = DBEngine.Workspaces(0).Databases(0)

  sSQL = "SELECT DISTINCTROW OrderDetails.OrderID, " _
    & "OrderDetails.ProductID, " _
    & "Products.ProductName, " _
    & "OrderDetails.UnitPrice, " _
    & "OrderDetails.Quantity, " _
    & "OrderDetails.Discount, " _
    & "CCur(OrderDetails.UnitPrice*Quantity) AS ExtendedPrice " _
    & "FROM Products INNER JOIN OrderDetails " _
    & "ON Products.ProductID = OrderDetails.ProductID " _
    & "ORDER BY OrderDetails.OrderID;"


  #If DEBUG1 Then
    MsgBox "sSQL: " & sSQL
  #End If

  Set rs = db.OpenRecordset(sSQL, DB_OPEN_DYNASET)
```

Compiler directives make it easy to include or exclude blocks of code from an application.

All the keywords beginning with the pound sign (#) are seen only by the VBA compiler. These keywords (`#Const`, `#If`, `#Else`, and `#End If`) constitute directives to the VBA compiler to include (or exclude) certain statements in the compiled version of your project.

continued

continued

The #Const directive you see in the preceding figure can appear anywhere in the module as long as it's placed 'above the #If directive. The logical place for the #Const is in the module's declaration section, since #Const values are global to the module. In the figure, the compiler constant is set to True, which means the statements between #If and #End If will be compiled into the application's VBA project. In this case, the MsgBox statement is processed and appears in the user interface. Removing the #Const directive (perhaps by commenting it out) or setting its value to False suppresses the MsgBox statement.

Compiler directives also can be used for statements other than MsgBox. You could, for example, use compiler directives to conditionally compile features, additional help, or other capabilities into an application. Compiler directives are particularly effective for suppressing MsgBox statements that are used for debugging purposes and must be squelched before giving the application to users. You can easily reactivate MsgBox statements by setting the #Const statement to True.

Perhaps the biggest impediment to using compiler constants is that the #Const statement is module-level in scope. A compiler constant declared in one module is not seen by other modules in the application. This means that you must add compiler constants to every module in which you want to employ conditional compilation.

Access provides the Conditional Compilation Arguments text box in the General tab of the application's Project Properties dialog box (Tools⇨ *Application Name* Properties) to get around this constraint. As shown in the following figure, you use the Conditional Compilation Arguments text box to specify any number of compiler constants that apply to the entire application. These settings make it very easy to toggle conditional compilation from a single location in the application, instead of changing the #Const statements in every module.

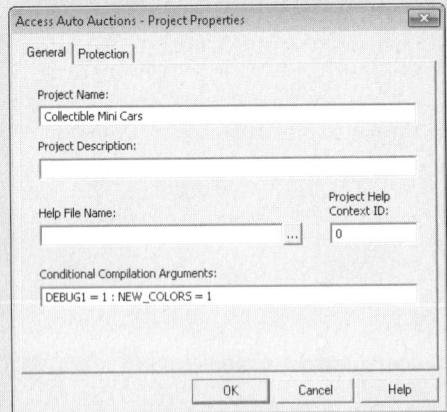

The Project Properties dialog box provides a convenient way to set conditional compilation arguments for the entire application.

Conditional Compilation Arguments and other settings set in the Project Properties dialog box are relevant only to the current application. Unlike the options you set in the Options dialog box (accessible from the Tools menu), the Project Properties settings are not shared among multiple Access applications.

Tip

In the preceding figure, notice that the values assigned to the Conditional Compilation Arguments are all numeric. Assigning zero to a Conditional Compilation Argument sets the argument's logical value to False; any nonzero value is interpreted as True. You can't use the words True and False in the Conditional Compilation Arguments text box. Setting the value to 0 (false) means that you can leave all the conditional compilation directives in your code. Setting the value to false effectively disables them, allowing your code to execute as if they don't exist.

If you're confused about the conflicting terminologies applied to the VBA conditional compilation feature, you're not alone. In a VBA code module, you assign conditional compilation constants using the #Const keyword, yet in the Project Properties dialog box, you set Conditional Compilation Arguments. Also, you assign the True and False keywords to conditional compilation constants in a VBA module, but use 1 and 0 to assign True and False, respectively, to Conditional Compilation Arguments. This is one place where the terminology and syntax used for the same purpose are quite different in different parts of an Access VBA project.

In case you're wondering, the name you apply to a compiler constant is anything you want it to be. The example in this section uses DEBUG1 merely as a convenience, but it could have been MyComplierConstant, Betty, DooDah, or any other valid constant name.

Using Debug.Print

The second commonly used debugging statement is using Debug.Print to output messages to the Immediate window. (Print is actually a method of the Debug object.) Figure 14.12 shows how the sSQL variable appears in the Immediate window.

Use Debug.Print to output messages to the Immediate window.

Unlike the MsgBox statement, you don't have to do anything special to suppress the Debug. Print output from the user interface. The output of Debug.Print only goes to the Immediate window, and because end users never see the Immediate window, you don't have to worry about a user encountering debug messages.

The problems with Debug.Print are obvious from Figure 14.12. Long strings don't wrap in the Immediate window. Also, the Immediate window must be visible in order for you to view its output. But these limitations are relatively harmless and you'll frequently use Debug.Print in your applications.

Note

Some people have reported that excessive numbers of Debug.Print statements can slow an application. Even though the Immediate window is not visible, Access executes the Debug.Print statements that it finds in its code. You may want to consider surrounding each Debug.Print statement with the compiler directives described in the "Compiler directives" sidebar to remove them from the end user's copy of the application.

Using the Access Debugging Tools

Microsoft Access features a full complement of debugging tools and other capabilities. You use these tools to monitor the execution of your VBA code, halt code execution on a statement so that you can examine the value of variables at that moment in time, and perform other debugging tasks.

Running code with the Immediate window

Open the Immediate window (also called the Debug window) by choosing View ➪ Immediate or by pressing Ctrl+G. You can open the Immediate window any time (for example, while you're working on a form's design). You'll sometimes find it useful to test a line of code or run a procedure (both of which are supported by the Immediate window) while you're working on a form or report.

The Immediate window is shown in Figure 14.13. The Immediate window permits certain interactivity with the code and provides an output area for Debug.Print statements. The basic debugging procedures include stopping execution so that you can examine code and variables, dynamically watching variable values, and stepping through code.

FIGURE 14.13

Get to know the Immediate window! You'll use it a lot in Microsoft Access.

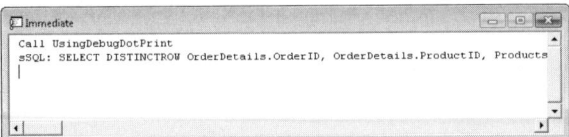

One of the most basic uses of the Immediate window is to run code, such as built-in functions, or subroutines and functions that you've written. Figure 14.14 shows several examples that have been run in the Immediate window.

FIGURE 14.14

Running code from the Immediate window is a common practice.

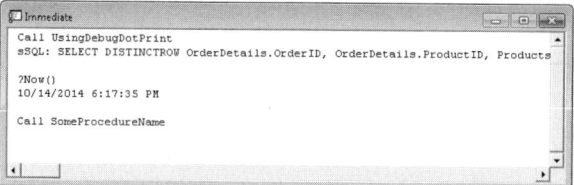

The first example in Figure 14.14 shows the same convention used to run a function (UsingDebugDotPrint) that's been added to the VBA project. You see the result of the function's execution (a long SQL statement), as long as the function is declared with the `Public` keyword, and any arguments required by the function are provided.

The `Now()` function has been run from the Immediate window, returning the current date and time. The question mark (?) in front of the `Now()` function name is a directive to the Immediate window to display (or print) the value returned by the `Now()` function.

The third example in Figure 14.14 (SomeProcedureName) shows calling a subroutine from the Immediate window. Because subroutines don't return values, the question mark is not used. The `Call` keyword is optional when calling subroutines, but it's often included for clarity.

Suspending execution with breakpoints

You suspend execution by setting a *breakpoint* in the code. When Access encounters a breakpoint, execution immediately stops, allowing you to switch to the Immediate window to set or examine the value of variables.

Setting a breakpoint is easy. Open the code window and click on the gray Margin Indicator bar to the left of the statement on which you want execution to stop (see Figure 14.15). Alternatively, position the cursor on the line and click on the Breakpoint ribbon button. The breakpoint itself appears as a large brown dot in the gray bar along the left edge of the code window and as a brown highlight behind the code. The text of the breakpoint statement appears in a bold font.

Tip
You can change all these colors and font characteristics in the Modules tab of the Options dialog box.

Removing a breakpoint involves nothing more than clicking on the breakpoint indicator in the Margin Indicator bar. Breakpoints are also automatically removed when you close the application.

Setting a breakpoint is easy.

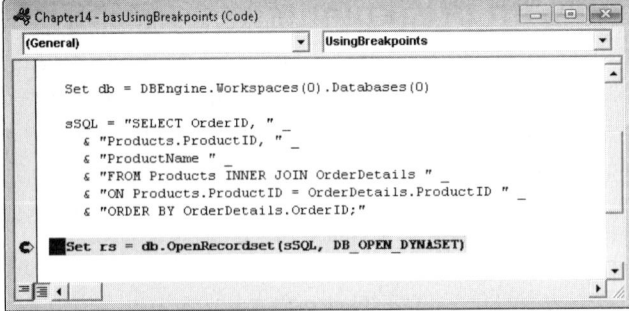

When execution reaches the breakpoint, Access halts execution and opens the module at the breakpoint (see Figure 14.16). You now use the Immediate window (see the preceding section) to examine the values of variables and perform other operations, or use any of the other debugging tools described in the "Using the Access Debugging Tools" section. Neither the code window nor the Immediate window are modal, so you still have full access to the development environment.

Execution stops on the breakpoint.

Figure 14.17 illustrates two techniques for viewing the values of variables while execution is stopped at a breakpoint. The Locals window contains the names and current values of all the variables in the current procedure. If you want to see the value of a variable in a slightly different format, use the print command (?) in the Immediate window to display the variable's value.

FIGURE 14.17

The Immediate window contains a lot of valuable information.

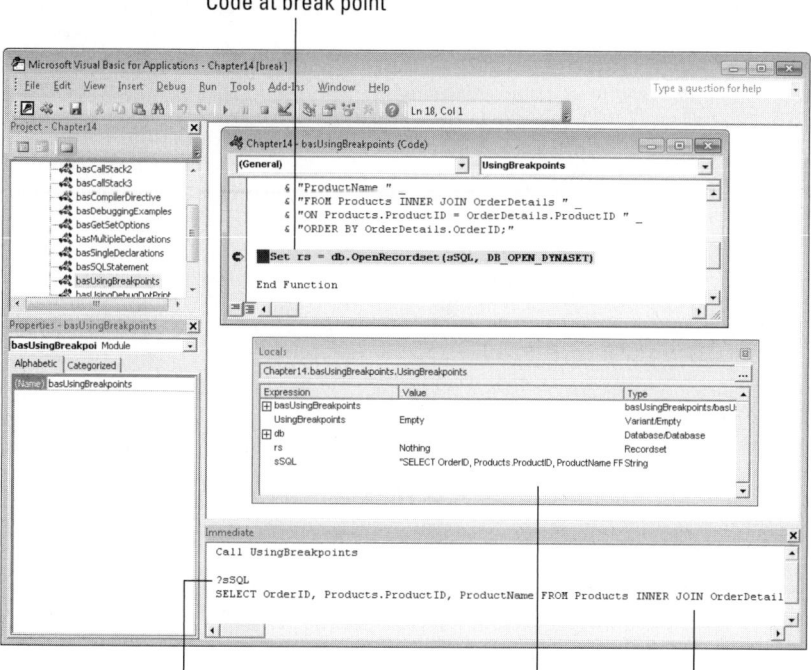

Code at break point

Using ? to display variable's value · Locals window · Immediate window

The most fundamental operation at a breakpoint is to walk through the code, one statement at a time, enabling you to view what's happening to the application's logic and variables. After you've reached a breakpoint, you use a few keystroke combinations to control the execution of the application. You're able to step through code one statement at a time, automatically walk through the local procedure, or step over the procedure and continue execution on the "other side" of the procedure.

In Figure 14.18, a breakpoint has been inserted near the top of the `FillRecordset1()` function. When execution reaches this statement a breakpoint asserts itself, allowing you to take control of program execution.

Using Stop statements instead of setting breakpoints

An alternative to setting breakpoints is to use Stop statements. The Stop statement halts execution but is more permanent than breakpoints. A Stop statement, like any other VBA statement, persists from session to session until explicitly removed. You can, however, surround the Stop statement with conditional compilation expressions and toggle their action by changing the value assigned to a conditional compilation constant. The following figure illustrates using the Stop statement.

Using Stop is a bit dangerous, however. Because Stop is an executable statement, unless it's carefully controlled with compiler directives, deleted, or commented out, your application will, literally, *stop executing* in front of a user. You're probably better off using regular breakpoints than Stop statements in most situations.

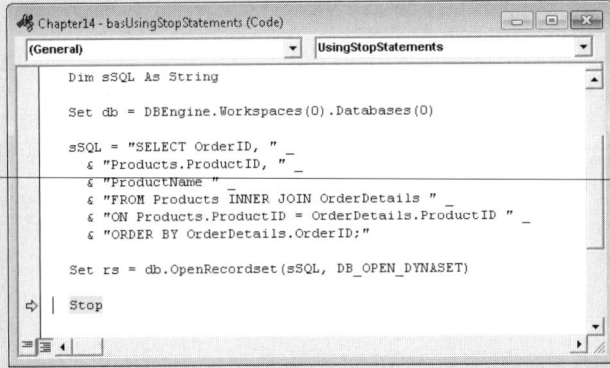

Stop statements are a type of permanent breakpoint.

Insert a breakpoint near the location of the code you want to step through.

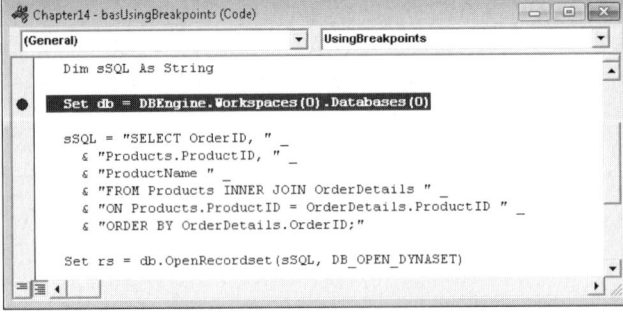

In Figure 14.19, the break has occurred and I've clicked on the Step Into button (or pressed F8). The Step Into button executes the next statement in the program's flow of execution. In this case, the SQL statement is composed and assigned to sSQL. If I wanted to view the value of sSQL at this point, I could flip to the Immediate window (Ctrl+G) and use ?sSQL to print its value in the Immediate window. I could also have a watch set on sSQL and view its value in the Watch window (described in the "Setting watches with the Watches window" section, later in this chapter).

FIGURE 14.19

Step Into executes one line at a time.

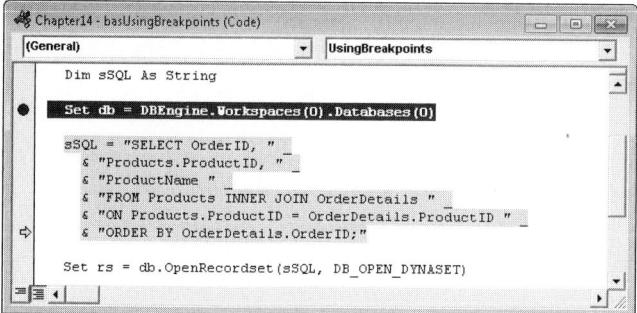

Notice the execution pointer (a yellow arrow) in the Margin Indicator bar pointing at the last line of the SQL statement. This arrow tells you where execution is actually stopped. The line pointed to by the arrow has not yet executed, so any action performed in the statement has not occurred.

Consecutive clicks on the Step Into button (or pressing F8) walks through the code one statement at a time. If a statement includes a call to a child procedure, you'll be taken to that procedure and walked through it. If you want, you can use the Step Over button (or press Shift+F8) to step "through" the child routine. If you've previously debugged the child routine and you're sure it contains no errors, there is no reason to walk through its code. The code in the called routine is actually executed when you click on the Step Over button, changing any variables involved.

When you're satisfied that you don't need to continue walking through the code in the child procedure, click on the Step Out button (or press Ctrl+F8) to complete the procedure. The Step Out button is handy if you've stepped into a called routine and you're sure there's nothing interesting going on in it.

One very nice feature in the Access VBA window is the Auto Data Tips option in the Modules tab in the Options dialog box. With this option selected, you're able to view the value of any variable in a tooltip-like window by hovering the mouse pointer over the variable's name in the module window (see Figure 14.20).

FIGURE 14.20

Auto Data Tips are a powerful tool for debugging.

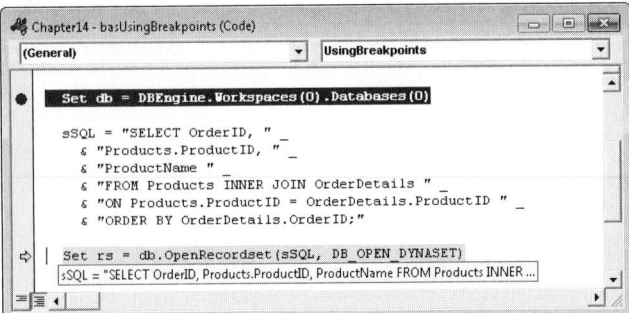

The Auto Data Tips display you see by hovering the mouse over a variable is very dynamic. The value shown in Auto Data Tips changes whenever the variable is assigned a new value. Because hovering the mouse is easy to do, you don't have to use the Immediate window to view every variable in your code.

Note

The Auto Data Tips option must be selected in the Modules tab in order for the data tip you see in Figure 14.20 to appear. (See the "Auto Data Tips" section, earlier in this chapter, for more on this option.)

One very nice feature of breakpoints is that the execution pointer (the yellow arrow in the left margin) is movable. You can use the mouse to reposition the pointer to another statement within the current procedure. For example, you can drag the pointer to a position above its current location to re-execute several lines of code.

You can easily reposition the execution pointer in such a way that your code's execution is invalid, such as moving it into the body of an If...Then...Else statement, or into the middle of a loop. Also, moving the pointer to a position *lower* in the code may mean that variables aren't set correctly or an important bit of code is ignored. Overall, though, the ability to easily re-execute a few lines of code is a valuable debugging aid.

Looking at variables with the Locals window

The Locals window (View ➪ Locals Window) shows all variables that are currently in scope, saving you from having to examine each variable one at a time. The variable's name, its data type, and its current value are displayed.

Notice the items in the Locals window in Figure 14.21. Any line in the Locals window that begins with a plus sign will unfold to reveal more information. For example, you can set a breakpoint on the End Function statement at the bottom of the function to halt execution so that you can examine the results of the `rs` assignment statement. Unfolding the `rs` entry in the Locals window reveals all the properties of the `rs` object and its contents (see Figure 14.21).

Use the Locals window to examine the values of complex objects.

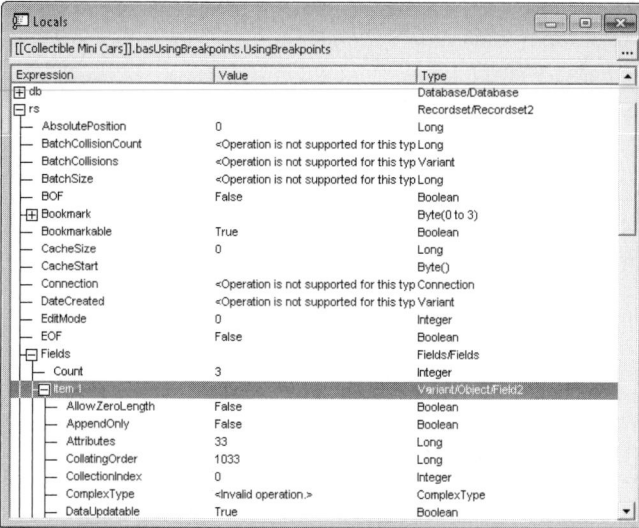

One powerful feature of the Locals window is that you can set the values of simple variables (numeric, string, and so on) by clicking on the Value column in a variable's row and typing in a new value for the variable. This makes it very easy to test how various combinations of variable values affect your application.

In the preceding section, I tell you how to move the execution point within a procedure by dragging the yellow arrow with the mouse. By changing the value of a variable and moving the execution point to different places in the procedure, you can verify that the code executes as expected. Directly manipulating variables is much easier than other methods of testing the effect of outliers and unexpected values.

Setting watches with the Watches window

The Locals window can be overrun with variables in a large application or in an application with many variables in scope. The Watches window enables you to specify just which variables you want to monitor as you single-step through your code. The value of a watched variable changes dynamically as the code runs. (You need to be at some kind of breakpoint, of course, to actually see the values.) The advantage of using the Watches window is that the variables displayed don't have to be from the local procedure. In fact, the variables in the Watch window can be from any part of the application.

Setting a watch is more complicated than using the Locals window or setting a breakpoint:

1. In the Watches window, click on the Watch tab.

2. The Add Watch dialog box (see Figure 14.22) appears.

The Add Watch dialog box includes some powerful options.

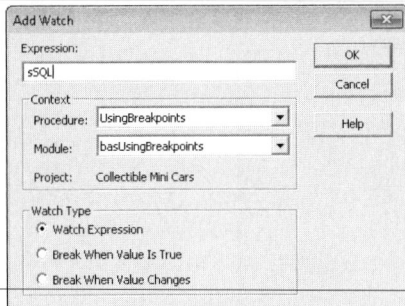

3. Enter the name of the variable or any other expression in the Expression text box.

The Add Watch dialog box includes some important options. In addition to the name of a variable or expression (an expression might be something like sSQL = " "), there are options for specifying the module and procedure within the module to watch. In Figure 14.23, the Add Watch dialog box is set up to watch the sSQL variable in all procedures in all modules.

At the bottom of the Add Watch dialog box are the following options:

- **Watch Expression:** The variable's value will dynamically change in the Watch window. You must use an explicit breakpoint or Stop statement in order to observe the value of the watched variable.

- **Break When Value Is True:** This option asserts a break whenever the value of the watched variable or expression becomes True. If you set the expression to sSQL = " ", a breakpoint occurs whenever the value of the sSQL variable changes to an empty string.

- **Break When Value Changes:** This directive causes Access to halt execution whenever the value of the variable or expression changes. Obviously, this setting can generate a *lot* of breakpoints!

Caution

Use watches wisely. You don't want to be breaking into program execution too frequently or you'll never get through the code. On the other hand, you don't want to overlook some important change in the value of a variable because you didn't set a watch appropriately.

Figure 14.23 shows the Watches window in action. The sSQL variable is displayed for all procedures in all modules.

FIGURE 14.23

The Watches window reveals all of a variable's details.

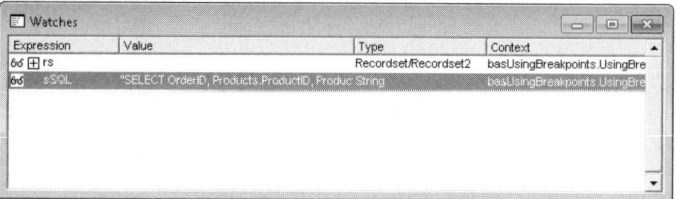

Tip

The Watches window can "float" or be docked at any side of the VBA editor window. If you don't like the Watches window's current position, use its title bar to drag it to another location. As you drag the window to a docking position, a gray rectangle appears where Access thinks you want to dock the window. Just release the mouse button when you have the window positioned in its new location, and Access will either dock the window or leave it floating freely, as you directed. The Watches window will be in the same position the next time you open the VBA editor window.

If you don't like the "docking" behavior, right-click anywhere within the body of the Watches window and deselect the Dockable option.

Using conditional watches

Although watching variables in the Locals window or Watches window can be entertaining, you can spend a lot of unproductive time hoping to see something unexpected happen. You'll probably find it much more efficient to set a *conditional watch* on a variable, and instruct the VBA engine to break when the condition you've established is met.

The Add Watch dialog box (see Figure 14.24) accepts a Boolean (true or false) expression, such as CustomerId=99 in the text box near the top. You specify where in the application (which procedures and which modules) the expression is applied, and you tell Access what you want the VBA engine to do when the expression is evaluated. For my purposes, I want execution to break when the expression CustomerID=99 is True.

The conditional watches you set up through the Add Watch dialog box are added to the Watches window. The watch expression appears in the Watches window's Expression column.

You can use conditional watches in other ways, too, such as using compound conditions (X = True And Y = False), and forcing a break whenever a value changes from the value set in the Expression text box. The small example illustrated in Figure 14.22 only hints at the capabilities possible with conditional watches.

FIGURE 14.24

A conditional watch halts execution when the expression `CustomerID=99` is true.

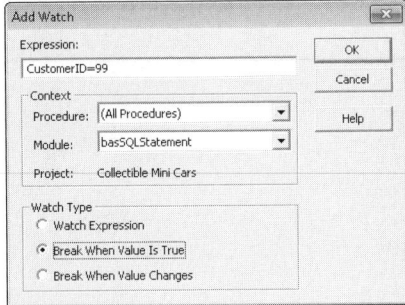

Tip

The Watches window is more than a static display. If needed, you can click on an item in the Expression column and change a watched expression. For example, let's say you set up a watch containing an expression as `TotalSale > 100` **and directed the watch to assert a breakpoint as soon as this expression becomes true. You may find that the breakpoint occurs much too often for your testing purposes. Instead of deleting the watch expression and starting over, you can easily modify the expression, replacing 100 with 200 or any other value you'd like to try.**

You can have as many watches as you want, but, as with all other debugging tools, the watches are removed when you exit Access.

Tip

If, while working with conditional watches, you find a particular expression useful, you may want to write it down for future use.

Using the Call Stack window

The last debugging tool I'll examine is a bit more difficult to understand because it involves "multiple dimensions" of execution. In many Access applications, you'll have procedures that call other procedures that call still other procedures. To my knowledge, there is no practical limit on the number of procedures that can be sequentially called in a VBA project. This means you may have a "tree" of procedures many levels deep, one level of which is causing problems in your application. This situation is particularly true in the case of an application that has been modified many times, or when little thought was given to optimizing how the code in the application is used.

Even so, some very carefully designed applications end up with deeply nested code, making it difficult to understand how all the code ties together.

Imagine a function that performs a common operation (such as calculating shipping costs) in an application. As a general rule, rather than include this function in every module in the application, you'll put the function into a single module, declare it with the `Public` keyword so that it's recognized and used by the entire application, and then call it from whichever procedure needs a sales tax calculation.

Furthermore, imagine that this application has many such functions and subroutines, each calling the other, depending on the application's logic at that moment. Finally, imagine that users report that the shipping fee appears to be incorrectly calculated under some conditions but not others.

You could single-step through all the code in the application, hoping to discover the cause of the erroneous shipping fee. However, this approach wouldn't be efficient. You'd be much better off setting a conditional watch on an important variable within the shipping fee function, forcing the code to break when the condition is `True`. Then open the Call Stack window (see Figure 14.25) to view the path that the VBA engine has taken to reach this particular point in the code.

FIGURE 14.25

The Call Stack window shows you how the execution point reached its current position.

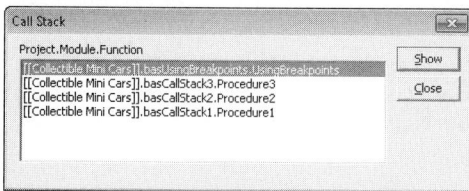

The bottom entry in the Call Stack window (`[[Collectible Mini Cars]].basCall-Stack1.Procedure1`) indicates that `Procedure1` (contained in module `basCallStack1`) was the first function called. The entry above it (`[[Collectible Mini Cars]].basCall-Stack2.Procedure2`) indicates that `Procedure1` call `Procedure2` (contained in `basCall-Stack2`) and so on. You can quite easily trace the path that the VBA code has taken to reach the current breakpoint.

Double-click on any of the items listed in the Call Stack to be taken to the statement that sent execution to the next procedure. Using the Call Stack window in conjunction with conditional watches enables you to stop code wherever relevant, and to diagnose how code has executed up to the breakpoint.

Summary

This chapter takes a quick look at the important topic of debugging Access VBA code. The techniques you apply and the tools you use in debugging your code are highly individual choices. Not all developers feel comfortable using the Immediate window to watch variables. Not every developer uses breakpoints and the Step buttons to stop and control execution. At the same time, it's nice to know that these tools are available for you to use when you're ready!

This chapter ends the section on VBA programming in Microsoft Access. You'll see many different ways of using VBA code to strengthen and enhance your Access applications in the following parts and chapters of this book.

The next part revisits the basic application-building tasks you read about in the first part of this book. The next several chapters explain many of the most important aspects of application development, such as using external data in your Access applications, creating advanced queries, and building complex forms and reports. These chapters take the basic skills explained in the first two parts of this book, and extend your understanding of Access application development.

Using Access Data Macros

A major new feature in Access 2010 is the ability to add data macros to your native Access tables. A data macro is logic you attach to a table to enforce business rules at the table level. In some ways a data macro is similar to a validation rule, except that a validation rule is rather unintelligent. All a validation rule can do is display a message to the user. Validation rules can't modify data or determine whether corrective action is needed. Data macros are specifically provided to allow you to manage data-oriented activity at the table level.

Most often, data macros are used to enforce business rules — such as a value can't be less than some threshold — or to perform data transformation during data entry. The real value of data macros is that they're in effect wherever the table's data is used. For example, if a data macro is attached to the sales table, any time the sales data is displayed on a form or report, the data macro is at work, watching for changes to the data and automatically controlling what happens to the table's data.

On the CD-ROM

This chapter uses a database named `Chapter15.accdb`**. If you haven't already copied it onto your machine from the CD, you'll need to do so now. This database contains the tables, forms, reports, and macros used in this chapter.**

Introducing Data Macros

Beginning with Access 2007, macros have played a more significant role in many Access applications. For a very long time, macros were considered the poor cousin to VBA statements. Although in many ways VBA and macros

IN THIS CHAPTER

Creating data macros

Understanding table events

Building macros

Understanding macro limitations

were equivalent in their capabilities, macros have always been considered inferior to VBA for handling an application's logic.

For example, up until Access 2007, the only options for opening a form when a button is clicked were to use VBA code (DoCmd.OpenForm "FormName") or to use a macro that ran the OpenForm macro action.

The problems with traditional Access macros were considerable:

- **Macros existed as separate database objects, so keeping track of the macros in effect on a particular form was often difficult.** Because there was no direct connection between a form (or a report, for that matter) and a macro, it was easy to break the macro by deleting or renaming it. VBA code encapsulated within the form's code module never had this problem.

- **There was no way to trap or handle errors in macros.** In versions of Access prior to 2007, macros would simply stop running and display an error dialog box if something unexpected happened. These interruptions were unwelcome by users, particularly because there was, most often, nothing a user could do to correct the problem or prevent it from happening again. VBA code has always featured strong error handling and could often provide a default value or instruct the user what to do in the event of a problem.

- **Macros were unable to work with code.** There was no way for a macro to loop through a recordset, for example, to sum field values or detect out-of-range data. VBA code is well-suited for data-management tasks and includes all the looping constructs necessary to iterate over recordsets.

Microsoft dramatically improved macros in Access 2007 by adding error handling and allowing temporary variables during a macro's execution. These two new features went a long way toward making macros more acceptable to serious Access developers and allowed macros to be used in situations where macros were considered unacceptable in earlier Access versions.

Access 2007 also introduced the concept of *embedded macros*. An embedded macro is (typically) a small macro attached directly to a control event on a form or report. The macro runs every time the event is triggered, such as when a user clicks on a button or when a report's detail section is formatted. Embedded macros eliminate the objection that macros were always external to the form or report they serviced.

Access 2010 continues the improvement and expansion of Access macro capabilities. In Chapter 30, I cover some of the details of using the new Access editor, as well as looping and trapping errors in macros. This chapter specifically covers data macros, which add intelligence directly to Access tables.

Data macros are intended to make it easier to ensure consistent data handling throughout an application. Because data macros are applied at the table level, the exact same action happens each time the table's data is updated. Although the subset of actions available to data macros is considerably smaller than user interface macros, when carefully crafted and implemented, data macros are a powerful addition to Access applications.

There are many different ways to use data macros in Access 2010, including the following:

- Verifying that a customer's payments are up to date before allowing additional charges to be made

- Automatically calculating shipping costs or sales taxes as part of a sales table

- Ensuring that a field's value falls within required limits before the record is updated in the database

- Keeping a log of changes to a products table

Although these same rules are easily applied at the application level, the logic enforcing these rules must be repeated every time the data is used by the application. Having these relatively simple actions implemented at the data level means that the user interface logic (VBA code and macros) can focus on more complex operations.

Looking at How Data Macros Are Created

In general, macros are created by stringing together a number of macro *actions*, each of which performs a simple operation, such as setting the value of a field in a record.

Cross-Reference

In Chapter 30, you'll read about user interface macros, which are primarily used to control the user interface (opening forms and reports, responding to button clicks, and so on) and are an alternative to automating Access with VBA code.

Access 2010 data macros share some of the advanced constructs available to user interface macros, such as branching (the `If` action) and looping through recordsets (the `ForEachRecord` action). Together, these constructs and the macro actions available to data macros combine to make a powerful tool for Access data management.

Access 2010 data macros use the same macro editor used to create embedded and user interface macros. Once you master the macro editor, you'll use it for all macro development and macro management. The primary difference is that the action catalog (described later in this section) contains different actions, depending on the context. By far the richest variety of macro actions is available to user interface macros because they support a much greater variety of activity than data macros do.

Using the Macro Designer

The details of table events and macro actions are discussed in the following sections. In the meantime, let's take a look at the Access 2010 Macro Designer to see how data macros work, and how you use the Macro Designer to construct data macros.

Cross-Reference

In Chapter 30, you'll learn more details of the Macro Designer's features; in this chapter, we use the Macro Designer as a tool only for constructing data macros.

Adding data macros to a table is quite easy. In fact, an Access table doesn't even have to be in Design view — you can add data macros to a table displayed as a datasheet, if you like. The data macros you construct for a table are in effect immediately, so you can easily work on a macro and observe how well the macro works without compiling or switching between Design view and Datasheet view.

For this example, let's assume that the Collectible Mini Cars company uses a standard markup of 66.66 percent on its products. This means that a product's wholesale cost is multiplied by 1.6666 to yield the default selling price of an item. Collectible Mini Cars has found that a 66.66 percent markup provides the margin necessary for them to offer volume discounts, special sales, and significant discounts to selected buyers while remaining profitable.

The default selling price can always be overridden by manually entering a new price in the RetailPrice field. The 1.6666 just serves as the starting point for a product's selling price.

The problem to be solved with a data macro is updating the retail price of a product any time the product's cost is changed. Although this could be done quite easily with code or a macro behind Access forms, consider the issue if there were dozens of different forms where the product's cost might be changed. The same code or macro would have to be added in many different places, contributing to development and maintenance costs. Also, there is always the chance that one or more forms would not be updated should Collectible Mini Cars ever decide on a different approach for setting the default retail price of its products.

Using a data macro attached directly to the Products table simplifies development and maintenance of the application's forms and reports. Because the business rule (multiplying cost by 1.6666) is enforced at the data layer, every form, report, and query using the Products data benefits from the data macro. Also, if the cost is ever changed by VBA code or a user interface macro, the selling price is automatically updated appropriately.

With the Products table open in Datasheet view, click on table ribbon tab to show table events (see Figure 15.1). Notice that five events — Before Change, Before Delete, After Insert, After Update, and After Delete — are available to the table.

FIGURE 15.1

Every Access table includes five data-oriented events.

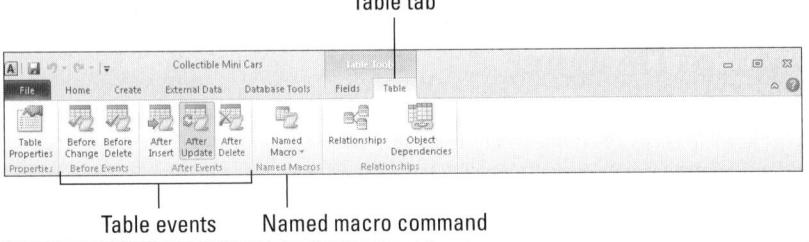

Double-clicking on the After Update ribbon command opens the Macro Designer (shown in Figure 15.2). Initially, at least, there's not much to look at.

FIGURE 15.2

Initially, the Macro Designer is not much to look at.

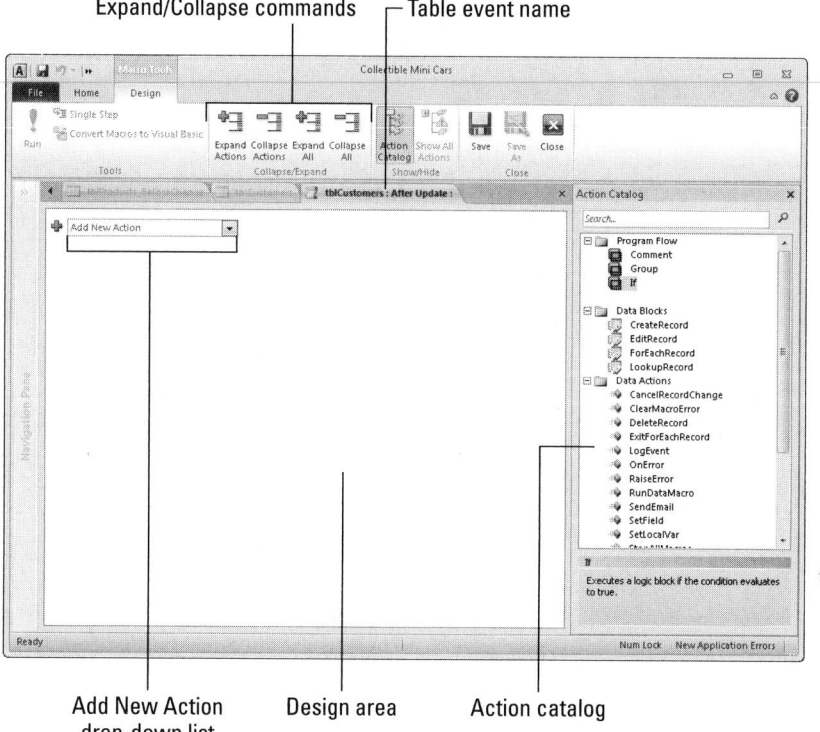

The large rectangle to the left is the macro design area. This is where you place macro actions. On the right side is the Action Catalog, a hierarchical list of all macro actions currently available. The only indication of which table event is being programmed is in the main Access window caption, and in the tab above the macro design area. With a macro open in the design area, the ribbon contains several tools you use when working with the macro. Notice that you can collapse or expand macro sections, save the macro currently under construction, and close the Macro Designer.

The ribbon you see in Figure 15.2 is exactly the same as seen when working with embedded or stand-alone user interface macros. The main differences between what is shown here and in Chapter 30 is that, when building user interface macros, more options are available to you. For example, all the items in the Tools group at the far left of the ribbon are currently grayed out. Data macros don't provide the option of single-stepping through macro actions or converting to VBA code. Data macros are intended to be relatively simple, short, and to-the-point, rather than large and complex.

The same view is obtained somewhat differently if the table is in Design view. If the table is in Design view, select the Create Data Macros command from the Design ribbon tab, and select a table event from the drop-down list that appears (see Figure 15.3).

Selecting a table event with a table in Design view.

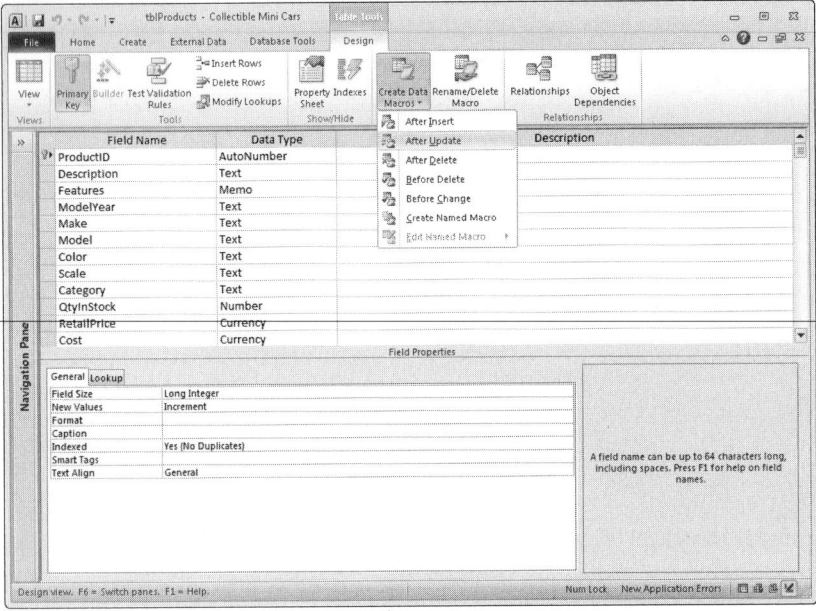

In either case, the Macro Designer opens as shown in Figure 15.2. in Figure 15.2, the table's `AfterUpdate` event has been selected. When the Access tabbed interface is used, the table's name and selected event appears in the Macro Designer's tab. If the overlapping windows interface is selected, this information appears in the Access main window's caption.

In Figure 15.1 and again in Figure 15.3, notice the Named Macro option. A *named macro* is just like a data macro attached to a table event. The only difference is that a named macro is "free floating" and not specifically tied to a particular event. A named macro is meant to be called from an event macro and typically implements logic that is common to a table's fields. Consider the business rule described earlier. If more than one data macro in a table might change a product's wholesale cost, you might create a named macro to handle updating the `RetailPrice` field. The named macro could then be called by any of the table's other data macros so that every macro within the table handles the update in the same way.

Using the Action Catalog

The Action Catalog on the right side of the Macro Designer serves as the repository of macro actions you add to your data macros. The contents of the Action Catalog depend entirely on which table event has been selected, so its appearance varies considerably while you work with Access macros.

Program flow

At the top of the Action Catalog are certain program-flow constructs you apply to your macros. When working with data macros, the only program-flow constructs available are comments, groups, and If blocks. Comments help document your macros and should be used if the macro's logic is not easily understood.

A *macro group* provides a way to wrap a number of macro actions as a named entity. The group can be independently collapsed (you'll see collapsed macro sections in the "Adding macro items" section, later in this chapter), copied, and moved around within a macro. A macro group is not, however, an executable unit. Instead, it's simply meant to provide a convenient way to establish a block of macro actions to simplify your view of the macro in the Macro Designer.

The If block adds branching logic to a macro. You've seen several examples of the VBA If... Then...Else construct in other chapters, and a macro If is no different. Double-click or drag the If onto the macro's design surface (see Figure 15.4) to define a block of macro actions that are executed only when the condition specified in the text box at the top of the If block is true.

In Figure 15.4, the body of the If block executes only when the Cost field is set to a value less than zero. There are many other ways to handle this situation, including using a validation rule, but an If block attached to the Product table's AfterUpdate event is automatic and requires no effort on the part of the user.

In the lower-right corner of the If block are options to add an Else or an Else If to the If block. Use these options to extend the If block to include other conditions you want to check as part of the same If block.

Data blocks

The Data Blocks group of macro actions (except for Lookup Record) is only available for "after" events. As you'll read in the "Data actions" section, later in this chapter, the "before" events are meant to be very fast and lightweight, so they don't provide for CPU-intensive operations such as adding or editing new records.

Each of the data-block constructs includes an area for adding one or more macro actions. The data block performs all the macro actions as part of its operation. In other words, you set up the data block you want to perform (for example, EditRecord), and then add the actions you want to execute as part of the block.

FIGURE 15.4

The `If` block conditionally executes macro actions.

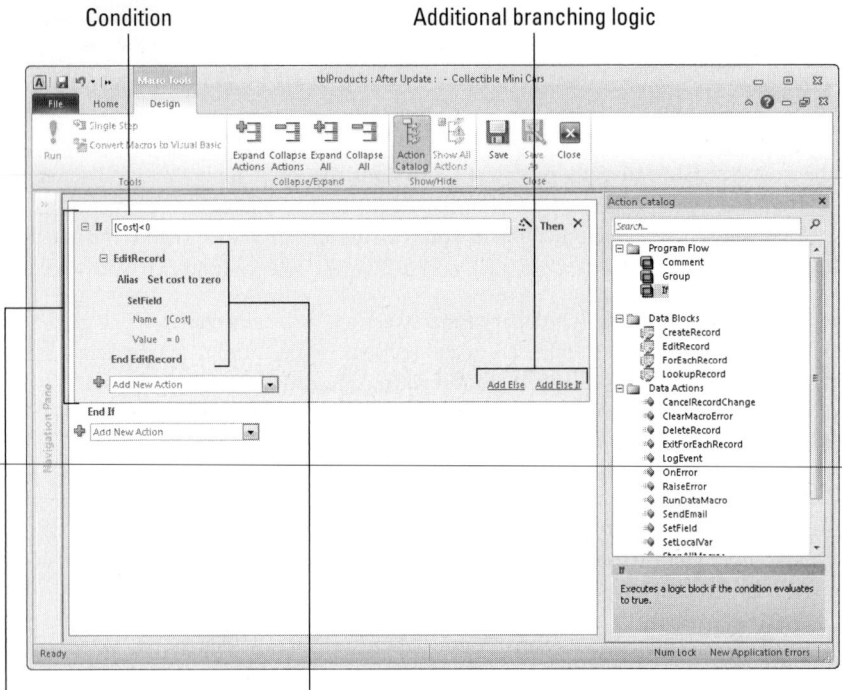

Data blocks may also be nested. You could, for example, set up a `ForEachRecord`, and then run the `CreateRecord` block, adding records to another table with data contained in the records returned by the `ForEachRecord`.

The data-blocks macro actions are

- `CreateRecord`: The `CreateRecord` action provides a way to add a record to the current table (which is rarely done) or to another table (which is more typical). An example of using `CreateRecord` is building a log of all changes to the Products table. The `CreateRecord` macro action can add a new record to a table, populating fields in the record with data passed from the current table. The reason `CreateRecord` is not often used to add a record to the current table is that recursion can occur. Adding a new record to the current table triggers events such as `AfterInsert` (described in the "After events" section, later in this chapter), which may run the `CreateRecord` action again and again.

Figure 15.5 also shows how IntelliSense helps you compose the expressions used in data macros. In this case, the Name property requires a fully-qualified field reference, and as soon as you start typing in a table name, a list of tables in the database appears. After you select a table, the field names in the table appear as shown in Figure 15.5. Although not all macro properties support this level of IntelliSense, most expressions are relatively easy to compose properly.

CreateRecord adds a new record to any table in the database.

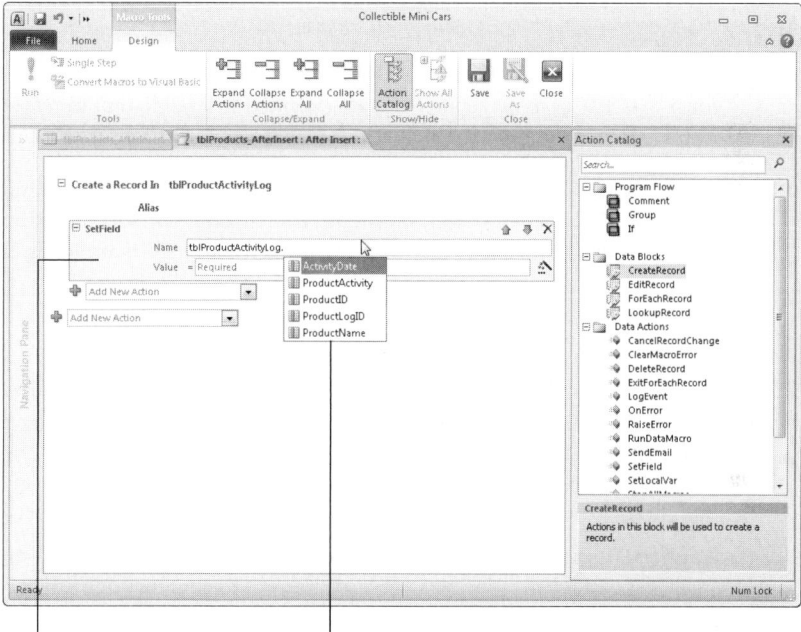

Set Field macro action   IntelliSense for Name property

- EditRecord: As its name implies, EditRecord provides a way to change the content of an existing record in the current, or another, table. EditRecord is ideal for situations such as adjusting inventory levels when a product is sold or returned, or calculating sales tax or shipping costs when the quantity field has been provided.

- ForEachRecord: The ForEachRecord action is a looping construct. Given the name of a table or query, ForEachRecord can perform an operation on every record in the recordset. The action can be an update using the SetField action (described in the next section), can copy data, or can perform a mathematical operation on the data in the recordset. The ForEachRecord block has a macro action included within the block to make it easy to specify the action you want this block to perform. And, you can stack multiple macro actions within the ForEachBlock to perform more-complex operations.

- LookupRecord: The LookupRecord action is quite simple and easy to understand. LookupRecord returns a record found in a table and provides a macro action area for specifying the actions you want to perform on the returned record.

Data actions

The next topic to discuss are the *actions* a data macro can take. You've already read that a data macro consists of one or more actions that are executed as a single unit in response to a table event. You need a good understanding of the variety of macro actions available to data macros.

Not all these actions are available to every table event. The BeforeChange and BeforeDelete (described in the "Before events" section, later in this chapter) support only a subset of these actions because many actions are computationally intensive (such as updating or adding records), and the "before" events are meant to be very fast and lightweight.

Here are the data macro actions:

- DeleteRecord: As its name implies, DeleteRecord deletes a record in a table (without confirmation from the user). Obviously, DeleteRecord must be carefully used to prevent deleting valuable data from the application. A typical use of DeleteRecord would be as part of an archiving operation, where data is a table is copied into another table (perhaps a linked SQL Server table) and then deleted from the current table.

- CancelRecordChange: EditRecord and CreateRecord both make irrevocable changes to a record. CancelRecordChange, in conjunction with an If block, allows a data macro to cancel the changes made by EditRecord and CreateRecord before the changes are committed to the database.

- ExitForEachRecord: The ForEachRecord loops through a recordset returned from a table or query, enabling the data macro to make changes to the recordset's data or scan the data for "interesting" values. There are many situations where a data macro may need to escape from a ForEachRecord loop before it has run to the end of its recordset. For example, consider a data macro that searches for a certain value in a table, and once the value is found, there is no need to continue the loop. The ExitForEachRecord is typically executed as part of an If block (also discussed in the next section) and is executed only when a certain condition is true.

- LogEvent: Every Access 2010 application includes a hidden USysApplicationLog table (this table is hidden by virtue of the USys prefix in its name). USysApplicationLog is used to record data macro errors and can be used to log other information as well. The LogEvent macro action is specifically designed to add a record to USysApplicationLog anytime you want from a data macro. The only field in USysApplicationLog that can be written using LogEvent is Description, a memo type field. The other fields in USysApplicationLog (Category, Context, DataMacroInstanceID, ErrorNumber, ObjectType, and SourceObject) are provided by the macro itself.

- SendEmail: This macro action, obviously, sends an e-mail using the default Windows e-mailer (usually Microsoft Office Outlook). The arguments for SendEmail are: To, CC, BCC, Subject, and Body. SendEmail is quite useful in certain situations, such as automatically dispatching an e-mail when an error condition occurs, or when a product's inventory level falls below some threshold.

- SetField: The SetField action updates the value of a field in a table. The arguments to SetField include the table and field names, and the new value to assign to the field. SetField is not available to BeforeChange and BeforeDelete table events.

- SetLocalVar: Access 2010 macros are able to use local variables for passing values from one part of a macro to another. For example, you might have a macro that looks up a value in a table and passes the value as a variable to the next macro action. SetLocalVar is an all-purpose variable declaration and assignment action that creates a variable and assigns a value to it.

- StopMacro: The StopMacro action interrupts the currently executing macro, causing it to terminate and exit. Most often used in conjunction with an If data block, or in the destination of an OnError macro action, there are no arguments to StopMacro.

- StopAllMacros: This macro action is parallel to StopMacro, except that it applies to all currently executing macros. Macros may run asynchronously because table events might launch multiple macros at one time, or a macro might call a named macro as part of its execution.

- RunDataMacro: This macro action is very simple. Its only argument is the name of some other data macro that Access runs. RunDataMacro is useful in situations where a certain data macro performs some task that another data macro finds useful. Instead of duplicating the macro's actions, it's simpler just to call the macro and allow it to perform its actions as a single operation.

- OnError: The OnError macro action is the heart of Access 2010 macro error handling. OnError is a directive that tells Access what to do in the event an error occurs during a macro's execution. The first argument (GoTo) is required, and is set to either Next, Macro Name, or Fail. Next directs Access to simply ignore the error and continue execution at the macro action following the action that caused the error.

Unless another OnError is positioned within the data macro, OnError GoTo Next tells Access to ignore all errors in the data macro, and continue execution regardless of whatever errors occur. The Macro Name directive names a macro you want to jump to in the event of an error. The destination of Macro Name is a named macro, which is just a collection of macro actions not attached to a table event. The Macro Name destination could be a named macro within the current table, or in another table.

- `RaiseError`: The `RaiseError` macro action passes an error up to the user interface layer. An example is using `RaiseError` on a `BeforeChange` event to validate data before it's committed to the database. `RaiseError` passes an error number and description to the application, adding the error details to `USysApplicationLog`.

- `ClearMacroError`: Once an error has been handled by running the `RaiseError` macro action or redirecting execution to a named macro, `ClearMacroError` resets `MacroError`, the macro error object, and prepares Access for the next error.

Discovering Table Events

There are five different macro-programmable table events: `BeforeChange`, `BeforeDelete`, `AfterInsert`, `AfterUpdate`, and `AfterDelete`.

These events are designated as "before" and "after" events. The *before events* occur before changes are made to the table's data, while the *after events* indicate that successful changes have been made.

Before events

The `"before"` events (`BeforeChange` and `BeforeDelete`) are very simple and support only a few macro actions. They support the program flow constructs (`Comment`, `Group`, and `If`) and just the `LookupRecord` data block. The only macro data actions they provide are `ClearMacroError`, `OnError`, `RaiseError`, `SetLocalVar`, and `StopMacro`.

The `BeforeChange` event is similar to the `BeforeUpdate` event attached to forms, reports, and controls. As its name implies, `BeforeChange` fires just before the data in a table is changed by the user, a query, or VBA code.

`BeforeChange` gives you a chance to look at new values in the current record and make changes if needed. By default, references to a field within a `BeforeChange` or `BeforeDelete` data macro automatically refer to the current record.

`BeforeChange` is an excellent opportunity to validate user input before committing values to a table. A simple example is shown in Figure 15.6. In this case, the default value of the `Description` field in `tblProducts_BeforeChange` is set to `Description`. If the user fails to change the `Description` field while adding a new record to the table, the `BeforeChange` event updates the field to `Please provide description`.

The `BeforeChange` event can't interrupt the user with a message box or stop the record from updating in the underlying table. All `BeforeChange` can do is set a field's value or set a local macro variable's value before the record is added or updated in the table.

FIGURE 15.6

Using BeforeChange to update a field

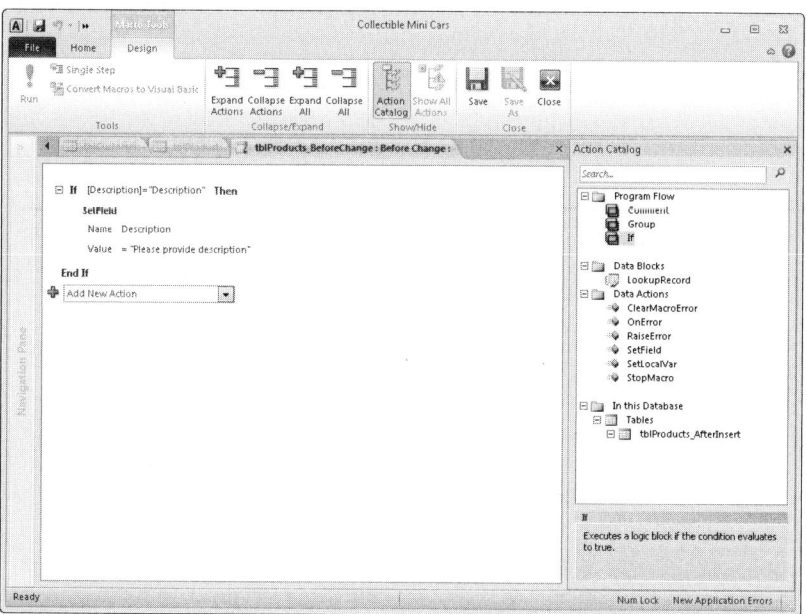

BeforeChange fires for both updates to existing records and new record insertions into the table. Access provides the IsInsert property that tells the macro whether the current change is the result of inserting a new record or because a record is being updated. Figure 15.7 shows how IsInsert can be used within an If block to ensure the BeforeChange fired as the result of a new record inserted into the table.

Figure 15.7 also illustrates that program-flow blocks (like If) can be nested. The outer If block checks the value of IsInsert, while the inner If conditionally sets the Description field value.

The BeforeDelete event is parallel in almost every regard to BeforeChange, so no examples are given here. Use BeforeDelete to verify that conditions are appropriate for deletion. As with BeforeChange, the BeforeDelete event can't prevent a record's deletion, but it can set a local variable or raise an error if conditions warrant.

FIGURE 15.7

Using `IsInsert` to determine if `BeforeChange` fired as the result of adding a new record.

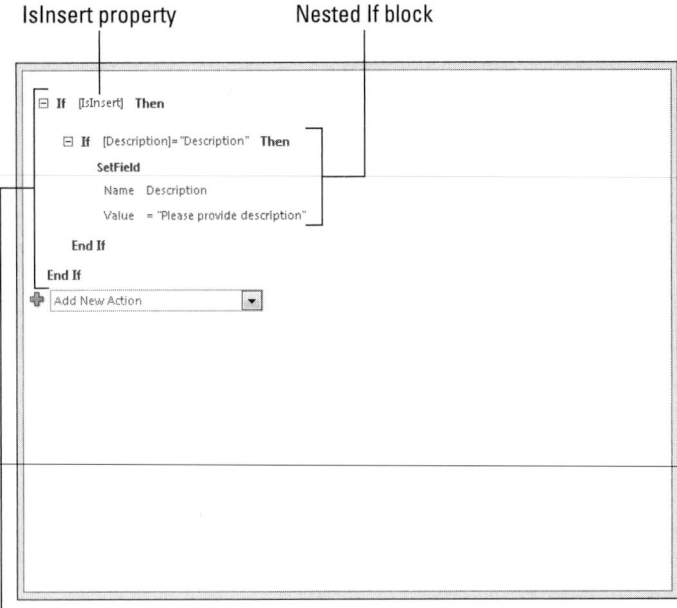

After events

The "after" events (`AfterChange`, `AfterInsert`, and `AfterDelete`) are more robust than their "before" counterparts. Each of these events supports the entire family of data-macro actions (`DeleteRecord`, `SetField`, `SendEmail`, and so on), so it's likely that you'll frequently use these events as the basis of your data macros.

Most important, perhaps, is that the "after" events can use the `ForEachRecord` macro block to iterate over recordsets provided by tables or queries. This ability makes these events ideal for scanning a table for consistency or to add a record to a log table or perform some other compute-intensive updates.

Figure 15.8 shows a typical use of the `AfterInsert` event. The `AfterInsert` event fires whenever a new record is added to a table. The new record has already been committed to the table and `AfterInsert` is used to update a table name `tblProductActivityLog`.

FIGURE 15.8

Using `AfterInsert` to add a record to `tblProductActivityLog`

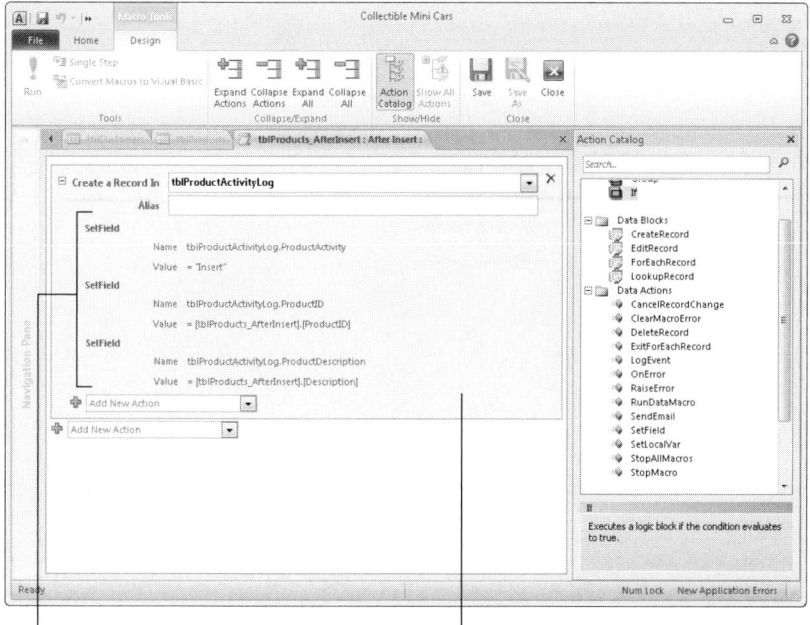

Setting fields in the new record   Create Record data block

In Figure 15.8, notice that three fields (`ProductActivity`, `ProductID`, and `ProductDescription`) in `tblProductActivityLog` are being updated as part of the `CreateRecord` data block. The `ProductID` is an `AutoNumber` field in `tblProducts_AfterInsert`. The `CreateRecord` block has already added the record to the table, so the new record's `ProductID` value is available to this data macro. Therefore, when the `SetField` macro action updates the `ProductID` field in `tblProductActivityLog`, the new product record's ID is successfully added to the log table.

`tblProductActivityLog` (shown in Figure 15.9) contains several fields (such as `ActivityDate`) that are set by default values specified in the table's design. `ActivityDate` is set to the current date by a default assignment in the field's properties, so there is no need to set the `ActivityDate` field with the `AfterInsert` data macro.

FIGURE 15.9

A typical log table updated with an `AfterInsert` data macro

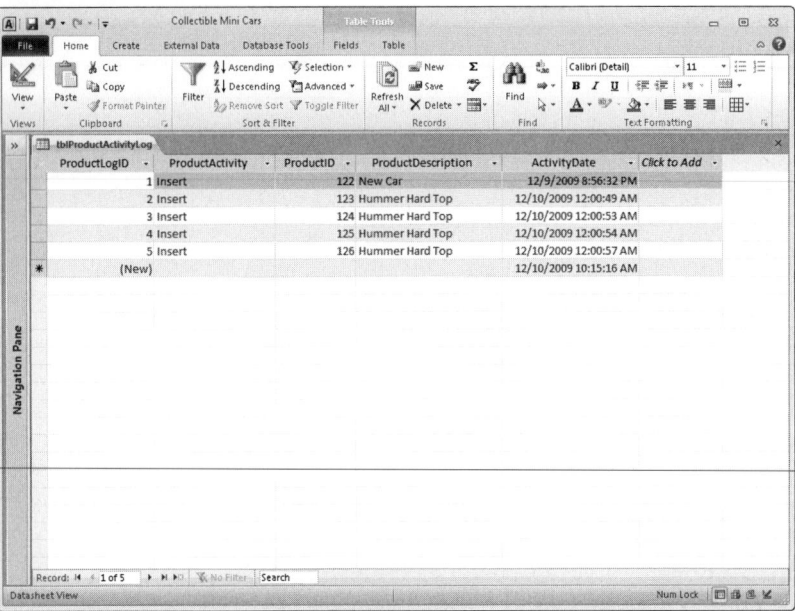

The `AfterInsert` data macro runs whenever a record is added to the table. Similar data macros can be added to the table's `AfterUpdate` and `AfterDelete` to log other changes to the table. You'll notice that `tblProductActivityLog` includes a text field named `ProductActivity` containing different changes (`Insert`, `Update`, `Delete`) occurring to the table.

Building Macros

You've seen several pictures of the Macro Designer, but let's take a closer look at how data blocks and macro actions are added to the design surface, and explore some of the options for managing macro objects once they're added to a macro's design.

Adding macro items

Program-flow items, data blocks, and macro actions are added to the design surface by double-clicking their entry in the Action Catalog, or by dragging them from the Action Catalog onto the macro surface.

When you double-click an item, it's added to the macro in its most logical destination. For example, in Figure 15.10, an `If` flow item has been added to a blank macro.

Adding an `If` block to a new macro

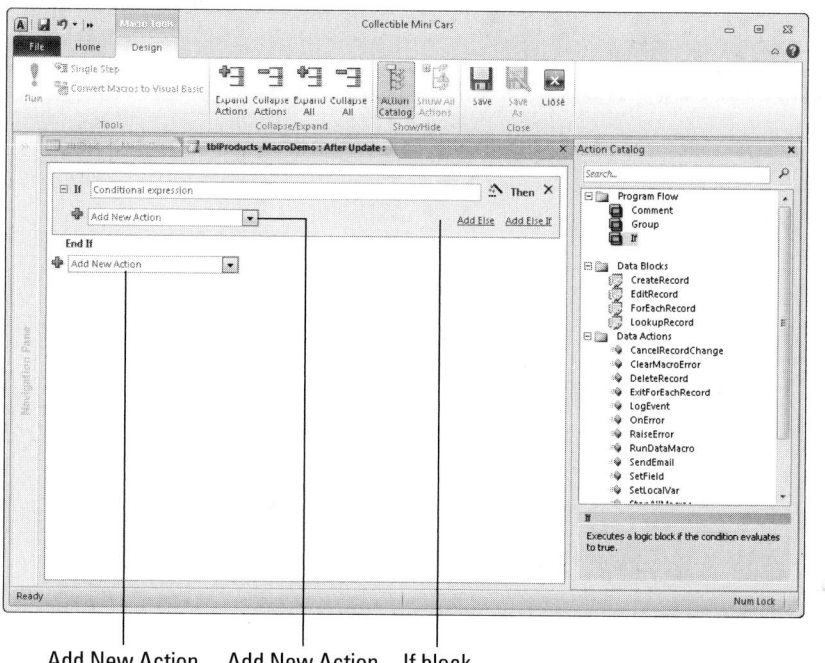

Add New Action   Add New Action   If block
(outside If block)   (inside If block)

In Figure 15.10, notice that the `If` block is highlighted with a gray background indicating the extent of the `If` block. Even though the input cursor is positioned in the Conditional expression box, double-clicking the `SetLocalVar` macro action adds it within the body of the `If` block, as shown in Figure 15.11. When you drag an item from the Action Catalog, you can drop it exactly where you want it in the macro's design.

Figure 15.11 can be a bit confusing because of the change from Figure 15.10. The `SetLocalVar` action is now highlighted with the gray background, and the border around the `If` block has disappeared. You have to watch for the `If` statement that begins the `If` block and the `End If` that ends the block to know its extent.

FIGURE 15.11

SetLocalVar has been added to the body of the If block

Beginning of If block

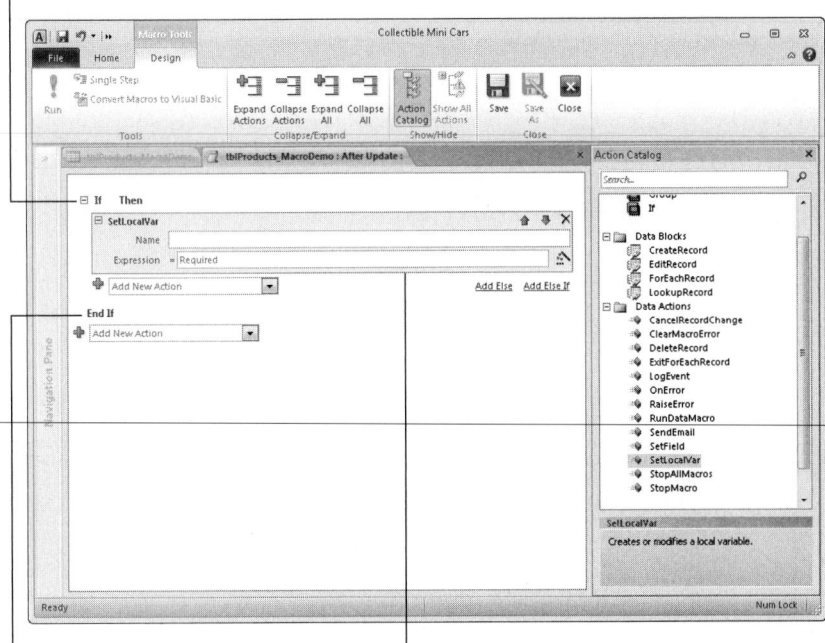

End of If block   SetLocalVar action within If block

You wouldn't be able to save this macro in its current condition. The If block requires its conditional expression, and none of the properties of SetLocalVar have been set. Figure 15.12 shows this macro with the conditional expression provided and the required SetLocalVar properties filled in.

Although the macro in Figure 15.12 doesn't do anything significant, we can use it to demonstrate other features of the Macro Designer.

FIGURE 15.12

A simple macro that updates a local variable

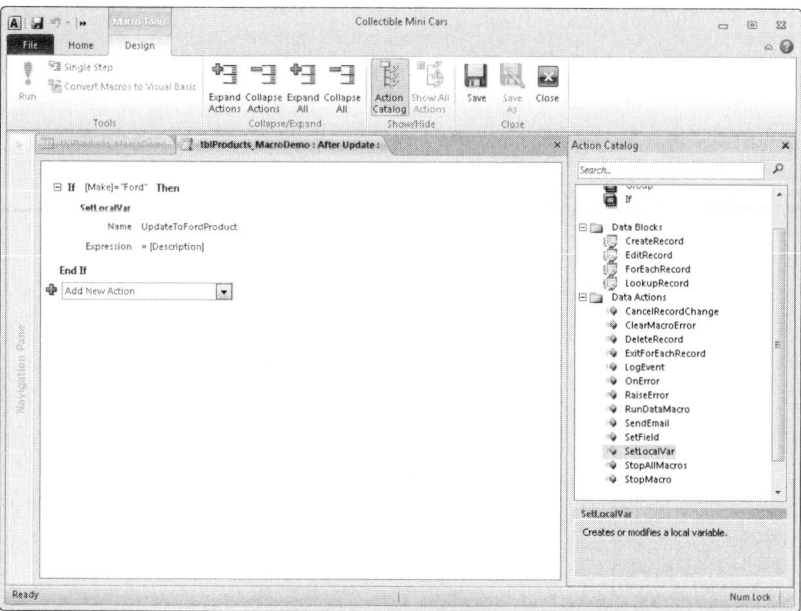

Manipulating macro items

In Figure 15.13, notice that, when the If block is selected, not only is the block highlighted with a gray background, but a delete icon (a graphical *X*) appears in the upper-right corner. You use the *X* to delete the currently selected item (block, macro action, and so on) and remove it from the macro. The macro deletes the item without confirmation, so be sure not to accidentally click the Delete icon.

In Figure 15.13, although you can't see it, the mouse is hovering over the SetLocalVar action. As the mouse hovers over an item, green up-and-down arrows appear to the right of the item's area. You use these buttons to adjust the item's position within a macro. For example, in a macro containing multiple actions, you may find that the macro runs incorrectly because the actions aren't ordered properly. Use the up and down arrows to reposition the actions into the correct sequence.

FIGURE 15.13

Hovering the mouse over `SetLocalVar`

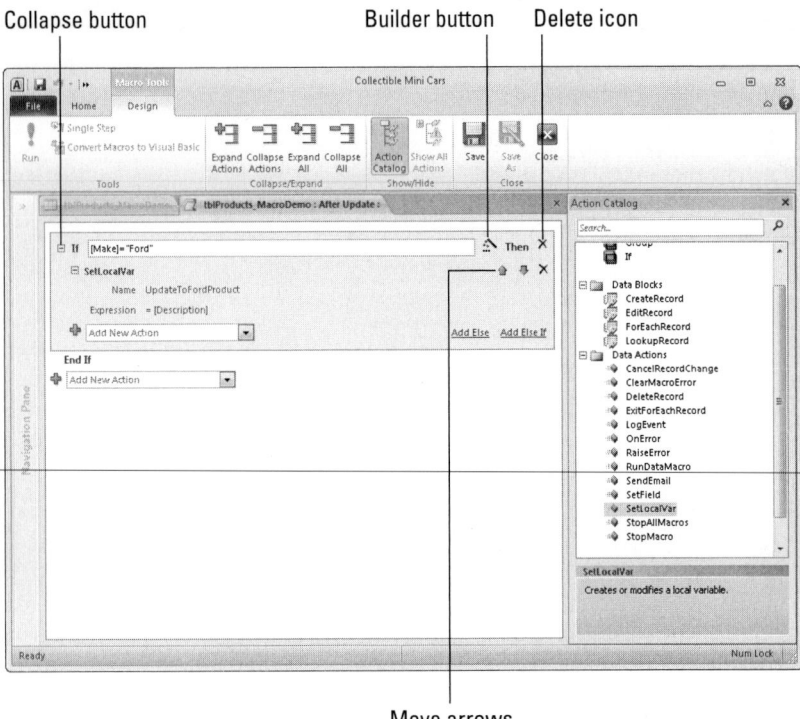

Also, in Figure 15.13, notice the Builder button to the right of the `If` statement's conditional expression box. This button opens the familiar Expression Builder (shown in Figure 15.14) used in many places in Access.

Macro items (blocks, actions, and so on) can be copied and pasted within the macro. In Figure 15.15, the `SetLocalVar` macro action has been copied (using the right-click context menu or by pressing Ctrl+C) and pasted (with the context menu or by pressing Ctrl+V) to a location below the `If` block. This action could've also been pasted within the `If` block, if necessary. You can't have two local variables with the same name, so in Figure 15.14 the Name box is selected, making it easy to assign the new variable's name.

FIGURE 15.14

The Expression Builder helps construct complex expressions.

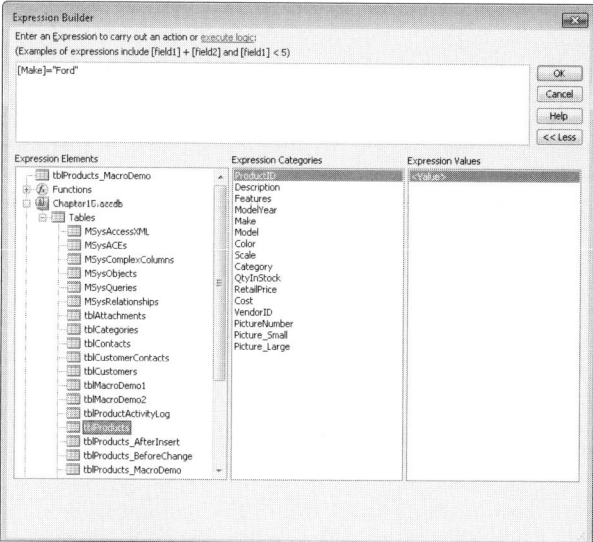

FIGURE 15.15

A copied macro item can be pasted almost anywhere within a macro.

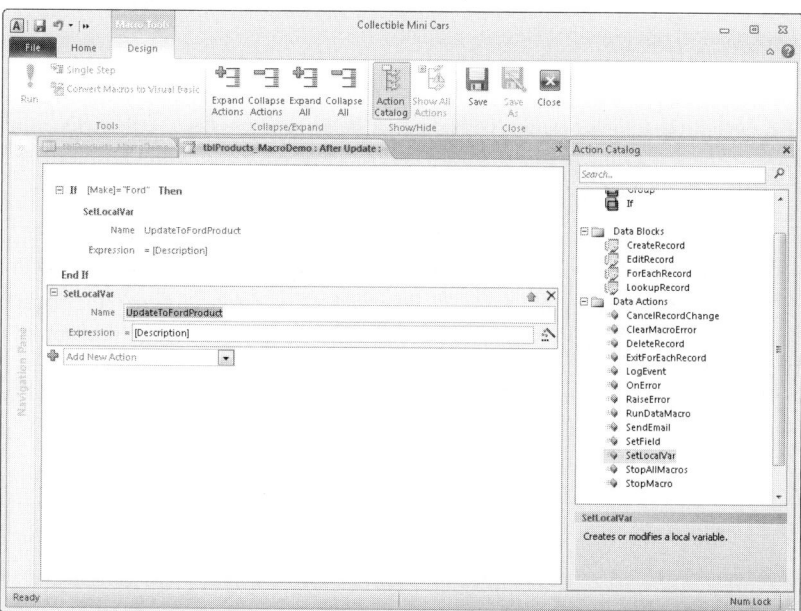

Moving macro items

In Figure 15.16, two more If blocks have been added to the macro. Each If block sets a separate local variable and doesn't do much else. Let's assume this arrangement isn't going to work for this macro and these items must be rearranged.

A simple macro with three If blocks

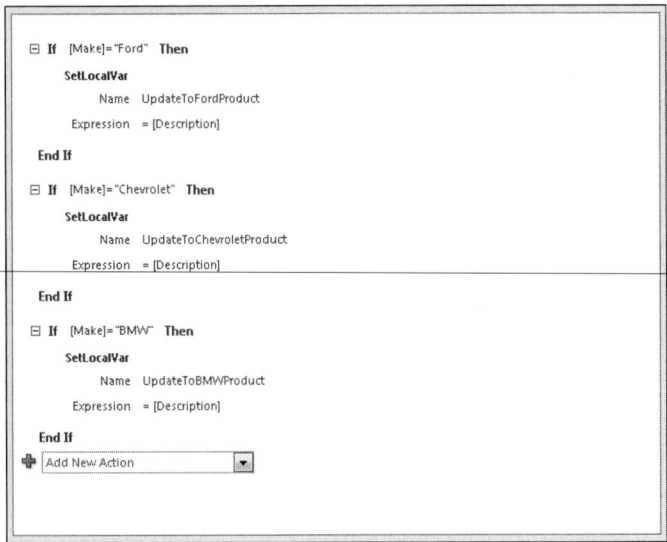

Macro items can be dragged into a new position with the mouse. This process is a little tricky because it's very easy to drag the wrong item away from its proper position. Carefully position the mouse pointer near the top of the target item, click with the mouse, and drag the item to its new location.

In Figure 15.17, the Chevrolet block is being dragged to a position between the BMW and Ford blocks. A horizontal bar (labeled "Position indicator" in Figure 15.17) indicates where the dragged item will be dropped when the mouse button is released. A gray shadow box indicates that you're dragging an item to a new location. Although hard to see in this figure, the shadow box contains the text of the dragged item so that you know what you're actually dragging with the mouse.

FIGURE 15.17

Dragging an item to a new location

Position indicator   Shadow box

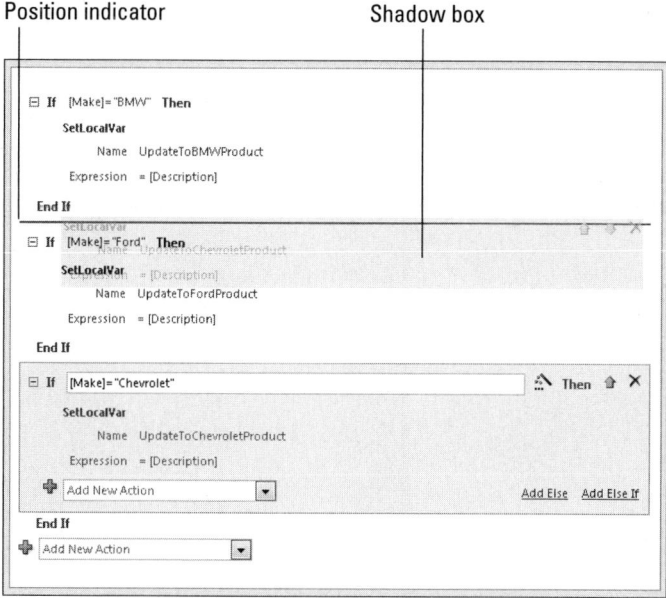

Collapsing macro items

Individual items in a macro can be collapsed to simplify the Macro Designer's surface. Each item is accompanied by a collapse/expand button to the left of its name in the designer. Clicking this button either expands or collapses the item to just one or two lines in the Macro Designer.

Figure 15.18 shows the demo macro with all three `If` blocks collapsed. Each `If` block occupies two lines, greatly simplifying the view.

Collapsing items makes them somewhat easier to drag to new locations, so consider using the collapse button when dragging large items.

Collapsed items help simplify the Macro Designer surface

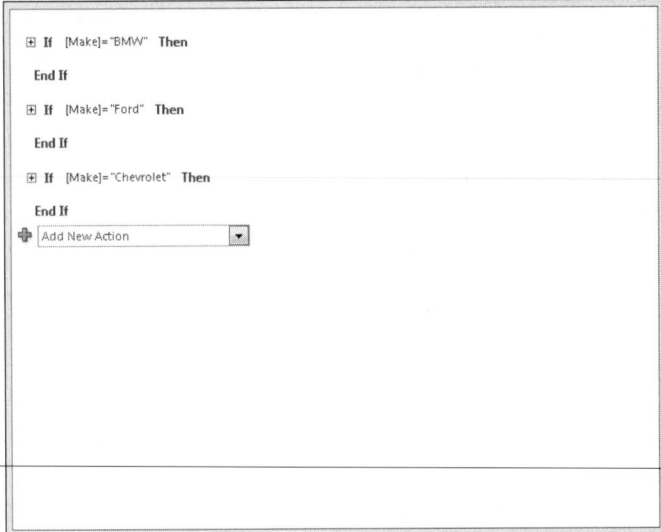

Saving a macro as XML

A completely hidden feature of Access 2010 data macros is the ability to copy them from the Macro Designer and paste them into a text editor as XML. Access internally stores macros as XML, and copying a macro actually means copying its XML representation.

There are a couple reasons you may want to save a macro as XML:

- **To e-mail the macro to someone else.**
- **To archive it as a backup.** Because each table contains only one copy of each event macro (`AfterUpdate`, for example) there's no easy way to set aside a copy of the macro before embarking on changes to the macro's logic.

Figure 15.19 shows a simple macro's XML pasted into Windows Notepad.

The XML saved in a text file can be pasted right into the Macro Designer surface and Access will display it as usual. The paste action works exactly as it does in Microsoft Word or a plain text editor. The pasted macro actions appear exactly where the cursor is when the paste is initiated.

Saving a macro as XML

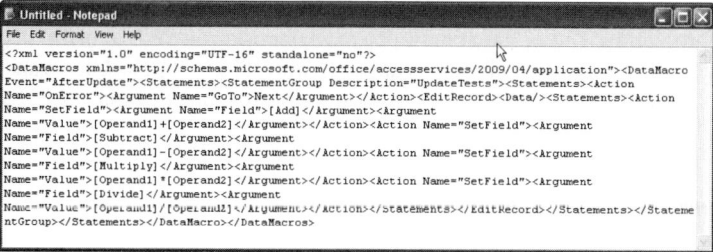

Recognizing the Limitations of Data Macros

As powerful as they are, data macros can't do everything. For example, data macros have no user interface at all. Data macros can't display a message box and can't open a form or report. Your ability to communicate with the user interface from a data macro is very limited, so data macros can't be used to notify users of problems or changes to data in tables. Displaying a user interface (such as a message box) would extract a serious performance penalty, particularly during bulk updates or inserts. Data macros are meant to run invisibly, with the highest possible performance.

Data macros are attached directly to Access tables and not to individual fields. If you have a situation where more than a few fields must be monitored or updated, the macro may become quite complex. Using the `If` block construct is a good way to conditionally execute blocks of macro statements.

The Macro Designer supports only one macro at a time. You must come to a stopping point on the current macro before closing it and opening another data macro.

Similarly, the Macro Designer is modal. You can't leave the Macro Editor without closing and saving (or not saving) the current macro. This restriction makes it difficult to view a table's data when working on a data macro's logic. As always, careful planning is a good idea when considering adding a data macro to a table.

Data macro execution doesn't occur on the back end in a split-database paradigm. Although the data macro resides in the table in the back-end database, the data macro is only executed in the front end.

Data macros can't work on multi-value or attachment fields. If it's important to use logic to control these data types, you must use traditional user-interface macros or VBA.

Access 2010 data macros are not supported on linked tables. If the table in an Access database is linked to SQL Server, you can't write data macros for the table. You must use traditional user interface macros or VBA code for this purpose.

Data macros can't call VBA procedures. One of the primary objectives for data macros is to make them portable to SharePoint when an Access application is upsized. Any calls to VBA procedures are sure to fail because there is no way to convert VBA to JavaScript in the SharePoint environment.

Cross-Reference

Publishing an Access database to SharePoint is discussed in Chapters 34 and 35.

Data macros don't support transactions. Every field and record update is executed immediately, and there's no way to roll back multiple table changes.

Finally, data macros are not compatible with earlier versions of Access. An Access 2007 application (with Service Pack 1 installed) can read, but not write to, Access 2010 tables containing data macros. You could, if necessary, use Access 2010 data macros to maintain tables intended for backward compatibility. These data macros would automatically update the "backward compatibility" tables every time a change (insert, update, or delete) is made to a Access 2010 table. Access 2007 and earlier versions would either link to or import data from the backward-compatibility tables.

Summary

This chapter has taken a brief look at the Access 2010 data-macros feature. Access has never before supported the capability of executing programmable logic in response to changes at the table level. Server-based databases like SQL Server have long had triggers that perform these tasks in their databases, and Access developers have waited a long time for similar capabilities in Access.

Access data macros support a rich set of program-flow, data-block, and macro-action items. When properly applied to Access tables, data macros provide you with valuable options and features, such as validating data, maintaining update logs, and calculating derived values — all at the table level.

When properly used in Access 2010 applications, data macros are capable of reducing the amount of VBA code required for managing data while adding considerable consistency to an application's data handling.

Part III

More-Advanced Access Techniques

Microsoft Access is a very sophisticated database-development system. Although many casual Access developers never move beyond building simple forms and reports, you can do much more with Microsoft Access if you know how. The chapters in this part cover many, but not all, of the capabilities possible with Microsoft Access. The topics in these chapters range from creating advanced queries and integrating Access with other applications, to controlling the user interface and manipulating data with the VBA programming language.

This section of this book contains many examples that show how to use these techniques in Microsoft Access applications. You'll make good use of this book's CD as you work through the examples presented in these chapters.

This part also includes a chapter on multiuser database development. As you'll soon see, there are considerations in multiuser applications that never arise in single-user environments. You'll have to keep these principles and concerns in mind as you work on applications destined for multiuser environments to ensure that your applications don't confuse users or cause data loss as one user overwrites another user's work.

IN THIS PART

Chapter 16
Working with External Data

Chapter 17
Importing and Exporting Data

Chapter 18
Advanced Access Query Techniques

Chapter 19
Advanced Access Form Techniques

Chapter 20
Advanced Access Report Techniques

Chapter 21
Building Multiuser Applications

Chapter 22
Integrating Access with Other Applications

Chapter 23
Handling Errors and Exceptions

Working with External Data

So far, you've worked with data in Access tables found within the current database. In this chapter, you explore the use of data from other types of files. You learn to work with data from database, spreadsheet, HTML, and text-based files. After I describe the general relationship between Access and external data, I explain the major methods of working with external data: linking and importing/exporting.

On the CD-ROM

This chapter uses the `Chapter16.accdb` database as well as several other files that you'll use for linking. If you haven't already copied these files onto your machine from the CD, you'll need to do so now.

Note that, because the point of this chapter is to show how Access works with external data, there are examples of external data that you need to copy to your machine. Unfortunately, when working with external data, Access requires an exact path to each file — it can't work with relative paths. That means that when you copy `Chapter16.accdb` to your machine, it won't work until you relink the various external files. I show you how to do that in this chapter. For now, be aware that the following tables are linked to the files indicated:

IN THIS CHAPTER

Looking at the types of external data and methods for working with them

Linking your Access database to external data

Using linked tables

Linking to external data sources with code

Table	External File Type	Filename(s)
CONTACTS	dBase 5.0	CONTACTS.DBF, CONTACTS.DBT, Contacts.INF, CONTACTS.MDX
Customers	Excel	CollectibleMiniCars.xls
CustomerTypes	HTML	CustomerTypes.html
Sales	Paradox 3.X	Sales.DB
tblSales	Access	Chapter16_Link.accdb
tblSalesLineItems	Excel 8.0	tblSalesLineItems.xls
tblSalesPayments	Access	Chapter16_Link.accdb
xlsProducts	Excel 8.0	Products.xls

The data linked or imported into Access applications comes in a bewildering variety of formats. There is no practical way to document every possible type of import or linking operation in a single chapter. Therefore, this chapter discusses the essential steps required to import or link to external data, and gives a few examples demonstrating how these processes are performed in Microsoft Access, instead of filling page after page with examples that may or may not be relevant to your work.

As you'll soon see, knowledge of the external data format is critical to a successful import or linking operation. You must have some notion of the external data format before you can successfully import data into your Access application or incorporate the data into an Access database through linking. This chapter points out many of the issues involved if you choose to import or link to external data; it's intended to serve as a guide as you perform these operations in your Access applications.

Looking at How Access Works with External Data

Exchanging information between Access and another program is an essential capability in today's database world. Information is usually stored in a wide variety of application programs and data formats. Access, like many other products, has its own native file format, designed to support referential integrity and provide support for rich data types, such as OLE objects. Most of the time, Access alone is sufficient for the job. Occasionally, however, you need to move data from one Access database file to another or use data from another program's format.

Types of external data

Access can use and exchange data among a wide range of applications. For example, you may need to get data from other database files (such as FoxPro or dBASE files) or get information from a SQL

Server, Oracle, or even a text file. Access can move data among several categories of applications, including other Windows applications, Macintosh applications, other database management systems, text files, and even mainframe files.

Ways of working with external data

Often, you need to move data from another application or file into your Access database, or vice versa. You might need to get information you already have in an external spreadsheet file. You can reenter all that information by hand or have it automatically imported into your database.

Access has tools that enable you to exchange data with another database or spreadsheet file. In fact, Access can exchange data with more than 15 different file types:

- Access database objects (all types)
- dBASE
- Microsoft FoxPro
- Text files
- Lotus 1-2-3
- Microsoft Excel
- ODBC databases (Microsoft SQL Server, Sybase Server, Oracle Server, and other ODBC-compliant databases)
- HTML tables, lists, and documents
- XML documents
- Microsoft Outlook
- Microsoft Exchange documents
- Microsoft SharePoint
- Microsoft Word Merge documents
- Rich Text Format documents

Access works with these external data sources in several ways:

- **Linking:** Creates a connection to a table in another Access database or links to the data from a different database format
- **Importing:** Copies data from a data source, another Access database, or another application's database file into an Access table
- **Exporting:** Copies data from an Access table into a text file, another Access database, or another application's file

There are distinct differences among the three methods:

- **Linking uses the data in its current file format (such as Excel or FoxPro).** The link to data remains in its original file. The file containing the link data should not be moved, deleted, or renamed. Otherwise, Access won't be able to locate the data the next time it's needed. If moving or renaming the linked data source is unavoidable, Access provides tools for relinking to the source.

- **Importing makes a copy of the external data and brings the copy into the Access database.** The imported data is converted to the appropriate Access data type, stored in a table, and managed by Access from that point on.

- **Exporting makes a copy of the data in the Access database and puts the copy into the file format of another application.** The exported data can be used by the other application from that point on.

Each method has clear advantages and disadvantages, covered in the following sections.

When to link to external data

Linking in Access enables you to work with the data in another application's format — thus, sharing the file with the existing application. If you leave data in another database format, Access can read the data while the original application is still using it. This capability is useful when you want to work with data in Access that other programs also need to work with. However, there are limitations as to what you can do with linked data. For example, you can't update data in a linked Excel spreadsheet or a linked text file. The ability to work with external data is also useful when you use Access as a front end for a SQL Server database — you can link to a SQL Server table and directly update the data, without having to batch-upload it to SQL Server.

Access databases are often linked to external data so that people can use Access forms to add and update the external data, or to use the external data in Access reports.

You can link to the following types of data in Access:

- Other Access tables (`.accdb`, `.accde`, `.accdr`, `.mdb`, `.mda`, `.mde`)
- Excel spreadsheets
- Exchange documents
- Outlook documents
- FoxPro
- dBASE
- Text files
- HTML documents
- SharePoint Team Services
- ODBC databases

Caution

Access is capable of linking to HTML tables and text tables for read-only access. You can use and look at tables in HTML or text format; however, the tables can't be updated and records can't be added to them using Access.

A big disadvantage of working with linked tables is that you lose the capability to enforce referential integrity between tables (unless all the linked tables are in the same external Access database, or all are in some other database management system that supports referential integrity). Linked tables may exhibit somewhat poorer performance than local tables. Depending on the source, and the location of the source data, users might experience a noticeable delay when they open a form or report that is based on linked data.

Performance issues become more pronounced when joining linked and local data in a query. Because Access is unable to apply optimization techniques to foreign data, many joins are inefficient and require a lot of memory and CPU time to complete. However, Access's outstanding ability to work with so many different types of external data makes it the ideal platform for applications requiring these features.

When to import external data

Importing data enables you to bring an external table or data source into a new or existing Access table. By importing data, Access automatically converts data from the external format and copies it into Access. You can even import data objects into a different Access database or Access project than the one that is currently open. If you know that you'll use your data in Access only, you should import it. Generally, Access works faster with its own local tables.

Note

Because importing makes another copy of the data, you might want to delete the old file after you import the copy into Access. Sometimes, however, you'll want to preserve the old data file. For example, the data might be an Excel spreadsheet still in use. In cases such as this, simply maintain the duplicate data and accept that storing it will require more disk space (and that the two files are going to get out of sync).

One of the principal reasons to import data is to customize it to meet your needs. After a table has been imported into an Access database, you can work with the new table as if you'd built it in the current database. With linked tables, on the other hand, you're greatly limited in the changes you can make. For example, you can't specify a primary key or assign a data-entry rule, which means that you can't enforce integrity against the linked table. Also, because linked tables point to external files, which Access expects to find in a specific location, it can make distributing your application more difficult.

Data is frequently imported into an Access database from an obsolete system being replaced by a new Access application. When the import process is complete, the obsolete application can be removed from the user's computer.

Working with data in unsupported programs

Although uncommon, you might occasionally need to work with data from a program that isn't stored in a supported external database or file format. In cases such as this, the programs usually can export or convert their data into one of the formats recognized by Access. To use the data in these programs, export it into a format recognized by Access and then import it into Access.

For example, many applications can export to the dBASE file format. If the dBASE format is not available, most programs, even those on different operating systems, can export data to delimited or fixed-width text files, which you can then import into Access.

Tip

If you'll be importing data from the same source frequently, you can automate the process with a macro or a VBA procedure. This can be very helpful for those times when you have to import data from an external source on a regular schedule or you have complex transformations that must be applied to the imported data.

When to export internal data

Exporting data enables you to pass data to other applications. By exporting data, Access automatically converts data to the external format and copies it to a file that can be read by the external application. As has already been mentioned, sometime you must import data into Access as opposed to just linking to the external data source if you want to be able to modify the data. If you still need to be able to work with the modified data in the external application, you have little choice but to create a new file by exporting the modified data.

A common reason to export data is to because you want to share the data with other users who don't have Access installed.

Linking External Data

As the database market continues to grow, the need to work with information from many different sources will escalate. If you have information captured in a SQL Server database or an old dBase table, you don't want to reenter the information from these sources into Access. Ideally, you want to open an Access table containing the data and use the information in its native format, without having to copy it or write a translation program to access it. In many cases, the capability of accessing information from one database format while working in another is often an essential starting point for many business projects.

Using code to copy or translate data from one application format to another is both time-consuming and costly. The time it takes can mean the difference between success and failure. Therefore, you want an intermediary between the different data sources in your environment.

Access can simultaneously link to multiple tables contained within other database systems. After an external file is linked, Access stores the link specification and uses the external data as if it were contained in a local table. Access easily links to other Access database tables as well as to non-Access database tables such as dBASE and FoxPro. A recommended practice is to split an Access database into two separate databases, for easier use in a multiuser or client-server environment.

Linking to external database tables

In the "Ways of working with external data" section, earlier in this chapter, you saw a list of database tables and other types of files that Access links to. Access displays the names of linked tables in the object list and uses a special icon to indicate that the table is linked and not local. An arrow pointing to an icon indicates that the table name represents a link data source. Figure 16.1 shows several linked tables in the list. (The icon indicates that the file is linked. The icon also indicates which type of file is linked to the current Access database. For example, Excel has an *X* symbol in a box and dBASE tables have a *dB* symbol.)

FIGURE 16.1

Linked tables in an Access database. Notice that each linked table has an icon indicating its status as a linked table.

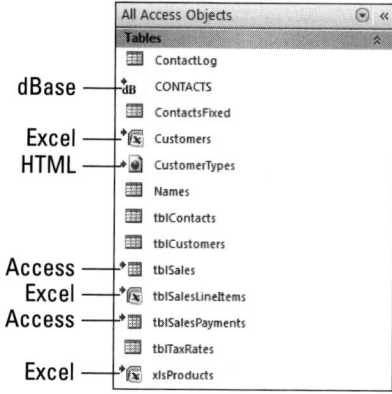

After you link an external database table to your Access database, you use it as you would any other table. For example, Figure 16.2 shows a query using several linked tables: `tblCustomers` (a local Access table), `tblSales` (a linked Access table), `tblSaleLineItems` (from an Excel file), and `xlsProducts` (from another Excel file). As you can see, there's nothing that distinguishes the fact that the tables are from external sources — Access treats them no differently from any other tables.

FIGURE 16.2

A query using externally linked tables

Local Access table   Linked Excel worksheet

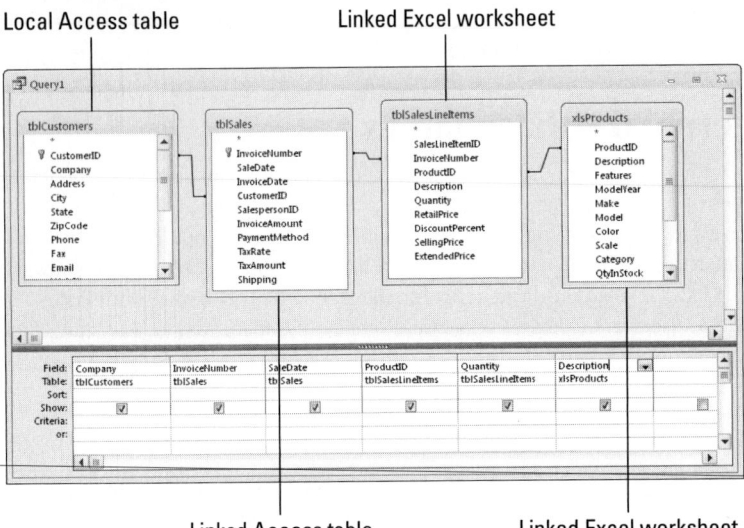

Linked Access table   Linked Excel worksheet

This query shows the potential benefit of linking to a variety of data sources and seamlessly displays data from internal and linked tables. Figure 16.3 shows the datasheet returned by this query. Each column in this datasheet comes from a different data source.

FIGURE 16.3

The datasheet view of externally linked data

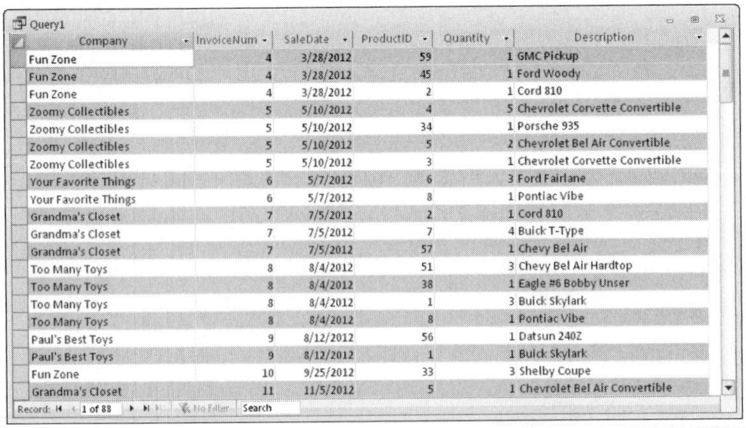

Figure 16.3 illustrates an important concept regarding using linked data in Access. Users will not know, nor will they care, where the data resides. All they want is to see the data in a format they expect. Only you, the developer, understand the issues involved in bringing this data to the user interface. Other than the limitations of linked data (explained in the next section), users won't be able to tell the difference between native and linked data.

Note

After you link an external table to an Access database, you should not move the source table to another drive or directory. Access doesn't bring the external data file into the `.accdb` file; it maintains the link via the file-name and the file's path. If you move the external table, you have to update the link using the Linked Table Manager, explained in the "Viewing or changing information for linked tables" section, later in this chapter.

Limitations of linked data

Although this chapter describes using linked data as if it existed as native Access tables, certain operations can't be performed on linked data. Plus, the prohibited operations depend, to a certain extent, on the type of data linked to Access.

These limitations are relatively easy to understand. Linked data is never "owned" by Access. External files that are linked to Access are managed by their respective applications. For example, an Excel worksheet is managed by Microsoft Excel. It would be presumptive — and dangerous — for Access to freely modify data in an Excel worksheet. For example, because many Excel operations depend on the relative positions of rows and columns in a worksheet, inserting a row into a worksheet might break calculations and other operations performed by Excel on the data. Deleting a row might distort a named range in the Excel worksheet, causing similar problems. Because there is no practical way for Access to understand all the operations performed on an external data file by its respective owner, Microsoft has chosen to take a very conservative route and not allow Access to modify data that might cause problems for the data's owner.

The following list describes the limitations of linked data:

- **Excel data:** Existing data in an Excel worksheet can't be changed, nor can rows be deleted or new rows be added to a worksheet. Excel data is essentially treated in a read-only fashion by Access.

- **Text files:** For all practical purposes, data linked to text files is treated as read-only in Access. Although the data can be used in forms and reports, you can't simply and easily update rows in a link text file, nor can you delete existing rows in a text file. Oddly enough, you can *add* new rows to a text file; presumably, this is because new rows won't typically break existing operations the way that deleting or changing the contents of an existing row might.

- **HTML:** HTML data is treated exactly as Excel data. You can't modify, delete, or add rows to an HTML table.

- **dBASE:** Because these are database files, you can pretty much perform the same data operations on dBASE tables as you can on native Access tables. This general statement applies only if a primary key is provided for each dBASE table.

- **ODBC:** ODBC is a data-access technology that uses a driver between an Access database and an external database file, such as Microsoft SQL Server or Oracle. Generally speaking, because the linked data source is a database table, you can perform whatever database operations (modifying, deleting, adding) you would with a native Access table, provided the table has a unique index defined. (I discuss ODBC database tables in some detail in the "Linking to ODBC data sources" section later in this chapter.)

Linking to other Access database tables

Access easily incorporates data located in the other Access files by linking to those tables. This process makes it easy to share data among Access applications across the network or on the local computer. The information presented in this section applies to virtually any Access data file you linked to from an Access database. Later in this chapter, you'll see short sections explaining the differences between linking to an Access table and linking to each of the other types of data files recognized by Access.

Note

A very common practice among Access developers is splitting an Access database into two pieces. One piece contains the forms, reports, and other user-interface components of an application, while the second piece contains the tables, queries, and other data elements. There are many advantages to splitting Access databases, including certain performance benefits as well as easier maintenance. You can read about splitting Access databases in Chapter 21. The process of linking to external Access tables described in this section is an essential part of the split database paradigm.

After you link to another Access table, you use it just as you use any table in the open database (with the exception that it can't be used in a relationship to other tables not in the source database). Follow these steps to link to tblSalesPayments in the Chapter16_Link.accdb database from the Chapter16.accdb database file:

1. Open the Chapter16.accdb database.

2. Select the External Data ribbon, and then choose Access as the type of data you want to link.

   The Get External Data dialog box (shown in Figure 16.4) appears.

3. Click the Browse button to open the Windows File Open dialog box. Locate the Chapter16_Link file, and click Open.

   The File Open dialog box closes and you're taken back to the Get External Data dialog box.

4. Click OK in the Get External Data dialog box.

   The Link Tables dialog box enables you to select one or more tables from the selected database (in this case, Chapter16_Link). Figure 16.5 shows the Link Tables dialog box open on Chapter16_Link.accdb.

5. Select tblSalesPayments and click OK.

   Double-clicking the table name won't select the table — you must highlight it and then click OK.

FIGURE 16.4

Use the Get External Data dialog box to select the type of operation you want to perform on the external data sources.

Import

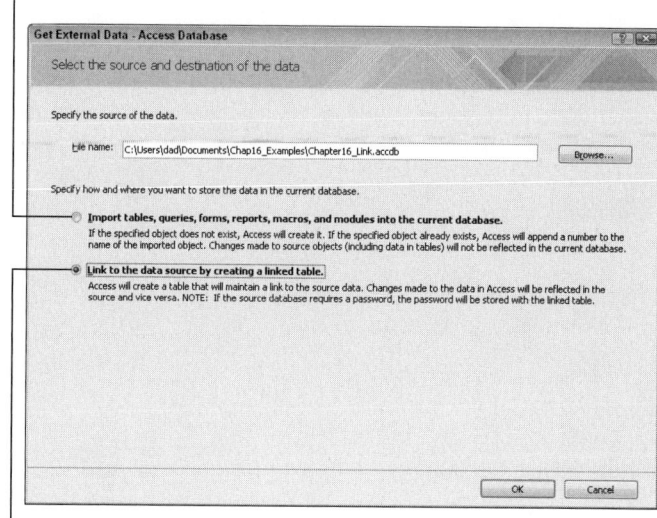

Link

FIGURE 16.5

Use the Link Tables dialog box to select the Access table(s) for linking.

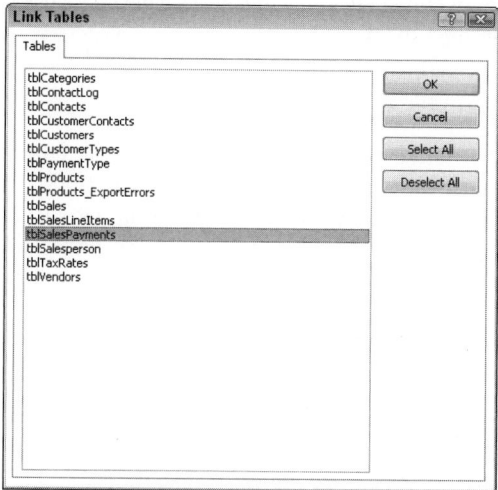

After you link `tblSalesPayments`, Access returns to the object list and shows you the newly linked table. Figure 16.6 shows `tblSalesPayments` linked to the current database. Notice the special icon attached to `tblSalesPayments`. This icon indicates that this table is linked to an external data source. Hovering over the linked table with the mouse reveals the linked table's data source.

FIGURE 16.6

The Navigation Pane with `tblSalesPayments` added. Notice the icon indicating that this is a linked table.

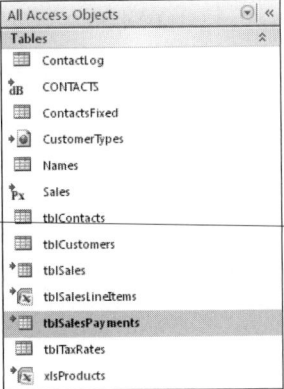

Tip

You can link more than one table at a time by selecting multiple tables before you click the OK button in the Link Tables dialog box. Clicking the Select All button selects all the tables. Note that, once you've selected all the tables, you can click on individual selections to unselect them.

Linking to ODBC data sources

One significant advance with regard to data sharing is the establishment of the Open Database Connectivity (ODBC) standard by Microsoft and other vendors. ODBC is a specification that software vendors use to create drivers for database products. This specification lets your Access application work with data in a standard fashion across many different database platforms. If you write an application conforming to ODBC specifications, then your application will be able to use any other ODBC-compliant back end.

For example, say you create an Access application that uses a Microsoft SQL Server database back end. The most common way to accomplish this requirement is to use the SQL Server ODBC driver. After developing the application, you find that one of your branch offices would like to use the application as well, but they're using Oracle as a database host. If your application has conformed closely to ODBC syntax, then you should be able to use the same application with Oracle by acquiring an Oracle ODBC driver. Not only are vendors supplying drivers for their own products, but there are now software vendors who only create and supply ODBC drivers.

Cross-Reference

Linking to ODBC sources is discussed in detail in Chapter 37. In that chapter, you'll learn about setting up ODBC data sources and linking to those sources. Although SQL Server is used as the example in Chapter 37, the same principles apply to all ODBC data sources.

Linking to xBase files

Unlike Access, dBASE and FoxPro (and other xBase systems) store each table as a separate file with a `.dbf` extension. Each `.dbf` file may be accompanied by an `.ndx` or `.mdx` file containing the indexes associated with the dBASE table.

When you link to a dBASE table, Access might ask you if you want to link to the index file associated with the dBASE table. In almost every case, you'll want to include the index file in the linking operation. Otherwise, the dBASE data will be read-only and not updatable.

One other significant difference between Access and dBASE is that table and field names are much shorter in dBASE than they are in Access, and they're almost always expressed in all uppercase characters.

Linking to dBASE or other xBase data files is much like linking to an external Access table. The main difference is that you select dBASE or FoxPro from the Files of Type drop-down list in the File Open dialog box. Also, because each xBase file is a table, you don't have to specify which table to link. Otherwise, the processes are virtually identical.

On the CD-ROM

This book's CD includes a dBASE IV file named CONTACTS.dbf containing a copy of the Contacts table from the Collectible Mini Cars application. You might want to use this file to practice linking the base tables.

Linking to non-database data

You can also link to non-database data, such as Excel, HTML, and text files. When you select one of these types of data sources, Access runs a Link Wizard that prompts you through the process.

Linking to Excel

The main issues to keep in mind when linking to Excel data are

- An Excel `.xls` spreadsheet file might contain multiple worksheets. You must choose which worksheet within a workbook file to link (unless you're using named ranges).

- You may link to named ranges within an Excel worksheet. Each range becomes a separate linked table in Access.

• Excel columns may contain virtually any type of data. Just because you have successfully linked to an Excel worksheet doesn't mean that your application will be able to use all the data contained in the worksheet. Because Excel doesn't limit the types of data contained in a worksheet, your application may encounter multiple types of data within a single column of a linked Excel worksheet. This means that you may have to add code or provide other strategies for working around the varying types of data contained in an Excel worksheet.

On the CD-ROM

This book's CD contains an Excel spreadsheet created by exporting the Products table from the Collectible Mini Cars application. Use this file to practice linking to Excel data, keeping in mind that, in practice, the data you're likely to encounter in Excel spreadsheets is far more complex and less orderly than the data contained in the Products.xls file.

By linking to an Excel table, you can update its records from within Access or any other application that updates Excel spreadsheets.

Follow these steps to link to the Excel Products.xls spreadsheet:

1. In the Chapter16 database, click the Excel button on the External Data ribbon.

    The Get External Data dialog box (shown in Figure 16.7) appears.

2. In the Get External Data dialog box, select Link to the Data Source by Creating a Linked Table, and click Browse.

    The same Get External Data dialog box is used for both import and link operations. So, be sure the correct operation is selected before continuing.

Cross-Reference

Importing data into Access is discussed in Chapter 17.

3. Click the Browse button to the right of the filename box.

    The File Open dialog box appears.

4. Locate and open the Excel file.

    You're returned to the Link Spreadsheet Wizard (see Figure 16.8).

    Notice that the Link Spreadsheet Wizard contains options for selecting either worksheets or named ranges within the workbook file. In this example, there are three different worksheets (named Products, Sales, and Contacts) within the spreadsheet file.

5. Select the Products worksheet for this demonstration.

6. The Link Spreadsheet Wizard walks you through a number of different screens where you specify details such as First Row Contains Column Headings and the data type you want to apply to each column in the Excel worksheet.

7. The last screen of the Link Spreadsheet Wizard asks for the name of the newly linked table. The linked table is established as you click the Finish button and are returned to the Access environment.

The first screen of the Get External Data dialog box

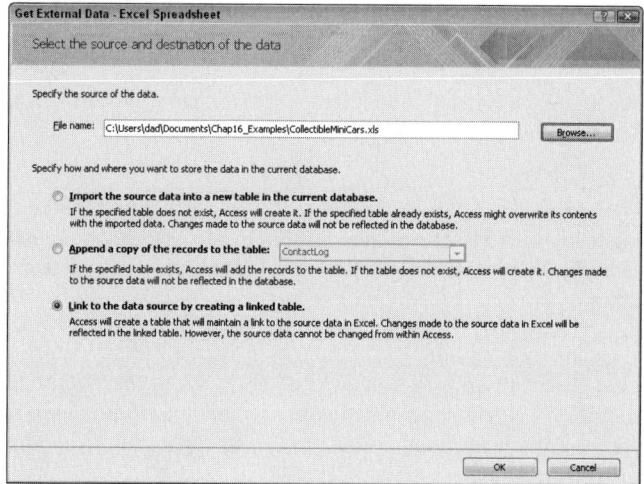

The main Link Spreadsheet Wizard screen

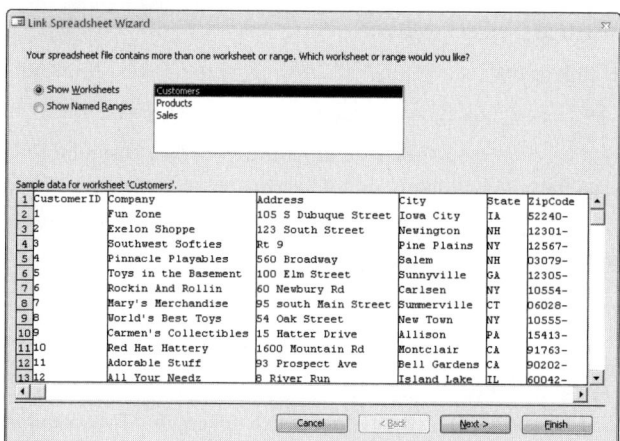

As with so many other things in database development, many decisions involved in linking to external data sources are based on how the data is to be used in the application. Also, the names you provide for fields and other details have a direct impact on your application.

Linking to HTML files

Linking to data contained in HTML documents is not covered in detail in this book because of the rather severe limitations imposed by Access on this process. For example, Access is unable to retrieve data from an arbitrary HTML file. The data must be presented as an HTML table, in a row-and-column format, and the data has to be relatively clean (absent any unusual data or mix of data, such as text, image, and numeric data combined within a single HTML table).

You're likely to encounter problems if more than one HTML table appears on the page, or if the data is presented in a hierarchical fashion (parent and child data).

Tip

All things considered, linking to arbitrary HTML documents is hit-or-miss at best. You're much better off linking to an HTML document specifically prepared as a data source for your Access application than trying to work with arbitrary HTML files.

Plus, if someone is going to the trouble of creating specialized HTML documents to be used as Access data sources, producing comma-separated values (CSV) or fixed-width text files is probably a better choice than HTML. Comma-separated values, where the fields in each row are separated by commas, is a very common way to move data from one application to another. CSV and fixed-width file types are discussed in the next section.

Having said that, the process of linking HTML data is very similar to linking to Excel spreadsheets:

1. Select the More drop-down list in the External Data tab and select HTML Document from the list.

   The Get External Data dialog box appears.

2. Select the Link to the Data Source by Creating a Link Table option, and click Browse.

   The File Open dialog box appears, enabling you to search for the HTML file you want to link.

   From this point on, the process of linking to HTML data is similar to linking to other types of data files, including providing field names and other details of the linked data.

   Figure 16.9 shows the first screen of the Import HTML Wizard. Click the Advanced button in the lower-left hand corner to get to the Import Specification screen (shown in Figure 16.10), where you can provide the field names and other details.

On the CD-ROM

This book's CD includes a very simple HTML file named `CustomerTypes.html`. The data in this file is, perhaps, overly simplistic, but it gives you the opportunity to practice linking to HTML documents. Because of the wide variety of ways that data is stored in HTML documents, it isn't possible to generalize an approach to linking to HTML data. However, as you gain proficiency with the ability to link to external data sources, you might find linking to HTML a valuable addition to your Access skills.

FIGURE 16.9

The Import HTML Wizard screen showing the data in the HTML file

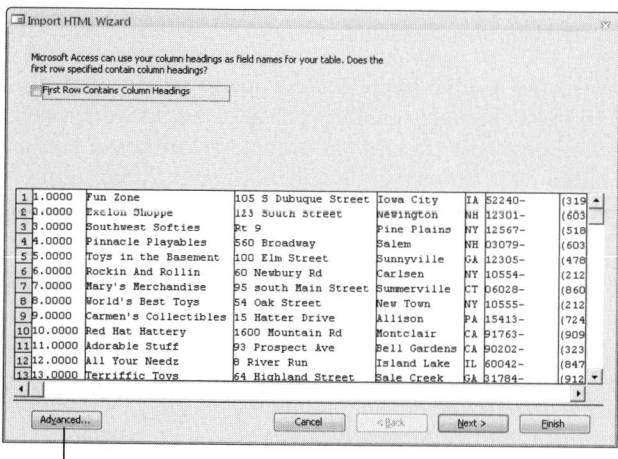

Click to provide field names and other details

FIGURE 16.10

The Import HTML Wizard screen that is used to name the column headings (field names) for the linked table

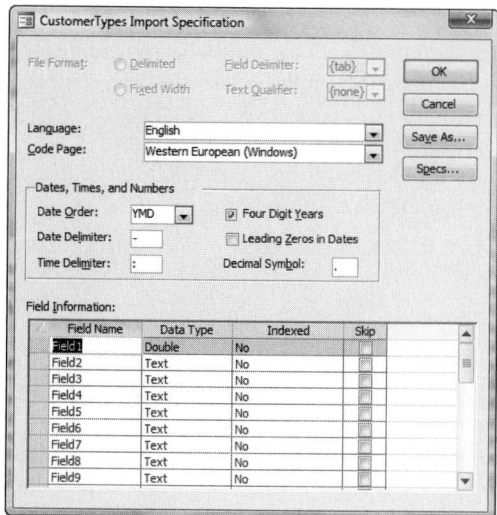

Linking to text files

A far more common situation than linking to HTML files is linking to data stored in plain text files. Most applications, including Microsoft Word and Excel, are able to publish data in a variety of text formats. The most common formats you're likely to encounter are

- **Fixed width:** In a fixed-width text file, each line represents one row of a database table. Each field within a line occupies exactly the same number of characters as the corresponding field in the lines above and below the current line. For example, a `Last Name` field in a fixed-width text file might occupy 20 characters, while a phone number field may only use 10 or 15 characters. Each data field is padded with spaces to the right to fill out the width allocated to the field. Figure 16.11 shows a typical fixed-width file open in Windows Notepad.

FIGURE 16.11

A typical fixed-width text file

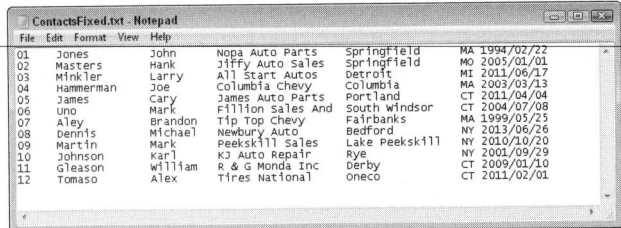

- **Comma-separated values (CSV):** Comma-separated values are somewhat more difficult to understand than fixed width. Each field is separated from the other fields by a comma character (,), and each field occupies as much space is necessary to contain the data. Generally speaking, there is little blank space between fields in a CSV file. The advantage of CSV files is that the data can be contained in a smaller file because each field occupies only as much disk space as necessary to contain the data.

  CSV files can be difficult to read when opened in Windows Notepad. Figure 16.12 shows a typical CSV text file.

FIGURE 16.12

CSV data is more compact than fixed-width text, but it's more difficult to read.

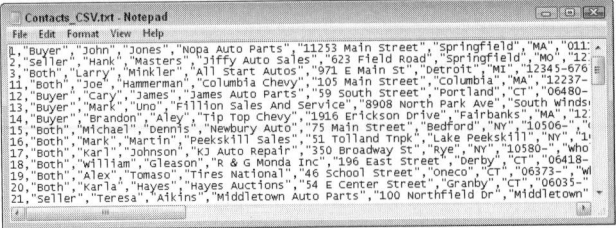

Text files are often used as intermediate data-transfer vehicles between dissimilar applications. For example, there might be an obsolete data-management system in your environment that is incompatible with any of the link or import data types in Access. If you're lucky, the obsolete system is able to output either fixed-width or CSV files. Linking to or importing the fixed-width or CSV files might be the best option for sharing data with the obsolete system. At the very least, much less time is required linking or importing the data than would be involved in rekeying all the information from the obsolete system into Access.

Follow these steps to link to the Contacts text file:

1. Open the Chapter16.accdb database and select the External Data ribbon.

2. Click on the Text File button.

   The Get External Data dialog box appears.

3. Be sure the Link to the Data Source by Creating a Link Table option is selected, and then click Browse.

   The File Open dialog box appears.

4. Locate the text file (either Contacts_FixedWidth.txt or Contacts_CSV.txt) and click Open.

5. Dismiss the other dialog boxes that appear.

   You'll be taken to the Link Text Wizard dialog box.

   Generally speaking, Access makes a pretty good guess at how the data in the file is delimited. Linking to text data involves nothing more than clicking Next and verifying that Access has correctly identified the data in the file.

On the CD-ROM

Rather than show or describe each of the dialog boxes in the Link Text Wizard, link to Contacts_CSV.txt and Contacts_FixedWidth.txt, both included on this book's CD.

As you'll see when you link to these files, about the only input required from you is to provide a name for each of the fields Access finds in the text files. If you're lucky, the text file includes field names as the first row in the text file. Otherwise, linking to text files will likely require that you specify names for each field.

Working with Linked Tables

After you link to an external table from another database, you use it just as you would any another Access table. You use linked tables with forms, reports, and queries just as you would native Access tables. When working with external tables, you can modify many of their features (for example, setting view properties and relationships, setting links between tables in queries, and renaming the tables).

One note on renaming linked tables: Providing a different name for the table inside of Access does not change the name of the file that is linked to the application. The name that Access refers to a link table is maintained within the Access application and doesn't influence the physical table that's linked.

Setting view properties

Although an external table is used like another Access table, you can't change the structure (delete, add, or rearrange fields) of an external table. You can, however, set several table properties for the fields in a linked table:

- Format
- Decimal places
- Caption
- Input mask
- Unicode compressions
- IME sequence mode
- Display control

Setting relationships

Tip

Access enables you to set permanent relations at the table level between linked non-Access tables and native Access tables through the Relationships Builder. You can't, however, set referential integrity between linked tables, or between linked tables and internal tables. Access enables you to create forms and reports based on relationships set up in the Relationships Builder, such as building a SQL statement used as the RecordSource **property of a form or report.**

Linking to external Access tables maintains the relationships that might exist between the external tables. Therefore, when linking to a back-end database, the relationships you've established in the back end are recognized and honored by the front-end database. This is a good thing, since it means that the rules you've defined will be enforced regardless of how many front ends are created to use the tables.

Optimizing linked tables

When working with linked tables, Access has to retrieve records from another file. This process takes time, especially when the table resides on a network or in an SQL database. When working with external data, optimize performance by observing these basic rules:

- **Avoid using functions in query criteria.** This is especially true for aggregate functions, such as DTotal or DCount, which retrieve all records from the linked table before performing the query operation.
- **Limit the number of external records to view.** Create a query using criteria that limit the number of records from an external table. This query can then be used by other queries, forms, or reports.

- **Avoid excessive movement in datasheets.** View only the data you need to in a datasheet. Avoid paging up and down and jumping to the first or last record in very large tables. (The exception is when you're adding records to the external table.)

- **If you add records to external linked tables, create a form to add records and set the DataEntry property to True.** This makes the form an entry form that starts with a blank record every time it's executed. Data-entry forms are not pre-populated with data from the bound table. Using a dedicated data entry form is much more efficient than building a normal form, populating it with data from the linked source, and then moving to the end of the linked data just to add a new record.

Deleting a linked table reference

Deleting a linked table from the object list is a simple matter of performing three steps:

1. In the object list, select the linked table you want to delete.

2. Press the Delete key, or right-click on the linked table and select Delete from the shortcut menu.

3. Click OK in the Access dialog box to delete the file.

Note

Deleting an external table deletes only its name from the database object list. The actual data is not deleted from its source location.

Viewing or changing information for linked tables

Use the Linked Table Manager Wizard to update the links when you move, rename, or modify tables or indexes associated with a linked table. Otherwise, Access won't be able to find the data file referenced by the link.

1. Select the External Data ribbon and click the Linked Table Manager button.

    The Linked Table Manager dialog box (shown in Figure 16.13) appears, enabling you to locate the data files associated with the linked tables in the database.

2. Click the check box next to a linked table and click OK.

    Access verifies that the file can't be found, and the Select New Location dialog box appears.

3. Find the missing file and reassign the linkage to Access.

    If all the files are already linked correctly, clicking OK makes Access verify all the linkages associated with all the selected tables.

    If you know all of the linked data sources have been moved, select the Always Prompt for a New Location check box, and then click OK. Access then prompts you for the new location, and links all the tables as a batch process. You'll find this operation much faster than linking one or two tables at a time.

FIGURE 16.13

The Linked Table Manager enables you to relocate external tables that have been moved.

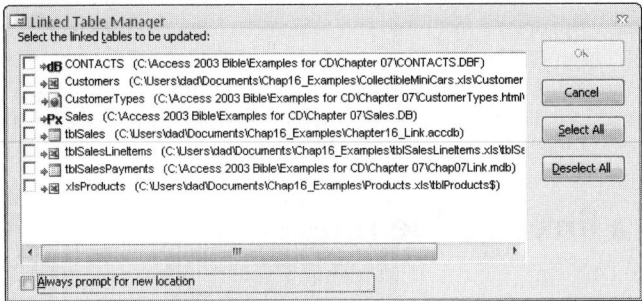

Note

If the Linked Table Manager Wizard is not present on your computer, Access automatically prompts you to provide the original Office CD so that Access can install the wizard. This may happen if you didn't instruct Office to install the Additional Wizards component during the initial installation process.

Using Code to Link Tables in Access

This section describes how to link tables to your Access application in code, instead of using the Access menus. It would be nice if you could just make the link once at development time and be done with the whole process. Occasionally, however, you might want to attach tables on the fly, to avoid losing a link. Testing your links whenever your application starts is a good practice — that way, you can keep users from facing any crashes or error messages. You'll find some examples of these routines in this section.

Note

The following code examples use DAO instead of ADO. For purposes such as linking tables, DAO works considerably faster than ADO, and is simpler to implement. The reason DAO is faster than ADO for simple operations such as linking tables is because DAO doesn't involve the overhead associated with declaring, instantiating, and discarding ActiveX controls. Because DAO is a much simpler object model, you'll find DAO is, arguably, a better fit for simple operations such as linking tables, although ADO might be a better choice for complex data management operations.

The Connect and SourceTableName properties

Open `Chapter16.accdb` and press Ctrl+G to open the Immediate window. Then, in the Immediate pane of the Immediate window, type the following:

```
? CurrentDB.TableDefs("tblContacts").Connect
```

You receive a zero-length string (" ") as the returned value. If, however, you type the following:

```
? CurrentDB.TableDefs("xlsProducts").Connect
```

you receive a much different result. Access returns a long string that looks something like this (although the path indicated at the end of this string may point to a different location):

```
Excel 8.0;HDR=NO;IMEX=2;DATABASE=C:\Data\CollectibleMiniCars.xls
```

In the first case, tblContacts is part of the current database, and Access finds it without any trouble. xlsProducts, on the other hand, is linked to an external Excel file. The Connect property of the xlsProducts contains information that Access uses to physically locate the Excel file and form a link to it.

The difference between the Connect property for tblContacts and xlsProducts is where the tables originate. The Connect property of an Access table found within the current database is a zero-length string because the table originates in the local database. There's nothing to connect to, or more appropriately, by default, the connection always exists. However, your ODBC, Excel, and linked Access data sources will always have a Connect property that explicitly tells Access what type of data is contained in the linked data source, and where the data source file can be found.

The Connect property string is composed of a number of different parameters, some of which are required, depending on the type of external data you're using. If you're accessing one of the Indexed Sequential Access Method (ISAM) formats that Access directly supports (Excel, dBASE, FoxPro, and so on), the Connect string is much more abbreviated, taking this form:

```
Object.Connect="Type;DATABASE=Path"
```

where *Object* is the name of the object variable for your TableDef, and *Type* is the type of database you're connecting to, such as dBASE IV, Excel 8.0, Text, and so on.

The Path parameter can be the complete path to the file, not including the filename itself, or it might include the filename as well, depending on the type of data source. For example, when connecting to another Access table, you include the entire path, like C:\Access\Samples\Nwind.mdb. The same is true of an Excel file.

When connecting to a dBASE file, however, you have to tell Access only the *path* to the file, not the .dbf file itself. The difference is in whether the object you'll be connecting to exists within another object, or whether the table is the file that you're going after. That's where the SourceTableName property comes in.

The SourceTableName property tells Access which object to take data from. If you want to connect to a dBASE file, you want your table definition to come from the .dbf itself. If, however, you're connecting to an Excel file, you might want the table to be based on a range of cells or a single worksheet within the .xls file, not the entire spreadsheet. Connecting to another Access .accdb or .mdb is the same way. To link to the Customers table in Northwind.accdb, your Connect string tells Access that the value of the DATABASE parameter is C:\Access\Samples\Northwind.mdb and that the SourceTableName property of your TableDef is

Customers. If you want to connect to a dBASE file named NewEmp.dbf located in the root directory of C:, you tell Access that the DATABASE is C:\ and the SourceTableName is NewEmp.dbf.

The AttachExcel() function (listed below) shows you how to connect to a named range within an Excel spreadsheet. To connect to a spreadsheet, you have to specify what kind of spreadsheet it is, where the spreadsheet file exists, and the range you want to connect to. You can use either a named range or a range of cells (such as A1:B20). You can also tell Access that the spreadsheet you're connecting to contains field names in the first row. The default for this parameter is Yes.

To use the AttachExcel() function, the calling procedure must pass the spreadsheet name, the new name for the Access table, and a valid Excel range name. To attach the range named Names from the spreadsheet EmpList.xls and give the attached table the name ExcelDemo, use the following statement:

```
Call AttachExcel("Emplist.xls", "ExcelDemo", "Names")
```

On the CD-ROM

The following function is located in the basAttachExcel module in Chapter16.accdb on the book's companion CD-ROM.

The AttachExcel() function returns a Boolean value reporting whether the Excel file was successfully attached (True) or not (False):

```
Function AttachExcel( _
    ByVal sFileName As String, _
    ByVal sTableName As String, _
    ByVal sRangeName As String _
    ) As Boolean
  Const conCannotOpen = 3432
  Const conNotRange = 3011
  Const conTableExists = 3012
  Dim db As DAO.Database
  Dim td As DAO.TableDef
  Dim sConnect As String
  Dim sMsg As String
  Dim sFunction As String
  On Error GoTo HandleError
  AttachExcel = False
  sFunction = "AttachExcel"
  ' Check for existence of worksheet:
  sFileName = CurDir() & "\" & sFileName
  ' If the file isn't found, notify
  ' the user and exit the procedure:
  If Len(Dir(sFileName)) = 0 Then
    MsgBox "The file " & sFileName _
        & " could not be found"
    MsgBox "Please move the file to " _
```

```
                  & CurDir() & " to continue"
          Exit Function
      End If
      Set db = CurrentDb
      ' Create a new tabledef in the current database:
      Set td = db.CreateTableDef(sTableName)
      ' Build Connect string:
    sConnect = "Excel 8.0;HDR=YES;DATABASE=" & sFileName
      td.Connect = sConnect
      ' Specify Range Name sRangeName:
      td.SourceTableName = sRangeName
      ' Append new linked table to TableDefs collection:
      db.TableDefs.Append td
      'Return True:
      AttachExcel = True
  ExitHere:
      Exit Function
  HandleError:
      Select Case Err
        Case conCannotOpen
            sMsg = "Cannot open " & sFileName
        Case conTableExists
            sMsg = "The table " & sTableName & _
                " already exists."
        Case conNotRange
            sMsg = "Can't find the " & sRangeName & " range."
        Case Else
            sMsg = "Error#" & Err & ": " & Error$
      End Select
      MsgBox sMsg, vbExclamation + vbOKOnly, _
          "Error in Procedure " & sFunction
      AttachExcel = False
      Resume ExitHere
  End Function
```

Connect strings and source table names are more involved when you're using ODBC data sources. For example, when you connect to a SQL Server ODBC data source, you have the option of specifying the type of source you'll be using (ODBC), the data source name (DSN), the application you're using, the table within the data source that contains the data you want, the workstation using the application, and a user ID and password. Not all these parameters are available to every ODBC data source, so you need to consult your ODBC driver manual to find out what you can and can't use.

By the way, you might not want to hard-code a user ID and password in your connect string but instead use some combination of Access and a customized security setup that allows you to capture a user's ID and password when the user logs in to your application and then pass those values dynamically.

One final example I've included in this section is one that shows you how to connect to a text file. As I mention in the "Linking to text files" section, earlier in this chapter, you can link to delimited or fixed-width text files. Linking to a text file follows the same process as the previous examples; the biggest difference is the DSN parameter. Before you can link to a text file, you must create an import specification that tells Access what the file looks like.

In previous versions of Access, you created import/export specs only when you imported or exported fixed files. But, beginning with Access 2007, you can create a spec for delimited files as well. If you use the Import Wizard, Access creates an import specification for you. The connect string for a text file is the name of the import spec you've created. The Database parameter is the path to the file, and the SourceTableName property is the filename you want to link to, without the file extension.

Import specifications are very convenient when data must be periodically linked or imported. For example, your users might require a weekly update from an external data source, or ad hoc linking from text files attached to e-mail messages. Once the import specification is prepared, it can be used over and over again without modification.

On the CD-ROM

The following function is located in the basLinkText module in Chapter16.accdb on this book's companion CD-ROM.

```
Function LinkText( _
    ByVal sFileName As String, _
    ByVal sDSN As String, _
    ByVal sFMT As String, _
    ByVal sHDR As String, _
    ByVal sIMEX As String, _
    ByVal sTableName As String _
    ) As Boolean
Dim db As DAO.Database
Dim td As DAO.TableDef
Dim x As Integer
Dim sType As String
Dim sPath As String
Dim sPathAndFileName As String
Dim sDatabase As String
Dim sConnect As String
Dim sMsg As String
Dim sFunction As String
Const conTableExists = 3012
On Error GoTo HandleError
    LinkText = False
    sFunction = "LinkTxt"
    ' Check for existence of file:
    sPath = CurDir() & "\"
    sDatabase = sPath & sFileName
    If Len(Dir(sDatabase)) = 0 Then
```

```
        MsgBox "The File " & sFileName & _
                "could not be found"
        MsgBox "Copy the file to " & CurDir() _
                & " to continue"
      Exit Function
    End If
    ' Create Tabledef:
    Set db = CurrentDb
    Set td = db.CreateTableDef(sTableName)
    sType = "Text;"
    sDSN = "DSN=" & sDSN & ";"
    sFMT = "FMT=" & sFMT & ";"
    sHDR = "HDR=" & sHDR & ";"
    sIMEX = "IMEX=" & sIMEX & ";"
    sDatabase = "DATABASE=" & sPath
    sConnect = sType & sDSN & sFMT & sHDR & sIMEX & sDatabase
    td.Connect = sConnect
    td.SourceTableName = sFileName
    db.TableDefs.Append td
    LinkText = True
ExitHere:
    Exit Function
HandleError:
    Select Case Err
      Case conTableExists
          sMsg = "The table " & sTableName _
                & " already exists."
      Case Else
          sMsg = "Error#" & Err & ": " & Error$
    End Select
    MsgBox sMsg, vbExclamation + vbOKOnly, _
          "Error in Procedure " & sFunction
    LinkText = False
    Resume ExitHere
End Function
```

Assuming you've created an import link specification named `EmployeeImport Link Specification`, the following statement uses the `LinkText()` function to link data from the `Empimp.txt` file to a new table named `EmployeeLink`.

On the CD-ROM

The sample database, `Chapter16.accdb`**, already contains this import link specification and the** `LinkText()` **function. The text file** `ImpFixed.txt`**, which contains fixed-length data, is also found on the companion CD.**

Use a statement like the following to link `ImpFixed.txt` to a table named `EmployeeLink`:

```
LinkText("ImpFixed.txt", _
    "EmployeeImport Link Specification", _
    "Fixed", "NO", "2", "EmployeeLink")
```

To import a comma-delimited text file named `ImpDelim.txt` (also found on the companion CD-ROM) for which you have created a corresponding import link specification, you can use the following statement:

```
LinkText("ImpDelim.txt", _
    "EmployeeImport Link Specification Delimited", _
    "Delimited", "NO", "2", "EmployeeLink2")
```

As you can see, there are dozens of combinations you can use when linking to external data sources. The connect strings for each can get a little confusing, but there is a way to make connecting easy. If you pretend you're an end user and use the wizards, the process can be a lot easier. Once you step through the process of linking the table you want using the Link Wizard, open the Debug window and query the `Connect` and `SourceTableName` properties of the table you've linked. Then you'll have all you need to build the VBA code for doing the same thing programmatically. Just copy the `Connect` string from the Debug window and paste it into your procedure.

Checking links

You (or, more accurately, your users) will at some point encounter a situation where a linked table in one of your applications becomes unavailable. For example, suppose your application links to a SQL Server database and the network goes down. One of your users, who doesn't know the network is down, sits at his workstation and tries to pull open the application. As soon as he tries to access data from the attached table, an error occurs and your uninformed user panics. Here's another common scenario: Suppose your application is linking to an Excel spreadsheet, but someone decides to clean up a directory and moves, renames, or deletes the spreadsheet. Again, an error occurs when someone tries to access data from the linked table. You might not be able to prevent these situations, but you can plan for them ahead of time.

The following function, `CheckLinks`, should probably be run as a startup routine for your application, or in addition to any procedures you run when your application is accessed. Pass `CheckLinks` the name of an attached table, and test to see if the link is still valid. All the procedure does is try to open the table as a recordset. If the `OpenRecordset` method fails, either the table doesn't exist in the database or the link has been lost. All this function has to do is flash a descriptive message to the user and a return value to announce that the application should proceed no further.

On the CD-ROM

The following function is located in the `basTestLinks` module in `Chapter16.accdb` on the book's companion CD-ROM.

Cross-Reference

The last portion of the error handler dealing with ODBC data sources is explained in Chapter 37.

```
Function TestLink(sTablename As String) As Boolean
  Dim db As DAO.Database
  Dim rs As DAO.Recordset
  Dim iStartODBC As Integer
  Dim iEndODBC As Integer
  Dim sDataSrc As String
  Dim iODBCLen As Integer
  Dim sMessage As String
  Dim iReturn As Integer
On Error GoTo HandleError
  Set db = CurrentDb
  'Open a recordset to force an error:
  Set rs = db.OpenRecordset(sTablename)
  'If the link is valid, exit the function:
  TestLink = True
ExitHere:
  If Not rs Is Nothing Then
    rs.Close
    Set rs = Nothing
  End If
  Exit Function
HandleError:
  'If the link is bad, determine what the problem
  'is, let the user know, and exit the function:
  Select Case Err
     Case 3078    'Table doesn't exist:
        sMessage = "Table '" & sTablename _
             & "' does not exist in this database"
     Case 3151    'Bad link
        'Extract the name of the ODBC DSN
'to use in your custom error message:
        iStartODBC = InStr(Error, "to '") + 4
        iEndODBC = InStr(Error, "' failed")
        iODBCLen = iEndODBC - iStartODBC
        sDataSrc = Mid$(Error, iStartODBC, iODBCLen)
        sMessage = "Table '" & sTablename _
             & "' is linked to ODBC datasource '" _
             & sDataSrc _
             & "', which is not available at this time."
     Case Else
        sMessage = Err.Description
  End Select
  iReturn = MsgBox(sMessage, vbOKOnly)
  'Return failure:
  TestLink = False
  Resume ExitHere
End Function
```

Summary

Linking to external data sources is an essential requirement for many Access applications. Microsoft Access is equipped to deal with virtually any type of external data, including obsolete database types such as dBASE, as well as more modern data types like HTML and XML.

With few exceptions, linking to virtually any external data source requires very few steps on the part of a developer. The Access linking wizards are very similar, regardless of the data type involved in the link operation. The code required to automatically link to external data sources is not extensive and is easily incorporated into Access applications. Access also provides tools such as the Linked Table Wizard to help you manage linked tables in your applications.

Chapter 17 deals with the important topic of importing data into Access applications. Although the process is very similar to linking to external data sources, importing permanently copies the data into an Access database. As you'll see in Chapter 17, virtually the same steps are required to import data as were required to link to external data.

Importing and Exporting Data

In Chapter 16, you discovered how Access is used to link to external data sources and files. A link allows you to view data stored in an Oracle database, an XML file, or many other databases and data formats. So, in the case of linking, Access is used as an interface to data stored outside of Access.

In this chapter, I show you that importing and exporting are quite different from linking. An import process adds data to an Access database from some external source, such as an XML file. An export from Access means you create something outside the Access database, like an XML or Excel file containing data stored in Access.

IN THIS CHAPTER

Selecting the import and export options that are right for you

Creating import specifications

Exporting to external tables and files

On the CD-ROM

This chapter uses various files for importing, plus two Access databases: `Chapter17_1.accdb` **and** `Chapter17_2.accdb`**. Both databases are used for importing and exporting examples. If you haven't already copied these files onto your machine from the CD, you'll need to do so now. The CD also contains a number of auxiliary files in different formats (**`.xls`**,** `.xml`**,** `.dbf`**,** `.txt`**, and so on). Be sure to copy these to your computer as well.**

Looking at Your Options for Importing and Exporting

Before examining the processes of importing and exporting, let's take a brief look at the various options for importing and exporting data with Access.

Microsoft Access is often described as a "landing pad" for many types of data. What this means is that Access can use and exchange data among a wide range of applications. For example, you might need to get data from other databases, such as FoxPro, or dBASE. Or you might need to obtain information from SQL Server or Oracle, a text file, or even an XML document. Access can move data among several categories of applications, database engines, and even platforms (mainframes and Macintosh computers).

Open the Chapter17_1.accdb database in Access, and click the External Data ribbon tab (see Figure 17.1). You'll see the following groups: Import, Export, Collect Data, and Web Linked Lists.

FIGURE 17.1

The External Data tab hints at the variety of external data sources available to Access.

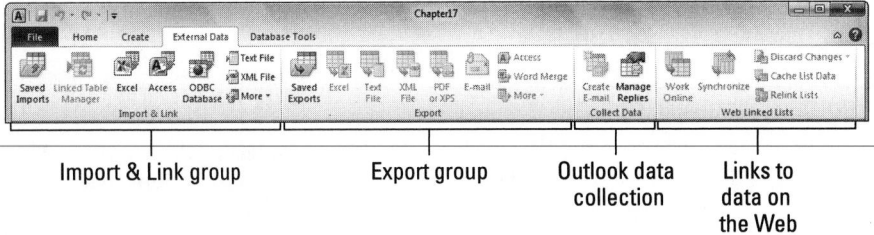

The Import group includes the following options:

- **Saved Imports**
- **Linked Table Manager**
- **Excel**
- **Access**
- **ODBC Database**
- **Text File**
- **XML File**
- **More:** Click this button to open the More drop-down list, which has the following options:
  - SharePoint List
  - Data Services
  - HTML document
  - Outlook folder
  - dBase File

The Export group includes the following options:

- **Saved Exports**
- **Excel**
- **Text File**
- **XML File**
- **PDF or XPS**
- **E-mail**
- **Access**
- **Word Merge**
- **More** Click this button to open the More drop-down list, which has the following options:
  - Word
  - SharePoint List
  - ODBC Database
  - HTML Document
  - dBase File

Obviously, Microsoft has well-prepared Access for its role as a "landing pad for data."

Importing External Data

An import copies external data into an Access database. The external data remains in its original state, but, after the import, a copy exists within Access. When you import a file (unlike when you link tables), you copy the contents from an external source into an Access table. The external data source is not changed during the import. No connection to the external data source is maintained once the import process is complete.

You can import information to new or existing tables. Every type of data can be imported to a new table. However, some types of imports — such as spreadsheets and text files — may have to be imported into existing tables, because text files and spreadsheets don't necessarily have a table structure compatible with Access.

Importing from another Access database

You can import items from a source database into the current database. The objects you import can be tables, queries, forms, reports, macros, or modules. Import an item into the current Access database by following these steps:

1. Open the destination database you want to import into.

In this case, open the Chapter17_1.accdb database.

2. Click the External Data tab.

3. Click the Access option in the Import section, and then click on the Browse button to select the filename of the source database (`Chapter17_2.accdb`).

   The Import Objects dialog box (shown in Figure 17.2) appears. It gives you options for importing a database object.

Note

When working with an external Access database, you can import any type of object, including tables, queries, forms, reports, macros, and VBA code modules.

FIGURE 17.2

Many types of Access database objects can be imported from one Access database into another.

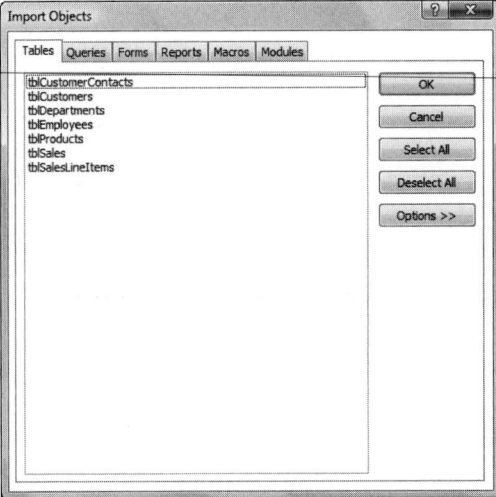

4. Select a table, and click OK.

   If an object already exists in the destination database, then a sequential number is added to the name of the imported object, distinguishing it from the original item. For example, if `tblDepartments` already exists, the new imported table is named `tblDepart-ments1`.

   The Get External Data – Save Import Steps dialog box appears, with a very useful feature that allows you to store the import process as a saved import, as shown in Figure 17.3.

5. Provide a name for the import process to make it easy to recall the saved import's purpose.

   You can execute the saved import again at a later date by clicking the Saved Imports button in the Import group of the External Data ribbon tab (see Figure 17.4).

FIGURE 17.3

The Saved Import Steps feature lets you save frequently executed import processes for future use.

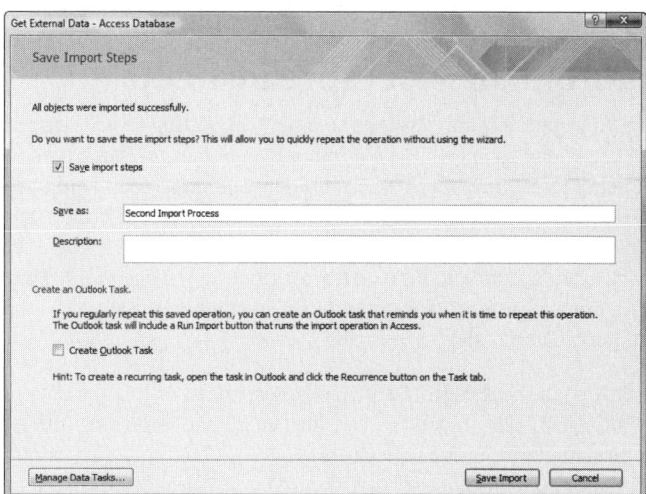

FIGURE 17.4

The Saved Imports feature lets you rerun previous saved import processes.

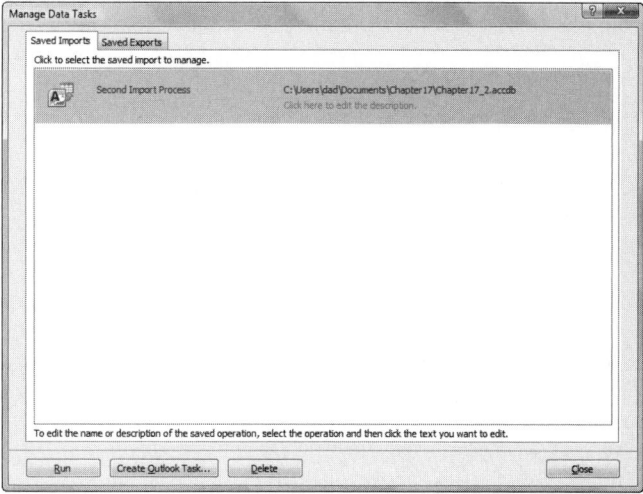

Tip

The Manage Data Tasks dialog box includes the Create Outlook Task button to set up the import procedure as a scheduled Outlook Task. This is a very convenient way to automatically execute the import process on a regular schedule.

Importing from an Excel spreadsheet

You can import data from Excel spreadsheets to a new or existing table. The primary rule when importing Excel data is that each cell in a column must contain the same type of data. When you're importing Excel data, Access guesses at the data type to assign to each field in the new table based on the first few rows of Excel data (other than column headings). An import error may occur if any Excel row past the first row contains incompatible data. In Figure 17.5, the Age column should contain all numeric data, but it contains a text description of the age of 49. This is likely to cause an error during the import process. The data in Row 5 should be changed so that the entire column contains numeric data (as shown in Figure 17.6).

You can import or link all the data from an Excel spreadsheet, or just the data from a named range of cells. Naming a range of cells in your spreadsheet can make importing into Access easier. Often a spreadsheet is formatted into groups of cells (or *ranges*). One range may contain a listing of sales by customer, for example, while another may include total sales for all customers, totals by product type, or totals by month purchased. By providing a range name for each group of cells, you can limit the import to just one section of the spreadsheet data.

FIGURE 17.5

Access can import data from an Excel spreadsheet, but there are some restrictions.

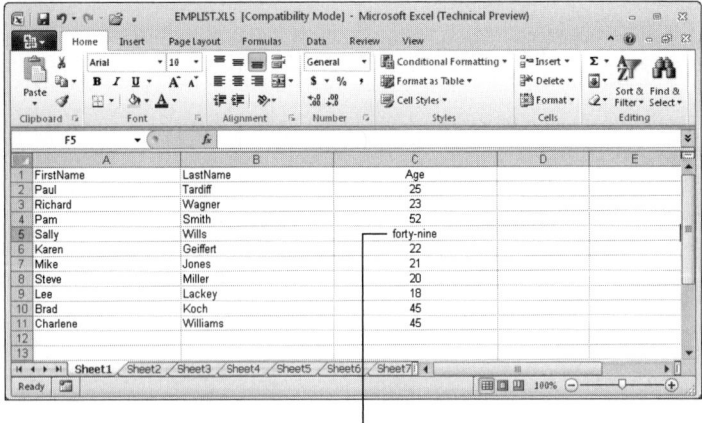

This data will cause import problems

FIGURE 17.6

Excel worksheet columns should contain consistent data.

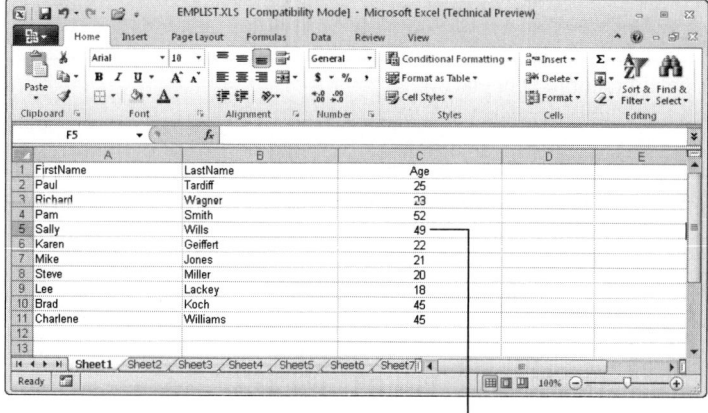

Data has been corrected

To import the Excel `emplist.xls` spreadsheet, follow these steps:

1. Click the Excel button in the Import group on the External Data tab.

2. Browse to the Excel file and click OK.

3. The first Import Spreadsheet Wizard screen (shown in Figure 17.7) shows lists of worksheets or named ranges in the Excel spreadsheet. Select a worksheet or named range and click Next.

FIGURE 17.7

The Import Spreadsheet Wizard

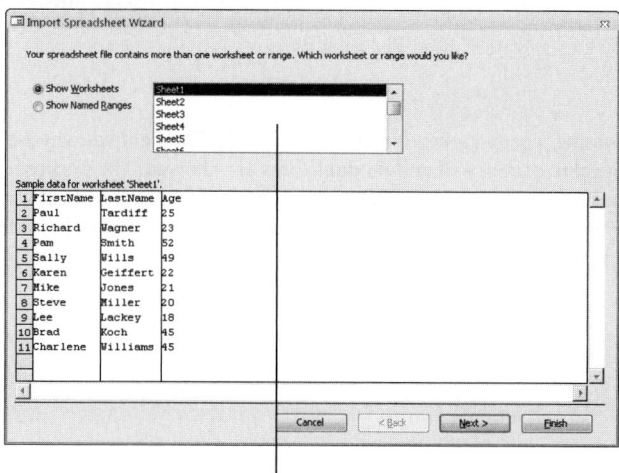

An Excel workbook may contain multiple worksheets and ranges

4. On the next screen (shown in Figure 17.8), select the First Row Contains Column Headings check box and click Next.

FIGURE 17.8

Does the first row contain column headers?

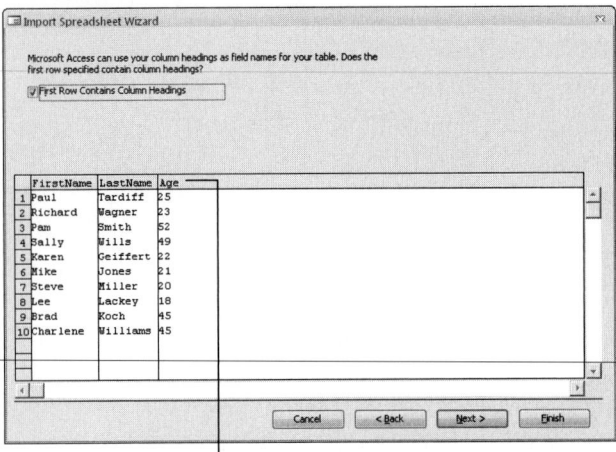

Column headings will become field names in the new table

Normally you don't want the Excel column headings stored as field data. Access uses the column headings as the field names in the new table.

5. On the next screen (shown in Figure 17.9), you can override the default field name and data type, remove fields from the import, and create an index on a field. When you're done, click Next.

6. On the next screen, set a primary key for the new table (see Figure 17.10) and click Next.

A primary key uniquely identifies each row in a table.

Caution

Be somewhat wary when choosing a primary key for the imported file. The field you choose must conform to the rules of primary keys: No value can be null and no duplicates are allowed. The purpose of a table's primary key is to uniquely identify the rows in the table, so if no column in the Excel spreadsheet is appropriate for this purpose, it's probably best to let Access add a default primary key field. The primary key added by Access is always an AutoNumber and always conforms to data normalization rules.

FIGURE 17.9

You can override any of the default settings Access has chosen.

Override default field name   Override default data type

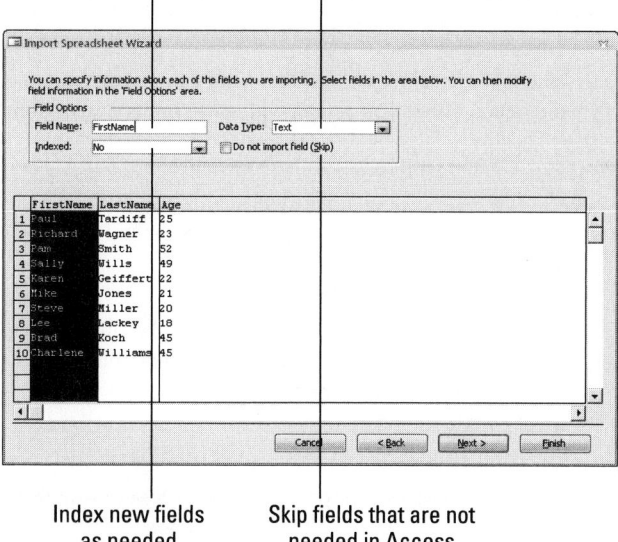

Index new fields
as needed

Skip fields that are not
needed in Access

FIGURE 17.10

Specify a primary key for the new table.

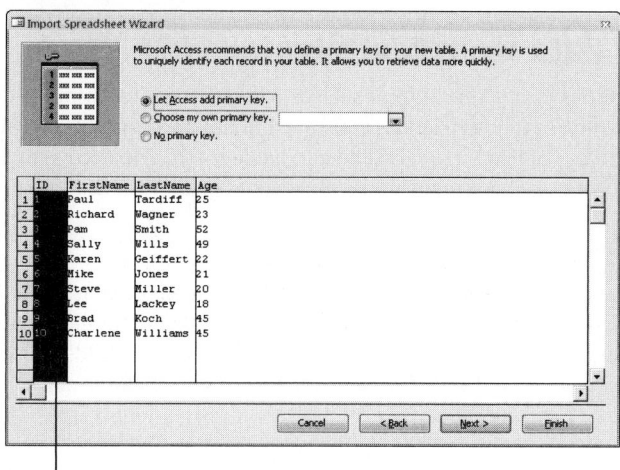

Access adds the primary key column by default

Cross-Reference
Primary keys are discussed in Chapters 2 and 3.

> **7.** Specify the new table's name and click Finish.

Caution
Importing an Excel file with the same name as a linked Excel file could cause problems. Give the newly imported table a new name to avoid issues, unless you actually intend to replace an existing table.

> **8.** If you want, save the import process for later execution.
>
> The new table now appears in the Access Navigation Pane.

Importing a SharePoint list

SharePoint lists are candidate data sources for Access databases. Because SharePoint lists reside on Web servers, SharePoint data is accessible across the Internet to qualified users. This gives Access the ability to share data virtually anywhere in the world.

Cross-Reference
Microsoft has dramatically enhanced Access 2010's ability to integrate with Microsoft SharePoint Services. In fact, this capability is so important that this book devotes all of Part V to documenting SharePoint integration. Chapter 33 shows how to consume SharePoint data in Access, and Chapters 34 and 35 describe the powerful new ability to publish an Access database on a SharePoint server.

Because SharePoint is increasingly deployed on corporate intranets, Access is guaranteed to continue as a major player in enterprise environments.

Importing data from text files

There are many reasons for text file output, such as B2B (business-to-business) data transfers. Also, mainframe data is often output as text files consumed in desktop applications. Access can import from two different types of text files: delimited and fixed-width. The Access Import Text Wizard assists you in importing or exporting both delimited and fixed-width text files.

Delimited text files

In *delimited text files* (sometimes known as *comma-delimited* or *tab-delimited text files*), each record is on a separate line in the text file. The fields on the line contain no trailing spaces, normally use commas or tab characters as field separators, and might have certain fields that are enclosed in *delimiters* (such as single or double quotation marks). Here's an example of a comma-delimited text file:

```
1,Davolio,Nancy,5/1/14 0:00:00,4000
2,Fuller,Andrew,8/14/14 0:00:00,6520
3,Leverling,Janet,4/1/14 0:00:00,1056
```

```
4,Peacock,Margaret,5/3/15 0:00:00,4000
5,Buchanan,Steven,10/17/15 0:00:00,5000
6,Suyama,Michael,10/17/15 0:00:00,1000
7,King,Robert,1/2/14 0:00:00,1056
8,Callahan,Laura,3/5/14 0:00:00,1056
9,Dodsworth,Joeseph,11/15/14 0:00:00,1056
```

Notice that the file has nine records (rows of text) and five fields. A comma separates each field. In this example, text fields are not delimited with double quotation marks. Notice also that the rows are different lengths because of the variable data within each row.

To import a delimited text file named `ImportDelim.txt`, follow these steps:

1. Open the `Chapter17_1.accdb` database.

2. Select the External Data tab.

3. Click Text File in the Import group.

4. Find the `ImportDelim.txt` file using the Browse button, select it, and click OK.

   The first screen of the Import Text Wizard (shown in Figure 17.11) appears.

FIGURE 17.11

The first screen of the Import Text Wizard

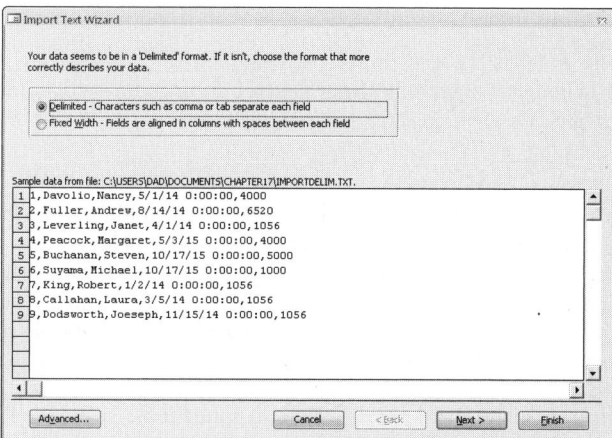

The Import Text Wizard displays the data in the text file and lets you choose between delimited or fixed-width.

5. Select Delimited and click Next.

   The next screen of the Import Text Wizard (shown in Figure 17.12) appears.

As you can see in Figure 17.12, this screen enables you to specify the separator used in the delimited file.

A *separator* is the character placed between fields in a delimited text file. The separator is often a comma or semicolon, although it can be another character.

FIGURE 17.12

The second Import Text Wizard screen

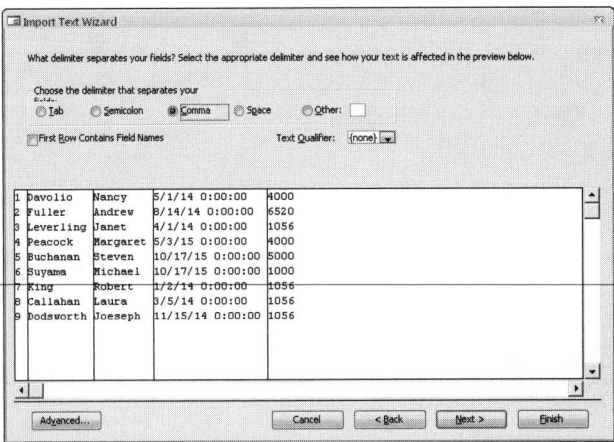

6. Select the delimiter that separates your fields. If an uncommon delimiter is used, select Other and enter the delimiter in the Other box.

Caution

There can be a problem with the separator used if any of the fields in the text file contain the separator character as data. For example, if you use a comma to delimit fields, and one of the fields is Acme Widgets, Inc., Access will have a problem importing the file. The solution is to wrap text fields in double quotes ("Acme Widgets, Inc.") so that the comma is not misinterpreted as a field separator. This use of double quotes is referred to as the text qualifier. Most often single- or double-quote marks are used for this purpose and usually resolve issues with special characters contained within data fields.

7. If the first row contains field names for the imported table, select the First Row Contains Field Names check box. When you're done with this screen, click Next.

The next few screens are very similar to the steps involved when importing Excel worksheets. You can change field names, specify a primary key, and save the import for future use. Save the imported text file with a descriptive Access table name.

Access creates the new table, using the text file's name by default. The new table appears in the Access Navigation Pane.

Tip

To specify a field containing no data in a delimited file, leave no characters between the commas (not even a space character). An empty field at the end of a row is indicated by a comma at the end of the line.

Fixed-width text files

Fixed-width text files also place each record on a separate line. However, the fields in each record are fixed in length. Fields are padded with trailing spaces to maintain spacing within each line, as shown in Figure 17.13.

FIGURE 17.13

A typical fixed-width text file

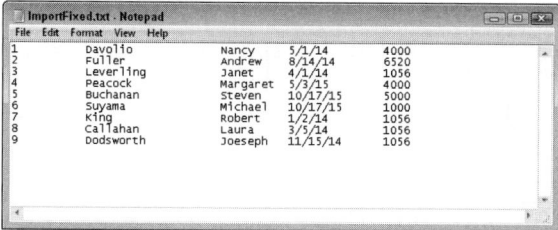

Notice that the fields in a fixed-width text file are not separated by delimiters. Instead, they start at exactly the same position in each record, and each record has exactly the same length.

Text values, such as first and last names, are not surrounded by quotation marks. There is no need for delimiting text values because each field is a specific width. Anything within a field's position in a row is considered data and does not require delimiters.

Note

If the Access table being imported has a primary key field, the text file cannot have any duplicate primary key values. If duplicate primary keys are found, the import will report an error and fail to import rows with duplicate primary keys.

To import a fixed-width text file, follow these steps:

1. Open the Chapter17_1.accdb database.

2. Select the External Data tab.

3. Click Text File in the Import group.

4. Find the ImportFixed.txt file using the Browse button, select it, and click OK.

   The first screen of the Import Text Wizard (refer to Figure 17.11) appears. The Import Text Wizard displays the data in the text file and lets you choose between delimited or fixed-width.

5. Select Fixed Width and click Next.

The next screen of the Import Text Wizard (shown in Figure 17.14) appears.

FIGURE 17.14

The Import Text Wizard screen for fixed-width text files

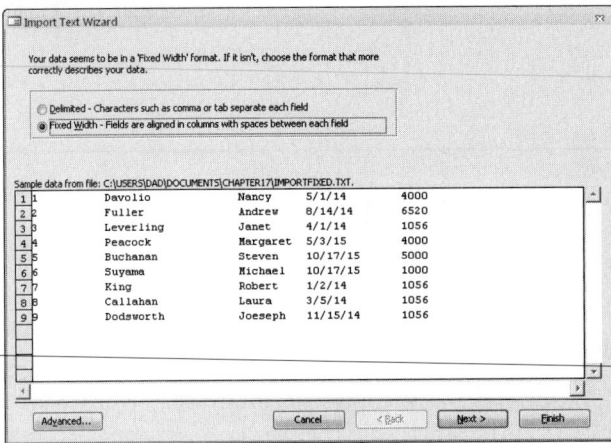

6. Adjust field widths as needed (see Figure 17.15).

Access guesses at the best breaks to use for fields, based on the most consistent spacing across rows. In this case, the field breaks are very consistent. If necessary, however, use the mouse to grab a dividing line and move it left or right to change the width of fields in the file.

FIGURE 17.15

Access guesses at field breaks in the fixed-width file.

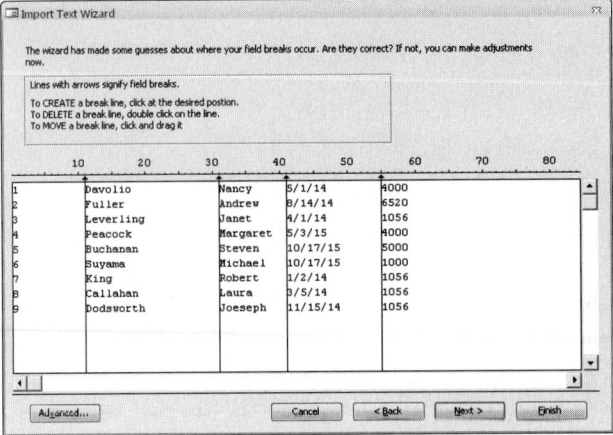

7. Click the Advanced button at the bottom of the wizard.

The Import Specification dialog box (shown in Figure 17.16) appears.

FIGURE 17.16

The Import Specification dialog box for importing a fixed-width text file

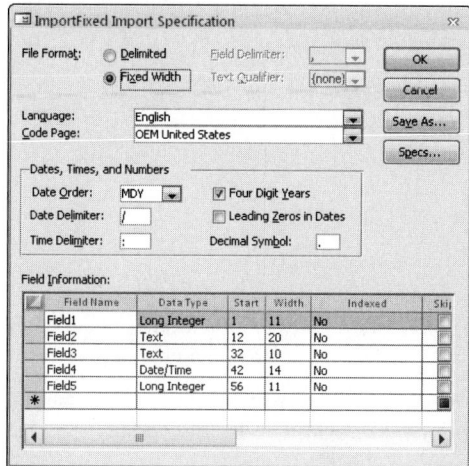

The Import Specification dialog box lets you specify formats for dates, times, field names, indexing, and data types. (For detailed information on this dialog box, see the nearby sidebar.)

8. Ensure that the Date Order is set to MDY and the Four Digit Years check box is selected.

9. Select the Leading Zeros in Dates check box.

10. Click OK to dismiss the Import Specification dialog box.

11. Walk through the remaining Import Text Wizard screens.

Importing an XML document

Importing XML documents is easy with Microsoft Access. XML is often used to transfer information between disparate platforms, databases, operating systems, applications, companies, planets, universes — you name it! XML is used for raw data, metadata (data descriptions), and even processing data. It's safe to say that most Access developers eventually import or export data in XML format.

Presenting XML in Access needs to be done in an odd way. You could easily import a simple XML document in your Access database. But the best way to find out how well Access uses XML is to begin by exporting something into XML.

Using the Import Specification dialog box

One advantage of using the Import Specification dialog box is the capability to specify the type of file to be imported from or exported to. The Language and Code Page drop-down lists determine the fundamental type of format. The Code Page drop-down list displays the code pages that are available for the selected language. For example, these choices are available when Language is set to English:

- OEM United States
- Unicode
- Unicode (Big-Endian)
- Unicode (UTF-7)
- Unicode (UTF-8)
- Western European (DOS)
- Western European (ISO)
- Western European (Windows)

The default for Windows installations is the Western European (Windows). You might need to set this value if the external file is in a language that doesn't use the Roman character set.

You can also specify the Field Delimiter option for delimited text files. Four built-in field-separator choices (semicolon, tab, space, and comma) are available in this combo box, or you can specify another character, if needed.

You can also specify the text qualifier used to surround text fields. Normally, text fields in a delimited file are enclosed by characters such as quotation marks that set the text data apart from other fields. This is useful for specifying numeric data like Social Security and phone numbers as text data rather than numeric.

The default text qualifier is a double quotation mark. The Text Qualifier drop-down list is actually a combo box, so you can enter a different delimiter in the text area.

When Access imports or exports data, it converts dates to a specific format (such as MMDDYY). You can specify how date fields are to be converted, using one of the six choices in the Date Order combo box:

- DMY
- DYM
- MDY
- MYD
- YDM
- YMD

These choices specify the order for each portion of a date. The D is the day of the month (1–31), M is the calendar month (1–12), and Y is the year. The default date order is set to the U.S. format (month, day, year). When you work with European dates, the order is often changed to day, month, and year.

You use the Date Delimiter field to specify the date delimiter character. The default is a forward slash (/), but you can change this to any other delimiter, such as a period. European dates are often separated by periods, as in 22.10.12.

Note

When you import text files with Date-type data, you must have a separator between the month, day, and year. Access reports an error if the field is specified as a Date/Time type and no delimiter is used. When you're exporting date fields, the separator is not needed.

With the Time Delimiter option, you can specify a separator (usually a colon) between the parts of time values in a text file. To change the separator, simply enter another in the Time Delimiter box.

Select the Four Digit Years check box to specify that the year portion of a date field is formatted with four digits. By checking this box, you can export dates that include the century (such as in 1981 or 2001). The default is to use four-digit years.

The Leading Zeros in Dates option specifies that date values include leading zeros. This means that date formats include leading zeros (as in 02/04/03), if needed.

Follow these steps to export data from Access to an XML file:

1. Open the `Chapter17_1.accdb` database.
2. Select the table to be exported.
3. Under the External Data tab, in the Export section, click the More drop-down button, and click XML File.
4. Browse to and select an XML file to export to, and click OK.

   The Export XML dialog box (shown in Figure 17.17) appears.

FIGURE 17.17

The Export XML dialog box

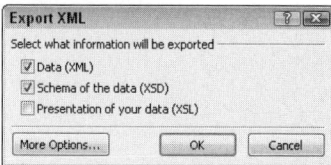

Although beyond the scope of this chapter, the Export XML Wizard includes options for specifying advanced options for the XML export process. Clicking on the More Options button opens a dialog box (see Figure 17.18) with several important XML settings.

FIGURE 17.18

Advanced XML export options

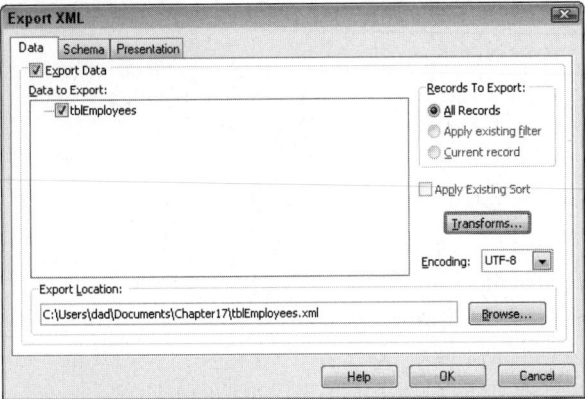

The data contained in an XML file may be relational or hierarchical. For example, a single XML file might contain information on both product categories and the products themselves. A *schema file* is needed for complex XML to be understood by other applications. Access automatically produces a schema file (.xsd extension) for data exported in XML format. Figure 17.19 shows the Schema tab of the Export XML dialog box.

FIGURE 17.19

Exporting XML schema information

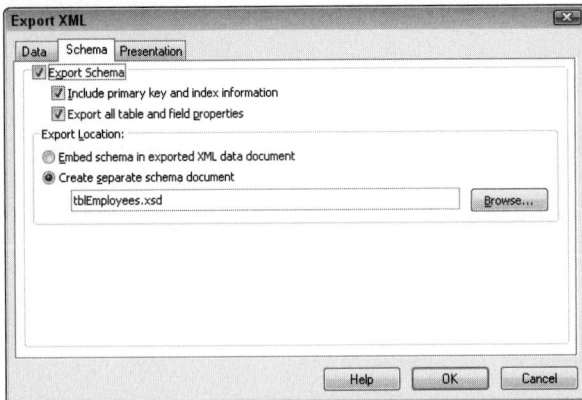

The XML schema file includes information such as the data type of each field and the source table's primary key and indexes.

A further refinement of the XML export process is to specify how the XML data should be presented in an application using the exported data. (The presentation is specified using HTML conventions.) In most cases, the XML presentation file (.xsl extension) is not needed because the XML consumer application displays the data as required by its users. Figure 17.20 shows the Export XML dialog box's Presentation tab. Notice that none of the options on this tab is selected by default.

XML presentation options

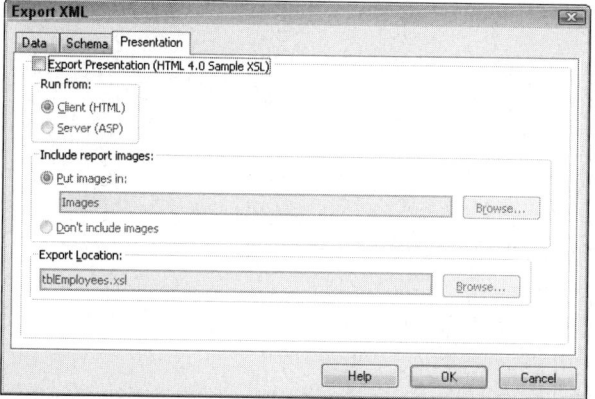

To import that same XML document just created, select the External Data tab, browse to the XML file in the Import section, and click OK. The process is similar to exporting, except in reverse.

Importing an HTML document

Access enables you to import HTML tables as easily as any other database, Excel spreadsheet, or text file. You simply select an HTML file to import and use the HTML Import Wizard. The HTML Import Wizard works exactly like the other import wizards described earlier in this chapter.

And just like demonstrating XML in the previous section, I'll do an HTML import in reverse as well. First, you export a table to generate an HTML file, then import the file back into Access to create a new table:

1. Open the Chapter17_1.accdb database.

2. Under the External Data tab, click the More drop-down button in the Export group and select HTML File.

3. Specify an HTML file as the export destination in the Export HTML dialog box (see Figure 17.21).

FIGURE 17.21

The HTML Export dialog

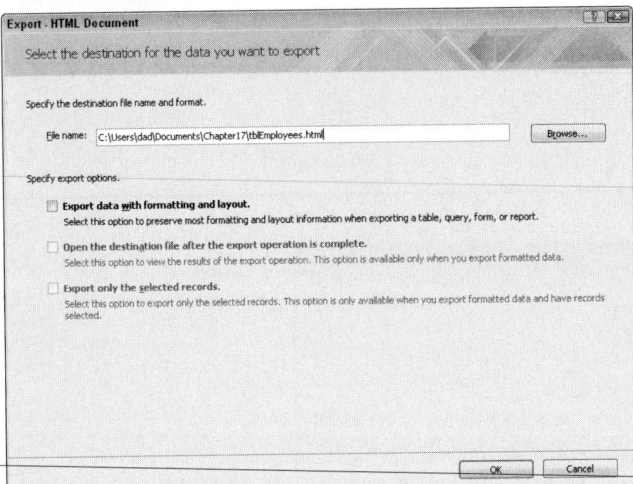

4. Follow the next screens to select your HTML output options, as well as your VBA macro export processing save options. Keep clicking until you finish.

   The HTML export is completed as soon as you click the OK button. No options other that what you see in Figure 17.21 are available when exporting HTML data.

Importing the HTML is simply the reverse of the export process.

The fundamental difference between importing XML and HMTL files is based on the basic difference between HTML and XML. The HTML import process imports data in much the same way as text files, using similar wizard options. XML, on the other hand, may include metadata and other description information.

Importing Access objects other than tables

You can import other Access database tables or any other object in another database, which means you can import an existing table, query, form, report, macro, or module from another Access database. You can also import custom toolbars and menus.

As a simple demonstration, follow these steps:

1. Open the Chapter17_1.accdb database.

2. Under the External Data tab, in the Import section, click the option to import from another Access database.

   The screen in Figure 17.22 appears. Notice that this dialog box enables you to specify whether to import database objects or link to tables in an external Access database.

FIGURE 17.22

The same wizard imports objects and links to external Access tables.

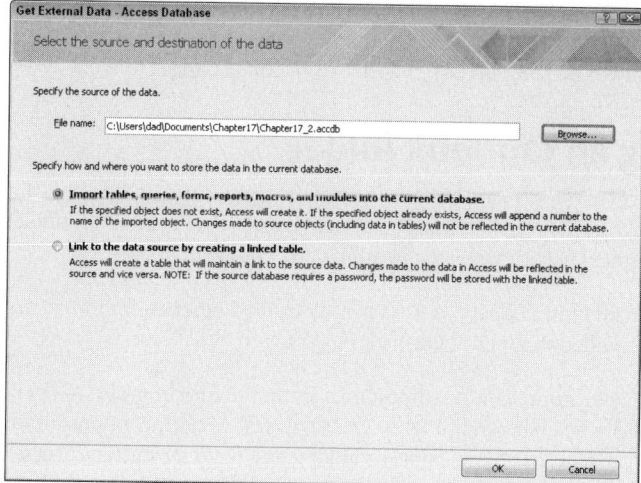

3. Browse to the Chapter17_2.accdb database and click OK.

Figure 17.23 shows that you can import every type of Access object.

FIGURE 17.23

Importing Access objects

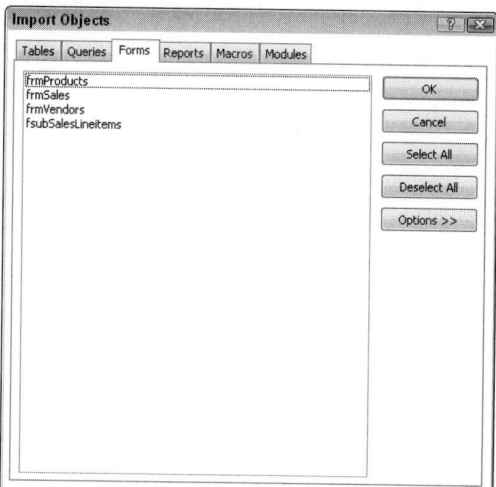

When including tables, queries, forms, reports, macros, or modules — all in the same import — you can select objects from each tab, and then import all the objects at once.

Notice also that the Import Objects dialog box includes options for importing table relationships, menus and toolbars, and other Access database objects. Importing (and exporting, for that matter) is an excellent way of backing up objects prior to making changes to them.

Importing an Outlook folder

An interesting Access import capability is the option to import data directly from Microsoft Outlook. Although most people think of Outlook as an e-mail system, Outlook supports a number of important business needs, such as scheduling and contact management.

When working with Outlook data, Access doesn't care whether an imported item is an e-mail or contact. Access handles all types of Outlook objects with equal ease.

Select Outlook Folder from the More drop-down list in the Import group to open the initial Outlook Folder import dialog box (shown in Figure 17.24). Access provides options for importing Outlook data, adding it to an existing Access table, or linking to it from the current Access database.

FIGURE 17.24

The initial Outlook import options

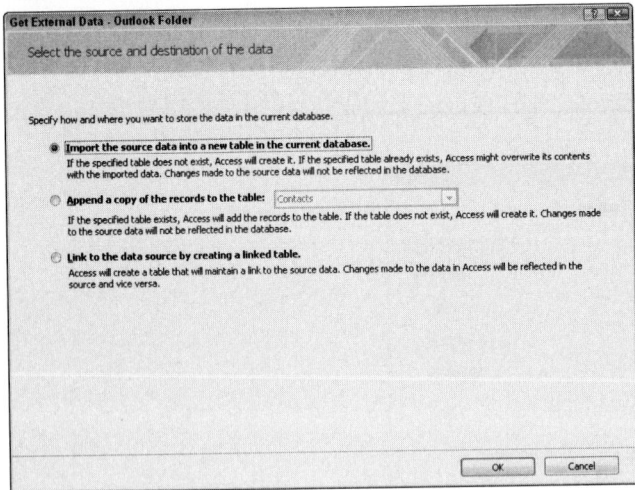

Selecting the import option opens the Import Exchange/Outlook Wizard (shown in Figure 17.25). As shown in this dialog box, Access can import Outlook e-mail, contacts, calendars, journals, and other folders.

Importing Outlook objects into Access

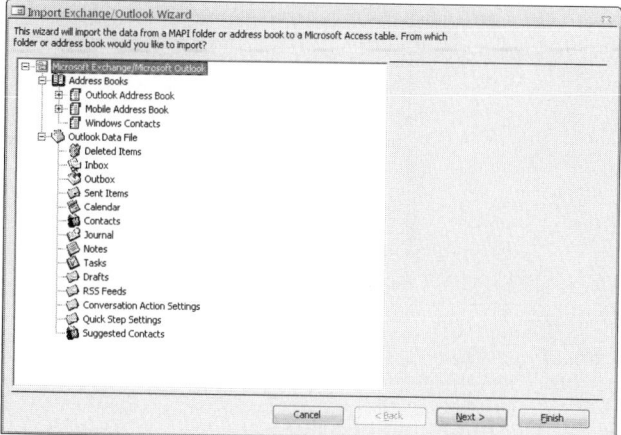

Depending on which item you select in the Import Exchange/Outlook Wizard, the remaining wizard screens walk you through the process of bringing Outlook data into Access. You can import Outlook data into a new or existing table, add a primary key, specify data types, and save the import process for later execution.

Importing dBase tables

dBase (currently a product of dataBased Intelligence, Inc.) has been around for many years. Although dBase's popularity has faded over time, because of its simplicity, the dBase format is used by many different applications (for example, Microsoft FoxPro). Access continues to support dBase import and export processes for developers needing access to these data sources.

dBase files can be imported directly into Access tables. The native dBase data types are converted to Access equivalents during the conversion.

You can import any dBASE III, dBASE IV, or dBASE 5 database table into Access. When browsing to the dBase file, select the correct dBase version in the Files of Type box in the lower-right corner of the File Open dialog box (shown in Figure 17.26).

FIGURE 17.26

Browsing to a dBase data file

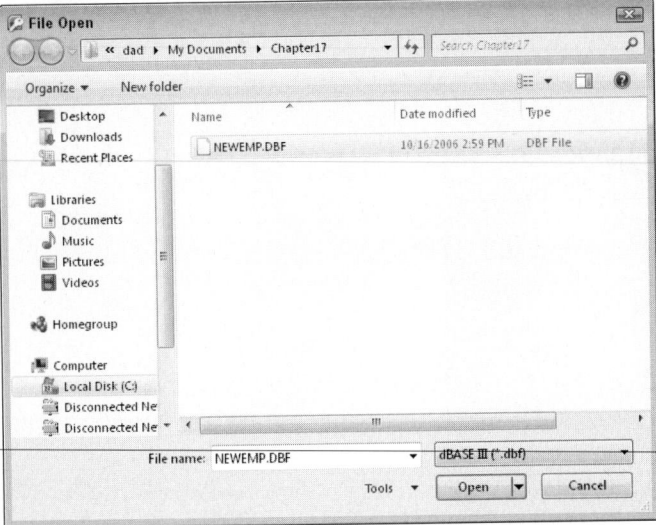

Table 17.1 lists how the dBase data types are converted to Access equivalents.

TABLE 17.1

Conversion of Data Types from dBASE to Access

xBASE Data Type	Access Data Type
Character	Text
Numeric	Number (property of Double)
Float	Number (property of Double)
Logical	Yes/No
Date	Date/Time
Memo	Memo

Note

When importing any dBASE database file in a multiuser environment, you must have exclusive use of the file. If other people are using it, you won't be able to import it.

Troubleshooting import errors

When you import an external file, Access might not be able to import one or more records, in which case it reports an error when it tries to import them. When Access encounters errors, it creates an Access table named Import Errors (with the user's name linked to the table name). The Import Errors table contains one record for each record that causes an error. You can use this table to determine which data caused the import issues.

Open the Import Errors table and try to determine why Access couldn't import all the records. If the problem is with the external data, you might need to edit it. If you're appending records to an existing table, the problem might be with the existing table. The table might need modifications (such as changing the data types and rearranging the field locations). After you solve the problem, erase the Import Errors file and import the data again.

Note

Access tries to import all records that don't cause an error. If you re-import the data, you might need to clean up the external table or the Access table before re-importing. If you don't, you might have duplicate data in your table.

Tip

If importing a text file seems to take an unexpectedly long time, it might be because of too many errors. You can cancel importing by pressing Ctrl+Break.

In most cases the Import Errors table contains just a few rows. You might be able to manually move the data from Import Errors to the destination table. If the Import Errors table contains numerous rows, you'll probably have to repair the input file (if possible) and repeat the import process, or modify the destination table to accommodate the data provided by the import file.

In more complex situations you might want to import the external data into a temporary table, and then use a query or VBA code to move the data to its final destination. Using a temporary table as an intermediate step is particularly helpful if the imported data is destined for more than one table in Access.

Import errors for new tables

An import error doesn't imply a problem with the data. It simply means that Access didn't understand something about the incoming data and needs you to inspect the questionable data and take corrective action. Access might not be able to import records into a new table for the following reasons:

- **A row in a text file or spreadsheet may contain more fields than are present in the first row.**

- **Data in the field can't be stored in the data type Access chose for the field.** This could be text in a numeric field — best case will import as zeros — or numeric trying to store in a date field.

- **On the basis of the first row's contents, Access automatically chose the incorrect data type for a field.** The first row is correct, but the remaining rows are blank.
- **The date order may be incorrect.** The dates are in YMD order, but the specification calls for MDY order. When Access tries to import 991201 (YYMMDD), it will report an error because it should be in the format of 120199 (MMDDYY).

Import errors for existing tables

Access might not be able to append records into an existing table for the following reasons:

- The data is not consistent between the file being imported and the existing Access table.
- Numeric data being entered is too large for the field size of the Access table.
- A row in a text file or spreadsheet may contain more fields than the Access table.
- The records being imported have primary-key values that duplicate existing primary keys in the destination table.

Exporting to External Formats

An export copies data from an Access table to some other application or data source, such as an XML document. The exported result uses the format of the destination data source and not the format of an Access database. You can copy data from an Access table or query into a new external file. You can export tables to several different sources.

Note
In general, anything imported can also be exported, unless otherwise stated in this chapter.

Exporting objects to other Access databases

When the destination of an export process is an Access database, you can export every type of Access object (tables, queries, forms, reports, and so on). To export an object to another Access database, follow these generic steps:

1. Open the source database and select an object to export.
2. Click the More button under the Export section of the External Data tab, and select Access Database as the export destination.

   The Export–Access Database dialog box appears.
3. Use the Browse button to locate the destination Access database.

Note
The target database can't be open, or else a locking conflict occurs.

4. Clicks OK, and the export process proceeds.

Note

Tables can be exported as data only or data and metadata.

5. If an object already exists in the target database, you'll be prompted whether you want to replace the object in the target database. If you don't, you can create a new object in the target database.

6. The last step of the wizard enables you to save the export configuration for future use.

    This option can be quite handy if you'll be frequently performing the same export process.

Note

If you try to export an object to another Access database that has an object of the same type and name, Access warns you before copying. You then have the option to cancel or overwrite.

Exporting through ODBC drivers

Exporting using an ODBC driver connection to another relational database is a simple process. You connect to the external database (in our case, an Oracle database). You then select a table to export as shown in Figure 17.27.

FIGURE 17.27

Exporting Access tables to an ODBC destination

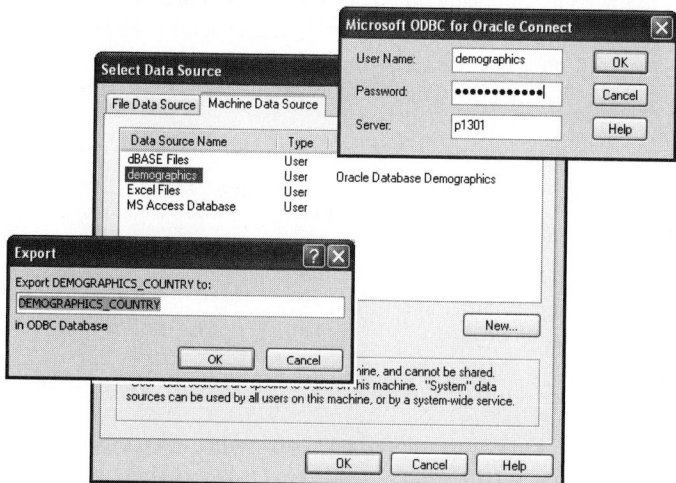

Functionality exclusive to exports

Access provides a number of special capabilities during exports. These special exports don't result in external data in the usual sense, but they make Access data accessible to external applications in some important ways.

These special export options are

- **Snapshot Viewer:** Exports to the Microsoft Access Snapshot format (`.snp`). This is a special, read-only format of an Access report, similar in concept to the Adobe PDF format.

- **Merge it with Microsoft Word:** Word documents can be produced as direct Access database exports.

Note

You can import from Word into Access by converting the Word document into a text file first. You could even use Word in combination with Excel to produce a delimited text file.

- **Microsoft Word Mail Merge:** A specialized Word document export function is that of Mail Merge using Word. In this case, you can create Word documents, for subsequent printing.

Summary

Access is unequaled in its ability to use data from many different sources. It imports and exports most common data file formats used by businesses around the world. This chapter covered many, but not all, of the import and export capabilities built into Micrsoft Access. These abilities, combined with the linked tables and other techniques discussed in Chapter 16 provide incredibly powerful options to Access developers.

Advanced Access Query Techniques

IN THIS CHAPTER

Using calculated fields

Creating queries that calculate totals

Performing totals on groups of records

Using different types of queries that total

Specifying criteria for queries that total

Creating crosstab queries

Specifying criteria for crosstab queries

Specifying fixed column headings for crosstab queries

I n this chapter, you work with more complex queries in greater detail than you did in earlier chapters. If you've followed through this book in order from the beginning, you've worked with select queries and parameters. Chapters 4 and 6 explain relatively simple select queries, in which you select specific records from one or more tables based on some criteria. You have not, however, worked with every option that can be used with Access queries.

As powerful and useful as select queries are, in many situations, you want queries that perform work on the returned data. As I explain in this chapter, Access queries are able to perform complex calculations, group data in ways that are important to users, and find unmatched and missing records.

This chapter covers several advanced ways to build and use Access queries. I cover totals queries that perform statistical calculations on returned data. You also find out about crosstab queries that show data in a number of different ways in a single datasheet. This chapter also explains some important query properties and other options you have when working with Access queries.

Select queries can specify criteria for single or multiple fields (including calculated fields) using multiple tables. Select queries may also work with wildcard characters and fields without a value (Is Null). Functions in queries can specify record criteria or create calculated fields. Finally, Access queries are a great tool for performing ad-hoc "what-if" scenarios.

This chapter focuses on four specialized types of advanced query techniques:

- **Calculated fields:** Creating new fields by performing calculations on the underlying data.

- **Number of records:** Finding a specific number of records returned by a query.
- **Total:** Calculate summary and other statistics on fields selected by the query.
- **Crosstab:** Summarize data in an easy-to-read, row-and-column format.

On the CD-ROM

This chapter uses the database named `Chapter18.accdb` on the CD-ROM accompanying this book. If you have not already copied it onto your machine from the CD, you should do so now.

Using Calculated Fields

Queries are not limited to displaying fields from tables. Your queries can also incorporate calculated fields that display the result of mathematical or other operations on the content of a field (or fields). A calculated field can be created in many different ways, including the following:

- Concatenating two text type fields using the ampersand (&).
- Performing a mathematical calculation on two numeric fields.
- Creating a new field based on data returned by an Access function.

In the next example, you create a calculated field, `DiscountPrice`, from the `Price` and `DiscountPercent` fields in `tblSalesLineItems`:

1. Create a new query containing `tblSalesLineItems`.
2. Add `InvoiceNumber`, `Description`, `Price`, and `DiscountPercent` to the QBE grid.
3. Move to an empty Field cell of the QBE pane.
4. Press Shift+F2 to open the Zoom box (or right-click and select Zoom).
5. Enter the following into the Zoom box (be sure to include the colon after DiscountPrice):

   `DiscountPrice: tblSalesLineItems.Price - tblSalesLineItems.Price * tblSalesLineItems.DiscountPercent`

   The Zoom box should look like Figure 18.1.

FIGURE 18.1

Creating a simple calculated field

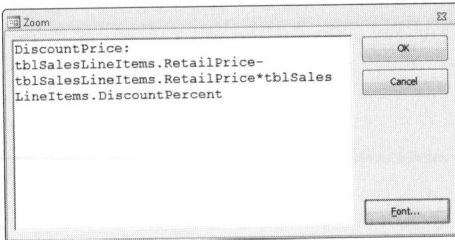

Note

Because you are using only one table, the name of the table is not required before each field name in the QBE grid. However, adding the table name in front of each field in the QBE grid is good practice to avoid issues in queries involving multiple tables. You could have just as easily typed DiscountPrice: Price - Price * DiscountPercent.

6. Click the OK button in the Zoom box (or press Enter) to return to the Design window.

7. Click the View button on the toolbar to see the new calculated field in the query results.

Your screen should look similar to Figure 18.2.

Figure 18.1 shows the expression from Step 5 being built in the Zoom window. DiscountPrice is the calculated field name for the expression. The field name and expression are separated by a colon.

FIGURE 18.2

The recordset containing the calculated DiscountPrice

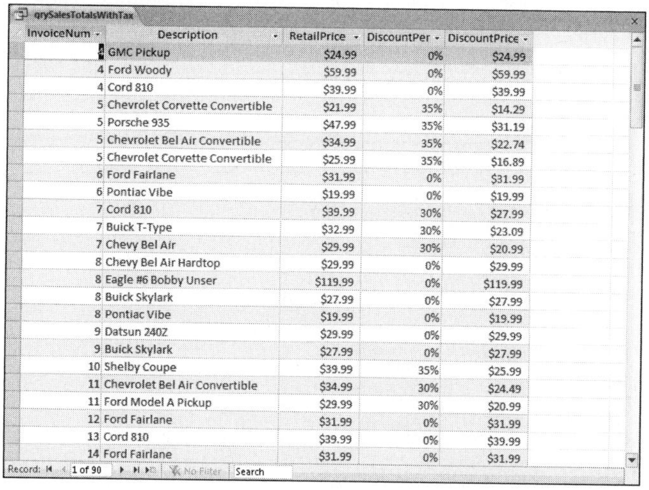

InvoiceNum	Description	RetailPrice	DiscountPer	DiscountPrice
	GMC Pickup	$24.99	0%	$24.99
4	Ford Woody	$59.99	0%	$59.99
4	Cord 810	$39.99	0%	$39.99
5	Chevrolet Corvette Convertible	$21.99	35%	$14.29
5	Porsche 935	$47.99	35%	$31.19
5	Chevrolet Bel Air Convertible	$34.99	35%	$22.74
5	Chevrolet Corvette Convertible	$25.99	35%	$16.89
6	Ford Fairlane	$31.99	0%	$31.99
6	Pontiac Vibe	$19.99	0%	$19.99
7	Cord 810	$39.99	30%	$27.99
7	Buick T-Type	$32.99	30%	$23.09
7	Chevy Bel Air	$29.99	30%	$20.99
8	Chevy Bel Air Hardtop	$29.99	0%	$29.99
8	Eagle #6 Bobby Unser	$119.99	0%	$119.99
8	Buick Skylark	$27.99	0%	$27.99
8	Pontiac Vibe	$19.99	0%	$19.99
9	Datsun 240Z	$29.99	0%	$29.99
9	Buick Skylark	$27.99	0%	$27.99
10	Shelby Coupe	$39.99	35%	$25.99
11	Chevrolet Bel Air Convertible	$34.99	30%	$24.49
11	Ford Model A Pickup	$29.99	30%	$20.99
12	Ford Fairlane	$31.99	0%	$31.99
13	Cord 810	$39.99	0%	$39.99
14	Ford Fairlane	$31.99	0%	$31.99

Save this query to use later, naming it qrySalesTotalsWithTax.

Note

You don't have to use the Zoom box to compose the expression defining a calculated field. You can just as easily type the expression directly into a Field cell in the QBE grid. However, many Access developers prefer using the Zoom box because expressions are sometimes quite long and complicated. The Zoom box makes it easy to see the entire expression without having to scroll through a Field cell in the QBE grid.

Calculated Fields and the Expression Builder

Access has an Expression Builder that helps you create any expression, such as a complex calculated field for a query. In the next example, you create a calculated field named DueDate that displays a date 45 days in the future, based on an invoice date in tblSales. You can use this date for a letter you plan to send to all buyers that have outstanding invoices:

1. Create a new query using tblSales from the Chapter18.accdb database and add InvoiceNumber, SaleDate, and InvoiceDate to the QBE pane.

2. Click an empty Field cell in the QBE pane, and then click the Builder button in the Query Setup group on the ribbon to open the Expression Builder (see Figure 18.3).

   In the next several steps, you use the DateAdd function in a calculated field. The DateAdd function adds a specified number of days, weeks, months, quarters, or years to another date. In this example, it is adding 45 days to the invoice date value.

3. Go to the Expression Elements area of the Expression Builder dialog box and expand the Functions tree.

The Expression Builder dialog box

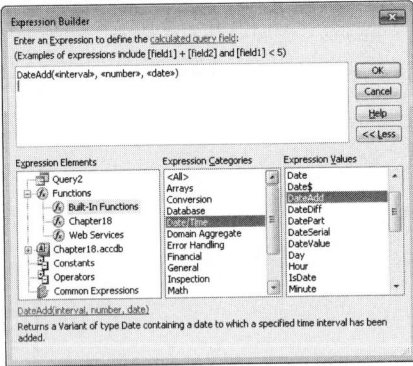

4. Select Built-in Functions in the Expression Elements area, then click on Date/Time in the Expression Categories area.

5. Select the DateAdd function (by double-clicking it) from the Expression Values area on the right.

   Access places the DateAdd function in the top window, with information about the three parameters needed by DateAdd.

6. Click the `<interval>` parameter in the window at the top and type "**d**" (a *d* in quotation marks).

7. Click `<number>` and replace it with 45 (see Figure 18.4).

The Expression Builder provides help for composing complex expressions.

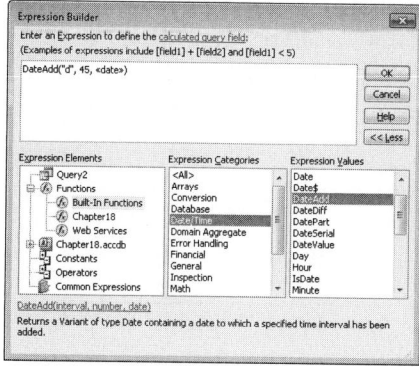

8. Click `<date>` to select it.

9. Go back to the Expression Elements window and expand `Chapter18.accdb`, expand the Tables tree, and then select `tblSales` by clicking it once.

   Access moves the parameter `<Value>` into the Expression Values area.

10. Double-click `InvoiceDate` in the Expression Categories area.

    Access places the table and field name in the last part of the DateAdd function in the top Expression Builder window.

11. Click OK to close the Expression Builder.

    Access returns to the QBE pane and places the expression in the cell for you.

12. Access assigns a name for the expression, automatically naming it `Expr1`. Change the field name to `DueDate` by highlighting `Expr1` and entering **DueDate**.

    If you perform these steps correctly and widen the column to display the entire expression, the cell should look like Figure 18.5. The `DateAdd()` function adds 45 days to the `InvoiceDate` in `tblSales`. The d signifies that you are working in days rather than months, weeks, or years.

FIGURE 18.5

A query creating the DueDate calculated field.

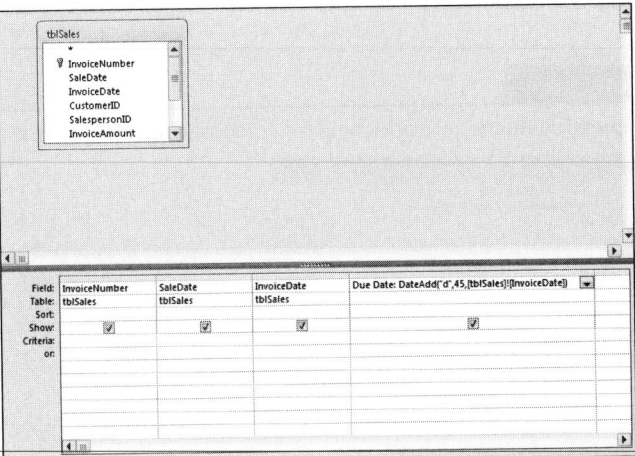

Clicking on the View button shows the query results containing the new calculated field. (This query is saved as qryCalculatedDueDate in the Chapter18.accdb sample database.)

Of course, you could have manually entered the DateAdd expression, but the Expression Builder is a valuable tool when you're creating complex, hard-to-remember expressions. The Expression Builder always shows all the parameters required by built-in functions and provides a nice tree view of available functions.

Counting Records in a Table or Query

The Count() function returns the number of records in a query's results. For example, to determine the total number of records in tblCustomers, follow these steps:

1. Start a new query using tblCustomers.

2. Click the first empty Field cell in the QBE pane.

3. Enter Count(*) in the cell.

   Access adds a default field name (Expr1). Your query's QBE pane should now look like Figure 18.6.

FIGURE 18.6

The QBE pane of a query using the Count(*) function

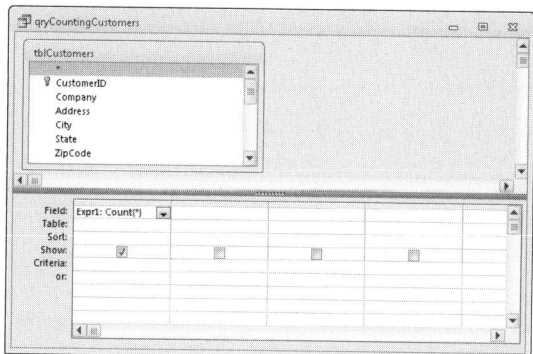

The datasheet now has a single cell that shows the number of records in tblContacts (see Figure 18.7). This query is included in the Chapter18.accdb database as qryCountingCustomers.

FIGURE 18.7

The datasheet of a Count(*) function for tblCustomers

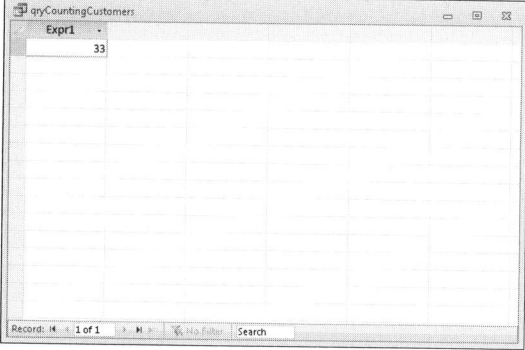

Because the Count() function counts the number of records returned by a query, it is the only field that can appear in the query's results. Although initially this may seem rather odd, there is no way a single query can display both a count of all records, and data from the records themselves.

Because of this limitation, the Count() function is almost always used to return information about the data in a database, rather than the data itself. After all, it is easy enough to create a second query that returns the data counted by Count(), if needed.

The Count (*) function can also be used to determine the total number of records that match a query's criteria. For example, the following example shows how many contacts you have in tblContacts that live in Connecticut:

1. Start a new query and select tblContacts.

2. Click the first empty Field cell in the QBE pane and enter Count (*) in the cell.

3. Double-click State in the table to add it to the query.

4. Deselect the Show cell for the State field.

5. Type CT in the Criteria cell for State.

6. Replace Expr1: in the first column with Customer Count in CT.

    Figure 18.8 shows how the query should look. Selecting Datasheet from the View button displays one cell in the datasheet containing the number of customers in Connecticut.

FIGURE 18.8

A query that shows the number of customers in CT

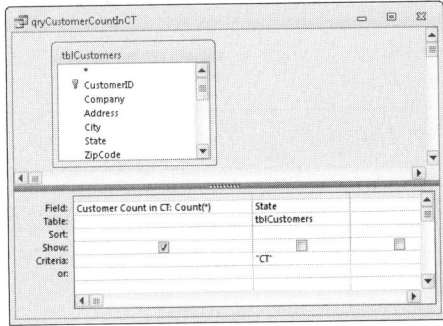

Remember that only the field containing the Count (*) function can be shown in the datasheet. Access reports an error if you try to display any additional fields.

Later in this chapter, you'll read about using grouping options to Access queries. Grouping enables you to perform aggregate operations (such as counting records) on *groups* of records. For example, grouping enables you to count all the products in each product category, or count the number of customers in each state.

Finding the Top (*n*) Records in a Query

Access provides the capability of finding the first (*n*) records (that is, a set number or percentage of its records) that meet a query's criteria.

Suppose that you want to identify the first 10 customers for 2012 — in other words, the first 10 sales of the year 2012. This is known as the top (*n*) records. Follow these steps to determine the first (top) 10 sales for 2012:

1. Create a new query using tblCustomers and tblSales.

2. Enter Between 1/1/2012 and 1/1/2013 as the criteria in the SaleDate field.

   Access automatically surrounds the dates with pound signs. You can, if you want, add the pound signs yourself as you enter the query's criteria.

3. Specify Ascending as the sort order for SaleDate.

4. Enter 10 in the Return box in the Query Setup group on the Design ribbon tab. (You could select another value such as 5 or 25 from the drop-down list, if desired.) Figure 18.9 shows the design of this query.

A query returning the first ten sales of the year

Number of records to return

Criteria restricts results to 2012

Caution

The expression you enter as the criteria depends on the regional settings (in Control Panel) on the user's computer. To be safe, you're better off entering dates in a format compatible with the computer's regional settings. For example, in many parts of the world, the date criteria in this example should be entered as 2012/1/1 and 2013/1/1 (or #2012/1/1# and #2013/1/1#, if you choose to include the pound signs yourself).

You're ready to run your query. Clicking the Query View button on the toolbar returns the first ten records in the recordset (see Figure 18.10). The actual records returned by this query on your computer may vary from those shown in Figure 18.10, depending on the data in the query's underlying tables.

FIGURE 18.10

Datasheet view of the top ten records in a query

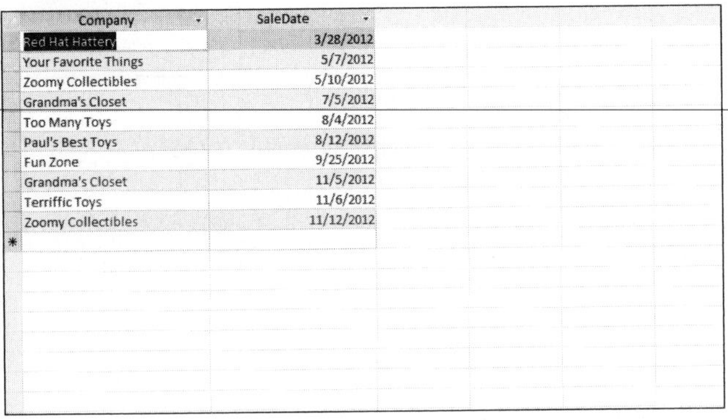

Company	SaleDate
Red Hat Hattery	3/28/2012
Your Favorite Things	5/7/2012
Zoomy Collectibles	5/10/2012
Grandma's Closet	7/5/2012
Too Many Toys	8/4/2012
Paul's Best Toys	8/12/2012
Fun Zone	9/25/2012
Grandma's Closet	11/5/2012
Terriffic Toys	11/6/2012
Zoomy Collectibles	11/12/2012

You can specify a percent or numeric value for the top (*n*) values of a query. This is very helpful when you want to see only a specific number of records. The Top option can be used with total queries, which you create later in this chapter, showing the top 5 percent, 15 percent, or any other value you want to specify. Perhaps you may want to see the top 10 percent in value of buyers in the system.

In the event of a tie (meaning, more rows fit the query's criteria than specified by the Top option) all the matching records are returned. This means that, in some cases, you'll see more records returned by a Top(*n*) query than expected.

How Queries Save Field Selections

When you open a query design, you may notice that the design has changed since you last saved the query. When you save a query, Access may rearrange (or even eliminate) fields on the basis of several rules. These rules apply if the Show box is not checked in the QBE pane:

- If the field has criteria specified, Access moves it to the rightmost columns in the QBE pane.

- Access may eliminate the field from the QBE pane unless it has sorting directives or criteria.

- If you create an expression using the Sum operator, Access changes it to an expression using the Sum function. This means that, from time to time, a query's appearance in the Query Designer changes as Access finds a more optimal way of performing the same operation you specified in the query's initial design.

Because of these rules, your query may look somewhat different after you save and reopen it. In this section, you learn how this happens (and some ways to prevent it).

Hiding (not showing) fields

Now and then, you may need to use a particular field as part of a query's criteria or for sorting purposes, but the field's values aren't needed in the query results. For instance, you might need a query for a report showing all the sales in the last 90 days, but you don't need the sales dates in the reports. Furthermore, you may want the sales by category, but don't need to see the actual category names in the report.

To hide, or exclude, a field from the query results, deselect the Show box under the field you want to hide. Figure 18.11 demonstrates this process. Notice that the State field is used to specify CT, NY, or MA. Because you don't need this field in the query results, deselect Show for the State field.

FIGURE 18.11

The easiest way to hide a field is to deselect the field's Show check box.

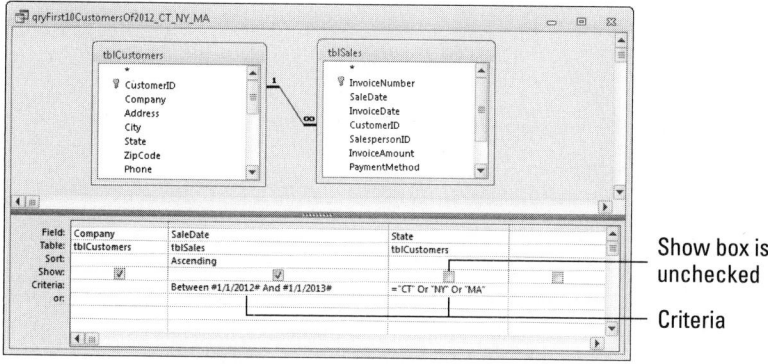

Show box is unchecked

Criteria

Renaming fields in queries

When working with queries, you can provide an alias for a field to describe the field's contents more clearly or accurately than the field's name in the underlying table. This new name is shown in the query's results. You may, for instance, want to join the city, state, and zip fields from a table as a single field named CSZ (City-State-Zip), rather than dealing with three separate fields on forms and reports. As you have already seen, an alias is useful for calculated fields or calculating totals. Access automatically assigns default names such as `Expr1` or `AvgOfWeight`, but it's easy to provide your own aliases for fields in Access queries.

Note

If you specified a Caption for the field in the table designer, this name is used in the query's results.

As you saw earlier with query fields created from expressions (such as `FullName: FirstName & " " & LastName`), field aliases are constructed by providing the field alias, followed by a colon and the expression specifying the field's contents. To create the CSZ aliased field, follow these steps:

1. Create a new query and select `tblCustomers`, and then add the `Company`, `Phone`, and `Fax` fields to the query.

2. Click in an empty column and enter the following expression:

    ```
    CSZ: [City] & ", " & [State] & "  " & [ZipCode]
    ```

    Figure 18.12 shows the new field and its alias. This query (`qryUsingFieldAlias`) is included in the `Chapter18.accdb` sample database.

FIGURE 18.12

A query field with the city, state, and zip code combined

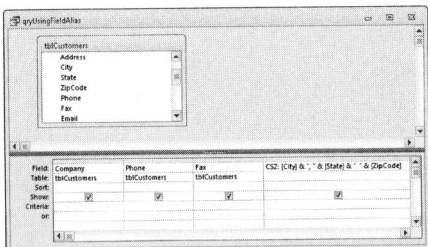

This same technique is easily applied to individual fields. Although, in most cases, the user never sees the actual field name, using an alias can make an application much easier to work with, especially if the field names in the underlying tables are abbreviated or technical in nature.

Tip

When naming a query field, delete any names assigned by Access (to the left of the colon). For example, be sure to remove the name Expr1 when you provide an alternate name for the calculated field.

If you rename a field, Access uses only the new name for the field's heading in the query's datasheet and does the same with the control source in forms and reports using the query. New forms or reports you create on the basis of the query use the new field name. (Access does not change the actual field name in the underlying table.)

When working with renamed fields, you can use an expression name (the new name you specified) in another expression within the same query. For example, many queries have a field called `FullName` that uses an expression to combine the first and last names fields. You created this type of field in an earlier query.

Note
When you work with aliased field names, you cannot have criteria that reference the field alias.

Generally speaking, Access accepts virtually any alias you provide, as long as it conforms to the naming rules applied to tables, fields, and other database objects. Do be aware, however, that loading up queries with a lot of aliases may cause problems later on. Because a field alias masks the name of the underlying field, it can be difficult to figure out the source of data on a form or report.

In most cases, unless there is a compelling reason to alias the name of a field, you only complicate maintenance efforts on any form or report using the query's data. In some situations, however, using field aliases is the only way to complete certain tasks. For instance, when you're upsizing an Access application to SQL Server, because of the stringent field naming requirements in SQL Server, you may use an aliasing query to convert the Access field names to names that are acceptable to SQL Server. Similarly, fields coming back to Access from SQL Server may be aliased to convert the field names to names recognized by the Access application. Rather than updating all the forms and reports in the Access application, it's easier to use an aliasing query to apply names recognized by the Access forms and reports to the SQL Server fields.

Query Design Options

Several specifiable default options are available when working with a query design. These options can be viewed and set by selecting File ➪ Options and then selecting the Object Designers tab. Figure 18.13 shows this Options dialog box.

These items are relevant to Access queries:

- Show Table Names
- Output All Fields
- Enable AutoJoin
- Query Design Font
- SQL Server Compatible Syntax (ANSI 92)

These options are detailed in Table 18.1.

FIGURE 18.13

The Object Designers tab of the Access Options dialog box

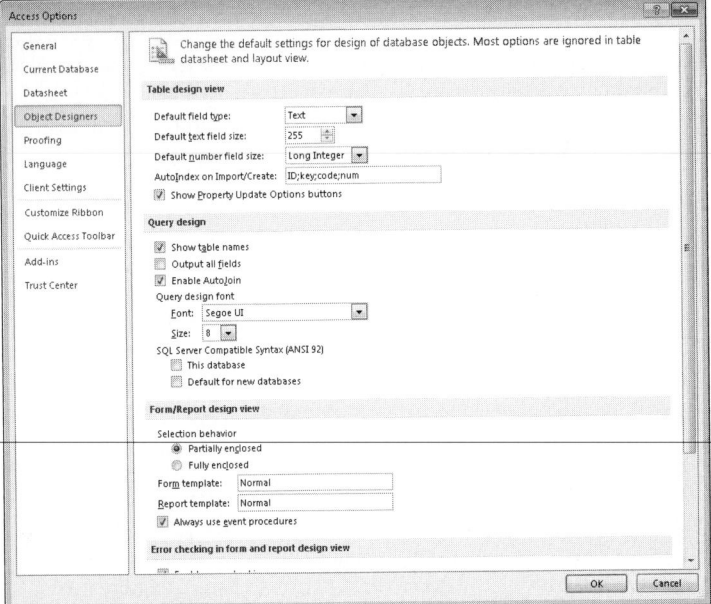

TABLE 18.1

Query Design Options

Option	Purpose	Default
Show Table Names	Shows the Table row in the QBE pane when set to Yes.	Yes
Output All Fields	Shows all fields in the underlying tables or only the fields displayed in the QBE pane.	No
Enable AutoJoin	Uses common field names to perform an automatic join between tables that have no relationships set to occur. The tables must have a field with the same name and type of data and one of the fields must be a primary key field.	Yes
Query Design Font	Used to set the Font type (name of font) and the size of the font used in queries.	Segoe 8
SQL Server Compatible	Select this database to enable ANSI-92 SQL query mode so that you can create and run queries using ANSI 92 SQL syntax. ANSI 92 is compatible with Microsoft SQL Server. Existing queries may not run correctly if you set this option after creating other queries.	No

Tip

When you set query design options, the options specify default actions for new queries only and do not affect the current query. To show table names in the current query, select View ⇨ Table Names from the main Query menu while designing the query.

Table 18.1 describes each Query design option and its purpose.

Setting Query Properties

While creating a query, you can set query properties a couple of different ways: click the Properties button on the ribbon or right-click the query's upper portion and choose Properties from the shortcut menu. The options you choose depend on the query type and on the table or field with which you're working.

Table 18.2 shows the query-level properties you can set for various types of Access queries. I cover each of these types of queries later in this chapter.

TABLE 18.2

Query-Level Properties

Property	Description	Select	Crosstab	Update	Delete	Make-Table	Append
Description	Text describing table or query	X	X	X	X	X	X
Default View	Values Datasheet, Pivot Table, or Pivot Chart	X	X				
Output All Fields	Show all fields from the underlying tables in the query					X	X
Top Values	Number of highest or lowest values to be returned					X	X
Unique Values	Return only unique field values					X	X
Unique Records	Return only unique records	X		X	X	X	X

continued

TABLE 18.2	(continued)						
Property	**Description**	**Select**	**Crosstab**	**Update**	**Delete**	**Make-Table**	**Append**
Source Database	External database name for all tables/queries in the query	X	X	X	X	X	X
Source Connect Str	Name of application used to connect to external database	X	X	X	X	X	X
Record Locks	Records locked while query runs (usually action queries)	X	X	X	X	X	X
Recordset Type	Which records can be edited: Dynaset, Dynaset (inconsistent updates), or Snapshot	X	X				
ODBC Time-out	Number of seconds before reporting error for opening DB	X	X	X	X	X	X
Filter	Filter name loaded automatically with query	X					
Order By	Sort loaded automatically with query	X					
Max Records	Max number of records returned by ODBC database	X					
Orientation	Set view order for fields from left-to-right or right-to-left	X	X	X	X	X	X
Subdatasheet Name	Identify subquery	X	X	X		X	X
Link Child Fields	Field name(s) in subquery	X	X	X		X	X
Link Master Fields	Field name(s) in main table	X	X	X		X	X

Property	Description	Select	Crosstab	Update	Delete	Make-Table	Append
Subdatasheet Height	Maximum height of subdatasheet	X	X	X		X	X
Subdatasheet Expanded	Records initially in their expanded state?	X	X			X	X
Filter On Load	Forms bound to query have Filter On Load set by default	X					
Order By On Load	Forms bound to query have Order By On Load set by default	X					
Column Headings	Fixed-column headings		X				
Use Transaction	Run action query in transaction?			X	X	X	X
Fail on Error	Fail operation if errors occur			X	X		
Destination Table	Table name of destination					X	X
Destination DB	Name of database					X	X
Dest Connect Str	Database connection string					X	X

Working with queries offers many options for how the fields can be displayed and properties for each specific type of query.

The remainder of this chapter works with advanced options for select queries.

Creating Queries That Calculate Totals

Many times, you want to find information in your tables based on data related to the total of a particular field or fields. For example, you may want to find the total number of contacts that are both buyers and sellers or the total amount of money each buyer has spent on products last year. Access supplies the tools to accomplish these queries without the need for programming.

Access performs totals calculations by using nine *aggregate functions* that let you determine a specific value based on the contents of a field. For example, you can determine the average price for products by type, the maximum and minimum price paid for a product, or the total count of all products purchased by customers in particular states. Performing each of these examples as a query results in a recordset based on the mathematical calculations you requested.

Cross-Reference
You have already worked with counts using the Count (*) function in the previous section.

To create a totals query, you use a new row in the Query by Example (QBE) pane — the Total row. The following section describes this handy tool in detail.

Showing and hiding the Total row in the QBE pane

To create a totals query, create a select query and then display the Total row of the QBE pane. You open the Total row by clicking on the Totals button in the Show/Hide group on the Design tab while a query is open in the Query Designer.

If the Table row is not present on your screen, open it by clicking the Table Names button in the Show/Hide group on the Design ribbon tab.

The Total row options

You can perform total calculations on all records or groups of records in one or more tables. To perform a calculation, you must select one of the options from the drop-down list in the Total row for every field you include in the query, including any hidden fields (with the Show option turned off). Figure 18.14 shows the drop-down list box opened in the Total row of the ProductID field.

Note
The query in Figure 18.14 is not included in the Chapter18.accdb example database.

FIGURE 18.14

The drop-down list box of the Total row

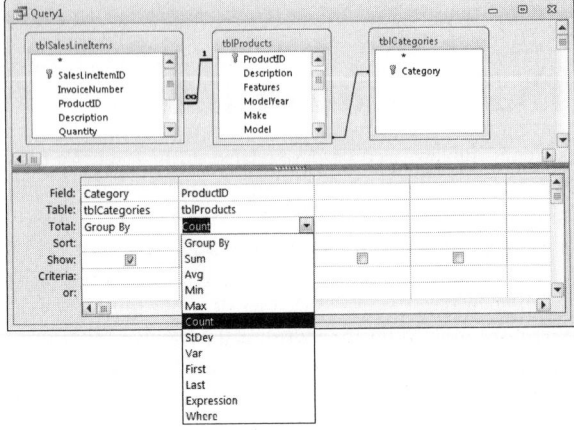

What is an aggregate function?

The word *aggregate* implies gathering together a mass (a group or series) of objects and working on the group of objects as a single entity. Therefore, an *aggregate function* takes a group of records and performs a mathematical operation over the entire group. The mathematical operation can be a count or a complex expression you specify.

The aggregates options can be divided into four distinct categories: Group By, Aggregate, Expression, and Query Criteria. Table 18.3 lists each category, its number of Total options, and its purpose.

TABLE 18.3

Four Types of Total Options

Category	Purpose of Operator
Group By	Groups common records together. Access performs aggregate calculations against the groups.
Aggregate	Specifies a mathematical or selection operation to perform against a field. There are nine different aggregate functions in Access 2010.
Expression	Groups several total operators together and performs the group totals.
Query Criteria	Filters records before performing an aggregate calculation against a field.

The following sections provide details about the options available in each aggregation options.

Group By

Totals queries can get complicated because of the variety of options and functions that may be used in a query. In all, there are nine different aggregate functions that may be applied to data in the query, and three other options that determine how the query works.

One of the fundamental operations in a totals query is Group By, which is applied to the field(s) used to group records in the underlying tables. For instance, consider a simple totals query that counts the number of orders placed by each customer. In this query, you want to group by the customer name and apply the Count aggregate function to the grouped records.

You use Group By to specify fields used to define the grouping applied to the other fields in the query. For example, in Figure 18.14, the Category field is set to Group By, which means that all the product records are grouped by the category field (all cars in one group, trucks in another, and so on) and the Count function is applied to each group. Group By is the default for fields as they are added to the QBE grid in a totals query. I discuss Group By in more detail in the "Specifying criteria for a Group By field" section, later in this chapter.

Expression

You use an expression to tell Access to derive a calculated field by using one or more aggregate functions in the Field cell of the QBE pane. For example, you may want to create a query that lists each customer and how much money the customer saved, based on the individual's discount rate. This query requires creating a calculated field that uses a sum aggregate against the Price field in tblSalesLineItems, which is then multiplied by the DiscountPercent field in tbl-SalesLineItems.

Cross-Reference

We discuss this type of calculation in detail in the section titled "Creating expressions for totals," later in this chapter.

Using a Where clause

The Where options tells Access that you want to specify a filter against other fields in the query. The filtering operation is performed before the aggregate functions are executed. For example, you may want to create a query that counts all products that cost more than $50. In this case, you would apply a Where clause to the RetailPrice field, and the query would then count only those products where the RetailPrice exceeds $50. This type of operation is also discussed in detail in the "Specifying criteria for a total query" section, later in this chapter.

One thing to notice is that it is possible to specify criteria for a field that is also set as a Group By field. Later in this chapter, in the "Specifying criteria for a Group By field" section, you'll see examples where a single field is used both for grouping and for filtering the query results.

Aggregate functions

You can choose from a total of nine aggregate functions: Sum, Avg, Min, Max, Count, StDev, Var, First, and Last. Each option performs an operation on the grouped data in the query (Table 18.4 describes how to use each option) and supplies the new data to a cell in the results. Aggregate options are what database designers think of when they hear the words *total query*.

For example, you may want to determine the maximum (Max), minimum (Min), and average (Avg) price of each type of product in tblProducts. There can be only one maximum value for all products. Several products may have the same maximum value, but only one price is the largest. You use aggregate queries to answer important business questions about the application's data.

You can also use Max, Min, or Avg to return a single aggregate value based on all the records in a table, without grouping the records.

Some of the aggregate options can be performed only against certain types of fields. For example, you cannot perform a Sum option against Text type data, nor can you use a Max option against an OLE object.

Table 18.4 lists each aggregate function, what it does, and which field types you can use with the option.

TABLE 18.4

Aggregate Options of the Total Row

Option	Finds	Field Type Support
Count	Count of non-null values in a field	AutoNumber, Number, Currency, Date/Time, Yes/No, Text, Memo, OLE object
Sum	Total of values in a field	Number, Currency, Date/Time, Yes/No
Avg	Average of values in a field	Number, Currency, Date/Time, Yes/No
Max	Highest value in a field	Number, Currency, Date/Time, Yes/No, Text
Min	Lowest value in a field	Number, Currency, Date/Time, Yes/No, Text
StDev	Standard deviation of values in a field	Number, Currency, Date/Time, Yes/No
Var	Population variance of values in a field	Number, Currency, Date/Time, Yes/No
First	Field value from the first record in a number, table, or query	Currency, Date/Time, Yes/No, Text, Memo, OLE object
Last	Field value from the last record in a number, table, or query	Currency, Date/Time, Yes/No, Text, Memo, OLE object

Make no mistake, however. Totals queries are among the most difficult database objects to design correctly. Virtually anything you might read or hear about Access totals queries (including this book) uses fairly simple examples to explain the principles behind totals queries. Because of the infinite variety of data in business applications, it's impossible to show complex real-world examples that are relevant to a significant portion of an audience. The good news is that users often require results that demand nothing more than summing or counting a few columns. Most often, you can achieve the desired results without too much difficulty. But, now and then, you encounter an issue that requires more than a simple response.

Unfortunately, no one rule of thumb always leads to a great query design. Very often, you end up with a compromise solution where some of the calculations are performed within a query, and more complicated work is performed using VBA code at the form or report level.

Performing totals on all records

You can use total queries to perform calculations against all records in a table or query. For example, you can find the total number of products in tblProducts, the average sale price, and the maximum and minimum retail price for each product category:

1. Add tblProducts and click the Totals button on the to open the Total: row in the QBE grid.
2. Add ProductID and SalePrice to the QBE grid.
3. Add SalePrice two more times to the QBE grid.
4. Select Count in the ProductID Total cell.

5. Select Avg, Min, and Max in the Total row of the three RetailPrice fields. Your query should look like Figure 18.15.

FIGURE 18.15

An aggregate query against records in tblProducts

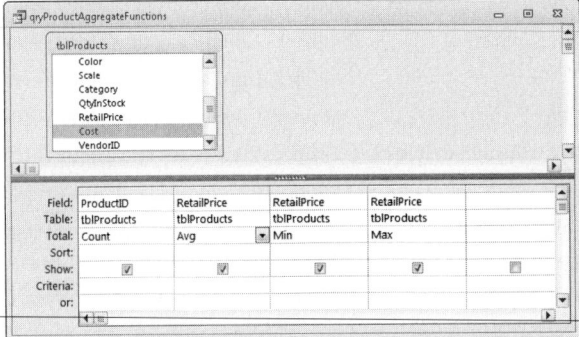

This query calculates the total number of records in tblProducts as well as the average, minimum, and maximum price for all products.

Name the query qryProductAggregateFunctions.

Note

The Count option of the Total cell can be performed against any field in the table (or query). However, Count excludes records that have a null value in the field you select. Therefore, you may want to count the table's primary key field (like ProductID) because the primary key cannot have any null values.

This query's results are shown in Figure 18.16. Notice that the recordset has only one record.

This record specifies the count, average, minimum, and maximum value for all products (regardless of type) in tblProducts. The query in Figure 18.16 (qryProductAggregateFunctions) is included in the Chapter18.accdb example database.

Note

Access creates default column headings for all total fields in a totals datasheet, as shown in Figure 18.16. The heading is a product of the total option and the field name. You can change a column heading name to something more appropriate by renaming the field in the QBE pane of the Design window as described in the section titled "Renaming fields in queries" earlier in this chapter.

This query was performed against all records in a table or query, and the query result consists of only one record.

FIGURE 18.16

This datasheet was created from a total query against tblProducts.

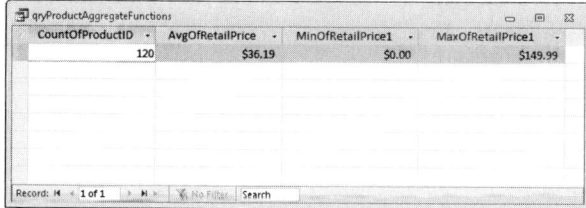

Performing totals on groups of records

Most of the time, you need to perform totals on a group of records rather than on all records. For example, you may need to calculate the query for each category of product. In other words, you want to create a group for each type of product (car, truck, motorcycle, and so on) and then perform the total calculations against each group.

Calculating totals for a single group

When you create your query, you specify which field or fields to use for grouping records and which fields to perform the totals against. Using the preceding example, to group on the Category field, select the Group By option in the Total cell:

1. Open the `qryProductAggregateFunctions` query in Design view.
2. Add the Category field to far left side of the QBE grid.
3. Make sure the Total cell for Category is set to Group By.

    The query in Figure 18.17 groups all like products together and then performs the calculations on each type of product. Unlike performing totals against all records, this query returns one record for each type of product. Figure 18.18 shows how the datasheet looks.

FIGURE 18.17

Totals against records grouped by product category

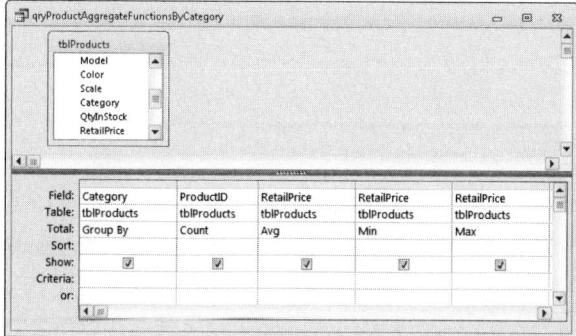

FIGURE 18.18

A totals query grouped by product category

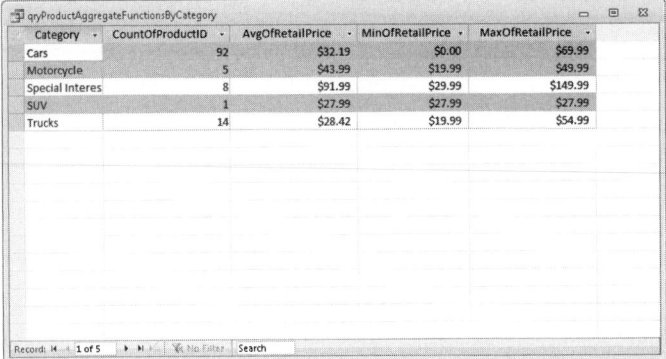

The recordset in Figure 18.18 has a single record for each type of product. The Group By field displays one record for each product type, in alphabetical order. The query shown in Figure 18.18 is included in the Chapter18.accdb database as qryProductAggregateFunctionsByCategory.

Calculating totals for several groups

You can perform group totals against multiple fields and multiple tables as easily as with a single field in a single table. For example, you may want determine the sales of each product category. This query requires information from tblProducts and tblSalesLineItems.

This query, shown in Figure 18.19, uses multiple tables and fields from each table. The query results are shown in Figure 18.20.

FIGURE 18.19

An aggregate query involving multiple tables

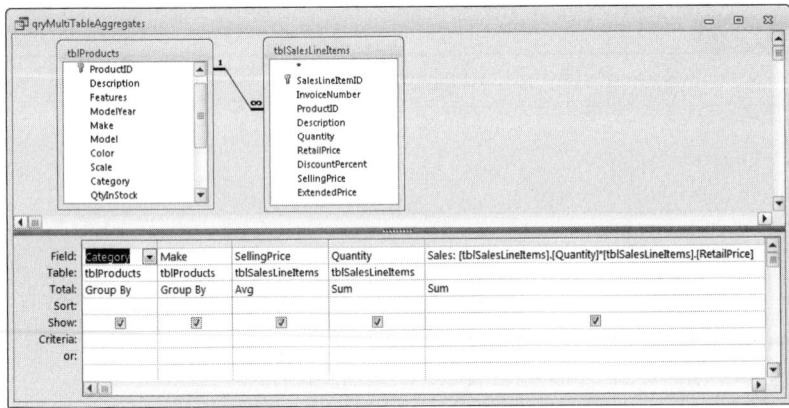

FIGURE 18.20

A datasheet of a multi-table aggregate query

Tip

You can think of the Group By fields in a total query as fields that specify the row headings of the datasheet. The Group By option creates the rows of the results in sorted order within each column.

Access groups records based on the order of the Group By fields in the QBE pane (from left to right). Therefore, you should pay attention to the order of the Group By fields. Although the order doesn't change the aggregate totals of the fields, the order of Group By fields does determine how the results are displayed in the datasheet. Placing Category before Make results in records ordered first by product category, and then by make (see Figure 18.21).

FIGURE 18.21

Changing the order of Group By fields

Make	Category	AvgOfSellingPrice	SumOfQuantity	Sales
Buick	Cars	$28.47	15	$476.85
Chevrolet	Cars	$25.14	26	$730.75
Cord	Cars	$33.71	20	$799.80
Datsun	Cars	$29.99	1	$29.99
Dodge	Cars	$18.84	2	$57.98
Ducati	Motorcycle	$27.49	1	$49.99
Ford	Cars	$28.05	40	$1,171.60
Ford	Trucks	$25.99	6	$175.94
GMC	Trucks	$21.24	5	$124.95
Honda	Special Interest	$106.87	11	$1,649.89
Lincoln	Cars	$50.66	3	$169.97
Mercedes	Cars	$35.74	5	$274.95
Mercury	Cars	$29.99	2	$59.98
Pontiac	Cars	$19.58	10	$239.65
Porsche	Special Interest	$36.79	4	$191.96
Shelby	Cars	$26.99	4	$159.96
SpecialInterest	Special Interest	$92.17	2	$218.98
Tucker	Cars	$25.99	3	$119.97
Volkswagen	Cars	$13.85	9	$197.91

Record: 1 of 19 No Filter Search

Changing the order of the Group By fields in a totals query enables you to look at data in new and creative ways.

Specifying criteria for a total query

In addition to grouping records for total queries, criteria to limit the records that will be processed or displayed in a total calculation can be specified. When you're specifying record criteria in total queries, several options are available:

- Group By
- Aggregate Total
- Non-Aggregate Total

Using a combination of these criteria types limits the scope of data returned by the query.

Specifying criteria for a Group By field

Criteria can be added to Group By fields in a query. These criteria limit the records included in the Group By field so that the calculations performed in other fields include only the filtered records. For instance, assume the sales manager is interested in the total sales to CT, NH, and NY, but not any other states. Figure 18.22 shows this query's design (see qryFilteredGroupBy in the database Chapter18.accdb).

FIGURE 18.22

Specifying criteria in a Group By field

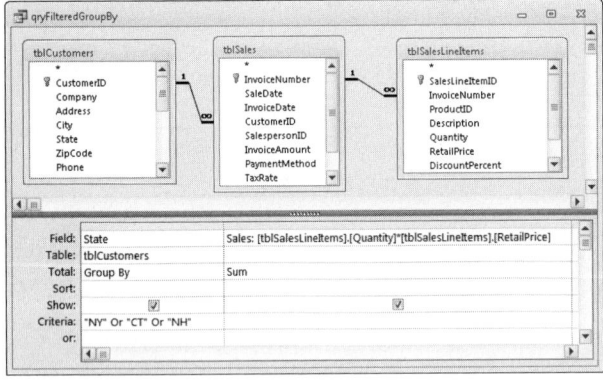

Without the criteria in the Group By field, qryFilteredGroupBy returns a record for every state.

Note

The query design in Figure 18.22 does not precisely match the design of `qryFilteredGroupBy` in the `Chapter18.accdb` example database. The difference occurred when the query in Figure 18.22 was closed and saved in the `Chapter18.accdb` database. The Query Optimizer rearranged the query's design so that the Sales total is calculated by applying the Sum function directly to the product of Quantity * RetailPrice. The records returned by the query are the same, regardless of how the Sum function appears in the query's design.

Specifying criteria for an Aggregate Total field

At times, you may want a query to calculate aggregate totals first and then display only those totals from the aggregate calculations that meet a specified criterion. More specifically, you may want to perform aggregate calculations against *all* records but return only records meeting some criteria. In effect, you're saying "I won't know which records I want to see until they're all totaled first. Then I want to see only those records that meet a particular criterion in my results."

For example, you may want a query to find the total sales by category, but only for categories with more than $1,000 in sales. This query should look like the one shown in Figure 18.23. Notice that > 2000 appears in the field summing product sales.

FIGURE 18.23

A query that filters returned records after grouping

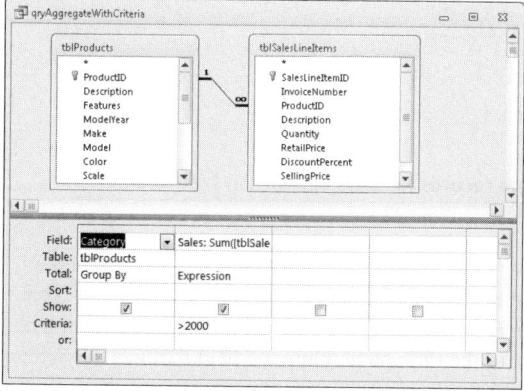

The query shown in Figure 18.23 (`qryAggregateWithCriteria`) is included in the `Chapter18.accdb` database.

Specifying criteria for a Non-Aggregate Total field

The preceding section showed you how to limit the records after performing the calculations against total fields. You also can specify that you want Access to limit the records based on a total field *before* performing total calculations. In other words, you can limit the range of records against which the calculation is performed. In this case, the field you want to use as a filter is not a Group By field.

For example, you may want to return sales totals only for the year 2012. Figure 18.24 shows `qry-AggregateByDate`. This query is very similar to the previous example except that `tblSales` has been added to include the `SaleDate`, and criteria is applied limiting `SaleDate` to the year 2012.

FIGURE 18.24

Specifying criteria for a Non-Aggregate field

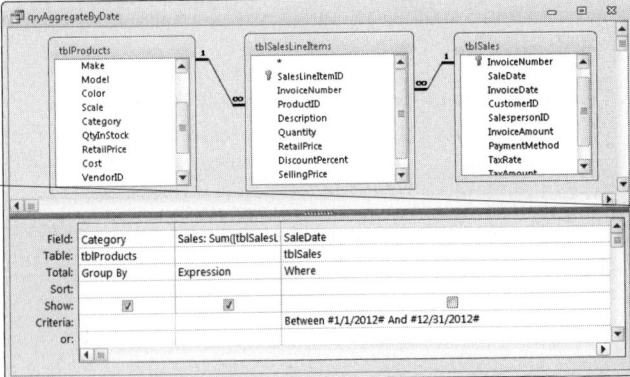

Note

In the query you just completed, Access displays only those records for sales between 1/1/2012 and 12/31/2012, inclusive. All other records are discarded.

Access automatically turns off the Show box for fields using Where as the Total option. Access knows these fields are used for filtering and are not expected to appear in the query results. If you try to turn on the Show cell, Access displays an error message. If you need to see the field contents in the datasheet, add a second copy of the field to the QBE pane. Only the field that has the Where condition in the Total row is not shown.

Creating expressions for totals

In addition to choosing one of the Access totals from the drop-down list, you can create your own aggregate expression based on any number of functions, such as Avg and Sum. Or you can base your expression on a calculated field composed of several functions, or on a calculated field that is based on several fields from different tables.

Suppose that you want to sum sales for each product category. I've shown you similar queries earlier in this chapter, but this time I'll perform the aggregation using an expression rather than using an option in the Total row:

1. Start a new query and add `tblProducts` and `tblSalesLineItems`.

2. Click the Totals button (the Σ) on the ribbon and add Category from `tblProducts` to the QBE grid. Leave its total option set at Group By.

3. In the empty column to the right of Category, add the following expression to the Field row:

   ```
   Sales: Sum(tblSalesLineItems.Quantity * tblSalesLineItems.
       RetailPrice)
   ```

4. Make sure Access has set the Total row for this column to `Expression`.

   Your query should be similar to Figure 18.25. Notice that the query uses two fields from `tblSalesLineItems` to create the Sales calculated field.

FIGURE 18.25

A query using an Expression Total

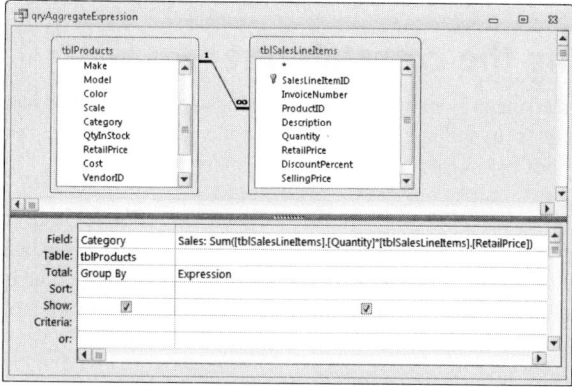

Clicking on the Datasheet button on the ribbon displays the datasheet shown in Figure 18.26. The Sales field is calculated by quantity and retail price from `tblSalesLineItems`, grouped by product category.

`qryAggregateExpression` is included in the `Chapter18.accdb` database.

A datasheet created by an Expression total

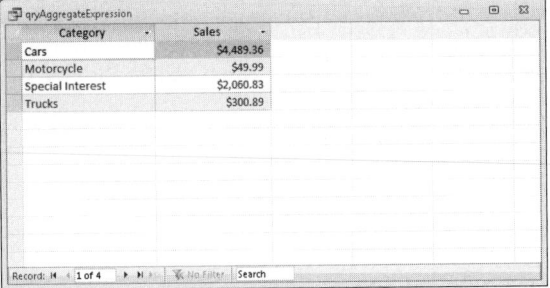

Creating Crosstab Queries

Access supports a specialized type of total query — the crosstab — that summarizes data in a row-and-column format.

Understanding the crosstab query

A *crosstab query* is a spreadsheet-like summary of the things specified by the row and column headers created from your tables. In this specialized type of total query, the Total row in the QBE pane is always active and cannot be toggled off in a crosstab query.

In addition, the Total row of the QBE pane specifies a Group By option for both the row and the column headings. Like other total queries, the Group By option specifies the row headings for the query datasheet and are based on the contents of the field. However, unlike other total queries, the crosstab query also obtains its column headings from values in a field rather than from table field names.

Note

The fields used as rows and columns must always have Group By in the Total row. Otherwise, Access reports an error when you attempt to display or run the query.

The datasheet itself contains a calculation (count, sum, average, and so on) in every cell (intersection of a row and a column). For instance, when basing a crosstab query on categories and products, the cells in the datasheet may contain a sum of all sales by category, by product.

For example, you may want to create a query that displays the average retail price of each product make, by category. For instance, say you want to see the average price of Ford cars, trucks, and SUVs. You want the make (Ford, for example) as the row heading, and the product category (car, truck, and so on) as the column heading, with each cell containing an average retail price for each make by category. Figure 18.27 shows the completed query (we build this query in the following discussion).

FIGURE 18.27

A crosstab query of product makes and categories

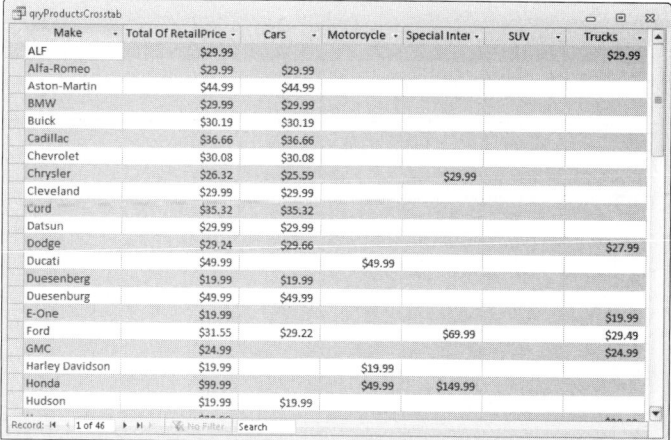

Make	Total Of RetailPrice	Cars	Motorcycle	Special Inter	SUV	Trucks
ALF	$29.99					$29.99
Alfa-Romeo	$29.99	$29.99				
Aston-Martin	$44.99	$44.99				
BMW	$29.99	$29.99				
Buick	$30.19	$30.19				
Cadillac	$36.66	$36.66				
Chevrolet	$30.08	$30.08				
Chrysler	$26.32	$25.59		$29.99		
Cleveland	$29.99	$29.99				
Cord	$35.32	$35.32				
Datsun	$29.99	$29.99				
Dodge	$29.24	$29.66				$27.99
Ducati	$49.99		$49.99			
Duesenberg	$19.99	$19.99				
Duesenburg	$49.99	$49.99				
E-One	$19.99					$19.99
Ford	$31.55	$29.22		$69.99		$29.49
GMC	$24.99					$24.99
Harley Davidson	$19.99		$19.99			
Honda	$99.99		$49.99	$149.99		
Hudson	$19.99	$19.99				

Record: 1 of 46 — No Filter — Search

Creating the crosstab query

After you have a conceptual understanding of a crosstab query, it is time to create one. By far, the easiest way to construct a crosstab query is with the Access Crosstab Query Wizard. The Crosstab Query Wizard is an excellent tool to help you create a simple crosstab query quickly. Select Query Wizard in the Macros and Code group on the Create tab to open the New Query dialog box (see Figure 18.28).

Access employs several Query Wizards, which are helpful additions to the query design surface. One such wizard is the Crosstab Wizard that helps you successfully create crosstab queries. Crosstabs are notoriously difficult to design by hand, and the Crosstab Wizard is a welcome aid when creating crosstabs.

FIGURE 18.28

Selecting the Crosstab Query Wizard from the New Query dialog box

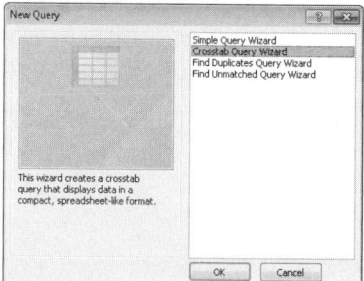

Select the table or query containing the data needed by the crosstab in the next wizard dialog box (see Figure 18.29). Notice that the Crosstab Wizard treats tables and queries as equivalent data sources. In some cases, you may have to construct a new query that provides the raw data needed by the crosstab's objective.

FIGURE 18.29

Selecting the crosstab's data source

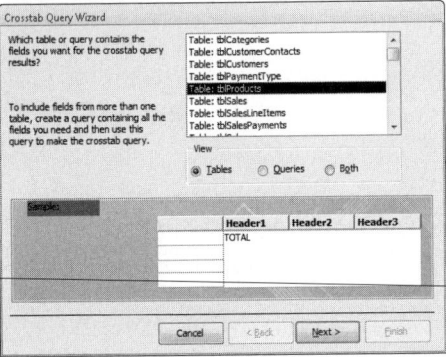

You specify the row headings (Ford, Chevrolet, Dodge, and so on) in the next Crosstab Wizard dialog box (see Figure 18.30). A little planning ahead of time makes this step, and the following steps, much easier.

FIGURE 18.30

Specifying the crosstab's row headings

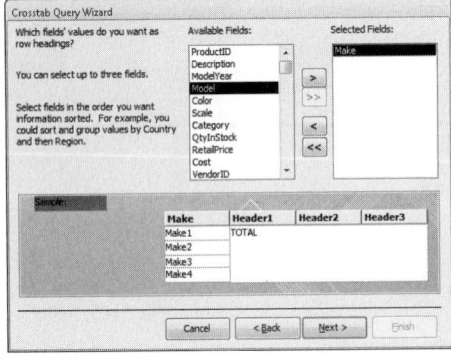

Predictably, the next Crosstab Wizard screen (see Figure 18.31) asks for the field to use as the column heading.

FIGURE 18.31

Specifying the crosstab's column heading field

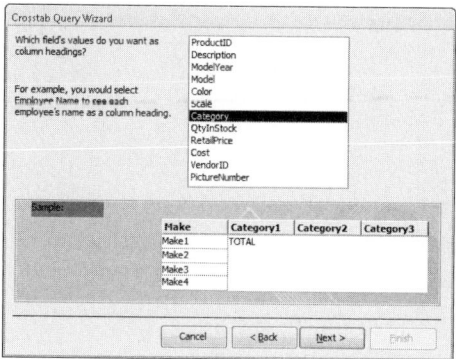

Next, you indicate the calculation you want the crosstab to perform on each cell in the crosstab's results (see Figure 18.32). In this case, the crosstab returns the retail prices of each product category (cars, trucks, and so on) for each product model (Chevrolet, Ford, and so on). I want the crosstab to calculate the average retail price of each field returned by the crosstab.

FIGURE 18.32

Specifying the calculation to be performed on each cell of the crosstab's records

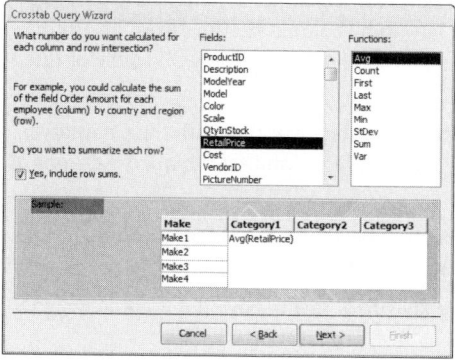

The last wizard screen (not shown) asks for the name of the new crosstab query. The results of this query are shown in Figure 18.33.

FIGURE 18.33

A typical crosstab query datasheet

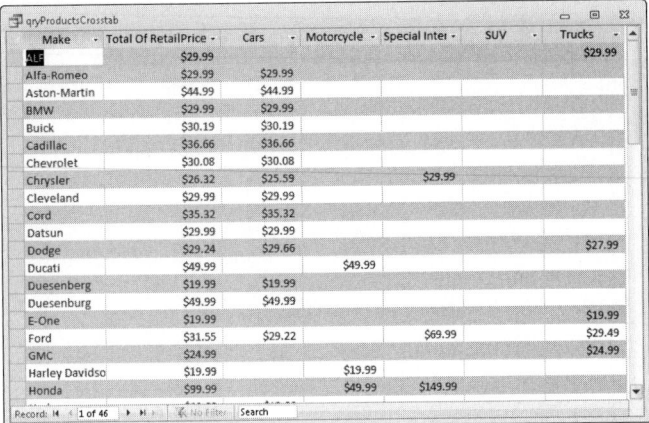

Crosstab queries are extremely powerful. The preceding example is exceedingly simple, but with a bit of additional work, valuable information can be obtained from the tables underlying the query. For instance, this crosstab could be extended by adding criteria that restrict records to a certain sales date interval or salesperson. You could use a query to combine certain information, such as sales by category and state, and then use it as input into a crosstab that calculates average sales by category by date.

The Crosstab Query Wizard has some limitations, however:

- To use more than one table for the crosstab query, you need to create a separate query that has the tables you need for the crosstab query. For example, you may have a Group By row heading from `tblCustomers` and a Group By column heading from `tblProducts` (Category). The Crosstab Query Wizard allows you to select only one table or query for the row and column heading.

- You can't specify the limiting criteria for the crosstab when working with the Crosstab Wizard. Use the wizard to build the crosstab, and then go in and set the query's criteria as a separate step.

- You cannot use a calculated field for row or column headings. In this case, add the calculated field to an intermediate query and use the query for the wizard.

- Column headings or column orders cannot be specified. Again, have the wizard create the query and then modify it.

Understanding Action Queries

So far, the queries I've covered are typical *select queries*. As the name implies, a select query *selects* records from a single table, or a number of tables, and arranges the selected records as a recordset. The recordset is then used by the application, most often as a data source for a form or report.

But, in most business situations, there is often a need to perform an *action* on a group of records, such as deleting inactive customers from the Customers table, or updating the retail price in every record in the Products table.

An action query is a type of query that performs an action (update, delete, and so on) against a group of records. The records are chosen selected as in any typical select query, and then the action is applied to the recordset.

Types of action queries

Action queries can't be created using the Access Query Wizard. An action query starts out as a select query that returns the set of desired records. When you're satisfied that the records are selected correctly, you convert the select query to an action query. Running the action query performs the operation on the records. Here are the four different types of Access action queries:

- **Update Query:** Updates data in an existing table. Update queries perform bulk maintenance on tables, such as adjusting product prices or customer discounts.

- **Make Table Query:** Makes a new database table from the selected records. For example, you may want to create an archive table of all inactive customer records.

- **Delete Query:** Deletes data in a specified table that matches a set of criteria (a filter). Extending the previous example, when the inactive customers have been archived as a separate table, you might use a delete query to remove the inactive customer records from the Customers table.

- **Append Query:** Adds new records to an existing table. For example, one of your former customers, whom you haven't heard from in several years, wants to make a purchase. You might use an append query to retrieve the customer's contact information and add it to the active Customers table.

Tip

You can quickly identify action queries in the Database window by the special exclamation point icon situation near the query name in the Navigation Pane. The icons next to the action queries in the Navigation Pane are miniatures of the action query icons as they appear in the ribbon (see the query icons in Figure 18.9).

Creating action queries

Creating an action query usually begins by creating a select query. You specify the fields for the query, add the query's criteria (if needed), and review the selected records by viewing the query as a datasheet. When you're satisfied that the query is selecting the appropriate records, return to Design view and choose the type of action (make table, update, or delete) you want to perform. When you run the query, the query modifies the selected records.

Creating an update action query

It's possible to individually update records in a table by using a form or by changing records in a query's datasheet. However, these approaches are impractical if there are many records to change. In addition, manual updates introduce transcription errors as you enter new text into fields.

The best way to handle this type of event is to use an update action query to change multiple records as a single operation. You save time and eliminate transcriptional errors that crop up in manually edited records.

Before embarking on a new action query, it's always a good idea to back up the tables affected by the query's action, if possible. Changes to Access databases can't be rolled back or undone, so the additional time required to copy a table (which can be as easy as selecting the table in the Navigation Pane, pressing Ctrl+C and then Ctrl+V, and accepting the default name for the copied table) is easily justified.

Let's create an update action query:

1. Create a very simple select query that selects the `RetailPrice` and `Category` fields from `tlbProducts`.

2. Use = `"trucks"` as the criteria for Category.

3. Select Datasheet View from the View drop-down list in the Results group in the Design ribbon tab to preview the records that will be updated.

4. Click the Select button in the Query Type group on the ribbon.

   Access adds the `Update To` row to the QBE grid.

5. Enter the following expression in the Update To cell in the RetailPrice field in the QBE grid:

   [RetailPrice] * 1.05

6. Click the Run button in the Results ribbon group.

   Access displays a message box indicating how many records will be updated, and asking you to verify the changes to be made to the database.

7. Either click OK to commit the changes, or click No to return to the query's Design view.

The completed update query is shown in Figure 18.34. Notice the similarities between this query and the select queries discussed in Chapter 4. In fact, the only indication that `qryUpdateRetailPrices` is an update query is the presence of the Update To row in the QBE grid.

FIGURE 18.34

A simple make-table query

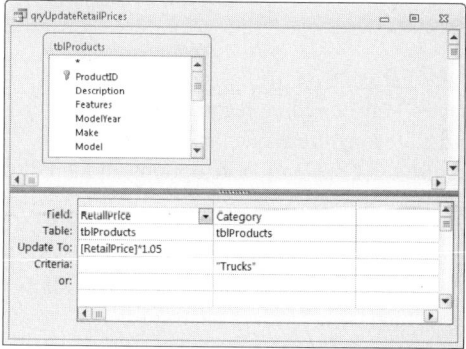

Creating a new table using a make-table query

Make-table queries are created following the same steps as update queries. The only difference is that, when you click the Make Table button in the Query Type, Access asks the name of the table to be created from the query's records.

Figure 18.35 shows a simple make-table query that selects all customers who have not placed an order for more than two years. The dialog box asking for the name of the new table is shown hovering over the query's design.

FIGURE 18.35

Specifying the name of the table created by the make-table query

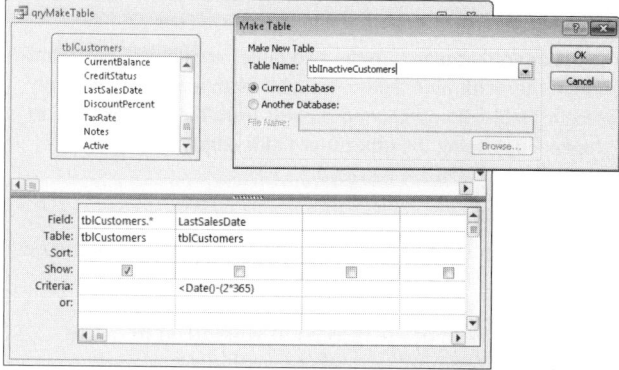

Creating queries to append records

As the word *append* suggests, an append query attaches or adds records to an existing table. An append query adds the records selected by the query to another table. You can append records to a table in the same database or in another Access database.

Append queries are useful for adding information to another table on the basis of some scoping criteria. Even so, append queries are not always the fastest way of adding records to another database. For example, if you need to append all fields and all records from one table to a new table, the append query is not the best way to do it. Instead, use the Copy and Paste options on the Edit menu when you're working with the table in a datasheet or form.

Append query creation follows the pattern already discussed for update and make-table queries. You start by building a select query that returns the desired records and clicking the Append button in the ribbon's Query Type group. Access asks you which table receives the records.

A good example of an append query is periodically adding inactive customers to `tblInactive-Customers`. In fact, the query you'd use is exactly the same as the previous example, except that you execute the query as an append, rather than as a make-table query.

When you're working with append queries, be aware of these rules:

- If the table you're appending records to has a primary key field, the records you add can't have Null values or duplicate primary key values. If they do, Access won't append the records and you'll get no warning. In many cases, the destination table doesn't need a designated primary key. Or, you may choose to use an AutoNumber primary key and let Access assign the key value to each record added to the destination table.

- If you use the asterisk (*) field in a field's row in Design view, you can't also use individual fields from the same table. Access assumes that you're trying to add field contents twice to the same record and won't append the records.

Note

When you're using the append query, only fields with names that match in the two tables are copied. For example, you might have a small table with six fields and another with nine fields. The table with nine fields has only five of the six field names that match fields in the smaller table. If you append records from the smaller table to the larger table, only the five matching fields are appended, leaving the other four fields empty.

Creating a query to delete records

Of all the action queries, the delete query is the most dangerous. Unlike the other types of queries you've worked with, delete queries irreversibly remove records from tables.

A delete action query can work with multiple tables to delete records. If you intend to delete related records from multiple tables, however, you should do the following:

1. Define relationships between the tables in the Relationships Builder.

2. Check the Enforce Referential Integrity option for the join between tables.

3. Check the Cascade Delete Related Records option for the join between tables (for one-to-one or one-to-many relationships).

When working with one-to-many relationships without defining relationships and turning Cascade Delete on, Access deletes records from one table at a time. Specifically, Access first deletes the *many* side (that is, the child records) of the relationship. Then you must remove the many table from the query and delete the records from the *one* side of the query.

This method is time-consuming and awkward. So, when you're deleting related records from one-to-many relationship tables, make sure that you define relationships between the tables and check the Cascade Delete box in the Edit Relationships dialog box. By doing this, you can delete from all related tables by creating a single Delete query.

No extensive description of a delete query is really necessary because the pattern is exactly the same as the other action queries. Start with a select query that retrieves the records you want to delete, preview the records in the query's Datasheet view, and then click the Delete button in the Query Type ribbon group. Access always confirms deletions when you execute the query by clicking on the Run button in the Results ribbon group.

Figure 18.36 illustrates a typical delete query. Its similarity to the update and make-table queries described earlier in this section should be obvious. In fact, the only difference between `qryDeleteQuery` and `qryMakeTable` is the presence of the Delete row, and the absence of the Sort and Show rows in the QBE grid in `qryDeleteQuery`.

FIGURE 18.36

A typical delete query

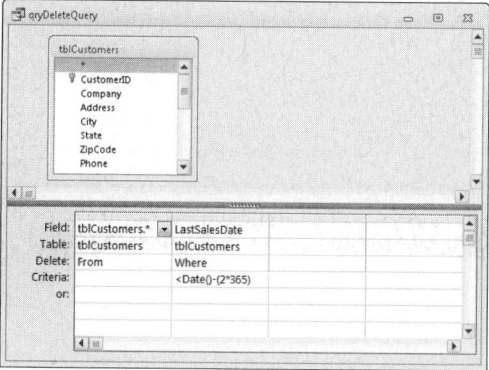

It deserves repeating that a delete query permanently and irreversibly removes the records from the database. You may want to use the query's design as an append query to provide a backup of the records before changing it to a delete query.

Running an action query

After you save an action query, you run it by double-clicking its name in the Navigation Pane. Access warns you that an action query is about to be executed and asks for confirmation before it continues with the query.

Alternatively, open the action query in design view, and use the Run command (the red exclamation point) in the Results group on the Design ribbon tab. Unless you know exactly what an action query will do, you may want to review the query's design before running it directly from the Navigation Pane, so the additional step of opening the query in Design view may protect your database from issues as the query runs.

Troubleshooting action queries

When you're working with action queries, you need to be aware of several potential problems. While you're running the query, any of several messages may appear, including messages that records were lost because of key violations or that records were locked during the execution of the query. This section discusses some of these problems and how to avoid them.

Data-type errors in appending and updating

If you try to enter a value that isn't appropriate for the specified field, Access ignores the incorrect values and inserts nulls into the fields. When you're working with append queries, Access appends the records, but fields might be blank because of data-type mismatches.

Key violations in action queries

When you try to append records to another database that has a primary key, Access won't append records that contain duplicate primary key values.

Access doesn't allow updating a record by changing a primary key value to an existing value. You can change a primary key value to another value under these conditions:

- The new primary key value doesn't already exist.
- The field value you're trying to change isn't related to fields in other tables.

Access doesn't enable you to delete a field on the *one* (parent) side of a one-to-many relationship without first deleting the records from the *many* (child) side.

Access doesn't enable you to append or update a field value that duplicates a value in a *unique index field*. A unique index field is a field that has the Index property set to Yes (No Duplicates).

Record-locked fields in multiuser environments

Access won't perform an action query on records locked by another user. When you're performing an update or append query, you can choose to continue and change all other values. But remember this: If you enable Access to continue with an action query, you won't be able to determine which records were left unchanged!

Text fields

When you're appending or updating to a text field that is smaller than the current field, Access truncates text data that doesn't fit in the new field. Access doesn't warn you that it has truncated the information.

Summary

This chapter has taken a look at just a few of the possibilities when using Access queries to perform calculations and data transformations. The benefit of performing these operations at the query level is that the calculations are performed dynamically, and consistently, no matter where the data is used.

Access totals queries provide many options for grouping, sorting, and filtering data before applying calculations to the data. Alternatively, calculations may be performed before filtering so that only certain records are returned by the query.

Finally, crosstabs are a powerful tool for summarizing data. When properly constructed, crosstab queries reveal patterns and valuable information not obvious from simple select queries. The ability to choose fields used as row and column headers, and the calculations to perform on the crosstab fields, is a powerful addition to your Access development toolkit.

Advanced Access Form Techniques

U ser interface is a term you hear frequently in discussions about computer software. In virtually all applications built with Microsoft Access, the user interface consists of a series of Access forms. If you intend to develop successful Access applications, you need to understand Access forms inside and out.

This chapter helps you improve your understanding of forms. First, I show you how to programmatically manipulate the many controls that constitute the building blocks out of which forms are constructed. I also show you some powerful ways to take advantage of subforms. I devote one section of the chapter to presenting a grab-bag of forms-related programming techniques that will help you create forms that elicit the best performance from Access and your computer. Then, I cover the Query by Form feature, which enables you to build an intuitive form-based interface between users and Access queries.

On the CD-ROM

This chapter uses examples in the Chapter19.accdb database and other files in the Chapter_19 folder on this book's CD. If you have not yet copied the contents of this folder to your computer, please do so now.

Setting Control Properties

The building blocks of Access forms are known as *controls*. The form design toolbox contains more than a dozen different types of controls from which you can build forms, including labels, text boxes, option groups, toggle

IN THIS CHAPTER

Setting properties for Access forms and controls

Using subforms in Access

Reviewing basic techniques for designing forms

Learning advanced Access forms techniques

Working with tab controls in Access forms

Collecting information with dialog boxes

buttons, option buttons, check boxes, combo boxes, list boxes, and other controls. Although this chapter doesn't discuss every type of Access form control in detail, it documents the most commonly used controls found in Access applications.

Each control on an Access form has a set of properties that determines the control's appearance and behavior. In Design view, you manipulate a control's property settings through its Property Sheet. To display the Property Sheet, right-click the object and click Properties in the pop-up menu, select the object and click the Properties button in the ribbon, or press the F4 key with the object selected. Once the Property Sheet is open, clicking any other control in the form displays the selected control's property settings. Figure 19.1 shows the Property Sheet for the command button named cmdNew on the Customers form (frmCustomers) in the Chapter19.accdb application.

FIGURE 19.1

The Property Sheet for the cmdNew command button

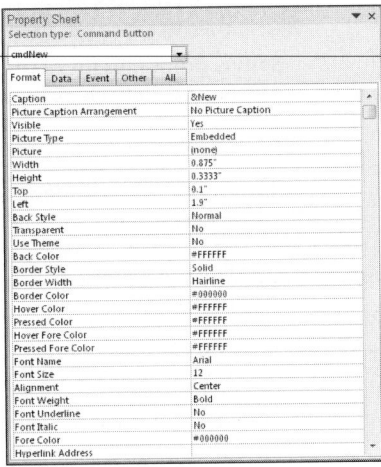

The form itself also has its own set of properties. If you display the Property Sheet in Design view before selecting a specific control, Access lists the form's properties in the Property Sheet, as indicated by the caption "Form" in the Property Sheet's title bar (see Figure 19.2). To display the form's properties in the Property Sheet after first displaying a control's properties, click a completely blank area in the form design window (outside the form's defined border).

FIGURE 19.2

The Property Sheet for the Customers form

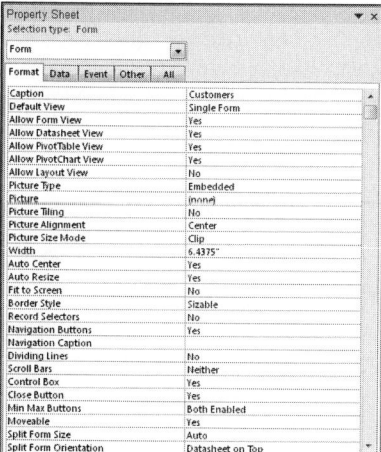

Customizing default properties

Whenever you use a tool in the form Design view toolbox to create a control, the control is created with a default set of property values. This may seem obvious, but what you may not know is that you can set many of these default values yourself. For example, if you want all list boxes in your form to be flat rather than sunken, it's more efficient to change the default SpecialEffect property to Flat before you design the form, instead of changing the SpecialEffect property for every list box individually.

To set control defaults, select a tool in the toolbox and then set properties in the Property Sheet without adding the control to the form. Notice that the title in the Property Sheet is Selection type: Default <ControlType>. As you set the control's properties, you're actually setting the default properties for that type of control for the current form. Instead of adding the control to the form, select another control (such as the Select control in the upper-right corner of the Controls group) to "lock down" the default settings. Then, when you reselect the control you want, you'll see that the control's default properties have been set the way you wanted. When you save the form, the property defaults you've set for the form's controls are saved along with the form.

In addition to saving you time while designing a form, customizing default properties can speed the saving and loading of forms. If most controls on the form use the default property settings, the saved form takes less space, saves faster, and subsequently loads faster when your application uses it (but doesn't save memory).

Manipulating controls at runtime

The form design capabilities of Access are so engaging that it's easy to lose sight of the fact that all Access controls are programmatically accessible at runtime. Changing the design of a form on the fly, based on input from the user, can sometimes be very convenient. For example, a list box that contains information that is relevant only some of the time doesn't have to be displayed all the time. Well-designed forms often hide irrelevant controls whenever possible. You can achieve this and similar functionality by assigning values to control and form properties at runtime.

Here are a few properties that are often good candidates for dynamic assignment at runtime:

- **The `Enabled` property:** If you want a control to be visible but grayed out, set the `Enabled` property to `False`. Clicking the grayed-out control has no effect. This technique enables you to maintain a consistent form design, and helps the user become familiar with the location of the controls on the form, but it prevents the user from selecting a control that's irrelevant to the current operation.

- **The `Visible` property:** You can easily toggle the display of any control by assigning `Yes` or `No` to the control's `Visible` property. While the control is invisible, it's also inactive and can't receive the focus. An invisible control can't respond to events. Making a control invisible is sometimes more appropriate than simply disabling the control, especially in the case of text, combo, or list boxes.

- **The `Caption` property:** By dynamically assigning values to a control's `Caption` property, the control can serve double- or triple-duty. This technique is especially useful when two command buttons serve mutually exclusive functions and don't need to appear on the form at the same time. For example, you might place a command button with the caption `&New Patient Data` on your application's main switchboard form. This button opens a form for adding a new record to your patient database. After the new patient data has been entered, but before the full transaction has been committed to the database, you could change the command button's caption to `&Edit Patient Data` using the button's `Caption` property. The code in the button's `Click` event procedure determines which task to perform based on the caption at the time the user clicks on the button.

    You can also use the active form's `Caption` property creatively to display information about the current record. Each time the current event occurs, assign a new value to the `Caption` property that contains pertinent information from the current record.

- **The `RowSource` property:** Use the `RowSource` property of a combo- or list-box control to synchronize the list contents with values in other controls in the active form. For example, if `txtDepartment` contains the value `Sales`, you can set the `cboPhoneList` combo box's `RowSource` property to show only members of the sales department in the combo box.

- **The `BackColor` and `ForeColor` properties:** Judicious use of color can be very effective in conveying important information. Access enables you to dynamically change the color of controls as they receive or lose focus, or to reflect a state of the data by changing the `ForeColor` and `BackColor` properties.

- **The** Left, Top, Width, **and** Height **properties:** Using these properties, you can control the position and dimensions of a control on the form.

- **The** MenuBar, ShortcutMenu, ShortcutMenuBar **properties:** If you have defined custom ribbons or shortcut menus, you can use these form properties to dynamically change the ribbon and shortcut menus as the user works with the application.

- **The Custom Ribbon ID:** If the current application includes custom ribbons, the ribbon IDs appear in this property's drop-down list. Access shows and hides the assigned ribbon as the form is opened and closed.

The SetProperty function can be used to set the value of any property of an open form or a property of controls on an open form:

```
Public Function SetProperty( _
    ByVal strFormName As String, _
    ByVal strCtrlName As String, _
    ByVal strPropName As String, _
    ByVal strNewValue As Variant) As Boolean
  Dim frmName As Form
  Dim strMsg As String
  Dim strFunction As String
  Dim strObjName As String
On Error GoTo HandleError
  SetProperty = False
  strFunction = "SetProperty"
  'If no control name is passed, must be a form:
  If Len(strCtrlName) > 0 Then
  'We fall through to this code if
  'strCtrlName is not an empty string.
  'Assign new control property value:
    strObjName = strCtrlName
  'If no form name provided,
  'exit procedure:
    If strFormName = "" Then
      Exit Function
    End If
    Set frmName = Forms(strFormName)
    frmName(strCtrlName).Properties( _
      strPropName) = strNewValue
    SetProperty = True
  Else
  'We fall through to this code if
  'strCtrlName is an empty string.
  'Assign new form property value:
    strObjName = strFormName
    Set frmName = Forms(strFormName)
    frmName.Properties(strPropName) = strNewValue
    SetProperty = True
  End If
```

```
ExitHere:
  Exit Function
HandleError:
  Select Case Err
    Case 2450
      strMsg = "'" & strFormName & "' is not an open form"
    Case 2465
      strMsg = "'" & strCtrlName _
        & "' is not a control on '" & strFormName & "'"
    Case 2465
      strMsg = "'" & strPropName _
        & "' is not a property of '" & strObjName & "'"
    Case Else
      strMsg = "Error#" & Err & ": " & Err.Description
    End Select
  MsgBox strMsg, vbExclamation + vbOKOnly, _
    "Error in Procedure " & strFunction
  SetProperty = False
  Resume ExitHere
End Function
```

This function takes four arguments:

- The name of the form
- The name of the control (if any)
- The name of the property to set
- The new value of the property

SetProperty returns True if the operation is successful and False if it is not. For example, to disable the button named GoToNew on frmEmployees, use the following statement:

```
intRetVal = SetProperty("frmEmployees", "GoToNew", _
"Enabled", False)
```

Although this task is easily done in code behind frmEmployees, SetProperty can be called from anywhere in the application. This means that, another form (perhaps a switchboard form) can easily control the enabled state the New button on frmEmployees.

To set the value of a form property, pass an empty string ("") as the control name. For example, use the following statement to set the frmEmployees form's caption (in the Chapter19.accdb database) to Sales Department:

```
intRetVal = SetProperty("frmEmployees", "", _
  "Caption", "Sales Department")
```

You can easily hide and show controls by adjusting a control's Visible property. You might want to hide certain controls (such as command buttons or text boxes) when they're irrelevant to the user's current task. You might also want to hide controls if the user isn't permitted to perform the operation (such as deleting an existing record). Rather than simply disabling the control (by setting its `Enabled` property to `False`), hiding the control makes it invisible to the user. Invisible controls are less likely to confuse users than controls that are visible but disabled. The following statement hides a command button named `cmdDeleteRecord` on the employees form:

```
intRetVal = SetProperty("frmEmployees", "cmdDeleteRecord", _
    "Visible", "False")
```

Reading control properties

If your application manipulates the control properties, at various times you'll need to read the value of a control's property. The following `GetProperty` function returns the value of any property of any open form or any property of any control in an open form. If the function encounters an error, it returns the value `ERROR`.

```
Public Function GetProperty( _
    ByVal strFormName As String, _
    ByVal strCtrlName As String, _
    ByVal strPropName As String) As Variant
  Dim frmName As Form
  Dim strMsg As String
  Dim strFunction As String
  Dim strObjName As String
On Error GoTo HandleError
  GetProperty = "ERROR"
  strFunction = "SetProperty"
  'If no control name is passed, must be a form:
  If Len(strCtrlName) > 0 Then
  'We fall through to this code if
  'strCtrlName is not an empty string.
  'Get control property value:
    strObjName = strCtrlName
    Set frmName = Forms(strFormName)
    GetProperty = _
      frmName(strCtrlName).Properties(strPropName)
  Else
  'We fall through to this code if
  'strCtrlName is an empty string.
  'If no form name provided,
  'exit procedure:
    If Len(strFormName) = 0 Then
      Exit Function
    End If
  'Get form property value:
    strObjName = strFormName
    Set frmName = Forms(strFormName)
    GetProperty = frmName.Properties(strPropName)
  End If
```

```
    ExitHere:
      Exit Function
    HandleError:
      Select Case Err
        Case 2450
          strMsg = "'" & strFormName & "' is not an open form"
        Case 2465
          strMsg = "'" & strCtrlName _
              & "' is not a control on '" & strFormName & "'"
        Case 2455
          strMsg = "'" & strPropName _
            & "' is not a property of '" & strObjName & "'"
        Case Else
          strMsg = "Error# " & Err & ": " & Err.Description
      End Select
      MsgBox strMsg, vbExclamation + vbOKOnly, _
        "Error in Procedure " & strFunction
      GetProperty = strMsg
      Resume ExitHere
    End Function
```

Notice that GetProperty returns a variant data type value. A variant is returned because the function might return a property object, or — in the event of a problem accessing the property — a string containing ERROR. If a runtime error is triggered by the GetProperty function, a string containing the error number and message is returned.

Working with Subforms

Subforms are indispensable for displaying information from two different tables or queries on the screen together. Typically, subforms are used where the main form's record source has a one-to-many relationship with the subform's record source. Many records in the subform are associated with one record in the main form.

Access uses the LinkMasterFields and LinkChildFields properties of the subform control to choose the records in the subform that are related to each record in the main form. Whenever a value in the main form's link field changes, Access automatically requeries the subform.

When creating a subform, you might want to display subform aggregate information in the master form. For example, you might want to display the count of the records in the subform somewhere on your main form. For an example of this technique, see the txtItemCount control in frm-CustomerSales in Chapter19.accdb. In this case the ControlSource expression in the txtItemCount control is

```
="(" & [subfPurchases].[Form]![txtItemCount] & " items)"
```

(Note that the equal sign needs to be included.) The result of this expression is shown in Figure 19.3.

FIGURE 19.3

Aggregate data from a subform can be displayed on the main form.

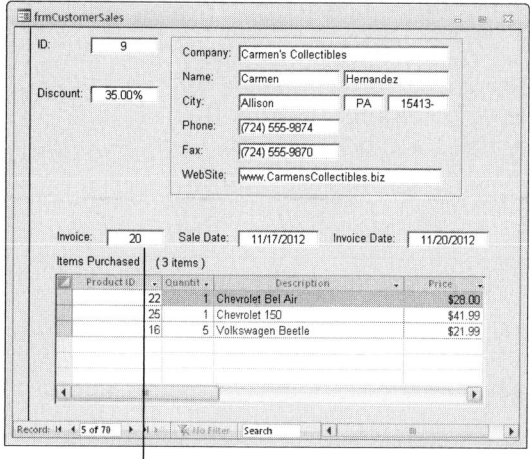

ControlSource is set to ="(" & [subfPurchases].[Form]!
[txtItemCount] & " items)"

Before you can put aggregate data in the master form, its value must be found in the subform. Place a text box wherever you want in the subform, and set its `Visible` property to `No` (`False`) so that it's hidden. Put an aggregate expression, such as `= Count([ProductID])`, into the `ControlSource` property of the hidden control.

In the main form, insert a new text box with `ControlSource` set to the following value:

```
=[Subform1].Form![Name-of-Aggregate-Control]
```

where *Subform1* is the name of the control on the main form that contains the embedded subform and *Name-of-Aggregate-Control* is the name of the control on the subform that contains the aggregate data.

The control on the main form updates each time you change its value in the subform.

Access treats a subform control in the same manner as other controls on the main form. You can set a subform control's properties, refer to it with a `GoToControl` command, and use code to set and read the values of controls on the subform. Use the following syntax versions to refer to subform properties, subform controls, and subform control properties, respectively:

```
Forms![FormName]![SubformControlName].Form.SubFormProperty
Forms![FormName]![SubformControlName].Form![ControlName]
Forms![FormName]![SubformControlName].Form![ControlName].ControlProperty
```

where *SubformControlName* refers to the name you've given the subform control, which is not necessarily the same as the name of the form as it appears in the Navigation Pane.

687

When using subforms within subforms, use the following syntax:

```
Forms![FormName]![SubformControlName]. _
    Form![SubSubformControlName].Form.SubSubFormProperty
Forms![FormName]![SubformControlName]. _
    Form![SubSubformControlName].Form.[ControlName]
Forms![FormName]![SubformControlName]. _
    Form![SubSubformControlName].Form.[ControlName] _
        .ControlProperty
```

Designing Forms

Following is a grab bag of form design tips that you might find handy. I hope they inspire you to come up with many more on your own!

Using the Tab Stop property

From time to time, you might place a control on a form that is intended to trigger a fairly drastic result, such as deleting a record, or printing a long report. If you want to reduce the risk that the user might activate this control by accident, you might want to make use of the Tab Stop property, which specifies whether you can use the Tab key to move the focus to the control.

For example, suppose you've placed a command button named cmdDelete on a form that deletes the current record. You don't want the user to click this button by mistake. Modify the Tab Stop property of cmdDelete to No to remove the button from the form's tab order (the default is Yes). A user will have to explicitly click on the button to activate it, and the user won't be able to accidentally choose it while entering data.

Tallying check boxes

If you ever need to count the number of True values in a check-box control, consider using the following expression:

```
Sum(Abs([CheckBoxControl]))
```

Abs converts every −1 to 1, and the Sum function adds them up. To count False values, use the following expression:

```
Sum([CheckBoxControl] + 1)
```

Each True values (−1) is converted to 0 and each False value (0) is converted to 1 before being summed.

Adding animation

Using the Timer event, you can pretty simply add animation to Access forms. You can move a control on the form at quick intervals or rapidly change the appearance of the control. To create the appearance of animation:

1. Embed a picture on the form.

2. Set the `TimerInterval` property of the form to `100`.

   The value represents the number of milliseconds between firing of the event.

3. Assign the following event procedure to the `Timer` event:

```
Private Sub Form_Timer()
   'Move the image down and to the right.
   ctlImage.Left = ctlImage.Left + 200
   ctlImage.Top  = ctlImage.Top  + 100
End Sub
```

Screen positions in VBA are given in twips — $1/1,440$ inch ($1/567$ centimeter). This event procedure moves the image in the `ctlImage` control down and to the right on the form every $1/10th$ of a second.

The `frmAnimation` form in `Chapter19.accdb` uses the technique described here to move an airplane bitmap across the form. A couple of other techniques are used to create a bit of animation. The following event procedure, associated with the `Timer` event, causes a bitmap of a pencil eraser to move back and forth by manipulating the `Image` control's `PictureAlignment` property. The procedure also causes a globe to spin by using the `Visible` property of three different bitmaps that are positioned one on top of the other:

```
Private Sub Form_Timer()
On Error Resume Next
  'Wiggle the eraser:
  If Eraser.PictureAlignment = 2 Then
    Eraser.PictureAlignment = 3
  ElseIf Eraser.PictureAlignment = 3 Then
    Eraser.PictureAlignment = 4
  ElseIf Eraser.PictureAlignment = 4 Then
    Eraser.PictureAlignment = 3
  End If
  '"Spin" the globe:
  If World1.Visible = -1 Then
    World1.Visible = 0
    World2.Visible = -1
  ElseIf World2.Visible = -1 Then
    World2.Visible = 0
    World3.Visible = -1
  ElseIf World3.Visible = -1 Then
    World3.Visible = 0
    World1.Visible = -1
  End If
  'Now move the plane:
Plane.Left = Plane.Left + 200
  Plane.Top = Plane.Top + 100
  If Plane.Left > 9000 Then
    Plane.Left = 0
    Plane.Top = 1440
  End If
End Sub
```

The `TimerInterval` property is set to `200` through the Property Sheet for the form, meaning that this code will execute every 200 milliseconds. Set it to a longer interval to slow down the animation.

Notice that the plane's position is reset as soon as the left margin of the plane exceeds 9,000 twips.

Using SQL for a faster refresh

You can generate faster combo-box refreshes on a form by making the control's row source a SQL statement instead of a query name. Complete the following steps:

1. Generate the query using the standard procedure.

2. Make the query the control's `RowSource` property and make sure the combo box is correctly populated.

3. When everything works correctly, display the query in Design view and select SQL from the View menu.

4. Cut and paste the SQL statement into the combo box's `RowSource` property.

Selecting data for overtyping

When users edit existing data in a form, they usually prefer to type over existing data without having to first select the existing data. The following function when triggered by each control's `GoFocus` event has this effect:

```
Function SelectAll()
  'Set the cursor to the beginning of the field.
  Screen.ActiveControl.SelStart = 0
  'Select all positions up to the last.
  'This will make a reversed image, which will be easier to see.
  Screen.ActiveControl.SelLength = _
    Len(Screen.ActiveControl)
End Function
```

Toggling properties with Not

A handy way to toggle properties that take Boolean values, such as the `Visible` property, is to use the `Not` operator. For example, the following VB statement toggles the object's `Visible` property, regardless of the actual value of the property:

```
Object.Visible = Not Object.Visible
```

For example, if `Visible` is `True`, its value is set to `False`, hiding the object. By using the `Not` operator, you don't have to test for the current value of the property.

`Chapter19.accdb` contains a simple form demonstrating this capability. `frmFlashingLabel` contains two label controls (`lblRed` and `lblBlue`) placed on top of one another. `lblRed's`

`Visible` property is initially set to `No`, making it invisible. Then the following code runs every time the form's `Timer` event fires:

```
Private Sub Form_Timer()
   lblRed.Visible = Not lblRed.Visible
   lblBlue.Visible = Not lblBlue.Visible
End Sub
```

This code simply alternates the `Visible` property of each of the label controls. Since `lblRed` was initially invisible, it's made visible in the first pass, and so on. Although there are many other ways to implement this form trick, this example adequately demonstrates the value of the `Not` operator when dealing with property values.

Caution
Be careful using flashing labels. They've been known to cause problems for people with epilepsy.

Creating an auto-closing form

If you want a form to close automatically as soon as the user moves to another form, do the following:

1. Create an event procedure for the `Deactivate` event that includes the following statement:

   `Me.TimerInterval = 1`

2. Create an event procedure for the `Timer` event that includes the following statement:

   `DoCmd.Close`

Your form automatically closes as soon as you go to any other form.

Setting up combo boxes and list boxes

Combo boxes and list boxes are powerful tools in your form-building toolbox, but they can be complicated to set up. When you build combo boxes and list boxes, it's important to keep in mind the distinction between `ControlSource` (the table or query field to and from which the control saves and loads data) and `RowSource` (the source of the data displayed in the list). Because combo and list boxes support multiple columns, they allow you to easily relate data from another table without basing your form on a query that joins the tables. This technique, which involves a bound combo- or list-box control that stores an ID number but displays names in a list, is used in the Organization combo box in the form named `frmContacts_Northwind` in `Chapter19.accdb`, as well as in several of the forms found in the Northwind sample database.

For example, suppose you're creating a form to display information about your clients and customers (your "contacts"), and you want to identify the organization with which these contacts are associated. In a well-designed database, you store only an organization ID number with each contact record, while you store the organization's name and other information in a separate table. You want your form to include a combo box that displays organization names and addresses in the list but stores organization ID numbers in the field. (For an example of this technique, see frmContacts_Northwind in Chapter19.accdb.)

To accomplish your design goal, create a multiple-column combo box. Set the ControlSource to the OrgID field (the field in the Contacts table that contains the organization ID number for each contact person). Set the RowSourceType property of the combo box to Table/Query. You could base the list on a table, but you want the list of names to be sorted; instead, set the RowSource property to a query that includes OrgID numbers in the first field, and organization names sorted ascending in the second field. The best way to do this is using the Query Builder for the RowSource property to create a SQL statement; alternatively, you can create and save a query to provide the list. In frmContacts_Northwind example (the Organization combo box), the RowSource query is as follows:

```
SELECT Organizations.OrgID, Organizations.Name,
Organizations.AddressLine1, Organizations.AddressLine2,
Organizations.City, Organizations.State,
Organizations.ZipCode, Organizations.Country
FROM Organizations ORDER BY Organizations.Name
```

Because you're interested in seeing all this data listed in the combo box, set the ColumnCount property to 8. You hide the OrgID column in a minute, but you need it in the combo-box RowSource because it contains the data that's saved by the control when a row is selected by the user. This column is identified by the combo box's BoundColumn property (set to 1 by default). The bound column containing ID numbers doesn't have to be visible to the user. The ColumnWidths property contains a semicolon-separated list of visible column widths for the columns in the drop-down list. Access uses default algorithms to determine the widths of any columns for which you don't explicitly choose a width. If you choose a width of 0 for any column, that column is effectively hidden from the user on the screen, but it isn't hidden from the rest of your forms, VBA code, or macros. In this case, you set the property to the following:

```
0";1.4";1.2";0.7";0.7";0.3;0.5";0.3"
```

This indicates to Access that you want the first column to be invisible and sets explicit column widths for the other columns.

The second column — in this case, the organization name — is the one against which the user's text input is matched. The first visible column in the combo box is always used for this purpose. Figure 19.4 shows the resulting drop-down list. Although this is a rather extreme example of loading a combo box with data, it effectively illustrates the power of the Access combo-box control.

When working with combo boxes, if you set the Limit to List property to Yes, the user is required to choose from only the entries in the drop-down list. You can then construct an event procedure for the control's NotOnList event to handle what should happen if a user enters a value not in the list. You might want to open a form into which the user can enter new information; or perhaps you want to display a message box that instructs the user what procedure to follow to add data.

FIGURE 19.4

The drop-down list for the Organizations combo box

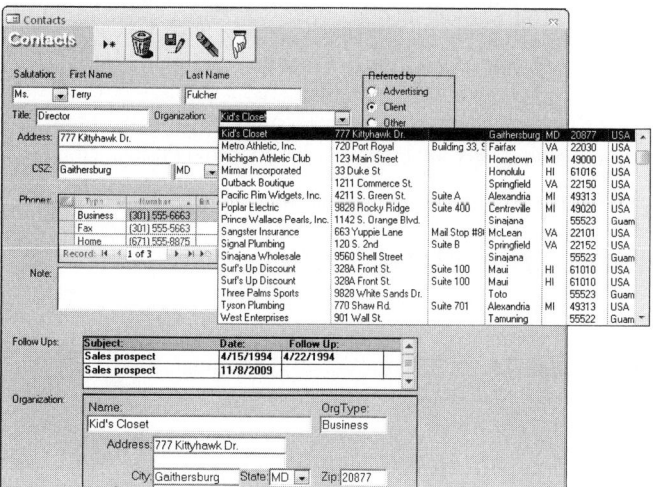

Determining whether a form is open

The following code shows a function that reports whether the form passed in as `strFName` is currently open. It simply enumerates all members of the `Forms` collection, looking to see if `strFName` matches the name of any open form.

```
Function IsFormOpen(strFName As String) As Integer
  'This function returns true if a form is open:
  Dim i As Integer
  'Assume False:
  IsFormOpen = False
  For i = 0 To Forms.Count - 1
    If Forms(i).Name = strFName Then
      IsFormOpen = True
      Exit Function
    End If
  Next
End Function
```

It's probably worth pointing out that when you use a form as a subform, it does not actually appear in the `Forms` collection, so that this function will not indicate that the form is open.

Tackling Advanced Forms Techniques

Access contains many powerful and exciting features in its forms design and user-interface capabilities. As you well know, the forms in your applications are the main component of the user interface. To a large extent, a user's perception of an application's ease of use and strength is determined by the attractiveness and effectiveness of its user interface. You'll be pleased to know that Microsoft has provided Access forms with significant capabilities to control the user interface. Many of these features have been in Access for a very long time but haven't been discovered by many developers.

Using the Page Number and Date/Time controls

Very often forms include the current date and time. Many developers add this information to a form or report with an unbound text box, and Date() function to return this information to the unbound text box. Access simplifies this process with the Date and Time commands on the Header/Footer group on the ribbon's Design tab (see Figure 19.5).

FIGURE 19.5

The Design tab contains essential tools when working with forms.

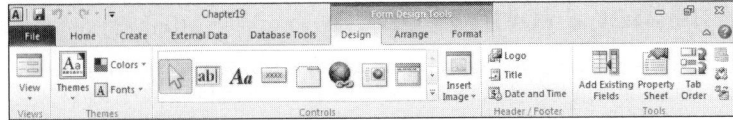

Figure 19.5 shows the ribbon when a form is in Design view.

When the date command is selected, Access displays the Date and Time dialog box (see Figure 19.6) to ask how you want the date and time formatted. After you make your selections and click OK, Access adds a form header containing the date and time formatted as you requested.

FIGURE 19.6

Tell Access how you want the date to appear.

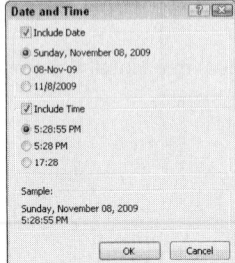

The Header/Footer group includes other commands for adding a logo (virtually any image file) and a title to the form header area. Using the Header/Footer controls in an application gives all the forms a consistent appearance (see Figure 19.7, which is `frmDialog` in the sample database).

The header control provides a consistent look to your Access forms.

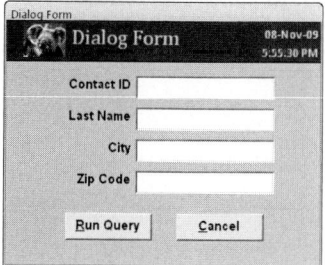

Using the Image control

A subtle and often overlooked performance issue in Access applications occurs when static images are added to forms. Images are often added to Access forms as OLE objects, which means that a certain amount of memory and disk space is required to maintain the image's connection to its parent application. This overhead is used even when the image is a company logo or other graphic that will not be changed or edited at runtime.

Access simplifies this process and provides a great deal more flexibility with the Image control. The Image control places an image frame onto a form or report, but does not burden the image object with the overhead associated with OLE objects. The Image control accepts virtually any type of image data type recognized by Windows (`.bmp`, `.pcx`, `.ico`, `.dib`, `.gif`, `.wmf`, `.jpg`, `.png`, `.tif` and so on), and enables you to specify the path to the image file at runtime in its `Picture` property. The Image control also accepts image data stored in an Access table, although it doesn't provide the flexibility of in-place editing.

Morphing a control

Surely one of the most frustrating problems when building Access forms is the need to specify the control type as a control is added to a form. For example, consider the issues involved when you add a list box to an Access form, specify the `ControlSource`, `RowSourceType`, `RowSource`, and other properties and then discover there's not enough room on the form for the list box. In this case, it seems the only solution is to remove the list box, add a combo box, and reset all the properties, even though the properties for the combo box are identical for the list box you just removed.

In Access, you can change a control to any other compatible type (a process sometimes called *morphing* the control). For example, a text box can be changed to a label, list box, or combo box. Simply right-click the control and select the Change To command from the shortcut menu to see the options. Figure 19.8 shows the options for changing a text-box control.

Access lets you change the type of a control without losing the properties you've already set.

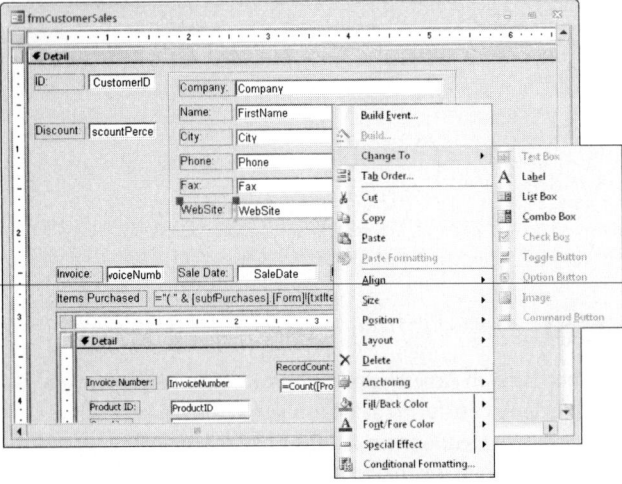

The choices you see in the shortcut menu are specific for the type of control you're changing. For example, an option button can be changed to a check box or toggle button, but not to a text box.

Using the Format Painter

Access includes a *format painter* that functions much like the same feature in Word. When creating a form, you set the appearance of a control (its border, font, special effects, like sunken or raised) and then click the Format Painter button on the Font group in the ribbon's Design tab to copy the properties to a special internal buffer. When you click another control of the same type, the appearance characteristics of the selected control are transferred to the second control. In Figure 19.9, the format properties of one text box are about to be "painted" onto the City text box. (The little paintbrush adjacent to the mouse pointer that tells you you're in Paint mode.)

You can lock the Format Painter by double-clicking its button in the Access ribbon. Note that not all properties are painted onto the second control. The size, position, and data properties of the control are not affected by the Format Painter. Only the most basic text properties are influenced by the Format Painter.

FIGURE 19.9

The Format Painter makes it easy to "paint" the appearance of a control onto other controls on a form.

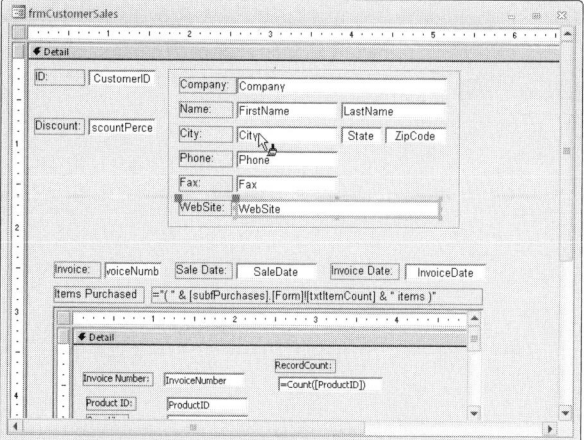

Offering more end-user help

Beginning with Office 4.x all Microsoft products have featured tooltip help — those little yellow notes that appear when you hold the mouse cursor over a control or button. (Microsoft calls these prompts *control tip help*.)

You add tooltips to Access forms by adding the help text to the control's `ControlTip Text` property (see Figure 19.10). By default the text in a tooltip doesn't wrap, but you can add a new line character by pressing Ctrl+Enter in the `ControlTip Text` property wherever you want the break to appear.

In general, you should consistently use tooltips throughout an application. After your users become accustomed to tooltips, they expect them on all but the most obvious controls.

Adding background pictures

Attractive forms are always a valuable addition to Access applications. It's difficult to add color or graphics to forms without obscuring the data contained on the form. Access makes it easy to add a graphic to the background of a form, much as a watermark might appear on expensive bond paper. The picture can contain a company logo, text, or any other graphic element. The picture is specified by the form's `Picture` property and can be embedded in the form or linked to an external file. If the picture is linked, the graphic displayed on the form changes anytime the external file is edited.

FIGURE 19.10

Tooltips help make your applications easier to use.

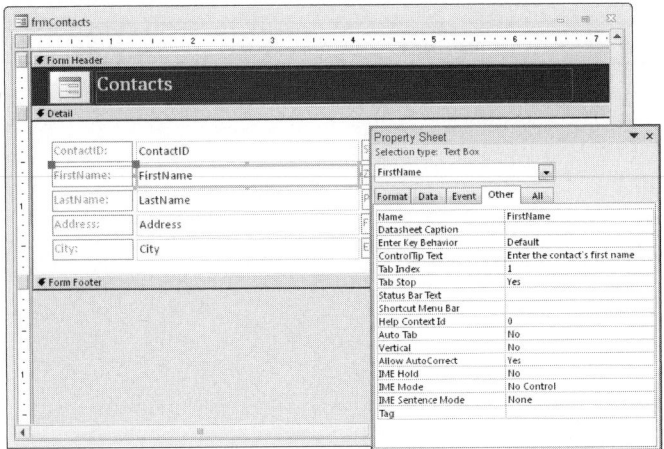

The picture can also be positioned at any of the form's four corners or centered in the middle of the form. Although the picture can be clipped, stretched, or zoomed to fit the dimensions of the form, you can't modify the picture to make it smaller (other than editing the image file, of course). Figure 19.11 shows a small background picture of an automobile positioned in the upper-right corner of frmCustomerSales.

FIGURE 19.11

A small .bmp file has been added to frmCustomerSales as the Picture property.

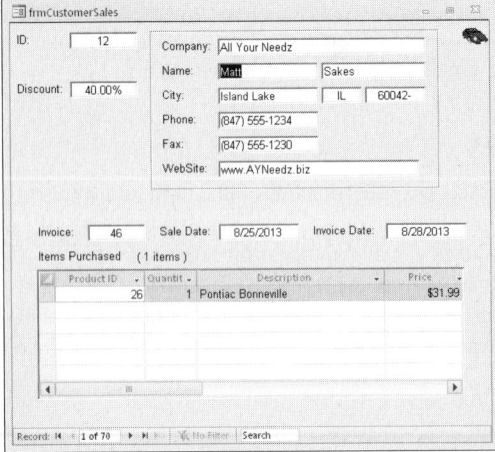

You can even make controls on a form transparent so that the form's background picture shows through the controls (see Figure 19.12). In this case (frmEmployees_Background), the background of each label control is set to Transparent, letting the form's background picture show through.

FIGURE 19.12

Transparent controls allow the background picture to show through.

It's easy to overdo the background picture added to Access forms, but, when carefully used, background pictures can make forms easier for users to understand.

Caution

Background pictures added to a form noticeably slow down the form's appearance on the screen. Generally speaking, you should use a background picture when the benefit provided by the picture outweighs the unavoidable performance degradation caused by the picture's presence.

Fine-tuning your form's behavior with form events

Form events allow you to fine-tune your form's behavior when filters are applied to or removed from the form's underlying data source.

ApplyFilter

The ApplyFilter event fires whenever the user applies a filter by clicking one of the filter buttons (Ascending, Filter, Selection, and so on) in the Sort & Filter ribbon group. You can use the ApplyFilter event to test the user's filtering criteria to make sure the filter makes sense. Use the form's Filter property to determine whether the filter being applied contains valid criteria, or to modify the Filter property in code.

You can also use the ApplyFilter event to hide certain fields that should not be viewed by all users, or to display a dialog box requesting additional identification information such as an extra password or username.

Finally, because `ApplyFilter` is triggered when the Remove Filter button in the Sort & Filter group is clicked, you can use this event to reveal hidden fields, reset the `Filter` property to its former value, and so on.

Filter event

The `Filter` event is similar to the `ApplyFilter` in that it's triggered whenever the user invokes one of the built-in form filtering options. The `Filter` event triggers before the `ApplyFilter` event and is useful for displaying your own filtering form, removing controls that should not be used in a filter by form session, and so on. Together the `Filter` and `ApplyFilter` events give you a great deal of control over user access to the built-in filtering capabilities in Access.

Using the Tab Control

A tab control provides several pages, each accessed through a tab at the top, bottom, or side of the dialog box. Figure 19.13 shows `frmCustomers`, a perfect example of a tabbed Access form. `frmCustomers` contains a tab control with three pages, allowing the form to contain many more controls than possible without the tab control. Each of the tabs along the top of the form reveals a different page of the form's data. Each page contains many controls. Figure 19.13 shows buttons, labels, and text boxes. Each control on the page behaves independently of all other controls on the form and can be accessed through Access VBA code as an independent unit.

FIGURE 19.13

The tab control allows a form to host a large amount of data.

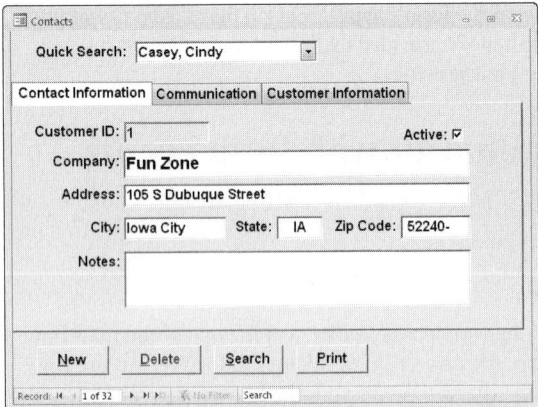

As you might guess, the tab control is fairly complex. It includes its own properties, events, methods, and object collections. You have to know and understand these items before you can effectively use the tab control in your applications.

Note

Developers often use the term tab when referring to the pages of a tabbed dialog box. In this chapter, the terms page and tab are used interchangeably.

A tab control consists of a number of `Page` objects, each a member of the control's `Pages` collection. Each page includes a `Controls` collection consisting of the controls that have been added to that page. A page is added to the `Pages` collection with the `Add` method of the `Pages` object; whereas a page is removed from the dialog box with the `Pages` object's `Remove` method. From the user interface, the quickest and easiest way to add or delete a page is to right-click the control and select the appropriate command from the shortcut menu (see Figure 19.14).

FIGURE 19.14

The tab control's shortcut menu contains relevant commands.

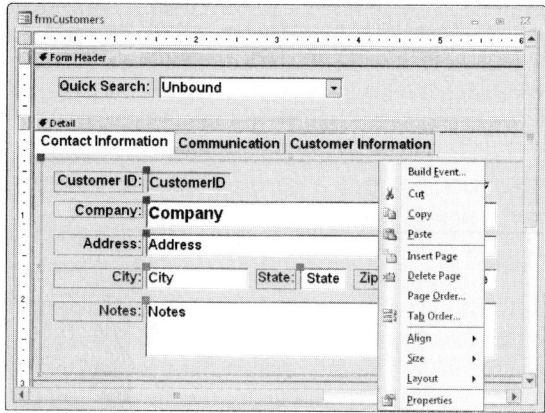

Using the `Insert Page` and `Delete Page` methods to add new pages or delete existing pages from a tab control is not very practical for a number of reasons:

- Both methods require the form to be in Design view before they're able to modify the tab control.

- The `Insert Page` method doesn't return a handle to the new tab. Therefore, it's difficult, if not impossible, to manipulate the properties of the new tab.

- The `Delete Page` method acts on the tab with the highest index and doesn't accept an index or page name as an argument. So, you have to be very careful to make sure you're actually removing the tab you think you are.

In addition to the `Insert Page` and `Delete Page` methods, the tab control contains the relevant properties shown in Table 19.1. Use these properties to tailor the tab controls in your applications to suit the needs of your users.

TABLE 19.1

Important Tab Control Properties

Property	Description
Caption	Applies to each page in the tab control. Provides the text that appears on the tab.
MultiRow	Applies to the tab control. Determines whether the tabs appear as a single row or as multiple rows. You can't specify how many tabs appear in each row. Instead, Access adds as many rows as necessary to display all tabs, given their respective widths.
Style	By default, tabs appear as tabs. The alternative (Buttons) forces the tabs to appear as command buttons.
TabFixedHeight	This value determines the height (in inches or centimeters, depending on the units of measurement settings in the Windows Control Panel) of the tabs on the control. When the TabFixedHeight is set to 0, the tab height is determined by the size of the font specified for the tab control.
TabFixedWidth	This value determines the width (in inches or centimeters) of the tabs on the control. Text that is too wide to fit on the tab when the TabFixedWidth value is set is truncated. When the TabFixedWidth is set to 0, the width of the tab is determined by the font size selected for the tab control and the text specified in the tab's Caption property.
Picture	Applies to each page on the tab control. The Picture property specifies an image (.bmp, .ico, or built-in picture) to display on the tab.

The tab control itself has a Value property that tells you which tab is selected. Value changes each time a tab is selected. Figure 19.15 shows frmTabControl2, a form included in Chapter19.accdb on this book's companion CD-ROM. This form demonstrates some of the properties of the tab control and its pages.

FIGURE 19.15

frmTabControl2 in the Chapter19.accdb example database demonstrates important tab control properties.

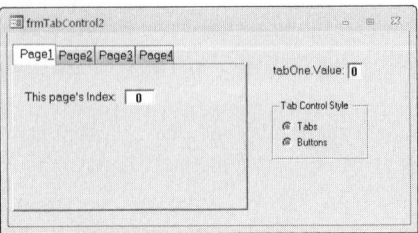

The Value property of a tab control indicates which page is currently selected. It returns an integer that indicates the position of the selected page in the Pages collection. For example, if the first page in a tab control is selected, the Value property returns 0, the index number of the first page in the `Pages` collection. If the second page is selected, the `Value` property returns 1, and so on. The page's position within the collection corresponds to the value of the `PageIndex` property for that page.

A tab control can contain virtually any type of control, including text boxes, combo and list boxes, option buttons and check boxes, and OLE objects. A tab control can even include other tab controls! Although a form can contain multiple tab controls, it's probably not a good idea to overload the user by putting more than one tab control on a form. After all, the reason you use tab controls in an application is to simplify the form by fitting multiple pages of controls within a single control. In most cases, there is no point in challenging the user with more than one tab control on a form.

Using Dialog Boxes to Collect Information

The dialog box is one of the most valuable user-interface components in Windows applications. When properly implemented, dialog boxes provide a way to extend the available screen space on the computer. Instead of having to place every text box, option button, and other user input control on the main form, dialog boxes provide a handy way to move some of these controls to a convenient pop-up device that is on the screen only when needed.

Dialog boxes usually collect a certain type of information, such as font attributes or hard-copy parameters. Dialog boxes are a valuable way to prefilter or qualify user input without cluttering the main form. Or use a dialog box to allow the user to enter query criteria before running a query that populates a form or report, or to gather information that is added to a report's header or footer area.

Although they are forms, dialog boxes should not look like or behave as other forms in the application do. Dialog boxes often pop up over the user's work. When properly implemented, dialog boxes also provide a means to simply cancel the query without breaking anything on the user's workspace.

A typical query form implemented as a dialog box is shown in Figure 19.16. This simple form gathers information that is used to query the database for order information.

FIGURE 19.16

A dialog box used to collect data for an ad hoc query

The relevant properties of this dialog box are outlined in Table 19.2.

TABLE 19.2

Property Settings for Dialog Forms

Property	Setting	Purpose
ScrollBars	Neither	Not needed.
NavigationButtons	No	Not needed.
PopUp	Yes	Keeps the form on top of other forms in the application.
Modal	Yes	Prevents the user from working with another part of the application until the dialog box is removed.
RecordSelectors	No	Not needed.
BorderStyle	Dialog	Specifies wide borders that can't be resized. Also removes Minimize and Maximize buttons.
ShortcutMenu	No	Not needed.

After these changes have been made, you have a form that's always on top of the user's work and won't leave the screen until the user clicks the Run Query or Cancel button.

There are a couple of rules you should follow when constructing dialog boxes. These rules ensure that your dialog boxes conform with the generally accepted behavior for Windows dialog boxes.

Composing the SQL statement

A temporary querydef object is created when the user clicks the Run Query button. Although you're simply opening the query on the screen, the temporary query could just as easily serve as the RecordSource of a form or report.

```
Private Sub cmdRunQuery_Click()
    Dim db As DAO.Database
    Dim QD As DAO.QueryDef
    Dim where As Variant
    Set db = CurrentDb
    'Delete existing dynamic query, trap error if it does not exist.
    On Error Resume Next
    db.QueryDefs.Delete ("MyQuery")
    On Error GoTo 0
    ' Note single quotes surrounding text
    ' fields [Ship Country]and [Customer ID].
' Note NO single quotes surrounding
    ' numeric field [Employee ID].
    where = Null
```

```
        If Not IsNull(txtContactID.Value) Then
          where = where _
            & (" [ContactID]= " & Me![txtContactID] & " ")
        End If
        If Not IsNull(txtLastName.Value) Then
          If Len(where) > 0 Then
            where = where _
              & (" OR [LastName]LIKE '" & Me![txtLastName] & "*' ")
          Else
            where = where _
              & (" [LastName]LIKE '" & Me![txtLastName] & "*' ")
          End If
        End If
      If Not IsNull(txtCity.Value) Then
          If Len(where) > 0 Then
            where = where _
              & (" OR [City] LIKE '" & Me![txtCity] & "*' ")
          Else
            where = where _
              & (" [City] LIKE '" & Me![txtCity] & "*' ")
          End If
        End If
        If Not IsNull(txtZipCode.Value) Then
          If Len(where) > 0 Then
            where = where _
              & (" OR [ZipCode] LIKE '" & Me![txtZipCode] & "*' ")
          Else
            where = where _
              & (" [ZipCode] LIKE '" & Me![txtZipCode] & "*' ")
          End If
        End If
        Set QD = db.CreateQueryDef("MyQuery", _
          "SELECT * FROM Contacts WHERE " & where & ";")
        DoCmd.OpenQuery "MyQuery"
        DoCmd.Close acForm, Me.Name
    End Sub
```

Notice that the SQL statement is built up with the contents of the text boxes on the form. Each text box's value is added only when the text box is not null. Also, the length of the query string is evaluated before adding to the SELECT clause. The OR clause is added only when the SELECT clause already contains a value so that the resulting SQL string looks something like this:

```
SELECT * FROM Contacts
WHERE ContactID = 17 OR City LIKE 'New*';
```

Using LIKE and an asterisk after the text added from the contents of the form's text boxes means that the SQL statement is quite inclusive. The previous example returns records where the ContactID is 17 and where the City begins with New (New York, New Haven, New Brunswick, and so on). Remove the asterisks and change the LIKE clause to the equal sign (=) to make the query very specific. When using the equal sign, the user is required to enter the full text for each value (New York, for example).

Adding a default button

There should be a button on the form that's automatically selected if the user presses the Enter key while the dialog box is open. The default button doesn't have to be selected by the user to be triggered; Access automatically fires the default button's Click event as the user presses the Enter key.

For example, the user enters 17 in the Customer ID text box and presses Enter. Unless a default button is specified, the input cursor simply drops down to the City text box. If you've designated the Run Query button as the dialog box's default, Access interprets the Enter key press as a Click event for the Run Query button.

Set the Run Query's Default property to Yes to make it the default for this dialog box. Only one button on a form can have its Default property set to Yes — if you move to the Cancel button and set its Default property to Yes, Access silently changes the Run Query's Default property to No.

Normally, the designated default button is on the left of the form. If you've arranged the command buttons vertically on a form, the top button should be the default.

You should select a button that won't cause trouble if accidentally triggered as the default for a form. For example, to avoid the risk of losing data, it's probably not a good idea to set a button that performs a delete action query as the default. In this case, you might decide to make the Cancel button the default.

Setting a Cancel button

The Cancel button on a form is automatically selected if the user presses the Esc key while the form is open. In most cases, you simply want the dialog box to disappear if the user hits the Esc key while the dialog box is open.

Set a button's Cancel property to designate it as the form's Cancel button. In this example, cmd-Cancel has been designated the dialog box's Cancel button. As with the default button, only one button on a form can be the Cancel button. Access triggers the Cancel button's On Click event whenever the user presses the Esc key.

Removing the control menu

After you've designated default and Cancel buttons, you have no need for the control menu button in the upper-left corner of the form. Set the form's Control Box property to No to hide the control menu button. When the control menu box is removed, the user will have to use the Cancel or Run Query buttons to remove the form from the screen.

Closing the form

The dialog box form remains on the screen on top of the query results. The following line was added to the Click event of the Run Query button to remove the form from the Access desktop:

```
DoCmd Close acForm, Me.Name
```

In some cases, however, you'll want to continue to reference information in the dialog box after the user is done with it. In these cases, you should hide the dialog box form, rather than close it. Use the following statement at the bottom of the Click event to hide the dialog box form as the query opens:

```
Me.Visible = False
```

As with any user-interface component, always completely test any dialog box. Because it "takes over" the user's desktop, you want to make sure the dialog box behaves as expected and doesn't impede or annoy the user in any way.

Summary

This chapter has assisted you in understanding Access forms. You now have a better grasp on the workings of the Access event model. You now know how to programmatically manipulate the many controls that constitute the building blocks out of which forms are constructed. You also have a larger bag of tricks from which to draw when you're building Access forms.

The advanced forms features in Microsoft Access boggle the mind. You probably won't use all the new form design tricks in your first Access 2010 application, but it's nice to know what you can do with this truly remarkable development platform.

20

Advanced Access Report Techniques

IN THIS CHAPTER

Organizing reports to present the data in a logical manner

Producing more attractive reports

Providing additional information about the report

Learning other approaches to enhance your presentation

Back in the bad old days, most computer-generated reports were printed on pulpy, green-bar paper in strict *tabular* (row-and-column) format. The user was expected to further process the data to suit his particular needs — often, a time-consuming process that involved manually summarizing or graphing the data.

Things have changed. Visually oriented businesspeople want useful, informative reports produced directly from their databases. No one wants to spend time graphing data printed in simple tabular format anymore. Today, users want the software to do much of the work for them. This means that reporting tools such as Microsoft Access must be able to produce the high-quality, highly readable reports that users demand.

Because Access is a Windows application, you have all the super-duper Windows facilities at your disposal: TrueType fonts, graphics, and a graphical interface for report design and preview. In addition, Access reports feature properties and an event model (although with fewer events than you saw on forms) for customizing report behavior. You can use the Visual Basic language to add refinement and automation to the reports you build in Access.

In this chapter, I provide some general principles and design techniques to keep in mind as you build Access reports. These principles will help make your reports more readable and informative.

Cross-Reference

This chapter does not discuss the basic process of building Access reports (see Chapter 9 for those details). Instead, this chapter describes a number of design techniques you can apply to Access reports using the skills described in Chapter 9.

On the CD-ROM

All of the examples presented in this chapter can be found in the `Chapter20.accdb` sample database on this book's CD-ROM. Please note that many of the figures in this chapter appear with the report Design view grid turned off to make the report design details easier to see.

Note

This chapter uses data from the Northwind Traders example database. The Northwind data is ideally suited for the example report described in this chapter and is a good model for most Access databases. The techniques described in the following sections should be adaptable to any well-designed database without too much trouble.

Grouping and Sorting Data

To be most useful, the data on a report should be well organized. Grouping data that's similar can reduce the amount of data presented, which makes it easier to find specific data. As you'll see in this section, the Access Report Builder offers a fair degree of flexibility in this regard.

Grouping data alphabetically

Data is often displayed with too much granularity to be useful. A report displaying every sale made by every employee arranged in a tabular format can be difficult to read. And, as you saw in the revised example, anything you do to reduce the overload of tabular reports can make the data more meaningful.

Sometimes even grouping data doesn't help much. Have you ever seen a book index where every major topic appeared in bold with minor topics within the major topic indented below the bold heading? Some book indexes use boldface for virtually *everything* (including topics with no subordinate subtopics below them), creating a confusing, hard-to-read page. A much better arrangement is to group data into alphabetically sorted groups. Dictionaries and encyclopedias use alphabetical groupings for their data. Imagine how difficult it would be to find a person's phone number if the data in a phone book weren't carefully grouped by the letters of the alphabet and then arranged into alphabetical order within the group!

The Group, Sort, and Total dialog box (which is opened by clicking the Group & Sort button in the Grouping & Totals group in the Design tab) controls how data is grouped on Access reports. Sorting alphabetically arranges the records in alphabetical order based on the first character of the company name, while grouping by company name creates a separate group for each company.

Clicking on the Add a Group button below the Sorting and Grouping area opens a list from which you choose a field to use for grouping data on the report. In Figure 20.1, both `CompanyName` and `OrderDate` have been selected, with `CompanyName` being grouped first and then `OrderDate` sorted within the company groups.

FIGURE 20.1

Alphabetical grouping is easy!

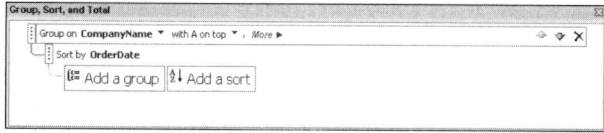

Typically, data is grouped on the entire contents of a field or combination of fields. Simple grouping on the CompanyName field means that all records for Bottom Dollar Markets appear together as a group and all the records for Ernst Handel appear together as another group. You can, however, override the default and group based on *prefix characters* by changing the Group On property in the Group, Sort, and Total dialog box.

Notice the More button in the CompanyName sorting bar in Figure 20.1. Clicking the More button reveals the sorting details you want to apply to the CompanyName field (see Figure 20.2). By default, text fields such as CompanyName are sorted alphabetically by the field's entire contents. You can, however, change this behavior to alter how Access applies grouping to the field's data (see Figure 20.3).

FIGURE 20.2

Many options are available to you for Grouping and Sorting

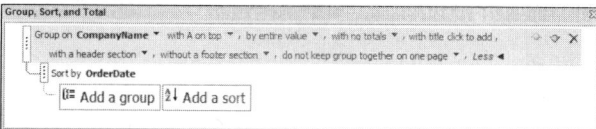

FIGURE 20.3

Modifying a text-base grouping

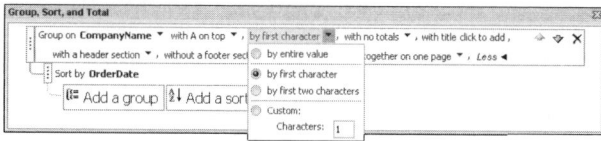

When you select by first character, the GroupInterval property tells Access how many characters to consider when grouping on prefix characters. In this case, the grouping interval is set to 1, meaning, "Consider only the *first* character when grouping." You could choose to group by the first character, the first two characters, or any number of characters in the field, depending on your requirements.

Notice also that the `CompanyName` field is set to ascending sort (with *A* on top), which causes alphabetic grouping starting at names beginning with *A* and progressing to names beginning with *Z*. With this combination of properties, all companies starting with *A* will be grouped together, those beginning with *B* will be in another group, and so on.

For this example, a slightly different report is used to illustrate prefix character grouping. This report (`rptSalesJanuarayAlpha1`, shown in Figure 20.3) shows purchases during the month of January, sorted by customer name. The order date, the order ID, and the employee filling the order are shown across the page. The result of the sorting and grouping specification in Figure 20.1 is shown in Figure 20.4. (`Hide Duplicates` has been set to `Yes` for the `CompanyName` field so that each customer appears only once in the list.)

FIGURE 20.4

A rearrangement of the data shown in Figure 20.13, later in this chapter

Northwind Sales: January

Company Name	Order Date	Order ID	Sales Person
Antonio Moreno Taquería	24-Jan-12	10365	Janet Leverling
Around the Horn	12-Jan-12	10355	Michael Suyama
Blondel pére et fils	19-Jan-12	10360	Margaret Peacock
Bon app'	22-Jan-12	10362	Janet Leverling
Bottom-Dollar Markets	17-Jan-12	10358	Steven Buchanan
	25-Jan-12	10367	Robert King
	30-Jan-12	10371	Nancy Davolio
Chop-suey Chinese	30-Jan-12	10370	Michael Suyama
Die Wandernde Kuh	04-Jan-12	10348	Margaret Peacock
	15-Jan-12	10356	Michael Suyama
Drachenblut Delikatessen	23-Jan-12	10363	Margaret Peacock
Eastern Connection	23-Jan-12	10364	Nancy Davolio
Ernst Handel	08-Jan-12	10351	Nancy Davolio
	26-Jan-12	10368	Andrew Fuller
Familia Arquibaldo	03-Jan-12	10347	Margaret Peacock
Furia Bacalhau e Frutos do Mar	09-Jan-12	10352	Janet Leverling
Galería del gastrónomo	25-Jan-12	10366	Laura Callahan

It's important to note that the data shown in Figure 20.4 is identical to the data shown in Figure 20.13. In fact, the same record source (`qrySalesJanuary`, shown in Figure 20.11, later in this chapter) is used for both of these reports. Often, a data rearrangement yields useful information. For example, you can easily see that Bottom-Dollars Market placed three orders in January, one with salesperson Steven Buchanan, one with Robert King, and one with Nancy Davolio.

Let's assume you want to refine the `rptSalesJanuaryAlpha1` report by labeling the groups with the letters of the alphabet. That is, all customers beginning with *A* (Antonio Moreno Tagueria and Around the Horn) are in one group, all customers beginning with *B* (Blondel père et fils, Bon app' and Bottom-Dollars Market) are in one group, and so on. Within each group, the company names are sorted in alphabetical order. The sales to each customer are further sorted by order date.

To emphasize the alphabetical grouping, a text box containing the first character for each group has been added to the report (see `rptSalesJanuaryAlpha2` in Figure 20.5). Although the data set in this example is rather small, in large reports such headings can be useful.

An alphabetic heading for each customer group makes the `rptSalesJanuaryAlpha2` report easier to read.

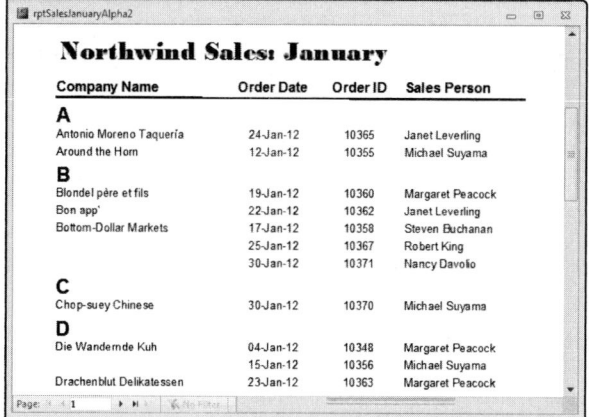

Adding the text box containing the alphabetic character is easy:

1. Choose View ⇨ Design.

2. Choose View ⇨ Sorting and Grouping.

   The Group, Sort, and Total dialog box appears.

3. Click on More, and ensure that `With a Header Section` is selected.

   This action adds a band for a group based on the `CompanyName` information (if it wasn't already there).

4. Expand the `CompanyName` group header and add an unbound text box to the `CompanyName` group header.

5. Set the text box's `Control Source` property to the following expression:

   `=Left$([CompanyName],1)`

6. Set the other text box properties (`Font`, `Font Size`, and so on) appropriately.

7. While you're grouping on the first character of the company name, you still need to ensure that company names are sorted correctly. Click Add a Sort and select the `CompanyName` field again. Click More to ensure that the entire field is going to be sorted, and that no header section will be added.

   When you're done, the report in Design view should appear as shown in Figure 20.6.

FIGURE 20.6

rptSalesJanuaryAlpha2 in Design view

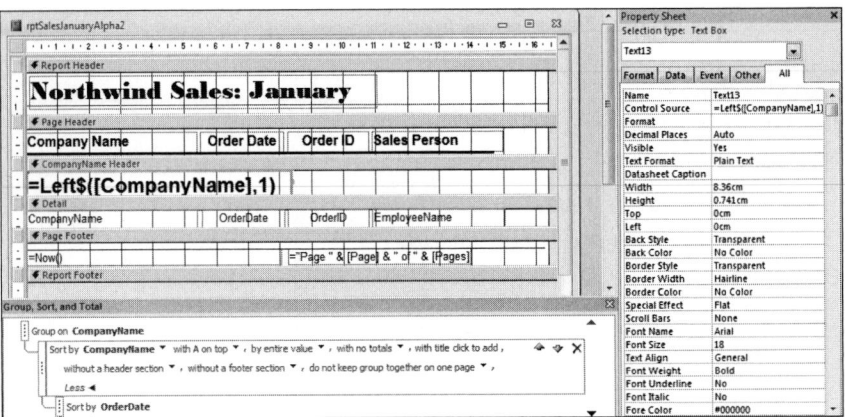

Notice the CompanyName group header that was added by the Group Header setting in the Group, Sort, and Total dialog box. The Property Sheet for the unbound text box is shown so you can see the expression used to fill the text box.

This little trick works because all the rows within a CompanyName group have the first character in common. Using the Left$() function to peel off the first character and use it as the text in the text box in the group header provides an attractive, useful heading for the CompanyName groups.

Grouping on date intervals

Many reports require grouping on dates or date intervals (day, week, or month). For example, Northwind Traders may want a report of January sales grouped on a weekly basis so that week-to-week patterns emerge.

Fortunately, the Access report engine includes just such a feature. An option in the Group, Sort, and Total dialog box enables you to quickly and easily group report data based on dates or date intervals. Just as I grouped data based on prefix characters in an earlier example, I can group on dates using the group's GroupOn property. Figure 20.7 shows the January sales report grouped by each week during the month. This report is named rptSalesJanuaryByWeek.

This report is easy to set up. Open the Group, Sort, and Total dialog box again and establish a group for the OrderDate field. Set the OrderDate GroupHeader option to Yes and drop down the Group On list (shown in Figure 20.8). Notice that Access is smart enough to present Group On options (Year, Qtr, Month, Week, and so on) that make sense for date/time fields like OrderDate. Selecting Week from this list instructs Access to sort the data on the OrderDate, grouped on a week-by-week basis. Note, though, that you still need to sort by the entire value of the OrderDate to ensure that they're in sequential order within the week.

FIGURE 20.7

The January sales data grouped by each week during the month

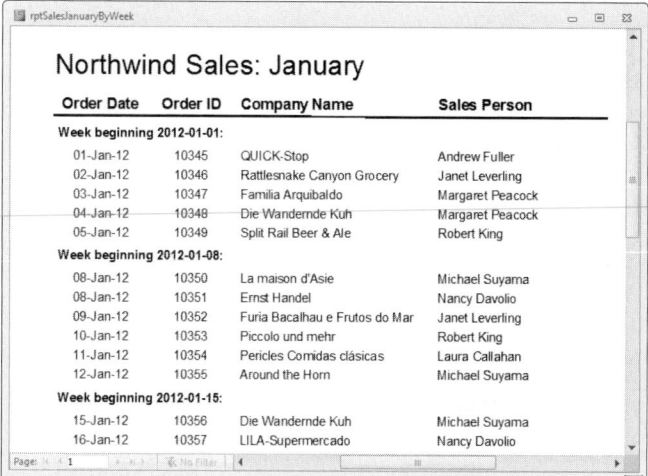

FIGURE 20.8

`OrderDate` is a date/time field, so the grouping options are relevant for date and time data.

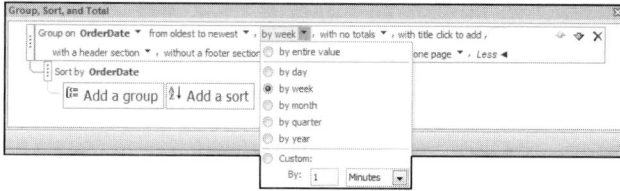

The label at the top of the group identifying the week (the first one reads `Week beginning 1/1/12:`) is the product of the following expression in an unbound text box in the `OrderDate` group header:

```
="Week beginning " & [OrderDate] & ":"
```

See the Design view of `rptSalesJanuaryByWeek` in Figure 20.9. Notice the unbound text box in the `OrderDate` group header. This text box contains the value of the order date that Access used to group the data in the `OrderDate` grouping.

FIGURE 20.9

The Design view of `rptSalesJanuaryByWeek`. Notice the expression in the `OrderDate` group header.

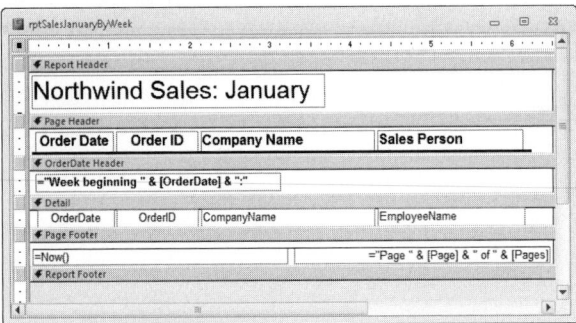

Hiding repeating information

An easy improvement to tabular reports is to reduce the amount of repeated information on the report. Figure 20.10 shows a typical tabular report (`rptTabularBad`) produced by Access, based on a simple query of the Northwind Traders data.

FIGURE 20.10

Simple tabular reports can be confusing and boring.

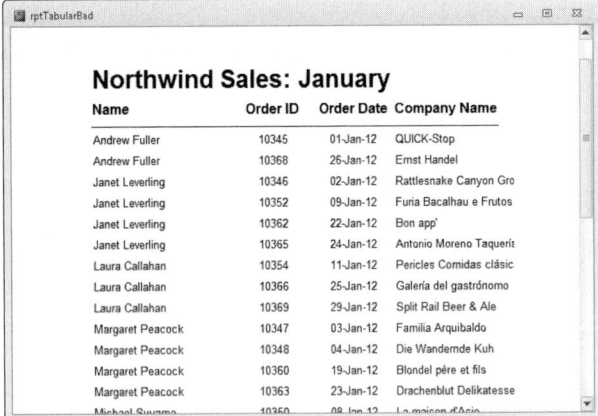

The report in Figure 20.10 was produced with the Access Report Wizard, selecting the tabular report format and all defaults. The query underlying this report selects data from the Customers, Orders, and Employees tables in `Northwind.accdb` and is shown in Figure 20.11. Notice that the data returned by this query is restricted to the month of January 2012. Also, the first and last names of employees are concatenated as the `Name` field.

FIGURE 20.11

The simple query underlying `rptTabularBad`

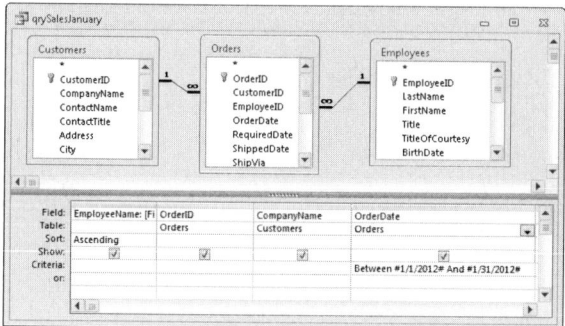

The query in Figure 20.11 (`qrySalesJanuary`) is used as the basis of several examples in this chapter.

You can significantly improve the report in Figure 20.10 simply by hiding repeated information in the Detail section. As soon as Andrew Fuller's name is given, there's no need to repeat it for every sale that Andrew made in January 2012. The way the data is arranged on `rptTabularBad`, you have to search for where one employee's sales data ends and another employee's data begins.

Making the change to hide the repeated values is very easy:

1. Open the report in Design view.
2. In the Detail section, select the `EmployeeName` field containing the employee's first and last names.
3. Open the property sheet for the `Name` field (see Figure 20.12).

FIGURE 20.12

The default property values sometimes lead to unsatisfactory results.

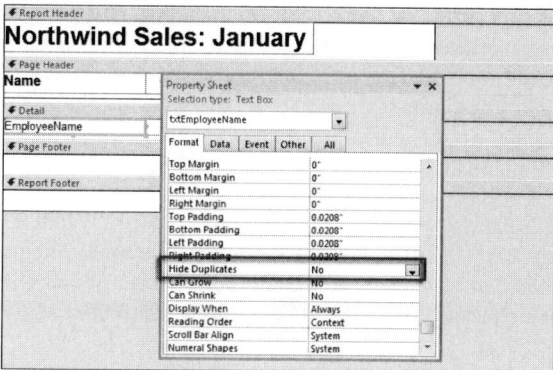

4. Change the `Hide Duplicates` property to `Yes`.

   The default is `No`, which directs Access to display every instance of every field.

5. Put the report back to Print Preview mode and enjoy the new report layout (shown in Figure 20.13).

   The report shown in Figure 20.13 is `rptTabularGood`.

FIGURE 20.13

Much better! Hide that repeating information.

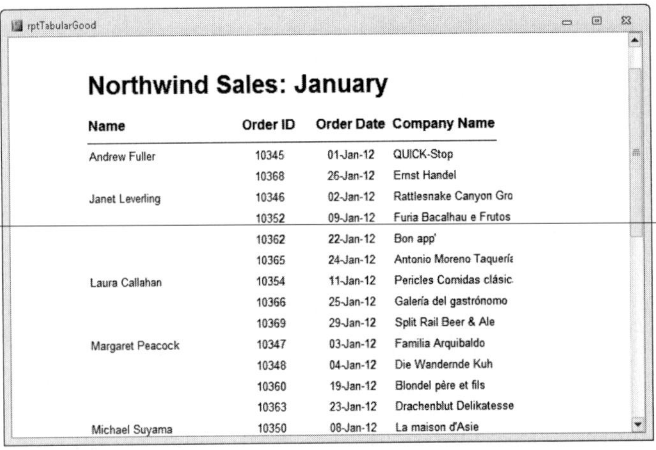

Name	Order ID	Order Date	Company Name
Andrew Fuller	10345	01-Jan-12	QUICK-Stop
	10368	26-Jan-12	Ernst Handel
Janet Leverling	10346	02-Jan-12	Rattlesnake Canyon Gro
	10352	09-Jan-12	Furia Bacalhau e Frutos
	10362	22-Jan-12	Bon app'
	10365	24-Jan-12	Antonio Moreno Taquerí
Laura Callahan	10354	11-Jan-12	Pericles Comidas clásic
	10366	25-Jan-12	Galería del gastrónomo
	10369	29-Jan-12	Split Rail Beer & Ale
Margaret Peacock	10347	03-Jan-12	Familia Arquibaldo
	10348	04-Jan-12	Die Wandernde Kuh
	10360	19-Jan-12	Blondel père et fils
	10363	23-Jan-12	Drachenblut Delikatesse
Michael Suyama	10350	08-Jan-12	La maison d'Asie

Distinguishing the sales figures for individual employees in Figure 20.13 is much easier than it is when the repeating information is printed on the report. Notice that no fancy programming or report design was required. A simple property-value change resulted in a much more readable and useful report. (Mainframe report designers working with traditional report writers would *kill* for a report as good looking as the one shown in Figure 20.13!)

The `Hide Duplicates` property only applies to records that appear sequentially on the report. As soon as Access has placed a particular `Name` value on the report, the name won't be repeated in records immediately following the current record. In Figure 20.13, the records are sorted by the `EmployeeName` field, so all records for an employee appear sequentially as a group. If the report were sorted by another field (for example, `OrderID` or `OrderDate`), the `Hide Duplicates` property set on the `Name` field would apply only to those instances where the employee's name coincidentally appeared sequentially in multiple records on the report.

The `Hide Duplicates` property can be applied to multiple controls within a report. As long as you understand that `Hide Duplicates` only hides subsequent duplicate values within a detail section, you should be able to achieve the results you expect. (Note, though, that you may occasionally run into unexpected results if only one of the multiple fields changes.)

Hiding a page header

Sometimes you need to display a page header or footer on just the first page of a report. An example is a terms and conditions clause in the header of the first page of an invoice. You want the terms and conditions to appear only on the first page of the invoice but not on subsequent pages.

Add an unbound text-box control to the report with its `ControlSource` property set to the expression `=HideHeader()`. Delete the text box's label and set the text box's text color to white and its border to transparent to make it invisible on the report.

Note
You can't actually set the control's `Visible` property to No; if you did, the control wouldn't be able to respond to events.

The `HideHeader()` function is as follows:

```
Function HideHeader()
   Reports![rptInvoice].Section(3).Visible = False
   'Section(3) is a reference to the
   'report page header reference
   HideHeader = True
End Function
```

The invisible text box can be placed virtually anywhere on the first page but is most logically located in the page footer. The assumption is that, because the page header is the first item printed on the page, you'll always get the first page header. Once the page footer containing the invisible text box has been processed, the page header's `Visible` property will be set to `False`, and the page header will not be seen on any other pages in the report.

Starting a new page number for each group

Sometimes a report will contain a number of pages for each group of data. You might want to reset page numbering to 1 as each group prints, so that each group's printout will have its own page-numbering sequence. For example, assume you're preparing a report with sales data grouped by region. Each region's sales may require many pages to print, and you're using the `ForceNewPage` property to ensure that grouped data doesn't overlap on any page. But how do you get the page numbering within each group to start at 1?

The report's `Page` property, which you use to print the page number on each page of a report, is a read/write property. This means that you can reset `Page` at any time as the report prints. Use the group header's `Format` event to reset the report's `Page` property to 1. Every time a group is formatted, `Page` will be reset to 1 by the following code:

```
Private Sub GroupHeader2_Format ()
   Me.Page = 1
End Sub
```

Use the Page property to display the current page number in the page header or footer as usual. For example, include the following expression in an unbound text box in the page footer:

```
= "Page " & [Me.Page]
```

Unfortunately, it's not nearly as easy to count the pages within a group so that you could put a "Page *x* of *y*" in the page footer, where *y* is the number of pages within the group.

Formatting Data

In addition to sorting and grouping data, you can make reports more useful by formatting them to highlight specific information. Numbering the entries or using bullets can make things stand out, as can using lines or spaces to separate parts of the report. Ensuring that the elements on the report are positioned in a consistent manner is important as well — you might have all the necessary data in a report, but poor presentation can leave a very negative impression on the users. The techniques discussed in this section will help you produce reports that are more professional looking.

Creating numbered lists

By default, the items contained on an Access report are not numbered. They simply appear in the order dictated by the settings in the Group, Sort, and Total dialog box.

Sometimes it would be useful to have a number assigned to each entry on a report or within a group on a report. You might need a number to count the items in a list or uniquely identify items in the list. For example, an order details report might contain an item number for each item ordered, plus a field for items ordered, showing how many things were ordered.

The Access Running Sum feature provides a way to assign a number to each item in a list on an Access report. For example, the Northwind Traders sales management has asked for a report showing the sum of all purchases by each customer during the month of January, sorted in descending order so that the top purchaser appears at the top. Oh, yes — and they want a number assigned to each line in the report to provide a ranking for the Northwind customers.

What an assignment! The query to implement this request is shown in Figure 20.14 (qryCustomerPurchasesJanuary). This query sums the purchases by each customer for the month beginning 1/1/12 and ending 1/31/12. Because the Purchases column is sorted in descending order, the customers buying the most product will appear at the top of the query results set. The OrderDate field is not included in the query results and is used only as the query's selection criterion (notice the *Where* in the Total row).

Although you could do much of this work at runtime using VBA to programmatically sum the values returned by the query or a SQL statement in the report's RecordSource property, you should always let the Access query engine perform aggregate functions. All Access queries are optimized when you save the query. You're guaranteed that the query will run as fast as possible — much faster than a filter based on a SQL statement in a report's RecordSource property.

FIGURE 20.14

An interesting query that sums data and sorts the query results in descending order of the sum.

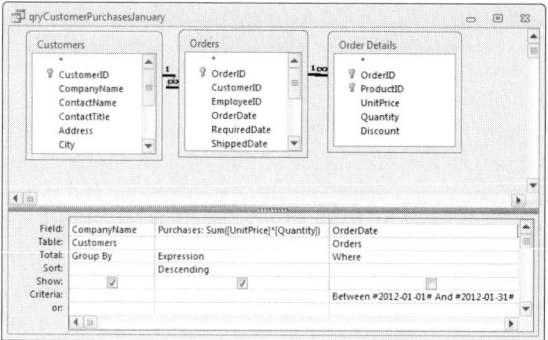

Tip

The Access Query Builder's aggregate functions perform flawlessly. Furthermore, Jet will perform the aggregate function exactly the same way every time the query is run. There is no reason you should be tempted to manually sum data when the query will do it for you.

The basic report (`rptUnNumberedList`) prepared from the data provided by `qryCustomer-PurchasesJanuary` is shown in Figure 20.15. All sorting options have been removed from the Group, Sort, and Total dialog box to permit the records to arrange themselves as determined by the query.

FIGURE 20.15

A straightforward report (`rptUnNumberedList`) produced with data from `qrySalesJanuary`

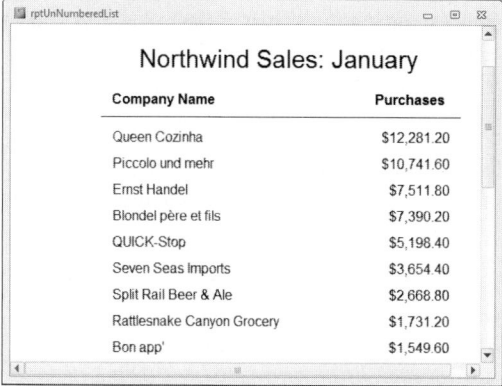

Adding a Ranking column to the simple report you see in Figure 20.15 is not difficult. Although the information that's shown in Figure 20.15 is useful, it's not what the user asked for.

To add a Ranking column to the report, use the RunningSum property of an unbound text box to sum its own value over each item in the report. When the RunningSum property is set to Over Group, Access adds 1 to the value in this text box for each record displayed in the Detail section of the report (RunningSum can also be used within a group header or footer). The alternate setting (Over All) instructs Access to add 1 each time the text box appears in the entire report. Add an unbound text box to the left of the CompanyName text box on the report, with an appropriate header in the Page Header area. Set the RecordSource property for the text box to =1 and the RunningSum property to Over All. Figure 20.16 shows how the Rank text box is set up on rptNumberedList.

FIGURE 20.16

The value in the unbound text box named txtRank will be incremented by 1 for each record in the report.

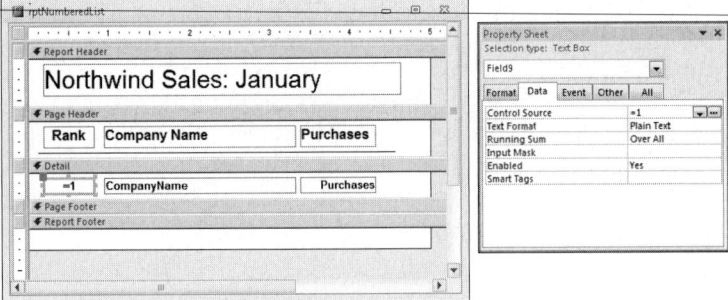

When this report (rptNumberedList) is run, the Rank column is filled with the running sum calculated by Access (see Figure 20.17). Once again, the data in this report is the same as in other report examples. The main difference is the amount of manipulation done by the query before the data arrives at the report and the additional information provided by the running sum.

Reports can contain multiple running sum fields. You could, for example, keep a running sum to show the number of items packed in each box of a multiple-box order while another running sum counts the number of boxes. The running sum starts at 0 (zero), hence the need to initialize it to 1 in the Control Source property on the Property Sheet.

You can also assign a running sum within each group by setting the RunningSum property of the unbound text box to Over Group instead of Over All. In this case, the running sum will start at zero for each group. So, be sure to set the ControlSource property of a group's running sum to 1.

FIGURE 20.17

The Running Sum column provides a ranking for each customer in order of purchases during January.

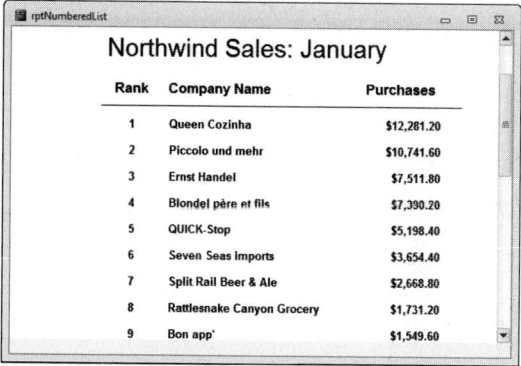

Adding bullet characters

You can add bullet characters to a list instead of numbers, if you want. Instead of using a separate field for containing the bullet, however, you can simply concatenate the bullet character to the control's RecordSource property — a much easier solution. Access will "glue" the bullet character to the data as it's displayed on the report, eliminating alignment problems that might occur with a separate unbound text box.

The design of rptBullets is shown in Figure 20.18. Notice the bullet character in the txtCompanyName text box as well as in the Property Sheet for this text box.

FIGURE 20.18

The bullet character is added to the ControlSource property of the txtCompanyName text box.

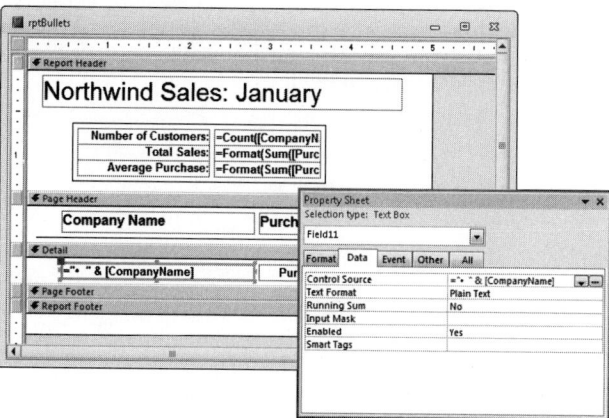

The bullet is added by exploiting a Windows feature. Position the text insertion character in the RecordSource property for the CompanyName field, hold down the Alt key, and type **0149**. Windows inserts the standard Windows bullet character, which you see in the property sheet. Looking at Figure 20.18, you can see that the bullet character is inserted correctly into the text box on the report. The expression you use in the ControlSource property is the following:

```
= " • " & [CompanyName]
```

where the bullet is inserted by the Alt+0149 trick.

You can produce the same effect by using the following expression in the text box:

```
= Chr(149) & " " & [CompanyName]
```

This expression concatenates the bullet character — returned by Chr(149) — with the data in the CompanyName field.

Note

This particular trick only works if the character set (such as Arial) assigned to the control (label or text box) includes a bullet character as the 149th ASCII character. Not all fonts accessible by Access applications include a bullet character, but popular typefaces such as Arial do tend to include this character.

The report now appears as shown in Figure 20.19. You might want to add a few extra spaces after the bullet to pad the white space between the bullet and the text. Because the bullet character and CompanyName field have been concatenated together in the text box, they'll be displayed in the same typeface. Also, adding the bullet character to the text box containing the company name guarantees that the spacing between the bullet and first character of the company name will be consistent in every record. When using proportionally spaced fonts such as Arial, it can sometimes be difficult to get precise alignment between report elements. Concatenating data in a text box eliminates spacing problems introduced by proportionally spaced characters. Note, though, that if the amount of text in the text box exceeds a single row, subsequent rows will not be indented.

FIGURE 20.19

Use a Windows feature to insert the bullet in front of the CompanyName field.

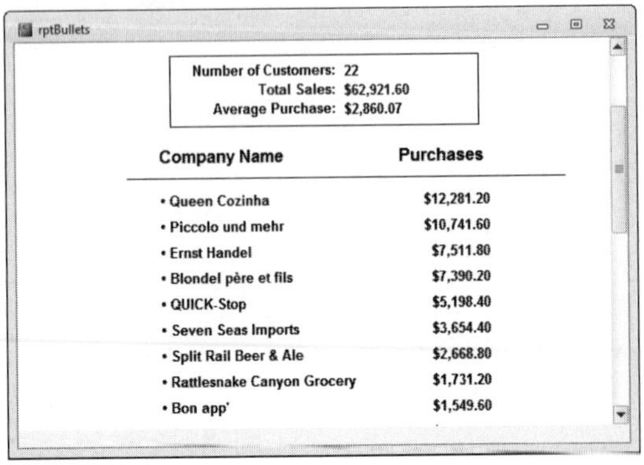

You might want to add other special characters to the control. For a complete display of the characters available in the font you've chosen for the text-box control, run `Charmap.exe`, the Windows Character Map application (see Figure 20.20). Be sure to select the font you've chosen for the text-box control. The only constraint on the characters you use on an Access report is that the font used in the text boxes on the report must contain the specified characters. Not all Windows TrueType character sets include all the special characters, like bullets.

Charmap is a useful tool for exploring Windows font sets.

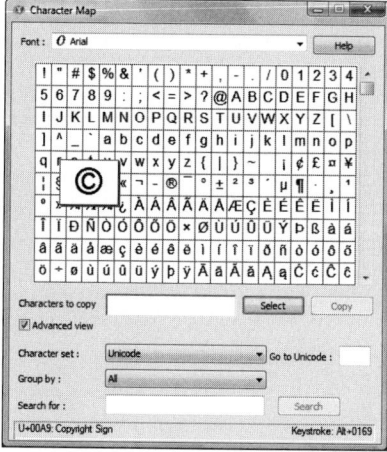

Charmap is quite easy to use. Select a font from the drop-down list at the top of the dialog box, and the main area fills with the font's default character set. Some character sets are incredibly large. For example, the Arial Unicode MS font includes more than 53,000 different characters, including traditional and simplified Chinese, Japanese Kanji, and Korean Hangul character sets.

Every character in a Windows font is accessible through the `Chr()` function. The page footer of `rptBullets` includes a text box filled with characters specified by the `Chr()` function. For example, the smiley face character is specified with `Chr(74)`. Some of the characters displayed by Charmap are identified only by their hexidecimal values. If the decimal value is not given, the hexidecimal value can be used with `Chr()` by using the `CInt()` function to convert the hex value to integer: `Chr(CInt("&H00A9"))` displays the familiar copyright symbol (©) when used to set the contents of a control set to the Arial font.

Adding emphasis at runtime

You might add a number of hidden controls to your reports to reduce the amount of clutter and unnecessary information. You can hide and show controls based on the value of another control. You hide a control, of course, by setting its `Visible` property to `False` (or `No`) at design time.

Only when the information contained in the control is needed do you reset the `Visible` property to `True`.

An example might be a message to the Northwind Traders customers that a certain item has been discontinued and inventory is shrinking. It's silly to show this message for every item in the Northwind catalog; including the number of units in stock, in conjunction with a message that a particular item has been discounted, might encourage buyers to stock up on the item.

Figure 20.21 shows `rptPriceList` in Print Preview mode. (You may have to right-click on the report name and select Print Preview from the context menu.) Notice that the Guarana Fantastica beverage product appears in italics, the price is bold italics, and the `Only 20 units in stock!` message appears to the right of the product information.

FIGURE 20.21

Can you tell Guarana Fantastica is on sale?

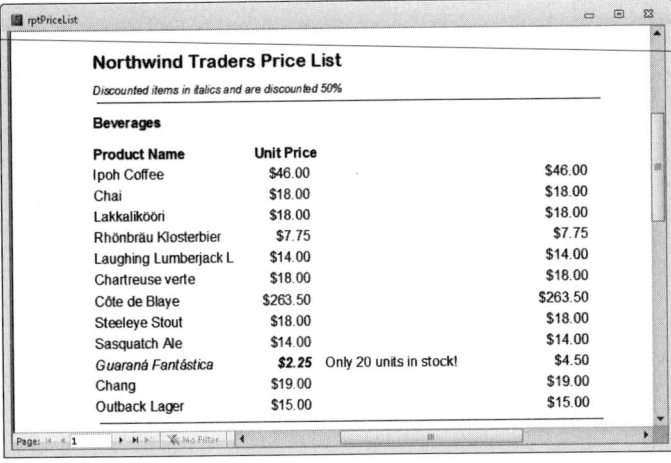

Figure 20.22 reveals part of the secret behind this technique. The visible unit price text box is actually unbound. This is the text box used to display the unit price to the user. Another text box is bound to the `UnitPrice` field in the underlying recordset, but it's hidden by setting its `Visible` property to No. Just to the left of the hidden `UnitPrice` field is a hidden check box representing the `Discontinued` field. `txtMessage`, which contains the `Only x units in stock!` message is also hidden.

FIGURE 20.22

rptPriceList in Design view reveals how this effect is implemented.

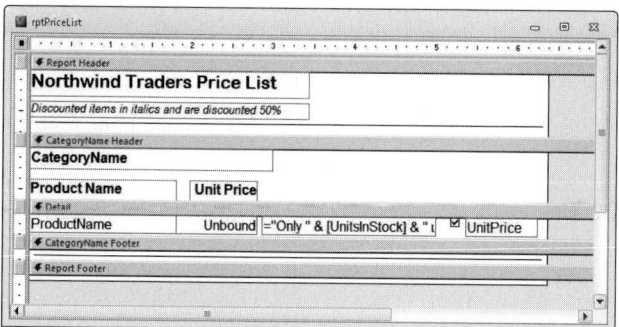

Use the Detail section's Format event to switch the Visible property of txtMessage to True whenever txtDiscontinued contains a true value. The code is quite simple:

```
Private Sub Detail_Format(Cancel As Integer,
    FormatCount As Integer)
  If Me![Discontinued] Then
    Me!txtProductName.FontItalic = True
    Me!txtPrice.FontItalic = True
    Me!txtPrice.FontBold = True
    Me!txtPrice = Me![UnitPrice] * 0.5
    Me!txtMessage.Visible = True
  Else
    Me!txtProductName.FontItalic = False
    Me!txtPrice.FontItalic = False
    Me!txtPrice.FontBold = False
    Me!txtPrice = Me![UnitPrice]
    Me!txtMessage.Visible = False
  End If
End Sub
```

In this code fragment, Me is a shortcut reference to the report. You must explicitly turn the italics, bold, and other font characteristics off when the product is not discontinued. Otherwise, once a discontinued product has been printed, all products following the discontinued product will print with the special font attributes. The font characteristics you set in a control's Property Sheet are just the initial settings for the control. If you change any of those properties at runtime, they stay changed until modified again. Similarly, txtMessage must be hidden after it's been displayed by setting its Visible property to False.

Avoiding empty reports

If Access fails to find valid records to insert into the Detail section of a report, all you'll see is `#Error` in the Detail section when the report is printed. To avoid this problem, attach code to the report's `Open` event that checks for valid records and sets a flag to cancel the print event if no records are found.

The `NoData` event is triggered when Access tries to build a report and finds no data in the report's underlying recordset. Using `NoData` is easy:

```
Private Sub Report_NoData(Cancel As Integer)
  MsgBox " There are no records for this report."
  Cancel = True
End Sub
```

The `Cancel = True` statement instructs Access to stop trying to open the report. The user will see the dialog box shown in Figure 20.23 and will avoid getting a report that can't be printed. (Open `rptEmpty` in `Chapter20.accdb` for this example.)

FIGURE 20.23

Better than `#Error` in all the text boxes in the report!

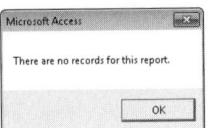

Because the `NoData` event is tied to the report itself, don't look for it in any of the report's sections. Simply add this code as the report's `NoData` event procedure and your users will never encounter a report full of `#Error` messages.

Avoiding null values in a tabular report

Null values in reports can cause errors, particularly when the field containing the null value is part of an expression in another control on the report. Instead of simply ignoring the null value and the resulting errors, you may decide that forcing a zero into the field is preferable.

The following expression in a numeric field's `ControlSource` property will solve this problem. In this expression, the field is contained in a text box named `txtField`:

```
=IIf(IsNull([Field]),0,[Field])
```

This immediate `If` statement sets the value of `txtField` to 0 if the value of `Field` (the data) is null; otherwise, `txtField` is set to the value of `Field`.

Alternatively, you could create the following function, which performs the same actions:

```
Function NullToZero(ByVal varValue as Variant)
  NullToZero = IIf(IsNull(varValue), 0, varValue)
End Function
```

This function accepts a value (like `Field`) as the `varValue` parameter and tests it with the `IIf`; then the function assumes the value of `varValue` or 0, depending on the result of the `IIf`. The benefit of using a VBA function is that you might want to perform some additional operation within the body of the function, such as substituting a value or logging or notifying the user of the null argument.

Properly handling nulls is so important that VBA includes a built-in `Nz()` function to automatically convert potentially null values to 0 or another value. The syntax of `Nz()` is

```
= Nz([Field], [ValueIfNull])
```

Typically, in a `ControlSource` property you'd provide 0 as the `ValueIfNull` argument:

```
= Nz([Field], 0)
```

Depending on your situation, you may not want to use 0 as the replacement for null values. For example, if you're multiplying two fields or variables together, converting one operand to 0 means the result of the multiplication is always zero. Using 1 as the `ValueIsNull` argument, at the very least, returns the other operand's value.

Inserting vertical lines between columns

You can easily add a vertical line to a report section whose height is fixed (like a group header or footer). Adding a vertical line to a section that can grow in height (like a Detail section on a grouped report) is more difficult. It's really difficult to get a vertical line between columns of a report (see `rptVerticalLines` in Figure 20.24). If you simply add a vertical line to the right side of a section of a snaking columns report, the line will appear to the right of the rightmost column on the page. You have to be able to specify where vertical lines will appear on the printed page.

Although you add most controls at design time, sometimes you have to explicitly draw a control as the report is prepared for printing. The easiest approach in this case is to use the report's `Line` method to add the vertical line at runtime. The following subroutine, triggered by the Detail section's `Format` event, draws a vertical line 3½ inches from the left printable margin of the report:

```
Sub Detail_Format ()
  Dim X1 as Single
  X1 = 3.5 * 1440
  Me.Line (X1, 0)-(X1, 10000)
End Sub
```

FIGURE 20.24

Vertical lines in `rptVerticalLines` help segregate data.

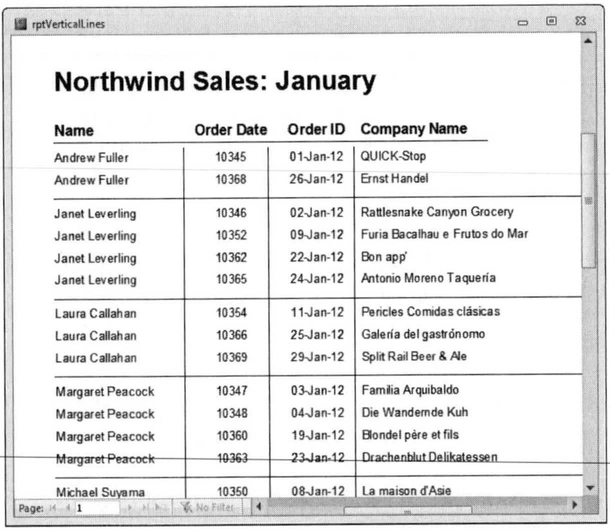

The syntax of the `Line` method is as follows:

```
object.Line (X1, Y1) - (X2, Y2)
```

The `Line` method requires four arguments. These arguments (X1, X2, Y1, and Y2) specify the top and bottom (or left and right, depending on your perspective) coordinates of the line. Notice that all calculated measurements on a report must be specified in twips (there are 1,440 twips per inch). In this case, X1 and X2 are the same value and I'm forcing the line to start at the very top of the Detail section (0) and to extend downward for 10,000 twips.

You might wonder why I'm using 10,000 as the Y2 coordinate for the end of the line. Access will automatically "clip" the line to the height of the Detail section. Because the line control doesn't contain data, Access won't expand the Detail section to accommodate the line you've drawn in code. Instead, Access draws as much of the 10,000-twip line as needed to fill the Detail section, and then it stops. The maximum value for Y2 is 32,767.

The same procedure could be used to draw horizontal lines for each section on the report. In the report example (`rptVerticalLines`) in the database accompanying this chapter (`Chapter20. accdb`), I've chosen to add line controls to the report instead. Using the `Line` control when the height of the report section is fixed (for example, in the group header and footer) is simply faster than drawing the line for each of these sections.

Adding a blank line every *n* records

Detail sections chock-full of dozens or hundreds of records can be difficult to read. It's easy to lose your place when reading across columns of figures and when the rows are crowded together on the page. Wouldn't it be nice to insert a blank row every fourth or fifth record in a Detail section? It's much easier to read a single row of data in a report (rptGapsEvery5th in Chapter20.accdb) where the records have been separated by white space every fifth record (see Figure 20.25).

Using white space to break up tabular data can make it easier to read.

Access provides no way to insert a blank row in the middle of a Detail section. You can, however, trick Access into inserting white space in the Detail section now and then with a little bit of programming and a couple of hidden controls.

Figure 20.26 reveals the trick behind the arrangement you see in Figure 20.25. An empty, unbound text box named txtSpacer is placed below the fields containing data in the Detail section. To the left of txtSpacer is another unbound text box named txtCounter.

FIGURE 20.26

This report trick uses hidden unbound text boxes in the Detail section.

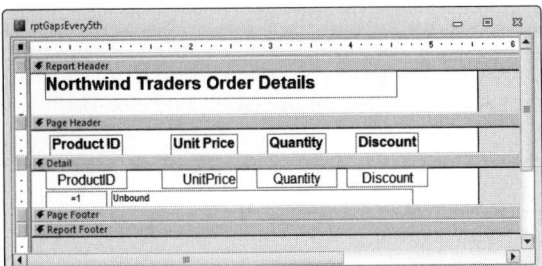

Set the following properties for txtSpacer, txtCounter, and the Detail section (see Table 20.1).

TABLE 20.1

Properties for the "Blank Line" Example

Control	Property	Value
txtSpacer	Visible	Yes
	CanShrink	Yes
txtCounter	Visible	No
	RunningSum	Over All
	ControlSource	=1
Detail1	CanShrink	Yes

These properties effectively hide the unbound txtSpacer and txtCounter controls, and permit these controls and the Detail section to shrink as necessary when the txtSpacer text-box control is empty. Even though txtSpacer is visible to the user, Access shrinks it to 0 height if it contains no data. The txtCounter control never needs any space because its Visible property is set to No, hiding it from the user.

The last step is to enter the following code as the Detail section's Format event procedure:

```
Sub Detail1_Format ()
  If (Me!txtCounter Mod 5) = 0 Then
    Me!txtSpacer = " "
  Else
    Me!txtSpacer = Null
  End If
End Sub
```

The `Format` event occurs as Access begins to format the controls within the Detail section. The value in `txtCounter` is incremented each time a record is added to the Detail section. The `Mod` operator returns whatever number is left over when the value in `txtCounter` is divided by 5. When `txtCounter` is evenly divisible by 5, the result of the `txtCounter Mod 5` expression is 0, which causes a space character to be assigned to `txtSpacer`. In this situation, because `txt-Spacer` is no longer empty, Access increases the height of the Detail section to accommodate `txtSpacer`, causing the "empty" space every fifth record to be printed in the Detail section. You never actually see `txtSpacer` because all it contains is an empty space character.

`txtCounter` can be placed anywhere within the Detail section of the report. Make `txtSpacer` as tall as you want the blank space to be when it's revealed on the printout.

Even-odd page printing

If you've ever prepared a report for two-sided printing, you may have encountered the need for knowing whether the data is being printed on the even side of the page or the odd side of the page. Most users prefer the page number to be located near the outermost edge of the paper. On the odd-numbered page, the page number should appear on the right edge of the page, while on the even-numbered side, the page number must appear on the left side of the page. How, then, do you move the page number from side to side?

The easiest way to determine whether the current page is even or odd is with the `Mod` operator with the following small function:

```
Function IsEven(iTest As Integer) As Integer
  If iTest Mod 2 = 0 Then
    IsEven = True
  Else
    IsEven = False
  End If
End Function
```

Assuming the page number appears in the Page Footer section of the report, you can use the page footer's `Format` event to determine whether the current page is even or odd, and move the text box containing the page number to the left or right side of the page accordingly.

The basic design of `rptEvenOdd` is shown in Figure 20.27. Notice that the `txtPageNumber` is right-aligned to ensure that the page number appears as close to the right margin as possible.

FIGURE 20.27

txtPageNumber moves from the right edge of the paper to the left edge of the paper.

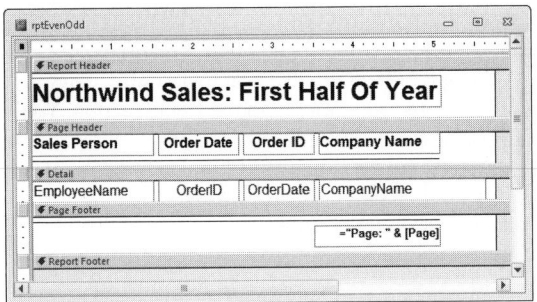

The Page Footer Format event procedure is a bit more involved than the IsEven function shown earlier. Because the Page Number text box is rather wide (we don't know how many pages are in the report, so the extra width ensures that there's adequate space in the box to accommodate almost any number), simply moving the text box to the left margin leaves the text in the text box too far to the right. You have to adjust the TextAlign property of txtPageNumber to shift the page number all the way to the left side of the text box. ALIGN_LEFT and ALIGN_RIGHT are integer constants set at 1 and 3, respectively, in the Declarations section of the report's code module.

```
Sub PageFooter1_Format ()
   If (Me.Page Mod 2) = 0 Then
      txtPageNumber.Left = 0
      txtPageNumber.TextAlign = ALIGN_LEFT
   Else
      txtPageNumber.Left = 3.5 * 1440
      txtPageNumber.TextAlign = ALIGN_RIGHT
   End If
End Sub
```

In this event procedure, any time the expression Me.Page Mod 2 is zero (meaning, the page number is even) the Left property of txtPageNumber is set to 0 and its TextAlign property is set to ALIGN_LEFT (1). On odd-numbered pages, TextAlign is set to ALIGN_RIGHT (3).

Notice how the Left property of txtPageNumber is set on odd-numbered pages. The expression 3.5 * 1440 is used to determine the Left property's setting. You may recall that, by default, all positioning information in Access Basic is done using twips as the unit of measure. There are 1,440 twips in an inch (or 567 twips in a centimeter), so this expression moves txtPageNumber to a position 3½ inches from the left print margin on the page. (Obviously, the position will depend on the width of the report.)

Like magic, this event procedure causes the Page Number text box to move from the right side on odd-numbered pages to the left side on even-numbered pages (see Figure 20.28).

FIGURE 20.28

txtPageNumber jumps from right to left.

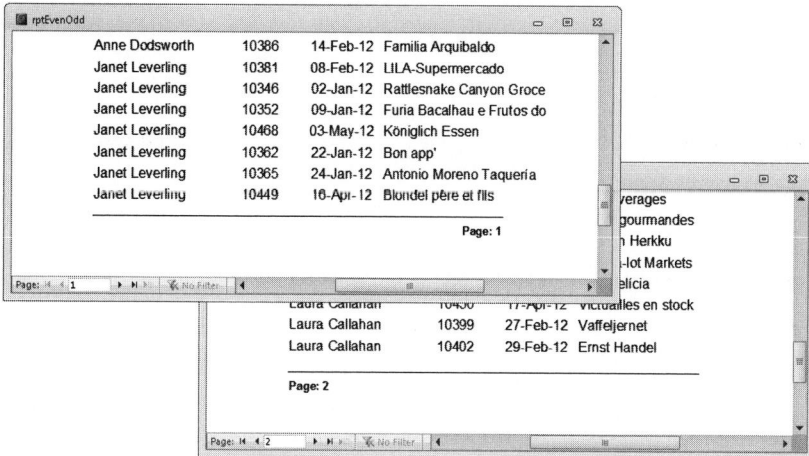

Using different formats in the same text box

On some reports, you may want the format of certain fields in a record to change according to the values in other fields on the report. A good example is a journal voucher report in a multicurrency financial system in which the voucher detail debit or credit amount format varies according to the number of decimal places used to display the currency value.

Unfortunately, a control in a Detail section of a report can have but a single format specified in its Property Sheet. Use the following trick to flexibly set the format property at run time. The FlexFormat() function uses the iFmt argument to return a string specifying the desired format:

```
Function FlexFormat (iFmt As Integer) As String
    Select Case iFmt
        Case 1 : FlexFormat = "##0.0;(##0.0)"
        Case 2 : FlexFormat = "##0.00;(##0.00)"
        Case 3 : FlexFormat = "##0.000;(##0.000)"
        Case 4 : FlexFormat = "##0.0000;(##0.0000)"
    End Select
End Function
```

Assume that the field to be dynamically formatted has its ControlSource set to [Amount]. The format of the Amount text box should vary depending on the value of the CurrDecPlaces field in the same record. CurrDecPlaces is an Integer data type. To use FlexFormat, change the ControlSource property of the Amount text box to the following:

```
=Format([Amount],FlexFormat([CurrDecPlaces]))
```

The Amount text box will be dynamically formatted according to the value contained in the CurrDecPlaces text box. This trick may be generalized to format fields other than currency fields. By increasing the number of parameters of the user-defined formatting function, the formatting can be dependent on more than one field, if necessary.

Centering the title

Centering a report title directly in the middle of the page is often difficult. The easiest way to guarantee that the title is centered is to stretch the title from left margin to right margin, and then click the Center Align button.

Easily aligning control labels

Keeping text boxes and their labels properly aligned on reports is sometimes difficult. Because a text box and its label can be independently moved on the report, all too often the label's position must be adjusted to bring it into alignment with the text box.

You can eliminate text-box labels completely by including the label text as part of the text box's record source. Use the concatenation character to add the label text to the text box's control source:

```
= "Product: " & [ProductName]
```

Now, whenever you move the text box, both the label and the bound record source move as a unit. The only drawback to this technique is that you must use the same format for the text box and its label.

Micro-adjusting controls

The easiest way to adjust the size of text boxes on a form in tiny increments is to hold down the Shift key and press the arrow key corresponding to Table 20.2.

TABLE 20.2

Micro-Adjustment Keystroke Combinations

Shift Combination	Adjustment
Shift+Left Arrow	Reduce width
Shift+Right Arrow	Increase width
Shift+Up Arrow	Reduce height
Shift+Down Arrow	Increase height

Another resizing technique is to position the cursor over any of the sizing handles on a selected control and double-click with the left mouse button. The control automatically "sizes to fit" the text contained within the control. This quick method can also be used to align not only labels but also text boxes to the grid.

To micro-adjust a control's position, hold down the Ctrl key as you press the arrows keys. The selected control will move in tiny increments in the direction indicated by the arrow keys you press.

Adding Data

When you're looking at data through forms, you can usually assume that the data is current. However, with printed reports, you don't always know if the data is old. Adding little touches like when the report was printed can help increase the usefulness of a report. In this section, I show you some techniques that will let you add additional information to the report to let the users know something of its origin.

Adding more information to a report

You probably know that the following expression in an unbound text box prints the current page and the number of pages contained in the report:

```
="Page " & [Page] & " of " & [Pages]
```

Both `Page` and `Pages` are report properties that are available at runtime and can be included on the report.

But consider the value of adding other report properties on the report. Most of the report properties can be added to unbound text boxes as long as the property is enclosed in square brackets. For the most part, these properties are only of value to you as the developer, but they may also be useful to your users.

For example, the report's `Name`, `RecordSource`, and other properties are easily added the same way. Figure 20.29 demonstrates how unbound text boxes can deliver this information to a report footer or some other place on the report.

FIGURE 20.29

`rptMoreInfo` demonstrates how to add more information to your reports.

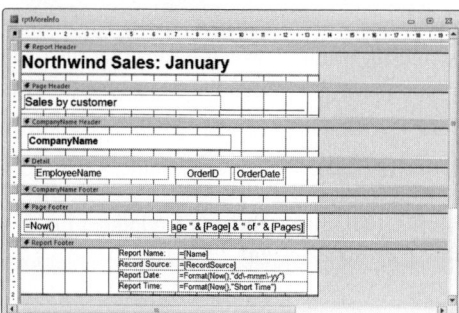

The inset in the lower-right part of Figure 20.29 shows the information provided by adding the four text boxes to this report. Very often, the user is not even aware of the name of a report — the only text the user sees associated with reports is the text that appears in the title bar (in other words, the report's Caption property). If a user is having problems with a report, it might be helpful to display the information you see in Figure 20.29 in the report footer.

Adding the user's name to a bound report

An unbound text box with its ControlSource set to an unresolved reference will cause Access to pop up a dialog box requesting the information necessary to complete the text box. For example, an unbound text box with its RecordSource set to the following displays the dialog box you see in the middle of Figure 20.30 when the report is run:

```
=[What is your name?]
```

Access displays a similar Parameter dialog box for each parameter in a parameter query. The text entered into the text box is then displayed on the report. (rptUserName in Chapter20.accdb on this book's companion CD-ROM demonstrates this technique.)

FIGURE 20.30

Use an unbound text box to capture useful information.

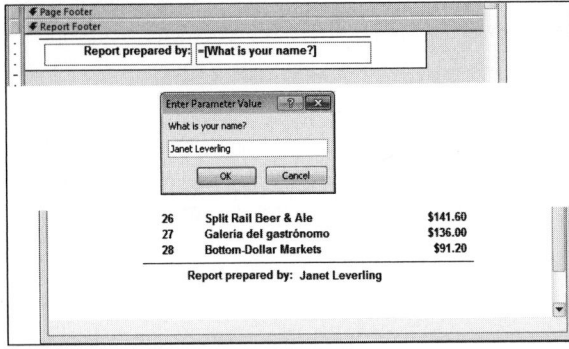

The unbound text box on the report can be referenced by other controls on the report. The Parameter dialog box appears before the report is prepared for printing, which means that the data you enter into the dialog box can be used in expressions, calculations, or the VBA code behind the report.

Cross-Reference

Chapter 27 describes the GetUserNameA Windows API call. This function returns the user's Windows login name and is the ideal way to capture the name of the person printing an Access report.

Trying More Techniques

As you've probably discovered by now, reporting in Access is a very large topic. I've included a few additional techniques that will help you make your reports even more flexible to users.

Displaying all reports in a combo box

The names of all the top-level database objects are stored in the `MSysObjects` system table. You can run queries against `MSysObjects` just as you can run queries against any other table in the database. It's easy to fill a combo box or list box with a list of the report objects in an Access database.

Choose Table/Query as the RowSource Type for the list box and put this SQL statement in the RowSource of your list box to fill the box with a list of all reports in the database:

```
SELECT DISTINCTROW [Name] FROM MSysObjects
WHERE [Type] = -32764
ORDER BY [Name];
```

The `-32764` identifies report objects in `MSysObjects`, one of the system tables used by Microsoft Access. The results are shown in Figure 20.31.

Note

Reports don't have to be open for this technique to work. `MSysObjects` **knows all the objects in the database, so no reports will escape detection using this technique.**

FIGURE 20.31

`frmAllReports` displays the reports in `Chapter20.accdb`.

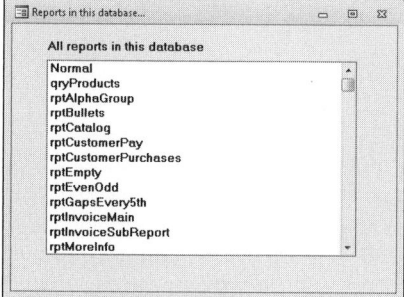

If you're using a naming convention for your database objects, use a prefix to show only the reports you want. The following code returns only those reports that begin with `tmp`:

```
SELECT DISTINCTROW [Name] FROM MSysObjects
WHERE [Type] = -32764 AND Left([Name], 3) = "tmp"
ORDER BY [Name];
```

Because MSysObjects stores the names of all database objects, you can return the names of the other top-level database objects as well. Just substitute the -32764 as the type value in the preceding SQL statement with the Table 20.3 values to return different database object types.

TABLE 20.3

Microsoft Access Object Types and Values

Object	Type Value
Local Tables	1
Linked tables (except tables linked using ODBC)	6
Linked tables using ODBC	4
Forms	–32768
Modules	–32761
Macros	–32766
Queries	5

To view the MSysObjects table, set the Show System Objects setting to Yes in the System Objects dialog box (which you can get to by right-clicking on the Navigation Pane's title bar, and selecting Navigation Options from the shortcut menu). MSysObjects does *not* have to be visible for this trick to work.

Note

Although Microsoft has gone on record that MSysObjects and the type values are not supported and are, therefore, prone to change at any time, Access has used the same type values for many, many years. It's unlikely Microsoft will drop the MSysObjects table or change the type values, but this trick is not guaranteed to work indefinitely.

Fast printing from queried data

A report that is based on a query can take a long time to print. Because reports and forms can't share the same recordset, once a user has found the correct record on a form it's a shame to have to run the query over again to print the record on a query. A way to "cache" the information on the form is to create a table (we'll call it tblCache) containing all the fields that are eventually printed on the report. Then, when the user has found the correct record on the form, copy the data from the form to tblCache, and open the report. The report, of course, is based on tblCache.

The query is run only once to populate the form. Copying the data from the form to tblCache is a very fast operation, and multiple records can be added to tblCache as needed. Because the report is now based on a table, it opens quickly and is ready to print as soon as the report opens.

Hiding forms during Print Preview

Very often, when you're using the overlapping windows user interface in Access, a report opened in Print Preview will be obscured by forms that are open on the screen. The easiest way to prevent forms from getting in the way during Print Preview is to simply hide them as the report opens, and then reveal them when the report is closed.

The `RunReport()` function opens a report for previewing and hides all open forms during Print Preview. To restore the forms after previewing the report, set the report's `OnClose` property to `=MakeFormsVisible( 1)`.

```
Function RunReport(RepName As String)
    Dim intErrorCode As Integer
    DoCmd.OpenReport RepName, acPreview
    intErrorCode = MakeFormsVisible(False)
End Function

Function MakeFormsVisible (YesNoFlag As Boolean)
    Dim intCounter As Integer
On Error GoTo HandleError
    For intCounter = 0 To Forms.Count - 1
        'If you want to make sure a hidden form is not
        'displayed, use the forms(intCounter).formname
        'statement to get the form name.
        Forms(intCounter).Visible = YesNoFlag
    Next intCounter
ExitHere:
    Exit Function
HandleError:
    Msgbox "Error " & Err.Number & ": " & Err.Description
    'Make sure all forms are restored if an error occurs.
    For intCounter = 0 To Forms.Count - 1
        Forms(intCounter).Visible = True
    Next
    Resume ExitHere
End Function
```

Using snaking columns in a report

When the data displayed on a report doesn't require the full width of the page, you may be able to conserve the number of pages by printing the data as snaking columns, as in a dictionary or phone book. Less space is wasted and fewer pages need to be printed, speeding the overall response of the report. More information is available at a glance and many people find snaking columns more aesthetically pleasing than simple blocks of data.

For the examples in this section, I need a query that returns more data than I've been using up to this point. Figure 20.32 shows the query used to prepare the sample reports in this section.

FIGURE 20.32

This query returns more detailed information than I've been using.

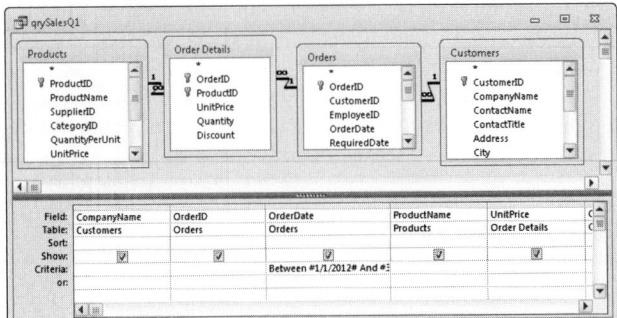

This query returns the following information: company name, order date, order ID, product name, unit price, and quantity for the period from January 1, 2012, to March 31, 2012.

The initial report design to contain this data is shown in Design view in Figure 20.33. This rather complex report includes a group based on the order ID for each order placed by the company, as well as a group based on the company itself. This design enables me to summarize data for each order during the quarter, as well as for the company for the entire quarter.

FIGURE 20.33

Notice how narrow the records in this report are.

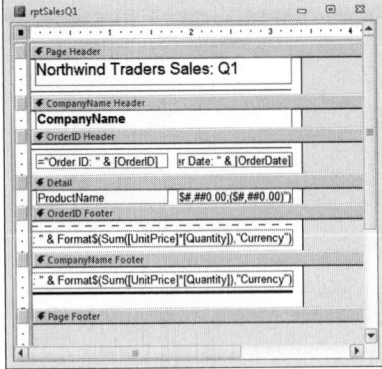

The same report in Print Preview mode is shown in Figure 20.34. Notice that the report really doesn't make good use of the page width available to it. In fact, each record of this report is only 3¼ inches wide.

FIGURE 20.34

The report makes poor use of the available page width.

Setting a report to print as snaking columns is actually part of the print setup for the report, not an attribute of the report itself. With the report in Design view, select the Page Setup tab in the Report Design Tools ribbon area, then click on the Columns button to open the Page Setup dialog box (shown in Figure 20.35) with the Columns tab selected. Change the Number of Columns property to 2. As you change Number of Columns from 1 to 2, the Column Layout area near the bottom of the Layout tab becomes active, showing you that Access has selected the Across, Then Down option to print items across the page first, and then down the page. Although this printing direction is appropriate for mailing labels, it's not what we want for our report. Select the Down, Then Across option to direct Access to print the report as snaking columns (see Figure 20.35).

When working with snaking columns, make sure the proper Column Layout option is selected. If you neglect to set the Column Layout to Down, Then Across, the snaking columns will be laid out horizontally across the page. This common error can cause a lot of confusion because the report won't look as expected (see Figure 20.36). The reports shown in Figures 20.36 and 20.37 are the same with the exception of the Column Layout setting.

FIGURE 20.35

Only a few changes are needed to produce snaking columns.

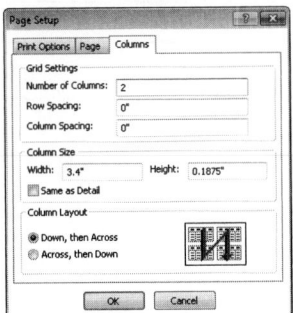

As long as the Same as Detail check box is *not* checked, Access intelligently adjusts the Column Spacing and other options to accommodate the number of items across that you've specified for the report. With Same as Detail checked, Access will force the columns to whatever width is specified for the columns in Design view, which might mean that the number of columns specified in the Number of Columns parameter won't fit on the page.

Figure 20.37 clearly demonstrates the effect of changing the report to a snaking two-column layout. Before the change, this report required 11 pages to print all the data. After this change, only seven pages are required.

FIGURE 20.36

The wrong Column Layout setting can be very confusing!

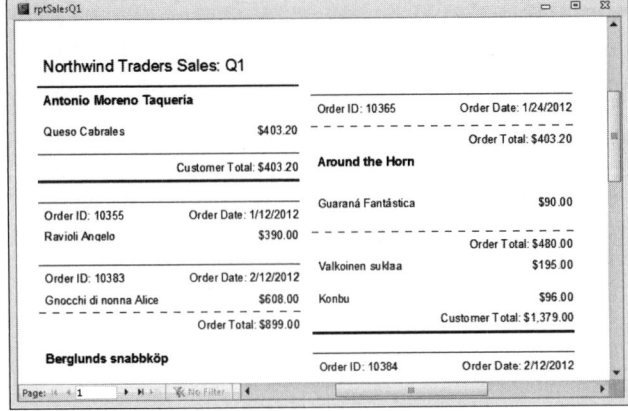

FIGURE 20.37

Snaking multiple columns conserve page space and provide more information at a glance.

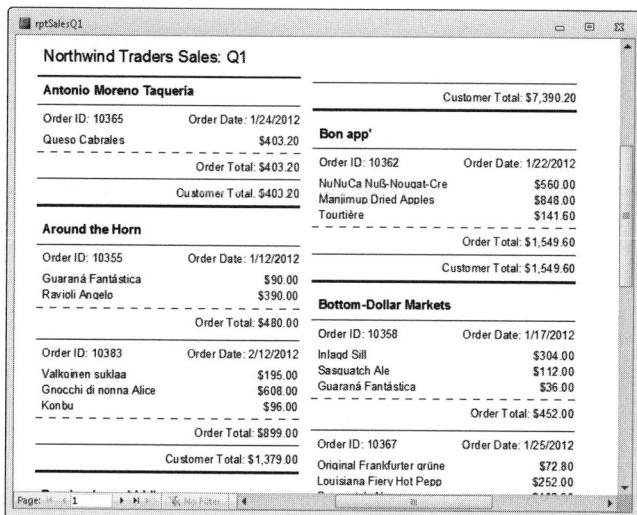

You may be wondering about the other print options in the Page Setup dialog box (refer to Figure 20.35). Here is a short description of each of the relevant settings in the Layout tab of the Page Setup dialog box:

- **Number of Columns:** Specifies the number of columns in the report. You should be aware that Number of Columns affects only the Detail section, Group Header section, and Group Footer section of the report. The Page Header section and Page Footer section are not duplicated for each column. When designing a multi-column report, you must keep the width of the design area narrow enough to fit on the page when multiplied by the number of columns you've selected. Most often, printing a report in landscape mode helps the width required for more than one column in a report.

- **Row Spacing:** Additional vertical space allowed for each detail item. Use this setting if you need to force more space between detail items than the report's design allows.

- **Column Spacing:** Additional horizontal space allowed per column. Use this setting if you need to force more space between columns in the report than the design allows.

- **Item Size – Same as Detail:** The column width and detail height will be the same as on the report in Design view. This property is useful when you need to fine-tune the column placement on a report (for example, when printing the data onto preprinted forms). Making adjustments to the report's design will directly influence how the columns print on paper.

- **Column Size – Width and Height:** The width and height of a column. These options are handy when printing onto preprinted forms to ensure that the data falls where you want it to.

- **Column Layout:** How the items are to be printed: either Across, Then Down or Down, Then Across.

In addition to these properties, be sure to take note of the New Row or Col property for the CompanyName Header section (see Figure 20.38). The values for New Row or Col are None, Before Section, After Section, Before & After. You use New Row or Col to force Access to (for example) start a new column immediately after a group footer or detail section has printed (see Figure 20.39). Depending on your reports and their data, New Row or Col may provide you with the flexibility necessary to make reports more readable.

FIGURE 20.38

Headers (and Footers) have properties that can be used to control actions when the grouping value changes.

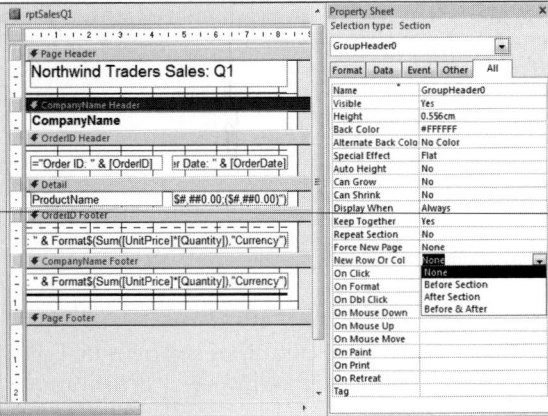

FIGURE 20.39

New Row or Col forces Access to start a column before or after a section.

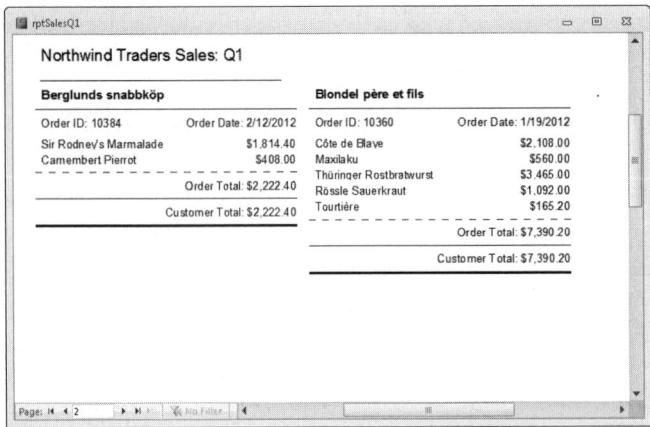

Keep in mind that the measurement units you see in the Page Setup ribbon tab are determined by the Windows international settings. For example, in Germany or Japan where the metric system is used, the units of measure will be centimeters instead of inches. Also, you must allow for the margin widths set in the Margins gallery, accessed from the Page Setup ribbon tab (see Figure 20.40).

FIGURE 20.40

All report page settings must consider the margin widths.

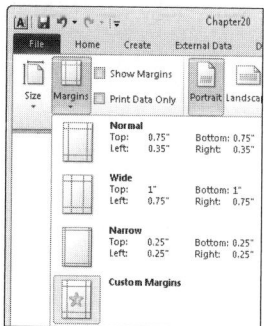

For example, if you specify a Column Size Width of 3.5" and the left margin is set to 1", this means the right edge of the column will actually fall 4½ inches from the left physical edge of the paper, or more than halfway across an 8½-x-11-inch sheet of paper printed in portrait mode. These settings will not allow two columns, each 3½ inches wide, to print on a standard letter-size sheet of paper. In this case, you might consider reducing the left and right margins until the 3½-inch columns fit properly. (Don't worry about setting the margins too small to work with your printer. Unless you're working with a nonstandard printer, Windows is pretty smart about knowing the printable area available with your printer and won't allow you to set margins too small.)

Exploiting two-pass report processing

In Chapter 9, we mention that Access uses a two-pass approach when formatting and printing reports. We'll now explore what this capability means to you and how you can exploit both passes in your applications.

The main advantage of two-pass reporting is that your reports can include expressions that rely on information available anywhere in the report. For example, placing a control with the Sum() function in a header or footer means that Access will use the first pass to accumulate the data required by the function, and then use the second pass to process the values in that section before printing them.

Another obvious example is putting an unbound text box in the footer of a report containing the following expression:

```
="Page " & [Page] & " of " & [Pages]
```

The built-in Pages variable (which contains the total number of pages in the report) isn't determined until Access has completed the first pass through the report. On the second pass, Access has a valid number to use in place of the Pages variable.

The biggest advantage of two-pass reporting is that you're free to use aggregate functions that depend on the report's underlying record source. Group headers and footers can include information that can't be known until the entire record source is processed.

There are many situations where aggregate information provides valuable insight into data analysis. Consider a report that must contain each salesperson's performance over the last year measured against the total sales for the sales organization, or a region's sales figures against sales for the entire sales area. A bookstore might want to know what portion of its inventory is devoted to each book category.

Figure 20.41 shows such a report. The Number of Customers, Total Sales, and Average Purchase information at the top of this report (rptSummary) are all part of the report header. In a one-pass report writer, the data needed to perform these calculations would not appear until the bottom of the page, after all the records have been processed and laid out.

A glance at rptSummary in Design view (see Figure 20.42) reveals that the text boxes in the report header are populated with data derived from these mathematical expressions:

```
Number of Customers: =Count([CompanyName])
Total Sales: =Format(Sum([Purchases]),"Currency")
Average Purchase: =Format(Sum([Purchases])/ _
        Count([CompanyName]), "Currency")
```

FIGURE 20.41

The summary information is part of the report's header.

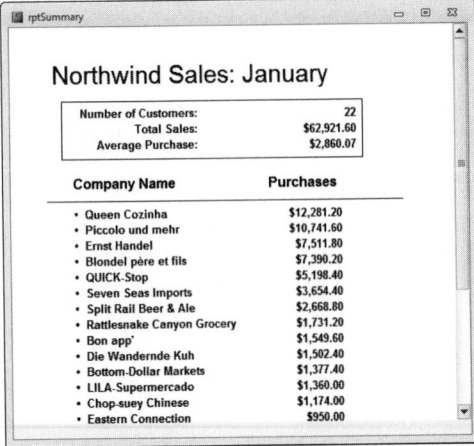

The Count() and Sum() functions both require information that isn't available until the entire report has been processed in the first pass. As long as Access can find the arguments provided to these functions (CompanyName and Purchases) in the underlying recordset, the calculations proceed without any action by the user.

rptSummary in Design view

Assigning unique names to controls

If you use the Report Wizard or drag fields from the Field List when designing your reports, Access assigns the new text boxes the same names as the fields in the recordset underlying the report. For example, if you drag a field named Discount from the field list, both the Name and ControlSource properties of the text box are set to Discount.

If another control on the report references the text box, or if you change the ControlSource of the text box to a calculated field, such as

```
=IIf([Discount]=0,"N/A",[Discount])
```

you'll see #Error when you view the report. This happens because Access can't distinguish between the control named Discount and the field in the underlying recordset named Discount.

You must change the Name property of the control to something like txtDiscount so that Access can tell the difference between the control's name and the underlying field.

Summary

This chapter examines a number of advanced report design concepts and techniques. Most of the "tricks" described in this chapter simply exploit the built-in properties and features of Access reports to yield more information or to make the reports easier to read. Anything you can do to help your users understand the data contained in their Access databases will be greatly appreciated, I'm sure!

The next several chapters explore some of the more interesting and challenging aspects of working with Microsoft Access. Chapter 21 takes on the issue of creating applications that will be simultaneously used by more than one person. Although multiuser applications may seem easy to produce, there's much more to them than meets the eye.

Chapter 22 explores *Automation*, the process of controlling one application (such as Microsoft Word) from another application (Microsoft Access, of course!). There you'll see how easy (or difficult!) it can be to share data between Windows applications and control printing and other operations with automation.

Building Multiuser Applications

You've created a really nifty application. After finishing your masterpiece, you tested, poked, and prodded it every which way imaginable. Finally, you gave it to your users, who tried it out and thought it was pretty nifty, too. Everything worked the way it was supposed to: The application's form navigation was smooth and quick, queries ran fast, and there were no errors during data entry.

So who is this guy on the other end of the phone line complaining about record locks? You didn't have any record-locking problems during testing. But then again, you didn't test your application in a multiuser environment. After all, Access is supposed to handle all those issues for you, right?

Almost, but not quite. There's a lot you need to know about using Access applications in multiuser environments before you can be confident that users won't encounter unwarranted record locks, frustration, and possible data loss.

This chapter shows you how to avoid some of the pitfalls of failing to plan for multiuser issues when developing applications in Microsoft Access. The key phrase here is *failing to plan.* In order to create a successful multiuser application, you must anticipate the environment in which the application will run (single-user, multiuser, desktop, network, and so on), and you must take into consideration what kind of database application you're developing (data entry, client-server, and so on). This chapter covers some of the planning issues you should keep in mind and ways to handle problems you might encounter, as well as explaining how to take advantage of Access's record-locking mechanism to prevent data loss or corruption when multiple users are trying to update records concurrently.

The Access record-locking mechanism is designed to prevent accidental data loss or corruption by controlling which of several users is able to make

IN THIS CHAPTER

Setting up your multiuser applications on a network

Determining how your Access database will be opened

Improving performance by splitting your Access database

Considering your locking options and handling locking errors

Getting more control over your application with unbound forms

updates to records in a database. Access security, on the other hand, prevents unauthorized users from viewing or changing not only the data, but the database objects such as forms and reports. Hand in hand, record locking and security combine to ensure the integrity of the application and its data.

Note

Access security was removed from the `.accdb` file format. It is, however, still available if you continue to use the `.mdb` file format.

Note

Some of the examples in this chapter are given using both ActiveX Data Objects (ADO) and Data Access Objects (DAO) syntax. Although ADO is superior to DAO for some purposes, many Access developers spend time maintaining applications written with DAO code. Because proper handling of multiuser issues is so important in many environments, I felt it was necessary to show both the proper ADO and DAO code involved with record locking.

Working on a Network

Multiuser applications require a network of some kind. Generally, the type of network you use doesn't matter. Multiuser issues are the same regardless of the underlying networking technology. The speed of your network, the location of your application's files, and the type of data source that you're accessing are all important considerations when planning your network installation. Although I've listed these as three separate items, they're all related to the fundamental issue of database performance.

No matter how well it's written, if your application performs poorly due to network bottlenecks, the *application* will get the blame, not the network.

Network performance

When you develop applications in Access, a good rule of thumb is to always plan for the lowest common denominator — that is, write your database applications as if they were going to be used on the most minimally equipped computer possible. Preparing databases that will be used in networked environments is no different. There are many different network topologies and speeds out there — everything from remote-access dial-up lines running on slow modems to megabit networks and dedicated T1 lines.

Tip

Plan ahead: If you're writing an application that will be used in a high-speed, low-traffic network environment, you can afford to be a little extravagant and less stringent in your control of record-locking issues. But if your application will be used by traveling salespeople dialing in over phone lines to retrieve customer and order information, your approach should be very conservative, and your design will have to accommodate the frequent updates that are likely in this scenario.

File location

File location can change the performance of your application more than you may think. Where you locate your files depends on the environment. For example, if your network contains diskless workstations, then you have no choice but to run the entire application from the server — an unfortunate but unavoidable choice. However, if each workstation has a hard disk with plenty of free space available, you might want to locate some files on the server and some on each workstation (although you probably should put all the files on each workstation except the data files that will be shared by all users).

Note

Splitting your database involves creating a back-end Access data file (`.accdb` or `.mdb`, containing data tables only) and a front-end database (an Access data file containing macros, code modules and form, report, and query objects). The split-database method of maintaining your applications has advantages in almost any environment, but it offers you even more advantages in a networked multiuser environment. (I cover the advantages of splitting Access databases in much greater detail in the "Splitting a Database for Network Access" section, later in this chapter.)

In the following sections, I cover some of the advantages and disadvantages of different file-location scenarios.

All files on the server

The primary advantage of locating all your application files on a server is that updating your application is easy because everything is in a single location. You can easily post a new `.accdb` or `.mdb` file on a file server or in a shared folder in a Windows network.

Caution

The disadvantages, however, far outweigh the advantage. Performance is poor because every read, write, or execute request must first cross the network to the server, and then a response must be sent back around the network to the client. This approach greatly increases network traffic, especially in an environment with many users. Try to avoid this scenario, if possible.

Distributed installation

A distributed installation is a good choice for most environments. In this design, you install a copy of Access and the front-end database on the user's local machine, leaving the back-end database application and linked data files on the server. Less network traffic is generated and less time is spent waiting for requests to be sent back and forth around the network. This installation allows for moderately simple upgrades because the majority of the most volatile files are in one central location.

One problem you may experience with this approach is decreased performance when several users access your application databases at the same time.

All files on the client

In this scenario, you have all executables — .exe files, .dll files, and application files — located on each client, and only data files are on the server. Your data files would be attached to your application database. You gain performance because network traffic and requests are kept to a minimum and because you don't have several users hitting the application at the same time — they're accessing only the data.

This scenario is not conducive to easy upgrades, however. In most cases, an application's front end changes most often. If the application is located on a client workstation, you'll have to go to each workstation and upgrade it individually (unless you're using some kind of distribution software, like Microsoft System Center Configuration Server).

Note

Microsoft's System Center Configuration Server (SCCS) is an add-on for network systems running Windows 2003 Server as the file server and either Windows 2000, Windows XP, Windows Vista, or Windows 7 on the user's desktop. SCCS enables the system administrator to install and manage software from a central location, making it much easier to upgrade operating system and application software on large networks.

Data sources

Access is a versatile development environment because of its ability to read many kinds of external data sources. This ability, however, can cause problems for your applications. Even if you're just reading a plain ol' Access .accdb or .mdb located on your sever, there are still issues to consider.

Access is a *client-centric* application. In many situations, when you execute a query against a table in an Access database located on your network, Access goes out to the server, brings back all the records needed to perform the query, and then processes the request on the client. The next time you get a chance, run a really big query on your workstation while watching the number of packets being sent to that address. It's fun to see your network utilization go from 35 percent to 90 percent just because of one query. All this traffic and the huge amount of data can kill performance.

This client-centric nature can be seen especially when using ODBC data sources. When working with ODBC databases, Access still acts the same way — but because ODBC is another layer that the Access database engine has to go through, performance can be even worse, especially when querying large recordsets.

When your users are off-site

With portable computing power increasing and becoming less expensive, more of your applications will have to be developed with remote or home users in mind. Although broadband Internet access is widely available, many users may still be using dial-up to access your company's network.

One approach to resolving this situation is to put as much of your application on the remote computer as possible. Executables across a dial-up line are unacceptable. The more you can put on the client, the fewer complaints you'll get.

ODBC and client-server applications are in high demand, so you have to find an acceptable solution to these performance problems. You can do a couple things to speed performance when using data sources other than native Access tables:

- **Use SQL pass-through.** SQL pass-through allows you to send a SQL statement (or a stored procedure name) to a host database to let it execute the request, returning only the result set (instead of the entire recordset) for local processing. This ability takes advantage of the host platform's capabilities, and it keeps network traffic down. The disadvantage to SQL pass-through is that you must use the host database's native SQL syntax instead of letting Access generate the SQL request for you. This makes your application less portable to other database platforms and doesn't let you take advantage of Access's Query by Example (QBE) facility; plus, you can't use parameters in your queries.

Note

A SQL pass-through query is not SQL Server specific. Any server database engine that understands SQL (Structured Query Language) can be the target of a SQL pass-through query.

- **Use transactions.** Transactions (the `BeginTrans` and `CommitTrans` methods of an ADO `Connection` object or DAO `Workspace` object) allow you to cache reads, edits, and updates in local memory instead of reading from or writing to disk or your external data source. If you know that you'll be doing several updates or reads within a VBA procedure, enclose the updates in transaction statements.

  Better performance is achieved because you don't have to wait on your request to be sent back around the network to your data source, and because all writes are done at one time (when the `CommitTrans` method is executed) instead of each time the `Update` method is executed.

  Listing 21.1 shows the use of transactions within a VBA procedure. (In the code editor, choose Tools ⇨ References to open the References dialog box, and then make sure that the `Microsoft Office 14.0 Access database engine Object Library` is selected.)

LISTING 21.1

Demonstrating DAO Transactions

```
Public Sub Transaction_DAO()
    Dim db As DAO.Database
    Dim ws As DAO.Workspace
    Dim rs As DAO.Recordset
On Error GoTo HandleError
    Set db = CurrentDb
    Set ws = DBEngine.Workspaces(0)
    Set rs = db.OpenRecordset("Employees", dbOpenTable)

    ' Begin transaction:
    ws.BeginTrans
    rs.MoveFirst
```

continued

LISTING 21.1 *(continued)*

```
    Do While Not rs.EOF
      rs.Edit
      rs![ReviewDate] = DateAdd("yyyy", 1, rs![HireDate])
      rs.Update
      rs.MoveNext
    Loop
    ' Commit transaction:
    ws.CommitTrans

ExitHere:
    rs.Close
    Set rs = Nothing
    Exit Function
HandleError:
    'Rollback transaction:
    ws.Rollback
    GoTo ExitHere
End Sub
```

Considering the Options for Opening a Database

By default, every time a user opens an Access database, other users are able to open and make changes to the data in the same database. The Shared mode of opening Access databases is great for most users because everyone is able to work with the data as if no one else were using the same tables and records. However, this Shared mode also leads to update conflicts when more than one user wants to simultaneously change the same record.

It's possible, however, to open the Access database for exclusive access, which prevents others from opening the database (and hence prevents update conflicts). While this may be necessary sometimes to prevent contention (say, if you're doing a large number of updates, or trying to replace the data in a table by importing from external data sources), in general it does make the database less usable, since users must now "take turns" using the database.

Note
Later in this chapter, I discuss the common practice of splitting an Access database application into front-end and back-end databases. The front-end contains all the user interface (forms and report) and the code and macros used by the application, while the back-end database (which is usually located on a file server) contains the tables. As you'll see in the "Splitting a Database for Network Access" section, a split database model offers significant advantages for multiuser environments. In the meantime, however, the current discussion refers only to a default, non-split .accdb or .mdb file.

You can easily change the open mode of an Access database. In the Open dialog box, select the Open Exclusive option (see Figure 21.1), which directs Access to open the database exclusively (for single-user access). When you don't select the Open Exclusive option, the database is opened for shared access, permitting simultaneous multiuser access to the data.

FIGURE 21.1

By default, Access databases are opened in Shared mode.

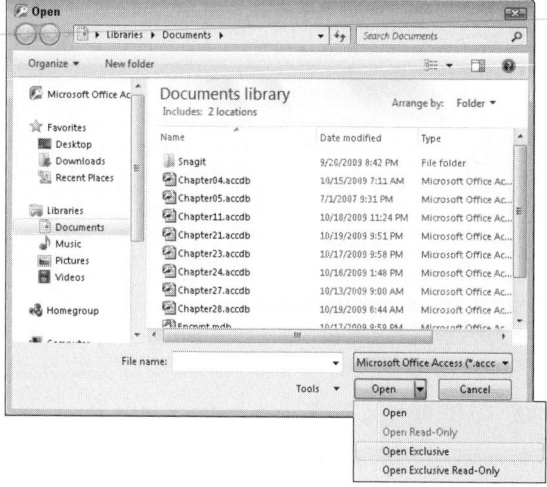

Tip

An essential step when working with multiuser databases is to make sure that the database in question has been opened for shared access. As you'll see in the "Default Open Mode" section later in this chapter, you can easily change the default open mode for Access databases.

Caution

As you'll see in the section "Splitting a Database for Network Access," a recommended practice is to split your application into a front-end database linked to a back-end database. Remember that, because it's the front-end database that the user actually opens, Open Exclusive only applies to the front-end database, not the back-end database where the data actually resides.

Listing 21.2 shows the ADO and DAO code necessary to open an Access database exclusively.

LISTING 21.2

Using ADO to Open a Database Exclusively

```
Public Sub OpenDatabaseTest_ADO()
    Dim cnn As ADODB.Connection
    Dim str As String
    str = "Provider=Microsoft.Jet.OLEDB.4.0;" _
        & "Data Source=C:\Data\MyDB.accdb"
    Set cnn = New ADODB.Connection
    cnn.Mode = adModeShareExclusive
    cnn.ConnectionString = str
    cnn.Open
    '... Your code goes here ...
    cnn.Close
    Set cnn = Nothing
End Sub

Public Sub OpenDatabaseTest_DAO()
    Dim db As DAO.Database
    Set db = DBEngine.OpenDatabase("C:\Data\MyDB.accdb", False)
    '... Your code goes here ...
    db.Close
    Set db = Nothing
End Sub
```

When opening a database with DAO code, you pass a parameter to the OpenDatabase method of the Workspace object to instruct the database engine which open mode to use. Notice that the False value is passed as the second argument to the OpenDatabase method in Listing 21.2.

The syntax of the DAO OpenDatabase method is

```
Set Database = Workspace.OpenDatabase (dbName _
        [, Exclusive] [, Read-only] [, Connect])
```

where:

- dbName is the name of the database to open
- Exclusive instructs Access whether to open dbName in exclusive or Shared mode. True means open the database exclusively; False means open in Shared mode.
- Read-only is a instruction telling Access to open the database in read-only mode.
- Connect is the connect string required by the ODBC database.

By default, a database opened with the OpenDatabase method is opened in Shared mode (Exclusive is False). You should, of course, specify either True or False as the Exclusive value.

Splitting a Database for Network Access

One common technique employed by many experienced Access developers working in multiuser environments is splitting the database into front-end and back-end components. This relatively simple operation can yield big benefits in terms of networked application performance and future maintenance on the application.

Detailing the benefits of splitting a database

There is at least one extremely good reason why you should consider splitting your Access databases. Although you can place a single copy of an .accdb or .mdb file onto a shared computer on the network, the performance degradation from such a design is considerable.

Using an Access database stored on a remote computer involves much more than simply moving data from the remote computer to the local machine. All the form, menu, and ribbon definitions must be transported to the local computer so that Windows can "construct" the user interface on the local computer's monitor. The Windows installation on the local computer must intercept and transmit any keyboard and mouse events to the remote computer so that the proper code will run in response to these events. Finally, the single copy of Access on the remote computer must fulfill all data requests, no matter how trivial or demanding. The impact of all these actions is compounded by increasing the number of users working with the same remotely installed copy of the database.

Fortunately, most of these issues disappear when the database application is split into front-end and back-end components. The local Windows installation handles the user interface from information stored in the front-end database. All code is run on the user's desktop computer, rather than on the remote machine. Also, the locally installed copy of Access is able to handle all local data requirements, while only those requests for remote data are passed on to the back-end database.

Before getting into the details of splitting a database, let's consider some of the problems associated with single-file databases. To begin with, unlike some other development systems, all the objects in an Access database application are stored in a single file, the familiar .accdb or .mdb you work with every day. Many other database systems like FoxPro for Windows maintain a number of different files for each application, usually one file per object (form, table, and so on). Although having to deal with multiple files complicates database development and maintenance somewhat, updating a single form or query involves nothing more than replacing the related file with the updated form or query file.

Updating an Access database object is somewhat more complicated. As you've probably discovered, replacing a form or query in an Access database used by a large number of users can be quite a problem. Replacing a form or other database object often requires hours of work importing the object into each user's copy of the database.

A second consideration is the network traffic inherent in single-file Access databases. Figure 21.2 shows an example of the problem. This figure illustrates a common method of sharing an Access database. The computer in the upper-left corner of the figure is the file server and holds the Access database file. Assume for a moment that the entire database is contained within a single .accdb on the file server, and the database has been enabled for shared data access. Each workstation in Figure 21.2 has a full copy of Access (or the Access runtime) installed.

FIGURE 21.2

A database kept on a file server can generate a large amount of traffic on the network.

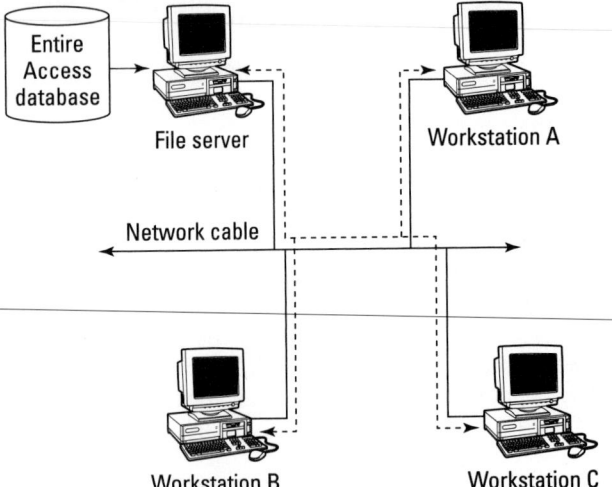

Now, what happens when the user on Workstation C opens the database? The Access installation on that machine must locate the .accdb on the file server, open that file, and start up the application. This means that any splash forms, queries, and other startup activities must take place across the network before the user is able to work with the database. Any time a form is opened or a query is run, the information necessary to fulfill the query must travel across the network, slowing the operation. (In Figure 21.2, the network load is indicated by a thick dashed line.)

The situation shown in Figure 21.2 is made even worse when more than one user is using the same database. In this case, the network traffic is increased by the queries, opening of forms, and other operations performed by each additional user's copy of Access. Imagine the dashed line getting thicker with each operation across the network.

The split-database model is illustrated in Figure 21.3. Notice that the back-end database resides on the server while individual copies of the front-end database are placed on each workstation. Each front-end database contains links to the tables stored in the back-end .accdb file. For performance reasons, the front-end databases may also contain certain tables that are more efficiently used from the local machine than when they're stored on the file server. The front-end databases also contain the forms, reports, queries, and other user-interface components of the application.

FIGURE 21.3

A database kept on a file server can generate a large amount of traffic on the network.

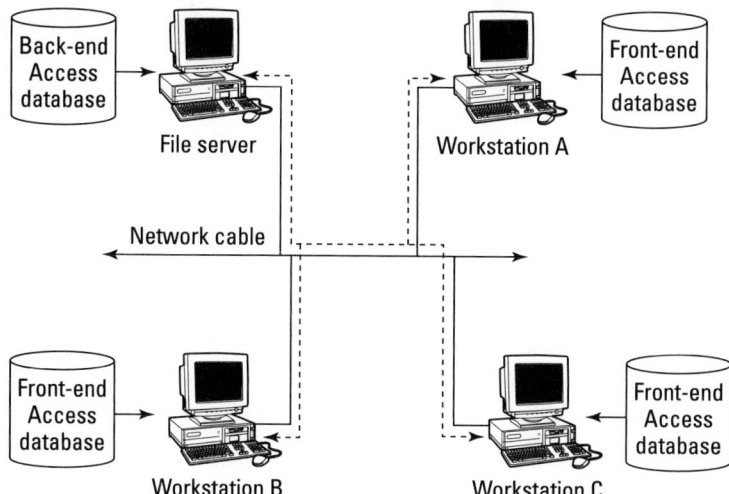

The network traffic is reduced in Figure 21.3 because only linking information and data returned by queries is moved across the network. A user working with the database application uses the forms, queries, reports, macros, and code stored in the local front-end .accdb file. Because the front end is accessed by a single user, response time is much improved because the local copy of Access is able to instantly open the database and begin the start-up operations. Only when actually running queries does the network traffic increase.

The second major benefit of the design in Figure 21.3 is that updating the forms, reports, and other application components requires nothing more than replacing the front-end database on each user's computer and reestablishing the links to the table in the back-end database. In fact, the design in Figure 21.3 supports the notion of customized front ends, depending on the requirements of the user sitting at each workstation. For example, a manager sitting at Workstation A might need access to personnel information that is not available to the people sitting at workstations B and C. In this case the front-end database on Workstation A includes the forms, queries, and other database objects necessary to view the personnel information.

Knowing where to put which objects

Not all tables need to be put into the back-end database. Generally speaking, objects that rarely change can be kept in the front-end database, while objects that change frequently should be kept in the back-end .accdb file. Keeping tables in the local .accdb reduces network traffic — there's no reason to move static data such as state abbreviations, city names, and zip codes across the network. The local tables require updating only when the data changes.

The local .accdb also contains all the user interface objects, including forms, reports, queries, macros, and modules. Keeping the user interface components on the local machine dramatically improves performance. You don't need to move forms, queries, or reports across the network — these objects are much more easily manipulated on the local machine than when accessed across the network.

All shared tables and tables that are changed at regular intervals really should be placed in the back-end database kept on the server. The server database is opened in Shared mode, making all its objects accessible to multiple users. The tables in the server database are linked to the front-end .accdb on each user's desktop. (There is no problem with simultaneously linking the same table to multiple databases.)

Obviously, with more than one person using the data within a table, the possibility exists that the same record will be edited by multiple users. The Access database engine handles this problem by locking a record as it's edited by a user. A lock contention occurs when more than one user tries to update the same record. Only one user will have "live" access to the record — all other users will either be locked or have their changes held up until the record holder is done making changes.

I explain the Access database locking mechanism in detail in the "Access's built-in record-locking features" section, later in this chapter

Using the Database Splitter add-in

The Database Splitter helps you split an application into front-end and back-end databases. This wizard enables you to build and test your database to your heart's content, and then lightens the burden of preparing the application for multiuser access.

As an experiment, let's take a look at splitting the Northwind Traders database into front-end and back-end .accdb files. You start the Database Splitter by choosing the External Data tab of the Access ribbon, and then clicking on the Move Data drop-down list and selecting Access Database. The opening wizard screen (see Figure 21.4) explains the actions of the Database Splitter and suggests that you make a backup of the database before proceeding.

FIGURE 21.4

The Database Splitter is a very simple wizard.

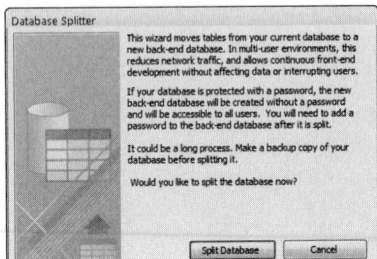

The only other information that the Database Splitter requires is where you want to put the back-end database. Figure 21.5 shows the familiar Explorer-style Create Back-end Database dialog box that lets you specify the location of the back-end `.accdb` file. By default, the back-end database has the same name as the original database with a _be suffix added to the name (for example, `MyDB_be.accdb`).

Tip

Plan to put the back end exactly where it will reside in the production environment. Because the front-end database will contain links to the back-end database, and because links are path-specific, the links would have to be refreshed if the back end were moved after being built by the Database Splitter.

FIGURE 21.5

Specify the permanent location of the back-end database in the Create Back-end Database dialog box.

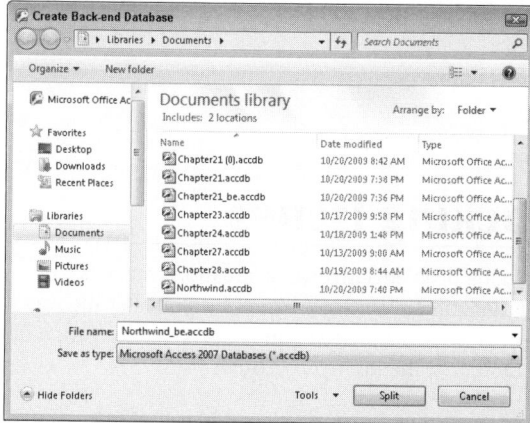

When you click on the Split button (refer to Figure 21.5), the Database Splitter creates the back-end database, exports all tables to it, deletes the tables in the local database, and creates links to the back-end tables. In other words, the Database Splitter performs precisely the same steps you'd have to perform manually if the Database Splitter weren't available.

Note

Be prepared for this process to take a little while, especially on large databases. Because Access has to create the new database, transfer tables to it, and create the links back to the original database, the splitting process can easily require more than a few minutes. Don't worry if the process appears to be taking longer than you expect — you'll be well rewarded for your efforts!

Also, keep in mind that the Database Splitter is rather simplistic, and tends to ignore system considerations such as available disk space. Make sure adequate disk space exists on the target machine to accommodate the back-end database.

Figure 21.6 shows the Access Database Explorer after splitting the Northwind Traders database. The back-end database only contains the tables exported from `Northwind.accdb`. Notice that the icons associated with all the tables in `Northwind.accdb` have been changed, indicating that they are now pointing to copies in the back-end database. You'll have to import any local tables from the back-end database before distributing the front end to the users.

FIGURE 21.6

The Database Splitter creates links for all tables in the database.

Finding the Key to Locking Issues

In multiuser environments, one of the most nagging problems involves a situation where two or more users try to access the same record at the same time. Although Access lets you alter the way it locks records using built-in options, the best cure for record-locking problems is a combination of Access's record-lock settings, careful planning, and error-handling procedures.

Access has long been criticized for its handling of record locks. Some of the older ISAM (Indexed Sequential Access Method) databases, and even some high-end server products, give you the ability to lock an individual row within a table or recordset. The advantage of this individual record-lock ability is its certainty: You know that only one person can access a record at a time. You can easily code procedures to handle single-record locks. In systems using record-locking schemes, it's easy to know which individual record is locked and handle lock contentions against that one record.

Access uses either row-level (record) locks or page locks. A page is a 4K-size section of your table that Access pulls into memory when you want to change a record within a table. When using page locking (which is a good option if performance is an issue), Access locks the entire 4K page containing the record. If the record is greater than 4K, Access locks as many 4K pages as necessary to lock all the record's data.

Page locking makes more efficient use of system resources by caching data locally, allowing you to have more responsive applications. The page-locking scheme in Access also corresponds to the locking behavior of high-end client-server database engines like SQL Server. After you've mastered the page-locking mechanisms in Access, you'll have a much better understanding of how locking works in client-server environments.

When using record-level locking, Access locks only the record currently being edited. Record-level locking is a good option when many users are editing and updating records simultaneously. The only lock contention that occurs in such a situation happens when two users happen to change the same record at the same time.

Note

Record-level locking is the default in Access. If you want to use page-level locking, choose File ⇨ Access Options ⇨ Advanced to open the Access Options dialog box (shown in Figure 21.7); then deselect the Open Databases by Using Record-Level Locking check box. In most environments, however, you'll find that record-level locking works just fine.

Tip

When you design your applications, the type of database application that you're creating should drive the locking strategy that you apply to your applications. Decision support or Executive Information System (EIS)–type applications usually don't need any locks (No Locks or Read-Only access), because most users only view data — they don't change or add new records to the underlying tables. However, if the records in your application are constantly changing as people add new records or edit existing data, your locking strategy will be more complex.

Access's built-in record-locking features

Access has several settings available at runtime and design time that you can change to control the locking behavior of your applications. The Access Options dialog box has an Advanced tab that contains record-lock settings for your databases (see Figure 21.7). Once set, these become the default behavior for your database and its objects. You can still change these defaults in code and in each form you create, though.

FIGURE 21.7

The Advanced tab in the Access Options dialog box

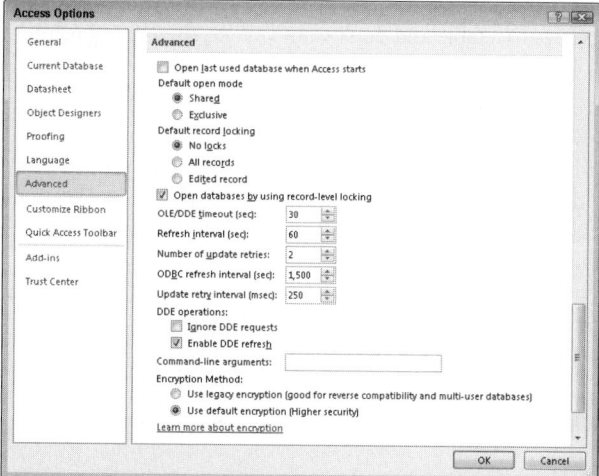

Default Open Mode

The Default Open Mode setting in the Advanced tab of the Access Options dialog box should always be set to Shared in multiuser applications (Shared is the default). After all, if everyone tried to open the application in Exclusive mode, no two users could use the database at the same time. You may use the Exclusive mode as the administrator to update files and tables, add forms, and so on.

Default Record Locking

Default Record Locking controls whether or how Access handles locking when your users add, edit, or change records within a recordset. Once set, the Default Record Locking setting applies globally to the objects you create within your database.

Note

The same settings exist within the Design view of forms, which will override the Default Record Locking settings of the Advanced tab.

Here are your Default Record Locking options:

- **No Locks:** This setting allows you or your users to add or edit a record without locking the page in which it exists. The only locking occurs during the split second when the update is actually written to the Access table. Thus, when No Locks is set, someone might be able to start an edit but might not be able to finish it. The No Locks setting is most appropriate in environments where users will be adding many records simultaneously. This setting allows all adds to be started and almost all updates to be committed (unless two people save the record at the same time). Your error-handling routines must anticipate the errors that occur when the record is committed. The No Locks setting is called *optimistic locking* because you have every expectation that the record commit will proceed without error.

- **All Records:** The All Records setting locks an entire recordset as long as the user has the table, form, or query open for viewing. This setting really has no practical use in a dynamic multiuser environment. The only time it should be used is when you're doing some kind of administrative updates to a table and don't want anyone else editing records while you're updating.

- **Edited Record:** Also called *pessimistic locking*, this setting locks a record when a user tries to obtain a record for editing. Access locks the record (or page) at the moment a user begins editing a record (as opposed to No Locks, which locks the page only at the instant the record is committed to the database). Pessimistic locking is appropriate in applications where data will be changed frequently but not added. In these environments, you don't want two users trying to edit the same record at the same time — if they do, one user has the potential to overwrite the changes of the other. With Edited Record locking on, your application can capture an error when the second user tries to obtain the lock for editing; the application then notifies the user to wait until the other user is finished.

Refresh Interval

In multiuser environments, data is extremely volatile because it can be changed by many different people during the course of a day or even an hour. You want users to see the most current data displayed on forms and datasheets, so that they don't make decisions based on information that is no longer valid. Refresh Interval tells Access how long to wait before refreshing the data displayed in a form or datasheet with current data. The default is 30 seconds, the minimum is 0 seconds, and the maximum is 32,766 seconds (which is roughly 9 hours).

Tip

In situations where data will be added or edited frequently, set the Refresh Interval fairly low (say, 3 seconds).

Note

Access doesn't requery the data; it only refreshes it. Requerying reissues the query behind the recordset displayed. To illustrate the difference, imagine that two users are editing data and one of the users deletes a record from a table that the other user is viewing. When Access refreshes the underlying table for the second user, the record viewed will display #Deleted in all the columns of the record. If the form or datasheet is queried again, the new recordset won't display the record at all because it no longer resides in the underlying table.

Number of Update Retries

When two users try to update the same record at the same time, Access captures the error and tries to recover using the Number of Update Retries setting. The Number of Update Retries setting tells Access how many times to attempt to update the record before it raises an error condition. The default is 2, the minimum is 0, and the maximum is 10.

Tip

In situations where you anticipate a high number of locking conflicts, set this option to a high number.

ODBC Refresh Interval

This setting is much like the Refresh Interval one, except that special considerations must be made when using external data sources. ODBC links can be slow, and queries executed against these back-end databases can consume a lot of time and increase network traffic. When you're using ODBC data sources, the ODBC Refresh Interval should be set higher than you would set the Refresh Interval of an Access database. The default is 1,500 seconds (25 minutes), much higher than the Refresh Interval default of 30 seconds. The ODBC Refresh Interval's maximum setting is much smaller, too: 3,600 seconds (1 hour).

Caution

Before setting this option, experiment with the speed of your queries and tables, and monitor network resources when you issue reads from your back end. Setting the ODBC Refresh Interval too low will really bog down the system as Access hits the ODBC data source looking for data changes.

Update Retry Interval

This option controls the period of time Access waits to retry a lock. Adjust this setting to accommodate the latency imposed by the network, slow computers, and other hardware constraints. The default is 250 milliseconds (one-quarter of a second), the minimum is 0 milliseconds, and the maximum is 1,000 milliseconds (1 second).

Tip

An unnecessarily long Update Retry Interval setting and a high Number of Update Retries setting can result in an uncomfortably long interval before the user sees a locking error message. In most cases, using the No Locks option (see "Default Record Locking," earlier) in conjunction with a brief Update Retry Interval setting and a minimum Number of Update Retries setting is adequate.

Record-lock error handling

Even though you plan ahead and set Access's default settings to a number you think will handle record-locking problems in your application, you're bound to encounter conflicts sometime. The more users you have hitting your application, the better the chances that you'll encounter a locking conflict. You can capture the errors that Access throws, however, and use VBA to communicate record-lock contention solutions to your users.

In an effort to correct some performance problems and locking conflicts in earlier versions of Access, Microsoft has developed Access so that it caches more data in memory and writes data to disk only after the cache has been filled (unless specified in the engine's Registry keys). Although these enhancements do increase performance, they can make it harder to trap lock errors on specific records. Here's an example: One person is changing data on Machine A. Another person is editing data on Machine B. Both users change the same record, but the record changed is cached in memory on Machine A along with several other records. Finally, Machine A runs out of cache space and flushes the cache to disk. Because a locking violation has occurred (even though time and records have long since passed the violation), Access flags an error. But because the record is being written along with several others, figuring out exactly which record lock caused the error is difficult.

Another problem with Access's caching behavior is latency. Because data is being stored in cache on each machine, changes that may have occurred to data on each machine won't be reflected to other users until the cache is flushed to disk.

In order to solve both of these problems, you must use explicit transactions in your procedures. Explicit transactions enclose each transaction with `Workspace.BeginTrans` and `Workspace.CommitTrans` (ADO transactions are managed by the `Connection` object).

Caution

You can encounter locking problems within your transactions, so be sure to provide adequate error handling.

You've gotten a taste of what can happen in your multiuser applications: Performance can suffer, and users can change each other's data and encounter errors when a locking conflict occurs. The good news is that you can plan for the errors, specifically by trapping for errors 3260, 3186, 3188, and 3197. The next sections explain what each of these errors means, and give you some routines to help you use them (instead of becoming their victim).

Error 3260: Couldn't update; currently locked by user . . .

Remember pessimistic locking (see the "Default Record Locking" section, earlier in this chapter)? Error 3260 most often occurs when pessimistic locking is enabled in an application. It occurs when a user tries to lock a record for editing but another user already has the record locked (because that person is editing it). You can choose to try again within your code, but one of the problems inherent in pessimistic locking is that a user can hold a record for editing for an indefinite period of time. This means that you have to provide a failure mechanism within your code just in case you can't obtain the lock after trying several times.

Before you waste time on edit procedures, make sure you can obtain a lock on the record you want to edit. You can check to see if the record is locked by forcing the error (if there is one). All you have to do is enable pessimistic locking and try to edit the desired record.

In an ADO application, pessimistic locking is implemented by setting the LockType parameter of the Recordset object's Open method:

```
rst.Open "Customers", _
    ActiveConnection:=conn, _
    CursorType:=adOpenForwardOnly, _
    LockType:=adLockReadOnly, _
    Options:=adCmdTableDirect
```

The enumerated values for LockType are shown in Table 21.1.

TABLE 21.1

Enumerated Values for LockType

Enumerated Constant	Numeric Value	Description
adLockBatchOptimistic	4	Specifies optimistic batch updates. This value is required for Batch Update mode.
adLockOptimistic	3	Optimistic locking on a record-by-record basis. The lock is applied only when the Update method is called.
adLockPessimistic	2	Pessimistic locking on a record-by-record basis. The lock is applied right after the user begins editing the record.
adLockReadOnly	1	The data is read-only.
adLockUnspecified	−1	No lock type is specified.

In a DAO environment, use the LockEdits property (a Boolean) of a Recordset object to specify the default record-locking behavior of a recordset. Set LockEdits to True to specify pessimistic locking:

```
MyRecordset.LockEdits = True
```

Set LockEdits to False for optimistic locking:

```
MyRecordset.LockEdits = False
```

Listing 21.3 creates a recordset based on the Northwind Traders Employees table and an EmployeeID passed to the function as an argument. It then sets record locking to pessimistic locking and tries to lock the record for editing. If the edit fails, the error handler (see the "A function to handle lock errors" section, later in this chapter) uses an empty loop to wait a few seconds before trying the edit again. After four tries, the edit fails and the user is notified of the failure.

LISTING 21.3

Pessimistic Locking in ADO

```
Public Sub PessimisticLocking_ADO(ID As Long)
    Dim cnn As ADODB.Connection
    Dim rs As ADODB.Recordset
    Dim str As String
    Dim lngTryCount As Long
On Error GoTo HandleError
    'Must use the Jet OLEDB provider
    'when opening an Access ACCDB file:
    str = "Provider=Microsoft.ACE.OLEDB.12.0;" _
        & "Data Source=C:\Data\Northwind.accdb"
    Set cnn = New ADODB.Connection
    cnn.ConnectionString = str
    cnn.Open
    str = "SELECT * FROM Employees " _
        & "WHERE EmployeeID = " & ID
    Set rs = New ADODB.Recordset
    'Open the recordset:
    rs.Open str, _
      ActiveConnection:=cnn, _
      CursorType:=adOpenForwardOnly, _
      LockType:=adLockPessimistic, _
      Options:=adCmdTableDirect
    'Try to update a field:
    rs.Fields("LastName") = UCase(rs.Fields("LastName"))
ExitHere:
    rs.Close
    Set rs = Nothing
    cnn.Close
```

```
      Set cnn = Nothing
      Exit Sub
 HandleError:
     'Update Retry Count:
     lngTryCount = lngTryCount + 1
     'Call ErrorRoutine, passing
     'in the number of retries:
     Select Case ErrorRoutine(lngTryCount)
         Case 3
             'Try again at the same statement
             'that caused the error:
             Resume
         Case 4
             MsgBox "Edit Canceled"
             GoTo ExitHere
     End Select
 End Function
```

Listing 21.4 performs the same operation as Listing 21.3, but this time on a local Employees table using DAO syntax and a somewhat different technique for referencing the LastName field in the recordset.

LISTING 21.4

Pessimistic Locking in DAO

```
Public Sub PessimisticLocking_DAO(ID As Long)
     Dim db As DAO.Database
     Dim rs As DAO.Recordset
     Dim strSQL As String
     Dim lngTryCount As Long
On Error GoTo HandleError
     Set db = CurrentDb
     strSQL = "SELECT * FROM Employees " _
           & "WHERE Employees!EmployeeID = " & ID
     Set rs = db.OpenRecordset(strSQL)
     'Set record locking to Pessimistic Locking:
     rs.LockEdits = True
     rs.Edit
     rs!LastName = UCase(rs!LastName)
     rs.Update
ExitHere:
     rs.Close
     Exit Sub
```

continued

LISTING 21.4   *(continued)*

```
HandleError:
     'Update Retry Count:
     lngTryCount = lngTryCount + 1
     'Call ErrorRoutine, passing
     'in the number of retries:
     Select Case ErrorRoutine(lngTryCount)
          Case 3
                'Try again at the same statement
                'that caused the error:
                Resume
          Case 4
                MsgBox "Edit Canceled"
                GoTo ExitHere
     End Select
End Function
```

The portion of code from `ErrorRoutine()` that handles this error is shown in the following listing. This code fragment contains an empty loop that provides a little bit of time for the lock to be released. As long as the value of `TryCount` is less than 10, the loop will be executed and the value of `ErrorRoutine()` is set to 3. If `ErrorRoutine()` has been called ten or more times, `ErrorRoutine()` is set to 4, which ends the attempt to rectify the situation.

```
     Case 3260
          ' Record is locked on another machine
          If TryCount < 10 Then
            For lngCounter = 0 To 15000
                  'Empty loop for short delay...
                DoEvents
            Next lngCounter
            ErrorRoutine = 3
          Else
             ParseError Err, Error
             ErrorRoutine = 4
          End If
```

Error 3186: Couldn't save; currently locked by user x on machine y

Sound familiar? This error is much like Error 3260 (see the preceding section), except for one difference: Error 3260 states that the record couldn't be updated; Error 3186 states that the record couldn't be saved. You can't update a record that you can't get a lock on for editing (pessimistic locking). But if you can get a lock on a record but not save it, it must be an optimistic record-locking error.

As an example, let's say two users are trying to edit the same record, but one is using pessimistic locking and the other is using optimistic locking. Both can pull the record into memory for updating because one of the two users is set to optimistic locking. If the user with optimistic locking tries to save while the pessimist is still editing, the optimist is likely to get Error 3186. The same could happen if two optimistic updates were committed at the same time (although this situation is less likely).

Listing 21.5 shows how to test for locking status on a record that's been obtained using optimistic locking. Actually, there's not much difference except that an edit takes place (`rs.Fields("Lastname") = UCase(rs.Fields("LastName"))`) using optimistic locking (`LockType:=adLockOptimistic`). Contrary to Listing 21.3, the error occurs as the record is updated instead of as it's edited. Again, when the error occurs, the global error handler is called to deal with the error.

LISTING 21.5

Optimistic Locking with ADO

```
Public Sub OptimisticLocking_ADO(ID As Long)
    Dim cnn As ADODB.Connection
    Dim rs As ADODB.Recordset
    Dim str As String
    Dim lngTryCount As Long
On Error GoTo HandleError
    str = "Provider= Provider=Microsoft.ACE.OLEDB.12.0;" _
        & "Data Source=C:\Data\Northwind.mdb"
    Set cnn = New ADODB.Connection
    cnn.ConnectionString = str
    cnn.Open
    str = "SELECT * FROM Employees WHERE " _
        & " EmployeeID = " & ID
    Set rs = New ADODB.Recordset
    'Open the recordset:
    rs.Open "Customers", _
      ActiveConnection:=cnn, _
      CursorType:=adOpenForwardOnly, _
      LockType:=adLockOptimistic, _
      Options:=adCmdTableDirect
    'Try to update a field:
    rs.Fields("LastName") = UCase(rs.Fields("LastName"))
ExitHere:
    rs.Close
    Set rs = Nothing
    cnn.Close
    Set cnn = Nothing
    Exit Sub
HandleError:
    'Update Retry Count:
    lngTryCount = lngTryCount + 1
```

continued

LISTING 21.5 *(continued)*

```
'Call ErrorRoutine, passing
'in the number of retries:
Select Case ErrorRoutine(lngTryCount)
    Case 3
        'Try again at the same statement
        'that caused the error:
        Resume
    Case 4
        MsgBox "Edit Canceled""
        GoTo ExitHere
    End Select
End Function
```

Again, a `Select Case` construct is used to handle the value returned by `ErrorRoutine()`. The function is stopped only when the value of `ErrorRoutine()` is 4. Here's the portion of `ErrorRoutine()` for handling Error 3186:

```
Case 3186
    ' Record is locked on another machine
    If TryCount < 10 Then
        For lngCounter = 0 To 15000
            'Empty loop for short delay...
            DoEvents
        Next lngCounter
        ErrorRoutine = 3
    Else
        ParseError Err, Error
        ErrorRoutine = 4
    End If
```

Tip

The code in this listing is identical to Listing 21.3. Because of the similarities between Error 3260 and Error 3186, they may be handled with the same logic. In fact, you can combine the `Case` routines for Error 3260 and Error 3186 into a single statement:

```
Case 3260, 3186:
```

Error 3188: Could not update; currently locked by another session on this machine

Error 3188 occurs when someone has more than one instance of a database open on the same machine and tries to lock the same record in both sessions. Error handling is simple for this error; it's included in the global error handler — `ErrorRoutine()` — in the `Chapter21.accdb` example database.

Tip

To keep this error from occurring altogether, try to keep users from starting more than one instance of your application. You can do this using the `FindWindow` API in your start-up routine. Check for a running instance of Access at start-up, and close the second instance if another is present.

The error handler called by both of these examples is really very simple. It merely reads the current error and uses a `Select Case` statement to decide what to do. The only errors I've included in this module — `modErrorHandlers` — relate to this chapter. You'll notice that the `ErrorRoutine` function has entries for Error 3186 and Error 3260. Each of these calls another subroutine, `ParseError`. `ParseError` (in module `modParseError`) accepts the error number and error message as arguments, and parses the user name and the machine name from Error 3260 and Error 3186. It doesn't matter which error has occurred because the parsing routine looks only for the `"user"` and `" on machine"` string values within the error message, so it's pretty generic. In fact, this same subroutine is called from both errors. You can make the default Access error message more descriptive, and you can also make use of the user ID and machine number within your error log (if you keep one). The code follows:

```
Public Sub ParseError(lngErr As Long, strError As String)
    Dim strUser As String
    Dim strMachine As String
    Dim lngUserStart As Long
    Dim lngMachineStart As Long
    Dim lngMachineEnd As Long
    lngUserStart = InStr(1, strError, "user") + 5
    lngMachineStart = _
        InStr(lngUserStart, strError, " on machine")
    lngMachineEnd = InStr(lngMachineStart, strError, ".")
    strUser = Mid$(strError, lngUserStart, _
        lngMachineStart - lngUserStart)
    strMachine = Mid$(strError, lngMachineStart + 12, _
        lngMachineEnd - (lngMachineStart + 12))
    MsgBox "The Record Could Not Be Locked " _
        & "Because It Is Locked On " _
        & strMachine & " By " & strUser
End Sub
```

Error 3197: Data has changed; operation stopped

Error 3197 can be one of the most confusing errors to an end user if it isn't captured through a VBA error handler. It usually occurs when optimistic locking is enabled in an application, but it may also occur in an environment containing mixed record-lock settings as well.

Here's an example: Mike starts an edit on his machine. During the course of the edit (Mike is a slow typist), Elizabeth starts and finishes an edit on the same record. This means that the underlying data that Mike is editing is no longer valid, so an error is flagged when he tries to save his changes. The resulting Access error message box is shown in Figure 21.8.

FIGURE 21.8

The Access error message for Error 3197

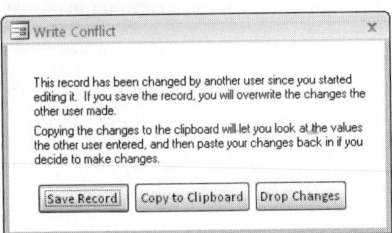

By default, Access gives the user (Mike, in this case) three choices:

- Save the record with the changes he has made.
- Copy the changes to the Clipboard.
- Abort the changes altogether.

The first and third options make sense, but the second option (Copy to Clipboard) has never seemed practical to me. Anyway, there are too many choices for the average user to make, especially when the options aren't self-explanatory.

The best option is to offer the user the option of saving his changes or terminating the edit, and then deliver the message in a format that's easy to understand. Besides providing a meaningful error message, you might want to offer to show your users the changes that have been made by refreshing the current form or opening a form based on the record that has been changed.

The actual error handling is straightforward. A record update throws an error the first time it's executed and your code traps the error. Then all you have to do is give the user the options you think best. If the user chooses to save the record, the update overwrites the other user's changes (unless another locking conflict occurs).

Listing 21.6 shows an example of this type of procedure. Like the previous examples, an edit is attempted, but if the edit fails, control is transferred to the error handler. However, in the previous examples the edit either failed or didn't fail after ten retries. `SaveChanges()` just gives the user a chance to overwrite or cancel. (Keep in mind that the message box asking the user whether to cancel or save is displayed by the `ErrorRoutine()` procedure.)

LISTING 21.6

Handling "Data Has Changed" Errors

```
Public Sub SaveChanges(ID As Long)
     Dim db As DAO.Database
     Dim rs As DAO.Recordset
```

```
    Dim sSQL As String
    Dim lngReturn As Long
On Error GoTo HandleError
    Set db = CurrentDb
    sSQL = "Select * from Employees where " _
        & "Employees![EmployeeID] = " & ID & ";"
    Set rs = db.OpenRecordset(sSQL)
    ' Set record locking to Pessimistic Locking
    rs.LockEdits = False
    rs.Edit   ' Try to lock the record for editing
    rs!LastName - "Smith"
    rs.Update
ExitHere:
    ' Exit The Procedure
    rs.Close
    Exit Sub
HandleError:
    'Notice that we're passing zero to ErrorRoutine.
    'This means not to attempt any retries:
    lngReturn = ErrorRoutine(0)
    Select Case lngReturn
      Case 3
          rs.Update
          MsgBox "Record Was Updated!"
      Case 4
          MsgBox "Edit Was Canceled!"
    End Select
    Resume ExitHere
End Sub
```

The portion of `ErrorRoutine()` for handling this error is shown here. Notice how the user is prompted for the action to be taken. The messaging in this routine is easier to understand than what you see in Figure 21.9, and the user's wishes are carried out in a more sophisticated manner than the default Access actions. Notice also that the option to copy the data to the Clipboard isn't provided because this routine assumes that the user wants to either save the record or abandon changes.

```
    Case 3197
        ' Offer the user a chance to cancel
        ' the edit or save the changes
        strMessage = "The record you are trying " _
            & "to save has been changed " _
            & "since your edit began" & vbCrLf & vbCrLf _
            & "Do you want to save it anyway?"
        lngReturn = MsgBox(strMessage, vbYesNo)
        Select Case lngReturn
            Case vbYes
```

```
            ErrorRoutine = 3
        Case vbNo
            ErrorRoutine = 4
    End Select
```

A function to handle lock errors

Many of the routines in the earlier code listings call an error-handling function named
ErrorRoutine(). Instead of each procedure having to trap and interpret every possible error,
many developers condense error handling as a single public function (such as ErrorRoutine),
and have the function trap and handle errors as they occur. Each procedure in the application is
responsible for trapping errors, but the errors are passed to ErrorRoutine for handling.
ErrorRoutine may notify the user, log the error, or simply ignore the error, depending on the
details of the error incident.

The ErrorRoutine function (shown in Listing 21.7) uses the Err object's Number property to
determine which locking error has occurred. It takes action based on the error number and the
TryCount parameter to appropriately handle record-locking problems. Most likely, you'll want to
modify each error number to suit your users and their environment.

As you'll see in Chapter 23, there is but a single Err object in any VBA project, such as a Microsoft
Access application. The Err object contains all the details of an error incident, and, because there
is only one Err object in the entire project, any routine (such as ErrorRoutine) can use the
information provided by the Err object.

ErrorRoutine accepts a single argument — TryCount — that instructs ErrorRoutine to
take specific actions depending on the value of TryCount. You saw this parameter passed to
ErrorRoutine in the previous sections.

LISTING 21.7

A Function to Handle Locking Errors

```
Public Function ErrorRoutine(TryCount As Long) As Integer
   Dim lngCounter As Long
   Dim lngReturn As Long
   Dim strMessage As String
   Select Case Err.Number
     Case 3021
          '3021-No Current Record.
          ' Let the error pass
     Case 3186
          '3186—Couldn't Save; currently
          'locked by user x on machine y:
          If TryCount < 10 Then
             For lngCounter = 0 To 15000
                'Empty loop for short delay...
```

```vb
          Next lngCounter
          ErrorRoutine = 3
        Else
          Call ParseError(Err, Error)
          ErrorRoutine = 4
        End If
    Case 3188
        '3188-Record is locked by another
        ' session on the same machine:
        MsgBox "The record could not be locked " _
            & "because it is locked on your machine"
    Case 3197
        '3197—Data has changed; Operation stopped.
        ' Offer the user a chance to cancel or save:
        strMessage = "The record you are trying " _
            & "to save has been changed " _
            & "since your edit began" & vbCrLf & vbCrLf _
            & "Do you want to save it anyway?"
        lngReturn = MsgBox(strMessage, vbYesNo)
        Select Case lngReturn
          Case vbYes
              ErrorRoutine = 3
          Case vbNo
              ErrorRoutine = 4
        End Select
    Case 3260
        '3260—Couldn't Update; currently
        'locked by user x on machine y:
        If TryCount < 10 Then
          For lngCounter = 0 To 15000
            'Empty loop for short delay...
          Next lngCounter
          ErrorRoutine = 3
        Else
          Call ParseError(Err, Error)
          ErrorRoutine = 4
        End If
    Case 3421
        '3421- Data type conversion error.
        strMessage = "This Add was canceled due " _
                    & "to a type conversion error"
        Call MsgBox(strMessage, vbOKOnly)
    Case Else
        strMessage = "The Error Number Was " & Err & " " & Error
        Call MsgBox(strMessage, vbInformation)
  End Select
End Function
```

Notice that `ErrorRoutine()` contains the error-handling segments for each of the errors discussed in the previous sections. `ErrorRoutine()` could be extended, of course, to include the `ParseError()` subroutine, error logging, and more extensive messaging, among other features.

Reducing Multiuser Errors with Unbound Forms

Everything in the previous discussion is relevant to any multiuser Access environment. However, when you use a *bound form* (a form with an attached recordset), you're more likely to encounter some of the negative situations mentioned. Bound forms are more prone to locking conflicts because all the fields in a bound form maintain "live" connections to the underlying data source. A bound form may lock the record in the underlying table as soon as the user begins changing data on a bound form, and doesn't release the lock until the edit is completed. Depending on the complexity of the data, and how quickly the user performs the update, the record lock may persist for several minutes or longer, leading to an increased chance of lock contention.

A common way to decrease the likelihood of encountering multiuser errors is to create and use unbound forms. Unbound forms have certain advantages and disadvantages, but they may be worth exploring if you want more control over your applications.

Unbound forms give you complete control over your user interface. All the updating, recordset navigation, editing, adding, and saving is executed by code, rather than by Access's default behavior. Record-locking errors are less frequent because the user has direct control over edits and updates, instead of relying on Access to do the dirty work.

Consider this scenario: Two users are sharing an Access application across a network. The database containing the tables is located on a file server on the network. The application uses a pessimistic locking strategy and the forms are directly bound to the underlying recordsets. Both users try to edit a particular record at the same time and — *bam!* — a locking error occurs. Why? Because when both users edit the record, only the *first* user gets to lock the record. The lock stays in effect until the record is updated in the recordset by the user who got there first. Meanwhile, the other user has to wait, and risk a lock contention error when saving the record.

However, when using unbound forms, editing a record on a form probably won't trigger record locks. There's nothing behind the form, so no recordset locks are established. When the user clicks the Save button, the application probably does a quick add or update to the recordset, only holding the lock for a fraction of a second. You're much less likely to hit a lock error with unbound forms.

You may, however, immediately see the disadvantages of this situation:

- Access does a lot for you when you bind forms to underlying recordsets. The less you let Access do, the more code you'll have to write. The more code you write, the more you have to maintain and update. The more you have to maintain, the less predictable your applications will become. It's a vicious cycle but one that may be necessary for complex applications.

- You can't use continuous forms when no recordset is attached to the form. Continuous forms can offer a very useful view of your data.

On the CD-ROM

The sample database for this chapter (Chapter21.accdb) includes a typical unbound Access form (shown in Figure 21.9). The form, named frmEmployees, works much like a bound form — you can navigate through all the records, and add, edit, and save data in the Employees table — but there is no data bound to this form. All the data-management work takes place in a collection of routines in the basUnboundMethods module.

In the following sections, I take you through each method and discuss how it works and how you can apply it to your own forms.

FIGURE 21.9

The unbound Employees form

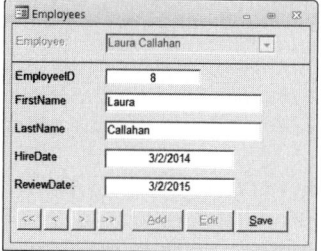

Creating an unbound form

Creating an unbound form doesn't take a lot of special skill — just some planning ahead of time and a few shortcuts. It's probably best to start by creating a bound form that looks and behaves as close to the finished product as possible. Why? Because all the form's controls are named by the fields they're bound to, controls keep the formatting set in the underlying tables, you don't have to set label captions, and so forth. The naming part is important, for reusability reasons that you'll discover as you populate controls with data.

After you've finished creating the look of the form, you move to the RecordSource property of the form and delete it. Tada! You now have an unbound form. Of course, it doesn't do anything, but it looks good.

Making an unbound form work

There are several events your form has to respond to, such as moving to a record, adding data, editing data, updating data, and so forth. To do this, I've created a separate routine that responds to each event. Each procedure accepts at least the name of the calling form and the recordset it's based on.

The Tag property

You tell the form what recordset you want to use by placing its name in the form's Tag property. The Tag property is unique in that it doesn't do anything. It's just a handy place to put some text that you intend to use in your VBA code. You can use the Tag property as a place to store information for later retrieval or to keep track of where you are in a process.

Here's a good example of what you can do with the Tag property: Suppose you want your application to have the ability to fill in each new record with data from the previous record. Using the Tag property, you can store the current record's values in each control's Tag property, and, upon moving to the next new record, fill in the form's controls with the values stored in the Tag. It's a whole lot easier than doing a lookup using a hidden field on a form and the Seek method on a clone of the form's recordset, which is an alternative I've seen some people use.

The Tag property was introduced way back in Access Version 2, but many developers don't know it exists or aren't sure what it's for. I encourage you to use this property often.

Opening the form

The first event you must respond to is the Open event of the form. When the Open event fires, two things need to be done to populate the unbound form:

- **Open the recordset filled with data displayed on the form.** You don't have to do this — you could just open a new recordset instance in each routine behind the form — but it's faster to just have a recordset open and waiting as the form opens.

- **Populate the form with data.** In fact, the form is populated with data from the very first record in the recordset. Again, you don't have to, but many times a user expects to see something on a form when it opens.

The Declarations section of the form contains two public variables, db (database) and rs (recordset). The form's Open event runs a very short procedure that sets the database and recordset variables to their proper values and calls the UnboundDisplay routine that loads the first record of the recordset into the form's fields:

```
Public db As DAO.Database
Public rs As DAO.Recordset
Private Sub Form_Open(Cancel As Integer)
    Dim iReturn As Integer
    Set db = CurrentDb
    Set rs = db.OpenRecordset("Employees")
    iReturn = UnboundDisplay(Me, rs)
End Sub
```

The real work begins in the UnboundDisplay routine. Like most of the unbound methods, this routine accepts the name of the form and the name of the open recordset as parameters. The key to making this practical is making your routines as reusable as possible — this is good practice anytime but especially in situations where you'll be doing the same type of action more than once.

For example, you shouldn't create routines that require a recordset named Employees, because the database may have unbound forms based on other tables that act the same way as the Employees form. UnboundDisplay is a reusable function. Because you created the form as a bound form first, the control names on the form should be the same as the field names in the recordset. And, because you have the recordset open, the names of the controls on your form are readily available. UnboundDisplay cycles through the recordset, setting the value of each form control equal to the value of its corresponding recordset field value.

The following listing shows the code for UnboundDisplay:

```
Function UnboundDisplay( _
    frm As Form, _
    frmRS As DAO.Recordset) As Integer
    Dim ctlName As String
    Dim lngReturn As Long
    Dim x As Integer
On Error GoTo HandleError
    ' Move to the first record in the table
    frmRS.MoveFirst
    ' Cycle through the recordset,
    ' setting thevalue of each control
    For x = 0 To frmRS.Fields.Count - 1
        ctlName = frmRS.Fields(x).Name
        frm.Controls(ctlName).Value = frmRS.Fields(x).Value
    Next x
Display_End:
    Exit Function
HandleError:
    ' If there's an error, switch to the error
    ' handling procedure:
    lngReturn = ErrorRoutine(0)
    GoTo Display_End
End Function
```

Navigating through records

A user can move through records on the Employee form in either of two ways:

- By using one of the navigation buttons I've created. (You can't use Access's navigation buttons on an unbound form.)
- By searching for a record using a combo box.

Using navigation buttons

The navigation buttons I've created are based on four routines, each of which work similarly. The UnboundMoveFirst and UnboundMoveLast routines accept the name of the form you're using and the open recordset as arguments. All they do is issue a MoveFirst or MoveLast method on the recordset variable to move to the desired location.

```
Function UnboundMoveFirst( -
    frm As Form, _
    frmRS As DAO.Recordset) As Integer
    Dim ctlName As String
    Dim x As Integer
    Dim lngReturn As Long
On Error GoTo HandleError
    frmRS.MoveFirst
    For x = 0 To frmRS.Fields.Count - 1
        ctlName = frmRS.Fields(x).Name
        frm.Controls(ctlName).Value = frmRS.Fields(x).Value
    Next x
ExitHere:
    Exit Function
HandleError:
    'Call ErrorRoutine, specifying zero retries:
    lngReturn = ErrorRoutine(0)
    GoTo ExitHere
End Function
```

Note

The code for UnboundMoveLast is not given here because it's nearly identical to UnboundMoveFirst. Simply use MoveLast instead of MoveFirst, and you've got UnboundMoveLast.

The UnboundMoveNext and UnboundMovePrevious procedures accept the name of the form and recordset, but they also include the employee ID of the currently displayed employee record. When you call the MoveNext or MovePrevious procedure, the function that was called sets the index of the recordset to the primary key and does a seek to place the cursor at the name of the employee whose record is displayed. If the record is found (If Not frmRS.NoMatch), you issue a MoveNext or MovePrevious method on the recordset to move to the desired record. The last step in the procedure is to update the controls on your form with data from the recordset.

Notice that the code in UnboundMoveNext fails if the MoveNext moves the record pointer off the end of the recordset. This issue will be trapped by the error handler, and UnboundMoveNext calls the ErrorRoutine procedure, passing 0 as its argument. The user sees a message (displayed from ErrorRoutine) that the operation failed.

Note

The code for UnboundMovePrevious is not given here because it is nearly identical to UnboundMoveNext. Simply use MovePrevious instead of MoveNext, and make a few other minor changes and you've got UnboundMovePrevious.

```
Function UnboundMoveNext( _
    frm As Form, _
    frmRS As DAO.Recordset,
    lValue As Long) As Integer
    Dim ctlName As String
    Dim x As Integer
```

```
        Dim lngReturn As Long
On Error GoTo MoveNext_Err
    'Move to the next employee record:
    frmRS.INDEX = "PrimaryKey"
    'Note: The Seek method works only on local tables:
    frmRS.Seek "=", lValue  'Search for displayed employee
    If Not frmRS.NoMatch Then
        ' Move to the next employee record
        frmRS.MoveNext
        For x = 0 To frmRS.Fields.Count - 1
            ctlName = frmRS.Fields(x).Name
            frm.Controls(ctlName).Value = _
                frmRS.Fields(x).Value
        Next x
    End If
MoveNext_End:
    Exit Function
MoveNext_Err:
    'Call ErrorRoutine, specifing zero retries:
    lngReturn = ErrorRoutine(0)
    GoTo MoveNext_End
End Function
```

Using a combo box

The second method for changing position within the form's recordset is with a combo box. cbo-Employee uses the employee's ID number, which is the bound column of the combo box. It's passed to the UnboundSearch function (shown here) as the variable lValue, which is called when the AfterUpdate event is triggered. UnboundSearch sets the recordset's index property to EmployeeID and then uses the Seek method to locate the employee chosen. If a match is found after using the Seek method, the now familiar looping routine is used to extract field values from the recordset and fill in the corresponding controls on the Employees form. The code is shown here:

```
Function UnboundSearch( _
    frm As Form, _
    frmRS As DAO.Recordset, _
    lValue As Long) As Integer
    Dim ctlName As String
    Dim x As Integer
    frmRS.Index = "PrimaryKey"
    'Note: The Seek method works only on local tables:
    frmRS.Seek "=", lValue
    If Not frmRS.NoMatch Then
        For x = 0 To frmRS.Fields.Count - 1
            ctlName = frmRS.Fields(x).Name
            frm.Controls(ctlName).Value = _
                frmRS.Fields(x).Value
        Next x
    End If
End Function
```

Editing data

The last action you need to provide for in your unbound form is editing. You must be able to add, remove, edit, and save data. The Employees form does all these things (except deletions, but that can be accomplished using the Delete method and the examples shown here). Although writing routines really isn't *that* involved, these routines are the reason that you created an unbound form in the first place. Because they don't take any action on the recordset until update time, your users shouldn't have trouble with locks.

When someone clicks on the Add button, a couple things happen:

- **The controls on the form are selectively enabled or disabled.** By default, this form is set to browse data, as evidenced by the disabled data-entry fields and disabled Save command button. When an add takes place, the data-entry fields and Save button are enabled, but everything else is disabled (to keep users from wandering until the add is successfully completed). When the user types information into form controls, he's really just typing the data into placeholders. No action has occurred in the recordset.

- **A value is set to indicate what kind of action is in progress.** To do this, the Save button's Tag property is set to Add. Later, this value will be retrieved and sent to the update routine.

When the Save button is clicked, its OnClick event runs the UnboundSave procedure, passing the procedure the value of the button's Tag property. Listing 21.8 shows the procedure.

LISTING 21.8

The UnboundSave Procedure

```
Function UnboundSave( _
     frm As Form, _
     frmRS As DAO.Recordset, _
     lValue As Long, _
     sAction As String) As Integer
     Dim ws As Workspace
     Dim ctlName As String
     Dim ctl As Control
     Dim x As Integer
On Error GoTo HandleError
     frmRS.LockEdits = False   ' Optimistic Locking
     Set ws = DBEngine.Workspaces(0)
     Select Case sAction
         Case "Add"
             ws.BeginTrans
             frmRS.AddNew
             For x = 0 To frmRS.Fields.Count - 1
                 ctlName = frmRS.Fields(x).Name
                 Set ctl = frm.Controls(ctlName)
```

```
            If ctl.Tag = "Key" Then 'Ignore key field
                'Do nothing...
            Else
                frmRS.Fields(ctlName).Value = ctl.Value
            End If
        Next x
    Case "Edit"
        frmRS.Index = "PrimaryKey"
        frmRS.Seek "=", lValue
        ws.BeginTrans
        frmRS.Edit
        For x = 0 To frmRS.Fields.Count - 1
            ctlName = frmRS(x).Name
            Set ctl = frm.Controls(ctlName)
            If ctl.Tag = "Key" Then
                'Do nothing...
            Else
                frmRS.Fields(ctlName).Value = ctl.Value
            End If
        Next x
    Case Else
        GoTo ExitHere
    End Select
    frmRS.Update
    ws.CommitTrans
ExitHere:
    Exit Function
HandleError:
    ws.Rollback
    GoTo ExitHere
End Function
```

Notice that every effort has been made to assure a successful update:

- Locking is set to optimistic locking (LockEdits = False).
- Transactions are used on the current workspace.
- The procedure uses a Select Case statement and the value passed from the Tag property to decide what action should be taken.

The update is essentially the reverse of the UpdateDisplay procedure, with a few exceptions:

- An AddNew (or Edit) method is invoked, and again you step through each field in the recordset's Fields collection, except this time you update values in the recordset instead of updating controls on the form.

- If you open the form and check the Tag property of the control EmployeeID, you'll see the string value Key. This lets the procedure know that this value should not be updated.

  Why? It's a counter — AutoNumber — and you can't update a counter. If you try, the routine will flag an error. After all the fields have been set, the update method is invoked. This is the only time a record-lock error can occur — this split second. If it does fail, which is unlikely, the procedure can roll back the transaction.

The process for editing a record is the same as the process for adding a record, except that the Tag property of the cmdSave command button is set to Edit, and the Seek method is used in the UnboundSave procedure to search for the record that has been edited. Once the match is found, the Edit method is invoked and the fields in the recordset are updated.

After the update is complete, the private form procedure EnableButtons is called (from the cmdSave button's OnClick event), and the appropriate fields are enabled/disabled.

Summary

Access is perfect for single-user database application development. It's also excellent in a multiuser environment, but there are more opportunities for things to go wrong in a multiuser environment. You have to do some careful planning before creating multiuser applications in order to assure their success. Consider network speed, number of users, type of application (data entry, decision support, point of sale, and so on), and update volume (high number of additions, high number of edits, high number of data selection) when planning and implementing a multiuser Access application. Only after extensive planning can you decide on the best approach for handling Access's record-locking behavior. You should decide which of the wide variety of options (retries and refresh rate, trapping errors, using bound or unbound forms, and so on) make the most sense for your users, and carefully apply those techniques to your applications.

Integrating Access with Other Applications

A s companies standardize their computer practices and software selec-tions, it's becoming more and more important to develop *total* solu-tions — in other words, solutions that integrate the many procedures of an organization. Usually, various business functions and processes are accomplished by using different software packages, such as Microsoft Word for document preparation, Microsoft Exchange Server and Microsoft Outlook for mailing and faxing, Microsoft PowerPoint for presentations, and Microsoft Excel for financial functions. If the organization for which you're developing has standardized on the Microsoft Office suite, you can leverage your knowledge of Visual Basic for Applications to enhance all these products.

Automation (formerly called *OLE Automation*) is a means by which an appli-cation can expose objects, each with its own methods and properties, that other applications can create instances of and control through code. Not all commercial applications support Automation, but more and more applica-tions are adopting Automation to replace the outdated Dynamic Data Exchange (DDE) interface. Consult with a specific application's vendor to find out whether it supports or plans to support Automation in the program.

Note

In this chapter the word *Automation* is capitalized to distinguish programmatic Automation from application automation (such as adding VBA code to a but-ton's Click event).

On the CD-ROM

This chapter uses a database named `Chapter22.accdb`. A Word template file, `Thanks.dotx`, is also included for use in this chapter. If you haven't already copied these files onto your computer from the CD, you need to do so now. Because this chapter relies on the use of VBA code, the Chapter 22 data-base includes the code and forms that are used by this chapter's examples.

Using Automation in Access

The Microsoft Office applications all support Automation. Using Automation, you create object references in your code that represent other applications (like Microsoft Word). By manipulating these objects (setting properties and calling methods), you control the referenced applications as though you were programming directly in them, which allows you to create seamless, tightly integrated applications.

Note

The macro security settings in the major Microsoft Office products (Word, Excel, and PowerPoint) may block access to their VBA projects to Automation servers such as Microsoft Access. When working with the examples in this chapter, you may need to adjust the settings in Microsoft Word's Trust Center to allow the Access Automation code to run against Word.

Understanding how Automation works

Each Automation-compliant application (such as Word or Excel) exposes an interface that enables the application to use Automation techniques to communicate with other applications. We never see the interface exposed by an application — it's only accessible by writing VBA code that attaches to the interface and uses the resources provided by the host (Word or Excel).

A good analogy for an Automation interface is the radio in your car. Most car radios feature controls that adjust the volume, station tuning, bass, treble, and other settings. Each of these controls is connected to the internal workings of the radio. You don't need to know anything about how radios work in order to rock out to your favorite tunes — you just need to know how to change the volume or tuner to a different station.

This is exactly how Automation works. An application (like Word) exposes an Automation interface. The code you write in Access defines *Automation objects* that connect to the interface, and you control Word by manipulating the properties and methods of the Automation objects. Applications that engage in Automation are often referred to as *servers* (Word, in this case) and *clients* (Access). The server provides the resources, and the client uses them.

Note

Automation is entirely a local process. You can't automate to an application on a remote computer. All the code and all the applications involved in an Automation scheme must run locally on the user's computer.

Perhaps the biggest challenge to developers using Automation is that the interface exposed by an Automation server is invisible. You only know it's there because VBA's IntelliSense reveals various methods to you. Even then, just knowing that the interface is there and knowing the names of the interface objects supported by the Automation server isn't necessarily enough. You need to know something about how the Automation server works, so that you can use the methods appropriately.

Knowing which of the exposed objects to use for a particular task can be daunting. Word 2010, for example, exposes more than 340 different objects in its Automation interface. Generally speaking, though, many highly productive tasks can be performed using only a fraction of the objects exposed in an application's Automation interface.

Creating Automation references

Applications supporting Automation provide information about their exposed objects in an *object library*. The object library contains information about an application's properties, methods, and classes. Each object in an application's Automation interface supports some aspect of the application's features. For example, Word's `Selection` object represents a the current selection in a window or pane, while the `Bookmarks` collection provides handles to all the bookmarks within a document.

When writing Automation code, you use *object variables* to represent the objects exposed by the Automation server's interface. Within your VBA code, you treat the object variable as if it were a literal instance of the Automation server. In the "Creating an instance of a Word object" section, later in this chapter, you'll see code that declares an object variable named `WordObj`. Once this variable has been connected to Microsoft Word, `WordObj` acts as if it *were* Microsoft Word. In other words, `WordObj` acts as a proxy for Microsoft Word within your code. In most cases, you begin by referencing the server application's object library. Referencing the library makes the exposed Automation interface accessible to your application. As you'll soon see, referencing an object library eases the process of writing VBA code against the interface. The reference also makes it possible to view the Automation interface in the VBA Object Browser.

Adding an object library reference is fairly easy. From the VBA code editor, choose Tools ⇨ References to open the References dialog box (see Figure 22.1). Each item in the References dialog represents an object library that is installed on the local computer (not all object libraries support Automation, however).

In Figure 22.1 notice that each item in the references list includes a checkbox. The items at the top of the list with filled check boxes (like Microsoft ActiveX Data Objects) are already referenced by the current application. In fact, Access requires references to several object libraries for its normal operation.

Note

Object libraries are routinely added to the files on a computer when the Automation server is installed. In fact, an Automation server's object library is almost certainly used by the server application in its normal operation. The objects, properties, and methods you use when automating Microsoft Word are exactly the same objects, properties, and methods that Word uses every time you work with it.

Use the scrollbar at the right side of the references list to locate the desired object library, and click its check box to add it as a reference to the current application.

Not all object libraries have obvious names. Sometimes the library name in the references list is not what you expect. Often a likely-looking library name turns out to be something entirely different. To further complicate things, some applications support more than one object library. In these cases, it is very helpful to have a good example to follow or, at least, to have good documenmation of an application's object library.

FIGURE 22.1

Early binding by setting references is the most efficient way to perform Automation.

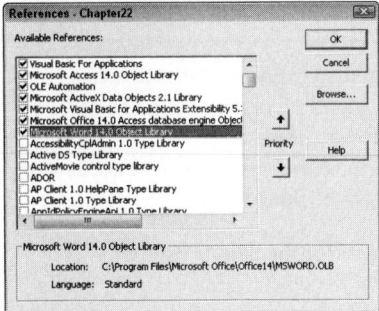

Note

Just because a library shows up in the list of References doesn't mean that it can be automated from Access (or at all).

Fortunately, Microsoft has done an outstanding job of documenting the object libraries supported by the Microsoft Office suite, and Automation example code is available from many sources such as books, magazines, and the Internet.

Binding your VBA object variables to objects in the Automation interface

The process of connecting your VBA object variables to objects exposed in an application's Automation interface is called *binding*. An Automation server's resources can't be used until its interface is bound to object variables in a client application.

The VBA programming language supports early and late binding:

- **Early binding** means you write VBA code that specifies the Automation server and directly bind object variables to the server's interface.

- **Late binding** means that the Automation server is not specified until runtime, and object variables are not bound to the server's interface until the VBA code executes on the user's desktop.

Early-binding an object

When you reference an object library, you're performing early binding. Automation code executes more quickly when early binding is used. Early binding means that, as Access starts up and the VBA project is loaded into memory, Windows provides a connection between Access and the Automation server. The connection between Access and the server is made before the user begins using the features exposed by the Automation server.

Referencing an object library means that you can use early binding to attach to objects exposed by the library. Once the object library is referenced, the VBA code editor uses IntelliSense — particularly Auto List Members and Auto Quick Info — to help you write effective code against the object library's contents.

For example, assume you've referenced the Microsoft Word libary, and the following statements appear in a VBA procedure:

```
Dim WordObj As Word.Application
Set WordObj - New Word.Application
```

The first statement declares an object variable (WordObj) as a Word.Application object type. Word refers to the referenced object library, and Application is one of the exposed object classes within the library.

The second statement instantiates the object variable. As this statement executes, VBA builds an instance of the Word.Application object in the computer's memory; this is the application's proxy, discussed in the "Creating Automation References" section, earlier in this chapter. Once the object instantiation is complete, VBA code is able to direct the Application object to perform work on behalf of the VBA project.

This process is called *early binding* because the Word.Application object is explicitly declared and instantiated. The object type is known before the application is even started. In the next section, you'll read about late binding, where the type of object is not known until the code actually executes.

Caution

For this chapter, you need to make sure that several object libraries are referenced. You may not initially have all four of the following references checked:

```
Microsoft DAO Object Library
Microsoft ActiveX Data Objects
Microsoft Word Object Library
Microsoft Office Object Library
```

If these libraries aren't active (or, visible at the top of the list), find them in the selection list box by scrolling to them, and verify that they're checked in the references list.

After you reference an Automation object library, you explicitly declare object variables from the referenced library. The VBA IntelliSense help feature displays the objects contained within the library as you type, as shown in Figure 22.2. After you select an object and enter a period, IntelliSense shows you the available classes within the object (see Figure 22.3).

FIGURE 22.2

IntelliSense provides insight into referenced object libraries.

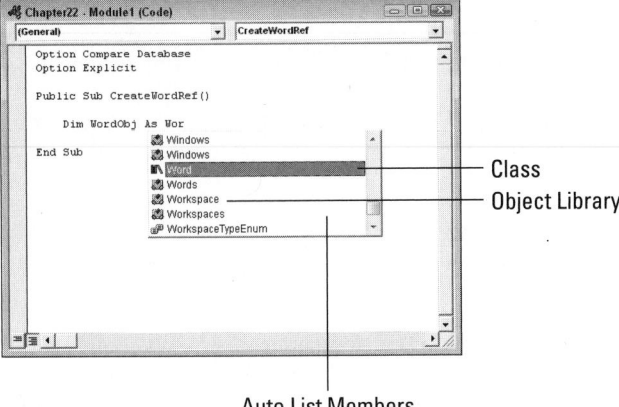

Auto List Members

FIGURE 22.3

The VBA IntelliSense feature makes it easy to use Automation servers.

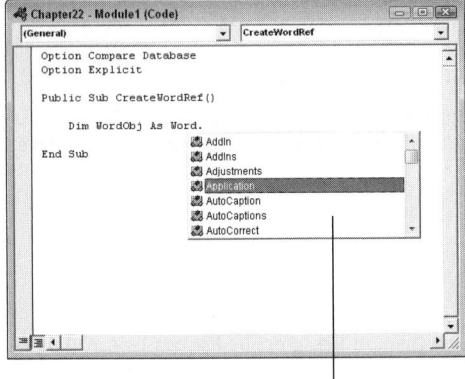

Auto List Members for an object

Late-binding an object

If you don't explicitly reference an object library by using the References dialog box, you can set an object's reference in code by first declaring a variable as an object and then using the Set command to bind the object variable to an Automation reference. This process is known as *late binding*.

For example, the following statements late-bind an object variable to the Microsoft Word Application object:

```
Dim WordObj As Object
Set WordObj = CreateObject("Word.Application")
```

Tip

If you create an object for an application that isn't referenced, an IntelliSense drop-down, such as the ones shown in Figures 22.2 and 22.3, will not appear.

Figure 22.2 shows the IntelliSense drop-down that appears immediately after you type New in the Dim statement. At this point, you can select one of the Application object name types displayed (such as Word) or enter a the name of a referenced object library.

In Figure 22.2, IntelliSense shows Word, which is a library, as indicated by the books icon in the Auto List Members list. This icon distinguishes a library object from a simple class object, such as VBProject. Object libraries contain classes, whereas simple classes contain properties, methods, and events. The class objects you see in Figure 22.2 (VBComponent, VBComponents, VBProject, and so on) are included within other libraries referenced by the Chapter22. accdb application.

Figure 22.3 shows the IntelliSense drop-down list that appears when you type a period after Word. This drop-down list displays all the objects exposed in the Word object libary. In this case, clicking the Application object completes the VBA statement.

Creating an instance of an Automation object

To perform an Automation operation, the operating system needs to start the application — if it isn't already started — and obtain a reference, or *handle*, to it. (Most Automation servers, like Word, expose an Application object.) The Application object exists at the top of the object library's object hierarchy and often contains many subordinate objects, as well.

Creating a new instance with New

Once an object variable is declared, you create an instance of the object with the New keyword. In the examples shown in Figures 22.2 and 22.3, the variable WordObj is set to a new instance of Word's Application object.

Caution

If you don't create a reference to the Automation server with the References dialog box, VBA doesn't recognize the variable's object type and generates an error on compile.

Every time you create an instance of an Automation server with the New keyword, a new instance of the application is started. If you don't want to start a new instance of the application, use the GetObject function (see the "Getting an existing object instance" section, later in this chapter).

Note

Not all Automation servers support the New keyword. Consult the specific Automation server's documentation to determine whether it supports the New keyword. If the New keyword is not supported, you must use the CreateObject function, which is discussed in the next section, to create an instance of the Automation server.

Creating a new instance with CreateObject

In addition to creating an instance of an object library by using the New keyword, you can create an instance of an object library by using the CreateObject function. You use the CreateObject function to create instances of object libraries that do not support the New keyword. To use the CreateObject function, first declare a variable of the type that you want to create. Then use the Set statement in conjunction with the CreateObject function to set the variable to a new instance of the object library.

Late binding is often used with Automation servers that don't support early binding, or when the users seldom work with the Automation server. In the latter case, a user may be better off with late binding because his computer spends the time setting up and binding to an Automation server only when it's needed. It's also a good idea if the application will be used by a number of users who may not all have the same version of the Automation server on their computers.

Here's a simple example of late-binding to Microsoft Outlook and displaying the Outlook calendar.

```
Public Sub DisplayOutlookCalendar()
    Dim ObjOutlook As Object
    Dim ObjNamespace As Object
On Error Resume Next
    'Late binding:
    Set ObjOutlook = GetObject(, "Outlook.Application")
    If Err.Number = 429 Then
        'Outlook is not running on this
        'computer, so start a new instance:
        Set ObjOutlook = CreateObject("Outlook.application")
    End If
    On Error GoTo 0  'Disable error trapping
    Set ObjNamespace = ObjOutlook.GetNamespace("MAPI")
    If ObjOutlook.ActiveExplorer Is Nothing Then
        ObjOutlook.Explorers.Add _
            (ObjNamespace.GetDefaultFolder(9), 0).Activate
    Else
        Set ObjOutlook.ActiveExplorer.CurrentFolder = _
            ObjNamespace.GetDefaultFolder(9)
        ObjOutlook.ActiveExplorer.Display
    End If
    Set ObjNamespace = Nothing
    Set ObjOutlook = Nothing
End Sub
```

This code runs rather slowly on most computers. The slow performance is not the result of late binding. Instead, it's because Outlook is a pretty big application and requires a lot of CPU cycles and memory to get up and running.

One very big difference between early and late binding is that late binding doesn't require an object library reference. When the code in this example runs, the VBA engine in Access passes the request for the `"Outlook.Application"` object to Windows, and Windows dynamically creates an instance of Outlook and provides the connection to Access.

Notice the quotes around `"Outlook.Application"`. This is not an object reference. Instead, `"Outlook.Application"` is the name of an Automation server as it exists in the Windows registry. Windows looks up `"Outlook.Application"` in the registry, finds the path to the Outlook executable, and performs the work of starting Outlook and connecting Outlook to Access.

An error is thrown if Outlook is not installed on the user's computer. In this case, no reference to Outlook exists in the system registry, and Windows can't resolve the reference to `"Outlook. Application"`.

Note

Did you notice that the code in this example does not specify a particular version of Outlook? One of the best features of Automation is that Windows uses whichever version of the Automation server is installed on the user's computer. The Automation server reference in the system registry point to the latest version of the server, without regard to the server's version. The only time you may need to specify a version is when the Automation code you've written uses features only available in a particular version of the server. To do this, you might use "Outlook.Application.10" or "Outlook.Application.12." Otherwise, keep references to Automation servers as generic as possible and let Windows take care of the details.

Getting an existing object instance

Using the `New` keyword or the `CreateObject` function creates a new instance of the Automation server (see "Creating an instance of an Automation object" section, earlier in this chapter). If you don't want a new instance of the server created each time you create an object, use the `GetObject` function. The format of the `GetObject` function is as follows:

```
Set objectvariable = GetObject([pathname][, class])
```

In this statement, *pathname* refers to a file (like a Word document) that is associated with an Automation server (in this case, Microsoft Word). For example, the following statement creates an instance of Word and loads a Word document named `MyDoc.doc` into Word:

```
Dim ObjWord As Object
Set ObjWord = GetObject("C:\MyDoc.doc", )
```

Notice that you don't have to provide a class name (`"Word.Application"`) because Windows is able to resolve the file's extension (`.doc`) to Microsoft Word. You'd need to provide the class name if there were more than one application on the user's computer that might be mapped to the file's extension.

The *pathname* parameter is optional. To use the *pathname* parameter, you specify a full path and filename to an existing file for use with the Automation Server.

Note

Have you noticed that `GetObject` is an example of late binding? Access doesn't care which application is going to open the file passed as the pathname argument, and Windows does all the work, in any case.

Using `GetObject` to instantiate an Automation server is a convenient way to open the server on a particular file. However, this statement will fail if the file specified by the pathname argument doesn't exist, or if the filename extension is omitted or not mapped to an application on the user's computer.

The class argument is optional, but it's used to clarify to Windows exactly which Automation server to instantiate and open. Consider a file such as `MyFile.txt`. Although Notepad is the default text editor on most computers, you might want to specify Word as the Automation server:

```
Dim ObjWord As Object
Set ObjWord = GetObject("C:\MyText.txt", "Word.Application")
```

Using late binding through the `GetObject` function is a convenient way to open Automation servers on arbitrary files. Consider an Access application that contains a list of different files, including Word and Excel file, images in `.jpg` and `.tiff` format, and `.mpg` and `.avi` video clips. Writing Automation code to work with all these file types could be a daunting task, but writing a few lines of code using late binding greatly simplifies the task.

Note

The specified document is opened in the server application. Even if you omit the parameter, you must still include the comma (,).

The `class` parameter is the same parameter that's used with the `CreateObject` function. See Table 22.1 for a list of some class arguments used in Microsoft Office.

TABLE 22.1

Class Arguments for Common Office Components

Component	Class Argument	Object Returned
Access	`Access.Application`	Microsoft Access `Application` object
Excel	`Excel.Application`	Microsoft Excel `Application` object
Excel	`Excel.Sheet`	Microsoft Excel `Workbook` object
Excel	`Excel.Chart`	Microsoft Excel `Chart` object
Word	`Word.Application`	Microsoft Word `Application` object
Word	`Word.Document`	Microsoft Word `Document` object

For example, to work with an existing instance of Microsoft Word, but not a specific Word document, you can use the following code:

```
Dim WordObj as Word.Application
Set WordObj = GetObject(, "Word.Application")
```

To get an instance of an existing Word document called `MyDoc.Docx`, on your `C:` drive, you can use the following code:

```
Dim WordObj as Word.Application
Set WordObj = GetObject("C:\MyDoc.Docx", "Word.Application")
```

Of course, this code is placed in a function or sub that you add to a code module.

Caution

The behavior of `GetObject` might have unexpected side effects. If, for example, Microsoft Word is already open on the user's computer, `GetObject` returns a handle to the running instance of Word, even if the user is working with Word at the same time that the Automation code runs. Obviously, this might cause confusion to the user as Word loads a new document and begins making changes to the document with no input from the user.

Working with Automation objects

After you have a valid instance of an Automation server, you manipulate the object as if you were working directly with the server application in Windows.

For example, when developing directly in Word, you can use the following code to change the directory that Word uses when opening an existing file:

```
Dim WordObj As Word.Application
Set WordObj = New Word.Application
WordObj.ChangeFileOpenDirectory "C:\My Documents\"
```

Note

Consult the development help for the Automation server (Word, Excel, and so on) for specific information on the objects, properties, and methods available.

Tip

When using Automation, avoid setting properties or calling methods that cause the Automation server to ask for input from the user via a dialog box. When a dialog box is displayed, the Automation code stops executing until the dialog box is closed. If the server application is minimized or behind other windows, the user might not even be aware that she needs to provide input and, therefore, might assume that the application is locked up.

Closing an instance of an Automation object

Most Automation object variables are closed when the variable goes out of scope. However, allowing an object to close itself doesn't necessarily free up all resources that are used by the object. In fact, it's possible that the object will continue to exist even after Access is shut down. Whenever possible, explicitly close the instance of the Automation object and set it to `Nothing`.

The best way to close an instance of an Automation object is to combine the two techniques, like this:

```
WordObj.Quit
Set WordObj = Nothing
```

`Nothing` is a value reserved for object variables and signals VBA that you're truly done with the variable. The VBA engine will do its best to remove all traces of the object variable from memory, reducing the chances of "memory leaks," which are so common to applications using Automation.

Looking at an Automation Example Using Word

Perhaps the most common Office application that is used for Automation from a database application like Access is Microsoft Word. Using Automation with Word, you can create documents containing information from Access databases. The following section demonstrates an example of merging information from an Access database with a Word document.

Ordinarily, you create a merge document in Word and bring field contents in from the records of an Access database. This method relies on using Word's `Bookmark` objects, which are replaced by the contents of Access database fields, and requires that you perform this action in Word — thus. limiting the scope and capability of the function.

The following example uses the Orders form, which calls a module named `WordIntegration`. The `WordIntegration` module contains a function named `MergetoWord()`, which uses the Word `Thanks.dotx` template file.

Note
When you try to run this example, make sure that the path for the template in the VBA code is the actual path in which the `Thanks.dotx` template file resides. This path may vary from computer to computer.

The items that are discussed in this Word Automation example include the following:

- Creating an instance of a Word object
- Making the instance of Word visible
- Creating a new document based on an existing template
- Using bookmarks to insert data

- Activating the instance of Word
- Moving the cursor in Word
- Closing the instance of the Word object without closing Word

This example prints a thank-you letter for an order based on bookmarks in the thank-you letter template (`Thanks.dotx`). Figure 22.4 shows the data for customers, Figure 22.5 shows the data entry form for orders, Figure 22.6 shows the `Thanks.dotx` template, and Figure 22.7 shows a completed merge letter.

Note

The example in this section does not use a built-in Word template. None of the Word templates appear to include bookmarks, and this example's code depends on carefully placed bookmarks in a template. Also, in the interest of keeping the example simple, this example uses a much smaller set of contacts and orders than is used in Collectible Mini Cars. However, the example is easily adapted to work with the Collectible Mini Cars customers and sales tables.

FIGURE 22.4

Customer data used in the following Automation example is entered on the Customers form.

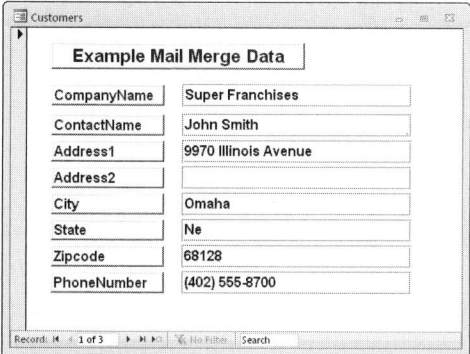

FIGURE 22.5

Each customer can have an unlimited number of orders. Thank-you letters are printed from the Orders form.

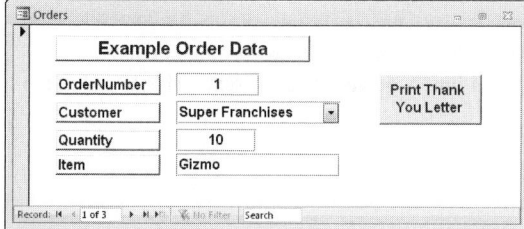

The bookmarks in Figure 22.6 are shown as grayed "I" icons on the Word document's surface. The bookmarks are normally not visible, but you can make them visible by using the File tab in the upper-left corner of the main Word window, choosing Options in the Backstage, and then selecting the Advanced tab. On the Advanced Options screen, make sure the Show Bookmarks check box is selected in the Show Document Content area. The bookmark names won't be visible — only the bookmark holders (locations) will be visible, as shown in Figure 22.6.

FIGURE 22.6

The `Thanks.dotx` template contains bookmarks where the merged data is to be inserted.

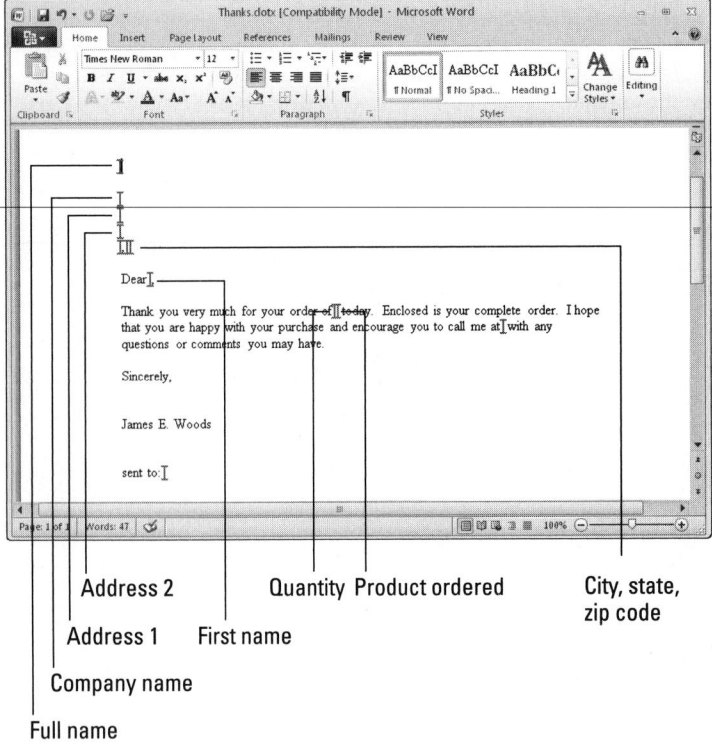

Full name

Company name

Address 1   First name

Address 2   Quantity Product ordered   City, state, zip code

Caution

If you click the Print Thank-You Letter button in Access while Word is open with an existing document that lacks the bookmark names specified in the code, the fields will simply be added to the text inside Word at the point where the cursor is currently sitting.

FIGURE 22.7

After a successful merge, all bookmarks have been replaced with their respective data.

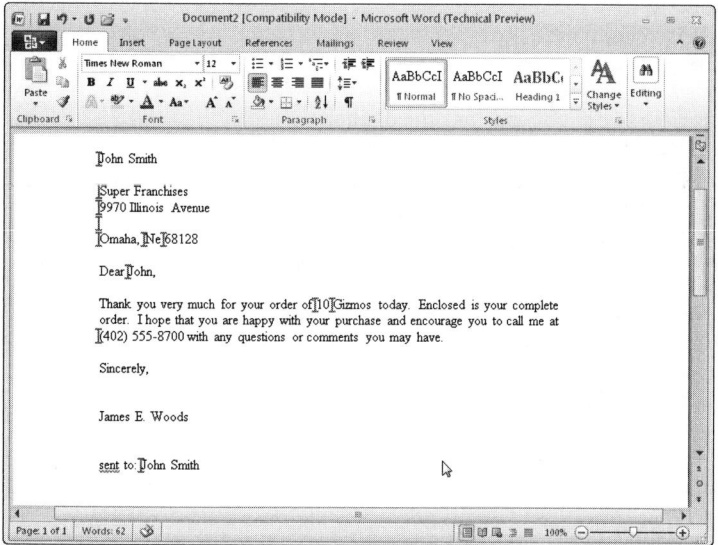

When the user clicks the Print Thank-You Letter button on the Orders form, Word generates a thank-you letter with all the pertinent information. The following code shows the `MergetoWord` function in its entirety so you can see in-depth how it works.

```
Public Sub MergeToWord()
    ' This method creates a new Word
    ' document using Automation.
On Error Resume Next
    Dim rsCust As New ADODB.Recordset
    Dim sSQL As String
    Dim WordObj As Word.Application
    Dim iTemp As Integer
    sSQL = "SELECT * FROM Customers " _
        & "WHERE CustomerNumber = " _
        & Forms!Orders![CustomerNumber]
    rsCust.Open sSQL, CurrentProject.Connection
    If rsCust.EOF Then
        MsgBox "Invalid customer", vbOKOnly
        Exit Function
    End If
    DoCmd.Hourglass True
    'Try to get a running instance of Word:
    Set WordObj = GetObject(, "Word.Application")
    If Err.Number <> 0 Then
```

```
         'An error is thrown if Word is not running,
         'so use CreateObject to start up Word:
         Set WordObj = CreateObject("Word.Application")
   End If
      'Make sure the user can see Word:
      WordObj.Visible = True
      'Warning:
      'Specify the correct drive and path to the
      'file named Thanks.dotx in the statement below:
      WordObj.Documents.Add _
         Template:="C:\Thanks.dotx", NewTemplate:=False
      With WordObj.Selection
         .GoTo what:=wdGoToBookmark, Name:="FullName"
         .TypeText rsCust![ContactName]
         .GoTo what:=wdGoToBookmark, Name:="CompanyName"
         .TypeText rsCust![CompanyName]
         .GoTo what:=wdGoToBookmark, Name:="Address1"
         .TypeText rsCust![Address1]
         .GoTo what:=wdGoToBookmark, Name:="Address2"
         If IsNull(rsCust![Address2]) Then
            .TypeText ""
         Else
            .TypeText rsCust![Address2]
         End If
         .GoTo what:=wdGoToBookmark, Name:="City"
         .TypeText rsCust![City]
         .GoTo what:=wdGoToBookmark, Name:="State"
         .TypeText rsCust![State]
         .GoTo what:=wdGoToBookmark, Name:="Zipcode"
         .TypeText rsCust![Zipcode]
         .GoTo what:=wdGoToBookmark, Name:="PhoneNumber"
         .TypeText rsCust![PhoneNumber]
         .GoTo what:=wdGoToBookmark, Name:="NumOrdered"
         .TypeText Forms!Orders![Quantity]
         .GoTo what:=wdGoToBookmark, Name:="ProductOrdered"
         If Forms!Orders![Quantity] > 1 Then
            WordObj.Selection.TypeText Forms!Orders![Item] & "s"
         Else
            WordObj.Selection.TypeText Forms!Orders![Item]
         End If
         .GoTo what:=wdGoToBookmark, Name:="FName"
         iTemp = InStr(rsCust![ContactName], " ")
         If iTemp > 0 Then
            .TypeText Left$(rsCust![ContactName], iTemp - 1)
         End If
         .GoTo what:=wdGoToBookmark, Name:="LetterName"
         .TypeText rsCust![ContactName]
         DoEvents
         WordObj.Activate
```

```
            .MoveUp wdLine, 6
        End With
        'Set the Word object to Nothing to free resources:
        Set WordObj = Nothing
        DoCmd.Hourglass False
    End Sub
```

The MergeToWord function uses the With construct to reduce the amount of code used to reference the object variable. All the property and method references within the body of the With... End With construct refer to the WordObj.Selection object. The WordObj object is set to Nothing at the end of the subroutine to remove the Word Automation server from memory.

Creating an instance of a Word object

The first step in using Automation is to create an instance of an object. The sample creates an object instance with the following code:

```
On Error Resume Next
...
Set WordObj = GetObject(, "Word.Application")
If Err.Number <> 0 Then
  Set WordObj = CreateObject("Word.Application")
End If
```

Obviously, you don't want a new instance of Word created every time a thank-you letter is generated, so some special coding is required. This code snippet first attempts to create an instance by using an active instance (a running copy) of Word. If Word is not a running application, an error is generated. Because this function has On Error Resume Next for error trapping, the code doesn't fail; instead, it proceeds to the next statement. If an error is detected (the Err.Number is not equal to 0), an instance is created by using CreateObject.

Cross-Reference
For information on handling errors, turn to Chapter 23.

Making the instance of Word visible

New instances of Word created with Automation code enables your application to exploit features of Word without the user realizing that Word is running. In this case, however, you want to let the user edit the merged letter, so Word needs to be made visible by setting the object's Visible property to True:

```
WordObj.Visible = True
```

Caution
If you don't set the object instance's Visible property to True, you may create hidden copies of Word that use system resources and never shut down. A hidden copy of Word doesn't show up in the Task tray or in the Task Switcher.

Creating a new document based on an existing template

After Word is running, a blank document is created. The following code creates a new document by using the `Thanks.dotx` template:

```
WordObj.Documents.Add _
    Template:="C:\Thanks.dotx", NewTemplate:=False
```

Note

The path must be set correctly in order to find the `Thanks.dotx` template on your computer.

The `Thanks.dotx` template contains bookmarks (refer to Figure 22.6) indicating where to insert data into the new Word document. To create a bookmark in Word:

1. Highlight the text that you want to make a bookmark.
2. In the Link group on Word's Insert ribbon, select the Bookmark command.
3. Enter the bookmark name.
4. Click Add.

Inserting data

The code uses the `Selection` object's `GoTo` method to move to bookmarks in the Word document. After moving to the bookmark, the text contained within the bookmark is selected. By inserting text (with Automation or by manually typing directly into the document), the code replaces the bookmark text. Use the `TypeText` method of the `Selection` object to insert text:

```
WordObj.Selection.Goto what:=wdGoToBookmark, Name:="FullName"
WordObj.Selection.TypeText rsCust![ContactName]
```

Note

You can't pass `Null` to the `TypeText` method. If the value may possibly be `Null`, you need to check ahead and make allowances. The preceding sample code checks the `Address2` field for a `Null` value and acts accordingly. If you don't pass text to replace the bookmark — even just a zero-length string (`" "`) — the bookmark text remains in the document. If you're okay with putting a zero-length string into the letter, you can always use the `Nz` function.

Activating the instance of Word

To enable the user to enter data in the new document, you must activate the Word application. If you don't make Word the active application, the user has to manually switch to Word from Access. Activate Word with the following statement:

```
WordObj.Activate
```

Tip

Depending on the processing that's occurring at the time, Access may take the focus back from Word. You can help to eliminate this annoyance by preceding the `Activate` method with a `DoEvents` statement. Note, however, that this strategy doesn't always work.

Moving the cursor in Word

You can move the cursor in Word by using the `MoveUp` method of the `Selection` object. For example, the following statement moves the cursor up six lines in the document:

```
WordObj.Selection.MoveUp wdLine, 6
```

Discarding the Word object instance

To release resources that are taken by an instance of an Automation object, you should always discard the instance. In this example, the following code is used to discard the object instance and remove it from memory:

```
Set WordObj = Nothing
```

This code removes the object instance but not the instance of Word as a running application. In this example, the user needs access to the new document, so closing Word would defeat the purpose of this function. You can, however, automatically print the document and then close Word. If you do this, you may even choose not to make Word visible during this process. To close Word without saving the changes, use the `Quit` method of the `Application` object, as follows:

```
WordObj.Quit SaveChanges:= wdDoNotSaveChanges
```

Inserting pictures by using bookmarks

You can perform other operations with bookmarks. Basically, anything that you can do within Word you can do by using Automation. The following code locates a bookmark that marks where a picture is to be placed and then inserts a `.bmp` file from disk. You can use the following code to insert scanned signatures into letters:

```
WordObj.Selection.Goto What:=wdGoToBookmark, Name:="Picture"
WordObj.ChangeFileOpenDirectory "D:\GRAPHICS\"
WordObj.ActiveDocument.Shapes.AddPicture _
 Anchor:=Selection.Range, _
 FileName:="D:\GRAPHICS\PICTURE.BMP", LinkToFile:=False,
 SaveWithDocument:=True
```

A brief word about named arguments

You likely noticed that the code example in the "Inserting pictures by using bookmarks" section uses some funny-looking arguments. For example:

```
WordObj.Selection.Goto What:=wdGoToBookmark, Name:="Picture"
```

This statement includes two named arguments (What and Name), a somewhat advanced VBA programming concept.

The named arguments in this statement are included to make it easy to understand the purpose of the statement. A named argument is comprised of the argument name (What or Name), followed by a colon and equal sign (:=), and then the value assigned to the argument.

Named arguments are most useful in cases where a procedure includes a lot of optional arguments and you aren't using all the optional arguments. When using named arguments, you don't have to use "placeholder" commas in the procedure call's argument list. For instance, the Selection object's GoTo method has four optional arguments, but the code example uses only two of those arguments. Using named arguments simplifies writing code that uses the GoTo method.

Using Office's macro recorder

Using Automation is not a difficult process when you understand the fundamentals. Often, the toughest part of using Automation is knowing the proper objects, properties, and methods to use. Although the online help for Automation servers such as Word and Excel can be useful, the easiest way to quickly create Automation code for Office applications like Word is to use Word's macro recorder.

Most Office applications have a macro recorder located on Word's Developer ribbon tab (see Figure 22.8). When activated, the macro recorder records all user actions, such as menu selections and button clicks, and creates VBA code from them.

FIGURE 22.8

The Word macro recorder is a powerful tool to help you create Automation code.

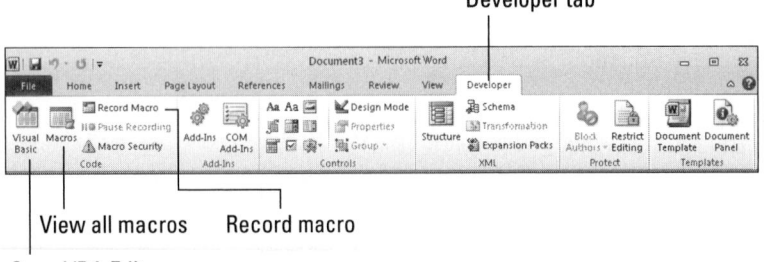

Tip

If you don't see the Developer tab in Microsoft Word, open Word Options from the Microsoft Office Button, click Word Options, and select the Customize Ribbon tab. On the right side of the Customize Ribbon dialog box, make sure the Developer check box is selected in the Main Tabs list.

After selecting Record Macro from the Developer ribbon's Code group, you must give your new macro a name (see Figure 22.9). In addition to a name, you can assign the macro to a button or keyboard combination and select the template (.dotm) file in which to store the macro.

After you enter a macro name and click OK, the macro recorder begins recording events. The Record Macro button (on the Developer ribbon tab) changes to Stop Recording while you are recording a macro. The arrow changes to an open pointer attached to a cassette, as shown in Figure 22.10. Stop recording events by clicking the Stop Recording button (the button with a square next to it). To pause recording events, click the Pause Recording button.

FIGURE 22.9

Enter a macro name and click OK to begin recording the macro. In this example, the macro is named MyMacro.

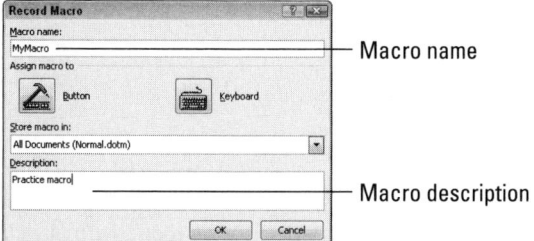

Macro name

Macro description

FIGURE 22.10

The Macro Recorder records all events until you click the Stop Recording button.

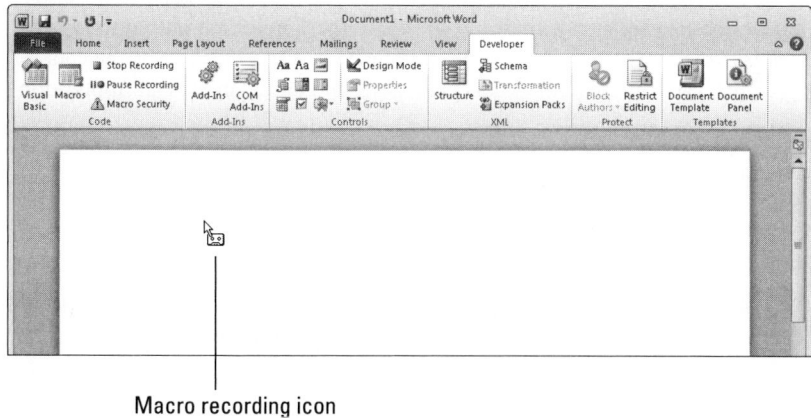

Macro recording icon

After you finish recording a macro, you can view the VBA code created by the macro recorder. To view the macro code, click the Macros button on the ribbon to display a list of all saved macros and select the macro that you recorded. Click the Edit button to display the VBA editor with the macro's code. Figure 22.11 shows the VBA editor with a macro that recorded the creation of a new document using the Normal template. The macro includes inserting a picture using the Picture from File command in the Insert ribbon's Illustrations group.

The VBA code recorded by Word's macro recorder

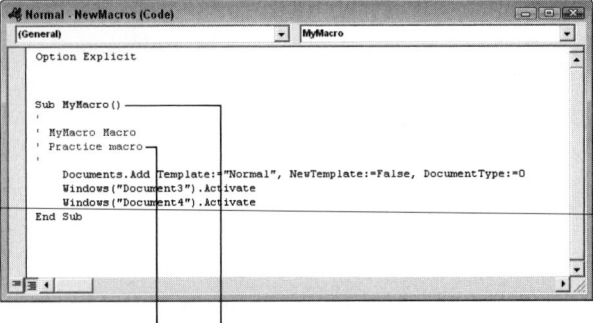

Macro description   Macro name

Most recorded Word macros make copious use of the Application object. The Application object is topmost in the object hierarchy exposed by Word. Even though the Application object may not be explicitly included in the VBA statements created by the macro recorder, it's the root of virtually all objects referenced by the macro. For example, the preceding macro uses the following code to create a new document:

```
Documents.Add Template:="Normal", _
   NewTemplate:= False, DocumentType:=0
```

Although this statement doesn't explicitly include a reference to the Application object, the Documents collection is owned by Application. To use this code for Automation, copy the code from the Word VBA editor, paste it into your Access procedure, and create an explicit Application object:

```
Dim WordObj as Word.Application
Set WordObj = New Word.Application
WordObj.Documents.Add Template:="Normal", _
   NewTemplate:= False, DocumentType:=0
```

The macro recorder enables you to effortlessly create long and complex Automation code without needing to read the Word or Excel documentation. Try using the macro recorder to generate VBA code instead of typing it from scratch.

Collecting Data with Microsoft Outlook

Access 2010 includes a new feature that lets you use Outlook to collect data from one or more users. This feature automatically creates a data-entry form in an Outlook e-mail message, gives you several options for sending, and then adds or modifies data in the database. This saves you lots of time when sending out surveys or updating contact information by letting users without access to your application do data entry.

The Collect Data feature in Microsoft Access is a powerful tool letting you separate some users from your applications If you want to add or update data to your database application, create a data-entry form, send it to the users you want data from, and then process the replies automatically or manually.

Note

The data collection process described in this section applies only to Outlook 2007 and 2010. Data collection doesn't work with Outlook 2003 and earlier versions.

Creating an e-mail

Creating an e-mail consists of a number of steps, which Access presents in a wizard when you click the Create E-mail button in the Collect Data group of the External Data ribbon (shown in Figure 22.12).

Tip

You must select a table or query in the Navigation Pane before creating an e-mail. You can't collect data if you have nowhere to store it.

FIGURE 22.12

Use the Collect Data group on the External Data ribbon to use Outlook to get information from users.

Create E-mail Manage Replies

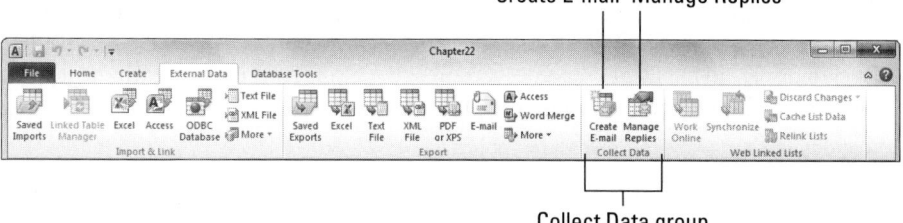

Collect Data group

Here are the steps for creating an e-mail:

1. Click the Customers table.

2. Click the Create E-Mail button.

   The Collect Data Wizard starts.

   The opening page of the wizard explains the new feature and the steps required to create an e-mail message.

3. Click Next to begin setting up the e-mail.

4. Choose the type of data-entry form you want to use to collect data.

   Your options are

   - **HTML:** The HTML form option creates an HTML e-mail message. The only requirement for the recipient is that his e-mail program supports HTML.

   - **Microsoft Office InfoPath:** The InfoPath form option creates an InfoPath form and requires the recipient to have both Outlook and InfoPath installed on her computer.

   For this example, click HTML form, and then click Next.

5. Choose whether you're collecting new data or updating existing data.

   Your options are

   - **Collect New Information Only:** Choose the Collect New Information Only option to send the recipient(s) a blank form. Any data collected from a blank form is appended to the database.

   - **Update Existing Information:** Choose the Update Existing Information option to send the recipient information to review and update. Any data collected from an update form overwrites older information in your table. You can update existing information only if the recipients' e-mail addresses are stored in the table.

   For this example, select Update Existing Information, and then click Next.

6. Select which fields you want to include in your form. You can also set the text of the label that appears next to each field and whether the field is read-only.

   For this example, add all the fields from the Customers table (shown in Figure 22.13). Then add spaces to each of the labels by clicking the field on the right, and changing the label to display in the Field Properties section of the form. Then click on each the field on the right, and select the Read Only check box. Then click Next.

7. Decide how you want to process the replies.

   Your options are

   - **Automatically Process Replies and Add Data to Customers:** Select this check box to let Outlook and Access do all the work from the Access Data Collection Replies folder in Microsoft Outlook.

   - **Only Allow Updates to Existing Data:** If you want to prevent records from being added, check the Only allow updates to existing data check box.

   For this example, check both check boxes, and then click Next.

FIGURE 22.13

Select the fields to add to the e-mail form; then set the caption and select the Read Only check box for each field.

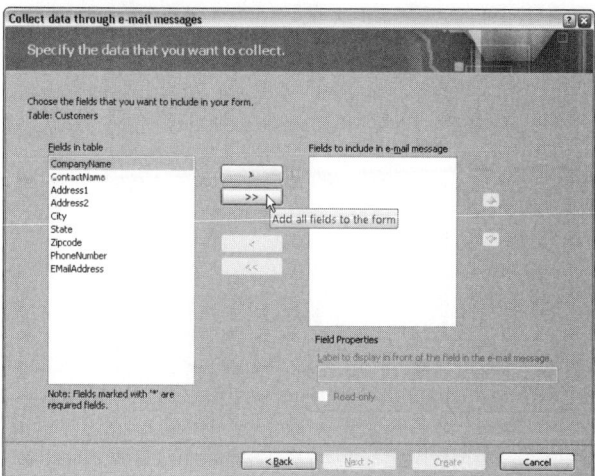

8. Specify the field in the database that contains the recipient's e-mail address.

   Your options are

   - **The Current Table or Query:** If the e-mail address is in the e-mail form's table or query, select the Current Table or Query option and select the field — in this example, the EMailAddress field.

   - **An Associated Table:** If the e-mail address is in an associated table, you have to select the Associated Table option. Then select the field in the current table that identifies who receives the e-mail, the associated table, and the field in the associated table that contains the e-mail address.

   For this example, select the current table, and then click Next.

9. Customize the e-mail message by typing a subject and introduction, and choosing whether you want the e-mail addresses in the To, Cc, or Bcc field (shown in Figure 22.14).

10. Accept the default settings, and click Next.

11. Review the instructions for managing the e-mails, and click Next again.

12. Verify the recipients, and create the e-mail.

13. Check all the recipients, and click Send to send the e-mail messages (shown in Figure 22.15).

FIGURE 22.14

Customize the e-mail message you're sending.

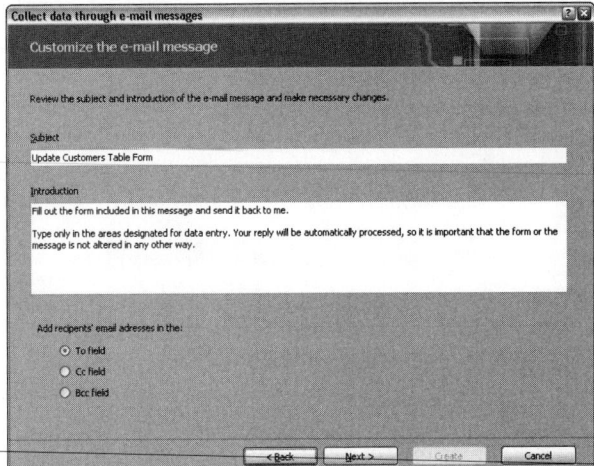

FIGURE 22.15

The resulting data-entry form sent to each recipient

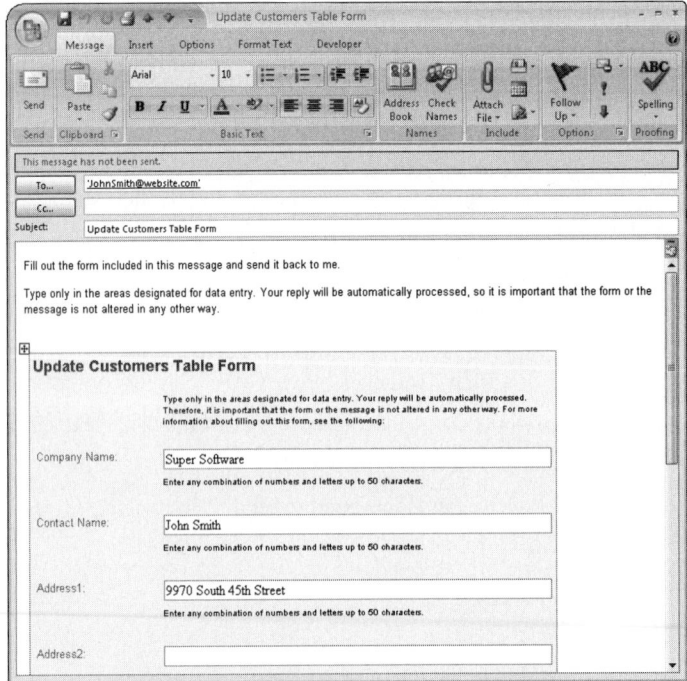

Note

These steps will vary if you make different choices from the ones I've suggested. For example, using InfoPath gives you a different look and functionality, and adding new data creates a blank form.

After creating the e-mails, you need to manage the replies, which the next section covers.

Managing replies

After sending an e-mail to collect data, click the `Manage Replies` button in the Collect Data group of the External Data ribbon (refer to Figure 22.12) to manage the e-mail messages you sent. The Manage Data Collection Messages dialog box (shown in Figure 22.16) lets you see which e-mails you sent and when you sent them, resend the messages, and delete the messages.

FIGURE 22.16

Use the Manage Data Collection Messages dialog box to manage replies to the e-mail forms you sent.

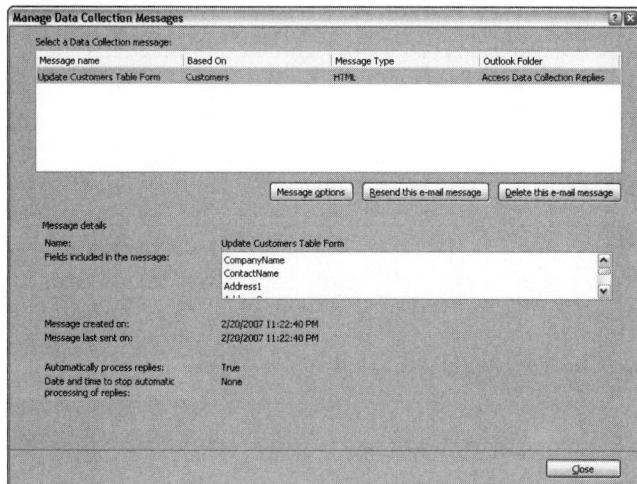

The list at the top of the dialog box shows the message details:

- Message name
- Table or query the e-mail is updating
- Message type
- Outlook folder where the replies are stored

The Message Details section at the bottom of the form displays information about the selected message:

- Fields included in the message
- Date and time the message was created and last sent
- Whether to process replies automatically
- Date and time to stop processing the replies

Click the Resend This E-Mail Message button to send the highlighted message again. This walks you through a few steps of the Create E-mail Wizard, letting you choose the same recipients or a different list of recipients. Follow the steps of the wizard to resend the message.

Click on the Delete This E-Mail Message button to stop processing replies to the message. If Outlook receives any replies to the message after you delete the message, it treats those messages as regular e-mail replies.

Choosing how to process replies

The Message Options button lets you customize the highlighted message. Click this button to display the Collect Data Using E-Mail Options dialog box (shown in Figure 22.17), which lets you specify the import settings and automatic processing settings.

Note
Changes you make to these settings don't affect the replies already in your Outlook mailbox.

FIGURE 22.17

Display the message options to customize the settings for importing and automatic processing of replies.

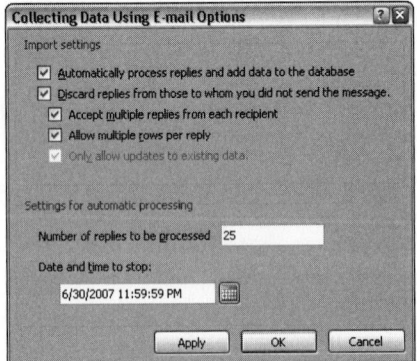

Select the Automatically Process Replies and Add Data to the Database check box to let Access and Outlook do all the work. This option lets Access process the replies as soon as they reach the Outlook Inbox. If you don't select this option, you must manually process the replies (see the "Manually processing replies" section, later in this chapter).

The Discard Replies from Those to Whom You Did Not Send the Message check box lets you process the replies from the original recipients of the e-mail. If this option is selected, replies from other recipients are stored in Outlook's destination folder, but they won't be automatically processed. You can, however, manually process the replies. Uncheck this option to automatically process all replies, regardless of who they're from.

If you choose to discard replies from non-original recipients, select the Accept Multiple Replies from Each Recipient check box to process all replies from each recipient. Deselect this check box to process only the first reply from each recipient; you can manually process — or delete — any subsequent replies.

Note

If you're using InfoPath, this option controls only the number of replies, not the number of records in a single reply. InfoPath lets users update multiple records in a single reply. With the check box deselected, Access only processes the first InfoPath reply and ignores any subsequent replies.

Select the Allow Multiple Rows per Reply check box if you're using InfoPath and you want to allow the recipients to add more records by clicking Insert a Row at the bottom of the e-mail message. Deselect this check box if you want to process only one record per reply.

Also, when using InfoPath, select the Only Allow Updates to Existing Data check box to ignore any new records the recipients add to the reply and process just the updates to existing records. If you want to allow recipients to add new records, clear this check box.

Automatically processing replies

The settings for automatic processing let you choose when to stop automatically processing replies. These settings apply only to the automatic processing of replies.

The Number of Replies to Be Processed text box lets you set the number of replies from all recipients that you want to automatically process. If you want to process all the replies, enter a large value in the text box. Replies received after you reach the specified value will be stored in the destination folder, but they won't be processed automatically. You can, however, manually process the replies.

The Date and Time to Stop option lets you pick a date and time to quit automatically processing the replies. Replies received after the specified date and time are stored in the destination folder, but aren't processed automatically. You can, however, manually process the replies. Leave this blank to process replies forever.

Manually processing replies

If you want to control which replies to process and when to process them, deselect the Automatically Process Replies and Add Data to the Database check box in the Collect Data Using E-mail Options dialog box (refer to Figure 22.17). You also need to manually process replies that aren't processed automatically, due to the import settings and settings for automatic processing, described in the previous sections.

To manually process each reply, you have to use Outlook 2007 or 2010. The replies reach your Outlook destination folder, but they aren't processed automatically. To process a reply manually, right-click the reply, and then click Export Data to Microsoft Office Access from the pop-up menu (shown in Figure 22.18). The resulting dialog box lets you verify the information being updated; click OK to process the data.

FIGURE 22.18

Process replies manually from Outlook.

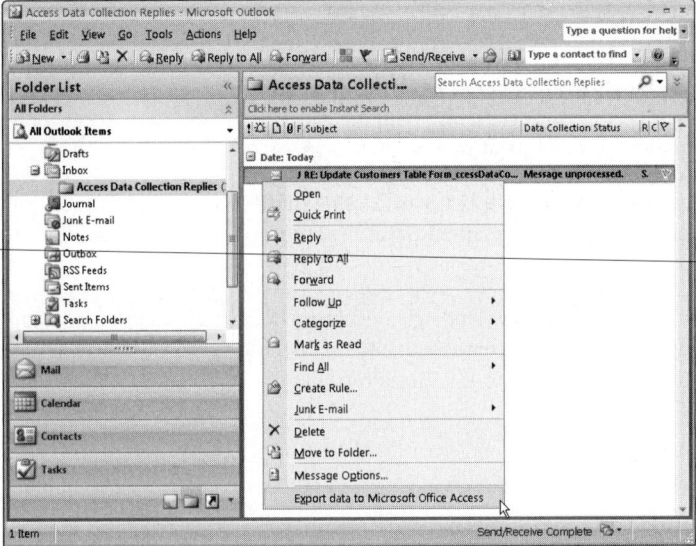

Summary

In this chapter, you learned how to use Automation to interact with other applications. You learned about the Automation references and how to create Automation objects. Then you used Automation to take control of the Word object to insert data from Access into a Word document using Word's bookmarks. You used Word's macro recorder to generate VBA code, so you don't have to learn Word's object model.

You also learned how to collect data using Microsoft Outlook 2007 and 2010. You walked through the steps to create an e-mail to update the data in the Customers table, sent the e-mail, and monitored the replies. Using Outlook and Access together lets you gather information from users without doing data entry or giving them access to your application.

Handling Errors and Exceptions

A ccess database applications prepared by even the very best developers have problems. By their very nature — when you consider table
and query design, forms and reports, and implementation details —
database applications are complicated. Plus, the VBA code written for databases often results in coding errors. If you're lucky, the problem and its
cause are obvious and easy to fix. If you're not so lucky, you know there's a
problem, but its source isn't immediately apparent. In the worst-case scenario, programming bugs are silently and perniciously damaging data — or
the representation of data in an application — without any warning.

This chapter looks at the types of errors you'll encounter in Access applications and tells you the steps you can take to uncover and repair these
critters.

Note

This chapter largely ignores the errors caused by poor design — those that
misrepresent data because of ill-designed queries, update and insert anomalies
caused by inappropriate use of referential integrity rules, and so on. For the
most part, the causes of design errors are rooted in failure to conform to database development best practices, misunderstanding Access query design, and
other causes. You have to pay careful attention to database design principles
in order to produce truly robust Access applications.

Note

There is no database for this chapter because the chapter contains only fairly
simple VBA code examples.

Dealing with Errors

We all have to deal with the errors that occur in our applications. Even the best-written code fails now and then, very often because of problems with data entry or poorly trained users. Other times, errors occur because we've written the code incorrectly, or we haven't adequately tested and debugged an application before distributing to users.

Errors fall into three basic categories: logical errors, runtime errors, and unanticipated errors.

Logical errors

Logical errors can be difficult to detect and remove. A logical error (also called a *bug*) often occurs because of some mathematical error: Perhaps data was misused in a recordset, maybe there is some other problem dealing with the data or program flow of the application, or maybe erroneous user input isn't properly captured by the application.

For example, let's say that a patient-management program assumes that the user has entered both a first name and a last name for a patient. A patient data-entry form contains text boxes for both these values. So far so good. But what if the user typing in the details doesn't enter something in both boxes? (There are all kinds of reasons this might happen — for example, maybe the user entered both the first and last names into the text box intended to hold only the last name.) An empty text box may contain a null value, unless a default value has been provided. A logical error is generated if the application then tries to use the patient's name in a lookup or sorting operation. If you're lucky, the user will notice the logical error. The user could be informed through the use of a pop-up dialog box or error message, and the missing data could be corrected before the data is committed to the database.

Other logical errors are created when, for instance, an application incorrectly calculates the days between dates, uses the wrong value in a division or multiplication operation, and so on. Virtually any time data is mishandled or inappropriately used in your application, a logical error is likely to occur as a result.

The obvious solution to the missing first name/last name situation is to add some VBA code to the form's `BeforeUpdate` event to verify that both a first name and a last name have been entered, and notify the user that one or both names are missing. Alternatively, the application may insert a default value such as "N/A" for the first and last names when either has been left blank.

Even so, a well-mannered application should detect errors when they occur, and handle them gracefully. Access, like most Windows applications, handles errors in a fairly unfriendly fashion, popping up a dialog box that may or may not adequately describe the error to the user. A carefully written application traps these errors before Access takes over, handling them without disturbing the user's workflow.

Runtime errors

If you get past the syntax checking using the VBA editor and your code compiles, you may still encounter errors. Those errors, which occur as the user works with an application, are generally referred to as *runtime errors*. Runtime errors occur for a multitude of reasons, such as unexpected data values (zero values or numbers that are too large to fit in the data type) or expected external files not being present. When a runtime error occurs, it results in one of following situations:

- A fatal error occurs, which causes the application to crash.
- An untrapped error occurs, and the default Access error dialog box appears.
- The error is handled by the application and your code takes care of the problem.
- An unanticipated application error occurs, which may or may not cause problems with your Access application.

I examine each of these situations in the following sections.

When fatal errors occur

A *fatal error* is a non-recoverable error and crashes the application. Fatal errors are generally the result of an operation outside the Access environment, and there is no way for Access to handle it. In most cases, your code won't be able to trap and respond to fatal errors. An example of this type of error is calling a poorly written Windows API function. As you'll see in Chapter 27, Windows API functions are extremely fussy about the type and number of parameters passed to them. Because Windows API functions execute outside of Access, there is no way for VBA code to trap an API error. In extreme cases, your users encounter the dreaded blue screen of death (BSOD), often seen when a computer is infected by a virus.

Tip

Because you can't do much about these fatal errors other than fix them, you should concentrate on the types of errors you can control.

When Access reports the error

Runtime errors often give no direct indication of a problem, such as a pop-up message on a screen. More likely, a runtime error is detected after the fact, when something with the data is discovered to be wrong. For instance, a report may contain blank text boxes when the user expects to see names and other data. This situation could even occur a long time after the data-entry error has occurred, and the error may occur many times before its discovery.

On rare occasions, runtime errors are traceable to a hardware failure such as a full disk or network problems, leading to the frequent "It's the *&#^ computer's fault!" complaint. Modern desktop computers are much more reliable than they were a few years ago, making this situation a rare occurrence. Many hardware failures, such as a hard-disk crash, are easily recognized by the user.

Other runtime errors may be less obvious and more difficult to deal with. For example, a network glitch may cause data loss or make lookup data temporarily unavailable. Running out of swap disk space makes Windows run erratically or crash. Many computers are equipped with marginal memory, making it difficult or impossible to run large queries or use the built-in Access wizards.

A good approach to avoiding runtime errors is to keep an Access database file well maintained by periodically running a compact and repair cycle:

1. Click the Office Button at the top-left of the Access window.

2. Select the Compact and Repair This Database option from the menu, as shown in Figure 23.1.

Compacting and repairing a database

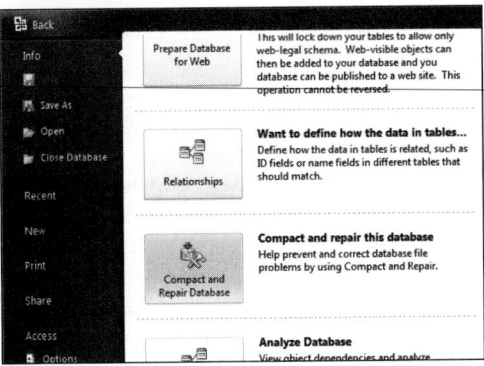

Best practices dictate frequent maintenance of an Access `.accdb` file, particularly if data is often deleted or modified. A compact and repair cycle helps to ensure physical integrity of the `.accdb` file on the hard disk.

When the application handles the errors

Access, Visual Basic, and the other VBA applications, such as Word and Excel, can handle errors for you. Unfortunately, the built-in error handling in most applications is not really intended for end users. Figure 23.2 shows a typical runtime error message produced by Access. Notice how unhelpful the message is — it includes technical expressions, such as *type mismatch* — and most users have no idea how to respond to this type of error message. Unless appropriate training has been provided, the user will likely guess at the correct action to take in response.

FIGURE 23.2

Built-in error messages usually are not helpful.

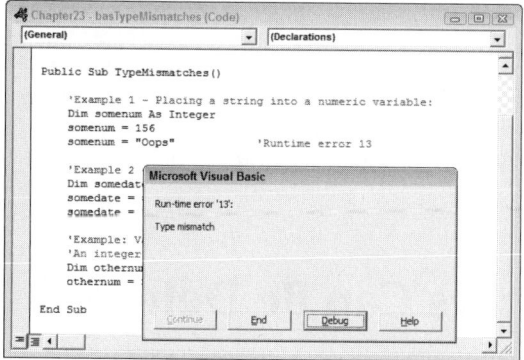

The error in Figure 23.2 occurs because the procedure declares and creates a string variable and a numeric variable and then tries to assign the numeric variable the value of the text string. The type mismatch occurs because you can't assign nonnumeric characters to a numeric variable.

The error message in Figure 23.2 reports Runtime error '13', which happens to be a type mismatch. Unless you know the cause of this problem, how does this message help you? Without a great deal of experience, how does the user know how to fix this type of problem? In fact, how do you determine what caused the problem? Clearly, this message box is not much help to a user who has entered character data into a text box that should be filled with a numeric value.

Notice the Debug button in Figure 23.2. The Debug button stops the program, opens the VBA code editor, and places a breakpoint on the offending statement (see Chapter 14 for more on breakpoints). The program is in a state of limbo. All the values of temporary variables are intact, and you can view them to help you solve the error. The End button causes the program to stop running, and the user can't use any tools to check the problem.

The error dialog box shown in Figure 23.2 appears for *untrapped errors*. This type of message can be good for development because problems can be traced to the specific line of code that caused the error. When you click the Debug button, the VBA window opens and highlights the guilty line of code. But this isn't the kind of interaction you generally want between your application's code and end users. For this reason, having an error handler in the VBA code and making the problem a *handled error* is much better. You may be able to prevent the user from seeing a problem by automatically taking corrective action as part of an error handler.

When unanticipated application errors occur

The last type of runtime error is the unknown or unanticipated application error. This is most often caused by a logical error in the code. Often, no error is displayed because the program is working exactly the way it was designed. For example, an endless loop occurs if you forget to advance a record pointer as you traverse a recordset or the condition ending a Do.Loop never happens. The problem is that the code is doing the wrong thing, even though it's executing as programmed.

A well-written application may prevent runaway, endless loops by counting how many times the loop has executed and forcing an end to the loop when the maximum value has been exceeded. Other sophisticated ways of handling unanticipated errors include keeping track of the number of times a particular function has been called, or monitoring how long it takes for a query to execute or a form or report to open. Such extreme measures are not necessary in the vast majority of Access applications, but you should be aware that there are solutions to virtually any unexpected application problem.

Identifying Which Errors Can Be Detected

Several hundred trappable errors can occur in VBA applications, but only a small portion of these hundreds of errors is likely to occur in your applications. The question is, then, which of the remaining 50 or 100 relevant errors should you trap in your applications?

Most developers begin simply and write an error handler that catches the most obvious errors. In the case of the navigation buttons on an Access or Visual Basic form, you should always trap the error that occurs when the user tries to move off either end of the recordset. Such an error is readily anticipated and is the result of normal navigation through a recordset.

However, consider a problem that makes it impossible for your application to create the recordset. There are many reasons why the OpenRecordset method may fail. Perhaps the table can't be found because it's been deleted or a link to the table is broken, or there could be an error in the SQL statement used to create the recordset and no records are returned. During development you may never see an error caused by an empty recordset because your test data is always available, and (during development) the OpenRecordset method never fails.

Experience will tell you which errors are expected as you write your VBA procedures. But, you should always prepare for the unexpected. Later in this chapter, you'll see how to add a general-purpose error handler to a VBA procedure. This general-purpose error handler catches all errors that occur within the procedure, and avoids the default error dialog box (refer to Figure 23.2).

What an error handler is

VBA provides extensive runtime-error-handling capabilities. You can add code to your applications to detect when an error occurs. Other code directs the program to handle anticipated errors in a predictable fashion. Still other code can catch unanticipated errors, automatically correcting the problem, preventing data loss, and reducing support costs. Although it may sound as though different coding techniques are needed for trapping different types of errors, VBA supports just one basic error-handling process, as described in the "Trapping Errors with VBA" section, later in this chapter.

Almost all error-handling routines in VBA programs require a three-step process:

1. Trap the error.
2. Redirect program flow to an error handler.
3. Direct program flow out of the error handler back to the main body of the procedure, or exit the procedure.

Note

All VBA error handling is done locally — that is, each procedure contains its own error-handling code. Although a procedure's error handler can call other functions and subroutines, the error handler exists entirely within the procedure causing the error. In fact, as I discuss later in this chapter, after you start implementing error handling, you need to include error-handling code in virtually every procedure in an application. An error that occurs in a procedure without error handling is passed back to the routine that called the procedure, easily causing confusion as to which procedure actually failed.

How to set a basic error trap

The VBA engine is constantly looking for problems and immediately notifies you when something unexpected happens. The default error message is generally technical in nature. A single line of VBA code is all that's necessary to intercept an error and redirect program flow to an error handler that provides a more user-friendly approach to error resolution.

The following procedure shows how error handling is implemented in VBA procedures:

```
Sub RoutineA()
On Error GoTo HandleError       'Trap the error
  MsgBox "Now in routine A"
ExitHere:
  MsgBox "Now leaving routine A"
  Exit Sub
HandleError:                    'Begin the error handler
  MsgBox "Error in routine A"
  Resume ExitHere               'Redirect out of error handler
End Sub
```

The On Error statement near the top of the procedure sets the error trap for the routine. Code near the bottom of the routine implements the error-handling mechanism for this subroutine. The error-handling code in this procedure is the very least you can include in your procedures to handle runtime errors effectively. The error-handling statements in this procedure are a template you can consistently use in all your VBA programs.

The On Error clause informs VBA that you want to override the default VBA error-handling system by sending execution to the location identified by the HandleError label. The GoTo *Label* statement is an unconditional branch (in the event of an error) to a label somewhere within the current procedure.

Note

A VBA label is nothing more than an identifier (such as `HandleError`) followed by a colon. A word by itself on a line in a VBA procedure is interpreted as the name of a procedure, variable, or VBA keyword, and VBA tries to evaluate it. When followed by a colon, the VBA interpreter understands that the word is actually a label and should not be executed or evaluated.

The `On Error` statement is a switch that disables the default VBA error handling. This statement switches the VBA engine away from its built-in error handling and redirects error handling to your code. After you set the error trap with the `On Error` statement, you suppress the appearance of the default Access error dialog boxes.

After an error occurs, the VBA engine's normal operation is suspended. Normal execution is directed to the error handler, and further error trapping is inhibited. If an error occurs in your error handler, VBA responds with its default behavior. Some resources (discussed in the next section) determine which error occurred and exactly where the error occurred. You also have several options as to where you want program flow to commence after the error handler has done its job.

Note

There is nothing special about the labels used in the error-handling statements. `HandleError` and `ExitHere` are just words; they convey no special meaning to Access or the VBA language engine. I use `HandleError` and `ExitHere` throughout this book simply because they're easily understood, but choose any label you want. In fact, you can use exactly the same labels in every VBA procedure. This fact makes it easier to copy and paste the error-handling template from one procedure to another in your Access application.

Trapping Errors with VBA

Several situations can cause a great deal of frustration for your application users:

- **A program that has been operating without a hint of trouble suddenly crashes, popping up a dialog box containing a contradictory or confusing error message.**

- **A program behaves inconsistently.** In one situation, the program operates in a predictable fashion, reliably churning out reports and displaying the results of calculations. Under other conditions, though, the program, operating on seemingly identical data, behaves erratically, stopping execution, or, perhaps, displaying the data in unexpected ways.

- **A program appears to be functioning properly but is in fact *corrupting* (unexpectedly changing the value of) data.** The program silently makes changes to the data or reports erroneous values without indicating that an error exists. For example, in a program that calculates currency exchange rates, the user of this program may believe the program is correctly calculating the monetary exchange values while, in fact, the program is actually reporting incorrect results.

Caution

The worst type of situation occurs when the values returned by the program appear to be correct but are, in fact, wrong.

Using VBA error-handling techniques, you can add code to your applications to prevent unexpected crashes or inconsistent behavior. Unfortunately, there is little you can do to correct a poorly programmed application, other than updating the application's code to correct the problem. If calculations are being performed incorrectly, there is little that the VBA engine can do to correct these types of errors. VBA code can be utilized to gracefully cater to unexpected behavior in Access.

Microsoft Access provides several basic programming elements used for catering to errors, including the following:

- The `Err` object
- VBA error-handling statements
- The `Error` event
- The ADO `Errors` collection

The following sections detail each of these program elements. As you read the following sections, notice that there are two types of errors in Access applications:

- **Application errors:** Application errors are generally caused by something in the user interface (incorrect data entry by the user, for example).
- **Database errors:** Database errors are thrown by the database engine (record locking problems, for instance). Database errors are generally caught by the Error event behind bound forms or are thrown by ActiveX Data Objects (ADO).

The Err object

The `Err` object is a part of the VBA language and is always present in Access applications. When an application error occurs, information about the error is stored in the `Err` object, enabling you to examine the `Err` object and learn the details of the error.

The `Err` object contains information about only the most recent error and does not contain information about any other error. This means that, if the current error was the result of a cascade of other errors, the only information available to you is the most recent error. When a new error occurs, the `Err` object is cleared and updated to include information about that most recent error.

The `Err` object has several properties, including `Number`, `Description`, and `Source`. The `Number` is the VBA number of the error. `Description` gives you a little more information about the error. The `Source` property is not normally very useful in Access applications, because it identifies the VBA project that generated the error, and in Access applications, the project name is the same as the name of the Access application by default.

The Err object also has two methods: Clear, to clear information from the Err object, and Raise, to force an error condition. The Raise method is often used to test error handlers to make sure they're catching specific errors.

The Description property returns the built-in description of the error that has occurred. The description is the same as the message displayed in the default error dialog box (such as Type mismatch — refer to Figure 23.2). Whether you choose to use this description is entirely up to you. Perhaps the most important property of the Err object is the Number associated with the error. The following listing shows how you might use the Err.Number property to determine which error has triggered the error handler:

```
Sub GenericProcedure()
On Error GoTo HandleError
    'Other VBA statements here
ExitHere:
    'Shut down statements here
    Exit Sub
HandleError:
    Select Case Err.Number
        Case 123
            'Handle error number 123
            Resume ExitHere
        Case 456
            'Handle error number 456
            Resume ExitHere
        Case 789
            'Handle error number 789
            Resume ExitHere
        Case Else  'Unanticipated error
            MsgBox Err.Number & " " & Err.Description
            Resume ExitHere
    End Select
End Sub
```

The Select Case statement in the error handler uses Err.Number to execute any of a number of responses to the error. The beauty of Select Case is that the error-handling code can be extended as far as necessary. There is no practical limit on the number of Case statements that can be contained within the Select Case construct, and multiple Err.Number values can be handled by a single Case statement.

In each Case construct, you choose whether to include the Resume ExitHere statement. For instance, perhaps Case 456 fixes the problem, and you really want the code to return to the statement that caused the error so that it can be executed a second time. In this case, rather than Resume ExitHere, use a simple Resume statement with no target label. Resume instructs VBA to go back to the statement that caused the problem and execute it again. (The different forms of the Resume statement are discussed in the "VBA Resume statements" section, later in this chapter.)

Obviously, the `Select Case` construct is not the only way to handle multiple error conditions. You could, for instance, use nested `If...Then...Else` and `If...Then...ElseIf` statements. However, you'll find that the `If` statement is not easily extensible and the logical flow through nested `If...Then...Else` statements can be difficult to follow.

In the "Resume *Label*" section, later in this chapter, you'll read about the special `Resume` statement you use to redirect program flow out of the error handler.

VBA error-handling statements

You've already seen several examples of the basic VBA statements for handling errors:

- `On Error`
- `Resume`

There are a number of forms of the `On Error` statement:

- `On Error GoTo` *Label*
- `On Error GoTo 0`
- `On Error Resume Next`

As you'll see in the section "VBA Resume statements" later in this chapter, there are also a number of forms of the `Resume` statement:

- `Resume`
- `Resume Next`
- `Resume` *Label*

An *error handler* is a section of code that is executed when some kind of an error occurs. The exact error can be specified or it can be general. Essentially, when an error is detected by an error trap, then the action defined by the error handler is taken.

There are numerous ways to deal with errors within forms, reports, and code. Each form and report, as well as each function and subroutine, can (and probably should) have an error-handling routine. It isn't unusual to see a good part of the development effort devoted to error handling. Probably the most common routine is the following:

```
Function SampleCode
    'Dim statements here
On Error GoTo HandleError
    'Insert functional code here
ExitHere:
  'Cleanup code goes here
  Exit Function
HandleError:
    'Error handler code here
```

```
       Msgbox Err.Description
       Resume ExitHere
   End Function
```

The On Error statement enables the error handler. In the event that an error occurs, execution branches to the first line after the HandleError label. This label could be any valid VBA label. The error-handler code would deal with the error and then either resume execution back in the body of the procedure or just exit the function or subroutine. The inclusion of the MsgBox statement in the error handler is a common way of informing the user what happened.

When an error occurs in a called function or a subroutine that doesn't have an enabled error handler, VBA returns to the calling procedure looking for an error handler. This process proceeds up the call stack until a procedure with an error handler is found. What this means is that an error thrown from a subordinate procedure may be handled by a higher-level procedure, making it difficult to know exactly which procedure triggered the error.

If no error handler is found, execution stops with the default Access error message displayed.

On Error GoTo *Label*

The On Error GoTo *Label* statement defines an error-handling code segment. On Error GoTo *Label* (such as On Error GoTo HandleError) is the standard error-handling directive described earlier in this chapter. Here is another example of using On Error GoTo *Label* within a VBA procedure:

```
   Sub LogMoreErrors()
      Dim db As DAO.Database
      Dim rs As DAO.Recordset
   On Error GoTo HandleError
      Set db = CurrentDb()
      Set rs = db.OpenRecordset("SELECT * FROM ErrorLog")
      'Put code here to use the information
      'retrieved from the ErrorLog table.
   ExitHere:
      rs.Close
      Exit Sub
   HandleError:
      MsgBox Err.Number & " " & Err.Description
      Resume ExitHere
   End Sub
```

On Error GoTo *Label* is, by far, the most common error trap you'll add to your VBA procedures. Because the GoTo statement defines an unconditional branch to the location specified by the *Label* clause, you're guaranteed that errors within the procedure will be handled by the error handler you've written.

Keep in mind that you're free to use any labels you wish as the targets of the On Error and Resume statements, as long as those labels actually exist in your procedure. The labels you see here — HandleError and ExitHere — were chosen simply because of the obvious purposes they serve. Using the same labels in all your VBA code makes it very easy to simply copy and paste the basic error-handling statements into all your procedures.

On Error GoTo 0

The On Error GoTo 0 statement disables error handling and returns Access to its default error-notification behavior. This statement also resets the properties of the Err object and defeats whatever error trap has been set in a procedure. The following procedure shows an example of using GoTo 0. After processing has bypassed the Delete method, the On Error GoTo 0 statement disables further error traps. This means any errors that occur after this statement will be handled by the default VBA error mechanism:

```
Sub DeleteTableDef()
   Dim db As DAO.Database
   Set db = CurrentDb()
   'Resume Next is described in the next section:
On Error Resume Next
   'The following statement throws an
   'error if tblTemp does not exist:
   db.TableDefs.Delete "tblTemp"
On Error GoTo 0
   'More code here
End Sub
```

Although in most cases it is not desirable to let VBA handle errors, one situation where you may choose to use On Error GoTo 0 is during the development process. Assume you're working on a complex procedure that has a number of different failure modes. You're never really sure you're trapping for all possible errors, so you may want to disable error handling temporarily so that you'll be sure to see all errors that occur past the error trap you've prepared. Later, when you're sure that you've captured all the possible errors thrown by the procedure, remove the On Error GoTo 0 statement and allow your error trap to handle errors within the procedure.

On Error Resume Next

The On Error Resume Next statement instructs Access to ignore errors in the code following the statement. Any errors that occur in the code following On Error Resume Next are simply ignored. No error-handling routine is called. The On Error Resume Next statement is useful if your code can safely ignore errors in the code immediately following the statement. In the two procedures that follow, should any error occur while attempting to delete the error log file, the rest of the routine continue to execute:

```
Sub DeleteTempFile()
On Error Resume Next
   Kill "C:\Temp.txt"
End Sub
```

In this example, the `Kill` statement is used to delete a temporary file that may or may not exist on the `C:` drive. `Kill` throws an error if the file does not exist, so `On Error Resume Next` is used as an easy way to safely ignore the "File not found" that may occur.

Caution

`On Error Resume Next` **must be used with caution. Once** `On Error Resume Next` **is set, Access ignores all errors until another error directive is encountered, as in this example:**

```
Sub DoSomething()
On Error Resume Next
  Kill "C:\Temp.txt"
On Error GoTo HandleError
  '... Other code here ...
End Sub
```

In this case, the `On Error Resume Next` **causes Access to ignore the error that occurs if the temporary file does not exist. Once execution is past this section of code, the** `On Error GoTo HandleError` **statement establishes the usual VBA error handler for the remainder of the procedure.**

Tip

It is probably best to reserve the `On Error Resume Next` **statement for situations where its special behavior is needed.**

VBA Resume statements

In earlier examples, you've seen the `Resume ExitHere` as a way to redirect processing out of a procedure's error handler. As with the `On Error` statement, there are a number of forms of the `Resume` statement:

- Resume
- Resume Next
- Resume *Label*

Using the `Resume` statement is all about gaining better and more effective program control over the occurrence of errors. In any of its forms, the `Resume` statement redirects processing to another location within the current procedure.

As a general rule, you shouldn't simply fall out of the error handler at the bottom of a procedure. You've probably noticed that the error handler usually appears near the bottom of a procedure. It's tempting to just let the `End Sub` or `End Function` statement after the error handler terminate the procedure after the error has been managed, but there are several problems with this approach:

- **The VBA error mechanism is left in an indeterminate state.** You'll recall that as soon as the error occurs, VBA enters a special "error" mode. This mode persists until the `Err.Clear` method is invoked or the VBA engine encounters a `Resume` statement, or until another error occurs. Even though the end of the procedure resets VBA's error mode, you shouldn't count on this happening, particularly in deeply nested procedure calls.

- **VBA procedures often open recordsets, establish object variables, and perform other tasks that may be left incomplete unless the procedures are shut down in a predictable fashion.** For instance, assume a procedure has opened a disk file and an error occurs. Unless the disk file is explicitly closed, you run the risk of damaging the disk's file structure. Using the Resume statement to redirect flow to the procedure's shutdown code provides a single point at which to close resources that are no longer needed.

Every VBA error handler should include some form of the Resume statement. This special VBA command instructs the VBA engine to clear the error condition and resume normal execution. Depending on how you write the Resume statement, you can redirect program execution to any of a number of different points within the procedure.

Note

The VBA GoTo statement will not work in place of Resume. GoTo is an unconditional branch to another location within the current procedure and does not reset the VBA engine error status.

Resume

The Resume statement (with no label) returns execution to the line at which the error occurred. The Resume statement is typically used when the user must make a correction, or when the error handler has repaired the problem causing the error. This might occur if you prompt the user for the name of a file to open and the user enters a filename that doesn't exist. You can then force the execution of the code back to the point where the filename is requested.

In almost all cases, the Resume keyword assumes that the error handler repairs the error condition. Otherwise, you'll find yourself in an endless loop. Unless the error condition is corrected, every time the line causing the error is executed, the error occurs again, triggering the Resume statement, causing the cycle to repeat itself an infinite number of times. The following procedure shows how the Resume statement fits into a robust error handler and how the Resume statement can simplify coding:

```
Public Sub ResumeDemo()
On Error GoTo HandleError
    'Statement causing error occurs here:
   Kill "C:\Temp.txt"
ExitHere:
   Exit Sub
HandleError:
   If MsgBox("Error! Try again?", vbYesNo) = vbYes Then
     Resume
   Else
     Resume ExitHere
   End If
End Sub
```

If the Temp.txt file cannot be found, processing jumps down to the error handler. A message box pops up with Yes and No buttons on it, asking the user whether to try again to delete the file.

If the user selects the Yes button (vbYes), the Resume statement forces processing back to the Kill statement. The cycle repeats itself until either the Temp.txt file becomes available and is deleted or until the user clicks the No button on the message box.

Resume Next

When your error handler corrects or works around the problem that caused the error, the Resume Next statement may be used. Resume Next returns execution to the statement immediately following the line at which the error occurred.

The assumption with Resume Next is that either the error handler corrected the error condition or that the error was relatively minor in nature and that it's appropriate for processing to simply continue at the statement following the error condition.

The following procedure shows how to use On Error Resume Next. As you saw earlier, this simple routine tries to delete a temporary file. If the file does not exist, an error is thrown and processing drops to the error handler. Within the error handler, if the error number is 53 ("File not found"), processing resumes at the first executable statement following Kill:

```
Public Sub ResumeNextDemo()
On Error GoTo HandleError
   'Statement causing error occurs here:
   Kill "C:\Temp.txt"
   'Other processing goes here
ExitHere:
   Exit Sub
HandleError:
   'Error 53 = "File not found"
   If Err.Number = 53 Then
     Resume Next
   Else
      'Handle other errors here
   End If
End Sub
```

This little demonstration illustrates how a single On Error GoTo statement, plus a little decision logic in the error handler, can protect the procedure from all kinds of errors, yet allows the code to simply ignore error 53 because this particular error is inconsequential to the application's execution.

Resume Label

Resume *Label* is the standard method for exiting an error handler. If you need to continue execution at someplace other than the line causing the error or the line immediately after the statement that caused the error, you should use the Resume *Label* statement. Resume *Label* directs execution to the location specified by the label argument.

The label must appear within the current procedure. You can't resume execution at a point outside of the currently executing procedure. You can certainly call other procedures from within an error handler, but execution always returns to the current procedure.

Note

When using error traps, one option is to redirect processing to an error trap and log the error to a log file. After that, you could always continue processing. The result is that processing is not halted and is often sufficient for situations where user intervention is not required.

One important aspect of Resume *Label* is that program execution is typically directed to the procedure's exit point. This gives you a handy place to put all the procedure's cleanup code, so that it executes regardless of whether an error occurs:

```
Sub LogErrors(iNumber As Integer, sDesc As String)
   Dim db As DAO.Database
   Dim rs As DAO.Recordset
On Error GoTo HandleError
   Set db = CurrentDb()
   Set rs = db.OpenRecordset("SELECT * FROM ErrorLog")
   rs.AddNew
   rs![TimeStamp] = Now()
   rs![Number] = iNumber
   rs![Description] = sDesc
   rs.Update
ExitHere:
   'These statements are executed regardless of whether
   'an error has occurred. This section provides a single
   'place in this procedure for cleanup code:
On Error Resume Next
   rs.Close
   Set rs = Nothing
   Exit Sub
HandleError:
   'Handle the error here
   Resume ExitHere
End Sub
```

In this short example, the statements following the ExitHere label are executed regardless of whether an error has occurred. You should always close recordset objects and set them to Nothing to conserve memory. These cleanup statements normally appear near the bottom of procedures, but in this example they're located midway through the subroutine. Execution of this procedure actually ends when the Exit Sub statement executes.

Caution

It should be recognized that the preceding example is incomplete. If the ErrorLog table doesn't exist, an error will be raised. You could choose to put logic in the HandleError section to create the ErrorLog table, and use Resume to return to the OpenRecordset statement. Note that if you don't do this, the recordset won't actually exist when the ExitHere section attempts to close it, so another error will be raised, creating an infinite loop.

The Error event

Access provides a special `Error` event when running a bound form or report. The `Error` event provides a nice way to trap an error that occurs in the database engine supplying data to the form or report. You need to create an event procedure for the `Error` event to trap these errors. The procedure looks like one of the following, depending on whether it was a form or a report:

```
Sub Form_Error(DataErr As Integer, Response As Integer)
    'Insert error handler here
End Sub

Sub Report_Error(DataErr As Integer, Response As Integer)
    'Insert error handler here
End Sub
```

There are two arguments for these subroutines:

- **DataErr:** `DataErr` is the error code returned by the Access database engine when an error occurs. Note that the `Err` object is superseded by `Error` event and is not helpful when this event is triggered by a problem with the data underlying the form or report. You must use the `DataErr` argument to determine which error occurred.

- **Response:** `Response` is set to either of the following constants by the procedure:

    - `AcDataErrContinue`: Ignore the error and continue without displaying the default Access error message.

    - `AcDataErrDisplay`: Display the default Access error message. (This is the default.)

    When you use `AcDataErrContinue`, you can then supply a custom error message or handler in place of the default error message.

The following is a typical `Form_Error` event procedure:

```
Private Sub Form_Error(DataErr As Integer, Response As Integer)
    Dim strMsg As String
    Select Case DataErr
      Case 7787  'OverwriteErr:
        strMsg = "You lose. Click on OK to see"_
          & "updates from other people."
        MsgBox strMsg, vbOKOnly + vbInformation
        Response = acDataErrContinue
      Case 7878 'DataChangedErr:
        strMsg = "Another user has changed this" _
          & "data while you were looking at it." _
          & vbCrLf & "Click OK to see " _
          & "the other user changes."
        MsgBox strMsg, vbOKOnly + vbInformation
        Response = acDataErrContinue
      Case Else
        'Default for any other errors:
        Response = acDataErrDisplay
    End Select
End Sub
```

This particular error-handling routine traps the errors on a bound form that occur when multiple users make simultaneous changes to the same record. The Access database engine raises the error, allowing the form to intelligently notify the user that a problem has occurred.

Notice how `DataErr` is examined to see if its value is 7787 or 7878 and an appropriate action (notifying the user of the problem) is taken to handle the problem. Response is set to `acData ErrContinue` to notify Access that the form's data error has been handled.

If any other error occurs, `Response` is set to `acDataErrDisplay`, allowing Access to present the user with the default error message. Hopefully, the user can make some sense of the error message or at least notify someone of the situation.

Keep in mind that the form and report `Error` event fires only in response to data errors raised by the database engine. The `Error` event is not related to problems caused by the user, other than inappropriate data entry and a failure to add or update the wrong kind of data in the database.

The ADO Errors collection

When an error occurs in an ADO object, an `Error` object is created in the `Errors` collection of the `Connection` object. These errors are referred to as *data access errors.* When an error occurs, the collection is cleared and the new set of `Error` objects is put into the collection. Although the collection exists only for the most recent data error event, a single event may generate several errors. Each of these errors is stored in the `Errors` collection. The `Errors` collection is an object of the `Connection` object, not ADO.

The `Errors` collection has one property, `Count`, which contains the number of errors or error objects. It has a value of zero if there are no errors. There are a few properties of the `Error` object. These include `Description`, `HelpContext`, `HelpFile`, `Number`, and `Source`. When there are multiple errors, the lowest-level error is the first object in the collection, and the highest-level error is the last object in the collection.

When an ADO error occurs, the VBA `Err` object contains the error number for the first object in the `Errors` collection. You need to check the `Errors` collection to see whether additional ADO errors have occurred.

In the following code, you find an error handler that can be used in a procedure that deals with an ADO connection. When an error occurs, the code following the label `HandleError` runs and first checks to see if the `Error` object contains any items. If it does, it checks to see if the error is the same as the `Err` object. If it is the same, the error was an ADO error and `strMessage` contain the descriptions of all the errors in the `Errors` collection. If it isn't an ADO error, the error occurred at the application level and the single `Err.Description` value is displayed:

```
Sub ADOTest()
   Dim cnn As New ADODB.Connection
   Dim errX As ADODB.Error
   Dim strMessage As String
On Error GoTo HandleError
```

```
      'Insert your code here
ExitHere:
  Exit Sub
HandleError:
  If cnn.Errors.Count > 0 Then
    If Err.Number = cnn.Errors.Item(0).Number Then
      'Error is an ADO Connection Error:
      For Each errX In cnn.Errors
        'Loop through the Errors collection, displaying
        'the description of each Err object:
        strMessage = strMessage & Err.Description & vbCrLf
      Next errX
      MsgBox strMessage, , "ADO Error Handler"
    End If
    Resume ExitHere
  Else
    'The error is a VBA Error:
    MsgBox Err.Description, vbExclamation, _
      "VBA Error Handler"
    Resume ExitHere
  End If
End Sub
```

Summary

This chapter surveys the important topic of adding error handling in Access applications. All VBA hosts (Access, Word, Excel, and so on) use identical error-handling paradigms. This means that all the code you saw in this chapter is applicable to any VBA host application.

Error handling is enabled with the On Error keywords. The typical error-handling process is to trap the error, redirect program execution to the code segment handling the error, and then resume out of the error handler. Most procedures use the Resume statement to redirect program flow to a common exit point in the procedure. The code following the exit label performs any cleanup (closing and discarding object variables, closing files that are open, and so on) and is executed regardless of whether an error occurs in the procedure.

Part IV

Professional Database Development

The chapters in this part cover issues that concern professional database developers, including "bullet-proofing" Access databases, enhancing the user interface with toolbars and menus, and using some advanced programming techniques such as the Windows Application Programming Interface (API).

This part builds on the information provided in earlier chapters. In this part, you'll find answers to many questions and problems facing Access developers, such as identifying a user as the user logs on to an application, exploiting object-oriented programming with the VBA language, and using advanced data-management techniques with ActiveX Data Objects (ADOs).

Some developers will never use many of the capabilities described in this part. However, far too often, even advanced developers overlook the capabilities provided by a system like Microsoft Access simply because they're too busy or too involved in other work to truly learn what Access is capable of. This part takes you on a tour of some of the high-end features provided by Microsoft Access so that you'll know they're there, and you'll have a blueprint for using these capabilities in your own applications.

IN THIS PART

Chapter 24
Optimizing Access Applications

Chapter 25
Advanced Data Access with VBA

Chapter 26
Bulletproofing Access Applications

Chapter 27
Using the Windows Application Programming Interface

Chapter 28
Object-Oriented Programming with VBA

Chapter 29
Customizing Access Ribbons

Chapter 30
Using Access Macros

Chapter 31
Distributing Access Applications

Optimizing Access Applications

W hen Microsoft introduced 32-bit Access, a number of new performance concerns came part and parcel with the new features and functions. Microsoft continues to make a conscious effort to enhance the performance of the Access database engine, as well as compilation techniques and features such as the formerly undocumented Decompile command. The end result is that Microsoft has helped to ease your burden, but in no way has it completely taken that burden from you.

Tip

The published minimum RAM requirement for a computer to run Access on Windows XP (SP2 or later), Windows Server 2003 (or higher), or Windows Vista or Windows 7 is 256MB — with an emphasis on *minimum.* **If you plan to do serious development with Access, you should have at least 512MB to 1GB of RAM or, preferably, 2GB or more.**

With today's computers and memory prices, this amount of memory is a valuable investment. In fact, simply adding more memory will increase speed much more than changing your processor speed, because Access must use the hard drive as a virtual memory area if it doesn't have enough memory. Hard drives are slow, and big hard drives are even slower — regardless of the processor speed.

Understanding Module Load on Demand

One of the great features of Visual Basic for Applications (VBA), the core language of Microsoft Access, is its *load on demand* functionality. Using load on demand, Access loads code modules only as they're needed or referenced. In

IN THIS CHAPTER

Taking advantage of VBA's Load on Demand functionality

Deciding which file format to use

Using `.accde` **databases for better performance**

Achieving better performance through compilation

Increasing the absolute speed of your application

Increasing the perceived speed of your application

Using special techniques with large databases

early versions of Access, on-demand loading of modules wasn't fully realized because referencing a procedure in a module loaded the entire module's potential *call tree* (all the modules containing procedures that *might* be called by the procedure). With Access, the load on demand feature truly does help reduce the amount of RAM needed and helps your program run faster.

Tip

Because Access doesn't unload code after it has been loaded into memory, you should periodically close your application while you develop. When developing, most of us have a tendency to open and work with many different procedures in many different modules. These modules stay in memory until Access is closed, which can lead to performance degradation.

Organizing your modules

When any procedure or variable is referenced in your application, the entire module that contains the procedure or variable is loaded into memory. To minimize the number of modules loaded into memory, you need to organize your procedures and variables into logical modules. For example, it's a good idea to place all global variables in the same module. If only one global variable is declared in a module, the entire module is loaded into memory. By the same token, you should put only procedures that are always used by your application (such as start-up procedures) into the module containing the global variables.

Note

In the discussion that follows, the term procedure is used to mean either a function or a sub.

Pruning the call tree

The call tree for a procedure contains any additional procedures that the current or procedure has referenced within it, as well as those referenced by the newly loaded procedures, and so on. Because a procedure may reference numerous additional procedures stored in different modules, based on the action taken by the procedure, this loading of all potentially called procedures takes a lot of time and memory.

Remember that when a procedure is called, the entire module in which that procedure is stored is placed in memory.

Therefore, a potential call tree consists of all the procedures that *could* be called by the current procedure that you're calling. In addition, all the procedures that could be called from *those* procedures and so forth are also part of the potential call tree. For example:

1. If you call procedure A, the entire module containing procedure A is loaded.

2. Modules containing variable declarations used by procedure A are loaded.

3. Procedure A has lines of code that call procedures B and C — the modules containing procedure B and procedure C are loaded. (Even if the call statements are in conditional loops and are never executed, they're still loaded because they could *potentially* be called.)

4. Any procedures that could be called by procedure B and procedure C are loaded, as well as the entire modules containing those potential procedures.

5. And so on and so on. . . .

Fortunately for all Access developers, this complete loading of a potential call tree has been addressed in Access 2010. Access now automatically compiles modules on demand, instead of loading the entire potential call tree.

Note

You can turn off the Compile on Demand option if you prefer, making Access compile all modules at one time. You do this in the VBA program rather than in Access. (Access links directly to VBA's development environment for working with VB code.)

To check the status of the Compile on Demand option, follow these steps:

1. In the VBA editor window, choose Tools ➪ Options.

   The Options dialog box appears.

2. Select the General tab, and either check or uncheck the Compile On Demand check box (see Figure 24.1).

FIGURE 24.1

For maximum performance, leave the Compile On Demand check box selected.

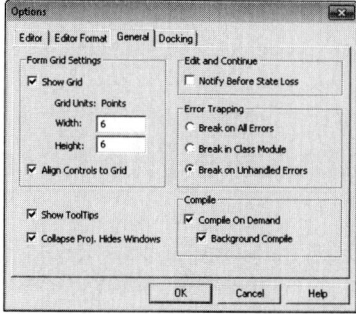

3. Click OK.

With the Compile on Demand option selected, Access loads only the portion of the call tree required by the executed procedure. For example, if you call procedure A in module A, any modules that contain procedures referenced in procedure A are loaded and compiled. However, Access doesn't take into consideration procedures that may be called from other procedures in module A, and it doesn't look at the potential call tree of the modules loaded because one of their procedures is referenced in procedure A. Because Access loads modules one level deep from the executed procedure's immediate call tree— and *not* the module's call tree — your applications should load and execute somewhat faster than they did in previous versions.

Even though Access has made a significant improvement in the way modules are loaded and compiled, you can still reduce the number of modules loaded and compiled. For example, never place infrequently called procedures in a module with procedures that are called often. Be aware, though, that organizing your procedures like this might make your modules less logical and harder to conceptualize. For example, you might have a dozen functions that perform various manipulations to contact information in your application. Ordinarily, you might make one module called modContacts and place all the contact-related procedures and variables into this one module. Because Access loads the entire module when one procedure or variable in it is called, you might want to separate the contact-related procedures into separate modules — one for procedures that are frequently used and one for procedures that are rarely called.

Tip

Keep in mind that all modules with procedures that are referenced from a different module are loaded when the procedure is called. In your application, if any of your common procedures reference a procedure that isn't frequently used, place the infrequently used procedure in the same module as the common procedures to prevent a different module (containing the uncommon procedure) from being loaded and compiled. You may even decide to use more than two modules if you have very large amounts of code in multiple procedures that are rarely called. Although breaking related procedures into separate modules may make your code a bit harder to understand, it can greatly improve the performance of your application.

To take full advantage of Compile on Demand, you have to carefully plan your procedure placement. Third-party tools can be invaluable for visualizing where all the potential calls for various procedures are located. An Internet search with Google, Bing, or Yahoo! for terms such as "Microsoft Access documenter" or "Access database documenter" should return valuable information.

Using the .accdb Database File Format

Since its inception, Microsoft Access has used a database engine named Jet (an acronym for Joint Engine Technology). Beginning with Access 2007 the Microsoft Access development team wanted to add significant new features to Access, such as multi-variable and attachment fields. Because the new features were so significant, it wasn't possible to retrofit Jet with the code necessary to support the new features. As a result, Microsoft developed an entirely new database engine, the Access Connectivity Engine (ACE), for Access 2007, 2010, and future versions of Access.

Access 2010 supports several file formats, including the following:

- Access 2007 .accdb format
- Access 2002–2003 .mdb format
- Access 2000 .mdb format
- Access 97 .mdb format

The Access .accdb format supports several new features, such as multivalued fields and attachments, not available in previous versions (.mdb). The new file format can't be opened or linked to earlier versions of Access (although you can link tables in earlier versions to an .accdb file). The .accdb file format doesn't support replication or user-level security. If you need to use an Access 2010 database with earlier versions of Access or use replication or user-level security, you must use the .mdb file format.

You can open and even run Access 97 database files, but you can't make any design changes in the Access 97 .mdb file. You can open Access 2002–2003 and Access 2000 database files and make any desired changes to them. However, you'll only be able to use features specific to those versions. Some of the new Access features won't be available, particularly those features that rely on the ACE database engine.

The default database file format in Access 2007 and 2010 is .accdb. You can convert a database saved in a previous format by opening the database in Access 2010, clicking the File menu in the upper-left corner of the main Access screen to open the Access Options dialog box, and selecting the Share tab. The Share tab (see Figure 24.2) includes a number of options for saving the current database in a number of different Access formats (.accdb, 2002–2003 .mdb, 2000 .mdb, and so on), or saving individual objects, such as forms or reports, in .pdf or .xps formats.

FIGURE 24.2

The Share tab under the File menu lets you save the current database in a number of different file formats.

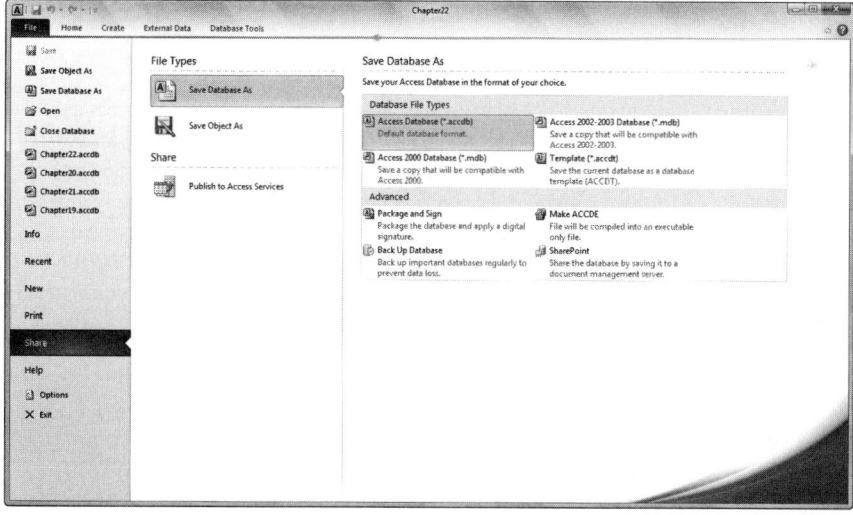

Tip

Change the default Access file format for new files by opening the Access Options dialog box, selecting the General tab (see Figure 24.3), and selecting the file format you'd like to use from the Default File Format drop-down list. When you're creating a new database, you can always select a different file format to use. The default selection simply makes it easier to work with a particular format if necessary.

FIGURE 24.3

Choose the default Access file format on the General tab of the Access Options dialog box.

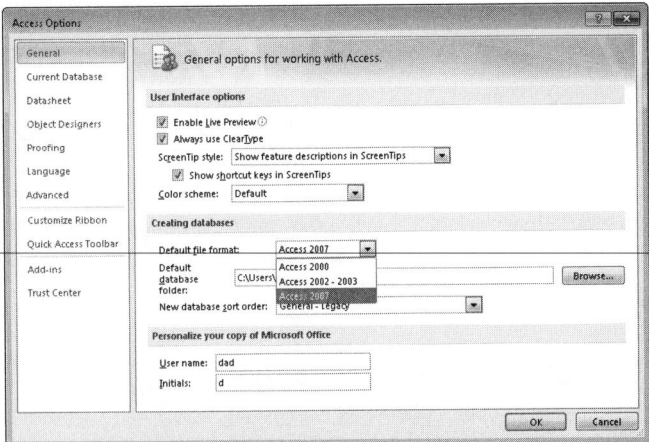

The Access 2007 file format should be used only in an Access environment where all users are using Access 2007 or 2010. In addition to complete compatibility with all Access 2007 and 2010 features, you may experience some performance advantages when using the Access .accdb file format with larger databases. However, you should stay with the Access 2002–2003 file format for compatibility with a mixed environment of Access 2002, 2003, 2007, or 2010 users. In a mixed environment of Access 2000, 2002, 2003, 2007, or 2010 users; stay with the Access 2000 file format. An Access 2003, 2007, or 2010 program can attach to Access 97 data files, but if you're trying to accommodate Access 97 users, you cannot upgrade the Access 97 data files.

Distributing .accde Files

One way to ensure that your application's code is always compiled is to distribute your database as an .accde file. When you save your database as an .accde file, Access compiles all code modules (including form and report modules), removes all editable source code, and compacts the database. The new .accde file contains no source code but continues to work because it does contain a compiled copy of all your code. Not only is using an .accde file a great way to secure your source code, but it also allows you to distribute databases that are smaller (because they contain no source code) and always keep their modules in a compiled state. Because the code is always in a compiled state, less memory is used by the application, and you suffer no performance penalty for code being compiled at runtime.

In addition to not being able to view existing code because it's all compiled, the following restrictions apply:

- You can't view, modify, or create forms, reports, or modules in Design view. You can, however, create and modify tables and queries in an .accde file.

- You can't add, delete, or change references to object libraries or databases.

- You can't change your database's VBA project name by using the Options dialog box.

- You can't import or export forms, reports, or modules. Note, however, that tables, queries, and macros can be imported from or exported to non-.accde databases.

Tip

If you want to create a demo of your application — and if you don't want the users to be able to see your code or form and report designs — you should create an .accde file. Because the designs of your forms, reports, and all code modules are simply not present (they're stored in a compiled version only), you don't have to worry about someone stealing or even modifying your designs and code. An .accde file is also good for distributing your work in environments where you don't want the user to change your designs.

Because of these restrictions, it may not be possible to distribute your application as an .accde file. For example, if your application creates forms at runtime, you wouldn't be able to distribute the database as an .accde file.

Caution

You have no way to convert an .accde file back into a normal database file, so always save and keep a copy of the original database! When you need to make changes to the application, you must open the normal database and then create a new .accde file before distribution. If you delete your original database, you won't be able to access any of your objects in Design view.

To create an .accde file, follow these steps:

1. Save and close all the database objects.

   If you don't close these objects, Access tries to close them for you, prompting you to save changes where applicable. When working with a shared database, all users must close the database; Access needs exclusive rights to work with the database.

Tip

Since Access can't convert an application into an .accde if it can't compile it, you may want to compile your application first.

2. Select the Make ACCDE command on the File menuShare ribbon (refer to Figure 24.2).

   The Save As dialog box appears.

3. Specify a name, drive, and folder for the database.

   Don't try to save the .accde file with the same filename (including the filename extension) as the original database.

Caution

Don't delete or overwrite your original database! You can't convert an .accde file to a normal database, and you can't edit any objects in an .accde file. If you delete or otherwise lose your original database, you'll never again be able to access any of the objects in the design environment.

Note

You can create an .accde file only if you first convert the database into the Access .accdb format. If the file is in an Access 2002–2003 format, you can create an .mde file — the Access 2002–2003 equivalent to an .accde file.

Understanding the Compiled State

Understanding how Access performs Compile on Demand is critical to achieving maximum performance from your Access application. However, it's also paramount that you understand what compilation is and what it means for an application to be in a compiled state.

Access has two types of code — code that you write and code that Access understands and executes. Before a VBA procedure is executed, the code must be run through a *compiler* to generate code in a form that Access understands — called *compiled code*.

Access lacks a true compiler and, instead, uses partially compiled code and an interpreter. A true compiler converts source code to machine-level instructions, which are executed by your computer's CPU. Access converts your source code to an intermediate state that it can rapidly interpret and execute. The code in the converted form (compiled code) is known as being in a *compiled state*.

If a procedure is called that isn't in a compiled state, the procedure must be compiled and the compiled code passed to the interpreter for execution. In reality, as previously stated, this doesn't happen at the procedure level, but at the module level. When you call a procedure, the module containing the procedure and all modules that have procedures referenced by the called procedure are loaded and compiled. You can manually compile your code, or you can let Access compile it for you on the fly. It takes time to compile the code, however, so the performance of your application suffers if you let Access compile it on the fly.

In addition to the time required for Access to compile your code at runtime, uncompiled programs use considerably more memory than compiled code does. When your application is completely compiled, only the compiled code is loaded into memory when a procedure is called. If you run an application that is in a decompiled state, Access loads the decompiled code and generates the compiled code as needed. Access doesn't unload the decompiled code as it compiles, so you're left with two versions of the same code in memory.

Even on computers with large amounts of installed memory, loading both the compiled and uncompiled versions of modules takes more time than loading compiled modules alone.

There is one drawback to compiled applications: They use a bit more hard drive space than their decompiled versions because both the compiled and decompiled versions of the code are stored on the hard drive.

Hard drive space shouldn't often be a problem, but if you have an application with an enormous amount of code, you can save hard drive space by keeping it in a decompiled state. Remember that a trade-off is made between hard drive space used and the performance of your database. Most often, when given the choice, a user would rather give up a few megabytes of hard drive space in exchange for faster applications.

Tip

You can use this space-saving technique to your advantage if you need to distribute a large application and your recipients have a full development version of Access. By distributing the uncompiled versions, you need much less hard drive space to distribute the application, and the end users can compile it again at their location. If you're going to do this, you should put the entire application into a decompiled state. I cover fully decompiling an application in the "Using the decompile option" section, later in this chapter.

Putting your application's code into a compiled state

You have only one way to put your entire application into a compiled state: In the VBA editor window, on the Modules toolbar, choose Debug ➪ Compile *Database Name* (see Figure 24.4). You must have a module open to access the Debug menu. Generally, you should always use the Compile *Database Name* command to ensure that all the code is saved in a compiled state. Complex applications may take a long time to compile, and, in general, you may choose to compile your Access projects only before distributing to end users or before performing benchmark tests.

FIGURE 24.4

Compile *Database Name* is the only way to fully compile your application.

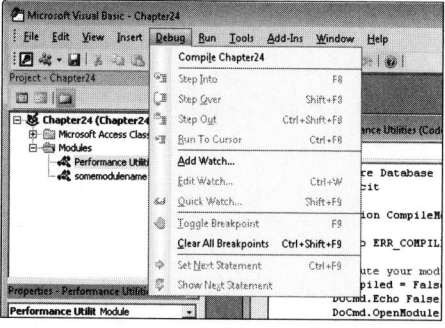

Note

When you choose Debug ⇨ Compile Database Name, you see the name of your project. This is the name that you used to save your database file the first time that it was created or saved. If you later rename the database file, the project name doesn't change. You can change it by choosing Tools ⇨ Properties in the module window; the database Properties dialog box contains the database name setting.

Access has a Background Compile option. Figure 24.1 shows this option under Compile on Demand — the default value for this option is True (selected). This option tells Access to compile code in the background rather than to compile it all at one time.

Tip

It is especially important to close your application after performing a Compile Database Name. To compile all your modules, Access needs to load every module into memory. All this code stays in memory until you close Access.

Losing the compiled state

In the past, one of the greatest roadblocks to optimizing Access applications has been the fact that an application could be uncompiled very easily. When the Access application was in an uncompiled state, Access had to constantly compile code as it was called. In fact, losing the compiled state was so easy to do in previous versions of Access that it would often happen without developers even realizing that they'd done it.

In Access 2010, only portions of code affected by certain changes are put into an uncompiled state — not the entire application. By itself, this is a tremendous improvement over previous versions of Access.

The following actions cause portions of your code to be uncompiled:

- Saving a modified form, report, control, or module. (If you don't save the modified object, your application is preserved in its previous state.)
- Adding a new form, report, control, or module, including adding new code behind a form.
- Deleting or renaming a form, report, control, or module.
- Adding or removing a reference to an object library or database by using the References command on the Tools menu.

Okay, so you think that you have a handle on code that loses its compiled state? Well, here are a couple of gotchas to consider:

- If you modify objects — such as reports or forms — at runtime through VBA code, portions of your application are put into an uncompiled state when the objects are modified. (Wizards often do this.)
- If your application creates objects like reports or forms on the fly, portions of your application are put into an uncompiled state when the objects are created. (Wizards often do this as well.)

Caution

When you change a project name (but not the filename), the entire application loses its compiled state. Because of this, you should change the project name only if absolutely necessary, and you should compile your database immediately after making the change.

Distributing applications in a compiled or uncompiled state

When distributing your Access application, you need to take several issues into consideration.

Distributing source code for your application

First and foremost, if you distribute source code and allow users to modify or add objects, you must make the users aware of the compilation issues. If your users don't fully comprehend what's happening with the application's compiled state, you can be sure that you'll receive complaints that the application is getting slower and slower over time.

Putting an application in an uncompiled state

If your application is the type that will be frequently changing its compiled state (due to creating forms and reports dynamically), or if end users will often make changes to the application's objects, or if distributed file size is an issue, you may want to consider distributing the database in a fully uncompiled state.

Follow these steps to put an application into an uncompiled state:

1. Create a new database.
2. Import all your application objects into the new database.
3. Compact the new database.

In the "Using the decompile option" section, later in this chapter, I tell you how to decompile the project manually.

Storing commonly used code in a library

After your application is finished and ready for distribution, you may want to consider placing all commonly used code into a *library database* (an external database referenced by an Access application database). A slight performance overhead is incurred by calling library code rather than accessing it directly in the parent application, but the library code will never be put into a decompiled state. This technique can greatly increase an application's performance and keep the performance relatively consistent over time.

The first step for using an external library is to create an external database and import all the application's code modules.

Caution

Any library procedures declared as Private are not accessible to the calling application, so carefully plan what you want to expose (declare as Public) and don't want to expose to other databases.

After you create the library database, you have to reference it in the application database (which is the database that your users will run). To create a reference, first open any module in your application in the VBA editor. With a module open in Design view, a new command — References — is available on the Tools menu (see Figure 24.5). Select the References command to open the References dialog box (see Figure 24.6).

FIGURE 24.5

The References option appears on the Tools menu only when you have a module open and selected in Design view and no code is currently running.

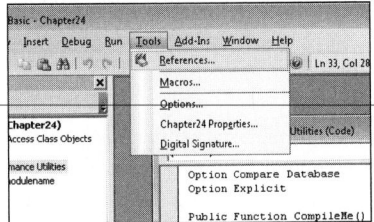

FIGURE 24.6

The References dialog box is where you reference different types of libraries.

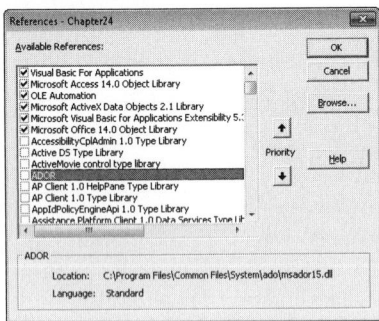

When making a reference to another Access database you may need to browse for the database. After you've selected the external Access database, it shows up in the References dialog box with a selected check box to indicate that it's referenced.

To remove a reference, open the References dialog box again and deselect the referenced item by clicking its check box. After you've made all the references that you need to make, click OK.

After a database is referenced, you can call the procedures in the referenced database as if they exist in your application database. The referenced database always stays in a compiled state unless it's directly opened in Access and modified.

Creating a library reference for distributed applications

If you're distributing your application, references stay intact only if the calling database and the library database are in the same path. For example, if the main database is in C:\myapp on your machine, and if the library database is in C:\myapp\library, the reference remains intact as long as the library database is located in C:\myapp\library. If the path won't remain consistent upon distribution, your application's users must manually adjust the reference or you must create the reference with VBA code.

The following procedure creates a reference to the file whose name is passed as an argument. In order for this function to work, the full filename with path must be passed:

```
bResult = CreateReference("C:\My Documents\MyLib.accdb").
```

The function is

```
Public Function CreateReference(strFileName As String) _
    As Boolean
  Dim ref As Reference
On Error GoTo HandleError
  Set ref = References.AddFromFile(strFileName)
  CreateReference = True
ExitHere:
  Exit Function
HandleError:
  MsgBox Err & ": " & Err.Description
  CreateReference = False
  Resume ExitHere
End Function
```

Tip

You can verify that a reference is set by using the ReferenceFromFile function. To verify a reference, pass the function, the full path, and the filename like this:

```
bResult =    ReferenceFromFile("C:\Windows\System32\mscal.ocx")
```

Here's the function, which returns True if the reference is valid and False if it isn't:

```
Public Function ReferenceFromFile(strFileName As String) _
    As Boolean
  Dim ref As Reference
On Error GoTo HandleError
  For Each ref In References
    If StrComp(ref.FullPath, strFileName) = 0 Then
      ReferenceFromFile = True
      Exit For
```

```
      End If
   Next ref
ExitHere:
   Exit Function
HandleError:
   MsgBox Err & ": " & Err.Description
   ReferenceFromFile = False
   Resume ExitHere
End Function
```

With the References collection, the primary concern of using and distributing libraries — losing references upon distribution — is now gone. However, library databases still have one major drawback: Access libraries don't support circular references. This means that the code in your library databases can't reference variables or call procedures that exist in your parent database.

Whether you distribute your application as one database or as a primary database that uses library databases, if your applications are *static* (they don't allow modification of objects by end users or wizards and don't perform object modifications on themselves), you should always distribute the databases in a fully compiled state so that your users experience the highest level of performance.

Improving Absolute Speed

When discussing an application's performance, the word *performance* is usually synonymous with speed. You'll find two types of speed in software development:

- **Absolute:** Absolute speed is how quickly your application performs a function, such as running a certain query. Absolute speed can be measured in units of time.

- **Perceived:** Perceived speed is how end users perceive an application's performance. This phenomenon of perceived speed is often the result of visual feedback provided to the user while the application performs a task. Whereas absolute speed can be measured, perceived speed is very subjective. (For more on perceived speed, see the "Improving Perceived Speed" section, later in this chapter.)

Among the most important steps for increasing absolute speed are the following:

- **Keeping your application in a compiled state:** As was discussed in the "Distributing .accde Files" section, converting your .accdb file to an .accde file is a good way to ensure that the code is always in a compiled state.

- **Organizing your procedures into "smart" modules:** As was discussed in the "Understanding Module Load on Demand" section, separating procedures into modules based on how frequently they'll be used is a good approach.

- **Opening databases exclusively:** You should always open a database exclusively in a single-user environment. If your database is a *standalone application* (meaning that nothing is shared over a network), opening the database in exclusive mode really boosts performance. If the database runs on a network and is shared by multiple users, the database can't be opened exclusively. (Actually, the first user can open it exclusively, but no other user can access the database until the first user closes it.) The preferred method for running an application in a network environment is to run Access and the main .accdb file locally, and then link to a shared database containing the data on the server.

Cross-Reference

The process of opening a database exclusively is explained in detail in Chapter 21.

To open a database exclusively in Access, in the Open dialog box click the Open button down arrow and select Open Exclusive (see Figure 24.7).

FIGURE 24.7

Selecting the Open Exclusive option when opening an Access database

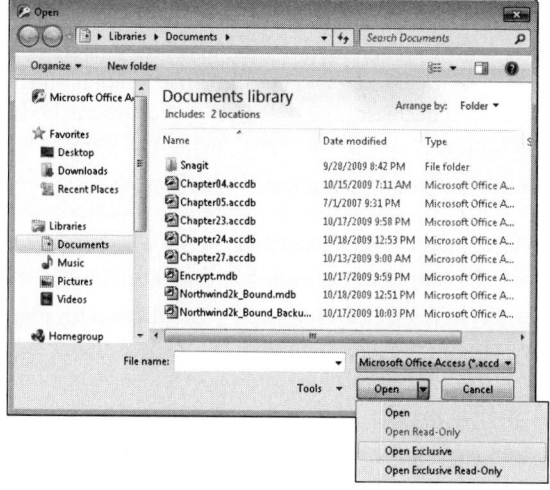

Tip

If you always want to open a database exclusively, you can make this the default setting. Click the Microsoft Office button and select Access Options. In the Access Options dialog box, select the Advanced tab. Change the Default Open Mode to Exclusive if you always want to open a database exclusively. (The Default Open Mode is otherwise set to Shared.)

- **Compacting databases regularly:** An often-overlooked way of maximizing a database's performance is to routinely compact the database. When records are deleted from an Access database, the hard drive space that held the deleted data is not recovered until a compact is performed. In addition, a database becomes fragmented as data is modified in the database. Compacting a database defragments the database and recovers hard drive space.

Note

Although databases should be compacted regularly, that does not mean they should be compacted every time they're used. I advise against using the Compact on Close option.

All the preceding methods are excellent (and necessary) ways to help keep your applications running at their optimum performance level, but these aren't the only tasks that you can perform to increase the absolute speed of your application. Almost every area of development, from forms to modules, can be optimized to give your application maximum absolute speed.

Tuning your system

One important aspect of performance has nothing to do with the actual application design — that is, the computer on which the application is running. Even though it's impossible to account for all the various configurations your clients may have, you can do some things for your computer and recommend that end users do them for theirs:

- **Equip the computer with as much memory as possible.** This step often becomes an issue related to the cost of purchasing and installing the computer memory. However, as memory prices continue to decrease, one of the most effective methods of increasing the speed of Access applications is to add additional memory to the user's computer.

- **Close all applications that aren't being used.** Windows makes it very handy to keep as many applications loaded as you want — on the odd chance that you may need to use one of them. Although Windows XP, Windows Vista, and Windows 7 are very good at handling memory for multiple applications, each application still uses computer resources.

- **Make sure that your Windows swap file is on a fast drive with plenty of free space.** If possible, you should also set the minimum hard drive space available for virtual memory to at least twice the physical RAM installed and make it a permanent swap file.

- **Defragment the hard drive often.** Defragmenting a hard drive allows data to be retrieved in larger sections, thus causing fewer reads and less repositioning of the read heads.

Getting the most from your tables

The preceding sections documented many technical issues that should be reviewed to improve application speed, but sometimes it's advantageous to get back to the basics when designing your applications. Tools like Access enable novices to create relational databases quickly and easily, but they don't teach good database design techniques in the process. (An exception to this statement is the Table Analyzer Wizard. Click the ribbon's Database Tools tab, then click the Analyze Table command in the Analyze group to start the Table Analyzer Wizard.)

Caution

Even though the Table Analyzer Wizard offers suggestions that are often helpful in learning good design technique, its recommendations should never be taken as gospel. The Table Analyzer has proven to be wrong on many occasions.

Entire volumes of text have been devoted to the subject of database theory. Teaching database theory is certainly beyond the scope of this chapter (or even this book). However, you should be familiar with many basics of good database design.

Creating efficient indexes

Indexes help Access find and sort records faster and more efficiently. To find data, Access looks up the location of the data in the index and then retrieves the data from its location. You can create indexes based on a single field or on multiple fields. Multiple-field indexes enable you to distinguish between records in which the first field may have the same value. If they're defined properly, multiple-field indexes can be improve the performance of queries. This is because Microsoft's Rushmore query optimization (the technology that Jet uses to optimize the speed at which queries execute) knows how to use multiple-field indexes.

Cross-Reference

For more on indexes, turn to Chapters 2 and 3.

Deciding which fields to index

People new to database development typically make two mistakes: First, not using indexes and, second, using too many indexes (sometimes putting an index on every field in a table). Both of these mistakes are serious. Sometimes a table with too many indexes may give *slower* performance than a table with no indexes. Why? When a record is saved, Access must check every index in the table, taking time and using a considerable amount of disk space. The time used is rarely noticed with a few indexes, but a lot of indexes can require a huge amounts of time for updates.

In addition, indexes can slow some action queries (such as append queries) because the indexes for updated fields need to be updated while performing the query's operations. Figure 24.8 shows the index property sheet for a sample `tblContacts` table.

FIGURE 24.8

Indexing common search fields like `ZipCode`, `CustomerType`, and `TaxLocation`

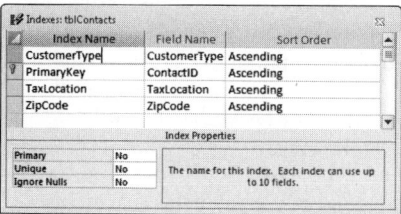

When you create a primary key for a table, the field (or fields) used to define the key is automatically indexed. You can index any field unless the field's data type is Memo or OLE Object. You should consider indexing a field if any of the following rules apply:

- The field's data type is Text, Number, Currency, or Date/Time.

- You anticipate searching for values stored in the field.

- You anticipate sorting records based on the values in the field.

- You will join the field to fields in other tables in queries.

- You anticipate storing many different values in the field. (If many of the values in the field are the same, the index may not significantly speed up searches or sorting.)

When defining an index, you have the option of creating an ascending or descending index. Ascending indexes are the default. But a descending index can be valuable in the case of fields such as dates, where the field may be sorted in descending order so that more recent dates appear at the top of the query's results.

Using multiple-field indexes

When frequently searching or sorting by multiple fields at the same time, you can create an index on the combined fields. For example, if you often set criteria for LastName and FirstName fields in the same query, it makes sense to create a multiple-field index on both fields.

When sorting a table by a multiple-field index, Access first sorts by the first field defined for the index. If the first field contains records with duplicate values, Access then sorts by the second field defined for the index, and so on. This creates a drill-down effect. For a multiple-field index to work, a search criterion *must* be defined for the first field in the index, but not for additional fields in the index. In the preceding example, if you wanted to search for someone with the last name Jones, but you didn't specify a first name to use in the search, the multi-field index wouldn't be used. If you need to perform searches on individual fields in a multiple-field index, you should create an index for each field in addition to the multiple-field index. It's not necessary to create an additional index for the first field in the multi-field index.

Getting the most from your queries

The performance problems of many Access applications result from query design. Database applications are all about looking at and working with data, and queries are the heart of determining what data to look at or work with. Queries are used to bind forms and reports, fill list boxes and combo boxes, make new tables, and perform many other functions within an Access application. Because they're so widely used, optimize your queries is extremely important.

A query that is properly designed can provide results minutes to hours faster than a poorly designed query that returns the same result set. Consider the following:

- When designing queries and tables, you should create indexes for all fields that are used in sorts, joins, and criteria fields. Indexes enable Jet to quickly sort and search through your database.

- When possible, use a primary key in place of a regular index when creating joins. Primary keys don't allow nulls, and they give the query optimizer more ways to use the joins.

- Limit the columns of data returned in a select query to only those you need. If you don't need the information from a field, don't return it in the query. Queries run much faster when returning less information.

Tip

If you need to use a field for a query condition and it isn't necessary to display the field in the results table, deselect the View check box to suppress displaying the field and its contents.

- When you need to return a count of the records returned by an SQL statement, use Count(*) instead of Count([FieldName]) because Count(*) is considerably faster. Count(*) counts records that contain null fields; Count([FieldName]) checks for nulls and disqualifies them from the count. This means that Count doesn't count records that have a null in the specified field.

Tip

You may also replace FieldName with an expression in the Count function, but this slows down the function even further.

- Avoid using calculated fields in nested queries. A calculated field in a subordinate query considerably slows down the top-level query. You should use calculated fields only in top-level queries, and even then, only when necessary.

- When you need to group records by the values of a field used in a join, specify the Group By for the field that is in the same table that you're totaling. You can drag the joined field from either table, but using Group By on the field from the table that you're totaling yields faster results.

- Domain aggregate functions (such as DLookup or DCount) that are used as expressions considerably slow down queries. Instead, you should add the table to the query or use a subquery to return the needed information.

- As with VBA code modules, queries are compiled. To compile a query, the query optimizer evaluates the query to determine the fastest way to execute the query. If a query is saved in a compiled state, it runs at its fastest speed the first time that you execute it. If it isn't compiled, it takes longer the first time because it must be compiled, but then it runs faster in succeeding executions. To compile a query, run the query by opening it in Datasheet view and then close the query without saving it. If you make changes to the query definition, run the query again after saving your changes, and then close it without saving it.

- If you really want to squeeze the most out of your queries, experiment by creating your queries in different ways (such as specifying different types of joins). You'll be surprised at the varying results.

Getting the most from your forms and reports

Forms and reports can slow an application by taking a long time to load or process information. You can perform a number of tasks to increase the performance of forms and reports.

Minimizing form and report complexity and size

One of the key elements to achieving better performance from your forms and reports is reducing complexity and size, which you can accomplish by

- **Minimizing the number of objects on a form or report:** The fewer objects used, the fewer resources needed to display and process the form or report.

- **Reducing the use of subforms:** When a subform is loaded, two forms are in memory — the parent form and the subform. Use a list box or a combo box in place of a subform whenever possible.

- **Using labels instead of text boxes for hidden fields because text boxes use more resources than labels do.** Hidden fields are often used as an alternative to creating variables to store information. (Remember, though, that you cannot use labels as parameters for queries.)

Tip

You can't write a value directly to a label like you can to a text box, but you can write to the labels caption property using VBA like this: `Label1.Caption = "MyValue"`.

- **Moving some code from a form's module into a standard module:** This enables the form to load faster because the code doesn't need to be loaded into memory. If the procedures that you move to a normal module are referenced by any procedures executed upon loading a form (such as in the form load event), moving the procedures won't help because they're loaded anyway as part of the potential call tree of the executed procedure.

- **Not overlapping controls on a form or report.**

- **Placing related groups of controls on form pages:** If only one page is shown at a time, Access doesn't need to generate all the controls at the same time.

- **Using a query that returns a limited result set for a form or report's RecordSource rather than using a table or underlying query that uses tables:** The less data returned in the `RecordSource`, the faster the form or report loads. In addition, you should return only those fields actually used by the form or report. Don't use a query that gathers fields that won't be displayed on the form or report (except for a conditional check).

Using bitmaps on forms and reports

Bitmaps on forms and reports make an application look attractive and can also help convey the purpose of the form or report (as in a wizard). However, graphics are always resource-intensive, so you should use the fewest possible number of graphic objects on your forms and reports. This helps to minimize form and report load time, increase print speed, and reduce the resources used by your application.

Often you'll display pictures that a user never changes and that are not bound to a database. Examples of such pictures include your company logo on a switchboard or static images in a wizard. When you want to display images like these, you have two choices:

- **Use an Image control.** If the image never changes, use an Image control. Image controls use fewer resources and display faster.
- **Use an Unbound Object Frame.** If you need the image to be a linked or embedded OLE object that you can edit, use an Unbound Object Frame.

Tip

If you have an image in an Unbound Object Frame that you no longer need to edit, you can convert the Unbound Object Frame to an Image control by right-clicking the control and choosing Change To ⇨ Image from the pop-up menu.

Tip

When you have forms that contain unbound OLE objects, close the forms when they aren't in use to free up resources. Also, avoid using bitmaps with many colors — they take considerably more resources and are slower to paint than bitmaps of the same size with fewer colors.

Note

If you need to display an unbound OLE object but don't want the user to be able to activate it, set its `Enabled` property to `False`.

Speeding up list boxes and combo boxes

It's important to pay attention to list boxes and combo boxes when optimizing your application. You can take a number of steps to make your combo boxes and list boxes run faster:

- When using multipage or tabbed forms containing list boxes or combo boxes on more than one page, don't set the `RowSource` of the list boxes or combo boxes until the actual page containing the control is displayed.

- Index the first field displayed in a list box or combo box. This enables Access to find entries that match text entered by the user much faster.

- Although it's not always practical, try to refrain from hiding a combo box's Bound column. Hiding the Bound column causes the control's searching features to slow down.

- If you don't need the search capabilities of AutoExpand, set the AutoExpand property of a combo box to No. Access is then relieved of constantly searching the list for entries matching text entered in the text portion of the combo box.

- When possible, make the first nonhidden column in a combo or list box a text data type, and not a numeric one. To find a match in the list of a combo box or list box, Access must convert a numeric value to text to do the character-by-character match. If the data type is text, Access can skip the conversion step.

- Often overlooked is the performance gain achieved by using saved queries for `RecordSource` and `RowSource` properties of list boxes and combo boxes. A saved query gives much better performance than an SQL `SELECT` statement because an SQL query is optimized on the fly.

Getting the most from your modules

An area where you'll often be able to use smart optimization techniques is in your modules. For example, in code behind forms, use the Me keyword when referencing controls. This approach takes advantage of the capabilities of Access. Using Me is faster than creating a form variable and referencing the form in the variable. Other optimization techniques are simply smart coding practices that have been around for many years. Try to use the optimum coding technique at all times. When in doubt, try different methods to accomplish a task and see which one is fastest.

Tip

Consider reducing the number of modules and procedures in your application by consolidating them whenever possible. A small memory overhead is incurred for each module and procedure that you use, so consolidation may free up some memory. When doing this, though, keep in mind the discussion in the "Understanding Module Load on Demand" section.

Using appropriate data types

You should always explicitly declare variables using the Dim function instead of arbitrarily assigning values to variables that haven't been dimmed. To make sure that all variables in your application are explicitly declared, choose Tools ⇨ Options in the VBA editor window, select the Editor tab, and then set the Require Variable Declarations option on the tab.

Note

If you forgot to set the Require Variable Declarations option before you started coding, you'll need to add the line of code Option Explicit to the top of each existing module.

Tip

Use integers and long integers rather than singles and doubles when possible. Integers and long integers use less memory, and they take less time to process than singles and doubles do. Table 24.1 shows the relative speed of the different data types available in Access.

TABLE 24.1

Data Types and Their Mathematical Processing Speed

Data Type	Relative Processing Speed
Integer/Long	Fastest
Single/Double	Next to fastest
Currency	Next to slowest
Variant	Slowest

In addition to using integers and long integers whenever possible, you should also use integer math rather than precision math when applicable. For example, to divide one long integer by another long integer, you can use the following statement:

```
x = Long1 / Long2
```

This statement is a standard math function that uses floating-point math. You can perform the same function by using integer math (the backward slash specifies integer division):

```
x = Long1 \ Long2
```

Of course, integer math isn't always applicable. It is, however, commonly applied when returning a percentage. For example, the following expression returns a percentage:

```
x = Total / Value
```

However, you can perform the same function using integer division by first multiplying the Total by 100 and then using integer division like this:

```
x = (Total * 100) \ Value
```

You should also use string functions ($) where applicable. When you're manipulating string variables, use the string functions (for example, Str$()) as opposed to their variant counterparts (Str()). If you're working with variants, use the non-$ functions. Using string functions when working with strings is faster because Access doesn't need to perform type conversions on the variables.

When you need to return a substring by using Mid$(), you can omit the third parameter to have the entire length of the string returned. For example, to return a substring that starts at the second character of a string and returns all remaining characters, use a statement like this:

```
strReturn = Mid$(strMyString, 2)
```

When using arrays, use dynamic arrays with the Erase and ReDim statements to reclaim memory. By dynamically adjusting the size of the arrays, you can ensure that only the amount of memory needed for the array is allocated.

Tip

In addition to using optimized variables, consider using constants when applicable. Constants can make your code easier to read and won't slow your application.

Writing faster routines

You can make your procedures faster by optimizing the routines that they contain in a number of ways. By keeping performance issues in mind as you develop, you'll find and take advantage of situations like the ones discussed here.

Some Access functions perform similar processes but vary greatly in execution time. You probably use one or more of these regularly, and knowing the most efficient way to perform these routines can greatly affect your application's speed:

- The `IIF()` function is much slower than `If...Then...Else`.

- The `With` and `For Each` functions accelerate manipulating multiple objects and their properties.

- Change a variable with `Not` instead of using an `If . . . Then` statement. (For example, use `x = Not(y)` instead of `If y = True then x= False`.)

- Instead of comparing a variable to the value `True`, use the value of the variable. (For example, instead of `If X = True then . . .`, use `If X then . . .`)

- Use the `Requery` method instead of the `Requery` action. The method is significantly faster than the action.

- When using OLE automation, resolve references by declaring variables as specific object types, rather than creating object references at runtime by using the `GetObject` or `CreateObject` functions. For example, in Chapter 22 you saw how to create object variables using the following syntax:

```
Dim WordObj As Word.Application
```

This statement is considerably faster than using `CreateObject`:

```
Set WordObj = CreateObject("Word.Application")
```

Using control variables

When referencing controls on a form in code, there are some very slow and some very fast ways to use references to controls. The slowest possible way is to reference each control explicitly, requiring Access to sequentially search for the control on the form. For example:

```
Forms![frmSales]![SaleDate] = something
Forms![frmSales]![InvoiceDate] = something
Forms![frmSales]![SalespersonID] = something
```

If the code is in the code module behind `frmSales`, you can use the `Me` reference. The `Me` reference substitutes for `Forms![formname]` and is much faster because it can go right to the form:

```
Me![SaleDate] = something
Me![InvoiceDate] = something
Me![SalespersonID] = something
```

If your code is not stored behind the form but is in a module procedure, you can use a control variable like the following:

```
Dim frm as Form
set frm = Forms![frmSales]
frm![SaleDate] = something
```

```
frm![InvoiceDate] = something
frm![SalespersonID] = something
```

This way, the form name is looked up only once.

An even faster way is to use the With construct:

```
With Forms![frmSales]
  ![SaleDate] = something
  ![InvoiceDate] = something
  ![SalespersonID] = something
End With
```

Using field variables

The preceding technique also applies to manipulating field data when working with a recordset in VBA code. For example, a typical loop looks something like this:

```
...
Do Until tbl.EOF
  MyTotal = MyTotal + tbl![OrderTotal]
  tbl.MoveNext
Loop
```

If this routine loops through many records, you should use the following code snippet instead:

```
Dim MyField as Field
...
Set MyField = tbl![OrderTotal]
Do Until tbl.EOF
  MyTotal = MyTotal + MyField
  tbl.MoveNext
Loop
```

This code executes much faster than explicitly referencing the field in every iteration of the loop.

Increasing the speed of finding data in code

Use the FindRecord and FindNext methods on indexed fields. These methods are much more efficient when used on indexed fields. Also, take advantage of bookmarks when you can. Returning to a bookmark is much faster than performing a Find to locate the data.

Listing 24.1 is an example of using a bookmark. Bookmark variables must be dimmed as variants, and you can create multiple bookmarks by dimming multiple variant variables. The following code opens tblCustomers, moves to the first record in the database, sets the bookmark, moves to the last record, and finally repositions back to the bookmarked record. For each step, the debug. print command shows the relative position in the database.

LISTING 24.1

Using a Bookmark to Mark a Record

```
Public Sub BookmarkExample()
   Dim rs As DAO.Recordset
   Dim bk As Variant
   Set rs = Workspaces(0).Databases(0).OpenRecordset( _
     "tblContacts", dbOpenTable)
   'Move to the first record in the database:
   rs.MoveFirst
   'Print the position in the database:
   Debug.Print rs.PercentPosition
   'Set the bookmark to the current record:
   bk = rs.Bookmark
   'Move to the last record in the database:
   rs.MoveLast
   'Print the position in the database:
   Debug.Print rs.PercentPosition
   'Move to the bookmarked record:
   rs.Bookmark = bk
   'Print the position in the database:
   Debug.Print rs.PercentPosition
   rs.Close
   Set rs = Nothing
End Sub
```

Eliminating dead code and unused variables

Before distributing your application, remove any *dead code* (code that isn't used at all) from your application. You'll often find entire procedures or even modules that once served a purpose but are no longer called. Also, it's quite common to forget to remove variable declarations after removing code using the variables. By eliminating dead code and unused variables, you reduce the memory your application uses and the time required to compile code at runtime.

Other things that you can do to increase the speed of your modules include opening any add-ins that your application uses for read-only access and replacing procedure calls within loops with in-line code. Also, don't forget one of the most important items: Deliver your applications with the modules compiled.

Increasing network performance

The single most important action that you can take to make sure that your networked databases run at peak performance is to run Access and the application database on the user's computer and link tables to the shared network database. Running Access over the network is much slower than running it locally.

When using Jet or ACE as the database engine, an Access application can run only so fast. With Jet or ACE, each time you open a table, run a query, or perform an operation on data, all the data referenced by the process or query must be moved from the data database (assuming that you've split your program and data database files) to the computer running the program. This may mean moving a lot of data across the network. In contrast, an Access project using the Microsoft SQL Server or SQL Server Express Edition can use stored procedures to minimize network traffic, drastically speeding up most Access applications.

Tip

If you're working with large amounts of data, consider using SQL Server as your back-end database file.

Improving Perceived Speed

Perceived speed is how fast your application appears to run to the end user. Many techniques can increase the perceived speed of your applications. Improving perceived speed usually involves supplying visual feedback to the user while the computer is busy performing some operation, such as updating a percent meter when Access is busy processing data.

Using a splash screen

Most Windows programs employ a splash screen, as shown in Figure 24.9. Most people think that the splash screen is simply to show the product's name and copyright information, but this isn't entirely correct. The splash screen contributes to the perceived speed of an application. It shows the user that something is *happening,* and it gives users something to look at for a few seconds while the rest of the application loads.

FIGURE 24.9

A splash screen to display product and version information

Note

In large applications, you may even display a series of splash screens with different information, such as helpful hints, instructions on how to use the product, or even advertisements. These are often called billboards.

To create a splash screen, create a basic form with appropriate information, such as your application name, logo, and user registration. Next, set this form as the Display Form in the Current Database options. You then want to call any initialization procedures from the On Open event of the splash form. A good splash screen should automatically disappear after a few seconds.

The code necessary to close a splash screen is very simple:

```
Private Sub Form_Timer()
    DoCmd.Close
End Sub
```

Set the form's Timer property to the number of milliseconds for which you want to display the splash screen.

Cross-Reference

For more information on splash screens and setting Current Database options (including the Display Form), see Chapter 31.

Keep in mind the following when using splash screens:

- **Minimize code in start-up forms.** Use only code that is absolutely necessary to display your start-up form and use a light form if possible.

Note

A light form is one that doesn't contain a class module. They're smaller and typically load and are displayed faster than forms with class modules. Also, because they require no storage space for a class module, they can decrease the size of your database. Possible disadvantages of using lightweight objects is that they do not appear in the Object Browser, and you cannot use the New keyword to create a new instance of the object.

- **The start-up form should call only initialization procedures.** Be careful about call trees — you don't want your start-up form to trigger the loading of many modules in your application.

Loading and keeping forms hidden

If you have frequently-displayed forms, consider hiding them rather than closing them. To hide a form, set its Visible property to False. When you need to display the form again, set its Visible property back to True. Hidden forms consume memory, but they display more quickly than forms that are loaded each time they're viewed. In addition, if you're *morphing* a form or report (changing the way it looks by changing form and control properties), keep the form hidden until all changes are made so that the user doesn't have to watch the changes take place.

Using the hourglass

Use the hourglass cursor when your application performs a task that may take a long time. The hourglass mouse pointer shows the user that the computer is busy and not locked up. Set the Hourglass cursor like this:

```
DoCmd.Hourglass True 'Use False to return to default cursor
```

Using the built-in progress meter

In addition to using the hourglass, you should consider using the Access progress meter when performing long routines in a procedure. The progress meter gives constant feedback that your application is busy, and it shows the user progress in the current process.

On the CD-ROM

`Chapter24.accdb` illustrates two types of progress meters. The first is the standard Microsoft Access progress meter displayed in the Access status bar; the second is a colored rectangle displayed on a pop-up form.

The `Chapter24.accdb` sample database includes a number of forms which show the use of two types of progress meters. Each uses a different type of progress meter but all run the same processing code. The code creates a 50,000-record `SampleData` table, and the progress meters show the progress of the operation. Each of the examples uses a simple form with several text-box controls and a button to start the process.

The following code demonstrates how to use the status-bar progress meter to show the meter starting at 0 percent and increasing to 100 percent, 1 percent at a time. The first example is `ProgressMeterUsingBuiltInAccessMeter`.

Caution

If you don't display the status bar, you won't see the built-in progress meter when it runs.

The code to initialize, update, and remove the meter is shown in Figure 24.10.

FIGURE 24.10

Code to run the status-bar progress meter

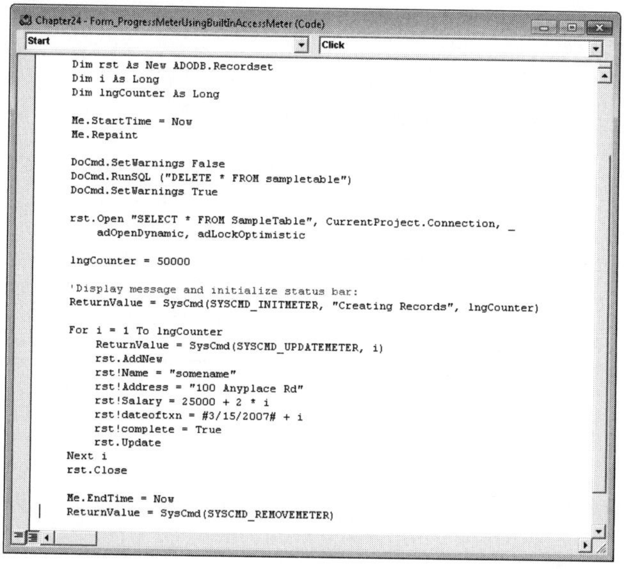

```
Dim rst As New ADODB.Recordset
Dim i As Long
Dim lngCounter As Long

Me.StartTime = Now
Me.Repaint

DoCmd.SetWarnings False
DoCmd.RunSQL ("DELETE * FROM sampletable")
DoCmd.SetWarnings True

rst.Open "SELECT * FROM SampleTable", CurrentProject.Connection, _
    adOpenDynamic, adLockOptimistic

lngCounter = 50000

'Display message and initialize status bar:
ReturnValue = SysCmd(SYSCMD_INITMETER, "Creating Records", lngCounter)

For i = 1 To lngCounter
    ReturnValue = SysCmd(SYSCMD_UPDATEMETER, i)
    rst.AddNew
    rst!Name = "somename"
    rst!Address = "100 Anyplace Rd"
    rst!Salary = 25000 + 2 * i
    rst!dateoftxn = #3/15/2007# + i
    rst!complete = True
    rst.Update
Next i
rst.Close

Me.EndTime = Now
ReturnValue = SysCmd(SYSCMD_REMOVEMETER)
```

The first step for using the percent meter is initializing the meter by calling the `SysCmd` function:

```
ReturnValue = SysCmd(acSysCmdInitMeter, "Creating Records", lngCounter)
```

`acSysCmdInitMeter` is an Access constant that tells the function to initialize the meter. The second parameter is the text to appear at the left side of the meter. Finally, the last value is the meter's maximum value (in this case, 100); for example, if you were iterating through a loop of 50,000 records, you might set this value to 50,000. Then you can pass the record count at any time to the `SysCmd` function and Access decides what the meter shows.

After the meter is initialized, pass a value to update the meter. Call the `SysCmd` function again and pass it the `acSysCmdUpdateMeter` constant and the new meter value. *Remember:* The value that you pass to the function is not necessarily the percent displayed by the meter — it can be the number of records processed or any number that represents a percentage from 1 to 100. For example, the meter displays 25 percent if 50,000 records are being processed and the update value is 12,500.

```
ReturnValue = SysCmd(acSysCmdUpdateMeter, i)
```

Remove the meter from the status bar after all the records are processed:

```
ReturnValue = SysCmd(acSysCmdRemoveMeter)
```

The progress meter displayed in the status bar is shown in Figure 24.11.

FIGURE 24.11

The Access status-bar progress meter

Creating a progress meter as a pop-up form

Open `ProgressMeterCallingEveryRecord` and click the Search button to see a progress meter implemented as a pop-up form. The bar grows from 0 percent to 100 percent.

The Progress Meter form in progress is shown in Figure 24.12.

FIGURE 24.12

A graphical progress meter

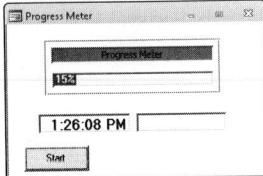

This progress meter has some advantages over the standard Microsoft Access progress meter. The status-bar progress meter isn't always as visible as you'd like. The status bar is always at the bottom of the screen and is easily overlooked by a user, whereas the pop-up progress meter pops up in the middle of the screen and is always visible to the user. Plus, the speed of the pop-up meter can be controlled by updating the meter every *x* percent.

The progress meter form is created from a few simple controls. It contains a rectangle control, two label controls, and option group controls. In Figure 24.12, the rectangle is showing 15 percent completed. The width of the rectangle is manipulated by the program used to display the meter's progress. The width is reset to 0 when the progress meter starts, and it's slowly built back to its original length.

The code for the progress meter is shown in Figure 24.13.

FIGURE 24.13

The Progress Meter form call to the pop-up progress meter

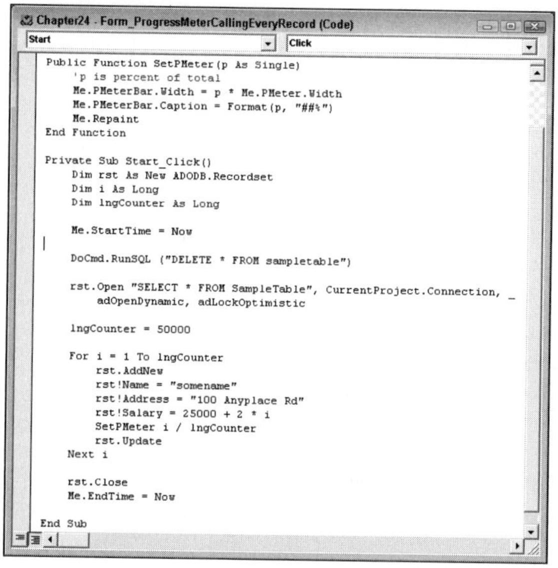

The code that calls the meter is one simple line buried in the middle of the iteration loop, passing the iteration number and total number of iterations expected. In this example, i is being processed and lngCounter is 50,000.

```
SetPMeter i / lngCounter
```

The function SetPMeter consists of only three lines — one to display the rectangle and manipulate its width, one to display the caption on the bar as it grows inside the rectangle, and one to repaint the screen each time so that the bar is animated:

```
Public Function SetPMeter(p As Single)
  'p is percent of total:
  Me.PMeterBar.Width = p * Me.PMeter.Width
  Me.PMeterBar.Caption = Format(p, "##%")
  Me.Repaint
End Function
```

Speeding up the progress meter display

This routine is called whenever you want to update the progress meter. Generally, you should call the progress meter only when it's likely to be updated. If you know that you have 1,000 records, you might call the meter every 10 records, but if you have 10,000 records, you might call the meter every 100 records.

Although this code is simple, it isn't the best option. In fact, because this code calls the progress meter for every record, it's much slower than the built-in progress meter. A better approach is to call the progress meter every few records:

```
If (i / lngCounter) * 100 = Int((i / lngCounter) * 100) Then
  SetPMeter i / lngCounter
End If
```

The If statement checks to see whether the calculation of the completion percentage is an *integer* (whole number). This calls the progress meter function (SetPMeter) that moves the progress meter rectangle and displays the percentage completed. It's called only 100 times to move the rectangle; even though the If statement is run 50,000 times, you might wonder why the If statement is faster. The reality is that the If statement takes very few resources to process, but a function that changes the width of a rectangle or control, writes to the screen, and then repaints the screen uses a lot of resources — as evidenced by the time to process falling by 90 percent.

Follow these steps to integrate the Progress Meter into your application:

1. Import the Progress Meter form into your application.
2. Change the code behind the form to interact with your application.

Working with Large Access Databases

When someone mentions large databases in Microsoft Access, he's generally thinking about a database containing tables holding hundreds of thousands of records. Although this is a large database, another definition is a database containing hundreds or thousands of objects — tables, queries, forms, reports, and lots of VBA modules. Although you can sometimes solve data performance problems by using SQL Server as the database engine, you'll probably have a much more complex problem dealing with applications containing many queries, forms, reports, and modules.

If your database has hundreds of objects, especially forms and reports, you may have run into problems that cause your database to exhibit strange behavior, including

- Not staying compiled
- Growing and growing, even after compiling and compacting
- Running more slowly over time
- Displaying the wrong record in linked subforms
- Displaying compile errors when you know that the code is correct
- Frequent database corruption

Compacting your database doesn't always work as advertised. Compiling and saving all modules takes a long time. After you compact and open the database, the database is uncompiled again. If you work with large databases, chances are good that you've had these experiences. This section shows how to solve these problems and get your databases up and running fast again.

Understanding how databases grow in size

Many things can cause a database to grow. Each time that you add an object to an Access database (.accdb) file, it gets larger. And why shouldn't it? You're certainly using more space to define the properties and methods of the object. Reports and forms take up a lot of space because of the properties associated with forms and reports and their controls. Table attachments (links) and queries take up very little space, but VBA code grows proportionally with the number of forms and reports. Storing data in a program database (rather than in a linked back-end database) also takes up space.

Many other things cause a database to grow: Each time you add another new form or report, more space is used. Each time you add a new control and define some properties, even more space is used. When you define any event in a form or report that contains even a single line of VBA code, more overhead is used, because the form or report is no longer a lightweight object. This requires more space and resources than a form or report containing no VBA code. Embedded images in forms and reports also use space. Embedded OLE data, such as pictures or sound, use more space than unbound objects or images.

Every time you make a change to any object — even a simple one — a duplicate copy of the object remains in the database file until you compact the database. Within a few hours of work, Access databases can begin to grow larger and larger. If the database contains thousands of lines of VBA code, the database can grow to two or three times its original size very quickly, especially when it's compiled and before it's compacted.

Recognizing that compiling and compacting may not be enough

As you add, delete, and modify objects, Access doesn't always clean up after itself. You've probably learned that, after you make changes to your objects, especially VBA code, you should open any module and choose Debug ➪ Compile *Database Name,* save the module, and close the VBA editor window. After you do this, click the Microsoft Office button, select the Info tab, and click the Compact and Repair This Database button. This action compacts the database with the same name and reopens the database.

Tip
If you prefer a less aggressive approach, close the database first and compact the database to a different name, effectively creating a compacted backup. You can then start working with the new database, or delete the old one and rename the new database to the original name.

Compiling and compacting may not be enough to solve some of the problems mentioned in the preceding section. Databases have been known to grow in size after compiling and compacting — even without adding new objects, code, or data. Sometimes, strange things happen to databases without a good explanation. The database might not compile code properly if the database is too large, or you might see compile errors on perfectly written code. The database might run slowly even if there's nothing wrong. There are a more few techniques to use, even when you think you're out of options.

Rebooting to get a clean memory map

Strange behavior in any program often gets better when you reboot your computer. Access applications are particularly prone to *memory leaks* (situations that arise when the application is unable to release memory it's acquired so that the operating system can use it for other purposes), especially if you're going in and out of form, report, and module design and using a lot of data objects (mostly recordsets).

If you don't want to reboot, at least close your database and exit Access as a first step in resolving a problem.

Fixing a corrupt form by removing the record source

Sometimes, you may have a form that doesn't run properly. Try opening the form in Design view and removing its record source. Then close and save the form, reopen it in Design view, and restore the record source. When the record source of an Access form or report is changed, it forces various pieces of internal code behind the form to be rebuilt and may help resolve the issue.

Creating a new database and importing all objects

Having your database as clean as possible is important. Although I'm not sure if gremlins crawl into some obscure portion of the database file, I am sure that you can't import or export resident gremlins. A technique that often proves successful is to create a new database and import all the objects from the original database. Access makes it easy to import all of a database's objects:

1. Open a new empty database.

2. Select the External Data ribbon tab.

3. Click the Access option on the Import group.

4. Select the database you're having problems with.

5. Ensure that the Import Tables, Queries, Forms, Reports, Macros, and Modules into the Current Database option is selected.

6. Click OK.

7. Click on Select All for each of the relevant tabs shown in Figure 24.14.

8. Click OK.

If you have any custom menus and toolbars, import/export specifications, or Navigation Pane groups, remember to select the appropriate items in the Import Objects dialog box (shown in Figure 24.14). If the old database contains custom database properties, you have to create them again because they can't be imported.

Caution

If you use externally referenced libraries or add-ins, you must manually reference these libraries in the new database. Choose Tools ⇨ References in the VBA editor to do this. As well, you'll need to reset any of options specified on the Current Database tab, such as Application Title, Display Form, and so on (choose File ⇨ Access Options).

FIGURE 24.14

Importing database objects (the Options button has been pressed in this case)

Using the decompile option

A little known start-up, command-line option is called /decompile. You may have seen other Access command-line options, such as /nostartup, /cmd, and /compact. The /decompile option starts Access in a special way and, when a database is opened, saves all VBA modules as text. This works with module objects and all the code behind forms and reports.

To decompile your application, follow these steps:

1. Go to the Windows Start menu Run command.

   The Run window appears.

2. In the Open text box, type **msaccess /decompile** (see Figure 24.15), and click Open.

3. Open your application as you normally would, holding down the Shift key while you click on OK.

   This prevents start-up forms or autoexec macro processes from running. You don't want the database to run code that forces even a single module to be compiled.

FIGURE 24.15

Starting Access with the decompile command-line option

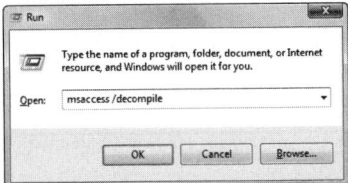

Access appears to start as usual, but the database may take several minutes to open if it contains a lot of data or VBA code. At this point, the real question is whether the database gets sufficiently smaller, runs faster, and stays compiled after it's compiled and compacted.

4. After the database window is displayed, close Access.

   Don't just close the database window — actually exit Microsoft Access.

5. Restart Access.

6. Open your database, open any module, and choose Debug⇨Compile *Project Name*.

7. After the database compiles, close the module, return to the Access window, and compact and repair the database.

   You should find that Access runs these procedures much faster than usual.

The six steps to large database success

If you're ready to release your application for a real test by the users, follow these steps to insure a clean-running system:

1. Reboot your computer to clean up memory.

2. Create a new Access database and import all the objects.

3. Restart Access by using the /decompile option while holding down the Shift key. Close Access after the database window is displayed.

4. Restart Access normally while holding down the Shift key.

5. Compile the database.

6. Compact and repair the database.

By releasing a clean, fully compiled and compacted system, your application runs faster and has fewer technical or maintenance problems.

Caution

Make sure that you immediately exit Access after it finishes decompiling and then start Access again before running Compile Project Name or Compact and Repair Database.

Detecting an uncompiled database and automatically recompiling

Making sure that a database is always in a compiled state is very important. If you release a database as an .accdb file, your customers may make changes to the application and then complain because it's running slowly. Although some of your customers may be serious developers, most often the users who make changes to Access databases don't understand compiling or compacting a database.

Tip

To see if your database is compiled, open the Visual Basic window for any module, display the Debug window at the bottom of the editor, and type ? IsCompiled, as shown in Figure 24.16. If the database is compiled, it displays True. If it's in a decompiled state, it displays False.

To solve this problem of changes being made by users who don't understand compiling or compacting a database, you can create an interface that automatically detects whether the database is not in a compiled state and then gives the user the option of compiling the application. This automatic detection runs each time the database is opened. The user still has to compact the database, but the form takes care of compiling the database, the part many users have trouble comprehending.

One line of code can be added anywhere in your program to detect an uncompiled application and start the process:

```
If IsCompiled() = False Then DoCmd.OpenForm "MessageImprovingPerformance"
```

FIGURE 24.16

Checking to see if an Access database is compiled

The form is displayed (see Figure 24.17) if the application isn't compiled. Users are given the choice of recompling or proceeding without compilation.

FIGURE 24.17

A form to help the user compile your application

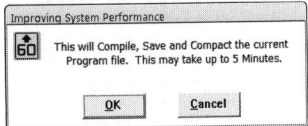

The compile and compact code is shown in Figure 24.18.

FIGURE 24.18

A module to automatically compile and compact your database

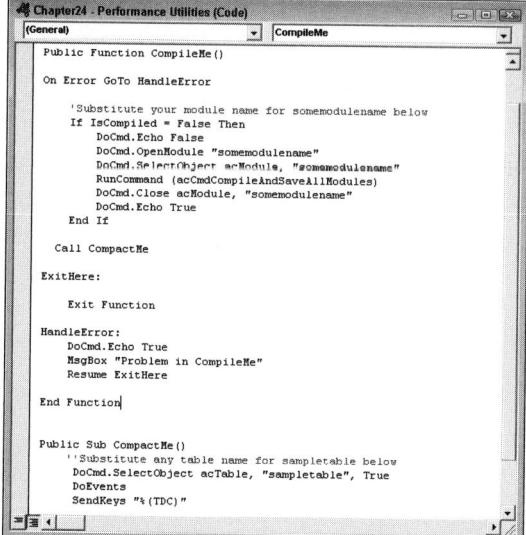

```
Chapter24 - Performance Utilities (Code)
(General)                          CompileMe

   Public Function CompileMe()

   On Error GoTo HandleError

       'Substitute your module name for somemodulename below
       If IsCompiled = False Then
           DoCmd.Echo False
           DoCmd.OpenModule "somemodulename"
           DoCmd.SelectObject acModule, "somemodulename"
           RunCommand (acCmdCompileAndSaveAllModules)
           DoCmd.Close acModule, "somemodulename"
           DoCmd.Echo True
       End If

   Call CompactMe

   ExitHere:

       Exit Function

   HandleError:
       DoCmd.Echo True
       MsgBox "Problem in CompileMe"
       Resume ExitHere

   End Function

   Public Sub CompactMe()
       ''Substitute any table name for sampletable below
       DoCmd.SelectObject acTable, "sampletable", True
       DoEvents
       SendKeys "%(TDC)"
```

Making small changes to large databases

When you're making lots of changes to a database, you're constantly opening and closing objects. Work with a copy of the database, and then when you have the changes just the way you want, export the changed objects to the production database. (An exported object with the same name as an object in the production database is exported with a 1 at the end of its name.) You can then delete the original object in the production database, and rename the exported objects. New objects are exported with their name intact.

The fewer changes to a large database, the better off you are. By following the tips and techniques in this section, you'll have fewer problems and be more productive.

Summary

In this chapter, you learned techniques to improve the performance and operation of your database. You learned how to set up tables, queries, forms, and reports to optimize performance. You saw techniques to take a problem database and turn it into a working database. You even used methods to make the user think an application is running faster.

Through judicious use of the techniques discussed in this chapter, you can increase the performance of your Access application to the highest level possible.

Advanced Data Access with VBA

In the previous few chapters, you learned the basics of Access programming, reviewed some built-in VBA functions, and experienced the various VBA logical constructs. You learned about DAO and ADO and how to access data in tables and queries through SQL recordsets. You also learned a lot about forms and queries.

In this chapter, you use all this knowledge and learn how to display selected data in forms or reports using a combination of techniques involving forms, Visual Basic code, and queries.

On the CD-ROM

In the `Chapter25.accdb` database, you'll find several forms to use as a starting point, and other completed forms to compare to the forms you change in this example. All the examples use a modified version of `frmProducts` and `tblProducts`.

IN THIS CHAPTER

Using a combo box to find a record on a form

Using the form's filter options

Adding an Unbound Combo Box to a Form to Find Data

When viewing an Access form, you often have to page through hundreds or even thousands of records to find the record or set of records you want to work with. You can teach your users how to use the Access "find" features, what to do to see other records, and so on, but this defeats the purpose of a programmed application. If you build an application, you want to make it easier for your users to be productive with your system, not teach them how to use the tools built into Microsoft Access.

Figure 25.1 shows `frmProducts` with an additional control at the top — a combo box that is not bound to any data in the form. The unbound combo box is used to directly look up a record in `tblProducts` and then display the record in the form using a bit of code. This chapter shows several ways to build this combo box and use it as a quick way to find records in the form.

FIGURE 25.1

The `frmProductsExample1` form with an unbound combo box

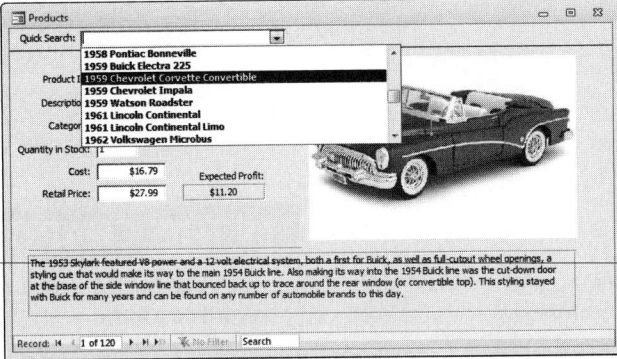

The design for the combo box is shown in Figure 25.2. Notice that the `Control Source` property is empty. This indicates that the combo box is not bound to any field in a table and is used only by the form, not to change data in the underlying database.

FIGURE 25.2

The Property Sheet for the unbound combo box control

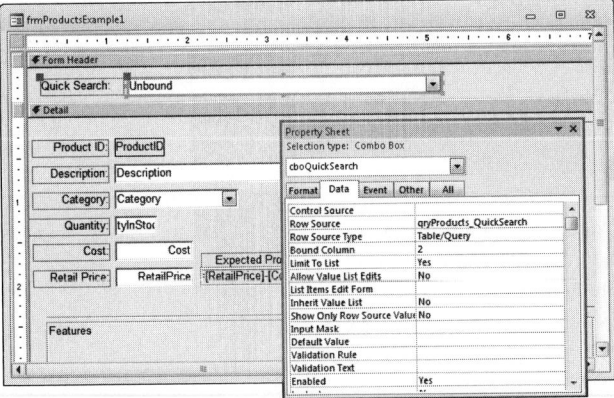

The combo box contains two columns selected by the query shown in Figure 25.3. The first column, LongDescription, joins ModelYear and Description from tblProducts. The second column is the ProductID field in tblProducts. The ProductID column serves as the bound column for the combo box and is the value returned by the combo box when a row is selected in the combo box. The second column's width is 0, which hides the column when the combo box list is pulled down.

Note

In the code examples that follow, you'll see references to cboQuickSearch.Value. Keep in mind that the value of the combo box is the Product ID of the item selected in the combo box.

FIGURE 25.3

The query behind the Row Source property of cboQuickSearch

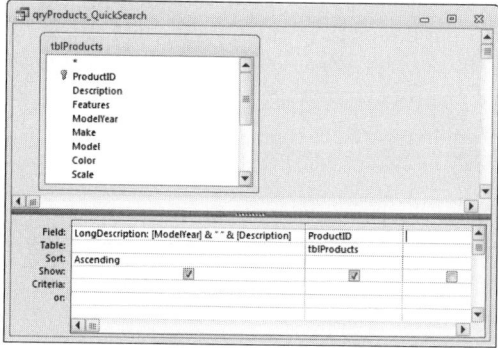

This combo box is used for several of the examples in this chapter. Next you see how to find records in a variety of ways using the combo box and the code behind it.

Using the FindRecord method

Let's take a look how the quick search combo box on frmProductsExample1 works. Selecting a product category from cboQuickSearch fires the AfterUpdate event. Code in the AfterUpdate event procedure performs the search on the form, and the form instantly displays the selected record.

The FindRecord method locates a record in the form's bound recordset. This is equivalent to using the binoculars in the Access ribbon to find a record in a datasheet.

When performing a search on a datasheet, you begin by clicking on the column you want to search, perhaps LastName. Next, you click on the binoculars in the ribbon to open the Find and Replace dialog box, and enter the name you want to find in the recordset. Access knows to use the LastName field because that's the column you selected in the datasheet. When you enter **Smith** as the search criteria, Access moves the datasheet record pointer to the first row that contains Smith in the `LastName` field.

When you use code to search through the contents of a bound Access form, you actually perform these same steps using VBA statements.

Follow these steps to create an `AfterUpdate` event procedure behind the combo box:

1. Display `frmProductsExample1` in Design view, click `cboQuickSearch`, and press F4 to display the Property Sheet.

2. Select the Event tab and select the `AfterUpdate` event.

3. Click the combo box arrow in the `AfterUpdate` event property and select `Event Procedure`.

4. Click the Builder button that appears in the right side of the property.

   The procedure appears in a separate VBA code window. The event procedure template (`Private Sub cboQuickSearch_AfterUpdate()...End Sub`) is automatically created in the form's code module. As you've learned, whenever you create an event procedure, the name of the control and event are part of the subprocedure.

5. Enter the four lines of code exactly as shown in Figure 25.4.

FIGURE 25.4

Using the `FindRecord` method to find a record

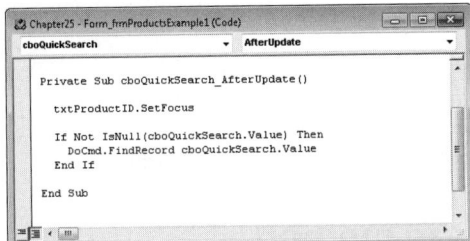

The first line is

```
txtProductID.SetFocus
```

This statement moves the cursor to the `txtProductID` control. Just as you need to manually move the cursor to a column in a datasheet in order to use the Find icon in the Access ribbon, you must place the cursor in the bound control you want to use as the search's target. In this case, you're moving the cursor to the control containing the `ProductID` value because the search will look for a particular `ProductID` in the form's bound recordset.

The next block of code is

```
If Not IsNull(cboQuickSearch.Value) Then
    DoCmd.FindRecord cboQuickSearch.Value
End If
```

This block of code first checks to make sure that `cboQuickSearch` contains a value (is not null) before using the `FindRecord` method. If a value is found in the combo box, `FindRecord` uses the combo box's value (which is the selected item's Product ID) to search for the selected product's record. Access matches the value in `cboQuickSearch` with the `ProductID` in the recordset bound to the form.

The first value found by the `FindRecord` method is determined by a series of parameters, including whether the case is matched and whether the search is forward, backward, or the first record found. Enter `DoCmd.FindRecord` in the code window and press the spacebar, to see all available options. The `FindRecord` method finds only one record at a time, while allowing all other records to be viewed.

Using a bookmark

The `FindRecord` method is a good way to search when the control you want to use to find a record is displayed on the form. It's also a good way if the value being searched for is a single value. However, many times multiple values are used as lookup criteria. A *bookmark* is another way of finding a record.

`frmProductsExample2` contains the code for this example.

Figure 25.5 shows the combo box's `AfterUpdate` event procedure. This code uses a bookmark to locate the record in the form's recordset matching the search criteria.

The first several lines are

```
Dim rs As DAO.Recordset
Dim strCriteria As String
If IsNull(cboQuickSearch) Then
    Exit Sub
End If
Set rs = Me.RecordsetClone
```

The first two lines declare a recordset named `rs` and a string named `strCriteria`. These will be used later in the code. Next, the procedure ends if `cboQuickSearch` is null, which means the user didn't actually select anything in the combo box. The following line sets the recordset to a copy of the form's bound recordset (the `RecordsetClone`).

A `RecordsetClone` is exactly what its name implies: an in-memory clone of the form's recordset that you can use when searching for records. If you used the form's bound recordset instead, your search will move the current record away from the record displayed in the form. If the search target is not found in the form's bound recordset, the form ends up positioned at the last record in the bound recordset, which is sure to confuse users.

FIGURE 25.5

Using a `RecordsetClone` bookmark to find a record

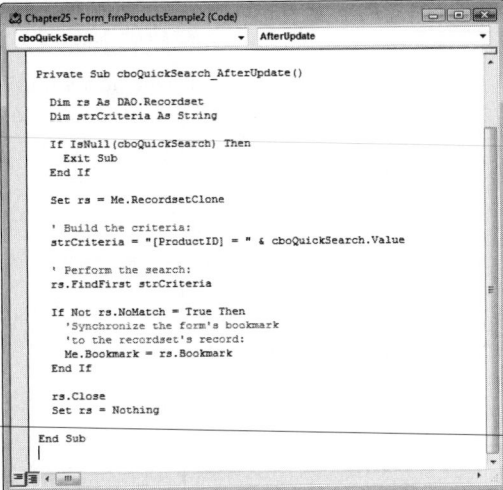

The `Recordset` object's `FindFirst` method requires a search string containing criteria to look up in the recordset. (Yes, that's correct — you're actually asking the `RecordsetClone` to search itself for a record, based on some criteria.)

The criteria string can be as complicated as needed. The following statement concatenates "`[ProductID] = `" with the value of `cboQuickSearch`:

```
strCriteria = "[ProductID] = " & cboQuickSearch.Value
```

The value of `Me!cboQuickSearch` is then added to the string. Assuming the value of cbo-QuickSearch is 17, `strCriteria` is now

```
[ProductID] = 17
```

Note

The criteria string works only because `ProductID` is a numeric field. If it were text, quotes would be required around the value, as in

```
strCriteria = "[ProductID] = '" & Me!cboQuickSearch.Value & "'"
```

so that the criteria would actually be

```
[ProductID] = '17'
```

Tip

Creating criteria in code is sometimes a complicated process. The objective is to build a string that could be copied into a query SQL window and run as is. Often, the best way to create a criteria string is to build a query, switch to SQL view, and copy the SQL into a VBA code window. Then, break the code's WHERE clause into field names and control values, inserting concatenation operators and delimiters as needed around string and date values

After the criteria string is completed, you use the recordset's FindFirst method to search for the record in the RecordsetClone. The following line uses the FindFirst method of the recordset, passing the criteria string as the argument:

```
rs.FindFirst strCriteria
```

Note

You don't have to create a Criteria variable and then set the criteria string to it. You can simply place the criteria after the rs.FindFirst method, like this:

```
rs.FindFirst "ProductID = " & cboQuickSearch.Value
```

However, when you have complex criteria, it may be easier to create the criteria separately from the command that uses the criteria string so you can debug the string separately in the query editor.

The next lines are used to determine whether the record pointer in the form should be moved. Notice the Bookmark property referenced in the following code block. A *bookmark* is a stationary pointer to a record in a recordset. The FindFirst method positions the recordset's bookmark on the found record.

```
If Not rs.NoMatch = True Then
  Me.Bookmark = rs.Bookmark
End If
```

If no record was found, the recordset's NoMatch property is True. Because you want to set the bookmark if a record *is* found, you need the computer equivalent of a double negative. Essentially, it says if there is "not no record found," and then the bookmark is valid. Why Microsoft chose NoMatch instead of Match (which would reduce the logic to If rs.Match Then...) is a mystery to everyone.

Here's an alternative way to write the logic for checking the NoMatch property:

```
If rs.NoMatch = False Then
  Me.Bookmark = rs.Bookmark
End If
```

If a matching record is found, the form's bookmark (Me.Bookmark) is set to the found recordset's bookmark (rs.Bookmark) and the form repositions itself to the bookmarked record. This does not filter the records — it merely positions the form's bookmark on the first record matching the criteria. All other records are still visible in the form.

The last lines of code simply close and discard the recordset.

Note

Criteria can be as complex as you need them to be, even involving multiple fields of different data types. Remember that strings must be delimited by single quotes (not double quotes, because double quotes surround the entire string), dates are delimited by pound signs (#), and numeric values are not delimited.

The `FindFirst` or `Bookmark` method is preferable to using `FindRecord` because it allows for more complex criteria and doesn't require the control being searched to be visible. You don't have to preposition the cursor on a control to use the recordset's `FindFirst` method.

Note

In case you're wondering, the recordset created from the form's `RecordsetClone` property is a DAO-type recordset. Only DAO recordsets support the `FindFirst`, `FindLast`, `FindNext`, and `FindPrevious` methods. There is no reason for Microsoft to re-architect Access forms (and reports, for that matter) to use ADO-type recordsets. The DAO model works very well when working with bound forms and reports.

Filtering a Form

Although using the `FindRecord` or `FindFirst` methods allow you to quickly locate a record meeting the criteria you want, it still shows all the other records in a table or query recordset and doesn't necessarily keep all the records together. Filtering a form lets you view only the record or set of records you want, hiding all non-matching records.

Filters are good when you have large recordsets and want to view only the subset of records matching your needs.

You can filter a form with code or with a query. I cover both approaches in this section.

With code

Figure 25.6 shows the two lines of code necessary to create and apply a filter to a form's recordset. Each form contains a `Filter` property that specifies how the bound records are filtered. By default, the `Filter` property is blank and the form shows all the records in the underlying recordset.

FIGURE 25.6

Code for filtering and clearing a filter behind a form

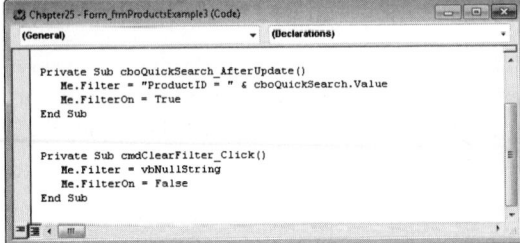

The first line of code sets form's `Filter` property:

```
Me.Filter = "ProductID = " & cboQuickSearch.Value
```

Notice that this is exactly the same string used as the criteria passed to the recordset's `FindFirst` property.

The second line of code (`Me.FilterOn = True`) turns on the filter. You can put all the criteria that you want in a filter property, but unless you explicitly set the `FilterOn` property to `True`, the filter is never applied to the form's recordset. The filter hides all the records that do not meet the criteria, showing only the records meeting the filter's value.

```
Me.FilterOn = True
```

Whenever you turn on a filter, it's useful to provide a way to turn the filter off. If you look at the top of Figure 25.6, you can see a small button (`cmdClearFilter`) next to the combo box. This button turns off the filter and sets the form's `Filter` property to an empty string (`vbNullString`). The second procedure shown in Figure 25.6 is the button's `Click` event procedure:

```
Private Sub cmdClearFilter_Click()
    Me.Filter = vbNullString
    Me.FilterOn = False
End Sub
```

Caution

If you create a form filter and then save the form design with the filter set, the filter is saved with the form. The next time the form is opened, the filter is active. It's a good practice to set the form's `Filter` property to an empty string as the form closes. The following code uses the form's `Close` event procedure to clear the filer:

```
Private Sub Form_Close()
    Me.FilterOn = False
    Me.Filter = vbNullString
End Sub
```

With a query

You might want to have one form control another. Or you might want a recordset to display selected data based on ad hoc criteria entered by the user. For example, each time a report is run, a dialog box is displayed and the user enters a set of dates or selects a product or customer. One way to do this is to use a parameter query.

Creating a parameter query

A parameter query is any query that contains criteria based on a reference to a variable, a function, or a control on a form. Normally, you enter a value such as **SMITH**, **26**, or **6/15/12** in a criteria entry area. You can also enter a prompt such as **[Enter the Last Name]** or a reference to a control on a form such as **Forms!frmProducts![cboQuickFind]**.

The Chapter25.accdb database contains a parameter query named qryProductParameter-Query.

The simplest way to create a parameter query is to create a select query, specify the query's criteria, and run the query to make sure it works. Then change the criteria to the following:

```
Like [<some prompt>] & "*"
```

or:

```
Like "*" & [<some prompt>] & "*"
```

where *some prompt* is the question you want to ask the user. Figure 25.7 shows a parameter query that prompts the user whenever the query is run to enter the Product Category.

FIGURE 25.7

Creating a simple parameter query

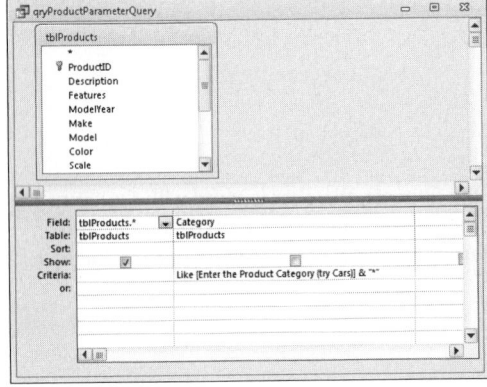

Anytime the query is run, even if it's used as the record source for a form or report or the row source for a list or combo box, the parameter dialog box is displayed — and depending on what is entered, the query criteria filters the query results. Figure 25.8 shows the parameter dialog box open, asking for the product category value required by the query.

You may remember learning that the Like operator allows for wildcard searches. For example, if you want to filter the query records for any product category that starts with "car" (or "CAR"), you enter **CAR** in the parameter dialog box. Without the parameter, you would have to enter **Like "CAR*"** in the criteria area of the query. Also, because the wildcard (*) is included as part of the parameter, users don't have to include the wildcard when they respond to the parameter dialog box.

FIGURE 25.8

Running the parameter query

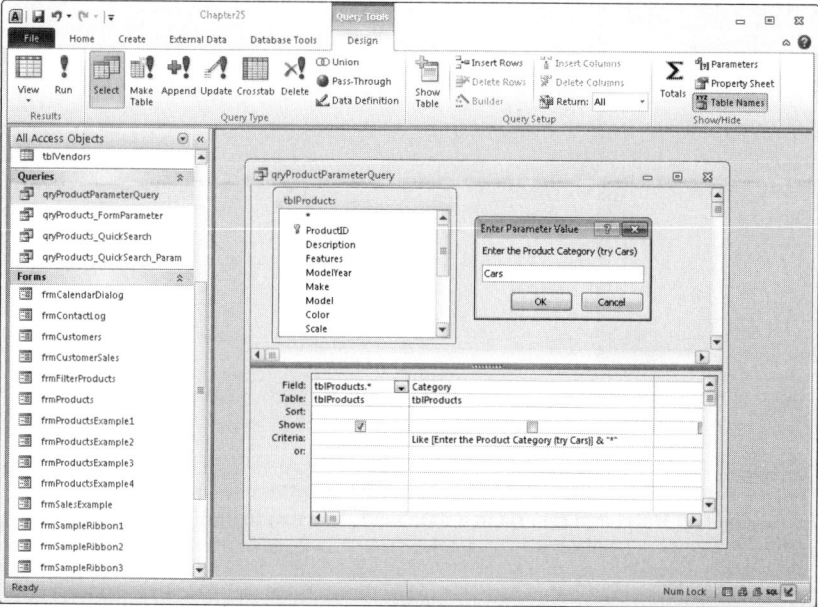

Tip

You can use the wildcards * (anything after this position) and ? (one character in this position) with a `Like` operator in any query or SQL string.

Note

If SQL Server Compatible Syntax (ANSI 92) is selected (File ⇨ Options, then select the Object Designers tab), or if ADO is being used to run the SQL statement, the wildcards are % (anything in this position) and _ (one character in this position)

A consequence of adding the asterisk to the parameter is that, if the user doesn't enter a parameter value, the criteria evaluates to `"LIKE *"`, and the query returns all records. Leaving the asterisk out of the criteria expression results in no returned records if the user fails to provide a product category.

Figure 25.9 shows the Query Parameters dialog box (opened by right-clicking the query's upper area and selecting Parameters from the shortcut menu). You use the Query Parameters dialog box to specify parameters that require special consideration, such as date/time entries or specially formatted numbers. One text entry has been entered in the Query Parameters dialog box to show how it works. You enter the parameter text and choose the parameter's data type.

FIGURE 25.9

The Query Parameters dialog box

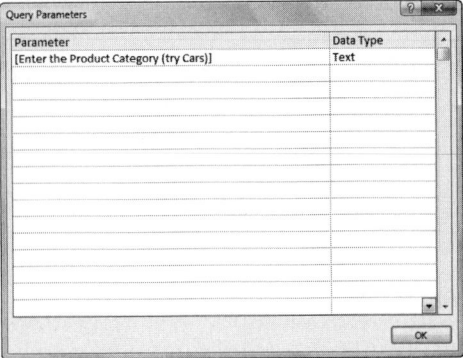

Tip

If you want to add more-complex parameters, such as a range of dates, use an expression such as Between [Enter the Start Date] and [Enter the End Date] as a criteria in a date field. This would display two separate parameter dialog boxes and then filter the date value appropriately.

Unfortunately, Access parameter queries don't provide a way to supply default values for parameters. Your best bet is to always include the asterisk in your criteria expression so that, if the user closes the parameter dialog box without entering a value, the query will return all record because the criteria expression will resolve to `Like "*"`.

Caution

You can only use Like "*" with text fields. For numeric fields, you can set the criteria to [My Prompt] OR ([My Prompt] IS NULL). Just be certain that both occurrences of My Prompt are typed identically. (Copy-and-paste is a good idea.)

Creating an interactive filter dialog box

The problem with parameter queries is that they're only suitable for simple parameters. The users have to know exactly what to type into the parameter dialog box, and if they enter the parameter incorrectly, they won't see the results they expect. Also, using parameter queries for entering complex criteria is fairly difficult.

A better technique is to create a simple form, place controls on the form, and reference the controls from a query as parameters. In other words, the query uses the form's controls to get its parameter values. This is a huge advantage to the users because the controls can help the user select the criteria by presenting lists or drop-down menus of the acceptable parameter values. Plus, code can be added to each control's `AfterUpdate` event to validate the user's input to ensure that the query will actually run. The content of controls like combo boxes or list boxes can be dynamic and contain actual values from the underlying tables. This means that the criteria controls might contain only the names of customers who've placed orders, or product categories actually in the database at the moment.

Figure 25.10 shows `frmFilterProducts` in Design view. `cboCategory` is filled with the data from `qryCategories`, which sorts the records in `tblCategories` in alphabetical order.

FIGURE 25.10

Creating a dialog box for selecting records

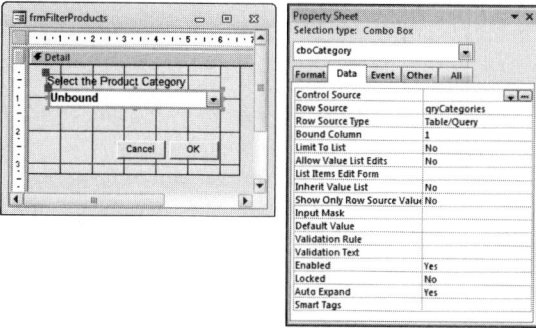

`cboCategory`'s `DefaultValue` property is set to `Cars` because this is the most commonly used criteria for the Products form. In this case, `LimitToList` is set to `No` because I want to force users to select only from the categories actually in `tblCategories`.

Figure 25.11 shows `qryProductsFormReference`. This query selects all fields in `tblProducts` based on the category retrieved from `cboCategory` on `frmFilterProducts`. Notice the criteria expression in the `Category` column:

    `= [Forms]![frmFilterProducts]![cboCategory]`

One very nice new feature in Access 2010 is that, as you type the form reference into the criteria box, IntelliSense helps you choose the control on the form to use (you can see this in effect in Figure 25.11). Unlike previous versions of Access, in which you had to know the exact name of the form and its controls, Access 2010 helps you out when composing this expression.

As the query runs, it automatically retrieves the criteria value from `cboCategory`. The combo box returns `Cars`, unless the user has choosen a different category.

FIGURE 25.11

Creating a query that references a form control

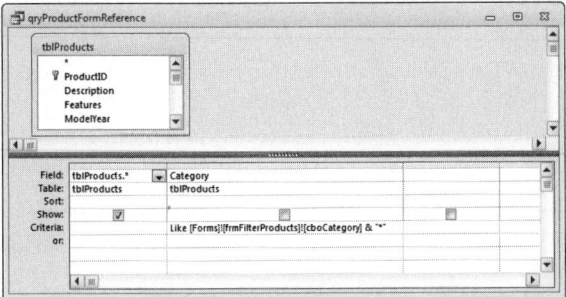

In normal operation, the user selects a product category from `frmFilterProducts` and clicks OK. Code behind the button opens `frmProductsExample4`, which is bound to `qry Products_FormParameter`. The criteria for the `Category` field in `qryProducts_ FormParameter` looks up the selected value in `cboCategory` on `frmFilterProducts`, and magically `frmProductsExample4` opens with just the selected product category loaded.

The only issue facing developers working with tightly integrated database objects like this (in this case, `frmFilterProducts`, `qryProducts_FormParameter`, and `frmProducts Example4`) is that it may not be obvious that the objects work together. Removing or modifying any of these objects might break the workflow, or cause problems for the users.

You might choose to use a naming convention that implies the relationship between the two forms and the query, such as giving each item the same name, but with different prefixes. Or, you could use the custom groups in the Access Navigation Pane, and add the objects to a single group. Very often things that are obvious to you — the original designer and developer — may not be as clear to someone else, so it pays to take advantage of simple techniques that help document your applications.

Linking the dialog box to another form

The `frmFilterProducts` dialog box (you saw this back in Figure 25.10) does more than just create a value that can be referenced from a query. It also contains code to open `frmProducts Example4`.

Figure 25.12 shows the `cmdCancel_Click` and `cmdOK_Click` event procedures behind the Cancel and OK buttons found on `frmFilterProducts`.

The `cmdOK_Click` event procedure code opens `frmProductsExample4`, sets the focus on it, and then re-queries the form to make sure that the latest selection is used on the form. The `SetFocus` method is necessary to move focus to the form that is opened. The `Requery` method isn't strictly required, because a form automatically re-queries its record source the first time it's opened. However, if the form is already opened — for example, if you use the dialog box a second time to search for another record — the `Requery` method ensures that the form displays fresh data.

Using the With keyword

The With keyword is used to save execution time by not referencing the controls on the form explicitly (that is, directly) — for example, Forms!frmProductsExample4.SetFocus. This syntax requires Access to search alphabetically through the list of forms in the database container. If there are 500 forms (and some large systems have this many or more) and the form name started with z, this would take a considerable amount of time. Because there is more than one reference to the form, this process would have to take place multiple times. The With command sets up an internal pointer to the form so that all subsequent references to controls, properties or methods (like Requery or SetFocus) of the form are much faster.

When you use the With keyword and reference the form name, you simply use a dot (.) or an exclamation point (!) to reference a control, property, or method just like the Forms!FormName was first. You can see this in Figure 25.12.

For each With, you must have an End With.

FIGURE 25.12

Creating a dialog box that opens a form

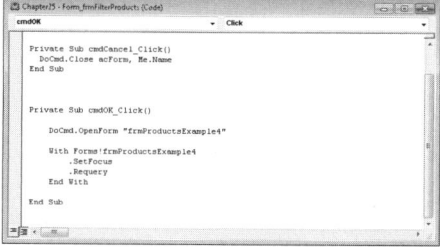

Although not implemented in frmFilterProducts, the cmdOK_Click event procedure could also contain a DoCmd.Close statement to close the dialog box after it has opened frmProduct Example4. Or, you may elect to keep the dialog box open to make it easy for users to select another product category to view.

Summary

This chapter examines several fairly advanced techniques for working with data on Access forms. In each case, a few lines of VBA code is all you need to make a form more efficient and effective for users.

I showed you several different filtering and searching techniques for bound Access forms. Each bound Access form includes a `RecordsetClone` property that references the set of records bound to the form. You saw how a recordset's `FindFirst` method and `Bookmark` property work together to locate and display data selected by the user.

You also reviewed the process of building parameter queries that include the parameter as part of the query's design, and another example where the parameter references a control on a dialog box.

The techniques described in this chapter greatly extend the utility of Access forms and empower users to quickly look up data without having to learn the built-in filtering and searching features of Access forms.

Bulletproofing Access Applications

One of my favorite old movies is *Desk Set* (1957), starring Spencer Tracy and Katharine Hepburn. In the film, Spencer Tracy plays a computer consultant responsible for installing a large computer system in Katharine Hepburn's office. Typical of computers in older movies, the massive wall-to-wall mainframe featured in *Desk Set* understands plain-English queries ("How many ounces of gold were mined in South Africa in the last ten years?") and is equipped with a galaxy of flashing lights that indicate when the machine is "thinking." And, of course, the machine and its software work flawlessly, delivering the requested information in seconds (after much clicking, clacking, and spinning of the huge tape drives, of course).

As we all know, Hollywood's vision of computer systems has always been far from reality. Even today, in the 21st century, computers still can't "understand" plain-English commands, hardware still doesn't perform flawlessly, and users still have trouble getting their applications to do what they want and need them to do. Most important, software can't be made to anticipate what the user wants. How many times have you heard people complain that they know the computer can do what they want, but they just can't get it to happen?

The objective of this chapter is to describe a development philosophy that leads to highly reliable and secure databases that protect the valuable data entrusted to them. As you'll see, often you need to limit the user's interaction with the Access environment in order to protect the data. Data must be validated as it is input by the user to prevent inappropriate values from distorting the user's interpretation of the information contained in the database. Other techniques described in this chapter make Access applications easier to learn and use, reducing the possibility that a simple misunderstanding harms the data.

IN THIS CHAPTER

Defining bulletproofing

Identifying the features of bulletproofed applications

Understanding that bulletproofing goes beyond code

Tip

In this chapter, the expressions end user, user, client, and customer all mean the same thing: the person or group of people using the application you've created. Although the terms client and customer are normally applied to the parties who pay to have the application produced, thinking of all users as clients should be your first step toward producing bulletproof applications. Always think of your users as the important people they are, and your work will reflect a conscientious attitude and a professional approach.

Introducing Bulletproofing

Advanced database systems like Access bring valuable data and information directly to the user's desktop. Unlike traditional mainframe and midrange databases, very often the data contained in an Access database resides on the user's computer or is only slightly removed by being situated on a file server on a local area network (LAN). In either case, the valuable data contained in an Access database can be exposed to potential loss or corruption by well-meaning users.

For example, unless you have added appropriate data validation to the applications you build, it's far too easy for a user to enter "bad" data into the database, causing errors later on. Or if you haven't applied adequate levels of security to the application, an unauthorized user may accidentally (or intentionally) change sensitive data. At the very least, database security prevents unauthorized users from viewing confidential information. When applied to their fullest, the Access security features will ensure that valuable data is not accessed by any but the most trusted and reliable users.

By one definition, *bulletproofing* an application means applying safeguards to an application's data through various techniques and methods. A good way to do this is by making sure that you trap all errors, preventing crashes and unexpected behavior. This book assumes that you're already a good programmer who understands that properly handling errors is a required part of any database development project.

Cross-Reference

If you aren't already familiar with handling errors, Chapter 23 explains what is needed to effectively handle the exceptions that inevitably occur in database applications.

Looking at the Characteristics of Bulletproofed Applications

Although, as a developer, you want to provide users with maximum flexibility, you simply can't allow full access to the entire database environment. Providing users with unrestricted access to tables, queries, forms, and other database objects, inevitably leads to chaos. Through mischief or ignorance, changes that damage the database's structure and logic will most certainly occur. Only the most disinterested and unimaginative user will resist the temptation to "improve" the forms and reports you've carefully crafted.

Perhaps the most important step to bulletproofing applications is to provide end users with the Access runtime environment, described later in this chapter. The Access runtime provides full support — well, *almost* full support — of all the features you build into Access databases without giving end users the tools needed to change the underlying database structures. (Unrestricted access to tables could mean deletion or modification of multiple records. Even though Access warns of most changes to data, an untrained user may ignore these warnings and proceed with the changes.)

Applications that have been bulletproofed protect the data through a number of techniques:

- **Rock-solid construction:** No database exhibiting unexplained crashes, general protection faults (GPFs), or other instabilities can be considered bulletproof. First and foremost, an Access application must be reliable and free from programming bugs that lead to crashes or other undesirable behavior.

Cross-Reference
Chapter 14 explains how to use the built-in debugging tools and how to test a database to improve its reliability.

- **Self-documenting behavior:** Built-in security features — helpful text on the screen, warning messages that caution the user when something dangerous is about to happen, and context-sensitive help to explain how the application is meant to be used — guide the user.

- **A controlled flow through the application:** Controlling an application's flow channels the user through the application in a logical sequence that's best suited to the way in which the application was envisioned being used.

- **Error handling that stops otherwise damaging actions on the part of the user:** You shouldn't let a user destroy, delete, or modify data without understanding what's happening. Whenever possible, warn the user before making an irreversible action.

- **Feedback so that the user is never left in the dark about the database status:** Long operations are indicated by progress meters, an hourglass cursor, or other visual indicators.

Identifying the Principles of Bulletproofing

Bulletproofing means much more than simply writing the right VBA code in your Access programs. You need the right attitude — one that leads to the careful, methodical approach necessary to succeed in bulletproofing your applications. In other words, you need to approach your development as a professional.

In this section, I give you some guidelines to follow to bulletproof your applications. (If you're already employing these procedures in your applications, you can look at this section as a series of friendly reminders.)

Building to a specification

All databases are meant to solve some problem experienced by users. The problem might be an inefficiency in their current methods or an inability to view or retrieve data in a format they need. Or you may simply be converting an obsolete database to a more modern equivalent. The effectiveness of the solution you build will be judged by how well it resolves the problem the users are having. Your best guarantee of success is to carefully plan the application before building any table, query, or form. Only by working to a plan will you know how well the application will solve the user's problem.

Most Access development projects follow this general sequence of events:

1. Define the problem.

   Something is wrong or inadequate with the current methods — a better system is needed and Access appears to be a good candidate to produce the new system.

2. Determine the requirements.

   Interviews with the client yield a description of the basic features the program should provide. The product of these discussions is the *design specification,* a written document that outlines and details the application.

3. Finalize the specifications.

   Review the design specifications with the client to ensure accuracy and completeness.

4. Design the application.

   The developer uses the initial design specification to design the basic structure of the database and its user interface.

5. Develop the application.

   This is where most developers spend most of their time. You spend a great deal of time building the tables, queries, forms, and other database objects needed to meet the specification produced in Step 2.

6. Test.

   The developer and client exercise the application to verify that it performs as expected. The application is tested against the requirements defined in the design specification, and discrepancies are noted and corrected for Step 6.

7. Distribute and roll out.

   After the application's performance has been verified, it's distributed to its users. If necessary, users are trained in the application's use and instructed on how to report problems or make suggestions for future versions.

Many Access developers dive right into development without adequately defining the application's objectives or designing the database's structure. Unless the application is incredibly simple, a developer who doesn't work to a specification will surely end up with a buggy, unreliable, and trouble-prone database.

Another major error is allowing the database to stray too far from the initial design specification. Adding lots of bells and whistles to an otherwise simple and straightforward database is all too tempting. If implementation digresses too far from the design specification, the project may fail because too much time is spent on features that don't directly address the users' problems. This is one of the reasons for the third step (Finalize the specifications). The developer and the user are essentially entering into a contract at that point, and you might want to include a process to be followed in order for either party to make changes to the specification once it's been agreed upon.

Before any work begins, most professional application developers expect the client to submit a written document describing the intended application and specifying what the program is expected to do. A well-written design specification includes the following information:

- **Expected inputs:** What kind of data (text, numeric, binary) will the database have to handle? Will the data be shared with other applications like Excel or another database system? Does the data exist in a format that is easily imported into an Access database, or will the data have to be re-keyed at runtime? Will all the data always be available? Is there a chance that the type might vary? For example, birth dates are obviously dates, but what happens if you know the year of birth but not the month or day?

- **User interface:** Will the users be comfortable with simple forms, or will they need custom menus and ribbons, and other user-interface components? Is context-sensitive online help required?

- **Expected outputs:** What kind of reports are needed by the user? Will simple select queries be adequate to produce the desired results, or are totals, crosstabs, and other advanced queries necessary as well?

The whole point of a design specification is to avoid adding unplanned features that decrease the database's reliability without contributing to its utility. Writing a design specification before beginning the actual implementation will consistently yield the following benefits:

- **A guide to development effort:** Without some kind of design specification, how can you possibly know whether you're building an application that truly meets the client's expectations? As you work through the development phase, you can avoid adding features that don't contribute to the application's objectives and concentrate on those items that the client has identified as having priority.

- **Verification that the application meets expectations:** All aspects of the application must be tested to verify its operation. The best way to conduct testing is to confirm that all design objectives have been met and that no unexpected behavior is observed during the testing phase.

- **Minimization of design changes during implementation:** Many problems can be avoided by sticking to the specification. One of the easiest ways to break an application is to add new features not included in the original design. If the application was properly planned, the specified features will have been designed to work together. Introducing new features after development has begun most likely will result in a less reliable system.

Overall, a well-written design specification provides the basis for creating tight, bulletproof applications that fulfill the user's requirements. At the conclusion of the project, the finished database can be compared to the design specification, and its effectiveness in addressing the original problem can be objectively evaluated. Without a design specification written at the beginning of a project, you have no valid measure of how well the application resolves the problem that inspired the project in the first place.

Becoming one with documentation

Even the best-written Access application will fail if users don't fully understand how to use it. And it's not just the user interface that needs to be understood: the logic of what happens when the user clicks a particular button needs to be understood both by at least some of the users as well as by any technical support staff who might be involved with the application.

While many developers dislike writing documentation, leaving it as a last step that they hopefully won't have time for because they've moved onto another project, documentation really is a "necessary evil."

Documenting the code you write

Over time, changes or additions might be required to the application. Even if you're the one making those changes, the passage of time since you originally wrote the code might mean that even *you* have problems understanding exactly what the code does. Imagine how much harder it'll be if someone else has to figure it out!

Include comments, use naming conventions, and provide logical names for your procedures and variables. Don't, for example, accept the default names that Access provides for database objects such as forms and controls. The default names are simply a convenience for simple applications and shouldn't be used in professional-quality work.

Figure 26.1 is an example of clear commenting and documenting. Imagine even this small section of code without comments, and it's easy to see how important documentation is.

Cross-Reference
The chapters in Part II describe many valuable Access programming techniques.

Documenting the application

The applications you deliver to end users should be accompanied by printed documentation that explains how the applications are meant to be used. End-user documentation doesn't have to include descriptions of the internal structure or logic behind the user interface. It should, however, explain how the forms and reports work, describe things the users should avoid (for example, changing existing data), and include printouts of sample reports. Use screenshots to illustrate the documentation.

FIGURE 26.1

Well-documented code is easier to maintain and is less likely to lead to coding errors.

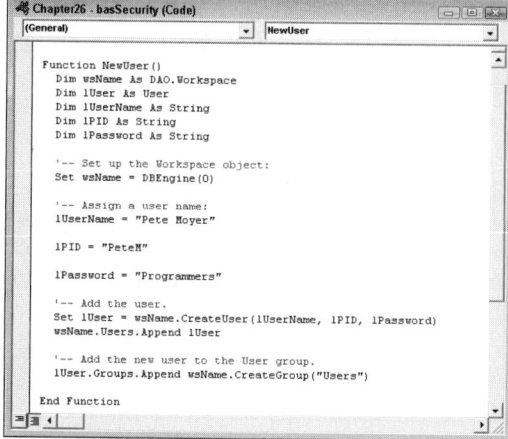

Tip

Be sure the documentation includes the exact version number in the title or footer so that users can verify that the documentation is the right version for the software they're using.

The users of your applications will benefit from the online help you build into the database. Online help, of course, means everything from the ToolTips you attach to the controls on a form to status-bar text, to sophisticated context-sensitive and "What's This" help you see in many Microsoft products.

Tip

It's often useful to have a user write the actual user documentation (in conjunction with the developer, of course). In this way, you can ensure that it's written in language that the users understand.

Considering your users

How you develop your application depends on what the users want the application to do for them. What may not be as obvious is that you also need to consider the capabilities and knowledge of your users when you design the forms and reports. This is especially important when deciding on what sort of feedback you'll provide to the users if an error occurs (or even to confirm that the normal program flow is occurring).

What they know

If you know in advance that the majority of your users are relatively unskilled or untrained, or that they won't have a lot of on-site support, you should ensure that the messaging and Help file in the application are very detailed (sometimes referred to as "overengineering"). On the other hand, if the users are relatively experienced in computing, you won't have to do as much hand holding.

One valuable technique used by many developers is to keep messages such as the one you see in Figure 26.2 in a table within the database. Figure 26.3 shows such a table and a message box displaying a message contained in this table.

On the CD-ROM

This table and the accompanying form (`frmMessageDemo`) are included in this chapter's example database (`Chapter26.accdb`) on this book's CD-ROM.

Note

Just to be clear, `frmMessageDemo` isn't actually a form you'd necessarily include in your application (unless you created a version that allowed the users to change the actual error messages). It's included here simply to provide a convenient way to see what messages have been included in the application, and how they'll look to the end user.

FIGURE 26.2

The messages you provide your users don't have to be extensive or sophisticated.

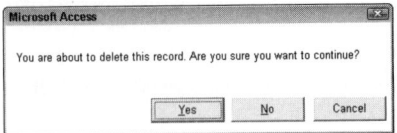

FIGURE 26.3

A simple message table and message box containing help text

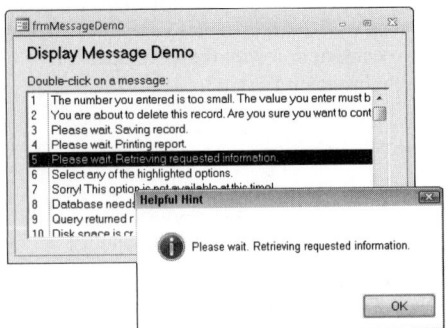

In practice, the `MessageID` is used to reference a particular message in this table. You could store the `MessageID` in the `Tag` field of a control or form and invoke the message when some error has occurred or when the user presses a button on a form. The message could also be displayed in the

Access status bar or in a designated message area on a form. The code required to display a message stored in this table is quite simple:

```
Public Function DisplayMessage(iMsgNumber As Long)
   Dim sMsg As String
   Dim sSQL As String
   Dim db As DAO.Database
   Dim rs As DAO.Recordset
   Set db = CurrentDb()
   sSQL = "SELECT * FROM tblMessages "
       & "WHERE MessageID = " & iMsgNumber & ";"
   Set rs = db.OpenRecordset(sSQL)
   MsgBox rs("Message"), vbInformation, "Helpful Hint"
End Function
```

The beauty of this little messaging system is that you could easily add a form to the application that permits users to add to the message list or change the existing text messages. Because the MessageID field is an AutoNumber, new messages are sequentially numbered without dealing with primary-key collisions. You'll also have to provide a form that sets a control or form's Tag property whenever a new message has been added to the database.

With a bit more work, you could provide each string in multiple languages. Each row would include the message in a different language (English, Spanish, French, and so on), and the SQL statement used to extract the message would indicate which language to use:

```
sSQL = "SELECT * FROM tblMessages " _
    & "WHERE MessageID = " & iMsgNumber & " " _
    & "AND Language = " & LanguageCode & ";"
```

You could extend the messaging concept a bit and provide multiple levels of help. For example, a novice user receives more extensive help than a more experienced user, while an expert should be able to turn off help completely.

What they want

The people using your applications have a number of basic needs that must be met. The applications you produce are expected to save time and/or money, produce new business, replace obsolete paper methods, reduce staffing requirements, or improve data reliability. Your applications may be expected to meet several or all of these objectives. Whatever the situation, you should have a firm understanding of what your users need. The better you understand the client's goals, the more you can concentrate on the aspects of the application that are critical to users.

Getting the application to the users

Once the application has been developed, you have to get a copy of that application to each of the users who require it. Because the application you developed requires a copy of Microsoft Access to be installed on each user's computer (as well as any ActiveX controls that you may be using), it may not be as easy as simply giving each user a copy of the .accdb (or .accde) file.

Using professional installation tools

The days of distributing an application as zipped files on a floppy disk are long gone. Microsoft Windows has become so popular that every possible type of user is working with applications running under some version of Windows. This means that many end users are people with virtually no computer experience, and you can't expect them to create directories, unzip files, and create program icons on their own.

In many cases, an Access application is simply copied across a network or copied to a CD-ROM or DVD. Other times, a more formal distribution package is needed by users. Chapter 31 explains the process of preparing Access applications for distribution to remote users. The Microsoft Office Package and Sign tool includes a very nice deployment wizard that walks you through all the steps necessary to build an effective distribution package. Figure 26.4 is an example of an application setup screen that will guide the user through the application's installation.

FIGURE 26.4

A professional-quality installation program adds a welcome touch to most applications.

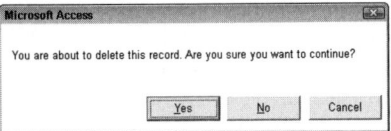

Tip

The user's first impression of your work is often based on how easily the application installs. If the user encounters problems or can't understand how to get the program installed on his computer, you're off to a bad start with the very people you've worked so hard to please.

Providing the Access runtime module to users

Although Access is included in the Microsoft Office Professional package, it's probably not a good idea to give the full development environment wide distribution in your organization. The most direct approach to preventing users from modifying the design of tables, forms, and other database objects is to give them only the Access runtime version. Although the runtime program requires the same memory and disk space as the full development environment, all the menu options required to modify database objects have been removed and are not accessible to users. In the runtime environment, even the Database window is hidden.

Note

Distributing the Access runtime module to the users does not offer any protection to the application. Any user can simply take a copy of the `.accdb` file and open it on a computer that has the full version of Access installed.

Tip

As a registered owner of the Access Developer Extensions (an Access add-in available for download from `http://msdn.microsoft.com`), you're permitted to distribute as many copies of the Access runtime and its support files as needed.

When you follow Microsoft's guidelines as you prepare a distributable application, your users may not even be aware that they're using Microsoft Access. You can modify or hide the runtime's title bar, menus, toolbars, dialog boxes, and other components to create a highly customized environment for your application.

Enabling the users to actually use the application

Even after the application has been distributed to the users, there are still steps you may have to perform in order for the users to be able to take advantage of the application. The most basic issue is providing them with a way to open the application to use it, but depending on how your application was built, you may also have a requirement to get information from the users, be it the first time they use the application or every time.

Making the application easy to start

You shouldn't expect users to locate the Access data file (`.accdb` or `.mdb`) or to choose File ⇨ Open in Access to invoke the application. Adding items to the Windows Start menu or to a program group isn't difficult. When properly implemented, a program icon creates the impression that the application exists as an entity separate from Access, and endows it with a status equivalent to Word, Excel, or other task-oriented programs.

Creating a program icon isn't difficult. Many freeware and shareware versions of icon editors are available online, enabling you to create entirely new icons. The `Chapter26.accdb` example database comes with its own program icon (`Earth.ico`) for you to experiment with. You designate the program icon in the Access start-up options (see the "Using start-up options" section, later in this chapter) or by setting a program icon in Windows Explorer.

Follow these steps to establish a Windows shortcut for an Access database application:

1. In the Microsoft Office program folder (usually `C:\Program Files\Microsoft Office\Office14`) locate `MSACCESS.EXE`.

2. Right-click on `MSACCESS.EXE` and select Create Shortcut from the context menu.

3. Press F2 while the shortcut is highlighted and enter a new caption for the icon.

4. Press Alt+Enter to open the shortcut's Properties dialog box.

   Alternatively, right-click on the icon and select Properties from the shortcut menu.

   The Properties dialog box for the icon appears.

5. Select the Shortcut tab in the Properties dialog box and add a complete path reference to the application's `.accdb` or `.mdb` file to the Target text box.

Caution

Be sure not to delete or alter the path to the Access executable file.

In Figure 26.5 the application database's path is `C:\Data\MarketingContacts.accdb` Notice that the Target text box contains the path to the Access executable.

Note

If the path to the database includes spaces, it's necessary to put double-quotes around the full path.

FIGURE 26.5

It's easy to get Access to automatically open a database from a shortcut icon.

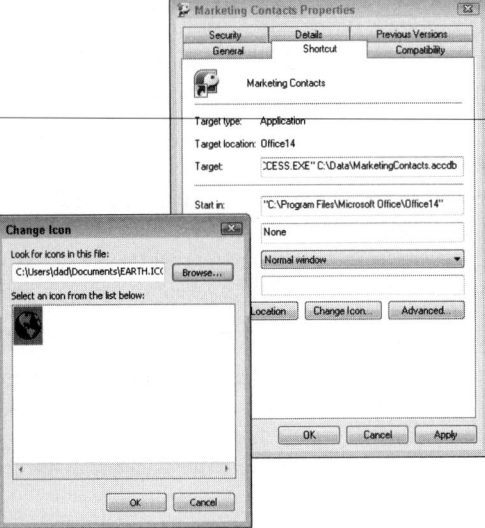

6. Click the Change Icon button.

    The Change Icon dialog box appears

7. Click the Browse button and navigate to the icon file (`.ico` extension) you want to use (see Figure 26.6).

8. Drag the shortcut to the computer's desktop or Quick Launch toolbar to provide a convenient way to start the Access application.

FIGURE 26.6

A colorful icon can make an application easy to find in a crowded folder or desktop.

Tip

Windows 7 adds the ability to pin an application to the taskbar at the bottom of the window. Right-click on an application icon and select Pin to Taskbar from the shortcut menu. Pinning an application icon to the taskbar is a convenient way to make an application available at all times.

Using start-up options

When properly designed, users shouldn't even be aware that they're working with Microsoft Access.

Choose File ⇨ Access Options to get to the Access Options dialog box (shown in Figure 26.7). To hide the Navigation pane, select the Current Database tab, and replace the default menus and ribbons with application-specific menus and ribbons. These options give the application control from the start, instead of having to wrest control away from the user once things are under way.

Figure 26.7 illustrates the first step to simplifying the user interface. The Current Database tab of the Access Options dialog box includes options for hiding the Navigation Pane, disabling the default ribbons, and trapping the built-in "special keys" (like Ctrl+F6) that might otherwise confuse users.

For example, notice the Application Icon text box in Figure 26.7. The icon file (`.ico`) that you specify in this text box is used in the Access title bar, replacing the default form icon you see in Figure 26.8. The same icon appears at the top of reports displayed in Print Preview.

The icon you assign to an Access application's shortcut doesn't affect the Access application itself. The icon you assign to the shortcut on the Windows desktop or in a program folder doesn't show up in the Access title bar and doesn't appear on the Windows taskbar. You must specify an icon in the database's Current Database tab to see the icon in the Access title bar.

Tip

The user can bypass all the start-up options by holding down the Shift key as the database opens. (The start-up must proceed normally for Access to display a custom icon.) See the "Disabling start-up bypass" section, later in this chapter, to see how you can disable this Access feature. After you've disabled the start-up bypass, only the most sophisticated user will be able to reinstate the bypass feature.

FIGURE 26.7

The Current Database tab of the Access Options dialog box helps you simplify the user interface.

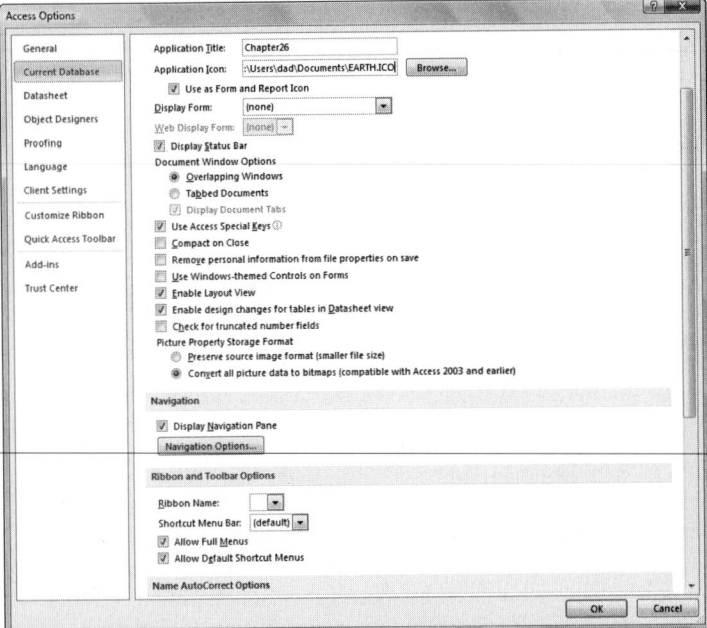

FIGURE 26.8

The application icon you specify in the Current Database tab replaces the default icons in form and report title bars.

Using a login form

The user's name or ID can be valuable information, even if user information isn't part of a security scheme. In the "Maintaining usage logs" section later in this chapter, you'll read about logging activity during a database session to provide an audit trail that helps determine what went wrong and who was responsible when failures occur as people work with the database. The login information you see in Figure 26.9 can be an invaluable aid to deciphering the audit trail.

FIGURE 26.9

Capture useful information on the login form.

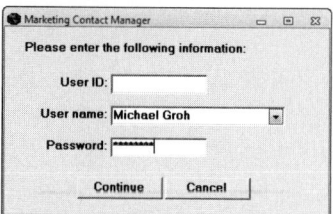

The login information should also include the date and time the user logged in to the application. You shouldn't make the user enter this information, though. The built-in Now() function returns the current system date and time and can be used in any logging features you build into the application.

Confirm the user ID and password from the login form with data stored in a hidden table. You could even include code to temporarily link to the password table in an "administration" database that resides in another location on the network. Store the user ID from the login form in a global variable to use in error logs, send e-mail messages, or stamp records with the user's identification.

In any case, set the Modal property of the login form to Yes (True) to prevent the user from accessing any other part of the application until the user ID, user name, and password have been verified.

Tip

Use the predefined Password value for the Password text box's InputMask property to display an asterisk for each character entered into this box.

Although a simple login form such as the one you see in Figure 26.10 doesn't deter a determined hacker or sophisticated user, the average user will comply with the request for the user information on this form. When used in conjunction with the BypassSetupKey property (which prevents the user from using the Shift key to bypass the start-up options) described in the "Disabling start-up bypass" section, later in this chapter, a startup form such as you see in Figure 26.10 provides a reliable login procedure for most applications.

Making a splash with a splash screen

Although a splash screen (also called a *start-up form*) might not sound like a bulletproofing technique, one aspect of professional application development is providing high-quality information to the user in a timely fashion. An appropriately designed splash screen gives the user such valuable information as the version number of the database application, the user name (or login ID), the date the database was most recently replicated, and so on. A simple splash screen is shown in Figure 26.10.

FIGURE 26.10

A splash screen confirms information about the application.

Very little code is needed to close a splash screen:

```
Private Sub Form_Timer()
    DoCmd.Close
End Sub
```

Set the form's `Timer` property to the number of milliseconds delay before closing the splash screen.

Controlling the flow of information

Applications exist to meet specific user requirements. Often a series of steps will have to be followed in order to accomplish certain tasks. It's important that the application be built in a way to facilitate the user progressing from form to form during their activities.

Adding switchboards to the application

Switchboard forms are an invaluable way of keeping users focused on using the database as intended. A switchboard form presents the user with a limited number of choices for working with the application and makes the application easier to use. You could, for example, use the user's login information to determine which of a number of switchboard forms to use. A manager with a higher level of privileges might be given a form with more options than a clerical worker.

Figure 26.11 shows the switchboard form from the Collectible Mini Cars database. Each button in this switchboard triggers some action within the database or leads to another switchboard form.

Controlling the ribbons

In most applications, you don't want the user to have access to ribbon commands that perform actions you don't want the users to be able to do. If, for example, users were able to access the export or import commands in the External Data ribbon, they might be tempted to experiment with exporting and importing data, which could have serious repercussions on the security and integrity of the data stored in the database.

FIGURE 26.11

Switchboard forms control a user's access to the application.

Removing default ribbon command options requires a bit of work, but it's worth the trouble. Actually, you don't remove ribbon items as much as you replace the built-in ribbons with custom ribbons that become part of the database.

Cross-Reference

Chapter 29 explains how to create custom ribbons containing virtually any built-in or custom commands or functions.

In addition, Access allows you to easily modify the Quick Access Toolbar in the upper-left corner of the Access environment. Figure 26.12 shows the Quick Access Toolbar tab of the Access Options dialog box, which you open by choosing File ⇨ Option.

FIGURE 26.12

Creating a custom Quick Access toolbar in Access isn't too difficult.

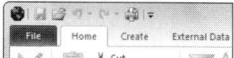

Hiding the Navigation Pane and removing menus

Access includes the Navigation Pane as a way to choose the various objects included in the database. Although it's critical that you have this navigation ability as a developer, it may be confusing to your users, so you should consider hiding the Navigation Pane in your application, as well as any other navigation menus Access includes by default.

Notice the Display Navigation Pane check box, the Allow Full Menus check box, and the Allow Built-in Toolbars check box in the start-up dialog box in Figure 26.7. When not selected, these check boxes hide the Navigation pane and remove the built-in menus from the Access environment. This means, of course, that your application will be totally reliant on the switchboard forms and toolbars you create, but it's a good way to control the user's access to the environment.

Displaying one form at a time

If appropriate for your application, you'll probably want to restrict the user to working with a single form to avoid problems by allowing forms to be opened only through your switchboard. Many inexperienced users are confused by the multiple document interface (MDI) paradigm used by Access. Having too many forms open on the screen can lead the user to jump from task to task in no particular order.

As an alternative to displaying a single form at a time, you can also use the Modal property to force a form to retain the focus during some operation. A good example is selecting from a number of reports to print. Once the user has decided to print a report, you might want to keep him focused on that task, instead of allowing him to jump back to the data-entry form. With access to both printing and data entry, the user might start a print job, jump back to data entry as the print job begins (to make changes to the data), and then wonder why the printout doesn't include the changes made after the printing has begun. Or Access might lock the records the user is trying to change during the print event.

Choosing the user-interface style

Early versions of Access provided only a single type of user interface — overlapping windows view. Beginning with Access 2007, and now in Access 2010, you have the choice of using the traditional overlapping windows view or the new Tabbed Documents interface. Choose File ⇨ Options to open the Access Options dialog box; select the Current Database tab; and then, under Document Windows Options, select either Overlapping Windows or Tabbed Documents (refer to Figure 26.7).

Choosing which user interface paradigm to use is a rather important decision because the choice you make applies to all forms and reports in the application, with the exception of free-floating modal dialog forms. Modal dialogs are always detached from other objects in the user interface and stay on the screen until explicitly dismissed by the user.

Tabbed Documents

The Tabbed Documents interface is ideal for users working with more than one object (form or report) at a time. In the Tabbed Documents interface, forms and reports can't lie on top of one another, unless explicitly designed to do so. You're assured that the user can see all the controls on a user interface object (form or report) without having to move another object out of the way.

You can, if needed, force a form or report to float on top of the Tabbed Documents interface by setting its Popup property to True. This trick enables you to display information in the pop-up form while the user views data on the Tabbed Documents interface.

Overlapping Windows

The Overlapping Windows interface has its advantages as well. Because of the variety of `BorderStyle` property settings and the ability to remove the Min, Max, and Close buttons on a form, you have a high degree of control over a user's access to a form or report. With the Overlapping Windows interface, you can easily force a user to interact with just one form at a time. Very often, this is the ideal way to ensure that a user has completed a particular task (such as data entry) before moving on to another part of the application.

Keeping the user informed

An uninformed user is a dangerous user. Keep the user informed of the database status through the hourglass mouse cursor, message boxes, status-bar text, and progress meters. A simple progress meter can keep a user from frustration during long queries or printouts. The last thing you want a user doing is hitting keys in a panic, thinking the application has crashed or is hung up.

Also, always warn the user when something dangerous (like a Delete query that removes data from the database) is about to happen. You don't have to inform users of trivial or expected actions, but make them aware when irreversible changes are being made.

Getting your message across with a message box

One of the easiest ways to communicate (but sometimes the most annoying to the user) is with the `MsgBox` function. Although message boxes are easy to add to applications, they're always modal and require the user to acknowledge the message before it's dismissed. Message boxes can disrupt the workflow if the user is constantly required to dismiss message boxes containing low-value information. In fact, flooding a user with silly message boxes containing unimportant information may cause a user to ignore truly important messages.

On the other hand, in many situations, message boxes are invaluable. A message box can be used to obtain confirmation before performing an irreversible action or to deliver important information.

The `MsgBox` function accepts a number of parameters that specify the message text, which buttons to display on the message box, and the text to display in the message-box title bar. The `MsgBox` function returns a value indicating which button displayed on the message box has been clicked by the user. The syntax of `MsgBox` is as follows:

```
MsgBox(Prompt[, Buttons][, Title][, HelpFile, Context])
```

where the function parameters are

- **Prompt:** The message displayed in the message box. `Prompt` can be a maximum of approximately 1,024 characters. Separate lines in `Prompt` with a carriage return character (`Chr(13)`), a linefeed character (`Chr(10)`), or a carriage return/linefeed character combination (`Chr(13) & Chr(10)`) between the lines. (Access provides the `vbCrLf` intrinsic constant that combines both a carriage return and a line feed, as well as a `vbNewLine` intrinsic constants.)

- **Buttons:** A numeric expression that defines the number and type of buttons to display in the message box, the icon style to use, which button to use as the default button, and the modality of the message box. The Buttons parameter completely defines the nature of the message box; therefore, there are many different values for this parameter. Table 26.1 contains all the possible values. If omitted, the default value for Buttons is 0.

- **Title:** The text to display in the title bar of the message box. If you omit the title, the name of the application is used in the title bar.

- **HelpFile:** A string that is the name of the Help file to use to provide help for the dialog box. If the HelpFile parameter is provided, the Context parameter must also be provided.

- **Context:** The help context number assigned to the message-box help topic. If the Context parameter is provided, HelpFile must also be provided.

Table 26.1 lists the valid values for the Buttons parameter. When more than one button or setting is required, sum the Constant values and pass the total to the MsgBox() function.

TABLE 26.1

MsgBox Button Constants

Button Constant	Value	Description
vbOKOnly	0	Display only the OK button.
vbOKCancel	1	Display the OK and Cancel buttons.
vbAbortRetryIgnore	2	Display Abort, Retry, and Ignore buttons.
vbYesNoCancel	3	Display Yes, No, and Cancel buttons.
vbYesNo	4	Display Yes and No buttons.
vbRetryCancel	5	Display Retry and Cancel buttons.
vbCritical	16	Display Critical Message icon.
vbQuestion	32	Display Warning Query icon.
vbExclamation	48	Display Warning Message icon.
vbInformation	64	Display Information Message icon.
vbDefaultButton1	0	The first button in the message box is default.
vbDefaultButton2	256	The second button in the message box is default.
vbDefaultButton3	512	The third button in the message box is default.
vbDefaultButton4	768	The fourth button in the message box is default.
vbApplicationModal	0	Make the message box application modal — the user must respond to the message box before continuing work in the current application.
vbSystemModal	4096	Make the message box "System modal" — all applications are suspended until the user responds to the message box.

The `Button` value you provide `MsgBox` can be a combination of several options. For example, the following command pops up a message box containing the famous `Are you sure?` message seen in many Windows applications. The message box contains Yes, No, and Cancel buttons:

```
iRetVal = MsgBox("Are you sure?", _
     vbQuestion + vbYesNoCancel, "Confirm, please")
```

Alternatively, a number can be used in place of the VBA intrinsic constants. The following statement is equivalent to the previous example:

```
iRetVal = MsgBox("Are you sure", 35, "Confirm, please")
```

The 35 is the sum of `vbQuestion (value = 32)` and `vbYesNoCancel (value = 3)`. You'll find using the VBA intrinsic constants is more self-explanatory. Figure 26.13 shows a variety of different error message boxes. Generally speaking, you'll want to use the built-in intrinsic constants (like `vbYesNo`) instead of their numeric equivalents (`32`). Using intrinsic constants always results in more readable code.

FIGURE 26.13

Message boxes come in a variety of sizes and display a number of different icons.

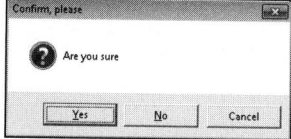

`MsgBox()`, like all VBA functions, returns a value. The value returned depends on which button displayed on the message box is clicked by the user. By default, a message box contains a single OK button and the return value of the `MsgBox()` function is 1 when the OK button is clicked. Not surprisingly, Microsoft provides an intrinsic constant for every value returned by the `MsgBox` function. The return values of the different message-box buttons are shown in Table 26.2.

Tip

If you don't care about which button the user selected, you can use MsgBox as a sub. To do this, simply omit the parentheses around the arguments passed to MsgBox.

On the CD-ROM

The form named `frmMsgBoxDemo` in the `Chapter26.accdb` example database contains a number of different message boxes and command buttons. You'll see how the different VBA constants influence the command buttons displayed in message boxes and how each type of message box returns a different value.

TABLE 26.2

MsgBox Return Values

Button Pressed	Constant Returned	Value Returned
OK	vbOK	1
Cancel	vbCancel	2
Abort	vbAbort	3
Retry	vbRetry	4
Ignore	vbIgnore	5
Yes	vbYes	6
No	vbNo	7

Creating and using a progress meter

Access provides a built-in progress meter in the status bar at the bottom of the main Access window. This progress meter is a green or blue rectangle that grows horizontally as a long-running process is executed by Access.

Setting up and using a progress meter requires an initializing step, and then incrementing the meter to its next value. As you increment, you don't just increment a counter that is managed by SysCmd. You must explicitly set the meter's value to a value between 0 and the maximum you set at initialization.

On the CD-ROM

The following code and demonstration is contained in a form named frmSysCmdDemo in the Chapter26. accdb database.

Use the acSysCmdInitMeter constant to initialize the meter. You must pass some text that is used to label the meter as well as the meter's maximum value:

```
Private Sub cmdInitMeter_Click()
  Dim vRetVal As Variant
  MeterMax = 100
  vRetVal = SysCmd(acSysCmdInitMeter, _
      "Reading Data", MeterMax)
End Sub
```

When this subroutine is run, the Access status bar appears, as shown in Figure 26.14.

FIGURE 26.14

The progress meter after initialization

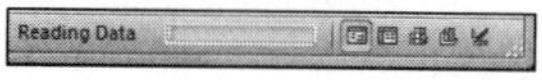

Incrementing the meter is a little tricky. In the following subroutine, the global variable `MeterInc` is incremented by 10 and the meter's position is set to the value of `MeterInc`.

```
Private Sub cmdIncrementMeter_Click()
  Dim vRetVal As Variant
  MeterInc = MeterInc + 10
  vRetVal = SysCmd(acSysCmdUpdateMeter, MeterInc)
End Sub
```

Figure 26.15 shows the progress meter after five increments. It's easy to see that the meter has moved a distance proportional to the value of `MeterInc` after being incremented five times.

FIGURE 26.15

The progress meter midway in its movement

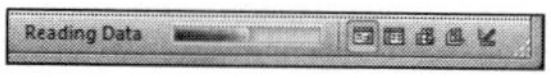

You'll have to choose values for the progress meter's maximum and increment settings in your application. Also, be sure to update the progress meter at appropriate intervals, such as every time one-tenth of a process has run (assuming, of course, that you know ahead of time how many items will be processed or how long an operation may take).

A meter is a valuable way of keeping the user informed of the progress of a lengthy process. Because you control its initial value and the rate at which it increments, you're able to fairly precisely report the application's progress to its users.

The only issue with the default Access progress meter is that it appears at the very bottom of the screen and is easily overlooked by users. Also, if the status bar is hidden through the Display Status Bar option on the Current Database tab of the Access Options dialog box (refer to Figure 26.7), the progress meter can't be seen at all.

Tracking down problems

So you've developed your great application, deployed it to all the users, and everyone's happy using it. Not that I'm suggesting you didn't do a good job developing the application, but it's possible (in fact, likely) that one or more users may get errors when using the application. When that happens, it's useful to have some techniques to help determine what went wrong.

Checking for obvious hardware errors

Whenever possible, you should monitor how much disk space, memory, and other resources are available to the application. You can avoid many problems encountered by users simply by testing to confirm that adequate disk space exists. An Access data file can completely fill up a small hard disk over time, causing the application (and Windows itself) to fail. All the error messages you see in Figure 26.16 were caused by running out of disk space on the computer.

FIGURE 26.16

Careful planning will help to avoid the unpleasant events that trigger these error messages.

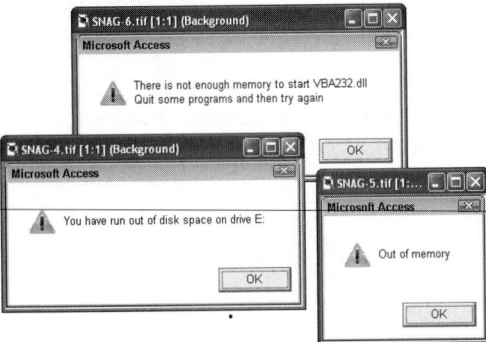

Unfortunately, the VBA language built into Access doesn't provide functions for checking free disk space or available memory. You have to resort to Windows API calls to interrogate the system for this information.

Cross-Reference

Chapter 27 explains how to call Windows API functions from your databases.

Note

You may be wondering why inadequate disk space leads to the memory errors you see in Figure 26.16. Windows uses disk space as virtual memory when all the physical memory (RAM) on the machine has been used. Windows creates virtual memory by allocating disk space to use as a swap file to temporarily store things that otherwise must be stored in memory. Windows continues allocating available disk space until nothing is left, leading to the "memory" error messages in Figure 26.16. To the application, there is no difference between running out of physical memory or swap space — a memory error is a memory error, regardless of the cause.

Maintaining usage logs

Usage logs capture information such as the user's name or ID, the date, and the time. They provide valuable information, especially if an error occurs. Although you can easily record too much information, a properly designed usage log will permit you to pinpoint whether a certain type of error always seems to occur when a particular user is working with the system or when a certain query is run.

The logging information you add to a database might include updating a time stamp on records in a table when changes are made. Be aware, however, that the more logging you do, the slower the application becomes. The log information will cause the database to grow as well, unless the log information is stored in another location.

You can even tailor the level of logging to suit individual users or groups of users. Using the information captured on a login form, the application can determine at start-up what level of logging to impose during the session. To make reviewing the logs much easier, you can even log to a table located in an external database in a different location on the network.

Usage logs can also provide an excellent way to perform a postmortem on an application that doesn't operate properly. If you have logging in each subroutine and function that might fail at runtime, you can see exactly what happened at the time an error occurred, instead of relying on the user's description of the error.

Logging can produce undesirable results when errors occur. For example, an error that causes an endless loop can easily consume all available disk space on the user's computer if each iteration of the loop adds a message to an error log. Use logging wisely. You may want to add logging to *every* procedure in an application during the beta-test process, and reduce the number of calls to the logging procedure just before distributing the application to its users. You may even provide some way that users can turn on logging if they encounter a reproducible problem in a database application.

You can easily activate or deactivate the calls to logging before distributing the application to users using the compiler directives described in Chapter 10. For example, the following call to the Logger() function will be ignored if the DEVELOPMENT constant has not been defined in the application.

```
#If DEVELOPMENT Then
   Logger("Begin function TestuserInput()  ", Now())
#End If
```

During the development cycle, include the following statement in the Declarations section of the form module, and calls to Logger() will be enabled. Before compiling and distributing to the user, either comment out this statement or set the DEVELOPMENT constant to 0.

```
#Const DEVELOPMENT = 1
```

The function shown in the following listing provides an elementary form of error logging. LogError() writes the following information to a table named tblErrorLog:

- The current date and time
- The procedure name that produced the error
- The error number
- The error description
- The form that was active at the time the error occurred (may be null if no form is open)

- The name of the control that was active at the time the error occurred (may be null if no control is selected)

```
Function LogError (ProcName As String, _
      ErrNum As Integer, ErrDescription) As Integer
   Dim MyDB As DAO.Database
   Dim tblErr As Table
   Set MyDB = CurrentDB()
   Set tblErr = MyDB.OpenTable("tblErrorLog")
   tblErr.AddNew
   tblErr("TimeDateStamp") = Now
   tblErr("ErrorNumber") = ErrNum
   tblErr("ErrorDescription") = ErrDescription
   tblErr("ProcedureName") = ProcName
   ' The following may be null if no form
   ' or control is currently active.
   tblErr("FormName") = Screen.ActiveForm. Name
   tblErr("ControlName") = Screen.ActiveControl. Name
   tblErr.Update
   tblErr.Close
End Function
```

This simple subroutine adds to an existing table named tblErrorLog. What you do with the data in this table is up to you. You may, for example, trigger a hard copy of the error log's report at the end of a session, or e-mail the report to a database administrator. A sophisticated application would create tblErrorLog at the first instance of a logged error and then check for the existence of tblErrorLog at the end of the session.

tblErrorLog contains the fields listed in Table 26.3.

TABLE 26.3

The Structure of tblErrorLog

Field Name	Data Type
TimeDateStamp	Date/Time
ErrorNumber	Long Integer
ErrorDescription	String 255
ProcedureName	String 64
FormName	String 64
ControlName	String 64

The ProcedureName, FormName, and ControlName fields are 64 characters in length — long enough to accommodate the longest possible names for these Access database objects. Error descriptions are usually short, but you want to provide as much space as possible to hold them.

A prototype of using `LogError()` is shown in the following subroutine. Notice that the `LogError()` function is triggered by the subroutine's error handler. After the error is logged, you handle the error by other code that may be needed.

```
Sub MySubroutine
  On Error GoTo MyErrorHandler
  <Your code goes here>
  Exit Sub
MyErrorHandler:
  LogError("MySubroutine", Err.Number, Err.Description)
  <Handle error here>
  Resume
End Sub
```

The most critical items in the error log are the date and time, the error number, and the error description. The procedure name is useful, but it has to be hard-coded for each procedure (subroutine or function) you log with `LogError()`.

Securing the environment

Obviously a serious Access application must be secured from unauthorized users. The built-in user-level security system (enforced by the Jet database engine, not by Access) provides multiple levels of security. You can, for example, secure a single database object (form, table, report) from individuals, groups, or individuals within groups. A user can even have multiple levels of security (provided the user has been assigned multiple login names). All the Access security objects, their properties, and methods are accessible throughout Access Visual Basic code.

User-level security is only available in the `.mdb` database format. The `.accdb` format provides other types of data protection, such as password-protected strong encryption, that is not available in the `.mdb` format. As a developer, you'll have to decide whether user-level security or strong encryption is needed to protect the data in your Access applications.

Setting start-up options in code

The options you set on the Current Database tab of the Access Options dialog box (refer to Figure 26.7) apply globally to every user who logs into the database. There are times when you want to control these options through start-up code instead of allowing the global settings to control the application. For example, a database administrator should have access to more of the database controls (menus, the Navigation pane) than a data-entry clerk has.

Almost every option you see in the Options screen can be set through code. As you'll see in the "Setting property values" section, you can use Access VBA to control the settings of the `Application` object properties listed in Table 26.4.

TABLE 26.4

Start-up Option Properties of the Application Object

Startup Option	Property to Set	Data Type
Application title	AppTitle	dbText
Application icon	AppIcon	dbText
Display form	StartupForm	dbText
Display database window	StartupShowDBWindow	dbBoolean
Display status bar	StartupShowStatusBar	dbBoolean
Menu bar	StartupMenuBar	dbText
Shortcut menu bar	StartupShortcutMenuBar	dbText
Allow full menus	AllowFullMenus	dbBoolean
Allow default shortcut menus	AllowShortcutMenus	dbBoolean
Allow built-in toolbars	AllowBuiltInToolbars	dbBoolean
Allow toolbar changes	AllowToolbarChanges	dbBoolean
Allow viewing code after error	AllowBreakIntoCode	dbBoolean
Use Access special keys	AllowSpecialKeys	dbBoolean

Depending on the user name (and password) provided on the login form, you can use VBA code in the splash screen or switchboard form to set or reset any of these properties. Clearly these properties have a lot to do with controlling the Access environment at start-up.

Be aware that many of the database options in Table 26.4, such as AppIcon, require restarting the Access database before they take effect.

Disabling start-up bypass

In old versions of Access, developers used the AutoExec macro to do things like hide the database container, open a start-up form, and execute some start-up code. The problem was that any user could easily bypass the AutoExec macro by holding down the Shift key while opening the database.

The Access start-up properties provide some relief from reliance on start-up macros and other routines. Unfortunately, the user is still able to bypass your carefully designed start-up options by holding down the Shift key as the application starts. Bypassing your start-up routines, of course, will reveal the application's design and objects that you've hidden behind the user interface.

Fortunately, the Access designers anticipated the need for bulletproofing an application's start-up by providing a database property named AllowBypassKey. This property, which accepts True or False values, disables (or enables) the Shift key bypass at application start-up.

Note

Because `AllowBypassKey` **is a developer-only property, it isn't built into Access databases. You must create, append, and set this property sometime during the development process. Once appended to the database's Properties collection, you can set and reset it as needed.**

Here's the code you need to implement the `AllowBypassKey` property:

```
Function SetBypass(BypassFlag As Boolean) As Boolean
'Returns True if value of AllowBypassKey
'is successfully set to BypassFlag.
  On Error GoTo SetBypass_Error
  Dim db As DAO.Database
  Set db = CurrentDb
  db.Properties!AllowBypassKey = BypassFlag
SetBypass_Exit:
  Exit Function
SetBypass_Error:
  If Err = 3270 Then
    'AllowBypassKey property does not exist
    'in this database, so add it now:
    MsgBox "Appending AllowBypassKey property"
    db.Properties.Append _
        db.CreateProperty("AllowBypassKey", _
        dbBoolean, BypassFlag)
    SetBypass = True
    Resume Next
  Else
    'Some other error
    MsgBox "Unexpected error: " & Error$ _
        & " (" & Err & ")"
    SetBypass = False
    Resume SetBypass_Exit
  End If
End Function
```

This function first tries to set the `AllowBypassKey` property to whatever value is passed in as `BypassFlag`. If the attempt to set the property generates an error, indicating that the `AllowBypassKey` property doesn't exist, the error trap checks to see if the error value is 3270. If it is, the `AllowBypassKey` property is created and appended to the database's Properties collection after being set to the `BypassFlag` value.

If the error is anything other than 3270, the function simply exits and doesn't try to resolve the problem. Refer to Chapter 23 for more information on trapping and handling errors.

On the CD-ROM

The `AllowBypassKeyDemo` **objects (**`frmAllowBypassKeyDemo` **and** `basAllowBypassKey`**) in the** `Chapter26.accdb` **sample file on this book's companion CD-ROM demonstrate how to set and use the** `AllowBypassKey` **property. The** `frmAllowBypassKeyDemo` **form contains two toggle buttons that alternately enable or disable the bypass feature.**

Setting property values

You use the `Application` object's `SetOption` method to set each of these properties, and the `GetOption` method to retrieve the current value. The syntax of the `SetOption` method is

```
Application.SetOption OptionName, Setting
```

where *OptionName* is the name of an option in Table 26.4, and *Setting* is one of a number of different data types, depending on the option being manipulated with *SetOption*.

In most cases, unless the property has already been set in the Access Options dialog box, the property hasn't been appended to the `Application` object's Properties collection. You must make sure the property exists before trying to set its value in code. The following function sets the value of a start-up property, creating and appending the property to the `Application` object's Properties collection if the property doesn't exist:

```
Function AddStartupProperty(PropName As String, _
    PropType As Variant, PropValue As Variant) _
    As Integer
    'Consult the Access online help for the PropName
    'and PropType for each of the startup options.
    'Adding a property requires the appropriate
    'PropType variable or the property creation fails.
    Dim MyDB As DAO.Database
    Dim MyProperty As DAO.Property
    Const _PropNotFoundError = 3270
    Set MyDB = CurrentDB
    On Error GoTo AddStartupProp_Err
    'The following statement will fail if the
    ' property named PropName doesn't exist.
    MyDB.Properties(PropName) = PropValue
    AddStartupProperty = True
AddStartupProp_OK:
    Exit Function
AddStartupProp_Err:
    'Get here if property doesn't exist.
    If Err = _PropNotFoundError Then
        'Create the new property and set it to PropValue
        Set MyProperty = MyDB.CreateProperty(PropName, _
            PropType, PropValue)
        'You must append the new property
        'to the Properties collection.
        MyDB.Properties.Append MyProperty
        Resume
    Else
        'Can't add new property, so quit
        AddStartupProperty = False
        Resume AddStartupProp_OK
    End If
End Function 'AddStartupProperty
```

Using `AddStartupProperty()` is quite easy. You must know the exact property name and data type of the property before invoking `AddStartupProperty()`. The following subroutine demonstrates how to set a start-up property with `AddStartupProperty()`:

```
Sub cmdAddProperty_Click()
  Dim iRetVal As Integer
  iRetVal = AddStartupProperty("AppTitle", dbText,
      "Marketing Contact Management")
  iRetVal = AddStartupProperty("AppIcon", dbText,
      "C:\My Documents\World.ico")
End Sub
```

Notice that both the `AppTitle` and `AppIcon` properties are string data types (`dbText`).

Tip

Use the `RefreshTitleBar` method to see the changes made by setting either the `AppTitle` or `AppIcon` property. The syntax of `RefreshTitleBar` is simple:

```
Application.RefreshTitleBar
```

Getting property values

Getting the value of a property is much easier than setting a property's value. The `GetOption` method returns the value of a property. The syntax of `GetOption` is as follows:

```
vRetVal = GetOption(PropertyName)
```

where `vRetVal` is a variant and `PropertyName` is the name of a property in Table 26.4. The following code fragment shows how to use the `GetOption` method to read an option property:

```
Dim vRetVal As Variant
' Get the current setting.
vRetVal = Application.GetOption("Project Name")
```

A variant is used to capture the return value because of the different data types used for start-up properties. Also, a property that has not yet been set may be null, and the variant is the only type of variable that can accept null values without error.

Protecting your database

As has already been explained, bulletproofing an application means safeguarding the application's data. Ideally, you want to prevent errors from occurring, not simply be able to identify when errors occur and recover from them.

The next few sections discuss a number of techniques you can use in an attempt to minimize the ability of the user to make mistakes. I'll also talk a little about safeguarding the Access environment, so that user can't go "behind the scenes" and introduce problems.

Building bulletproof forms

You can take several steps to make each form in an application virtually bulletproof:

- **Remove the Control Box, Min, Max, and Close buttons from the form at design time.** Your users will be forced to use the navigation aids you've built into the application to close the form, ensuring that your application is able to test and verify the user's input. When using the tabbed documents interface, the Min and Max buttons don't apply. The Close button is represented by an X at the far right of the tab above the form's body. Removing the Close button from a tabbed form disables the X in the tab but doesn't actually remove it.

- **Always put a Close or Return button on forms to return the user to a previous or next form in the application.** The buttons should appear in the same general location on every form and should be consistently labeled. Don't use Close on one form, Return on another, and Exit on a third.

- **Set the ViewsAllowed property of the form to Form at design time.** This setting prevents the user from ever seeing a form as a datasheet.

- **Use modal forms where appropriate.** Keep in mind that modal forms force the user to respond to the controls on the form — the user can't access any other part of the application while a modal form is open.

- **Use your own navigation buttons that check for EOF (End of File) and BOF (Beginning of File) conditions on bound forms.** Use the OnCurrent event to verify information or set up the form as the user moves from record to record.

- **Use the StatusBarText property on every control, to let the user know what's expected in each control.** The Control TipText property should also be set on all relevant controls.

Note

For the StatusBarText to be used, the status bar must be displayed (see Figure 26.7).

- **Disable the Del key or trap the OnDelete event to confirm deletions.** You can disable the Del key by creating an AutoKeys macro to remap it to a harmless action, and you can put use the form's BeforeDelConfirm event to have the users confirm deletions.

Validating user input

One of the most important bulletproofing techniques is to simply validate everything the user enters into the database. Capturing erroneous data input during data entry is one of the most import safeguards you can build into your applications. In many cases, you can use the table-level validation (determined by each field's ValidationRule and ValidationText properties), but in many other cases you'll want more control over the message the user receives or the actions taken by the database in response to erroneous input.

One of the major problems with the ValidationRule property is that it isn't checked until the user actually tabs to the next control, making it impossible to capture bad data entry. You're much better off in many cases validating entries in code. Very often you'll want to validate all controls on a form from the form's `BeforeUpdate` event instead of individually checking each and every control on the form.

Using the /runtime option

If you're not concerned with protecting your application, and you just want to prevent users from mistakenly breaking your application by modifying or deleting objects, you can force your application to be run in Access's *runtime mode*. When a database is opened in Access's runtime mode, all the interface elements that allow changes to objects are hidden from the user. In fact, while in runtime mode, it's impossible for a user to access the Navigation pane.

When using the runtime option, you must ensure that your application has a start-up form that gives users access to any objects you want them to access. Normally, this is the main menu or main switchboard of your application.

Tip

To assign a form as a start-up form, open the database that you want to use, click the Microsoft Office button, select Access Options, and select the Current Database tab. Under Application Options, set the Display Form drop-down list to the form you want to be the start-up form for the application. Start-up forms are covered in more depth in the "Making a splash with a splash screen" section, earlier in this chapter.

Earlier in this chapter, in the "Making the application easy to start" section, you read how to create a Windows shortcut that launches an Access application. Forcing runtime behavior in Access is quite easy. Simply add the `/runtime` switch after the reference to the database file in the shortcut properties, as shown in Figure 26.17.

FIGURE 26.17

Adding the `/runtime` switch to a shortcut

Tip

If your database has a password associated with it, the user will still be prompted to enter the password prior to opening the database.

New Feature

Access contains a new data file extension — .accdr — that automatically opens your Access database in run-time mode when it's opened. Change your database file's extension from .accdb to .accdr to create a locked-down version of your Access database. Change the extension back to .accdb to restore full functionality.

Encrypting or encoding a database

When security is of utmost importance, one final step that you need to take is to encrypt or encode the database. Microsoft Access 2010 uses strong encryption, based on the RC4 and large key values, to secure the data and contents of Access 2010 databases.

Follow these steps to encrypt an Access 2010 .accdb database:

1. Open an existing .accdb database (Chapter26.accdb) exclusively.

2. Click the File button in the upper-left corner of the screen, and select the Encrypt with Password command on the Info tab (see Figure 26.18).

FIGURE 26.18

Choosing to encrypt an Access database

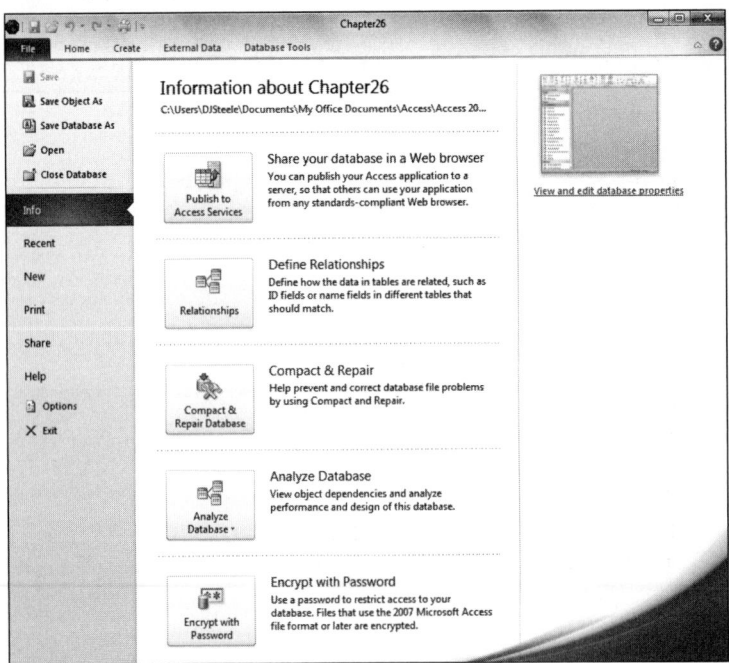

3. In the Password field, type the password that you want to use to secure the database (see Figure 26.19).

Access does *not* display the password; instead, it shows an asterisk (*) for each letter.

Providing a password to encrypt an Access database

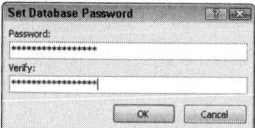

4. Retype the same password in the Verify field and click OK.

An encrypted database looks like any other Access application to its users. There is no outward difference in the appearance of the application's forms or reports after encryption. The only difference is that the user is required to provide the password each time the database is opened.

When encrypting a database, however, be aware of the following drawbacks:

- **Encrypted databases don't compress from their original size when used with compression programs, such as WinZip or sending it to a compressed (zipped) folder.** Encryption modifies the way that the data is stored on the hard drive so compression utilities have little or no effect.

- **Encrypted databases suffer some performance degradation (up to 15 percent).** Depending on the size of your database and the speed of your computer, this degradation may be imperceptible.

Also, be aware that encrypting a database makes it impossible to access the data or database objects without the proper password. Always maintain an unencrypted backup copy of the database in a secure location in the event that the password is lost or accidentally changed. There is no "universal" password for decrypting an encrypted Access database, and because strong encryption is used by Access 2010 there is no way to decrypt the database without the proper password.

Removing a database password

Follow these steps to remove the password from an encrypted database, and restore it to its previous, unencrypted state.

1. Open the encrypted .accdb database (for example, Chapter26.accdb) exclusively.

2. Click the File button in the upper-left corner of the screen, and select the Decrypt Database command on the Info tab (see Figure 26.20).

FIGURE 26.20

Choosing to remove a password from an encrypted Access database.

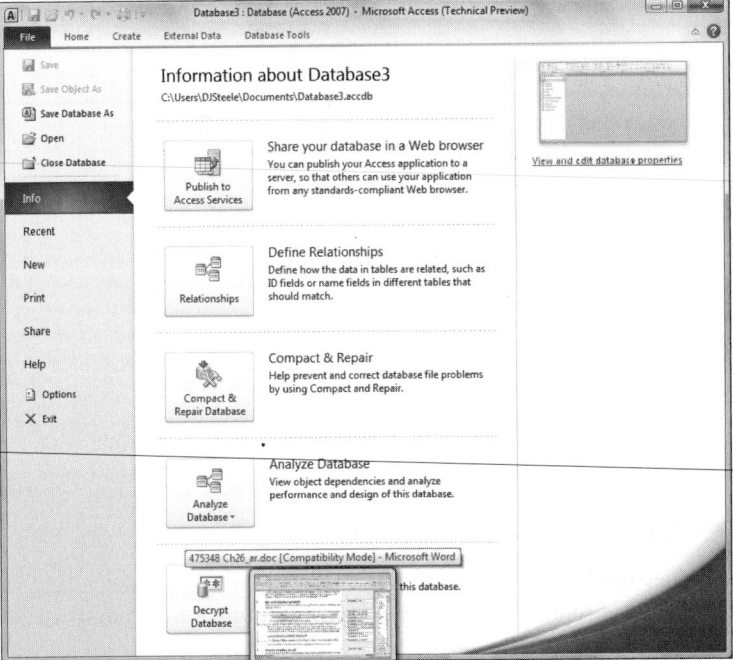

The Unset Database Password dialog box appears (see Figure 26.21).

FIGURE 26.21

Providing a password to remove a password from an encrypted Access database.

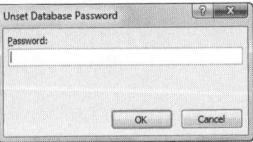

3. Enter the database password and click OK.

Protecting Visual Basic code

You control access to the VBA code in your application by creating a password for the Visual Basic project that you want to protect. When you set a database password for a project, users are prompted to enter the password each time they try to view the Visual Basic code in the database.

Note

A Visual Basic project refers to the set of standard and class modules (the code behind forms and reports) that are part of your Access database.

1. Open any standard module in the database.

   For this example, open the `basSalesFunctions` module in `Chapter26.accdb`.

2. In the Visual Basic Editor, choose Tools ➪ Chapter26 Properties.

   The Project Properties dialog box appears.

3. Select the Protection tab (shown in Figure 26.22).

FIGURE 26.22

Creating a project password restricts users from viewing the application's Visual Basic code.

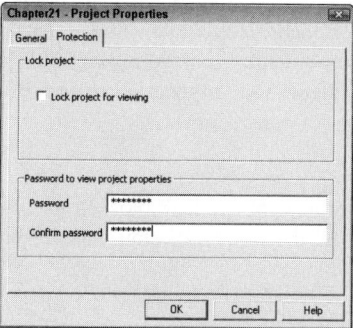

4. Select the Lock Project for Viewing check box.

5. Enter a password in the Password text box.

   Access does *not* display the password; instead, it shows an asterisk (*) for each letter.

6. Type the password again in the Confirm Password text box and click OK.

   This security measure ensures that you don't mistype the password (because you can't see the characters that you type) and mistakenly prevent everyone, including you, from accessing the database.

After you save and close the project, users attempting to view the application's code must enter the password. Access prompts for the project password only once per session.

A more secure method of securing your application's code, forms, and reports is to distribute your database as an .accde file. When you save your database as an .accde file, Access compiles all code modules (including form modules), removes all editable source code, and compacts the database. The new .accde file contains no source code but continues to work because it contains a compiled copy of all your code. Not only is this a great way to secure your source code, but it also enables you to distribute databases that are smaller (because they contain no source code) and always keep their modules in a compiled state.

Understanding macro security

You've probably had experience at some point with a virus attack on your computer. Or most likely, you know someone who has. It goes without saying that installing and running a virus scanning utility on your workstation, and keeping its virus signatures up to date, are imperative. Even though you may be very careful about keeping your virus scanner up to date, new viruses crop up all the time. So, you have to be proactive about protecting your applications and sensitive data from exposure to these kinds of attacks.

When you run forms, reports, queries, macros, and VBA code in your application, Microsoft Access uses the Trust Center to determine which commands may be unsafe and which unsafe commands you want to run. From the Trust Center's perspective, macros and VBA code are "macros" and shouldn't be trusted by default. Unsafe commands could allow a malicious user to hack into your hard drive or other resource in your environment. A malicious user could possibly delete files from your hard drive, alter the computer's configuration, or generally create all kinds of havoc in your workstation or even throughout your network environment.

Each time a form, report, or other object opens, Access checks its list of unsafe commands. By default, when Access encounters one of the unsafe commands, it blocks the command from execution. To tell Access to block these potentially unsafe commands, you must enable sandbox mode.

Enabling sandbox mode

Sandbox mode allows Access to block any of the commands in the unsafe list it encounters when running forms, reports, queries, macros, data access pages, and Visual Basic code:

1. Open Access, click the Microsoft Office button, and select Access Options.

   The Access Options dialog box appears.

2. Select the Trust Center tab, and then click Trust Center Settings.

   The Trust Center dialog box appears.

3. Select the Macro Settings tab (shown in Figure 26.23).

4. Select either Disable All Macros without Notification or Disable All Macros with Notification.

FIGURE 26.23

Enabling all macros

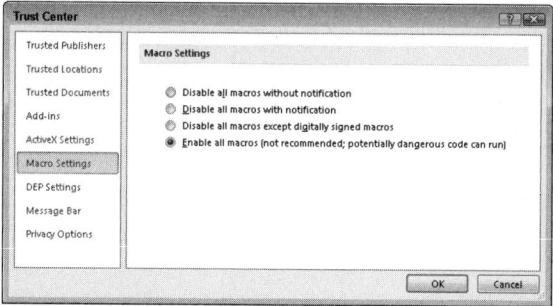

5. Restart Access to apply the security change.

The Macro Settings tab provides four levels of macro security:

- **Disable All Macros without Notification:** All macros and VBA code are disabled and the user isn't prompted to enable them.

- **Disable All Macros with Notification:** All macros and VBA code are disabled and the user is prompted to enable them.

- **Disable All Macros Except Digitally Signed Macros:** The status of the macro's digital signature is validated for digitally signed macros. For unsigned macros, a prompt displays advising the user to enable the macro or to cancel opening the database.

- **Enable All Macros (Not Recommended; Potentially Dangerous Code Can Be Run):** Macros and VBA code are not checked for digital signatures and no warning displays for unsigned macros.

A *digital signature* (contained within a *digital certificate*) is an encrypted secure file that accompanies a macro or document. It confirms that the author is a trusted source for the macro or document. Digital signatures are generally implemented within large organizations that are willing to fund the expense of purchasing and maintaining digital signatures. You, or your organization's IT department, can obtain a digital certificate through a commercial certification authority, like VeriSign, Inc., Adobe Systems, or DocuSign. Search `http://msdn.microsoft.com` for "Microsoft Root Certificate Program Members" to obtain information on how to obtain a digital certificate.

If you're sure of the security of your database, you can select the Enable All Macros setting. As its name implies, Enable All Macros allows all VBA code (and macros) to run, unchallenged, in an Access application. If there is a reasonable chance an application may run untrusted VBA code or macros, choose one of the alternate security settings: Disable All Macros without Notification, Disable All Macros with Notification, and Disable All Macros except Digitally Signed Macros. For most applications, however, during the development and maintenance cycles you'll probably use the Enable All Macros setting so that all the code and macros in the application executes without interrupting you with permissions dialog boxes.

If you or your organization has acquired a digital certificate, you can use it to sign your Access projects:

1. Open the Access database to digitally sign; then access any module to open the Visual Basic Editor.

2. Choose Tools ⇨ Digital Signature from the Visual Basic Editor menu.

   The Digital Signature dialog box opens, as shown in Figure 26.24.

FIGURE 26.24

Digitally signing an Access project

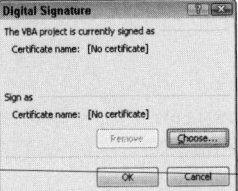

3. Click Choose to display the Select Certificate dialog box and select a certificate from the list, as shown in Figure 26.25.

FIGURE 26.25

Choosing a digital certificate

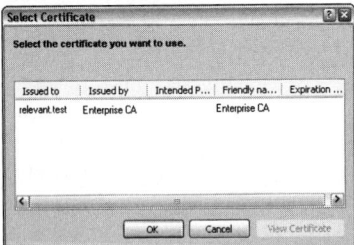

4. Select the certificate to add to the Access project.

5. Click OK to close the Select Certificate dialog box, and click OK again to close the Digital Signature dialog box and save the security setting.

Note

Don't sign your Access project until the application has been thoroughly tested and you don't expect to make any further changes to it. Modifying any of the code in the project invalidates the digital signature.

Tip

To prevent users from making unauthorized changes to the code in your project, be sure to lock the project and apply a project password.

The Trust Center

The Trust Center is where you can find security and privacy settings for Microsoft Access. The Trust Center replaces the Security dialog box in previous versions of Access. To display the Trust Center, click the Microsoft Office Button and click Access Options to open the Access Options dialog box. Select the Trust Center tab, and then click Trust Center Settings.

Here's a description of each section and what it controls:

- **Trusted Publishers:** Displays a list of trusted publishers — publishers where you clicked Trust all documents from this publisher when encountering a potentially unsafe macro — for Microsoft Office. To remove a publisher from this list, select the publisher; then click Remove. Trusted publishers must have a valid digital signature that hasn't expired.

- **Trusted Locations:** Displays the list of trusted locations on your computer or network. From this section, you can add, remove, or modify folders on your computer that will always contain trusted files. Any file in a trusted location can be opened without being checked by the Trust Center. You can also choose not to allow network locations and to disable all Trusted Locations and accept signed files.

- **Trusted Documents:** When Trusted Documents is selected, the name of the Access application is added to a special area in the system registry on the user's computer. Then, each time the application is used, it is recognized as a *trusted document,* and all the macros, code, and other elements of the application are enabled without interrupting the user's workflow.

- **Add-ins:** Lets you to set up how Access handles add-ins. You can choose whether add-ins need to be digitally signed from a trusted source and whether to display a notification for unsigned add-ins. You can also choose to disable all add-ins, which may impair functionality.

- **ActiveX Settings:** Lets you set the security level for ActiveX Controls.

- **Macro Settings:** Lets you set the security setting for macros not in a trusted location. (For more information on Macro Settings, see the previous section on sandbox mode.)

- **DEP Settings:** Allows you enable Data Execution Prevent mode.

- **Message Bar:** Lets you set whether to display the message bar that warns you about blocked content, or to never show information about blocked content.

- **Privacy Options:** Lets you choose how Microsoft Office Online communicates with your computer. You can set options to use Microsoft Office Online for help, show featured links at startup, download files to determine system problems, and sign up for the Customer Experience Improvement Program.

Continuing to improve the product

A developer's work is never done. Most likely, you came up with new ideas as you built the basic application, or your clients pestered you with improvement requests as they beta-tested the interim builds. Although avoiding "off-spec" changes that interfere with the main development effort is important, you should record these ideas and use them as starting points for the next iteration of the product.

In many cases, improvements to the application consist of enhancements to the user interface. If you discover that users misunderstand how to enter data, perhaps you need to add more label text to the forms to serve as guidance. Or if people complain that the application is hard to use, you might have to add more menu options or use more "plain English" throughout the program.

In the "Maintaining usage logs" section, earlier in this chapter, you read about building usage logs into your applications. A properly designed and maintained usage log provides invaluable information about how the database is being used. You might be surprised by how often errors occur, or how rarely a particular form or report is used. Any feedback you get from your users or the application itself will help you as you begin the next phase of what might turn out to be an endless project.

Summary

This chapter has taken a quick look at the steps required to bulletproof Access applications. Although entire books could be written on this important subject, the concepts presented in this chapter are all you need for most Access applications.

Obviously, bulletproofing a database application takes a lot of time. Validating all the data entry on every form or adding status-bar messages to every control in an application isn't easy. But the time you spend bulletproofing your databases will be paid back many times over in reduced support calls and happier users.

Using the Windows Application Programming Interface

Access and Visual Basic for Applications (VBA) help you develop powerful applications. Using the Windows application programming interface (API), you can take full advantage of the Windows graphical user interface (GUI) to create your own windows (forms), dialog boxes (message boxes), list boxes, combo boxes, command buttons, and so on. These objects make your application a *Windows* application. And that's what this chapter is all about.

Although this chapter concentrates on the API included with Windows, the concepts are applicable to other APIs as well, such as the Open Database Connectivity (ODBC) API, the Messaging Application Programming Interface (MAPI), and the Telephony Application Programming Interface (TAPI).

What the Windows API Is

The Windows API is a set of built-in code libraries extending the Windows interface. Access makes these libraries available to you and simplifies their use. The API libraries include functions that allow you to create windows, check systems resources, work with communications ports, send messages to applications, and access the Registry, among other things.

These functions hook directly into the internal workings of Windows. Although Access and VBA let you reach a great many of these hooks transparently, there are still some you can't get to without writing your application in the C programming language or referencing the Windows API directly. Access and VBA give you everything you need to tap into this collection of hundreds of functions. You only need to know how they work and what to look for.

IN THIS CHAPTER

Introducing the Windows application programming interface (API)

Learning when you'll use the Windows API

Looking at documentation sources for dynamic link libraries (DLLs)

Writing VBA code for the Windows API

Practicing API programming with examples

The API functions are written in libraries that can be *dynamically linked* to Windows applications. Typically, the functions are contained in dynamic link libraries (DLLs, or `.dll` files), but they can also be in `.exe`, `.drv`, and `.ocx` files.

Dynamic linking is a method of making functions available to your applications without hard-coding them into the executable (`.exe`) file. In many compiled languages, the code referenced by an application during development is included in the final product when the executable file is produced. Binding a library into an application's executable file is called *static linking* (also known as *early binding,* because the libraries are bound into the executable early in the executable's life). Static linking makes for tightly integrated code, but it can also be difficult to manage. The same type of function may be included in several applications, which can take up space on your user's hard drive. In addition, if you need to update or enhance your application, you have to replace the entire `.exe`, making those enhancements more difficult to execute.

Dynamic linking, on the other hand, allows you to store a library of code in one place (a DLL) and reference functions from that library only when they're needed at runtime. (Dynamic linking is sometimes called *late binding,* because the library routines are bound to the executable "late" in the executable's life.)

Using DLLs has several advantages:

- It keeps unneeded code out of memory. When calling a function from a DLL, the code takes up memory only when it's being used. The memory is reclaimed when the called function is unloaded.

- As a developer, you can create a host of applications. Rather than include the same code in each application, you can include only one copy of the DLL and call the functions from all your applications. This gives your applications a smaller footprint.

- It allows you to update or enhance just the DLL, without replacing all the applications that use its code.

Although you can't create DLLs in Microsoft Access, you can certainly use functions stored in the DLLs underlying Microsoft Windows. As you'll see in the "How to Use the Windows API" section, later in this chapter, calling functions stored in the Windows DLLs involves following certain rules. Generally speaking, you must declare a Windows API call before using it in your code, and most API functions are rather fussy about the parameters used in the VBA statements calling them. But overall, the benefits to be gained from using the API functions greatly outweigh the relatively short learning curve necessary to master them.

Reasons to Use the Windows API

There are many reasons why you should consider using the Windows API (and other application programming interfaces). Here are a few, in addition to the ones listed in the preceding section.

Common code base

In establishing the Windows API, Microsoft has made a common library of code available to your Access and Visual Basic applications. You can count on the fact that, if Windows is installed, the Windows API and its 500-plus functions are available. You don't have to distribute or check for these code modules — they exist on every Windows machine. You also know that any time Microsoft adds functionality to one of its DLLs, that functionality is available to all your applications.

Tested and proven code

If you develop applications professionally, then you know that time is paramount. Getting your application to market before a competitor or getting an application up and running in your own installation can give your company the competitive edge. Every module of code you or your programmers produce takes time to develop and time to test. The functions included in the API libraries are already tested and proven. They exist on hundreds of thousands — even millions — of machines all over the world.

A good example is the `GetPrivateProfileString` function. This function retrieves an entry from an application's `.ini` file. Yes, Access VBA has tremendous string manipulation and file input/output (I/O) capabilities, but why waste time writing and testing a function to do what `GetPrivateProfileString` already does? Let the API take some of the burden off your programming staff and allow them to concentrate on more important business issues. As you'll see in the "GetPrivateProfileStringA" section, later in this chapter, `GetPrivateProfileString` is easy to use — much easier than writing an equivalent function in Access VBA.

Cross-platform compatibility

Microsoft's strategy for the future of its operating systems includes the convergence of its code base. All editions of Microsoft Windows use the Win32 API, which makes the applications you write for one platform portable to others. Almost all Win32 API declarations are available across all platforms, which gives you an extended user base and keeps you from rewriting much of your code to fit each kind of installation.

Smaller application footprint

Making use of the DLLs included with Windows keeps you from distributing the same code within your applications. This, in turn, keeps the size of your applications smaller. Users appreciate the consideration you put into helping them manage their hardware resources.

Application consistency

Users are familiar with common dialog boxes, such as the File Find, and font selection dialog boxes. These dialog boxes are actually displayed by API functions and are available to any application needing the resources provided by these dialog boxes. The Windows API provides your

Access applications with the ability to display dialog boxes that are consistent with other Windows applications and work exactly as your users expect.

DLL Documentation

Windows ships with a large number of DLLs, and many application vendors distribute their own DLLs with their applications. Microsoft has documented its core DLLs so that developers can experience the advantages listed in the preceding section. Of course, this strategy has benefited Microsoft as well. By making it easier for programmers to write applications for Windows, Microsoft has made Windows the most popular development platform.

Not every vendor documents its DLLs, however. Many consider the DLLs distributed with their applications as proprietary property, so they don't make the interfaces for those applications available to the public.

Caution

If a vendor doesn't formally release documentation for its libraries, using them is usually not good practice, even if some outside documentation exists. A vendor could remove or change functions within a library without notification, making any applications that you've based on them unreliable at best, unusable at worst.

Finding the documentation

Microsoft has released Software Development Kits (SDKs) for many of its products, including ODBC, MAPI, and, of course, Win32. These kits contain not only general product information but also documentation for the core DLLs included in the products. They comprise a wealth of resources, documenting each function, argument, return value, data type, and so on. You can purchase the SDKs directly from Microsoft, or, if you're a member of the Microsoft Developer Network (MSDN), you can get them with the MSDN library, where they're included.

Making sense of the documentation

The good news: Microsoft releases documentation of its APIs. The bad news: The Windows API documentation is pretty cryptic and designed primarily to be used by C and C++ programmers. Most of Microsoft's high-level product documentation assumes that you're already an experienced developer. The "official" API documentation from Microsoft is not for the faint of heart.

The hardest part of understanding API documentation is deciphering data types. Many books, articles, and the Microsoft documentation have standards for referring to data types. When you know what kind of data type is being referred to, and how that type translates to Access, the battle is mostly over.

The C/C++ programming languages contain many different data types, most of which have Access VBA equivalents and some of which do not. Occasionally, the arguments included with API functions are structures composed of several different data types. Table 27.1 shows each C/C++ data type, its size, and its Access VBA equivalent.

Comparing C/C++ and VBA Data Types

C Type	Size	VBA Data Type
char	8 bits	String * 1
short	16 bits	Integer
int	32 bits	Long
long	32 bits	Long
float	32 bits	Single
double	64 bits	Double
UINT	32 bits	Long
ULONG	32 bits	Long
USHORT	16 bits	Integer
UCHAR	8 bits	String * 1
DWORD	32 bits	Long
BOOL	32 bits	Boolean
BYTE	8 bits	Byte
WORD	16 bits	Integer
HANDLE	32 bits	Long
LPTSTR	32 bits	No equivalent
LPCTSTR	32 bits	No equivalent

All these data types become important when examining both the SDKs and other API references for VBA. You'll have to know what kind of data type the function is expecting and match it with a compatible type in your Access applications. Listing 27.1 shows how the `GetPrivateProfile-String` function is declared in the API reference of the Win32 SDK and how to decipher each argument declared.

SDK Reference for GetPrivateProfileString

```
DWORD GetPrivateProfileString(
  LPCTSTR  lpszSection,      // points to section name
  LPCTSTR  lpszKey,          // points to key name
  LPCTSTR  lpszDefault,      // points to default string
  LPTSTR   lpszReturnBuffer, // points to destination buffer
  DWORD    cchReturnBuffer,  // size of destination buffer
  LPCTSTR  lpszFile          // initialization filename
);
```

Listing 27.2 shows the same declaration using Basic syntax instead of C/C++ syntax. Notice how the C/C++ data types are converted to their VBA equivalents.

LISTING 27.2

Visual Basic Declaration for GetPrivateProfileString

```
Declare Function GetPrivateProfileStringA lib "Kernel32"( _
        ByVal lpszSection As String,
        ByVal lpszKey As String, _
        ByVal lpszDefault As String, _
        ByVal dwReturnBuffer As Long, _
        ByVal cchReturnBuffer As Long, _
        ByVal lpszFile As String) As Long
```

Caution

You must declare the correct data types in your applications. Failure to do so can result in the dreaded General Protection Fault, crashing your Access application. If you don't declare variables of the proper size (such as using an integer when a long is specified), your function calls might overwrite memory locations allocated to other applications. Using inappropriate data types as parameters to API functions is the most common cause of problems when using the Windows API.

In Listing 27.2, notice the prefix attached to each argument passed to the functions. These are standard prefixes used throughout most of the API documentation you'll find. Some of the more common prefixes are shown in Table 27.2.

TABLE 27.2

Common Windows API Argument Prefixes

Prefix	C/C++ Data Type	VBA Data Type
lpsz	Long pointer to a null terminated string	String
dw	DWORD	Long
w	WORD	Integer
hWnd	HANDLE	Long
b	BOOL	Long
l	LONG	Long

Sometimes you'll encounter situations where a function uses a data type that you aren't familiar with or may not have even heard of. Most likely, the parameter being passed is a *data structure,* which is a fancy term for "user-defined data type." If that term sounds familiar, then you're probably thinking about the Access VBA Type statement. Data structures are usually a collection of fields allocated contiguously (next to each other in memory). The Type statement in Access VBA is compatible with its C/C++ Struct counterpart, as long as the fields declared within the structure are compatible. Listing 27.3 shows the data structure passed in the GetVersionEx API and its Access VBA equivalent.

LISTING 27.3

OSVERSIONINFO Structure

```
'C-type OSVERSIONINFO structure syntax
typedef struct _OSVERSIONINFO{
    DWORD dwOSVersionInfoSize;
    DWORD dwMajorVersion;
    DWORD dwMinorVersion;
    DWORD dwBuildNumber;
    DWORD dwPlatformId;
    TCHAR szCSDVersion[ 128 ];
} OSVERSIONINFO;
'VBA-typedef for OSVERSIONINFO
Private Type OSVERSIONINFO
    dwVersionInfo As Long
    dwMajorVersion As Long
    dwMinorVersion As Long
    dwBuildNumber As Long
    dwplatformID As Long
    szVersion As String * 128
End Type
```

Recognizing what you can't do with the API

I hesitate to place anything in this paragraph, because as soon as I do, someone will find a way to prove me wrong. Programmers are an inventive bunch. But a few things are difficult to do when converting APIs to VBA. One is converting APIs that make use of a Callback function. Sometimes APIs make calls to other functions that process messages and then return values back to the calling API. To do this, you must be able to pass the address of the entry point of the function. Access doesn't provide a way to handle this situation. However, some people have developed their own DLLs that specifically handle these types of situations. Never say never.

How to Use the Windows API

If you've made it this far, congratulations! The concept of APIs can be a little intimidating. Once you understand the concepts, however, using them is as easy as calling any other function or subroutine from Access VBA.

The Declare statement

In order to use an API in your Access application, you must first tell Access the name of the API function and where to find it. You do this within the declarations section of a module using the `Declare` statement. The `Declare` keyword notifies VBA that what follows is not part of VBA but exists outside of the current application. A prototype `Declare` statement is shown here:

```
Declare [Function|Sub] FunctionName Lib "LibraryName" _
        Alias "AliasName" (ArgumentList) As DataType
```

The `Declare` statement has several parts, all of which are discussed in the following sections.

Note

The `Declare` statement is sometimes referred to as an API function prototype because it serves as the prototype for all calls to the API function.

Function or Sub

APIs can be in the form of a function or a subroutine, just like Access VBA procedures. A function returns a value back to the calling code, while a subroutine does not. When an API function returns a value, good programming practice requires the calling procedure to check the return value to verify that the function completed as expected. The vast majority of Windows API calls are functions, so you rarely have to deal with the distinction between functions and subs.

Function name

The function name you use in the `Declare` statement can be one of two things:

- **The actual name of the API function you'll be using as declared in the library:** For instance, if you were going to use `GetPrivateProfileString`, listed in the "Making sense of the documentation" section, earlier in this chapter, you would use `GetPrivateProfileStringA` as the function name.
- **The name of the function as you would like to use it within your code.**

Tip

`GetPrivateProfileStringA` is a long function name, especially if you're going to be using the function frequently within your code. You might want to shorten its name to `GetString` instead. You can do this by using the `Alias` parameter discussed in the "Alias 'AliasName'" section, later in this chapter.

Lib "LibraryName"

The library name is simply the name of the DLL that contains the API function or subroutine that you're declaring. This parameter tells Access where to find the function. If the DLL is not a standard Windows DLL, or the DLL has been moved to another location, you'll have to specify the complete path of the DLL. The LibraryName parameter must be enclosed in quotations but is not case sensitive.

Most Windows DLLs are located in the System32 folder within the main Windows folder (usually C:\Windows). If the DLL path is not given in the Declare statement, the VBA interpreter first looks for the DLL in the System32 folder, and then in the Windows folder. In the rare event that you're using a DLL located anywhere else on your computer, you should specify the path to the DLL as part of the LibraryName clause in the API function's declare statement.

Alias "AliasName"

The Alias clause lets you call an API function by some other name, if needed. In such a case, the FunctionName parameter is the new name you assign to the function, and the Alias clause identifies the original function name. In the following example, the Declare prototype is prefixed with api to indicate that it is an API function call, and not the usual VBA function name:

```
Declare Function apiGetPrivateProfileString _
    Lib "Kernel32" Alias "GetPrivateProfileStringA"
```

In this example, apiGetPrivateProfileString is the function name you'll use in your VBA code, and it's an alias for GetPrivateProfileStringA.

There are several reasons why using an alias is a good idea. In the preceding example, the alias provides a way to apply a naming convention (the api prefix) to the declared API function. Occasionally, you'll encounter API functions that begin with an underscore, such as _lopen or _lread. Access VBA procedures cannot begin with an underscore, so these functions must be aliased. Another reason to alias your function names is to avoid the possibility of declaring a function using a name that already exists in your Access application or in its libraries. If you try to declare a function with a name that already exists, you'll receive an error: Ambiguous Name Detected: FunctionName.

Tip

Like library names, the aliased function name (GetPrivateProfileStringA, in this example) must always be enclosed in quotations. The alias reference (GetPrivateProfileStringA) is always case sensitive and must be spelled exactly like the function name it references in the DLL.

ArgumentList

The ArgumentList is composed of the elements that the function expects to receive from you in order to do its job. When you declare a function, you must declare the same number of arguments in the function declaration that the function's documentation specifies. If you don't, you'll receive runtime error 49: Bad DLL calling convention. The same error occurs if you pass incompatible arguments to an API function.

Note

The arguments in the argument list are only placeholders. It doesn't matter what you name them, although most developers assign them the same name specified in the SDK documentation. The argument list simply tells Access what to expect when the function is called so that it can check the arguments and their data types. Access does not, however, check the type declarations against the actual library, so it's up to you to assign the correct data types to your arguments.

ByVal or ByRef?

When you assign arguments to a declaration statement, you must decide how the API expects to receive the arguments. By default, when Access passes an argument, it does so by reference, or ByRef. This means that Access passes the memory *address* of the variable to the function it's calling. When a function receives the address of an argument, it can change the value stored at that address, which may or may not be desirable. When you pass an argument by value, or ByVal, you're telling Access to pass only the variable's *value* to the function. When a function receives only the value of an argument, it can use only that value to do its job. Passing an argument by value is usually desirable because it ensures that the variables used in your application keep a stable value.

Here's an example of using the ByVal keyword:

```
Declare Function apiGetTempPath Lib "Kernel32" _
    Alias "GetTempPathA" (ByVal BufferSize As Long, _
    ByVal lpszReturnBuffer As String) As Long
```

There is always an exception to the rule, and the exception in this case is string variables. Access VBA and C++ handle strings differently. C++ expects to receive pointers to strings that are terminated with a null value; Access VBA does not. This means that you must pass the string by value (ByVal). As I said earlier, passing an argument by value passes the data stored in the variable instead of the memory address — except when you pass strings. When you pass a string using the ByVal option, you pass the address of the variable, which means the function can change the value passed to it by manipulating what's stored at the memory address.

In the case of API calls, it's a good thing that strings are always passed with the ByVal qualifier. An API function can't return a string value, so you must give the function permission to alter a memory location in order to retrieve a string value from an API. You do this by specifying that the argument is to be passed by value. Notice that lpszReturnBuffer is a pointer to a string that GetTempPathA uses to place the path that Windows uses for temp files; it's being passed as an address. BufferSize, on the other hand, is a variable that contains the length of the string being passed as lpszReturnBuffer.

A final note on passing strings: Many API functions expect to receive addresses to string values. Most of the time, these functions expect a minimum number of bytes to be allocated for the string value. In order to fulfill these requirements, you must know in advance how many bytes the function expects in the string, and you must expand your string variables to that length before passing the string. You can do this using the VBA String$() function. The String function fills a string variable with a fixed number of characters. In the following example, strMyString is filled with 20 spaces:

```
Dim strMyString As String
strMyString = String$(20," ")
```

The preceding code fills the fixed-width string variable `strMyString` with 20 spaces. You can achieve the same result by declaring the string with the number of characters already allocated:

```
Dim strMyString * 20
```

Caution

If you don't allocate enough space for an API function to write a string, it could end up writing over another application's data, causing an error. It's very difficult to know how many characters an API will accept, so a safe way to declare your string variables is to allocate 255 characters to string variables. Most functions will not pass a string larger than 255 characters.

As DataType

Any API call that is a function returns a value. A subroutine does not. The value returned by a function is usually a value that you use in your application, or it's an error number. For example, many functions return zero, or `ERROR_SUCCESS` if the function completes successfully. In this case, if the value returned is not zero (indicating that the API call failed to execute properly), you should provide an error-handling routine to deal with the function's failure.

Other functions, such as `GetPrivateProfileStringA`, return a numeric value indicating the number of characters copied into a string buffer. Therefore, if `GetPrivateProfileStringA` completes successfully, you use its return value and the `Left$()` function to extract the returned string from a string buffer.

```
StringVar = Left$(StringBuffer, ReturnValue)
```

If the value returned by `GetProfileStringA` is 0, of course, it means that no string was found in the `.ini` file.

The data type specified for the return value must be compatible with the data type specified in the API function's documentation.

Wrapper functions

You rarely directly program API functions. API calls frequently require complicated arguments, and the values returned by API functions most often require interpretation before they can be used.

Many developers use wrapper functions to resolve these issues. A *wrapper function* is a simple VBA procedure that provides the API call with all the parameters it needs, as well as converting the values returned by the API function to a format the application can use. Your VBA code calls the wrapper function, which, in turn, calls the API function. The wrapper function returns the transformed value provided by the API function.

What is this "hwnd" thing?

Many Windows API functions use a parameter named hwnd. Hwnd is a long integer value that Windows uses to keep track of graphical objects on the computer's screen. Every object on the screen (windows, buttons, text boxes, and so on) has an hwnd value, and many API calls require this value before they can operate on the object.

Microsoft has made hwnd very easy to get for most Access objects. Many Access objects include hwnd among their properties. You won't see hwnd in the property window, but it's there just the same. Use Me.hwnd to pass the hwnd of an Access form, or MyControl.hwnd (for example, txtLastName. hwnd) to pass the hwnd of a control to an API call requiring this important value.

The "API Examples" section, later in this chapter, provides typical wrapper functions for the API calls documented in this chapter. All that's needed to utilize an API call is to include the API function's Declare statement, as well as the VBA wrapper function accompanying the API declaration. Then call the VBA wrapper function as you would any function such as Format() or Now(). VBA wrappers protect your application from the sometimes ugly and tedious code needed to properly process API calls.

API Examples

Here comes the fun part. At the beginning of this chapter, I reviewed several different uses for the Windows API. From here to the end of the chapter, you'll see some examples of different types of APIs, how to declare them, what you would use them for, error messages you may encounter, and so on.

On the CD-ROM
All the examples in this chapter are included on the companion CD-ROM in the Chapter27.accdb example database. The code examples in Chapter27.accdb are contained in a module named basAPIFunctions. This module contains all the raw declarations and working functions you see described in this chapter.

The System Information dialog box (shown in Figure 27.1), which you open from the Access 2010 Options menu, contains useful information, including information about the operating system and the computer's hardware. The code in basAPIFunctions uses Windows API calls to populate the API Demo form (frmAPIDemo) included in the Chapter27.accdb example database (see Figure 27.2).

Caution
Whenever you're working with API functions, frequently save your work. Because you're working deep within the Windows system, application errors can occur — especially when you're first learning how to make these calls.

FIGURE 27.1

The System Information dialog box

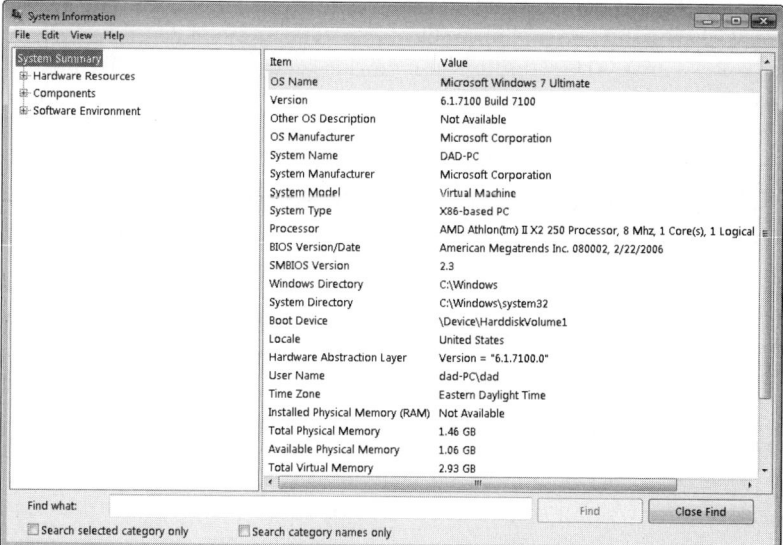

FIGURE 27.2

The API Demo form from `Chapter27.accdb` on the companion CD-ROM

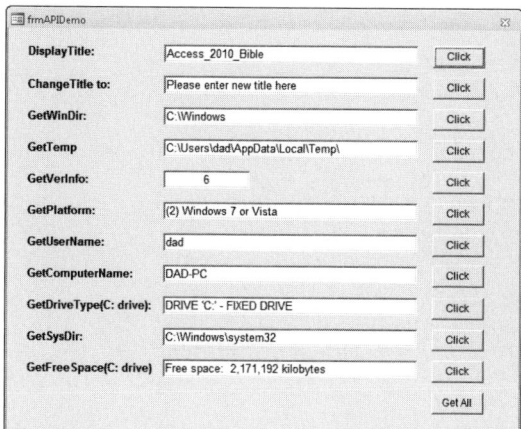

Retrieving system information

The Windows API provides a number of functions that you'll find useful for retrieving information about the Windows system, the hardware, and other software that may be running on the computer. This information is often useful for avoiding problems like running out of disk space or trying to write data to a CD-ROM drive. These functions also provide handy information, like the location of the Windows and temporary directories.

GetCommandLineA

`GetCommandLine` returns the command line used to start up the current application. This may be useful if you need to know whether the shortcut used to start an Access application included references to a macro or VBA procedure.

```
Declare Function apiGetCommandLine _
    Lib "kernel32" _
    Alias "GetCommandLineA" () As Long
```

When run from the immediate window in Access VBA, the function returns the full path, including the executable name, for Microsoft Access. The command line is returned in quotation marks.

The following function serves as a wrapper around `GetCommandLineA`:

```
Declare Sub CopyMemory _
    Lib "kernel32" _
    Alias "RtlMoveMemory" ( _
    pDst As Any, _
    pSrc As Any, _
    ByVal ByteLen As Long _
)
Declare Function lstrlen _
    Lib "kernel32" _
    Alias "lstrlenA" ( _
    ByVal lpString As Long _
) As Long
Function GetCommandLine() As String
    Dim RetStr As Long
    Dim SLen As Long
    Dim Buffer As String

    'Get a pointer to a string containing the command line:
    RetStr = apiGetCommandLine
    'Get the length of that string:
    SLen = lstrlen(RetStr)
    If SLen > 0 Then
        'Create a buffer:
        GetCommandLine = Space$(SLen)
        'Copy to the buffer:
        CopyMemory ByVal GetCommandLine, ByVal RetStr, SLen
    End If
End Function
```

Although not strictly necessary, the GetCommandLine wrapper trims leading and trailing spaces from the string returned by the apiGetCommandLine declaration. Very often, API functions return strings that are padded with extra characters, and the extra characters should be trimmed off of the wrapper's return value.

In Chapter27.accdb, GetCommandLine is used to retrieve the path to MSAccess.exe.

GetWindowsDirectoryA

GetWindowsDirectoryA retrieves the path to Windows and stores it in a string buffer.

```
Declare Function apiGetWindowsDirectory _
    Lib "Kernel32" _
    Alias "GetWindowsDirectoryA"( _
    ByVal lpszReturnBuffer As String, _
    ByVal lpszBuffSize As Long) As Long
```

The return value is the length of the string copied into the buffer. If the buffer isn't long enough, the return value is the length required. But if the function fails, GetWindowsDirectoryA returns zero.

Here's a function wrapper that uses the GetWindowsDirectoryA API function:

```
Function GetWindowsDirectory() As String
    Dim WinDir As String * 255
    Dim WinDirSize As Long
    Dim RetVal As Long
    WinDirSize = Len(WinDir)
    RetVal = apiGetWindowsDirectory(WinDir, WinDirSize)
    If RetVal > 0 Then
      GetWindowsDirectory = Left$(WinDir, RetVal)
    Else
      GetWindowsDirectory = vbNullString
    End If
End Function
```

In the GetWindowsDirectory wrapper, notice that the API function's return value (RetVal) is used as an argument to the Left$ function to extract the Windows folder name from the WinDir string. If RetVal is zero, an empty string (vbNullString) is returned instead.

GetTempPathA

The GetTempPathA function retrieves the path to the directory where temp files are stored and places it in a string buffer.

```
Declare Function apiGetTempPath _
    Lib "Kernel32" _
    Alias "GetTempPathA"( _
    ByVal BufferSize As Long, _
    ByVal lpszReturnBuffer As String) As Long
```

The return value is the length of the returned string. Like `GetWindowsDirectory`, if the buffer isn't long enough, the return value is the length required to hold the temp path. If the function fails, the return value is zero.

The wrapper for `GetTempPathA` properly interprets the return values when the API function is called.

```
Function GetTempDir() As String
    Dim Buffer As String * 255
    Dim BufferSize As Long
    Dim RetVal As Long
    BufferSize = Len(Buffer)
    RetVal = apiGetTempPath(BufferSize, Buffer)
    If RetVal > 0 Then
      GetTempDir = Left$(Buffer, RetVal)
    Else
      GetTempDir = vbNullString
    End If
End Function
```

GetVersionExA

`GetVersionEx` returns the version number of the Windows installation on the user's computer.

```
Declare Function apiGetVersion _
    Lib "Kernel32" _
    Alias "GetVersionExA"( _
    ByRef osVer As OSVERSIONINFO) As Long
```

Notice that the GetVersionExA API function uses a data structure named OSVERSIONINFO as one of its arguments. Notice that OSVERSIONINFO is passed by reference, which means that the API function changes the contents of the data structure. GetVersionExA returns much of its data by setting the members of OSVERSIONINFO to the values returned by Windows. Here's the definition of OSVERSIONINFO:

```
Private Type OSVERSIONINFO
    dwVersionInfo As Long
    dwMajorVersion As Long
    dwMinorVersion As Long
    dwBuildNumber As Long
    dwplatformID As Long
    szVersion As String * 128
End Type
```

The OSVERSIONINFO can be interpreted like this: dwVersionInfo is the length, in bytes, of the data structure. dwMajorVersion is 6 for Windows Vista and Windows 7. The build number is a value that is used mostly by Microsoft internally.

dwPlatformID is a long integer representing the platform on which the application is running. The dwPlatformID constants are declared as follows:

```
Const VER_PLATFORM_WIN32S = 0
Const VER_PLATFORM_WIN32_Windows = 1
Const VER_PLATFORM_WIN32_NT = 2
```

Chapter27.accdb on the CD-ROM uses the GetVersionEx function to display the current version of Windows in the system information using the following two functions. One retrieves the platform number, while the other gets the major and minor versions.

```
Function GetVersion() As Long
    Dim RetVal As Long
    Dim VersionNo As OSVERSIONINFO
    Dim lngVer As Long
    Dim Version As String
    VersionNo.dwVersionInfo = 148
    RetVal = apiGetVersion(VersionNo)
    Version = VersionNo.dwMajorVersion & "." _
        & VersionNo.dwMinorVersion
    lngVer = CLng(Version)
    GetVersion= lngVer
End Function
```

The GetPlatform wrapper function calls the same API declaration but uses the values returned in the OSVERSIONINFO structure to compose a string indicating that the Windows version installed on the computer.

```
Function GetPlatform()
    Dim RetVal As Long
    Dim VersionNo As OSVERSIONINFO
    Dim Platform As String
    VersionNo.dwVersionInfo = 148
    RetVal = apiGetVersion(VersionNo)
    Select Case VersionNo.dwPlatformID
        Case VER_PLATFORM_WIN32S
            Platform = "Windows 3.x"
        Case VER_PLATFORM_WIN32_Windows
            Platform = "Windows 98 or Lower"
        Case VER_PLATFORM_WIN32_NT
            Platform = "Windows NT"
        Case VER_PLATFORM_WIN32_NT_2
            Platform = "Windows XP, Vista, or 7"
        Case Else
            Platform = "Unknown"
    End Select
    GetPlatform = Platform
End Function
```

GetUserNameA

The `GetUserNameA` function retrieves the name of the user currently logged on to the system and places it in a string buffer.

```
Declare Function apiGetUserName _
    Lib "Advapi32" _
    Alias "GetUserNameA"( _
    ByVal Buffer As String, _
    BufferSize As Long) As Long
```

If the function is successful, it returns TRUE, and the length of the returned string is placed in the `BufferSize` variable.

The user name returned by the `GetUserName` API function has nothing to do with the user logged in to Access — Windows doesn't know anything about the Access users or groups and doesn't monitor who's logged in to an Access database. The following wrapper function tells you exactly who logged on to the computer:

```
Function GetUserName() As String
    Dim UserName As String * 255
    Dim NameSize As Long
    Dim RetVal As Long
    NameSize = Len(UserName)
    RetVal = apiGetUserName(UserName, NameSize)
    GetUserName = Left$(UserName, NameSize - 1)
End Function
```

GetComputerNameA

The `GetComputerNameA` function is very similar to `GetUserNameA`. It returns the network name of the local computer.

```
Declare Function apiGetComputerName _
    Lib "Kernel32" _
    Alias "GetComputerNameA"( _
    ByVal Buffer As String, _
    BufferSize As Long) As Long
```

`GetComputerNameA` retrieves the name of the current computer system. If the function fails, its return value is zero; otherwise, the return value is 1, and the `BufferSize` argument returns the number of characters copied to the `ComputerName` string variable. The `GetComputerName` function is a wrapper for the `GetComputerNameA` declaration and returns a string containing the name of the computer.

```
Function GetComputerName() As String
    Dim ComputerName As String * 255
    Dim NameSize As Long
    Dim RetVal As Long
    NameSize = Len(ComputerName)
```

```
      RetVal = _
          apiGetComputerName(ComputerName, NameSize)
      If RetVal > 0 Then
        GetComputerName = Left$(ComputerName, NameSize)
      Else
        GetComputerName = vbNullString
      End If
  End Function
```

GetDriveTypeA

From time to time, you may need to know what types of hard disks and optical drives are installed on a user's computer. You wouldn't want to, for instance, try writing to an optical drive on the user's computer unless you knew it was capable of read/write operations. The GetDriveTypeA API function returns a value indicating the type of drive specified by the lpszPath parameter.

```
Declare Function apiGetDriveType Lib "Kernel32" _
    Alias "GetDriveTypeA"( _
    ByVal lpszPath As String) As Long
```

You pass the function the path to the drive you want to test, and GetDriveTypeA returns a long integer value representing the drive type. The following constants can be used to determine the drive type:

```
Const DRIVE_UNKNOWN = 0
Const DRIVE_NOT_AVAILABLE = 1
Const DRIVE_REMOVABLE = 2
Const DRIVE_FIXED = 3
Const DRIVE_REMOTE = 4
Const DRIVE_CDROM = 5
Const DRIVE_RAMDISK = 6
```

Read/write optical drives (such as a CD-RW or DVD-RW drive) and USB thumb drives are reported as DRIVE_REMOVABLE.

The following function cycles through each drive possibility and prints its type in the debug window using the constants listed earlier and GetDriveTypeA:

```
Function GetAllDriveTypes() As String
    Dim DriveInfo As String
    Dim PathName As String
    Dim intChar As Integer
    Dim RetVal As Long
    Dim DriveType As String
    For intChar = 65 To 90
        ' The backward slash is not required,
        ' but does not interfere with this API call.
        ' The colon is required, however:
        PathName = Chr$(intChar) & ":\"
```

```
            RetVal = apiGetDriveType(PathName)
            Select Case RetVal
                Case DRIVE_UNKNOWN
                    DriveType = "DRIVE '" & PathName & _
                        "' - UNKNOWN"
                Case DRIVE_NOT_AVAILABLE
                    DriveType = "DRIVE '" & PathName & _
                        "' - NOT AVAILABLE"
                Case DRIVE_REMOVABLE
                    DriveType = "DRIVE '" & PathName & _
                        "' - REMOVEABLE DRIVE"
                Case DRIVE_FIXED
                    DriveType = "DRIVE '" & PathName & _
                        "' - FIXED DRIVE"
                Case DRIVE_REMOTE
                    DriveType = "DRIVE '" & PathName & _
                        "' - NETWORK DRIVE"
                Case DRIVE_CDROM
                    DriveType = "DRIVE '" & PathName & _
                        "' - CDROM; DRIVE"
                Case DRIVE_RAMDISK
                    DriveType = "DRIVE '" & PathName & _
                        "' - RAM DRIVE"
                Case Else
                    RetVal = 0
            End Select
            Debug.Print DriveType
            RetVal = 1
        Next intChar
    End Sub
```

GetVolumeInformationA

The GetVolumeInformationA function returns information about the file system and volume information for a valid path.

```
    Declare Function apiGetVolumeInformation _
        Lib "Kernel32" _
        Alias "GetVolumeInformationA"( _
        ByVal lpszPath As String, _
        ByVal lpVolNameBuffer As String, _
        ByVal lpVolumeNameSize As Long, _
        lpVolSerialNo As Long, _
        lpMaxFileLen As Long, _
        lpSystemFlags As Long, _
        ByVal lpSysNamebuffer As String, _
        ByVal lpSysNameBufSize As Long) As Long
```

lpMaxFileLen is the maximum number of characters allowed for a filename on the particular file system. lpSystemFlags indicates whether the volume is compressed, whether filenames are case sensitive, and whether the volume supports file-based compression. The return value is 1 if successful, 0 if not.

The GetVolumeInformation wrapper function accepts a valid path name and a 1 or 2 indicating whether to return the volume name or file system information, respectively.

```
Function GetVolumeInfo(PathName As String, _
    Selection As Integer) As String
    Dim VolName As String * 255
    Dim BufferSize As Long
    Dim VolSerNo As Long
    Dim MaxFileLen As Long
    Dim SysFlags As Long
    Dim SysName As String * 255
    Dim SysBufSize As Long
    Dim RetVal As Long
    Const Get_Volume_Name = 1
    Const Get_File_System = 2
    BufferSize = Len(VolName)
    SysBufSize = Len(SysName)
    RetVal = apiGetVolumeInformation(PathName, _
        VolName, BufferSize, VolSerNo, MaxFileLen, _
            SysFlags, SysName, SysBufSize)
    If Selection = 1 Then
        GetVolumeInfo = "Volume Name: " & Trim(VolName)
    Else
        If Selection = 2 Then
            GetVolumeInfo = "File System: " & Trim(SysName)
        End If
    End If
End Function
```

GetSystemDirectoryA

GetSystemDirectoryA returns the Windows system directory for the current machine.

```
Declare Function apiGetSystemDirectory _
    Lib "Kernel32" _
    Alias "GetSystemDirectoryA"( _
    ByVal ReturnBuffer As String, _
    uiBufferSize As Long) As Long
```

Upon success, the function returns the number of characters contained in the ReturnBuffer argument. GetSystemDirectoryA returns zero if unsuccessful. GetSystemDirectory is a wrapper utilizing GetSystemDirectoryA to return the Windows installation folder.

```
Function GetSystemDirectory() As String
    Dim ReturnBuffer As String * 255
    Dim BufferSize As Long
    BufferSize = Len(ReturnBuffer)
    Dim RetVal As Long
```

```
            RetVal = _
                apiGetSystemDirectory(ReturnBuffer, BufferSize)
            GetSystemDirectory = _
                Left$(ReturnBuffer, RetVal)
        End Function
```

Going over general-purpose Windows API functions

The Win32 API has many functions to manipulate individual windows within applications like Access. A few of these functions are discussed in the following sections. The `DisplayTitle()` function under Listing 27.5 and Listing 27.6 uses several of the API functions as an example.

GetParent

The `GetParent` function returns a handle to a window's parent. You might use this call to get a handle on an Access application's parent window.

```
    Declare Function apiGetParent _
        Lib "User32" Alias "GetParent"( _
        ByVal hWnd As Long) As Long
```

When passed a valid window handle, `GetParent` retrieves the handle (`hwnd`) of the child window's parent. The function returns a `Null` value if it's unsuccessful.

GetWindowTextA

`GetWindowTextA` returns the title-bar text of a window, given its `hwnd` property.

```
    Declare Function apiGetWindowText _
        Lib "User32" _
        Alias "GetWindowTextA"( _
        ByVal hwnd As Long, _
        ByVal lpszCaption As String, _
        ByVal CaptionSize As Long) As Long
```

Occasionally, you may want to capture the text that appears in the title bar of a particular window or the text displayed on a control. `GetWindowTextA` captures the text of the handle of the window or control that has been passed and places it in the `lpszCaption` argument.

GetClassNameA

`GetClassNameA` returns the class of the specified window.

```
    Declare Function apiGetClassName _
        Lib "User32" _
        Alias "GetClassNameA"( _
        ByVal hwnd As Long, _
        ByVal lpClassName As String, _
        ByVal ClassSize As Long) As Long
```

The window's handle is passed as an argument, and the function places the window's class name in the string lpClassName. The function returns the number of characters copied to the string buffer if it's successful, 0 if not.

The DisplayTitle wrapper function (see Listing 27.5) uses GetParent and GetClassNameA to cycle through the windows and controls of an open Access form until the Access application form (class Omain) is located. It then captures the text displayed in the title bar, using GetWindowTextA, and displays the text in a message box.

LISTING 27.5

Returning the Caption Bar Text for a Window

```
Sub DisplayTitle()
    Dim RetVal As Long
    Dim Parent As Long
    Dim lngRet As Long
    Dim Caption As String * 128
    Dim CaptionSize As Long
    Dim WinHwnd As Long
    Dim Class As String * 6
    Dim ClassSize As Long
    CaptionSize = Len(Caption)
    ClassSize = Len(Class)
    WinHwnd = Me.hwnd
    Do Until Trim(Class) = "OMain"
        Parent = apiGetParent(WinHwnd)
        lngRet = apiGetClassName(Parent, Class, ClassSize)
        WinHwnd = Parent
    Loop
    RetVal = apiGetWindowText( _
        Parent, Caption, CaptionSize)
    MsgBox Left$(Caption, RetVal)
End Sub
```

Notice that the Do...Loop in the middle of DisplayTitle searches for a window with a class name of OMain. The very first version of Microsoft's desktop database project was named Omega, and this very early precursor to Microsoft Access lives on as the class name applied to the Access main window.

SetWindowTextA

Use SetWindowTextA to change the caption displayed in a window's title bar.

```
Declare Function apiSetWindowText _
    Lib "User32" _
```

```
Alias "SetWindowTextA"( _
ByVal hwnd As Long, _
ByVal lpszCaption As String) As Long
```

SetWindowTextA is much like altering the Caption property of a form. Many people find they want to change the caption of the Access main window to make their applications look more professional. The function in Listing 27.6 cycles through the windows and controls of an Access application until it finds the Access application form (class Omain), and then it changes the title-bar text.

LISTING 27.6

Changing the Title-Bar Text for a Window

```
Function ChangeTitle()
    Dim RetVal As Long
    Dim Parent As Long
    Dim lngRet As Long
    Dim Caption As String * 128
    Dim CaptionSize As Long
    Dim NewCaption As String
    Dim WinHwnd As Long
    Dim Class As String * 6
    Dim ClassSize As Long
    NewCaption = "My New Application Title"
    CaptionSize = Len(caption)
    ClassSize = Len(class)
    WinHwnd = Me.hwnd
    Do Until Trim(class) = "OMain"
        Parent = GetParent(WinHwnd)
        lngRet = apiGetClassName(Parent, Class, ClassSize)
        WinHwnd = Parent
    Loop
    RetVal = apiSetWindowText(Parent, NewCaption)
End Function
```

SetWindowTextA returns 1 when successful, 0 when it fails.

Manipulating application settings with the Windows API

In the past, software vendors and Microsoft have used .ini files to control the settings of their applications. The system.ini and win.ini files controlled almost everything in older versions of Windows. Back then, each application had an .ini file containing sections, string values, key names, and integer values that related to everything from screen color to network protocols.

Although many vendors still use application-specific .ini files for their applications, more recent versions of Windows use the System Registry for most settings. The Win32 API comes with everything needed to control System Registry settings.

However, you may find it much simpler to use .ini files for storing persistent information (such as configuration data) needed by your Access applications. One huge advantage that .ini files have over the System Registry is that a user can use Notepad or Word to change the contents of an .ini file, and changing an application's .ini file won't affect any other application on the computer.

This section demonstrates the use of .ini functions for Win32.

GetPrivateProfileStringA

GetPrivateProfileStringA function retrieves a value from a private (application-specific) .ini file.

```
Declare Function apiGetPrivateProfileString _
    Lib "Kernel32" _
    Alias "GetPrivateProfileStringA" ( _
    ByVal lpszSection As String, _
    ByVal lpszKey As String, _
    ByVal lpszDefault As String, _
    ByVal lpszReturnString As String, _
    ByVal dwReturnSize As Long, _
    ByVal lpszFilename As String) As Long
```

It is passed the section, key, and .ini filename and retrieves the value for the key. If a Null value is passed as a key, all the entries for the section are retrieved. If a specified key is not found, the value passed as lpszDefault is returned. If the function is successful, it returns the number of characters copied into the string buffer lpszReturnString. Sections, keys, and values are illustrated in the following examples.

```
[section]
key=string
```

The next example uses the CurentProject.Path property to retrieve the path for Access and uses it as the path for the test.ini file. It then uses the GetPrivateProfileStringA API function to retrieve a string value for the AppTitle key.

```
Function GetPrivateProfileString() As String
    Dim Section As String
    Dim KeyName As String
    Dim Default As String
    Dim ReturnBuffer As String
    Dim Filename As String
    Dim BufferSize As Long
    Dim RetVal As Long
    Dim IniPath As String
```

```
        IniPath = CurrentProject.Path & "\"
        Filename = IniPath & "TEST.INI"
        Section = "Settings"
        KeyName = "AppTitle"
        Default = "Not Found"
        ReturnBuffer = String$(128, 0)
        BufferSize = Len(ReturnBuffer)
        RetVal = apiGetPrivateProfileString(Section, _
            KeyName, Default, ReturnBuffer, _
            BufferSize, Filename)
        GetPrivateProfileString = ReturnBuffer
    End Function
```

GetPrivateProfileIntA

The GetPrivateProfileIntA function returns an integer value from an application-specific
.ini file.

```
    Declare Function apiGetPrivateProfileInt _
        Lib "Kernel32" _
        Alias "GetPrivateProfileIntA"( _
        ByVal lpSection As String, _
        ByVal lpszKey As String, _
        ByVal dwDefault As Long, _
        ByVal lpszFilename As String) As Long
```

GetPrivateProfileIntA accepts a Section, KeyName, default, and filename like
GetPrivateProfileStringA but does not accept a string buffer. If the function is successful,
it returns the integer value. The GetTitleSetting wrapper shows how to use GetPrivate
ProfileIntA:

```
    Function GetTitleSetting() As Long
        Dim Section As String
        Dim KeyName As String
        Dim Default As Long
        Dim Filename As String
        Dim RetVal As Long
        Dim IniPath As String
        IniPath = CurrentProject.Path & "\"
        Filename = IniPath & "TEST.INI"
        Section = "Settings"
        KeyName = "TitleBar"
        Default = 1
        RetVal = apiGetPrivateProfileInt( _
            Section, KeyName, Default, Filename)
        GetTitleSetting = RetVal
    End Function
```

GetProfileStringA

GetProfileStringA is very much like GetPrivateProfileStringA.

```
Declare Function apiGetProfileString _
    Lib "Kernel32" _
    Alias "GetProfileStringA"( _
    ByVal lpszSection As String, _
    ByVal lpszKey As String, _
    ByVal lpszDefault As String, _
    ByVal lpszReturnString As String, _
    ByVal dwReturnSize As Long) As Long
```

This function behaves like GetPrivateProfileStringA, except it does not accept a filename as an argument. GetProfileStringA works only with the win.ini file, located in the Windows installation folder. Notice that you don't have to tell GetProfileStringA where Windows is installed. GetProfileStringA is able to find the Windows installation folder without any help.

WritePrivateProfileStringA

WritePrivateProfileStringA writes information to a private (application-specific .ini file):

```
Declare Function apiWritePrivateProfileString _
    Lib "Kernel32" _
    Alias "WritePrivateProfileStringA"( _
    ByVal lpszSection As String, _
    ByVal lpszKey As String, _
    ByVal lpszSetting As String, _
    ByVal lpszFilename As String) As Long
```

Like GetPrivateProfileStringA, this function receives a section, KeyName, default, and filename as arguments. But it also accepts the value you want to place in the .ini file in the lpszSetting argument. If the function is successful, it returns a nonzero value; otherwise, it returns zero.

The WritePrivateString() wrapper function writes new title-bar text to a specified .ini file by using the CurentProject.Path property and using the returned command line, plus the filename, as the full path to the .ini file:

```
Sub WritePrivateString()
    Dim Section As String
    Dim KeyName As String
    Dim Value As String
    Dim FileName As String
    Dim RetVal As Long
    Dim Setting As Long
    Dim PathName As String
```

```
        Dim lenPath As Integer
        Dim IniPath As String
        IniPath = CurrentProject.Path & "\"
        Filename = IniPath & "TEST.INI"
        Section = "Settings"
        Setting = GetTitleSetting()
        Select Case Setting
            Case 1
                KeyName = "AppTitle"
                Value = "Microsoft Access - " & GetUserName()
                RetVal = apiWritePrivateProfileString( _
                    Section, KeyName, Value, FileName)
                Value = "2"
                KeyName = "TitleBar"
                RetVal = apiWritePrivateProfileString( _
                    Section, KeyName, Value, FileName)
            Case 2
                KeyName = "AppTitle"
                Value = "My Access Application"
                RetVal = apiWritePrivateProfileString( _
                    Section, KeyName, Value, FileName)
                KeyName = "TitleBar"
                Value = "1"
                RetVal = apiWritePrivateProfileString( _
                    Section, KeyName, Value, FileName)
            Case Else
        End Select
    End Sub
```

WriteProfileStringA

`WriteProfileStringA` behaves much like `WritePrivateProfileStringA`, except it doesn't accept a filename as a parameter:

```
Declare Function apiWriteProfileString _
    Lib "Kernel32" _
    Alias "WriteProfileStringA"( _
    ByVal lpszSection As String, _
    ByVal lpszKey As String, _
    ByVal lpszSetting As String) As Long
```

Like `GetProfileStringA`, this function only works on the `win.ini` file. If the function completes successfully, a nonzero value is returned; if not, zero is returned.

Summary

In this chapter, you've gotten a look at how you can go beyond Access's limits by digging into the interior of Windows. The Windows API is a great way to add extra functionality to your applications. There are close to 1,000 different functions built into Windows that allow you to control your application settings, communications, Registry settings, and network functions.

In this chapter, you learned:

- What the API is and how you use it
- How to write Windows function `Declare` prototypes
- How to write function wrappers to make using the API functions easier
- A number of practical API calls that work well for Access applications

Using Windows API functions is a rewarding way to add sophisticated features to your Access application that can't be accomplished by VBA programming alone.

Object-Oriented Programming with VBA

A major goal in all modern application development is to produce robust, reusable code. Microsoft Access 2010 provides a number of ways to make code more reusable, from simple importing or exporting of code modules to building runtime code libraries.

This chapter covers one approach to creating code modules that you can reuse from any Access database. The code modules we describe in this chapter define new types of objects for your Access applications. These objects include properties and methods, and you can copy the objects into other Access applications or add them to Access code libraries.

The objects you create enforce modular, object-based programming. You've likely noticed how Access is based on the concept of objects. Microsoft defines just about everything in an Access application — forms, controls on forms, reports, and other visible parts of your programs — as some kind of object.

In addition, any number of hidden objects (such as table relationships) are lurking in your program. These objects are one of the ways in which Access is modular in nature. Each built-in Access object (such as a table, query, or form) performs some task in the application.

In this chapter, I dive into the important topic of object-oriented programming (OOP) in Access. Here you'll learn what objects are and how to use them in your applications. You'll also find out how to build your own objects using Access VBA code.

Although this chapter discusses objects such as forms and controls as examples, the emphasis is on the technology of creating and using custom objects in your Access applications. You create custom objects in your applications by adding code to a special class module.

IN THIS CHAPTER

Getting acquainted with object-oriented programming

Looking at how you can benefit from object-oriented programming

Making use of property procedures

Extending a class by adding properties and methods

Understanding events

Making use of class events

Note

In the lexicon of object-oriented programming, a class is a code element that defines an object. A good analogy for a class module is the engineering specification that defines a car or airplane. You create an object using the class as its specification. You add code to the class module to define the object's properties and methods. Modifying the code in a class module modifies how the object defined by the class module behaves.

On the CD-ROM

This chapter uses the database `Chapter28.accdb`. If you haven't already copied it onto your machine from the CD, you'll need to do so now.

Introducing Object-Oriented Programming

The world is filled with objects. The car you drive, the computer you use, and the radio you listen to are all examples of objects. Some objects, such as a desk lamp, are relatively simple, while other objects, such as a stealth bomber, are considerably more complex.

In addition to physical objects, the world is filled with objects you can't feel or touch. Electricity, sound, and light are all examples of objects people can produce, measure, and use, but you can't sense them as physical entities. An object's visible characteristics have little to do with its value to people. The electricity coursing through your computer's circuitry can be as valuable as the car you drive, under the right conditions.

You'll find any number of visible and invisible objects in most Access databases. And, just as with the objects that make up our environment, the invisible objects in an Access database can be as valuable as the forms, menus, and ribbons the user sees.

Getting to know objects

An Access object is a programmable entity of one sort or another. The `Err` object is an example of an invisible, but valuable, object built into Access. You use the `Err` object's properties (`Number`, `Description`, and so on) to determine which error has occurred. The `Clear` method resets the `Err` object, preparing it for the next error to occur. Even though the `Err` object never appears on an Access form or report, it has an important role in every professional Access application.

Understanding what objects are

Although there's an endless variety of objects, all objects have features in common:

- **An object is a programmable entity.** Most objects contain a number of properties you can read or set at runtime.

- **Most objects include methods you can execute to perform tasks.** An object's properties and methods define the object's interface to the rest of the program.

You can write custom objects to adapt to changing environments and user requirements. Most often, you can exploit an object's programmable nature by changing its properties and invoking its methods. But you can engineer a custom object in such a way that the object automatically adapts to differing conditions by running different internal routines.

You can create most object types multiple times in an application. Each time you create the object, Access assigns it a unique name to distinguish it from other instances of the object. In other words, a single Access program can host more than one instance of the object, with each object operating independently of the others (possibly even cooperating with the other objects) and maintaining its own set of properties and other data.

For example, say the Northwind Traders database (included with Microsoft Access) contains a Product object. The class module supporting the Product object defines the Name, Supplier, UnitPrice, and other properties of the product. There are any number of Product objects in the Northwind Traders database, each with its own name, price, and supplier.

To carry the analogy further, another class module might define a ProductInventory collection object that contains a number of Product objects. The ProductInventory class would feature a Count property that tells you how many Product objects are in the collection. The Product Inventory class module might contain a Sell method that deducts a certain Product item from the ProductInventory.

Using objects in applications

Every time you've written code setting a label's Caption property or returning the contents of a text box's Value, you've worked with objects. Although a label or text-box control is a simple type of object, the principles behind these objects are the same as using more complex and intelligent objects that you create yourself.

The following Access VBA code shows a series of statements that are typical of how you'd use objects in Access applications:

```
Dim MyObject As ObjectClass
Set MyObject = New ObjectClass
'Setting a property of the object:
MyObject.SomeProperty = SomeValue
'Invoking a method of the object:
MyObject.SomeMethod
```

Some of this code might seem a little strange, especially the statement where MyObject is assigned to a New ObjectClass. As you'll see later in this chapter, all this statement does is create a new object named MyObject that's based on the ObjectClass class.

In this code, the name of the object is ObjectName and its object class (described in the next section) is ObjectClass. You declare the object in the Dim statement and the New keyword *instantiates* (creates) it. SomeProperty is a property of the object, and SomeMethod is a method of the object.

Defining objects with class modules

You define an object by the code in a class module. You add that class module to your Access application, and then add the property and method code to a module before using the object that the class module defines. The name of the class module is the name of the object's class.

A class module is a special type of code module. Access recognizes the module as the definition of an object and lets you create new instances of the object from the code in the module. Any of the object's special features — including properties, methods, and events — are exposed as procedures tagged with the `Public` keyword in the class module. You should declare any code in the class module you intend for only the object to use, and that you won't expose to the outside world, with the `Private` keyword.

Each object you create from the class module is an instance of an object class. For example, the Nissan Sentra is a particular class of automobile. The Nissan Sentra that your Uncle Joe owns is a particular instance of the Nissan Sentra class of automobile. Even though Uncle Joe's car looks pretty much like every other Nissan Sentra, certain attributes of his car set it apart from all the other Nissan Sentras on the road.

Carrying the car analogy a bit further, consider the properties and methods of the automobile object class. A car has a color property that defines the color of the car's exterior. It's likely that the color of any car matches the color applied to other cars produced by the car's manufacturer. A car also has a vehicle identification number (VIN) that isn't shared with any other car anywhere in the world.

An object's property values, therefore, are a combination of values shared with other objects of the same class and values unique to the particular instance of the class. In fact, there must be a property or some other attribute of the object that sets it apart from all other instances of the same type of object in the application. Otherwise, Access can't know which instance you're referring to in your code.

If you were to construct a `Product` class module, you'd include properties such as `Name` (a string), `UnitPrice` (a currency data type), `UnitsInStock` (an integer or long integer), `ReorderLevel` (also an integer or long integer), and `Discontinued` (a Boolean value). Depending on how you planned to use the product object in the application, you might add properties to contain the quantity per unit, the category ID, and other information relevant to the application. You'd also want to add the `ProductID` property to uniquely identify each instance of the product object.

You may have noticed that all the properties I mention in the preceding paragraph correspond to the fields in the `Products` table in the Northwind Traders database. In fact, often each instance of the object represents a record contained in a database table.

Because you're constructing the class in VBA code, you can add any properties necessary to support the application and the data you're constructing. When you build Access classes, you have access to all the power and utility available through the Access data types and features. Adding new public procedures to the class module extends the properties and methods available to the object.

You can, therefore, define new data types to accommodate whatever peculiarities your application requires.

In the class module, private variables handle property values. As you can see in the "Exploring property-value persistence" section, later in this chapter, the mechanism for implementing properties is part of the special attributes of class modules. You have to follow certain rules and coding conventions (see the "Creating simple product properties" section, later in this chapter) to successfully implement properties in Access class modules.

In addition to properties, most objects support a number of methods, which are the actions that the class performs. An airplane has a number of rather obvious methods: ascend, descend, and land, among others. The classes you construct in Access implement whatever functionality you want the class's objects to support. The Product object we describe earlier might have Sell or Discount methods not shared with a Customer object in the same database.

The methods of a custom object exist as public procedures (functions and subroutines) in the class module. And, just as with properties, you have the full power and flexibility of VBA at your disposal as you write the methods of your custom classes.

Looking at a simple class module

Most often, the classes in your applications will model some real-world object, such as customers, contacts, employees, and products. Your knowledge and understanding of the physical object translate directly into Access VBA code and become the properties and methods of the Access objects you create from the class module's code.

This chapter's database (Chapter28.accdb) implements a Product class similar to the one we describe in the previous sections. The product class module — clsProduct1 — in Chapter28.accdb includes the properties in Table 28.1 and the methods in Table 28.2.

TABLE 28.1

Example Properties in the Chapter28.accdb Database

Name	Data Type	Description
ProductID	Long Integer	The product's ID
Name	String	Name of the product
Supplier	String	Name of the company supplying the product
UnitPrice	Currency	Customary selling price of the product
UnitsInStock	Integer	Current stocking level of the product
ReorderLevel	Integer	Minimum stocking level before reordering
Discontinued	Boolean	True if the product has been discontinued

TABLE 28.2

Product Class Methods Used in the Example Database

Name	Purpose
Sell	Sells a quantity of the product
Discount	Reduces the selling price of the product instance

The `Product` class object in `Chapter28.accdb` doesn't completely model a real product. You can add many other properties and methods to this class to more effectively model a real product, but this simple class does show you how to approach modeling a physical object in Access.

You can describe the product you'd create from the class like this: A product `Name` and `ProductID` identify the product. A certain manufacturer (the `Supplier`) produces the product, and the product is intended to be sold for a certain unit price (`UnitPrice`). Northwind Traders keeps track of the number of units in stock (`UnitsInStock`) and has determined the minimum number of units to keep in stock (`ReorderLevel`). The manufacturer may discontinue a product, in which case its `ReorderLevel` is set to zero and the `UnitsInStock` is allowed to decrease to zero as items are sold. Periodically, a product may be sold (the `Sell` method) and may also be discounted through the `Discount` method.

Adding a class module to a database

You can open a new class module in one of two ways:

- In the editor window, choose Insert ⇨ Class Module.
- In the Other group of the Access Create ribbon tab, select the Macro drop-down list, and choose Class Module.

Tip

It's a good idea to click on the Save button on the Code Editor toolbar and assign a name to the class module early in its development cycle. The class name should be descriptive but not excessively long. Finally, the name should be meaningful to you — users never see the name of the class, so use a name that means something to you or another developer.

The name you provide for the class module becomes the name of the object's class when creating objects from the class module (see Figure 28.1). The name of the class module is similar to the names you've given other objects in your databases.

The class module is in the code editor window in Figure 28.1. Notice that the class module looks just like any other module in the editor window. Your only indication that it isn't a normal module is the tiny icon in the left corner of the module as it appears in the code editor. It's a little box icon, instead of the tinkertoy icon you see in standard modules.

FIGURE 28.1

You'll use the name you provide for the class module as the object's class name (`clsProduct` in this case).

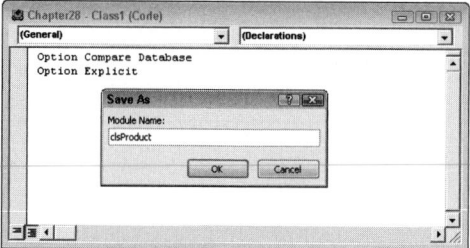

Creating simple product properties

The easiest way to establish the properties of a class, and the technique you'll use in your first class example, is to simply declare each of the properties as a public variable in the `clsProduct1` class module. Adding a public variable to a class module creates a new property for the class. The variable's public scope makes it accessible to other routines in the database. In the "Using Property Procedures" section, later in this chapter, you'll see an alternate way to create properties for your class modules.

```
Public ProductID As Long
Public Name As String
Public Supplier As String
Public UnitPrice As Currency
Public UnitsInStock As Integer
Public ReorderLevel As Integer
Public Discontinued As Boolean
```

Figure 28.2 shows the class module after you've added the public variables.

FIGURE 28.2

Public variables in a class module become properties.

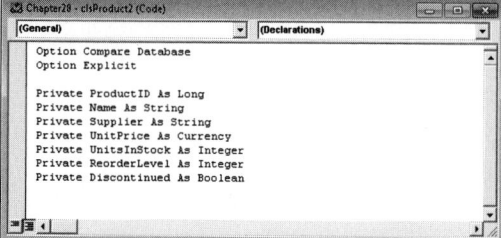

Access treats each public variable in a class module as a property of the objects created from the class. Because you declare the public variables in a class module, Access uses the variables as properties of the class's objects without further work on your part. Figure 28.3 shows how IntelliSense displays the properties in the Auto List Members drop-down list in a module using an object created from the class.

FIGURE 28.3

IntelliSense shows you the properties and methods created for the new object class.

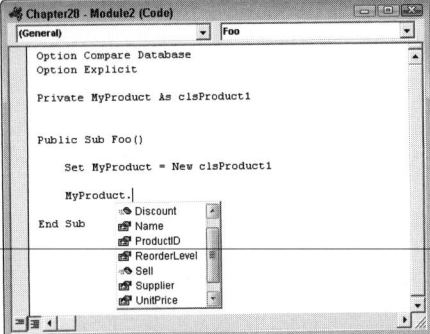

Because the object's properties are variables in the class module, the names you assign to these items must conform to VBA's variable naming requirements:

- Property names must be 64 or fewer characters.
- Property names can contain only alphanumeric characters and the underscore character.
- Property names must begin with an alphabetic character and can never begin with the underscore character or a number.

Tip

The names you provide for an object's properties and methods should be descriptive and easy to recognize.

Creating methods

The `clsProduct1` class includes two methods: `Sell` and `Discount`. These methods, like all object methods, define actions supported by the objects created from the class. Each method is nothing more than a public procedure in the object's class module.

- **Sell:** The following code example shows the procedure implementing the `Sell` method. Because all procedures in a class module are public by default, the `Public` keyword is optional and you add it to the `Sell` method to clarify the status of the procedure.

```
Public Sub Sell(UnitsSold As Integer)
  Me.UnitsInStock = Me.UnitsInStock - UnitsSold
End Sub
```

Notice there's nothing special about the Sell method. There's no special declaration for this procedure, nor is there reference to its status as a method of the class. Methods are an example of how Access treats class modules differently from simple code modules. As long as you haven't declared the procedure (sub or function) with the Private keyword (remember that the Public keyword is the default), Access treats the procedure as a method of the objects created from the class module.

Because it's a subroutine, the Sell method doesn't return a value. If you declare it as a function, it could return any valid Access data type. The Sell procedure requires an argument specifying how many items were sold.

Note

Notice the use of the Me keyword in the previous code example. In this context, Me refers to the object instance created from the class module.

You may have noticed an obvious bug in the Sell method. If the UnitsSold is larger than the UnitsInStock, the UnitsInStock value will be a negative number after the method runs. To fix this bug, you must add a couple of lines of code to the method:

```
Public Sub Sell(UnitsSold As Integer)
  If UnitsSold > Me.UnitsInStock Then
    Exit Sub
  End If
  Me.UnitsInStock = Me.UnitsInStock - UnitsSold
End Sub
```

This change causes the Sell method to simply exit and not deduct any units when the UnitsSold value would result in a negative value for the UnitsInStock.

On the CD-ROM

Obviously, you can add much more to the Product class. I've included the complete class module in the Chapter28.accdb example database as the clsProduct1 module in the Modules tab of the database.

- **Discount:** The Discount method is similar to Sell:

```
Public Sub Discount(Percent As Integer)
  If Percent < 1 _
  Or Percent > 99 Then
    Exit Sub
  End If
  Me.UnitPrice = _
    Me.UnitPrice - ((Percent / 100) * Me.UnitPrice)
End Sub
```

In this case, the method ends immediately if the Percent is less than 1 or larger than 99. Otherwise, the object's UnitPrice property is discounted by an expression derived from the Percent and current UnitPrice.

Eventually, with enough work and attention to detail, you can refine the product class to the point where it would support all the features and requirements of a real product sold by Northwind Traders. Other classes could model other data in the Northwind database such as customers, employees, and orders. In the "Recognizing the Benefits of Object-Oriented Programming" section, later in this chapter, you'll see some of the advantages of using class modules in your Access applications.

Using the product object

After you've assembled the class module from properties and methods, you can create new objects from the class. Figure 28.4 shows frmProductUnbound, a form included in Chapter28. accdb, the database accompanying this chapter. The text boxes along the left side of this form display the object's properties. The buttons to the right side of this form invoke the object's methods.

FIGURE 28.4

frmProductUnbound creates an object from clsProduct1 and provides an interface to its properties and methods.

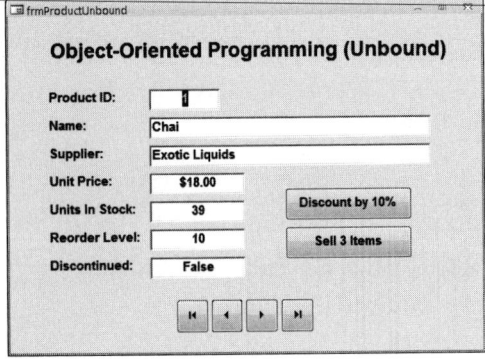

Creating a new product object requires you to use the New keyword. This statement is one way to create a new instance of a product object from the clsProduct1 class module:

```
Private Product As New clsProduct1
```

Alternatively, you can first declare the Product object, and then instantiate as separate statements. For example, place this statement in the module's Declarations section to establish the clsProduct1 object:

```
Private Product As clsProduct1
```

The object instantiates in the form's Load event procedure:

```
Set Product = New clsProduct1
```

Tip

I prefer using separate statements for declaration and instantiation, because it isn't possible to trap errors when declaration and instantiation are processed as a single statement. If you use a single statement for declaration and instantiation, your application may exhibit instability in some situations.

The code creates the new instance of the Product object when the New keyword executes. The code behind frmProductUnbound uses the two-statement approach to creating the Product object: In frmProductUnbound, you declare the product in the form's Declarations section as a module-level variable, and then the object instantiates during the form's Load event. Therefore, the Product object is available as soon as the form opens on the screen, and it's accessible to all the code behind the form.

The code in the form's Load event procedure also fills a recordset object with records from tbl-Products. You then use this recordset to set the Product object's properties. A private subroutine named SetObjectProperties retrieves values from the recordset and sets the object's properties to those values:

```
Private Sub SetObjectProperties()
    'Set the product object's properties:
    With Product
        .ProductID = rs.Fields("ProductID").Value
        .Name = rsFields("ProductName").Value
        .Supplier = rsFields("Supplier").Value
        .UnitPrice = rsFields("UnitPrice").Value
        .UnitsInStock = rsFields("UnitsInStock").Value
        .ReorderLevel = rsFields("ReorderLevel").Value
        .Discontinued = rsFields("Discontinued").Value
    End With
End Sub
```

After you create the product, you can reference its properties and methods. References to the product object's properties are similar to property references anywhere else in VBA. This statement retrieves the current value of the product's UnitPrice property and assigns it to the text box named txtUnitPrice on frmProductUnbound:

```
txtUnitPrice.Value = Product.UnitPrice
```

You can find a number of similar statements in the form's FillForm procedure:

```
Private Sub FillForm()
    'Fill the form with the product's properties:
    txtID.Value = Product.ProductID
    txtName.Value = Product.Name
    txtSupplier.Value = Product.Supplier
    txtUnitPrice.Value = Product.UnitPrice
    txtUnitsInStock.Value = Product.UnitsInStock
    txtReorderLevel.Value = Product.ReorderLevel
    txtDiscontinued.Value = Product.Discontinued
End Sub
```

frmProductUnbound makes several property assignments from the form's Load event procedure. The following code listing shows the entire Form_Load sub from frmProductUnbound.
Notice how the code builds the recordset, makes the property assignments, and fills the text boxes
on the form through the SetObjectProperties and FillForm procedures.

```
Private Sub Form_Load()
    Set Product = New clsProduct1
    Set rs = CurrentDb.OpenRecordset("tblProducts")
    If rs.RecordCount > 0 Then
        Call SetObjectProperties
        Call FillForm
    End If
End Sub
```

Similarly, selling a product involves using the object's Sell method. The code below shows how a
form might use the Sell method. Notice that the code passes a parameter: txtNumberToSell.
The user has entered the number of items to sell into a text box named txtNumberToSell. That
value becomes the UnitsSold argument for the Sell method I mentioned in the "Looking at a
simple class module" section, earlier in this chapter.

```
Private Sub cmdSell_Click()
    Product.Sell txtNumberToSell
    Call FillForm
End Sub 'cmdSell_Click
```

The FillForm procedure is called to refresh the form's contents after the Sell method executes.

Creating bulletproof property procedures

In many cases, assigning an invalid value to a property results in a runtime error or other bug. If
you're lucky, the invalid value causes the application to halt and display an error message to the
user. It's much worse to have the application continue operating as if nothing is wrong when, in
fact, the class module is working with invalid data. The best situation is when the class module
itself validates property values as they're assigned, instead of waiting until the properties are used
by forms, reports, and code in the application.

For example, consider a banking application that calculates exchange rates for foreign currency
deposited in the bank's vault. A class module is the ideal vehicle for handling foreign currency
exchange calculations. Keeping these calculations in a class module isolates these complicated routines from the rest of the application and makes it easy to maintain the calculations as currency
values fluctuate. And, because class modules support IntelliSense, it's much easier to work with
objects defined by class modules than public procedures stored in standard modules.

Ideally, the exchange rate class module wouldn't accept invalid exchange ratios or would check the
exchange ratios that the user inputs at runtime. Perhaps the class module could check online
sources such as *The Wall Street Journal* or other financial publications to verify that the data the
user input is correct.

Property errors might occur if the code passes a string when a numeric value is required or when a property value is less than zero. The following strategies help bulletproof properties and avoid run-time errors:

- **Set default property values if the code passes an inappropriate data type.** Use a conversion routine to correct the value, if possible.

- **Use private procedures in the class module to validate data types.** These data-validation routines are often class-specific

- **Use error trapping everywhere in the class module, especially on the class's properties and methods.** The property procedures and methods (the public procedures in the class) are where most unexpected behaviors occur.

Tip

Keep in mind that a basic principle of using object-oriented programming is encapsulating functionality. Whenever possible, you should include anything that affects how the class operates in the class module. Keeping the property validation, method error handling, and other features in the class module makes the class more portable and reusable.

Encapsulation isn't well implemented in the `clsProduct1` example presented in this section. For example, the form's code retrieves the data, and assigns values to the product object's properties. A better approach would be to have all the data management performed by the class itself, isolating the form from the data-management operations. A form using a properly constructed class shouldn't have to know which database table contains the product data; instead, the form should be a strict consumer of the product data.

Recognizing the Benefits of Object-Oriented Programming

You might be wondering why it's important to bother with objects. What are the advantages of Access object-oriented programming? Why complicate things by introducing the complexity of building and maintaining custom objects when traditional procedural programming techniques have worked so well in your Access applications?

You've already seen how Access's object-based programming benefits database developers. You do all the Access data access through Data Access Objects (DAO) or ActiveX Data Objects (ADO) recognized by the Access database engine. Other built-in Access objects such as forms and controls include properties you can easily manipulate at design time. As the application runs, these properties determine the object's behavior. Creating a form or report requires nothing more than dropping control objects on the form or report's surface and setting properties to bind the control to data and establish the control's appearance.

Encapsulating functionality

The greatest benefit from using objects is *encapsulation,* which is the ability to wrap all aspects of the object's functionality into an entity. For example, dropping a text box onto an Access form adds several new properties, methods, and events to the form. The text-box control encapsulates all the relevant properties (for example, `ForeColor`, `BackColor`, and so on), methods (for example, `SetFocus`), and events (for example, `BeforeUpdate`, `LostFocus`, and so on) required to support a text-box type of object. Although you add these new items to the form, you can access the new properties, methods, and events through the new text-box control.

The text-box control encapsulates everything a text data-entry control requires to do its job. In addition, Access text-box controls incorporate many hidden capabilities, such as binding to a data source, applying validation rules, and so on. In other words, there's a lot going on in the humble text-box control that you probably seldom recognize or appreciate.

A custom Access object lets you encapsulate complex activities and tasks as a simple, compact entity you can use in any other Access database. An encapsulated object is often much easier to maintain than a traditional module or VBA procedure. Because the object contains all its functionality as a single entity, there's just one module for you to modify or maintain as you make improvements to the program.

Although you can't create new form controls using the Access object-oriented development tools, you can add many capabilities to your applications through class modules alone. Custom objects don't have to be controls displayed in the user interface. They include code modules that perform specific tasks, encapsulating all the logic necessary to support the object's job within an application.

For example, most applications include extensive data-validation routines. Depending on the type of data the user enters, data validation ranges from one line of code to extensive modules containing dozens or hundreds of lines of code. Using Access's OOP features, you can wrap all data-validation routines into a single object that you can use by setting its properties and invoking its methods.

Simplifying programming tasks

Custom objects, therefore, provide a simplified interface to complex operations. When properly designed and implemented, you can use the custom objects you create in Access in virtually any compatible VBA programming system, exposing the same properties and methods you work with when incorporating the objects in your Access databases.

Once you've decided what properties and methods should be exposed by your object, you need to add them to the class module. The simplest way to add properties to a class is to include public variables within the class module. In fact, anything declared with the `Public` keyword is exposed by the class as either a property or a method. In the "Creating simple product properties" section, earlier in this chapter, you can see public variables used to define properties. The following sections explain using property procedures, a more robust and sophisticated way to define properties, and explain in detail the requirements and rules governing the properties in a class.

The mix of properties (and their data types), methods (and the arguments accepted or returned by the methods), and the events supported by a class are referred to as the class's *interface*. A developer working with an object created from a class module is typically unable to access the class's interface, and not the code within the class (unless, of course, the class's creator and the developer working with the class are the same person). Very often, class modules are bundled as Access libraries, or distributed as .mde or .accde files, and the interface is the only hint a developer has of the operations supported by the class (unless printed or online documentation accompanies the class).

Managing a class's interface

A class's interface is revealed by the Object Browser (press F2 with the code editor window open). Figure 28.5 shows the Object Browser open to the Product2 class, revealing the properties, methods, and events supported by this class.

FIGURE 28.5

The Object Browser reveals a class's interface.

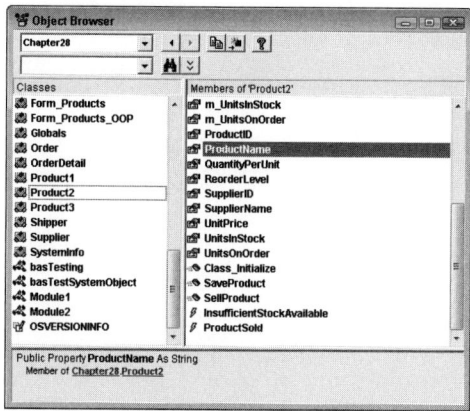

At the bottom of the Object Browser, you can see that ProductName is defined as a public property and is a string data type. This area is where you'd see that a property is read-only or write-only. Also, all private elements are identified accordingly. Finally, notice how all the property variables are sorted together because of the m_ prefix. (You can read about property variables in the "Using Property Procedures" section, later in this chapter.)

Figure 28.6 illustrates one of the most valuable aspects of object-oriented programming. Notice how the IntelliSense Auto List Members drop-down list shows you all the appropriate interface elements as soon as the object is identified and the dot is typed. This is a huge benefit to anyone working with your class module.

FIGURE 28.6

The Auto List Members drop-down list makes it easy to select an object's properties or methods.

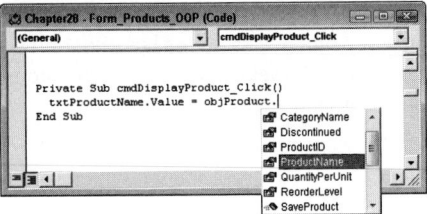

Furthermore, if you position the input cursor anywhere within the property name (such as ProductName) and press Shift+F2, the class module opens, showing you the code associated with the property (see Figure 28.7).

FIGURE 28.7

Shift+F2 shows you the code associated with an object's property.

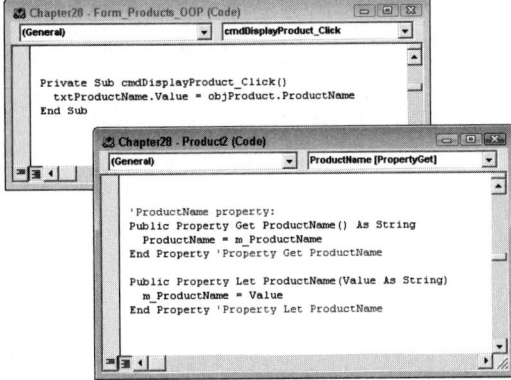

The class module's VBA code must be available for the Shift+F2 shortcut to work, of course. If the class has been bundled as an .mde or .accde file or is otherwise unavailable, Shift+F2 will not work.

Note

In case you're wondering, the Shift+F2 shortcut works in any Access module, not just class modules.

Generally speaking, object-oriented programming techniques are most often applied to unbound applications. Although you can build an Access application with a mix of bound, unbound, and object-oriented techniques, using bound forms misses one of the main advantages of object-oriented programming: control over how the data is used in the application. Most developers turn to object-oriented programming techniques because they want more control over how the data is used by their applications. Using bound forms negates many of the following advantages of using object-oriented programming techniques without really adding anything of value to the project:

- **Programming flexibility:** Bound forms hide the data acquisition and display processes, so you lose the opportunity to take control of these operations.

- **Encapsulation:** There's nothing (data-wise) to encapsulate on a bound form. The data exists in the form's recordset, so you can't add new properties or methods to a class that acts as the data's container.

Also, most developers using object-oriented programming techniques are fairly advanced and are comfortable building unbound applications. The extra code involved in building classes containing properties and methods is not a hindrance to the majority of advanced Access developers.

Following the rules

There are two cardinal rules that you must obey when applying object-oriented programming techniques. I didn't make up these rules, but I know from personal experience that you're asking for trouble when you fail to pay adequate attention to them.

- **Never reveal a user interface component, such as a message box, from a class module.** This rule is perhaps less important in Access applications than in other systems, but ignoring this rule may cause problems later on.

  Here's why this is important: Consider a class that opens a message box to the user, indicating that a problem has arisen. Although this works fine in Access environments, this practice may cause problems if the class is ported to other environments.

  All Access applications run locally on the user's computer. Therefore, opening a dialog box from an Access class module is guaranteed to open on the user's computer. In an Access application, there's no way to cause a message box to appear on another computer.

  However, other development platforms support the notion of *remoting* (running code on an application server). Most often, the remoted component is implemented as a set of compiled classes, and if one of those classes opens a dialog box, the dialog box opens on the remote application server.

  In this case, the application freezes in front of the user, and the user has no idea what happened. All the user knows is that the code stopped running. The code on the remote machine has stopped running, waiting for a response to the dialog box that has opened on the application server.

  For obvious reasons, you're not going to make many friends if your application causes an application server to stop running!

- **Preserve the class's interface as the class is updated.** You can add to the interface by introducing new properties, methods, and events, but you should never alter the data type of existing properties or method arguments, or remove an event from a class module.

continued

continued

It's very difficult to know where a class might be used, and once a class has been distributed, any changes to the class might break code in many different places without warning.

Sometimes it's impossible not to change a property's value or modify a method's arguments. As an example, users might require an additional argument to be passed to the SellProduct method so that shipping charges can be accurately calculated. Unless you take care to preserve backward compatibility, the consumer code referencing the original version of the SellProduct method is sure to fail.

One technique I recommend to ensure backward compatibility is to duplicate the property or method, suffixing a numeric value to its name. For example, you might add SellProduct1 to the class module, leaving the unchanged, original SellProduct for older code. New code will use the updated SellProduct1 to take advantage of the shipping charges calculation.

Using Property Procedures

The concept of property procedures is fundamental to object-oriented programming. As the name implies, a *property procedure* is a VBA procedure that defines a property for a class. Most classes contain several to many property procedures.

Note

Property procedures are always public by default. Even if you omit the Public keyword, your property procedure is exposed to the other elements of your applications. You should, however, always use the Public keyword to clarify the property procedure's scope. It never hurts to be very explicit in your code.

Looking at the types of property procedures

There are three types of property procedures:

- **Property Get:** Retrieves the value of a property. A Property Get works very much like any function and follows the same pattern as any VBA function.

- **Property Let:** Assigns a new value to the property. Property Let works only for simple data types such as numeric, strings, and date properties.

- **Property Set:** Assigns a value to an object property. You would use a Property Set for a property defined as a recordset or other object data type.

The concepts behind property procedures are illustrated in Figure 28.8. Each time your code references a property, the class module responds by running the appropriate property procedure.

FIGURE 28.8

Each time you read or write an object's properties, the class module runs a property procedure.

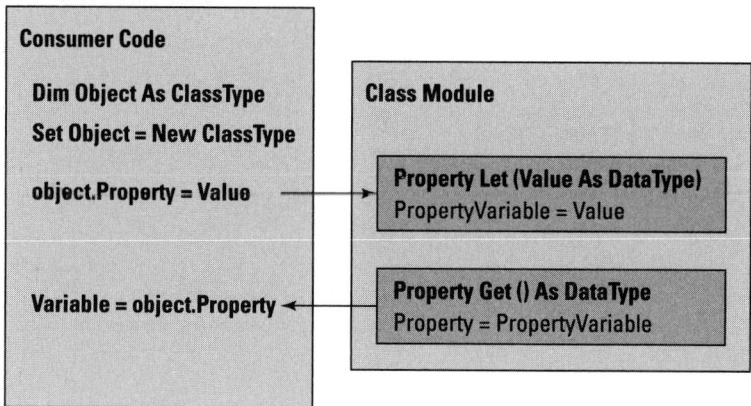

I explain the syntax of each of these procedures in the following sections.

Read/write, read-only, and write-only

The properties you add to your classes can be read/write, read-only, or write-only, depending on how you expect the property to be used.

- **Read/write:** Including both a `Property Get` and a `Property Let` (or `Property Set`) makes a property read/write. The `Property Get` lets a consumer read the property's value, while the `Property Let` (or `Property Set`) lets a value (or object) be assigned to a property.

- **Read-only:** Omitting the `Property Let` (or `Property Set` for object properties) makes a property read-only. A consumer can read the property's value through the `Property Get` procedure but can't assign a new value to the property.

  Obviously, because there is no way to assign a value to a read-only property, the class must provide the read-only property's value. This is often done by extracting a value from a database, or from the System Registry, or by reading a value from an `.ini` file or the operating system. Because a `Property Get` is a procedure, you can add any logic your class requires to obtain the property's value.

- **Write-only:** Omitting a `Property Get` makes a property write-only. You may decide to use a write-only property for sensitive information such as passwords and login identities. Making a write-only property is an excellent way to preserve the security of sensitive data. Write-only properties are also used to provide a class with information that it needs to support its activities, such as a connection string or database name.

Property Let

The Property Let procedure assigns a value to a property. The property's value is passed into the procedure as an argument, and the value is then assigned to the class module's private variable that stores the property's value.

The following example is a prototype for any `Property Let` procedure:

```
Public Property Let <PropertyName>(Value As <DataType>)
  <PrivateVariable> = Value
End Property
```

Tip

The property's argument can be named anything you want. I always use `Value` as the argument name. Consistently using `Value` is simpler than assigning a meaningful name to the argument and is consistent with how property values are assigned to built-in Access properties.

The following example is from the `Employee` class module:

```
Public Property Let LastName(Value As String)
  m_LastName = Left$(Value, 20)
End Property
```

This small example hints at the power of property procedures. Notice that the `Value` argument is a string. The statement within the property procedure assigns only the 20 leftmost characters of the `Value` argument to the `m_LastName` variable. This is because the `LastName` field in the Northwind Employees table only accepts 20 characters. Many database systems generate errors if more characters are sent to a field than the field can hold.

Tip

Adding a little bit of logic to a property procedure can go a long way toward bulletproofing an application.

Property Set

The syntax of `Property Set` is parallel to the `Property Let` procedure. The only difference is that the argument is an object data type, and the VBA `Set` keyword is used for the assignment within the body of the `Property Set`. The following is an example of hypothetical `Property Set` procedure that accepts a recordset object and assigns it to a private variable named `m_Products`:

```
Public Property Set Products(Value As ADO.Recordset)
  If Not Value Is Nothing Then
    Set m_Products = Value
  End If
End Property
```

In this small example, the argument is validated before it is assigned to the private variable.

Property Get

This is the basic syntax of the Property Get:

```
Public Property Get <PropertyName>() As <DataType>
  <PropertyName> = <PrivateVariable>
End Property
```

Notice the similarities between a Property Get and a VBA function. The Property Get is declared as a particular data type, and the property is assigned a value within the body of the property. The syntax is identical to any VBA function.

This is the Property Get from the Employee class module in the example application accompanying this chapter:

```
Public Property Get LastName() As String
  LastName = m_LastName
End Property
```

The Property Get executes whenever the property's value is assigned to a variable or otherwise used by the application. For example, the following VBA statement executes a Property Get named LastName in the Employee class module (objEmployee has been declared and instantiated from the Employee class):

```
strLastName = objEmployee.LastName
```

Notice that this statement doesn't directly reference the Property Get. Because the obj Employee object was created from the Employee class, the VBA engine knows to run the Property Get because a variable is assigned the value of the LastName property. In other words, the VBA engine gets the LastName property value from the class.

In this example, the Property Get is very simple and only returns the value of the private variable. However, you could have a much more complex Property Get that performs data transformation on the value or retrieves the value from a database file, an .ini file, the operating system, or some other source.

This example also illustrates the simplified programming possible with object-oriented techniques. A single VBA statement in the application's consumer code is enough to run whatever complex operation is necessary to retrieve the value of the property. The consumer is never aware of the logic supporting the property.

Exploring property-value persistence

At this point, you know that properties can be read/write, read-only, or write-only. What hasn't been explained is where the property persists the value when the property is written, and where the property gets its value when the property is read.

In a VBA project, property-value persistence is mediated through private variables contained within the class module. Generally speaking, each property is accompanied by a private variable that is the same data type as the property. This means that a property that reads or writes a string value will be accompanied by a private string variable, and each date property will be accompanied by a private date variable.

As you saw in the previous section, the property variables are either assigned or returned by the property procedures. A property variable should be given a name that indicates which property owns the variable. In the examples accompanying this chapter, each property variable has exactly the same name as its property, and is tagged with an m_ prefix. For example, the property variable for the CustomerID property is named m_CustomerID. Furthermore, because the CustomerID property is a string, m_CustomerID is also a string.

There are cases, of course, where a property is not accompanied by a variable. For example, a read-only property may extract the value from a database file or retrieve it from the operating system. Or, the property might be write-only, in which case the property may act immediately on the value passed to the property procedure, and no storage is necessary.

Heeding property procedure rules

Two rules apply to property procedures:

- **The name assigned to a property procedure is the name of the property.** Therefore, you should use a descriptive, helpful name for all your properties. Typically, a developer using objects created from a class you create doesn't have access to the VBA code in the class and has to rely on the names you've assigned to its properties and methods for guidance.

- **The data type of the Property Let, Property Get, and the private variable must coincide.** For example, if the property is defined as a string, the private variable must be a string. Figure 28.9 illustrates this concept.

  Note the following points in Figure 28.9:

  - The property variable is declared as some data type (labeled "A" in Figure 28.9).

  - The argument to the Property Let procedure is the same data type as the property variable ("B" in Figure 28.9).

  - The property variable is assigned its value in the body of the Property Let ("C" in Figure 28.9).

  - The Property Get procedure returns the same data type as the property variable ("D" in Figure 28.9).

  - The Property Get is assigned the value of the property variable ("E" in Figure 28.9).

  You'll get the following error if the data type assigned by the property procedures does not coincide:

Definitions of property procedures for the same property are inconsistent, or property procedure has an optional parameter, a ParamArray, or an invalid Set final parameter.

FIGURE 28.9

The property variable data type must coincide with the property's data type.

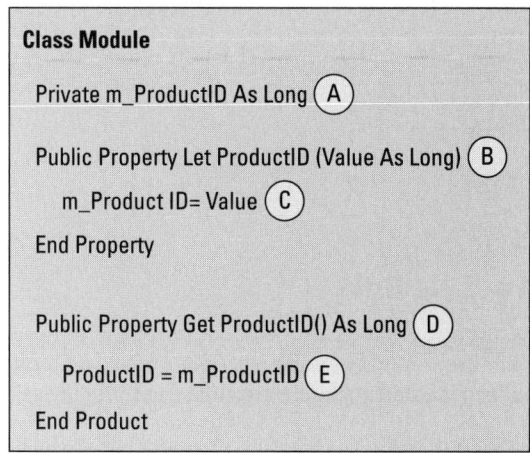

```
Class Module

 Private m_ProductID As Long (A)

 Public Property Let ProductID (Value As Long) (B)
    m_Product ID= Value (C)
 End Property

 Public Property Get ProductID() As Long (D)
    ProductID = m_ProductID (E)
 End Product
```

Caution

Although you can use an incorrectly typed private variable for your property procedures, you'll encounter side-effect bugs if the variable doesn't match the data type used for the property procedures.

Modifying the Product Class

Earlier in this chapter, I built a simple product class representing a Northwind product. The initial class is included in the Access .accdb file accompanying this chapter as the clsProduct1 class module. In this section, I extend the initial class (as the clsProduct2 class module) by making its properties more intelligent and useful.

Specifically, this section extends the property procedures within the Product class module, and adds methods to the module. I also expand the basic application by adding a few other classes needed to support the Northwind Traders application.

The example application accompanying this chapter includes a form named Products_OOP, which is based on the Products form included with Northwind Traders (see Figure 28.10). This form utilizes the majority of OOP techniques described in this chapter and can serve as a model for your OOP endeavors.

FIGURE 28.10

The `Products_OOP` form demonstrates unbound object-oriented techniques.

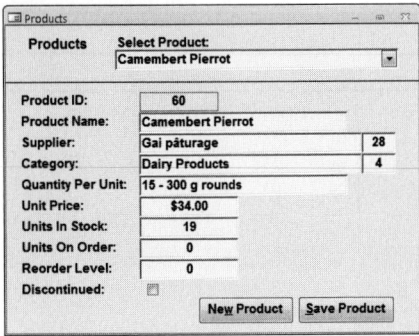

Retrieving product details

The first enhancement to the `Product` class is to update the process of retrieving product details, given a particular `ProductID`. In the initial example, the user selected a product from a combo box, and the form used an inline SQL statement to extract the details for the selected product.

The problem with having the form directly manage data is that the form (which is the consumer of the product data) has to know a great deal about how the product data is stored. The form holds a hard-coded SQL statement, creates a recordset with product data, and then assigns the recordset's data to the product object's properties. This is far too much to entrust to the user interface.

Consider an application with perhaps hundreds of forms. Using the design described in the previous paragraph, each form in the application has to manage its own data. Changing anything in the database means many different changes have to be made to the user interface, greatly complicating maintenance.

Two of the primary objectives of object-oriented programming are code-reuse and data abstraction. We all know and understand code reuse: Write the code once, and use it many different places. Data abstraction is a bit more complex, but it's based on the notion that each layer of an application (data management, business logic, and user interface) should do what it does best, and not have to worry about other parts of the application. The data layer should concern itself with getting data into and out of the data source. The business logic should concern itself with the rules that drive the application, and the user interface presents data from the user and manages the application's interaction with the user.

Bundling all those operations behind or within a form violates the notion of data abstraction. Every form in a bound application knows everything about the data managed by the form. Although this works well in small applications where complete control over the data is relatively unimportant, larger, more ambitious applications generally require significant control over the data.

Looking at the new ProductID property

The ProductID property enhancement is quite simple, even though the implementation requires a bit of code. The Property Get procedure simply returns the value of m_ProductID, as described earlier in this document. The real change comes with the Property Let.

The enhancements work like this: If a value greater than zero is assigned to the ProductID property, the class retrieves all the product details matching the assigned ProductID. Each product detail selected from the database is assigned to the corresponding product property. If a value zero or less is assigned, the class assumes the product entity is a new product, and default values are assigned to each property.

The updated Product class is utilized behind a form named Products_OOP.

The code contained in the ProductID Property Let is fairly extensive. It begins by opening a recordset against the ProductID value, and then determines whether any data was selected. A small bit of logic then either assigns the found data to the property variables or sets the property variables to default values:

```
Public Property Let ProductID(Value As Long)
  Dim db As DAO.Database
  Dim rs As DAO.Recordset
  m_ProductID = Value
  If m_ProductID <= 0 Then
    Exit Property
  End If
  Set db = CurrentDb()
  Set rs = db.OpenRecordset( _
    "Products")
  'Seek the Product record matching
  'the m_ProductID value.
  rs.FindFirst "ProductID =" & m_ProductID
If Not rs.NoMatch Then
    'Assign database data to object properties:
    If IsNull(rs.Fields("ProductName").Value) Then
      m_ProductName = vbNullString
    Else
      m_ProductName = rs.Fields("ProductName").Value
    End If
<This pattern is repeated for each property>
  Else 'Product not found!
    'Assign default values to
    'each property variable:
    m_ProductName = vbNullString
    m_SupplierID = -1
    m_CategoryID = -1
    m_QuantityPerUnit = vbNullString
    m_UnitPrice = -1
    m_UnitsInStock = -1
    m_UnitsOnOrder = -1
```

```
        m_ReorderLevel = -1
        m_Discontinued = False
        'Also assign default value to ProductID.
        'This will serve as a signal to the consumer
        'that a product was not found:
        m_ProductID = -1

        'An alternate approach would be to raise an
        'event telling the consumer that the product
        'could not be found.
    End If
End Property 'Property Let ProductID
```

This is a good example of encapsulation. Instead of requiring a consumer of the Product class to select the product data, the Product class easily supplies the data through the ProductID setting.

This small example also illustrates one of the major benefits of object-oriented programming: In a well-designed application, the only way to retrieve product data should be through the Product class. No other portion of the application needs to know anything about where the product data is stored, how to select or insert product data, and so on. In the future, should the need arise to change the product data source, only the Product class is updated, and all other portions of the application continue to function as before, without any changes.

Consider the time savings in a large application where the product data is used in dozens or even hundreds of different places. Good object-oriented design enforces modular programming and provides significant efficiencies when maintaining medium to large applications.

Adding a new property to provide extra information

One of the things that bothers me about the Northwind Traders application is that it relies very heavily on Access-only constructs. In particular, most of the tables, when viewed in Datasheet view, display related data. For example, opening the Products table in Datasheet view shows the product category and supplier information, and not the ID values associated with each of these items. The supplier name is shown in the Products table because the lookup properties of the SupplierID field are set to display a combo box containing the supplier names.

I've found these constructs to be confusing to users, especially people new to Access. Most people, when they see the supplier's name in the Products table, expect to find the supplier name among the data stored in the table. However, the only type of supplier information in the Products table is the SupplierID. If the supplier name is required, you must extract it the from the Suppliers table, using the SupplierID as the criterion.

An enhancement to the Product class is to make the supplier and category names accessible as read-only properties. You probably can guess how this is done: Simply extract this information from the respective tables, using the property variables for the SupplierID and CategoryID properties.

Here's the Property Get procedure for the new SupplierName property. The Property Get for the CategoryName property is virtually identical:

```
Public Property Get SupplierName() As String
  Dim varTemp As Variant
  If m_SupplierID <= 0 Then
    SupplierName = vbNullString
    Exit Property
  End If
  varTemp = DLookup("CompanyName", "Suppliers", _
    "SupplierID = " & m_SupplierID)
  If Not IsNull(varTemp) Then
    SupplierName = CStr(varTemp)
  Else
    SupplierName = vbNullString
  End If
End Property
```

The `Property Get` uses DLookup to retrieve the `CompanyName` from the `Suppliers` table that matches the `m_SupplierID` property variable. The property variable is first checked to make sure its value is greater than zero, and the property ends if this condition is not met.

The `SupplierName` property is an example of how a class module can be enhanced by introducing new properties — read-only, write-only, or read/write — that provide functionality not otherwise available. Again, the consumer of the class doesn't have to know anything about the underlying data structures, and all the data management is handled through the class module.

Adding a new method to the product class

In the "Recognizing the Benefits of Object-Oriented Programming" section, earlier in this chapter, I discussed some of the advantages of encapsulation. Another major advantage of encapsulation is that, because all data operations required by the entity are contained within the class, it's quite easy to update business logic.

Assume that the hypothetical `SellProduct` method (introduced in the "Following the rules" sidebar, earlier in this chapter) has to be updated to accommodate a new sales tax. Whichever technique you use to update the method, the end result is the same. Because the method is an integral part of the class, there is only one update needed to update all uses of the `SellProduct` method in the application.

The previous section dealt with an update to the `ProductID` property. In the new `ProductID` `Property Let`, the property variable was assigned –1 when it appeared that the product was a new product. Here's how the `SaveProduct` method would handle the various values of the `m_ProductID` variable:

```
Public Function SaveProduct() As Boolean
  Dim db As DAO.Database
  Dim strSQL As String
On Error GoTo HandleError
  Set db = CurrentDb()
  If m_ProductID > 0 Then
    'Update existing record:
```

```
            strSQL = _
                "UPDATE Products SET " _
              & "ProductName = '" & m_ProductName & "'" _
              & "SupplierID = " & m_SupplierID _
              & "CategoryID = " & m_CategoryID _
              & "QuantityPerUnit = '" _
              & m_QuantityPerUnit & "'" _
              & "UnitPrice = " & m_UnitPrice _
              & "UnitsInStock = " & m_UnitsInStock _
              & "UnitsOnOrder = " & m_UnitsOnOrder _
              & "ReorderLevel = " & m_ReorderLevel _
              & "Discontinued = " & m_Discontinued _
              & "WHERE ProductID = " & m_ProductID
        Else
          'Insert new record:
          strSQL = _
                "INSERT INTO Products (" _
              & "ProductName," _
              & "SupplierID, " _
              & "CategoryID," _
              & "QuantityPerUnit, " _
              & "UnitPrice," _
              & "UnitsInStock, " _
              & "UnitsOnOrder," _
              & "ReorderLevel, " _
              & "Discontinued " _
      & ")VALUES(" _
              & m_ProductName & ", " _
              & m_SupplierID & ", " _
              & m_CategoryID & ", " _
              & m_QuantityPerUnit & ", " _
              & m_UnitPrice & ", " _
              & m_UnitsInStock & ", " _
              & m_UnitsOnOrder & ", " _
              & m_ReorderLevel & ", " _
              & m_Discontinued & ")"
        End If
    db.Execute strSQL
        SaveProduct = True
    ExitHere:
        Exit Function
    HandleError:
        SaveProduct = False
        Resume ExitHere
    End Function
```

The code in the SaveProduct method is straightforward. If the m_ProductID variable is larger than zero, the record in the Products table matching the ProductID is updated. Otherwise, a new record is inserted into the Products table.

Learning about Class Events

There are two very important built-in events that accompany every Access class module: Initialize and Terminate. As you'll soon see, these two events provide invaluable assistance in many object-oriented programming projects.

Using class events is one thing that's completely different from using standard code modules. Not only do class modules maintain their own data states, but they provide events that offer a great deal of control over how the data is initialized and cleaned up within the class.

The Class_Initialize event procedure

Very often, the property variables or other resources used by a class need to be initialized, or set to some beginning state. Other than adding a method to trigger initialization, it might not seem obvious how to add initialization operations to your classes.

For example, let's say you create a class module that needs to have a recordset open the entire time the class is used. Perhaps it's a class where the data needs to be frequently selected from a database. Frequently opening and closing connections and recordsets can be an unnecessary drain on performance. This is especially true when the selected data set doesn't change from operation to operation. It'd be much more efficient to open the recordset one time, leave it open while the class is being used, and then close it at the conclusion of the session.

That's where the class's Initialize event comes in. The Initialize event fires whenever an object is instantiated from the class module. In the following consumer code example, the Class_Initialize event procedure runs when the object is set to a new instance of the class:

```
Dim objProduct As Product
Set objProduct = New Product
```

Select Class from the object drop-down list in the VBA editor, and then select the Initialize event from the Events drop-down list. You don't have to do anything else other than add the code you want to run when an object is instantiated from your class module. Figure 28.11 shows an example of a Class_Initialize event procedure in the Product class.

The sequence indicated by the numbers in Figure 28.11 are

- The object is instantiated in (A). Before this statement is completed by the VBA engine, the Class_Initialize event is invoked.

- Notice that Class_Initialize (B) is a private subroutine. It's owned by the class, and executes independently of the consumer code. No arguments are passed to Class_Initialize.

- In C, execution is passed back to the consumer code when Class_Initialize ends.

- Finally, at D, execution recommences in the consumer code at the statement following the object instantiation.

FIGURE 28.11

The Class_Initialize event procedure runs whenever an object is instantiated from the class module.

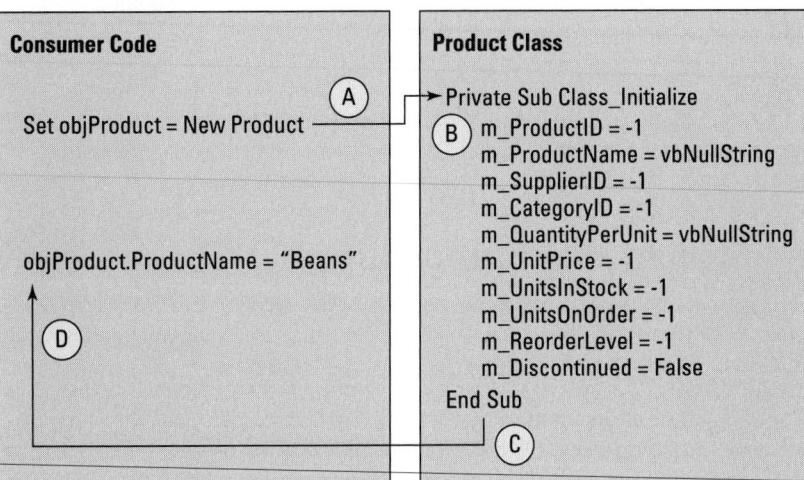

In this small example, you'll notice that numeric property variables are set to −1, rather than VBA's default of zero for numeric variables. This is because certain logic in the class module uses −1 to determine when certain states — such as when the user is entering a new product — are in effect.

The Class_Terminate event procedure

The opposite of the Initialize event is the Terminate event. The Terminate event fires whenever an object created from the class is set to Nothing, or goes out of scope. In the following code fragment, the Class_Terminate event procedure runs when the object is set to Nothing:

```
Set objProduct = Nothing
```

Use the Terminate event to clean up your class module. For example, if a Database or Recordset object has been opened but hasn't been closed by the class, use the Terminate event to perform these operations.

The Terminate event fires as the statement dismissing the object runs, not after. VBA processes one statement at a time, no matter where the statement takes the execution point. Therefore, when the Set objProduct = Nothing executes, the Class_Terminate event procedure runs before the statement ends. This sequence ensures that the class is cleaned up before execution is returned to the code using the class. This process is illustrated in Figure 28.12.

FIGURE 28.12

The `Class_Terminate` event procedure passes control back to the consumer code when it ends.

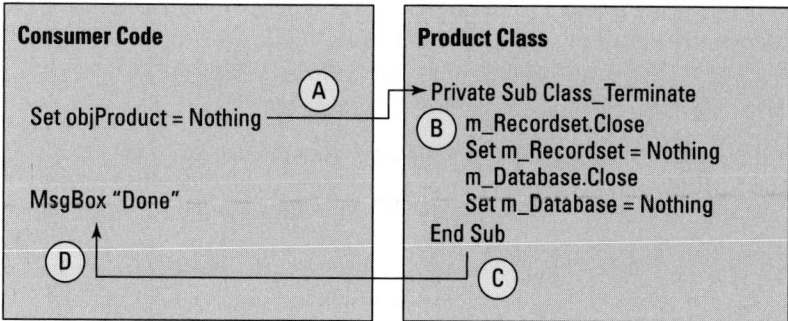

Just as with the `Class_Initialize` event procedure, the sequence of `Class_Terminate`'s execution is important:

- In A, the object is set to `Nothing`, or goes out of scope. Before the statement causing these states executes, control is passed to `Class_Terminate`.

- Just as you saw with `Class_Initialize`, notice that `Class_Terminate` (B) is a private subroutine. It's owned by the class and executes independently of the consumer code. No arguments are passed to `Class_Terminate`.

- Execution is passed back to the consumer code at C, when `Class_Terminate` ends.

- In D, execution recommences in the consumer code at the statement following the object's dismissal.

Adding Events to Class Modules

Everyone is familiar with the interfaces supported by the objects built into Microsoft Access. A `TextBox` object, for example, supports `ForeColor` and `BackColor` as properties. The `DoCmd` object provides a wide variety of methods (such as `OpenForm`) that perform a number of essential actions in Access applications.

Beginning with Access 2000, developers have been able to add events to the class modules in their applications. (Although Access 97 supported class modules with properties and methods, Access 97 didn't provide for custom events in class modules.) Adding events to your class modules is an excellent way to enhance and strengthen the object-oriented elements you add to your applications.

Learning about events in Access

Events are a bit more complex than properties or methods. Even though you constantly use events in your applications, you never see an event (because events don't exhibit a user interface), and under most circumstances, you don't deliberately invoke an event through your code. Events just sort of happen when a user clicks on a command button or tabs off of a control. Events are just there — you use them as needed.

A reasonable analogy for events is the ringer on your cellphone. Your phone rings whenever someone wants to talk to you. The ring alerts you to the incoming call, and you decide whether to respond to the ring or ignore it.

From an object-oriented perspective, you add events to your objects so that the object has some way of notifying its consumer that something has happened within the object or has happened to the object. For example, consider a data-management object that reads and writes data from a data source. The properties are easy to understand and may include the path to the data source, the name of a table, and an ID value to use when extracting or saving data.

In this case, you may add an event to the data-management object that's triggered when the data source is unavailable, or when a record matching the ID value can't be found. Using events is much cleaner and more direct than relying on errors to be thrown when the data-management object fails to complete its task.

Recognizing the need for events

To my knowledge, there is no limit on the number of events you can add to a class module. You declare events in a class module's header, and invoke the events within the class's properties and methods.

This process may make more sense if you consider a property procedure built in the "Adding a new property to provide extra information" section, earlier in this chapter:

```
Public Property Get SupplierName() As String
  Dim varTemp As Variant
  If m_SupplierID <= 0 Then
    Exit Property
  End If
  varTemp = DLookup("CompanyName", "Suppliers", _
    "SupplierID = " & m_SupplierID)
  If Not IsNull(varTemp) Then
    SupplierName = CStr(varTemp)
  End If
End Property
```

This property procedure returns the name of a product supplier, given the SupplierID (notice that the SupplierID is obtained through the class-level m_SupplierID variable). The SupplierName property assumes that the m_SupplierID property variable has already been set through the SupplierID Property Let procedure. The If...End If at the top of this procedure handles cases where the m_SupplierID variable has not been properly set to a value greater than zero.

So far, so good. But, what happens if the SupplierID can't be found in the supplier table? The only way the class's consumer can determine that the supplier does not exist is by examining the value of the SupplierName property. If the SupplierName property is an empty string, the consumer can assume the supplier cannot be found in the supplier table and notify the user accordingly.

The problem with this scheme is that a lot of work is left up to the consumer. The consumer must first set the SupplierID property, then ask for the SupplierName property, and then finally examine SupplierName to see if a nonzero-length string was returned by the SupplierName Property Get.

One of the basic tenets of object-oriented programming is that a class module should encapsulate most, if not all, of the processing required by the entity represented by the class. In the case of the Product class, a consumer shouldn't be required to examine a property's return value to verify its validity. The class should notify the consumer when a problem (such as missing or invalid data) arises within the class.

And, that's one of the primary purposes of events. The InvalidSupplierID event is invoked whenever the class determines that a problem exists with the SupplierID value supplied by the consumer code.

Creating custom events

Events must be declared within a class module. Although an event declaration may occur anywhere within a VBA module, it only makes sense to position event declarations near the top of the module where they're easily seen by other developers. An event declaration is actually quite simple:

```
Public Event InvalidSupplierID()
```

That's all there is to an event declaration. The Public keyword is needed, of course, to expose the event to the class's consumers. In effect, the Public keyword adds the event to the class's interface. The Event keyword, of course, specifies that the declaration's identifier — InvalidSupplierID — is an event and should be managed by VBA's class module hosting mechanism.

You might recall that I've asserted that class modules were special in a number of regards. Events are clearly one of the special characteristics of VBA class modules.

A quick look through the Object Browser at the class module (see Figure 28.13) shows that the class's interface does, indeed, include the InvalidSupplierID event.

FIGURE 28.13

The `InvalidSupplierID` event appears in the Object Browser.

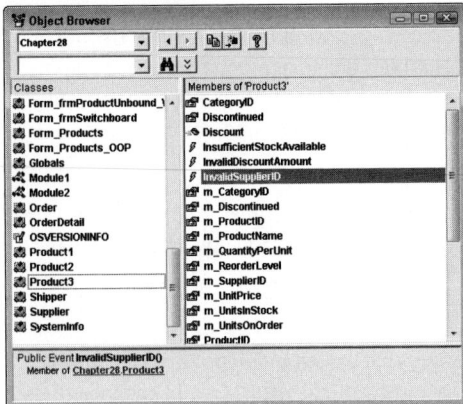

You'll notice a couple other events — `InsufficientStockAvailable` and `ProductSold` — in the `Product` class module. I've added the other events in exactly the same manner as the `InvalidSupplierID` event. An event declaration is all that's required to add an event to a class's interface. The class module never even has to trigger an event shown in the Object Browser.

Raising events

An event that is never invoked by a class module's code isn't much use to anybody. Events are typically triggered (or raised) whenever circumstances indicate that the consumer should be notified.

Raising an event requires a single line of code:

```
RaiseEvent <EventName>(<Arguments>)
```

I discuss event arguments in the "Passing data through events" section, later in this chapter. In the meantime, take a look at raising the `InvalidSupplierID` event from the `SupplierName` Property Get:

```
Public Property Get SupplierName() As String
  Dim varTemp As Variant
  If m_SupplierID <= 0 Then
    RaiseEvent InvalidSupplierID()
    Exit Property
  End If
  varTemp = DLookup("CompanyName", "Suppliers", _
    "SupplierID = " & m_SupplierID)
  If Not IsNull(varTemp) Then
    SupplierName = CStr(varTemp)
  Else
```

```
        RaiseEvent InvalidSupplierID()
    End If
End Property
```

The SupplierName property raises the InvalidSupplierID under two different situations: when the SupplierID is zero or a negative number, and when the DLookup function fails to locate a record in the Suppliers table.

There is no requirement that consumer code respond to events raised by class modules. In fact, events are very often ignored in application code. I doubt you've ever written code for every single event raised by an Access TextBox control, and custom events raised from class modules are no different.

But, again, that's one of the nice things about object-oriented programming: You can add as many events as needed by your classes. Consumer code working with your classes can ignore irrelevant events and trap only those events that are important to the application.

Trapping custom events

Just about the only place where event-driven programming with Access classes becomes tricky is when it's time to capture events (also called *sinking* events) in consumer code. There are a number of rules governing event consumption:

- **The class hosting events must be declared within another class module.** It shouldn't be surprising that events can only be captured by code within class modules. After all, class modules are special critters and have capabilities beyond simple code modules. You've never seen a stand-alone VBA code module directly respond to events raised by controls on an Access form, so there's no reason to expect a plain code module to be able to consume events raised by the classes you add to an application.

  However, a plain code module can very well create and use objects derived from class modules. It's just that VBA code modules can't capture events raised from class modules.

  This requirement is not quite as onerous as it first appears. After all, every form and report module is a class module. That means that forms and reports are ready-built for consuming the events thrown by your class modules.

- **The object variable created from the class must be module-level and can't be declared within a procedure.** There's no way to capture an event from within a procedure. Procedures know nothing about objects, and there's no provision for hooking a locally declared object variable to its events.

  When you look at the class module behind a form, it becomes obvious why object variables must be module-level before their events can be sunk by consumer code. You've seen the typical Access form module (shown in Figure 28.14). Notice what appears in the code module's event list when an object variable has been declared with the WithEvents keyword.

FIGURE 28.14

The `WithEvents` keyword instructs VBA to watch for events raised from the object's class module.

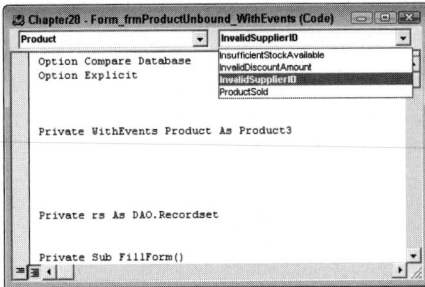

As you'd expect, selecting an event from the `Product` object's event list opens a new event procedure, enabling you to write code in response to the event. The `Product_InvalidSupplierID` event procedure notifies the user whenever the `Product` class determines that the `SupplierID` value cannot be used by the class.

Obviously, the code in the event procedure runs whenever the corresponding event is raised from the object's class module. The consumer doesn't have to explicitly check the value returned by the `SupplierName` property. Instead, the event procedure linked to the `InvalidSupplierID` handles the event and takes appropriate action.

Also, because the same event can be raised from multiple places within the class module, a single event procedure may handle many different situations related to a single problem within the class module.

I suspect that, behind the scenes, Access does exactly the same thing for built-in objects such as text boxes and command buttons. As soon as you add a control to an Access form, you're able to add code to event procedures hooked into the control's events.

- **The object variable declaration must include the WithEvents keyword.** The keyword `WithEvents` is how Access knows that it needs to monitor events raised by the class to enable you to include code to react to the events.

Passing data through events

You probably noticed that the event declaration example given earlier in this chapter included a set of empty parentheses:

```
Public Event InvalidSupplierID()
```

What may not be obvious is that event arguments may be added within the parentheses:

```
Public Event ProductSold(Quantity As Integer)
```

The `RaiseEvent` statement includes a value for the event argument:

```
RaiseEvent ProductSold(UnitsSold)
```

Event declarations may include multiple arguments and can pass any valid VBA data type, including complex data such as recordsets and other objects.

The ability to pass data through event arguments is an incredibly powerful tool for developers. A class module can directly communicate with its consumers, passing whatever data and information is necessary for the consumer to benefit from the class's resources.

Exploiting Access class module events

You can add custom events to Access forms and to raise those events from code within the form. Custom events are declared with exactly the same syntax as declaring events within any class module and are raised with the `RaiseEvent` statement. The only tricky part is sinking custom events raised by a form in another form's module.

Custom events can be exploited as a way to convey messages and data between forms. Recently, I responded to a reader's question about dialog boxes with a relatively lengthy explanation of modally opening the dialog box, hiding the dialog box when the user was ready to return to the main form, and then reading a custom property from the hidden dialog box. Although this technique works well, it requires quite a bit of planning and preparation.

The dialog box operation can be more simply implemented by adding a custom event to the dialog form that is raised by the dialog form and sunk by the main form. Information entered by the user on the dialog form is passed to the main form as an event argument. The event is raised when the user closes the dialog form and the information passed as the event argument is captured by the main form. There is no need for the main form to close or otherwise manage the dialog form.

Let's start with the dialog form that raises a custom event. The dialog form is shown in Figure 28.15.

FIGURE 28.15

This form uses a custom event to pass data back to the main form.

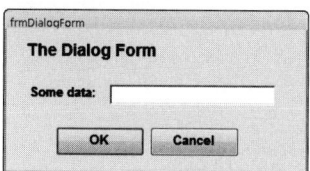

The user types something into the text box and clicks either OK or Cancel. The OK button passes the text box's contents to the main form, while the Cancel button passes a `"No data"` message, indicating that the user dismissed the dialog box without entering any data.

Here's all the code behind this simple dialog box:

```
Public Event FormClosing(Message As String)
Private Sub cmdOK_Click()
   DoCmd.Close acForm, Me.Name
End Sub
Private Sub cmdCancel_Click()
   txtSomeData.Value = Null
   DoCmd.Close acForm, Me.Name
End Sub
Private Sub Form_Close()
   If Not IsNull(txtSomeData.Value) Then
      RaiseEvent FormClosing(txtSomeData.Value)
   Else
      RaiseEvent FormClosing("No data")
   End If
End Sub
```

A public event named FormClosing is declared at the top of the dialog form's module. This event returns a single argument named Message. The cmdOK_Click event procedure closes the form, while the cmdCancel_Click event clears the contents of the text box named txtSome-Data before closing the form.

The FormClosing event is raised by the dialog form's Close event procedure, ensuring that the event is raised whenever the form is closed. If the txtSomeData is not Null, the value of the text box is passed by the FormClosing event, while a default message is passed if the text box's value is Null.

No other code is needed by the dialog form, and the form is allowed to close normally because the FormClosing event fires just before the form disappears from the screen.

The main form is shown in Figure 28.16.

FIGURE 28.16

The main form sinks the custom event raised by the dialog form.

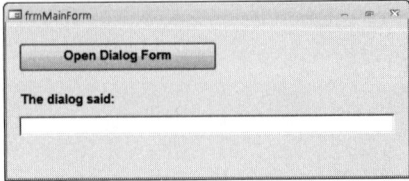

The code behind the main form is also quite simple. Notice the WithEvents keyword applied to the form object's declaration:

```
Private WithEvents frm As Form_frmDialogForm
Private Sub cmdOpenDialogForm_Click()
  Set frm = New Form_frmDialogForm
  frm.Visible = True
End Sub
Private Sub frm_FormClosing(Message As String)
  txtDialogMessage.Value = Message
End Sub
```

The dialog form must be declared as a module-level variable behind the main form. The WithEvents keyword notifies the VBA engine that you want the main form to capture (or sink) events raised by the frm object.

Also notice that the form's class name is Form_frmDialogForm. This is the name of the class module behind frmDialogForm, and it's the entity that actually raises the event. From the perspective of the VBA project driving the application, the form's surface is just a graphic interface and has nothing to do with the class module that supplies the logic driving the form.

The WithEvents keyword is almost magical. Once you've qualified an object declaration with WithEvents, the name of the object appears in the drop-down list at the top of the class module, and the object's events appear in the right drop-down list (see Figure 28.17).

All Access developers are familiar with how the object drop-down list shows all the controls placed on the surface of an Access form, as well as an entry for the form itself. In this case, the object drop-down list shows the form object declared with the WithEvents keyword in addition to controls on the form's surface.

In this case, the form object named frm is declared and instantiated, and it's completely controlled by the main form. The main form captures the dialog form's events and uses the data passed through the FormClosing event. The main form could just as easily reference other properties of the dialog form.

FIGURE 28.17

The WithEvents keyword enables the main form's class module to capture events raised by the object.

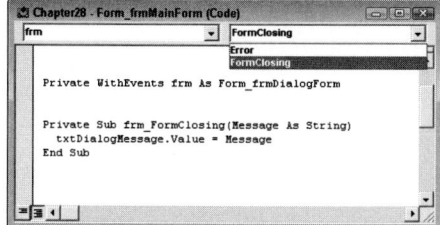

Access forms are objects

It's important to understand that every Access form is actually an object created from a class and is not a physical entity stored within the .accdb file. Most people think of forms as UI objects that are maintained somewhere within the .accdb file and used as needed. In reality, each form is stored as a class, and Access instantiates a form object and displays the form on the screen whenever you work with the form's class. In Design view, Access presents you with an editable interface to the form's class, and you work with the form's properties.

Interestingly enough, the code behind an Access form is nothing more than a property of the form's class. The code behind an Access form is, itself, a class. There is nothing in the object-oriented paradigm supported by Access that prohibits a class from containing another class.

Note

This technique eliminates the infamous bang-dot notation that Access developers have suffered with for so many years. Treating a form as an OOP object eliminates a lot of overhead from the code behind the main form.

Summary

This chapter has taken on the important topic of creating and using object classes. Access's object-oriented features are a powerful way to encapsulate functionality, letting you design modular applications that are easy to create and maintain. Breaking complex features into discrete objects is a powerful way to incrementally build applications from a series of components, each of which performs a single job in the application.

Property procedures and class events are at the core of any OOP project. Object-oriented programming enforces modular programming, and the only access a consumer has to an entity's data is through a class's interface. Assigning a value to an object's property can run hundreds of lines of code in the class module, greatly simplifying programming tasks on the consumer side.

Also, because encapsulation means that all of an object's logic is contained within its class module, maintenance is much simpler than with traditional linear programming practices.

There's a lot to think about and learn when you begin using object-oriented programming in database applications. Sometimes the rewards are a bit difficult to see at first, but once you begin using OOP in your applications, you'll wonder how you got along without it!

In case you're wondering, class modules, properties, methods, and events are very similar in .NET applications. The major difference is that the .NET framework adds many, many capabilities that are not possible in VBA classes. However, the OOP code you write in Access would be quite comfortable in a .NET application.

Customizing Access Ribbons

U nless you've been working with Access 2007, the Office ribbon will be entirely new to you. In fact, the ribbon is the distinguishing characteristic of the Office 2007 and 2010 applications. The toolbars and menus were an effective user interface when working with a variety of tasks and operations, but the CommandBars model used in versions of Access prior to 2007 was quite complex, and sometimes difficult to program. The ribbon introduces an entirely new way of working with user interface components.

The ribbon is quite unlike traditional toolbars or menus, and supports features not possible with toolbars and menus. As you will soon see, customizing Access ribbons is a very different process than using CommandBars to compose toolbars and menus in previous versions of Access.

On the CD-ROM

In the `Chapter29.accdb` database, you can find several database objects needed to support the techniques described in this chapter. You can't see the `USysRibbons` table until you right-click the Navigation Pane, select Navigation Options, and select the Show System Objects check box in the Navigation Options dialog box.

Why Replace Toolbars and Menus?

Unlike previous version of Access where developers used CommandBar objects to build toolbars and menus, Access developers work with the ribbon object. The *ribbon* is the large, horizontal control that stretches across the top of the main Access window. A ribbon is a complex entity, consisting of a number of nested controls that support the functions previously provided by toolbars and menus.

IN THIS CHAPTER

Learning about the new Access ribbon

Working with the default ribbon

Examining ribbon architecture

Studying ribbon controls

Learning the XML necessary to construct ribbons

Adding VBA callbacks

Unlike toolbars and menus in older Access versions, Access 2007 and 2010 support a single ribbon. All of the older versions of Access (version 2003 and earlier) had multiple toolbars and menus, and Access automatically swapped toolbars and menus, depending on the current task performed by the user. Access 2003, for instance, included a total of 29 different toolbars, many of which were virtually identical except for a few controls here and there. The menuing system in Access 2003 was similarly complex, with many different menu bar configurations, all dependent on the user's current activity.

Access 2007 and 2010 perform similar magic on the ribbon. The ribbon automatically transforms to support the user's current activity. For instance, when you're working with a table in Datasheet view, the ribbon displays controls for filtering, searching, and sorting datasheet fields, whereas opening a report in Print Preview mode causes the ribbon to show controls for printing and adjusting margins. Access takes care of all of the complexity of rearranging the controls on the ribbon to suit the current task.

The older CommandBars model (see Figure 29.1), although complex and somewhat difficult to work with, featured a complete object model that included several different object types, with properties, methods, and events. Although a considerable amount of work was involved in building CommandBar-based toolbars and menus, a developer working with CommandBar objects benefited from IntelliSense and online help that documented each type of CommandBar control.

FIGURE 29.1

Developers working with Access CommandBars were limited in their choice of controls.

In addition to the difficulty of programming the complex CommandBar model, CommandBar-based toolbars and menus were somewhat limited in their abilities. Because of their rather "flat" construction, many developers had to resort to deeply nested menus and toolbars buttons that didn't do much more than open dialog boxes that actually performed the task the user required. Many users complained about the difficulty they had learning how to use custom menus, especially if they were not particularly well-planned and constructed.

In addition, some users had tremendous trouble with movable toolbars and menus. By default, the CommandBar objects in previous versions of Access were not only movable, but they could also be docked at the top, bottom, or either side of the main Access screen. Users often complained that, after they accidentally moved a toolbar or menu, it would "stick" to one side or the other of the main Access screen, and they couldn't figure out how to move it back to its original location. Also, even though the convention was to always place a menu CommandBar above a toolbar CommandBar, it was easy to swap these positions, contributing to a user's confusion.

The ribbon (see Figure 29.2), which is shared by all of the Office applications, is an innovative approach to dealing with the problem of flat toolbars and menus. Perhaps the first thing a new users notices about the ribbon is how large it is: It's considerably taller than the toolbar/menu combination common in previous versions of Access. And at first glance, its differences from earlier user interface tools quickly become apparent.

FIGURE 29.2

The ribbon is a new paradigm for Access developers and users.

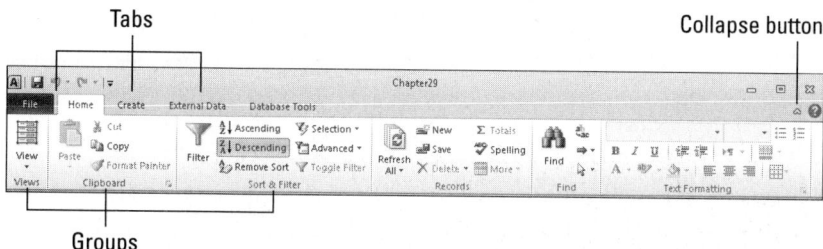

First of all, the Access ribbon supports tabs that separate categories of tasks into logical groupings. Each tab may contain a number of groups that further define task categories. Within a group, many different types of controls — both large and small — that actually perform tasks required by the user might appear.

Microsoft's objectives for introducing ribbons in Office included simplifying the user interface by eliminating overly complex menus, with their fly-outs, drop-down lists, and other conventions made necessary by the limitations of toolbars and menus. Admittedly, the ribbon consumes more vertical space on the screen than the old menus and toolbars did, but the benefits of having all controls visible at one time greatly outweigh this relatively minor issue.

If users still want more vertical space on the screen, the Access 2010 ribbon includes a "collapse" button (which looks like an upward-pointing arrow) at the far right of the ribbon, just to the left of the help button. While collapsed, the ribbon still displays the tab captions so the user can quickly re-open the ribbon to access controls that are needed while working in the Access environment.

Another benefit of the ribbons is that you can use different size controls within a group. This means that you can use a large icon for frequently-performed operations, and smaller icons for less common tasks. The Office ribbon automatically adjusts the sizes of controls as the user resizes the main Access window. For instance, if the user chooses to make the Access window narrower than it is by default, the ribbon changes buttons to icons, removing the labels next to the buttons to conserve space. Ultimately, if the window is made small enough, the ribbon collapses horizontally to just groups with no visible controls (see Figure 29.3).

FIGURE 29.3

The Office ribbon resizes controls to accommodate the width of the Access window.

One final benefit of the ribbon to developers is that you can compose the XML for ribbons in any qualified text editor. You don't have to use a development tool such as Visual Studio to compose ribbon XML. In this chapter, we use the Microsoft Web Developer Express, a free download from Microsoft at www.microsoft.com/express/vwd/. This tool has several advantages over using a plain text editor such as Windows Notepad. In the Visual Web Developer editor, XML is displayed with different colors signifying XML tags, keywords, and identifiers. Also, Visual Web Developer is smart about XML, and flags poorly formed XML statements with the familiar red squiggles Microsoft Word places under misspelled words.

A complete explanation of Visual Web Developer Express is beyond the scope of this chapter, but because Access does not include a qualified XML editor, you need access to an external tools such as Visual Web Developer for composing your ribbon XML. Because Visual Web Developer is a free download, and because it does such a fine job of composing XML statements, it is the ideal tool for Access developers to use when developing ribbon XML.

Hopefully, Microsoft will include an XML editor or a drag-and-drop ribbon designer in a future Access version. In the meantime, we have to manually create the XML for custom ribbons.

Because the XML syntax is used to create and customize Access ribbons, the exact same XML syntax is used by all the Office applications. Also, because you compose XML in a file outside of Access, it is possible to work on a ribbon without disturbing users working with the application. As you will soon see, updating the XML driving an Access ribbon is a relatively simple process and does not require importing or exporting database objects.

At some point, Microsoft will inevitably provide a developer interface for creating and customizing Access ribbons. It is safe to assume that this tool will be made available as an Access add-in and will provide the same or similar functionality as Microsoft Visual Web Developer Express. Therefore, the sections of this chapter describing how to compose the XML for Access ribbons will be applicable even after a ribbon customization tool becomes available from Microsoft.

The section titled "Developing Custom Access Ribbons" later in this chapter discusses the details of building custom Access ribbons. In the meantime, however, we should spend some time understanding the variety of controls and other features that are possible with Access ribbons. The differences between toolbars and menus and the Access ribbon are significant, and the following sections help explain exactly what can be done with the Office ribbon.

New controls for Access ribbons

The Access ribbon supports many more types of controls then the older command bars. In previous versions of Access, the type and variety of controls you could add to menus and toolbars were severely limited. Most toolbars included buttons, and a few other types of controls like drop-down lists, but there were very few options for adding complex or sophisticated controls to command bars.

Access ribbons can contain buttons, text boxes, labels, separators, check boxes, toggle buttons, edit boxes, and even controls nested within other controls. This chapter has only enough room to explore a few of these controls, but you can find examples showing how to utilize virtually every type of ribbon control in Access on the Microsoft Office Web site (http://office.microsoft.com).

Access features some very interesting controls to use on your custom ribbons. These controls are used in the default Access ribbon and are accessible to the custom ribbons you add to your applications. These controls have no analogues in older versions of Access and are completely new to Access.

SplitButton

The *SplitButton* is similar to a traditional button in an Access interface. What makes the SplitButton different is that it is, quite literally, split vertically or horizontally into two different controls. The left or top side of the control works as any other button and responds to a single click. The right or bottom side of the button includes an arrow that, when clicked, reveals a selection list of single-select options.

The example SplitButton in Figure 29.4 reveals a list of reports when the downward-pointing arrow is clicked.

FIGURE 29.4

The SplitButton is a powerful ribbon control.

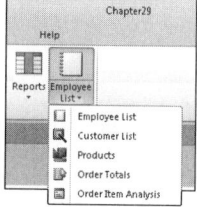

Only one option in the SplitButton list can be selected. As soon as an item in the list is selected, the SplitButton closes and the action selected by the user is performed.

The button portion of the SplitButton control is independently programmable.

DropDown

The *DropDown* is shown in Figure 29.5. Although the DropDown looks very much like a combo box, they are not the same type of object. Notice that the items in the drop-down list in Figure 29.4 include not only text (Clear All Filters, Filter By Form, and so on), but also an image and ToolTip help (not shown in Figure 29.5) associated with each item.

FIGURE 29.5

The DropDown control simplifies a user's selections.

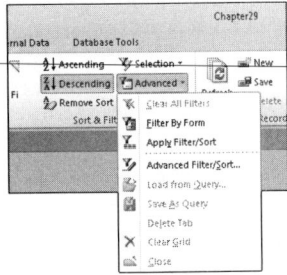

Only one item in the list can be selected at a time, providing an easy-to-understand interface for your users, when a limited number of options exist.

The SplitButton and DropDown are very similar in many ways. They both expose a list when clicked and present a list of single-select items. The main difference is that a SplitButton is, literally, split into two portions (horizontal or vertical), whereas the DropDown simply drops down the list when clicked.

Gallery

The *Gallery* presents the user with an abbreviated view of different options for formatting and other tasks. Figure 29.6 shows a Gallery of famous fictional characters.

Gallery controls are used extensively in Access for displaying options such as ForeColor, BackColor, and font selections.

FIGURE 29.6

The Gallery provides the user with a preview of the options.

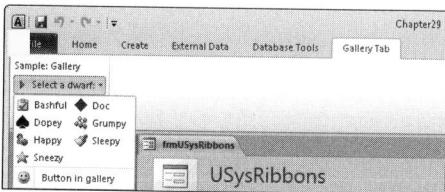

SuperTips

One last Access ribbon control is the *SuperTip*. The SuperTip is very similar to the ToolTip used in previous versions of Access. A SuperTip is relatively large and contains text that you specify, helping the user understand the purpose of a control. The SuperTip, shown in Figure 29.7, appears as the user hovers the mouse over a control on the ribbon.

FIGURE 29.7

The SuperTip provides helpful information to the user.

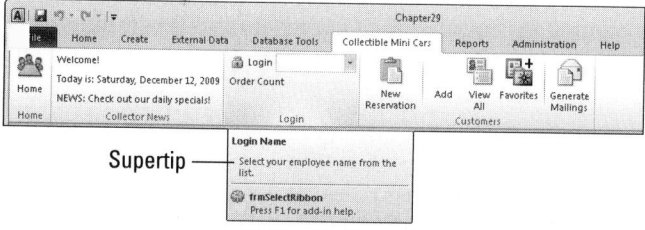

The SuperTip example in Figure 29.7 is included in the Main1 ribbon example in the `Chapter29.accdb` database. Use `frmSelectRibbon`, choose Main1 from the list by double-clicking, and view the Collectible Mini Cars tab on the sample ribbon.

You see examples of creating several types of ribbons controls in the following sections of this chapter. In addition, the Collectible Mini Cars database accompanying this chapter (`Chapter29.accdb`) includes several other examples that are not discussed in this chapter. You are encouraged to take a look at these examples and to use them in your own Access ribbons if you find them useful.

Working with the Access Ribbon

We begin our discussion of the Access ribbons by briefly touring a custom ribbon built for the Collectible Mini Cars (shown in Figure 29.8) database. Later in this chapter, you see how this ribbon was constructed, but in the meantime, just tour the ribbon, its controls, and its behaviors.

FIGURE 29.8

A custom ribbon built for the Collectible Mini Cars database

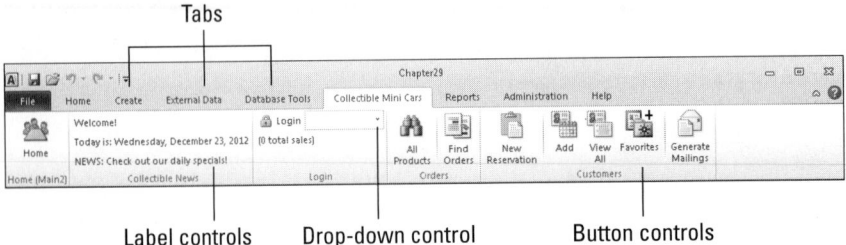

Tabs

Label controls   Drop-down control   Button controls

This sample ribbon (Main2) was constructed by modifying a sample ribbon distributed by Microsoft during the Access 2010 beta. You are almost always better off starting with a good example ribbon than constructing a ribbon entire from scratch. You will find numerous examples of ribbons on the companion CD for this book. The Chapter29.accdb example database includes more than 20 partial and complete ribbons for your experimentation and development.

Oddly enough, the default Access ribbon is inaccessible to developers. You cannot easily customize the default Access ribbon. Instead, you have to build an identical ribbon from scratch and customize your hand-built ribbon. As we discuss later in this chapter, it isn't very difficult to construct a custom ribbon entirely from built-in ribbon controls, but considerable time is required to identify the default Access ribbon tabs, groups, and controls, and then reference those items from a custom ribbon.

Note

The Main2 ribbon (and, most of the other example ribbons in the Chapter29.accdb database) is configured to add its tabs to the tabs already on the screen from the default Access ribbon. When you select Main2 from frmSelectRibbon, notice that four new tabs appear instantly to the right of the tabs already displayed in the Access ribbon. Moving off of frmSelectRibbon closes the Main2 ribbon, making it easy to see how a custom ribbon influences the Access user interface.

Tabs

The Collectible Mini Cars ribbon contains four tabs: Collectible Mini Cars, Reports, Administration, and Help. The main tab (Collectible Mini Cars) contains the operations most frequently conducted by the Collectible Mini Cars application users, whereas the other tabs contain less frequently used controls.

Groups

Each tab in the Collectible Mini Cars ribbon includes a number of groups. Figure 29.8 shows the Collectible Mini Cars tab that contains the Home, Collectible News, Login, Orders, and Customers groups. A tab can contain numerous groups, but you should take care not to overload a tab with too many groups. It's much better to add additional tabs as needed, rather than add so many groups that a user is confused.

Controls

In Figure 29.8, each group contains a variety of controls. For instance, the Home group contains a single large button labeled Home, whereas the Customers group contains five different buttons. A DropDown control is located within the Login group, whereas the Collectible News group includes three different label controls.

Managing the ribbon

By default, the ribbon is always open on the screen. However, the ribbon, with all its controls, and tabs, is quite large, and may be in the way while users work with an application. You can easily collapse the ribbon by double-clicking any tab. Single-clicking any tab brings the ribbon back again, at least temporarily. The ribbon will "auto-collapse" until you double-click a tab to restore the ribbon to its uncollapsed state.

Any forms or reports that are open as the ribbon is collapsed and expanded are moved up or down so that their positions (relative to the ribbon) remain the same. For example, a form that is open right below the ribbon moves upward to occupy the same distance between the top of the form and the bottom of the ribbon area (see Figure 29.9).

FIGURE 29.9

Objects move up or down to accommodate the ribbon as it's opened and closed.

Tabs are moved upward when ribbon collapses

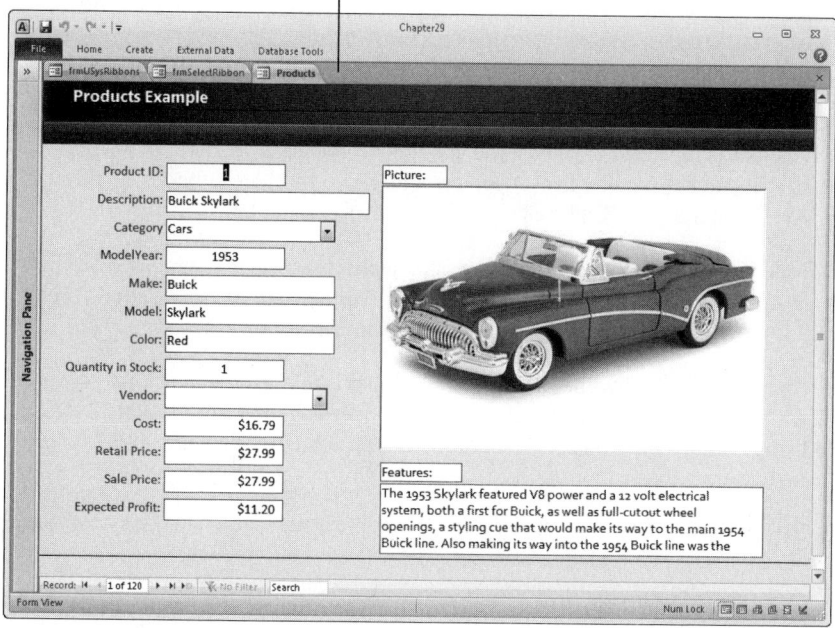

Figure 29.9 shows the Access 2010 tabbed interface and how the tabs maintain their distance from the bottom of the ribbon while the ribbon is collapsed. The same can be said when using the overlapping windows interface. Collapsing or expanding the ribbon causes each floating window in the Access work area to move upward or downward to maintain a consistent distance from the bottom of the ribbon.

Working with the Quick Access Toolbar

You may have noticed the new Quick Access Toolbar in the upper-left corner of the main Access screen (see Figure 29.10 — the Quick Access toolbar is somewhat enlarged in this figure to make it easier to see), just to above the File tab. The Quick Access toolbar remains visible at all times in Access and provides a handy way to give your users quick access to commonly performed tasks such as opening a database file or sending an object to a printer.

FIGURE 29.10

The Quick Access Toolbar remains on the screen at all times.

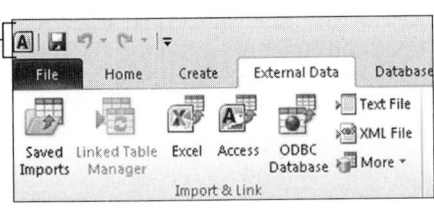

The Quick Access toolbar is fully customizable. You can quickly and easily add any of a large number of operations to the Quick Access toolbar. Also, the controls you add are applicable either to the current database, or to all Access databases.

The easiest way to add a command to the Quick Access toolbar is to locate the command on the Access ribbon, right-click it, and select Add to Quick Access Toolbar from the shortcut menu that appears. Access adds the selected item to the rightmost position in the Quick Access toolbar.

A more flexible approach to modifying the Quick Access toolbar is to open the Quick Access Toolbar customization screen by clicking the File tab in the upper-left corner of the main Access screen and clicking the Options button near the bottom of the Backstage. Then, select the Quick Access Toolbar item from the Access Options list to open the Customize the Quick Access Toolbar screen (see Figure 29.11).

FIGURE 29.11

You can easily add new commands to the Quick Access Toolbar.

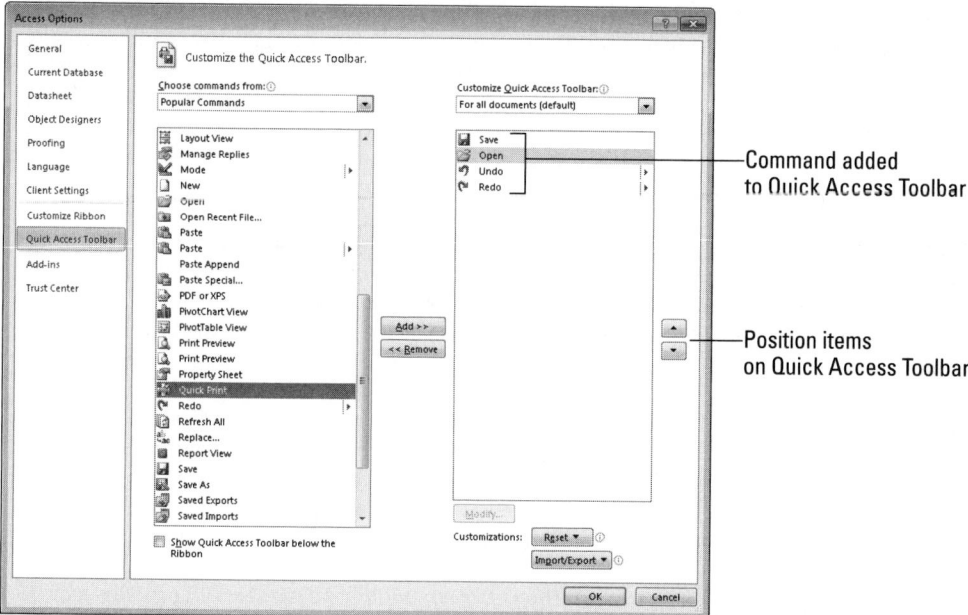

The list on the left side of the screen contains items representing every command available in Microsoft Access, categorized as Popular Commands, Commands Not in the Ribbon, All Commands, and Macros. You select the command category from drop-down control above the list. The category list also contains entries for all of the ribbon tabs in Access (File, Home, External Data, and so on). Selecting an item from this drop-down list reveals the commands within that category.

The Quick Access toolbar provides a handy way for you to control which commands the users access as they work with your Access applications. The tasks available to the Quick Access toolbar include operations such as backing up the current database, converting the current database to another Access data format, viewing database properties, and linking tables.

Because the Quick Access toolbar is visible to all users, be sure not to include commands (such as Design View) that may be confusing to users or harmful to your applications. Because the Quick Access toolbar is easy to customize, it's not difficult to add the commands you need at the time you need them, instead of leaving them visible to all users all of the time.

Use the right- and left-pointing arrows in the Quick Access toolbar designer to move an item from the list on the left to the list on the right. The Quick Access toolbar designer is quite smart. After a command has been added to the Quick Access toolbar, the command is no longer available to be added again, so you can't add the same command more than once.

The Quick Access toolbar designer also contains up and down arrows to the right of the selected list that enable you to reorder the left-to-right appearance of the Quick Access toolbar commands.

Be warned that you can add virtually any number of commands to the Quick Access toolbar. When more commands are contained than the Quick Access toolbar can display, scroll arrows appear at the far right side. However, because the whole idea of the Quick Access toolbar is to make commands quickly available to users, there is no point in loading up the Quick Access toolbar with dozens of commands that only make it more difficult for the user.

Editing the Default Access Ribbon

An entirely new feature in Access 2010 is the ability to edit the default Access ribbon. Changes made to the ribbon stay with Access on the machine where the changes were made, but an option to export modifications is available in the ribbon designer.

The Customize the Ribbon window (see Figure 29.12) uses the "two list" paradigm, just like the Quick Access Toolbar designer, except that the ribbon designer is a bit more complex. You select the category of ribbon you want to modify (File Tabs, Main Tabs, Macros, All Commands, Popular Commands, and so on) from the drop-down above the list on the left side, and then use the left- and right-pointing buttons between the lists to add or remove items from the ribbon.

From the perspective of Access, there is just one ribbon, but it has a number of Main tabs on it: Print Preview, Home, Create, External Data, Database Tools, Source Control, and Add-Ins. Within a Main tab are a number of groups such as Views, Clipboard, and Sort & Filter. You cannot add or remove tabs or commands from the default ribbon, but you can remove individual groups.

You can take away entire built-in groups, but you can't remove individual commands within a group. You can use the buttons below the right list to add new custom tabs or to add new groups within existing ribbon tabs, and then add commands to the custom group. Using a new custom tab or group is the only way to add commands from the left list to the ribbon definition on the right side.

You can't add commands directly to tabs. Commands must reside within groups on a tab. It's easy to add a command to a group: Select the command from the list on the left, select the custom group to receive the command in the list on the right, and click the right-pointing arrow between the lists.

If your objective is to take "dangerous" commands away from your users, you have to remove the built-in group containing the bad command, add a custom group, move it to the appropriate tab, and then add only the commands you want your users to have in the group. Right-click the new group and select Rename from the shortcut menu, or select the new group and click the Rename button under the Customize the Ribbon list. The Rename dialog box appears (see Figure 29.13). Use this dialog box to assign a new name to the group and select the group's icon.

FIGURE 29.12

The Ribbon Designer is a new feature in Access 2010.

Command Category drop-down list

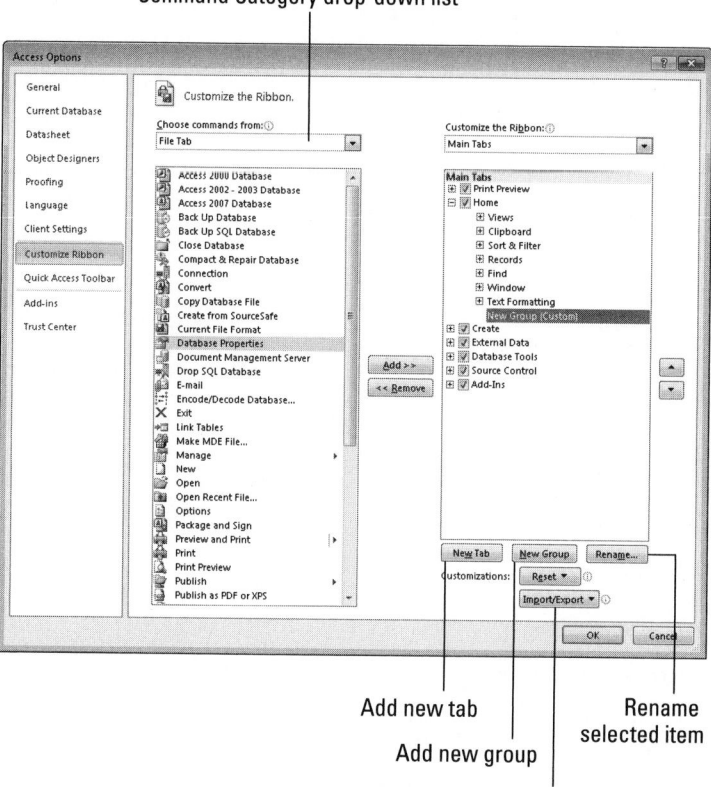

Add new tab

Add new group

Import or export modifications

Rename
selected item

You can hide built-in ribbon tabs if you prefer. Notice the check boxes next to the items in the list on the right side of Figure 29.12. Deselecting a box next to a tab hides the tab from the user. If the tab contains commands the user must have, you can add a custom tab (with the New Tab button under the Customize the Ribbon list on the right side of Figure 29.12), and then add custom groups as needed. Finally, add the necessary commands to the custom groups.

In many cases, simply hiding tabs is probably easier than removing them from the ribbon. If they are hidden, you can easily restore their visibility later on, if you need to.

The ribbon designer includes up-and-down arrows at the far right side for repositioning tabs and groups within tabs. You could, for instance, add a custom group (or use an existing group) and move the most commonly-used commands into it with the up-and-down arrow keys.

Renaming a custom group and setting the group's icon

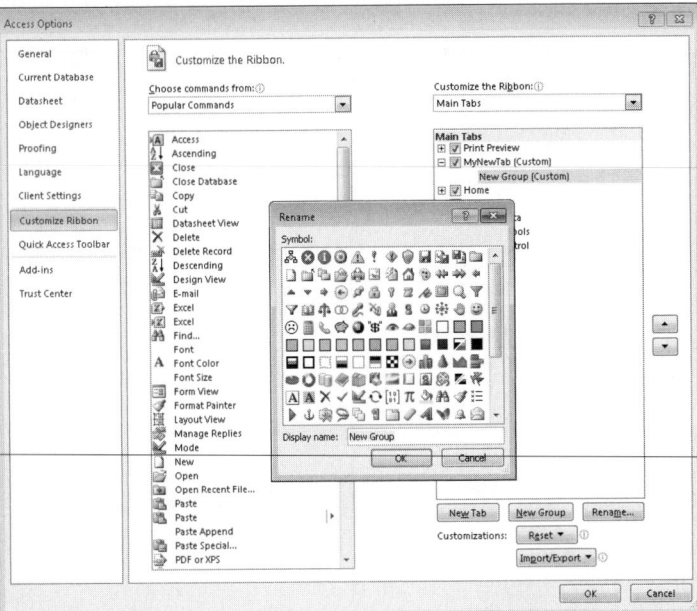

If the changes you've made don't work out as expected, use the Reset button below the Customize the Ribbon list to return the built-in ribbon to its original state. The Reset button (notice its drop-down arrow in Figure 29.12) lets you reset the entire ribbon or just the selected tab.

Use the Import/Export button below the Customize the Ribbon list to export the customizations you've make to the ribbon as an external file. Alternatively, the list that appears when you click the Import/Export button includes a command to import a customization file and apply it to your ribbon. Not surprisingly, the customization file is in XML format, and is shared by all of the Office 2010 applications.

Using a customization file should make it easy to apply custom ribbon changes to all users working with an Access 2010 application. It's also a great way to back up the changes you've made if you need to reapply the changes later on. You could, for instance, set up the ribbon exactly as you want your users to see it, export the customization, and then reset the ribbon to its original state so that you have access to all ribbon features during your development cycle.

Developing Custom Access Ribbons

Ribbons are not represented by a programmable object model in Access. Each ribbon is defined by XML statements contained in a special table named USysRibbons. Access uses the information it finds in the XML to compose and render the ribbon on the screen.

The ribbon creation process

Briefly, creating custom ribbons is a five-step process:

1. Design the ribbon and compose the XML that defines the ribbon.
2. Write VBA callback routines (described in the following section) that support the ribbon's operations.
3. Create the USysRibbons table.
4. Provide a ribbon name and add the custom ribbon's XML to the USysRibbons table.
5. Specify the custom ribbon's name in the Access options screen.

None of these steps is particularly intuitive, especially when it comes to composing the XML and writing callback routines. Your best bet is to find an example that is reasonably close to what you want and customize its XML to suit your purposes.

Using VBA callbacks

A *callback* is code that is passed to another entity for processing. Each procedure you write to support operations on a ribbon is passed to the "ribbon processor" in Access that actually performs the ribbon's actions. This is very unlike the event-driven code you've been working with in Access. Clicking a button on a form *directly* triggers the code in the button's Click event procedure. A ribbon's callback procedure is linked to the ribbon, but is internally processed by Access and does not directly run in response to the click on the ribbon.

To fully understand this process, imagine that Access contains a process that constantly monitors activity on the ribbon. As soon as the user clicks a ribbon control, the ribbon processor springs into action, retrieving the callback procedure associated with the control and performing the actions specified in the callback.

This means that there are no Click, DblClick, or GotFocus events associated with Access ribbons. Instead, you bind a callback to a ribbon control through the XML that defines the ribbon. Each ribbon control includes a number of action attributes that can be attached to callbacks, and the ribbon processor takes over when the user invokes a control's action.

Here is an example. The following XML statements define a button control on a ribbon:

```
<button id="ViewProducts"
    label="All Products"
    size="large"
    imageMso="FindDialog"
    onAction="OpenProductsForm"
    tag="frm ProductsDisplay"/>
```

(These lines appear as a single statement in the XML code behind the Collectible Mini Cars Main2 ribbon.)

Notice the onAction attribute in this XML code. Notice also that the onAction attribute is set to onOpenFormEdit. The onAction attribute is similar to the events associated with a form's controls. Each interactive ribbon control (buttons, SplitButtons, and so on) include the onAction attribute. The callback procedure (onOpenFormEdit, in this example) assigned to the on Action attribute is passed to the ribbon processor when the control's action occurs.

A control's attributes may appear in any order within the control's XML, but they must be spelled correctly. XML is notoriously case sensitive, so attributes must be entered exactly as you see in the examples in this chapter and in the Chapter29.accdb example database. And, attribute values (like "FindDialog") must be surrounded by double or single quote characters.

Notice that the button control does not contain a click event. Instead, each interactive control's onAction attribute handles whatever action is expected by the control. In the case of a button, the action is a user clicking the button, whereas for a text box, the action is the user typing into the text box. Both of these controls include the onAction attribute, but onAction means something different for each control.

Note

Be aware that onAction is not an event. It is just an XML attribute that points to the callback procedure tied to the ribbon control. The callback procedure runs whenever the user interacts with the control. In this case, the ViewProducts button's callback procedure is invoked when the user clicks on the button.

Ribbon controls have several other important attributes, such as imageMso, screenTip, and super-tip. These attributes are described in the "Adding Ribbon Controls" section, later in this chapter.

Tip

You probably want to see any errors generated by your custom ribbon during development. By default, ribbon error reporting is disabled, and you must enable it before you see error messages thrown by the ribbon. Click the File tab in the upper-left corner of the main Access screen and choose the Options button at the bottom. Next, select the Client Settings tab in the Options dialog box and scroll down to the General section. Make sure the Show Add-In User Interface Errors check box is selected; click OK at the bottom of the dialog box. The error messages generated by the ribbon are invaluable debugging aids (see Figure 29.14). Without these messages, you have no idea what has failed in your custom ribbons.

FIGURE 29.14

An error message thrown by a custom Access ribbon

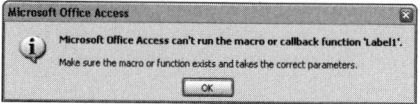

The Ribbon Hierarchy

The ribbon itself is a fairly complex structure and is hierarchical in nature. At the top level are the tabs you see along the top of the ribbon. Each tab contains one or more groups, each containing one or more controls. The ribbon is highly adaptable to your current tasks, so the description that follows may not be exactly the same as you see on your screen:

- **Tabs:** The top object in the ribbon hierarchy. You use tabs to separate the most fundamental operations into logical groups. For instance, the default Access ribbon contains four tabs: Home, Create, External Data, and Database Tools.

- **Groups:** The second highest object in the ribbon hierarchy. Groups contain any of the number of different types of controls and are used to logically separate operations supported by a ribbon tab. In Figure 29.15, the Home tab contains six groups: Views, Clipboard, Sort & Filter, Records, Find, and Text Formatting.

- **Controls:** In Figure 29.15, notice the variety of controls within each group on the Home tab. The Views group contains a single control, while the Text Formatting group contains 18 different controls. Normally, the controls within a group are related to one another, but this is not a hard and fast rule.

FIGURE 29.15

The default Access ribbon

As you design your custom Access ribbons, you should keep the basic ribbon hierarchy in mind. Microsoft has spent a great deal of time experimenting with and testing the Office ribbon paradigm, and it works well for a wide variety of applications.

One of the principles employed in Access ribbons is that there is virtually no limit to the number of objects at each level of the ribbon hierarchy. This means that you can add virtually any number of tabs to a custom ribbon. Obviously, too many tabs or too many groups can become a real problem for your users. Generally speaking, you should design your ribbons in a conservative manner, including only the items at each level that your users actually need.

Getting Started with Access Ribbons

As mentioned before, creating and customizing ribbons is very different than working with CommandBars in earlier versions of Access. Creating Access ribbons is, at a minimum, a five-step process. Each of these steps is described in detail in the following sections. Later you'll see many more examples of these steps.

Step 1: Design the ribbon and build the XML

As with most database objects, the first step to creating a new Access ribbon is to design it carefully on paper. If you are converting an existing toolbar or menu to an Access ribbon, you have a pretty good idea of the controls and other items to add to the ribbon.

The XML document you create for your ribbon mirrors the design you've laid out. Perhaps the most challenging aspect of composing the ribbons XML is visualizing how the ribbon will look, based on the XML behind it. There are no visual cues in a ribbon XML document that hint at the ribbon's appearance when rendered in Access. Experience will be your best guide as you work with ribbon customization, and sometimes trial and error is the only way to achieve a desired objective.

As a final point, Access is extremely fussy about the XML used to compose ribbons. There is no "parser" in Access that validates the XML as a ribbon is rendered. If an error exists in the XML document, Access refuses to render the ribbon, or the ribbon will be missing elements defined in the XML. Most often, the only way you know that an error exists in your ribbon XML code is that Access loads the default ribbon instead of your custom ribbon.

Inevitably, ribbon development in Access requires a number of back-and-forth cycles in which you modify the XML, transfer it to Access, and view the results. You have no real way of really knowing how well your XML will work as a ribbon specification until Access renders the ribbon on the screen.

The section titled, "The Basic Ribbon XML," later in this chapter, describes the fundamental XML statements required by Access ribbons.

See the section titled, "Using Visual Web Developer" later in this chapter to see how to use the Express edition to compose the XML driving your Access ribbons. Also, several sections in this chapter discuss the XML necessary to define ribbons, tabs, groups, and controls.

Step 2: Write the callback routines

Before writing any callback code for Access ribbon controls, you must reference the Microsoft Office 14.0 Object Library in the References dialog box (select Tools ➪ References, and select the check box next to Microsoft Office 14.0 Object Library). Otherwise, the VBA interpreter will have no idea how to handle references to ribbon controls.

As we described earlier in this chapter, callback routines are similar to event procedures, but do not directly respond to control events. Each type of callback routine has a specific "signature" that must be followed in order for the ribbon processor to locate and use the callback. For instance, the prototype onAction callback signature for a button control is

```
Public Sub OnAction(control as IRibbonControl)
```

The prototype onAction callback for a check box is

```
Public Sub OnAction(control As IRibbonControl, _
    pressed As Boolean)
```

Even though these callbacks support the same onAction control attribute, because the controls are different, the signatures are different. Clicking a button is just that — click once, and the action is done. In the case of a check box, a click either selects (pressed = True) or deselects (pressed = False) the control. Therefore, an additional parameter is required for check boxes.

These procedures are just prototypes and do not apply to any particular control on a ribbon. In practice, the callback procedure for a control is usually named after the control to distinguish it from callback procedures for other controls. For example, the actual callback for the ViewProducts button described in the "Using VBA callbacks" section, earlier in this chapter, might be:

```
Public Sub OpenProductsForm(control As IRibbonControl)
    'Called from ViewProducts ribbon button
    DoCmd.OpenForm "frmProducts"
End Sub
```

Notice that this procedure's declaration matches the prototype for a button control's onAction callback procedure. Although not required, this procedure even contains a comment that identifies the ribbon control that calls the routine.

Callback routines must be declared with the Public attribute, or they can't be seen by the Access ribbon process.

The name you apply to callback routines is entirely your choice, as long as the procedure's declaration matches the control's onAction signature. Obviously, the procedure's name must match the value you assign to the control's onAction attribute, and documenting the procedure's relationship to a ribbon control is very helpful when it comes time to modify the ribbon or the callback.

The complete callback procedure for a simple button might be

```
Public Sub OnAction(control As IRibbonControl)
    DoCmd.OpenForm "frmMyForm", , , , acNormal
End Sub
```

The callback procedure for the check box uses the pressed parameter to determine which path to take through the procedure:

```
Public Sub onAction(control As IRibbonControl, _
    pressed As Boolean)
    If pressed = True Then
        DoCmd.OpenForm "frmHelp"
    Else
        DoCmd.Close acForm, "frmHelp"
    End If
End Sub
```

We've been focusing on the onAction callback, but many other callbacks exist. Here is the XML definition of a simple Label control:

```
<labelControl id="lblTodaysDate" getLabel="onGetLabel"/>
```

Notice the getLabel attribute. The callback signature of the getLabel attribute is

```
Public Sub onGetLabel(control as IRibbonControl, ByRef label)
```

The Label control is passed as the IRibbonControl parameter, and the label's contents are passed as the (variant) label parameter. Notice that the label parameter is passed by reference, allowing the callback to modify the parameter's value. An example procedure for filling a label with the current date is

```
Public Sub onGetLabel(control as IRibbonControl, ByRef label)
    label = "Today is: " & FormatDateTime(Date, vbLongDate)
End Sub
```

The attribute linked to this callback is getLabel, which designates the procedure that fills the label's text at runtime. The name of the callback (onGetLabel) can be anything, but it makes good sense to provide it with a name that links it to the control's getLabel attribute.

Notice that none of these callback procedures discussed so far reference the control by name. This means that you have to write a uniquely named callback for each control, or use a single callback for multiple similar controls. Several of the Collectible Mini Cars callbacks use the control's id property to determine which control has triggered the callback:

```
Public Sub onGetLabel(control As IRibbonControl, ByRef label)
    Select Case control.id
      Case "lblWelcome"
        label = GetWelcomeMessage()
      Case "lblToday"
        label = "Today is: " & FormatDateTime(Date, vbLongDate)
      Case "lblOrderCount"
        label = GetSalesCountString()
      Case "lblCompany"
        label = "Name: " & DLookup("Company", "tblContacts")
```

```
        Case "lblCompanyLocation"
          label = "Location: " & DLookup("City", "tblContacts") _
            & ", " & DLookup("State", "tblContacts")
      End Select
    End Sub
```

A control's id property, of course, is the name assigned to the control in the XML:

```
<labelControl id="lblCompanyName" getLabel="onGetLabel"/>
<labelControl id="lblCompanyLocation" getLabel="onGetLabel"/>
```

Because the id properties are different, both of these Label controls use the same callback procedure. The callback uses the id to determine which label has triggered the callback.

Because the getLabel attribute specifies where the control gets its text, the getLabel attribute could be just as easily written as follows:

```
<labelControl id="lblHello" label="Hello!"/>
```

In this case, no callback is used, and the label is filled with a literal text string.

Step 3: Create the USysRibbons table

Access looks for a table named USysRibbons to see whether there are any custom ribbons in the current database application. This table does not exist by default, and, if present, contains the XML that defines the custom ribbons in the application.

Note

USysRibbons is hidden in the Navigation Pane by virtue of the USys prefix in its name (any database object with USys as the first four characters of its name is automatically hidden in the Navigation Pane). If you want to see USysRibbons in the Navigation Pane, you must enable Show System Objects in the Navigation Options: Right-click on the Navigation Pane title bar, select Navigation Options, and select Show System Objects in the lower-left corner of the Navigation Options dialog box.

USysRibbons is very simple, and contains only three fields, shown in Table 29.1.

TABLE 29.1

The USysRibbons Table Design

Field	Data Type
ID	AutoNumber
RibbonName	Text 255
RibbonXML	Memo

The ID field just keeps track of the ribbons in the table. The RibbonName is used to specify which ribbon Access should load at startup (described in Step 5 later in this chapter), whereas RibbonXML is a memo field (with a maximum size of 65,000 characters) containing the XML that defines the ribbon.

Because USysRibbons is a table, your Access database may actually include the definitions of many different custom ribbons. However, only one custom ribbon can be active at a time. In the section titled "Managing Ribbons," later in this chapter, we cover how to invalidate an existing ribbon and load a new ribbon in its place.

You might find good reasons to add additional fields to USysRibbons, if necessary. For instance, you could add a Notes or Comments field that helps another developer understand how the ribbon should be used. You could also add a modification date and other fields that help track changes to your custom ribbons. If you modify USysRibbons, be sure not to remove or rename the three required fields (ID, RibbonName, and RibbonXML). These three fields must exist in USysRibbons and must be named correctly for your custom ribbons to work.

Step 4: Add XML to USysRibbons

Figure 29.16 shows the XML, in a Microsoft Visual Web Developer window, for a very simple Access ribbon.

FIGURE 29.16

The XML required for a very simple Access ribbon

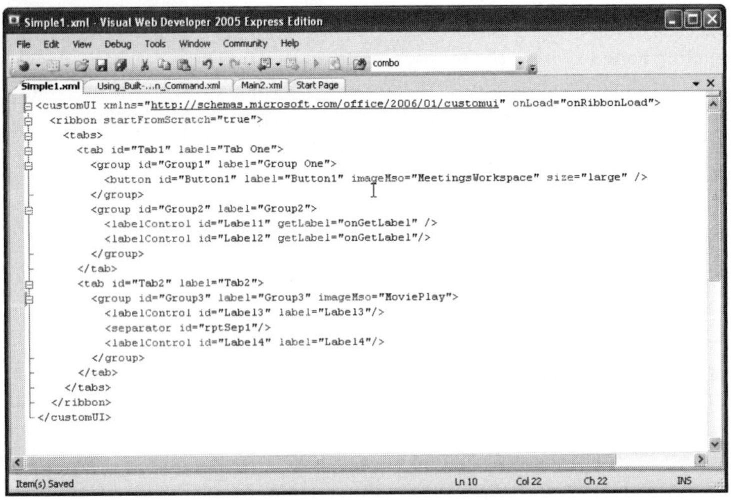

The ribbon produced with this XML is shown in Figure 29.17.

The simple Access ribbon created with the XML in Figure 29.16

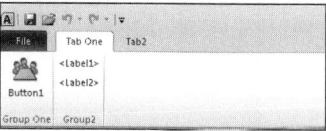

The XML for the Simple1 ribbon is included in the USysRibbons table in Chapter29.accdb. To use this ribbon, set the Custom Ribbon Id value in the Current Database options to Simple1 and restart the application.

In Figure 29.16, notice the absence of red squiggles, indicating improperly formed XML. Visual Web Developer flags any obvious XML errors (such as unmatched tags) by underlining suspicious passages with red squiggles.

Keep in mind that the Visual Web Developer locates syntax errors, but cannot detect problems with the XML's logic. Incorrect references, misplaced or missing attributes, and other problems with the XML's content can still prevent your XML code from working as expected.

Notice the very top line of XML (<?xml version="1.0" encoding="utf-8"?>) in Figure 29.16. This line is automatically added to every XML document created with Visual Web Developer and is not really needed by Access ribbons. However, no harm is caused if this line is copied into the USysRibbons table.

Copying the XML from an editor such as Visual Web Developer to USysRibbons is a simple process. Highlight the XML, making sure to include the very top (<customUI...) and bottom (</customUI>) tags. Then, switch to Access, open the USysRibbons table, and paste the XML into the RibbonXML column of a new row. Finally, provide a RibbonName for the new ribbon (see Figure 29.18).

In Figure 29.18, notice that additional columns (Results and RibbonDescription) have been added to USysRibbons, in addition to the required fields (ID, RibbonName, and RibbonXml). The additional fields are displayed on frmUSysRibbons (shown in Figure 29.19) to help document each ribbon in the Chapter29.accdb example database. The additional fields in no way affect the ribbons stored in USysRibbons.

FIGURE 29.18

Copying the XML to USysRibbons and naming the new ribbon

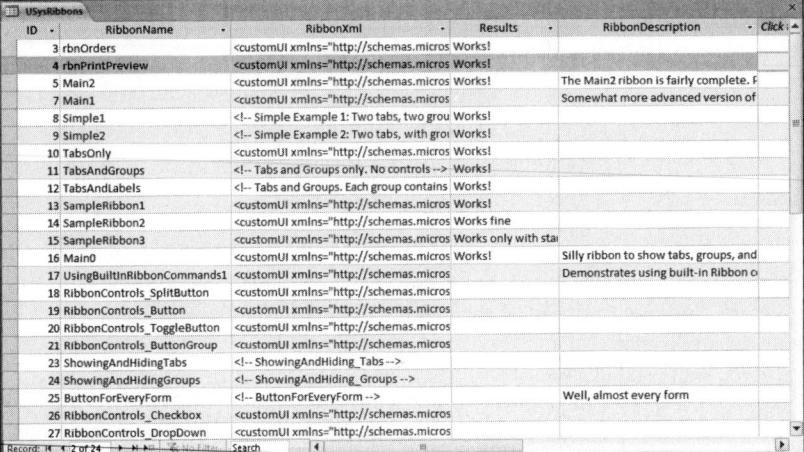

FIGURE 29.19

frmUSysRibbons displays the information stored in the USysRibbons table.

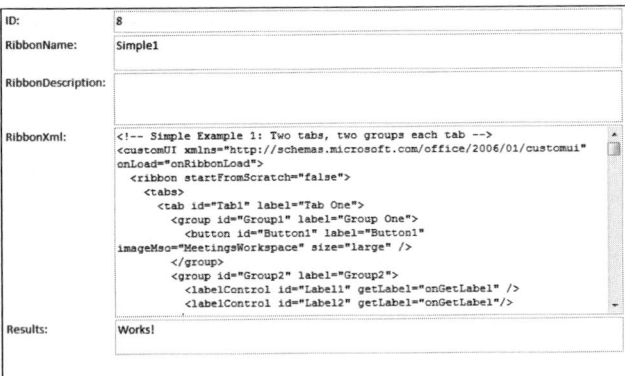

Step 5: Specify the custom ribbon property

The last step, before restarting the application, is to open the Current Database properties (File ➪ Options ➪ Current Database), scroll to the Ribbons and Toolbar Options section, and select the name of the new ribbon from the RibbonName combo box (see Figure 29.20). The combo box's list contains only the names of custom ribbons in USysRibbons that were in the table as Access started (apparently Access only reads USysRibbons one time as Access opens a database), so it does not contain the name of the new ribbon. You have to type the ribbon's name into the combo box, or restart the application and let Access find the new ribbon in USysRibbons.

FIGURE 29.20

Specifying the new custom ribbon in the Current Database options dialog box

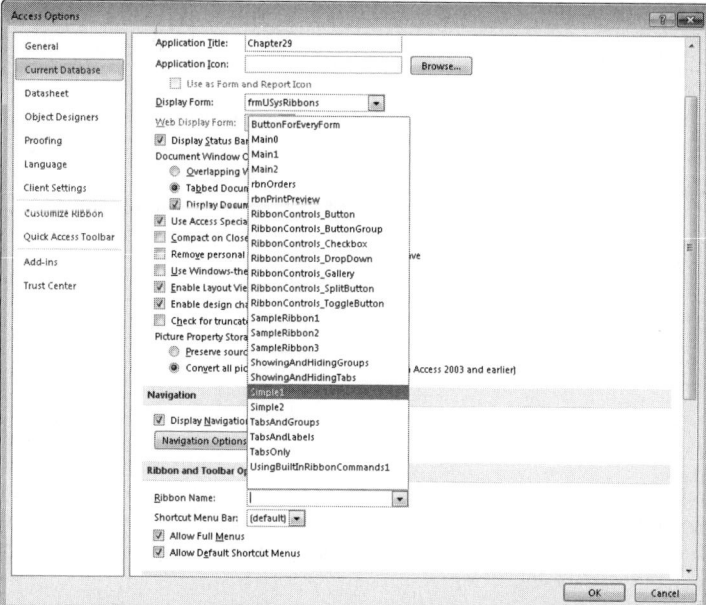

The Basic Ribbon XML

Take a closer look at the basic XML required by Access ribbons. The following XML represents a prototype ribbon (line numbers have been added to make the discussion following this XML easier to understand):

```
1  <?xml version="1.0" encoding="utf-8"?>
2  <!-- This is a comment in the ribbon's XML -->
3  <customUI xmlns="http://schemas.microsoft.com/office
   /2006/01/customui" onLoad="onRibbonLoad">
4    <ribbon startFromScratch="true">
5      <tabs>
6        <tab id="tab1" ...
7          <group id="group1" ... >
8            ... Controls go here ...
9          </group>
10       </tab>
11       <tab id="tab2" ...
12         <group id="group2" ... >
13           ... Controls go here ...
14         </group>
```

```
15         ... Repeat Groups ...
16      </tab>
17         ... Repeat Tabs ...
18    </tabs>
19   </ribbon>
20 </customUI>
```

The first statement (`<?xml version="1.0" encoding="utf-8"?>`), as discussed before, is added by Visual Web Developer, and does not affect Access ribbons. It is completely your choice whether to keep this line or not in the `USysRibbons` table. Line 2 shows how to add a comment to a ribbon's XML code. The `<!--` and `-->` are standard commenting tags for XML documents.

Line 3 (beginning with `<customUI...`) specifies an XML *namespace* (`xmlns`), an XML document that predefines acceptable tags for the XML statements that follow. The Office namespace defines the Office ribbon constructs (tabs, groups, controls, and so on) and enables IntelliSense in the Visual Web Developer editor. Every ribbon defined in the RibbonXML field in USysRibbons must start with this statement, so be sure it's included.

Note

Beginning with Office 2010, you have another option for the `CustomUI` tag. The tag you see in the preceding code applies to ribbons intended to be used in Access 2007 or 2010. If you are building a ribbon and you know (for sure!) that it will only be used with Access 2010 (perhaps to take advantage of new features in Access 2010), you can use the following CustomerUI statement:

```
<customUI xmlns="http://schemas.microsoft.com/office/2009/07/customui">
```

The statement in line 4 is rather important. The `startFromScratch` directive notifies Access that we are building an entire ribbon from scratch, rather than starting with the default Access ribbon and taking things away. Depending on your situation, the majority of your custom ribbons may be built from scratch because the default Access ribbon knows nothing about the forms, reports, and other objects and operations in your database. Also, the default Access ribbon contains commands that may be dangerous to your application's integrity. For instance, a user could open a form, report, or table in design view and make changes without your being aware of it. Removing these commands from the user interface is a first line of defense for your applications.

When `startFromScratch` is set to `false`, your custom ribbon definition is added to the default Access ribbon to the right of the built-in tabs. Because Access only includes four tabs by default, you may have enough room for your additional tabs without overcrowding the ribbon.

The `<tabs>` (line 5) and `</tabs>` (line 18) tags indicate the beginning and end of the tabs on the ribbon. Ribbons are hierarchical, with tabs containing groups which contain controls. The tabs, therefore, are the highest-level objects within a ribbon and enclose all other ribbon objects.

Line 6 defines the left-most tab on the ribbon. In this example, the tab's name is `tab1`. The other attributes for this tab are not shown, but are implied by the ellipsis (`...`). The ending tag for `tab1` is located on line 10.

Line 7 begins the definition of the first group on `tab1` and line 9 ends this group. Within the group are the controls displayed by the group.

The rest of this prototype ribbon is simple repetition of the first few items.

Note
Remember: XML is case-sensitive. Be careful to use exactly the same case and spelling for all references in your XML as well as in the callback code driving the ribbon.

Adding Ribbon Controls

The previous section presented a simple prototype ribbon. In this example, the controls were indicated by `... Controls go here ....` on lines 8 and 13. Take a moment and look at the actual XML construction of a few common ribbon controls.

Specifying imageMso

Most, but not all, ribbon controls include an `imageMso` attribute that specifies the picture attached to the control. You are not able to provide simple references to image files; instead, you must use an `imageMso` identifier for this purpose. Every ribbon control in the Office 2010 applications has an associated `imageMso` value. You use these values on your custom Access ribbon controls and provide a label that tells your users the exact purpose of the control.

There are two ways to obtain the `imageMso` for a particular ribbon control. The first method is with the ribbon designer described earlier in this chapter. Use the Customize the Ribbon window to open a particular ribbon, use the drop-down in the upper left of the designer to select the ribbon category containing the ribbon command, and hover the mouse over the command's entry in the list (see Figure 29.21).

The `imageMso` for the Find command (`FindDialog`) is shown in parentheses in the ToolTip that appears near the selected command.

The second way to discover `imageMso` values is with the `imageMso_Galleries.accdb` example database on this book's CD. The ribbon in this database includes every Office ribbon icon, arranged as a number of Gallery ribbon controls (see Figure 29.22). Hovering the mouse over an icon in a Gallery shows the icon's `imageMso`. The ribbon Galleries in `imageMso_Galleries.accdb` are divided among 6 different ribbons, each containing 5 or 6 galleries, each with 100 icons. The Office application family has so many icons that they could not all fit on a single ribbon.

When looking up an icon's `imageMso`, be sure to check the other ribbon Galleries. `imageMso_Galleries.accdb` includes a form (`frmSelectRibbonGallery`) that dynamically adds a ribbon icon Gallery to the main as you select a button.

FIGURE 29.21

Using the ribbon designer to obtain a ribbon command's `imageMso` attribute.

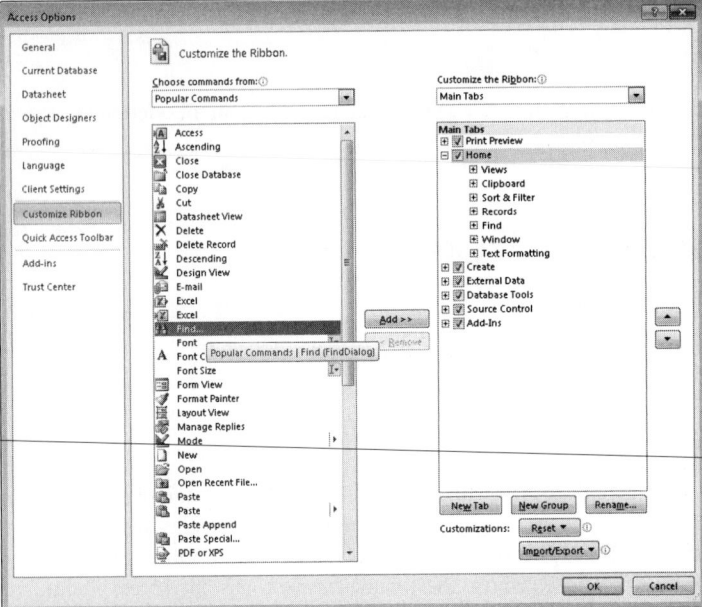

FIGURE 29.22

Looking up an icon's `imageMso` with `imageMso_Galleries.accdb`

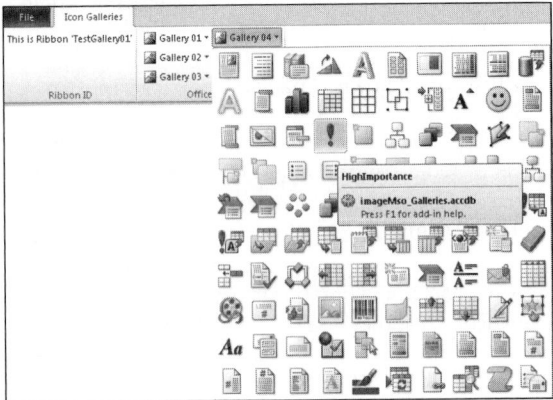

The `imageMso_Galleries` example database includes `frmSelectRibbonGallery` (shown in Figure 29.23) to dynamically load any of the six Gallery ribbons in the database. Select a Gallery using the buttons on this form, and the Gallery tab appears to the right of the default Access ribbon tabs.

FIGURE 29.23

`frmSelectRibbonGallery` dynamically loads the ribbon Galleries in `imageMso_Gallery.accdb`

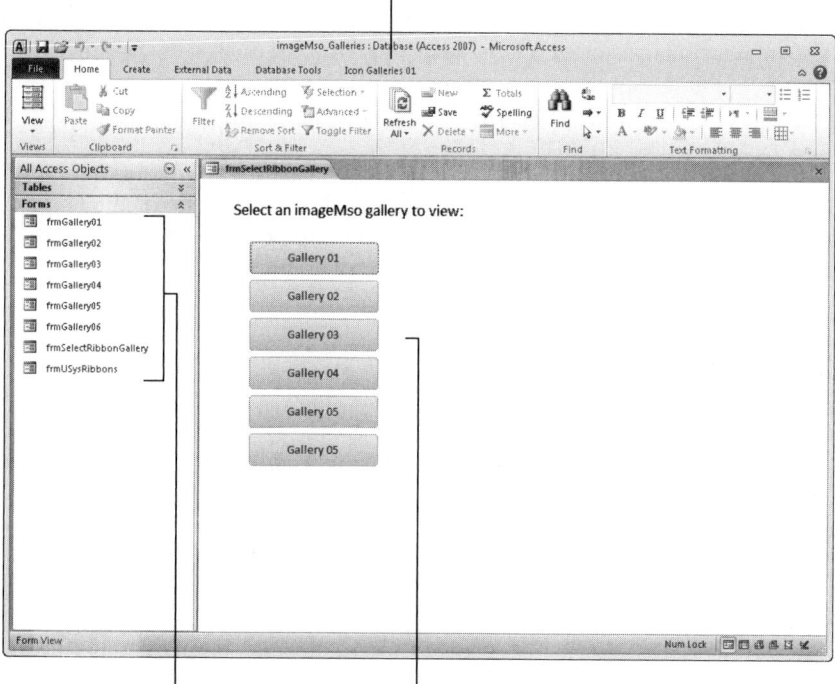

imageMso_Galleries also include a form for each of the ribbon Galleries. Opening any of these forms (`frmGallery01`, `frmGallery02`, and so on) dynamically loads the ribbon associated with the form. (A form's custom ribbon is specified by the form's Ribbon Name property.)

The Label control

The Label control is, by far, the simplest and easiest to add to a ribbon. A ribbon label is completely analogous to a label you add to an Access form. It contains either hard-coded text or text that is generated by a callback procedure.

Here is a sample label definition:

```
<group id="grpFonts" label="Settings">
  <labelControl id="lbl1" label="Font Things" />
  <separator id="s1"/>
  <labelControl id="lc2" label="Choose Font Settings" />
  <check box id="chk1" label="Bold" onAction="SetBold"/>
  <check box id="chk2" label="Italics" onAction="SetItalics"/>
</group>
```

This XML contains three labels, a separator, and two check boxes. The text in each of these labels is hard-coded, rather than returned by a callback procedure. Earlier, in the "Step 2: Write the callback routines" section, you read how to use the getLabel attribute to specify a callback that returns a label's text.

The Button control

The Button control is, perhaps, the most useful and fundamental of all of the ribbon controls. A button is very simple. A button has a label, an imageMso attribute for setting the button's image, and an onAction attribute that names the callback routine. An example of button XML is

```
<button id="MyButton1" size="large"
    label="MyButton1"
    imageMso="OutlookGlobe"
    onAction="nyi" />
```

The nyi referenced in the onAction attribute is a simple procedure in the Chapter29.accdb sample database, and stands for not yet implemented. This procedure is just a placeholder for you to insert your own callback routine. The Button ribbon control does not support double-click actions, so tying a button to a callback procedure is very simple.

Separators

A separator is a graphical element that divides items in a group, as shown in Figure 29.24. Separators contain no text and appear as a vertical line within a group. By themselves, they're not very interesting, but they graphically separate controls that would otherwise be too close within a group.

FIGURE 29.24

Separators provide a way to divide controls within a group.

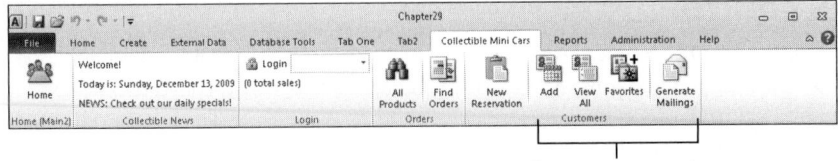

Separator controls

The XML code for the separators in Figure 29.24 is

```
<group id="grpCustomers" label="Customers">
  <button id="cmdNewReservation" ...
  <separator id="sep2"/>
  <button id="cmdAddCustomer" label="Add" ...
  <button id="cmdViewCustomers" label="View All"
  <button id="cmdFavorites" label="Favorites" ...
  <separator id="sep3"/>
  <button id="cmdMailings" label="Generate Mailings"...
</group>
```

The XML statements have been shortened to make it easier to see the separator placement. grp-Customers contains two separators.

The only requirement for separators is that each be assigned a unique ID value.

Check boxes

Check boxes are effective to allow the user to select any of a number of different options. Check boxes are not mutually exclusive, so the user can choose any of the check boxes within a group without affecting other selections.

Check boxes are established much like any other ribbon control:

```
<tab id="tabOutdoor" label="Outdoor">
  <group id="grpSports" label="Sports" ...>
    <check box id="chk04" label="Baseball" .../>
    <check box id="chk05" label="Basketball" .../>
    <separator id="sep1"/>
    <check box id="chk06" label="Tennis" .../>
    <check box id="chk07" label="Water Polo" .../>
  </group>
  <group id="grpCamping" label="Camping Supplies">
    <check box id="chk08" label="Tent" .../>
    <check box id="chk09" label="Granola" .../>
    <check box id="chk10" label="Lantern" .../>
    <separator id="sep2"/>
    <button id="btn" imageMso="StartTimer"
      size="large" label="A Big Button" />
  </group>
</tab>
```

We removed code and replaced it with ellipsis characters to improve clarity of this example XML.

The tab produced by this XML code is shown in Figure 29.25 and is included in the Simple2 example ribbon in the Chapter29.accdb database.

FIGURE 29.25

Check boxes are a good choice when the user needs to be able to select among a number of options.

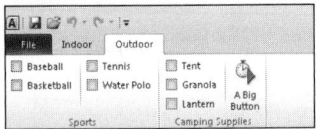

The ribbon check boxes you see in Figure 29.25 work exactly as you would expect. The check boxes may be selected individually, or in any combination. Check boxes are not mutually exclusive, and each check box has its own onAction attribute.

The DropDown control

The DropDown control is more complex than the label, button, and check box examples we've covered. It includes a list of items for the user to choose from. Therefore, a DropDown has a number of attributes that define its appearance, as well as callbacks that populate its list:

```
<dropDown
  id="ddLogin"
  label="Login" supertip="Select your employee name..."
  screentip="Login Name"
  getItemCount="onGetLoginCount"
  getItemLabel="onGetLogins"
  imageMso="Private"
  onAction="onLogin">
</dropDown>
```

The id, label, screentip, and imageMso attributes define the DropDown control's appearance. The getItemCount and getItemLabel populate the DropDown's list. onAction specifies the callback that handles the control's action.

The VBA callbacks for a typical DropDown are shown in the following code. Two primary callbacks are required for a DropDown. The first sets the count of items to appear in the list, and the second actually populates the list.

```
Public Sub onGetLoginCount( _
    control As IRibbonControl, ByRef count)
    count = Nz(DCount("*", "tblSalesPerson"), 0)
End Sub
Public Sub onGetLogins( _
    control As IRibbonControl, index As Integer, ByRef label)
    Dim strName As String
    strName = Nz(DLookup("SalespersonName", _
        "tblSalesPerson", "SalesPersonID = " & index + 1), "")
    label = strName
End Sub
```

The first callback (onGetLoginCount) gets the count of items to be placed on the DropDown's list. Notice the ByRef count parameter. This parameter tells the DropDown how many items to accommodate on its list.

The second procedure (onGetLogins) actually retrieves the items for the list. In this case, the procedure pulls the SalesPerson name field from tblSalesPerson using DLookup. onGet-Logins is called by the DropDown multiple times; the exact number of calls is determined by the count value established by onGetLoginCount.

The onGetLogins routine cheats a little bit to supply this information. Notice the index parameter passed to this routine. Index tells the procedure which slot on the drop-down list is being filled when the procedure is called. The DLookup adds 1 to this value and extracts the name of the sales person whose ID matches this value. This means that the SalesPersonID values have to be sequential, starting with 1, or this procedure will fail.

Extracting data with nonsequential ID values, or where the ID value is non-numeric, requires a bit more work. You could, for instance, create a sorted recordset of the values you want on the list. Then, using the index parameter, advance through the recordset to the record requested by the DropDown.

An accurate count of values to add to the DropDown is important. The DropDown has no way, other than the count parameter, to know how many items to expect. Setting a count too low means that not all items will be added, whereas setting the count too high means that list contains blank spaces. If, for instance, you set the count to 10 items, but only 5 are available, the DropDown's list contains the five items, but also five blank spaces.

The SplitButton Control

The SplitButton control is very useful in situations where the user may select from a number of different options, but one option is used more frequently than the others. An example might be a number of reports, one of which is commonly printed, and the others are printed only periodically (a SplitButton example is shown in Figure 29.4).

The items on a SplitButton's list are contained within <menu> and </menu> tags. Whatever controls (within reason, of course) that appear within these tags show up in the SplitButton's list. The definition of the default button portion of a SplitButton lies outside of the <menu> and </menu> tags. In the following code fragment, MyButton1 is the default button, whereas the other buttons (MyButton2, MyButton3, and so on) occupy the SplitButton's list.

```
<customUI xmlns="http://schemas.microsoft.com/office/2006/01/
    customui">
  <ribbon startFromScratch="true">
    <tabs>
      <tab id="RibbonControls" label="RibbonControls">
        <group id="MyGroup" label="Split button">
          <splitButton id="MySplitButton" size="large">
            <button id="MyButton1"
              imageMso="ModuleInsert"
```

```
                      label="Button1"
                      onAction="nyi" />
                  <menu id="MySplitMenu" itemSize="large">
                    <button id="MyButton2"
                      imageMso="OutlookGlobe"
                      label="Button2"
                      onAction="nyi" />
                    <button id="MyButton3"
                      imageMso="OutlookGears"
                      label="Button3"
                      onAction="nyi" />
                    <button id="MyButton4"
                      imageMso="Organizer"
                      label="Button4"
                      onAction="nyi" />
                  </menu>
                </splitButton>
              </group>
            </tab>
          </tabs>
        </ribbon>
      </customUI>
```

This ribbon xml example produces the SplitButton shown in Figure 29.26. This example is contained in the `RibbonControls_SplitButton` example in the `Chapter29.accdb` database.

FIGURE 29.26

SplitButtons are a very useful ribbon control.

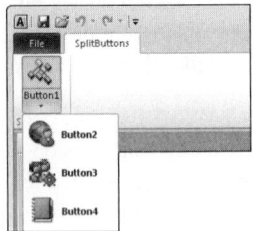

Using Visual Web Developer

Microsoft Visual Web Developer, Express Edition (VWD) is a free downloadable tool provided by Microsoft to aid your efforts to build Web sites. Visual Web Developer is used to produce entire Web sites and individual files. The XML code you see in this chapter was written and modified using Visual Web Developer's XML editor.

Begin by downloading VWD from `http://msdn.microsoft.com/vstudio/express/vwd/` and installing it on your computer. When you first launch it, VWD presents a rather intimidating opening screen (see Figure 29.27).

Visual Web Developer's opening screen

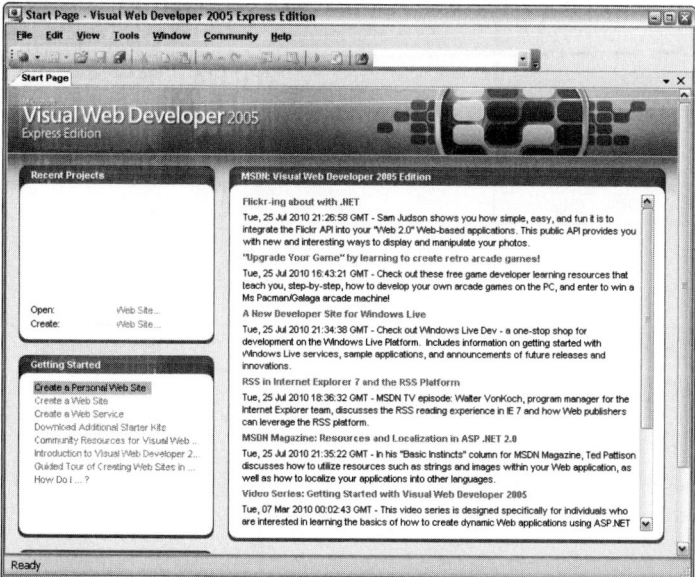

The opening screen contains links to Web sites and pages related to using VWD, as well as navigation aids to help you organize and manage Web sites created with VWD.

For this demonstration, choose File ➪ New File to open the New File dialog box (see Figure 29.28).

Notice that VWD is proficient at creating any of a number of different file types, including XML. Selecting the XML option opens the XML editor (see Figure 29.29), ready for your Access ribbon XML code.

And, that's about all there is to VWD as far as working with XML. The primary advantage of using a tool such as VWD is that it understands XML and performs basic syntax checking to help you compose valid XML. Also, VWD supports multiple open documents at one time, making it quite easy to copy XML from one window and paste into another. And, although you can't tell from the figures in this book, the XML code in Figure 29.29 is color-coded to indicate which words are keywords, which are identifiers, and which are XML tags.

Together, these features make VWD a compelling addition to any developer's toolkit.

FIGURE 29.28

The Visual Web Developer New File dialog box

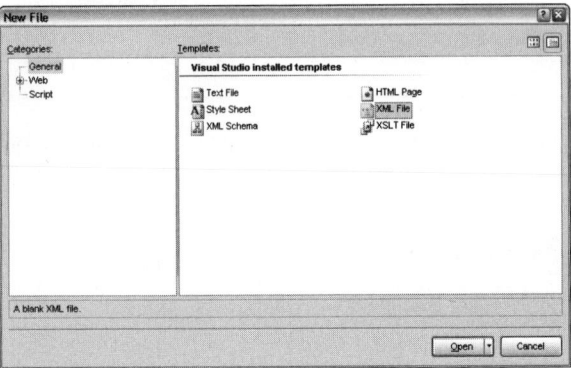

FIGURE 29.29

The XML editor in Visual Web Developer

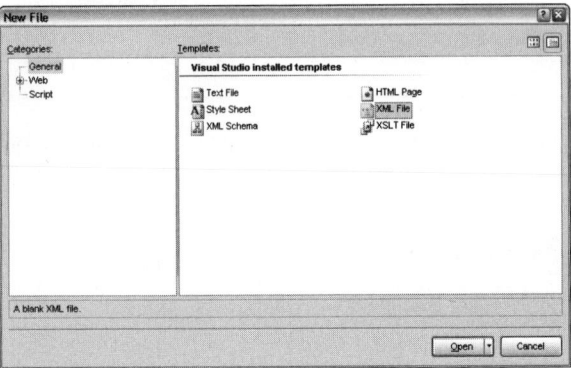

Managing Ribbons

From time to time, you may find it necessary to replace a ribbon with another one while the user works with an application. So far, all the examples you've seen are loaded as Access starts and stay on the screen as long as the user works with the application. We haven't yet covered the steps involved in closing one ribbon and opening another.

You don't really close a ribbon. Instead, you *invalidate* it, causing Access to discontinue managing the ribbon. The syntax for invalidating a ribbon is

```
Ribbon.Invalidate
```

The problem is knowing which ribbon to invalidate. Microsoft suggests you cache a reference to a ribbon each time it is opened, and then use that reference to invalidate the ribbon should the need arise. You may have noticed the onLoad attribute of the prototype ribbon in the section titled, "The Basic Ribbon XML," earlier in this chapter:

```
<customUI xmlns="http://schemas...." onLoad="onRibbonLoad">
```

(Some text has been removed from this statement for clarity's sake.)

The onLoad attribute specifies a callback that supports the ribbon's startup activities. You can use the onLoad callback to cache a reference to the ribbon.

Begin by establishing a public object variable that will point to the ribbon:

```
Public gobjRibbon As IRibbonUI
```

Next, use the object variable to store a reference to the ribbon during startup:

```
Public Sub onRibbonLoad(ribbon As IRibbonUI)
  'Cache a copy of the Ribbon:
  Set gobjRibbon = ribbon
End Sub
```

The gobjRibbon object variable remains in scope while the application is used. If you need to invalidate the ribbon, simply invoke the Invalidate method:

```
gobjRibbon.Invalidate
```

Of course, after you invalidate a ribbon, you want to replace it with another. Invalidating a ribbon does not remove it from the screen. Unless you overwrite it with another ribbon, it stays on the screen, taking up space, but not really doing anything.

Use the Access Application object's LoadCustomUI method to load a different custom ribbon:

```
Application.LoadCustomUI( _
    CustomUI_Name As String, CustomUI_XML As String)
```

The `CustomUI_Name` and `CustomUI_XML` are extracted from the `USysRibbons` table:

```
Public Function LoadRibbons(strName As String)
  Dim strXML As String
  strXML = DLookup("RibbonXML", "USysRibbons", _
    "RibbonName= '" & strName & "'")
  Call Access.Application.LoadCustomUI(strName, strXML)
End Function
```

Access should instantly replace the invalidated ribbon with the ribbon specified by the `strName` and `strXML` values passed to `LoadCustomUI`.

Completely Removing the Access Ribbon

Assume, for a moment, that there are perfectly legitimate reasons why you don't want to use the Access ribbons in your applications. Perhaps you've developed a set of effective switchboard forms, or have mimicked the old style toolbars and menus with borderless forms. Or, your applications are entirely forms-driven and don't need the flexibility provided by toolbars and ribbons.

Here's how you can completely remove ribbons from the Access interface:

1. Create a new table called `USysRibbons`, if you haven't already done so.

2. If creating the USysRibbons table for the first time, add three fields, ID (AutoNumber), RibbonName (text) and RibbonXML (Memo).

3. Create a new record with the RibbonName set to Blank.

    It doesn't really matter what you call it.

4. Then add the following XML to the RibbonXML column:

    ```
    <CustomUI xmlns="http://schemas.microsoft.com/office/2006
    /01/CustomUI">
     <Ribbon startFromScratch="true"/>
    </CustomUI>
    ```

5. Restart the database.

6. Click the File tab and select the Options button in the Backstage.

7. Click the Current Database tab and scroll to the Ribbon and Toolbars area.

8. In the Ribbon and Toolbars area, set the `Ribbon Name` to `Blank` (the same name you specified for the RibbonName column in Step 3).

9. Close and re-open the database.

This process sets up a dummy ribbon named `Blank` that contains no tabs, no groups, and no controls. In effect, you're telling Access to put up an empty ribbon, which simply removes the ribbon from the Access user interface.

Summary

This chapter documented the process of creating custom ribbons in Access. At the time this chapter was written, Access did not include a developer tool for customizing ribbons. Therefore, this chapter describes building ribbons from scratch, using an XML editor to compose the XML that defines a custom ribbon, adding the USysRibbons table to Access, and copying the XML into USysRibbons.

This chapter also reviewed several of the most common Access ribbon controls. We covered how to add controls such as labels, buttons, check boxes, and separators to Access ribbons. Access supports many other types of ribbon controls, and you are encouraged to investigate the wide variety of available controls.

Using Access Macros

Macros have been a part of Access since the beginning. As Access evolved as a development tool, the Visual Basic for Applications (VBA) programming language became the standard in automating Access database applications. Macros in previous versions of Access lacked variables and error handling, which caused many developers to abandon macros altogether. Access 2010 has these capabilities (added in Access 2007), which make macros a better alternative to VBA than in previous versions. If it's a slow day and you don't feel like writing VBA code, or if you aren't a VBA guru but you still want to customize the actions that your application executes, then building structured macros is the answer.

On the CD-ROM

This chapter uses a database named `Chapter30.accdb`. If you haven't already copied it onto your machine from the CD, you'll need to do so now. This database contains the tables, forms, reports, and macros used in this chapter.

An Introduction to Macros

A *macro* is a tool that allows you to automate tasks in Access. It's different from Word's Macro Recorder, which lets you record a series of actions and play them back later. (It's also different from Word in that Word macros are actually VBA code, whereas Access macros are something very different.) Access macros let you perform defined actions and add functionality to your forms and reports. Think of macros as a simplified, step-wise programming language. You build a macro as a list of actions to perform, and you decide when you want those actions to occur.

IN THIS CHAPTER

Getting acquainted with macros

Working with multi-action macros

Using submacros for actions that are frequently required

Making decisions with conditions

Using temporary variables

Handling errors and debugging your macros

Understanding embedded macros

Comparing macros to VBA

Cross-Reference

For more information on Word's Macro Recorder, see Chapter 22.

Building macros consists of selecting actions from a drop-down list, and then filling in the action's *arguments* (values that provide information to the action). Macros let you choose actions without writing a single line of VBA code. The macro actions are a subset of commands VBA provides. Most people find it easier to build a macro than writing VBA code. If you're not familiar with VBA, building macros is a great stepping-stone to learning some of the commands available to you while providing added value to your Access applications.

Suppose you want to build a main form with buttons that open the other forms in your application. You can add a button to the form, build a macro that opens another form in your application, and then assign this macro to the button's Click event. The macro can be a stand-alone item — which appears in the Navigation Pane — or an embedded object that is part of the event itself (see the "Embedded Macros" section).

Creating a macro

A simple way to demonstrate how to create macros is to build one that displays a message box that says Hello World! To create a new standalone macro, click the Client Macro button on the far right of the Create ribbon's Other group (shown in Figure 30.1).

FIGURE 30.1

Use the Create ribbon to build a new standalone macro.

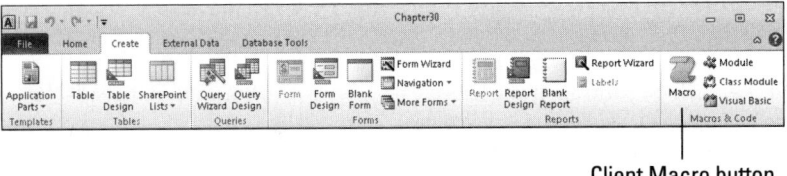

Client Macro button

Clicking the Client Macro button opens the macro design window and displays the Macro Tools ribbon (shown in Figure 30.2). Initially, the macro design window is almost featureless. The only thing in the macro window is a drop-down list of macro actions.

To the right of the macro window, you may see the Action Catalog. There are dozens of different macro actions, and knowing which action to use for a particular task can be an issue. The Action Catalog provides a tree view of all available macro actions and helps you know which action is needed to perform a particular task. I'll give you a closer look at the Action Catalog later in this chapter.

FIGURE 30.2

The macro design window displaying the Macro window and Action catalog

Macro Tools tab

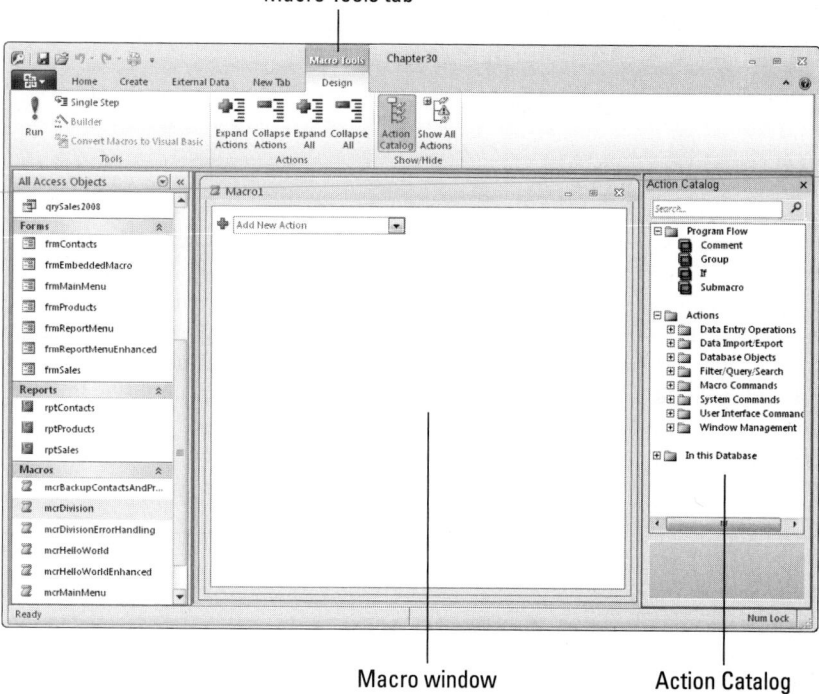

Macro window   Action Catalog

Select MessageBox from the drop-down list in the macro window. The macro window changes to display an area where you input the arguments (Message, Beep, Type, and Title) associated with the MessageBox action.

Set the arguments as follows:

- **Message:** Hello World!
- **Beep:** No
- **Type:** None
- **Title:** A Simple Macro

Your screen should look similar to Figure 30.3. The Message argument defines the text that appears in the message box and is the only argument that is required and has no default. The Beep argument determines whether a beep is heard when the message box appears. The Type argument sets which icon appears in the message box: None, Critical, Warning?, Warning!, or Information. The Title argument defines the text that appears in the message box's title bar.

FIGURE 30.3

The Hello World macro uses the `MessageBox` action to display a message.

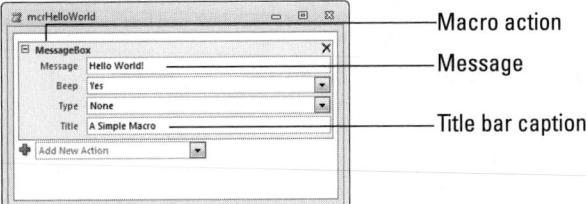

—Macro action

—Message

—Title bar caption

To run the macro, click the Run button in the Design ribbon's Tools group. (The Run button looks like a big red exclamation point at the far left of the ribbon.) When you create a new macro or change an existing macro, you'll be prompted to save the macro. In fact, you must save the macro before Access runs it for you. When prompted, click yes to save it, provide a name such as `mcrHelloWorld`, and click OK. The macro runs and displays a message box with the arguments you specified (shown in Figure 30.4).

FIGURE 30.4

Running the Hello World macro displays a message box.

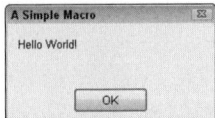

You can also run the macro from the Navigation Pane. Close the macro design window and display the Macros group in the Navigation Pane. Double-click on the `mcrHelloWorld` macro to run it. You'll see the same message box that displayed when you ran the macro from the design window.

Notice that the message box always appears right in the middle of the screen, and blocks you from working with Access until you click OK. These are built-in behaviors of the message box object, and are identical in every regard to a message box displayed from VBA code.

When you're satisfied with the Hello World macro, click on the close button in the upper-right corner of the macro window to return to the main Access window.

Assigning a macro to an event

When you're creating macros, you probably don't want end users using the Navigation Pane to run them — or worse, running them from the macro design window. Macros are intended for you to automate your application without writing VBA code. In order to make an application easy to use, assign your macros to an object's event.

The most common event to which you might assign a macro is a button's Click event. Follow these steps to create a simple form with a button that runs mcrHelloWorld:

1. Click the Create tab on the ribbon, and then click the Form Design button in the Forms group.

2. In the form's Design ribbon, deselect the Use Control Wizards option in the Controls group.

   For this example, you don't want to use a wizard to decide what this button does.

3. Click the Button control and draw a button on the form.

4. Set the button's Name property to cmdHelloWorld.

   Press F4 to open the button's Property Sheet if it isn't visible on the screen.

5. Set the button's Caption property to Hello World!.

6. Click the drop-down list in the button's On Click event property, and select mcr HelloWorld from the list (shown in Figure 30.5).

FIGURE 30.5

Set any object's event property to the macro to trigger that macro when that event occurs.

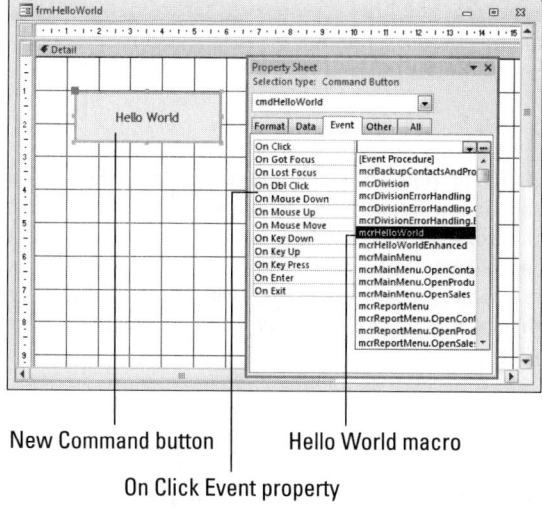

New Command button | Hello World macro

On Click Event property

That's all there is to creating and running a macro. Just select the action, set the action arguments, and assign the macro to an event property.

Tip

You aren't limited to the button's `Click` event. If you want a macro to run every time a form loads, set the `On Load` event property of the form to the macro's name. Select the Event tab on any object's Property Sheet to see the available events.

Note

Historically, there has been quite a bit of confusion about the names of events and their associated event properties. An event is always an action, such as `Click`, while its event property is `OnClick` or `On Click`. Conceptually, they're almost the same thing, but in technical terms, an event (like `Click` or `Open`) is an action supported by an Access object (like a form or command button), and an event procedure (`OnClick` or `OnOpen`) is how the event is attached or bound to the object.

Multi-Action Macros

The true power of macros comes from performing multiple actions at the click of a button. Creating a macro that runs a series of action queries is better than double-clicking each action query in the Navigation Pane — you might forget to run one or you may run them out of proper sequence.

For this next example, the `Chapter30.accdb` contains two delete queries that remove data from two different tables — `tblContacts_Backup` and `tblProducts_Backup`. `Chapter30.accdb` also includes two append queries that copy records from `tblContacts` and `tblProducts` to the backup tables. Table 30.1 shows the macro actions and action arguments for `mcrBackupContactsAndProducts` (a portion of which is shown in Figure 30.6).

Note

If all the actions don't appear in the Action drop-down list, click on the Show All Actions command in the Show/Hide group of the macro's Design ribbon. Some macro actions require a trusted database or enabling macros through your security settings. Also, some macro actions are considered unsafe because they modify data in the database or perform actions that may cause damage to the application if used incorrectly. Macro actions that are considered unsafe are indicated by a warning icon (which looks like an inverted yellow triangle containing an exclamation point) in the macro designer. By default, Access only displays trusted macro actions that run regardless of the security settings.

TABLE 30.1

mcrBackupContactsAndProducts

Action	Action Argument	Action Argument Setting
Hourglass	Hourglass On	Yes
SetWarnings	Warnings On	No

Action	Action Argument	Action Argument Setting
Echo	Echo On	No
	Status Bar Text	Step 1: Deleting Data
OpenQuery	Query Name	qryDeleteContactsBackup
	View	Datasheet
	Data Mode	Edit
OpenQuery	Query Name	qryDeleteProductsBackup
	View	Datasheet
	Data Mode	Edit
Echo	Echo On	No
	Status Bar Text	Step 2: Appending Data
OpenQuery	Query Name	qryAppendContactsBackup
	View	Datasheet
	Data Mode	Edit
OpenQuery	Query Name	qryAppendProductsBackup
	View	Datasheet
	Data Mode	Edit
Echo	Echo On	Yes
	Status Bar Text	<Leave Blank>
SetWarnings	Warnings On	Yes
Hourglass	Hourglass On	No
MessageBox	Message	Contacts and Products have been archived.
	Beep	Yes
	Type	Information
	Title	Finished Archiving

Here's a look at the actions this macro performs:

- Hourglass: This action changes the cursor to an hourglass or a pointer using the Hourglass On argument. For macros that may take a while to run, set this argument to Yes at the beginning of the macro and to No at the end of the macro. Be sure not to forget to set Hourglass off at the conclusion of the macro. Otherwise, the hourglass cursor stays on indefinitely.

- **SetWarnings**: This action turns the system messages on or off using the `Warnings On` argument. When running action queries, you'll be prompted to make sure you want to run the action query, asked if it's okay to delete these 58 records, and then asked again for the next action query. Set `Warnings On` to `No` at the beginning of the macro to turn these messages off — assuming you'll click OK or Yes in each message box. Set it back to `Yes` at the end of the macro.

  Again, don't forget to turn warnings back on at the conclusion of the macro. Once warnings are turned off, the user won't get confirmation messages from Access on important actions like record deletions until warnings are re-enabled.

- **Echo**: This action shows or hides the results of a macro while it runs using the `Echo On` argument. Set it to `No` to hide the results of the macro or `Yes` to show the results. Set the `Status Bar Text` argument to give the user an indication of what's happening. This is useful in longer-running macros to know where in the process the macro is.

  The Echo command "freezes" the screen so that the user isn't aware of activities performed by the macro. `Echo` is much like `Hourglass` and `SetWarnings` — be sure to restore the Echo status to `Yes` so that Access resumes its normal appearance. If Echo is not turned back on, the user may think the application has "locked up" because of a problem.

- **OpenQuery**: This action is the heart of the `mcrBackupContactsAndProducts` macro. OpenQuery opens a select or crosstab query or runs an action query. The `Query Name` argument contains the name of the query to open or run. The `View` argument lets you pick the view — Datasheet, Design, Print Preview, PivotTable, or PivotChart — for a select or crosstab query. The `Data Mode` argument lets you choose from Add, Edit, or Read Only to limit what users can do in a Select query. The `View` and `Data Mode` arguments are ignored for action queries.

The heart of the macro is the four `OpenQuery` actions that run the four action queries. `qryDeleteContactsBackup` and `qryDeleteProductsBackup` clear the contents of `tblContacts_Backup` and `tblProducts_Backup`, so the current data can be copied into them. `qryAppendContactsBackup` and `qryAppendProductsBackup` append data from `tblContacts` and `tblProducts` into the backup tables.

You could easily build this macro just using the four `OpenQuery` actions, but running it would be cumbersome, especially if one of the queries took a few minutes — or hours — to run. Use the `Hourglass`, `SetWarnings`, `Echo`, and `MessageBox` actions to eliminate the need for user interaction and to let the user know what's happening and when the macro has completed its activity.

FIGURE 30.6

`mcrBackupContactsAndProducts` archives data from the live tables into the backup tables.

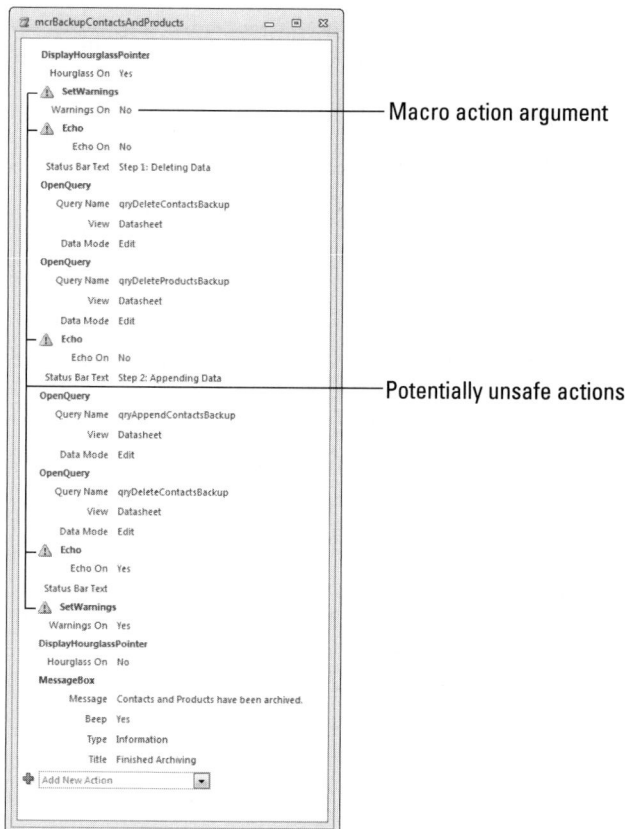

Macro action argument

Potentially unsafe actions

Submacros

When automating your application with macros, you might easily get carried away filling the Navigation Pane with a bunch of little macros for opening every form and every report. *Submacros* are the equivalent of subroutines. If you have a series of actions that are performed in a number of places, ideally you only want one copy, so that you need to make changes only in one place. Submacros give you that capability: You define the series of actions in one place as a submacro, and then invoke that submacro wherever it's needed. Only the submacro object appears in the Navigation Pane, rather than multiple smaller macros.

The macro action drop-down list contains Submacro as an entry. While working on a macro, selecting Submacro from the action list adds an area to the macro where you can input the actions associated with the submacro.

Without using submacros, you'd have to create three separate macros to automate a main menu form with three buttons that open frmContacts, frmProducts, and frmSales. Using submacros, just create a single top-level macro that contains three submacros. Each of the submacros opens one form. Only the top-level macro appears in the Navigation Pane. Table 30.2 shows the submacro names, the actions, and submacro actions for mcrMainMenu.

TABLE 30.2

mcrMainMenu

Submacro	Action	Action Argument	Action Argument Setting
OpenContacts	OpenForm	Form Name	frmContacts
		View	Form
		Filter Name	<Leave Blank>
		Where Condition	<Leave Blank>
		Data Mode	<Leave Blank>
		Window Mode	Normal
OpenProducts	OpenForm	Form Name	frmProducts
		View	Form
		Filter Name	<Leave Blank>
		Where Condition	[ProductID]=3
		Data Mode	Read Only
		Window Mode	Dialog
OpenSales	OpenForm	Form Name	frmSales
		View	Layout
		Filter Name	qrySales2008
		Where Condition	<Leave Blank>
		Data Mode	Edit
		Window Mode	Icon

Figure 30.7 illustrates the submacro concept. A new macro is under construction. The developer has selected Submacro from the Add New Action list, provided a name (OpenContacts) for the submacro, and filled in its properties.

Next, the developer selected Submacro a second time from the Add New Action list, and provided OpenProduct as its name. None of the arguments for the second submacro has been filled in.

The confusing thing about submacros is that you see two Add New Action lists in Figure 30.7. One is at the very bottom of the main macro, while the second is inside the second submacro. The submacro that is currently being developed (OpenProducts) is enclosed in a box, while the completed submacro (OpenContacts) at the top of the main macro is not contained in a box.

FIGURE 30.7

Using submacros to individually open three forms

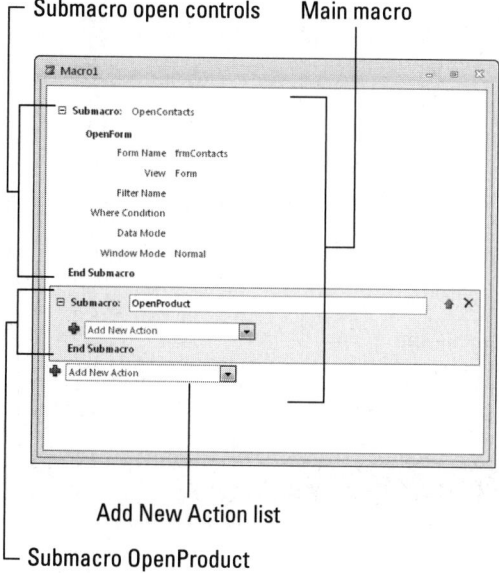

Submacro open controls · Main macro

Add New Action list

Submacro OpenProduct

Note

In Figure 30.7, notice the small minus sign to the left of Submacro in the first line of the macro. The minus sign is there to show you that the submacro is currently expanded so that you can see all the steps in the submacro. Clicking on the minus sign collapses the macro to a single line, which lets you view more of the macro and its actions in a single glance. Several figures in this chapter show macros with portions collapsed (identifiable by the small plus sign to the left), so don't be confused if it appears that portions of a macro illustrated in a figure appear to be missing.

To implement a macro using submacros, create a form (`frmMainMenu`) with three buttons — in this case, `cmdContacts`, `cmdProducts`, and `cmdSales`. Then set the `On Click` event properties of these buttons as follows (see Figure 30.8):

Button name	On Click event property
cmdContacts	mcrMainMenu.OpenContacts
cmdProducts	mcrMainMenu.OpenProducts
cmdSales	mcrMainMenu.OpenSales

FIGURE 30.8

The submacro names appear after the macro object in the event property drop-down list.

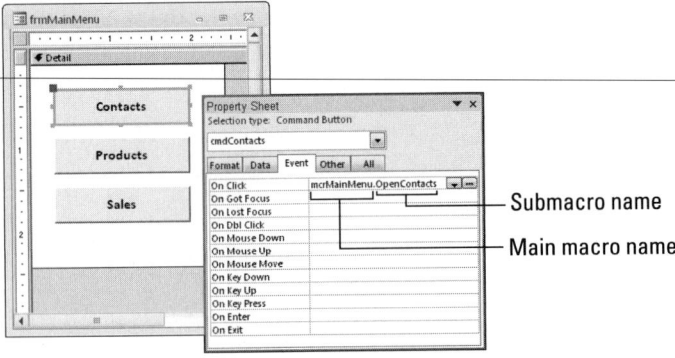

Open `frmMainMenu` in Form view and click the Contacts button; `frmContacts` opens and displays all the records. Click the Products button to display `frmProducts`, which only displays one record. Click the Sales button to display `frmSales` in a minimized state, which displays the sales made in 2012.

To see why these forms open differently, take a look at the action arguments for the `OpenForm` action:

- `Form Name`: This argument is the name of the form you want the macro to open.
- `View`: This argument lets you select which view to open the form in: Form, Design, Print Preview, Datasheet, PivotTable, PivotChart, or Layout. For this example, `frmContacts` and `frmProducts` open in Form view, while `frmSales` opens in Layout view.
- `Filter Name`: This argument lets you select a query or a filter saved as a query to restrict and/or sort the records for the form. For this example, this argument is set to `qry-Sales2012` for the `OpenSales` macro. `qrySales2012` is a query that outputs all the fields in the table and only displays sales between 1/1/2012 and 12/31/2012. This query also sorts the records by `SaleDate`.

- `Where Condition`: This argument lets you enter a SQL `Where` clause or expression that selects records for the form from its underlying table or query. For this example, this argument is set to `[ProductID]=3` for the `OpenProducts` submacro, which only shows one record when you open `frmProducts`.

- `Data Mode`: This argument lets you choose the data-entry mode for the form. Select Add to only allow users to add new records, Edit to allow adding and editing of records, or Read Only to allow only viewing of records. This setting only applies to forms opened in Form view or Datasheet view, and overrides settings of the form's `AllowEdits`, `AllowDeletions`, `AllowAdditions`, and `DataEntry` properties. To use the form's setting for these properties, leave this argument blank. For this example, `frmProducts` opens in read-only mode, while `frmContacts` and `frmSales` allow editing.

- `Window Mode`: This argument lets you choose the window mode for the form. Select Normal to use the form's properties. Select Hidden to open the form with its `Visible` property set to `No`. Select Icon to open the form minimized. Select Dialog to open the form with its `Modal` and `PopUp` properties set to `Yes` and `Border Style` property set to `Dialog`. For this example, `frmContacts` opens normally, `frmProducts` opens as a dialog box, and `frmSales` opens minimized.

Cross-Reference
For more information on form properties, see Chapter 8.

Note
When you run a macro with submacros from the Navigation Pane, only the first submacro executes.

If you're careful in planning your macros, you can create one top-level macro object for each form or report, and use submacros for each action in the form or report you want to perform. Submacros let you limit the number of macros that appear in the Navigation Pane and make managing numerous macros much easier.

Conditions

Submacros let you put multiple groups of actions in a single macro object, but a *condition* specifies certain criteria that must be met before the macro performs the action. You can enter any expression in the macro's condition column that evaluates to `True/False` or `Yes/No`. If the expression evaluates to `False`, `No`, or `0`, the action will not execute. If the expression evaluates to any other value, the action is performed. Click the Conditions button in the Show/Hide group on the macro's Design ribbon to display the Condition column in the macro window.

Opening reports using conditions

To demonstrate conditions, use `frmReportMenu` (shown in Figure 30.9), which contains three buttons and a frame control (`fraView`) with two option buttons: Print and Print Preview. Clicking Print sets the frame's value to 1; clicking Print Preview sets the frame's value to 2.

The macro that opens the reports uses submacros, as well as the Condition column. Table 30.3 shows the submacro names, conditions, actions, and action arguments for mcrReportMenu (a portion of which is shown in Figure 30.10), which opens one of three reports. The Filter Name and Where Condition arguments are blank for each OpenReport action.

frmReportMenu uses a frame to select the view in which to open the Contacts, Products, and Sales reports.

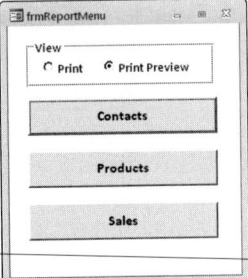

mcrReportMenu

Submacro Name	Condition	Action	Action Argument	Action Argument Setting
OpenContacts	[Forms]![frmReportMenu]![fraView]=1	OpenReport	Report Name	rptContacts
			View	Print
			Window Mode	Normal
	[Forms]![frmReportMenu]![fraView]=2	OpenReport	Report Name	rptContacts
			View	Print Preview
			Window Mode	Normal
OpenProducts	[Forms]![frmReportMenu]![fraView]=1	OpenReport	Report Name	rptProducts
			View	Print Preview
			Window Mode	Normal

Submacro Name	Condition	Action	Action Argument	Action Argument Setting
	[Forms]![frmReportMenu]![fraView]=2	OpenReport	Report Name	rptProducts
			View	Print Preview
			Window Mode	Normal
OpenSales	[Forms]![frmReportMenu]![fraView]=1	OpenReport	Report Name	rptSales
			View	Print Preview
			Window Mode	Normal
	[Forms]![frmReportMenu]![fraView]=2	OpenReport	Report Name	rptSales
			View	Print Preview
			Window Mode	Normal

FIGURE 30.10

mcrReportMenu uses an If action to open reports in Print or Print Preview view.

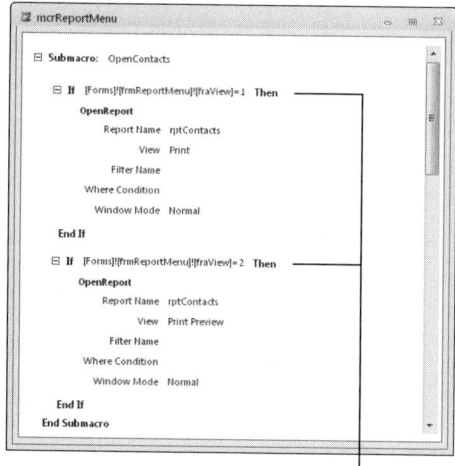

If macro action

To implement this macro, set the On Click event properties of the buttons (cmdContacts, cmdProducts, and cmdSales) on frmReportMenu as follows:

Button name	On Click event property
cmdContacts	mcrReportMenu.OpenContacts
cmdProducts	mcrReportMenu.OpenProducts
cmdSales	mcrReportMenu.OpenSales

The If macro action in mcrReportMenu has two expressions that look at fraView on frmReportMenu to determine if Print or Print Preview is selected:

- [Forms]![frmReportMenu]![fraView]=1: Print view selected
- [Forms]![frmReportMenu]![fraView]=2: Print Preview view selected

If Print is selected on frmReportMenu, the OpenReport action with the View arguments set to Print executes otherwise, if Print Preview is selected on frmReportMenu, the OpenReport action with the View arguments set to Print Preview executes. This structure is set up for each submacro in mcrReportMenu.

Multiple actions in conditions

If you want to run multiple actions based on a condition, add multiple actions within the If and End If actions. Figure 30.11 illustrates this concept.

FIGURE 30.11

Mutliple actions within If and End If actions execute as a group.

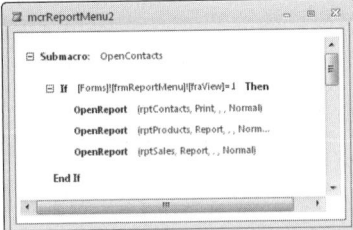

Conditions let you selectively run actions based on other values in your application. Use the If macro action to reference controls on forms or reports, and other objects and determine which actions to execute.

Temporary Variables

In previous versions of Access, you could use variables only in VBA code. Macros were limited to performing a series of actions without carrying anything forward from a previous action. Beginning with Access 2007, three new macro actions — SetTempVar, RemoveTempVar, and RemoveAllTempVars — let you create and use temporary variables in your macros. You can use these variables in conditional expressions to control which actions execute, or to pass data to and from forms or reports. You can even access these variables in VBA to communicate data to and from modules.

Enhancing a macro you've already created

A simple way to demonstrate how to use variables in macros is to enhance the Hello World example created earlier in this chapter (see "Creating a macro," earlier in this chapter). Table 30.4 shows the macro actions and action arguments for mcrHelloWorldEnhanced (shown in Figure 30.12).

The SetTempVar action has two arguments: Name and Expression. The Name argument (MyName in this example) is simply the name of the temporary variable. The Expression argument is what you want the value of the variable to be. In this example, the InputBox() function prompts the user for his name.

TABLE 30.4

mcrHelloWorldEnhanced

Action	Action Argument	Action Argument Setting
SetTempVar	Name	MyName
	Expression	InputBox("Enter your name.")
MessageBox	Message	="Hello " & [TempVars]![MyName] & "."
	Beep	Yes
	Type	Information
	Title	Using Variables
RemoveTempVar	Name	MyName

The MessageBox action's Message argument contains the following expression:

```
="Hello " & [TempVars]![MyName] & "."
```

This expression concatenates the word Hello with the temporary variable MyName, created in the SetTempVar action of the macro. When referring to a temporary variable created with the SetTempVar action, use the following syntax:

```
[TempVars]![VariableName]
```

FIGURE 30.12

mcrHelloWorldEnhanced uses the SetTempVar action to get a value from the user and display it in a message box.

Setting a temporary variable

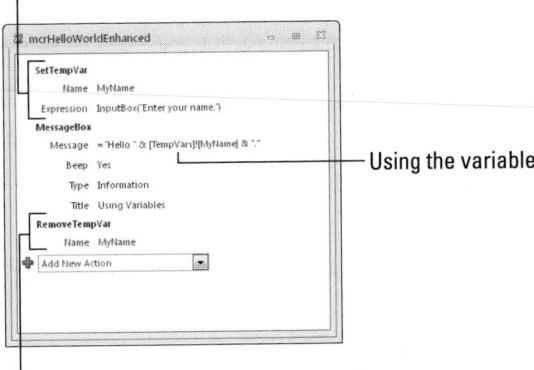

Using the variable

Removing the temporary variable

Cross-Reference

For more information on string concatenation using the ampersand (&), see Chapter 5.

The RemoveTempVar action removes a single temporary variable from memory — in this example, MyName. You can only have 255 temporary variables defined at one time. These variables stay in memory until you close the database, unless you remove them with RemoveTempVar or RemoveAllTempVars. It's a good practice to remove temporary variables when you're done using them.

Caution

Using the RemoveAllTempVars action removes all temporary variables created with the SetTempVar action. Unless you're sure you want to do this, use the RemoveTempVar action instead.

Temporary variables are global. Once you create a temporary variable, you can use it in VBA procedures, queries, macros, or object properties. For example, if you remove the RemoveTempVar action from mcrHelloWorldEnhanced, you can create a text box on a form and set its Control Source property as follows to display the name the user entered:

```
=[TempVars]![MyName]
```

Using temporary variables to simplify macros

Using temporary variables, you can sometimes eliminate steps from a macro. You can get the form or report name from another control on a form. With a temporary variable, you eliminate the need for creating a structure of multiple OpenForm or OpenReport actions. You can also use more than one variable in a macro.

For this example, use `frmReportMenuEnhanced` (shown in Figure 30.13), which contains the same `fraView` shown in Figure 30.9, but adds a combo box (`cboReport`), which contains a list of reports to run. The Run Command button executes `mcrReportMenuEnhanced`, which doesn't use submacros to decide which report to open.

FIGURE 30.13

`frmReportMenuEnhanced` uses a combo box to select which report to open.

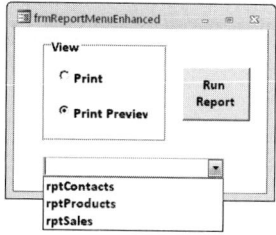

Table 30.5 shows the conditions, actions, and action arguments for `mcrReportMenuEnhanced` (shown in Figure 30.14), which opens one of three reports.

TABLE 30.5

mcrReportMenuEnhanced

Condition	Action	Action Argument	Action Argument Setting
	SetTempVar	Name	ReportName
		Expression	[Forms]![frmReportMenuEnhanced]![cboReport]
	SetTempVar	Name	ReportView
		Expression	[Forms]![frmReportMenuEnhanced]![fraView]
[TempVars]![ReportView]=1	OpenReport	Report Name View Window Mode	=[TempVars]![ReportName] Print Normal
[TempVars]![ReportView]=2	OpenReport	Report Name View Window Mode	=[TempVars]![ReportName] Print Preview Normal
	RemoveTempVar	Name	ReportName
	RemoveTempVar	Name	ReportView

FIGURE 30.14

mcrReportMenuEnhanced uses temporary variables to open the report in Print or Print Preview view.

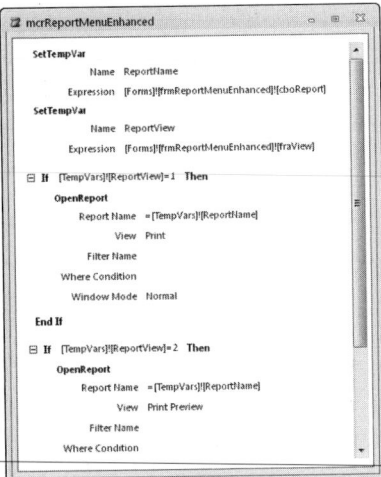

The first two SetTempVar actions in mcrReportMenuEnhanced set the values of the temporary variables — ReportName and ReportView — from cboReport and fraView on frmReportMenuEnhanced. The OpenReport actions use the temporary variables in the Condition column and for the Report Name argument. When using temporary variables as a setting for an argument, you must use an equal (=) sign in front of the expression:

```
=[TempVars]![ReportName]
```

There are still two OpenReport actions in this macro. Certain arguments — such as View — don't allow the use of temporary variables in expressions. Because one of your variables is a setting for the report's view, you still have to use the Condition column to decide which view to open the report in.

The last two RemoveTempVar lines remove the temporary variables — ReportName and ReportView — from memory. Because these variables probably won't be used later on in the application, it's important to remove them.

Using temporary variables in macros gives you far more flexibility in Access 2007 and 2010 than in previous versions. You can use these variables to store values to use later on in the macro, or anywhere in the application. Just remember that you only have 255 temporary variables to use, so don't forget to clean up after yourself by removing them from memory once you're finished using them.

Using temporary variables in VBA

You may start out using macros to automate your application, but over time, you may begin using VBA code to automate and add functionality to other areas. What do you do with the temporary variables you've already implemented with macros? Well, you don't have to abandon them; instead, you can use them directly in your VBA code.

To access a temporary variable in VBA, use the same syntax used in macros:

```
X = [TempVars]![VariableName]
```

If you don't use spaces in your variable names, you can omit the brackets:

```
X = TempVars!VariableName
```

Use the previous syntax to assign a new value to an existing temporary variable. The only difference is to put the temporary variable on the left side of the equation:

```
TempVars!VariableName = NewValue
```

Use the `TempVars` object to create and remove temporary variables in VBA. The `TempVars` object contains three methods: `Add`, `Remove`, and `RemoveAll`. To create a new temporary variable and set its value, use the `Add` method of the `TempVars` object as follows:

```
TempVars.Add "VariableName", Value
```

Use the `Remove` method of the `TempVars` object to remove a single temporary variable from memory:

```
TempVars.Remove "VariableName"
```

Tip

When adding or removing temporary variables in VBA, remember to put the variable name in quotation marks.

To remove all the temporary variables from memory, use the `RemoveAll` method of the `TempVars` object as follows:

```
TempVars.RemoveAll
```

Any VBA variables you create are available to use in your macros, and vice versa. Any variables you remove in VBA are no longer available to use in your macros, and vice versa. Using temporary variables, your macros and VBA code no longer have to be independent from each other.

Error Handling and Macro Debugging

In previous versions of Access, if an error occurred in a macro, the macro stopped execution, and your users saw an ugly dialog box (shown in Figure 30.15) that didn't really explain what was going on. If they were unfamiliar with Access, they quickly became disgruntled using the application. The lack of error handing in macros is one main reason many developers use VBA instead of macros to automate their applications.

FIGURE 30.15

Errors in macros cause the macro to cease operation.

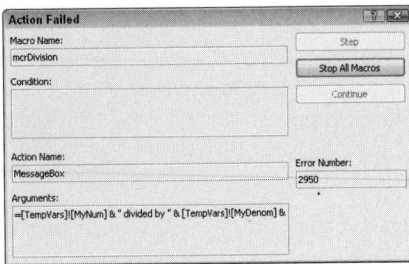

A common error that's easy to demonstrate is the divide-by-zero error. For the next example, mcrDivision (shown in Figure 30.16) contains two temporary variables — MyNum and MyDenom — set with the InputBox() function asking for a numerator and denominator. The MessageBox action shows the result — [TempVars]![MyNum]/[TempVars]![MyDenom] — in a message box and the RemoveTempVar actions remove the variables from memory.

FIGURE 30.16

mcrDivision divides the numerator by the denominator and generates an error when the denominator is zero.

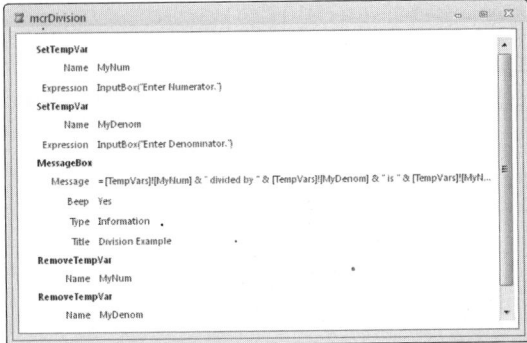

Run the macro and enter **1** for the numerator and **2** for the denominator; the macro runs and displays a message box saying 1 divided by 2 is 0.5. Run the macro again and enter **0** in the denominator; a divide-by-zero error occurs and the macro stops running. Without error handling, the two RemoveTempVar actions won't run and won't remove the temporary variables from memory.

If an error occurs in another macro — such as a string of action queries — any queries after an error occurs won't run. Adding error handling to your macros allows you to choose what to do when an error occurs while a macro's running.

The OnError action

The OnError action lets you decide what happens when an error occurs in your macro. This action has two arguments: Go to and Macro Name. The Go to argument has three settings and the Macro Name argument is used only with one of these settings, described as follows:

- **Next:** This setting records the details of the error in the MacroError object but does not stop the macro. The macro continues with the next action.

- **Macro Name:** This setting stops the current macro and runs the macro in the Macro Name argument of the OnError action.

- **Fail:** This setting stops the current macro and displays an error message. This is the same as not having error handling in the macro.

The VBA equivalents of these settings are as follows:

```
On Error Resume Next       'Next
On Error Goto LABELNAME     'Macro Name
On Error Resume 0          'Fail
```

The simplest way to add error handling to a macro is to make OnError the first action and set the Go to argument to Next. This will cause your macro to run without stopping, but you won't have any clue which actions ran and which ones didn't.

Instead, create an error-handling structure. Table 30.6 shows the macro names, actions, and action arguments for mcrDivisionErrorHandling (shown in Figure 30.17).

TABLE 30.6

mcrDivisionErrorHandling

Macro Name	Action	Action Argument	Action Argument Setting
	OnError	Go to	Macro Name
		Macro Name	ErrorHandler
	SetTempVar	Name	MyNum
		Expression	InputBox("Enter Numerator.")
	SetTempVar	Name	MyDenom
		Expression	InputBox("Enter Denominator.")
	MessageBox	Message	=[TempVars]![MyNum] & " divided by " & [TempVars]![MyDenom] & " is " & [TempVars]![MyNum]/[TempVars]![MyDenom]

(continued)

TABLE 30.6 *(continued)*

Macro Name	Action	Action Argument	Action Argument Setting
		Beep	Yes
		Type	Information
		Title	Division Example
	RunMacro	Macro Name	mcrDivisionErrorHandling.Cleanup
ErrorHandler	MessageBox	Message	="The following error occurred: " & [MacroError].[Description]
		Beep	Yes
		Type	Warning?
		Title	="Error Number: " & [MacroError].[Number]
	ClearMacroError		
	RunMacro	Macro Name	mcrDivisionErrorHandling.Cleanup
Cleanup	RemoveTempVar	Name	MyNum
	RemoveTempVar	Name	MyDenom

FIGURE 30.17

mcrDivisionErrorHandling uses the OnError action to display a user-friendly error message and remove the temporary variables.

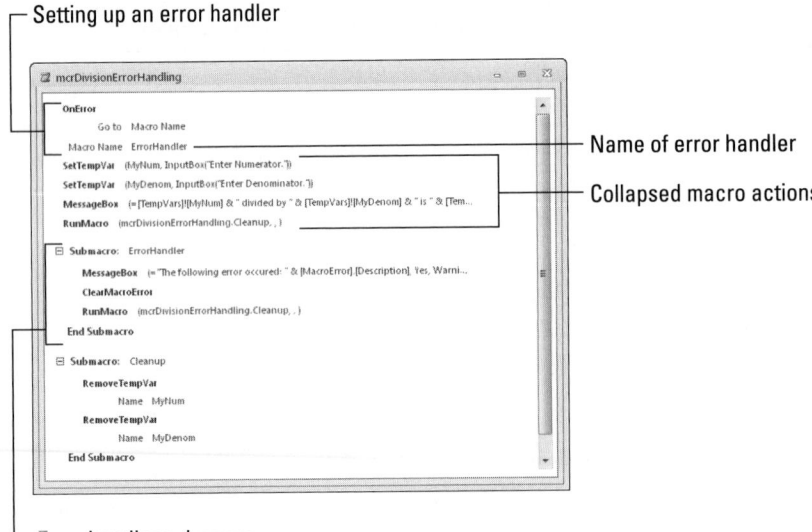

Setting up an error handler

Name of error handler

Collapsed macro actions

Error handler submacro

The first `OnError` action in the macro lets Access know to move to the submacro `ErrorHandler` when an error occurs. If an error occurs (by entering 0 as the denominator), the macro stops and moves to the `ErrorHandler` submacro. The `ErrorHandler` submacro displays a message box — using the `MacroError` object (described in the next section) to display the error's description in the `Message` and the error's number in the `Title`, using the following expressions:

```
[MacroError].[Description]
[MacroError].[Number]
```

After the error handler's message box, the `ClearMacroError` action clears the `MacroError` object. The `RunMacro` action moves execution to the macro's `Cleanup` submacro. The `Cleanup` section of the macro removes the temporary variables.

Note

There's no Resume functionality in macro error handling. If you want to run additional code after the error-handling actions, you must use the `RunMacro` action in the error-handling submacro to run another macro, or place the actions in the error handler.

The `RunMacro` action also appears after the `MessageBox` action in the main section of the macro. Because you're using submacros, the macro stops after it reaches the `ErrorHandler` submacro. In order to force the cleanup of the temporary variables, use the `RunMacro` action to run the `Cleanup` submacro. Otherwise, you'd have to put the `RemoveTempVar` actions in the main section and in the `ErrorHandler` section of the macro.

The MacroError object

The `MacroError` object contains information about the last macro error that occurred. It retains this information until a new error occurs or you clear it with the `ClearMacroError` action. This object contains a number of read-only properties you can access from the macro itself or from VBA. These properties are as follows:

- `ActionName`: This is the name of the macro action that was running when the error occurred.

- `Arguments`: The arguments for the macro action that was running when the error occurred.

- `Condition`: This property contains the condition for the macro action that was running when the error occurred.

- `Description`: The text representing the current error message — for example, Divide by Zero or Type Mismatch.

- `MacroName`: Contains the name of the macro that was running when the error occurred.

- `Number`: This property contains the current error number — for example, 11 or 13.

Use the `MacroError` object as a debugging tool or to display messages to the user, who can then relay that information to you. You can even write these properties to a table to track the errors that occur in your macros. Use this object within an `If` action to customize what actions execute based on the error that occurs. When used in combination with the `OnError` action, it gives you additional functionality by handling errors, displaying useful messages, and providing information to you and the user.

Debugging macros

Trying to figure out what's going on in a macro can be difficult. The `OnError` action and `MacroError` object make debugging Access macros easier than in previous versions. There are other tools and techniques that are useful when debugging macros. Use the following list as a guideline for troubleshooting macros.

- **Single Step:** Click the Single Step button in the macro design ribbon's Tools group to turn on Single Step mode. The Macro Single Step dialog box (shown in Figure 30.18) lets you see the macro name, condition, action name, arguments, and error number of a macro action before the action executes. From this dialog box, click Step to execute the action, Stop All Macros to stop the macro from running, or Continue to finish the macro with Single Step mode turned off.

FIGURE 30.18

Use the Macro Single Step dialog box to step through a macro.

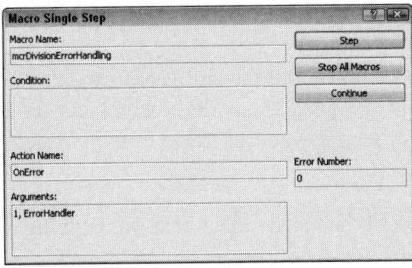

- `MessageBox`: Use the `MessageBox` macro action to display values of variables, error messages, control settings, or whatever else you want to see while the macro is running. To see the value of a combo box on a form, set the `Message` argument as follows:

  `[Forms]![frmReportMenuEnhanced]![cboReport]`

- `StopMacro`: Use the `StopMacro` action to stop the macro from executing. Insert this action at any point in the macro to stop it at that point. Use this in conjunction with the debug window to check values.

- **Debug window:** Use the debug window to look at any values, temporary variables, or properties of the `MacroError` object after you stop the macro. Press Ctrl+G to display the code window after you stop the macro. Just type a question mark (?) and the variable or expression you want to check the value of, and press Enter. Here are some examples of expressions to display in the Debug window:

```
? TempVars!MyNum
? MacroError!Description
? [Forms]![frmReportMenuEnhanced]![cboReport]
```

These techniques are similar to ones you'd use when debugging VBA code. You can step through sections of code, pause the code and look at values in the debug window, and display message boxes to display variables or errors that occur. Granted, you don't have all the tools available — such as watching variables and `Debug.Print` — but at least you have the new `MacroError` object to provide the information you need to figure out what's going wrong.

Cross-Reference

For more information on error handling, see Chapter 23. Debugging VBA code is covered in Chapter 14.

Embedded Macros

An *embedded macro* is stored in an event property and is part of the object to which it belongs. When you modify an embedded macro, you don't have to worry about other controls that might use the macro because each embedded macro is independent. Embedded macros aren't visible in the Navigation Pane and are only accessible from the object's Property Sheet.

As an example, let's say you want to add a command button to a form that opens a report. You could use a global macro (one that's in the Navigation Pane) to open the report, or you could add an embedded macro to the command button.

Embedded macros are trusted. They run even if your security settings prevent the running of code. Using embedded macros allows you to distribute your application as a trusted application because embedded macros are automatically prevented from performing unsafe operations.

One big change in Access 2007 and 2010 is that, when you use a wizard to create a button, it no longer creates an event procedure — it creates an embedded macro. So if you're used to running a wizard and using the wizard's VBA code for another purpose, you'll have to abandon that technique. Using embedded macros instead of code accomplishes two things:

- It allows you to quickly create a distributable application.

- It allows users not familiar with VBA code to customize buttons created with wizards.

Follow these steps to create an embedded macro that opens `frmContacts`:

1. Click the Create tab on the ribbon, and then click the Form Design button in the Forms group.

2. In the form's Design ribbon, deselect the Use Control Wizards option in the Controls group. For this example, you don't want to use a wizard to decide what this button does.

3. Click the Button control and draw a new button on the form.

4. Set the button's `Name` property to `cmdContacts` and the `Caption` property to `Contacts`.

5. Display the Property Sheet for `cmdContacts`, select the Event tab, and then click the `On Click` event property.

6. Click the builder button — the button with the ellipsis (...).

   The Choose Builder dialog box (shown in Figure 30.19) appears.

FIGURE 30.19

Use the builder button in the event property to display the Choose Builder dialog box to create an embedded macro.

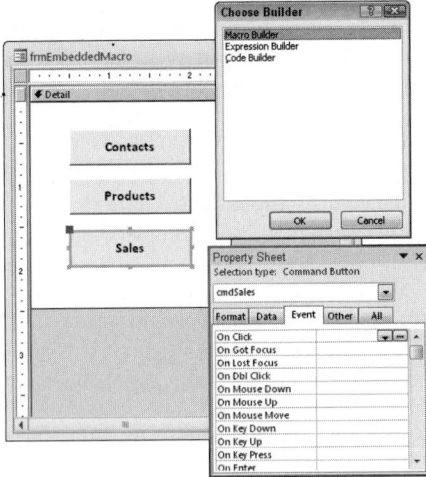

7. Choose Macro Builder and click OK to display the macro window (shown in Figure 30.20).

8. Add the `OpenForm` action to the macro, and then set the `Form Name` argument to `frmContacts`.

9. Close the embedded macro, and click OK when you're prompted to save the changes and update the property.

   The `On Click` event property of `cmdContacts` now displays `[Embedded Macro]`.

FIGURE 30.20

An embedded macro doesn't have a name. The title bar displays the control and the event in which the macro is embedded.

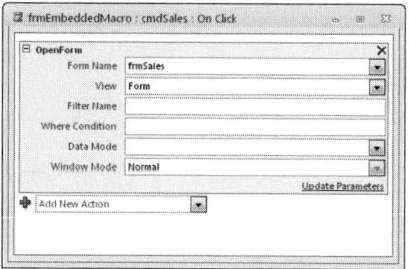

Using an embedded macro has some advantages over using an event procedure containing VBA code. If you copy the button and paste it on another form, the embedded macro goes with it. You don't have to copy the code and paste it as a separate operation. Similarly, if you cut and paste the button on the same form (for example, moving it onto a Tab control), you don't have to reattach the code to the button.

Embedded macros offer another improvement to macros in previous versions. If you automate your application with embedded macros, and import a form or report into another database, you don't have to worry about importing the associated macros into the database as well. By using embedded macros, all the automation moves with the form or report. This makes maintaining and building applications easier.

Macros versus VBA Statements

In Access, macros often offer an ideal way to take care of many details, such as running reports and forms. You can develop applications and assign actions faster using a macro because the arguments for the macro actions are displayed with the macro (in the bottom portion of the macro window). You don't have to remember complex or difficult syntax.

Several actions you can accomplish with VBA statements are better suited for macros. The following actions tend to be more efficient when they're run from macros:

- Using macros against an entire set of records with action queries — for example, to manipulate multiple records in a table or across tables (such as updating field values or deleting records)
- Opening and closing forms
- Running reports

Note

The VBA language supplies a `DoCmd` object that accomplishes many macro actions. Under the surface, `DoCmd` runs a macro task to accomplish the same result provided by a macro action. You could, for example, specify `DoCmd.Close` to run the `Close` macro action and close the currently active form.

Choosing between macros and VBA

Although macros sometimes prove to be the solution of choice, VBA is the tool of choice at other times. You'll probably want to use VBA rather than macros when you want to

- **Create and use your own functions.** In addition to using the built-in functions in Access, you can create and work with your own functions by using VBA code.

- **Use Automation to communicate with other Windows applications or to run system-level actions.** You can write code to see whether a file exists before you take some action, or you can communicate with another Windows application (such as a spreadsheet), passing data back and forth.

- **Use existing functions in external Windows Dynamic Link Libraries (DLLs).** Macros don't enable you to call functions in other Windows DLLs.

- **Work with records one at a time.** If you need to step through records or move values from a record to variables for manipulation, code is the answer.

- **Create or manipulate objects.** In most cases, you'll find that creating and modifying an object is easiest in that object's Design view. In some situations, however, you may want to manipulate the definition of an object in code. With a few VBA statements, you can manipulate virtually any and all objects in a database, including the database itself.

- **Display a progress meter on the status bar.** If you need to display a progress meter to communicate progress to the user, VBA code is the answer.

- **Macros are required by Access Web databases.** Access 2010 supports a new type of database that is used only in SharePoint 2010. A "Web-enabled" database requires the use of macros instead of VBA for all of its forms and reports.

Converting existing macros to VBA

After you become comfortable with writing VBA code, you may want to rewrite some of your application macros as VBA procedures. As you begin this process, you quickly realize how mentally challenging the effort can be as you review every macro in your various macro libraries. You can't merely cut the macro from the macro window and paste it into a module window. For each condition, action, and action argument for a macro, you must analyze the task it accomplishes and then write the equivalent statements of VBA code in your procedure.

Fortunately, Access provides a feature that converts macros to VBA code automatically. One of the options in the Save As dialog box is Save As Module. You can use this option when a macro file is highlighted in the Macros object window of the Database window. This option enables you to convert an entire macro group to a module in seconds.

To try the conversion process, convert the `mcrHelloWorldEnhanced` macro used earlier in this chapter. Follow these steps to run the conversion process:

1. Click the Macros group in the Navigation Pane.

2. Select `mcrHelloWorldEnhanced`.

3. Click the Microsoft Office button, and then click Save As.

   The Save As dialog box (shown in Figure 30.21) appears.

FIGURE 30.21

Saving a macro as a module

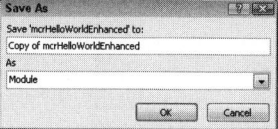

Access assigns a default name for the new module as "Copy of" followed by the macro name.

4. Enter a name for the new module and select Module for the As option.

5. Click OK to display the Convert Macro dialog box (shown in Figure 30.22).

FIGURE 30.22

The Convert Macro dialog box

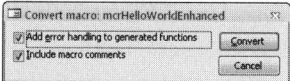

6. Select the options that include error handling and macro comments, and click Convert.

   Access briefly displays each new procedure as it's converted. When the conversion process completes, the `Conversion Finished!` message box appears.

7. Click OK to display the new module in the VBA Editor (shown in Figure 30.23).

   Access names the new module `Converted Macro- mcrHelloWorldEnhanced`.

FIGURE 30.23

The newly converted module

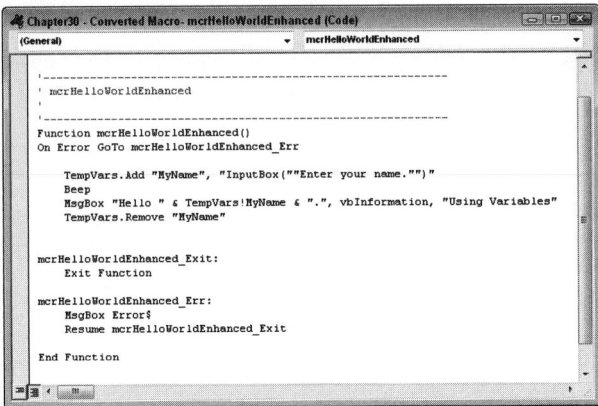

```
Chapter30 - Converted Macro- mcrHelloWorldEnhanced (Code)
(General)                                    mcrHelloWorldEnhanced

' --------------------------------------------------------------
' mcrHelloWorldEnhanced
'
' --------------------------------------------------------------
Function mcrHelloWorldEnhanced()
On Error GoTo mcrHelloWorldEnhanced_Err

    TempVars.Add "MyName", "InputBox(""Enter your name."")"
    Beep
    MsgBox "Hello " & TempVars!MyName & ".", vbInformation, "Using Variables"
    TempVars.Remove "MyName"


mcrHelloWorldEnhanced_Exit:
    Exit Function

mcrHelloWorldEnhanced_Err:
    MsgBox Error$
    Resume mcrHelloWorldEnhanced_Exit

End Function
```

When you open the VBA editor for the new module, you can view the procedure created from the macro. Figure 30.23 shows the mcrHelloWorldEnhanced function that Access created from the mcrHelloWorldEnhanced macro.

At the top of the function, Access inserts four comment lines for the name of the function. The Function statement follows the comment lines. Access names the function, using the macro library's name (mcrHelloWorldEnhanced).

When you specify that you want Access to include error processing for the conversion, Access automatically inserts the On Error statement as the first command in the procedure. The On Error statement tells Access to branch to other statements that display an appropriate message and then exit the function.

The statement beginning with DoCmd is the actual code that Access created from the macro. The DoCmd methods run Access actions from VBA. An action performs important tasks, such as closing windows, opening forms, and setting the value of controls.

If you're new to VBA and want to learn code, a good starting point is converting your macros to modules. Just save your macros and modules, and then look at the VBA code to become familiar with the syntax. The new macro features in Access 2007 and 2010 makes it harder to decide whether to use macros or VBA.

Summary

In this chapter, you learned how to create a variety of different macros, from simple macros with one action to complex macros containing many different actions that run only under certain conditions. Using macro names, you saw how one macro object can hold many macros. You also compared macros to VBA and converted a macro to a VBA module.

The addition of temporary variables allows you to store values for use anywhere in your application, including VBA code. The new error-handling actions let you gracefully stop a macro when an error occurs. These new features also make troubleshooting macros easier. You also created a trusted embedded macro, which is stored in the control and moves around with the control.

Distributing Access Applications

You're lucky if you have the luxury of developing only single-user, in-house applications and you never have to worry about distributing an application within a company or across the country. Most developers have to prepare an Access application for distribution sooner or later. You don't even have to develop commercial software to deal with distribution — when you develop an application to be run on a dozen workstations in one organization, you need to distribute your application in some form or other.

This chapter covers the issues relevant to distributing Access applications. However, because some of these items — such as error handling and splitting tables — are covered in detail elsewhere in this book, this chapter focuses primarily on setting database options when preparing your application for distribution.

You need to be concerned with many issues when preparing an Access application for distribution. Distributing your application properly not only makes installing and using the application easier for the end user, but also makes updating and maintaining the application easier for you, the application's developer. In addition, the support required for an application is greatly decreased by properly preparing and packaging the database and associated files for distribution.

IN THIS CHAPTER

Setting options for your current database

Making sure your application works before you distribute it

Putting the finishing touches on your application

Hardening your application

On the CD-ROM
This chapter uses the `Chapter31.accdb database`. If you haven't already copied it onto your machine from the CD, you'll need to do so now.

Tip
Most of the techniques described in this chapter have been applied to the sample database. In order to open it so that you can see the options, open Access first, then hold down the Shift key while you click on the name of the database to open. Don't release the Shift key until the database has opened.

Defining the Current Database Options

Access databases have a number of options that simplify the distribution process. You can access these database options by clicking the Microsoft Office Button, selecting Access Options, and selecting the Current Database tab (shown in Figure 31.1). You can still use an Autoexec macro to execute initialization code, but the Current Database options enable you to set up certain aspects of your application, thus reducing the amount of startup code that you have to write. It's very important to correctly structure these options before you distribute an Access application.

FIGURE 31.1

The Current Database options enable you to take control of your application from the moment a user starts it.

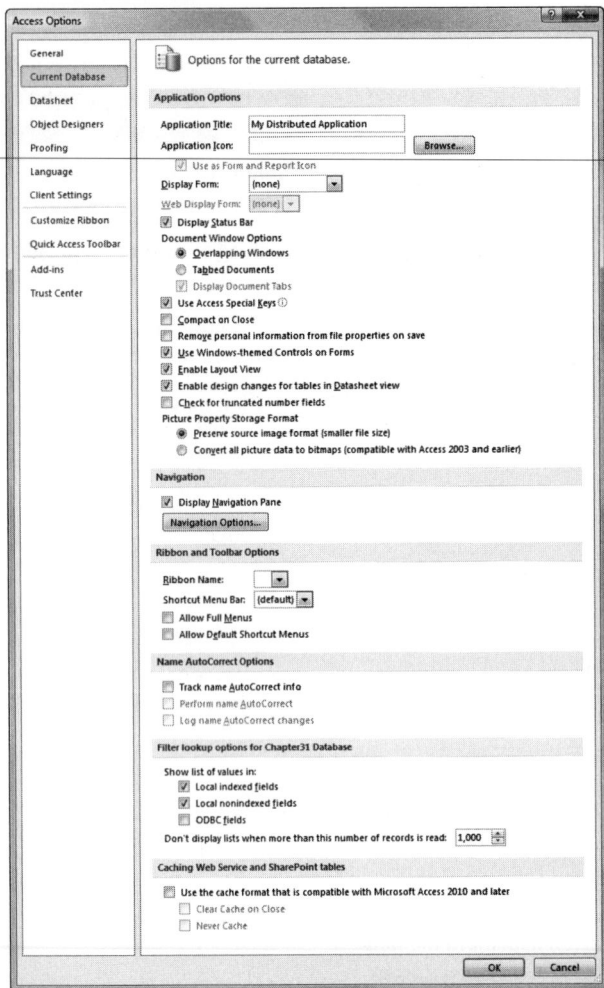

New Feature
The Current Database options replace the Startup dialog box from previous versions of Access.

Tip
Setting the Current Database options saves you many lines of code that you would ordinarily need in order to perform the same functions and enables you to control your application's interface from the moment the user starts it. Always verify the Current Database options before distributing your application.

Application options

The settings in the Application Options section let you define parameters for your database as an application.

Application Title

The text that you provide in the Application Title field displays on the main Access window's title bar. The Application Title is also the text that's displayed in the Windows task bar when the application is open and running.

Tip
You should always specify an application title for your distributed applications. If you don't, the database name and "Access" appear on the title bar of your application.

Application Icon

The icon that you specify in the Application Icon field displays on the title bar of your application and in the task switcher (Alt+Tab) of Windows. If you check the Use as Form and Report Icon box, this icon is also displayed when a form or report is minimized.

If you don't specify your own icon, Access just displays the default Access icon, so you might want to provide an application-specific icon for your application. Using special program icons helps your users distinguish between different Access applications.

Tip
You can create small bitmaps in Windows Paint and use a conversion tool to convert a `.bmp` file to the `.ico` file format. You can also create icons using other graphics programs or search for application icons online.

Display Form

The form you select in the Display Form drop-down list automatically opens when Access starts the application. When the form loads, the `Form Load` event of the display form fires (if it contains any code), reducing the need to use an Autoexec macro.

Tip
Consider using a splash screen (see the "A splash screen" section, later in this chapter) as your startup display form.

Display Status Bar

Deselect the Display Status Bar check box to remove the status bar from the bottom of the Access screen. (This option is selected by default.)

Tip

The status bar is an informative and easy-to-use tool because it automatically displays key states (such as Caps Lock and Scroll Lock), as well as the Status Bar Text property for the active control. Instead of hiding the status bar, you should make full use of it and disable it only it if you have a very good reason to do so.

Document Window Options

Under Document Window Options, you can choose how the forms and reports look in your distributed application. Your options are

- **Overlapping Windows:** Overlapping Windows retains the look of previous versions of Access, letting you look at multiple forms at once.

- **Tabbed Documents:** Tabbed Documents uses a single-document interface (shown in Figure 31.2) similar to recent versions of Internet Explorer.

FIGURE 31.2

A database with the Tabbed Documents option selected. The tabs let you select which Access object to work with.

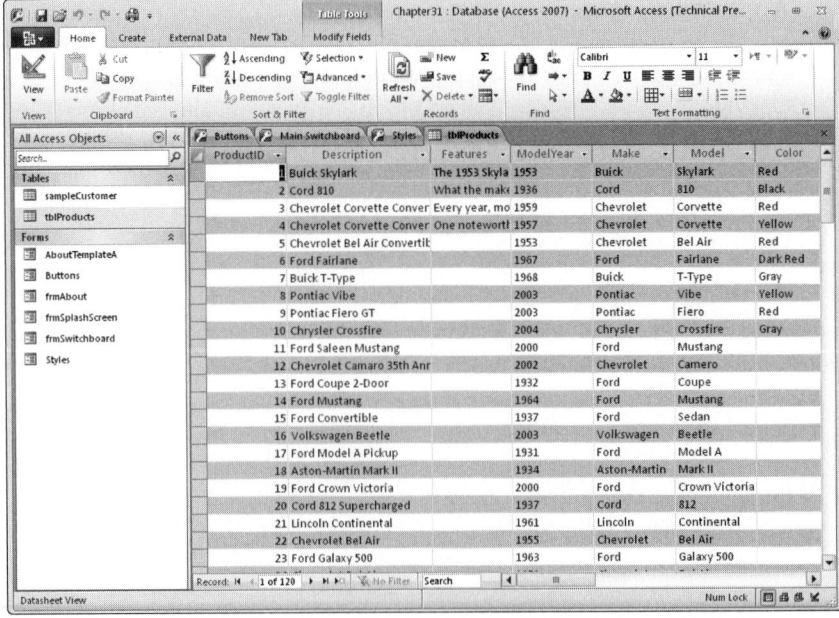

You must close and reopen the current database for the changes to take effect.

The Display Document Tabs check box is only available when you select Tabbed Documents; it turns on or off the tabs that appear at the top of any open database object. This setting turns off only the tabs and does not close tabbed objects themselves.

Use Access Special Keys

If you select this option, users of your application can use accelerator keys that are specific to the Access environment in order to circumvent some security measures, such as unhiding the Navigation Pane. If you deselect this option, the following keys are disabled:

- **F11:** Use this key to show the Navigation Pane (if hidden).
- **Ctrl+G:** Use this key to open the Immediate window in the Visual Basic Editor.
- **Ctrl+Break:** In Access projects, use this key to interrupt Access while retrieving records from the server database.
- **Alt+F11:** Use this key to start the VBA Editor.

Tip
It's a good idea to deselect the Access Special Keys check box when distributing the application, in order to prevent users from circumventing the options you select. Otherwise, users might inadvertently reveal the Navigation Pane or VBA code edition, leading to confusion and other problems.

Tip
When using the Access Special Keys property to disable Access's default accelerator keys, you can still use an AutoKeys macro to set your application's shortcut keys.

Compact on Close

Checking the Compact on Close check box tells Access to automatically compact and repair your database when you close it. Many Access developers use Compact on Close as a way to perform this vital maintenance process each time a user works with a database. You must close and reopen the current database in order for this change to take effect.

Cross-Reference
For more information on the benefits of compacting and repairing a database, see Chapter 24.

Caution
Keep in mind that compacting a large database might take a considerable amount of time. Plus, Compact on Close only affects the front-end database. Unless your application uses the front end for temporary tables or other operations that cause the front end to bloat, the Compact and Repair option may be of minimal benefit to your users.

Remove Personal Information from File Properties on Save

Checking this box automatically removes the personal information from the file properties when you save the file. You must close and reopen the current database for this change to take effect.

Use Windows-Themed Controls on Forms

Checking this box uses your system's Windows theme on the form/report controls. This setting only applies when you use a Windows theme other than the standard theme.

Enable Layout View

The Enable Layout View check box shows or hides the Layout View button on the Access status bar and in the shortcut menus that appear when you right-click on an object tab.

Note

Remember that you can disable the Layout view for individual objects, so even when you enable this option, Layout view may not be available for certain forms and reports.

Enable Design Changes for Tables in Datasheet View

The Enable Design Changes for Tables in Datasheet View check box allows you to make changes to your tables in Datasheet view, as opposed to having to be in Design view. Since you won't want your users to make any table changes at all, this should be unchecked.

Check for Truncated Number Fields

Checking this option makes numbers appear as "#####" when the column is too narrow to display the entire value. (This behavior has been in Excel for a long time.) Unchecking this box truncates values that are too wide to be displayed in the datasheet, which means that users see only a part of the column's value when the column is too narrow and might misinterpret the column's contents.

Picture Property Storage Format

Under Picture Property Storage Format, you can choose how graphic files are stored in the database. Your options are

- **Preserve Source Image Format (Smaller File Size):** Choose this option if you want to store the image in the original format, which also reduces the database size.
- **Convert All Picture Data to Bitmaps (Compatible with Access 2003 and Earlier):** Choose this option if you want to store all images as bitmaps, which increases the database size but keeps it compatible with previous versions of Access (Access 2003 and earlier).

Earlier versions of Access always stored images twice within the database. The first copy was the original format of the image file (such as .jpg), while the second copy was a bitmap used only to display the image on Access forms and reports. Because images were stored twice, early Access databases were prone to severe bloating when a lot of image data was stored in the .mdb.

You have the option to Preserve Source Image Format to conserve disk space by reducing the database file's size. (This option is only available in the .accdb file format.) When using this option,

Access only stores one copy of an image (in its original format) and dynamically generates a bitmap when the image is displayed on a form or report.

Navigation options

The settings in the Navigation section let you define parameters when navigating your database as an application.

The Display Navigation Pane check box

With most distributed applications, you might never want your users to have direct access to any of your tables, queries, forms, or other database objects. It's far too tempting for a user to try to "improve" a form or report, or to make some minor modification to a table or query. Rarely are users really qualified to make such changes to an Access database. Deselecting the Display Navigation Pane option hides the Navigation Pane from the user at startup.

Note

Unless you also deselect the Use Access Special Keys option (described earlier in this chapter), users can press F11 to unhide the Navigation Pane.

You must close and reopen the current database for this change to take effect.

The Navigation Options button

One nice addition to recent versions of Access is the ability to select which database options are exposed to users when the Navigation Pane is visible at startup. Clicking the Navigation Options button opens the Navigation Options dialog box (shown in Figure 31.3), which you use to change the categories and groups that appear in the Navigation Pane.

FIGURE 31.3

The Navigation Options dialog box

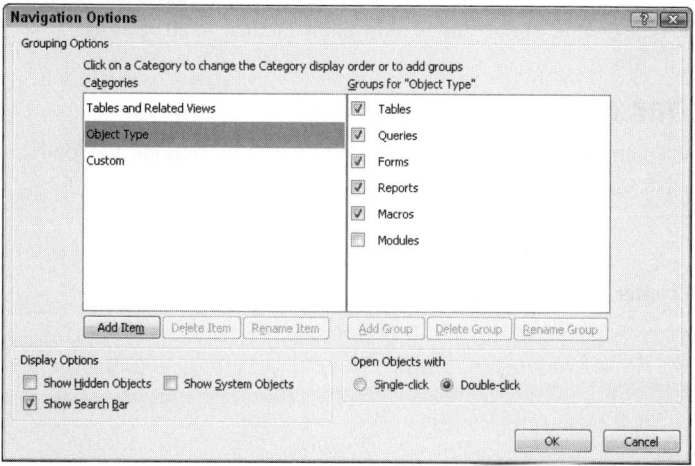

In the Grouping Options section, click on a category on the left side of the dialog box to change the category display order or to add groups to the right side of the dialog box. Click on the Object Type category to disable viewing of certain Access objects (tables, queries, forms, reports, macros, or modules).

In the Display Options section, you can select the Show Hidden Objects, Show System Objects, and Show Search Bar check boxes.

Tip

It's usually a good idea to hide the hidden and system objects, which you normally don't want to modify. (They're hidden for a reason!)

The Search Bar (shown in Figure 31.4), on the other hand, is useful in the Navigation Pane when you have a lot of objects and want to narrow the list to avoid excessive scrolling, so you should select the Show Search Bar check box. For example, if you wanted to see the forms that had the word Customer in them, you'd type Customer in the Search Bar to limit the tables shown in the Navigation Pane.

FIGURE 31.4

The Search Bar appears at the top of the Navigation Pane.

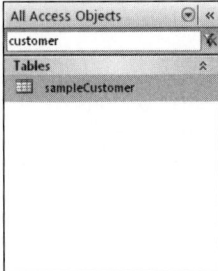

In the Open Objects With section, select Single-Click or Double-Click to choose how you open a database object. Double-Click is the default option and is most likely familiar to all your users.

Ribbon and toolbar options

The settings in the Ribbon and Toolbar Options section let you define custom ribbons and toolbars when using your database as an application.

Cross-Reference

Custom ribbon creation is explained in Chapter 29.

Ribbon Name

The Ribbon Name option lets you specify a customized (usually trimmed-down) version of the Access ribbon. If you don't supply a ribbon name, Access uses its built-in ribbon, which might be inappropriate for your application. The default ribbon contains many controls for modifying database objects, which might lead to problems with your users.

You must close and reopen the current database for this change to take effect.

Shortcut Menu Bar

Setting the Shortcut Menu Bar changes the default menu for shortcut menus (right-click menus) to a menu bar that you specify. Using custom shortcut menus that have functionality specific to your application is always preferable.

You must close and reopen the current database for this change to take effect.

Allow Full Menus

Checking the Allow Full Menus box determines whether Access displays all the commands in its menus or just the frequently used commands. If you supply custom menus for all your forms and reports and set the Menu Bar property to a custom menu bar, this setting has no effect.

You must close and reopen the current database for this change to take effect.

Allow Default Shortcut Menus

The Allow Default Shortcut Menus setting determines whether Access displays its own default shortcut menus when a user right-clicks an object in the Navigation Pane or a control on a form or report.

You must close and reopen the current database for this change to take effect.

Name AutoCorrect Options

Several chapters in this book mention the problems associated with changing the names of fundamental database objects such as tables and fields within tables. For example, if you change the name of a table, everywhere you refer to that table (a query, a control's `ControlSource` property, VBA code, a macro, and so on) becomes invalid, causing the application to malfunction.

Microsoft added the Name AutoCorrect feature to Access 2000 as a way of mitigating the problems that inevitably occur when database objects are renamed. Unfortunately, this feature has never worked quite as well as Microsoft had hoped. Primarily, Name AutoCorrect is a major drag on performance. Because Access must constantly monitor activity while Access is used, a database with this option selected runs noticeably slower than it does when the option is turned off. Plus, there are far too many places where an object's name may appear for an AutoCorrect feature to effectively capture every instance when the object is renamed. This is especially true of object names appearing in VBA code; many applications contain hundreds of thousands of lines of VBA code, making it virtually impossible to find and update every object reference.

Tip

The Name AutoCorrect option is turned on by default in Access applications. Unless you find this option useful in your projects, you should consider turning it off, as it has been in the `Chapter31.accdb` example accompanying this chapter.

Testing the Application before Distribution

After you finish adding features and have everything in place within your application, you should take some time to thoroughly test the application. Testing may seem obvious, but this step is overlooked by many developers, evidenced by the amount of buggy software appearing on the shelves of your local computer store. If you don't believe this to be true, check out the software support forums on the Internet — almost every major commercial software application has some patch available or known bugs that need to be addressed.

Distributing an application that is 100 percent bug-free is almost impossible. The nature of the software development beast is that, if you write a program, someone can — and will — find an unanticipated way to break it. Certain individuals seem to have a black cloud above their heads and can break an application (in other words, hit a critical bug) within minutes of using it. If you know of such people, hire them! They can be great assets when you're testing an application.

While working through the debugging process of an application, categorize your bugs into one of three categories:

- **Category 1: Catastrophic bugs:** These bugs are absolutely unacceptable — for example, numbers in an accounting application that don't add up the way they should or a routine that consistently causes the application to terminate unexpectedly. If you ship an application with known Category 1 bugs, prepare for a lynching party organized by your users!

- **Category 2: Major bugs that have a workaround:** Category 2 bugs are fairly major bugs, but they don't stop users from performing their tasks because some workaround exists in the application. For example, a button that doesn't call a procedure correctly is a bug. If the button is the only way to run the procedure, this bug is a Category 1 bug. But if a corresponding ribbon command calls the procedure correctly, the bug is a Category 2 bug. Shipping an application with a Category 2 bug is sometimes necessary. Although shipping a bug is officially a no-no, deadlines sometimes dictate that exceptions need to be made. Category 2 bugs will annoy users, but they shouldn't send them into fits.

Tip

If you ship an application with known Category 2 bugs, document them! Some developers have a don't-say-anything-and-act-surprised attitude regarding Category 2 bugs. This attitude can frustrate users and waste their time by forcing them to discover not only the problem, but also the solution. For example, if you were to ship an application with the Category 2 bug just described, you should include a statement in your application's README file that reads something like this: "The button on the XYZ form does not correctly call feature such-and-such. Please use the corresponding command such-and-such found on the ribbon. A patch will be made available as soon as possible."

- **Category 3: Small bugs and minor nits:** Category 3 bugs are small issues that don't affect the operation of your application. They may be caption or label misspellings or incorrect text-box colors. Category 3 bugs should be fixed soon, but they shouldn't take precedence over Category 1 bugs. They should take precedence over Category 2 bugs only when they're so extreme that the application looks completely unacceptable or when they cause enough trouble for users that a fix is quickly needed.

Categorizing bugs, and approaching them systematically, helps you create a program that looks and behaves the way its users think it should. Sometimes you may feel like you'll never finish your Category 1 list, but you will. You'll be smiling the day you check your bug sheet and realize that you're down to a few Category 2s and a dozen or so Category 3s! Although you might be tempted to skip this beta-testing phase of development, don't. You'll only pay for it in the long run.

Tip

It's often useful to have a user try to categorize the errors, as the developer may not always have sufficient objectivity. The users are also better at judging what impact a particular bug might have on their day-to-day activity.

Tip

Not all Access features are available when an application is run within the Access runtime environment. You can operate in the runtime environment and use the full version of Access to test for problems with your code and with the runtime environment by using the `/Runtime` command-line option when starting your Access application. Click Run on the Windows Start menu or create a shortcut.

The following command-line example starts Access and opens the Invoices database (if it's located at `D:\ MYAPPS\`) in the runtime environment (all this text appears as a single line in a shortcut's `Target` property):

```
"C:\Program Files\...\MSACCESS.EXE" /RUNTIME
C:\MYAPPS\INVOICES.ACCDB
```

Tip

Anytime there are spaces in the path name, it's necessary to include the entire path in quotes. In the example above, if the path to the database included blanks (`C:\Some Folder\Invoices.accdb`), it would have been necessary to uses quotes, as was done for the path to `MSACCESS.EXE`.

You should always test and debug your application in the runtime environment if you plan to distribute the application.

New Feature

Access recognizes a database filename extension — `.accdr` — that automatically starts an application in the runtime environment when it's opened. Change your database file's extension from `.accdb` to `.accdr` to create a "locked-down" version of the application, and change the extension back to `.accdb` to restore full functionality.

Polishing Your Application

When your application has been thoroughly tested and appears ready for distribution, spend some time polishing your application.

Giving your application a consistent look and feel

First and foremost, decide on some design standards and apply them to your application. This step is incredibly important if you want a professional look and feel to your applications. Figure 31.5 shows a form with samples of different styles of controls.

You can decide on any interface style that you like for your application. But after you decide on a style, use it consistently.

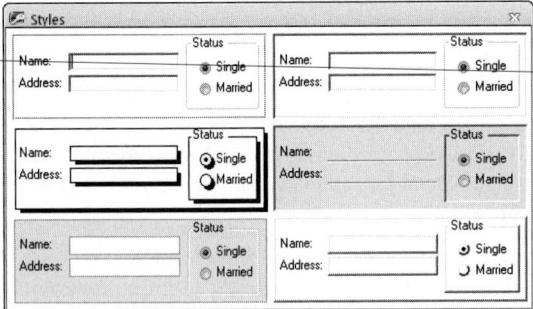

Your design decisions may include the following:

- Will text boxes be sunken, flat with a border, flat without a border, chiseled, or raised?
- What back color should text boxes be?
- What color will the forms be?
- Will you use chiseled borders to separate related items or select a sunken or raised border?
- What size will buttons on forms be?
- For forms that have similar buttons, such as Close and Help, in what order will the buttons appear?
- Which accelerator keys will you use on commonly used buttons, such as Close and Help?
- Which control will have focus when the form opens?
- How will the tab order be set?
- What will your Enter key property be for text boxes?

- Will you add some visual indication for when list boxes are multi-select and when they aren't?

- Will you add some visual indication for when combo boxes have their Limit To List property set?

Tip

Making your application look and work in a consistent manner is the single most important way to make it appear professional. For ideas on design standards to implement in your applications, spend some time working with some of your favorite programs and see what standards they use.

Caution

In the area of look and feel, copying from another developer is generally not considered plagiarism but is instead often looked upon as a compliment. Copying does not extend, however, to making use of another application's icons or directly copying the look and feel of a competitor's product; this is a very bad practice.

Adding common professional components

Most professional applications have some similar components. The most common components are the splash screen, an application switchboard, and an About box. These may seem like trivial features, but they can greatly enhance your application's appeal. They don't take much time to implement and should be included in all your distributed applications.

A splash screen

The splash screen (see Figure 31.6 for an example) not only aids in increasing perceived speed of an application but also gives the application a polished, professional appearance from the moment a user runs the program.

Getting Office Compatible

An application might be certified Office Compatible by meeting certain user-interface requirements specified by Microsoft. An Office-Compatible application uses the same menu structures as all the Office applications. In addition, ribbons are similar and, where applicable, have the same button image that Microsoft uses. Making an application look like an Office application saves the developer time by giving clear and concise guidelines for interface features, and it helps end users by reducing the learning curve of the application.

Although you might not want to have your application independently tested and certified Office Compatible, you might want to check out the specifications and use some of the ideas presented to help you get started designing your own consistent application interfaces.

FIGURE 31.6

A splash screen not only increases perceived speed of your application, but it also gives your application a professional appearance.

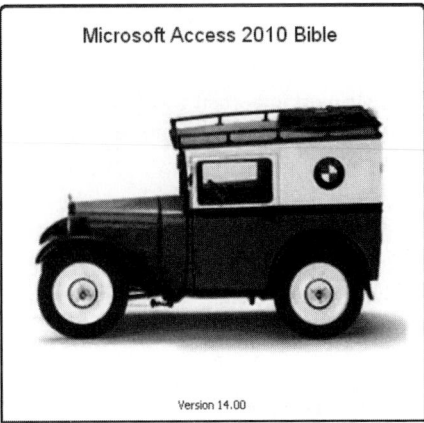

Microsoft Access 2010 Bible

Version 14.00

On the CD-ROM

Figure 31.6 shows the design window for a splash screen template that you can use when building your own applications. This form is included in the Chapter31.accdb **database. It's named** frmSplashScreen. **Import this form into your application and use it as a template for creating your own splash screen.**

Most splash screens contain information such as the following:

- The application's title
- The application's version number
- Your company information
- A copyright notice (© Copyright)

In addition, you might want to include the licensee information and/or a picture on the splash screen. If you use a picture on your splash screen, make it relevant to your application's function. For example, some coins and an image of a check could be used for a check-writing application. If you want, you can also use clip art for your splash screen — just be sure that the picture is clear and concise and doesn't interfere with the text information presented on your splash screen.

To implement the splash screen, have your application load the splash form before it does anything else. (Consider making your splash screen the Display Form in the Application Options, described earlier in this chapter.) When your application finishes all its initialization procedures, close the form. Make the splash form a light form and convert any bitmaps that you place on your splash screen to pictures in order to decrease the splash form's load time.

An application switchboard

An application switchboard is essentially a steering wheel for users to find their way through the functions and forms that are available in the application. Use the switchboard itself as a navigation form, using buttons to display other forms, as shown in the switchboard example in Figure 31.7. This is the switchboard named `frmSwitchboard` created for the Collectible Mini Cars database in this book.

The switchboard provides a familiar place where users can be assured that they won't get lost in the application.

The switchboard provides a handy way to navigate throughout the application.

Tip

Make sure that the switchboard redisplays whenever the user closes a form.

An About box

The About box (like the one shown in Figure 31.8) contains your company and copyright information, as well as the application name and current version. Including your application's licensee information (if you keep such information) in the About box is also a good idea.

The About box serves as legal notice of ownership and makes your application easier to support by giving your users easy access to the version information. Some advanced About boxes call other forms that display system information. You can make the About box as fancy as you want, but usually a simple one works just fine.

Making the most of pictures

Most users love pictures, and most developers love to use pictures on buttons. Studies have shown that clear and concise pictures are more intuitive and are more easily recognized than textual captions. Most developers, however, are not graphic artists and usually slap together buttons made from any clip-art images that are handy. These ugly buttons make an application look clumsy and unprofessional. In addition, pictures that don't clearly show the function of the button make the application harder to use.

Select or create pictures that end users will easily recognize. Avoid abstract pictures or pictures that require specific knowledge to understand them. If your budget permits, consider hiring a professional design firm to create your button pictures. A number of professional image galleries and tools to create and edit buttons are available.

Picture buttons that are well thought out can really make your application look outstanding, as well as make it easier to use.

FIGURE 31.8

An About box provides useful information to the user and protects your legal interests.

On the CD-ROM

Figure 31.8 shows an About box template form that you can use when building your own applications. This form is included in the `Chapter31.accdb` database. It's named `AboutTemplateA`. Import this form into your application and use it as a template for creating your own About box.

The About box should be accessible from a Help menu or from a button on your switchboard form. The submenu title should be About My Application. Of course, substitute *Your program name here* with your application's actual name.

Bulletproofing an Application

Bulletproofing (or hardening) an application is the process of making the application more stable and less prone to problems caused by unskilled users. Bulletproofing involves trapping errors that can be caused by users, such as invalid data entry, attempting to run a function when the application is not ready to run the function, and allowing users to click a Calculate button before all necessary data has been entered. Bulletproofing your application is an additional stage that should be completed in parallel with debugging, and should be performed again after the application is working and debugged.

Cross-Reference

Chapter 26 discusses many bulletproofing techniques in addition to those discussed here.

Using error trapping on all Visual Basic procedures

An error-handling routine gives you a chance to display a friendly message to the user, rather than some unintuitive default message box. Figure 31.9 shows a message box with a runtime error "2102," which is unintuitive; however, it also shows a more-detailed message of a form missing or misspelled. The user won't know the name of the form or if it's misspelled or missing. An error-handling routine is needed to provide the user with a more informative and meaningful error message than what's shown in Figure 31.9.

An error message resulting from a procedure with no error-handling routine

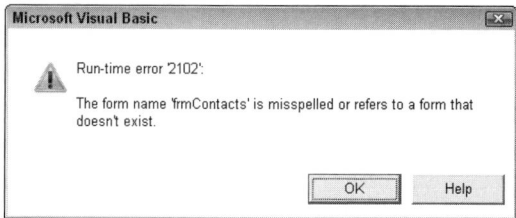

One of the most important elements of bulletproofing an application is making sure that the application never *crashes* — that is, never ceases operation completely and unexpectedly. Although Access provides built-in error processing for most data-entry errors (for example, characters entered into a currency field), automatic processing doesn't exist for VBA code errors. You should include error-handling routines in every VBA procedure, as described in Chapter 23.

When running an application at runtime, any untrapped error encountered in your code causes the program to terminate completely. Your users can't recover from such a crash, and serious data loss might occur. Your users have to restart the application after such an application error.

Separating tables from the rest of the application

You should separate your code objects (forms, reports, queries, modules, and macros) from your table objects. Many benefits are gained from distributing these objects in separate `.accdb` files:

- Network users benefit from speed increases by running the code `.accdb` (the database containing the queries, forms, macros, reports, and modules) locally and accessing only the shared data on the network.

- Updates can easily be distributed to users.

- Data can be backed up more efficiently because disk space and time aren't used to continuously back up the code objects.

All professionally distributed applications — especially those intended for network use — should have separate code and data database (`.accdb`) files.

Documenting the application

Most developers don't like to write documentation — not only is it no fun, but it can be quite frustrating and time-consuming. Also, every time a change is made to the application, the application's documentation needs updating. But putting in the time and effort now to prepare thorough documentation can save hours of technical support time down the road. Even if you don't plan to distribute a full user's manual, take time to document how to perform the most common functions in your application. If you've created shortcuts, make sure to share them with the users.

Cross-Reference
Chapter 26 discusses documentation in more detail.

Summary

In this chapter, you learned how to set up the Current Database options, which make your application professional looking and more difficult for the nosey user to poke around in. You learned how to restrict components users can interact with, as well as how to simulate the runtime environment with the `/runtime` switch or the `.accdr` extension.

You also reviewed testing and polishing procedures that make your application less likely to break after you distribute it. You revisited error handling and bulletproofing as additional methods to make a solid application. Preparing your database for distribution might take a bit more time, but you'll be thankful you spent the time on it when your deployment goes smoothly.

Part V

Access and Windows SharePoint Services

IN THIS PART

Chapter 32
Understanding Windows
SharePoint Services

Chapter 33
Integrating Access with
SharePoint

Chapter 34
Converting Access Objects to
SharePoint

Chapter 35
Deploying Access Applications
to SharePoint

Access continues to grow as an integral part of enterprise data management. Important capabilities have been added with each new release of Microsoft Access. Even though Access is not a strong tool for creating or driving Web sites, Access 2010 includes outstanding capabilities for publishing Access data and application objects on Microsoft SharePoint servers.

The most significant of these new capabilities is integration with Microsoft SharePoint Services. Access 2010 seamlessly shares data with SharePoint, using SharePoint Lists as linked tables. This means that your Access 2010 applications can provide data to users anywhere in the world. SharePoint data linked to Access databases is completely updatable and can be displayed on Access forms and reports.

Access 2010 carries integration with SharePoint a step farther. You're actually able to push Access objects to SharePoint as native SharePoint objects. This means that any user with permission to log on to a SharePoint server can work with a SharePoint-hosted Access application, without a local copy of Access or Microsoft Office installed on his computer.

The chapters in Part V position SharePoint as an enterprise-collaborative platform and explain the process of integrating Access with SharePoint. Starting with simple data sharing, the chapters in Part V progress to publishing Access applications on Microsoft Office SharePoint Services (MOSS) as native SharePoint applications.

Understanding Windows SharePoint Services

IN THIS CHAPTER

Getting familiar with SharePoint

Working with SharePoint Lists

Looking at different types of SharePoint sites

Throughout this book you've been reading about the many, many changes and new features that Microsoft has added to Access 2010. As exciting and interesting as these new capabilities are, they pale in comparison to the ability to upsize Access applications to Windows SharePoint Server (WSS). Each recent version of Access has demonstrated greater and greater ability to integrate with SharePoint, but always at the data level. Not until Access 2010 have you been able to upsize an Access application to actually run as a SharePoint Web site.

Upsizing Access databases to SharePoint is discussed in Chapters 34 and 35. Chapter 33 discusses sharing data with SharePoint sites, and this chapter discusses SharePoint and explains how Access developers can use the features provided by SharePoint.

Access and SharePoint can be tightly integrated, seamlessly sharing data across corporate intranets and the Internet. Access data can be linked or copied from data sources located on a SharePoint site. SharePoint data linked to Access appears as any other linked table, with the exception of somewhat slower data access because of the latency introduced by accessing remote data on a SharePoint server.

Although a lot of this chapter might sound as though I'm promoting SharePoint, given the expanded role that Access 2010 is sure to play in SharePoint installations, you'll be glad to have some background in SharePoint applications in this book. As you'll see in the chapters following this one, virtually any SharePoint data is accessible to Access applications, and Access 2010 makes it possible for the first time to migrate Access applications to the SharePoint platform. Microsoft is clearly planning a close relationship between Access and SharePoint for a long time to come.

On the CD-ROM

This chapter uses the `Chapter32.accdb` database. If you haven't already copied it onto your machine from the CD, you'll need to do so now.

Introducing SharePoint

SharePoint is Microsoft's premier collaborative environment, providing tools for sharing documents, calendars, messages, and other information across networks. SharePoint provides security, user authentication, logging, and other administrative features. SharePoint is implemented as a Web application. SharePoint Server runs on a Web server, using SQL Server as the back-end database for the pages and documents.

SharePoint is not a general-purpose Web development tool. It's almost always deployed on corporate intranets and used exclusively by the company's employees. Given that, it's not surprising that SharePoint's features focus on workgroup and corporate needs, such as sharing calendars, documents, and messages.

Access 2010 provides tools that enable you to publish Access applications as SharePoint Web sites. This means that Access data, forms, and reports are available anywhere SharePoint 2010 is deployed. Because SharePoint is almost entirely an intranet tool, your ability to expose Access applications as "Web sites" is limited to SharePoint's installations.

Understanding SharePoint is complicated by the variety of terms applied to SharePoint and SharePoint deployments. Microsoft hasn't helped things by changing the product's name several times over its history.

Microsoft uses the expression *Microsoft SharePoint Products and Technologies* to encompass all aspects of SharePoint, SharePoint tools, and SharePoint usage. Microsoft continues to aggressively expand SharePoint's capabilities and to enhance all the ways that companies can use SharePoint on their intranets.

The SharePoint Server product is Microsoft Office SharePoint Services (MOSS), which provides the server-side support for SharePoint sites. MOSS must be installed on a server operating system, such as Microsoft Windows Server 2003; it can't be installed on Windows XP, Windows Vista, Windows 7, or Windows Server 2008.

The previous name for Microsoft Office SharePoint Services was Microsoft SharePoint Portal Services. Microsoft is apparently positioning SharePoint as an extension and companion to the Office suite of applications.

SharePoint is deployed on a company's network as a series of SharePoint *sites*. Sites can be nested within other sites in a hierarchical fashion. Figure 32.1 shows a typical top-level page in a SharePoint site.

FIGURE 32.1

A typical SharePoint top-level page

Navigation menus   Search controls

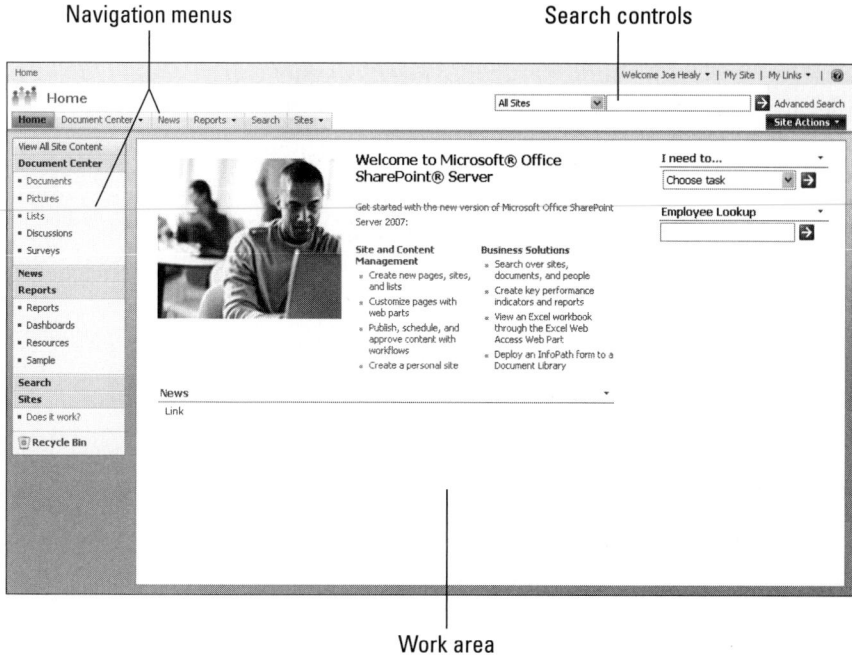

Work area

SharePoint data is stored and displayed as *lists,* which are conceptually equivalent to database tables. SharePoint lists store and display all manner of data, including messages, documents, files, images, and threaded conversations. SharePoint lists are displayed as pages, with navigation aids along the top and left side of the list (see Figure 32.2).

A SharePoint site is a logical grouping of pages and subsites. Each SharePoint site consists of a number of pages, each of which implements some type of SharePoint list or other object. In Figure 32.2, a phone number list occupies the page's work area. Just above the list is a navigation "bread-crumb trail," a common Web page navigation aid.

As with any other Web site, a SharePoint user has no direct interaction with the SharePoint Server that delivers the page content to her computer. The SharePoint site, or an individual page within the site, is accessible through a URL that the user types into her Web browser's address box.

FIGURE 32.2

A SharePoint page displaying a list of phone numbers

Navigation "bread crumbs"　　　　　　　　　　Image area

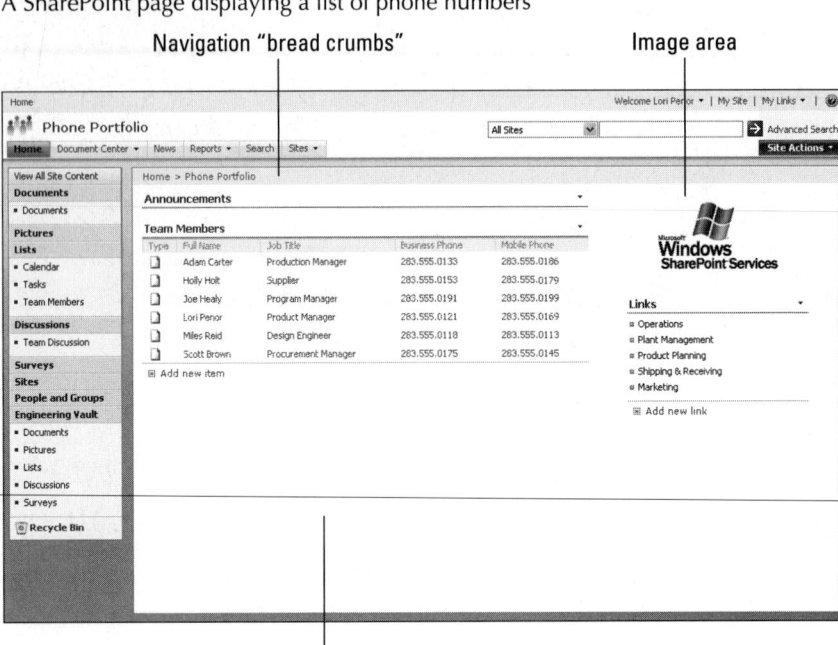

SharePoint list

Reviewing Various Types of SharePoint Sites

Although SharePoint is most frequently used for sharing documents and calendars, and other content-management tasks, SharePoint is frequently applied to many other applications. In fact, Microsoft provides a wide variety of application templates that can be modified to suit specific implementation requirements.

Here's a partial list of the available SharePoint templates:

- Business Performance Reporting
- Classroom Management
- Clinical Trial Initiation and Management
- Competitive Analysis Site
- Discussion Database
- Disputed Invoice Management

- Employee Activities Site

- Employee Self-Service Benefits

- Employee Training Scheduling and Materials

- Integrated Marketing Campaign Tracking

- Manufacturing Process Management

- New Store Opening

- Product and Marketing Requirements Planning

- Request for Proposal

- Sports League

- Team Work Site

- Timecard Management

SharePoint is frequently used, for example, to handle the documentation required for product development. A SharePoint site devoted to a development project easily handles the project initiation, tracking, and progress reporting tasks. Because SharePoint easily handles virtually any type of document, project drawings, videos, schematics, photographs, and so on can be added to the project's SharePoint site for review and comment by project members.

Companies often use SharePoint for distributing human-resource and policy documents. Because SharePoint provides user- and group-level security, it's quite easy to grant a particular department access to a SharePoint page while denying other users access to the same site.

SharePoint also logs changes to documents, and supports a check-in/check-out paradigm for controlling who is eligible to make changes to existing documents, and who is allowed to post new documents and files.

Some of the most common SharePoint deployments are storing of version-controlled documents, such as Word document and Excel worksheets. In many environments, e-mail is used for passing documents back and forth between users. The potential for mixing up different versions of the same document is considerable. Also, storing multiple copies of the same document takes up a lot of disk space. Because SharePoint provides a single source for storing, viewing, and updating documents, many of these issues are eliminated entirely.

Working with SharePoint Lists

The primary storage object in SharePoint is the *list*. Although conceptually similar to database tables, there are significant differences, and the differences have an impact on how Access works with SharePoint data.

SharePoint lists consist of rows and columns of data. Each column holds a particular type of data such as text, a date, or an object (such as a photo). From this simplistic perspective, SharePoint lists are analogous to Access tables.

But, unlike Access tables, SharePoint lists are not relational. There is no way to directly relate data in two different SharePoint lists, or to query multiple SharePoint lists to find related data. Also, you can't add validation rules to individual SharePoint list columns, or to the list as a whole. You can, however, restrict values in list columns to ensure that a list contains valid data.

When linking SharePoint data (as described in Chapter 33), you're somewhat limited in your use of the SharePoint data in an Access application. Because the data is not relational, and because there are no primary keys in SharePoint lists, you can't easily create meaningful relationships between linked SharePoint lists and Access tables.

However, as you'll see in Chapter 33, there is still plenty you can do with SharePoint data. A linked SharePoint list is fully editable. You can update or delete existing rows in the SharePoint list, or add new rows as needed.

Also, a common use of SharePoint data in Access is to populate reports, or to combine SharePoint data with Access data. Because of the ability to create ad hoc joins in Access queries, you can create reports with data from both sources.

Looking at a SharePoint Web Site

Before going into the detail of describing how Access integrates with SharePoint technology, you need to picture a typical SharePoint Web site.

Perhaps the most common use of SharePoint is storing shared documents and other files. SharePoint keeps track of files from the moment they're added to a list until they're removed or deleted. Figure 32.3 shows a short list of several different types of files in a SharePoint document library.

In Figure 32.3, notice that the library contains several different types of documents. Each row in the document list includes an icon indicating the document's type, the document's name, the size of the document, and the name of the person who added the document to the list. The library also includes tracking information ("In progress," "Approved") for each item.

SharePoint document libraries support a check-in/check-out paradigm. Only one person at a time is able to check out a document for changes. Although not shown in Figure 32.3, SharePoint records when a document is checked in or out, and keeps track of the individuals making changes. SharePoint can even be instructed to roll back document changes to an earlier version, if necessary.

Figure 32.4 shows a group calendar with multiple appointments. Users can be assigned permissions to view or update calendar contents, and SharePoint calendars can be tied to personal calendars in Outlook.

One particularly strong feature in SharePoint is its support for discussion lists. Discussions can be configured as blogs (where new discussion topics are added in a linear fashion) or threaded (where replies to postings can branch out in new directions). Figure 32.5 shows a task list and team discussions.

FIGURE 32.3

A SharePoint document library

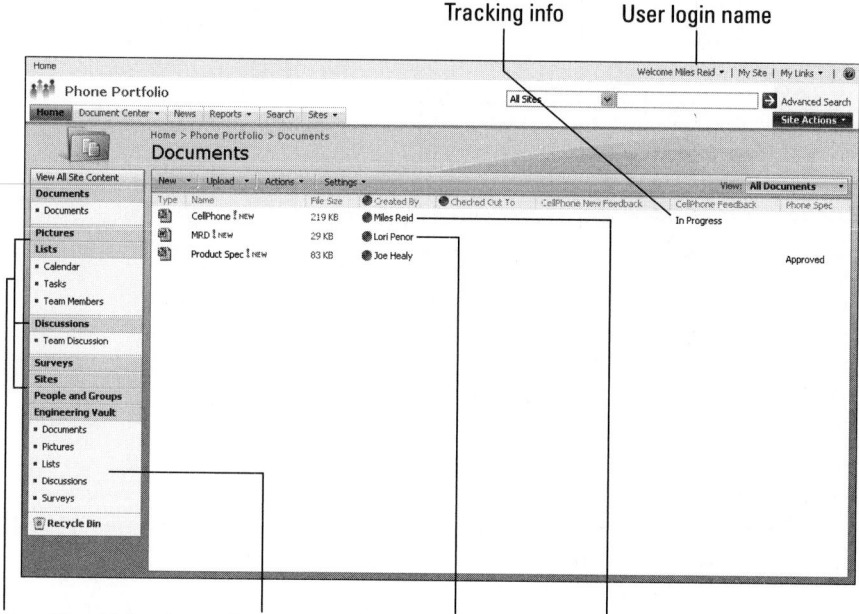

Other SharePoint sites   SharePoint lists   Word document   PowerPoint document

FIGURE 32.4

A calendar SharePoint Services Web site

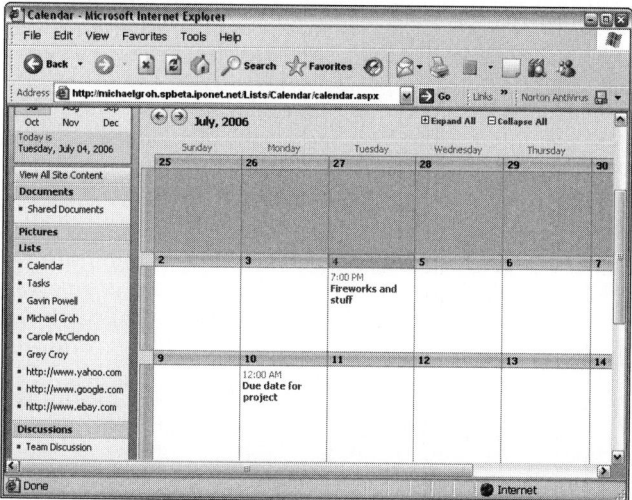

FIGURE 32.5

Tasks and discussions in SharePoint

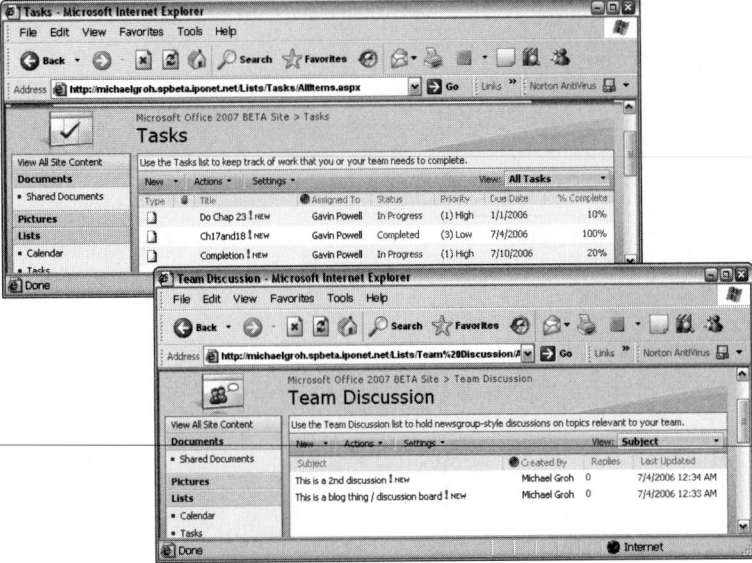

Editing SharePoint list items

Figures 32.6 and 32.7 shows how easily an item in a SharePoint list (in this case, a calendar) can be changed. All the relevant information is presented in a single screen. You add a new item, edit an existing item, or delete an item, through this same screen.

SharePoint can manage virtually any type of data you want to share with other people. Although this example concerns a specific project, SharePoint is suitable for many other purposes. For example, a Boy Scout troop could use a SharePoint site hosted by a commercial service provider for keeping track of its members and their merit badges. A bowling club could maintain tournament schedules and player rankings as SharePoint lists. Many professional organizations use SharePoint for maintaining calendars and membership lists.

FIGURE 32.6

Adding, changing, or deleting an item in a SharePoint site

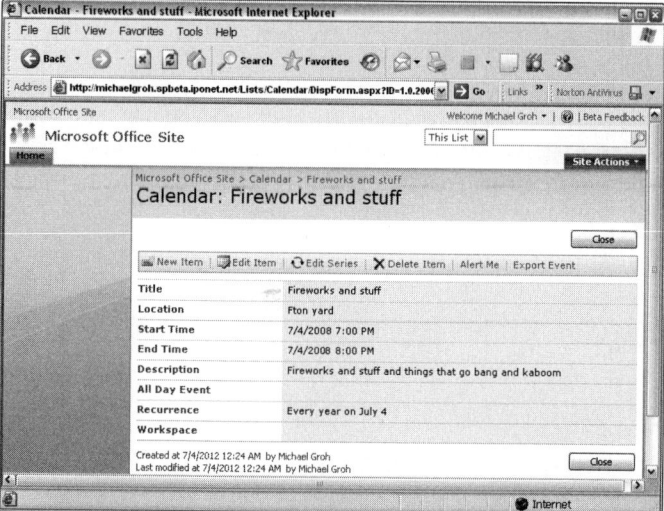

FIGURE 32.7

Adding a calendar item in a SharePoint Services Web site

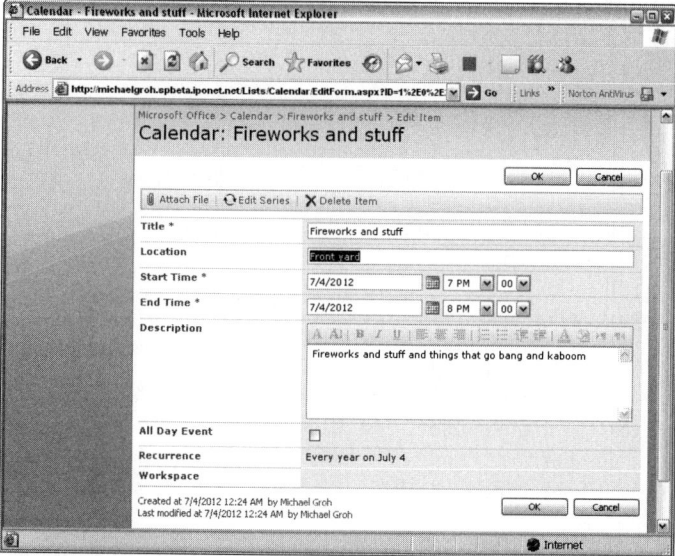

Creating SharePoint lists

One of the most significant features of SharePoint is that end users can add or modify SharePoint lists without a lot of training. Although a certain skill level is required to manage a SharePoint site (adding new users, assigning permissions, setting up the site's basic design, and so on), adding a new list is a simple task.

Figure 32.8 shows how a new list is added to a SharePoint site. The user clicks on the `Documents` link in the menu at the left of the SharePoint window to move to the `All Site Content` page. The All Site Content page is a "switchboard" of all the different libraries and lists in the site. This particular SharePoint site currently contains libraries for documents, images, and pages.

FIGURE 32.8

The All Site Content page of a SharePoint site

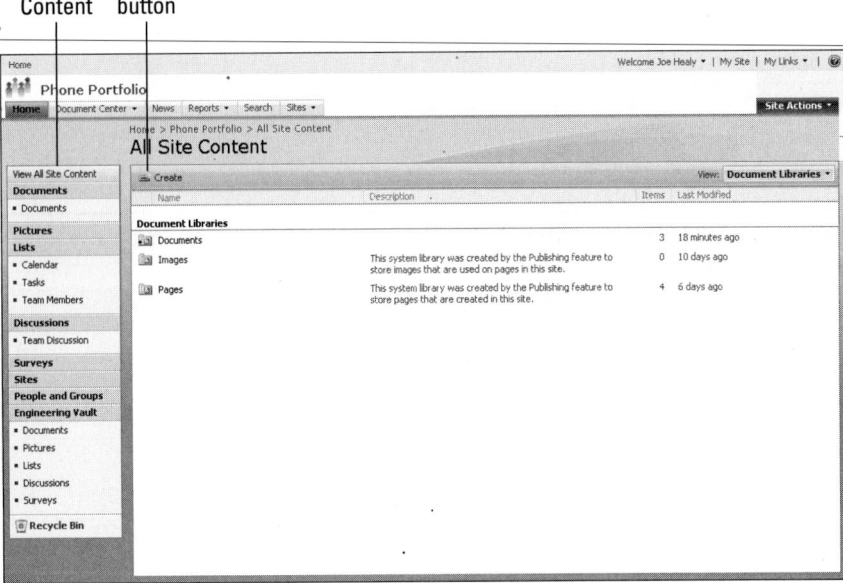

The user wants to add a wiki page to the SharePoint site. A wiki is similar to an old-fashioned bulletin board where anyone with access to the site is able to post messages, links to articles, documents, pictures, and any other content they want to make available to other users. Site members can post comments or feedback to the items left on the wiki.

A SharePoint wiki is just another type of SharePoint list. The main difference is that SharePoint doesn't limit the items posted to a wiki the way restrictions made can be imposed on an image or document library.

The user clicks on the Create button in the menu immediately above the libraries list in the All Site Content page (see Figure 32.8) to display the gallery of SharePoint page types (see Figure 32.9). SharePoint supports a wide variety of page types, including document and wiki libraries, contact lists, and calendars.

FIGURE 32.9

The SharePoint page gallery

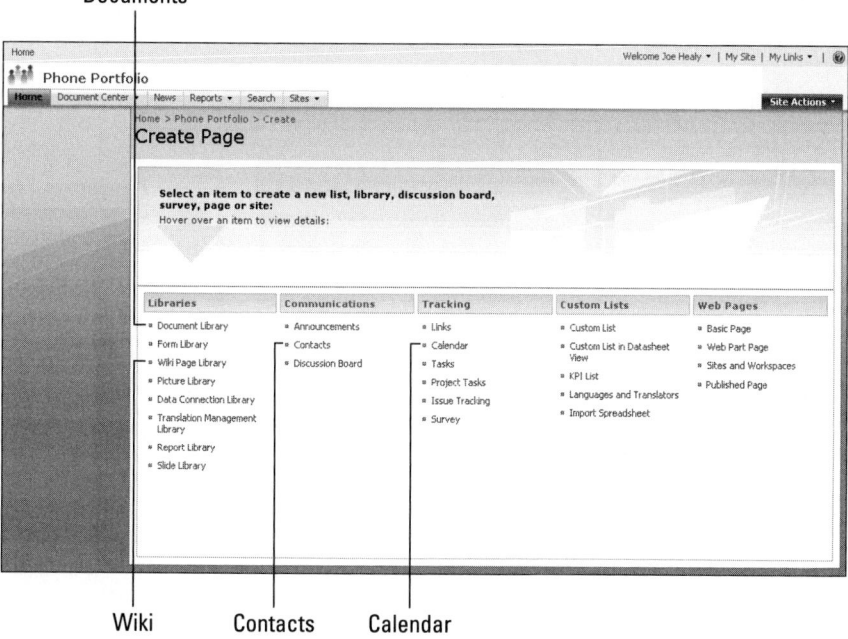

Documents

Wiki   Contacts   Calendar

SharePoint easily supports multiples of any type of SharePoint list. For example, a professional organization might have a calendar of events and another calendar of board meetings, with different permissions and entirely different items on each.

In this case, the user wants to add a public wiki where the SharePoint site members can make suggestions for future events. She double-clicks on Wiki Page Library in the Libraries list to open the New properties page. In Figure 32.10 the user is providing the new wiki's name, and (optionally) a description of the wiki. By default the new wiki is accessible from the Quick Launch navigation menu at the left side of all the SharePoint pages in the site. But, if needed, the wiki's presence in the Quick Launch list can be suppressed by changing the navigation option below the description box. If the wiki is hidden from the Quick Launch, an alternate method, such as a hyperlink on another page, should be provided to access the wiki page.

FIGURE 32.10

Providing the wiki's properties

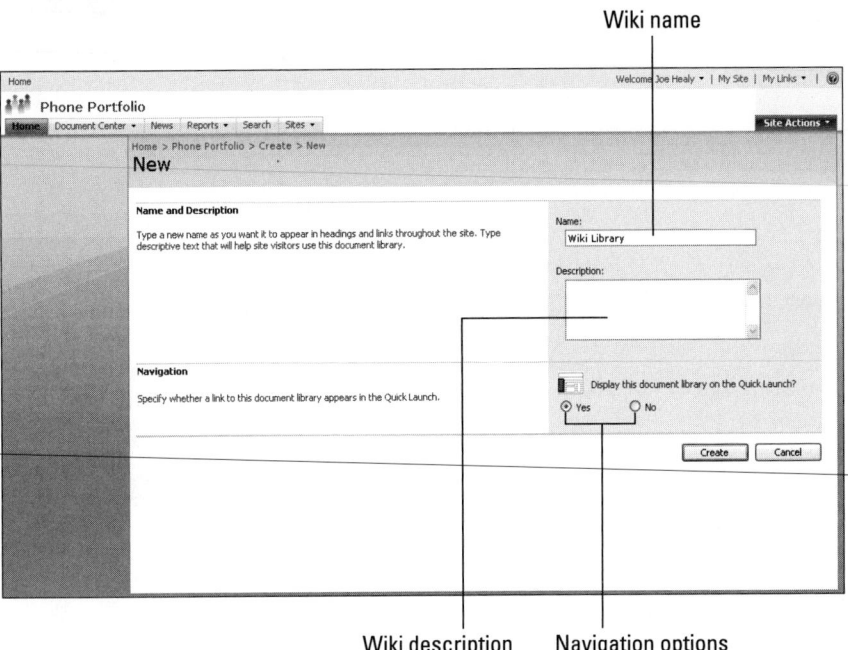

Wiki name

Wiki description   Navigation options

The new wiki is shown in Figure 32.11. Of course, because the wiki is new, there are no items in the list. But, notice the headings (Type, Name, Modified By, and so on) in the wiki list. These headings give you an idea of the variety of data that can be added to a wiki.

The new wiki open in SharePoint

Wiki entry on Quick Launch menu

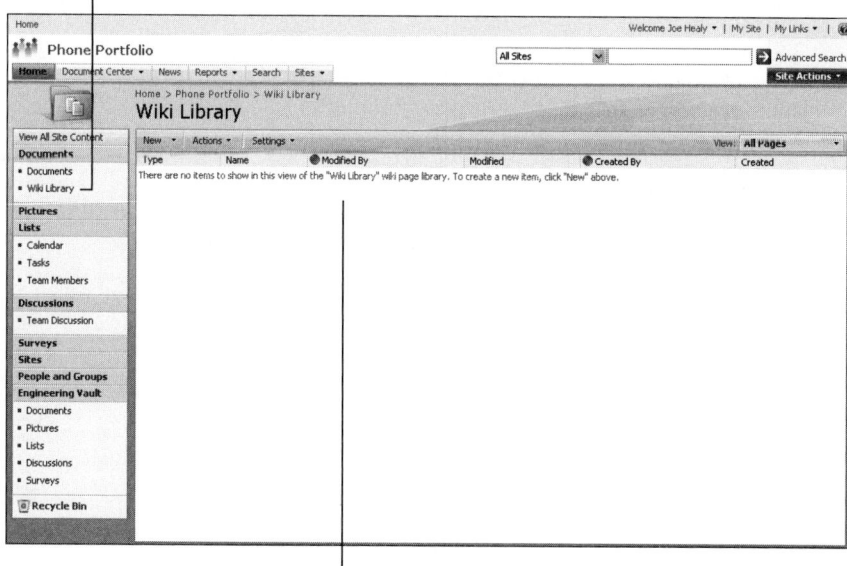

New wiki list

Summary

SharePoint Services are a major advance for Access developers. Microsoft is very clearly committed to SharePoint, and the ability to integrate Access and SharePoint data will only increase over time. SharePoint provides a flexible, secure, efficient, Web-accessible data repository, and provides security, versioning, and other valuable features to organizations and workgroups.

SharePoint integration is just one more example of Microsoft's commitment to enhancing Access's ability to integrate with diverse data sources. Although the other Microsoft Office applications also integrate with SharePoint, it's a sure bet that Access will take a dominant role when working with SharePoint. With its ability to provide the users with powerful forms and informative reports, Access is a natural tool to use when building SharePoint client-side interfaces. The next several chapters provide details of integrating Access 2010 with SharePoint. You'll see how to incorporate SharePoint data in Access applications, and how to migrate properly prepared Access applications to a SharePoint server.

Integrating Access with SharePoint

S everal of the previous chapters of this book have touched on different data sources for Access. You've seen how Access supports importing, linking, and exporting data. Microsoft Access has no equal when it comes to sharing data with other applications.

This chapter explains how to use Microsoft SharePoint as a data source for Access applications. Microsoft has taken great pains to ensure that Access and SharePoint interoperate seamlessly, providing Access developers with a rich source of data accessible from anywhere on the Internet.

SharePoint data are stored as *lists*. SharePoint lists can be exported from, and imported into, Access applications. SharePoint lists are available from any SharePoint site, sharing data across the Internet. In earlier chapters, you read about the SharePoint basics, about the services provided by SharePoint Services, and how various types of applications can be implemented using SharePoint. Additionally, you read about how a SharePoint Web site and Access can integrate with each other.

Linking to SharePoint lists makes data stored on a SharePoint Web site appear as linked tables in Access. From a data perspective, linking to a SharePoint list is no different than linking to a SQL Server database table or other remote data source. The only difference (from the user's perspective) may be a slight delay as data is transferred from a remote SharePoint site to Access and back.

Essentially, SharePoint is a way of sharing data over the Internet. Quite literally, SharePoint represents an Internet address from which data can be shared between multiple applications. Those applications can be virtually anywhere on the Internet. Most SharePoint installations, however, are strict *intranet* applications and are only accessed from within a company on its

IN THIS CHAPTER

Considering SharePoint as a data source

Understanding the SharePoint and Access interfaces

Using SharePoint data on Access forms

Displaying SharePoint data in Access reports

Looking at SharePoint collaborative applications

private LAN (local area network). SharePoint is not a general-purpose tool for building Web sites, and SharePoint pages lack many of the features expected of public Web sites.

This chapter takes a more generic look at using SharePoint data than previous chapters. The intent of this chapter is to show how to use SharePoint as a reliable and valuable source of data for Access applications.

When linked to an Access application, SharePoint data is available to all other users of that SharePoint site. This means that the data input by Access users at their workstations may be viewed and updated by other users who have access to the SharePoint site. Also, you can consider Access as a consumer of SharePoint data. Access becomes a feature-rich front-end application, using remote SharePoint data as if the data were located locally. The user notices nothing out of the ordinary. From the Access user's perspective, a SharePoint-hosted Access application looks like any other Access application and contains the same data-entry screens and reports as any other Access database.

Note

SharePoint is commonly used for intranet applications running on local area networks (LANs), rather than across the Internet. SharePoint provides many features that aren't needed in a pure Web context, such as sorting lists and searching for keywords. Also, SharePoint pages have too many constraints on them to make SharePoint a general-purpose Web development tool. For example, by default, SharePoint pages have a navigation panel along the left side, a menu bar across the top, and a large area to the right of the navigation panel for the page's main content. Although SharePoint pages can be coerced into almost any layout, the effort required to customize a SharePoint page is considerably larger than a traditional ASP.NET page.

On the CD-ROM

This chapter uses the database named `Chapter33.accdb`. If you haven't already copied this file onto your machine from the CD, do so now. You need access to either SharePoint Server 2007 or 2010 to experiment with the data sharing techniques described in this chapter. Earlier versions of SharePoint support limited data sharing with Access, but do not support updating linked SharePoint lists from Access.

Introducing SharePoint as a Data Source

This chapter builds on previous chapters covering importing and exporting SharePoint lists, and includes close integration between Access and SharePoint Web sites. This chapter demonstrates the power and flexibility of using SharePoint data within Access applications. SharePoint data linked to an Access application is live, and reflects changes made by users almost instantly. In reality, SharePoint integration is one of the big stories (from Microsoft's perspective) in Access and Office 2010. Microsoft is busily enhancing the ability of Access and SharePoint to cooperate and share data. SharePoint services can be both local to a specific company, and even rented or leased from service providers. The data input into an Access application on a user's desktop is available to all SharePoint users. Similarly, when a user opens an Access report, at least a portion of the data may be hosted on a SharePoint site many thousands of miles away.

Note

You can find a commercial site, or perhaps even a free demonstration service, to experiment with. This book uses a Microsoft beta SharePoint 2010 Web site, which will not be available by the time you read this book. However, all of the capabilities described in this chapter (and the other chapters in Part V of this book) are available to anyone with access to SharePoint Server 2010.

Sharing Access Data with SharePoint

Building Access interfaces with SharePoint simply means going into an Access application, linking to SharePoint lists, and then writing forms and reports based on those linked tables. A linked SharePoint lists appears (to Access) as any other linked data source as described in Chapter 16 and other places throughout this book.

In addition, Access 2010 enables you to import SharePoint data directly into local Access tables. Although imported data is no longer connected to the SharePoint site, and is therefore "stale" compared to data remaining on the site, a snapshot of data from a SharePoint site may be useful in some situations.

Linking to SharePoint lists

The most fundamental data sharing between Access and SharePoint is for Access to link to a SharePoint list and use the data as with any other linked data source. The only difference is that because SharePoint does not support a wide variety of data types, the linked SharePoint lists are somewhat less flexible than links to, for instance, SQL Server tables.

Linking to a SharePoint list is much like linking to any other data source. Click the More drop-down button in the Import & Link group on the External Data tab to reveal the list of more advanced import and linking options (see Figure 33.1).

Select SharePoint List from the list of import and linking options, and Access opens the Get External Data – SharePoint Site dialog box (see Figure 33.2). The top portion of this dialog box shows a list of recently-visited SharePoint sites, and just below this list is a text box for entering the destination SharePoint site's URL. As you may recall from Chapter 32, a SharePoint site is accessible through a URL, and actually resides on a Web server, most often located on a LAN.

FIGURE 33.1

Preparing to link to a SharePoint list

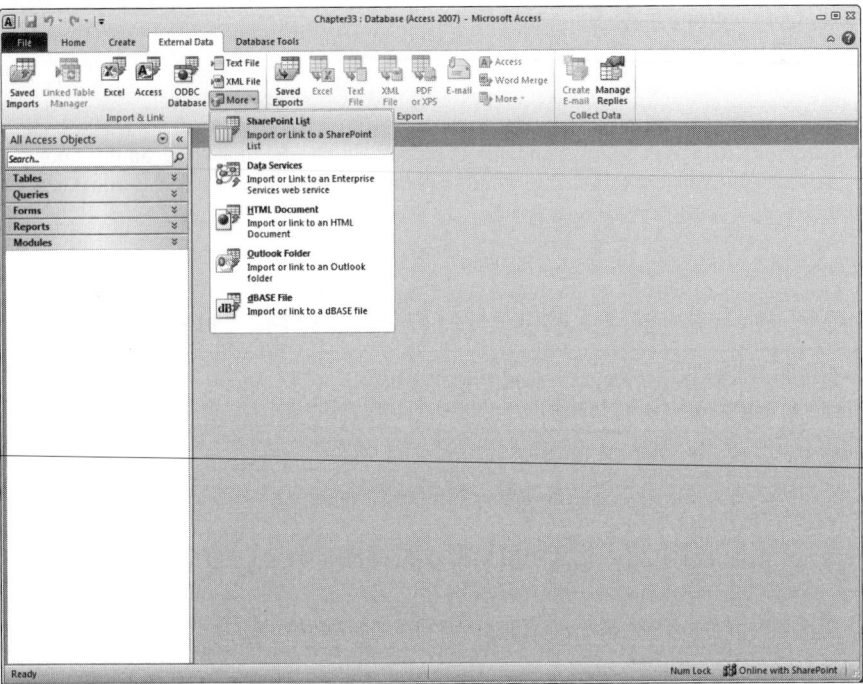

FIGURE 33.2

The Get External Data – SharePoint Site dialog box

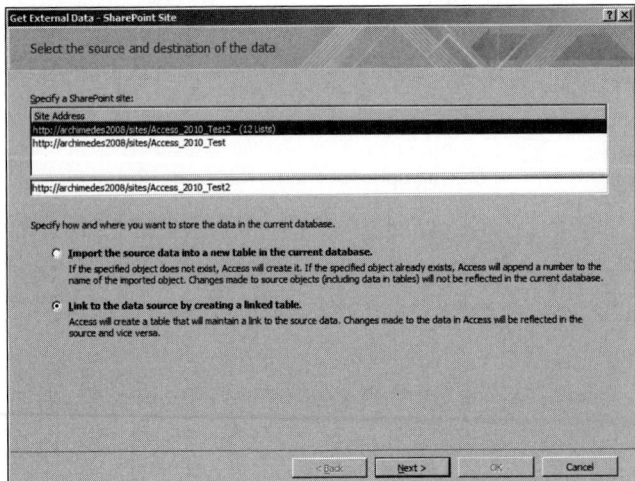

You must have appropriate permissions to link to a SharePoint list. In fact, without proper permissions, Access can't even display a list of SharePoint lists on the designated site. Figure 33.3 shows the standard SharePoint login dialog box, asking for the user's credentials. SharePoint users are recognized by their membership in Windows Active Directory services and their inclusion in designated SharePoint groups. These topics are beyond the scope of this book, but you should be aware that access to SharePoint sites and SharePoint data is protected by processes similar to any other Windows application.

FIGURE 33.3

The SharePoint 2010 login dialog box

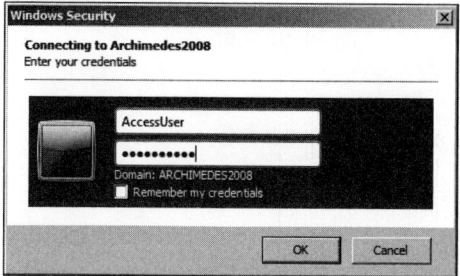

After providing appropriate SharePoint credentials, the user is presented with a list of SharePoint lists in the designated SharePoint site. Each item in the list is accompanied by a check box. In Figure 33.4, only the Calendar SharePoint list is selected for linking, but you can select multiple lists as well.

FIGURE 33.4

Selecting a SharePoint list for linking

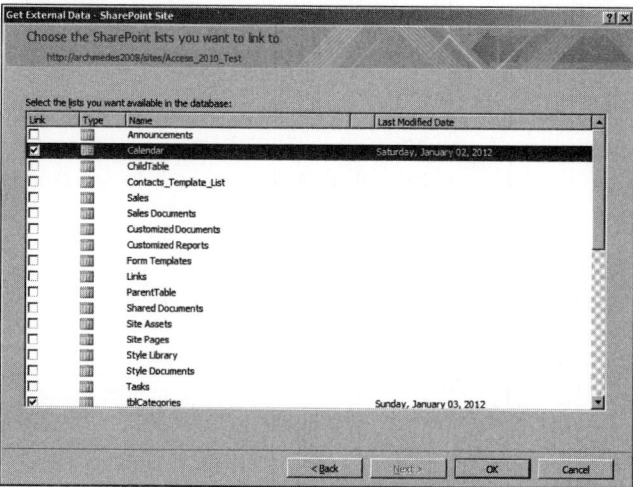

Figure 33.5 shows the linked SharePoint list displayed as an Access datasheet. The data in the linked table is compatible with Access, and you can build queries, forms, and reports against this data if needed. You could, for instance, build a billing system around the SharePoint calendar, specifying when invoices are to be sent to customers and when payments are received. Although the linked Calendar list only accepts data related to SharePoint's calendar features, an Access query could combine data from the calendar (event title, date, description, and so on) with information stored in Access tables (sales dates, invoice amounts, customer addresses, and so on).

FIGURE 33.5

A linked SharePoint list appears much like any other Access table.

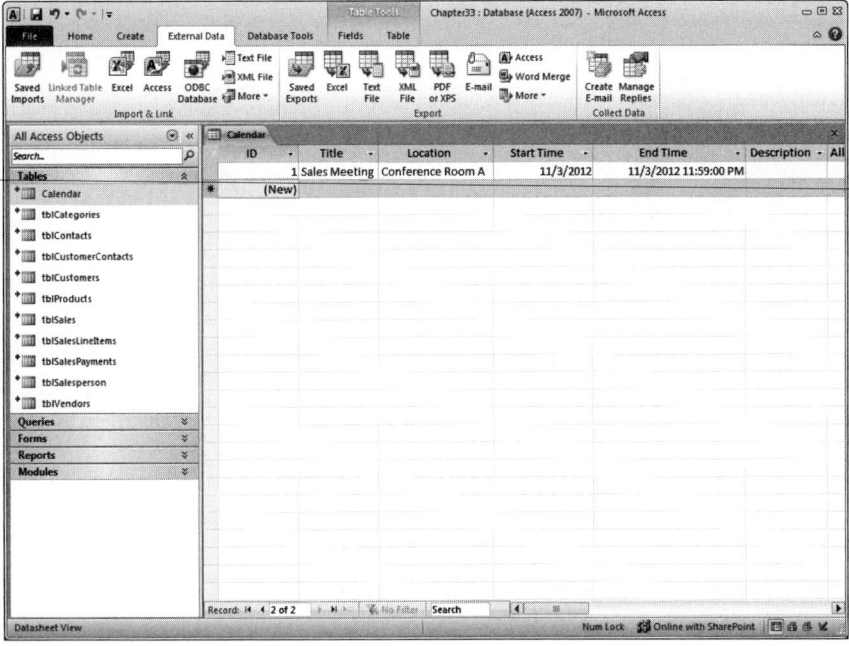

The calendar item you see in the linked table in Figure 33.5 is shown in SharePoint's calendar format in Figure 33.6. Nothing about the calendar suggests that its data is shared with an Access application.

Linking to a SharePoint calendar is a good example of tight integration between Access and SharePoint users. People familiar with SharePoint are likely to know and understand the SharePoint calendar feature. The ability to link to a SharePoint calendar from Access and to work with its data like any other linked table is a powerful capability.

Many other SharePoint features, such as Tasks, Announcements, and document libraries, that are similarly accessible to Access applications.

FIGURE 33.6

The SharePoint calendar displaying the event scheduled in the Access table

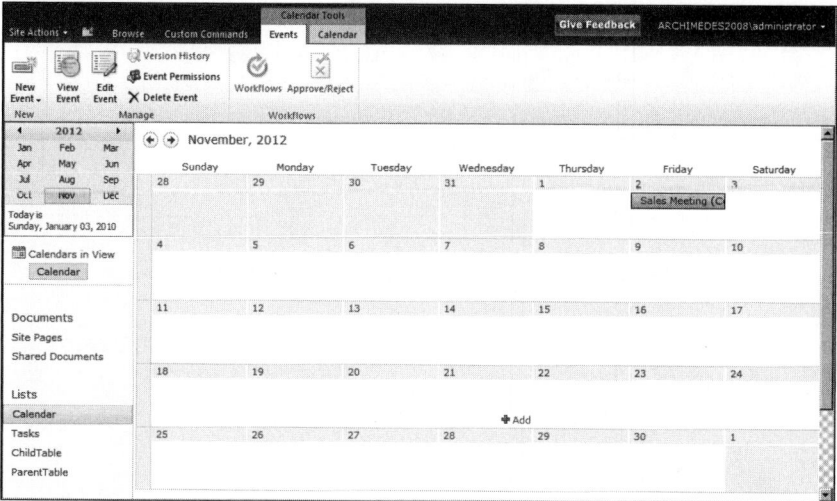

Note

Rather than requiring the user to log in each and every time she uses SharePoint data, after a user's SharePoint credentials have been established, Access creates a UserInfo table containing information about the user and her role in SharePoint. Although the user has to provide a password to initially access SharePoint, the UserInfo table is a repository of additional information about the user. The UserInfo table resides within Access, which means that it's available before the user logs in to SharePoint. This enables Access to provide SharePoint with the user information as the user logs in to SharePoint.

Exporting Access tables to SharePoint

Sometimes you need to transfer data from Access to SharePoint so that SharePoint users have access to the same data as Access users. The first example exports a table from Access to SharePoint:

1. Open the Chapter33.accdb example database.

2. Open the tblCustomers table, or just highlight tblCustomers in the Navigation Pane.

   When you open the table, the Access ribbon changes by adding a few more controls.

3. Select the More drop-down list in the Export group on the ribbon's External Data tab and click SharePoint List (shown in Figure 33.7).

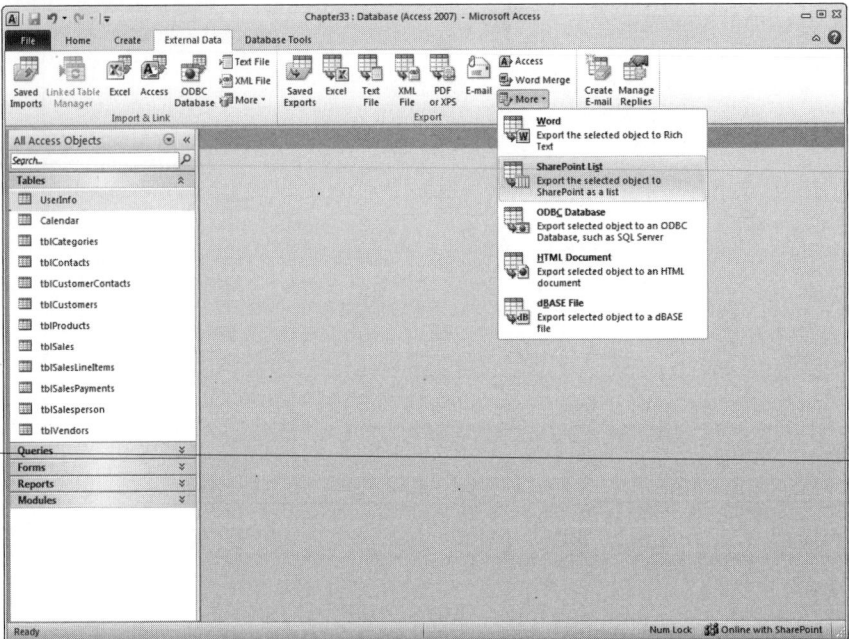

FIGURE 33.7

Selecting SharePoint as the export destination

The SharePoint Site Wizard starts.

4. Enter the SharePoint site URL.

The site used in this chapter is shown in Figure 33.8.

Note

The URL shown in these figures will not be available by the time you read this book. Be sure to use the URL of a SharePoint site available to you as you experiment with SharePoint integration.

The objective is to create a SharePoint list for selected tables in your Access database.

5. Click OK.

6. If you are prompted for a login, enter a valid user name and password.

Enter a valid SharePoint user name and password. The SharePoint login dialog box shown in Figure 33.9 is very similar to the dialog box in Figure 33.3. The difference is that the dialog box in Figure 33.9 requires only the user's password because the user name was previously cached.

FIGURE 33.8

Selecting the destination SharePoint site

Recently visited SharePoint sites

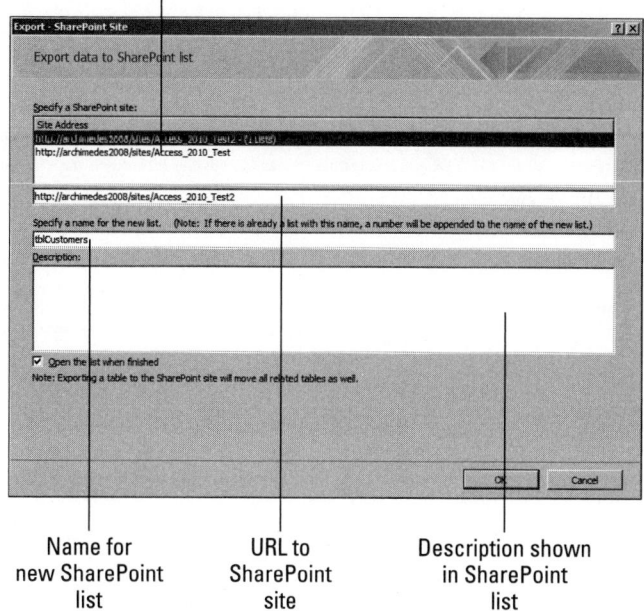

Name for   URL to   Description shown
new SharePoint   SharePoint   in SharePoint
list   site   list

FIGURE 33.9

The SharePoint login dialog box

As the wizard progresses, you see a small dialog box indicating the progress of the conversion process. The dialog box means that the Access table design is being copied to SharePoint and a new SharePoint list is being created. When the conversion is complete, the new SharePoint list is displayed in your default Web browser (see Figure 33.10).

FIGURE 33.10

The new SharePoint list created from an Access table

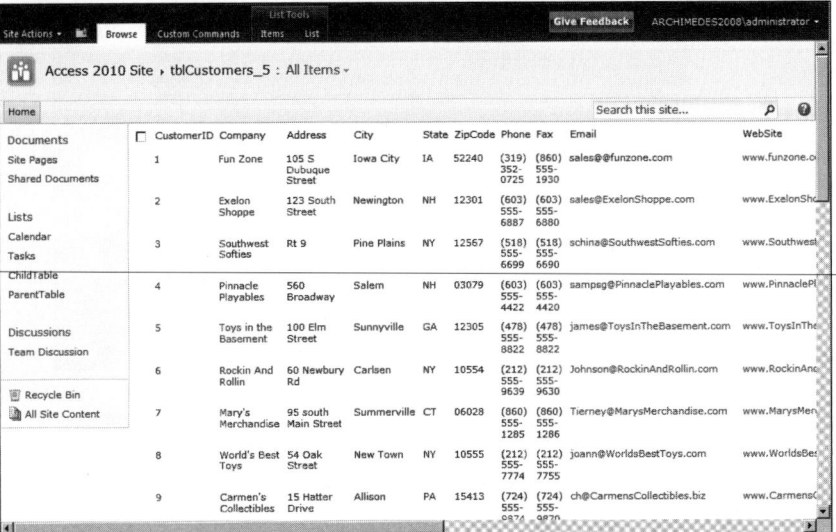

7. If you receive any errors or warnings, check the Show Details box in the wizard's dialog box, and read the information that is displayed.

8. Click the Close button in Access to dismiss the Export to SharePoint dialog box.

When the export process is complete, the data exists in two places: in the original Access table, and as a SharePoint list. The two data stores are not connected, so if changes are made in either location, the other application does not see the change.

Certain fields do not export well to SharePoint. For instance, an OLE Object field is simply left empty on the SharePoint side and contains no data. But most other field data types are properly translated into compatible SharePoint columns and populated with data from the Access table. Table 33.1 shows how Access data types are translated to compatible column types in SharePoint. Notice that far fewer types of data are available in SharePoint lists than in Access tables. The data types in Table 33.1 are applied any time an Access table is exported to SharePoint.

TABLE 33.1

SharePoint Data Type Conversion

Access Data Type	Converted Type in SharePoint
AutoNumber	Number
Text	Single line of text
Memo	Multiple lines of text, limited to 8,192 characters
All Number Types (Byte, Integer, Long Integer, Single, Double, Decimal)	Number
Date/Time	Date and Time
Currency	Currency
Yes/No	YesNo
OLE Object	Single line of text
Calculated	Calculated
Hyperlink	Hyperlink or Picture

Moving Access tables to SharePoint

Rather than simply exporting Access tables to SharePoint, another approach to data sharing is to move all of the tables in an Access application to SharePoint as a single export operation and link the new SharePoint lists back to the Access application. All of the tables in the Access database are moved to SharePoint and linked back to Access in a single process. The end result of the process is an Access application with its back-end data managed by Microsoft SharePoint. This process is analogous to using the Upsizing Wizard to migrate an Access application to SQL Server (the Upsizing Wizard is described in Chapter 38).

The advantage of moving Access tables to SharePoint is that both SharePoint and Access users have access to the same data. Changes in either environment are immediately seen in the other. Depending on user requirements, this level of integration may provide the best use of the data while giving users access to Access's superior user interface and reporting tools.

Moving Access tables to SharePoint is not one of the import/export features of Access 2010. Instead, the commands necessary to move the entire set of Access tables to SharePoint are on the Database Tools ribbon tab (see Figure 33.11).

Clicking the SharePoint button in the Move Data ribbon group opens the Export Tables to SharePoint Wizard dialog box shown in Figure 33.12. This dialog box is similar to the Export — SharePoint Site dialog box in Figure 33.8, except that you need less information when exporting all of an Access database's tables to SharePoint. In fact, the only information that you need is the URL of the destination SharePoint site. Access handles the rest.

FIGURE 33.11

The Move Data ribbon group contains some important wizards.

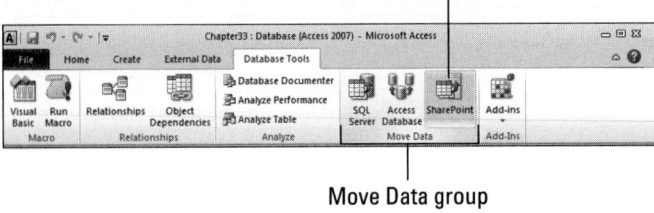

SharePoint export command

Move Data group

FIGURE 33.12

The Export Tables to SharePoint Wizard dialog box specifies the destination SharePoint site.

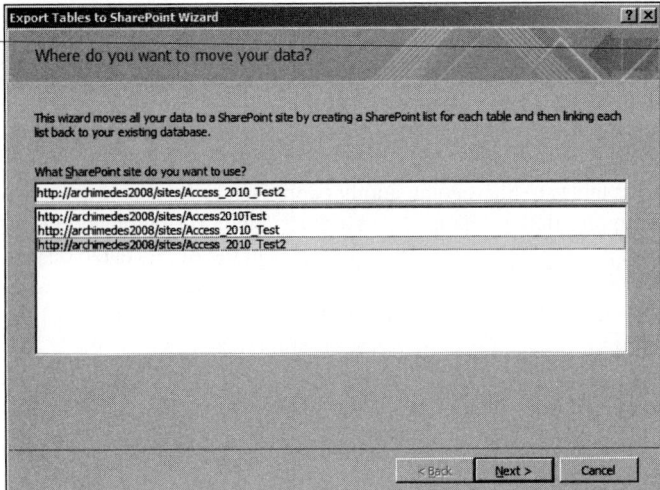

The Next button initiates the export process, which may take more than a few minutes, depending on the number of tables in the Access database, the volume of data in each record, and the efficiency of the SharePoint server hardware and software. You may also be asked for your SharePoint user name and password because SharePoint must verify that you have the proper permissions to create objects in the destination SharePoint site.

The newly created SharePoint lists are given the same name. The export might fail if an Access table name does not conform to SharePoint naming rules. For example, Access table names may contain spaces and limited punctuation characters, while SharePoint tables are plain text with no spaces. If the export fails, it's likely to be caused by a list-naming violation.

At the conclusion of the process, all the tables in the Access database have been moved to SharePoint and linked back to the Access application (see Figure 33.13). Notice that the icon next to each table name has changed to indicate that the table is now linked and not contained locally. Just as with other export processes, you are able to save the export steps for future use. Access also makes a backup of the Access database file prior to the export process so that you can revert to the prior state, if necessary.

After executing the Export to SharePoint Wizard, tables are linked from Access to SharePoint.

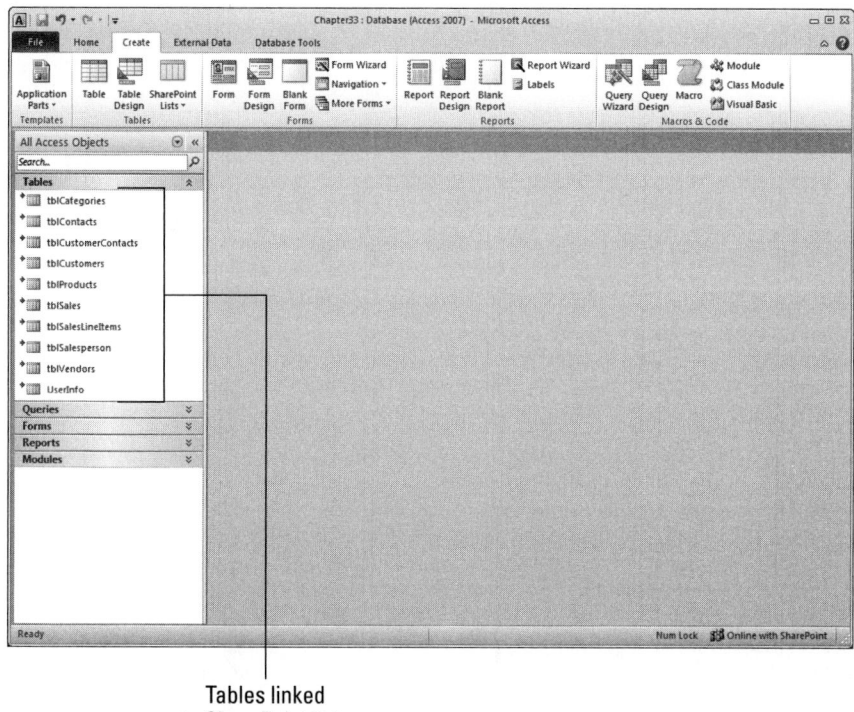

Tables linked
to SharePoint lists

The icons indicating linked SharePoint lists look very much like Access table icons. Each linked list is accompanied by an arrow, and the color of the icon has changed to a yellowish-orange color. Otherwise, the icons look much like any linked table.

All of the queries, forms, and reports are based on the linked tables and should function as before, with a few exceptions. Because of incompatibilities between Access and SharePoint data, not every Access data type migrates to SharePoint. The incompatible fields are created in the SharePoint list, but they are added to the SharePoint list as text columns and are left empty.

Export issues are reported in a table named Move to SharePoint Site Issues, with one row for each problem (a single Access field may generate multiple rows in the issues table). Most export problems are traceable to data incompatibility issues, but other situations exist.

For instance, while exporting the tables in `Chapter33.accdb`, a `Duplicate output destination 'Title'` error was reported on `tblCustomerContacts`, and the export failed. None of the tables in this database were exported to SharePoint because of the error. It turns out that this error occurred because `Title` is a reserved word in SharePoint. Every custom list in SharePoint includes a Title column that cannot be deleted or renamed, making it impossible to add a second column named Title in a list.

Figure 33.14 shows the tables copied from Access to the SharePoint site. The tables and their data are now stored and managed by SharePoint Services. All that is left in the Access database are logical links to the SharePoint Web site. The tables and data are no longer stored in the Access database.

Tables added from Access to SharePoint

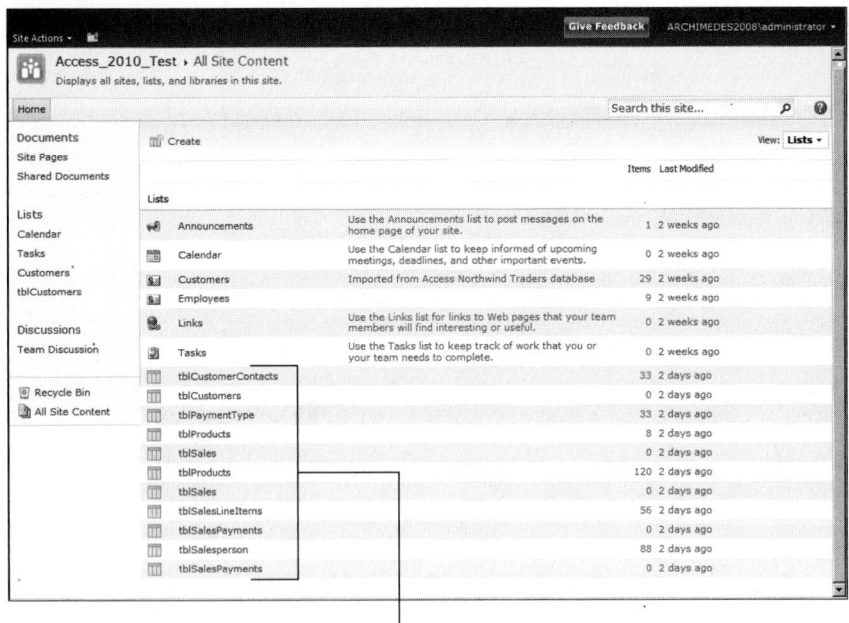

Exported Access tables

During the export process, several fields are added to the SharePoint list that are required for list management on the SharePoint side. These fields are available in the linked table in Access, but are not included in any of the queries, forms, or reports based on the table before it was exported to

SharePoint. These additional fields are listed in Table 33.2. It's possible that you may be able to make use of at least some of these columns, but by and large, they serve no purpose in an Access application.

TABLE 33.2

New Fields Added to the SharePoint List

SharePoint Field Name	Data Type
_OldId	Number (Double)
Content Type	Text
Workflow Instance ID	Text
File Type	Text
Modified	Date/Time
Created	Date/Time
Created By	Text
Modified By	Text
URL Path	Text
Path	Text
Item Type	Text
Encoded Absolute URL	Text

Using SharePoint Templates

In this chapter, we examined the options available when an Access database already exists and users require the same data on a SharePoint Web site. In its attempt to solidify the connection between Access and SharePoint, Microsoft has provided yet another approach to integrating Access applications with SharePoint.

Rather than exporting existing Access tables to SharePoint, or linking to SharePoint lists, this alternate technique involves building entirely new SharePoint lists within the Access environment. Access 2010 provides SharePoint list *templates,* which contain all the details necessary to build SharePoint lists, including column names and data types, and other list properties. When completed, the lists are already linked to Access and may serve as the basis for new forms and reports.

The SharePoint templates in Access 2010 cover a number of important business functions: Contacts, Tasks, Issues, and Events, as shown in Figure 33.15. In addition, the Custom list template (near the bottom of the list) allows adding virtually any combination of SharePoint-compatible columns to an otherwise blank list. The last item in the drop-down list (Existing SharePoint List) provides the same linking capability discussed in the section titled "Linking to SharePoint lists" earlier in this chapter.

FIGURE 33.15

SharePoint list templates available in Access

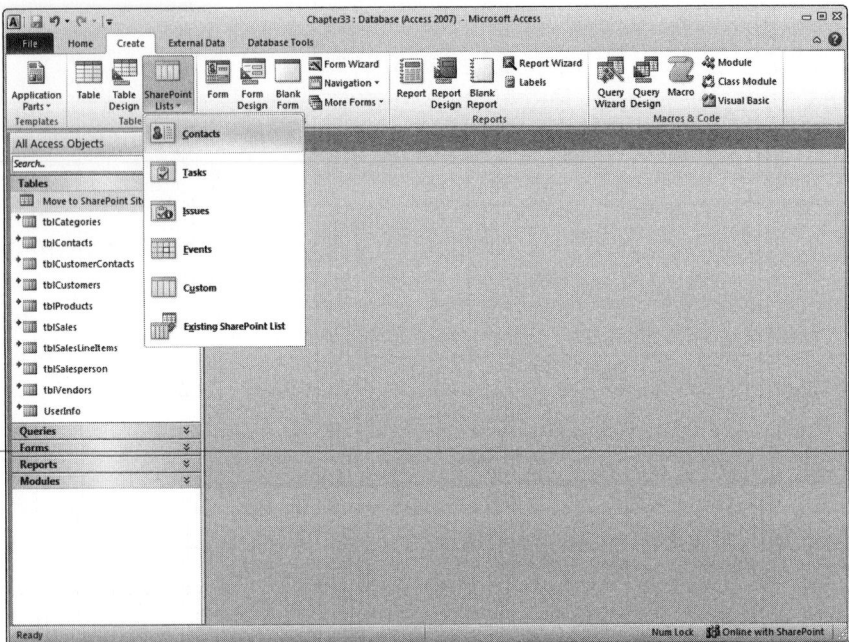

Selecting an item from the list of SharePoint list templates opens the Create New List dialog box (see Figure 33.16). Notice that you don't have an option to modify the template before you create it in SharePoint. This means, of course, that the list will include a predetermined set of columns, each set to a particular data type required for the list's operations.

You may be asked to provide SharePoint credentials as the new list is created. You need administrative rights to add lists to a SharePoint site, so even if you are able to link to a SharePoint list, you may not be entitled to create an entirely new list.

The newly-created SharePoint contacts list (with one contact added) is shown in Figure 33.17. There is nothing special about this list, so if you don't need some of the columns, you can remove them or add new columns if necessary.

FIGURE 33.16

The Create New List dialog box when creating a new SharePoint list from an Access template

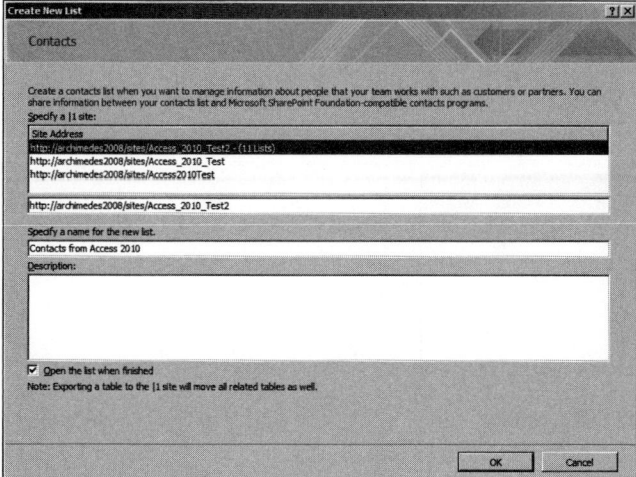

FIGURE 33.17

The new SharePoint list created from an Access template

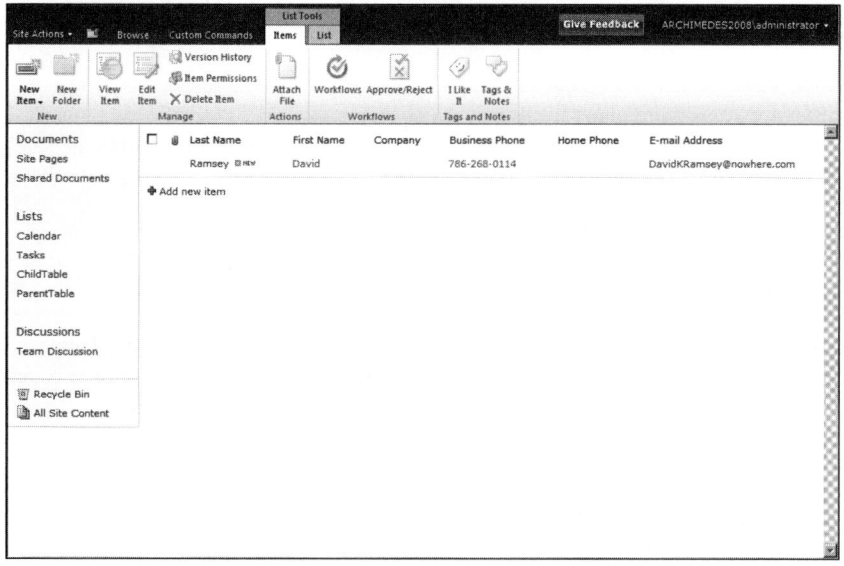

Figure 33.18 shows the Access view of the new SharePoint list. This linked table behaves like any other linked SharePoint list and allows the user to add, edit, or delete records as needed. The user, of course, needs proper SharePoint permissions to work with the data because it is hosted in SharePoint and not Access.

The Access view of the new SharePoint list

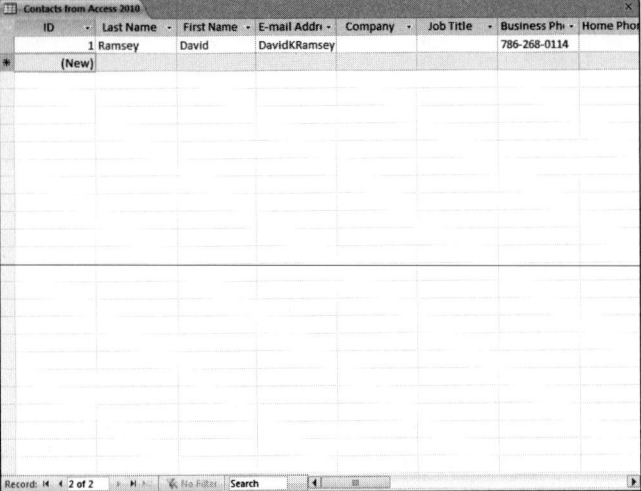

In the future, other application templates for Access may become available. Potential tracking application templates include customer service, projects and project management, marketing, sales channels and pipelines, student management, school and college student management, and others.

Summary

This chapter took a quick look at the potential benefits of combining data stored in SharePoint with Access forms and reports. Access enables you to seamlessly integrate with SharePoint Services, across the Internet or more locally on an intranet. The SharePoint data is available to any SharePoint user with the appropriate credentials (user name and password), and data security is provided by SharePoint Services.

Microsoft is aggressively and rapidly improving the performance in capability of SharePoint Services. The ability to share Access data with remote users through SharePoint will only increase over time. The next two chapters explain in detail Microsoft's plans to extend Access applications into the SharePoint environment, greatly enhancing SharePoint as a extensible platform for Access developers.

Understanding Access Services

A ccess 2010 introduces a new standard for Access application development. The new model is not quite full-blown Web development in the sense of producing public Web sites driven by large databases, but it does offer many new and exciting capabilities for Access developers.

For a long time, Microsoft has been emphasizing and promoting SharePoint as a platform for collaborative development. Chapters 32 and 33 explored some of the new and existing capabilities built into Access 2010 that enable Access users to seamlessly share data with SharePoint users. Because SharePoint must be hosted on a Web server and is accessible only through a Web browser, integrating Access data with SharePoint is the first step toward creating Access applications with a credible Web presence.

All the features and techniques described in Chapters 32 and 33 apply to Access 2007 and 2010. But this chapter is a departure from previous discussions because it is essentially a white paper on the Web capabilities built solely into Access 2010. The features described in this chapter require Access 2010 and are incompatible with any other version of Access. Also, a complete installation of SharePoint Server 2010 is required as the destination for Access Web apps. No other version of SharePoint includes Access Services, which is vital to these new capabilities.

IN THIS CHAPTER

Understanding managed applications

Introducing Access's Web publishing features

Looking at Access Services in SharePoint 2010

Explaining the limits of Access Web Services

Note

Although SharePoint 2010 is a requirement for migrating Access applications to the Web, this does not mean that SharePoint must be installed on your local network. Hundreds of service providers offer subscription-based SharePoint services. Many of these providers provide volume-based pricing, so the client pays less for a low-volume site and more for a site that receives a lot of hits. Subscribing to a commercial SharePoint service provider may be the fastest and most affordable way to host Access applications on SharePoint. The only caveat is that the commercial service provider must offer SharePoint 2010, and not an earlier version.

On the CD-ROM

This chapter uses the database named Chapter34.accdb. If you haven't already copied this file to your machine from the CD, you'll need to do so now. You'll also need access to SharePoint Server 2007 or 2010 to experiment with the data-sharing techniques described in this chapter. Earlier versions of SharePoint support limited data sharing with Access but do not support updating linked SharePoint lists from Access.

Explaining Managed Applications

Access has long been relegated to a role as a workgroup and departmental database development system. In spite of its outstanding user interface and report tools, Access's reliance on a database file that can be corrupted or lost due to hardware failure or accidentally (or purposefully) deleted has made Access a hard sell in many environments.

Traditionally, IT departments are charged with maintaining a company's mission-critical database systems. These systems — whether implemented as SQL Server, Oracle, DB2, or another server database — require professional management, including careful design, periodic backups, and maintaining user and group permissions. The objectives of large-scale database systems are to ensure the availability and integrity of the data.

The objectives of departments and business units (even small businesses), on the other hand, are flexibility and access to data. Time is money, and waiting for an IT department to develop a user interface or a new report in a development tool such as Visual Studio.Net can be a costly. Many business units prefer using Access because of its ability to quickly turn user requirements into bona fide, completed applications.

The problem comes when a business unit wants to store mission-critical data in an Access data file on a file server or (worse) on a user's desktop or laptop computer. Without proper management, it is easy to lose data due to a hard disk crash or a stolen laptop.

Furthermore, without careful data synchronization, different copies of a database can exist in multiple locations. As a result, Access reports can't be trusted because no one is sure whether a report reflects the state of the company's data.

There is a trade-off between an expensive, large, carefully managed application such as a .NET Windows or Web form application running on top of SQL Server and a smaller, lighter, and more agile application built with Microsoft Access. Even when an Access application is built around data stored in SQL Server, providing access to the data through a Web browser is difficult at best. In most cases, users must work with SQL Server data through a LAN and depend on SQL Server database administrators (DBAs) to provide permissions to the data and other support to the Access front ends as needed.

Managed applications (such as server-based database systems) offer many advantages to businesses and organizations. However, these same businesses and organizations also benefit from the flexibility and agility of unmanaged applications written with Microsoft Access.

Looking at Web Publishing in Access

Ideally, users would have fast, simple access to their data, without the constraints of large database systems such as SQL Server. Although linking to SQL Server database tables from Access applications removes the problems caused by multiple copies of the database on different computers and provides a high degree of database security, users often depend on database administrators for simple tasks such as developing stored procedures to sort or filter data in various ways.

Microsoft's solution to the conflicting needs of business users and IT departments is to provide tools in Access 2010 that allow Access developers to *publish* Access applications on SharePoint sites. When you publish a properly prepared Access application to SharePoint, users benefit from simple and easy access to their data and retain the ability to view and work with the data in either Access forms or SharePoint lists. The data in a published Access application is centralized and stored in SharePoint lists. The SharePoint data is secure because users must be granted permission to use SharePoint, but after they provide their user name and password, the SharePoint data is accessible through any Web browser. Chapter 35 covers this process in detail, and explains the changes required in an Access application to make Access object compatible with SharePoint.

An Access application residing on a SharePoint server represents a single point of maintenance, which is a major benefit for developers. To modify a form or report, it must be copied from SharePoint to a local Access installation, where the changes are made. Only one developer at a time can take out a form or report, and when the object is returned to SharePoint, all users receive the updated object the next time they use the application.

Why SharePoint?

Many developers question why Microsoft chose to make Access Web development reliant on SharePoint Services. If the intent is to make Access a bona fide Web development tool, doesn't it make sense to incorporate true Web development capabilities into Access, like Microsoft did with Visual Studio, many years ago?

When Microsoft examined the issues involved, it quickly became clear that adding credible Web development capabilities to Access wasn't practical. Many of us forget that a Web site is far more than just HTML pages. Security, performance, and data integrity issues must be considered.

For instance, Jet (or ACE, for that matter) is unsuitable as a Web database system. You cannot coerce the multiuser, stability, and capacity requirements of a public Web site into an .accdb database. The architecture is wrong, and making it right would require rewriting ACE for the Web environment.

Leveraging SharePoint features

Microsoft chose SharePoint as the platform for Access Web publishing because of the significant features built into SharePoint, including the following:

- **Security:** SharePoint supports users and groups of users. Users and groups may be granted or denied access to various parts of a SharePoint Web site, and designated users may be granted permission to add, delete, or modify the site.

- **Versioning:** SharePoint automatically maintains a version history of objects and data. Changes can be rolled back to an earlier state at virtually any time. The ability to roll back changes can be granted to individual users, and DBA support is not required.

- **Recycle bin:** Deleted data and objects are held in a recycle bin so that they may be recovered. Unlike Access, in which every deletion or change is permanent, SharePoint supports an undo feature for its data.

- **Alerts:** Users and groups can be sent e-mail when specific data in a SharePoint list is added, deleted, or changed. If granted the proper permissions, users can manage their own alerts.

- **End-user maintenance:** SharePoint sites are meant to be maintained by their users, without the intervention of IT departments. Although SharePoint pages are not as flexible as typical Web pages, a SharePoint developer is able to add or remove features from pages, change fonts, headings, colors, and other attributes of pages, create subsites and lists, and perform many other maintenance and enhancement tasks.

- **Other features:** Every SharePoint site includes a number of features, such as a calendar, a task list, and announcements, that users may turn off or remove.

The ability of users to maintain a SharePoint site is a major difference between a SharePoint site and a Web site built with a tool such as ASP.NET. The Web pages in a .NET Web site are tightly bound to the compiled code that manages the site. A user cannot change an ASPX page because it is stored on a Web server, and (in most cases) the code behind the page must be recompiled when changes are made to the page's interface.

Publishing Access applications to SharePoint

Publishing an Access application to SharePoint is a multistep process. Fortunately (as you'll see in Chapter 35), Access 2010 includes wizards and helpers to guide you through the process.

Because of the variety of methods and architectures that you can use when publishing to SharePoint, reducing the process to a list of steps to perform every time you publish an Access application to SharePoint is difficult. Chapter 35 covers some of these options in detail, so I'll describe only the most basic publishing process here.

In most cases, you will start with a completed, working Access application. In the Backstage area, click the Publish to Access Services button or click the Share button on the left side of the Backstage area (see Figure 34.1) to open the Access Services Overview area (shown in Figure 34.2).

FIGURE 34.1

The Backstage area with the Publish to Access Services button and the Share button

Publish to Access Services button

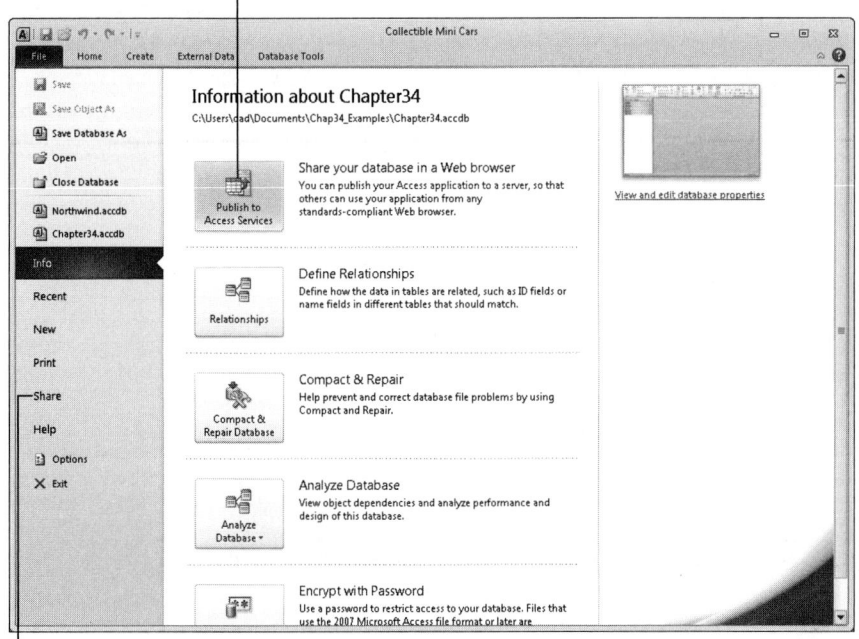

Share button

Note that the Publish to Access Services button in Figure 34.2 is disabled. You must run Compatibility Checker before this button is enabled. As its name implies, Compatibility Checker examines the application for issues that may prevent it from publishing to SharePoint without error. Unless the application is extremely simple, containing just a few tables, queries, forms, and reports and very little code, it is unlikely that it will pass Compatibility Checker the first time around. Chapter 35 discusses the most common compatibility failures and what you can do to resolve these issues so that your application will successfully publish to SharePoint Services.

At the conclusion of a successful publishing process, the current Access application remains intact. All tables and other database objects are converted to Web-compatible versions (more on this in Chapter 35) but are not removed from the current application. You retain the published Access application because you will use it in the future to maintain the Web version of the application. You make changes to the Access version of the application and resynchronize the database objects with their SharePoint counterparts.

FIGURE 34.2

The Access Services Overview area in the Backstage area

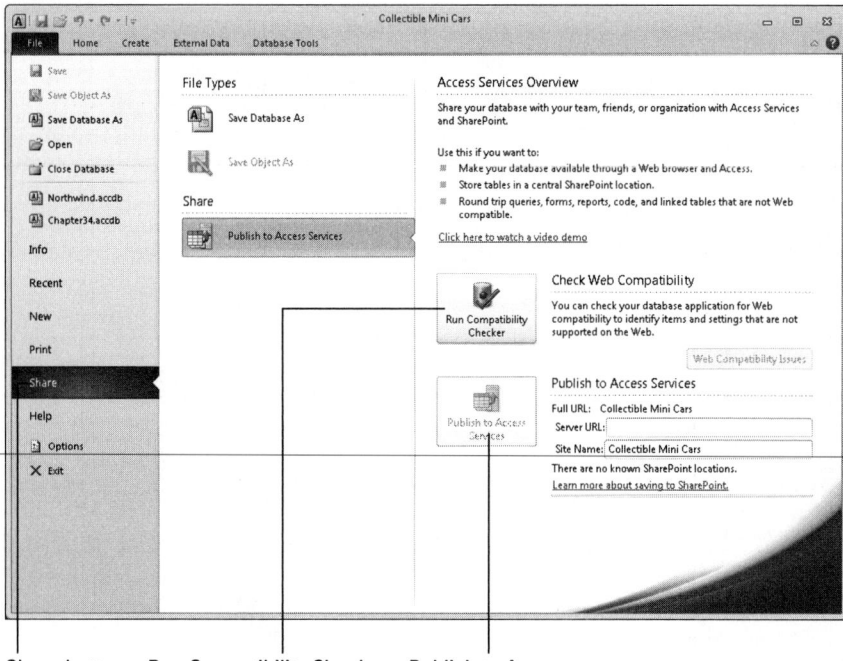

Share button   Run Compatibility Checker   Publish to Access
button   Services button

Understanding Access Services

Previously in the chapter, you read that only SharePoint Server 2010 supports the full range of Access Web publishing options. This is because SharePoint Server 2010 is the first version to support *Access Services*, the server-side support necessary for hosting Access applications in SharePoint.

Access applications are built in Access, of course, using essentially the same tools as in previous versions of Access. When the application is published to SharePoint, Access Services renders the ASPX pages necessary to display the Access application in a Web browser. In other words, Access Services is the driving force behind SharePoint-hosted Access applications.

Access Services also compiles and executes the queries in the Access Web application and directs the queries against the SharePoint lists containing the data. Access Services also synchronize updates between versions of the Access application on a developer's desktop and the version stored in SharePoint (these steps are described in detail in Chapter 35).

Perhaps the most important role played by Access Services is maintaining the relational nature of the tables exported to SharePoint when an Access application is published to SharePoint. SharePoint itself is not relational in the sense that we expect and require in a database. Although SharePoint supports *lookup* columns, this ability is more a convenience to link data in one list to another list, not to enforce referential integrity.

Access Services provides the logic required to join list data and maintain referential integrity between lists, as long as the relationships between tables are defined before the Access application is published to SharePoint.

Access Services uses hidden SharePoint lists to manage the formal relationships between Access tables as the tables are migrated to SharePoint. If, for instance, you have established a one-to-many relationship between a customers table and a sales table, Access Services manages this relationship on the SharePoint side through entries in hidden SharePoint lists. As a result, you will not be able to delete a customer record without first handling the customer's sales records.

However, SharePoint does not have a "relationships" screen. Instead, as described in Chapter 35, you use Access as the database designer to make updates to the application's schema and resynchronize the changes with the database previously published to SharePoint.

Access Services in SharePoint 2010 also provides data caching. Rather than relying on the native ability of SharePoint to locate and deliver data, Access Services provides a middle-tier caching service that stores data that is likely to be consumed by the application and delivers the data much more quickly than SharePoint alone. The caching is transparent to users and developers, and no configuration options exist for setting up the cache or modifying its parameters.

The Access Services layer filters data in a query before adding it to the cache. This means that queries that include a WHERE clause are guaranteed to run more quickly and make better use of Access Services' caching than a query that selects all rows from the underlying table(s). As with any database application, you should plan on using query predicates (the WHERE clause) when possible to minimize the amount of data that moves between the data store (in this case, SharePoint lists) and the user interface.

Examining Access Web Application Limits

Access Web applications are not the best solution for public-facing Web sites, and are better suited in departmental or workgroup environments. Certain limitations mean that the Access/SharePoint Web option is targeted for specific situations. These limitations are discussed in the following sections.

Not public-facing

The limitations of Access Web applications are determined more by SharePoint than anything in Access itself. For instance, SharePoint does not support anonymous access to SharePoint sites. Users are expected to log on to a SharePoint site, using a valid user name and password (SharePoint uses Windows Active Directory services to identify users).

Although workarounds exist for this limitation, it can be difficult to restrict users to only certain portions of a SharePoint application. In general, after a user is authenticated by SharePoint's security system, the user is able to access the lists, calendars, and other features supported by the SharePoint site. Restricting users means determining which features should be allowed for which sets of users, and individually setting permissions for those features throughout the SharePoint site. Most Web applications, on the other hand, present only the features the developer has specified.

SharePoint was never meant to be a general-purpose Web development tool; instead, it was designed and built primarily as a collaborative platform for sharing data and documents. This means that SharePoint pages are built from templates, rather than from free-form HTML. As a result, all SharePoint pages share certain appearance features (see Figure 34.3).

FIGURE 34.3

A typical SharePoint page

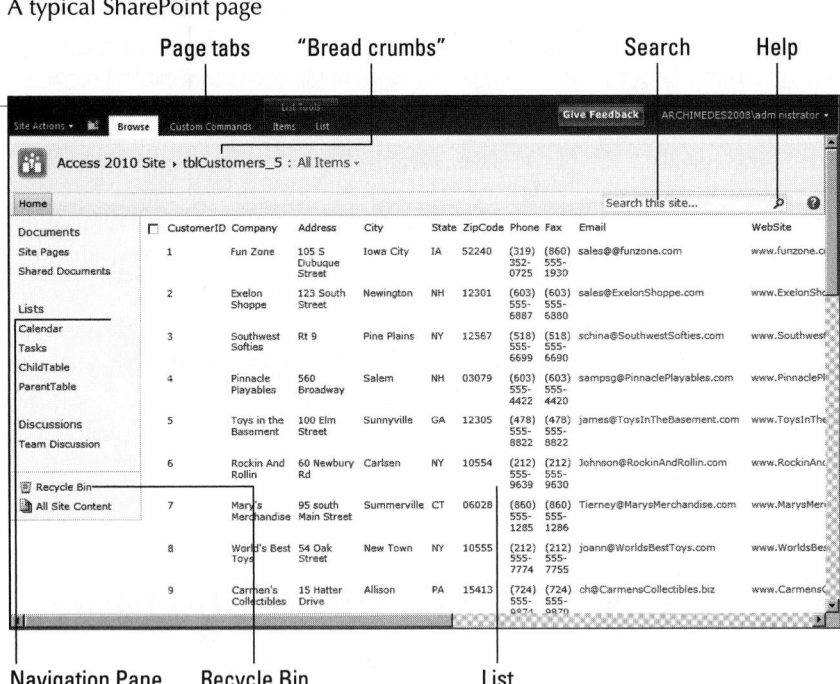

In most cases, the similarities between pages hosted on different SharePoint sites are an asset, not a hindrance. After a user is familiar with SharePoint and SharePoint pages, no further instruction is needed, so users are productive more quickly than with applications where each page is different. Common tasks such as adding a new item to a list or editing an existing item are the same in every SharePoint page.

You can customize colors, fonts, and some other appearance attributes of a SharePoint page. The basic layout, however, with the Navigation Pane at the left, a ribbon and "breadcrumbs" at the top, and an items list to the right of the Navigation Pane, are common to all SharePoint pages.

If absolutely necessary, you can create a custom page template from scratch, or from an existing template, and use it on a SharePoint site. But because most SharePoint sites are used on an intranet for a specialized audience, the default page layout usually works quite well.

Fewer than 20,000 rows of data

Although SharePoint is not a high-performance database system, users have performance expectations when using any Access application. Microsoft has determined that the best performance (even with the data caching provided by Access Services) is achieved when the upsized Access application contains no more than 3 tables containing 20,000 rows of data each, and no more than 20 tables containing 1,000 rows of data each. In relatively small applications, the best performance is achieved when one main table contains 10,000 or fewer rows and 10 to 20 other tables have fewer than 1,000 rows of data.

Larger applications are good candidates for more traditional Web development, using tools such as ASP.NET and SQL Server. These development platforms are geared toward large-scale, high-performance, data-driven Web sites. However, Web development with .NET and SQL Server is, in general, considerably more expensive and time-consuming than upsizing Access database applications to SharePoint.

Microsoft is blunt in suggesting that applications with more than 40,000 rows in any one table are not good candidates for SharePoint-hosted Access applications. As you'll see in Chapter 35, you can create hybrid Access applications that incorporate some aspects of SharePoint hosting, but more work is required of the developers creating these applications.

Modest transactional requirements

A major benefit of traditional Web applications is that they can be scaled to virtually any audience. The main performance bottleneck for most Web applications is the Web server and its software. Web site performance issues can usually be resolved by adding more hardware and using load-balancing techniques to distribute user demand over multiple database servers. A well-designed Web application (such as Amazon.com) can service many thousands of users simultaneously with acceptable performance.

A SharePoint-hosted Access Web application is not a great platform (even on an intranet) for environments where hundreds of users are constantly adding to or updating data. Although SharePoint uses SQL Server as its underlying database, database updates are considerably slower than when working directly with SQL Server tables through linked Access tables or stored procedures.

In other words, a SharePoint-hosted Access database should not be used for applications requiring high-volume data entry features. Instead, the SharePoint-hosted Access application would be used ideally for moderate database updates and reporting.

Summary

The process of publishing Access applications to SharePoint involves much more than has been discussed in this chapter. My intent was to explain some of the reasoning behind the decision to use SharePoint as the Web platform for Access applications and the implications inherent in using SharePoint for this purpose.

When all goes well, an Access database can be migrated to SharePoint in a few minutes. However, as you will see in Chapter 35, many things may go wrong in the process. Also, large applications that contain a lot of database objects and data take quite a while to publish on Access Services in SharePoint. Successfully publishing a moderate-sized Access application to SharePoint may require a few days of work resolving the compatibility issues flagged by Compatibility Checker.

Deploying Access Applications to SharePoint

A ccess 2010 provides significant new features for developers working on applications that must be shared among many users. In particular, Microsoft is exploiting the features provided by SharePoint Services to extend the reach of Access to situations where Access hasn't been a viable platform.

SharePoint Services provides an excellent platform for Access databases because it comes with many valuable built-in resources that don't have to be added to Access. These resources include a logon and user authentication process, versioning (the ability to roll back to earlier versions), a recycle bin, and navigation tools. SharePoint 2010 is required for the techniques described in this chapter, but many corporations using the Windows operating system already have SharePoint installed, so upgrading to SharePoint 2010 should not be a barrier to adoption of these techniques.

The good news for Access developers is that you don't have to become a SharePoint expert to use these techniques. All that is needed is the URL to a SharePoint server and proper permissions to create SharePoint sites on the server. All the development work is performed in Access 2010, and access to the SharePoint user interface is needed only to verify that the Access objects are reaching their destinations as expected.

On the CD-ROM

This chapter uses the `Chapter35.accdb` database, before the application of any upsizing techniques described in the text. If you haven't already copied this file to your machine from the CD, you'll need to do so now. You'll also need access to SharePoint Server 2010 to experiment with the data-sharing techniques described in this chapter.

IN THIS CHAPTER

Understanding your options when deploying to SharePoint

Resolving issues detected by Compatibility Checker

Looking at SharePoint Deployment Options

It should come as no surprise that Microsoft provides more than one way to deploy Access applications to SharePoint. In their eagerness to encourage developers to consider SharePoint as a platform for Web deployment, Microsoft suggests at least three ways to publish Access databases to SharePoint: table exporting, enhanced table exporting, and publishing to SharePoint.

Cross-Reference
Exporting Access tables to SharePoint is covered in Chapter 34, while this chapter discusses remaining options.

Enhanced table exporting option

In Chapter 33, you saw an example of the simplest of these options: exporting all the tables in an Access 2010 application to a SharePoint site as SharePoint lists. The newly created lists were then linked back to the Access application.

Simply moving the Access tables to SharePoint resolves one of the major complaints about Access. Moving tables into a managed application like SharePoint means that the tables are professionally backed up, protected by SharePoint's security system, and accessible to authorized SharePoint users. The same protection is obtained by upsizing to SQL Server (as described in Chapter 38), but most users are prohibited from viewing or working with the data in a SQL Server database.

The second way to publish an Access database to SharePoint is using the enhanced table exporting technique. This method duplicates the first several steps outlined in Chapter 33 but carries the process one important step further:

1. Open the `Chapter35.accdb` example database.

   The database before deployment is shown in Figure 35.1.

2. Select SharePoint from the Move Data group on the Database Tools ribbon group.

   Access opens the Export Tables to SharePoint Wizard (see Figure 35.2).

3. Specify an existing SharePoint site to receive the tables exported from Access.

   In Figure 35.2, the site is specified as `http://archimedes2008/sites/Access_Bible_Chapter35`.

FIGURE 35.1

The Chapter35.accdb database before deployment

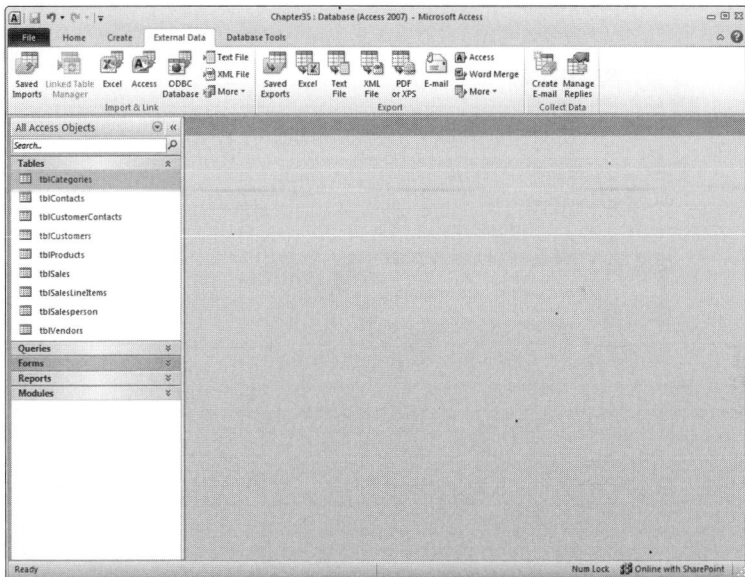

FIGURE 35.2

Access with the Export to SharePoint Wizard open

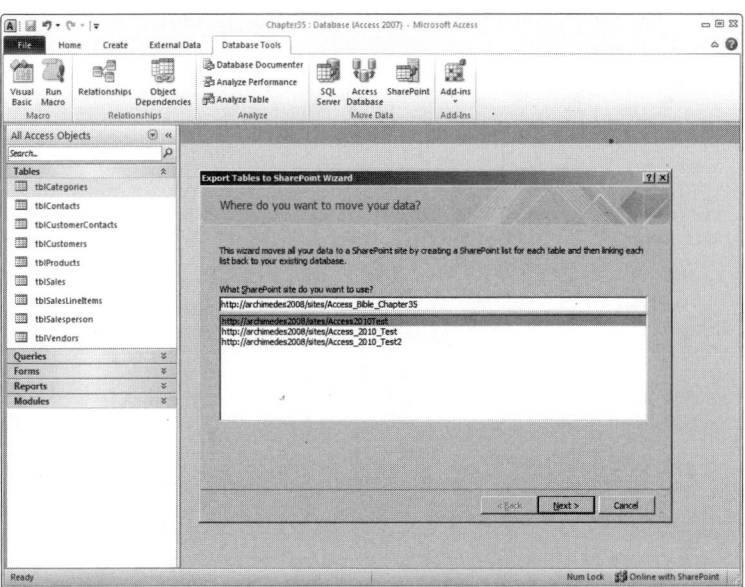

4. Click the Next button.

SharePoint opens the logon dialog box (shown in Figure 35.3), which requests your SharePoint user name and password.

FIGURE 35.3

SharePoint requests the user's credentials.

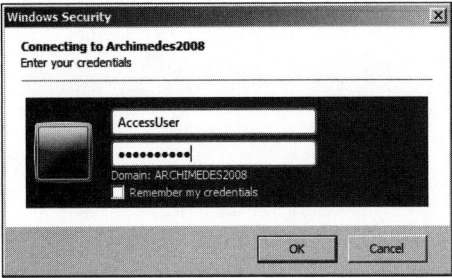

5. Enter your user name (if not already known to SharePoint) and password.

As soon as SharePoint verifies your credentials, the export starts (see Figure 35.4). The export process may take some time, depending on the complexity of the database and the size of its tables.

FIGURE 35.4

Access keeps you informed during the export process.

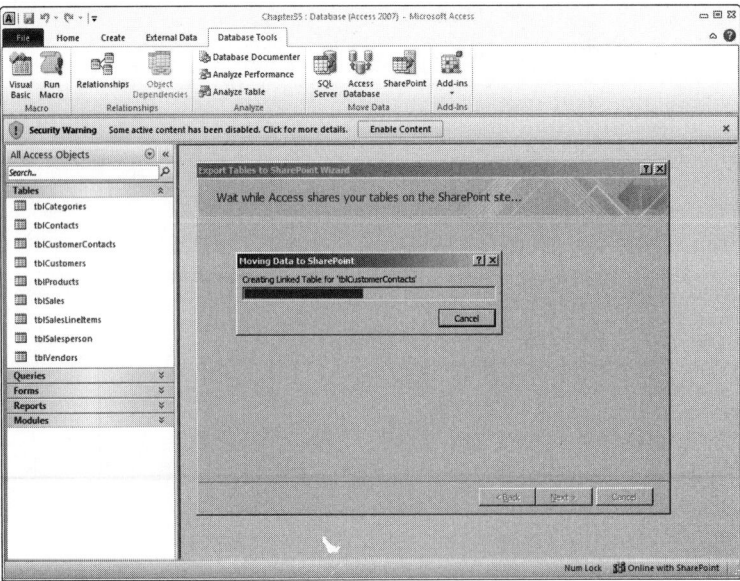

6. The export fails the first time through because of a "Duplicate output destination" error on `tblCustomerContacts` (see Figure 35.5).

   Correct the issue by changing the name of the Title field in `tblCustomerContacts` to `ContactTitle` and repeating Steps 1 through 5. Note that you may not be asked for your SharePoint credentials a second time.

FIGURE 35.5

The Move to SharePoint Issues table helps explain errors during the export process.

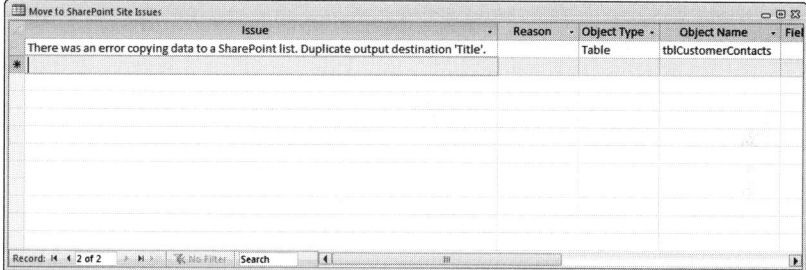

If all goes well, Access creates a backup of the current database, submits the database's tables to SharePoint, and displays the dialog box shown in Figure 35.6.

FIGURE 35.6

Success at last!

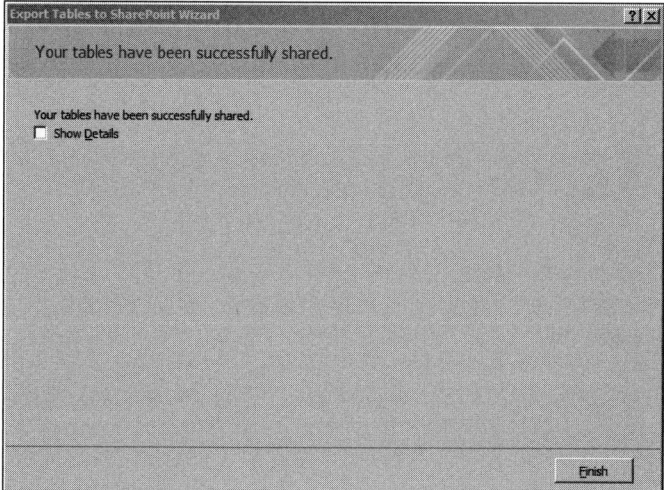

Access builds a link for each table to the newly created SharePoint list (see Figure 35.7).

FIGURE 35.7

The local tables are replaced with links to SharePoint lists.

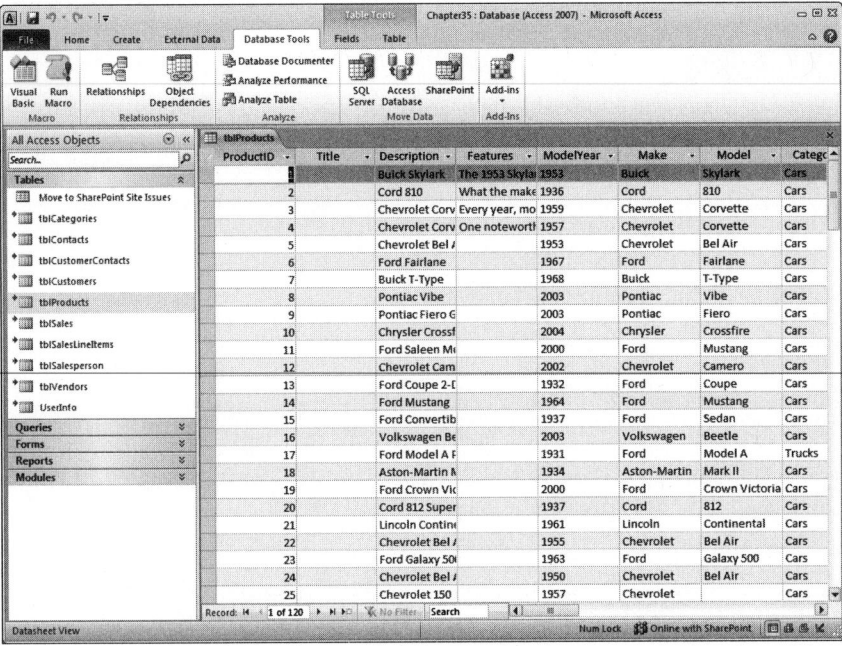

The table shown in Figure 35.7 is hosted in SharePoint as a standard SharePoint list. As discussed previously, working with this data in Access is no different than using a linked SQL Server table, except this same table is available to authorized SharePoint users, as shown in Figure 35.8.

The formatting in Figure 35.8 looks strange because the Features column is a memo field containing a lot of data. You can resolve this minor issue by adjusting the column width and height in SharePoint (a process not described here).

The data in the SharePoint list is fully editable. Authorized users can change existing rows, delete existing rows, and add new rows. Access users see the changes in SharePoint when their datasheets, forms, and reports are refreshed.

The products table as a SharePoint list

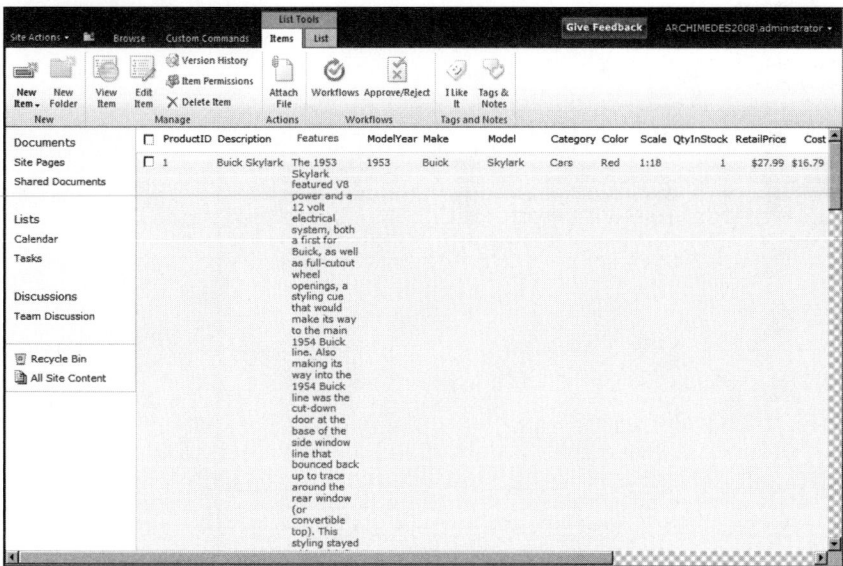

If an export error occurs, Access creates a new table named Move to SharePoint Site Issues that contains a row for each export error. The information in the Move to SharePoint Site Issues table tells you which field in which table failed to export, and why. The table does not suggest how to correct the issue, but in most cases a simple export such as this fails because of data or name incompatibilities between Access and SharePoint. Very often, changing the name of a field (as in this example) is enough to allow the export to proceed.

In spite of the apparent success of the export process just described, several issues were recorded in the Move to SharePoint Site Issues table (see Figure 35.9). None of these issues were fatal to the export process, and all issues may be resolved on the Access side, if necessary.

For instance, one reported issue is that the Picture_Small field was not exported to SharePoint. Because the pictures are important to the users, it would be helpful to come up with a solution. One approach is to set up an Access table that contains only a product ID and the corresponding product picture. You then use a query to join the picture table to the linked products table so that forms and reports still receive the Picture_Small field and display it the same as before the export. Because tblProducts is now a linked table, it's not possible to create a formal one-to-one relationship between tblProducts and tblProductPictures, but Access easily handles an ad-hoc join between tables in a query.

FIGURE 35.9

The final export issues list

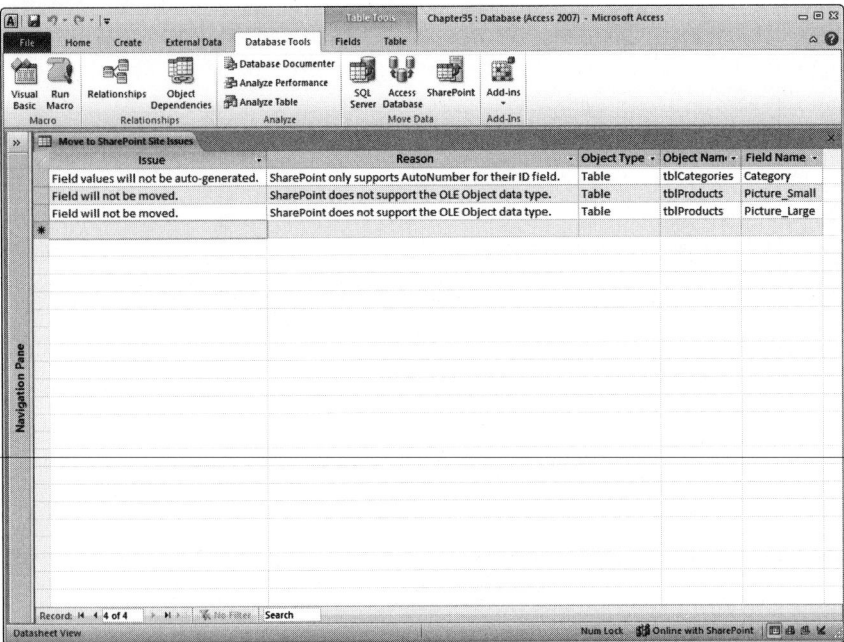

An alternate approach, and one that must be completed before exporting the tables to SharePoint, is to add an Attachment field to tblProducts and use it to store the product pictures. Oddly enough, Attachment fields export to SharePoint without a problem, so the picture can be seen both in SharePoint and in Access. This solution requires changing the queries, forms, and reports in the Access application to use the new Attachment field instead of the former Small_Picture field.

In spite of the errors shown in Figure 35.9, the Access application continues to function as before. During the export process, proxy fields are added to the SharePoint lists as placeholders for the fields that cannot be exported to SharePoint. These fields are typed as "Single line of text" in SharePoint and allow the Access queries, forms, and reports to function as before, even though no data is shown in bound controls on the forms and reports. In this example, you have to devise a solution for the missing SharePoint data before users are able to see the product pictures.

Keep in mind, however, that if you change the name of a field or make other changes to an Access table during the export process, you will have to correct your queries, forms, reports, VBA code, and other database objects. If you make changes, test the application before proceeding with the export because you will have less control over the table's design after the export is complete.

So far, this deployment technique simply duplicates the process described in Chapter 33. The next steps complete the deployment process and make the entire Access application available to all authorized SharePoint users:

1. In SharePoint, open the Shared Documents document library, and click the Add new document link.

   SharePoint opens the Upload Document dialog box, shown in Figure 35.10.

FIGURE 35.10

SharePoint allows you to upload entire Access database files.

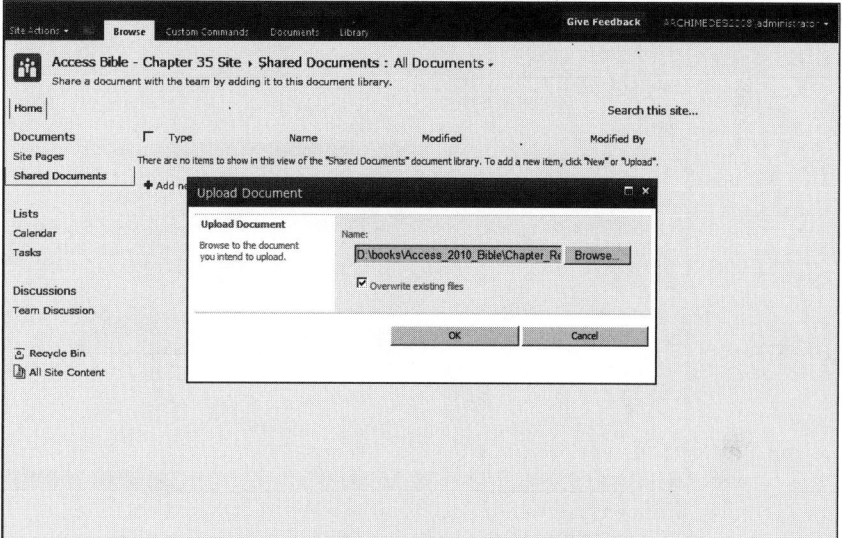

2. Browse to the Access database file and import it to SharePoint.

3. Open the Access database by double-clicking its entry in the Shared Documents list.

   SharePoint opens the Open Document dialog box shown in Figure 35.11.

   The Access application opens on the user's desktop, ready for use.

FIGURE 35.11

SharePoint provides options for opening the Access database.

Access application

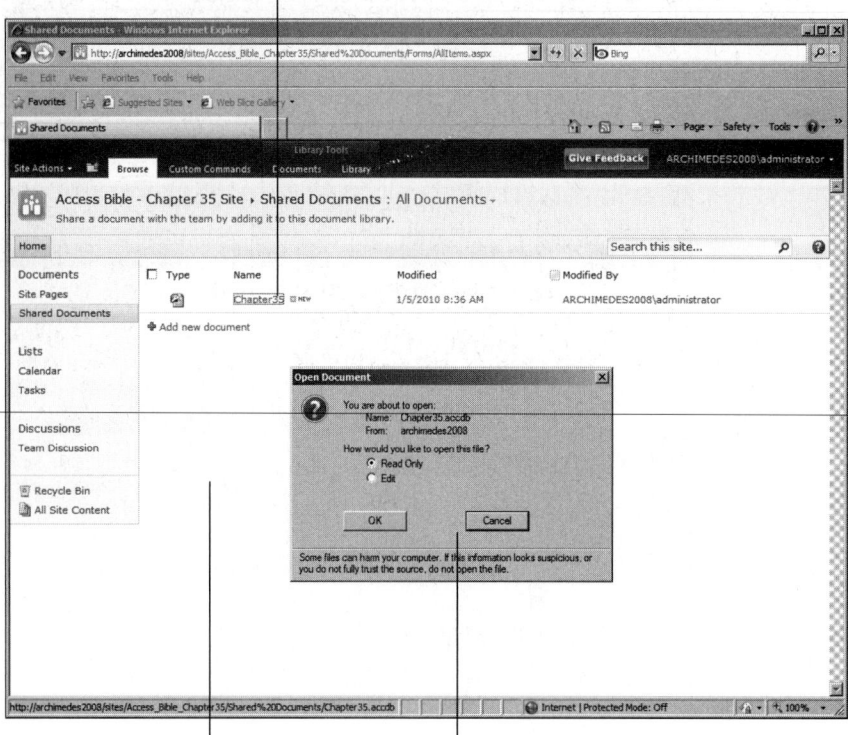

Shared Documents list   Open Document dialog box

The options presented by SharePoint allow users to copy the application to their computer in read-only or edit mode. Read-only mode simply means that the application's design cannot be modified in the copy. The user is still able to work with the application's data. Use the Edit option if you want to make changes to the Access application's design. The editable version of the application is shown in Figure 35.12.

If you choose to copy the database in read-only mode (keep in mind that *read-only* refers to the application's *design,* and not the data in the database), you may receive a security warning message that SharePoint is trying to write to your computer's file system. You may need to add the Access Services application's URL to the Trusted Sites in Internet Explorer to avoid this warning message.

FIGURE 35.12

The Access application copied from SharePoint in edit mode

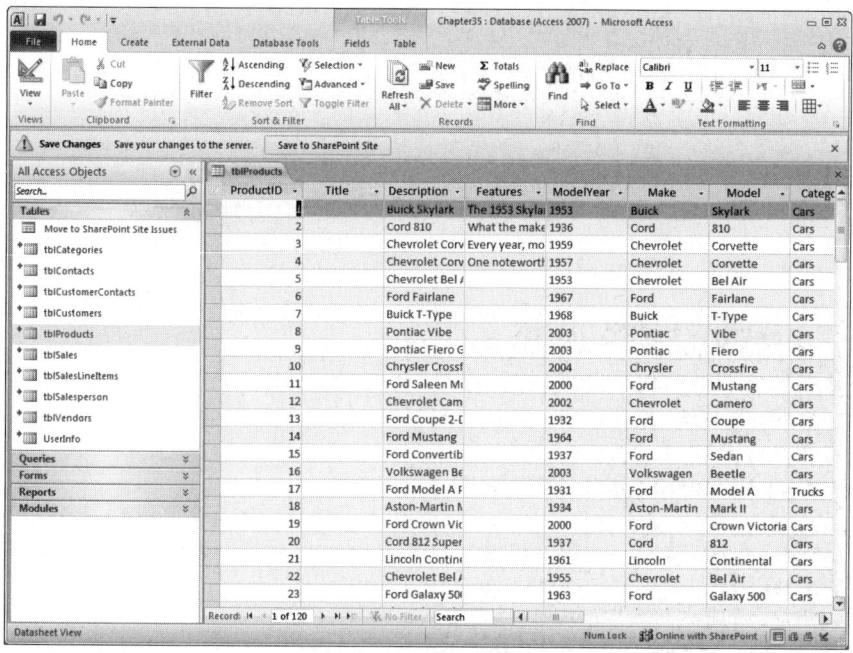

Note that the Access user interface includes a button to copy the changes you make to the application back to SharePoint. Data changes are automatically reflected in SharePoint because all tables are linked to SharePoint lists. You must explicitly submit your application changes, however, to SharePoint before other users see them.

The technique described in this section provides a number of benefits to users and the application. The data is protected by virtue of its existence as SharePoint lists. Users cannot access the data unless they are authorized SharePoint users. Also, users must be granted access to the Shared Documents library before they can open the stored Access application. (The Access application can be stored in a different document library if a higher level of security is required. The Shared Documents library is accessible to all SharePoint users by default.)

Furthermore, presumably the SharePoint site is managed and periodically backed up by system administrators. No working .accdb file can be accidentally deleted or overwritten, and a single copy of the data is shared by all users.

This technique works fine with Access 2007 and SharePoint 2007. Access is able to move tables to SharePoint and link back to the Access application, and SharePoint easily accommodates an Access application as an item in a document library.

Publishing to SharePoint option

The option described in the preceding section has a few problems. Foremost, perhaps, is the fact that users must copy the Access application to their desktop before they can work with it. When dealing with a large `.accdb` file, the copy process may take a few minutes. Also, nothing prevents users from copying an editable version of the `.accdb` file and making changes to it on their desktop. This means that the application may be damaged by a well-meaning user who tries to improve the application by moving things around or renaming a database object.

What is really needed, then, is a SharePoint deployment technique that essentially eliminates the `.accdb` file. If users have no access to the database file, they are left working with the user interface and logic provided by SharePoint. Ideally, a copy of Access (even the runtime) doesn't need to be installed on the user's computer, and the application is run instead in a Web browser.

Understanding publishing to SharePoint deployment

The next deployment option is, perhaps, the most significant new feature in Access 2010. In the following example, an entire Access application is *published* to SharePoint. Specifically, the Access application is published to Access Services running within SharePoint. All the forms, reports, and other database objects in the Access application move into SharePoint, preserving the investment in the Access application. Tables are converted to SharePoint lists (as in the preceding example), and other Access database objects are converted to SharePoint analogs. Queries, for instance, are converted to SharePoint *workflow* objects, because workflows incorporate the logic necessary to select and transform data in SharePoint lists. Forms are expressed as SharePoint Web pages, and macros and VBA code are translated to JavaScript. (Using JavaScript enables the pages to be viewed in virtually any Web browser.)

The user works with the Access application from within SharePoint. The tables, queries, and underlying elements are hidden from the user and are handled by Access Services in SharePoint. All forms are expressed as Web pages, and reports are implemented as SQL Server Reporting Services (SSRS) reports. Any user (with proper SharePoint credentials) can access the application through a Web browser, and the Access runtime is not needed on the user's desktop.

You, as the developer, retain a special copy of the Access application on your desktop. Although the master definition of the application resides on SharePoint, you make changes to the application, including tables, queries, forms, reports, and code, on your desktop and synchronize the changes with SharePoint.

The publishing to SharePoint technique is different from the deployment techniques used in previous versions of Access and, frankly, requires some adjustment. The first time you see a familiar

Access form rendered as a Web page inside a browser, with none of the usual Access user interface objects (such as the Navigation Pane) visible, is an eye-opening experience.

Revisiting Access Services

In Chapter 34, and again in this chapter, you see several references to *Access Services*. As described previously, Access Services is an intrinsic part of SharePoint Server 2010 and is responsible for enabling Access applications to be published to SharePoint. An important part of Access Services is how it supports collaborative development, which means that more than one developer can make changes to an application at the same time.

One issue developers encounter when working with Access is that everything is stored in a single database file. Without resorting to workarounds, it is difficult for two people to work on two different parts of an Access application without each person stepping on the other's work. Access Services makes collaborative development simpler and easier. When an Access application is published to SharePoint, Access Services *serializes* (converts to a text stream) each Access object and stores it separately in SharePoint. As you'll see later in this chapter, this design makes it possible to "check out" a single object, make changes to the object, and sync it back to SharePoint without touching the other objects in the application. In this way, Access Services plays a role as a source code controller, allowing more than one person to work on an application at the same time.

Using Compatibility Checker

When starting on an upsizing process, you begin with a working, completed Access application. Access provides all the tools necessary for SharePoint deployment, and you need to do nothing in SharePoint, other than making sure a destination SharePoint site is available.

Many things can interfere with the deployment process. For example, many Access applications have complex logic in VBA procedures, and the Publish to SharePoint Wizard cannot always convert this complex logic to JavaScript. Also, advanced features such as ActiveX controls may not have .NET analogs, and the wizard cannot provide an appropriate substitute.

Microsoft provides Compatibility Checker to help you detect and respond to issues that interfere or inhibit the publish to SharePoint operation. Unless the application is simple and contains a small amount of data, Compatibility Checker is virtually guaranteed to reveal issues. Compatibility Checker is so important to the publishing process that the Publish to Access Services button in the Backstage area is disabled until Compatibility Checker has scanned the application and found no issues.

Running Compatibility Checker is quite easy. Click the File tab in the upper-left corner of the Access screen to open the Backstage area. Then, in the Backstage area, click the Publish to Access Services button or the Share button (in the Navigation Pane to the left of the Backstage area) to open the Access Services Overview area (see Figure 35.13).

FIGURE 35.13

Running Compatibility Checker is a requirement when publishing to SharePoint.

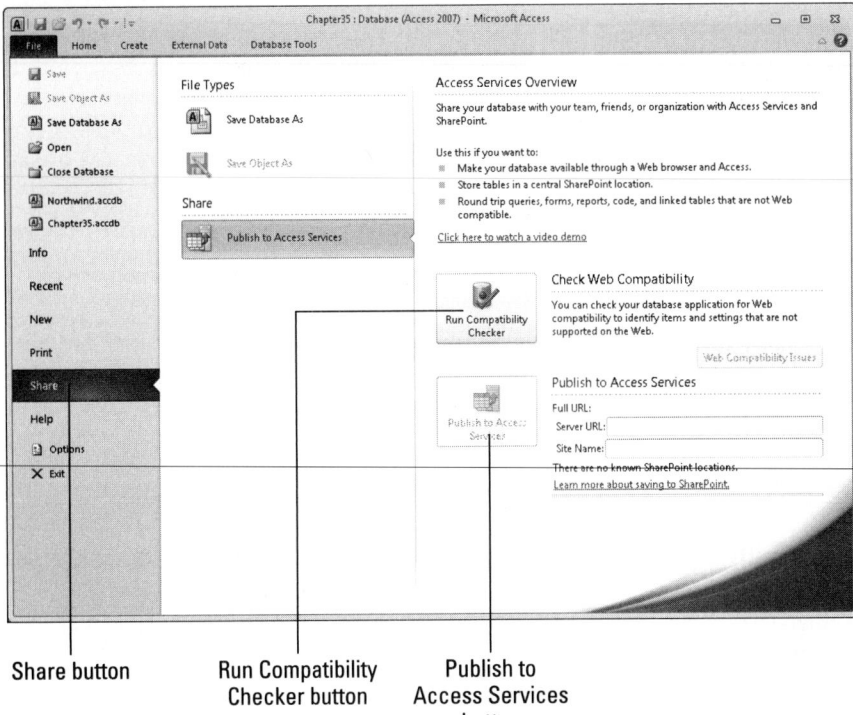

Share button   Run Compatibility   Publish to
                      Checker button   Access Services
                                                   button

After running Compatibility Checker, the Backstage area looks different (see Figure 35.14). Because incompatibilities were found, the Web Compatibility Issues button is enabled, and a message is displayed explaining that the database is incompatible with SharePoint.

The Chapter35.accdb application generated six errors: two are issues with fields in tbl Products and the others are related to the table relationships in the database. Figure 35.15 shows the Web Compatibility Issues table containing these six errors.

The Issue Type ID column in the Web Compatibility Issues table is important. The items in this column are hyperlinks to a Microsoft Web site describing the error (see Figure 35.16). Microsoft did a good job of documenting compatibility errors, and the ability to jump directly to an issue's explanation and suggested solution is useful.

FIGURE 35.14

The Web Compatibility Issues button shows you the problems that are keeping the application from publishing.

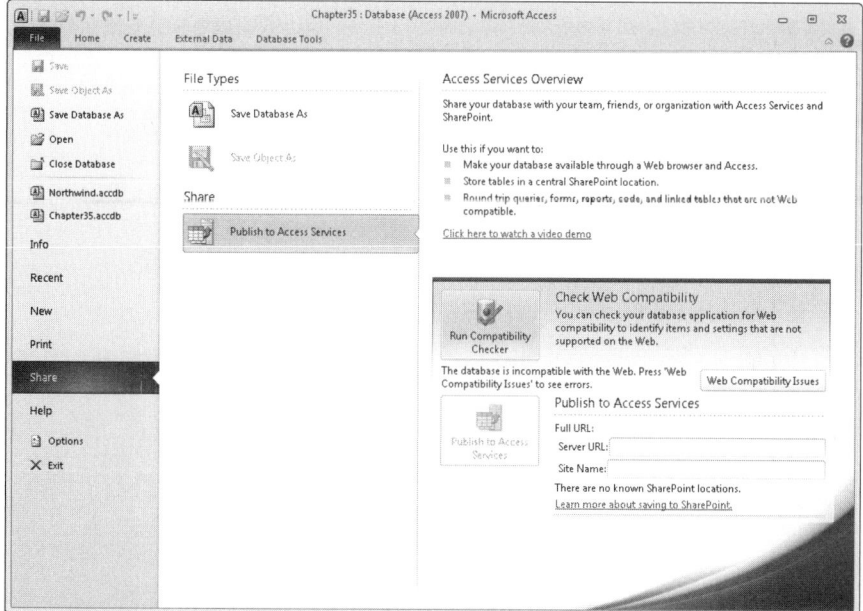

FIGURE 35.15

The Web Compatibility Issues table lists all the compatibility issues detected by Compatibility Checker.

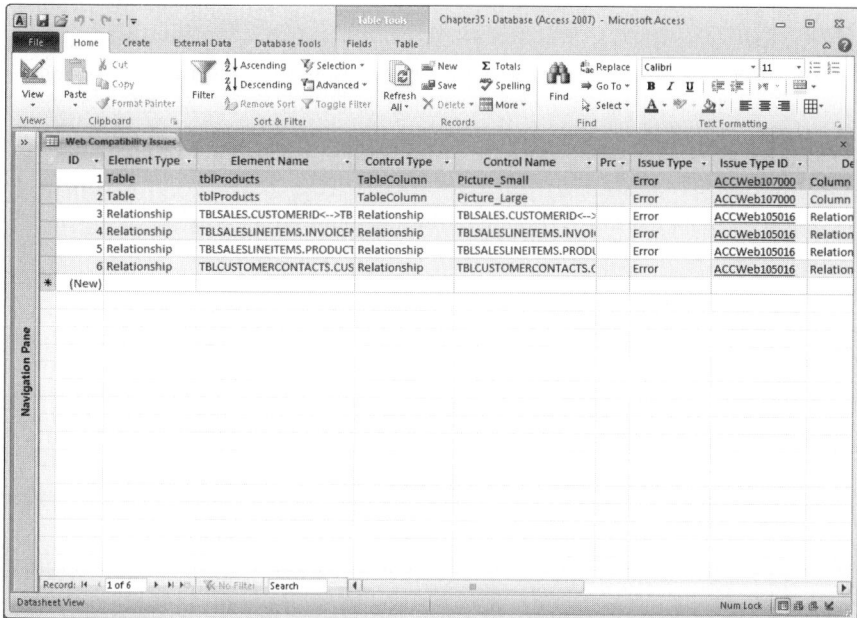

FIGURE 35.16

The online help for compatibility issues is quite comprehensive.

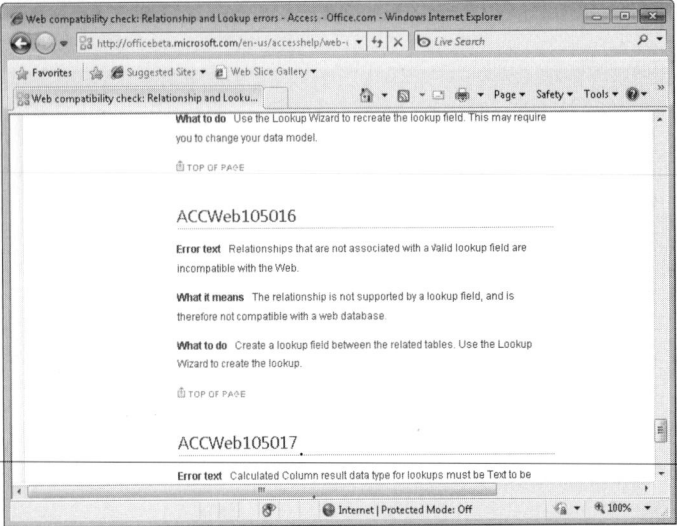

Repairing the error caused by the OLE Object fields in tblProduct (Picture_Small and Picture_Large) is easy. For this example, the data type of each of these fields was changed to Text, but in a production environment you'd probably want to convert these fields to the Attachment data type and add the product picture to these fields.

The relationships issues are a bit different, and more complex, that simple data type incompatibilities. On the SharePoint side, relationships are managed as *lookups* from one table to another. Using the relationship between tblCustomers and tblSales as an example, first delete the relationship between these tables in the Relationships window (opened from the Database Tools ribbon tab). Next, open tblSales in design view and change the data type of the CustomerID field from Number (Long Integer) to Lookup Wizard, which opens the Lookup Wizard dialog box (see Figure 35.17).

You specify the source table for the lookup field in the next Lookup Wizard screen (shown in Figure 35.18). In our case, we specify tblCustomers as the source of the CustomerID field.

FIGURE 35.17

SharePoint requires that you replace formal relationships with lookups.

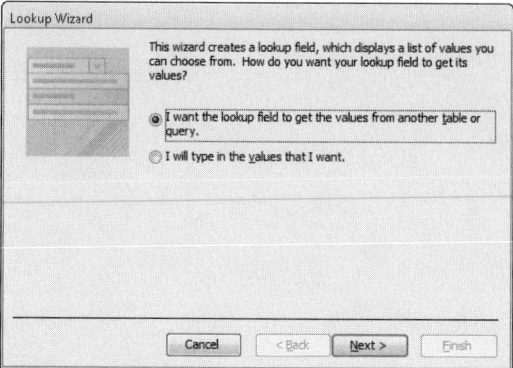

FIGURE 35.18

Specify the source of the lookup field's value in this Lookup Wizard screen.

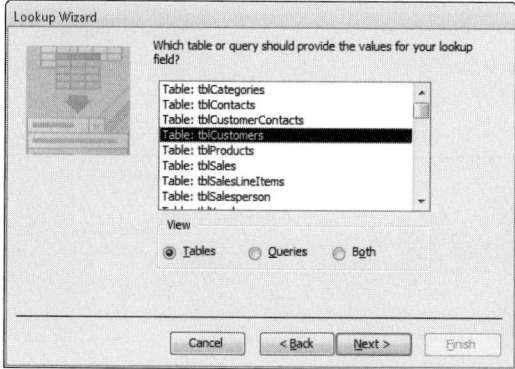

The next Lookup Wizard screen (shown in Figure 35.19) is where we specify which field in tbl-Customers supplies values for the CustomerID field in tblSales.

FIGURE 35.19

Specify the field used to populate the lookup field in tblSales.

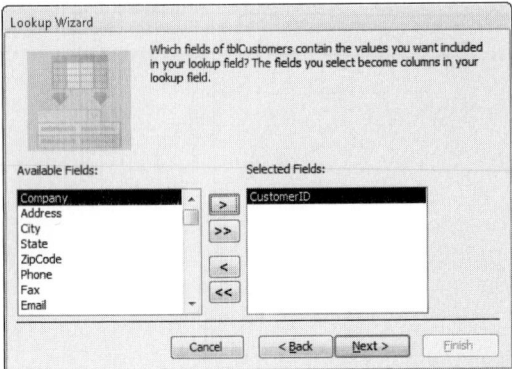

The last screen of interest in the Lookup Wizard is shown in Figure 35.20. We want to make sure that data integrity is enforced between tblSales and tblCustomers. This means we want Access to make sure that any value entered in the CustomerID is matched in tblCustomers. This rule ensures that no record in tblSales is orphaned by the user entering an ID value that doesn't match an existing customer.

FIGURE 35.20

Make sure the Enable Data Integrity check box is selected.

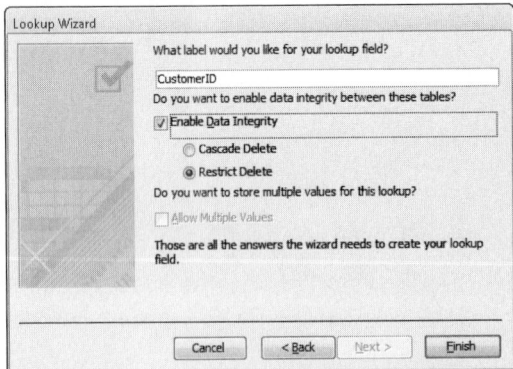

The change to tblSales is superficial. The only visible difference is that tblCustomers now appears as a drop-down list (see Figure 35.21). Because we chose to enforce data integrity on the lookup, the user must select a CustomerID value from this list when adding new customers.

Access uses a drop-down list for the CustomerID lookup field in tblSales.

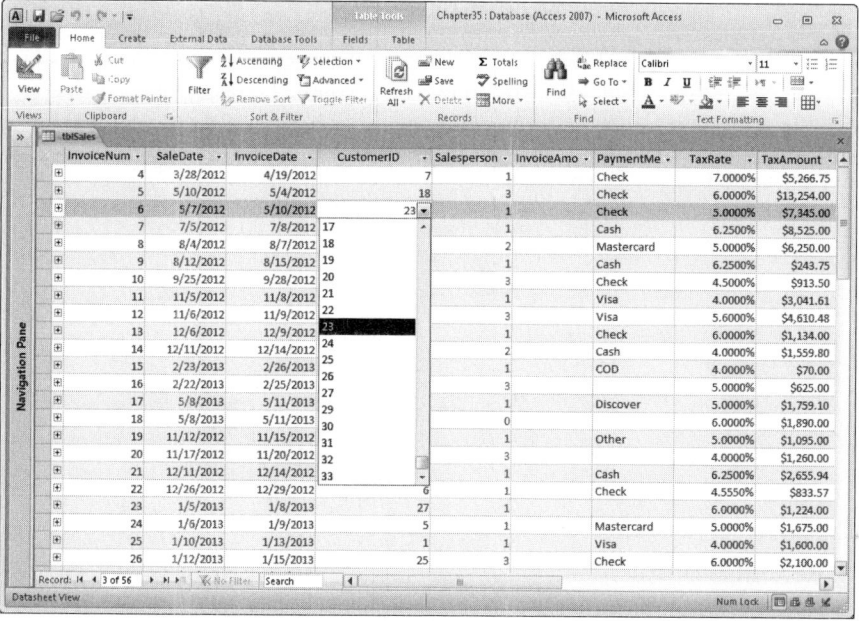

Compatibility Checker is quite thorough. Even a simple Access application may generate dozens of items that must be corrected before publishing to Access Services. The section titled "Dealing with Compatibility Checker Problems," later in this chapter, describes some of the more common issues reported by Compatibility Checker and suggests ways to resolve these issues.

After correcting the problems reported in the Web Compatibility Issues table, run Compatibility Checker again (and again, if necessary!) until "The database is compatible with the Web" message appears just below the Compatibility Checker button and the Web Compatibility Issues button remains disabled (see Figure 35.22).

FIGURE 35.22

Eventually, Compatibility Checker delivers good news!

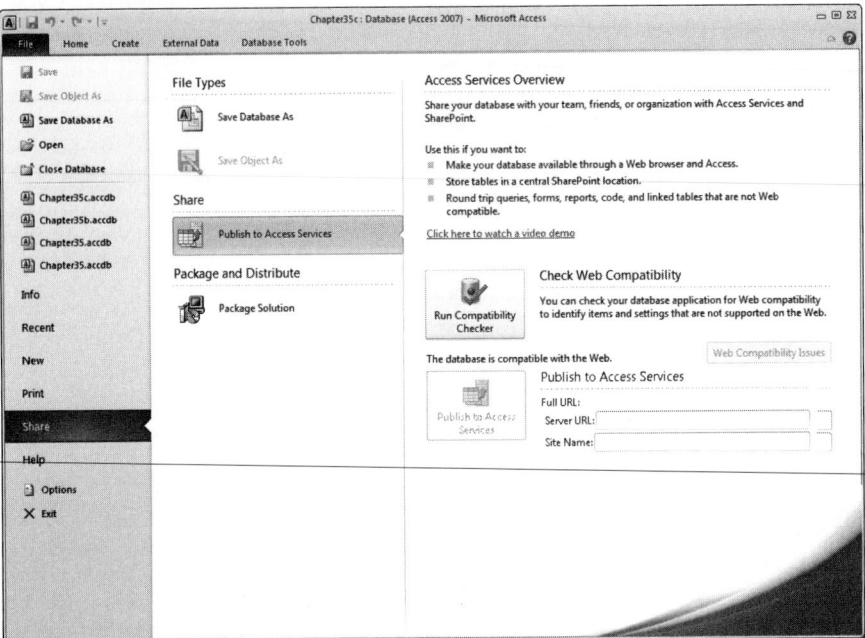

Publishing to SharePoint

After the setup, the preparation, and dealing with compatibility issues, the final step of publishing an Access 2010 application to SharePoint is anticlimactic. Access will publish the database to a *subsite* within an existing SharePoint site. The SharePoint administrator should provide you with a destination site on a SharePoint server and the permissions to create new SharePoint sites before you can proceed with a publishing operation.

Enter the URL to the parent SharePoint site in the Server URL text box, and the name you want to give to your Access Services site in the Site Name text box. In Figure 35.23, the parent URL is http://archimedes2008/sites/, and the Access Services site is MyPublishedSite. Access Services builds the MyPublishedSite (under the parent site) during the upsizing process.

FIGURE 35.23

Enter the parent site URL and the name for the new Access Services site.

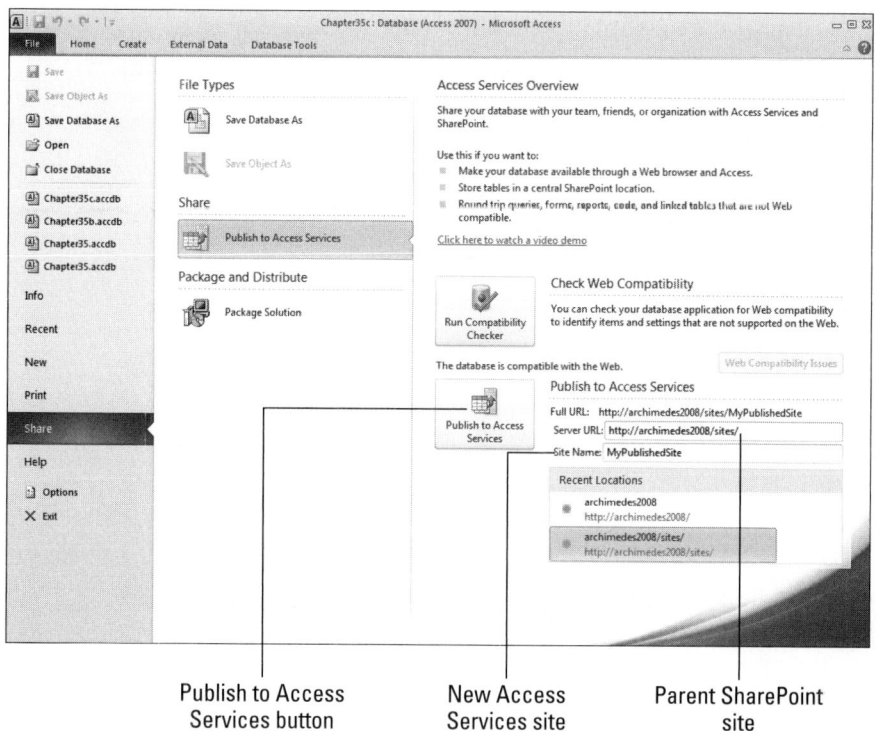

Publish to Access   New Access   Parent SharePoint
Services button   Services site   site

Click the Publish to Access Services button to launch the Publishing Wizard. Access displays the dialog box shown in Figure 35.24, which tracks the publishing progress. Access makes a copy of the application before beginning the publishing process, so you can always return to the previous version, if necessary.

At the conclusion of the process, Access displays the dialog box shown in Figure 35.25.

FIGURE 35.24

Access keeps you informed during the publishing process.

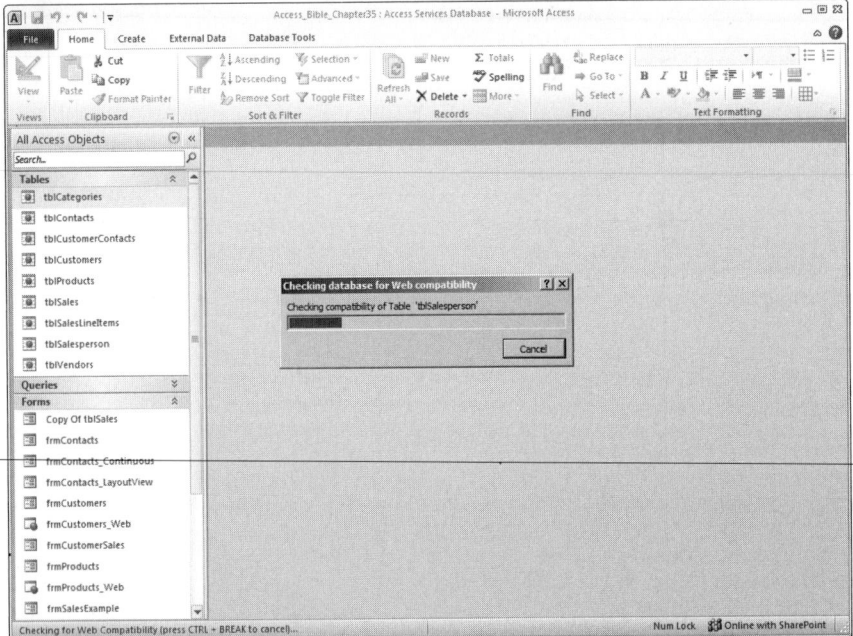

FIGURE 35.25

The publishing process has succeeded at last!

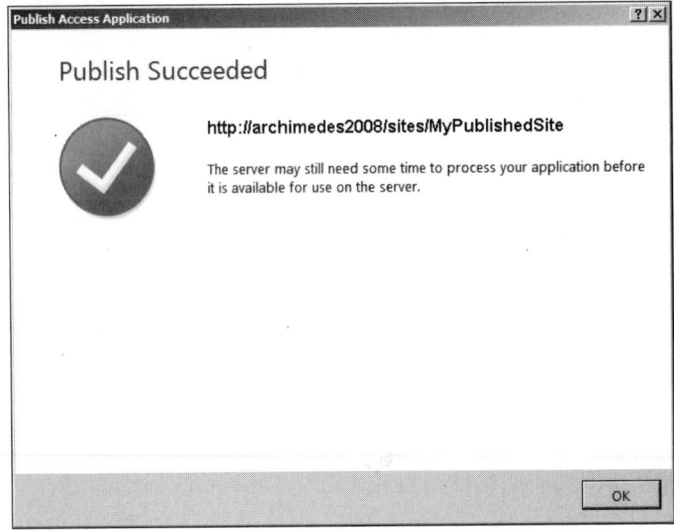

At this point, Access Services has accepted all the tables, queries, and other schema objects and has converted them to SharePoint analogs. The forms, reports, and other objects are moved to the SharePoint site but are not converted to Web versions. We can verify the presence of the new Access Services site by going to SharePoint and opening All Site Content view (see Figure 35.26). The All Site Content page is opened by clicking on the All Site Content link in the SharePoint Navigation Pane.

FIGURE 35.26

The All Site Content view in SharePoint shows the new Access Services site.

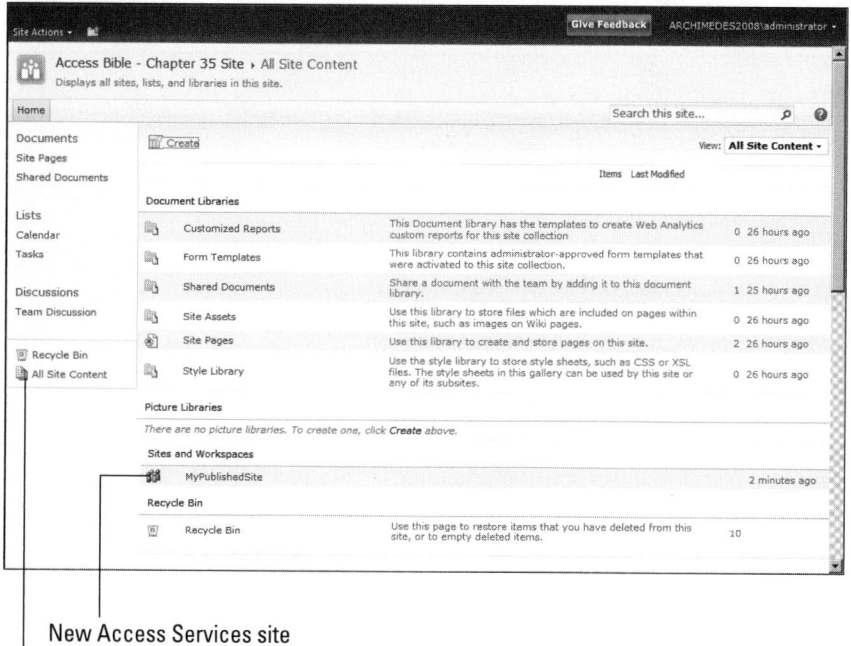

New Access Services site

All Site Content link

Clicking the MyPublishedSite link opens a SharePoint view of the site (see Figure 35.27). Note the upsized Access tables in the top portion of the screen and the migrated Access forms and reports in the lower area. SharePoint users could open any upsized Access tables, but the forms and reports are still *client-side objects* and remain in the Access .accdb file. Client-side objects are not usable in the SharePoint environment. You must use the create and publish new Web versions of the forms and reports you intend for your users to work with in SharePoint.

FIGURE 35.27

FIGURE 35.27

The new Access Services site

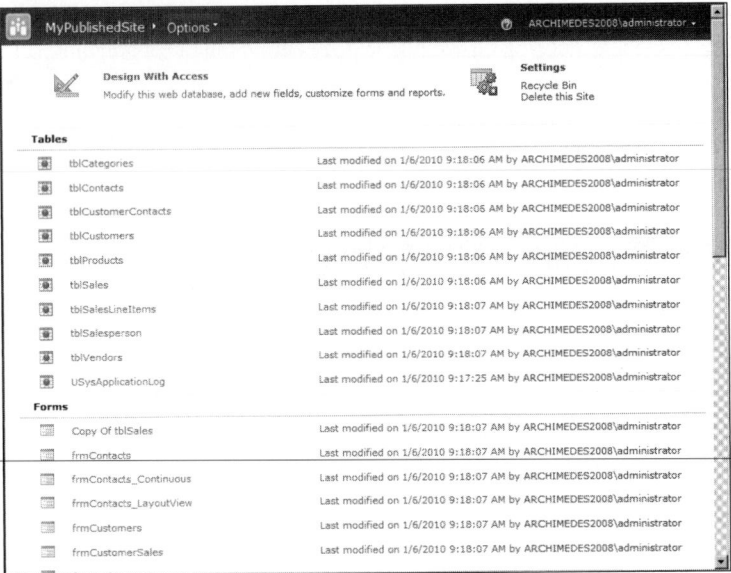

Returning to Access, the next step is to being adding new objects (forms and reports) to the Access Services database. Users browsing to the Access Services site see the view shown in Figure 35.26, which is not a useful application at this point. We need the forms and reports the users will work with and a navigation form to help users select which form or report they want to use.

The first thing to note in Access is that the ribbon has changed (see Figure 35.28). It now displays a number of buttons and controls for creating and working with Web objects. We can't directly use Access client forms in SharePoint, so each form that users need in SharePoint must be created from scratch.

FIGURE 35.28

The Access ribbon now displays Web commands.

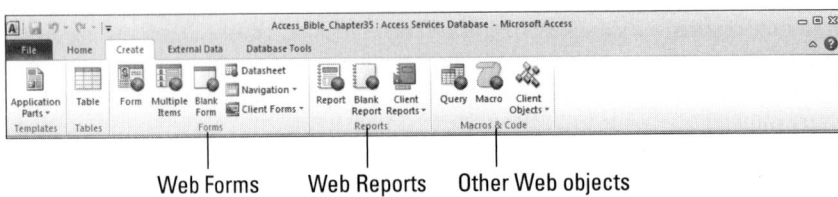

The easiest way to create an Access form is to select a table or query in the Navigation Pane and click the Form button in the Forms ribbon group. By default, Access creates a bound form in layout view (see Figure 35.29). In general, the table format used by layout view is acceptable to most users familiar with data displayed in a Web form, and layout view is a fast and easy way to produce a Web form for the Access Services application. You can always go back and add a more elaborate version of the form later.

FIGURE 35.29

A quick and easy Web form for the Access Services application

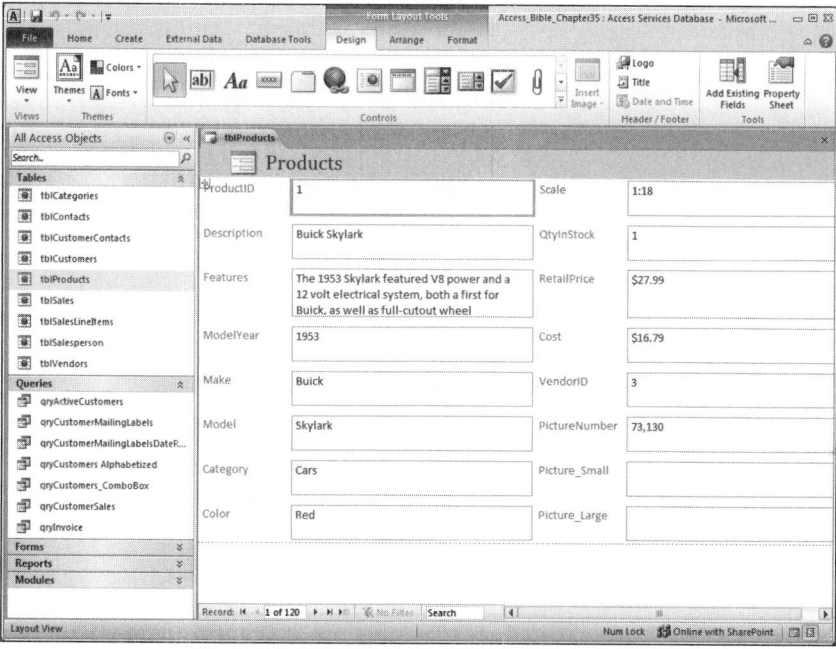

Note the following things about the environment in Figure 35.28. The text in the title bar of the Access window identifies the application as an Access Services Database. This is a clear indication that the application is no longer a standard Access application.

In the Navigation Pane, each table icon is marked with a globe, indicating that these tables are Access Services tables in SharePoint. Opening these tables in Access is like opening any linked table. The data appears exactly as it did before the publishing process. One difference, however, is that — unlike other linked tables — the Access Services table's design is fully editable in Access. In fact, your only means of modifying the design of a table (or adding a new table) published to Access Services is by making the change in the Access client.

You'll recall from previously in this chapter that when users browse to the new SharePoint site created by the publishing process, they see only the list of items exported to SharePoint. They do not see a user interface, a switchboard, or a navigation aid, and nothing shows them where to start.

Microsoft addresses this issue with the new Navigation Web form. This is a simple templated form that lets you quickly build a switchboard for your Web (or traditional) application. Start by selecting Navigation from the Forms group on the Create ribbon tab (see Figure 35.30). In Figure 35.30, we're selecting the Horizontal Tabs design, but you may need or prefer one of the other designs.

FIGURE 35.30

The Navigation form is a new feature in Access 2010.

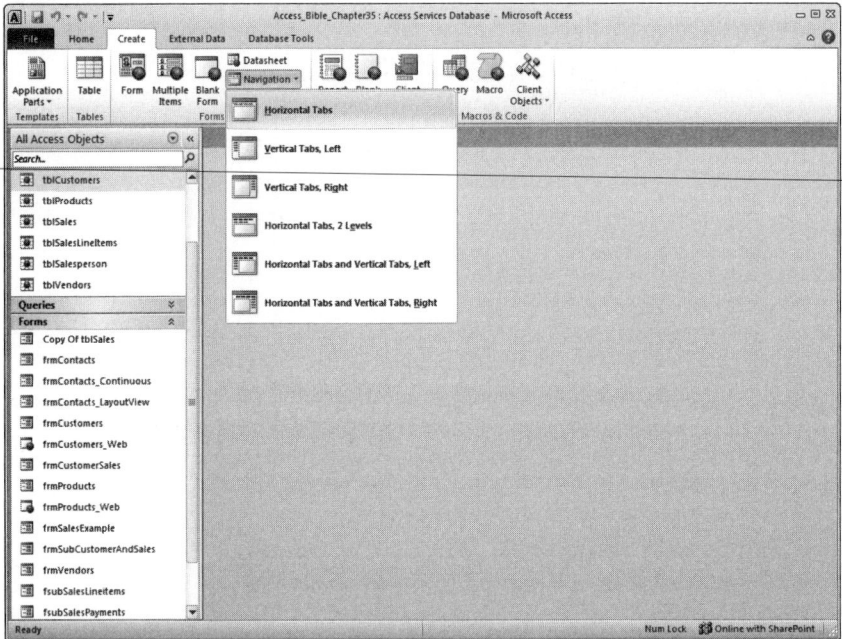

When completed, this navigation form will display a number of tabs across the top of the form. Clicking a tab reveals the form or report indicated by the caption of the selected tab. The navigation form is easy to build. Click a tab, type the tab's caption, and then choose the tab's form from the drop-down list in the `Navigation.TargetName` property (see Figure 35.31).

FIGURE 35.31

Specify the target form or report for each tab in the navigation form.

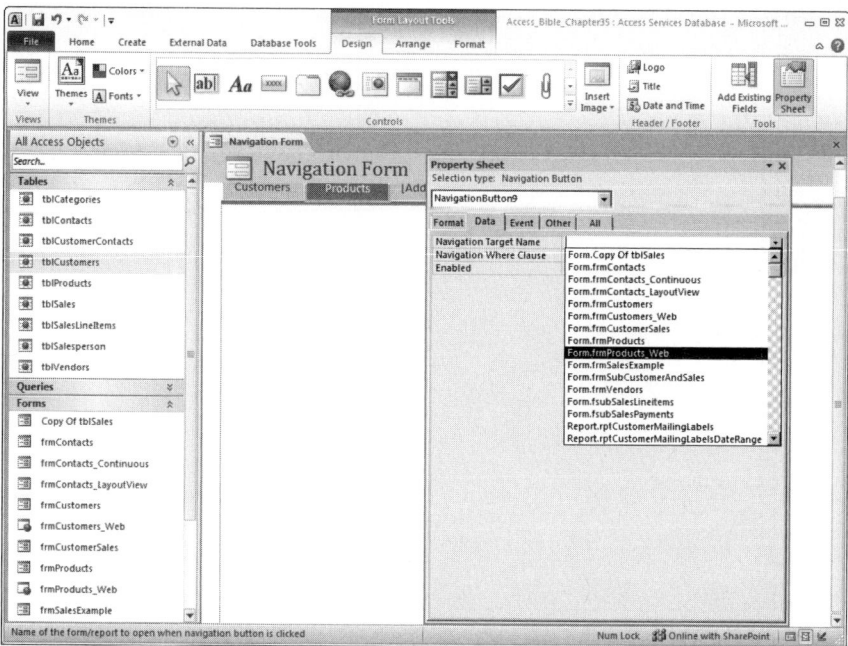

Next, save the form (in Chapter35.accdb, the form is named webNavigationForm): Click the File tab in the upper-left corner of the Access window to open the Backstage area, and click the Options button near the bottom of the screen. Select Current Database, and set the Web Display Form to the name of the new navigation form, as shown in Figure 35.32.

The Web Display Form is added to the Current Database properties when you publish the Access application to SharePoint.

The last step in this long process is to resynchronize your desktop copy of the Access application with the Access Services version. In the Backstage area, click the Sync All button (see Figure 35.33), and Access synchronizes the changes you just made with the application in SharePoint. During this process, you'll see a dialog box similar to that shown in Figure 35.24, except this time it tells you that it's synchronizing your changes with Access Services.

FIGURE 35.32

Set the Web Display Form property to the navigation form's name.

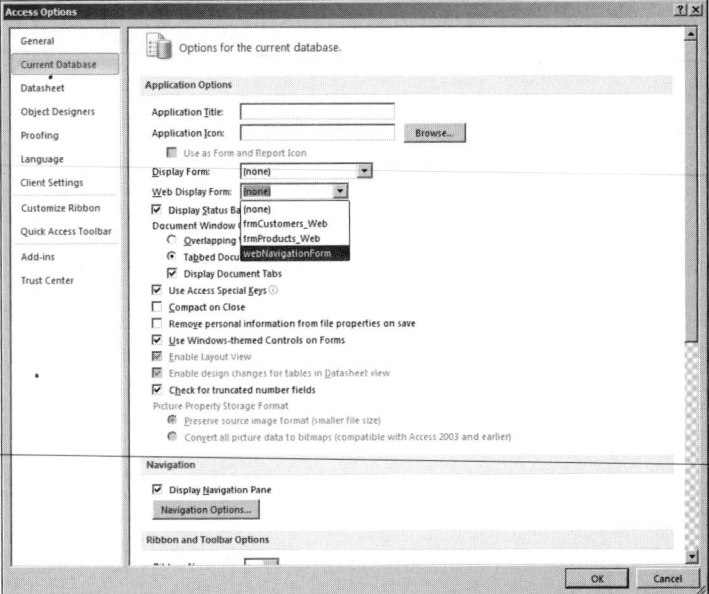

At this point, the application has been successfully published to SharePoint Access Services. The tables, relationships, queries, and other infrastructure are hosted by SharePoint. Users have a form or two to work with and a navigation form to help them get to the forms they need. Figure 35.34 shows the Access Services application hosted in SharePoint when a user browses to the site's URL.

You use the same desktop version of the Access application for maintenance. You make changes to tables, queries, forms, and so on just as you did before the publishing process, and you resynchronize the changes so that users can see them. Users will have to provide a username and password when logging on to SharePoint, but that should not be an obstacle to authorized users.

FIGURE 35.33

Resynchronize with the Access Services version after making changes to the desktop copy.

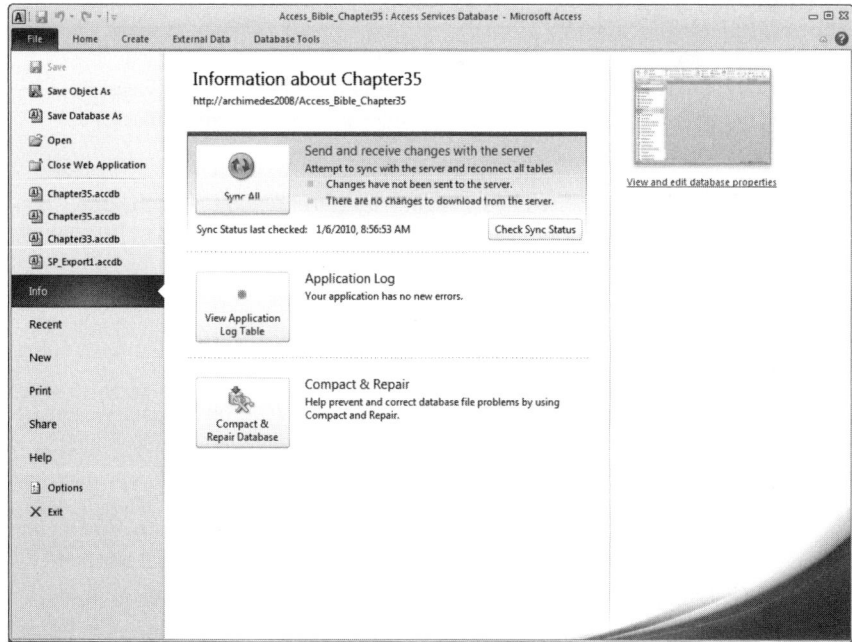

FIGURE 35.34

An Access 2010 application running in SharePoint under Access Services

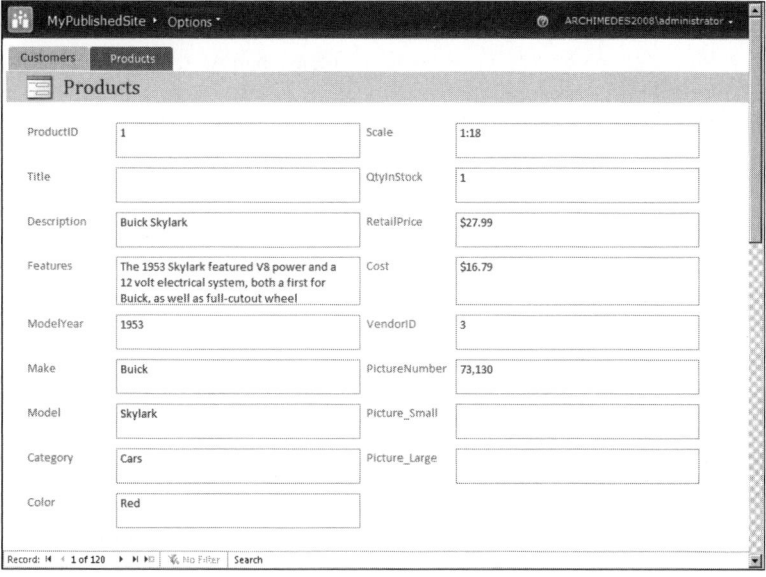

Dealing with Compatibility Checker Problems

Compatibility Checker does a good job of flagging Access 2010 database issues that will cause problems when publishing the application to SharePoint. Virtually every part of an Access application may cause compatibility issues, from a table's design to the actions in a simple macro.

The issues caught by Compatibility Checker are not suggestions for making the application better. You are required to correct the issues reported by Compatibility Checker; otherwise the publish to Access Services process will not succeed.

Some of the most common problems reported by Compatibility Checker are described in this section.

General errors

General errors, by and large, are caused by problems with object names. An object name might contain punctuation or other illegal characters, or there may be a problem with an object named as the target of an OpenForm or OpenReport command.

For example, as explained in the "Object name violations" section, later in this chapter, there is a fairly large number of characters that cannot be included in object names. Most of the issues discussed in this section are easily resolved, while others may require significant work on your part.

References to other database objects cannot be the names of client-side objects. For instance, you can't have a report that is based on a query that has not been published to SharePoint, and you can't have a button on a Web form that opens a report that hasn't been published to SharePoint.

Relationship and lookup errors

Many different types of errors are caused by Access table relationships. Because Access Services uses a different technique for maintaining relationships between tables than Access itself, many conventions commonly followed in Access applications do not apply or must be modified to conform to SharePoint's requirements.

Incompatible fields

SharePoint supports fewer data types than Access, so fields containing data such as OLE objects must be handled differently. The only acceptable field data types are Text, Number, Currency, Yes/No, Date/Time, Calculated field, Attachment, Hyperlink, Memo, and Lookup.

Table relationships

Most table relationships in Access Services are based on lookup fields. You may have to convert some relationships to lookup fields, as described in the "Using Compatibility Checker" section, earlier in this chapter. Also, the field in the parent table used to populate the lookup in the child table must be the parent table's primary key.

Primary key constraints

All primary keys must be AutoNumber fields. Access Services uses long integers exclusively as primary keys, so if any table contains a primary key that is not a long integer, you must update the table accordingly.

Lookup field issues

Foreign key fields in child tables are called lookup fields in Access Services, or at least, Access Services uses lookup fields to reference the primary keys in parent tables. This means that a lookup field (a foreign key field in a child table) must be one of the following data types: Text, Date/Time, Number, or Calculated field that returns a text value.

A lookup field used to form a relationship to another table can be a *value list* (a hard-coded list of values). If you choose to use a value list for a lookup field, the value list must contain at least one item. This means that you must include a dummy value in the value list if you plan to populate the lookup list with code at runtime.

The source table for a lookup list (that is, the parent table) must exist when the Access application is published to SharePoint. You won't be able to create the parent table at runtime and backfill the foreign key values after building the parent table.

An expression used to populate a lookup field list must reference a single table. You can't use an expression that includes more than one table.

Form and report errors

Most errors reported by Compatibility Checker are caused by differences in the controls used on Access forms and reports and their Web equivalents. Access features a rich set of form and report controls, and only a subset of those controls are supported on the Web.

Unsupported form controls

Certain controls are not compatible with the Web. These controls are ActiveX, Chart, Hyperlink, EmptyCell, Image, FrameLine, OLEDocument, OptionButton, OptionGroup, PageBreak, Rectangle, and ToggleButton. The acceptable controls are CheckBox, ComboBox, CommandButton, Form, FormDetail, FormFooter, FormHeader, Image, Label, ListBox, NavigationButton, NavigationControl, Page, Subform, TabList, TextBox, and WebBrowser. If your forms use any of these controls, you'll have to redesign the forms to remove these controls.

Problems with form events

SharePoint does not accept all form events. The only form events that are compatible with Access Services are AfterUpdate, OnApplyFilter, OnChange, OnClick, OnCurrent, OnDblClick, OnDirty, and OnLoad. If your forms use code attached to any other events, the forms will have to be redesigned.

Control issues

Form and report headers and footers cannot contain bound controls. You have to move bound controls to the body of the form or report or replace bound controls with unbound equivalents.

Unsupported report controls

The list of unsupported report controls is surprisingly long. This is probably because Access Services reports are expressed as SSRS (SQL Server Reporting Services) reports and are therefore limited to the set of controls supported by SSRS. The unsupported controls are ActiveX Controls, Attachment, Bound Object Frame, Button, Chart, ComboBox, Insert Page Break, Remove Page Break, Insert Page, ListBox, Option, Option Group, Rectangle, Subform, Subreport, Toggle Button, and Unbound Object Frame.

The supported controls on Access Services reports are CheckBox, Detail, Empty Cell, Group Footer, Group Header, Hyperlink, Image, Label, Page Footer, Page Header, Report, Report Footer, Report Header, and TextBox.

Reports do not support events

All event procedures must be removed from reports. SSRS reports do not support events.

Reports do not support subreports

Subreport controls must be removed from reports.

Object name violations

SharePoint has a problem with object names that contain punctuation. If any of your forms, reports, or controls include the following punctuation characters, they must be removed before publishing:

/ \ : * ? "" < > | # <TAB> { } % ~ &

Query errors

Some queries are incompatible with Access Services. For instance, you may have to reconstruct some queries to remove references to custom VBA functions, or to simplify queries that use sub-queries. In particular, Access Services has a hard time dealing with queries that reference same-named fields in multiple tables, so you may have to rename fields in your tables to accommodate this issue.

Problems with SQL statements

Access Services can't evaluate SQL statements in queries for many reasons. The SQL statement may, for instance, reference a Web-incompatible object. If Access Services can't evaluate the object, the SQL statement is invalid. The best way to resolve SQL issues is to review the SQL statement in Access Query Designer. Very often, the issue becomes obvious because Query Designer fails to display the query's details in the QBE grid.

Query join issues

The fields used to define joins between tables in a query must be compatible. Both fields must be the same data type, such as text or numeric.

Invalid expression errors

Queries sometimes contain expressions that cannot be evaluated by Access Services. If a query fails Compatibility Checker but otherwise seems valid, look closely at the query's SQL statement to see whether all the expressions are properly composed.

Invalid query name

Query names cannot begin with an equal sign (=) or include a period (.). Query names also cannot include any of the following punctuation and special characters: exclamation mark (!), square brackets ([]), <Enter> or <TAB>, or any of the following symbols:

/ \ : * ? " < > | # { } % ~ &

Queries cannot include subqueries

Access Services is unable to evaluate subqueries (queries used as input to other queries). You'll have to rewrite queries that use subqueries before publishing them to SharePoint.

Macro errors

Macros are another common source of compatibility errors. Most often, macro incompatibilities stem from using macro actions that are unavailable in Access Services or whose names conflict with SharePoint reserved words.

Reserved word collisions

The following words are reserved in SharePoint. Do not use the following words as the names of database objects (tables, fields, forms, reports, queries, and so on): UserInfo, Lists, Docs, WebParts, ComMd, Webs, Workflow, WFTemp, Solutions, Report Definitions, and MSysASO.

Incompatible macro actions

In addition to these issues, many macro actions are not compatible with Access services. You may have to rewrite macros to eliminate these macro actions or convert macros to VBA procedures to work around this limitation. The invalid macro actions include AddMenu, ApplyFilter, ApplyOrderBy, Beep, CopyDatabase, CopyObject, DeleteObject, DisplayHourGlassPointer, Echo, EmailDatabaseObject, FindNextRecord, FindRecord, GoToPage, ImportExportData, LockNavigationPane, MaximizeWindow, MinimizeWindow, MoveAndSizeWindow, NavigateTo, OpenDataAccessPage, OpenDiagram, OpenFunction, OpenModule, OpenQuery, OpenStoredProcedure, OpenTable, OpenView, OutputTo, PrintOut, Quit, Rename, RepaintObject, Restore, RunApp, RunCommand (all options other than UndoRecord, SaveRecord, and DeleteRecord), RunCode, RunSavedImportExport, RunSQL, SearchForRecord, SelectObject, SendKeys, SetDisplayedCategories, SetMenuItem,

SetValue, SetWarnings, ShowToolbar, SingleStep, TransferSharePointList, TransferSpreadsheet, TransferSQLDatabase, and TransferText.

The following is the list of acceptable macro actions: SetOrderBy, BrowseTo, ClearMacroError, CloseWindow, GoToControl, GoToRecord, MessageBox, OnError, OpenForm, OpenReport, RefreshRecord, RemoveAllTempVars, RemoveTempVar, Requery, RunCommand (only UndoRecord, SaveRecord, and DeleteRecord), RunDataMacro, RunMacro, SetFilter, SetLocalVar, SetOrderBy, SetProperty, SetTempVar, StopAllMacros, and StopMacro.

Schema errors

Schema errors include all the things that may be wrong with table design, table properties, field data types, field properties, and other aspects of the database's data structures.

Lookup field issues

Many schema errors are caused by problems with lookup fields. These procedures explain how to launch the Lookup Wizard in datasheet view to correct these problems by creating or modifying a lookup field.

In lookup fields using value lists, all items on the list must be text.

Previously in this chapter, you read about the common error "A primary key which is a lookup is incompatible with the Web." This error requires removing the existing relationship between the child and parent tables, and converting the foreign key field in the child table to a lookup field type. The easiest way to do this is with the Lookup Field Wizard.

Field data type issues

The only valid data types for Access Services are Text, Number, Currency, Yes/No, Date/Time, Calculated, Attachment, Hyperlink, Memo, and Lookup.

Primary key issues

All primary keys must be AutoNumbers. Composite keys are not supported in Access Services.

Attachment field limitations

Attachment fields are supported in Access Services, but only one Attachment field is permitted in each table. If multiple Attachment fields exist in an Access table, combine the fields by moving all the attachments from one field into the other field.

Calculated field issues

The only valid data types produced by calculated fields are Text, Number, Currency, Yes/No, and Date/Time.

Table field issues

Fields in Access Services tables can contain a maximum of 220 fields. This number is less than the 255 fields permitted in Access tables, so you may have to redesign tables if the maximum column count is exceeded.

Table name issues

The following are reserved words in SharePoint and cannot be used as table names: UserInfo, Lists, Docs, WebParts, ComMd, Webs, Workflow, WFTemp, Solutions, Report Definitions, and MSysASO.

Custom field formats are not compatible

Your tables cannot contain any custom formats for currency and dates (such as "MM/dd/yyyy") in field properties. You must use the predefined formats (Long Date, Short Date, and so on). The only numeric formats acceptable to Access Services are General Number, Percent, and Standard.

Unique property must be false

The Unique property must be set to false for the following data types: Memo, Yes/No, and Hyperlink.

AutoNumbers are reserved for primary keys

No field, other than a table's primary key, can be an AutoNumber. Access Services reserves the AutoNumber data type for primary keys only.

Summary

This chapter has looked at the new publish to SharePoint feature in Access 2010. The upsized application runs in Access Services, a new SharePoint resource that permits relational tables, queries, and other database objects to behave like a traditional Access application.

The publish to SharePoint technique described in this chapter is applicable only to Access 2010 and SharePoint 2010. You will not be able to publish an Access 2007 application to SharePoint unless you open it in Access 2010.

Part VI

Access as an Enterprise Platform

Over its many versions, Access has increasingly been used in enterprise environments. No other desktop database provides access to as many different data sources as Microsoft Access, yet supports an attractive, easy-to-use interface. Access has been used to create every conceivable type of database application, from managing kids' soccer teams to handling accounts receivable for Fortune 500 companies.

Each version of Access has extended previous capabilities as an enterprise development platform while introducing new features geared to client-server database applications. Access 2010 seamlessly integrates with all current versions and editions of SQL Server without sacrificing performance or ease of use. Even beginning developers can succeed in working with large SQL Server databases using Microsoft Access as a development tool.

The chapters in Part VI explain client-server computing from the Access developer's perspective. I explain the essential SQL Server features and technologies involved when consuming SQL Server data on Access forms and reports, or when upsizing an existing Access database to SQL Server. In these chapters, you'll learn about SQL Server data types, SQL Server stored procedures, and how to integrate server data with your Access applications.

IN THIS PART

Chapter 36
Client/Server Concepts

Chapter 37
SQL Server as an Access Companion

Chapter 38
Upsizing Access Databases to SQL Server

Client/Server Concepts

H istorically, the term *client/server* has been applied to two-tier computer systems. The fundamental characteristic of a client/server system is that tasks are partitioned between two different computers. One computer (the *server*) is primarily involved in providing some kind of service, while another computer (the *client*) is usually charged with supporting a user interface and interacting with the user.

There are many kinds of servers: file servers, application servers, Web servers, printer servers, mail servers, and (the subject of this chapter) database servers. The term *server* applies to both hardware and software. In a hardware context, a server is (usually!) an exceptionally well-equipped computer, with a lot of memory (often in excess of 16GB), large hard disks (several terabytes is not uncommon in database servers), and an operating system that is specifically designed for managing many, many resource requests at one time.

Server computers are often arranged as *clusters* or *farms,* where multiple computers, using their specialized operating systems, work together as a single, really big computer. When working with a server cluster, a user isn't aware that more than a single computer is at work.

Server operating systems and software offer features and capabilities not found in desktop operating systems. Generally speaking, server software is specifically designed for multiuser operation, and provides greater security, memory access, and optimization techniques not usually found in desktop software.

Server software typically involves applications that are meant to be shared among multiple users. An application like SharePoint is a good example. A properly designed and maintained SharePoint installation can service hundreds of simultaneous users with only minor performance issues.

IN THIS CHAPTER

Distinguishing between the client and the server

Understanding multi-tiered computer systems

Understanding how Access fits into client/server architecture

A client/server environment is typically used to service a single company, using a local area network (LAN), or sometimes a wide area network (WAN), where many, many client computers communicate with a single server computer. The server computer, quite literally, serves up information and services. The client computer consumes information provided by the server computer. Of course, there is a two-way interaction between the client computer and the server computer, such that client computers can also send information back to server computers.

The classic example of client/server computing is the relationship between your computer and a Web server handling requests for a Web page. Your computer and its Web browser are the client. The Web server hosting the Web page is the server. You don't need to know anything about the Web server, its location, the server software it's running, or anything else, to use the Web page. Even if a software add-in is required to display or run a particular Web page, most often the add-in installation occurs automatically.

In this scenario, the Web server is responsible for retrieving the HTML, images, and other resources required by the Web page, and your Web browser is responsible for rendering the HTML into the page you see on the screen. The Web browser is also responsible for accepting your input (mouse clicks, keyboard entry, and so on) and transmitting the input to the Web server.

Very often, as in this case, the client is an active participant, and runs executable code on the client machine. In the case of a Web browser, the code might include JavaScript or VBScript embedded on the page, ActiveX controls included in the page's display, or other controls such as Flash Player.

From the perspective of browsing a Web page, the Internet is nothing more than a wide-area network connecting computers through the TCP/IP networking protocol. Each computer running a Web browser is a client connecting to resources provided by Web servers. Most often, very little data is stored on the client computers, while vast amounts of data may be kept on the Web servers. The primary purpose of the Web browser application running on the client computers is to provide an interface to the data provided by the Web servers.

In an Access environment, client/server architecture includes environments where an Access database communicates with a server database engine (usually Microsoft SQL Server) running on a remote server computer, or even running on the same computer as Access.

Looking at the Parts of Client/Server Architecture

A client/server setup is essentially one or more client computers (workstations) running some kind of application. That client application is connected (usually through a network) to a server computer. The client application's features — such as input screens and reports — provides an interface to the data managed on the server computer. In many client/server environments, the only activity that occurs on the client computer is the interaction between the user and the application.

Figure 36.1 illustrates one possible client/server architecture deployed in a corporate environment. Everything is connected to the central server computer. A single server computer (which may be a cluster or Web server farm) provides local access to client computers across a local intranet. At the same time, the server provides access to remote computers across the Internet. The same data is shared by all users, whether local or remote. All the client computers, the Internet browsers shown in the cloud, and even the printer are effectively client applications of one form or another.

Note

The printer shown in Figure 36.1 outputs reports sent by both client computers and the server computer. In this case, a printer is a client to the server computer, as well as a resource provided by the server.

Alternatively, the computers in the Internet cloud in Figure 36.1 may be other Web servers that indirectly provide data to the client computers connected to the server computer. The actual connections between the computers in Figure 36.1 are somewhat conceptual, and the distinction between client and server depends on which computer is accessing data stored on another computer.

FIGURE 36.1

A common client-server computer-system layout

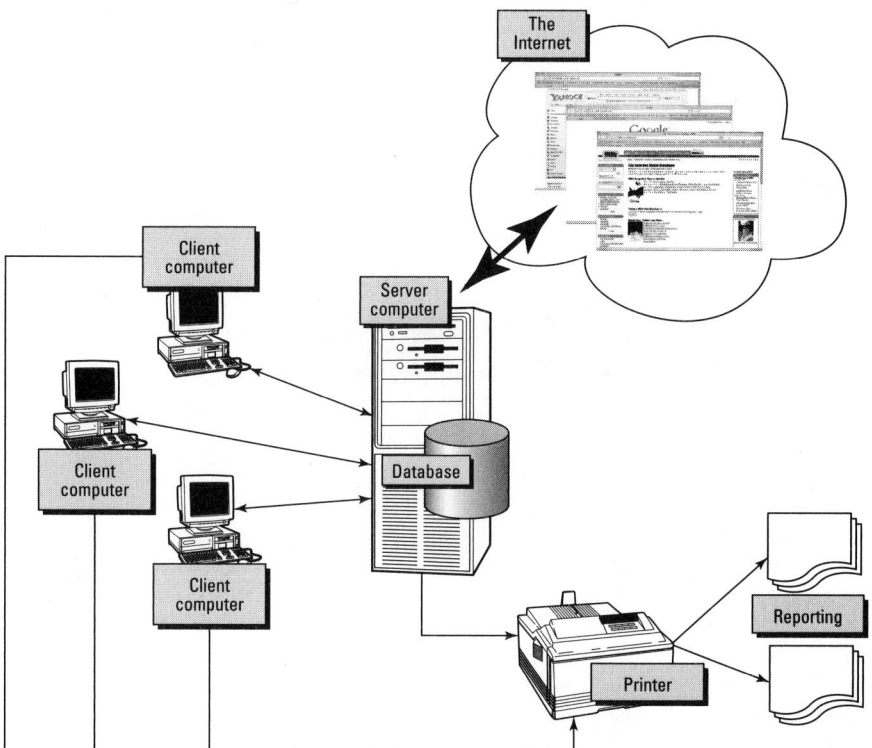

If you're a user sitting at the leftmost client computer and your application is using data stored in the database on the server computer, you're obviously working in a tight client/server system. If, however, your application needs data stored on a remote computer located on the Internet, the server computer (at least temporarily) becomes a client with regard to the remote server machine.

Very often, the distinction between client and server is not entirely clear. In the case of an Access application working with data stored in SQL Server, however, Access is always the client and SQL Server is always the server.

Applications

Figure 36.1 illustrates how the terms *client* and *server* are used when considering a computer system as a whole. A client may be physically located near the server computer, or it may be very distant and accesses the server through the Internet.

An *application* is a program running locally on a client computer. The application performs the operation of connecting the client computer to a server computer. The server computer can be somewhere on the local network or located on the Internet. Figure 36.2 and Figure 36.3 show two different applications.

From these figures, it's not clear exactly where the data displayed on the forms is stored. When properly implemented, the user is unaware of whether the data is stored locally or remotely in a server application. The data could be sourced from SQL Server or SharePoint, or it could be more local as linked tables in a back-end Access database file, or contained entirely within the current .accdb file.

FIGURE 36.2

An automobile products application entry screen (an Access form)

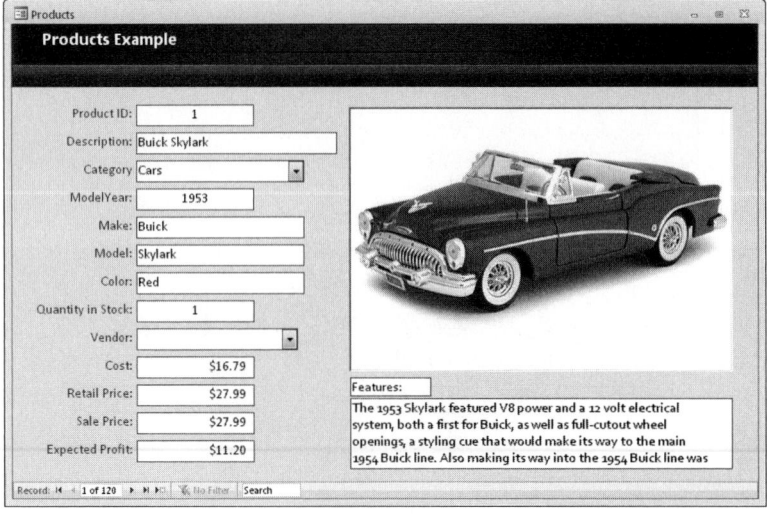

FIGURE 36.3

A contacts application entry screen (an Access form)

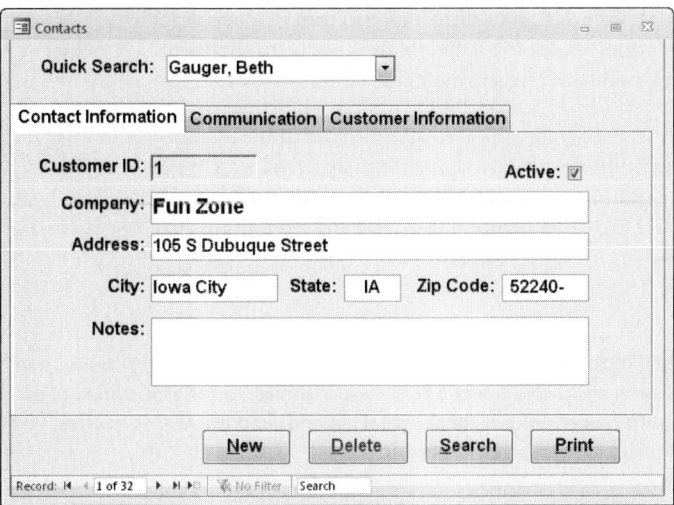

The back office

You might have heard the term *back office* used to refer to the computers that store a company's data. The back-office portion of a client/server system is normally unseen by the users of client computers. More than one server computer can be involved in a single application. Server computers can be running databases, such as SQL Server or Oracle. Server computers can be used to transfer data between database servers and client applications. These intermediary computers may be Web servers, application servers, or file servers.

Big companies spend a lot of money and human resources on their back-office computer systems. Not only is the hardware considerably more expensive than desktop computers, but professional administrators are needed to keep the machines up and running with a minimum of problems. Also, because the data stored in database servers is usually mission-critical to the company's operation, high levels of security must be applied to the server hardware and software to protect the integrity of the data.

The database

A database is used primarily to store data. In general, larger and more scalable database engines like SQL Server provide features well beyond the capabilities of Microsoft Access. Depending on installation and configuration details, SQL Server databases easily exceed terabytes in size and can service hundreds or thousands of simultaneous users.

One particular difference between a server database engine like SQL Server and Access is with respect to specialized database objects supported by server database engines. These specialized database objects are *stored procedures, user-defined functions,* and *triggers. Stored procedures* are much like VBA procedures, except the statements they contain consist of SQL language commands. A SQL Server *user-defined function* is a type of stored procedure that returns a value, much like an Access VBA function, while a *trigger* is a SQL statement attached to a SQL Server table that runs in response to changes to the table's data. Access data macros are very, very similar to SQL Server triggers and are, in fact, often referred to as triggers in Access tables.

A *stored procedure* is a block of commands that operates against data in the database. A *user-defined function* is similar to a stored procedure except that it returns a single value. A *trigger* is an event detector, which executes a sequence of commands when a specific event occurs with the database. These objects add intelligence and logic that determines how data stored in the database is handled by the database server.

Note

Stored procedures are almost always written in the standardized structured query language (SQL) common to all server database engines. The SQL you see in an Access query's SQL view is similar to the SQL syntax used by SQL Server, but there are many, many differences. Except for the smallest and simplest Access queries, you can't copy Access SQL code and use it in a SQL Server stored procedure.

Access has its equivalent of stored procedures, functions, and triggers, in the form of data macros, modules, and class modules.

- **Data macros:** Access 2010 introduces *data macros,* which are code elements attached directly to fields in Access tables. Data macros behave much like SQL Server triggers, in that data macros are fired whenever data is added, deleted, or changed in an Access table. A data macro attached to an Access field or table is in effect anywhere the data is used: on a form, on a report, on a query, or in VBA code.

Cross-Reference

For more information on data macros, turn to Chapter 15.

- **Modules and class modules:** Modules and class modules are blocks of VBA code, stored within an Access database. You've seen many examples of VBA code in other chapters in this book, so no further explanation is necessary.

These three objects all perform a similar function to that of stored procedures in a server database: They execute sequences of commands in response to changing conditions in an Access database. Those commands typically act on data stored within an Access database, but they can do much more, such as modify the user interface or interact with the user.

In reality, an Access database is not suitable for the extreme processing requirements of large groups of users, public-facing Web sites, or massive amounts of data. Microsoft never intended Access to be an enterprise database system. The challenging role of enterprise data management is better suited to specialized server database engines like SQL Server and Oracle Database.

Microsoft intends for Access to be used primarily as a single-user or workgroup database system, and not as a database engine driving large Web sites or supporting applications used by hundreds or thousands of simultaneous users. Access processes its data locally, on the user's computer. When an Access database is split, and the back-end `.accdb` resides on a file server, Access pulls data from the back-end database, and processes it on the user's computer. The file-based database model is not suitable for many environments outside of personal and workgroup computing.

In contrast, server database engines like SQL Server and Oracle, process data on the server computer, and deliver requested data to the client application. Neither SQL Server nor Oracle provides any kind of user interface; they both rely entirely on other software to support end-user application requirements. The client-side application is responsible for supporting the user interface and responding to user input. This division of operations is the primary difference between a file-oriented database system like Access and a server database engine like SQL Server.

Access's role in client/server computing

Access fulfills a rather unique dual role of database administration and application development. As you'll see in Chapters 37 and 38, Access is well suited as both an administrative tool for working with SQL Server databases, and an application development tool. With few exceptions, developing Access applications that use SQL Server data is identical to building the same applications using data stored in Access `.accdb` files.

The Access Database Engine doesn't provide the multiuser/multitasking capabilities of SQL Server. For example, in addition to relying on stored procedures, databases like SQL Server and Oracle also support highly specialized database objects, such as the following:

- **View:** A stored query definition containing no data. A view doesn't contain data, but it delivers data when the view is requested by a client application. In many ways, a SQL Server view is analogous to an Access Select query. An Access application treats a SQL Server view as if it were a table, even though the data is dynamically selected from the underlying tables as the view is requested.

- **Clustered index:** A special type of index that maintains the physical order of records in a table to match the table's primary index.

- **Identity fields:** Maintains sequential index counters. Typically used to generate surrogate primary keys for creation of new records in a table in a relational database. Identity fields are very similar to Access AutoNumber fields.

Note
A surrogate key is where an integer identifier is used to replace a primary key in a table.

- **Temporary table:** Used to temporarily store data, usually for intermediary steps in larger operations. SQL Server temporary tables exist only while a stored procedure is running; they're used to temporarily hold data used by the stored procedure. Temporary tables may be used by more than one SQL Server stored procedure at a time.

- **Partitioning and parallel processing:** Physical splitting of tables into separate partitions, including parallel processing on multiple partitions, or individual operations performed on individual partitions. Table partitioning is particularly useful with very large tables when only a portion of the data is likely to be queried at one time. Querying a small portion of a table is called *partition pruning*.

Even though the Access Database Engine and Jet don't support the advanced features in SQL Server, Access supports truly sophisticated forms and report builders. And even though SQL Server supports a rather nice reporting tool (SQL Server Reporting Services, or SSRS), the features of SSRS pale in comparison to Access reports. And, as I've said, SQL Server has no user-interface builder or design at all (other than database-management tools). SQL Server is entirely dependent on other applications, such as Access, SharePoint, and Visual Studio, for providing end users with interfaces for viewing and working with data.

A huge improvement of the Access Database Engine over the Jet database engine is that the Access Database Engine has built-in integration with SharePoint Services. The Access Database Engine handles all the complexity of communicating with SharePoint operating on a remote server located across the Internet.

Cross-Reference
For more on SharePoint Services, see Chapter 33.

Web servers and application servers
On a most basic level, a Web server and an application server perform exactly the same function. They both play a role as a processing and pooling funnel between application computers and back-end server computers.

Figure 36.4 illustrates that the difference between the computers shown in Figure 36.1 and those shown in Figure 36.4 is a difference of scale and scalability. In Figure 36.4, there is much more interrogation and direct access to the database on the single-server computer. A single-server computer is limited as to how much load it can manage without causing performance problems for its users. Even if the server computer in Figure 36.4 is a large cluster of physical servers, it's probably doing too much work as a database server, a Web server, and a reporting server at the same time.

Overloading a database server can be prevented by using intermediary servers. In Figure 36.5, the load on the central server has been distributed among dedicated Web, application, and database servers. Although more expensive to initially install and configure, and more expensive to maintain in the long term, a distributed system provides much higher performance overall. Each server in Figure 36.5 is optimized for its particular task, and, as long as the loads directed to each server are managed properly, users benefit from much better application performance.

FIGURE 36.4

A database server can be overloaded by too many users.

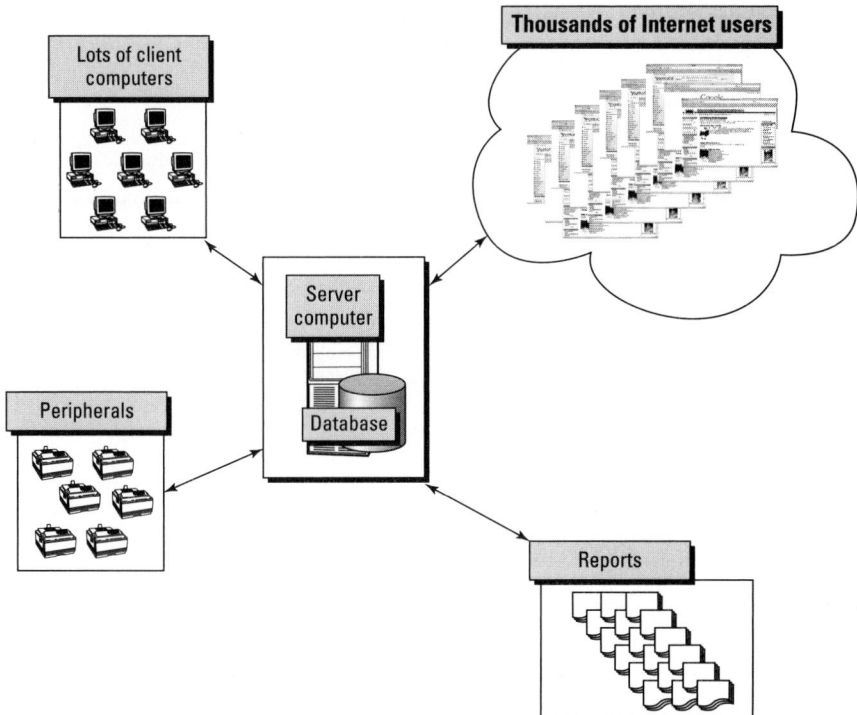

Application servers are typically used to serve applications in large-scale client/server environments. Application servers often perform "load balancing" by directing user requests to server computers that are less busy than heavily used servers. A Web server is used to serve applications in an Internet environment and may simultaneously service many hundreds of users. A Web server is generally focused on managing Web requests by sharing database server connections among many Internet users. Web servers use *connection pooling* to share the database and other resources among all the concurrent Web connections.

FIGURE 36.5

Web and application server computers manage back-end server access.

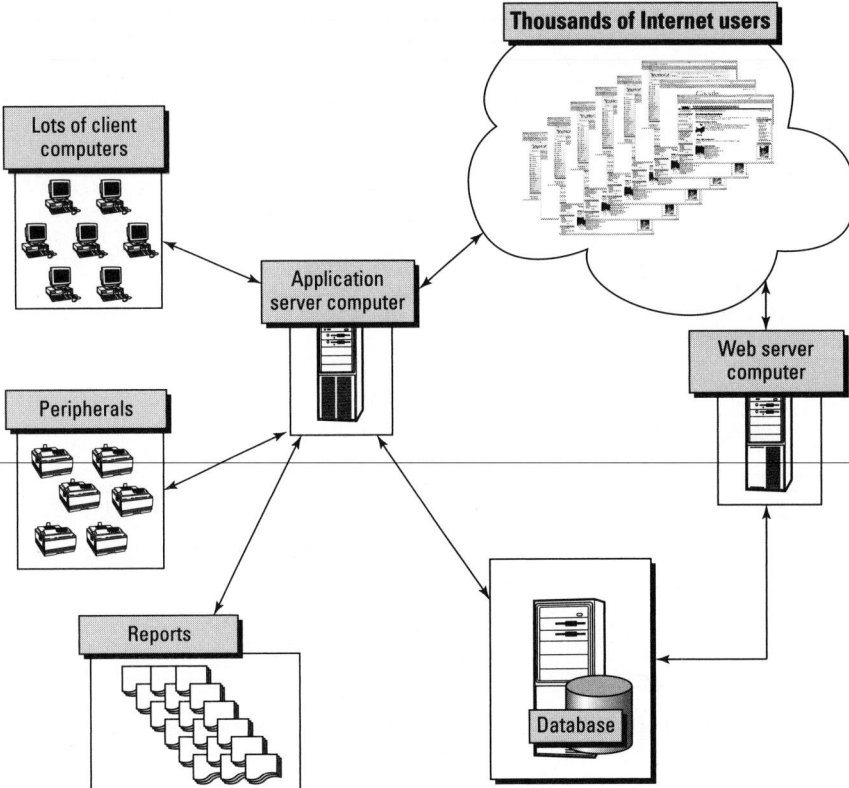

An application server is less often used for connection pooling than Web servers are because the number of connections is much reduced. An application server is better suited for maintaining frequently used data in a dedicated computer, in addition to managing load balancing.

Making Sense of Multi-Tier Architecture

Database systems can be thought of as consisting of three major components: the data, the business logic that determines how data is handled by the application, and a user interface that interacts with the user. Each of these three components is a *tier* of a multitier system.

A tier is a logical construct. It's a way of segregating an application's activities. Very often, the tier is physical as well as logical, but physical tier separation is not a requirement of client-server applications.

Other database architectures involve two tiers and sometimes only a single tier. Most Access applications are written as single-tier database applications. Access forms and reports are most often bound directly to a data source, and very often the specification for extracting the data is contained within the `ControlSource` properties of the forms, reports, and controls in these applications.

An unbound Access application that uses VBA code to extract data and populate forms can be considered a two-tier database application, but even then, reports are almost always directly bound to a record source in the database.

Also, unless data macros are used for managing data in an Access 2010 table, the data tier in an Access application is not an active participant in a multi-tier database system.

Two-tier systems

Most client/server database systems have been built as two-tier systems. This type of architecture is typical of a company running one or only a few applications, against a database across a LAN. The fundamental characteristic of a client/server system is that the system's work is partitioned between the client and the server computers. Typically, the client handles all the user interaction (user interface, keyboard, mouse, and so on) while the server handles the data access.

In case you're wondering, splitting an Access database into front and back ends is *not* considered client/server. One of the fundamental characteristics of client/server databases is that processing takes place on both the client end and the server end of the application. The front-end processing is primarily involved with managing and maintaining the user interface, which involves interacting with the user, validating the user's input, and preparing the data for delivery to the database engine. The server-side processing includes extracting and manipulating data before sending to the client side, as well as receiving data sent from the client and storing that data in the database tables.

When an Access database has been split into two pieces and the portion containing the tables has been moved to another computer, no processing ever takes place on the back-end computer. You don't have to install software on the "server" computer in order to place the back-end database on it. Access is, and has always been, a file-based database system. The `.accdb` file used by an Access application is really nothing more than a data file, much as a Word document or Excel workbook is contained within a file. No processing is required on the part of the computer holding the file in order for Access to use the data stored within the `.accdb` file.

Three-tier systems

A three-tier computer system divides processing one step farther than two-tier architecture. An example of a three-tier system is where the Web servers and application servers come into use. In this case, the resulting architecture is the same as that shown in Figure 36.5, and for all the same reasons described previously.

Many client/server databases are written as three-tier systems. The data-management tier runs on the database server computer, while the user interface is managed on the client-side workstation. The business logic is often split between the client and server computers. Data validation, user notification, and data transformation often take place within the user interface, usually in the programming code under the forms and reports. The server computer may also implement business logic in the form of user-defined functions and stored procedures that validate and verify data before storing it in the database's tables. Additionally, triggers in each table might apply certain business rules or transformations at the lowest possible data level.

Putting It All Together: Access, Client-Server, and Multiple Tiers

Access is really a combination of an application development system, database development tools, and a database engine. The target markets for Access as a database development system are workgroups, small to medium businesses, and individual users.

Most often, client-side applications that use server-provided data are built with tools like Visual Studio .NET or the Java programming language. These development systems provide no database capabilities themselves, yet they support all the features needed by client-side database applications. A relatively simple application written in Visual Basic .NET or Microsoft Access is able to work with millions of records of data stored in SQL Server, without having to support all the database operations supported by a server database engine.

Now, just imagine a scenario with an Access database on a single desktop computer. Then add an application or two, or maybe a dozen different applications, each one written in a different development system (Access, VB.NET, Microsoft Excel, and so on). Then imagine a single Access .accdb file trying to simultaneously service dozens, even hundreds of users. This is a prescription for disaster because it's really not the kind of environment best-suited for an Access .accdb database.

Microsoft has never represented Access as a strong candidate for an application servicing large numbers of simultaneous users. Instead, Microsoft has always primarily positioned Access as a single-user or workgroup database system. Over time, of course, the capabilities built into Access have improved to the point that Access is now a valid tool for building client-side applications that hook into server-provided data. As mentioned earlier in this chapter and in Part V, Access seamlessly consumes data provided by SharePoint, no matter where that data is located. Similarly, Access is also able to use data managed by Microsoft SQL Server or Oracle, located on the local network or anywhere on the Internet.

Access has severe limitations in client/server environments and, realistically, can't be used to drive an Internet site. Even in large-scale computer systems, however, a tool like Access plays an important role as a front-end development tool for server data.

Note

As mentioned earlier, splitting an Access database into front- and back-end pieces doesn't constitute client/server, even if the back end is located remotely. The defining characteristic of client/server computing is that the application's work is partitioned between the client and server computers. In the case of a split Access database, no processing occurs on the computer storing the back-end `.accdb` file. Access doesn't even have to be installed on the file server. There is no computing going on at the remote computer on behalf of the Access application. The back-end `.accdb` is nothing more than a data file, much like a Word document or Excel spreadsheet kept on a file server.

However, when an `.accdb` is upsized to SQL Server (see Chapter 38), SQL Server actively manages the upsized data. When a query is opened in Access, Access requests the data from SQL Server, and SQL Server either retrieves the data directly or runs a stored procedure that produces the data requested by Access. Client/server always involves processing on both ends of the relationship.

Access as a database repository

Access is used as a database repository throughout this book. The basic relational database consists of tables containing fields and records, and the ability to establish and enforce relationships between those tables. The application layer of an Access database adds commands allowing changes to data and commands allowing reading of data. Access has all this, and then some. Figure 36.6 shows a picture of data stored in an Access table.

FIGURE 36.6

A database repository stores fields in records within tables.

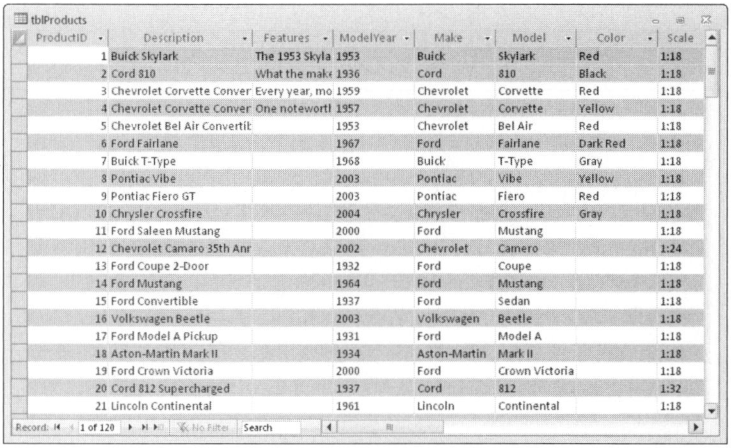
tblProducts

ProductID	Description	Features	ModelYear	Make	Model	Color	Scale
1	Buick Skylark	The 1953 Skyla	1953	Buick	Skylark	Red	1:18
2	Cord 810	What the mak	1936	Cord	810	Black	1:18
3	Chevrolet Corvette Conver	Every year, mo	1959	Chevrolet	Corvette	Red	1:18
4	Chevrolet Corvette Conver	One notewortl	1957	Chevrolet	Corvette	Yellow	1:18
5	Chevrolet Bel Air Convertil		1953	Chevrolet	Bel Air	Red	1:18
6	Ford Fairlane		1967	Ford	Fairlane	Dark Red	1:18
7	Buick T-Type		1968	Buick	T-Type	Gray	1:18
8	Pontiac Vibe		2003	Pontiac	Vibe	Yellow	1:18
9	Pontiac Fiero GT		2003	Pontiac	Fiero	Red	1:18
10	Chrysler Crossfire		2004	Chrysler	Crossfire	Gray	1:18
11	Ford Saleen Mustang		2000	Ford	Mustang		1:18
12	Chevrolet Camaro 35th Anr		2002	Chevrolet	Camero		1:24
13	Ford Coupe 2-Door		1932	Ford	Coupe		1:18
14	Ford Mustang		1964	Ford	Mustang		1:18
15	Ford Convertible		1937	Ford	Sedan		1:18
16	Volkswagen Beetle		2003	Volkswagen	Beetle		1:18
17	Ford Model A Pickup		1931	Ford	Model A		1:18
18	Aston-Martin Mark II		1934	Aston-Martin	Mark II		1:18
19	Ford Crown Victoria		2000	Ford	Crown Victoria		1:18
20	Cord 812 Supercharged		1937	Cord	812		1:32
21	Lincoln Continental		1961	Lincoln	Continental		1:18

Record: 1 of 120 No Filter Search

Figure 36.7 shows an Access table's design, detailing the fields, data types, and field specifications.

FIGURE 36.7

A database repository stores data in tables with field and data-type definitions.

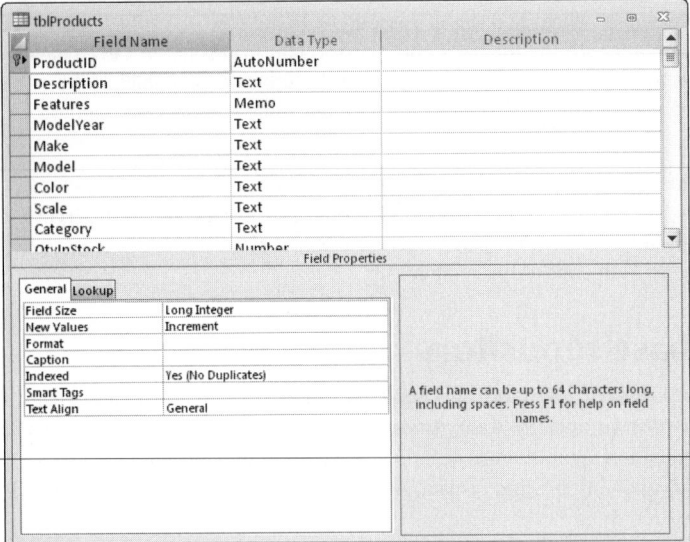

Figure 36.8 shows relationships established and enforced between various tables inside an Access database.

FIGURE 36.8

A relational database allows relationships between related tables.

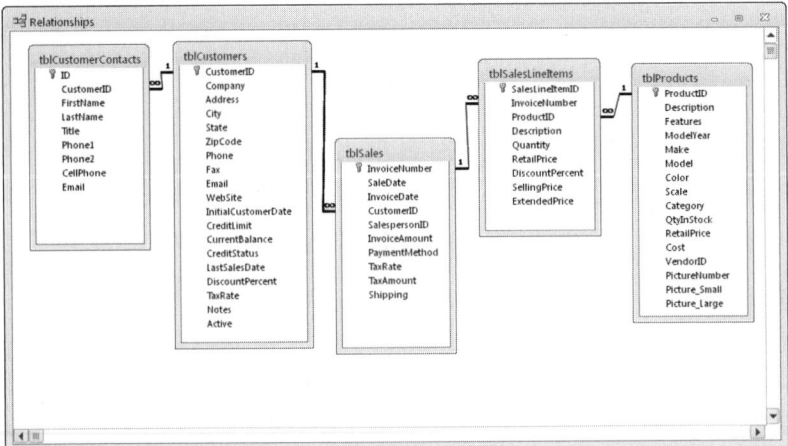

Cross-Reference
Table relationships are covered in Chapter 3.

Access as an Internet database

Although an Access database can be used to drive an Internet site, this practice is not recommended. The Access Database Engine just can't hold up to hundreds of simultaneous requests, particularly when data is being modified in the database. Performance is sure to suffer, and database corruption is virtually guaranteed in such an environment. For any measure of scalability, something like SQL Server is best. And SharePoint is increasingly a viable data repository for Access applications, or, at the very least, portions of the data provided by an Access application. Using SharePoint Services and Access in tandem might allow adequate servicing of a small-scale Internet database, or perhaps a localized company or educational intranet.

Summary

This chapter has provided the basis for understanding the differences between an Access desktop application and a full-blown client/server database produced with a database engine such as SQL Server. Access is a fine development tool for producing client-side user interfaces to server-provided data. Access's excellent report writer, its superior forms designer, and VBA code combine to produce powerful and useful front ends for SQL Server data.

The user is unaware whether the data in an Access form or report resides on his desktop computer, on the local network, or across the Internet. This level of remote data integration wasn't practical with older Access databases, but it's been made possible by the features built into recent versions of Microsoft Access.

SQL Server as an Access Companion

IN THIS CHAPTER

Linking to SQL Server tables

Understanding SQL Server database objects

Microsoft has increasingly positioned Access as a gateway to SQL Server data. SQL Server, of course, is Microsoft's flagship enterprise database engine, and it's frequently used to drive mission-critical applications for tens of thousands of companies around the world. Because of its excellent scalability, fault tolerance, transaction logging, and other features, SQL Server is often used as the data store behind large Web sites, for data warehousing, and for business intelligence purposes.

Depending on installation specifics, SQL Server is able to serve many thousands of users simultaneously. From SQL Server's perspective, an Access application making requests for data is just another user — and it's treated no differently from any other client.

Access projects are used to create and maintain SQL Server Express databases, or SQL Server Enterprise databases. You can also use an Access project to create the user-interface objects and forms, reports, macros, and modules that utilize data from SQL Server. The database window for a project looks very similar to the Access database window you're already accustomed to. In fact, creating the user-interface objects is virtually the same as creating them in Access.

On the CD-ROM

This chapter uses a database named Chapter37.accdb. If you haven't already copied it onto your machine from the CD, you'll need to do so now. The CD also includes Chapter37.mdf and Chapter37.ldf, the SQL Server database files to attach to a SQL Server instance on your computer.

In general, SQL Server Express automatically installs on the same computer you use for development. Even though SQL Server is a server database, by default SQL Server Express installs as a client-side service retaining all its database server features.

Note

SQL Server Express is a free download from Microsoft. (www.microsoft.com/express/sql). **You can use it as a development and deployment database server for your Access applications if you don't have access to a SQL Server Enterprise installation.**

Before beginning this chapter, keep in mind that the architecture discussed in the following sections uses SQL Server to store data and Access to build the user interface, the application's reports, and the logic controlling the application's behavior and features.

This chapter examines a number of different ways to use SQL Server data in Microsoft Access applications. Although there are no SQL Server object designers (tables, stored procedures, views, and so on) in the .accdb file format, you can use Open Database Connectivity (ODBC) to link to SQL Server data objects. However, if you choose to use the Access 2000 .adp data file format you have access to a full range of tools specifically designed to work with SQL Server data. You can edit existing or create new SQL Server tables, stored procedures, and views when using the .adp file format.

Downloading SQL Server Express

Microsoft is vitally interested in developers learning and using SQL Server. But, the truth is that acquiring and installing the "full" versions of SQL Server can be a daunting process. As a server application, SQL Server is relatively expensive to license, and its hardware requirements are rather extensive. Not to worry! Microsoft has a wonderful gift available to you, free for the downloading.

SQL Server Express is a somewhat stripped-down version of SQL Server intended to be used as a database engine for smallish workgroup applications, and as a test platform for developers working on SQL Server front-end applications. You may freely download and install SQL Server Express, to use on your computer, and even bundle it with applications you distribute to users.

SQL Server Express works and behaves exactly like SQL Server Enterprise, its much bigger brother. SQL Server Express supports all the data types, stored procedures, triggers, and other database objects used in SQL Server Enterprise. In fact, migrating a SQL Server Express database to SQL Server Enterprise involves nothing more than disconnecting from SQL Server Express and connecting the database files to SQL Server Enterprise.

The primary differences between the standard editions of SQL Server and SQL Server Express is that SQL Server Express databases are limited to 4GB in size (twice that of Access!), and SQL Server Express doesn't support some of the more advanced features of SQL Server Standard and Enterprise editions. Otherwise, the database engines in all editions of SQL Server are identical.

You really owe it to yourself and your users to take a look at SQL Server Express. At the time of publication, the official home of SQL Server Express is www.microsoft.com/express/sql, or do a Web search for "SQL Server Express download."

Caution

Be aware, however, that when you create an `.adp` file in Access (File ➪ New ➪ Browse, then select ADP from the Save as Type drop-down list), you're actually creating an Access 2000–format data file. This isn't a big issue for most developers, but you may encounter situations where Access features can't be supported in an application because the file is not an `.accdb`.

Also, when working in an `.adp` file, you won't be able to create local tables or queries. The `.adp` file format is specifically designed to work as a front-end to SQL Server data.

Connecting to SQL Server

There are several ways for Access to use SQL Server data:

- Using the `.adp` file format discussed earlier in this chapter
- Using ADO code to programmatically open a SQL Server database and work with its data

Cross-Reference

For more on ADO, turn to Chapter 25.

- Linking to SQL Server tables and using them as if they were tables linked to another Access database

The remainder of this chapter covers this third option. As you'll soon see, working with SQL Server data through linked tables is no different from using tables linked to any other data source.

One of the most fundamental operations with any large-scale multiuser database engine, such as SQL Server, is connecting to the database. Connecting directly to SQL Server, using SQL Server front-end tools is quite easy. All that's required is a connection to SQL Server, and Access does the rest.

Introducing connection strings

The specification used to communicate with a database is called a *connection string*. A connection string is made up of a number of things:

- **Host name:** The host is the computer where the database server resides.
- **Database name:** The name of a database on the server. SQL Server supports multiple databases in a single installation, as well as multiple SQL Server installations on a single computer. Now and then, a SQL Server installation services a single database for each database server.
- **Authentication:** A user name and password are used for security. In some environments, the user name and password can use an operating system user name and password. In other cases, a user name and password can be part of the database software itself.

The easiest way to connect to a SQL Server database may be to use a command-line shell utility called SQLCMD that comes with both SQL Server and SQL Server Express (look in the `C:\Program Files\Microsoft SQL Server\90\Tools\Binn` folder). SQLCMD provides a simple, command-driven interface to SQL Server. Although not practical for managing complex databases, SQLCMD provides a simple way to verify a SQL Server installation.

The options for SQLCMD are shown in Figure 37.1.

FIGURE 37.1

The SQLCMD utility has numerous options.

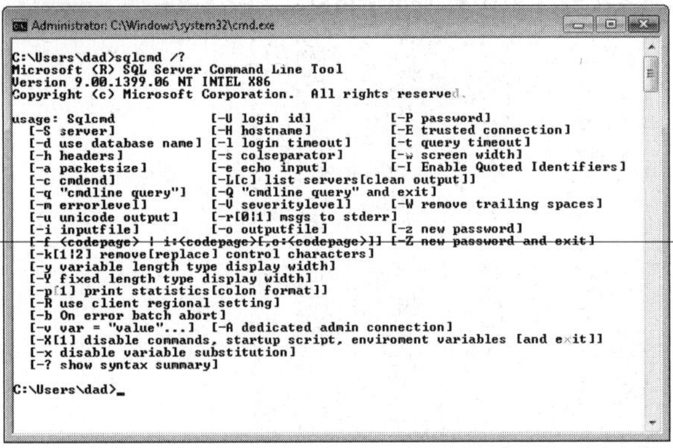

Figure 37.1 shows the two most significant options, which are -S server (the computer on which SQL Server is running), and -d use database name (the name of a database within the SQL Server installation).

Note

The name of the server in Figure 37.1 (-S server) is a SQL Server instance name, not the name of a computer. When installing SQL Server, the default name applied to the SQL Server instance is the name of the host computer. Also, by default, SQL Server security is set to use the user's Windows login name and password as authentication. In other words, SQL Server uses Windows security and the name of the machine on the network.

When using the SQLCMD utility, the easiest way to communicate with a SQL Server database is with the following command to get to a specific SQL Server installation:

```
sqlcmd -S mycomputer
```

Use the following more refined command to connect to a specific database, within a specific SQL Server installation:

```
sqlcmd -S mycomputer -d mydatabase
```

Figure 37.2 shows two connection screens for a tool called SQL Server Management Studio (which can be downloaded from the same site as SQL Server Express). The screen on the left is connecting to a SQL Server on a remote computer called DAD-PC, using a SQL Server stored user name and password to authenticate. The screen on the right side of Figure 37.2 is on the local computer, using the Windows user name to authenticate.

Connecting to a SQL Server in the Management Studio

SQLCMD is not practical as a user interface to a SQL Server database. It is, instead, a tool for verifying a SQL Server installation, testing login names and passwords, and performing other admin tasks.

Connecting to SQL Server from Access

Creating a connection between Access and SQL Server environments requires a little something extra, as opposed to just a simple database connection, because both Access and SQL Server are autonomous environments that must work together. As with many relational databases running under Windows, drivers are used to allow tools such as SQL Server and Access to communicate. As is common with many Microsoft software tools and toys, special drivers are created to facilitate communication between different software products. These drivers can be used to connect tools such as Excel and Access to an Oracle or DB2 database or, in this case, an Access database connected to SQL Server.

The drivers in question fall into a number of categories and include ODBC, Object Linked Embedding (OLE), and native drivers. Native drivers are often the best and fastest way to connect to server database engines, but they tend to be less generic and adaptable, and usually apply to one specific product or database. Many of these drivers are produced by Microsoft because they all run under Windows operating systems. Some vendors do produce their own ODBC and OLE drivers, though.

Let's focus on the ODBC driver allowing Access to communicate with a SQL Server. How do you deal with an ODBC driver? You have to create an ODBC data source, often called a *Data Source Name* (DSN), then reference the DSN from within Access. Once configured, a DSN remains on the local computer and is available to any ODBC-compliant application, such as Microsoft Access. The DSN contains enough information about the ODBC data source that the Access database engine (Jet or ACE) is able to use the ODBC driver to communicate with SQL Server.

Create a data source as follows:

1. Go to Windows Start menu, and choose Settings ⇨ Control Panel.

2. In the Control Panel, double-click the Administrative Tools option, and select Data Sources (ODBC).

   The three ODBC configuration options are

   - **User DSN:** A User DSN applies to a specific user on the client computer on which the User DSN is created.

   - **System DSN:** A System DSN is similar to a User DSN, except it applies over a network (to a certain extent).

   - **File DSN:** A File DSN creates a connection configuration (a connection string), for a database, into a file on your client computer.

Tip

Of these three options, the File DSN is the best choice in most situations. Because the connection information is stored in a file (the default location for DSN files is `C:\Program Files\Common Files\ODBC\Data Sources`**), you can easily share a DSN configuration with other users.**

Sharing a File DSN is easy: Simply locate the DSN on your machine and attach it to an e-mail, or move it to a common location on the network. User DSNs and System DSNs are actually stored in the computer's Registry, and must be manually set up on each computer needing access to an ODBC data source.

Essentially, what you're doing in this situation is creating a link from Access to data that is stored in SQL Server. Therefore, tables are maintained in SQL Server, and the front-end application (queries, forms, reports, VBA code, and so on) is maintained in Access. In Chapter 17, you examined importing tables into Access, making copies of data from a SQL Server database, and creating complete copies of data in Access. In this case, you want to simply link between Access and SQL Server because data are maintained in SQL Server, and not copied to Access.

A DSN specifies a data source (like SQL Server) and a database managed by the data source. Referencing a DSN from an application (like Access) provides the application with a direct path to the database. All the tables in the database are accessible through the DSN. The logic required to actually retrieve the data from the database is provided by the ODBC driver. Access knows nothing about SQL Server, but it knows a lot about working with an ODBC driver.

The following steps describe how to set up a DSN that connects to an ODBC data source:

1. Select the External Data ribbon tab, and click the ODBC Database button in the Import & Link group (shown in Figure 37.3).

FIGURE 37.3

Linking to an ODBC data source

ODBC data sources

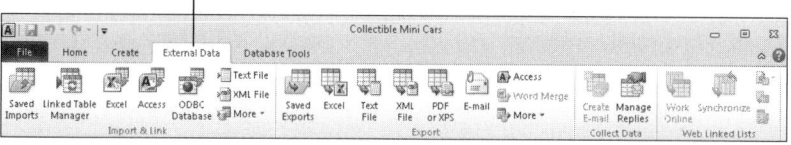

Access opens the Get External Data – ODBC Database dialog box (shown in Figure 37.4).

FIGURE 37.4

Linking to an external table

Import tables

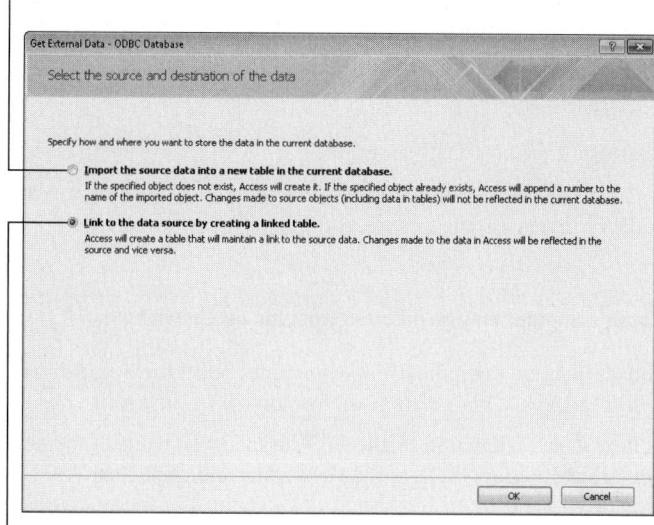

Link to external data source

2. Select the Link to the Data Source by Creating a Linked Table option, and click OK.

The Select Data Source dialog box (shown in Figure 37.5) appears.

FIGURE 37.5

Selecting a data source type

Enter a new DSN name

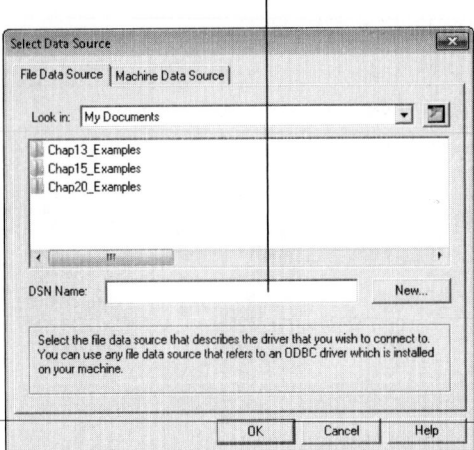

Each item (if any) in the list box on this dialog box is a configured DSN pointing to an ODBC data source. In this case, there are no DSNs configured, so the list is empty.

The options are to link to a File Data Source, a User Data Source, or (possibly) a System DSN to communicate between Access and SQL Server. You'll see a System Data Source tab in the Select Data Source dialog box when a System DSN is available on your computer.

3. Click New because no DSN yet exists.

   The Create New Data Source Wizard (shown in Figure 37.6) appears. It contains a list of all ODBC drivers installed on the computer.

Note

The drivers you see on your computer may be different from the list shown here.

4. Scroll all the way down the list of drivers and select the SQL Server driver (ignore the SQL Native Client driver for now), and click Next.

5. The next screen (shown in Figure 37.7) asks for the name of the new DSN. Type **CollectibleMiniCars_SQL** as the DSN name and click Next.

   The final screen of the Create New Data Source Wizard contains just a Finish button, and is not shown here.

FIGURE 37.6

Select the SQL Server ODBC driver from the list of installed drivers.

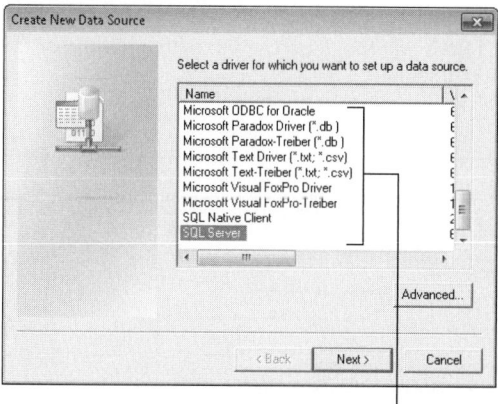

All ODBC drivers installed on local computer

FIGURE 37.7

Providing a name for the new DSN

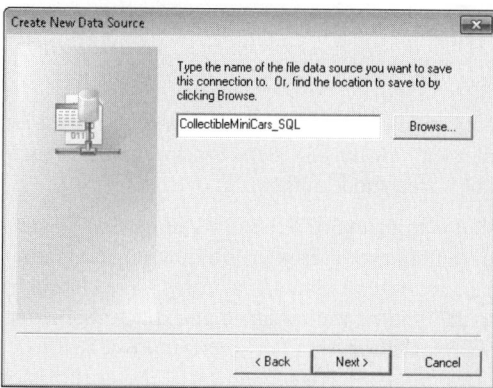

6. Click Finish to complete the first phase of creating a SQL Server DSN.

At this point, you've created a new data source named DSN using the SQL Server ODBC driver. You still have to connect the DSN to a SQL Server instance and database within the instance. The next dialog box you see depends on the ODBC driver you selected in Step 4. In the case of the SQL Server driver, you must specify the SQL Server instance and the database for the DSN.

The description in Figure 37.8 is not essential, but you must provide the SQL Server instance name. You'll experience a delay when you drop down the list of SQL Server instances at the bottom of this dialog box. The dialog box actually goes out across the network and retrieves the names of all the SQL Server installations it can find. Depending on the size of the local network, the delay can be up to a minute or more.

FIGURE 37.8

Specifying the DSN name and SQL Server instance

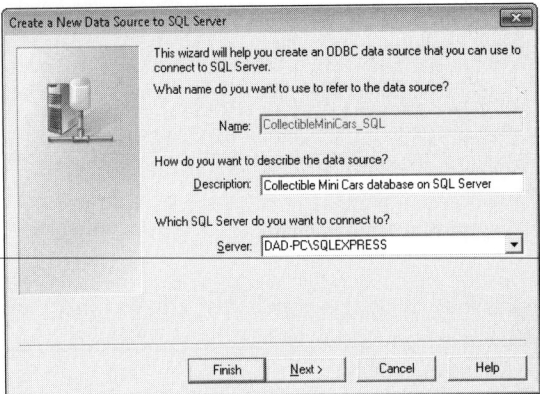

7. Click Next after selecting a SQL Server instance.

8. You specify the authentication mode for the DSN connection in the next dialog box (see Figure 37.9). Depending on how the SQL Server installation was configured, you may need to use NT login or mixed-mode authentication.

The default settings shown in Figure 37.9 assume you have a SQL Server with operating system authentication. (SQL Server uses your Windows login name and password to authenticate you and grant permission to its databases.) The alternative (mixed-mode authentication) means that you've been assigned an explicit user name and password for the selected SQL Server installation.

9. Specify the authentication mode and click Next.

10. Select the DSN's database in the next dialog box.

The drop-down list at the top of the dialog box contains the names of all the databases managed by the SQL Server instance selected in Figure 37.8. In Figure 37.10, the CollectibleMiniCarsSQL database is selected for the new DSN.

By default, the DSN's database is set to master, a system database used by SQL Server to manage its internal information. Check the Change the Default Database To check box to enable the database drop-down list so that you can select a working data source for the DSN and click Next.

FIGURE 37.9

Selecting the SQL Server authentication mode

NT login authentication

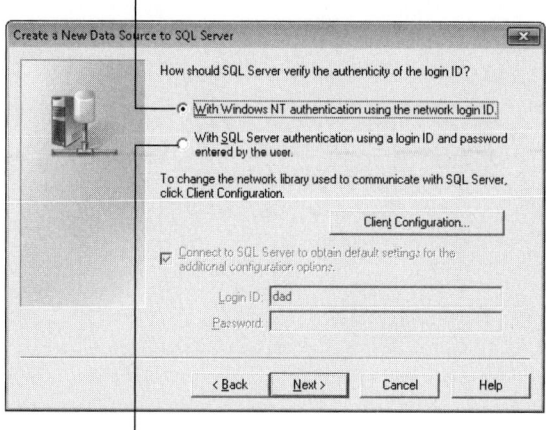

Mixed-mode authentication

FIGURE 37.10

Selecting the DSN's database

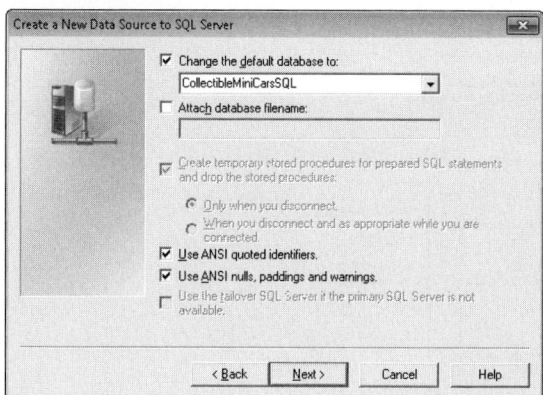

The final DSN Wizard screen (shown in Figure 37.11) contains a number of settings that rarely need changing.

FIGURE 37.11

The final DSN configurations for a SQL Server connection

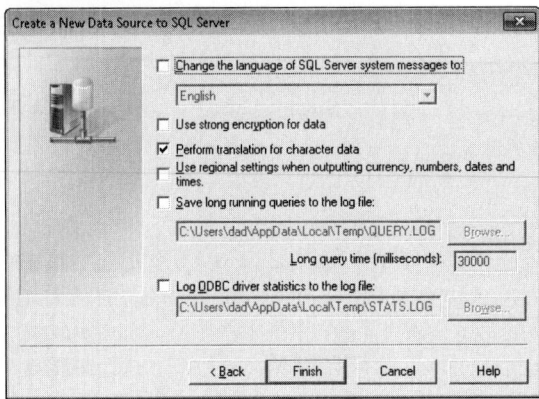

11. Click Finish to open the confirmation dialog box (shown in Figure 37.12).

FIGURE 37.12

Testing the new DSN connection

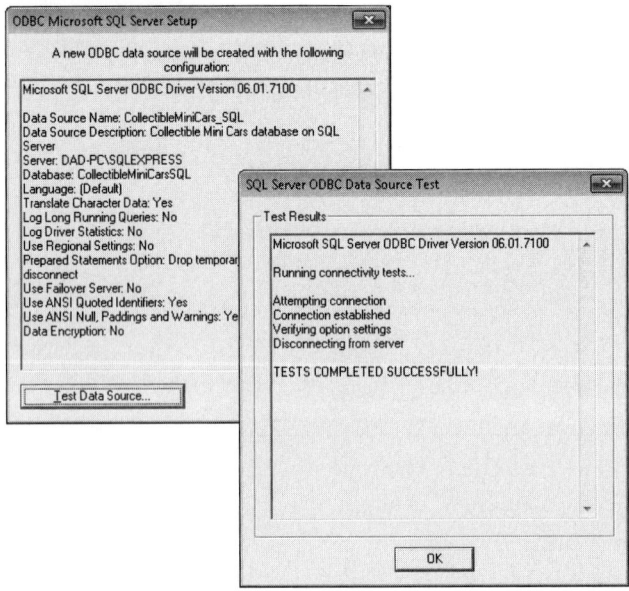

The confirmation dialog box includes a Test Data Source button. Clicking this button verifies the DSN's ability to connect to the selected SQL Server instance and database. The test will fail if any of the parameters specified by the DSN Setup Wizard are incorrect for the selected SQL Server data source.

If the connection fails, it's likely that the DSN's authentication mode is incorrect for the SQL Server instance. You may need to contact a database administrator or a network administrator for help configuring the DSN's connection details.

Tip

SQL Server is rather fussy about its name. Prior to SQL Server 2000, SQL Server assumed the same name as its host computer because only one instance of SQL Server could be installed on a computer. However, beginning with SQL Server 2000, a single computer can host multiple SQL Server installations, so the name you use to reference a SQL Server instance is a bit more complex. The syntax used to reference a SQL Server instance is MyComputer\MySQLServerInstance, where MyComputer is the name of the host computer, and MySQLServerInstance is the instance you want to reference.

If only a single SQL Server instance is installed on the local computer, you may be able to specify (local) **as the name of the server. Otherwise, you'll have to provide the name of the computer and the SQL Server instance name as described in the preceding paragraph.**

After creating, configuring, and testing the new DSN, you'll be returned to the Select Data Source dialog box (refer to Figure 37.5). The only difference this time is that the DSN Name box is filled in with the name of the new DSN you built with the DSN Wizard. Keep in mind that a DSN is a Windows resource and is not owned by Access. Any ODBC-compliant application on the computer can use the DSN you just created. Access makes the creation process easier by incorporating the DSN Wizard into the Access user interface.

The next step is to link to a table in the SQL Server database:

1. If the Select Data Source dialog box is not open, use the ODBC Databases button on the External Data tab to open it (see Figure 37.13).

FIGURE 37.13

The new DSN appears in the DSN list in the Select Data Source dialog box.

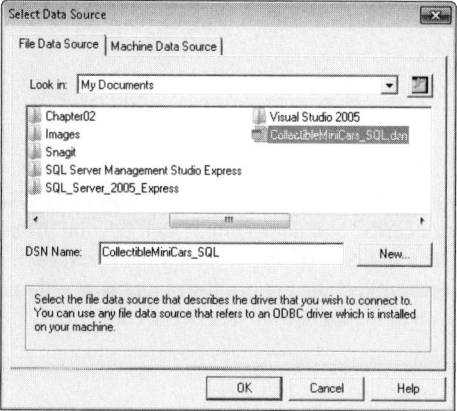

2. If you don't see the DSN you created earlier, use the Browse button to the right of the Look In text box to locate it. Then click OK.

The Link Tables dialog box (shown in Figure 37.14) appears, enabling you to select SQL Server tables to link to your Access database.

Note

If this dialog box doesn't appear, or if you encounter an error while waiting for this dialog box, there may be a problem with the DSN.

FIGURE 37.14

Selecting tables from a SQL Server database

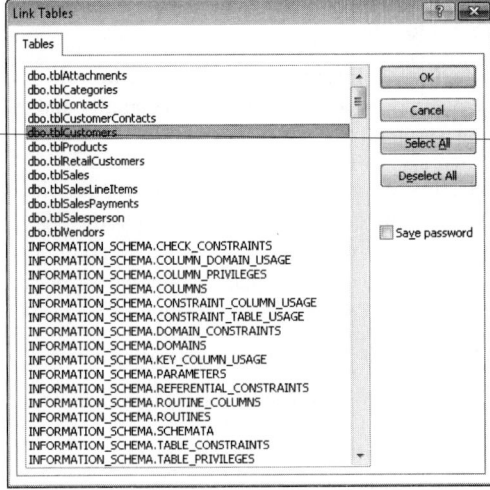

Ignore all the system tables (prefixed with sys or INFORMATION_SCHEMA) in the Link Tables dialog box. The tables you're interested in are generally at the top of the list in the Link Tables dialog box.

In Figure 37.14, the Customers table has been selected. This table was actually upsized from the Collectible Mini Cars database earlier.

3. Click OK to close the Link Tables dialog box and link to the selected table(s).

Note

dbo is shorthand for database owner and is the default prefix for all objects within a SQL Server database. A full explanation of SQL Server authentication, security, and ownership is well beyond the scope of this chapter. For the meantime, it's enough to understand that SQL Server supports multiple users, each of whom is identified by a name. When a user creates a SQL Server object, he creates the object with either his own name prefix, or with the default dbo prefix, depending on how SQL Server security is configured.

Depending on whether the SQL Server contains a primary key, you may or may not see the dialog box shown in Figure 37.15. When working with linked tables, Access needs a unique identifier in the SQL Server table so that updates in Access are properly performed in SQL Server. In the case of the linked products table in Figure 37.15, the logical choice is to use the `ProductID` as the unique identifier. In some cases, you may have to closely examine the data in the SQL Server table to determine which field, or combination of fields, to use as the unique identifier.

FIGURE 37.15

Selecting a unique identifier in the SQL Server table

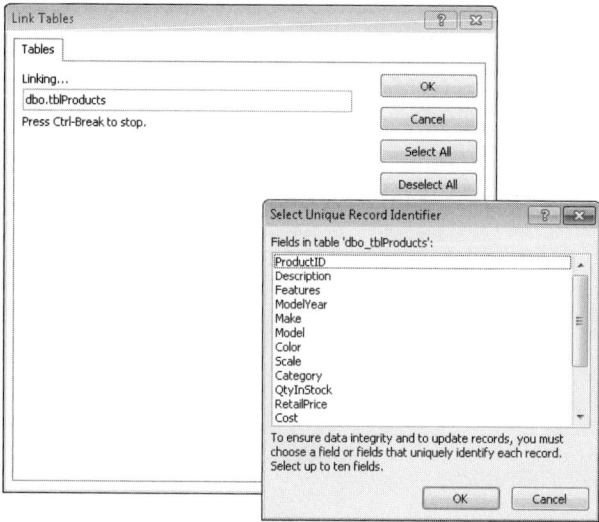

Figure 37.16 shows the main Access window with a number of local Access tables and linked SQL Server tables in the Navigation Pane, and a linked table open in the Access work area to the right of the Navigation Pane. The globe icon next to the linked tables in Figure 37.15 indicates that SQL Server is the data source for these files. Other data sources use different icons, so you always know where the data in your Access applications is hosted. Notice also that the table names are prefixed with dbo_ in the Access Navigation Pane. (The tables are not renamed in SQL Server, however.)

As you can see, connecting from Access to a SQL Server database is really quite simple, even though a number of steps are involved. The main advantage of using ODBC to link to SQL Server tables should be evident from Figure 37.16. Access makes no distinction between a SQL Server table located on a remote database server and an Access table located in the current database. Furthermore, there is no reason why an Access database can't simultaneously connect to multiple data sources.

FIGURE 37.16

A table linked from Access to SQL Server is named dbo_TableName by default.

Local tables

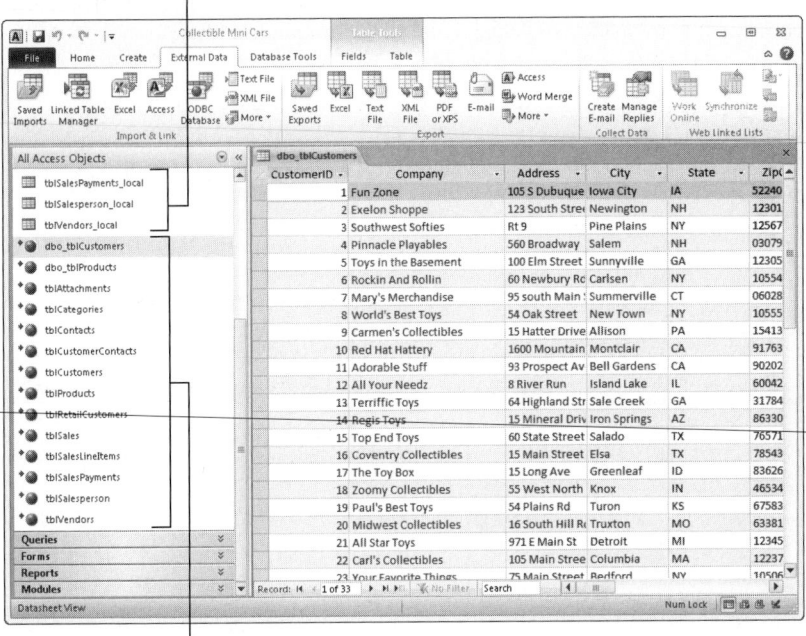

Linked SQL Server tables

The ability to link to many different data sources is a fundamental advantage of using Microsoft Access over other desktop database systems. Access and SQL Server integrate particularly well, and users are seldom aware that they're using data hosted in a remote database in a properly maintained Access application.

Working with SQL Server Objects

SQL Server contains many types of objects that are not supported in Access.

SQL Server supports database objects such as stored procedures, functions, and triggers. So far in this chapter, I've only covered using Access tables linked to SQL Server tables, but most SQL Server databases include more than just tables.

There are two approaches to sharing SQL Server data at the table level:

- **Import SQL Server tables into Access.** Any changes to the Access copy of the table won't be reflected in SQL Server. And any changes to the same tables in SQL Server will require a refresh in Access, which means a complete re-import of the table. It may be possible to use VBA code to create an automatic update process, but such a scheme may not perform well when you're working with large sets of data.

- **Link to tables that remain within SQL Server.** Linked Access tables can update SQL Server data because the table and data actually reside in SQL Server, not in Access. In fact, the interaction between an Access table linked to SQL Server is so seamless that most users are unaware that they're working with remote data.

Cross-Reference

Data types and a comparison between Access and SQL Server data types is covered in Chapter 36. Chapter 36 covers upsizing, which means moving tables from Access to SQL Server, and then linking the upsized tables back to the Access database. This chapter deals with top-level objects, such as tables and views, and not the structure of those objects (the fields within tables). The real task of this chapter is to show which SQL Server objects can be accessed from Microsoft Access.

Using SQL Server tables from Access

The Access .accdb database with linked SQL Server tables looks as shown in Figure 37.16.

As shown in Figure 37.17, some tables are local Access tables, and some tables are linked to SQL Server. The dbo_Employees1 table was imported from the Northwind Traders database on SQL Server. This table and its data reside entirely in Access; they aren't connected to SQL Server in any way.

As you can see in Figure 37.17, a new record is being added to dbo_Employees1. The new record is not present in the SQL Server database because the table resides within Access. Because the dbo_Employee1 table is not connected to SQL Server, updating the SQL Server table has to be done using an append query to add the record to the linked dbo_Employees table.

There is no automatic refresh for *imported* tables in either direction.

Linked data, on the other hand, is (more or less) constantly synchronized between the two databases. Keeping the data synchronized is a rather expensive process. The Access database engine has to monitor SQL Server for changes, and when the user indicates a need to see the freshest data, the database engine retrieves the most recent set of data from SQL Server.

Figure 37.18 shows a simple SQL statement in SQL Server Management Studio (the user interface tool most commonly used to work directly with SQL Server). This statement adds a new record to the Northwind Employees table. Just below the SQL editor area is a grid showing that the new record has been added to the Employees table.

FIGURE 37.17

Adding a new record to an Access copied table

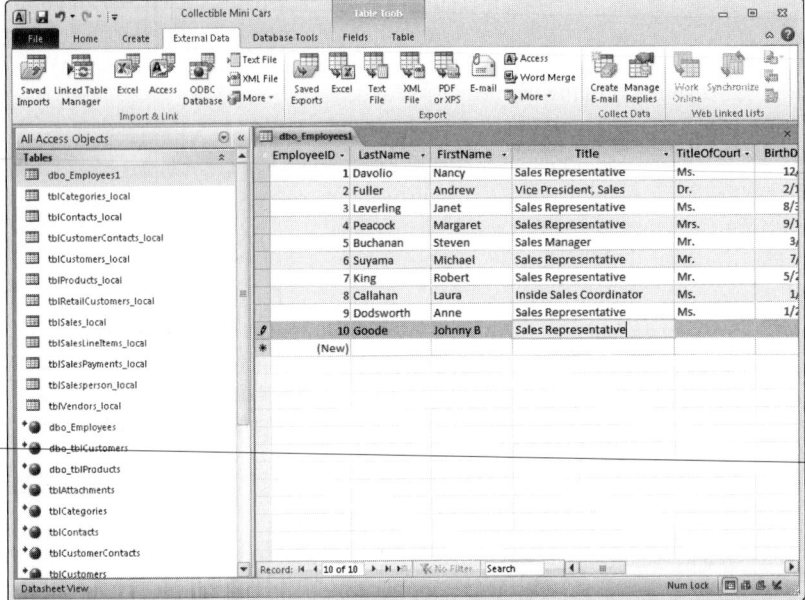

FIGURE 37.18

Making changes directly to SQL Server tables

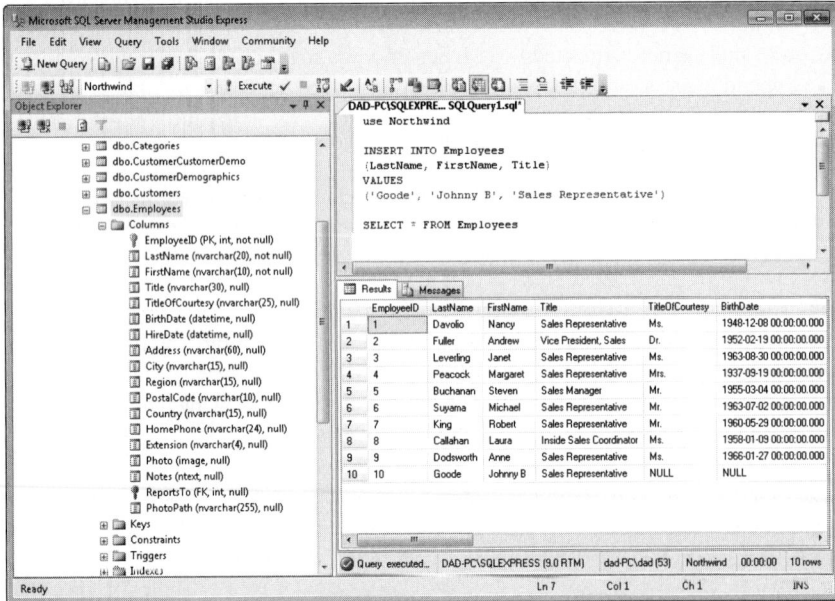

This is the script used in Figure 37.17:

```
USE NORTHWIND
INSERT INTO Employees
(LastName, FirstName, Title)
VALUES
('Goode', 'Johnny B', 'Sales Representative')
SELECT * FROM Employees
```

After running this short SQL script in SQL Server and pressing F5 in Access to refresh the datasheet view of dbo_Employees (or closing and re-opening the table), dbo_Employees now shows the record just added in SQL Server (see Figure 37.19).

FIGURE 37.19

SQL Server changes are automatically reflected in linked Access tables.

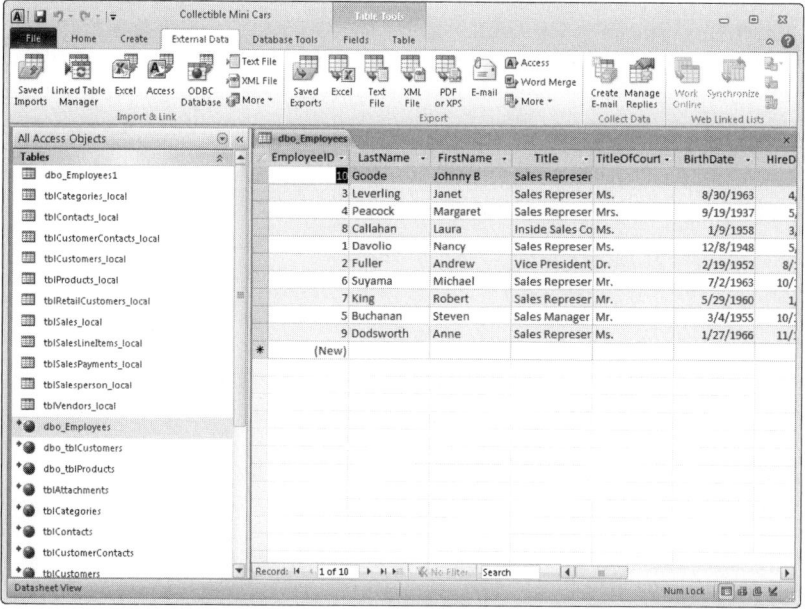

The imported SQL Server table (dbo_Employees1) does not contain the new record added to SQL Server. The table would have to be re-imported from SQL Server, or code could be used to search for records present in SQL Server but not in Access.

Views

Another object used in SQL Server databases is called a *view*. A view is really a stored query that joins tables and filters data. Essentially, when you create a form in Access, you're creating a query behind that form. A SQL Server view object creates a table-like object based on a SQL statement that may join tables, sort the data, and perform other fundamental operations on the data as it's selected. When a client application references the view, SQL Server executes the SQL statements, producing a table-like dataset of the data.

The result is that an Access query can be executed against a SQL Server view, as if the view were a table. When the view is accessed in an Access SELECT command, SQL Server executes the view's SQL statement against the tables underlying the view and the records returned to the client.

Figure 37.20 shows the creation of a SQL Server view. This view joins the products and categories tables, but only where the product has not been discontinued.

Creating a view in SQL Server

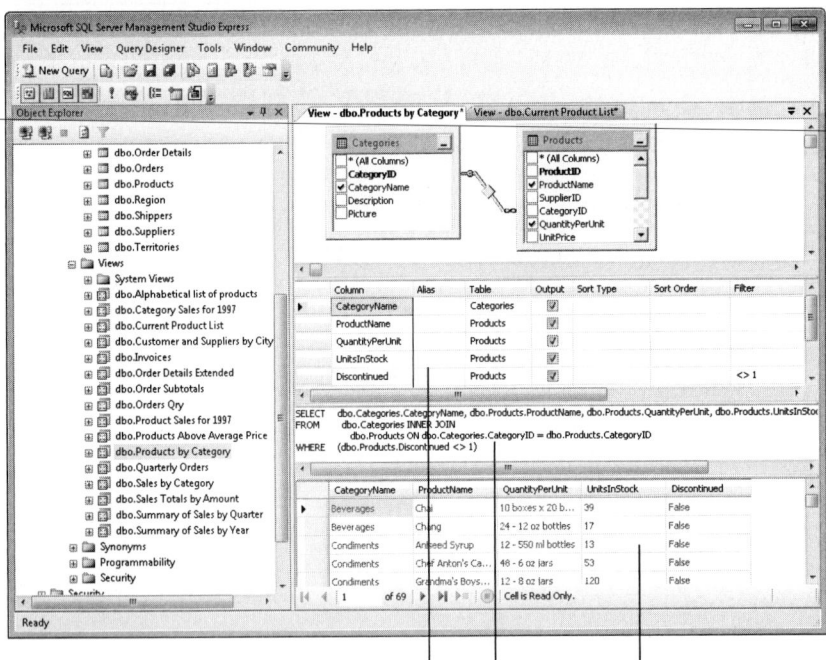

Table contents   SQL statement   Execution results

From Access's perspective, this view is just another SQL Server table. This view can be linked just like a native SQL Server table, as shown in Figure 37.21.

In this particular case, during the linking process the product and category names were chosen to uniquely identify each row. The unique identifier is needed so that, when data in the view is changed in Access, Access can tell SQL Server which row has been updated. Without a unique identifier, it would be impossible for Access to reliably update SQL Server data.

FIGURE 37.21

A SQL Server view is equivalent to an Access datasheet.

Stored procedures

Although superficially similar to Access queries, SQL Server stored procedures often perform significant data processing at the database engine level. SQL Server's SQL dialect is capable of looping, using variables and temporary tables, calling any of hundreds of different built-in SQL Server functions (such as returning the current date and time), and performing many other tasks.

Note

Stored procedures, functions, and triggers are not queries. A stored procedure is a block of SQL statements that are executed as a single entity.

One use of stored procedures is as handy containers for storing the SQL statements used throughout an application. Instead of writing SQL statements in your application code, you can store them in the database as stored procedures, calling them from your code in much the same way that you call a VBA function. Here are some of the many benefits of stored procedures:

- They can contain multiple SQL statements.
- They can call another stored procedure.
- They can receive parameters and return a value or a result set.

- They're stored in a semi-compiled, interpretive state on the database server, so they execute faster than if they were embedded in your code. In other words, stored procedures are typically not compiled into a relational database as binary code, but they're usually pre-parsed, and partially pre-executed, making for faster execution.

- They're stored in a common container in your application so that others can maintain them more easily because there is less database access code.

- After a stored procedure has been added to a SQL Server database, it's accessible to any client application using that database. This means that an Access desktop database application will execute the exact same logic as a Web application written with Visual Studio .NET, if they both use the same stored procedure to access data.

Here are some of the disadvantages of stored procedures:

- Overuse of stored procedures tends to place too much business logic into a database. This can sometimes make number-crunching-type business logic execute in a database very slowly. Some types of processing are best left to application coding, which is often much better suited to intense calculations.

- Overuse of stored procedures for data access can sometimes cause serious issues with network performance.

SQL Server stored procedures are usually executed through ADO code. Here is a small example of calling a SQL Server stored procedure:

```
Public Sub StoredProcTest()
    Dim cnn As ADODB.Connection
    Dim cmd As ADODB.Command
    Dim rs As ADODB.Recordset
    sConnect= "driver={sql server};" _
        & "server=DAD-PC\SQLEXPRESS;" _
        & "Database=Northwind;UID=;PWD=;"
    ' Establish connection.
    Set cnn = New ADODB.Connection
    cnn.ConnectionString = sConnect
    cnn.Open
     ' Open recordset.
    Set cmd = New ADODB.Command
    cmd.ActiveConnection = cnn
    cmd.CommandText = "sp_MyProc"
    cmd.CommandType = adCmdStoredProc
    cmd.Parameters.Refresh
    cmd.Parameters(1).Value = 10
    Set rs = cmd.Execute()
    'Use the recordset's data here...
    ' Process results from recordset, then close it.
    rs.Close
    Set rs = Nothing
End Sub
```

This code is intended simply to show how ADO is able to run a SQL Server stored procedure, retrieve the procedure's return value as a recordset, and then use the recordset in Access. In this particular case, the connection to SQL Server is made through the ADO provider, and not through ODBC.

Triggers

A *trigger* is a bit of SQL code that executes when some action occurs on a table in a database. Typically, triggers execute as before (FOR in SQL Server), as after (AFTER in SQL Server), and as instead of (INSTEAD OF in SQL Server) triggers. As the name implies, a before trigger fires *before* data is changed in the table, while an after trigger files *after* the data has changed.

The biggest danger with triggers is that they can be recursive, calling themselves over and over, resulting in serious performance problems. For example, consider an AFTER trigger that changes data in a table. If the change invokes the trigger a second time, an endless recursive loop may occur.

Creating a trigger is very similar to a procedure or a function. This example creates an entry in a log file every time a new product is added:

```
USE test
CREATE TRIGGER LogEntries ON Products
    FOR INSERT
        INSERT INTO LogFile(id,event)
        VALUES(<autocounter>,'New product added');
```

Summary

This chapter has taken a look at some of the capabilities possible when Access is partnered with SQL Server. Although some of the techniques used to access SQL Server have changed in Access, the same capabilities are available as in previous versions of Access.

In many ways, Access is the ideal interface tool for SQL Server data. SQL Server provides a high level of data security, the ability to service thousands of simultaneous users, and advanced data-management tools such as log files, stored procedures, views, and triggers. Also, the storage capacity of SQL Server installations is practically unlimited. Many SQL Server installations manage billions of records, making all that data available to qualified client applications such as Microsoft Access.

Upsizing Access Databases to SQL Server

The Access Upsizing Wizard provides a quick and easy way to upsize Access data to a SQL Server database. Either SQL Server Express or full server-based SQL Server can be the target of an Access upsizing process. The SQL Server database file created during the upsizing process is exactly the same, regardless of which edition of SQL Server is used.

The Upsizing Wizard automatically creates an *Access Data Project* (a special type of Access data file that allows you to work directly with a SQL Server database). In Chapters 16 and 37 you saw the simplest and quickest method of upsizing Access data to SQL Server: simply linking SQL Server data to an existing Access application (presumably, the SQL Server data was imported into SQL Server using SQL Server Integration Services [SSIS]). Although this option moves your data to a client-server architecture, it takes you only part of the way. Even though the data now resides in a client-server database, the linked tables in the existing *Access front end* (the forms, reports, and data-access pages) continue to use the Microsoft Jet database engine to retrieve information from the database.

Access Data Projects (ADPs) are frequently used to create and maintain SQL Server databases (from here on usually referred to simply as SQL Server). You can also use an ADP to create the user-interface objects and forms, reports, macros, and modules, which get their data from SQL Server. The ADP user interface looks very much like the standard Access database window you're already accustomed to. In fact, creating the user-interface objects is virtually the same as creating them in Access.

IN THIS CHAPTER

Considering SQL Server Express as an Access database engine

Understanding Access ADP databases

Working with the Access Upsizing Wizard

On the CD-ROM

This chapter uses `Chapter38.accdb` database on this book's CD. If you haven't already copied it onto your machine from the CD, you'll need to do so now. You'll also need access to some version of SQL Server (Standard, Enterprise, or Express) if you intend to practice upsizing Access databases to SQL Server.

Before beginning this chapter in earnest, you need to keep in mind a few things about transferring data to SQL Server. When upsizing an Access database to SQL Server, SQL Server takes over data-management tasks. All the tables, queries, and other data-oriented objects are contained within the SQL Server database. An Access `.adp` file is not much more than an interface to the SQL Server database, and contains the forms, reports, VBA code, and other user-interface components.

The good news is that if you're moving from an existing Access front end to SQL Server, you don't have to build these objects from scratch. The Access Upsizing Wizard does most of the work for you, preserving the work you've already invested in the user interface of your Access application.

Using linked SQL Server tables in an Access front end can be an acceptable solution for many small-workgroup environments. However, for environments with large numbers of users or where large volumes of data are processed, you need a solution that utilizes client-server architecture in both the front-end and back-end databases.

Cross-Reference

Although this chapter focuses on upsizing an Access database to SQL Server, a very common technique for using SQL Server data in an Access application is to use ODBC to link to SQL Server tables. Chapter 37 discusses this process, and shows how to access SQL Server data from a standard Access `.accdb` file. The `.adp` file created by the Upsizing Wizard is actually an Access 2000 format data file, but it features all the user-interface enhancements seen in the `.accdb` data file type.

Introducing SQL Server Express

This chapter makes many references to SQL Server Express Edition. Client-server databases, and their differences from a file-based database system like Microsoft Access, are discussed in Chapters 36 and 37. But those chapters really didn't describe SQL Server in detail or explain why SQL Server is so important to Access developers.

SQL Server is Microsoft's premier database engine for enterprise, Web, and large database systems. SQL Server is just an engine, with a minimal interface necessary to create and maintain databases and database objects. There is no provision for building user interfaces or reporting features in SQL Server.

Because SQL Server is scalable — from tiny individual desktop list managers to multi-terabyte databases serving thousands of simultaneous users — it's the database engine of choice for many small and large companies. Large SQL Server installations can be *clustered,* allowing multiple servers to work together as a single, huge computer system. There is no practical limit on the number of tables, stored procedures, and other objects in a SQL Server database, and each table can have a virtually unlimited number of records.

SQL Server also provides significant security for its databases. The SQL Server security system directly incorporates with Windows Active Directory, which means that (depending on configuration) SQL Server may recognize a user by virtue of their Windows login and membership in Active Directory groups, or may require each user to log in each time a SQL Server database is accessed from an application. Because the physical SQL Server database resides only on an application server, there is little chance an unauthorized user is able to access data stored in SQL Server or abscond with an entire SQL Server database.

For all these reasons, SQL Server is the natural destination for Access databases that have outgrown the practical limits of a file-based database, or databases that must be shared with more users than is practical using the Access database engines.

Microsoft provides SQL Server Express as a practical server-based database engine for moderate-size databases. Because SQL Server Express is binary-compatible with full SQL Server, no conversion is necessary to move a SQL Server Express database to full SQL Server. All you have to do is detach the database files from the Express edition and attach the file to the full edition.

SQL Server Express contains exactly the same core code as all SQL Server editions and works with exactly the same format database files as SQL Server Enterprise. The data file format, Transact-SQL syntax, security architecture, and other specifications are the same in SQL Server Express and SQL Server Enterprise. The primary difference between these database engines is that SQL Server Express does not include several of the more-advanced features (such as full text searches) that SQL Server Enterprise includes. Also, SQL Server Express supports databases up to 4GB in size; SQL Server Enterprise supports databases in excess of 500,000TB.

SQL Server Express includes SQL Server Management Studio and SQL Server Reporting Services. Furthermore, unlike the Microsoft Database Engine (MSDE) that preceded SQL Server Express, the Express edition does not contain the performance throttle that inhibited more than a few connections to MSDE. Consult the SQL Server Express pages (`www.microsoft.com/Express/SQL`) on the Microsoft Web site for more details.

SQL Server Express is the ideal database engine for small workgroups and individuals wanting to make the leap into client-server architecture. And the price is definitely right! SQL Server Express is a free download from the Microsoft MSDN site (`www.microsoft.com/express/sql/default.aspx`).

Installing SQL Server Express Edition is painless. Download either the 32- or 64-bit version for your computer and install using all the default settings. The memory, hard disk, and other hardware requirements for SQL Server Express Edition are somewhat more stringent than for Microsoft Office, but they should be met by most desktop and laptop computers today.

Upsizing Access and the Upsizing Wizard

Today, many organizations are becoming more and more dependent on their database applications to manage everyday business operations, and these applications are growing both in volume of data and number of users. Applications that you might have developed using Microsoft Access even in the past year or two might be starting to strain the organization's network. At the same time, client-server databases like SQL Server are becoming more popular — even with smaller businesses — because these databases become easier to install, use, and maintain.

You may have been advised recently of a new mandate that all new applications must conform to client-server technology only: No file-server database management allowed. Having already invested a significant amount of your budget into the Access applications that you've developed, you're naturally concerned that the move to client-server architecture might require a major rewrite.

Fortunately, with Access and its Upsizing Wizard, you can provide a relatively simple and inexpensive solution that retains a significant amount of the original development effort while providing a database that conforms to client-server methodology.

You can automatically convert the tables stored in an existing Microsoft Access database (.accdb or .mdb) to a client-server database using the Microsoft Access Upsizing Wizard. The Upsizing Wizard takes an Access .accdb database, and creates an equivalent SQL Server database with the same table structures, data, and most other attributes of the original database. The Upsizing Wizard re-creates table structures, indexes, validation rules, defaults, autonumbers, and relationships, and takes advantage of the latest SQL Server functionality wherever possible.

Before upsizing an application

Prior to converting an application using the Upsizing Wizard, do the following:

- **Back up your database.** Although the Upsizing Wizard doesn't remove any data or database objects from your Access database, it's always a good idea to create a backup copy of an Access database before upsizing it.

- **Ensure that you have enough hard-drive space.** At a minimum, you need enough hard-drive space to store the new SQL Server database. Plan to allow at least twice the size of your Access database to allow room for future growth. If you expect to add a lot of data to the database, allow a corresponding amount of free disk space on the destination drive.

- **Set a default printer.** You must have a default printer assigned, because the Upsizing Wizard creates a report snapshot as it completes the conversion.

SQL Server should be started automatically by the SQL Server Express installation. If SQL Server is not currently running, use the SQL Server Management Studio Express that was installed along with SQL Server Express to start SQL Server. The upsizing process needs a running SQL Server instance.

If, on the other hand, you're using a SQL Server instance running on another computer on the network, it's almost surely up and running, and there's nothing more for you to do.

Running the Upsizing Wizard

After you've completed the steps to prepare for the conversion (see the preceding section), you're ready to upsize your application. First, open the Microsoft Access database that you want to convert. This example upsizes the database for this chapter (Chapter38.accdb — make sure you use the original copy).

Note

Keep in mind that the result of the Upsizing Wizard is a brand-new Access .adp file already linked to the SQL Server database created by the Upsizing Wizard. Your original .accdb file remains unchanged.

Notice that the following steps accept all the default options provided by the Upsizing Wizard. Accepting all defaults is the best way to ensure that the upsized version of your application works exactly as the .accdb version. The Upsizing Wizard creates a SQL Server database that mirrors the .accdb in almost every regard, including table and field names, data types, and validation rules.

1. Open the Access database for this chapter (Chapter38.accdb).
2. Select the Database Tools tab.
3. Select the SQL Server option from the Move Data section.

   The first dialog box of the Upsizing Wizard is shown in Figure 38.1.

FIGURE 38.1

Upsizing from Access to SQL Server

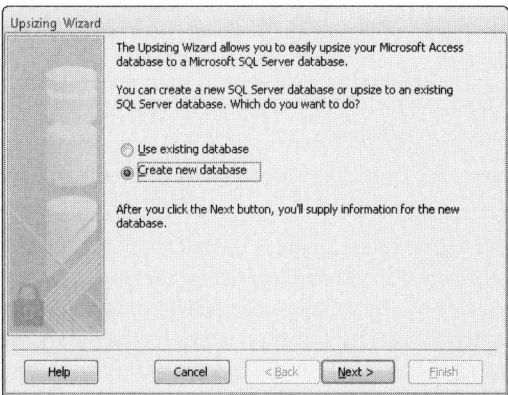

Notice that the Create New Database option has been selected in this dialog box. Selecting the Use Existing Database option requires an existing SQL Server database as the target of the upsizing process. For the purposes of this demonstration, assume that you're upsizing an Access database to take advantage of the features provided by SQL Server, and you're creating a brand-new SQL Server database to use as the data source for an existing Access application.

4. The second dialog box of the Upsizing Wizard asks for the location of the SQL Server installation you want to use.

   In Figure 38.2, a SQL Server Express database has been selected running on a computer named "DELL6000." The Upsizing Wizard creates a new database on the selected server, containing replicates of all the database objects (except for forms, reports, modules, and macros) in the current database.

FIGURE 38.2

Specifying the SQL Server installation to receive the new database.

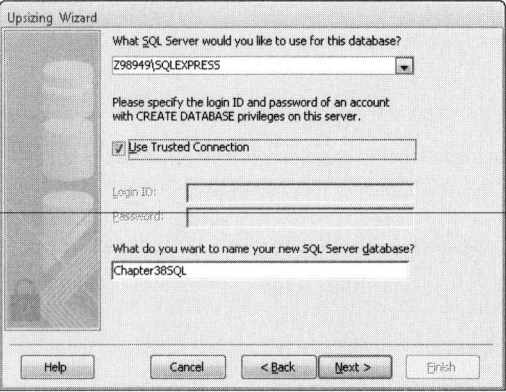

5. The third dialog box (shown in Figure 38.3) allows you to select which tables to export to the SQL Server database.

   Again, our scenario is to completely upsize an Access application to SQL Server, so all tables have been selected in this dialog box.

6. The next screen (shown in Figure 38.4) asks for a lot of details on the table attributes that you want to upsize.

   Generally speaking, if you've added an index or validation rule to an Access table, you want the same attributes in a corresponding SQL Server table. Therefore, all the options are selected on this dialog box by default. The Use DRI option is selected by default because DRI (Declarative Referential Integrity) is much closer to the Access model of table relationships than using triggers to maintain referential integrity. Using triggers means that each table requires *triggers* (SQL statements that are executed whenever data in a SQL Server table is changed) that ensure the proper relationships between tables are maintained. Using triggers to manage referential integrity requires considerably more work than DRI but is preferred in some situations, particularly situations where the database administrator (DBA) prefers triggers over DRI for performance reasons.

FIGURE 38.3

Selecting tables for the upsizing operation

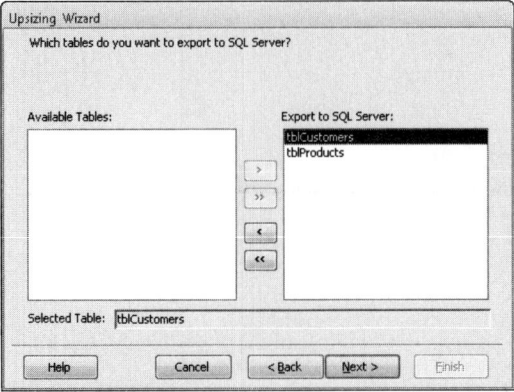

FIGURE 38.4

Specifying the table details for the upsizing process

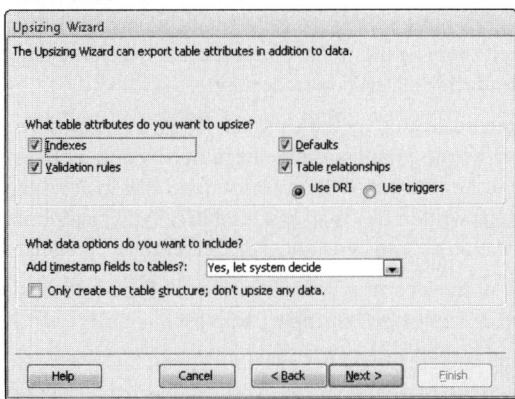

7. The next screen (shown in Figure 38.5) allows you to either specify a new Access .adp file, or simply link the upsize SQL Server tables to the current database.

   Because our scenario is to completely upsize an Access application to SQL Server, and because we want to use the SQL Server application for managing the tables and other database objects on SQL Server, Figure 38.5 shows the Creating New Access Client/Server Application option selected. The default name for the upsized .adp file is the same as the current Access database with a CS suffixed.

Choosing how you want your Access application upsized

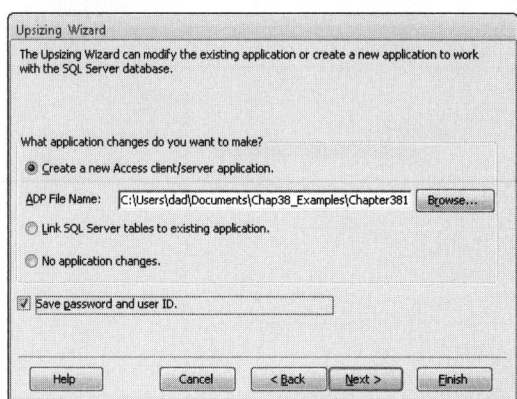

You could just as easily have decided to simply upsize the tables without making changes to the current Access database file. This might be a good option if the intent were to create copies of the Access tables in SQL Server so that other users, working with other SQL Server client-side applications, could use the same data. However, because the data is copied to SQL Server, there would be no connection between the data remaining in the Access application and the data seen by other users.

The SQL Server database created by the Upsizing Wizard is accessible to any qualified SQL Server user. Just because the data came from Access doesn't mean that the data can only be used in an Access context. Other users will be able to access the upsized Access data using applications written in Visual Studio .NET, Web pages built with ASP .NET, and any other application able to consume SQL Server data (like SharePoint).

8. The final dialog box of the Upsizing Wizard (shown in Figure 38.6) asks whether you want to (in this case, at least) open the new `.adp` file.

   If, instead of upsizing and creating a new `.adp` file, you had chosen to upsize the tables and link them back to the current database, you would be returned to the database. But, for the purposes of this demonstration, go ahead and open the new `.adp` file. The alternative (Keep the Database file open) means that Access creates the new `.adp` file but leaves the current database open in front of you. You may prefer keeping the database open if you know you have other work to perform in the existing database.

The final Access Upsizing Wizard dialog box

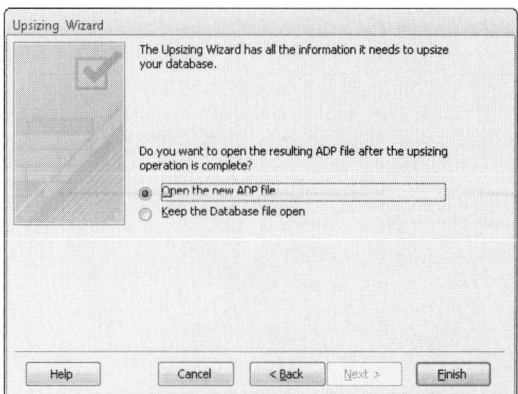

If, instead of upsizing all the Access tables to SQL Server, you had chosen Link SQL Server Tables to Existing Application, the Upsizing Wizard would have modified your Access database to work with the new SQL Server database. Queries, forms, reports, and data-access pages are automatically linked to the data in the new Microsoft SQL Server database. The Upsizing Wizard renames the tables to be upsized with the suffix `_local` and leaves them intact. For example, if you upsize a table called `Customers`, the table is renamed `Customers_local` in your Access database. Then, the Upsizing Wizard creates a linked SQL Server table named `Customers`.

Upsizing the entire Access application to an Access project connected to a SQL Server database converts your application to a true client-server implementation. However, if you've been developing only Access databases until this point, you'll find client-server development is quite different. The Upsizing Wizard takes you only part of the way. The Upsizing Wizard doesn't make any changes to modules and macros. You might also need to make changes to your tables and queries to reach full functionality in the new architecture.

Typically, the conversion process requires no more than a few minutes to complete, but the elapsed time depends entirely on the size and complexity of the upsized Access database. A message box displays the progress of the conversion, as shown in Figure 38.7.

Note

An error message will be displayed if the Upsizing Wizard encounters referential integrity errors during the conversion process. You can click Yes to proceed with the conversion if you encounter an error message. Any problem data is not converted to the new database. If you don't want to omit the problem data, you must click No to cancel the conversion process.

FIGURE 38.7

Waiting for the Upsizing Wizard to complete the conversion process

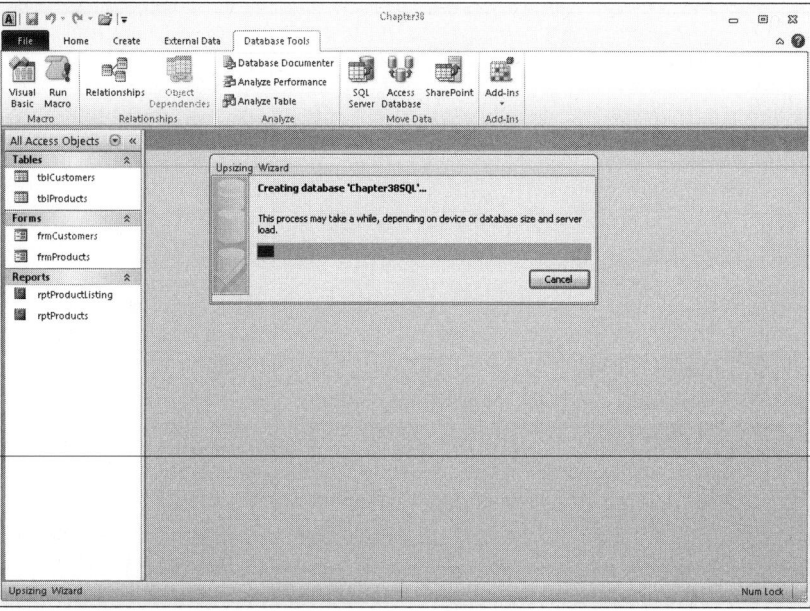

When the conversion process completes, the Upsizing Wizard automatically displays a report snapshot of the upsizing process. An example of the report snapshot is shown in Figure 38.8. The report snapshot includes information about each step of the conversion process for your application. The Upsizing Wizard report contains information about the following:

- Database details, including database size
- Upsizing parameters, including what table attributes you chose to upsize and how you upsized
- Table information, including a comparison of Access and SQL Server values for names, data types, indexes, validation rules, defaults, triggers, and whether timestamps were added
- Any errors, including database or transaction log full; inadequate permissions; device or database not created; table, default, or validation rule skipped; relationship not enforced; query skipped (because it can't be translated to SQL Server syntax); and control and record-source conversion errors in forms and reports

FIGURE 38.8

The Upsizing Wizard report

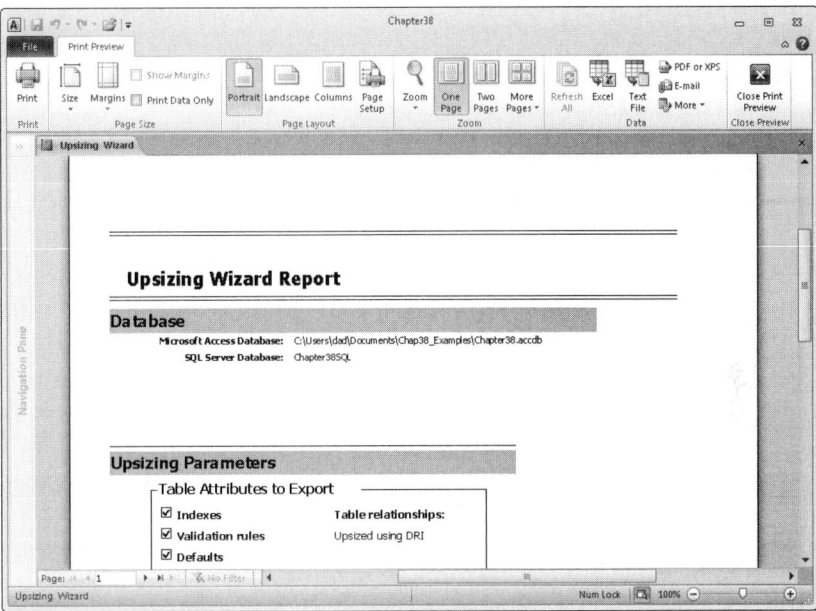

The Upsizing Wizard Report is a good place to start when verifying the upsize process. The report tells you which Access database objects must be manually re-created in SQL Server and which tasks could not be completed by the wizard. A typical example of conversion failure is an Access query that contains a reference to a custom VBA procedure. There is no way for the Upsizing Wizard to recreate VBA logic in a SQL Server database, so you'll have to prepare a workaround after the upsizing task is complete.

Working with an Access ADP file

After you're finished reviewing the report, close it. When you close the report, the Upsizing Wizard automatically loads the new Access project. The Access Upsizing Wizard migrates the native Access objects into their corresponding objects in the new Access project. Although Access projects are organized into the same object groupings (tables, queries, forms, reports, and so on), ADP objects differ significantly in how they work compared to native Access. Here are the characteristics of ADP objects and how they differ from the Access objects you work with in an .accdb database:

- **Tables:** Individual tables are converted to SQL Server tables. Data types are converted to their corresponding SQL Server data types.

Cross-Reference
Refer to the next section, "Comparing Access to SQL Server data types," for a listing of SQL Server data types and how they compare to native Access data types.

- **Queries:** Queries are converted into views, stored procedures, and functions according to the following rules:

  - Select queries that don't have an ORDER BY clause or parameters are converted to views.

  - Action queries are converted to stored-procedure action queries. Access adds SET NOCOUNT ON after the parameter declaration code to make sure the stored procedure runs.

  - Select queries that use either parameters or an ORDER BY clause are converted to user-defined functions. If necessary, the TOP 100 PERCENT clause is added to a query that contains an ORDER BY clause.

  - Parameter queries that use named parameters maintain the original text name used in the Access database and are converted either to stored procedures or inline user-defined functions.

- **Forms and reports:** Converted with no changes. The RecordSource property of a form or report still points to the same database object as before, except that in an .adp file, the table is hosted by SQL Server.

- **Ribbons:** Converted with no changes.

- **Macros and modules:** Converted with no changes.

To take full advantage of SQL Server and an Access project, you need to make some fairly significant changes to your newly converted application. Although the Upsizing Wizard tries to make its best guess as to the most efficient conversion approach, you should review the table and query designs and revise them as necessary. Record sources and control sources for forms and reports are converted without any changes. In an implementation with a large number of users, you don't want to bind forms and reports directly to a table or even a query.

Note
If you're converting an application created in an earlier version of Access, you may also need to manually convert code from Data Access Objects (DAO) to ActiveX Data Objects (ADO) in your modules.

It is important to understand that an Access `.adp` file doesn't contain linked tables. The tables in an Access `.adp` file are equivalent to any Access table. The only difference is that the table's data is provided by SQL Server and not by the Access Database Engine. And, because the tables are hosted by SQL Server, the data types available to you are somewhat different from the way they are in a native Access database. Figure 38.9 shows the user interface of the Access ADP created earlier in this chapter. Notice how similar it is to any Access application.

FIGURE 38.9

An Access ADP looks like any other Access 2010 application.

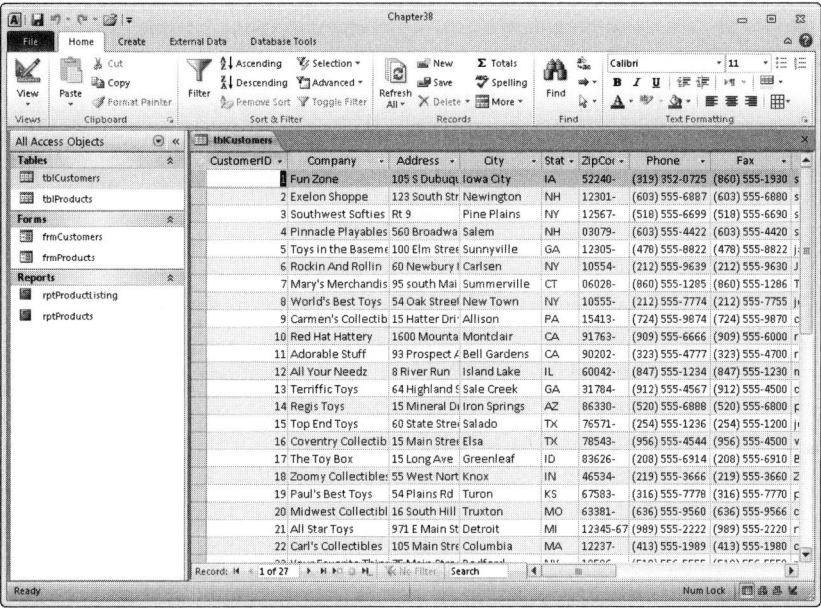

Comparing Access to SQL Server data types

Opening an upsized `.adp` table in Design view quickly reveals a significant difference between Access and SQL Server. In Figure 38.10, the `Customers` table has been open in Design view. Notice that SQL Server provides many more different field data types and that the properties at the bottom of the table designer include items such as `Precision`, `Scale`, and `Identity`. These are all SQL Server constructs, yet they're accessible from within the Access developer interface.

FIGURE 38.10

SQL Server field data types in an ADP database are considerably different from the way they are in Access.

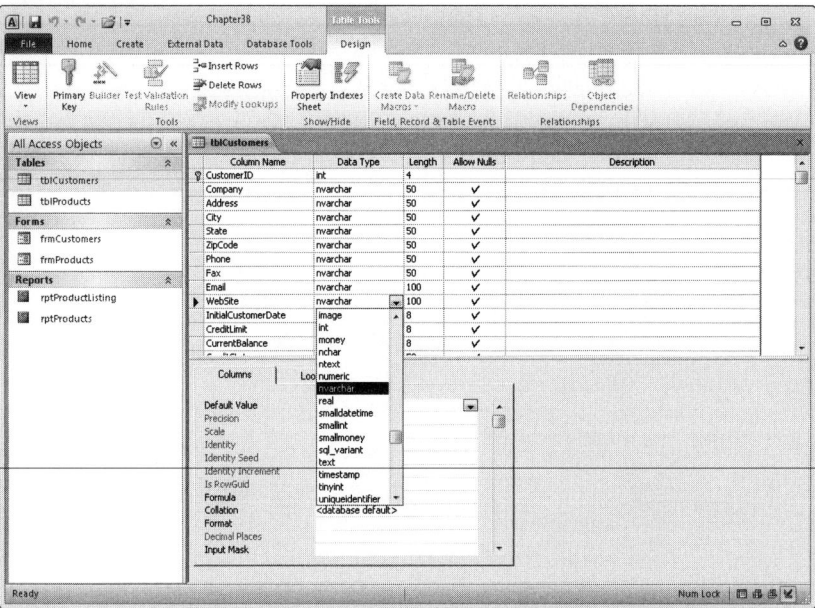

The data types available in Access are described in Table 38.1.

TABLE 38.1

The Details of Access Data Types

Data Type	Used to Store	Limitations/Restrictions
Text	Alphanumeric data (text and numbers)	Stores up to 255 characters.
Memo	Alphanumeric data (text and numbers)	Stores up to 2GB of data (the size limit for all Access databases), if you fill the field programmatically. Remember that adding 2GB of data causes your database to operate slowly.
		If you enter data manually, you can enter and view a maximum of 65,535 characters in the table field and in any controls that you bind to the field.
		When you create databases in the Access file format, Memo fields also support rich-text editing.

Data Type	Used to Store	Limitations/Restrictions
Number	Numeric data	Uses a Field Size setting that controls the size of the value that the field can contain. You can set the field size to 1, 2, 4, 8, or 16 bytes.
Date/Time	Dates and times	Stores all dates as 8-byte double-precision integers.
Currency	Monetary data	Stores data as 8-byte numbers with precision to four decimal places. Use this data type to store financial data and when you don't want Access to round values.
AutoNumber	Unique values created by Access when you create a new record	Stores data as 4-byte values; typically used in primary keys.
Yes/No	Boolean (true or false) data	Uses –1 for all Yes values and 0 for all No values.
OLE Object	Images, documents, graphs, and other objects from Office and Windows-based programs	Stores up to 2GB of data (the size limit for all Access databases). Remember that adding 2GB of data causes your database to operate slowly. OLE Object fields create bitmap images of the original document or other object, and then display that bitmap in the table fields and form or report controls in your database.

For Access to render those images, you must have an OLE server (a program that supports that file type) registered on the computer that runs your database. If you don't have an OLE server registered for a given file type, Access displays a broken image icon. This is a known problem for some image types, most notably `.jpg` images.

As a rule, you should use Attachment fields for your `.accdb` files instead of OLE Object fields. Attachment fields use storage space more efficiently and are not limited by a lack of registered OLE servers. |
| Hyperlink | Web addresses | Stores up to 1GB of data. You can store links to Web sites, sites or files on an intranet or local area network (LAN), and sites or files on your computer. |
| Attachment | Any supported type of file | New to Access `.accdb` files. You can attach images, spreadsheet files, documents, charts, and other types of supported files to the records in your database, much like you attach files to e-mail messages. You can also view and edit attached files, depending on how the database designer sets up the Attachment field. Attachment fields provide greater flexibility than OLE Object fields, and they use storage space more efficiently because they don't create a bitmap image of the original file. |

Table 38.2 shows the equivalent SQL Server data type for each Access data type.

TABLE 38.2

Comparison of Access and SQL Server Data Types

Microsoft Access Data Type	SQL Server Data Type
Yes/No	Bit
Number	tinyint, smallint, int, bigint: Very small integers up to very large integers. Smaller data types use less bytes and occupy less physical space.
	real, float: Real numbers and floating point numbers are the same thing.
	decimal[(18,0)]: A decimal defaults to 2 decimal places but can be sized up to 18 bytes with no decimals.
	numeric[(18,0)]: Can be a specified length as for decimal.
Currency	money, smallmoney
Date/Time	datetime, smalldatetime, timestamp
AutoNumber	int (with identity property defined)
Text	char(10), varchar(50), varchar(n), varchar(MAX): ASCII (8-bit) character set string variables.
	nchar(10), nvarchar(50), nvarchar(n), nvarchar(MAX): Unicode (16-bit) character set string variables.
	char: Fixed-length string, usually short and known sizes, where string is padded up to fixed length regardless of value.
	varchar(50-n): Variable-length strings where no padding is added for shorter strings.
	MAX: Used for extremely large values
Memo	text and ntext: Large variable text strings stored in binary form. ntext stores unicode character set.
OLE Object	Image: Intended specifically for storing images in binary form
Attachment	No equivalent
Hyperlink	No equivalent
Lookup Wizard...: based on a query or multiple literal values	No equivalent
No equivalent	binary(50), varbinary, varbinary(50), varbinary(MAX)
No equivalent	uniqueidentifier
No equivalent	xml: XML data type for storing both content and functionality of XML documents.
No equivalent	sql_variant: A variable data type, except it does not allow text, ntext, image, or timestamp.

Although the Upsizing Wizard maps Access data types to SQL Server data types, there are other conversion issues you need to be aware of. If the Upsizing Wizard Report indicates that a table has been skipped, examine the field names in each of the Access tables to ensure that they adhere to the following constraints:

- The first character must be a letter or the @ sign.

- The remaining characters may be numbers, letters, the dollar sign ($), the number sign (#), or the underscore (_).

- Spaces are allowed, but the Upsizing Wizard will insert brackets ([ ]) around the field name.

- The name must not be a Transact-SQL keyword. SQL Server reserves both the uppercase and lowercase versions of keywords.

To verify SQL Server reserved words, go to http://msdn.microsoft.com, and search for Transact-SQL Reference and SQL-Server Language Reference.

If any field name in an Access table fails to follow these guidelines, the Upsizing Wizard is not able to upsize the table. The Upsizing Wizard Report informs you that the table has been skipped. However, the wizard does not always provide the reason the table was skipped. When you review the report, you can refer to this section to review the field-naming rules.

In addition to field-name constraints, the Upsizing Wizard also fails to upsize a table if it encounters any of these situations:

- The field size between two fields participating in an Access relationship is not exactly the same for both fields.

- There is no unique index.

- There is a unique index on a field and the Required property is set to No.

- More than two foreign keys are defined on a single table.

- An Access database may contain data that are invalid in SQL Server. Date must be no earlier than 1/1/1753 to be compatible with SQL Server. (Access supports a much wider range of dates, all the way back to 1/1/100.)

After you're finished reviewing the report, close it. When you close the report, the Upsizing Wizard displays the modified Access application.

Note

You might notice that all Access text data types are upsized to SQL Server nvarchar columns. This may cause a problem in some situations. The nvarchar data type supports Unicode (16-bit) character sets (as does Access), which means every character requires 16 bits (2 bytes) of data storage, instead of 8 bits (1 byte). Upsizing very large Access tables containing lots of text fields could, conceivably, overwhelm the 4GB limit on the SQL Server Express database file. However, because an Access database is limited to 2GB, this is, at best, a remote possibility.

Figure 38.11 shows the upsized SQL Server database open in Management Studio Express. The column properties of the Contacts table are displayed in the Summary tab of the Management Studio interface, showing the data types the Upsizing Wizard selected for each field in the original Contacts table.

FIGURE 38.11

The tables in the upsized database from within SQL Server Management Studio Express

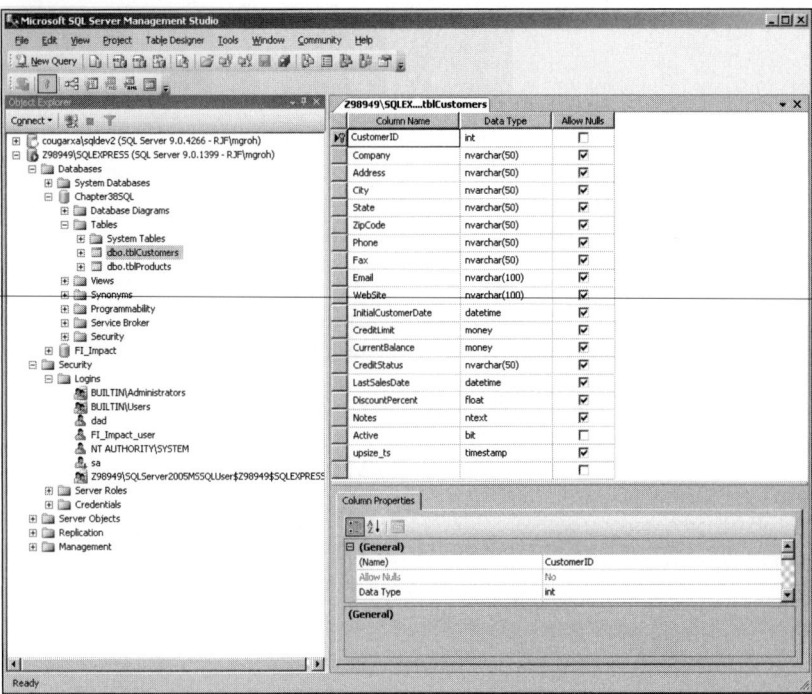

Summary

This chapter has surveyed the process of upsizing Access applications to SQL Server, using the Access .adp data file format as upsized database output. SQL Server alleviates many issues that have long vexed Access developers, such as database corruption, record lock contention, and poor performance when more than a few users make simultaneous updates.

Furthermore, upsizing to SQL Server immediately makes Access data accessible to any application connecting to SQL Server, including Web sites and Microsoft SharePoint Services. It's hard to over-emphasize how important this aspect of the upsizing process is to Access developers. The data that your users input into their desktop Access applications is instantly accessible anywhere in the world, to anyone with access to SharePoint or another application connected to the SQL Server database.

This chapter also discussed the SQL Server Express Edition. SQL Server Express is a free download from Microsoft's Web site. Outside minimal registration requirements, it can be used by anyone wanting to take advantage of the SQL Server database architecture and features. Unlike MSDE, which preceded SQL Server Express, the Express edition does not include the performance throttle that inhibited more than five or six connections to MSDE. This means that SQL Server Express is the ideal upgrade path for workgroup applications that have outgrown the Access Database Engine's capabilities.

Part VII

Appendixes

I conclude the book with several appendixes to serve as reference material as you work with Microsoft Access 2010.

Appendix A covers the Access 2010 specifications, and includes information such as the limits (database size, number of database objects, maximum number of rows in an Access table, and so on) of Access objects. Appendix A also includes the specifications for SQL Server Express Edition.

Appendix B provides a description of the most important new features in Access 2010. This version of Access includes more changes than any other recent version of Microsoft Access, both in the user interface and in capabilities facing developers, and I analyze many of these changes for you in Appendix B.

Appendix C describes the contents of the book's CD.

IN THIS PART

Appendix A
Access 2010 Specifications

Appendix B
What's New in Access 2010

Appendix C
What's on the CD-ROM

Access 2010 Specifications

This appendix shows the limits of Microsoft Access database files, tables, queries, forms, reports, and macros. Please be aware the values given in this appendix are subject to change, and refer to Microsoft's Web site (www.microsoft.com) for the latest information on these specifications.

The maximum database size, number of columns, and other limits on Access databases are more than adequate for the vast majority of Access applications. In most cases, when an Access database application exceeds these limits, there is some underlying design issue that is inappropriately driving the application toward these limits. In the vast majority of cases, careful review of an application's design reveals a flaw in the database's implementation. The flaw eventually causes the application to bump up against the table or column limits for Access databases.

For example, the maximum number of columns in an Access database table is 255. Many Access developers would like to see Microsoft raise the maximum number of columns in Access tables to 1,000 or more. However, in virtually every case I've ever looked at, a perceived need for more columns in a table is the result of improper normalization more than anything else.

In many cases, improperly normalized data stems from importing data directly from Microsoft Excel into Access. Excel users are accustomed to simply adding new columns to accommodate their needs without regard to considering the impact of the additional columns on the data the worksheet contains.

Cross-Reference
Refer to Chapter 3 to review the steps for normalizing data.

Very few Excel users understand the need to break out "child" data (like phone numbers and addresses) into separate worksheets to minimize data maintenance. And they shouldn't be concerned — after all, Excel is a spreadsheet, not a database, even though many Excel users work with Excel worksheets as if they were database tables.

Recent versions of Excel allow more than 16,000 columns in a single worksheet. Inevitably, you'll be asked to import a humongous Excel worksheet into access, or to link to an Excel spreadsheet so reports can be produced and printed in Access. You'll find that you can't import or link to Excel spreadsheets when the Excel column count exceeds 255. Don't blame Access! Instead, look for workarounds, such as segmenting the Excel data into named ranges and importing or linking the named ranges separately. Sure, it'll be a hassle, but there's no reason Microsoft should abandon the performance and utility of a relational database system (like Access) just to accommodate the infrequent situation in which Access's database limits seem unfair or inappropriate.

Another common suggestion is to increase the maximum database size beyond the current 2GB limit. There are several workarounds to this issue, such as linking a front-end database to multiple back-end databases. Although linking to multiple back-end databases can impose serious performance problems on some queries (databases have trouble joining tables from diverse data sources because relationships can't be properly established between tables in different database files), carefully planning how the data is distributed among the back-end databases should minimize these issues.

And, of course, linking to *blob* (binary large object) data such as images and video clips, is a much more efficient use of database space than embedding the data directly into the database.

Generally speaking, if you have a database that contains more than 2GB of data that can't be handled by splitting out as multiple back-end databases or other tricks, it's probably time to consider upsizing to SQL Server. Because its database size is 4GB, SQL Server Express might help with the initial move. The Access upsizing tools are very easy to use and virtually foolproof. And SQL Server Express is a free download and may be freely distributed with your Access applications.

Cross-Reference

Turn to Chapter 38 for more on the Access upsizing tools.

Always keep in mind that Access is a file-based database system. The Access database file, whether it's an .accdb, an .mdb, or any other type, is just a Windows file. Access databases don't support logging, rollbacks, archiving, or other administrative tasks intended to protect a database's data. There is a point at which it really doesn't make good business sense to continue storing vast amounts of mission-critical data in a file-based database system. Server database systems (like SQL Server) provide all the tools necessary to properly administer and protect very large amounts of data.

Microsoft Access Database Specifications

Databases

Attribute	Maximum
`.accdb` or `.mdb` file size, including all database objects and data	2GB, minus space needed for system objects (Because your database can include attached tables in multiple files, its total size is limited only by available storage capacity.)
Total number of objects in a database (tables, queries, forms, reports, and so on)	32,768
Number of modules, including modules attached to forms and reports	1,000
Number of characters in object names	64
Number of characters in a database password	14
Number of characters in a user name or group name	20
Number of concurrent users	255

Tables

Attribute	Maximum
Number of characters in a table name	64
Number of characters in a field name	64
Number of fields in a record or table	255
Number of open tables	2,048, including system tables opened by Microsoft Access internally. Also includes linked tables.
Table size	2GB (minus space needed for system objects). There is no set limit on the number of rows in an Access table.
Number of characters in a Text field	255
Number of characters in a Memo field	65,535 when entering data through the user interface; 1GB when entering data programmatically
Size of OLE object field	1GB
Number of indexes in a record or table (including composite indexes, primary key indexes, and other indexes)	32, including single-field and composite indexes, and indexes created internally for maintaining table relationships

continued

TABLE A.2 *(continued)*

Attribute	Maximum
Number of fields in an index or primary key	10
Number of characters in a validation message	255
Number of characters in a validation rule (including punctuation and operators)	2,048
Number of characters in a table or field description	255
Number of characters in a record	4,000 (excluding Memo and OLE Object fields)
Number of characters in a field property setting	255

TABLE A.3

Queries

Attribute	Maximum
Number of tables in a query	32
Number of enforced relationships	32 per table, minus indexes that are on the table for the fields or combinations of fields that are not involved in the relationship
Number of fields in a recordset	255
Maximum recordset size	1GB
Sort limit	255 characters in one or more fields
Number of levels of nested queries	50
Number of characters in a cell of the design grid	1,024
Number of characters in a parameter name for a parameterized query	255
Number of ANDs in a WHERE or HAVING clause	99
Number of characters in a SQL statement	Approximately 64,000

TABLE A.4

Forms and Reports

Attribute	Maximum
Number of characters in a label	2,048
Number of characters in a text box	65,535
Form or report width	22.75 inches (57.79 centimeters)
Section height	22.75 inches (57.79 centimeters)

Attribute	Maximum
Height of all sections plus section headers in Design view	200 inches (508 centimeters)
Number of levels of nested forms or reports	7 (form-subform-subform)
Number of fields/expressions you can sort or group on (reports only)	10
Number of headers and footers in a report	1 report header/footer, 1 page header/footer, 10 group headers/footers
Number of printed pages in a report	65,536
Number of characters in a SQL statement that is the Recordsource or Rowsource property of a form, report, or control (both .mdb and .adp)	32,750
Number of controls or sections you can add over the lifetime of the form or report	754
Number of characters in a SQL statement that serves as either the RowSource property of a form or report or the ControlSource property of a control	32,750

TABLE A.5

Macros

Attribute	Maximum
Number of actions in a macro	999
Number of characters in a condition	255
Number of characters in a comment	255
Number of characters in an action argument	255

Microsoft SQL Server Express Specifications

With the exception of database size, the values in this table apply equally to Microsoft SQL Server 2005 and 2008 Express Edition. The maximum size of a SQL Server 2005 or 2008 Express database is 4GB.

The maximum size of data managed by SQL Server 2008 editions (other than Express Edition) is practically unlimited because of SQL Server's ability to be configured as clustered database servers. Any single SQL Server installation (other than the Express and Compact editions) is 524TB.

SQL Server 2008 Express Edition is a 32-bit application. It runs in a 32-bit process space when run on 64-bit operating systems.

Table A.6 includes the specifications for SQL Server 2008 Express Edition only. The other SQL Server 2008 editions are similar in most regards, with the exception of maximum database size. Also, there are some differences in limits between the 32- and 64-bit versions of SQL Server 2008. These variations make it difficult to include every limit for every edition of SQL Server 2008.

TABLE A.6

Microsoft SQL Sever Express Capacities

SQL Server Database Engine Object	Maximum Size or Number for SQL Server 2008 Express
CPU core utilization	1 (SQL Server Express does not utilize more than one CPU core on multi-core machines.)
Maximum memory utilization	1GB
Batch size	65,536 × network packet size
Bytes per short string column	8,000
Bytes per GROUP BY, ORDER BY	8,060
Bytes per index key	900
Bytes per foreign key	900
Bytes per primary key	900
Bytes per row	8,060
Bytes in source text of a stored procedure	Lesser of batch size or 250MB
Bytes per varchar(max), varbinary(max), xml, text, or image column	1,073,741,823
Characters per ntext or nvarchar(max) column	536,870,910
Clustered indexes per table	1
Columns in GROUP BY, ORDER BY	Limited only by number of bytes
Columns or expressions in a GROUP BY WITH CUBE or WITH ROLLUP statement	10
Columns per index key	16
Columns per foreign key	16
Columns per primary key	16
Columns per base table	1,024
Columns per SELECT statement	4,096
Columns per INSERT statement	1,024
Connections per client	Maximum value of configured connections

SQL Server Database Engine Object	Maximum Size or Number for SQL Server 2008 Express
Database size	4GB
Databases per instance of SQL Server	32,767
File groups per database	32,767
Files per database	32,767
File size (data)	4GB (not including log file size)
File size (log)	2TB
Foreign key table references per table	253
Identifier length (in characters)	128
Instances per computer	16
Length of a string containing SQL statements (batch size)	65,536 × network packet size
Locks per connection	Maximum locks per server
Locks per instance of SQL Server	Up to 2,147,483,647
Nested stored procedure levels	32
Nested subqueries	32
Nested trigger levels	32
Non-clustered indexes per table	999
Parameters per stored procedure	2,100
Parameters per user-defined function	2,100
REFERENCES per table	253
Rows per table	Limited by available storage
Tables per database	Limited by number of objects in a database
Partitions per partitioned table or index	1,000
Statistics on nonindexed columns	30,000
Tables per SELECT statement	256
Triggers per table	Limited by number of objects in a database
User connections	32,767
XML indexes	249

What's New in Access 2010

S uperficially, Access 2010 looks much like Access 2007. The some-what-controversial ribbon is still there, and the old Database window has been replaced by the Navigation Pane. Other than a few new items on the ribbon, you might think that Access 2010 is just a minor upgrade to 2007.

But, just as Access 2007 added significant new features, Access 2010 also complicates the developer's life, but in ways that most people welcome.

Many of the following descriptions cover features that were introduced in Access 2007. I've left those discussions in for people who are transitioning to Access 2010 from an older version. Understanding these changes is particularly important for anyone not familiar with the ribbon and how the ribbon works.

IN THIS APPENDIX

Reviewing the changes and enhancements for the developer in Access 2010

Looking at what's new in table design

Understanding the new form and report options

Learning the importance of SharePoint integration

The User Interface

Although the Access 2010 user interface is much like Access 2007, certain changes have been made to make Access easier and more intuitive to use. The Access 2010 user interface is shown in Figure B.1.

FIGURE B.1

The Access 2010 interface

As you can see, our old friend Northwind has an entirely new look. The biggest change in the Access 2007 interface was replacing the traditional nested menus in favor of a more tabular, every-thing-in-front-of-you system called the *ribbon*. In Access 2010, Microsoft replaced the round Office button with a simpler File tab. Selecting the File tab reveals the Backstage area (shown in Figure B.2).

The Backstage simplifies the ribbon by providing a landing pad for common administrative tasks. The options you see in the Backstage depend on which tab is selected (the Info tab is selected in Figure B.2). Notice that the Info tab in Figure B.2 includes administrative tasks such as compacting and repairing the database, as well as the all-new for 2010 Share Your Database in a Web Browser. This latter feature is described in the "Publish Access to the Web" section, later in this appendix.

The ribbon is designed to be contextual so that everything you need is there when you need it. Functions such as Font, Records, and Sort & Filter are grouped together and make the ribbon a welcome change.

Access 2010 provides a very nice, easy-to-use interface for customizing the Access ribbon (see Figure B.3). Access 2007 only provided a way to customize the Quick Access Toolbar in the upper-left corner of the main Access screen. Access 2010 extends this capability by including the entire Access ribbon as a customizable object.

FIGURE B.2

The Backstage replaces the former File dialog box.

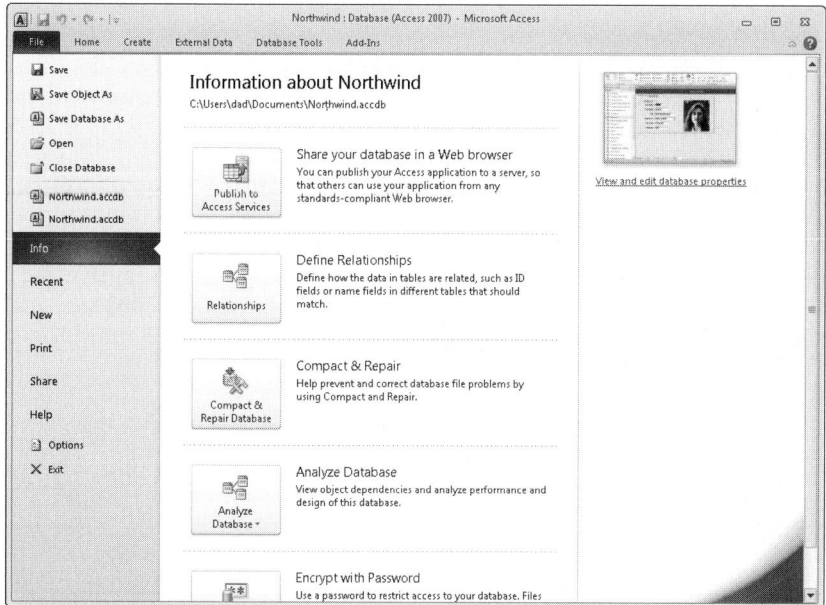

FIGURE B.3

Access 2010 includes an editor for modifying the ribbon.

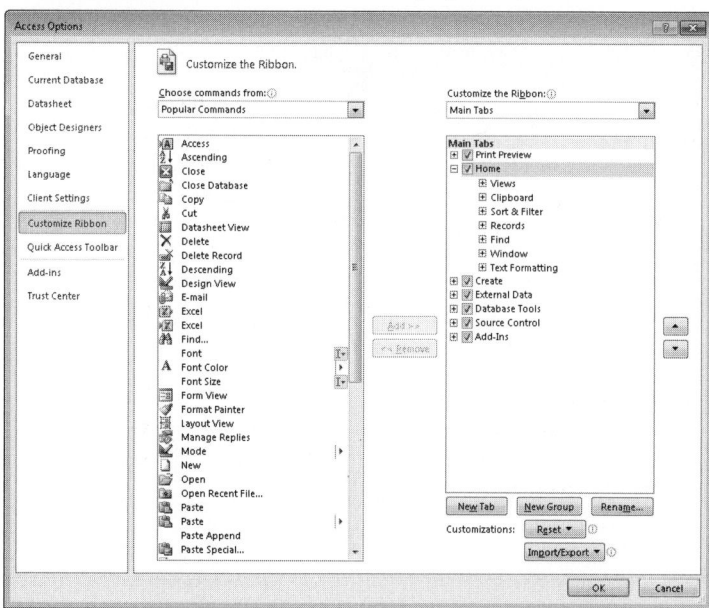

The list on the left side of the customization area includes selectable commands that can be added to any of the built-in ribbon tabs. Commands may be added to an existing group within the tab, or a new group can be created and positioned within the tab. In addition, entirely new tabs can be added to the ribbon and built from the commands in the selection list.

Macros (but not VBA functions) may also be added to the ribbon. If you want to trigger VBA code from the ribbon, you have to create a custom ribbon using XML code as well as using the ribbon's "callback" model for the VBA procedures.

Another organizational feature for the user interface is the use of a tab system for open objects (tables, forms, queries, and so on) instead of independent, floating windows. No more looking for an object through various task bar and menu items. Each open object occupies a tab for easy reference. Figure B.4 shows three different objects (Home, Order List, and Employee List) open in the tabbed workspace. Even though the Customers table is currently displayed in the tabbed area, any of the other open objects (Home, Order List, and Employee List) is quickly accessible through its corresponding tab.

Figure B.4 also shows the Navigation Pane in its collapsed state, which allows much more room for the active form or report in the work area. The ribbon can also be collapsed (as shown in Figure B.5) to allow more vertical space for forms and reports.

FIGURE B.4

The new tabbed interface is very efficient.

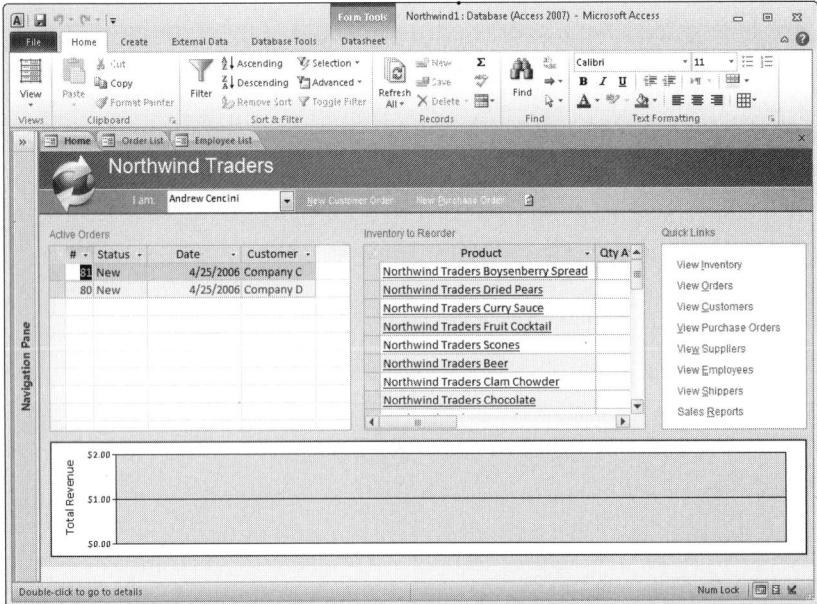

FIGURE B.5

The Access 2010 ribbon is collapsible to provide more vertical space for forms and reports.

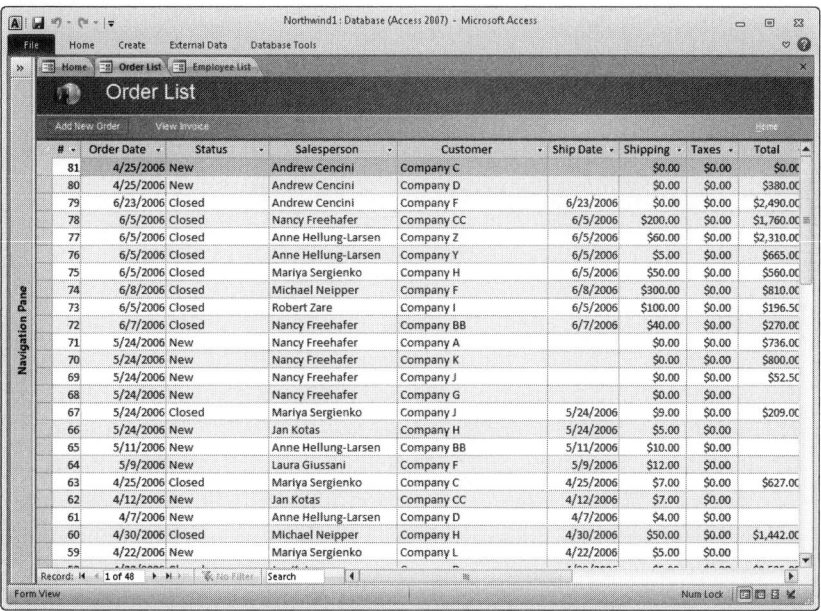

With the ribbon collapsed, there is actually *more* space for forms and reports than the old menu-and-toolbar paradigm allowed in earlier versions of Access.

The Navigation Pane has also been enhanced to allow the user to view objects by create date, modified date, dependencies, or custom groups. The Navigation Pane docks at the left side of the screen so that you have more room to work. You can also collapse the Navigation Pane by clicking on the left-pointing arrows in the upper-right corner, if you need more room to work on a form or report. Figure B.6 shows some of the options available for viewing database objects in the Access 2010 Navigation Pane.

The new Navigation Pane replaces the old Database window.

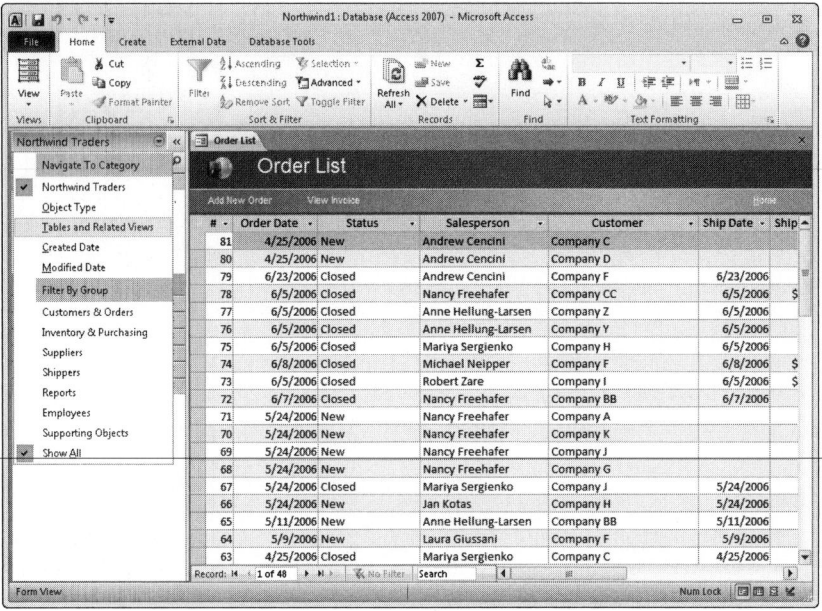

Publish Access to the Web

Starting with Access 2010 developers have the option of publishing a prepared Access database to SharePoint services. Instead of simply sharing data with SharePoint users, the new feature actually converts Access objects (tables, forms, and so on) to their SharePoint equivalents, and pushes the objects to a SharePoint server. Users are then able to access the application through a URL, rather than as a traditional file-based application.

Tables

A table is a table is a table, but new features make life easier and faster. Access 2007 and 2010 tables support rich-text formatting in memo fields and multivalue fields, as well as automatic formatting of data pasted from Excel. If you paste an Excel date field into a new table, Access recognizes it and formats the field as the Date/Time data type. It's a simple change, but it really does help with initial table design.

Another welcome addition is the alternating color option in Access 2007 and 2010. Creating a "green bar" look for your datasheets is now a snap and makes reviewing data and forms that much easier and appealing for the end user.

Access 2007 and 2010 tables support the attachment data type. An attachment field accepts virtually any type of Windows file, and stores it in the `.accdb` database file without conversion. A single attachment field may contain multiple files, of different types. Attachments are very useful for storing files that are logically related (such as project files, including Word documents, Excel spreadsheets, Visio drawings, and so on).

Perhaps the most significant addition to Access 2010 tables is the ability to add data macros to a table. A data macro is much like any other macro except that it's bound to a table and triggered when certain data events (Before Change, Before Delete, After Insert, and so on) occur with the table and its data. Data macros are an excellent way to enforce business rules, transform data, and perform other operations involving the table's data. Data macros travel with the table to which they're attached, regardless of where the table is used in an Access application. Data macros are entirely transparent to the user and provide very granular control over a table and its data.

Datasheet View

Datasheet view is an excellent tool for reviewing, modifying, or verifying your data. The new enhancements include embedding filters and simple mathematical expressions as part of the view itself.

Filtering is now contextual to the field type you choose and many new point-and-click sorts are available. Figure B.7 shows the filters Access supports for date fields. Similar filters are available for numeric and text data, as well.

You can also click on a field within a row and get additional sort-and-filter options based on the field's content. Figure B.8 shows a few of the filtering options for text data.

FIGURE B.7

Datasheet view supports a number of powerful filtering and sorting options.

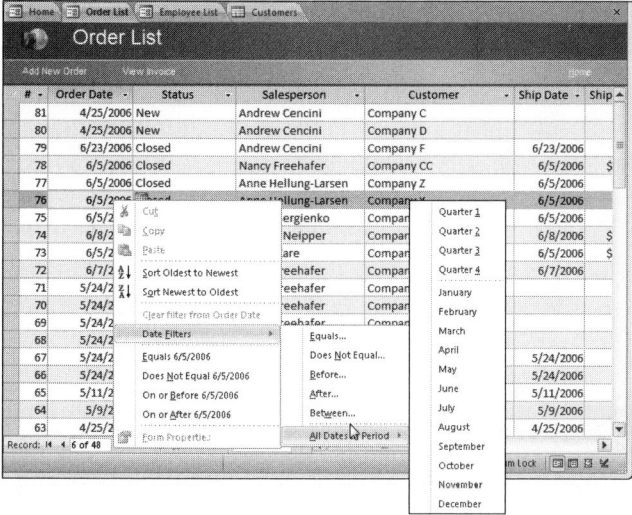

FIGURE B.8

Selecting Text Filters reveals filtering options useful for text, rather than dates or numbers.

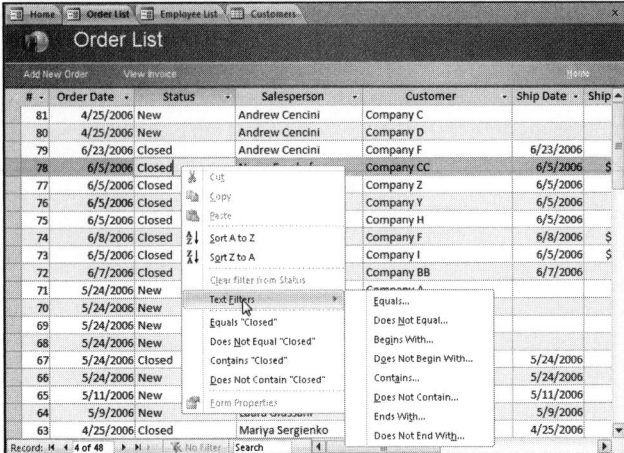

Along with filtering, you can now get totals for a column right from Datasheet view. These totals will also apply as you filter down through the records — *very* cool! Figure B.9 shows the Totals row added to the bottom of a datasheet. Notice that the Totals row (which is opened by clicking on the Totals button on the ribbon) appears below the data contained within the datasheet, and does not interfere with the datasheet's data. The Totals row is easily turned on or off through a ribbon button.

FIGURE B.9

Clicking on the Totals ribbon button adds a Totals row to Datasheet view.

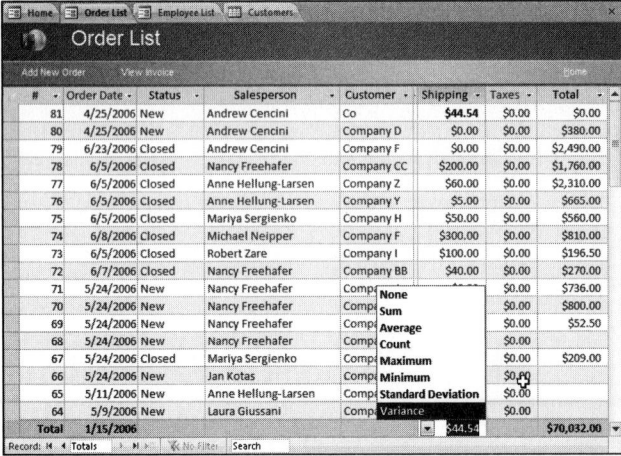

Fields can easily be added from Datasheet view, and there is now a Field Template pane from which you can choose a field complete with name, data type, length, and pre-populated properties. You can also set up your own field templates and standard definitions to share with a workgroup or department.

Forms

With the expanded field list task pane, you can now add fields that are part of the recordset, as well as fields from other tables that are not. Access will automatically set up any relationships that are required as you drag the field onto the form. A split view is available to show both the Form view and Datasheet view on the same form. The datasheet can be placed on the top, bottom, left, or right side of a split form. Form design has been greatly enhanced with a new view called Layout view. With Layout view, you can perform many of the most common form edit tasks while looking at the data on the form itself as opposed to the standard form design option, which does not display the recordset.

If you're tired of the same old colors and options, you'll really enjoy the new format and color options. Access now has almost 40 standard themes that can be applied to new or existing forms. Each theme specifies the fonts, font sizes and colors, and many control colors and other appearance attributes of the form. A theme can be applied to a single form or to all forms in the application. Custom themes are easily created from forms in an application and are saved as discrete files in the Office Themes folder. A portion of the themes supported by Access 2010 is shown in Figure B.10.

FIGURE B.10

Access 2010 comes with a wide variety of built-in themes for forms and reports.

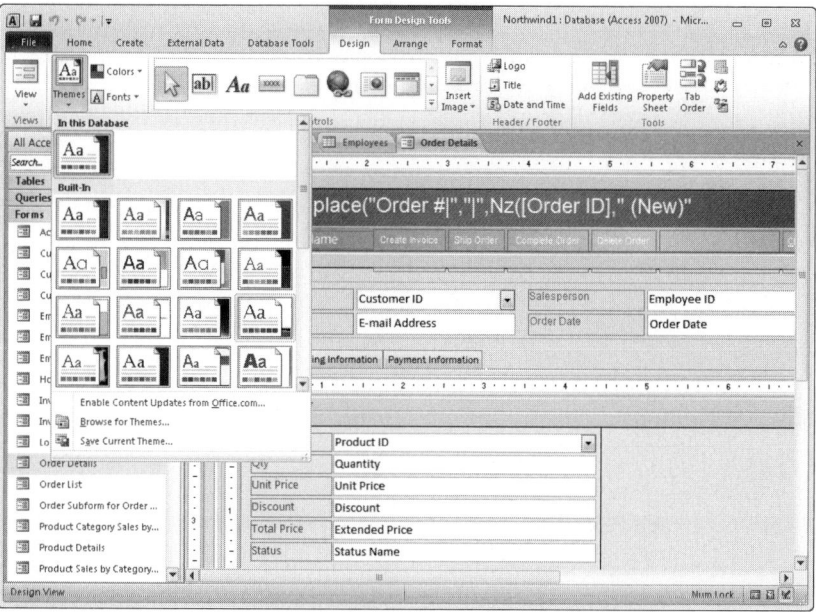

Themes are shared by all the Office applications, so you can have a corporate theme that is applied to Access forms and reports, Word documents, and Excel spreadsheets.

One particularly useful new feature in Access 2010 is the set of *application parts* (similar to form templates) that can be added to an application (see Figure B.11). Application parts are pre-built forms and other application objects that come complete with the controls and embedded macros necessary to support common application requirements. For example, the Message Box application part is a complete Yes/No/Cancel-style message box, while the Dialog application part is a customizable dialog box that is easily adapted to use wherever a dialog box is required by an application.

A powerful option on forms is the ability to embed macros within forms and controls. These are traditional Access macros that become part of the form, report, or control object just like a form's module. Embedded macros are somewhat limited in their functionality but are trusted by the new security features of Access.

Also added is a calendar date picker for all date/time formats. The date picker is activated through a simple control property; its appearance may be turned on or off through VBA code or a macro.

FIGURE B.11

Application parts provide templates that support common application features.

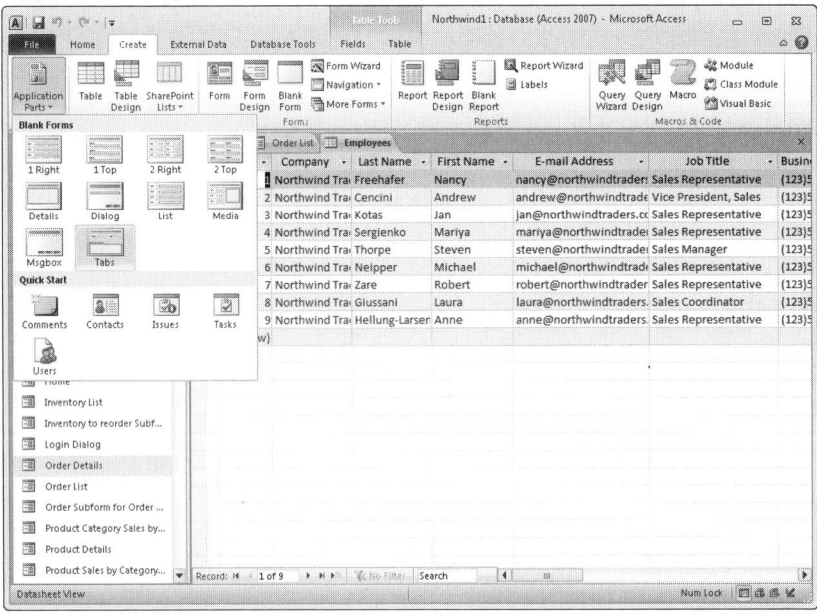

Reports

Reports offer all the new features of forms but also include additional group, sort, and total features. Sorting and grouping can be applied and automatically viewed in Report view. Simple group totals and sums can be added to a section by selecting the section and selecting a Sum Field option. No need to create a calculated control. Figure B.12 shows the new Group & Sort area, and how you set up a report group in Access 2010.

Access 2010 reports come with a number of built-in summary and other totals controls.

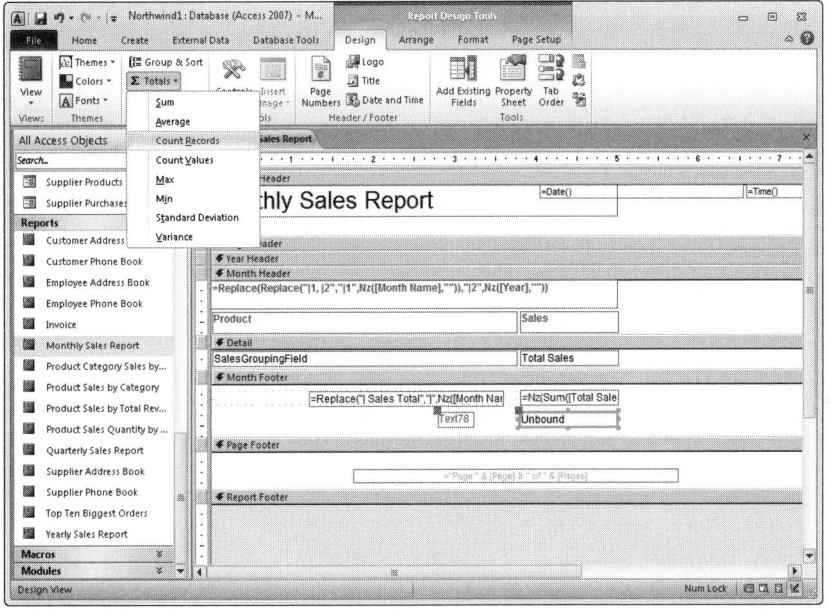

Macros

Microsoft is placing a large emphasis on macros in Access 2010. Much of this has to do with the new security model. Certain macro actions, such as opening forms and reports, are considered "safe" and are permitted to run without any adjustments to the default Access security settings. These macros may be embedded in forms, reports, and controls to automate many common database operations.

Macros now include error handling, better debugging, and the ability to assign values to the variables. This is a big change over previous versions of Access and may be difficult for many advanced developers to embrace. One neat feature of the new macros is the ability to schedule macros to run through Outlook. This is a very powerful feature for automatic imports, exports, or report generation.

Most important, perhaps, is the new macro editor (shown in Figure B.13). The new macro editor is much easier to use than in previous versions of Access. All the available macro actions are listed in the Action Catalog on the right side of the macro editor, while the macro itself is displayed as a top-down, hierarchical listing of macro actions and their properties.

The macro editor provides a friendly user interface for building macros.

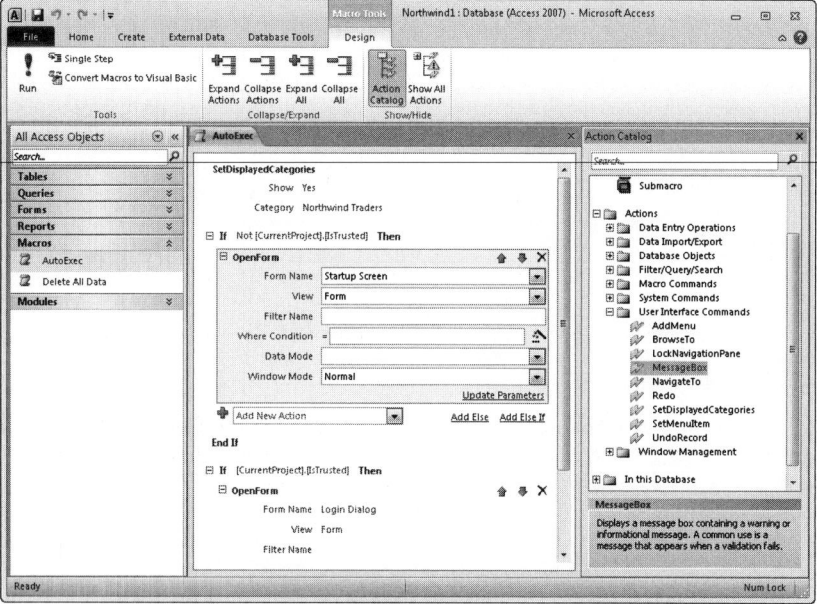

In Figure B.13, the OpenForm action is being added to the AutoExec macro. Notice that all the properties for the OpenForm action are visible in one place, and the position of OpenForm, relative to other actions in the macro, is obvious and easily understood. What can't be shown in this figure are the colors applied to various objects and text in the macro editor. Comments are green, as are the up and down arrows used for repositioning a macro action within the editor.

The same macro editor is used when creating embedded macros for form and report controls, or data macros attached to Access tables.

Security

User-level security has been removed from Access (except when using the older .mdb file format) in favor of the new trusted security model that relies on trusted folders and sandbox mode for any other applications. The enhanced macro functionality is further designed to allow users the most functionality through it. In a nutshell, the plan is to implement most or all your application's logic as the new embedded macro so that the application will be trusted and run under the new model. This may prove difficult to implement in certain environments.

For users who require user-level security, Access 2010 works with older-format .mdb files without conversion or enabling. This means you can continue to use an Access 2000, 2002, or 2003 .mdb file, complete with user-level security, in Access 2010 without changes.

Access databases may now be password-protected with strong encryption. The password is not stored within the database file (this feature applies only to the .accdb file format), and the password must be provided to Access when a user tries to open the database.

Access database encryption is based on the Windows Cryptographic API.

SharePoint

SharePoint Services are being used to provide functionality to enterprise applications over a SharePoint Server for functionality such as revision history, permission setting, and recovery of deleted records.

SharePoint data residing on distant Web servers is available to local Access applications with no special requirements other than a fast Internet connection. Access users (with the appropriate security credentials) are able to view, update, and add to SharePoint data as if the data resided on their desktop computer, no matter where the SharePoint server is hosted.

Specifically prepared Access 2010 databases may be "published" to SharePoint 2010 sites. A Web-enabled Access application contains only the forms, reports, controls, and other objects that are compatible with SharePoint. Web-enabled Access applications can't directly access data outside of the SharePoint environment and are somewhat less capable than their desktop equivalents.

Even so, the ability to build database applications in Access 2010 and make the applications available to authenticated SharePoint users, is a powerful and compelling feature of Access 2010.

SharePoint is sure to grow in importance and prominence in environments where instant access to remote data is a high priority.

Summary

Access 2010 represents a large number of new and changed features, all of which present challenges for Access developers. The new interface requires some adjustments to your way of thinking, but it's considerably more efficient for many common tasks. Developers already familiar with Access 2007 should have no problem transitioning to Access 2010. Anyone moving to Access 2010 from versions earlier than 2007 will require some adjustments, but the rewards and benefits of the new environment are considerable.

In spite of the new features, the loss of user-level security, replication, and the fact that ribbons replace toolbars and menus may prove to be an obstacle for some developers. Ribbons require a new way of thinking. Because ribbons are defined by XML, there's nothing to look at during development, and VBA code is not directly attached to ribbon controls. However, the majority of users *love* the ribbon, and Office-style ribbons are appearing in more and more applications instead of traditional toolbars and menus.

Overall, the new interface and new features are welcome changes in Access 2010. I hope you'll find Access 2010 as interesting and productive as I have.

What's on the CD-ROM

This appendix provides you with information on the contents of the CD that accompanies this book. For the latest and greatest information, please refer to the ReadMe file located at the root of the CD. Here is what you'll find:

- System requirements
- Using the CD
- What's on the CD
- Troubleshooting

IN THIS APPENDIX

Using the CD-ROM

Knowing what's included on the CD

Solving common problems

System Requirements

Make sure that your computer meets the minimum system requirements listed in this section. If your computer doesn't match up to most of these requirements, you may have a problem using the contents of the CD.

- A 500 MHz or higher processor
- 256MB or more of RAM
- A monitor with a screen resolution of at least 1,024 x 768 pixels
- Windows 7 (32- or 64-bit), Windows Vista (32- or 64-bit with Service Pack 1), Windows XP (with Service Pack 3), Windows Server 2003 R2 with MSXML 6.0, or Windows Server 2008 with (32- or 64-bit Service Pack 2).
- 3GB of free disk space (for installation of Microsoft Office 2010) or 1.5GB of free disk space (for installation of Microsoft Office Access 2010 alone)

- SharePoint Services running on Windows 2003 Server (with Service Pack 1), or Windows 2008 Server (with Service Pack 2), as a minimum, if you want to take advantage of the SharePoint collaborative features

- A SharePoint 2010 Server running the Access services, if you want to publish Access objects to SharePoint

- A CD-ROM or DVD drive, depending on your Office 2010 installation media

Using the CD

To access the content from the CD, follow these steps:

1. **Insert the CD into your computer's CD-ROM drive.**

   A window appears displaying the License Agreement.

   Note: The interface won't automatically launch if you have autorun disabled. In that case, click Start ⇨ Run (for Windows Vista or Windows 7, Start ⇨ All Programs ⇨ Accessories ⇨ Run). In the dialog box that appears, type **D:\Start.exe**. (Replace D with the proper letter if your CD drive uses a different letter. If you don't know the letter, see how your CD drive is listed under My Computer.) Click OK.

2. **Read through the license agreement, and then click the Accept button if you want to use the CD.**

   The CD interface appears.

What's on the CD

The following sections provide a summary of the materials you'll find on the CD.

Example files

Example files will be installed into a directory named `Access 2010 Bible`, or you can choose any directory in which to install these files. Below this directory will be subdirectories named `Chapter_01`, `Chapter_02`, and so on through `Chapter_38`. Each subdirectory contains all the files necessary to follow the examples in the corresponding chapter.

A few chapters have no examples, and do not have a corresponding folder on the book's CD. Most chapters contains a single Access 2010 database file with an `.accdb` extension, such as `Chapter30.accdb`, while some folders contain multiple Access database files and auxiliary files used for the chapter's examples.

Also, a few chapters include Access 2000–format `.mdb` data files to demonstrate Access 2010 features that are only supported in the older database file formats.

Many chapters also use additional database files, graphics, document files, or help files as found in each chapter subdirectory and explained at the beginning of each chapter.

You'll also find links on the CD to a Wiley Web site to download any later corrections to the material.

eBook version of *Access 2010 Bible*

The complete text of the book you hold in your hands is provided on the CD in Adobe's Portable Document Format (PDF). You can read and quickly search the content of this PDF file by using Adobe's Acrobat Reader, also included on the CD.

Shareware programs are fully functional, trial versions of copyrighted programs. If you like particular programs, register with their authors for a nominal fee and receive licenses, enhanced versions, and technical support.

Freeware programs are copyrighted games, applications, and utilities that are free for personal use. Unlike shareware, these programs do not require a fee or provide technical support.

GNU software is governed by its own license, which is included inside the folder of the GNU product. See the GNU license for more details.

Trial, demo, or evaluation versions are usually limited either by time or functionality (such as being unable to save projects). Some trial versions are very sensitive to system date changes. If you alter your computer's date, the programs will "time out" and no longer be functional.

Troubleshooting

If you have difficulty installing or using any of the materials on the companion CD, try the following solutions:

- **Turn off any antivirus software that you may have running.** Installers sometimes mimic virus activity and can make your computer incorrectly believe that it is being infected by a virus. (Be sure to turn the antivirus software back on later.)

- **Close all running programs.** The more programs you're running, the less memory is available to other programs. Installers also typically update files and programs; if you keep other programs running, installation may not work properly.

- **Reference the ReadMe:** Please refer to the ReadMe file located at the root of the CD-ROM for the latest product information at the time of publication.

If you have trouble with the CD-ROM, please call the Wiley Product Technical Support phone number at (800) 762-2974. Outside the United States, call 1(317) 572-3994. You can also contact Wiley Product Technical Support at `http://support.wiley.com`. John Wiley & Sons will provide technical support only for installation and other general quality-control items. For technical support on the applications themselves, consult the program's vendor or author.

To place additional orders or to request information about other Wiley products, please call (877) 762-2974.

Index

Symbols and Numerics

& (ampersand)
    any character or digit required, 67
    concatenation operator, 173, 178–179, 188, 422
    continuation character, 419
    optional character indicator, 64
    in select queries, 188
* (asterisk)
    filling empty spaces, 60
    multiplication operator, 174, 188
    new record indicator, 221–222
    in select queries, 188
    wildcard character, 181, 195–198, 477
"..." (double quotes)
    around returned strings, 178
    literal text indicator, 60, 194
    text qualifier, 620, 624
= (equal sign)
    assignment operator, 422
    equal operator, 176, 188
    in select queries, 188
! (exclamation point)
    displaying input masks, 67
    in With keyword, 895
    left-aligning a display, 60
    left-aligning text, 60
> (greater-than sign)
    convert to uppercase, 64, 67
    Date comparison operator, 152
    greater-than operator, 177, 188
    in select queries, 188
– (hyphen)
    input mask separator, 67
    range indicator, 181
    in select queries, 188
    subtraction operator, 173–174, 188
< (less-than sign)
    convert to lowercase, 64, 67
    Date comparison operator, 152
    less-than operator, 177, 188
    in select queries, 188
(pound sign)
    Date comparisons, 152
    hyperlink indicator, 65–66
    optional digit indicator, 67
    placeholder, 62
    wildcard character, 181
? (question mark)
    optional letter indicator, 67
    wildcard character, 181, 195–198
/ (slash)
    date delimiter, 625
    division operator, 174, 188
    input mask separator, 67
    integer division operator, 175
    in select queries, 188
    separating time elements, 63
: (colon)
    compiler argument separator, 414
    date/time separator, 67
    time element separator, 63
, (comma)
    field separator, 620
    thousands separator, 62, 67
. (period)
    date delimiter, 625
    decimal points, 62, 67
    in With keyword, 895
    table and field name separator, 174
; (semicolon)
    input mask separator, 67
    SQL end-of-statement indicator, 484
< > (angle brackets)
    not-equal operator, 176, 188, 198–199
    in select queries, 188
[ ] (square brackets)
    around field names, 476–477
    pattern indicator, 181
    referencing fields, 192–193
    table and field name notation, 174

Index

@ (at sign), required character indicator, 64

\ (backslash), literal text indicator, 60, 67

^ (caret), exponentiation operator, 175

$ (dollar sign), formatting currency fields, 62

= (equal sign), `Date` comparison operator, 152

! (exclamation point), `Not` operator, 195–198

>= (greater-than, equal), greater-than-or-equal-to operator, 177

<= (less-than, equal), less-than-or-equal-to operator, 177

% (percent sign), formatting percentages, 62

+ (plus sign), addition operator

    calculating fields, 173

    concatenating strings, 173, 179

    description, 173

    in select queries, 188

(pound signs), in numeric fields, 1088

'...' (single quotes), criteria string indicator, 194

_ (underscore), continuation character, 389, 418–419

∞ (infinity symbol), table joins, 159, 161

0 (zero)

    placeholder, 62

    required digit indicator, 67

1NF (first normal form), 95–97

2NF (second normal form), 97–102

3NF (third normal form), 102

9, optional digit indicator, 67

A

a, optional letter or digit indicator, 67

A, required letter or digit indicator, 67

absolute speed. *See also* optimizing applications; perceived
      speed.

    changing variables, 864

    closing unused applications, 856

    combo boxes, 861

    compacting databases, 855–856

    comparing variables, 864

    control variables, 864–865

    data types, 862–863

    dead code, removing, 866

    definition, 854

    defragmenting hard drives, 856

    `For Each` function, 864

    field variables, 865

    finding data in code, 865–866

    `FindNext` method, 865–866

    `FindRecord` method, 865–866

    forms, 859–861

    `With` function, 864

    `IIF` function *versus* `If...Then...Else`, 864

    list boxes, 861

    marking records with bookmarks, 866

    memory, 856

    modules, 862–866

    network performance, 866–867

    overview, 854–855

    queries, 858–859

    reports, 859–861

    `Requery` method *versus* `Requery` action, 864

    resolving references, OLE automation, 864

    routines, 863–866

    swap files, 856

    table indexes, 856–858

    tuning the system, 856

    unused variables, removing, 866

`.accdb` files

    format description, 844–846

    security, 752

`.accdb` files, SharePoint deployment

    copying the file, 1145

    eliminating the file, 1156–1173

`.accde` files

    application demos, 847

    converting to normal database files, 847

    creating, 847–848

    distributing, 846–848

    restrictions, 847

`.accdr` files, 1093

accelerator keys, enabling, 1087

Access 2010 Bible, eBook on the CD-ROM, 1269

Access Data Projects (ADPs). *See* ADPs (Access Data
      Projects).

access errors, 837–838

Access Options dialog box, 650

Access ribbon. *See* the ribbon.

Access Services

    overview, 1140–1141. *See also* SharePoint.

    SharePoint deployment, 1157

Action Catalog, 557–562

action queries

    creating, 671–675

    data-type errors, 676

    definition, 133

    key violations, 676

record-locked fields in multiuser environments, 676

running, 675–676

troubleshooting, 676

truncating text data, 676

types of, 671

updating records, 672–673

`ActionName` property, 1073

actions, macro

cursor, changing to hourglass, 1054–1055

`Echo`, 1055, 1056

hiding/showing macro results, 1055, 1056

`Hourglass`, 1054–1055

for `mcrBackupContactsAndProducts` macro, 1054–1057

`MessageBox`, 1055

messages, displaying, 1055

opening a query, 1055, 1056

`OpenQuery`, 1055, 1056

`SetWarnings`, 1054–1055, 1056

system messages, enabling/disabling, 1054–1055, 1056

`Activate` event, 457, 461

`ActiveConnection` parameter, 510–512

ActiveX Data Objects (ADO). *See* ADO (ActiveX Data Objects).

ActiveX settings, 937

Add Watch dialog box, 546–548

adding

class modules to databases, 974–975

commands to Quick Access Toolbar, 1018–1019

data macros to tables, 554

data to reports, 737–738

descriptions to fields, 54–55

dialog box pages, 701

logos to forms, 695

macro items to data macros, 566–569

QBE grid to fields, 156

queries, 137

tables to queries, 136, 160

text boxes to reports, 352–359

user names to reports, 738

adding controls to forms

buttons, 385–386

with the `Controls` group, 267–268

with the Field List, 268–271

overview, 266–267

adding date/time to

forms, 694

reports, 372

adding fields to

forms, 315–316

queries, 138–140, 156

tables, 41

adding page numbers to

forms, 694

reports, 353

adding records to

datasheets, 220–223, 231, 234

forms, 231

adding records to tables

with data macros, 558–559

in Datasheet view, 88

external linked tables, 599

with forms, 88

primary keys, 119

with VBA code, 517

add-ins, trusted, 937

`AddNew` method, 517

`Address` property, 66

`adLockBatchOptimistic` constant, 769

`adLockOptimistic` constant, 769

`adLockPessimistic` constant, 769

`adLockReadOnly` constant, 769

`adLockUnspecified` constant, 769

ADO (ActiveX Data Objects)

versus DAO, 486, 507

data access errors, 837–838

methods, 486–487

optimistic locking, 773–774

overview, 485–488

pessimistic locking, 769–771

properties, 486–487

ADO object model

clearing from memory, 491

`Command` object, 492–494

`Connection` object, 489–492

`ConnectionString` property, discovering, 491–492

diagram, 488

ADO object model, `Recordset` object. *See also* recordsets.

`ActiveConnection` parameter, 510–512

`adOpenDynamic` cursor, 497

`adOpenForwardOnly` cursor, 497

`adOpenKeyset` cursor, 497

`adOpenStatic` cursor, 497

`BOF` (beginning-of-file indicator), 497–498

`CancelUpdate` method, 512

counting records, 498–499

Index

ADO object model, `Recordset` object (*continued*)
  current record pointer, 495
  cursor type, specifying, 496–497
  `CursorType` parameter, 510–512
  `CursorType` property, 496–497
  `Edit` method, 512
  EOF (end-of-file indicator), 497–498
  `MoveNext` method, 497–498
  `MovePrevious` method, 497–498
  navigating recordsets, 495
  `Open` method, 510–512
  opening a table, 510
  overview, 494–495
  `RecordCount` property, 498–499
  `RecordsetNavigation` procedure, 495
  `Source` parameter, 510–512
  `Update` method, 512
adOpenDynamic cursor, 497
adOpenForwardOnly cursor, 497
adOpenKeyset cursor, 497
adOpenStatic cursor, 497
.adp file type, 5
ADP objects, *versus* Access objects, 1233–1235
ADPs (Access Data Projects), 1223. *See also*
        Upsizing Wizard.
AfterDelConfirm event, 458–459
AfterEventUpdate event procedure, 509–513
AfterFinalRender event, 464
AfterInsert event, 458–459
AfterLayout event, 464
AfterRender event, 464
AfterUpdate event, 458–459, 460
aggregate functions
  datasheets, 247–248
  Excel spreadsheets, 247–248
aggregate functions, in queries
  Aggregate option, 655
  aggregate total fields, criteria for, 663
  Aggregate Total fields, criteria for, 663
  averaging field values, 657
  Avg option, 657
  Count option, 657, 658
  counting field values, 657
  crosstab queries, 666–670
  definition, 655
  Expression option, 655, 656
  expressions for totals, 664–666
  First option, 657
  first/last field values, finding, 657

Group By fields, criteria for, 662
Group By option, 655, 661–662
highest/lowest field values, finding, 657
Last option, 657
Max option, 657
Min option, 657
non-aggregate total fields, criteria for, 663–664
population variance, calculating, 657
QBE pane, hiding/showing `Total` row, 654
Query Criteria option, 655
standard deviation, calculating, 657
StDev option, 657
Sum option, 657
summary of, 656. *See also specific functions*.
Total row options, 654
totaling all records, 657–658
totaling field values, 657
totaling groups of records, 659–662
Var option, 657
Where options, 656
Aggregate option, 655
aggregate total fields, criteria for, 663
Aggregate Total fields, criteria for, 663
alerts, SharePoint, 1138
aliases (field names)
  referencing, 649
  specifying, 144–145
Align Center command
  Datasheet ribbon, 220
  Form ribbon, 293
Align Left command
  Datasheet ribbon, 220
  Form ribbon, 293
Align Right command
  Datasheet ribbon, 220
  Form ribbon, 293
aligning
  control labels, 736
  controls, 275–277, 314
  data in datasheets, 220–221, 241
  displays, 60
  pictures on forms, 308
  report control labels, 736
  snapping to the grid, 276–277
  text, 60, 220, 293
All Access Objects option, 36
All Records option, 766
ALL SQL predicate, 478
Allow Additions property, 310

`Allow Datasheet View` property, 306

Allow Default Shortcut `Menus` check box, 1091

`Allow Deletions` property, 310

`Allow Edits` property, 310

`Allow Filters` property, 310

`Allow From View` property, 306

Allow Full Menus check box, 1091

`Allow Layout View` property, 306

`Allow PivotTable View` property, 306

`AllowBypassKey` property, 925

`AllowZeroLength` property, 60, 70–71

alphabetical report headings, 712–714

alphanumeric data type. *See* `Memo` data type; `Text` data type.

alternate displays, 34

Alternate Fill/Back Color command, 220

always on top

    dialog boxes, 704

    forms, 310

Always Use Event Procedures option, 391

ampersand (`&`)

    any character or digit required, 67

    concatenation operator, 173, 178–179, 188, 422

    continuation character, 419

    optional character indicator, 64

    in select queries, 188

`am/pm:`, lowercase 12-hour format, 64

`AMPM:`, uppercase 12-hour format, 64

And operator

    across fields in a query, 208–212

    Boolean logic, 180

    with Or operator, 211–212

    results of, 182

    in select queries, 188

    specifying a range, 204–205

angle brackets (`< >`)

    not-equal operator, 176, 188, 198–199

    in select queries, 188

animation, forms, 688–690

anomalies, 99, 103

anonymous site access, SharePoint, 1141

`a/p:`, lowercase 12-hour format, 64

`A/P:`, uppercase 12-hour format, 64

API function prototype. *See* `Declare` statement.

Append Data to Existing Table button, 87

Append Query action queries, 671, 674

application icon, specifying, 1085

Application Icon field, 1084, 1085

Application options, 1084, 1085–1089

application parts, 1262

application programming interface. *See* Windows API.

application servers, *versus* Web servers, 1190–1192

Application Title field, 1084, 1085

applications

    See also bulletproofing applications

    See also distributing applications

    See also network applications

    See also optimizing applications

    See also user interface

    See also VBA

    client/server architecture, 1186–1187

    delivering to users, 905–907

    ease of starting, 907–909

    error handling, 822–823. *See also* debugging; troubleshooting.

    starting in runtime environment, 1093

    testing, 524–525

`ApplyFilter` event, 458–459, 699–700

architecture, client/server

    Access, as database repository, 1195–1196

    Access, as Internet database, 1197

    Access's role in, 1189–1190

    applications, 1186–1187

    back office, 1187–1192

    clustered indexes, 1189

    connection pooling, 1191–1192

    databases, 1187–1189

    defining characteristics, 1195

    identity fields, 1189

    load balancing, 1191–1192

    multi-tiered, 1192–1194

    parallel processing, 1190

    partition pruning, 1190

    partitioning, 1190

    versus splitting a database, 1193

    stored procedures, 1188. *See also* class modules; data macros.

    system layout, 1184–1186

    temporary tables, 1189

    three-tiered, 1193–1194

    tiers, 1193

    triggers, 1188. *See also* class modules; data macros.

    two-tiered, 1193

    user-defined functions, 1188. *See also* class modules; data macros.

    views, 1189

    Web servers, 1190–1192

argument prefixes, DLLs, 944

`ArgumentList` parameter, 947–949

Index

arguments
  macro error handling, getting, 1073
  macros, 1050
  named, VBA, 447–448
  passing `ByVal` *versus* `ByRef`, 948
`Arguments` property, 1073
`As DataType` parameter, 949
asterisk (*)
  filling empty spaces, 60
  multiplication operator, 174, 188
  new record indicator, 221–222
  in select queries, 188
  wildcard character, Access, 181, 195–198
  wildcard character, SQL, 477
at sign (@), required character indicator, 64
`AttachExcel` function, 602–603
`Attachment` data type, 49, 54
attachment fields
  data macros, 575
  limitations, 1178
  overview, 88–89
`Auto Center` property, 307
Auto Data Tips option, 412, 529, 543–544
Auto Indent option, 411
Auto List Members feature, 396
Auto List Members option, 411, 528
Auto Quick Info feature, 396–397
Auto Quick Info option, 411–412, 528
`Auto Resize` property, 307
Auto Syntax Check option, 411, 525–527
AutoCorrect feature, turning off, 41
AutoForm, 253
AutoFormat feature, 332
AutoIndex option, 72–73
automatic data-type validation, 224–225
automatic number increments. *See* `AutoNumber` data type.
automatic numbering, skipping numbers, 53. *See also*
        `AutoNumber` data type.
Automation
  object libraries, 791–792
  object variables, 791–792
  overview, 790–791
Automation, Outlook example
  collecting data, 811–818
  creating e-mail, 811–815
  managing e-mail replies, 815–818
Automation, Word example
  activating Word instances, 805
  bookmarks, 807

  creating documents based on templates, 806
  creating Word instances, 805
  discarding Word instances, 807
  displaying Word, 805
  hidden copies of Word, 805
  inserting data, 806
  inserting pictures, 807
  moving the cursor, 807
  named arguments, 808
  Office macro recorder, 808–810
  overview, 800–805
Automation objects
  class arguments for Office components, 798
  closing instances, 800
  creating instances of, 795–797
  getting instances of, 797–799
  manipulating, 799
  user input, 799
Automation references
  binding objects, 792–795
  creating, 791–792
  early binding, 792–794
  late binding, 794–795
`AutoNumber` data type
  converting from other data types, 57
  converting to `Number`, 58
  converting to `Text`, 58
  overview, 53
  problems, 1179
  purpose, 48
  storage size, 49
`AutoNumber` fields
  editing, 232, 296
  example, 55
  `Required` property, 70–71
AutoOrder button, 313–314
averaging field values, 657
Avg option, 657

B

back office, 1187–1192
`BackColor` property, 682
back-end data macro execution, 575
background, pictures as, 307
background color, modifying, 239–241
backslash (\), literal text indicator, 60, 67

Backstage area
    Compatibility Checker, 1158
    illustration, 28
    new features, 1254
    overview, 27
    SharePoint, 1139–1140
banded reports. *See also* sections, of reports.
    definition, 340
    Detail section, 341–342, 344
    Group Footer section, 341–342, 344
    Group Header section, 341–342, 343–344
    overview, 340–342
    Page Footer section, 341–342, 344–345
    Page Header section, 341–342, 343
    Report Footer section, 341–342, 345
    Report Header section, 341–342, 343
`BeforeDelConfirm` event, 458–459
`BeforeInsert` event, 458–459
`BeforeQuery` event, 464
`BeforeRender` event, 464
`BeforeScreenTip` event, 464
`BeforeUpdate` event, 458–459, 460
`Between...And` operator
    range indicator, 184, 188, 205–206
    in select queries, 188
binding to a data source. *See also* connecting.
    bound controls, 266, 285
    bound forms, 304
    in reports, 346–348
binding VBA object variables to Automation references,
    792–795
Blank Form command, 252
blank lines, inserting in reports, 731–733
blank pages, on reports, 349, 372
`BOF` (beginning-of-file indicator), 497–498
bookmarks
    finding data, 885–888
    inserting pictures in Word, 807
    marking records, 866
`Boolean` data type, VBA, 428
`Border Style` property, 307, 360
borders
    dialog boxes, 704
    forms, 307
    reports, transparent, 360
`BorderStyle` property, 704
bound controls, 266, 285

bound forms. *See also* unbound forms.
    connecting to data sources, 304
    creating, 304
    multiuser errors, 780–788
branching
    `Case Else` clause, 404
    definition, 401
    `Else` statements, 402
    `ElseIf` clause, 402–403
    `If...Then...Else...Endif` statements, 401–403
    `If...Then...Endif` statements, 401–403
    overview, 401
    `Select Case...End Select` statements, 403–404
Break on all Errors option, 411
breakpoints, 539–544. *See also* `Stop` statements.
bugs. *See also* testing.
    See also Compatibility Checker
    See also debugging
    See also error handling
    See also testing
    See also troubleshooting
    definition, 524. *See also* debugging; logical errors;
        troubleshooting.
    severity levels, 1092–1093
bulleted lists, 723–725
bulletproofing applications
    characteristics of, 898–899
    continuous improvement, 938
    documenting applications, 1100
    error trapping on Visual Basic procedures, 1099
    overview, 898
    separating tables from applications, 1099–1100
bulletproofing applications, principles of
    building to specification, 900–902
    development process, 900
    documentation, 902–903
bulletproofing applications, security
    bulletproofing forms, 928
    digital certificates, 935–936
    digital signatures, 935
    encoding, 930–931
    encryption, 930–931
    macros, 934–938
    passwords, removing, 931–933
    privacy settings, 937–938
    property values, getting, 927
    property values, setting, 926–927

bulletproofing applications, security *(continued)*
    runtime mode, forcing, 929–930
    sandbox mode, 934–936
    settings, 937–938
    start-up bypass, disabling, 924–927
    start-up option properties, 924
    start-up options, setting, 923–924
    Trust Center, 937–938
    validating user input, 928–929
    VBA code, 933–934
bulletproofing applications, troubleshooting
    hardware errors, 920
    inadequate disk space, 920
    memory errors, 920
    usage logs, 920–923
    virtual memory, 920
bulletproofing applications, user considerations
    application delivery, 905–907
    ease of starting, 907–909
    forms, displaying one at a time, 914
    information flow, 912–915
    installation tools, 906
    login forms, 910–911
    menus, removing, 913–914
    messages, 915–918
    Navigation Pane, hiding, 913–914
    Overlapping Windows interface, 915
    passwords, hiding, 911
    progress meters, 918–919
    ribbons, 912–913
    splash screens, 911–912
    start-up options, 909–912
    switchboard forms, 912
    Tabbed Documents interface, 914
    understanding user needs, 904–905
    user-interface style, choosing, 914–915
    Windows shortcuts, 907–909
bulletproofing property procedures, 980–981
business rules, enforcing. *See* data macros; data validation
        rules.
Button controls on the ribbon, 1038
buttons. *See also specific buttons.*
    adding to forms, 385–386
    dialog boxes, defaults, 706
ByRef argument passing, 948
Byte size numeric fields, 52
ByVal argument passing, 948

C

C, any character or digit optional, 67
c:, General Date format, 63
caching, troubleshooting, 768–769
calculated controls
    creating, 316
    description, 266
    editing, 296
    updating tables, with VBA code, 513–516
calculated field issues, 1178
calculated fields
    creating, 638–639
    editing, 232
    expressions in, 640–642
    removing, 102–104
calculations
    on numeric fields, 18
    with queries, 134
    on values containing commas, 174
calendars (SharePoint), linking to, 1122–1123
Call Stack window, 548–549
Call statement, 437
call tree, pruning, 842–844
callbacks
    overview, 1023–1025
    writing, 1027–1029
calling
    VBA functions, 436
    VBA procedures, 437
    VBA subroutines, 436
Cancel button
    dialog boxes, 706
    Edit Relations window, 122
    Tab Order dialog box, 313–314
canceling record changes with data macros, 560
CancelRecordChange action, 560
CancelUpdate method, 512
Caption property
    dynamic setting, 682
    for form title bars, 306
    naming conventions, 285
    setting at runtime, 682
    tab labels, setting, 702
captions
    form title bars, 306
    formatting, 68–69
    maximum length, 68–69
    navigation buttons, on forms, 309

caret (^), exponentiation operator, 175
Cartesian products, creating, 169–170
cascading
    deletes, 123–125
    updates, 123–125
case conversion
    date/time fields, 64
    with input masks, 67
    text and memo fields, 64
Case Else clause, 404
case sensitivity
    Access, 48
    alias references, 947
    SQL keywords, 476
    VBA variable names, 423
    XML for the ribbon, 1035
CD-ROM
    accessing files, 1268
    contents, 1268–1269
    eBook version of *Access 2010 Bible*, 1269
    example files, 1268–1269
    installing, 1268
    support for, 1270
    system requirements, 1267–1268
    troubleshooting, 1269–1270
cell gridlines
    hiding/showing, 220, 239, 293
    modifying appearance of, 240
    snapping to the grid, 276–277
centering
    forms, 307
    report titles, 736
Change event, 460
changing. *See* editing; modifying; updating.
check boxes. *See also* controls; *specific check boxes*.
    on the ribbon, 1039–1040
    tallying true responses, 688
    toggling values, 231
Check for Truncated Number Fields check box, 1084,
        1088
checking table links, 606–607
CheckLInks function, 606–607
child/parent table relationships, 108–110
class events, 997–999
class interfaces, managing, 983–985
class modules. *See also* events; OOP (object-oriented
        programming); Product class.
    adding to databases, 974–975
    bulletproofing property procedures, 980–981

defining objects, 972–973, 978–980
for forms, displaying, 311
methods, 976–978
naming, 974–975
overview, 973–974
properties, 975–976
Class_Initialize event procedure, 997–998
Class_Terminate event procedure, 998–999
ClearMacroError action, 562
Click event, 455, 460
client-centric network applications, 754–756
client/server architecture
    Access, as database repository, 1195–1196
    Access, as Internet database, 1197
    Access's role in, 1189–1190
    applications, 1186–1187
    back office, 1187–1192
    clustered indexes, 1189
    connection pooling, 1191–1192
    databases, 1187–1189
    defining characteristics, 1195
    identity fields, 1189
    load balancing, 1191–1192
    multi-tiered, 1192–1194
    parallel processing, 1190
    partition pruning, 1190
    partitioning, 1190
    versus splitting a database, 1193
    stored procedures, 1188. *See also* class modules; data
        macros.
    system layout, 1184–1186
    temporary tables, 1189
    three-tiered, 1193–1194
    tiers, 1193
    triggers, 1188. *See also* class modules; data macros.
    two-tiered, 1193
    user-defined functions, 1188. *See also* class modules;
        data macros.
    views, 1189
    Web servers, 1190–1192
Clipboard group
    Access 2010 ribbon, 36
    copying tables, 86–88
    Datasheet ribbon, 220
    Form ribbon, 292
    Form view, 292
Close button, displaying on forms, 307
Close Button property, 307
Close event, 457, 461

Index

closing
> forms, 469–470, 691
> ribbons, 1045–1046

clustered indexes, 1189

CmdBeforeExecute event, 464

CmdEnabled event, 464

CmdExecute event, 464

code
> looping through, 404–406
> storing, 851–853

code editors. *See* VBA editor.

code window
> editing VBA modules, 393
> ribbon, 393
> splitting, 393
> toolbar, 393

collapsing
> macro items, 573–574
> the ribbon, 1011
> submacros, 1059

collection items, VBA
> counting, 407
> looping through, 408–410
> naming conventions, 407
> number of, effects on performance, 408
> referencing, 407

collections, Access
> definition, 486
> naming conventions, 486

collections, VBA
> Count property, 407
> counting items in, 407
> definition, 406
> Item property, 407
> looping through, 408–410
> Name property, 407
> naming conventions, 407
> properties of, 407

colon (:)
> compiler argument separator, 414
> date/time separator, 67
> time element separator, 63

color
> background, modifying, 239–241
> control background/foreground, 682
> formatting output, 61
> highlighting alternate records, 220, 239–241
> in reports, 331–335, 368–369
> specifying, 61

color coding
> breakpoints, 539
> comments, 419–420
> identifiers, 419–420
> keywords, 419–420
> syntax errors, 526

Column Headings property, 653

columnar reports, 321–322

columns (database). *See* fields.

columns (report)
> layout, specifying, 745
> number of, specifying, 745
> snaking, 741–747
> spacing, specifying, 745
> vertical lines between, 729–730

combo boxes. *See also* controls; list boxes.
> absolute speed, 861
> creating, 74–76
> displaying reports, 739–740
> forms, 691–693
> selecting items from lists, 299–300
> synchronizing list contents, 682
> unbound forms, network applications, 785

comma (,)
> field separator, 620
> thousands separator, 62, 67

Command Button Wizard, 385–386

command line, getting, 952–953

Command object, 492–494

command-line arguments, 414–415

Command-Line Arguments option, 414–415

commands
> Alternate Fill/Back Color, 220
> Blank Form, 252
> Datasheet, 253
> Decrease Horizontal, 277
> Decrease Vertical, 277
> Equal Horizontal, 277
> Equal Vertical, 277
> Form, 252, 253–254
> Form Design, 252
> Form Wizard, 252, 254–257
> Format Painter, 292–293
> Group, 278–279
> Increase Horizontal, 277
> Increase Vertical, 277
> menu display, customizing, 1091
> Modal Dialog, 253
> More Forms, 252

Multiple Items, 253
Navigation Form, 252
Pivot Table, 253
PivotChart, 253
Print Preview, 249
Remove Sort, 243
on the ribbon, customizing defaults, 1020–1022
Select, 220
Selection, 243–244
Snap to Grid, 276–277
Split Form, 253
commands, Align Center
    Datasheet ribbon, 220
    Form ribbon, 293
commands, Align Left
    Datasheet ribbon, 220
    Form ribbon, 293
commands, Align Right
    Datasheet ribbon, 220
    Form ribbon, 293
commands, Copy
    Datasheet ribbon, 220
    Form ribbon, 292
commands, Cut
    Datasheet ribbon, 220
    Form ribbon, 292
commands, Gridlines
    Datasheet ribbon, 220
    Form ribbon, 293
commands, Paste
    Datasheet ribbon, 220
    description, 233
    Form ribbon, 292
commands, Paste Append
    Datasheet ribbon, 220
    description, 233
    Form ribbon, 292
commands, Paste Special
    Datasheet ribbon, 220
    description, 233
    Form ribbon, 292
comma-separated values (CSV)
    importing text files, 618–623
    linking to, 596–597
comments
    color coding, 419–420
    forms, 311
common code base, 941
Compact and Repair button, 874–875

Compact on Close check box, 1084, 1087
compacting databases
    absolute speed, 855–856
    on closing, 1087
    with Compact and Repair button, 874–875
comparison operators
    > (greater than), 177, 188
    >= (greater-than, equal), 177
    = (equal sign), equal, 176, 188
    < (less-than sign), less-than, 177, 188
    <= (less-than, equal), less-than-or-equal-to, 177
    < > (angle brackets), not-equal, 176, 188, 198–199
    list of, 176
    precedence, 186
Compatibility Checker
    See also bugs
    See also debugging
    See also error handling
    See also testing
    See also troubleshooting
    Backstage area, 1158
    data integrity, enforcing, 1162–1163
    enabling Publish to Access Service button,
        1139–1140
    online help, 1160
    running, 1157–1158
    successful completion, 1163–1164
Compatibility Checker, SharePoint deployment
    attachment field limitations, 1178
    AutoNumber data type problems, 1179
    Backstage area, 1158
    calculated field issues, 1178
    control issues, 1176
    data integrity, enforcing, 1162–1163
    field data type issues, 1178
    form errors, 1175–1176
    form event problems, 1175
    general errors, 1174
    incompatible custom field formats, 1179
    incompatible fields, 1174
    incompatible macro actions, 1177–1178
    invalid expression errors, 1177
    invalid query names, 1177
    issues, displaying, 1158–1159
    lookup errors, 1174–1175
    lookup field issues, 1175, 1178
    macro errors, 1177–1178
    object name violations, 1176
    online help, 1160

Index

Compatibility Checker, SharePoint deployment (*continued*)
    primary key constraints, 1175
    query errors, 1176–1177
    query join issues, 1177
    relationship errors, 1174–1175
    relationship issues, 1160–1161
    report errors, 1175–1176
    reports do not support events, 1176
    reserved word collisions, 1177
    running, 1157–1158
    schema errors, 1178–1179
    SQL statement problems, 1176
    subqueries in queries, 1177
    successful completion, 1163–1164
    table field issues, 1179
    table name issues, 1179
    table relationships, 1174
    Unique property problems, 1179
    unsupported form controls, 1175
    unsupported report controls, 1176
Compatibility Checker problems
    attachment field limitations, 1178
    AutoNumber data type problems, 1179
    calculated field issues, 1178
    control issues, 1176
    field data type issues, 1178
    form errors, 1175–1176
    form event problems, 1175
    general errors, 1174
    incompatible custom field formats, 1179
    incompatible fields, 1174
    incompatible macro actions, 1177–1178
    invalid expression errors, 1177
    invalid query names, 1177
    issues, displaying, 1158–1159
    lookup errors, 1174–1175
    lookup field issues, 1175, 1178
    macro errors, 1177–1178
    object name violations, 1176
    primary key constraints, 1175
    query errors, 1176–1177
    query join issues, 1177
    relationship errors, 1174–1175
    relationship issues, 1160–1161
    report errors, 1175–1176
    reports do not support events, 1176
    reserved word collisions, 1177
    schema errors, 1178–1179
    SQL statement problems, 1176

    subqueries in queries, 1177
    table field issues, 1179
    table name issues, 1179
    table relationships, 1174
    Unique property problems, 1179
    unsupported form controls, 1175
    unsupported report controls, 1176
compatibility with older databases
    converting old files, 32–33
    Database Enhancement dialog box, 32–33
    enabling obsolete databases, 32
    overview, 31
Compile on Demand option
    checking status of, 843
    compiled state, 848–854
    Options dialog box, 411, 530
    overview, 843–844
    turning off, 843
compiled state
    creating, 849–850
    distributing applications, 851–854
    library databases, 851–853
    library references, 851–853
    losing, 850–851
    overview, 848–854
    storing code, 851–853
compiler directives, 413–414, 535–537
compiling
    code, conditional compilation, 535–537
    databases, 874–875
    VBA code, 532–534
    VBA procedures, 397
composite primary keys, 77, 118
compound controls, in reports, 356–358
compound object names, naming conventions, 40
concatenating strings
    & (ampersand), concatenation operator, 173, 178–179,
        188, 422
    + (plus sign), addition operator, 173, 179
Condition property, 1073
conditional compilation, 535–537
Conditional Compilation Arguments option,
        413–414
conditional processing
    Case Else clause, 404
    definition, 401
    Else statements, 402
    ElseIf clause, 402–403
    If...Then...Else...Endif statements, 401–403

If...Then...Endif statements, 401–403
overview, 401
Select Case...End Select statements, 403–404
conditions for macro error handling, getting, 1073
conditions for macro execution
mcrReportMenu macro, example, 1062–1063
multiple actions, 1064
opening reports with, 1061–1064
confirming deletions
AfterDelConfirm event, 458–459
BeforeDelConfirm event, 458–459
MsgBox function, 470–471
Connect event, 464
Connect property, 600–606
connecting data. *See* join tables; table relationships.
connecting to data sources. *See also* binding.
ADO Connection object, 489–492
ConnectionString property, 491–492
connecting to SQL Server
from Access, 1203–1214
connection strings, 1201–1203
creating a data source, 1204
DSN, setting up, 1205–1211
File DSN, 1204
linking to tables, 1211–1214
ODBC configuration options, 1204
System DSN, 1204
User DSN, 1204
Connection object, 489–492
connection pooling, 1191–1192
connection strings, 1201–1203
ConnectionString property, discovering, 491–492
#Const compiler directive, 413–414
#Const directive, 535–537
Control Box property, 307
control menu
displaying on forms, 307
removing, 706
control properties
defaults, customizing, 681
GetProperty function, 685–686
getting, 685–686
control properties, setting
dynamically at runtime, 682–685
in Layout view, 312
overview, 284–285, 679–681
SetProperty function, 683–685
Control Source property, 284
control tip help, 697

control totals, reports, 344–345
control variables, absolute speed, 864–865
controls. *See also specific controls.*
aligning, 275–277, 314
background color, 682
bound, 266, 285
categorizing, 264–265
copying, 281
custom ribbons, 1017
customizing ribbons, 1025–1026
data-entry forms, 22
definition, 264
deleting, 281
deleting groups, 279
deselecting, 272
disabling, 682
event procedures, modifying, 390–391
foreground color, 682
formatting, 462–463
forms, unsupported, 1175
graying out, 682
grouping, 278–279
hiding/showing, 463
labeling, 279–280
list of, 265. *See also specific controls.*
morphing, 695–696
moving, 271–272, 274–275
naming conventions, 285–286
overview, 264
positioning, 683
RecordSource property, 271
resizing, 273–274, 683
selecting, 271–272
SharePoint deployment issues, 1176
sizing handles, 271–272
snapping to the grid, 276–277
type, modifying, 270, 280–281
unbound, 266, 285
VBA event procedures, 459–460, 462–463
visibility, hiding/showing, 682, 684
controls, adding to forms
with the Controls group, 267–268
with the Field List, 268–271
overview, 266–267
controls, calculated
creating, 316
description, 266
editing, 296
updating tables, with VBA code, 513–516

Index

controls, editing. *See also* properties.
   modifying appearance of, 277–278
   protected controls, 296
controls, reports
   aligning labels, 736
   compound, 356–358
   expressions in text controls, 353
   formatting, 358
   hiding/showing, 463, 725–727
   label control properties, 359–360
   label controls, moving, 356–358
   label controls, pasting, 356
   label controls, resizing, 354
   micro-adjusting, 736–737
   modifying text, 351–352
   moving between sections, 365–366
   naming conventions, 285–286, 749
   page breaks, 367
   placing, 350–351
   and report page breaks, 367
   selecting with the mouse, 357–358
   text, modifying, 351–352
   text, moving, 356–358
   text-box control properties, 359–360
   text-box controls, resizing, 360–361
   totals, 344–345
   unsupported, 1176
controls, the ribbon
   Button, 1038
   check boxes, 1039–1040
   DropDown, 1014, 1040–1041
   Gallery, 1014–1015
   help, 1015
   imageMso, specifying, 1035–1037
   Label, 1037–1038
   resizing, 1012
   separators, 1038–1039
   SplitButton, 1013–1014, 1041–1042
   SuperTips, 1015
Controls group, 265–268
ControlSource property, 691–693
Convert All Picture Data option, 1084, 1088–1089
converting case
   date/time fields, 64
   with input masks, 67
   text and memo fields, 64
converting data types, 57–58

converting to SQL Server
   forms, 1234
   issues, 1239
   macros, 1234
   modules, 1234
   queries, 1234
   reports, 1234
   ribbons, 1234
Copy command
   Datasheet ribbon, 220
   Form ribbon, 292
copying. *See also* cutting/copying/pasting.
   .accdb file, SharePoint deployment, 1145
   controls, 281
   formats, 292–293
   OLE objects, 296–297
   pictures, 296–297
   tables to another database, 87
   tables within a database, 86–87
Count function, 642–644
Count option, 657, 658
Count property, 407
counting
   collection items, 407
   field values, 657
   null values, 658
   records in recordsets, 498–499, 642–644
Create button, 122
Create New button, 122
Create ribbon, 1050
Create ribbon tab, 42
Created Date option, 35
CreateObject function, 796
CreateRecord action, 558–559
creating. *See also* reports, creating.
   action queries, 671–675
   Automation references, 791–792
   compiled state, 849–850
   custom events, 1001–1002
   data-entry forms, 11–12
   datasheets, 10
   forms, 11–12, 290
   macros, 1050–1052
   primary keys, 115–116, 118–119
   Product class, 972–974
   queries, 10–11, 135–138
   ribbons, 1023
   SharePoint lists, 1112–1115

an SQL Server data source, 1204
table relationships, 119–125
unbound forms for network applications, 781
creating databases. *See also* designing databases.
default name, 30
naming databases, 29–30
new database screen, 29
tblCustomers database, 55
templates, 26–27
creating tables. *See also* designing tables.
Create ribbon tab, 42
Datasheet view, 42–43
Fields ribbon tab, 43
Table button, 42
Table Design button, 42, 43–45
creating VBA elements
event procedures, 397–399, 437–441
functions, 441–442
modules, 391–392
procedures, 395, 397–399, 436
subroutines, 437–441
cross-platform compatibility, 941
cross-products of tables. *See* Cartesian products.
crosstab queries, 133, 666–670
Crosstab Query Wizard, 667–670
cross-table products. *See* Cartesian products.
CSV (comma-separated values)
importing text files, 618–623
linking to, 596–597
Currency data type
automatic validation, 224–225
converting to Number, 58
converting to Text, 58
default value, 59
description, 53
entering, 226
group headers, 363
purpose, 48
storage size, 49
VBA, 428
currency fields, formatting, 61
Currency format, 61
Current Database options
accelerator keys, enabling, 1087
application icon, specifying, 1085
Application Icon field, 1084, 1085
Application options, 1084, 1085–1089
Application Title field, 1084, 1085

Check for Truncated Number Fields check box,
1084, 1088
Compact on Close check box, 1084, 1087
compacting the database on closing, 1087
Convert All Picture Data option, 1084,
1088–1089
Current Database tab, 1084
Display Form drop-down list, 1084, 1085
Display Status Bar check box, 1084, 1086
Document Window options, 1084, 1086–1087
Enable Design Changes check box, 1084, 1088
Enable Layout View check box, 1084, 1088
forms, selecting, 1085
layout view, enabling, 1088
overlapping windows, specifying, 1086–1087
personal information, removing on save, 1088
Picture Property Storage Format option, 1084, 1088–
1089
pictures, specifying storage format, 1088–1089
Preserve Source Image Format option, 1084,
1088–1089
Remove Personal Information check box, 1084, 1088
status bar, displaying, 1086
tabbed documents, specifying, 1086–1087
table changes, enabling, 1088
title bar text, specifying, 1085
truncated numeric fields, checking for, 1088
Use Access Special Keys check box, 1084, 1087
Use Windows-Themed Controls on Forms check box,
1084, 1088
Windows themes, enabling, 1088
Current Database tab, 1084
Current event, 458–459
current record pointer, 495
cursor
changing to hourglass, 1054–1055
type, specifying, 496–497
CursorType parameter, 510–512
CursorType property, 496–497
custom field formats, incompatibilities, 1179
Custom option, 34
Custom Ribbon ID property, 311
Customize the Ribbon window, 1020–1021
customizing the ribbon, limitations, 1016
customizing the ribbon defaults
commands, 1020–1022
Customize the Ribbon window, 1020–1021
groups, 1020–1022
importing/exporting customizations, 1022

Index

customizing the ribbon defaults (*continued*)
    renaming groups, 1020–1022
    resetting to original, 1022
    tabs, 1020–1022
    with Visual Web Developer, 1042–1044
customizing ribbons
    building XML, 1026
    controls, 1025–1026
    creating a ribbon, 1023
    custom property, specifying, 1032–1033
    designing ribbons, 1026
    error reporting, enabling, 1024
    getLabel attribute, 1028
    groups, 1025–1026
    hierarchical structure, 1025–1026
    OnAction attribute, 1024
    tabs, 1025–1026
    USysRibbons table, adding XML, 1030–1032
    USysRibbons table, creating, 1029–1030
    VBA callbacks, overview, 1023–1025
    VBA callbacks, writing, 1027–1029
customizing SharePoint pages, 1143
Cut command
    Datasheet ribbon, 220
    Form ribbon, 292
cutting/copying/pasting. *See also* copying.
    data in datasheets, 220, 231–233
    macro items, 569–571
Cycle property, 311

D

d:, formatting day of the month, 63
DAO (Data Access Objects)
    versus ADO, 486, 507
    linking tables, 600–606
    methods, 486–487
    overview, 485–488, 499–500
    pessimistic locking, 770–771
    properties, 486–487
DAO object model
    Database object, 502
    DBEngine object, 501
    diagram, 500
    Field objects, 506
    QueryDef object, 503–505
    Recordset object, 505–506
    security, 501

TableDef object, 502–503
transaction tracking, 501
Workspace object, 501
dash. *See* hyphen.
data. *See also* datasheets; normalization.
    back-end data files, 32
    definition, 6
    designing, 16–18
    in local tables, 32
    rows, SharePoint maximum, 1143
data access with VBA, filtering data in forms
    with code, 888–889
    interactive filter dialog boxes, 892–894
    With keyword, 895
    linking dialog boxes, 894
    with queries, 889–895
    wildcards, 890–891
data access with VBA, finding data in forms
    bookmarks, 885–888
    FindRecord method, 883–885
    unbound combo boxes, 881–883
data actions, 560–562
data aggregation, 247–248
Data Blocks actions, 557–560
data entry, datasheets
    * (asterisk), new record indicator, 221–222
    adding new records, 220–223
    automatic data-type validation, 224–225
    Currency data, 226
    Date/Time data, 225
    input masks, 225
    Memo data, 226–227
    Number data, 226
    OLE Object data, 226
    text data, 225
data entry, forms
    controls, 22. *See also specific controls.*
    creating, 11–12
    designing, 22
    graphical objects, 22
    labels, 22
    overview, 11–12
    text-box data-entry fields, 22
Data Entry property, 310
data events, 452
Data Execution Prevent (DEP) mode, 937
data integrity. *See* referential integrity.

data macros. *See also* macros; VBA.
  Action Catalog, 557–562
  adding records to tables, 558–559
  adding to tables, 554
  back-end execution, 575
  calling VBA procedures, 576
  canceling record changes, 560
  `CancelRecordChange` action, 560
  `ClearMacroError` action, 562
  `CreateRecord` action, 558–559
  data actions, 560–562
  Data Blocks actions, 557–560
  `DeleteRecord` action, 560
  deleting records, 560
  editing records, 559
  `EditRecord` action, 559
  error handling, 561
  error logging, 560–561
  `ExitForEachRecord` action, 560
  `ForEachRecord` action, 560
  limitations of, 575–576
  with linked tables, 576
  `LogEvent` action, 560–561
  `LookupRecord` action, 560
  looping through recordsets, 560
  Macro Designer, 553–562
  macro groups, 557
  for multi-value or attachment fields, 575
  `OnError` action, 561
  overview, 551–553
  passing values with local variables, 561
  program flow, 557–560
  `RaiseError` action, 562
  rasing errors, 562
  resetting errors, 562
  for returned records, 560
  `RunDataMacro` action, 561
  running other data macros, 561
  saving as XML, 574–575
  `SendEmail` action, 561
  sending email, 561
  `SetField` action, 561
  `SetLocalVar` action, 561
  `StopMacro` action, 561
  terminating, 561
  updating field values, 561
data macros, macro items
  adding, 566–569
  collapsing, 573–574

  copying and pasting, 569–571
  dragging and dropping, 572–573
  moving, 572–573
data macros, table events
  before, 562–566
  after, 564–566
  `AfterChange` event, 564–566
  `AfterDelete` event, 564–566
  `AfterInsert` event, 564–566
  `BeforeChange` event, 562–564
  `BeforeDelete` event, 562–564
`Data Mode` argument, 1061
data object models. *See* ADO (ActiveX Data Objects); DAO
       (Data Access Objects).
`Data` properties, 283
data sources
  for forms, specifying, 309
  network applications, 754–756
data sources, binding to. *See also* connecting.
  bound controls, 266, 285
  bound forms, 304
  in reports, 346–348
data types
  `Attachment`, 49, 54
  DLLs, 943–945
  `Hyperlink`, 49, 54
  Lookup Wizard, 49, 54
  SharePoint, 1127
  validation, automatic, 224–225
  VBA *versus* C/C++, 943–945
data types, Access
  absolute speed, 862–863
  converting to other types, 57–58
  converting to SharePoint types, 1127
  corresponding VBA types, 429
  for fields, 45, 48–50
  indexing, 50
  list of, 49. *See also specific types.*
  for phone numbers, 50
  processing speeds, 862
  property procedures, 990–991
  for Social Security numbers, 50, 51
  sorting, 50–51
  versus SQL Server, 1235–1240
  storage requirements, 50
  for telephone numbers, 51
  for zip codes, 51

Index

data types, `AutoNumber`
  converting from other data types, 57
  converting to `Number`, 58
  converting to `Text`, 58
  overview, 53
  problems, 1179
  purpose, 48
  storage size, 49
data types, `Currency`
  automatic validation, 224–225
  converting to `Number`, 58
  converting to `Text`, 58
  default value, 59
  description, 53
  entering, 226
  group headers, 363
  purpose, 48
  storage size, 49
  VBA, 428
data types, `Date/Time`
  automatic validation, 224–225
  converting to `Text`, 58
  description, 53
  entering, 225
  group headers, 362
  leading zeros, enabling, 625
  purpose, 48
  storage size, 49
data types, `Memo`
  converting to `Text`, 58
  indexing, 50
  overview, 52
  purpose, 48
  sorting, 50
  storage size, 49
data types, `Number`. *See also* numeric fields.
  converting from `AutoNumber`, 58
  converting to `Currency`, 58
  converting to `Text`, 58
  default value, 59
  group headers, 363
  overview, 52–53
  purpose, 48
  storage size, 49
data types, `OLE Object`
  converting to other data types, 58
  description, 54
  indexing, 50, 73

  sorting, 50, 147
  types of data stored, 49
data types, `Text`
  converting from `AutoNumber`, 58
  converting from `Date/Time`, 58
  description, 51
  group headers, 362
  purpose, 48
  storage size, 49
data types, VBA variables
  `Boolean`, 428
  corresponding Access data types, 428
  `Currency`, 428
  `Date`, 428
  `Decimal`, 428
  default, 426, 430
  `Double`, 428
  `Integer`, 428
  `Long`, 428
  `Object`, 428
  `Single`, 428
  specifying, 422
  `String`, 428
  supported by VBA, 428
  `Variant`, 428, 430
data types, `Yes/No`
  automatic validation, 224–225
  converting to `Text`, 58
  description, 53
  purpose, 48
  storage size, 49
data validation rules
  `AllowZeroLength` property, 70–71
  business rules, enforcing, 69
  date/time data, limiting to a range of dates, 70
  error messages, 69
  input, 69–70
  nonexistent data, 71
  required data, indicating, 70
  `Required` property, 70
  specifying, 49
  unknown data, 71
  `Validation Rule` property, 69
  `Validation Text` property, 69
  zero-length data, allowing, 70–71
Database Enhancement dialog box, 32–33
`Database` object, 502

database objects. *See also specific objects.*
  data-entry forms, 11–12
  datasheets, 10
  display forms, 11–12
  macros, 10
  modules, 10
  queries, 10–11
  reports, 12
Database Splitter wizard, 762–764
dataBased Intelligence, Inc., 631
databases
  See also fields
  See also records
  See also tables
  See also Upsizing Wizard
  compacting, 874–875, 1087
  compiling, 874–875
  computerized *versus* manual filing systems, 4–5
  default file format, 845–846
  definition, 4–5
  file types, 5
  flat file, 95–97, 104–105. *See also* spreadsheets.
  naming conventions, 8, 29–30
  opening exclusively, 756–758
  RDBMS (relational database management system), 5
  recompiling automatically, 877
  recreating, 874–875
  specifications, 1247
  versus spreadsheets, 92–94
  uncompiled, detecting, 877–878
databases, dBase
  browsing to, 631–632
  data type conversions, 632
  importing from multi-user environments, 631–632
  linking to, 587
databases, optimizing
  average size, 872
  compacting, 874–875
  compiling, 874–875
  corrupted forms, 874
  decompile option, 876
  growth rate, 873
  memory leaks, 874
  minimizing changes, 879
  pre-release steps, 877
  rebooting, 874
  recompiling automatically, 877
  recreating, 874–875
  uncompiled databases, detecting, 877–878

databases, splitting for network applications
  benefits of, 759–761
  Database Splitter wizard, 762–764
  definition, 753
  placing objects, 761–762
DataChange event, 464
data-entry forms. *See* forms, data entry.
DataSetChange event, 464
Datasheet button, 262
Datasheet command, 253
Datasheet Formatting dialog box, 240
Datasheet ribbon
  Align Center command, 220
  Align Left command, 220
  Align Right command, 220
  Alternate Fill/Back Color command, 220
  Clipboard group, 220
  Copy command, 220
  Cut command, 220
  Find group, 220
  Gridlines command, 220
  Home tab, 219–221
  Paste Append command, 220
  Paste command, 220
  Paste Special command, 220
  Records group, 220
  Size to Fit Form button, 220
  Sort & Filter group, 220, 242–246
  Switch Windows button, 220
  Text Formatting group, 220–221
  Views group, 219
  Window group, 220
Datasheet view
  deleting records, 234–235
  description, 42–43
  enabling, 306
  illustration, 42
  new features, 1259–1261
  switching to, 291, 300
Datasheet window
  overview, 217
  padlock icon, 223
  pencil icon, 223
  record pointers, 223
Datasheet window, navigating. *See also* Navigation Pane.
  within a datasheet, 218
  finding specific values, 228–229
  keystrokes for, 218
  Navigation buttons, 218–219

Index

Datasheet window, navigating (*continued*)
    overview, 227
    between records, 227–228
datasheets
    aligning data, 220–221
    coloring alternate records, 220
    creating, 10
    cutting/copying/pasting data, 220
    data aggregation, 247–248
    data sources, 216
    definition, 10
    displaying data, 10
    fields, 216–217
    find and replace records, 220
    Find group, 220
    forms, 262
    go to a specific record, 220
    gridlines, hiding/showing, 220
    highlighting alternate records, 220
    illustration, 216
    justifying data, 220–221
    line breaks, inserting, 231
    modifying, 10
    navigating, 599
    opening, 221
    overview, 215–216
    printing, 248–249
    records, 216–217
    Records group, 220
    resizing, 220
    Size to Fit Form button, 220
    summing rows and columns, 247–248
    Switch Windows button, 220
    text formatting, 220–221
    Text Formatting group, 220–221
    totals calculation, 247–248
    views, switching, 219
    Window group, 220
    windows, switching, 220
datasheets, data entry
    * (asterisk), new record indicator, 221–222
    adding new records, 220–223
    automatic data-type validation, 224–225
    Currency data, 226
    Date/Time data, 225
    input masks, 225
    Memo data, 226–227
    Number data, 226

OLE Object data, 226
    text data, 225
datasheets, displaying records
    field display width, modifying, 237
    hiding/showing records, 237
    rearranging fields, 235–236
    record display width, modifying, 238
    resizing field width, 237
    resizing record height, 238
datasheets, modifying data
    adding records, 234
    aligning data, 241
    background color, modifying, 239–241
    coloring alternate records, 239–241
    copying and pasting, 231–233
    deleting records, 234–235
    display fonts, modifying, 239
    editing techniques, 231
    field display width, modifying, 237
    freezing records, 242
    gridlines, hiding/showing, 239
    gridlines, modifying appearance of, 240
    hiding/showing fields, 241
    highlighting alternate records, 239–241
    protected fields, 231
    rearranging fields, 235–236
    record display width, modifying, 238
    replacing existing values, 230, 233–234
    resizing field width, 237
    resizing record height, 238
    saving changes, 242
    undoing changes, 231
datasheets, records
    * (asterisk), new record indicator, 221–222
    adding, 220–223
    automatic data-type validation, 224–225
    deleting, 220
    filtering, 220, 242–246
    hiding, 220, 238
    saving, 220, 223
    sorting, 220, 242–243
data-type errors, action queries, 676
Date data type, VBA, 428
Date fields
    comparison operators, 152
    data entry, 298
    importing/exporting, 624–627
    query selection criteria, 151–152
    selection criteria for, 151–152

Date Order option, 624–625
Date Picker control, 298
date/time
    adding to forms, 694
    data type for, 51
    in datasheets, 231
    date delimiter character, specifying, 625
    duration, 51
    in forms, 231
    limiting to a range of dates, 70
    regional format, setting, 646
    in reports, 362, 372
    storing, 51
    time delimiter character, specifying, 625
    two-digit years *versus* four-digit, 212
    validation rules, 70
date/time, formatting
    : (colon), separating time elements, 63
    / (forward slash), separating time elements, 63
    am/pm:, lowercase 12-hour format, 64
    AMPM:, uppercase 12-hour format, 64
    a/p:, lowercase 12-hour format, 64
    A/P:, uppercase 12-hour format, 64
    built-in formats, 62–63
    c:, General Date format, 63
    custom formats, 63–64
    d:, formatting day of the month, 63
    dd:, formatting day of the month, 63
    ddd:, formatting day of the week, 63
    dddd:, formatting day of the week, 63
    ddddd:, Short Date format, 63
    dddddd:, Long Date format, 63
    General Date format, 63
    h:, formatting hours, 64
    hh:, formatting hours, 64
    input masks, creating, 68
    Long Date format, 63
    Long Time format, 63
    m:, formatting month of the year, 63
    Medium Date format, 63
    Medium Time format, 63
    mm:, formatting month of the year, 63
    mmm:, formatting month of the year, 63
    mmmm:, formatting month of the year, 63
    n:, formatting minutes, 64
    nn:, formatting minutes, 64
    q:, formatting quarter of the year, 63
    s:, formatting seconds, 64
    Short Date format, 63

Short Time format, 63
ss:, formatting seconds, 64
tttt:, Long Time format, 64
w:, formatting day of the week, 63
ww:, formatting week of the year, 63
y:, formatting day of the year, 63
yy:, formatting two digit year, 63
yyyy:, formatting four digit year, 63
Date/Time data type
    automatic validation, 224–225
    converting to Text, 58
    description, 53
    entering, 225
    group headers, 362
    leading zeros, enabling, 625
    purpose, 48
    storage size, 49
Day property, 362
dBase databases
    browsing to, 631–632
    data type conversions, 632
    importing from multi-user environments, 631–632
    linking to, 587
DBEngine object, 501
DblClick event, 455, 460
dbo prefix, 1212
dd:, formatting day of the month, 63
ddd:, formatting day of the week, 63
dddd:, formatting day of the week, 63
ddddd:, Short Date format, 63
dddddd:, Long Date format, 63
Deactivate event, 457, 461
dead code, removing, 866
debug window, 1075. *See also* Immediate window.
debugging
    See also bugs
    See also Compatibility Checker
    See also error handling
    See also testing
    See also troubleshooting
    color-coding syntax errors, 526
    compiling on demand, 530
    forcing variable declaration, 527–528
    object hierarchy, displaying, 528
    stopping for errors, 529
    syntax checking, 525–527
    variable values, displaying, 529
    variables out of context, 528

Index

debugging, macros
  debug window, 1074
  error information, displaying, 1074
  `MessageBox` action, 1074
  Single Step dialog box, 1074
  stepping through code, 1074
  `StopMacro` action, 1074
  stopping macro execution, 1074
debugging, tools and techniques
  Add Watch dialog box, 546–548
  breakpoints, 539–544. *See also* `Stop` statements.
  Call Stack window, 548–549
  color coding, 539
  compiler directives, 535–537
  conditional compilation, 535–537
  `#Const` directive, 535–537
  `#Else` directive, 535–537
  `#End If` directive, 535–537
  error messages, 534–535
  help for syntax, 528–529
  help for variables, 543–544
  `#If` directive, 535–537
  Immediate window, 399–401, 538–539, 541
  Locals window, 544–545
  `MsgBox` statement, 534–535
  `Print` method, 537–538
  printing messages, 537–538
  stepping through code, 543–544
  `Stop` statements, 542. *See also* breakpoints.
  tracing execution path, 549
  variables in scope, displaying, 544–545
  watches, setting, 545–547
  Watches window, 545–548
`Decimal` data type, VBA, 428
decimal places, formatting, 62
`Decimal` size numeric fields, 52
`DecimalPlaces` property, 59
declarations section, VBA, 394, 427
`Declare` statement
  `ArgumentList` parameter, 947–949
  arguments, passing `ByVal` *versus* `ByRef`, 948
  `As DataType` parameter, 949
  `FunctionName` parameter, 946
  functions *versus* subroutines, 946
  `LibraryName` parameter, 947
  purpose, 946
  strings, maximum length, 949
  syntax, 946

declaring VBA variables
  declarations section, 394, 427
  explicitly, 424, 430
  forcing explicit declaration, 394, 411, 431
  implicitly, 423, 430
  importance of, 424
  overview, 421–425
decompile option, 876
decomposition, 99
`Decrease Horizontal` command, 277
`Decrease Vertical` command, 277
default data type, VBA, 426, 430
Default Open Mode option, 766
Default Record Locking option, 766
`Default View` property, 306, 651
`DefaultValue` property, 59
defragmenting hard drives, 856
`Delete` event, 458–459
`Delete Page` method, 701
`Delete Query` action queries, 671, 673–675
Delete Rows button, 46
`DeleteRecord` action, 560
deleting. *See also* removing.
  controls, 281
  dialog box pages, 701
  fields, 41, 56
  groups of controls, 279
  records, 46
  records with data macros, 560
  table relationships, 126
  tables, 86
  text boxes from reports, 354–355
deleting records
  across multiple tables, 518–521
  checking deletion status, 515–516
  Datasheet view, 234–235
  `Delete` method, 517–518
  Delete Rows button, 46
  enabling, 310
  with VBA code, 517–521
deletion anomalies, 103
deletion confirmation
  `AfterDelConfirm` event, 458–459
  `BeforeDelConfirm` event, 458–459
  Design tab, 46
  with event procedures, 458–459, 470–471
  status, checking, 458–459
denormalization, 102–104

DEP (Data Execution Prevent) mode, 937

dependency, 98

deploying applications. *See* distributing applications; SharePoint deployment.

`Description` property, 651, 1073

descriptive names, naming conventions, 40

deselecting controls, 272

Design tab, 45–47, 314

Design view, 37, 292

designing databases, five-step method. *See also* databases.
    data design, 16–18
    foreign keys, 20–21, 114. *See also* primary keys.
    form design, 22
    linking tables, 20–22
    needs analysis, 14
    normalization, 20, 22
    numeric field calculations, 18
    overall design, 13–14
    overview, 13. *See also specific steps.*
    primary keys, 20–21. *See also* foreign keys.
    report design, 14–16
    table design, 19–22
    unique identifiers, 20–21

designing databases, normalizing data
    1NF (first normal form), 95–97
    2NF (second normal form), 97–102
    3NF (third normal form), 102
    calculated data, removing, 102–104
    decomposition, 99
    deletion anomalies, 103
    denormalization, 102–104
    dependency, 98
    flat-file approach, 95–97
    insertion anomalies, 103
    overview, 94–95
    redundant or repetitive data, 95–97
    splitting into tables, 97–102
    update anomalies, 99, 103

designing databases, overview, 92–94

designing databases, primary keys
    adding records to tables, 119
    benefits of, 117
    choosing, 115–116
    composite, 118
    creating, 115, 119
    definition, 105
    deriving, 116
    designating, 118–119
    importance of, 115

    indexed tables, 117
    natural, 118–119
    null values, 113
    single, 118
    surrogate, 118–119

designing databases, referential integrity
    application-specific, 126–127
    cascading deletes, 123–125
    cascading updates, 123–125
    definition, 112
    enforcing, 119–125
    entity integrity, 115
    ignoring, 123
    null values in primary keys, 113
    orphaned records, 114
    overview, 112–113
    primary keys matching foreign keys, 114
    table conflicts, resolving, 124

designing databases, table relationships. *See also* join tables.
    connecting data, 105–107. *See also* primary keys.
    creating, 119–125
    deleting, 126
    equi-joins, 122–125
    flat-file databases, 104–105
    join tables, 111
    join type, specifying, 122–125
    many-to-many, 110–111
    one-to-many, 108–110
    one-to-one, 107–108
    outer joins, 122–125
    parent/child, 108–110
    viewing, 125–126

designing dialog boxes
    always on top, 704
    borders, 704
    Cancel buttons, 706
    closing the form, 707
    for collecting information, 703–707
    control menu, removing, 706
    default buttons, 706
    deleting pages, 701
    filtering criteria, 700
    inserting pages, 701
    modality, 704
    property settings, 704

designing dialog boxes, tab control
    labels on tabs, 702
    overview, 700–703
    pictures on tabs, 702

Index

designing dialog boxes, tab control (*continued*)
  selected tabs, identifying, 702
  tab size, setting, 702
  tabs, as command buttons, 702
designing forms
  animation, 688–690
  automatic closing, 691
  background pictures, 697–699
  bound to SQL statements, 690
  combo boxes, 691–693
  common objects, 22
  control tip help, 697
  ControlSource *versus* RowSource, 691–693
  date/time, adding, 694
  for faster refresh, 690
  filtering options, 699–700
  form events, 699–700
  format painter, 696–697
  image control, 695
  inserting *versus* overtyping user input, 690
  list boxes, 691–693
  logos, adding, 695
  morphing controls, 695–696
  open state, determining, 693
  page numbers, adding, 694
  Tab key behavior, 22
  tallying true check box responses, 688
  toggling properties, 690–691
designing tables. *See also* creating tables.
  example, 44–45
  process overview, 41
  Table Design button, 42, 43–45
  Table Design window, 44–45
Dest Connect Str property, 653
Destination DB property, 653
Destination Table property, 653
Detail section, 341–342, 344, 370–371
development process, 900
dialog boxes. *See also specific dialog boxes.*
  interactive filters, 892–894
  linking to forms, 894
dialog boxes, designing
  always on top, 704
  borders, 704
  Cancel buttons, 706
  closing the form, 707
  for collecting information, 703–707
  control menu, removing, 706
  default buttons, 706

  deleting pages, 701
  filtering criteria, 700
  inserting pages, 701
  modality, 704
  property settings, 704
digital certificates, 935–936
digital signatures, 935
Dim keyword, 421, 425–426
dimensions. *See* resizing.
Dirty event, 458–459, 460
disabled fields, editing, 232
Disconnect event, 464
Display Form drop-down list, 1084, 1085
display forms. *See* forms, data display.
Display Navigation Pane check box, 1089
Display Status Bar check box, 1084, 1086
Display Text property, 66
displaying
  fields in queries, 145–147
  recordsets, 140–141
  selected data, 134
displaying data. *See* datasheets; forms; reports.
displaying fields
  field display width, modifying, 237
  rearranging fields, 235–236
  resizing field width, 237
displaying records
  display width, modifying, 238
  height, modifying, 238
  hiding/showing records, 237
DISTINCT SQL predicate, 478–479
DISTINCTROW SQL predicate, 479–480
distributed installation, network applications, 753
distributing applications. *See also* SharePoint deployment.
  in compiled state, 851–854
  Name Autocorrect options, 1084, 1091–1092
  table/field names, automatic correction, 1091–1092
  testing requirements, 1092–1093
distributing applications, Current Database options
  accelerator keys, enabling, 1087
  application icon, specifying, 1085
  Application Icon field, 1084, 1085
  Application options, 1084, 1085–1089
  Application Title field, 1084, 1085
  Check for Truncated Number Fields check box, 1084, 1088
  Compact on Close check box, 1084, 1087
  compacting the database on closing, 1087
  Convert All Picture Data option, 1084, 1088–1089

Current Database tab, 1084
Display Form drop-down list, 1084, 1085
Display Status Bar check box, 1084, 1086
Document Window options, 1084, 1086–1087
Enable Design Changes check box, 1084, 1088
Enable Layout View check box, 1084, 1088
forms, selecting, 1085
layout view, enabling, 1088
overlapping windows, specifying, 1086–1087
personal information, removing on save, 1088
Picture Property Storage Format option, 1084, 1088–1089
pictures, specifying storage format, 1088–1089
Preserve Source Image Format option, 1084, 1088–1089
Remove Personal Information check box, 1084, 1088
status bar, displaying, 1086
tabbed documents, specifying, 1086–1087
table changes, enabling, 1088
title bar text, specifying, 1085
truncated numeric fields, checking for, 1088
Use Access Special Keys check box, 1084, 1087
Use Windows-Themed Controls on Forms check box, 1084, 1088
Windows themes, enabling, 1088
distributing applications, Navigation options
Display Navigation Pane check box, 1089
Navigation Options button/dialog box, 1089–1090
Navigation Pane, displaying, 1089
Navigation Pane options, displaying, 1089–1090
system objects, hiding, 1090
distributing applications, Ribbon and Toolbar options
Allow Default Shortcut Menus check box, 1091
Allow Full Menus check box, 1091
command display, customizing, 1091
custom ribbon, specifying, 1091
Ribbon Name option, 1091
Shortcut Menu Bar option, 1090–1091
shortcut menu defaults, specifying, 1090–1091
shortcut menu display, specifying, 1091
dividing lines, displaying
on forms, 306
Dividing Lines property, 306
DLLs (dynamic link libraries)
advantages of, 940
definition, 940
dynamic linking, 940
static linking, 940

DLLs (dynamic link libraries), documentation
argument prefixes, 944
finding, 942
understanding, 942–945
VBA data types *versus* C/C++ data types, 943–945
Document Window options, 1084, 1086–1087
documentation
applications, 1100
bulletproofing, 902–903
documents, trusted, 937
dollar sign ($), formatting currency fields, 62
Do...Loop statements, 404–405
Double data type, VBA, 428
double quotes ("...")
around returned strings, 178
literal text indicator, 60, 194
text qualifier, 620, 624
Double size numeric fields, 52
drive type, getting, 957–958
DropDown controls on the ribbon, 1014, 1040–1041
DSN, setting up, 1205–1211
duplicate names, naming conventions, 39
dynamic link libraries (DLLs). *See* DLLs (dynamic link libraries).
dynamic linking, 940. *See also* late binding.
Dynasets, 141

E

E+, formatting scientific notation, 62
e+, formatting scientific notation, 62
E-, formatting scientific notation, 62
e-, formatting scientific notation, 62
Each Value property
Currency data types, 363
Date/Time data types, 362
Number data types, 363
Text data types, 362
early binding, 792–794. *See also* static linking.
Echo action, 1055, 1056
Edit method, 512
Edit Relations window, 122
Edited Record option, 766
editing. *See also* code window; modifying.
AutoNumber fields, 232
calculated fields, 232
controls, 277–278, 296. *See also* properties.

Index

editing *(continued)*
  disabled fields, 232
  locked fields, 232
  multiuser locked records, 232
  records with data macros, 559
  SharePoint list items, 1110–1111
  unbound forms, network applications, 786–788
  VBA modules, 393
  VBA procedures, 399
editing data
  in forms, 295
  with queries, 134
editing datasheets
  current date/time, inserting, 231
  insertion point, moving, 231
  line breaks, inserting, 231
  protected, 231
  records, adding, 231
  records, deleting, 231
  saving the current record, 231
  selecting, 231
  techniques, 231
  toggling values, 231
  undoing changes, 231
  values, inserting, 231
  values, replacing, 231
editing forms
  current date/time, inserting, 231
  enabling, 310
  insertion point, moving, 231
  line breaks, inserting, 231
  protected, 231
  records, adding, 231
  records, deleting, 231
  saving the current record, 231
  selecting, 231
  techniques, 295
  toggling values, 231
  undoing changes, 231
  values, inserting, 231
  values, replacing, 231
Editor tab, 410–412, 525–530
editors. *See also* VBA editor.
  macros, 1264
  ribbons, 1254–1255
  XML, 1012
`EditRecord` action, 559
`#Else` directive, 535–537
`Else` statements, 402

`ElseIf` clause, 402–403
e-mail, sending with data macros, 561
embedded macros, 552, 1075–1077
embedded pictures *versus* linked, 307
`Enable AutoJoin` option, 650
Enable Design Changes check box, 1084, 1088
Enable Layout View check box, 1084, 1088
`Enabled` property, 682
encapsulation, 982
encoding, 930–931
encryption, 930–931
`#End If` directive, 535–537
endless loops, preventing, 405
end-user maintenance, SharePoint, 1138
`Enter` event, 460
entity integrity, 76, 115
EOF (end-of-file indicator), 497–498
`Equal Horizontal` command, 277
equal sign (=)
  assignment operator, 422
  `Date` comparison operator, 152
  equal operator, 176, 188
  in select queries, 188
Equal Vertical command, 277
equi-joins, 122–125, 165–166
`Err` object, 827–829
`Error 3186: Couldn't save...`, 772–774
`Error 3188: Could not update...`, 774–775
`Error 3197: Data has changed...`, 775–778
`Error 3260: Couldn't update...`, 769–772
`Error` event, 458–459, 461, 836–837
error events, 452
error handlers
  definition, 824–825
  exiting, 834–835
error handling. *See also* debugging; testing; troubleshooting.
  in Access, 821–822
  access errors, 837–838
  ADO objects, 837–838
  in applications, 822–823
  disabling, 831
  error messages, 822–823. *See also specific messages.*
  fatal errors, 821
  handled errors, 823
  identifying errors, 824–826
  logical errors, 820
  macros, 552
  runtime errors, 821–824

stopping for errors, 411
unanticipated errors, 823–824
untrapped errors, 823
error handling, data macros
ClearMacroError action, 562
error response, 561
logging errors, 560–561
OnError action, 561
RaiseError action, 562
raising errors, 562
resetting errors, 562
error handling, macros
ActionName property, 1073
arguments, getting, 1073
Arguments property, 1073
condition, getting, 1073
Condition property, 1073
Description property, 1073
error message, getting, 1073
error number, getting, 1073
macro action, getting, 1073
MacroError object, 1073–1074
MacroName property, 1073
mcrDivisionErrorHandling macro, 1071–1073
name of failed macro, 1073
Number property, 1073
OnError action, 1071–1073
overview, 1069–1070
error handling, trapping errors with On Error statements,
825–826
error handling, trapping errors with VBA
disabling error handling, 831
Err object, 827–829
Error events, 836–837
On Error GoTo 0 statements, 831
On Error GoTo Label statements, 830–831
On Error Resume Next statements, 831–832
error-handling statements, 829–835
ignoring errors, 831–832
overview, 826–827
Resume Label statements, 834–835
Resume Next statements, 834
Resume statements, 832–834
resuming after errors, 832–835
error messages. *See also* messages; MsgBox function; *specific messages.*
built-in, 822–823
data validation, 69

debugging technique, 534–535
macro error handling, getting, 1073
error numbers, macro error handling, 1073
error reporting, ribbons, 1024
error trapping on Visual Basic procedures, 1099
ErrorRoutine function, 778–780
Euro format, 61
even-odd page printing, 733–735
[Event Procedure] option
attaching event procedures, 397–398
creating event procedures, 439–441
event procedures as default development language, 391
event procedures. *See* VBA, event procedures.
event properties, 387. *See also* VBA event procedures; VBA procedures.
Event properties, 283
events. *See also* table events; VBA events; *specific events.*
assigning macros to, 1052–1054
class, 997–999
in class modules, 1005–1008
forms, 699–700
need for, 1000–1001
overview, 1000
passing data through, 1004–1005
raising, 1002–1003
events, custom
creating, 1001–1002
trapping, 1003–1004
Excel data, linking to, 587, 591–594, 602–603
exceptions. *See* error handling.
exclamation point (!)
displaying input masks, 67
in With keyword, 895
left-aligning a display, 60
left-aligning text, 60
Not operator, 195–198
Exit Do statements, 405
Exit event, 460
ExitForEachRecord action, 560
expanding submacros, 1059
explicit variables. *See also* implicit variables; VBA, variables.
effects on performance, 430
forcing, 394, 411, 431
forcing declaration, 411
versus implicit, 430
importance of, 424
syntax, 424
export errors, SharePoint deployment, 1151

Index

Export group, 611

exporting

    Access tables to SharePoint, 1123–1127

    ribbon customizations, 1022

exporting external data

    definition, 581

    HTML documents, 627–628

    versus linking and importing, 582

    Merge it With Microsoft Word option, 636

    Microsoft Word Mail Merge option, 636

    to other Access databases, 634–635

    `Snapshot Viewer` option, 636

    special options, 636

    through ODBC drivers, 635

    uses for, 584

    to XML files, 625–627

Expression Builder, 640–642

Expression option, 655, 656

expressions. *See also* operators.

    . (period), table and field name separator, 174

    [ ] (square brackets), table and field name notation, 174

    definition, 171

    field-name notation, 174

    in group headers, 369–370

    invalid, 1177

    in queries, 187–193

    table-name notation, 174

    in text controls, 353

    for totals, 664–666

eXtensible Markup Language (XML). *See* XML (eXtensible Markup Language).

external data. *See also* exporting external data; importing external data.

    file types supported, 581

    HTML tables, 583

    text tables, 583

    types of, 580

    unsupported programs, 584

External Data tab, 610–611

external tables, linking to. *See also* linked tables; linking tables.

    CSV (comma-separated values), 596–597

    data types supported, 582

    dBase databases, 587

    definition, 581

    disadvantages of, 583

    Excel data, 587, 591–594

    external database tables, 585–587

    fixed-width text files, 596–597

    HTML data, 587, 594–595

    versus importing and exporting, 582

    limitations of, 587–588

    non-database data, 591–594

    ODBC (Object Database Connectivity), 588, 590–591

    other Access databases, 588–590

    text data, 596–597

    text files, 587

    uses for, 582

    xBase files, 591

F

`Fail on Error` property, 653

`Fast Laser Printing` property, 311

fatal errors, 821

`Fetch Defaults` property, 310

`Field Delimiter` option, 624–625

`Field List`, 268–271, 315–316

field names

    automatic correction, 1091–1092

    SQL Server, 1239

`Field` objects, 506

field separators, importing text files, 620

field variables, absolute speed, 865

fields (columns). *See also* queries, fields; records; tables.

    adding to forms, 315–316

    aliases, 649

    column headings, modifying, 658–659

    data type conversion, 57–58

    data type issues, 1178

    data types, specifying, 45, 48–50. *See also specific types*.

    default size, 49

    definition, 8

    deleting, 41, 56

    descriptions, adding, 54–55

    disabled, 296

    display width, modifying, 237

    finding, 229–230

    hiding/showing, 241

    incompatibilities, 1174

    indexing, 72–73

    inserting in tables, 41, 55–56

    listing, 314–316

    locked, 296

    modifying, 41

    moving, 57

    naming, 45, 47–48

    navigating among, 294

rearranging, 235–236

renaming, 41, 57, 647–649

resizing, 57, 143–144

sequence of, 46

size, specifying, 49

updating with data macros, 561

values, definition, 8

fields (columns), displaying

field display width, modifying, 237

rearranging fields, 235–236

resizing field width, 237

fields (columns), properties

AllowZeroLength, 60

assigning, 58–59

Caption, 59

DecimalPlaces, 59

DefaultValue, 59

FieldSize, 59

Format, 59, 60–61

IMEMode, 60

IMESentence Mode, 60

Indexed, 60

Input Mask, 59

New Values, 59

Required, 60

setting, 45

SmartTags, 60

UnicodeCompression, 60

Validation Rule, 60

Validation Text, 60

Fields ribbon tab, 43

FieldSize property, 59

File button, 27–28

File dialog box, new features, 1255

File DSN, 1204

file formats supported, 844. *See also specific formats.*

file location, network applications, 753–754

File menu, 27–28

file system information, getting, 958–959

File tab, new features, 1254

file types, databases, 5

files, on the CD-ROM, 1267–1270

Filter by Form button, 246

Filter By Group option, 35–36

Filter event, 458–459, 700

Filter Name argument, 1060

Filter On Load property, 309, 653

Filter property, 309, 652

filtering

dialog boxes, 700

by form, 246

forms, 699–700

new features, 1259–1261

records, 242–246

filtering data in forms

with code, 888–889

interactive filter dialog boxes, 892–894

With keyword, 895

linking dialog boxes, 894

with queries, 889–895

wildcards, 890–891

filtering forms

enabling, 310

specifying records for, 309

at startup, 309

filtering selections, 475. *See also* WHERE clauses.

Find and Replace dialog box, 228–230

Find group

Datasheet ribbon, 220

Form ribbon, 293

finding

case sensitivity, 229

data in code, absolute speed, 865–866

fields, 229–230

and replacing records, 220, 228–230

specific values, 228–229

finding data in forms

bookmarks, 885–888

FindRecord method, 883–885

unbound combo boxes, 881–883

FindNext method, absolute speed, 865–866

FindRecord method, 865–866, 883–885

FindWindow API, 775

First option, 657

first/last field values, finding, 657

Fixed format, 61

fixed-width files, importing, 621–623

fixed-width text files, linking to, 596–597

flat-file databases, 95–97, 104–105. *See also* spreadsheets.

focus events, 452

fonts

modifying, 239

Query Design Font option, 650

screen *versus* printer, 308

footers, forms, 311–312

For Each function, absolute speed, 864

For Each statements, 409–410

Index

Force New Page property, 366–367
ForEachRecord action, 560
ForeColor property, 682
foreign keys. *See also* primary keys.
    definition, 20–21
    matching primary keys, 114
Form command, 252, 253–254
form controls
    naming conventions, 285–286
    unsupported, 1175
Form Design command, 252
Form Designer, 38
form errors, SharePoint deployment, 1175–1176
form events, SharePoint deployment, 1175
form layout, modifying controls. *See also* forms, properties.
    aligning controls, 314
    calculated controls, creating, 316
    control properties, 312
    fields, adding to forms, 315–316
    fields, listing, 314–316
    Layout view, 312–315
    tab order, specifying, 313–314
    text, formatting, 314
form modules, 390
Form Name argument, 1060
Form ribbon
    Align Center command, 293
    Align Left command, 293
    Align Right command, 293
    Clipboard group, 292
    Copy command, 292
    Cut command, 292
    Design tab, 314
    Design view, 292
    Find group, 293
    Format Painter command, 292–293
    Gridlines command, 293
    Home tab, 291–293
    Paste Append command, 292
    Paste command, 292
    Paste Special command, 292
    Records group, 293
    Size to Fit Form button, 293
    Sort & Filter group, 293
    Switch Windows button, 293
    Text Formatting group, 293
    Views group, 291–292
    Window group, 293

Form view
    Clipboard group, 292
    creating forms, 290
    enabling, 306
    Home ribbon tab, 291–293
    illustration, 290
    navigating among fields, 294. *See also* Navigation forms.
    navigating among records, 294
    overview, 289–291
    scrolling, 291
    switching to, 290, 291
    Views group, 291–292
Form Wizard command, 252, 254–257
Format event, 462–463
format painter, 696–697
Format Painter command, 292–293
Format properties, 59, 60–61, 283
formatting. *See also* reports, formatting.
    , (comma), thousands separator, 62
    . (period), decimal points, 62
    $ (dollar sign), formatting currency fields, 62
    % (percent sign), formatting percentages, 62
    # (pound sign), hyperlink indicator, 65–66
    # (pound sign), placeholder, 62
    0 (zero), placeholder, 62
    Address property, 66
    AllowZeroLength property, 70–71
    AutoIndex option, 72–73
    color, 61
    control captions, 68–69
    controls, 462–463
    currency fields, 61
    Currency format, 61
    decimal places, 62
    Display Text property, 66
    E+, formatting scientific notation, 62
    e+, formatting scientific notation, 62
    E-, formatting scientific notation, 62
    e-, formatting scientific notation, 62
    Euro format, 61
    Fixed format, 61
    form properties for, 306–309
    General Number format, 61
    Indexed property, 72–73
    indexing by table fields, 72–73
    input, 69–70
    Kanji conversions, 60
    numeric fields, 61–62
    Percent format, 61

placeholders, 62
Required property, 70
Scientific format, 61
Standard format, 61
Sub-Address property, 66
thousands separator, 62
Validation Rule property, 69
Validation Text property, 69
Yes/No fields, 65–66
formatting, date/time fields
: (colon), separating time elements, 63
/ (forward slash), separating time elements, 63
am/pm:, lowercase 12-hour format, 64
AMPM:, uppercase 12-hour format, 64
a/p:, lowercase 12-hour format, 64
A/P:, uppercase 12-hour format, 64
built-in formats, 62–63
c:, General Date format, 63
custom formats, 63–64
d:, formatting day of the month, 63
dd:, formatting day of the month, 63
ddd:, formatting day of the week, 63
dddd:, formatting day of the week, 63
ddddd:, Short Date format, 63
dddddd:, Long Date format, 63
General Date format, 63
h:, formatting hours, 64
hh:, formatting hours, 64
input masks, creating, 68
Long Date format, 63
Long Time format, 63
m:, formatting month of the year, 63
Medium Date format, 63
Medium Time format, 63
mm:, formatting month of the year, 63
mmm:, formatting month of the year, 63
mmmm:, formatting month of the year, 63
n:, formatting minutes, 64
nn:, formatting minutes, 64
q:, formatting quarter of the year, 63
s:, formatting seconds, 64
Short Date format, 63
Short Time format, 63
ss:, formatting seconds, 64
tttt:, Long Time format, 64
w:, formatting day of the week, 63
ww:, formatting week of the year, 63
y:, formatting day of the year, 63

yy:, formatting two digit year, 63
yyyy:, formatting four digit year, 63
formatting, input masks
: (colon), date/time separator, 67
, (comma), thousands separator, 67
. (period), decimal points, 67
; (semicolon), input mask separator, 67
A, required letter or digit indicator, 67
a, optional letter or digit indicator, 67
& (ampersand), any character or digit required, 67
\ (backslash), literal text indicator, 67
- (dash), input mask separator, 67
! (exclamation point), displaying input masks, 67
/ (forward slash), input mask separator, 67
> (greater-than sign), convert to uppercase, 67
< (less-than sign), convert to lowercase, 67
(pound sign), optional digit indicator, 67
? (question mark), optional letter indicator, 67
0 (zero), required digit indicator, 67
9 (nine), optional digit indicator, 67
C, any character or digit optional, 67
Input Mask property, 66–68
Input Mask Wizard, 67–68
L, required letter indicator, 67
phone numbers, 66–68
Social Security numbers, 66–68
formatting, memo fields
& (ampersand), optional character indicator, 64
@ (at sign), required character indicator, 64
> (greater-than sign), convert to uppercase, 64
< (less-than sign), convert to lowercase, 64
examples, 65
formatting, text fields
& (ampersand), optional character indicator, 64
@ (at sign), required character indicator, 64
> (greater-than sign), convert to uppercase, 64
< (less-than sign), convert to lowercase, 64
examples, 65
input masks, creating, 68
painting formats, 292–293
formatting reports
aligning control labels, 736
blank lines, inserting, 731–733
bulleted lists, 723–725
centering titles, 736
color, 368–369
column layout, specifying, 745
column spacing, specifying, 745

Index

formatting reports (*continued*)
  date and time, adding, 372
  Detail section adjustments, 370–371
  even-odd page printing, 733–735
  expressions in group headers, 369–370
  graphic rules, 368–369
  hiding/showing controls, 725–727
  horizontal lines between sections, 730
  item size, specifying, 745
  micro-adjusting controls, 736–737
  number of columns, specifying, 745
  numbered lists, 720–723
  overview, 367–368
  page header adjustments, 368–369
  Page Setup dialog box, 745–747
  report headers, creating, 371–372
  row spacing, specifying, 745
  at runtime, 735–736
  snaking columns, 741–747
  two-sided printing, 733–735
  vertical lines between columns, 729–730
  white space, inserting, 731–733
forms. *See also* controls; designing forms; subforms; VBA
      events, forms.
  absolute speed, 859–861
  always on top, 310
  assigning as start-up forms, 929–930
  border style, 307
  bulletproofing, 928
  buttons, adding, 385–386
  centering, 307
  class module, displaying, 311
  Close button, displaying, 307
  closing, 469–470
  commenting, 311
  confirming deletions, 470–471
  control menu, displaying, 307
  converting to reports, 316
  corrupted, 874
  creating, 290
  custom ribbon, specifying, 311
  data display, 11–12
  data events, 458–459
  data source, specifying, 309
  datasheet, 262
  Datasheet view, enabling, 306
  default values, retrieving, 310
  default view, specifying, 306
  displaying one at a time, 914

displaying selected data, 134
dividing lines, displaying, 306
edits, enabling, 310
footers, displaying, 311–312
Form view, enabling, 306
grids, specifying points per inch, 308
headers, displaying, 311–312
Help context ID, displaying, 311
Help file, specifying, 311
hiding *versus* closing, 868
Layout view, enabling, 306
login, 910–911
menu bar, specifying an alternative, 311
Min/Max buttons, displaying, 307
morphing, 868
movement, enabling, 308
multiple-item, 260–261
multi-table, editing, 310
naming, 256
Navigation, 257–260
navigation buttons, captioning, 309
navigation buttons, displaying, 306
new features, 1261–1262
new record content, specifying, 310
as objects, 1008
opening, 468–469
palette source, 308
printing, 300–301, 311
record deletion, enabling, 310
record locks, 310
Record Selector, displaying, 306
versus reports, 322
resizing, 263
resizing automatically, 307
saving, 256, 263
saving records, 300
screen fonts *versus* printer fonts, 308
scroll bars, displaying, 306
SharePoint deployment, creating, 1169–1170
shortcut menu bars, specifying an alternative, 311
shortcut menus, enabling, 311
sorting data, 309
specifications, 1248–1249
split, 261–262, 309
SQL Server conversions, 1234
startup display, selecting, 1085
switchboards, 912
Tab key behavior, specifying, 311
tabular, 260–261

tagging, 311
title bar caption, 306
toolbar, specifying, 311
verifying, 466–468
view orientation, 308
width, displaying, 307
forms, creating with
AutoForm, 253
Form command, 253–254
Form Wizard, 254 257
forms, data entry
controls, 22. *See also specific controls.*
creating, 11–12
designing, 22
graphical objects, 22
labels, 22
overview, 11–12
text-box data-entry fields, 22
forms, filtering
enabling, 310
specifying records for, 309
at startup, 309
forms, filtering data
with code, 888–889
interactive filter dialog boxes, 892–894
With keyword, 895
linking dialog boxes, 894
with queries, 889–895
wildcards, 890–891
forms, finding data
bookmarks, 885–888
FindRecord method, 883–885
unbound combo boxes, 881–883
forms, pictures
aligning, 308
as background, 307
display mode, specifying, 307
embedded *versus* linked, 307
tiling, 308
forms, properties
connecting to data sources, 304
creating bound forms, 304
for data, 309–310
displaying data, 304–305
for formatting, 306–309
list of, 306–311. *See also specific properties.*
overview, 301
Record Selector, removing, 305

setting, 302
title bar text, 303
forms, split
editing, enabling, 309
orientation, 309
printing, 309
resizing, 309
forms, Splitter Bar
displaying, 309
position, saving, 309
forms, submacros
data entry mode, specifying, 1061
filters, selecting, 1060
form name, specifying, 1060
opening view, specifying, 1060
queries, selecting, 1060
Where clause, inserting, 1061
window mode, specifying, 1061
Forms option, 36
For...Next statements, 405–406, 408–409
forward slash (/)
input mask separator, 67
separating time elements, 63
freezing records, 242
FROM clause, 480–484
FROM keyword, 475
FunctionName parameter, 946
functions
in query data, 598
in select queries, 192. *See also* operators, in queries.
versus subroutines, Windows API, 946
functions, VBA. *See also* VBA procedures.
calling, 436
creating, 441–442
definition, 380
description, 388–389
versus procedures, 436

G

Gallery controls, 1014–1015
General Date format, 63
General Number format, 61
General Protection Fault, 944
General tab, 530
GetClassNameA function, 960–961
GetCommandLineA function, 952–953
GetComputerNameA function, 956–957

Index

GetDriveTypeA function, 957–958
getLabel attribute, 1028
GetObject function, 797–799
GetOption method, 927
GetParent function, 960
GetPrivateProfileIntA function, 964
GetPrivateProfileStringA function, 963–964
GetProfileStringA function, 965
GetProperty function, 685–686
GetSystemDirectoryA function, 959–960
GetTempPathA function, 953–954
GetUserNameA function, 956
GetVersionExA·function, 954–955
GetVolumeInformationA function, 958–959
GetWindowsDirectoryA function, 953
GetWindowTextA function, 960
global modules. *See* standard modules.
global scope, 426
go to a specific record, 220
GotFocus event, 457, 460
graphic rules, in reports, 368–369, 730
graphical objects. *See also* pictures.
    data-entry forms, 22
    tracking, 950
graphs, data type. *See* OLE Object data type.
graying out controls, 682
greater-than, equal (>=), greater-than-or-equal-to
        operator, 177
greater-than sign (>)
    convert to uppercase, 64, 67
    Date comparison operator, 152
    greater-than operator, 177, 188
    in select queries, 188
Grid X property, 308
Grid Y property, 308
gridlines
    aligning objects with, 276–277
    forms, specifying points per inch, 308
    hiding/showing, 220, 239, 293
    modifying appearance of, 240
    snapping to, 276–277
Gridlines command
    Datasheet ribbon, 220
    Form ribbon, 293
Group By fields, criteria for, 662
Group By option, 655, 661–662
Group command, 278–279
group data, defining for reports, 326–327
Group Footer property, 362

Group Footer section, 341–342, 344
group footers, 361–364
Group Header property, 362
Group Header section, 341–342, 343–344
Group Interval property, 363
Group On property, 362
grouping
    controls, 278–279
    objects in the Navigation Pane, 34
grouping report data
    alphabetical headings, 712–714
    alphabetically, 710–714
    on date intervals, 714–716
    hiding page headers, 719
    hiding repeating information, 716–718
    intervals, 327
    into levels, 325–326
    resetting page numbers, by group, 719–720
grouping report data headers
    creating, 361–363
    deleting, 364
    expressions in, 369–370
groups, on ribbons, 1016, 1020–1022, 1025–1026

H

h:, formatting hours, 64
handled errors, 823
hardening. *See* bulletproofing.
hardware errors, troubleshooting, 920
Has Module property, 311
headers
    forms, 311–312
    page, 368–369, 719
    reports, 361–364, 719
headers, group
    Currency data type, 363
    Date/Time data type, 362
    expressions in, 369–370
    Number data types, 363
    Text data types, 362
Height property, 683
Hello World example, 1050–1052, 1065–1069
help
    Auto Data Tips option, 543–544
    Auto List Members, 396
    Auto Quick Info, 396–397
    for CD-ROM, 1270
    Compatibility Checker, 1160

control tips, on forms, 697
Intellisense, 395–397
for options, 396–397
for the ribbon, 1015
SuperTips, 1015
for syntax, 528–529
for variables, 543–544
help, VBA
Auto List Members, 396
Auto Quick Info, 396–397
Intellisense, 395–397
`Help Context ID` property, 311
`Help` file, specifying, 311
`Help File` property, 311
`hh:`, formatting hours, 64
`Hide Duplicates` property, 718
`HideHeader` function, 719
hiding
fields in queries, 145–147
system objects, 1090
hiding/showing
controls, 463, 682, 684
datasheet values, 231
fields, 241
form values, 231
forms in reports, 741
macro results, 1055, 1056
page headers, 719
records, 237
repeating report information, 716–718
report controls, 725–727
result fields, 647
highest/lowest field values, finding, 657
highlighting alternate records, 220, 239–241
Home tab
Access 2010 ribbon, 36
Datasheet ribbon, 219–221
Form ribbon, 291–293
Form view, 291–293
Hopper, Grace, 524
horizontal lines, in reports, 368–369, 730
`Hour` property, 362
hourglass, changing cursor to, 1054–1055
`Hourglass` action, 1054–1055
hourglass cursor, 868
HTML data, linking to, 583, 587, 594–595
HTML documents, exporting, 627–628
`hwnd` parameter, 950

`Hyperlink` data type, 49, 54
hyphen (-)
input mask separator, 67
range indicator, 181
in select queries, 188
subtraction operator, 173–174, 188

I

icons, application, 1085
identifiers, color coding, 419–420
identity fields, 1189
`#If` compiler directive, 413–414
`#If` directive, 535–537
`If...Then...Else...Endif` statements, 401–403
`If...Then...Endif` statements, 401–403
`IIF` function *versus* `If...Then...Else`, 864
`imageMso`, specifying, 1035–1037
`IMEMode` property, 60
`IMESentence Mode` property, 60
`Immediate` window, 399–401, 538–539, 541. *See also* debug window.
implicit variables. *See also* explicit variables; VBA, variables.
declaring, 423
effects on performance, 430
versus explicit, 430
`Import` group, 610
Import Specification dialog box, 624–625
importing external data. *See also* external tables, linking to.
Access objects, 628–630
canceling, 633
dBase tables, 631–632
definition, 581
error handling, 633
from Excel spreadsheets, 614–618
HTML documents, 627–628
versus linking and exporting, 582
from other Access databases, 611–613
Outlook folders, 630–631
with a scheduled Outlook task, 614
from SharePoint lists, 618
troubleshooting, 633–634
uses for, 583–584
XML documents, 625–627
importing external data, from text files
CSV (comma-separated values), 618–623
duplicate primary keys, 621
field separators, 620
fixed-width files, 621–623

Index

importing ribbon customizations, 1022
In operator, 184–185, 188, 203–204
inadequate disk space, 920
Increase Horizontal command, 277
Increase Vertical command, 277
indenting code, 411
indenting lines of code, 418
Indexed property, 60, 72–73
indexed tables, 117
indexing
    data types, 50
    fields, 72–73
    Memo fields, 73
    OLE Object fields, 73
indexing tables
    drawbacks, 83
    effect on performance, 81
    entry order, 79
    IgnoreNulls property, 82
    ignoring null values, 82
    importance of, 80–81
    indexes as primary keys, 82
    naming the index, 81
    natural order, 79
    overview, 78–79
    physical order, 79
    Primary property, 82
    properties, setting, 82–83
    simple indexes, 79
    table scans, 80–81
    Unique property, 82
    uniqueness, specifying, 82
    when to index, 83–84
infinity symbol (∞), table joins, 159, 161
information flow, 912–915
.ini files
    integer values, getting, 964
    string values, getting, 963–964, 965
    writing to, 965–966
INNER JOIN...ON expression, 480–484
inner joins. See equi-joins.
Input Mask property, 59, 66–68
Input Mask Wizard, 67–68
input masks
    creating, 67–68
    on Date/Time data, 225
    formatting with, 67
    Input Mask property, 66–68
    Input Mask Wizard, 67–68

    phone numbers, 66–68
    Social Security numbers, 66–68
insert mode *versus* overtyping, 690
Insert Page method, 701
Insert Rows button, 46
inserting
    data in Word, 806
    pictures in Word, 807
    records, 46
    records in databases, 88
insertion anomalies, 103
insertion point, moving, 231
installation tools, 906
installing CD-ROM files, 1267–1270
Integer data type, VBA, 428
Integer size numeric fields, 52
integrity of data. *See* referential integrity.
Intellisense, 395–397
interactive filter dialog boxes, 892–894
Interval property, 363
Is Not Null operator, 188, 206–208
Is Null operator, 185, 188, 206–208
Item property, 407

J

join issues, 1177
join tables. *See also specific types*.
    Cartesian products, creating, 169–170
    default, 165
    definition, 111
    description, 165
    equi-joins, 122–125, 165–166
    left outer, 166
    orphaned records, 166
    outer, 122–125, 166–167
    right outer, 166–167
    self-joins, 167–169
join tables, query joins
    ad hoc, 161–162
    auto-join line, 161
    Cartesian products, 161, 164
    creating, 160–161
    deleting, 164
    equi-joins, 160
    outer, 163
    type, specifying, 162–163
Join Type button, 122
justifying data in datasheets, 220–221

K

Kanji conversions, 60
Keep Together option, 363
key violations, action queries, 676
keyboard events, 452, 455, 457
KeyDown event, 455, 460
KeyPress event, 455, 460
keys. *See* foreign keys; primary keys.
KeyUp event, 455, 460
keywords
    color coding, 419–420
    VBA, 379

L

L, required letter indicator, 67
Label control, on the ribbon, 1037–1038
label control properties, 359–360
label controls
    moving, 356–358
    pasting, 356
    properties, 359–360
    resizing, 354
labeling controls, 279–280
labels. *See also* controls.
    aligning, 736
    data-entry forms, 22
    highlighting, 352
    mailing, 322–323
    reports, aligning, 736
    on tabs, 702
Last option, 657
last/first field values, finding, 657
late binding, 794–795. *See also* dynamic linking.
latency, troubleshooting, 768–769
Layout for Print property, 308
layout for reports
    adjusting, 330–331
    multiple-page display, 336–337
    Print Preview window, 335–337
    selecting, 329
Layout view
    enabling, 306
    modifying controls, 312–315
    purpose of, 292
layout view, enabling, 1088
Leading Zeros in Dates option, 625
leading zeros in numeric fields, 50

LEFT JOIN...ON expression, 480–484
left outer joins, 166
Left property, 683
less-than, equal (<=), less-than-or-equal-to operator, 177
less-than sign (<)
    convert to lowercase, 64, 67
    Date comparison operator, 152
    less-than operator, 177, 188
    in select queries, 188
library databases, 851–853
library references, 851–853
LibraryName parameter, 947
lifetime, VBA variables, 434–435
Like operator
    description, 179–180
    in select queries, 188
    similar string indicator, 188
    with wildcards, 181, 195–198
line breaks, inserting in forms, 231
lines, graphic. *See* graphic rules.
Link Child Fields property, 652
Link Master Fields property, 652
LinkChildFields property, 686
linked pictures *versus* embedded, 307
Linked Table Manager Wizard, 599–600
linked tables. *See also* external tables, linking to.
    data macros, 576
    external, adding records to, 599
    functions in query data, 598
    limiting external records, 598
    Linked Table Manager Wizard, 599–600
    modifying information, 599–600
    navigating datasheets, 599
    optimizing, 598–599
    relationships , setting, 598
    renaming, 597
    SQL Server conversions, 1235
    view properties, setting, 598
    viewing information, 599–600
linking
    Access to SharePoint lists, 1119–1123
    DAO tables, 600–606
    dialog boxes to forms, 894
    dynamic, 940. *See also* late binding.
    static, 940. *See also* early binding.
    subforms to parent forms, 686–687
linking tables. *See also* external tables, linking to; join tables.
    AttachExcel function, 602–603
    checking links, 606–607

Index

linking tables *(continued)*
  CheckLInks function, 606–607
  with code, 600–606
  Connect property, 600–606
  with DAO, 600–606
  Excel, 602–603
  foreign keys, 20–21
  keys, 20–21
  LinkText function, 604–606
  overview, 19–22
  primary keys, 20–21
  source table, specifying, 600–606
  SourceTableName property, 600–606
  to SQL Server, 1211–1214
  text files, 604–606
linking to
  CSV (comma-separated values), 596–597
  dBase databases, 587
  Excel data, 587, 591–594, 602–603
  external data, 582
  fixed-width text files, 596–597
  HTML data, 583, 587, 594–595
  non-database data, 591–594
  ODBC tables, 588, 590–591
  SharePoint calendars, 1122–1123
  SQL Server tables, 1211–1214
  text files, 587, 604–606
  text tables, 583
linking to external tables. *See also* linked tables; linking tables.
  CSV (comma-separated values), 596–597
  data types supported, 582
  dBase databases, 587
  definition, 581
  disadvantages of, 583
  Excel data, 587, 591–594
  external database tables, 585–587
  fixed-width text files, 596–597
  HTML data, 587, 594–595
  versus importing and exporting, 582
  limitations of, 587–588
  non-database data, 591–594
  ODBC (Object Database Connectivity), 588, 590–591
  other Access databases, 588–590
  text data, 596–597
  text files, 587
  uses for, 582
  xBase files, 591
LinkMasterFields property, 686

links to Internet resources. *See* Hyperlink data type.
LinkText function, 604–606
[list], wildcard character, 181
[!list], wildcard character, 181
list boxes. *See also* combo boxes; controls.
  absolute speed, 861
  forms, 691–693
  selecting items from lists, 299–300
  synchronizing list contents, 682
lists of values, comparing, 203–204
load balancing, 1191–1192
Load event, 457
load on demand, 841–842
local scope, 426
Locals window, 544–545
locations, trusted, 937
locked fields
  editing, 232, 296
  in multiuser environments, 676
locking
  records, 296, 310
  recordsets, 510–511
locking issues
  default, 765
  editing locked records, 232
  page-lock, 764–765
locking issues, record-lock
  All Records option, 766
  built-in features, 765–768
  Default Open Mode option, 766
  default options, 766–768
  Default Record Locking option, 766
  Edited Record option, 766
  No Locks option, 766
  Number of Update Retries option, 767
  ODBC Refresh Interval option, 767
  optimistic locking, 766, 769
  overview, 764–765
  pessimistic locking, 766, 769–772
  Refresh Interval option, 767
  Update Retry Interval option, 768
locking issues, record-lock error handling
  bound forms *versus* unbound, 780–788
  caching, 768–769
  Error 3186: Couldn't save..., 772–774
  Error 3188: Could not update..., 774–775
  Error 3197: Data has changed..., 775–778
  Error 3260: Couldn't update..., 769–772
  ErrorRoutine function, 778–780

latency, 768–769
overview, 768–769
LockType parameter, 769
LogEvent action, 560–561
logging errors, 560–561
logical errors, 820
logical operators. *See* operators, Boolean.
logical values. *See* Yes/No data type.
login forms, 910–911
logos, adding to forms, 695
Long data type, VBA, 428
Long Date format, 63
Long Integer size numeric fields, 52
Long Time format, 63
look and feel, consistency, 1094–1095
lookup errors, 1174–1175
lookup field issues, 1175, 1178
Lookup Wizard data type, 49, 54
LookupRecord action, 560
looping through recordsets, 560. *See also* branching.
losing compiled state, 850–851
LostFocus event, 457, 460
lowest/highest field values, finding, 657

M

m:, formatting month of the year, 63
Macro Designer, 553–562
macro editor, new features, 1264
macro recorder, 808–810
MacroError object, 1073–1074
MacroName property, 1073
macros. *See also* data macros; submacros; VBA; *specific macros.*
    arguments, 1050
    assigning to events, 1052–1054
    bulletproofing, 934–938
    code compatibility, 552
    conditions for execution, 1061–1064
    converting to VBA, 382–384, 1078–1080
    creating, 1050–1052
    definition, 10, 1049
    embedded, 552, 1075–1077
    error handling, 552
    errors, 1177–1178
    groups, 557
    Hello World example, 1050–1052, 1065–1069
    limitations of, 378, 552
    multi-action, 1054–1057

named, 556
naming, 1052
new features, 1256, 1263–1264
purpose of, 10
on ribbons, 1256
settings, 937
specifications, 1249
SQL Server conversions, 1234
temporary variables, 1065–1069
tracking, 552
versus VBA, 382
versus VBA statements, 1077–1078
macros, actions
    cursor, changing to hourglass, 1054–1055
    Echo, 1055, 1056
    hiding/showing macro results, 1055, 1056
    Hourglass, 1054–1055
    incompatibilities, 1177–1178
    macro error handling, getting, 1073
    for mcrBackupContactsAndProducts macro, 1054–1057
    MessageBox, 1055
    messages, displaying, 1055
    opening a query, 1055, 1056
    OpenQuery, 1055, 1056
    SetWarnings, 1054–1055, 1056
    system messages, enabling/disabling, 1054–1055, 1056
macros, debugging
    debug window, 1074
    error information, displaying, 1074
    MessageBox action, 1074
    Single Step dialog box, 1074
    stepping through code, 1074
    StopMacro action, 1074
    stopping macro execution, 1074
macros, error handling
    ActionName property, 1073
    arguments, getting, 1073
    Arguments property, 1073
    condition, getting, 1073
    Condition property, 1073
    Description property, 1073
    error message, getting, 1073
    error number, getting, 1073
    macro action, getting, 1073
    MacroError object, 1073–1074
    MacroName property, 1073
    mcrDivisionErrorHandling macro, 1071–1073

Index

macros, error handling *(continued)*
  name of failed macro, 1073
  `Number` property, 1073
  `OnError` action, 1071–1073
  overview, 1069–1070
mailing-label reports, 322–323
`Make Table Query` action queries, 671, 673
managed applications, 1136
manual filing systems *versus* computerized databases, 4–5
many-to-many table relationships, 110–111
margins of reports, specifying, 348–349
marking records with bookmarks, 866
mathematical operators. *See* operators, mathematical.
`Max` option, 657
`Max Records` property, 652
mcrBackupContactsAndProducts macro, 1054–1057
mcrDivisionErrorHandling macro, 1071–1073
mcrHelloWorldEnhanced macro, 1065
mcrMainMenu macro, 1058
mcrReportMenu macro, 1062–1063
mcrReportMenuEnhanced macro, 1067–1068
.mdb files, security, 752
`Medium Date` format, 63
`Medium Time` format, 63
Memo criteria, 193–195
Memo data, entering, 226–227
Memo data type
  converting to `Text`, 58
  indexing, 50
  overview, 52
  purpose, 48
  sorting, 50
  storage size, 49
Memo fields
  data entry, 297
  formatting, 64
  indexing, 73
  line breaks, inserting, 231
  sorting, 147
memory, absolute speed, 856
memory errors, troubleshooting, 920
memory leaks, 874
menu bar for forms, specifying an alternative, 311
`Menu Bar` property, 311
`MenuBar` property, 683
menus. *See also* the ribbon.
  removing, 913–914
  shortcut menu defaults, specifying, 1090–1091
  shortcut menu display, specifying, 1091

Merge it With Microsoft Word option, 636
message bar, displaying, 937
`MessageBox` action, 1055, 1074
messages. *See also* error messages; `MsgBox` function.
  error information, displaying, 1074
  informational, 915–918
  informational, displaying with actions, 1055
  printing, 537–538
  system, enabling/disabling, 1054–1055, 1056
methods. *See also specific methods*.
  creating, 976–978
  definition, 396
  `Product` class, 974, 995–996
micro-adjusting report controls, 736–737
Microsoft Office button. *See* File button.
Microsoft Word Mail Merge option, 636
migrating Access applications to the Web, 1135, 1138–1140
`Min Max Buttons` property, 307
`Min` option, 657
Min/Max buttons, displaying on forms, 307
minus sign. *See* hyphen.
`Minute` property, 362
`mm:`, formatting month of the year, 63
`mmm:`, formatting month of the year, 63
`mmmm:`, formatting month of the year, 63
`Mod`, modulo division operator, 175–176
Modal Dialog command, 253
`Modal` property, 704
Modified Date option, 35
modifying. *See also* editing.
  control appearance, 277–278
  control type, 270, 280–281
  datasheets, 10
  linked tables, 599–600
  VBA event procedures, 391
modifying, data in datasheets
  adding records, 234
  aligning data, 241
  background color, modifying, 239–241
  coloring alternate records, 239–241
  copying and pasting, 231–233
  deleting records, 234–235
  display fonts, modifying, 239
  editing techniques, 231
  field display width, modifying, 237
  freezing records, 242
  gridlines, hiding/showing, 239
  gridlines, modifying appearance of, 240
  hiding/showing fields, 241

1310

highlighting alternate records, 239–241
protected fields, 231
rearranging fields, 235–236
record display width, modifying, 238
replacing existing values, 230, 233–234
resizing field width, 237
resizing record height, 238
saving changes, 242
undoing changes, 231
modules
absolute speed, 862–866
database objects, 10
forms, 390
report, 390
SQL Server conversions, 1234
standard, 389–390
versus VBA procedures, 380
modules, class. *See also* events; OOP (object-oriented
programming); Product class.
adding to databases, 974–975
bulletproofing property procedures, 980–981
defining objects, 972–973, 978–980
for forms, displaying, 311
methods, 976–978
naming, 974–975
overview, 973–974
properties, 975–976
modules, VBA
creating, 391–392
definition, 380
editing, 393
form, 390
Option Explicit directive, 394
versus procedures, 380
report, 390
sections, 394
standard, 389–390
types of, 389–391
variable declarations section, 394, 427
Modules tab, 539, 543–544
monetary data type. *See* Currency data type.
Month property, 362
More Forms command, 252
morphing
controls, 695–696
forms or reports, 868
mouse events
for controls, 460
definition, 452

for forms, 457
for objects, 455
MouseDown event, 455, 460
MouseMove event, 455, 460
MouseUp event, 455, 460
MouseWheel event, 455
Moveable property, 308
MoveNext method, 497–498
MovePrevious method, 497–498
moving
Access tables to SharePoint, 1127–1131
controls, 271–272, 274–275
fields, 57
forms, enabling, 308
macro items, 572–573
text boxes on reports, 354–355
MsgBox function. *See also* error messages.
confirming deletions, 470–471
constants, 916
debugging technique, 534–535
informational messages, 915–918
parameters, 915–916
return values, 918
multi-action macros, 1054–1057
Multiple Items button, 260–261
Multiple Items command, 253
multiple-item forms, 260–261
MultiRow property, 702
multi-tiered architecture, 1192–1194
multi-value fields, data macros, 575

N

n:, formatting minutes, 64
Name Autocorrect options, 1084, 1091–1092
Name property, 285, 407
named arguments, 447–448, 808
named macros, 556
naming conventions
class modules, 974–975
collections, 407
compound object names, 40
controls, 285–286
databases, 8, 29–30
descriptive names, 40
duplicate names, 39
fields, 45, 47–48
fields and tables, automatic correction, 1091–1092
form controls, 285–286

Index

naming conventions (*continued*)
  forms, 256
  importance of, 39–40
  macros, 1052
  prefixes, 40
  property procedures, 990
  report controls, 285–286, 749
  spaces in names, 40
  SQL Server, 1211
naming conventions, VBA
  collections, 407
  overview, 432
  parameters, 442
  prefixes, 432
  procedures, 435–436
  spaces in names, 423
  subroutines, 435–436
  tags, 432
  variables, 394, 422–423
natural primary keys, 77, 118–119
navigating
  among fields, 294
  among records, 294
  datasheets, 599
  recordsets, 495
  unbound forms, network applications, 783–788
navigating, Datasheet window. *See also* Navigation Pane.
  within a datasheet, 218
  finding specific values, 228–229
  keystrokes for, 218
  Navigation buttons, 218–219
  overview, 227
  between records, 227–228
Navigation buttons, 218–219, 704
navigation buttons, on forms
  captioning, 309
  displaying, 306
  unbound forms, 783–785
Navigation Buttons property, 306
Navigation Caption property, 309
Navigation form, SharePoint deployment, 1170–1171
Navigation Form command, 252
Navigation forms, 257–260. *See also* Form view, navigating.
Navigation options
  Display Navigation Pane check box, 1089
  Navigation Options button/dialog box, 1089–1090
  Navigation Pane, displaying, 1089
  Navigation Pane options, displaying, 1089–1090
  system objects, hiding, 1090

Navigation Options button/dialog box, 1089–1090
Navigation Pane. *See also* Datasheet window, navigating.
  All Access Objects option, 36
  alternate displays, 34
  Created Date option, 35
  custom groups, 34
  Custom option, 34
  displaying, 1089
  Filter By Group option, 35–36
  Forms option, 36
  hiding, 913–914
  Modified Date option, 35
  new features, 1256–1258
  Object Type option, 34
  options, displaying, 1089–1090
  overview, 33
  Queries option, 36
  Reports option, 36
  Tables and Related Views option, 34–35
  Tables option, 36
needs analysis, 14
network applications. *See also* locking issues; SharePoint.
  all files on server, 753
  all files on the client, 754
  client-centric applications, 754–756
  data sources, 754–756
  distributed installation, 753
  file location, 753–754
  opening a database, 756–758
  performance, 752
  SQL pass-through, 755
  transactions, 755–756
network applications, splitting databases
  benefits of, 759–761
  Database Splitter wizard, 762–764
  definition, 753
  placing objects, 761–762
network applications, unbound forms
  versus bound forms, 780–781
  combo boxes, 785
  creating, 781
  editing data, 786–788
  navigating through records, 783–788
  navigation buttons, 783–785
  opening, 782–783
  overview, 780–781
  populating, 782–783
  specifying a recordset for, 782

networks
  local computer name, getting, 956–957
  performance, absolute speed, 866–867
new features
  application parts, 1262
  Backstage area, 1254
  Datasheet view, 1259–1261
  File dialog box, 1255
  File tab, 1254
  filtering options, 1259–1261
  forms, 1261–1262
  macro editor, 1264
  macros, 1263–1264
  macros on ribbons, 1256
  Navigation Pane enhancements, 1256–1258
  Office button, 1254
  publishing to the Web, 1258
  reports, 1263
  the ribbon, 1254–1257
  ribbon editor, 1254–1255
  security, 1265
  SharePoint, 1265
  tabbed interface, 1256
  tables, 1258–1259
  themes, 1261
  user interface, 1253–1258
New keyword, 795–797
New Query dialog box, 667–670
New Values property, 59
9, optional digit indicator, 67
nn:, formatting minutes, 64
No Locks option, 766
No option, 363
NoData event, 461–463
non-aggregate total fields, criteria for, 663–664
non-database data, linking to, 591–594
nonexistent data. See data validation rules.
Normal view, switching to Design view, 37
normalization
  1NF (first normal form), 95–97
  2NF (second normal form), 97–102
  3NF (third normal form), 102
  decomposition, 99
  definition, 9
  deletion anomalies, 103
  denormalization, 102–104
  dependency, 98
  designing databases, 20, 22
  flat-file approach, 95–97

insertion anomalies, 103
overview, 94–95
redundant or repetitive data, 95–97
splitting into tables, 97–102
update anomalies, 99, 103
Not Like operator
  comparing string expressions, 179–180
  dissimilar string indicator, 188
  in select queries, 188
Not operator
  Boolean logic, 180
  negating Boolean expressions, 183
  negation, 188
  searching for non-matching values, 198–199
  in select queries, 188
  toggling properties, 690–691
NotInList event, 460
Null values
  definition, 192
  in primary keys, 113
  in reports, avoiding, 728–729
  searching for, 206–208
  in Yes/No fields, 200
Number data
  automatic validation, 224–225
  entering, 226
Number data type. See also numeric fields.
  converting from AutoNumber, 58
  converting to Currency, 58
  converting to Text, 58
  default value, 59
  group headers, 363
  overview, 52–53
  purpose, 48
  storage size, 49
Number of Update Retries option, 767
Number property, 1073
numbered lists, 720–723
numbers, representing as text. See Text data type.
numeric criteria, 199–200
Numeric fields. See also Number data type.
  Byte size, 52
  calculations, 18
  Decimal size, 52
  Double size, 52
  formatting, 61–62
  Integer size, 52
  leading zeros, 50
  Long Integer size, 52

Index

Numeric fields (continued)
    query selection criteria, 151–152
    Replication ID size, 52
    Single size, 52
    size, specifying, 52–53
    wrong data type, 52

O

Object data type, VBA, 428
Object Designers tab, 650
object hierarchies, listing members of, 411
object hierarchy, displaying, 528
object libraries, Automation, 791–792
object list, sorting, 420
object name violations, 1176
Object Type option, 34
object variables, Automation, 791–792
object-oriented programming (OOP). See OOP
       (object-oriented programming).
objects. See also OOP (object-oriented programming).
    in applications, 971
    defining, 972–973, 978–980
    initializing, 997–998
    overview, 970–971
    terminating, 998–999
obsolete databases. See compatibility with older databases.
ODBC drivers, exporting through, 635
ODBC Refresh Interval option, 767
ODBC (Object Database Connectivity) tables
    configuration options for SQL Server, 1204
    linking to, 588, 590–591
ODBC Time-out property, 652
Office Backstage view. See Backstage area.
Office button, new features, 1254
Office Compatible certification, 1095
Office macro recorder, 808–810
OK button, 313–314
OLE Automation. See Automation.
OLE Object data, entering, 226
OLE Object data type
    converting to other data types, 58
    description, 54
    indexing, 50, 73
    sorting, 50, 147
    types of data stored, 49
OLE objects
    copying, 296–297
    inserting in forms, 296–297

query criteria, 201
resizing, 297
On Error GoTo 0 statements, 831
On Error GoTo Label statements, 830–831
On Error Resume Next statements, 831–832
On Error statements, trapping errors, 825–826
On Format event, 462–463
On Print event, 462–463
OnAction attribute, 1024
1NF (first normal form), 95–97
OnError action, 561, 1071–1073
one-to-many table relationships, 108–110
one-to-one table relationships, 107–108
online templates. See templates.
OnRetreat event, 462–463
OOP (object-oriented programming). See also class modules;
       events; objects; property procedures.
    benefits of, 981–986
    cardinal rules for, 985–986
    class events, 997–999
    Class_Initialize event procedure, 997–998
    Class_Terminate event procedure, 998–999
    description, 970
    encapsulation, 982
    managing class interfaces, 983–985
    simplifying tasks, 982–983
    user interfaces, revealing, 985
Open dialog box
    browsing to dBase files, 631–632
    exclusive database opening, 757, 855
Open event, 457, 461
Open method, 510–512
OpenContacts, 1058
OpenDatabase method, 758
OpenForm action, 1060–1061
opening
    CD-ROM files, 1267–1270
    datasheets, 221
    forms, 468–469
    queries with macro actions, 1055, 1056
    reports with conditions, 1061–1064
    ribbons, 1045–1046
    tables, 510
    unbound forms, network applications, 782–783
opening a database
    exclusively, 756–758
    network applications, 756–758
    for sharing, 756–758
OpenProducts, 1058

OpenQuery action, 1055, 1056
OpenSales, 1058
operands, definition, 171
operators. *See also* expressions.
    In (list comparison), 184–185, 188
    Between...And (range indicator), 184, 188
    Is Not Null (not-null value indicator), 188
    Is Null (null value indicator), 185, 188
operators, Boolean (logical)
    And, 180, 182, 188
    list of, 180
    Not, 183, 188
    Or, 182–183, 188
    precedence, 187
operators, comparison
    > (greater than), 177, 188
    >= (greater-than, equal), 177
    = (equal sign), equal, 176, 188
    < (less-than sign), less-than, 177, 188
    <= (less-than sign, equal), less-than-or-equal-to, 177
    < > (angle brackets), not-equal, 176, 188, 198–199
    list of, 176
    precedence, 186
operators, in queries
    And, 188, 204–205
    In, 188, 203–204
    > (greater than), 188
    & (ampersand), concatenate, 188
    * (asterisk), multiplication, 188
    * (asterisk), wildcard character, 195–198
    "..." (double quotes), literal indicator, 194
    = (equal sign), equal, 188
    ! (exclamation character), Not operator, 195–198
    – (hyphen), subtraction, 188
    < (less-than sign), less-than, 188
    + (plus sign), addition, 188
    ? (question mark), wildcard character, 195–198
    '...' (single quotes), criteria string indicator, 194
    / (slash), division, 188
    < > (angle brackets), not-equal, 188, 198–199
    [ ] (square brackets), referencing fields, 192–193
    Between...And, 188, 205–206
    Boolean, 188
    character criteria, 193–195
    comparison, 188
    complex criteria, 189–192
    complex queries, 212–213
    functions, 192
    Is Not Null, 188, 206–208

Is Null, 188, 206–208
Like, 188, 195–198
list of, 188
lists of values, 203–204
mathematical, 188
Memo criteria, 193–195
for multiple fields, 208–213
multiple values, specifying, 201–203
non-matching values, 198–199
Not, 188, 198–199
Not Like, 188
Null values, 192, 206–208
numeric criteria, 199–200
OLE object criteria, 201
And operator, 208–212
Or, 188, 201–203, 208–212
overview, 187
pattern searches, 197–198
ranges of values, 204–206
referencing fields, 192–193
select queries, 192–193
spaces, 196
string, 188
Text criteria, 193–195
true/false criteria, 200
wildcards, 195–198
operators, mathematical
    * (asterisk), multiplication, 174, 188
    ^ (caret), exponentiation, 175
    – (hyphen), subtraction, 173–174, 188
    + (plus sign), addition, 173, 179, 188
    / (slash), division, 174, 175, 188
    list of, 173
    Mod, 175–176
    overview, 172
    precedence, 185–186
    rounding, 175
operators, string
    & (ampersand), concatenation operator, 173, 178–179, 188
    * (asterisk), wildcard character, 181
    "..." (double quotes), around returned strings, 178
    – (hyphen), range indicator, 181
    # (pound sign), wildcard character, 181
    ? (question mark), wildcard character, 181
    [ ] (square brackets), pattern indicator, 181
    Like (similar strings), 179–180, 181, 188
    [list], wildcard character, 181
    [!list], wildcard character, 181

Index

operators, string (*continued*)
  list of, 178
  Not Like (dissimilar strings), 179–180, 188
  wildcards, 181
optimistic locking, 766, 769
optimizing applications. *See also* performance.
  .accdb file format, 844–846
  default database file format, 845–846
  load on demand, 841–842
  pruning the call tree, 842–844
  supported file formats, 844
optimizing applications, absolute speed
  changing variables, 864
  closing unused applications, 856
  combo boxes, 861
  compacting databases, 855–856
  comparing variables, 864
  control variables, 864–865
  data types, 862–863
  dead code, removing, 866
  definition, 854
  defragmenting hard drives, 856
  For Each function, 864
  field variables, 865
  finding data in code, 865–866
  FindNext method, 865–866
  FindRecord method, 865–866
  forms, 859–861
  With function, 864
  IIF function *versus* If...Then...Else, 864
  list boxes, 861
  marking records with bookmarks, 866
  memory, 856
  modules, 862–866
  network performance, 866–867
  overview, 854–855
  queries, 858–859
  reports, 859–861
  Requery method *versus* Requery action, 864
  resolving references, OLE automation, 864
  routines, 863–866
  swap files, 856
  table indexes, 856–858
  tuning the system, 856
  unused variables, removing, 866
optimizing applications, .accde files
  application demos, 847
  converting to normal database files, 847
  creating, 847–848

distributing, 846–848
  restrictions, 847
optimizing applications, Compile on Demand option
  checking status of, 843
  compiled state, 848–854
  overview, 843–844
  turning off, 843
optimizing applications, compiled state
  creating, 849–850
  distributing applications, 851–854
  library databases, 851–853
  library references, 851–853
  losing, 850–851
  overview, 848–854
  storing code, 851–853
optimizing applications, large databases
  average size, 872
  compacting, 874–875
  compiling, 874–875
  corrupted forms, 874
  decompile option, 876
  growth rate, 873
  memory leaks, 874
  minimizing changes, 879
  pre-release steps, 877
  rebooting, 874
  recompiling automatically, 877
  recreating, 874–875
  uncompiled databases, detecting, 877–878
optimizing applications, perceived speed
  definition, 867
  forms, hiding *versus* closing, 868
  hourglass cursor, 868
  morphing forms or reports, 868
  progress meter, 869–872
  splash screens, 867–868
optimizing databases
  average size, 872
  compacting, 874–875
  compiling, 874–875
  corrupted forms, 874
  decompile option, 876
  growth rate, 873
  memory leaks, 874
  minimizing changes, 879
  pre-release steps, 877
  rebooting, 874
  recompiling automatically, 877

recreating, 874–875
uncompiled databases, detecting, 877–878
option buttons, 231. *See also* controls.
option groups, 298–299. *See also* controls; radio buttons.
options, help for, 396–397
Options dialog box
    Auto Data Tips option, 412, 529, 543–544
    Auto Indent option, 411
    Auto List Members option, 411, 528
    Auto Quick Info option, 528
    Auto Syntax Check option, 411, 525–527
    Break on all Errors option, 411
    Compile on Demand option, 411, 530
    Editor tab, 410–412, 525–530
    General tab, 530
    Modules tab, 539, 543–544
    Require Variable Declaration option,
        411, 527–528
    Step Into button, 543
    Step Out button, 543
    Step Over button, 543
Option Explicit directive, 394
Or operations
    maximum number of, 203
    QBE (Query by Example) grid, 202–203
Or operator
    across fields in a query, 208–212
    Boolean logic, 180, 188
    with And operator, 211–212
    in queries, 188, 201–203
    results of, 183
ORDER BY clause, 475, 484
Order By On Load property, 309, 653
Order By property, 309, 652
orientation of reports, specifying, 348–349
Orientation property, 308, 652
orphaned records, 114, 166
Other properties, 283
outer joins, 122–125, 166–167. *See also* equi-joins.
Outlook, Automation example
    collecting data, 811–818
    creating e-mail, 811–815
    managing e-mail replies, 815–818
Output All Fields option, 650
Output All Fields property, 651
overall database design, 13–14
overlapping windows, specifying, 1086–1087
Overlapping Windows interface, 915
overtyping *versus* insert mode, 690

P

padlock icon, 223
page breaks, reports, 366–367
Page event, 461
Page Footer section, 341–342, 344–345
Page Header section, 341–342, 343
page headers, appearance adjustments, 368–369
page numbers (forms), 694
page numbers (reports)
    adding, 353
    in footers, 344–345
    resetting by group, 719–720
Page Setup dialog box, 745–747
page size, reports, 348–349
painting formats, 292–293
Palette Source property, 308
paper size, reports, 348–349
parallel processing, 1190
parameters, VBA
    definition, 388, 442
    naming conventions, 442
    passing to functions, 443–445
    sales tax calculation (example), 445–447
parent window handles, getting, 960
parent/child table relationships, 108–110
partition pruning, 1190
partitioning databases, 1190
passing values
    ByVal *versus* ByRef, 948
    with local variables, 561
passwords
    hiding, 911
    removing, 931–933
Paste Append command
    Datasheet ribbon, 220
    description, 233
    Form ribbon, 292
Paste command
    Datasheet ribbon, 220
    description, 233
    Form ribbon, 292
Paste Special command
    Datasheet ribbon, 220
    description, 233
    Form ribbon, 292
Paste Table As dialog box, 86–87
pasting. *See* cutting/copying/pasting.
pattern searches, 181, 197–198

Index

pencil icon, 223
perceived speed. *See also* absolute speed; optimizing
      applications.
   definition, 867
   forms, hiding *versus* closing, 868
   hourglass cursor, 868
   morphing forms or reports, 868
   progress meter, 869–872
   splash screens, 867–868
Percent format, 61
percent sign (%), formatting percentages, 62
performance. *See also* optimizing applications.
   implicit variables *versus* explicit, 430
   large collections, effects of, 408
   network applications, 752
period (.)
   date delimiter, 625
   decimal points, 62, 67
   in With keyword, 895
   table and field name separator, 174
permissions, SharePoint, 1121
personal information, removing on save, 1088
pessimistic locking, 766, 769–772
phone numbers
   data types, 50
   formatting, 66–68
Picture Alignment property, 308
Picture property, 307, 702
Picture Property Storage Format option,
      1084, 1088–1089
Picture Size Mode property, 307
Picture Tiling property, 308
Picture Type property, 307
pictures
   copying, 296–297
   form background, 697–699
   graphical objects, data-entry forms, 22
   graphical objects, tracking, 950
   image control, 695
   inserting in forms, 296–297
   inserting in Word, 807
   OLE Object data type, 49–50, 54, 58
   resizing, 297
   specifying storage format, 1088–1089
pictures, on forms
   aligning, 308
   as background, 307
   display mode, specifying, 307

embedded *versus* linked, 307
   tiling, 308
Pivot Table command, 253
pivot tables, 464
PivotChart command, 253
PivotChart view, 292
PivotTable events, 464
PivotTable view, 291
PivotTableChange event, 464
placeholders, 62
plagiarism, user interface, 1095
plus sign (+), addition operator
   calculating fields, 173
   concatenating strings, 173, 179
   description, 173
   in select queries, 188
Pop Up property, 310, 704
populating unbound forms, 782–783
population variance, calculating, 657
pound sign (#)
   Date comparisons, 152
   hyperlink indicator, 65–66
   optional digit indicator, 67
   placeholder, 62
   wildcard character, 181
pound signs (#####), in numeric fields, 1088
precedence
   Boolean operations, 187
   comparison operations, 186
   mathematical operations, 185–186
Prefix Characters property, 362
prefixes, naming conventions, 40, 432
Preserve Source Image Format option, 1084,
      1088–1089
previewing reports, 249, 335–340
primary keys. *See also* foreign keys.
   adding records to tables, 119
   benefits of, 117
   choosing, 115–116
   composite, 118
   composite, setting, 77
   constraints, 1175
   creating, 115, 119
   definition, 20–21, 105
   deriving, 116
   designating, 118–119
   duplicate, 621
   entity integrity, 76
   importance of, 115

importing text files, 621
indexed tables, 117
matching foreign keys, 114
natural, 77, 118–119
null values, 113
setting, 76–77
single, 118
specifying, 46
surrogate, 77, 118–119
Print event, 462–463
print events, 452
Print method, 537–538
Print Preview, 249, 335–340, 741
Print Preview command, 249
Print Preview window, 335–337
printer fonts, *versus* screen fonts, 308
printing. *See also* reports.
    datasheets, 248–249
    forms, 300–301, 311
    messages, 537–538
    recordsets, 153
    reports, 338–340
    table design, 84–85
privacy settings, 937–938
Private keyword, 427
private scope, 427, 432–434
problems. *See* error handling; troubleshooting.
procedures, VBA. *See also* VBA, event procedures; VBA
        functions; VBA subroutines.
    Call statement, 437
    calling, 437
    calling from data macros, 576
    compiling, 397
    creating, 395, 397–399, 436
    definition, 380
    editing, 399
    versus modules, 380
    naming conventions, 435–436
    scope, 432–434
    testing in Immediate window, 399–401
Product class. *See also* class modules; OOP (object-oriented
        programming).
    creating, 972–974
    methods, 974
    methods, adding, 995–996
    modifying, 991–996
    ProductID property, 993–994
    properties, 973

properties, adding, 994–995
retrieving product details, 992
ProductID property, 993–994
progress meters, 869–872, 918–919
Project Description option, 413
Project Name option, 413
Project Properties dialog box, 412–414
properties. *See also* control properties; fields (columns),
        properties.
    ActionName, 1073
    Address, 66
    Allow Additions, 310
    Allow Datasheet View, 306
    Allow Deletions, 310
    Allow Edits, 310
    Allow Filters, 310
    Allow From View, 306
    Allow Layout View, 306
    Allow PivotTable View, 306
    AllowBypassKey, 925
    AllowZeroLength, 60, 70–71
    Arguments, 1073
    Auto Center, 307
    Auto Resize, 307
    BackColor, 682
    Border Style, 307, 360
    BorderStyle, 704
    of a class, creating, 975–976
    Close Button, 307
    collections, 407
    Column Headings, 653
    Condition, 1073
    Connect, 600–606
    Control Box, 307
    Control Source, 284
    ControlSource, 691–693
    Count, 407
    CursorType, 496–497
    Custom Ribbon ID, 311
    Cycle, 311
    DAO, 486–487
    Data Entry, 310
    Day, 362
    DecimalPlaces, 59
    Default View, 306, 651
    DefaultValue, 59
    definition, 282
    Description, 651, 1073
    Dest Connect Str, 653

Index

properties (*continued*)
Destination DB, 653
Destination Table, 653
Display Text, 66
displaying, 282–283
Dividing Lines, 306
Enabled, 682
Fail on Error, 653
Fast Laser Printing, 311
Fetch Defaults, 310
FieldSize, 59
Filter, 309, 652
Filter On Load, 653
Filter on Load, 309
Force New Page, 366–367
ForeColor, 682
Format, 59
Format property, 60–61
forms, setting, 302
Grid X, 308
Grid Y, 308
Group Footer, 362
Group Header, 362
Group Interval, 363
Group On, 362
Has Module, 311
Height, 683
Help Context ID, 311
Help File, 311
Hide Duplicates, 718
Hour, 362
IMEMode, 60
IMESentence Mode, 60
Indexed, 60, 72–73
Input Mask, 59, 66–68
Interval, 363
Item, 407
Layout for Print, 308
Left, 683
Link Child Fields, 652
Link Master Fields, 652
LinkChildFields, 686
LinkMasterFields, 686
MacroName, 1073
Max Records, 652
Menu Bar, 311
MenuBar, 683
Min Max Buttons, 307
Minute, 362

Modal, 704
Month, 362
Moveable, 308
MultiRow, 702
Name, 285, 407
Navigation Buttons, 306
Navigation Caption, 309
New Values, 59
Number, 1073
ODBC Time-out, 652
Order By, 309, 652
Order By On Load, 309, 653
Orientation, 308, 652
Output All Fields, 651
Palette Source, 308
Picture, 307, 702
Picture Alignment, 308
Picture Size Mode, 307
Picture Tiling, 308
Picture Type, 307
Pop Up, 310, 704
Prefix Characters, 362
Product class, 973, 994–995
ProductID, 993–994
Qtr, 362
for queries, 651–653
Record Locks, 310, 652
Record Selectors, 306
Record Source, 309
RecordCount, 498–499
RecordSelectors, 704
Recordset Type, 310, 652
RecordSource, 271
Required, 60, 70–71
RowSource, 682, 691–693
Running Sum, 344
Save Splitter Bar Position, 309
Scroll Bars, 306, 704
Shortcut Menu, 311
Shortcut Menu Bar, 311
ShortcutMenu, 683, 704
ShortcutMenuBar, 683
SizeMode, 297
SmartTags, 60
Source Connect Str, 652
Source Database, 652
SourceTableName, 600–606
Split Form Datasheet, 309
Split Form Orientation, 309

`Split Form Printing`, 309
`Split Form Size`, 309
`Split Form Splitter Bar`, 309
`Style`, 702
`Sub-Address`, 66
`Subdatasheet Expanded`, 308, 653
`Subdatasheet Height`, 308, 653
`Subdatasheet Name`, 652
`Tab Index`, 314
`Tab Stop`, 314
`TabFixedHeight`, 702
`TabFixedWidth`, 702
tables, specifying, 46–47
`TabStop`, 22
`Tag`, 311, 782
for the `tblCustomers` field, 73–76
`Toolbar`, 311
`Top`, 683
`Top Values`, 651
`UnicodeCompression`, 60
`Unique Records`, 651
`Unique Values`, 651
`Use Default Paper Size`, 311
`Use Transaction`, 653
`Validation Rule`, 60, 69
`Validation Text`, 60, 69
`Value`, 702
viewing linked tables, setting, 598
`Visible`, 682, 684
`Week`, 362
`Width`, 307, 683
`Year`, 362
properties, `Caption`
    dynamic setting, 682
    for form title bars, 306
    naming conventions, 285
    setting at runtime, 682
    tab labels, setting, 702
properties, `Each Value`
    Currency data types, 363
    Date/Time data types, 362
    Number data types, 363
    Text data types, 362
`Property Get`, 986, 989
`Property Let`, 986, 988
property procedures. *See also* OOP (object-oriented
        programming).
    assigning values to, 986, 988
    bulletproofing, 980–981

data types, 990–991
getting, 986, 988–989
naming conventions, 990
`Property Get`, 986, 989
`Property Let`, 986, 988
`Property Set`, 986, 988
property value persistence, 989–990
read-only access, 987
read/write access, 987
rules, 990–991
setting, 986
write-only access, 987
`Property Set`, 986, 988
Property Sheet
    Data properties, 283
    displaying, 282–283
    Event properties, 283
    form properties, 302–311
    Format properties, 283
    Other properties, 283
    setting properties, 283
    tables, 46–47
Property Sheet button, 46–47
property values
    getting, 927
    persistence, 989–990
    setting, 926–927
protected fields, 231
pruning the call tree, 842–844
`Public` keyword, 426
public scope, 426, 432–434
public-facing Web sites, 1141–1143
Publish to Access Service button, enabling,
        1139–1140
publishers, trusted, 937
publishing to the Web
    new features, 1258
    SharePoint deployment, 1156–1157, 1164–1173

Q

`q:`, formatting quarter of the year, 63
QBE (Query by Example) grid
    columns, resizing, 143–144
    description, 137
    Or operations, 202–203
    resizing columns, 143
    table names, viewing, 155–156

Index

QBE (Query by Example) grid, fields
  adding, 156
  aliases, specifying, 144–145
  displaying, 145–147
  hiding, 145–147
  inserting, 144
  removing, 144
  selecting, 142
QBE pane, hiding/showing Total row, 654
Qtr property, 362
queries. *See also* QBE (Query by Example); SQL
      (Structured Query Language).
  absolute speed, 858–859
  adding, 137
  counting records, 642–644
  creating, 10–11, 135–138
  crosstab, 133
  definition, 130
  displaying selected data, 134
  errors, 1176–1177
  example, 11
  field aliases, 649
  filtering data, 889–895
  forms, displaying selected data, 134
  hiding result fields, 647
  invalid names, 1177
  join issues, 1177
  modifying data, 134
  for multiple tables, 153–157
  overview, 10–11, 130–133
  performing calculations, 134
  renaming fields, 647–649
  reports, displaying selected data, 134
  saving, 138, 153
  saving field selections, 646–649
  select, 133
  selection criteria, specifying, 134
  sorting records, 134
  specialized, 133
  specifications, 1248
  SQL Server conversions, 1234
  SQL statements, displaying, 136
  subqueries, 134
  top(*n*) records, 133, 644–646
  total, 133
  types of, 133
  uses for, 134

queries, action
  creating, 671–675
  data-type errors, 676
  definition, 133
  key violations, 676
  record-locked fields in multiuser environments, 676
  running, 675–676
  troubleshooting, 676
  truncating text data, 676
  types of, 671
  updating records, 672–673
queries, fields
  adding, 138–140, 156
  aliases, specifying, 144–145
  choosing, 134
  displaying, 145–147
  field lists, 159
  field selector, 142
  hiding, 145–147
  inserting, 144
  names, displaying, 136
  rearranging, 142–143
  removing, 144
  resizing columns, 143
  selecting, 142
  selecting in the QBE grid, 142
  updating, 158
queries, recordsets
  definition, 131
  displaying, 140–141
  overview, 134–135
  printing, 153
  sort order precedence, 148
  sorting, 147–149
queries, selection criteria
  for Date fields, 151–152
  definition, 149
  for Numeric fields, 151–152
  for Text fields, 150–151
  for Yes/No fields, 151–152
queries, tables
  adding, 136, 160
  choosing, 134
  creating, 134
  limitations, 156–158
  moving, 159
  multiple, 153–157
  names, viewing, 155–156

primary keys, editing, 156–158
removing, 136, 159–160
queries, updating
primary keys, 158
rules for, 157
Queries option, 36
Query by Example (QBE). *See* QBE (Query by Example).
Query Criteria option, 655
Query Design Font option, 650
Query Design ribbon
Append button, 138
Crosstab button, 138
illustration, 137
Make Table button, 138
Run button, 138
Save (in the Quick Access Toolbar) button, 138
Select button, 138
Show Table button, 138
Update button, 138
View button, 138
Query Designer
adding tables, 136, 160
creating queries, 135–138
Datasheet view, 136
description, 137
Design view, 136
displaying field names, 136
Enable Autojoin option, 650
Field List window, 136
field lists, 159
illustration, 136
join line, 158–159
launching, 135
moving tables, 159
options, 650
Output All Fields option, 650
QBE (Query by Example) grid, 137
Query Design Font option, 650
removing tables, 136, 159–160
Show Table Names option, 650
SQL Server Compatible option, 650
SQL view, 136
Query Designer, table/query pane
adding tables, 160
description, 137
field lists, 159
illustration, 136

join line, 158–159
moving tables, 159
removing tables, 159–160
Query event, 464
query joins. *See also* join tables.
ad hoc, 161–162
auto-join line, 161
Cartesian products, 161, 164
creating, 160–161
deleting, 164
equi-joins, 160
outer, 163
type, specifying, 162–163
QueryDef object, 503–505
question mark (?)
optional letter indicator, 67
wildcard character, 181, 195–198
Quick Access Toolbar. *See also* the ribbon.
adding commands, 1018–1019
illustration, 1018
modifying, 1018–1020

R

radio buttons, 298–299. *See also* option groups.
RaiseError action, 562
raising events, 1002–1003
RAM, minimum requirements, 841
RDBMS (relational database management system), 5
read-only properties, 987
read/write properties, 987
rearranging fields, 235–236
rebooting, 874
record display width, modifying, 238
Record Locks property, 310, 652
record pointers, 223
Record Selector, 305–306
Record Selectors property, 306
Record Source property, 309
RecordCount property, 498–499
record-lock. *See* locking issues, record-lock.
record-locked fields in multiuser environments, 676
records (rows). *See also* fields; tables.
coloring, 239–241
current position indicator, 295
in datasheets, 216–217
definition, 8
display width, modifying, 238
freezing, 242

Index

records (rows) (*continued*)
    highlighting, 220, 239–241
    inserting, 46
    locking, 296, 310
    navigating among, 294
    selecting, 220
    unique identifiers, 20–21
    values, definition, 8

records (rows), adding
    AddNew method, 517
    in datasheets, 231
    to external linked tables, 599
    in forms, 231
    to tables, with data macros, 558–559

records (rows), deleting
    in datasheets, 231
    Delete Rows button, 46
    enabling deletion, 310
    in forms, 231

records (rows), displaying
    display width, modifying, 238
    hiding/showing records, 237
    record display width, modifying, 238
    resizing record height, 238

records (rows), in datasheets
    * (asterisk), new record indicator, 221–222
    adding, 220–223
    automatic data-type validation, 224–225
    deleting, 220
    filtering, 220, 242–246
    hiding, 220, 238
    saving, 220, 223
    sorting, 220, 242–243

records (rows), saving
    in datasheets, 231
    in forms, 231, 300
    layout changes, 242

Records group
    Access 2010 ribbon, 36
    Datasheet ribbon, 220
    Form ribbon, 293

RecordSelectors property, 704

Recordset object, ADO object model
    ActiveConnection parameter, 510–512
    adOpenDynamic cursor, 497
    adOpenForwardOnly cursor, 497
    adOpenKeyset cursor, 497
    adOpenStatic cursor, 497
    BOF (beginning-of-file indicator), 497–498

    CancelUpdate method, 512
    counting records, 498–499
    current record pointer, 495
    cursor type, specifying, 496–497
    CursorType parameter, 510–512
    CursorType property, 496–497
    Edit method, 512
    EOF (end-of-file indicator), 497–498
    LockType parameter, 510–512
    MoveNext method, 497–498
    MovePrevious method, 497–498
    navigating recordsets, 495
    Open method, 510–512
    opening a table, 510
    overview, 494–495
    RecordCount property, 498–499
    RecordsetNavigation procedure, 495
    Source parameter, 510–512
    Update method, 512

Recordset object, DAO object model, 505–506
Recordset Type property, 310, 652
RecordsetNavigation procedure, 495
recordsets. *See also* Recordset object.
    beginning-of-file indicator, 497–498
    closing, 513
    counting records, 498–499, 642–644
    current database connection, 510–512
    current record pointer, 495
    cursor type, specifying, 496–497, 510–512
    data source, specifying, 510–512
    definition, 131
    displaying, 140–141
    empty, runtime error, 512
    end-of-file indicator, 497–498
    hiding fields, 647
    locking, 510–512
    navigating, 495, 497–498
    opening, 510–512
    overview, 134–135
    printing, 153
    saving updates, 512
    sort order precedence, 148
    sorting, 147–149
    specifying for unbound forms, 782
    updates, canceling, 512
    updating fields, 512
    view contents of, 493, 511–512
RecordSource property, 271
recycle bin, SharePoint, 1138

redundant or repetitive data, 95–97
`ReferenceFromFile` function, 853–854
referential integrity
    application-specific, 126–127
    cascading deletes, 123–125
    cascading updates, 123–125
    definition, 112
    enforcing, 119–125, 1162–1163
    entity integrity, 115
    ignoring, 123
    null values in primary keys, 113
    orphaned records, 114
    overview, 112–113
    primary keys matching foreign keys, 114
    SQL Server conversions, 1231
    table conflicts, resolving, 124
Refresh Interval option, 767
relational database management system (RDBMS), 5
relational databases, 5. *See also* databases.
relational operators. *See* comparison operators.
relationship errors, 1174–1175
relationships
    for linked tables, setting, 598
    SharePoint deployment issues, 1160–1164
relationships, between tables
    connecting data, 105–107
    creating, 119–125
    deleting, 126
    equi-joins, 122–125
    flat-file databases, 104–105
    join tables, 111
    join type, specifying, 122–125
    many-to-many, 110–111
    one-to-many, 108–110
    one-to-one, 107–108
    outer joins, 122–125
    parent/child, 108–110
    viewing, 125–126
Remove Personal Information check box,
    1084, 1088
Remove Sort command, 243
`RemoveAllTempVar` action, 1065–1068
`RemoveTempVar` action, 1065–1068
removing. *See also* deleting.
    fields from queries, 144
    personal information on save, 1088
    the ribbon, 1046
    submacros, 1065–1068

renaming
    fields, 41, 57, 647–649
    linked tables, 597
    ribbon groups, 1020–1022
    tables, 86
replacing ribbons, 1045–1046
Replication ID size numeric fields, 52
Report Design window, 337–338
report errors, 1175–1176
Report Footer section, 341–342, 345
Report Header section, 341–342, 343
report modules, 390
Report Wizard
    alternate formats, 337
    color schemes, 331–335
    group data, defining, 326–327
    group intervals, 327
    grouping levels, selecting, 325–326
    layout, adjusting, 330–331
    layout, selecting, 329
    multiple-page display, 336–337
    new reports, 324–325
    previewing the report, 335–340
    Print Preview window, 335–337
    printing the report, 338–340
    report design, opening, 329–330
    Report Design window, 337–338
    saving the report, 340
    sort order, selecting, 327–328
    summary options, selecting, 328–329
    themes, selecting, 331–333
reports. *See also* printing.
    absolute speed, 859–861
    adding data, 737–738
    columnar, 321–322
    control totals, 344–345
    controls, naming, 749
    controls, naming conventions, 285–286
    converting from forms, 316
    creating, 12
    designing, 14–16
    displaying in a combo box, 739–740
    displaying selected data, 134
    empty, avoiding, 728
    versus forms, 322
    hiding forms, 741
    hiding/showing controls, 463
    mailing-label, 322–323
    memo data, 51

Index

reports *(continued)*
- morphing, 868
- new features, 1263
- null values, avoiding, 728–729
- OLE data, 51
- opening with conditions, 1061–1064
- overview, 12
- page numbers, 344–345
- palette source, 308
- Print Preview, 741
- from queried data, 740
- sorting, 710–714
- specifications, 1248–1249
- SQL Server conversions, 1234
- summary calculations, 344
- tabular, 320
- two-pass processing, 747–749
- types of, 320–322
- Upsizing Wizard, 1232–1233
- user name, adding, 738
- VBA event procedures, 460–462

reports, banded. *See also* sections, of reports.
- definition, 340
- Detail section, 341–342, 344
- Group Footer section, 341–342, 344
- Group Header section, 341–342, 343–344
- overview, 340–342
- Page Footer section, 341–342, 344–345
- Page Header section, 341–342, 343
- Report Footer section, 341–342, 345
- Report Header section, 341–342, 343

reports, controls
- aligning labels, 736
- compound, 356–358
- expressions in text controls, 353
- formatting, 358
- hiding/showing, 463, 725–727
- label control properties, 359–360
- label controls, moving, 356–358
- label controls, pasting, 356
- label controls, resizing, 354
- micro-adjusting, 736–737
- moving between sections, 365–366
- naming conventions, 285–286, 749
- page breaks, 367
- placing, 350–351
- selecting with the mouse, 357–358
- text, modifying, 351–352

- text, moving, 356–358
- text-box control properties, 359–360
- text-box controls, resizing, 360–361
- totals, 344–345

reports, creating from scratch
- assembling the data, 324
- binding to a data source, 346–348
- compound controls, 356–358
- control text, modifying, 351–352
- controls, and page breaks, 367
- controls, formatting, 358
- controls, moving between sections, 365–366
- controls, placing, 350–351
- controls, selecting with the mouse, 357–358
- defining the layout, 323
- expressions, in text controls, 353
- group footers, creating, 361–363
- group footers, deleting, 364
- group headers, creating, 361–363
- group headers, deleting, 364
- grouping data, 361–366
- label control properties, 359–360
- label controls, moving, 356–358
- label controls, pasting, 356
- label controls, resizing, 354
- label text, highlighting, 352
- layout, defining, 348–349
- margins, specifying, 348–349
- orientation, specifying, 348–349
- overview, 323, 345–346
- page breaks, 366–367
- page numbers, 353
- page size, defining, 348–349
- paper size, specifying, 348–349
- sections, hiding/showing, 364
- sections, moving controls between, 365–366
- sections, resizing, 351–352, 365. *See also* banded reports.
- sorting data, 361–366
- text boxes, adding, 352–359
- text boxes, deleting, 354–355
- text boxes, moving, 354–355
- text boxes, resizing, 354
- text controls, moving, 356–358
- text-box control properties, 359–360
- text-box controls, resizing, 360–361
- transparent borders, 360
- units of measure, displaying, 349
- unwanted blank pages, 349, 372

reports, creating with Report Wizard
    alternate formats, 337
    color schemes, 331–335
    group data, defining, 326–327
    group intervals, 327
    grouping levels, selecting, 325–326
    layout, adjusting, 330–331
    layout, selecting, 329
    multiple-page display, 336–337
    new reports, 324–325
    previewing the report, 335–340
    Print Preview window, 335–337
    printing the report, 338–340
    report design, opening, 329–330
    Report Design window, 337–338
    saving the report, 340
    sort order, selecting, 327–328
    summary options, selecting, 328–329
    themes, selecting, 331–333
reports, formatting
    aligning control labels, 736
    blank lines, inserting, 731–733
    bulleted lists, 723–725
    centering titles, 736
    color, 368–369
    column layout, specifying, 745
    column spacing, specifying, 745
    date and time, adding, 372
    Detail section adjustments, 370–371
    even-odd page printing, 733–735
    expressions in group headers, 369–370
    graphic rules, 368–369
    hiding/showing controls, 725–727
    horizontal lines between sections, 730
    item size, specifying, 745
    micro-adjusting controls, 736–737
    number of columns, specifying, 745
    numbered lists, 720–723
    overview, 367–368
    page header adjustments, 368–369
    Page Setup dialog box, 745–747
    report headers, creating, 371–372
    row spacing, specifying, 745
    at runtime, 735–736
    snaking columns, 741–747
    two-sided printing, 733–735
    vertical lines between columns, 729–730
    white space, inserting, 731–733

reports, grouping data
    alphabetical headings, 712–714
    alphabetically, 710–714
    on date intervals, 714–716
    hiding page headers, 719
    hiding repeating information, 716–718
    resetting page numbers, by group, 719–720
reports do not support events, 1176
Reports option, 36
Requery method *versus* Requery action, 864
Require Variable Declaration option,
    411, 527–528
required data, indicating, 70
Required property, 60, 70–71
reserved word collisions, 1177
Resize event, 457
resizing. *See also* sizing handles, controls.
    columns, 143–144
    datasheets, 220
    field width, 237
    fields, 57
    forms, 263, 307
    label controls, 354
    record height, 238
    the ribbon, 1012
    split forms, 309
    text boxes on reports, 354, 360–361
resizing controls
    with properties, 683
    with sizing handles, 271–274, 273–274
Resume Label statements, 834–835
Resume Next statements, 834
Resume statements, 832–834
Retreat event, 462–463
retrieving system information, Windows API
    command line, 952–953
    drive type, 957–958
    file system information, 958–959
    local computer network name, 956–957
    parent window handles, 960
    temporary files path, 953–954
    title-bar text, 960
    user name, 956
    volume information, 958–959
    window class, 960–961
    Windows path, 953
    Windows system directory, 959–960
    Windows version, 954–955

Index

retrieving system information, Windows API examples
  `GetCommandLineA` function, 952–953
  `GetComputerNameA` function, 956–957
  `GetDriveTypeA` function, 957–958
  `GetSystemDirectoryA` function, 959–960
  `GetTempPathA` function, 953–954
  `GetUserNameA` function, 956
  `GetVersionExA` function, 954–955
  `GetVolumeInformationA` function, 958–959
  `GetWindowsDirectoryA` function, 953
revealing user interfaces, 985
the ribbon. *See also* Quick Access Toolbar.
  collapsing, 1011
  `Create` tab, 41–42
  custom, displaying, 1091
  customizing, 1016
  `Design` tab, 45–47
  `Fields` tab, 43
  groups, 36
  Home tab, 36
  illustration, 1011
  managing, 1017–1018
  new features, 1254–1257
  overview, 1009–1013
  removing, 1046
  SharePoint deployment, Web commands, 1168
the ribbon, controls
  `Button`, 1038
  check boxes, 1039–1040
  `DropDown`, 1014, 1040–1041
  `Gallery`, 1014–1015
  help, 1015
  `imageMso`, specifying, 1035–1037
  `Label`, 1037–1038
  resizing, 1012
  separators, 1038–1039
  `SplitButton`, 1013–1014, 1041–1042
  `SuperTips`, 1015
the ribbon, customizing defaults
  commands, 1020–1022
  `Customize the Ribbon` window, 1020–1021
  groups, 1020–1022
  importing/exporting customizations, 1022
  renaming groups, 1020–1022
  resetting to original, 1022
  tabs, 1020–1022
  with Visual Web Developer, 1042–1044

the ribbon, XML
  case sensitivity, 1035
  editors, 1012
  example, 1033–1035
  syntax, 1012
`Ribbon and Toolbar` options
  Allow Default Shortcut Menus check box, 1091
  Allow Full Menus check box, 1091
  command display, customizing, 1091
  custom ribbon, specifying, 1091
  Ribbon Name option, 1091
  Shortcut Menu Bar option, 1090–1091
  shortcut menu defaults, specifying, 1090–1091
  shortcut menu display, specifying, 1091
ribbon editor, new features, 1254–1255
Ribbon Name option, 1091
ribbons. *See also specific ribbons.*
  closing, 1045–1046
  code window, 393
  opening, 1045–1046
  replacing, 1045–1046
  SQL Server conversions, 1234
  user considerations, 912–913
ribbons, custom
  controls, 1017
  groups, 1016
  illustration, 1016
  specifying for forms, 311
  tabs, 1016
ribbons, customizing
  building XML, 1026
  controls, 1025–1026
  creating a ribbon, 1023
  custom property, specifying, 1032–1033
  designing ribbons, 1026
  error reporting, enabling, 1024
  `getLabel` attribute, 1028
  groups, 1025–1026
  hierarchical structure, 1025–1026
  `OnAction` attribute, 1024
  tabs, 1025–1026
  `USysRibbons` table, adding XML, 1030–1032
  `USysRibbons` table, creating, 1029–1030
  VBA callbacks, overview, 1023–1025
  VBA callbacks, writing, 1027–1029
`RIGHT JOIN...ON` expression, 480–484
right outer joins, 166–167
rounding, 175

routines, absolute speed, 863–866
rows (database). *See* records (rows).
rows (report), spacing, 745
RowSource property, 682, 691–693
rules (graphic), in reports, 368–369
RunDataMacro action, 561
Running Sum property, 344
runtime environment, starting applications in, 1093
runtime errors, 821–824
runtime mode, forcing, 929–930
/runtime switch, 929

S

s:, formatting seconds, 64
sandbox mode, 934–936
Save Splitter Bar Position property, 309
saving
    datasheet changes, 242
    forms, 256, 263
    queries, 138, 153
    records in forms, 231, 300
    reports, 340
    tables, 85
schema errors, 1178–1179
Scientific format, 61
scope, VBA procedures, 432–434
scope, VBA variables
    definition, 432
    global, 426
    local, 426
    private, 427, 432–434
    Private keyword, 427
    public, 426, 432–434
    Public keyword, 426
screen fonts *versus* printer fonts, 308
scroll bars, displaying on forms, 306
Scroll Bars property, 306, 704
scrolling forms, 291
searching. *See* finding; queries; SQL (Structured Query Language).
sections, of reports. *See also* banded reports.
    hiding/showing, 364
    moving controls between, 365–366
    resizing, 351–352, 365
security
    .accdb files, 752
    bulletproofing forms, 928

DAO, 501
digital certificates, 935–936
digital signatures, 935
encoding, 930–931
encryption, 930–931
macros, 934–938
.mdb files, 752
new features, 1265
passwords, removing, 931–933
privacy settings, 937–938
property values, getting, 927
property values, setting, 926–927
runtime mode, forcing, 929–930
sandbox mode, 934–936
settings, 937–938
SharePoint, 1138
start-up bypass, disabling, 924–927
start-up option properties, 924
start-up options, setting, 923–924
Trust Center, 937–938
validating user input, 928–929
VBA code, 933–934
security, applications
    bulletproofing forms, 928
    digital certificates, 935–936
    digital signatures, 935
    encoding, 930–931
    encryption, 930–931
    macros, 934–938
    passwords, removing, 931–933
    privacy settings, 937–938
    property values, getting, 927
    property values, setting, 926–927
    runtime mode, forcing, 929–930
    sandbox mode, 934–936
    settings, 937–938
    start-up bypass, disabling, 924–927
    start-up option properties, 924
    start-up options, setting, 923–924
    Trust Center, 937–938
    validating user input, 928–929
    VBA code, 933–934
segmenting data into tables. *See* normalization.
Select Case...End Select statements, 403–404
Select command, 220
SELECT keyword, 475, 476–477
select queries, 133

Index

selecting
  controls, 271–272
  fields, 475, 476–477, 484
  records in forms, 231
selecting data. *See* queries; SQL (Structured Query
        Language).
selecting from lists. *See* combo boxes; list boxes.
Selection Behavior option, 357
Selection command, 243–244
selection criteria, specifying, 134. *See also* queries; SQL
        (Structured Query Language).
SelectionChange event, 464
self-joins, 167–169
semicolon (;)
  input mask separator, 67
  SQL end-of-statement indicator, 484
SendEmail action, 561
separators on the ribbon, 1038–1039
servers. *See* client/server architecture.
SetField action, 561
SetLocalVar action, 561
SetOption method, 926–927
SetProperty function, 683–685
SetTempVar action, 1065–1068
SetWarnings action, 1054–1055, 1056
SetWindowTextA function, 961–962
SharePoint
  Access Services, 1140–1141
  alerts, 1138
  Backstage area, 1139–1140
  end-user maintenance, 1138
  managed applications, 1136
  migrating Access applications to the Web, 1135,
        1138–1140
  new features, 1265
  overview, 1104–1106
  Publish to Access Service button, enabling,
        1139–1140
  recycle bin, 1138
  security, 1138
  versioning, 1138
  Web publishing, 1137–1140
SharePoint, as a data source
  calendars, linking to, 1122–1123
  data type conversion, 1127
  exporting Access tables to SharePoint, 1123–1127
  linking Access to SharePoint lists, 1119–1123
  moving Access tables to SharePoint, 1127–1131
  overview, 1117–1119

  permissions, 1121
  SharePoint templates, 1131–1134
SharePoint, Web application limits
  anonymous site access, 1141
  maximum data rows, 1143
  public-facing sites, 1141–1143
  transactional requirements, 1143
SharePoint deployment. *See also* distributing applications.
  .accdb file, copying, 1145
  .accdb file, eliminating, 1156–1173
  Access forms, creating, 1169–1170
  Access ribbon, Web commands, 1168
  Access Services, 1157
  export errors, 1151
  Navigation form, 1170–1171
  publishing Access applications, 1156–1157, 1164–1173
  relationship issues, 1160–1164
  synchronizing desktop application with Access Services,
        1171–1173
  tables, enhanced export options, 1146–1156
SharePoint deployment, Compatibility Checker
  Backstage area, 1158
  data integrity, enforcing, 1162–1163
  online help, 1160
  running, 1157–1158
  successful completion, 1163–1164
SharePoint deployment, Compatibility Checker problems
  attachment field limitations, 1178
  AutoNumber data type problems, 1179
  calculated field issues, 1178
  control issues, 1176
  field data type issues, 1178
  form errors, 1175–1176
  form event problems, 1175
  general errors, 1174
  incompatible custom field formats, 1179
  incompatible fields, 1174
  incompatible macro actions, 1177–1178
  invalid expression errors, 1177
  invalid query names, 1177
  issues, displaying, 1158–1159
  lookup errors, 1174–1175
  lookup field issues, 1175, 1178
  macro errors, 1177–1178
  object name violations, 1176
  primary key constraints, 1175
  query errors, 1176–1177
  query join issues, 1177
  relationship errors, 1174–1175

relationship issues, 1160–1161
report errors, 1175–1176
reports do not support events, 1176
reserved word collisions, 1177
schema errors, 1178–1179
SQL statement problems, 1176
subqueries in queries, 1177
table field issues, 1179
table name issues, 1179
table relationships, 1174
Unique property problems, 1179
unsupported form controls, 1175
unsupported report controls, 1176
SharePoint lists
creating, 1112–1115
definition, 1105
editing list items, 1110–1111
wikis, creating, 1112–1115
working with, 1107–1108
SharePoint pages
customizing, 1143
examples, 1105, 1106
SharePoint Web sites
common examples, 1108–1111
definition, 1105
types of, 1106–1107
sharing over networks. See SharePoint.
Short Date format, 63
Short Time format, 63
Shortcut Menu Bar option, 1090–1091
Shortcut Menu Bar property, 311
Shortcut Menu property, 311
shortcut menus
defaults, specifying, 1090–1091
display, specifying, 1091
on forms, 311
ShortcutMenu property, 683, 704
ShortcutMenuBar property, 683
shortcuts, launching applications, 907–909
Show Table dialog box, 135–136, 138
Show Table Names option, 650
showing. See hiding/showing.
Single data type, VBA, 428
single primary keys, 118
single quotes ('...'), criteria string indicator, 194
Single size numeric fields, 52
Single Step dialog box, 1074

Size to Fit Form button
Datasheet ribbon, 220
Form ribbon, 293
SizeMode property, 297
sizing handles, controls, 271–272, 273–274. See also resizing.
slash (/)
date delimiter, 625
division operator, 174, 188
input mask separator, 67
integer division operator, 175
in select queries, 188
separating time elements, 63
SmartTags property, 60
snaking report columns, 741–747
Snap to Grid command, 276–277
snapping to the grid, 276–277
Snapshot Viewer option, 636
Social Security numbers
data types, 50, 51
formatting, 66–68
Sort & Filter group
Datasheet ribbon, 220, 242–246
Form ribbon, 293
illustration, 36
sort order
precedence, recordsets, 148
selecting for reports, 327–328
sorting
data on forms, 309
data types, 50–51
fields, 142–143, 235–236
Memo fields, 50, 147
numbers, 51
object lists, 420
OLE object fields, 147
with QuickSort ribbon, 243
records, 134, 220, 242–243
recordsets, 147–149
report data, 361–366, 710–714
reverting to original order, 243
selected records, 475, 484. See also ORDER BY clause.
with Sort & Filter group, 36
sound, data type. See OLE Object data type.
Source Connect Str property, 652
Source Database property, 652
Source parameter, 510–512
SourceTableName property, 600–606

Index

spaces
  displaying as characters, 60
  filling, 60
  in names, 40, 423
  in path names, 1093
  in search criteria, 196
  in VBA event names, 455
  in VBA variable names, 423
specialized queries, 133
specifications
  Access databases, 1247
  building to, 900–902
  forms, 1248–1249
  macros, 1249
  queries, 1248
  reports, 1248–1249
  SQL Server Express, 1250–1251
  tables, 1247–1248
specifying tables, 475
splash screens
  contents, 1096
  designing, 1095–1097
  effects on perceived speed, 867–868
  user considerations, 911–912
Split Form button, 261–262
Split Form command, 253
Split Form Datasheet property, 309
Split Form Orientation property, 309
Split Form Printing property, 309
Split Form Size property, 309
Split Form Splitter Bar property, 309
split forms, 261–262
SplitButton controls, 1013–1014, 1041–1042
Splitter Bar, 309
splitting
  code windows, 393
  VBA statements, 419
splitting databases
  benefits of, 759–761
  versus client/server architecture, 1193
  Database Splitter wizard, 762–764
  definition, 753
  placing objects, 761–762
spreadsheets. See also flat-file databases.
  aggregate functions, 247–248
  versus databases, 92–94. See also flat-file databases.
  importing from, 614–618

SQL (Structured Query Language). See also queries.
  * (asterisk), wildcard character, 477
  [ ] (square brackets), around field names, 476–477
  filtering selections, 475
  overview, 473–474
  selecting fields, 475, 476–477, 484
  sorting selections, 475, 484
  specifying tables, 475, 480–484
SQL keywords
  FROM, 475
  case sensitivity, 476
  ORDER BY clause, 475
  SELECT, 475, 476–477
  summary of, 475. See also specific keywords.
  WHERE clause, 475
SQL pass-through, network applications, 755
SQL predicates
  ALL, 478
  FROM clause, 480–484
  definition, 478
  DISTINCT, 478–479
  DISTINCTROW, 479–480
  INNER JOIN...ON expression, 480–484
  LEFT JOIN...ON expression, 480–484
  ORDER BY clause, 484
  RIGHT JOIN...ON expression, 480–484
  TOP, 480
  WHERE clause, 484
SQL queries, viewing, 474–475. See also queries.
SQL Server
  naming conventions, 1211
  overview, 1199–1200
SQL Server, connecting to
  from Access, 1203–1214
  connection strings, 1201–1203
  creating a data source, 1204
  DSN, setting up, 1205–1211
  File DSN, 1204
  linking to tables, 1211–1214
  ODBC configuration options, 1204
  System DSN, 1204
  User DSN, 1204
SQL Server Compatible option, 650
SQL Server Express
  downloading, 1200
  overview, 1224–1225
  specifications, 1250–1251

SQL Server objects
    stored procedures, 1219–1221
    tables, 1215–1217
    triggers, 1221
    views, 1217–1219
SQL statements
    ; (semicolon), end-of-statement indicator, 484
    maximum length, 484
    problems, 1176
    spanning multiple lines, 476
    viewing, 474–475
square brackets ([ ])
    around field names, 476–477
    pattern indicator, 181
    referencing fields, 192–193
    table and field name notation, 174
ss:, formatting seconds, 64
standard deviation, calculating, 657
Standard format, 61
standard modules, 389–390
start-up bypass, disabling, 924–927
Startup dialog box. *See* Current Database options.
start-up option properties, 924
start-up options, 909–912, 923–924
start-up screen, 26
statement continuation, VBA, 418–419
static linking, 940. *See also* early binding.
status bar, displaying, 1086
StDev option, 657
Step Into button, 543
Step Out button, 543
Step Over button, 543
stepping through code, 543–544, 1074
Stop statements, 542. *See also* breakpoints.
StopMacro action, 561, 1074
stopping for errors, 411, 529
stopping macro execution, 1074
stored procedures
    server database engines, 1188
    SQL Server, 1219–1221
storing code, 851–853
String data type, VBA, 428
string operators
    & (ampersand), concatenation operator, 173, 178–179,
        188
    * (asterisk), wildcard character, 181
    "..." (double quotes), around returned strings, 178
    – (hyphen), range indicator, 181

\# (pound sign), wildcard character, 181
? (question mark), wildcard character, 181
[ ] (square brackets), pattern indicator, 181
Like (similar strings), 179–180, 181, 188
[list], wildcard character, 181
[!list], wildcard character, 181
list of, 178
Not Like (dissimilar strings), 179–180, 188
wildcards, 181
strings, concatenating
    & (ampersand), concatenation operator, 173, 178–179,
        188, 422
    + (plus sign), addition operator, 173, 179
strings, maximum length, 429, 949
Structure and Data button, 86
Structure Only button, 86
Structured Query Language (SQL). *See* SQL (Structured
        Query Language).
Style property, 702
Sub-Address property, 66
Subdatasheet Expanded property, 308, 653
Subdatasheet Height property, 308, 653
Subdatasheet Name property, 652
subforms. *See also* forms.
    embedding, 258–259
    linking to parent forms, 686–687
    overview, 686–688
    properties, setting, 687
    within subforms, 688
submacros
    Data Mode argument, 1061
    expanding/collapsing, 1059
    Filter Name argument, 1060
    Form Name argument, 1060
    implementing, 1060
    for mcrMainMenu macro, 1058
    OpenContacts, 1058
    OpenForm action, 1060–1061
    OpenProducts, 1058
    OpenSales, 1058
    overview, 1057–1058
    View argument, 1060
    Where Condition argument, 1061
    Window Mode argument, 1061
subprocedures, VBA, 388
subqueries, 134, 1177
subroutines
    versus functions, Windows API, 946
    VBA, 380

Index

subroutines, VBA. *See also* VBA procedures.
  calling, 436
  components of, 436
  creating, 437–441
  definition, 380
  naming conventions, 435–436
  overview, 435–436
Sum option, 657
summary calculations in reports, 344
summary options, selecting for reports, 328–329
summing rows and columns, 247–248
summing values. *See* aggregate functions.
SuperTips, 1015
surrogate primary keys, 77, 118–119
swap files, absolute speed, 856
Switch Windows button
  Datasheet ribbon, 220
  Form ribbon, 293
switchboards
  creating, 912, 1097
  description, 1097
  user considerations, 912
synchronizing desktop application with Access Services,
    1171–1173
syntax checking, 411, 525–527
syntax errors, color-coding, 526
System DSN, 1204
system information, getting with Windows API
  command line, 952–953
  drive type, 957–958
  file system information, 958–959
  `GetCommandLineA` function, 952–953
  `GetComputerNameA` function, 956–957
  `GetDriveTypeA` function, 957–958
  `GetSystemDirectoryA` function, 959–960
  `GetTempPathA` function, 953–954
  `GetUserNameA` function, 956
  `GetVersionExA` function, 954–955
  `GetVolumeInformationA` function, 958–959
  `GetWindowsDirectoryA` function, 953
  local computer network name, 956–957
  parent window handles, 960
  temporary files path, 953–954
  title-bar text, 960
  user name, 956
  volume information, 958–959
  window class, 960–961
  Windows path, 953

  Windows system directory, 959–960
  Windows version, 954–955
system messages, enabling/disabling, 1054–1055
system objects, hiding, 1090
system requirements, CD-ROM, 1267–1268

T

`Tab Index` property, 314
Tab key behavior, specifying, 311
tab order, specifying, 313–314
Tab Order dialog box, 313–314
`Tab Stop` property, 314
tabbed dialog boxes
  labels on tabs, 702
  overview, 700–703
  pictures on tabs, 702
  selected tabs, identifying, 702
  tab size, setting, 702
  tabs, as command buttons, 702
tabbed documents, specifying, 1086–1087
Tabbed Documents interface, 914
tabbed interface, 37–38, 1256
`TabFixedHeight` property, 702
`TabFixedWidth` property, 702
Table button, 42
table columns. *See* fields.
table design. *See* creating tables; designing tables.
Table Design button, 42, 43–45
Table Design window, 44–45
table events
  before, 562–566
  after, 564–566
  `AfterChange` event, 564–566
  `AfterDelete` event, 564–566
  `AfterInsert` event, 564–566
  `BeforeChange` event, 562–564
  `BeforeDelete` event, 562–564
table indexes, absolute speed, 856–858
table names
  automatic correction, 1091–1092
  viewing, 155–156
table relationships
  connecting data, 105–107
  creating, 119–125
  deleting, 126
  equi-joins, 122–125
  flat-file databases, 104–105
  join tables, 111

join type, specifying, 122–125
many-to-many, 110–111
one-to-many, 108–110
one-to-one, 107–108
outer joins, 122–125
parent/child, 108–110
viewing, 125–126
table rows. *See* records.
`TableDef` object, 502–503
tables. *See also* creating tables; designing tables; updating
    tables.
adding records, 88
adding records to, 119
changes, enabling, 1088
conflicts, resolving, 124
copying, 86–88
copying to another database, 87
copying within a database, 86–87
definition, 6
deleting, 86
design, printing, 84–85
enhanced export options, 1146–1156
examples, 6, 7
exporting to SharePoint, 1123–1127
field issues, 1179
indexed, 117
moving to SharePoint, 1127–1131
name issues, 1179
new features, 1258–1259
overview, 6–7
properties, specifying, 46–47
Property Sheet, 46–47
relationships, SharePoint deployment, 1174
renaming, 86
saving, 85
separating from applications, 1099–1100
SharePoint deployment, 1146–1156
specifications, 1247–1248
specifying to SQL, 480–484. *See also* FROM keyword.
splitting data into, 97–102
SQL Server, 1215–1217
temporary, 1189
tables, linking
foreign keys, 20–21
keys, 20–21
overview, 19–22
primary keys, 20–21
tables, multiple, 8. *See also* normalization.
Tables and Related Views option, 34–35

Tables option, 36
tabs (ribbon), customizing, 1016, 1020–1022, 1025–1026
`TabStop` property, 22
tabular forms, 260–261
tabular reports, 320
`Tag` property, 311, 782
tagging forms, 311
tags, naming conventions, 432
`tblCustomers` database, 55, 73–76
technical support for CD-ROM, 1270
telephone numbers, data types, 51
templates
creating databases, 26–27
SharePoint, 1131–1134
temporary files path, getting, 953–954
temporary tables, 1189
temporary variables. *See also* macros; variables.
enhancing macros, 1065–1066
`mcrHelloWorldEnhanced` macro, 1065
`mcrReportMenuEnhanced` macro, 1067–1068
`RemoveAllTempVar` action, 1065–1068
`RemoveTempVar` action, 1065–1068
removing, 1065–1068
`SetTempVar` action, 1065–1068
setting, 1065–1068
simplifying macros, 1066–1068
uses for, 1065
in VBA, 1068–1069
testing
    See also bugs
    See also Compatibility Checker
    See also debugging
    See also error handling
    See also troubleshooting
VBA procedures in Immediate window, 399–401
testing applications
before distribution, 1092–1093
overview, 524–525
text boxes, on reports
adding, 352–359
control properties, 359–360
deleting, 354–355
moving, 354–355
resizing, 354, 360–361
text controls, expressions in, 353
`Text` criteria, 193–195
text data
entering, 225
numbers, sorting, 51

Index

Text data type
    converting from AutoNumber, 58
    converting from Date/Time, 58
    description, 51
    group headers, 362
    purpose, 48
    storage size, 49
Text data type, converting to
    Currency, 58
    Date/Time, 58
    Number, 58
    Yes/No, 58
Text fields
    formatting, 64
    line breaks, inserting, 231
    query selection criteria, 150–151
    size, specifying, 51
text files, importing
    CSV (comma-separated values), 618–623
    duplicate primary keys, 621
    field separators, 620
    fixed-width files, 621–623
text files, linking to, 587, 604–606
text formatting
    in controls, 314
    in datasheets, 220–221
Text Formatting group
    Access 2010 ribbon, 36
    Datasheet ribbon, 220–221
    Form ribbon, 293
text tables, linking to, 583
text-box data-entry fields, 22
themes
    new features, 1261
    selecting for reports, 331–333
    Windows themes, enabling, 1088
thousands separator, specifying, 62
3NF (third normal form), 102
three-tiered architecture, 1193–1194
tiers, architectural, 1193
tiling pictures on forms, 308
time data type. See Date/Time data type.
Time Delimiter option, 625
Time event, 688–690
Timer event, 457, 464
TimerInterval event, 464
timing events, 452

title-bar, forms
    captioning, 306
    specifying text for, 303
title-bar text
    getting, 960
    setting, 961–962
    specifying, 1085
Toolbar property, 311
toolbars. See Quick Access Toolbar; the ribbon.
ToolTips. See SuperTips.
Top property, 683
TOP SQL predicate, 480
Top Values property, 651
top(n) queries, 133
top(n) records, 644–646
total queries, 133
Total row options, 654
totaling values. See aggregate functions.
tracing execution path, 549
tracking
    DAO object model transactions, 501
    graphical objects, 950
    macros, 552
tracking macros, 552
transaction tracking, 501
transactional requirements, SharePoint, 1143
transactions, network applications, 755–756
transparent borders on reports, 360
trapping custom events, 1003–1004
triggers
    server database engines, 1188
    SQL Server, 1221
troubleshooting. See also debugging; error handling; testing.
    See also bugs
    See also Compatibility Checker
    See also debugging
    See also error handling
    See also testing
    action queries, 676
    CD-ROM, 1269–1270
    hardware errors, 920
    inadequate disk space, 920
    memory errors, 920
    usage logs, 920–923
    virtual memory, 920
troubleshooting, applications
    hardware errors, 920
    inadequate disk space, 920

memory errors, 920
  usage logs, 920–923
  virtual memory, 920
troubleshooting, record-lock errors
  bound forms *versus* unbound, 780–788
  caching, 768–769
  `Error 3186: Couldn't save...`, 772–774
  `Error 3188: Could not update...`, 774–775
  `Error 3197: Data has changed...`, 775–778
  `Error 3260: Couldn't update...`, 769 772
  `ErrorRoutine` function, 778–780
  latency, 768–769
  overview, 768–769
true/false criteria, 200
truncated numeric fields, checking for, 1088
truncating text data, 676
Trust Center, 937–938
`tttt:, Long Time` format, 64
2NF (second normal form), 97–102
two-pass report processing, 747–749
two-sided printing, 733–735
two-tiered architecture, 1193
`TypeText` method, 806

U

unanticipated errors, 823–824
unbound combo boxes, 881–883
unbound controls, 266, 285
unbound forms, network applications. *See also* bound forms.
  versus bound forms, 780–781
  combo boxes, 785
  creating, 781
  editing data, 786–788
  multiuser errors, 780–788
  navigating through records, 783–788
  navigation buttons, 783–785
  opening, 782–783
  overview, 780–781
  populating, 782–783
  specifying a recordset for, 782
underscore (_), continuation character, 389, 418–419
Undo button, 231
Undo event, 458–459, 460
undoing changes, 231
`UnicodeCompression` property, 60

unique identifiers, 20–21. *See also* foreign keys; primary keys.
`Unique` property problems, 1179
`Unique Records` property, 651
`Unique Values` property, 651
unknown input data. *See* data validation rules.
`Unload` event, 457
unsupported report controls, 1176
untrapped errors, 823
update anomalies, 99, 103
`Update` method, 512
`Update Query` action queries, 671, 672–673
`Update Retry Interval` option, 768
`Updated` event, 460
updating
  fields with data macros, 561
  records with action queries, 672–673
updating tables
  adding fields, 41
  deleting records, 41
  renaming fields, 41
updating tables, with VBA code
  adding records, 517
  ADO (ActiveX Data Objects), 509–513
  `AfterEventUpdate` event procedure, 509–513
  deleting records, 517–521
Upsizing Wizard
  ADP objects, *versus* Access objects, 1233–1235
  ADPs (Access Data Projects), 1223
  conversion issues, 1239
  data types, Access *versus* SQL Server, 1235–1240
  field names, 1239
  form conversions, 1234
  linked tables, 1235
  macro conversions, 1234
  module conversions, 1234
  query conversions, 1234
  referential integrity errors, 1231
  report conversions, 1234
  reports, 1232–1233
  ribbon conversions, 1234
  running, 1226–1233
  upsizing, prerequisites, 1226
usage logs, 920–923
Use Access Special Keys check box, 1084, 1087
Use Control Wizard button, 266
Use Default Paper Size property, 311
Use Transaction property, 653

Index

Use Windows-Themed Controls check box, 1084, 1088
user considerations
    application delivery, 905–907
    ease of starting, 907–909
    forms, displaying one at a time, 914
    information flow, 912–915
    installation tools, 906
    login forms, 910–911
    menus, removing, 913–914
    messages, 915–918
    Navigation Pane, hiding, 913–914
    Overlapping Windows interface, 915
    passwords, hiding, 911
    progress meters, 918–919
    ribbons, 912–913
    splash screens, 911–912
    start-up options, 909–912
    switchboard forms, 912
    Tabbed Documents interface, 914
    understanding user needs, 904–905
    user-interface style, choosing, 914–915
    Windows shortcuts, 907–909
User DSN, 1204
user input, validating, 928–929
user interface
    About box, 1097–1098
    consistent look and feel, 1094–1095
    design decisions, 1094–1095
    legal notices, 1097
    new features, 1253–1258
    Office Compatible certification, 1095
    pictures, 1097
    plagiarism, 1095
    revealing, 985
    splash screens, 867–868, 911–912, 1095–1097
    switchboards, 912, 1097
user name, getting, 956
user-defined functions, server database engines, 1188
user-interface style, choosing, 914–915
USysRibbons table, 1029–1032

V

validating data
    AllowZeroLength property, 70–71
    business rules, enforcing, 69
    date/time data, limiting to a range of dates, 70
    error messages, 69
    input, 69–70

    nonexistent data, 71
    required data, indicating, 70
    Required property, 70
    specifying, 49
    unknown data, 71
    Validation Rule property, 69
    Validation Text property, 69
    zero-length data, allowing, 70–71
validating user input, 928–929
Validation Rule property, 60, 69
Validation Text property, 60, 69
Value property, 702
values, definition, 8
values, inserting in
    datasheets, 231
    forms, 231
values, replacing in
    datasheets, 231
    forms, 231
Var option, 657
variable declaration, forcing
    Option Explicit directive, 394
    Require Variable Declaration option, 411, 431,
        527–528
variable declarations section, VBA modules, 394, 427
variables. *See also* temporary variables; VBA, variables.
    grouping by data type, 531–532
    out of context, 528
    in scope, displaying, 544–545
    values, displaying, 529
variables, absolute speed
    changing, 864
    comparing, 864
    control variables, 864–865
    field variables, 865
    unused, removing, 866
variables, debugging
    displaying variables in scope, 544–545
    forcing variable declaration, 527–528
    help, 543–544
    out of context, detecting, 528
    values, displaying, 529
Variant data type, VBA, 428, 430
variant variables, 423–424, 428, 430
VBA (Visual Basic for Applications). *See also* data access with
        VBA; data macros; macros; OOP (object-oriented
        programming).
    converting macros to, 1078–1080
    event properties, 387

extending, 387
keywords, 379
versus macros, 382, 1077–1078
name origins, 379
named arguments, 447–448
naming conventions, 432
overview, 378–379
submacros, 1068–1069
subprocedures, 388
variables, 380
VBA branching
Case Else clause, 404
definition, 401
Else statements, 402
ElseIf clause, 402–403
If...Then...Else...Endif statements, 401–403
If...Then...Endif statements, 401–403
overview, 401
Select Case...End Select statements, 403–404
VBA callbacks
overview, 1023–1025
writing, 1027–1029
VBA code
bulletproofing, 933–934
compiling, 532–534
grouping variables by data type, 531–532
organizing, 530–532
VBA collection items
counting, 407
naming conventions, 407
number of, effects on performance, 408
referencing, 407
VBA collections
Count property, 407
counting items in, 407
definition, 406
Item property, 407
looping through, 408–410
Name property, 407
naming conventions, 407
properties of, 407
VBA developer options
Auto Data Tips option, 412
Auto Indent option, 411
Auto List Members option, 411
Auto Quick Info option, 411–412
Auto Syntax Check option, 411
Break on all Errors option, 411
command-line arguments, 414–415

Command-Line Arguments option, 414–415
Compile on Demand option, 411
compiler directives, 413–414
Conditional Compilation Arguments option, 413–414
#Const compiler directive, 413–414
Editor tab, Options dialog box, 410–412
explicit variable declaration, forcing, 394, 411, 431
#If compiler directive, 413–414
indenting code, 411
object hierarchies, listing members of, 411
Options dialog box, 410–412
Project Description option, 413
Project Name option, 413
Project Properties dialog box, 412–414
Require Variable Declaration option, 411
stopping for errors, 411
syntax checking, 411
variable values, displaying, 412
VBA editor. *See also* editing.
& (ampersand), continuation character, 419
_ (underscore), continuation character, 418–419
comments, color coding, 419–420
identifiers, color coding, 419–420
indenting lines of code, 418
keywords, color coding, 419–420
object list, sorting, 420
splitting statements, 419
statement continuation, 418–419
VBA [Event Procedure] option
attaching event procedures, 397–398
creating event procedures, 439–441
event procedures as default development language, 391
VBA event procedures. *See also* VBA procedures.
attaching, 397–399
for controls, 459–460, 462–463, 466–468
as default development language, 391
definition, 387
identifying, 391
modifying, 391
for reports, 460–462
spaces, in event names, 455
VBA event procedures, creating
by copy and paste, 455
on forms, 456–459
methods for, 397–399
overview, 453–454
steps in, 439–441

Index

VBA event procedures, for forms
  closing forms, 469–470
  confirming deletions, 470–471
  creating, 456–459
  opening forms, 468–469
  verifying, 466–468
VBA events. *See also specific events.*
  categories of, 452
  data, 452
  error, 452
  focus, 452
  keyboard, 452, 455, 457
  list of, 455
  mouse, 452, 455, 457
  for pivot tables, 464
  print, 452
  sequence of, 465–466
  timing, 452
  triggering VBA code, 452–453
  windows, 452
VBA events, forms
  data changes, 465–466
  data management, 458–459
  focus changes, 465
  mouse activity, 466
  opening/closing, 465
VBA functions. *See also* VBA procedures.
  calling, 436
  creating, 441–442
  definition, 380
  description, 388–389
  versus procedures, 436
VBA help
  Auto List Members, 396
  Auto Quick Info, 396–397
  Intellisense, 395–397
VBA looping
  Do...Loop statements, 404–405
  For Each statements, 409–410
  endless loops, preventing, 405
  Exit Do statements, 405
  For...Next statements, 405–406, 408–409
  overview, 404
  With statements, 408–409
  terminating the loop, 405
  through code, 404–406
  through collection items, 408–410
  While clause, 404–405

VBA modules
  creating, 391–392
  definition, 380
  editing, 393
  form, 390
  Option Explicit directive, 394
  versus procedures, 380
  report, 390
  sections, 394
  standard, 389–390
  types of, 389–391
  variable declarations section, 394, 427
VBA objects. *See also* VBA collections.
  definition, 406
VBA parameters
  definition, 388, 442
  naming conventions, 442
  passing to functions, 443–445
  sales tax calculation (example), 445–447
VBA procedures. *See also* VBA, event procedures; VBA
    functions; VBA subroutines.
  Call statement, 437
  calling, 437
  calling from data macros, 576
  compiling, 397
  creating, 395, 397–399, 436
  definition, 380
  editing, 399
  versus modules, 380
  naming conventions, 435–436
  scope, 432–434
  testing in Immediate window, 399–401
VBA statements
  _ (underscore), continuation character, 389
  definition, 380
  example, 381
VBA subroutines. *See also* VBA procedures.
  calling, 436
  components of, 436
  creating, 437–441
  definition, 380
  naming conventions, 435–436
  overview, 435–436
VBA variables
  & (ampersand), concatenation operator, 422
  = (equal sign), assignment operator, 422
  assigning values to, 422
  case sensitivity of names, 423

Dim keyword, 421, 425–426
lifetime, 434–435
naming conventions, 394, 422–423
spaces in names, 423
storing expression results, 421
string, maximum size, 429
values, displaying, 412
variants, 423–424, 428, 430
VBA variables, data types
Boolean, 428
corresponding Access data types, 428
Currency, 428
Date, 428
Decimal, 428
default, 426, 430
Double, 428
Integer, 428
Long, 428
Object, 428
Single, 428
specifying, 422
String, 428
supported by VBA, 428
Variant, 428, 430
VBA variables, declaring
declarations section, 394, 427
explicitly, 424, 430
forcing explicit declaration, 394, 411, 431
implicitly, 423, 430
importance of, 424
overview, 421–425
VBA variables, scope
definition, 432
global, 426
local, 426
private, 427, 432–434
Private keyword, 427
public, 426, 432–434
Public keyword, 426
verifying data. *See* data validation rules.
verifying forms, 466–468
versioning, SharePoint, 1138
vertical lines between report columns, 729–730
video, data type. *See* OLE Object data type.
View argument, 1060
ViewChange event, 464

viewing data. *See* datasheets; forms; reports.
views
description, 1189
SQL Server, 1217–1219
switching, 219
Views group
Access 2010 ribbon, 36
Datasheet ribbon, 219
Form ribbon, 291–292
virtual memory, troubleshooting, 920
visibility, toggling on/off. *See* hiding/showing.
Visible property, 682, 684
Visual Basic for Applications (VBA). *See* VBA (Visual Basic for Applications).
Visual Basic.NET, 379
Visual Web Developer, customizing the ribbon, 1042–1044
volume information, getting, 958–959

W

w:, formatting day of the week, 63
watches
conditional, 547–548
setting, 545–547
Watches window
conditional watches, 547–548
description, 545
docking, 547
editing watched expressions, 548
floating, 547
maximum number of watches, 548
setting watches, 545–547
Web hosting. *See* Access Services; SharePoint.
Web publishing
new features, 1258
SharePoint deployment, 1156–1157, 1164–1173
Web servers *versus* application servers, 1190–1192
Week property, 362
WHERE clauses, 475, 484
Where Condition argument, 1061
Where options, 656
While clause, 404–405
white space, inserting in reports, 731–733
Whole Group option, 363
Width property, 307, 683
wikis, creating, 1112–1115

Index

wildcards
  * (asterisk), wildcard character, 181, 195–198
  # (pound sign), wildcard character, 181
  ? (question mark), wildcard character, 181, 195–198
  description, 181
  filtering data, 890–891
  Find and Replace dialog box, 228–230
  with Like operator, 195–198
  [list], wildcard character, 181
  [!list], wildcard character, 181
window class, getting, 960–961
Window group
  Access 2010 ribbon, 36
  Datasheet ribbon, 220
  Form ribbon, 293
Window Mode argument, 1061
Windows
  path, getting, 953
  system directory, getting, 959–960
  version, getting, 954–955
windows. *See specific windows.*
windows, switching, 220
Windows API
  application consistency, 941–942
  command line, getting, 952–953
  common code base, 941
  cross-platform compatibility, 941
  drive type, getting, 957–958
  file system information, getting, 958–959
  General Protection Fault, 944
  graphical objects, tracking, 950
  hwnd parameter, 950
  limitations of, 945
  local computer network name, getting, 956–957
  overview, 939–940
  parent window handles, getting, 960
  smaller application footprint, 941
  temporary files path, getting, 953–954
  tested and proven code, 941
  title-bar text, getting, 960
  title-bar text, setting, 961–962
  user name, getting, 956
  uses for, 940–942
  volume information, getting, 958–959
  window class, getting, 960–961
  Windows path, getting, 953
  Windows system directory, getting, 959–960
  Windows version, getting, 954–955
  wrapper functions, 949

Windows API, Declare statement
  ArgumentList parameter, 947–949
  arguments, passing ByVal *versus* ByRef, 948
  As DataType parameter, 949
  FunctionName parameter, 946
  functions *versus* subroutines, 946
  LibraryName parameter, 947
  purpose, 946
  strings, maximum length, 949
  syntax, 946
Windows API, DLL documentation
  argument prefixes, 944
  finding, 942
  understanding, 942–945
  VBA data types *versus* C/C++ data types, 943–945
Windows API, DLLs (dynamic link libraries)
  advantages of, 940
  definition, 940
  dynamic linking, 940
  static linking, 940
Windows API, .ini files
  integer values, getting, 964
  string values, getting, 963–964, 965
  writing to, 965–966
Windows API examples, general purpose functions
  GetClassNameA function, 960–961
  GetParent function, 960
  GetWindowTextA function, 960
  SetWindowTextA function, 961–962
Windows API examples, manipulating application settings
  GetPrivateProfileIntA function, 964
  GetPrivateProfileStringA function, 963–964
  GetProfileStringA function, 965
  WritePrivateProfileStringA function, 965–966
  WriteProfileStringA function, 966
Windows API examples, retrieving system information
  GetCommandLineA function, 952–953
  GetComputerNameA function, 956–957
  GetDriveTypeA function, 957–958
  GetSystemDirectoryA function, 959–960
  GetTempPathA function, 953–954
  GetUserNameA function, 956
  GetVersionExA function, 954–955
  GetVolumeInformationA function, 958–959
  GetWindowsDirectoryA function, 953
windows events, 452
Windows shortcuts, launching applications, 907–909
Windows themes, enabling, 1088
With First Detail option, 363

With function, absolute speed, 864
With keyword, filtering data, 895
With statements, 408–409
Word, Automation example
    activating Word instances, 805
    bookmarks, 807
    creating documents based on templates, 806
    creating Word instances, 805
    discarding Word instances, 807
    displaying Word, 805
    hidden copies of Word, 805
    inserting data, 806
    inserting pictures, 807
    moving the cursor, 807
    named arguments, 808
    Office macro recorder, 808–810
    overview, 800–805
Workspace object, 501
wrapper functions, 949
write-only properties, 987
WritePrivateProfileStringA function, 965–966
WriteProfileStringA function, 966
wrong data type. See data validation rules.
ww:, formatting week of the year, 63

X

xBase files, linking to, 591
XML (eXtensible Markup Language)
    files, exporting, 625–627
    saving data macros as, 574–575
XML, for the ribbon
    case sensitivity, 1035
    customizing, 1026

    editors, 1012
    example, 1033–1035
    syntax, 1012

Y

y:, formatting day of the year, 63
Year property, 362
years, two-digit versus four-digit, 212
Yes/No data type
    automatic validation, 224–225
    converting to Text, 58
    description, 53
    purpose, 48
    storage size, 49
Yes/No fields, 65–66
    Null values, 200
    query selection criteria, 151–152
yy:, formatting two-digit year, 63
yyyy:, formatting four-digit year, 63

Z

0 (zero)
    placeholder, 62
    required digit indicator, 67
zero-length data, allowing, 70–71
zip codes, data types, 51
Zoom dialog box, 297
Zoom window, 226–227

Wiley Publishing, Inc.
End-User License Agreement

READ THIS. You should carefully read these terms and conditions before opening the software packet(s) included with this book "Book". This is a license agreement "Agreement" between you and Wiley Publishing, Inc. "WPI". By opening the accompanying software packet(s), you acknowledge that you have read and accept the following terms and conditions. If you do not agree and do not want to be bound by such terms and conditions, promptly return the Book and the unopened software packet(s) to the place you obtained them for a full refund.

1. **License Grant.** WPI grants to you (either an individual or entity) a nonexclusive license to use one copy of the enclosed software program(s) (collectively, the "Software") solely for your own personal or business purposes on a single computer (whether a standard computer or a workstation component of a multi-user network). The Software is in use on a computer when it is loaded into temporary memory (RAM) or installed into permanent memory (hard disk, CD-ROM, or other storage device). WPI reserves all rights not expressly granted herein.

2. **Ownership.** WPI is the owner of all right, title, and interest, including copyright, in and to the compilation of the Software recorded on the physical packet included with this Book "Software Media". Copyright to the individual programs recorded on the Software Media is owned by the author or other authorized copyright owner of each program. Ownership of the Software and all proprietary rights relating thereto remain with WPI and its licensers.

3. **Restrictions on Use and Transfer.**

   (a) You may only (i) make one copy of the Software for backup or archival purposes, or (ii) transfer the Software to a single hard disk, provided that you keep the original for backup or archival purposes. You may not (i) rent or lease the Software, (ii) copy or reproduce the Software through a LAN or other network system or through any computer subscriber system or bulletin-board system, or (iii) modify, adapt, or create derivative works based on the Software.

   (b) You may not reverse engineer, decompile, or disassemble the Software. You may transfer the Software and user documentation on a permanent basis, provided that the transferee agrees to accept the terms and conditions of this Agreement and you retain no copies. If the Software is an update or has been updated, any transfer must include the most recent update and all prior versions.

4. **Restrictions on Use of Individual Programs.** You must follow the individual requirements and restrictions detailed for each individual program in the "About the CD" appendix of this Book or on the Software Media. These limitations are also contained in the individual license agreements recorded on the Software Media. These limitations may include a requirement that after using the program for a specified period of time, the user must pay a registration fee or discontinue use. By opening the Software packet(s), you agree to abide by the licenses and restrictions for these individual programs that are detailed in the "About the CD" appendix and/or on the Software Media. None of the material on this Software Media or listed in this Book may ever be redistributed, in original or modified form, for commercial purposes.

5. **Limited Warranty.**

   (a) WPI warrants that the Software and Software Media are free from defects in materials and workmanship under normal use for a period of sixty (60) days from the date of purchase of this Book. If WPI receives notification within the warranty period of defects in materials or workmanship, WPI will replace the defective Software Media.

   (b) WPI AND THE AUTHOR(S) OF THE BOOK DISCLAIM ALL OTHER WARRANTIES, EXPRESS OR IMPLIED, INCLUDING WITHOUT LIMITATION IMPLIED WARRANTIES OF MERCHANTABILITY AND FITNESS FOR A PARTICULAR PURPOSE, WITH RESPECT TO THE SOFTWARE, THE PROGRAMS, THE SOURCE CODE CONTAINED THEREIN, AND/OR THE TECHNIQUES DESCRIBED IN THIS BOOK. WPI DOES NOT WARRANT THAT THE FUNCTIONS CONTAINED IN THE SOFTWARE WILL MEET YOUR REQUIREMENTS OR THAT THE OPERATION OF THE SOFTWARE WILL BE ERROR FREE.

   (c) This limited warranty gives you specific legal rights, and you may have other rights that vary from jurisdiction to jurisdiction.

6. **Remedies.**

   (a) WPI's entire liability and your exclusive remedy for defects in materials and workmanship shall be limited to replacement of the Software Media, which may be returned to WPI with a copy of your receipt at the following address: Software Media Fulfillment Department, Attn.: *Microsoft Access 2010 Bible,* Wiley Publishing, Inc., 10475 Crosspoint Blvd., Indianapolis, IN 46256, or call 1-877-762-2974. Please allow four to six weeks for delivery. This Limited Warranty is void if failure of the Software Media has resulted from accident, abuse, or misapplication. Any replacement Software Media will be warranted for the remainder of the original warranty period or thirty (30) days, whichever is longer.

   (b) In no event shall WPI or the author be liable for any damages whatsoever (including without limitation damages for loss of business profits, business interruption, loss of business information, or any other pecuniary loss) arising from the use of or inability to use the Book or the Software, even if WPI has been advised of the possibility of such damages.

   (c) Because some jurisdictions do not allow the exclusion or limitation of liability for consequential or incidental damages, the above limitation or exclusion may not apply to you.

7. **U.S. Government Restricted Rights.** Use, duplication, or disclosure of the Software for or on behalf of the United States of America, its agencies and/or instrumentalities "U.S. Government" is subject to restrictions as stated in paragraph (c)(1)(ii) of the Rights in Technical Data and Computer Software clause of DFARS 252.227-7013, or subparagraphs (c) (1) and (2) of the Commercial Computer Software - Restricted Rights clause at FAR 52.227-19, and in similar clauses in the NASA FAR supplement, as applicable.

8. **General.** This Agreement constitutes the entire understanding of the parties and revokes and supersedes all prior agreements, oral or written, between them and may not be modified or amended except in a writing signed by both parties hereto that specifically refers to this Agreement. This Agreement shall take precedence over any other documents that may be in conflict herewith. If any one or more provisions contained in this Agreement are held by any court or tribunal to be invalid, illegal, or otherwise unenforceable, each and every other provision shall remain in full force and effect.